Hawaii
a travel survival kit

Glenda Bendure
Ned Friary

Hawaii – a travel survival kit

2nd edition

Published by
   Lonely Planet Publications
   Head Office: PO Box 617, Hawthorn, Vic 3122, Australia
   Branches: PO Box 2001A, Berkeley, CA 94702, USA
                 12 Barley Mow Passage, Chiswick, W4 4PH, UK

Printed by
   Colorcraft Ltd, Hong Kong

Photographs by
   Glenda Bendure & Ned Friary
   Front cover: Windsurfers at Waikiki's Fort DeRussy Beach, Oahu (Ned Friary)

First Published
   August 1990

This Edition
   February 1993

Although the authors and publisher have tried to make the information as accurate as possible, they accept no responsibility for any loss, injury or inconvenience sustained by any person using this book.

National Library of Australia Cataloguing-in-Publication Data

Bendure, Glenda.
   Hawaii, a travel survival kit.

   2nd ed.
   Includes index.
   ISBN 0 86442 164 8.

   1. Hawaii Guidebooks. I. Friary, Ned. II. Title. (Series: Lonely
   Planet travel survival kit).

919.6904

Glenda Bendure

Glenda grew up in California's Mojave Desert. Her first trip overseas was as a high school AFS exchange student to India.

Ned Friary

Ned grew up near Boston, studied Social Thought & Political Economy at the University of Massachusetts in Amherst and upon graduating headed west.

They met in Santa Cruz, California, where Glenda was completing her university studies and Ned was working with the forestry. In 1978, with Lonely Planet's first book *Across Asia on the Cheap* in hand, they hit the overland trail across southern Europe, through Iran and Afghanistan, and on to trains in India and treks in Nepal. The next six years were spent exploring Asia and the Pacific, with a home base in Japan where Ned taught English and Glenda landed a job as the editor of *Kansai Time Out*, an English-language monthly.

The first of many trips to Hawaii was in 1980, when they went straight from Osaka to the green lushness of Kauai, a sight so soothing for concrete-weary eyes that a two-week holiday turned into a four-month stay. Now living on Cape Cod in Massachusetts, they both write articles for magazines and newspapers in the USA and Asia and Glenda has a travel column in the *Cape Cod Times*.

Ned and Glenda are also the authors of Lonely Planet's *Micronesia – a travel survival kit* and of the Norway and Denmark chapters of LP's *Scandinavian & Baltic Europe on a shoestring*.

From the Authors

Many thanks to the people who helped us on this project: State Parks archaeologist Martha Yent; Linda Delaney from the Office of Hawaiian Affairs; Kathy Tachibana of the Nature Conservancy; Christina Meller, Na Ala Hele Program Manager; Jeanne Kirby of Greenpeace; Bill Puleloa, aquatic biologist for the Department of Land & Natural Resources; Daniel Kawaiaea, park ranger at Puukohola Heiau National Historic Site; Jean Greenwell of the Kona Historical Society; Jon Giffin of the Division of Forestry & Wildlife; Leon Bruno of the Lyman Museum in Hilo; Roy Damron of the Kona Reefers Dive Club; John P Lockwood, geologist at Hawaiian Volcano Observatory; Noelani Whittington of the Kohala Coast Resort Association; and to the Hawaii Visitors Bureau, in particular Lindy Boyes.

Thanks to friends Richard Heinisch, Glenn Thering and Ted Brattstrom, who hiked with us on the back trails of various islands; and also to D L Webber, Bernd Marks, Mark Schlagbohmer, Jim & Barbara Kershner, Rosemary Smith & family, Walter Ritte Jr, Bruno on Lanai and all the other helpful people we met along the way.

From the Publisher

This second edition of *Hawaii – a travel survival kit* was edited by Sharan Kaur, Katie Cody and Miriam Cannell. Thanks to Simone Calderwood for proofing, Sharon Wertheim for indexing and Tom Smallman for editorial support.

Sandra Smythe was responsible for the cover design, layout, mapping and illustrations. Trudi Canavan and Glenn Beanland also helped with the map corrections and Natalie Daykin, a work experience student, lent a hand with the map bromiding and illustrations.

Thanks also to those travellers who wrote in with information:

Tommy Aerts (Nl), Carol Austin (USA), Ann & Bob Babson (USA), Iris Barnett (USA), Ron & Kate Bauer (USA), Tim Blood (USA), Donald Brown (USA), Jane Campbell (Aus), Tommy & Brenda Carson (USA), Joyce Chizmadia (USA), Patricia Cuthbertson (USA), Fred Diamond (USA), Liz Dunn (USA), Mike & Annette Endres (USA), Mitzi Fedoroniak (C), David & Susan Felthous (USA), Debbie Fraser (Aus), Jens Griesang (D), Birgit & Lute Guderjahn (D), Kirby Guyer-Searles (USA), David Hill (UK), Joanne van Hoof (C), Amanda Horswill (USA), Philippa Hurman (C), Judy Jones (USA), Susan K E Jones (USA), Susan Kauai (USA), Allan Kempe (USA), Fritz Knott (D), Anne Krum (USA), Lucy Kunkel (Aus), Jean S Lai (USA), Roger Lasko (USA), Mary Catherine Lombard (USA), M Loveridge (Aus), Tony Mamo (USA), Bernd Marks (D), Lida Martin (USA), Danila & Talya Masri (USA), Don & Penny Merryman (USA), Hugh Montgomery (USA), Kate Murphy (USA), Luly Nakanishi (USA), Malin Nygren (Sw), Ron Ober (USA), Elke Obermeier (D), Martin & Susan Oogjen (USA), Vikki Patterson (USA), MIchael Pearson (UK), Arne Phillips (USA), Paul Rabe (USA), Sally Richards (USA), Irene Richardson (UK), Richard Rowlett (USA), Mary Jane Schock (USA), Keith Schwebel (USA), Michael Schyster (USA), Joseph Sidebottom (USA), Rick & Regina Steinkamp (USA), Mike Sutherland (USA), Lisa Tarleton (Aus), Alex & Michael Tboring (D), Maurice Thomas, Andrea Thomas (USA), John Thorvaldson (USA), Robert Tobin, David L Torzeski (USA), R Michael Tuggle (USA), Doug & Judith Urquhart (C), J B Van Vely (USA), Chas Wagner (USA), Ron & Christine Walkinshaw (USA), Bill Webber (UK), Miss D L Webber (UK), Eileen Winters (USA), Valeria Wissinger (C), Robert Woodward (USA), Ch. Xhaflaire (B), Franklin Young (USA)

Aus - Australia, B - Belgium, C - Canada, D - Germany, Nl - Netherlands, Sw - Sweden, UK - United Kingdom, USA - United States of America

Warning & Request

Things change – prices go up, schedules change, good places go bad and bad places go bankrupt – nothing stays the same. So if you find things better or worse, recently opened or long since closed, please write and tell us and help make the next edition better.

Your letters will be used to help update future editions and, where possible, important changes will also be included in a Stop Press section in reprints.

We greatly appreciate all information that is sent to us by travellers. Back at Lonely Planet we employ a hard-working readers' letters team to sort through the many letters we receive. The best ones will be rewarded with a free copy of the next edition or another Lonely Planet guide if you prefer. We give away lots of books, but, unfortunately, not every letter/postcard receives one.

Contents

Map Legend

BOUNDARIES

—·—·—·—	........International Boundary
—··—··—	...............Internal Boundary
┼┼┼┼┼┼┼	....National Park or Reserve
----------	.........................The Equator
....	.........................The Tropics

SYMBOLS

◉ NEW DELHI	......................National Capital
● BOMBAY	.........Provincial or State Capital
● Pune	................................Major Town
● Barsi	................................Minor Town
■	............................Places to Stay
▼	............................Places to Eat
✉	...................................Post Office
✈	....Airport
i	....................Tourist Information
⊖	.............Bus Station or Terminal
66	............Highway Route Number
☪ ✝ ⌂ ☩	...... Mosque, Church, Cathedral
∴	..........................Temple or Ruin
✚	......................................Hospital
☀	....Lookout
⚑	...........................Camping Area
⊓	.................................Picnic Area
⌂	............................Hut or Chalet
▲	........................Mountain or Hill
├─┤	........................Railway Station
═══	..............................Road Bridge
┼┼┼┼	...........................Railway Bridge
⇒ ⇐	.................................Road Tunnel
→) (←	............................Railway Tunnel
⌇⌇⌇	...................Escarpment or Cliff
⌣	....Pass
⊓⊓⊓	.............Ancient or Historic Wall

ROUTES

──────	.......Major Road or Highway
----------	.........Unsealed Major Road
──────	........................Sealed Road
- - - - - -	.....Unsealed Road or Track
════════	...........................City Street
┼┼┼┼┼┼	...................................Railway
●──◉──●	...................................Subway
....	.....................Walking Track
- - - - - -	.......................Ferry Route
┼┼┼┼┼┼	........Cable Car or Chair Lift

HYDROGRAPHIC FEATURES

	....................River or Creek
	.............Intermittent Stream
	........Lake, Intermittent Lake
	...........................Coast Line
	...................................Spring
	................................Waterfall
	.................................Swamp
	................Salt Lake or Reef
	.................................Glacier

OTHER FEATURES

	Park, Garden or National Park
	......................Built Up Area
	... Market or Pedestrian Mall
	.........Plaza or Town Square
	...............................Cemetery

Note: not all symbols displayed above appear in this book

Introduction

Hawaii's natural beauty is extraordinarily grand. Mark Twain fittingly called Hawaii 'the loveliest fleet of islands that lies anchored in any ocean'. Volcanic in origin, the Hawaiian islands are high and rugged, lushly green and cut by spectacular gorges and valleys. The beaches are beautiful, ranging from bleached white to jet black. The terrain is amazingly varied, climbing from lowland deserts to alpine mountain-tops, with everything from barren lava flows to tropical rainforest found in between.

. Hawaii is the world's most isolated archipelago, 2500 miles from the nearest land mass. Its isolation is so great that of the thousands of species of flora & fauna that have evolved here, over 90% exist no where else on earth.

Geologically it's also singularly unique.

Hawaii has the world's most active volcano (Kilauea), its largest dormant volcano (Haleakala), its highest mountain when measured from the sea floor (Mauna Kea) and its highest sea cliffs (on Molokai).

As one of the world's leading visitor destinations, Hawaii does have the expected mass tourism, high-rise hotels and crowded beaches. But that's only one side of it.

You can also find scores of untouristed areas and secluded beaches to explore, while your accommodation options include upcountry lodges, isolated resorts, B&B inns and oceanside cottages. And the best the islands have to offer is still free for hikers and backcountry campers.

The islands have some of the world's top surfing and windsurfing, as well as excellent conditions for snorkelling, swimming,

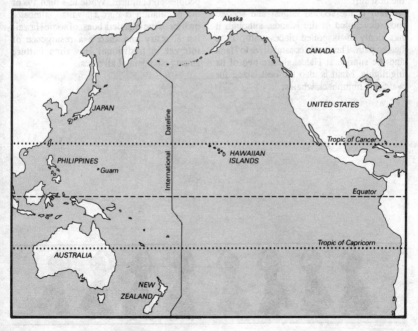

diving, bodysurfing and most other water sports.

Hawaii's climate is unusually pleasant for the tropics, as near-constant trade winds prevail throughout the year. Much of the time the rain falls as short daytime showers that are accompanied by rainbows.

Hawaii's six main islands all have lovely beaches and splendid scenery. Their leeward coasts are sunny, dry and desert-like, with white sands and turquoise waters. The mountainous windward sides have tropical jungles, cascading waterfalls and pounding surf. The uplands are cool and green, with rolling pastures, small farms and ranches.

Oahu is the most crowded and developed of the islands, with Waikiki still providing half the tourist accommodation in Hawaii. Honolulu has all the pluses and minuses of urban life, from congested traffic to good museums and lively nightlife. It has wonderful restaurants, with both inexpensive ethnic foods and gourmet cuisines. Oahu also has the best surf.

Maui is the second largest and second most developed of the islands, although it has plenty of unspoiled places well off the beaten path. The scenic coastal drive to Hana and the sunrise at Haleakala are two of its highlights. Maui is also the best island for watching humpback whales.

The Big Island has two things the others don't: snow and erupting volcanoes. There's room to move, with niches for cowboys, astronomers and traditional fishing villages, as well as alternative communities settling in on the side of lava flows.

Kauai has Hawaii's greenest scenery, a deeply cut canyon resembling a mini-Grand Canyon and the famous razorback cliffs of the Na Pali Coast.

While Kauai took a direct hit from powerful Hurricane Iniki in September 1992, and the scars from that storm will take some time to heal, it's still a special place that's well worth including in a Hawaii itinerary.

Molokai, the most Hawaiian of the islands, is charmingly rural and slow-paced. Lanai, the smallest island, is undergoing a jolting transition from an economy based on pineapple growing to a new identity as a luxury resort destination.

Hawaii is ethnically diverse with an appealing collage of East, West and Pacific peoples and cultures. While less than 1% of the population is pure Hawaiian, almost a quarter of the islanders boast of some Hawaiian ancestry and there's a resurgence of interest in traditional Hawaiian culture among islanders of all races.

Facts about the Country

HISTORY

Hawaii is the northern point of the huge triangle of Pacific Ocean islands known as Polynesia. The other two points are Easter Island to the south-east and New Zealand to the south-west.

The original settlers of Polynesia, which means 'many islands', apparently followed a long migratory path through South-East Asia, down through Indonesia and across Melanesia, before settling the Polynesian islands of Tonga and Samoa in about 1000 BC. Over the next 1500 years they migrated to the more distant islands of Polynesia, with Hawaii being one of the last areas settled.

Archaeological evidence indicates the first Polynesians arrived in Hawaii from the Marquesas between 500 and 700 AD. Among the links are ancient stone statues found on Hawaii's now uninhabited Necker Island which have striking similarities to statues found on the Marquesas.

When the first wave of Tahitians arrived in Hawaii in about 1000 AD they apparently conquered and subjugated the Marquesans, forcing them to build their temples, irrigation ditches and fishponds.

Hawaiian legends of a tribe of little people called *menehune* may well refer to the Marquesans. Indeed, the word 'menehune' is very similar to the Tahitian word for 'outcast'.

Ancient Hawaii

The earliest Hawaiians had simple animistic beliefs. Good fishing, a safe journey and a healthy child were all the result of being in tune with the spirits of nature. Their offerings

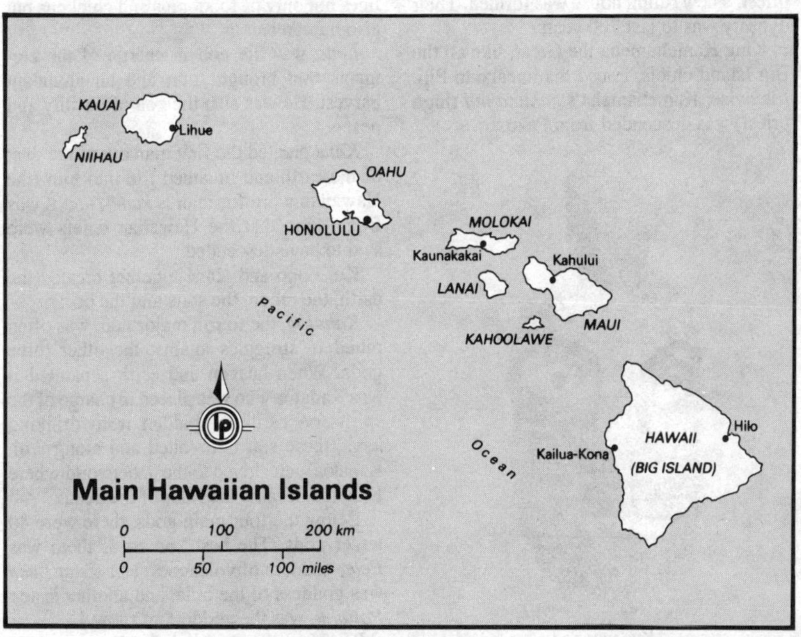

Main Hawaiian Islands

KAUAI
Lihue
NIIHAU

OAHU
HONOLULU
MOLOKAI
Kaunakakai
Kahului
LANAI
KAHOOLAWE
MAUI

Pacific

HAWAII
(BIG ISLAND)
Hilo
Kailua-Kona

Ocean

0   100   200 km
0   50   100 miles

to the gods consisted of prayers and a share of the harvest.

Around the 12th century, in a later wave of migration, a powerful Tahitian *kahuna* (priest), Paao, arrived on the Big Island. Convinced that the Hawaiians were too lax in their worship, Paao introduced the offering of human sacrifice to the gods and built the first *luakini heiau*, a type of temple where these sacrifices took place. He also established the *kapu* system of taboos which strictly regulated all social interaction.

The kapus forbade commoners from eating the same food or even walking the same ground as the *alii*, or royalty. A commoner who crossed the shadow of a king could be put to death. Kapus prohibited all women from eating coconuts, bananas, pork and certain fish.

Paao decided that Hawaii's blue-blood was too diluted and summoned the chief Pili from Kahiki (Tahiti) to establish a new royal lineage. With Pili as chief and Paao as high priest, a new ruling house was formed. Their dynasty was to last 700 years.

King Kamehameha the Great, like all the Big Island chiefs, traced his lineage to Pili. Likewise, Kamehameha's *kahuna nui* (high priest) was descended from Paao.

Ku - war god

Religion In the old Hawaiian religion there were four main gods: Ku, Lono, Kane and Kanaloa.

Ku was the ancestor god for all generations of humankind, past, present and future. He presided over all male gods while his wife, *Hina*, took charge of the females. When the sun rose in the morning, it was said to be Ku; when it set in the evening it was Hina. Like Yin and Yang, they were responsible for heaven and earth.

Ku had many manifestations, one as the benevolent god of fishing, *Ku-ula* (Ku of the abundant seas), and others as the god of forests and farming. People prayed to Ku when the harvest was scarce. At a time of drought or other such disaster, a temple would be built to appease Ku.

One of the most fearful of Ku's manifestations was *Kukailimoku* (Ku, the snatcher of land), the war god that Kamehameha the Great worshipped. The temples built for the worship of Kukailimoku were offered sacrifices not only of food, pigs and chickens but also human beings.

Lono was the god in charge of the elements that brought rain and an abundant harvest. He was also the god of fertility and peace.

Kane created the first man out of the dust of the earth and breathed life into him (the Hawaiian word for man is *kane*), and it was from Kane that the Hawaiian chiefs were said to have descended.

Ku, Lono and Kane together created the earth, the moon, the stars and the ocean.

Kanaloa, the fourth major god, was often pitted in struggles against the other three gods. When heaven and earth separated it was Kanaloa who was placed in charge of the spirits on earth. Forbidden from drinking kava, these spirits revolted and along with Kanaloa were driven to the underworld where Kanaloa became the ruler of the dead.

Below the four main gods, there were 40 lesser gods. The best known of them was *Pele*, goddess of volcanoes. Her sister *Laka* was goddess of the hula, and another sister, *Poliahu*, was the goddess of snow.

The Hawaiians had gods for all occupations

and natural phenomena. There was a god for the tapa maker and a god for the canoe builder, shark gods and mountain gods.

Heiaus The temples erected in ancient Hawaii, called *heiau*, were built in two basic styles, both of which were constructed of lava rock. One was a simple rectangular enclosure of stone walls built directly on the ground. The other was a more substantial structure built of rocks piled high to form raised terraced platforms. (The remains of both types can be found throughout the islands today.)

Inside the heiaus were prayer towers, taboo houses and drum houses. These structures were made of ohia wood, thatched with pili grass and tied with cord from the native olona shrub. Tiki, or god images, called *kii*, were carved of wood and placed around the prayer towers.

Heiaus were most commonly dedicated to Lono, the god of harvest, or Ku, the god of war. The heiaus built in honour of Ku were called luakini heiau and were the only ones where human sacrifices took place.

Heiaus were built in auspicious sites, often perched on cliffs above the coast or in other places thought to have *mana*, or 'spiritual power'. A heiau's significance lay not in the structure itself but focused on the mana of the site. When a heiau's mana was gone, it was abandoned.

The Makahiki According to legend, the god Lono rode a rainbow down from the heavens to a breadfruit grove above Hiilawe Falls in Waipio Valley where, in a paradise-like setting, he found Kaikilani, a beautiful princess surrounded by birds. They fell in love, married and moved across the island to Kealakekua Bay.

When Lono discovered that a chief was lusting after Kaikilani, he became enraged and beat Kaikilani who, as she lay dying, professed her faithful love for Lono alone. In his grief, Lono travelled restlessly around the island challenging every man he met to a wrestling match and other competitions.

After four months, a still disheartened Lono set sail on a canoe with a tall mast hung with sails made of finely woven Niihau mats. The huge canoe was laden with so much food that it took 40 men to carry it down to Kealakekua Bay. Lono promised to return one day on a floating island covered with trees and full of chickens and pigs.

The Hawaiians remembered Lono each year with a harvest festival, called the *makahiki*, which lasted from October to February. Numerous inter-island competitions similar to the Olympics were held, including outrigger canoe races, fishing and surfing tournaments, foot races, boxing and wrestling matches and *holua* (sled) racing. Even during wartime, fighting would be suspended for the four months of the makahiki, so that the games and festivities dedicated to Lono could proceed.

Captain Cook
The Hawaiian Islands were the last of the

Petroglyphs
Although the Hawaiians had no written history, they did leave petroglyphs cut into the lava. Many of these carved pictures are stylised stick figures depicting warriors with spears, barking dogs, birds, canoes and other decipherable images. Some are marks which may have recorded important events, calendars or genealogical charts.

The meanings and purposes behind Hawaiian petroglyphs are not well understood. Some may have been intentionally cryptic, while others may just be random graffiti or the carvings of a budding artist.

Most petroglyphs are found along ancient footpaths and may have been clustered at sites thought to have mana.

The Big Island has the greatest concentration of petroglyphs, with several large fields just a few minutes' walk from the road. ■

Polynesian islands to be 'discovered' by the West. Early European explorers who entered the Pacific around the tips of either Africa or South America centred their explorations in the southern hemisphere.

Although the English were the first *known* Western explorers to set foot on Hawaiian shores, there is speculation that the Spanish, whose Manila galleons had been making annual runs between Mexico and the Philippines since 1565, may have stumbled upon Hawaii and kept the discovery a secret.

British explorer Captain James Cook spent the better part of a decade exploring and charting most of the South Pacific before chancing upon Hawaii as he sailed from Tahiti in search of a north-west passage to the Atlantic.

On 18 January 1778 Cook spotted the islands of Oahu, Kauai and Niihau. The winds favoured approaching Kauai and on 19 January Cook's ships, the *Discovery* and the *Resolution*, sailed into Kauai's Waimea Bay. Cook named the Hawaiian archipelago the Sandwich Islands in honour of the Earl of Sandwich.

Cook was surprised to find that the islanders had a strong Tahitian influence in their appearance, language and culture. They sailed out in canoes to welcome the ships and were eager to trade fish and sweet potatoes for nails. The islanders were not interested in the useless beads and trinkets used successfully as barter elsewhere in the Pacific. The only thing they cared to exchange anything

for was metal, which was totally absent from their islands.

After two weeks of stocking provisions on Kauai and Niihau, Cook's expedition continued its journey north. Failing to find the fabled passage through the Arctic, Cook set sail back to Hawaii where his arrival date virtually coincided with that of his initial visit to the islands the year before.

This time he discovered the remaining Hawaiian islands. On 17 January 1779 Cook sailed into Kealakekua Bay on the Big Island where a thousand canoes came out to greet him.

When Cook went ashore the next day he was met by the high priest and guided to a temple lined with skulls. Everywhere the English captain went people fell face down on the ground in front of him to the chant of *Lono*.

As fate would have it, Cook had landed during the makahiki festival. The tall masts and white sails of Cook's ships and even the way he had sailed clockwise around the island all fitted the legendary descriptions of how the god Lono would reappear on the scene.

Whether the priests actually believed Cook was the reincarnated Lono or whether they just used his appearance to enhance their power and add a little flair to their festivities is unknown. What is clear is that Cook never realised that both of his arrivals to Hawaii had coincided with the makahiki festivals – he assumed this was the way things were in everyday Hawaii.

Fishponds
The Hawaiians had a well-developed aquaculture system with numerous coastal fishponds.

There were essentially two kinds of fishponds. One type was inshore and totally closed off from the sea, although generally close enough to have brackish water. These inshore ponds would be stocked with netted fry (young fish) and often had varying salinity levels which the Hawaiians took advantage of by cultivating different fish in different parts of the pond.

The other kind was a shoreline fishpond, created by building a long stone wall that paralleled the beach and curved back to shore at both ends. For these walled ponds the Hawaiians built *makaha*, or 'sluice gates', that allowed young fish to swim through but kept fattened fish from swimming back out. The fish in the pond could be easily netted at anytime.

Amaama (mullet) and *awa* (milkfish) were the two varieties of fish most commonly raised in these fishponds. Most fishponds were strictly for the alii, and commoners were not allowed to eat the fish raised in them. ■

There's little wonder Cook had a favourable impression of the islands. The islanders treated his crew with open hospitality. Hawaiian men invited the sailors to boxing matches and other competitions and the women performed dances and readily bedded down with them.

For men who had just spent months roaming inhospitable frozen tundra, this was paradise indeed.

The expedition's skilled artist, John Webber, was allowed to move freely in the villages. Today his detailed drawings of native people, costumes and village life constitute the best visual accounts of old Hawaii.

A few weeks after their arrival the crews had restocked all the supplies needed except firewood. Rather than scour the hillsides for wood Cook directed his men to haul on board the temple railings and wooden images from the harbourside temple dedicated to Lono. As Cook had been passed off as Lono himself, the priests didn't attempt to stop them.

On 4 February the English vessels and their crews headed north out of Kealakekua Bay for Maui, but ran into a storm off the north-west coast of the Big Island where the *Resolution* broke a foremast. Uncertain of finding a safe harbour in Maui, Cook decided to go back to Kealakekua to repair the mast – a decision which proved to be a fatal mistake.

When they arrived at Kealakekua Bay on 11 February the islanders quickly appeared with the usual provisions to barter. The ruling alii, however, seemed upset with the ships' reappearance.

Hawaiian Sports

Holua racing was ancient Hawaii's most exciting spectator sport. Racers would ride prone on narrow wooden sleds, racing at high speed down steep hills along furrows which had been covered with pili grass or ti leaves to make the surface smooth. Many of the holua slide paths were a mile or two long.

Hawaiians were heavy betters and often wagered on the holua races, as well as on foot races, surfing competitions and many other sports.

Surfing is a Hawaiian invention that was as popular in old Hawaii as it is today. When the waves were up, everyone was out. There were royal surfing grounds and spots for commoners as well. Boards used by commoners were made of breadfruit or *koa* (native hardwood) and were about six feet long. Only the alii were free to use the long *olo* boards, which were up to 16 feet in length and made of *wiliwili*, the lightest of native woods. The boards were highly prized possessions and were carefully wrapped in tapa cloth and suspended from the ceilings of homes.

Other popular Hawaiian games included *ulu maika*, in which rounded stone discs were rolled between two stakes, somewhat resembling bowling, and *moa pahee*, a similar game using a large wooden dart.

For the more passive, there was *konane*, a strategy game similar to checkers. Indentations were carved into a stone board to hold the pebbles of white coral and black lava that were used as playing pieces. ∎

Apparently the makahiki had ended and not only was Cook's timing inauspicious but so were the conditions of his return. This time he had arrived in an anti-clockwise direction and with a broken sail.

Thievery became a big problem and after a cutter was stolen, Cook ordered a blockade of Kealakekua Bay and then set off with a party of 11 men to the main village at the northern point of the bay. His intention was to capture the high chief Kalaniopuu and hold him until the cutter was returned. This was a tactic which Cook had used elsewhere in the Pacific and saw as reasonable diplomacy.

While Cook was en route to the village, a Hawaiian canoe attempting to sail out of the bay was fired upon by the English sailors. Unknown to Cook's crew the canoe was transporting a chief, Noekema, who was killed in the musket fire.

In the meantime Cook had reached Kalaniopuu's house and the chief had agreed to go with him. But as they walked down to the shore, Kalaniopuu's wailing wife ran after him and the old chief suddenly balked and attempted to get away. In the midst of it all, word of Noekema's death reached the village where a crowd quickly gathered.

Hoping to prevent bloodshed, Cook let the chief go, but the situation continued to escalate. As Cook was walking towards his boat, he shot at one of the armed Hawaiians who tried to block his way. The pistol misfired and the bullet bounced off the man's chest. The Hawaiians began to throw stones, and Cook ordered his men on shore to fire more shots.

Cook had always assumed, as had been the case on other Pacific islands, that if trouble developed his men could fire a few shots and the natives, upon seeing the blood, would run. Instead the Hawaiians, who were now in an angry frenzy, attacked rather than retreated.

The sailors in the boats fired another round as their captain began to make his way towards them over slippery rocks. Before they could reload, the crowd of Hawaiians moved in and Cook was struck on the head.

Stunned by the blow, he staggered into the shallows where the Hawaiians beat and stabbed him, passing the daggers to share in the kill. Four other sailors also died in the battle.

James Cook was intelligent, resourceful and popularly regarded as one of the finest and most humane explorers of all time. In this freak melee on a shore of the Sandwich Islands, his last discovery, the life of the greatest explorer and navigator of the century came to a bloody end.

Cook's men went on a rampage. They burned a village, beheaded two of their victims and rowed across the bay with the heads on poles.

Eventually Kalaniopuu made a truce and returned those parts of Cook's dismembered body he was able to find. The skull was returned but it had been stripped of its skin – a common practice bestowed upon great chiefs.

Cook's remains were buried at sea in a military funeral, at which time the Hawaiians placed a kapu on the bay and also held ceremonies of their own.

A week after Cook's 14 February death the two ships set sail, landing briefly on Oahu, Kauai and Niihau before finally leaving Hawaiian waters on 15 March 1779.

Cook and his crew left the Hawaiians a costly legacy in the iron that was turned into weapons, the introduced diseases that gained a rapid foothold and the birth of the first children of mixed blood. The crews also returned home with charts and maps that would allow others to follow in their wake and in Britain and Europe their stories and drawings were published, stirring the public's sense of adventure.

Some of Cook's crew returned to the Pacific leading their own expeditions. Among them was Captain George Vancouver who brought the first cattle and horses to Hawaii, and the ill-fated William Bligh who captained the *Bounty*.

Kamehameha the Great

At the time of Cook's arrival in Hawaii in 1778 the islands were divided into separate

Top: Kaina Keana'aina Hula Troupe, Big Island
Bottom: Hula dancers at Waimea Falls Park, Oahu

Top: Bird of Paradise
Left: Anthurium
Right: Hibiscus

warring chiefdoms. Kamehameha the Great, who by 1791 had become sole chief of the Big Island, was to become the first to unite all the Hawaiian Islands.

In 1795, after conquering Maui and Molokai, Kamehameha successfully invaded Oahu in the bloody battle of Nuuanu, and established his reign there as well.

Kamehameha made two attempts to invade Kauai, the only island not yet under his control. In 1796 his canoes were caught in a storm at sea and forced to turn back before ever reaching the island. In 1804, while Kamehameha was in Oahu again preparing for the invasion of Kauai, his warriors were struck by a decimating outbreak of a feverish disease, probably cholera, and the invasion plans were scrapped. The luck of the roll may have been Kauai's at the time, but Kamehameha's power was too obvious to ignore, so in 1810 Kauai agreed by treaty to accept Kamehameha's suzerainty.

The Sandalwood Trade

By the mid-1780s Hawaii was becoming a popular port of call for Yankee traders plying the seas between North America and China.

In the early 1790s American sea captains discovered Hawaii had great stocks of sandalwood, which were worth a premium in China. When the captains showed interest in it, Hawaiian chiefs readily began bargaining their wood away in exchange for weapons.

A lucrative three-way trade developed. From Hawaii the ships sailed to Canton and traded loads of sandalwood for Chinese silk and porcelain which was then carried back to New England ports and sold at high profit. In New England the ships were reloaded with goods to be traded to the Hawaiians.

Hawaii's forests of sandalwood were so vast at this time that the Chinese name for Hawaii was *Tahn Heong Sahn* – the 'Sandalwood Mountains'.

To try to maintain the resource Kamehameha eventually put a kapu on all sandalwood forests, giving himself total control over the trade. Even under Kamehameha's relatively shrewd management, the bulk of the profits ended up in the

sea captains' pockets. Payment for the sandalwood was in overpriced goods, originally cannons and rifles, and later exotic items such as European furniture.

While Kamehameha was careful not to use up all his forests or overburden his subjects, his successor, Liholiho, partially lifted the royal kapu, allowing island chiefs to get in on the action. The chiefs began purchasing foreign luxuries by signing promissory notes to be paid in future shipments of sandalwood.

To pay off the rising 'debts', the *makaainana* (commoners) were forced into virtual servitude. They were used like packhorses to cut and haul the wood, the sandalwood strapped to their backs with bands of ti leaves. The men who carted the wood were called *kua leho*, literally 'calloused backs' after the thick permanent layer of calluses which they developed. It was not uncommon for them to carry heavy loads 20 miles from the interior to ships waiting on the coast. Missionaries recorded seeing caravans of as many as 3000 men carting wood during the height of the trade.

In a few short years after Kamehameha's death Hawaii's sandalwood forests were exhausted. In a futile attempt to continue the trade, Oahu's Governor Boki, who had heard of vast sandalwood reserves in New Hebrides, set sail in November 1829 with 500 men on an ill-conceived expedition to harvest the trees. Boki's ship was lost at sea and the expedition's other ship, not too surprisingly, received a hostile welcome in New Hebrides.

In August 1830, 20 emaciated survivors sailed back into Honolulu Harbor. Boki had been a popular if troubled leader in a rapidly changing Hawaii. Hawaiians grieved in the streets of Honolulu when they heard of Boki's tragedy, and his death marked the end of the sandalwood trade.

End of the Old Religion

King Kamehameha died in 1819 at his Kamakahonu residence on the Big Island. The crown was passed to his reluctant son, Liholiho, who was proclaimed Kamehameha II. In reality the power was passed to Kaahumanu, who had been the favourite of Kamehameha's 21 wives.

Kaahumanu was an ambitious woman, determined to break down the ancient kapu system of taboos that restricted her powers. Less than six months after Kamehameha's death, Kaahumanu threw a feast for women of royalty at the sacred Kamakahonu compound. Although one of the most sacred taboos strictly forbade men from eating with women, Kaahumanu forcefully persuaded Liholiho to sit beside her and join in the meal.

It was an otherwise uneventful meal; not a single angry god manifested itself. But in that one act the old religion was cast aside, along with 600 years of taboos and restrictions. Hawaiians no longer had to fear being put to death for violating the kapus, and a flurry of temple smashing and idol burning immediately followed.

Those chiefs and kahunas who resisted were easily squelched by Liholiho using the powerful army which Kamehameha had left behind. It was the end of an era.

The Missionaries

On 19 April 1820 the brig *Thaddeus* arrived from Boston with the first of the Christian missionaries to Hawaii. By a twist of fate, they landed in Kailua Bay, a stone's throw from Kamakahonu, where six months earlier Kaahumanu had feasted the overthrow of the old religion.

It was a timely arrival for the missionaries. The loss of their religion and social structure had left the Hawaiians with a spiritual void into which the Christians zealously stepped.

The *Thaddeus* carried 23 Congregationalists, the first of 12 groups to be sent in the next three decades by the New England-based American Board of Commissioners of Foreign Missions (ABCFM). The leader of this initial group of missionaries was Hiram Bingham.

Dance & Music

Ancient Hula Perhaps nothing is more uniquely Hawaiian than the hula. There are many different schools of hula, all very disciplined and graceful in their movements. Before Western contact students spent years training in hula schools, sometimes moving to other islands to enrol with the masters.

Most ancient hula dances expressed historical events, legendary tales and the accomplishments of the great alii. Facial expressions, hip sway and dance steps all conveyed the story. They were performed to rhythmic chants and drum beatings, serving to connect with the world of spirits. Eye movement was very important; if the story was about the sun the eyes would gaze upward, if about the netherworld they would gaze downward.

One school, the *hula ohelo*, was very sensual, with movements suggesting the act of procreation.

Hula dancers wore tapa cloth, not the grass skirts which were introduced from Micronesia only a hundred years ago.

The Christian missionaries thought it all too licentious for their liking and suppressed it. The hula might have been lost forever if not for King Kalakaua, the 'Merrie Monarch', who revived it in the latter half of the 19th century.

Musical Instruments The *pahu hula*, a knee drum carved from a breadfruit or coconut log, with a sharkskin drum head, was used solely at hula performances. Other hula musical instruments include *ke laau* sticks used to keep the beat for the dancers; *iliili*, stone castanets; *puili*, rattles made from split bamboo; and *uliuli*, gourd rattles decorated with colourful feathers.

The Hawaiians were a romantic lot. Instruments used for courting included the *ohe*, a nose flute made of bamboo, and the *ukeke*, a musical bow with a couple of strings.

Ancient Crafts

Tapa Weaving In ancient Hawaii, women spent much of their time beating *kapa* (tapa cloth) or preparing *lauhala* for weaving.

Tapa made from the wauke (paper mulberry tree) was the favourite. The bark was carefully stripped, then beaten with a stick. The beaters were carved with different patterns which then became the pattern of the tapa. Dyes were made from charcoal, flowers and sea urchins.

The missionaries befriended Hawaiian royalty and made their inroads quickly. After Queen Kaahumanu became seriously ill, Sybil Bingham nursed her back to health. Shortly after, Kaahumanu showed her gratitude by passing a law forbidding work and travel on the Sabbath.

Up until this time the Hawaiians had no written language. Using the Roman alphabet the missionaries established a written Hawaiian language that allowed them to translate the Bible. They taught the Hawaiians to read and write and established the first 'American' high school west of the Rocky Mountains.

With encouragement from the missionaries, the Hawaiians quickly took on Western ways, Western clothing and Western laws.

Liholiho (Kamehameha II)

With Kaahumanu holding the real power, in November 1823 a floundering Liholiho set sail for England with his favourite wife to pay a royal visit to King George – although he failed to inform anyone in England of his plans.

When Liholiho arrived unannounced in London, misfitted in Western clothing and lacking in royal etiquette, the British press roasted him with racist caricatures. He never met King George. While being prepped in the social graces for their audience with the king, Liholiho and his wife came down with measles. They died in England within a few weeks of each other, in July 1824.

The Whalers

Within a year of the missionaries' arrival, whalers began arriving in Hawaiian ports. The first were mostly New England Yankees and a sprinkling of Gay Head Indians and Black men. As more ships came on line, men of all nationalities roamed Hawaiian ports.

Tapa had many uses in addition to clothing, from food containers to burial shrouds. After the missionaries introduced cotton cloth and western clothing, the art of tapa making slowly faded away. These days most of the tapa for sale in Hawaii is from Samoa, with bold designs. Hawaiian tapa was different, with more delicate patterns.

Lauhala Weaving Lauhala weaving uses the lau (leaves) of the hala tree. Preparing the leaves for weaving is hard, messy work as there are razor-sharp spines along the leaf edges and down the centre.

In old Hawaii, lauhala was woven into mats and floor coverings, but these days smaller items like hats, placemats and baskets are most common.

Wooden Bowls The Hawaiians had no pottery and made their containers using either gourds or wood. Wooden food bowls were mostly of kou or milo, two native woods which didn't leave unpleasant tastes.

Hawaiian bowls were free of designs and carvings. Their beauty lay in the natural qualities of the wood and in the shape of the bowl alone. Cracked bowls were often expertly patched with dovetailed pieces of wood. Rather than decrease the value of the bowl, patching suggested heirloom status and such bowls were amongst the most highly prized.

Featherwork & Leis The Hawaiians were known for their elaborate featherwork. The most impressive were the capes worn by chiefs and kings. The longer the cape, the higher the rank. Those made of the yellow feathers of the now extinct *mamo* bird were the most highly prized.

The mamo was a predominately black bird with a yellow upper tail. Around 80,000 mamo birds were caught to create the cape that King Kamehameha wore. It's said that bird catchers would capture the birds, pluck the desired feathers and release them unharmed. Feathers were also used to make helmets and *leis* (garlands).

The *lei palaoa*, a Hawaiian necklace traditionally worn by royalty, is made of finely braided human hair hung with a smoothly carved whale tooth pendant shaped like a curved tongue. Before foreign whalers, arrived many of these pendants were made of bone. ■

Most were in their teens or twenties, ripe for adventure.

Towns sprung up with shopkeepers catering to the whalers, and saloons, brothels and hotels boomed. Honolulu and Lahaina became bustling ports of call.

From 1825 to 1870 Hawaii was the whaling centre of the Pacific. It was a convenient waystation for whalers hunting both the Arctic and Japanese whaling grounds. At its peak, between 500 and 600 whaling ships were pulling into Hawaiian ports each year.

Whaling brought big money to Hawaii and the dollars spread beyond the whaling towns. Many Maui farmers got their start supplying the whaling ships with potatoes; Big Island cattle ranches grew with the demand for beef; and even the average Hawaiian could earn a little money by turning in sailors who had jumped ship.

Hawaiians themselves made good whalers and sea captains gladly paid a $200 bond to the Hawaiian government for each 'kanaka' allowed to join their crew. Kamehameha IV even set up his own fleet of whaling ships which flew under the Hawaiian flag.

Whaling in the Pacific peaked in the mid-1800s and quickly began to burn itself out. In a few short years all but the most distant whaling grounds were being depleted and whalers were forced to go farther afield to make their kills. By 1860 whale oil prices were dropping as an emerging petroleum industry was beginning to produce a less expensive fuel for lighting.

The last straw for the Pacific whaling industry came in 1871 when an early storm in the Arctic caught more than 30 ships by surprise, trapping them in ice floes above the Bering Strait. Although over 1000 seamen were rescued, half of them Hawaiian, the fleet itself was lost.

Sugar Plantations

Ko, or sugar cane, arrived in Hawaii with the early Polynesian settlers. While the Hawaiians enjoyed chewing the cane for its juices, they never refined sugar.

The first known attempt to produce sugar in Hawaii was in 1802 when a Chinese immigrant in Lanai boiled crushed sugar cane in iron pots. Other Chinese soon set up small sugar mills on the scale of neighbourhood bakeries.

In 1835 a young Bostonian, William Hooper, saw a bigger opportunity in sugar and set out to establish Hawaii's first sugar plantation. Hooper convinced Honolulu investors Ladd & Company to put up the money for his venture and then worked out a deal with Kamehameha III to lease 980 acres of land on Kauai for $300. His next step was to negotiate with the alii for the right to use Hawaiian labourers.

In the mid-1830s Hawaii was still largely feudalistic. Commoners were tied into subsistence fishing and agriculture and worked when needed for the alii. Therefore before Hooper could hire any work hands, he had to first pay the alii a stipend to free the Hawaiians from their traditional work obligations.

The new plantation system, which introduced the concept of growing crops for profit rather than subsistence, marked the advent of capitalism and the introduction of wage labour in Hawaii.

The sugar industry emerged at the same time whalers began arriving in force. Together they formed the root of Hawaii's moneyed economy.

By the 1850s sugar plantations were established on Maui, Oahu and the Big Island, as well as Kauai.

Sugar cane, a giant grass, only flourishes with abundant water, so plantations were limited to the rainier parts of Hawaii and even then were vulnerable to drought. In 1856 an 11-mile irrigation ditch was dug to bring mountain water to Lihue cane fields which were suffering from drought. While this Kauai ditch was intended as a rescue procedure, its success signalled plantation owners to the possibilities for diverting water to irrigate heretofore unsuitable lands. In the 1870s the 17-mile Hamakua Ditch was dug on Maui, the first of several extensive aqueducts that would carry millions of gallons of water daily from upland rainforests to water-thirsty plantations. They turned dry central plains into drenched cane fields. Today Hawaii is still criss-crossed with hundreds of miles of working ditches and aqueducts built a century ago – as well as 160,000 acres of cane.

In addition to the irrigation systems, the sugar companies built flumes and railroads to carry the cane from the fields to the mills. For over 100 years, sugar was the backbone of the Hawaiian economy.

Hawaii's Immigrants

As the sugar industry was booming, Hawaii's native population was in decline, largely as the result of diseases introduced by foreigners.

To expand their operations, the plantation owners began to look overseas for a labour supply. They needed immigrants who would be accustomed to working long days in hot weather and for whom the low wages being paid would seem like an opportunity.

In 1852 the plantation owners began recruiting labourers from China. In 1868 they went to Japan and in the 1870s they brought in Portuguese from Madeira and the Azores. After Hawaii's annexation to the USA in 1898 resulted in restrictions on Chinese immigration, plantation owners turned to Puerto Ricans and Koreans. The Filipinos were the last group of immigrants brought in to work the fields; the first wave came in 1906, the last in 1946.

Although these six ethnic groups made up the bulk of the field hands, South Sea islanders, Scots, Scandinavians, Germans, Galicians, Spaniards and Russians all came in turn.

Each group brought its own culture, food and religion. Chinese clothing styles mixed with Japanese kimonos and European bonnets. A dozen languages filled the air and a unique pidgin English developed through people's need to communicate with one another.

Conditions varied with the ethnic group and the period. At the turn of the century Japanese contract labourers were being paid $15 a month. After annexation, the contracts were considered indentured servitude and

were declared illegal under US law. Still, wages as low as $1 a day were common up until the 1930s.

In all, approximately 350,000 immigrants came to Hawaii to work on the sugar plantations. A continuous flow of immigrant workers was required to replace those who invariably found better options elsewhere. Although some workers came for a set period to save money and return home, others worked out their contracts and then moved off the plantations to farm their own plots or start their own businesses.

Plantation towns like Koloa, Paia and Honokaa grew up around the mills, with barber shops, fish markets, beer halls and bathhouses catering to the workers.

Some of the major immigrant populations – Japanese, Chinese, Filipino and Western European – came to outnumber the native Hawaiians. Together they created the unique blend of cultures that would continue to characterise Hawaii for generations to come.

Kamehameha III

Kamehameha III, the last son of Kamehameha the Great, ruled for 30 years from 1825 to 1854. In 1840 he introduced Hawaii's first constitution, both to protect his powers and adjust to changing times. The constitution established Hawaii's first national legislature and provided for a Supreme Court.

Kamehameha III was also responsible for passing the Great Mahele land act, establishing religious freedom and giving all male citizens the right to vote.

Hawaii's only 'invasion' by a foreign power occurred during Kamehameha's reign. In 1843, George Paulet, an upstart British commander upset about a petty land deal involving a British subject, sailed into Honolulu commanding the British ship *Carysfort* and seized Oahu for six months. In that short period, he Anglicised street names, seized property and began to collect taxes.

To avoid bloodshed, Kamehameha III stood aside as the British flag was raised and the ship's band played 'God Save the Queen'. Queen Victoria herself wasn't flattered.

After catching wind of the incident, she dispatched Admiral Richard Thomas to restore Hawaiian independence. Admiral Thomas re-raised the Hawaiian flag at the site of what is today Honolulu's Thomas Square. As the flag was raised Kamehameha III uttered the words *Ua mau ke ea o ka aina i ka pono*, meaning 'The life of the land is perpetuated in righteousness', which remains Hawaii's motto.

The Great Mahele

The Great Mahele of 1848 changed Hawaiian concepts of land ownership, for the first time allowing land to become a commodity that could be bought and sold.

Through this act the king, who had previously owned all the land, gave up title to the majority of it. Island chiefs were allowed to purchase some of the lands which they had controlled as fiefdoms for the king. Other lands, which were divided into three-acre farm plots called *kuleana*, were made available to all Hawaiians. In order to retain title, chiefs and commoners alike had to pay a tax and register the land.

The chiefs had the option of paying the tax in property and many did so. Commoners had no choice but to pay the taxes in cash. Although the act was intended to turn Hawaii into a country of small farms, in the end only a few thousand Hawaiians carried through with the paperwork and received kuleanas.

In 1850 land purchases were opened to foreigners. Unlike the Hawaiians, the Westerners jumped at the opportunity and before the native islanders could clearly grasp the concept of private land ownership, there was little land left to own.

Within a few decades, the Westerners, who were more adept at wheeling and dealing in real estate, owned 80% of all privately held lands, with the bulk of it in huge estates. Even many of the Hawaiians who had gone through the process of getting their own kuleana eventually ended up selling it to the *haoles* (Whites).

Hawaiians who had grown taro for generations suddenly became a landless people, and drifted into ghettos in the larger towns.

Although commoners had no rights to the land prior to the Great Mahele, they were free to move around and work the property of any chief. In return for their personal use of the land they paid the chief in labour or with a percentage of their produce. In this way they lived off the land. After the Great Mahele, they were simply *off* the land.

Kamehameha IV

Kamehameha IV had a short and rather confusing reign that lasted from 1855 to 1863. He tried to give his rule an element of European regality, à la Queen Victoria, and he and his consort, Queen Emma, established a Hawaiian branch of the Anglican Church of England. He also passed a law mandating all children be given a Christian name along with their Hawaiian name. The law stayed on the books until 1967.

Struggles between those wanting to strengthen the monarchy and those wishing to limit it marked Kamehameha IV's reign.

Kamehameha V

Kamehameha V's (1863-1872) major accomplishment was the establishment of a controversial constitution that gave greater power to the king at the expense of elected officials. It also restricted the right to vote.

Kamehameha V, who suffered a severe bout of unrequited love, was the last king from a royal lineage that dated back to the 12th century. From childhood he was enraptured by Princess Bernice Pauahi who in the end turned down his proposals, opting instead to marry American Charles Bishop. Jolted by the rejection, Kamehameha V never married, yet he also never gave up on the princess. Even on his death bed he offered Princess Bernice his kingdom, which she declined.

As the bachelor king left no heirs, his death in December 1872 brought an end to the Kamehameha dynasty. Future kings would be elected.

Lunalilo

King Lunalilo (1873-1874) had a short reign. His cabinet, made up largely of Americans, was instrumental in paving the way for a treaty of reciprocity with the USA.

Although the USA was the biggest market for Hawaiian sugar, US sugar tariffs ate heavily into profit margins. As a means of eliminating the tariffs, most plantation owners favoured the annexation of Hawaii to the USA.

The US government was cool to the idea of annexation, but it warmed to the possibility of establishing a naval base on Oahu. In 1872 General John Schofield was sent to assess Pearl Harbor's strategic value. He was impressed with what he saw – the largest anchorage in the Pacific – and reported his enthusiasm back to Washington.

Although native Hawaiians protested in the streets and the Royal Troops even staged a little mutiny, there would eventually be a reciprocity agreement that would cede Pearl Harbor to the USA in exchange for duty-free access for Hawaiian sugar.

King Kalakaua

King David Kalakaua (1874-1891) was Hawaii's last king. Although known as the 'Merrie Monarch', he ruled in troubled times.

The first challenge to his reign came on election day. His contender had been the dowager Queen Emma and when the results were announced her followers rioted in the streets, requiring Kalakaua to request aid from American and British warships which happened to be in Honolulu Harbor at the time.

Despite the initial turmoil, Kalakaua went on to become a great Hawaiian revivalist. He brought back the *hula*, turning around decades of missionary repression against the 'heathen dance', and composed the national anthem *Hawaii Ponoi*, which is now the state song. He also tried to ensure some self-rule for native Hawaiians, now a minority in their own land.

When Kalakaua left for his first trip overseas, scores of Hawaiians came to the waterfront weeping. The last king to leave the islands, Kamehameha II, had come back in a coffin.

While in America, Kalakaua met with President Ulysses Grant and persuaded him to accept the reciprocity treaty which the US Congress had been resisting. Kalakaua even managed to postpone the ceding of Pearl Harbor for eight years. He returned to Hawaii a hero, to the business community for the treaty and to the Hawaiians for simply making it back alive.

The king became a world traveller, visiting India, Egypt, Europe and South-East Asia. Kalakaua was well aware that Hawaii's days as an independent Polynesian kingdom were numbered. To counter the Western powers that were gaining hold of Hawaii, he made a futile attempt to establish a Polynesian-Pacific empire. On a visit with the emperor of Japan, he even proposed a royal marriage between his niece Princess Kaiulani and a Japanese prince but the Japanese declined.

Visits with other foreign monarchs gave Kalakaua a taste for royal pageantry. He returned to build Iolani Palace for what the haole business community thought was an extravagant $360,000. He was a lavish spender who was fond of partying and throwing public luaus.

Kalakaua incurred big debts and became increasingly less popular with the sugar barons whose businesses were now the backbone of the economy. They formed the Hawaiian League in 1887 and developed their own armies which stood ready to overthrow Kalakaua. The league presented Kalakaua with a list of demands and forced him to accept a new constitution strictly limiting his powers. It also limited suffrage to property owners, which by then excluded the vast majority of Hawaiians.

On 30 July 1889 about 150 Hawaiians attempted to overthrow the new constitution by occupying Iolani Palace. Called the Wilcox Rebellion after its part-Hawaiian leader, it was a confused and futile attempt and the rebels were forced to surrender.

Kalakaua died in San Francisco in 1891.

Queen Liliuokalani

Kalakaua was succeeded by his sister,

Liliuokalani, wife of Oahu's governor John Dominis.

Queen Liliuokalani (1891-1893) was even more determined than Kalakaua to strengthen the power of the monarchy. She charged that the 1887 constitution had illegally been forced upon King Kalakaua. The Hawaii Supreme Court upheld her contention.

In January 1893, as Liliuokalani was about to proclaim a new constitution to restore royal powers, a group of armed haole businesspeople occupied the Supreme Court and declared the monarchy overthrown. They announced a provisional government, led by Sanford Dole, son of a pioneer missionary. Wanting to avoid bloodshed, the queen stepped down.

The provisional government immediately appealed to the USA for annexation, while the queen appealed to the USA to restore the monarchy. Timing was in the queen's favour. Democrat president Grover Cleveland had just replaced a Republican administration and his sentiments favoured the queen.

Cleveland sent an envoy, James Blount, to investigate and determine what course of action the US government should take.

In the meantime he received Queen Liliuokalani's niece, Princess Kaiulani, who, at the time of the coup, had been in London being prepared for the throne. The beautiful 18-year-old princess eloquently pleaded the monarchy's case. She also made a favourable impression with the American press which largely caricatured those involved in the annexation as dour, greedy buffoons.

Cleveland ordered the American flag be taken down and the queen restored to her throne. However the provisional government, now firmly in power, turned a deaf ear, declaring that Cleveland was meddling in 'Hawaiian' affairs.

The new government, with Dole as president, inaugurated itself as the Republic of Hawaii on 4 July 1894.

In early 1895 a group of Hawaiian royalists attempted a counter revolution that was easily squashed in a fortnight. Liliuokalani was accused of being a conspirator and placed under arrest.

To humiliate her, she was tried in her own palace and referred to only as Mrs John O Dominis. She was fined $5000 and sentenced to five years of hard labour, later reduced to nine months of house arrest at the palace.

Liliuokalani spent the rest of her life in her husband's residence, Washington Place, one block from the palace. When she died in November 1917, all of Honolulu came out for the funeral procession. To most islanders, Liliuokalani was still their queen.

Annexation

With the Spanish-American War of 1898, Americans suddenly acquired a taste for expansionism.

Not only was Hawaii gifted with Pearl Harbor, but it took on a new strategic importance being midway between the USA and its newly acquired possession, the Philippines. Annexation of Hawaii passed in the US Congress on 7 July 1898. Hawaii would enter the 20th century as a territory of the USA.

In just over a century of Western contact the native Hawaiian population had been decimated by foreign diseases to which they had no immunities. It began with the venereal disease introduced by Captain Cook's crew in 1778. The whalers followed with cholera and smallpox, and Chinese immigrants, who came to replace Hawaiian labourers, brought leprosy. By the end of the 19th century, the native Hawaiian population had been reduced from an estimated 300,000 to less than 50,000.

Descendants of the early missionaries had taken over first the land and now the government. Without ever having fought a single battle against a foreign power, Hawaiians had lost their islands to ambitious foreigners. All in all, as far as the native Hawaiians were concerned, the annexation wasn't anything to celebrate.

The Chinese and Japanese were also uneasy. One of the reasons for the initial reluctance of the US Congress to annex Hawaii had been the racial mix of the islands' population. There were already restrictions on Chinese immigration to America, and restrictions on Japanese seemed likely to follow.

In a rush to avoid a labour shortage the sugar plantation owners quickly brought 70,000 Japanese immigrants into Hawaii. By the time the immigration wave was over the Japanese accounted for over 40% of Hawaii's population.

In the years since the reciprocity agreement, sugar production had increased tenfold. Those who ruled the land ruled the government and closer bonding with the USA didn't change the formula. In 1900, US President McKinley appointed Sanford Dole the first territorial governor.

WW I

Soon after annexation, the US Navy set up a huge Pacific headquarters at Pearl Harbor and built Schofield Barracks, the largest US army base anywhere. The military quickly became the leading sector of Oahu's economy.

The islands were relatively untouched by WW I, even though the first German prisoners of war 'captured' by the USA were in Hawaii. They were escorted off the German gunboat *Grier* which had the misfortune to be docked at Honolulu Harbor when war broke out.

The war affected people in Hawaii in other ways. Heinrich Hackfeld, a German sea captain long settled in the islands, had established Hawaii's most successful merchandise stores, B F Ehler's and Company. He had also developed a real estate empire rooted in sugar, purchasing Lahaina's Pioneer Mill, among other properties. He lost it all during WW I.

Anti-German sentiments forced Hackfeld to liquidate his holdings and American Factors (Amfac) took over his properties, renaming the stores Liberty House.

Pineapple & Planes

In the early 1900s pineapple emerged as Hawaii's second major export crop. James Dole, a cousin of Sanford, purchased the island of Lanai in 1922 and turned it into the

world's largest pineapple plantation. Although sugar remained king in export value, the more labour-intensive pineapple eventually surpassed it in terms of employment.

In 1936 Pan American flew the first passenger flights from the US mainland to Hawaii, an aviation milestone which ushered in the transpacific air age. Hawaii was now only hours away from the West Coast.

WW II

On 7 December 1941 a wave of Japanese bombers attacked Pearl Harbor, jolting the USA into WW II. The attack caught the US fleet totally by surprise, even though there had been warnings, some of which were far from subtle.

At 6.40 am the USS *Ward* spotted a submarine conning tower approaching the entrance of Pearl Harbor. The *Ward* immediately attacked with depth charges and sank what turned out to be one of five midget Japanese submarines launched to penetrate the harbour.

At 7.02 am a radar station on the north shore of Oahu reported planes approaching. Even though they were coming from the wrong direction, they were assumed to be American planes from the mainland.

At 7.55 am Pearl Harbor was hit. Within minutes the USS *Arizona* went down in a fiery inferno, trapping 1177 men beneath the surface. Twenty other US ships were sunk or damaged, along with 347 aircraft. More than 2500 people were killed.

It wasn't until 15 minutes after the attack that American anti-aircraft guns began to shell Japanese planes. The Japanese lost 29 aircraft in the attack.

Hawaii was placed under martial law and Oahu took on the face of a military camp. Already heavily militarised, vast tracts of Hawaii's land were turned over to the US forces for expanded military bases, training and weapons testing. Much of that land would never be returned. Throughout the war, Oahu served as the command post for US Pacific operations.

Following the attack on Pearl Harbor a

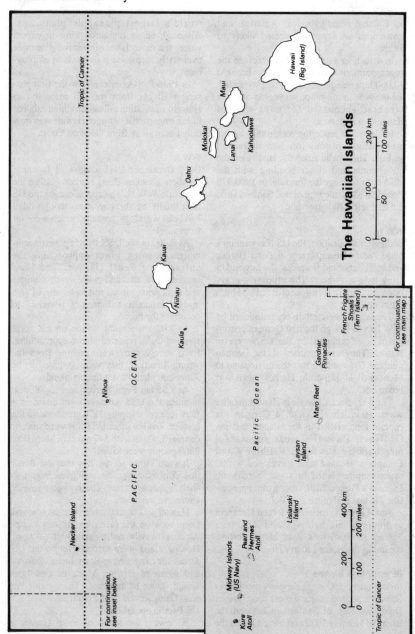

The Hawaiian Islands

For continuation, see inset below

For continuation, see main map

wave of suspicion landed on the *nisei* (people of Japanese descent) in Hawaii. While sheer numbers prevented the sort of internment practices that took place on the mainland, the Japanese in Hawaii were subject to interrogation and their religious and civic leaders were sent to mainland internment camps.

Japanese language schools were closed and many of the teachers arrested. Posters were hung in restaurants and other public places warning islanders to be careful about speaking carelessly in front of anyone of Japanese ancestry. Nisei were dismissed from posts in the Hawaiian National Guard and prevented from joining the armed services.

Eventually Japanese-Americans were allowed to volunteer for a segregated regiment, although they were kept on the mainland and out of action for much of the war.

During the final stages of the war, when fighting was at its heaviest, the nisei were given the chance to form a combat unit. Volunteers were called and more than 10,000 nisei signed up, forming two distinguished Japanese-American regiments. One of these, the 442nd Second Regimental Combat Team, which was sent into action on the European front, became the most decorated fighting unit in US history.

The veterans returned to Hawaii with different expectations. Many went on to college using the GI bill and today account for some of Hawaii's most influential lawyers. One of the veterans of the 442nd is Hawaii's senior US senator, Daniel Inouye, who lost an arm in the fighting.

Unionising Hawaii

The feisty mainland-based International Longshoremen's and Warehousemen's Union (ILWU) began organising Hawaiian labour in the 1930s.

After WW II, the ILWU organised an intensive campaign against the 'Big Five' – C Brewer, Castle & Cooke, Alexander & Baldwin, Theo Davies and Amfac – Hawaii's biggest businesses and landholders, all with roots in sugar.

The ILWU's six-month waterfront strike in 1949 virtually halted all shipments to and from Hawaii. The union went on to organise plantation strikes which resulted in Hawaii's sugar and pineapple workers becoming the world's highest paid.

The new union movement helped develop a political opposition to the staunchly Republican big landowners, who had maintained a stronghold on the political scene since annexation.

In the 1950s McCarthyism, the fanatical wave of anti-Communism which swept the mainland, spilled over to Hawaii. In the

---

The Creation Myth

The early Hawaiians were astutely tuned in to geological forces and knew the order in which the islands were created. Their creation story goes something like this:

Pele, the goddess of volcanoes and fire, was born of the marriage of earth and sky. She is both Creator and Destroyer (not unlike the Hindu god Shiva). Her eruptions of molten lava both build the mountains and wreak havoc over everything in their path.

Pele was driven from her home in the north-western shoals by a jealous older sister, Na Maka O Kahai, goddess of the seas. Pele fled to the south-east and built her home in a crater on Niihau, then on Kauai, then Oahu, and each island in turn. Each time she dug down into the fiery earth deeper than the time before, and each time she was chased away by her sister, the sea.

After being routed from her home on Haleakala on Maui, Pele crossed over to the Big Island. There she built her highest mountains yet and in their volcanic recesses made a home far from the reaches of Na Maka O Kahai.

The sea goddess, however, is still never far from Pele's doorstep. She persistently wears away at Pele's home, her waves taking on the lava, eroding it down and crushing it into sand.

In time Pele will again be forced to move on, but for now she makes her home deep in Kilauea, the most active volcano on earth. ∎

fallout, the leader of the ILWU in Hawaii, Jack Hall, was tried and convicted of being a Communist.

Post-War Hawaii

WW II brought Hawaii closer to the centre stage of American culture and politics.

The prospect of statehood had long been the central topic in Hawaiian political circles. Three decades has passed since Hawaii's first delegate to the US Congress, Prince Jonah Kuhio Kalanianaole, introduced the first statehood bill in 1919. It had received a cool reception in Washington at that time and there were mixed feelings in Hawaii as well. However by the time the war was over, opinion polls showed that two out of three Hawaiian residents favoured statehood.

Still, Hawaii was too much of a melting pot for many politicians to support statehood, particularly those from the segregated southern states. To the overwhelmingly White and largely conservative Congress, Hawaii's multiethnic community was too exotic and foreign to be thought of as American.

Congress was also concerned with the success of Hawaiian labour strikes and the growth of membership in the ILWU. It all combined to keep statehood at bay until the end of the 1950s.

Statehood

In March 1959, the US Congress finally passed legislation to make Hawaii a state. On 27 June a plebiscite was held in Hawaii, with more than 90% of the islanders voting for statehood. The island of Niihau was the only precinct to vote against it.

On 21 August 1959, after 61 years of territorial status, Hawaii became the 50th state of the USA.

GEOLOGY

The Hawaiian Islands are the tips of massive mountains, created by a crack in the earth's mantle which has been spewing out molten rock for 25 million years. The hot spot is stationary, but the ocean floor is part of the Pacific Plate which is moving north-west at the rate of about three inches a year. (The eastern edge of this plate is California's San Andreas fault.)

As weak spots in the earth's crust pass over the hot spot, molten lava bursts through as volcanoes, building underwater mountains. Some of them finally emerge above the water as islands.

Each new volcano eventually creeps northward past the hot spot which created it. The farther from the source, the lower the volcanic activity, until the volcano is eventually cut off completely and turns cold.

Once the lava stops it's a downhill battle. The forces of erosion – wind, rain and waves – slowly wash the mountains away. In addition, the settling of the ocean floor causes the land to gradually recede.

Thus the once mountainous Northwestern Hawaiian Islands, the oldest in the Hawaiian chain, are now low flat atolls that in time will be totally submerged.

The Big Island, Hawaii's southernmost island, is still in the birthing process. Its most active volcano, Kilauea, is directly over the hot spot. In its latest eruptive phase, which began in 1983 and still continues, Kilauea has pumped out more than two billion cubic yards of lava, making this the largest known volcanic eruption in Hawaii's history.

Less than 30 miles south-east of the Big Island, a new seamount named Loihi has already built up 15,000 feet on the ocean floor. The growing mounds of lava are expected to break the ocean surface within 10,000 years – however if it were to get hyperactive, it could emerge within a century or two.

In 1987 the Woods Hole Oceanographic Institution explored Loihi with *Alvin*, the same deepwater mini-sub that had discovered the *Titanic* wreck the year before. They measured Loihi's summit to be 3117 feet below the surface of the water.

Hawaii's volcanoes are shield volcanoes which form not by explosion but by a slow build-up of layer upon layer of lava. They rise from the sea with gentle slopes and a relatively smooth surface. It's only after eons of facing the elements that their surfaces become sharply eroded. It's for this reason that the Na Pali cliffs on Kauai, the oldest of the main islands, are the most jagged in Hawaii.

Hawaii's active volcanoes are Kilauea and Mauna Loa, both on the Big Island. The Big Island's Mauna Kea and Hualalei and Maui's Haleakala are dormant, with future eruptions possible. The volcanoes on all the other Hawaiian islands are considered extinct.

GEOGRAPHY

The Hawaiian Islands stretch 1523 miles in a line from Kure Atoll in the north-west to the Big Island in the south-east. Ka Lae, on the Big Island, is the southernmost point of the USA.

The equator is 1470 miles south of Honolulu and all the main islands are in the tropic of Cancer. Hawaii shares the same latitude as Hong Kong, Bombay and Mexico's Yucatan Peninsula.

Hawaii's eight major islands are, from largest to smallest, Hawaii (the Big Island), Maui, Oahu, Kauai, Molokai, Lanai, Niihau and Kahoolawe. They have a total land area of 6470 sq miles, which includes 96 small offshore islands with a combined area of less than three sq miles.

The Northwestern Hawaiian Islands lie scattered across a thousand miles of ocean west of Kauai. They consist of 28 islands in nine clusters with a total land area of just under three sq miles.

The Midway Islands, geographically in the Hawaiian archipelago but politically not part of the state of Hawaii, are not included in these figures.

In total, Hawaii is a bit smaller than Fiji and a bit larger than the US state of Connecticut.

Hawaii's highest mountain is Mauna Kea on the Big Island, which is 13,796 feet above sea level. According to the *Guinness Book of Records* it's the world's highest mountain (33,476 feet) when measured from the ocean floor. Mauna Loa, also on the Big Island, is Hawaii's second highest mountain, at 13,679 feet.

CLIMATE

Overall, Hawaii has great weather. It's balmy and warm, with northeasterly trade winds prevailing most of the year.

Average temperatures differ only about 7°F from winter to summer. Near the coast daily temperatures average a high of about 83°F and a low of around 68°F.

The rainiest time of the year is from December to March. Apart from the fact that winter has about twice the rainfall of summer, winter storms can also hang around for days. In summer the rain is more likely to fall as passing showers. This doesn't mean winter is a bad time to go to Hawaii, it just means the weather is more of a gamble.

Rainfall varies even more with location than with season. In places like Kailua-Kona, on the Big Island, you can sunbathe on the beach for all but a few days a year. At the same time you can watch typical afternoon showers pour on the hill slopes just a mile or two inland and know you're well beyond reach.

Hawaii's high volcanic mountains trap the trade winds that blow from the north-east, blocking their moisture-laden clouds and bringing abundant rainfall to the windward side of the islands. Hilo, the rainiest city in the USA with 130 inches annually, is on the windward side of the Big Island.

Conversely, the same mountains block the wind and rain from the southwesterly, or leeward side of the islands, so it's there you'll find the driest, sunniest conditions and the calmest waters. Leeward areas generally receive only 10 to 25 inches of rain a year.

During kona weather the winds blow from the south, a shift from the typical north-east trades. The ocean swell pattern also changes – dive spots suddenly become surfing spots and vice versa. Kona storms usually occur in winter and are very unpredictable.

The summits of Mauna Kea and Mauna Loa on the Big Island receive snow each winter and on some years Haleakala on Maui catches a short-lived snow cover as well. The lowest temperature ever recorded on Mauna Kea, Hawaii's coldest spot, was 11°F, while the highest temperature there was 66°F.

Temperature & Rainfall Charts

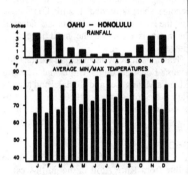

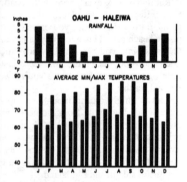

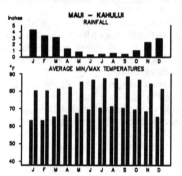

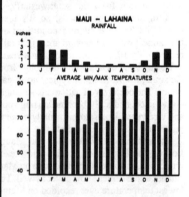

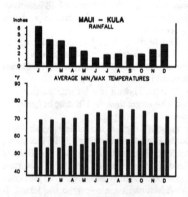

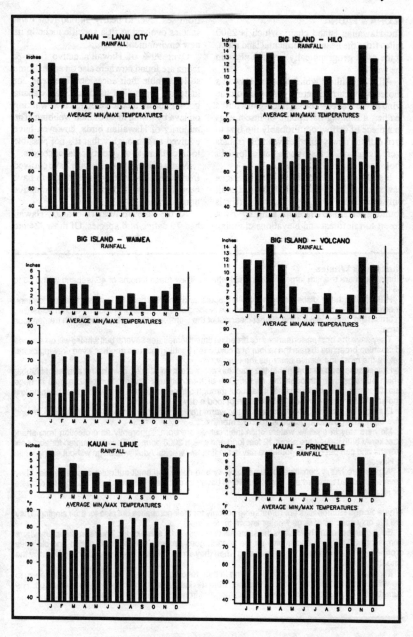

FLORA & FAUNA

The Hawaiian island chain, which is 2500 miles from the nearest continental land mass, is the most geographically isolated place in the world.

All living things which reached Hawaii's shores were carried across the ocean on the wind or the waves – seeds clinging to a bird's feather, a floating hala plant, or insect eggs in a piece of driftwood. Probably the first to arrive on the newly emerged volcanic islands were fern and moss spores, able to drift thousands of miles in the air.

It's estimated that before human contact a new species managed to take hold in Hawaii only once every 100,000 years. New arrivals found specialised habitats ranging from desert to rainforest and elevations climbing from sea level to nearly 14,000 feet. Each species evolved to fit a specific niche in its new environment.

Over 90% of Hawaii's native flora & fauna are found nowhere else on earth. Some still resemble their ancestors. The *nene*, for instance, looks like its cousin the Canada goose, but its feet have adapted to walking on lava by losing most of their webbing. The majority of Hawaiian birds, however, have evolved so thoroughly that it's not possible to trace them to any continental ancestors.

Many of Hawaii's birds may have evolved from a single species, as is thought to have been the case with over 30 species of native honeycreeper.

At the time of Western contact, Hawaii had 70 native bird species. Of those, 24 are

Humpback Whales

Humpbacks are the fifth largest of the great whales. They reach lengths of 45 feet and weigh 40 to 45 tons.

Humpbacks have distinctive long white flippers and knobby heads. They're great performers, known for their acrobatic displays which include arching dives, lobtailing, breaching and fin splashing. In breaching, humpbacks jump almost clear out of the water and then splash down with tremendous force.

They save the best performances for breeding time. Sometimes several bull whales will do a series of crashing breaches to gain the favour of a cow, often bashing into one another, even drawing blood, before the most impressive emerges the winner.

Humpbacks feed all summer in the plankton-rich waters off Alaska, developing a layer of blubber which sustains them through the winter. One of the toothless whales, humpbacks gulp in huge quantities of water and then strain it back out through a filter-like baleen in their mouths, trapping krill and small fish. They can eat close to a ton of food a day.

During their romantic winter sojourn in the warm tropical waters off Hawaii, humpbacks mate and give birth. The gestation period is 10 to 12 months.

Mothers stay in shallow waters once their calves are born, apparently as protection from shark attacks. At birth calves are about 12 feet long and weigh 3000 pounds. They are nursed for about six months and can put on 100 pounds a day in the first few weeks. Adult whales go without eating while in Hawaii.

Whales are highly sensitive to human activity and noise and seek out quiet coastal areas. They have abandoned areas where human activities have picked up and seem to have a particular distaste for jet skis.

Whale Songs Humpbacks are remarkable not only for their acrobatics but also for their singing. They are the only species of large whales known to do either.

Each member of the herd sings the same set of songs, in the same order. Their songs last anywhere from six to 30 minutes and evolve as the season goes on, with new phrases added and old ones dropped, so that the songs the whales sing when they arrive in Hawaii become different songs by the time they leave.

It's thought that the humpbacks don't sing in their feeding grounds in Alaska. When they return to Hawaii six months later they recall the songs from the last season and begin where they left off. The humpback's complex songs include the full range of frequncies audible to the human ear. ■

now extinct and an additional 36 are threatened with extinction.

Having evolved with limited competition and few predators, Hawaii's native species generally fare poorly amongst more aggressive introduced flora & fauna. They are also highly sensitive to habitat destruction.

When the first Polynesian settlers arrived, they weren't travelling light. They brought food and medicinal plants, chickens, dogs and pigs.

The pace of introducing exotic species escalated with the arrival of Westerners, starting with Captain Cook who dropped off goats and left some melon and pumpkin seeds. The next Western visitors left cattle and horses.

Prior to human contact, Hawaii had no land mammals at all except for monk seals and hoary bats. The introduction of free-ranging pigs, cattle and goats, who grazed and foraged at will, devastated Hawaii's fragile ecosystems and spelled extinction for many plants. Released songbirds and gamebirds spread avian diseases to which native Hawaiian birds had no immunity. Erosion, deforestation and thousands of introduced plants which compete with and choke out native vegetation have all taken their toll.

Today more than 25% of all endangered species in the USA are Hawaiian plants and animals. Of approximately 2400 different native plants, half are either threatened or endangered.

Hawaiian Monk Seal

The Hawaiian monk seal, so named for the cowl-like fold of skin at its neck and for its solitary habits, exists only in Hawaii. The species has remained nearly unchanged for 15 million years but is now in danger of dying out completely. Only about 1000 remain.

Hawaiian monk seals, which are sensitive to human disruption, breed and give birth primarily in the Northwestern Hawaiian Islands. In recent years, however, sightings of seals hauling themselves onto Kauai's beaches have increased.

Of the world's two other monk seal species, the Caribbean monk seal is already extinct and the Mediterranean monk seal numbers only in the hundreds.

Whales

Whales, the largest of the marine cetaceans, are air breathing, warm blooded, placental mammals that lactate and nurse their young. Basically there are two types: toothed whales, which use their teeth to catch and rip apart their prey; and baleen whales, which have rows of a horny elastic material, called baleen or whalebone, that hangs from the upper jaw and acts as a filter to extract food from the water.

Several types of whales frequent Hawaiian waters, although it is the migrating humpback that everyone wants to see. Luckily for whale watchers, humpback whales are coast-huggers, preferring waters with depths of less than 600 feet. Other migratory whales that pass by the islands on occasion include the fin whale, minke whale and right whale. All are baleen whales.

Hawaii's year-round resident whales, which are all toothed whales, include the sperm whale, false killer whale, pigmy killer whale, beaked whale, melon-head whale and, most common of all, the pilot whale. The latter is a small whale which often travels in large pods and, like most whales, prefers deep offshore waters.

Curiously, the early Hawaiians seem to have paid little attention to whales. They are not found in petroglyph drawings and there are virtually no legends about whales.

Humpback Whales Humpbacks, once one of the most abundant of the great whales, were hunted almost to extinction and are now an endangered species. Around the turn of the century an estimated 15,000 humpbacks remained. They were still being hunted as late as 1966 when the International Whaling Commission enforced a ban on their slaughter.

The entire population of North Pacific humpbacks is now thought to be about 2000.

More than half of those winter in Hawaii, while most of the others migrate to Mexico.

Humpbacks don't arrive in Hawaii en masse, but start filtering in around November. They can be found throughout the islands, although their most popular wintering spot is the shallow waters between Maui, Lanai, Molokai and Kahoolawe. The Kona Coast of the Big Island is another favoured spot, as is the Penguin Bank west of Molokai.

Humpbacks are protected by US federal law under the Marine Mammal Protection Act and the Endangered Species Act. Approaching within 100 yards of a humpback (300 yards in cow/calf waters) is prohibited and can result in a $25,000 fine. The rules apply to everyone, including boaters, jet skiers, swimmers and surfers, and are strictly enforced.

The humpback whale has been designated Hawaii's official marine mammal.

Dolphins

Dolphins, which are also marine cetaceans, are common to Hawaii. Spinner, bottlenose, slender-beaked, spotted, striped and rough-toothed varieties are all found in Hawaiian waters.

Dolphins are nocturnal feeders who often come into calm bays during the day to rest. Although it may seem tempting to swim out and join them, approaching the dolphins apparently can cause them to leave the bay prematurely, as well as subject swimmers to a hefty fine under the Marine Mammal Protection Act. This is a current controversy in Hawaii, as swimmers who claim that dolphins enjoy playing in the surf with humans are at odds against federal officials bent on enforcing laws against the harassment of marine mammals.

Incidentally, the *mahimahi* or 'dolphin' that you may come across on menus in Hawaii is not the mammal but a fish.

Environmental Groups

Sierra Club Legal Defense Fund The Sierra Club Legal Defense Fund is in the forefront pressing legal challenges against abuses to Hawaii's fragile environment.

In conjunction with Greenpeace, they've forced the state of Hawaii to prohibit jet skis in waters used by endangered humpback whales. On behalf of several environmental groups, including Greenpeace, the SCLDF has filed legal challenges to halt the Puna geothermal energy project on the Big Island, an ill-conceived undertaking that threatens one of Hawaii's last remaining lowland rainforests. One successful suit has enjoined all federal funding for the geothermal project until an environmental impact statement is carried out and a second suit now pending may force state funding to be withdrawn as well.

In another challenge, SCLDF took on the National Rifle Association and the state to force the removal of introduced mouflon game sheep from the slopes of Mauna Kea on the Big Island. The sheep were found to be the primary cause for the decline of a small, native honeycreeper called the *palila*.

It was the first time that habitat destruction was successfully defined as the 'taking' (meaning killing, harming or harassing) of an endangered species under the US Endangered Species Act. The State Department of Land & Natural Resources spent a bundle to fight the Sierra Club tooth and nail but finally lost after 10 years of legal action. The sheep have now been removed and the numbers of palila appear to be increasing. If you want to learn more about their present struggles, the Sierra Club Legal Defense Fund's Mid-Pacific office (☎ 599-2436) is at 212 Merchant St, Suite 202, Honolulu, HI 96813.

Nature Conservancy The Nature Conservancy of Hawaii is protecting Hawaii's rarest ecosystems by buying up vast tracts of land and working out long-term stewardships with some of Hawaii's biggest landholders.

One project included purchasing the Kipahulu Valley on Maui in conjunction with the state and turning the 11,000 acres over to the federal government to become part of Haleakala National Park. The Oheo Pools south of Hana are part of this land.

On Molokai the Nature Conservancy manages the rainforest at Kamakou and Pelekunu Valley on the island's wet northeast coast and the windswept Moomomi dunes on the dry north-west coast.

They also manage a crater above Hanauma Bay on Oahu, the Waikamoi rainforest on Maui, a native dryland forest in Lanai and a Kauai nesting site for the *ao* (Newell's shearwater), a threatened species once thought extinct.

For more information on guided hikes into Nature Conservancy preserves or to find out more about their projects contact the Nature Conservancy of Hawaii (☎ 537-4508), 1116 Smith St, Honolulu, HI 96817.

Na Ala Hele Of special interest to hikers and naturalists is the work of Na Ala Hele, a group affiliated with Hawaii's Department of Land & Natural Resources. Na Ala Hele was established in 1988 with the task of documenting public access to trails as part of a movement to preserve Hawaii's natural environment and cultural heritage. Na Ala Hele is comprised largely of volunteers, from trail workers to lawyers, who are trying to reestablish abandoned trails, some of which now run over private property. To gain the cooperation of landowners who are concerned with being sued should someone be injured crossing their property, legislation was introduced that shifts such liability to the state.

Na Ala Hele is now working on demonstration trails on each island, the most ambitious of which is a shoreline trail along a 35-mile stretch of the leeward coast of the Big Island. The group publishes a quarterly newsletter on the progress of their emerging trails. For more information write: Na Ala Hele, Department of Land & Natural Resources, 1151 Punchbowl St, Honolulu, HI 96813.

Other Environmental Groups There are over 150 environmental groups in Hawaii, ranging from chapters of international organisations fighting to save the rainforest to neighbourhood groups working to protect local beaches from impending development.

One of the broadest based is the Hawaii chapter of the Sierra Club, which has groups on all the main islands. Its activities range from political activism on local environmental issues to outings to eradicate invasive plants from native forests. The Sierra Club also maintains trails and leads guided hikes. For further information, see the individual island chapters.

Another active environmental group with scheduled outings is the Hawaii Audubon Society. For a calendar of upcoming field trips, most of which take place on Oahu, write to: Hawaii Audubon Society, 212 Merchant St, Room 320, Honolulu, HI 96813.

GOVERNMENT

Hawaii has three levels of government: federal, state and county. The seat of state government is in Honolulu.

Hawaii has a typical state government with executive power vested in the governor. The current governor, John Waihee, is Hawaii's first governor of Hawaiian ancestry. He is a Democrat and was reelected to a second four-year term in 1990.

The state's lawmaking body is a bicameral legislature. The Senate is comprised of 25 members, elected for four-year terms from the state's 25 senatorial districts. The House of Representatives has 51 members, each elected for a two-year term.

The legislature has a typical Hawaiian casualness. The regular legislative session, which convenes on the third Wednesday of January, meets for only 60 days a year. Special sessions of up to 30 days can be convened by the governor, but otherwise that's it.

Hawaii is the only US state to have a public education system run by the state, rather than county or town education boards. Education accounts for approximately one-third of the state budget. Hawaii is divided into four county governments, but unlike the mainland states, it has no municipal government. The city of Honolulu is part of Honolulu County which governs all of Oahu;

Hawaii County governs the Big Island; Kauai County governs Kauai and Niihau; and Maui County governs Maui, Molokai and Lanai.

While the leprosy colony of Kalaupapa on Molokai is called the 'county' of Kalawao, in actuality it has no county government and is under the jurisdiction of the Hawaii State Department of Health.

Each county has a mayor and county council. The counties provide services, such as police and fire protection, that on the mainland are usually assigned to cities. Development issues are usually decided at county level and are the central issue of most mayoral elections.

ECONOMY

Tourism is Hawaii's largest industry and accounts for about one-third of the state's income. Hawaii gets about seven million visitors a year. In total they spend almost $10 billion in the state, but not all at the same rate. In 1991, the 4.5 million visiting Americans spent an average of $137 a day, while the 1.5 million Japanese averaged $294 a day.

The second largest sector in the economy is the US military, pumping out $2.5 billion annually. Agriculture is a distant third.

Sugar and pineapple, which once formed the base of Hawaii's economy, are rapidly losing ground. Together in 1991 they accounted for $300 million in sales. Meanwhile diversified crops, defined as all crops except sugar and pineapple, have increased two-fold over the past decade and have a combined sales value of almost $200 million. Of this, Hawaii's 700 farms and nurseries sold $70 million in flowers, while macadamia nuts brought in another $41 million. Other sizeable crops included vegetables ($38 million), fruits ($25 million), and coffee and seed corn ($7 million each).

Not all of Hawaii's agricultural endeavours are legal. An estimated $5 billion worth of marijuana was confiscated in island police raids in 1991. While the police figures are based on an inflated street value that is higher than the price of gold, by almost anyone's estimate *pakalolo* (marijuana) is still the biggest cash crop on the islands.

Hawaii is moving to diversify its economy and one direction it's heading is into the area of high technology. The state is in the forefront of renewable energy research, including ocean thermal energy conversion. It's also home to some of the world's most powerful and sophisticated astronomy observatories. Aquaculture is another rapidly developing industry, and includes the raising of nori, freshwater prawns, 'Maine' lobsters and spirulina.

Hawaii's former agribusiness-based economy is in the midst of change. Hawaii's 'Big Five' companies – Amfac, Castle & Cooke, C Brewer, Theo Davies and Alexander & Baldwin – all had their origins in sugar, which is on the decline. The Big Five hold on to their plantations not so much for what's being produced on them, but for the potential they hold as future golf courses and condo developments – and bit by bit they're being sold off for those purposes.

Throughout the 1980s the islands underwent a major building boom, largely in resort developments and new subdivisions of exclusive housing. The boom was so rapid that island governments are still trying to catch up with it. Many regions that saw their populations nearly double now suffer from insufficiencies in basic infrastructure, including water supplies, hospitals and schools. While economic downturns in Japan and the US mainland have at least temporarily stalled the boom, the number of proposed construction projects remains staggering. In the long run, the construction crane, often said in jest to be Hawaii's state bird, doesn't appear to be endangered.

The cost of living is almost 20% higher in Honolulu than in the average US mainland city, while wages are 9% lower. For those stuck in service jobs, the most rapidly growing sector of the economy, it's tough to get by.

Native Hawaiians have the lowest median family income in Hawaii and are at the bottom of most health and welfare indicators, including high school drop-out rates, suicide rates and tragic death and major disease statistics. They also make up a disproportionately high percentage of the homeless who live out of their cars at a number of county beaches, particularly on Oahu.

Hawaiian Home Lands

In 1920, under the sponsorship of Prince Jonah Kuhio Kalanianaole, who was the Territory of Hawaii's congressional delegate, the US Congress passed the Hawaiian Homes Commission Act. The act set aside almost 200,000 acres of land for homesteading by native Hawaiians, who were by this time the most landless ethnic group in Hawaii. The land was but a fraction of the 1¾ million acres of government and crown lands that was taken from the Kingdom of Hawaii when the USA annexed the islands in 1898.

Under the legislation, people of at least 50% Hawaiian ancestry were eligible to apply for 99-year leases at $1 a year. Originally most of the leases were for 40-acre parcels of agricultural land, although more recently residential lots as small as a quarter of an acre have been allocated.

Hawaii's prime land, already in the hands of the sugar barons, was excluded from the act. Much of what was designated for homesteading was on far more barren turf.

Indeed, the first homesteading village, at Kalanianaole on Molokai, failed when the wells drew brackish waters and destroyed the newly established crops. Still many Hawaiians were able to make a go of it, settling homesteads on Oahu, the Big Island, Kauai, Maui and Molokai. Presently there are about 5000 native Hawaiian families living on 25,000 acres of homestead lands.

Like many acts established to help native Hawaiians, administration of the Hawaiian Home Lands has been riddled with abuse. The majority of the land has not been allocated to native Hawaiians but has been leased out to big business, ostensibly as a means of creating an income for the administration of the programme.

Parker Ranch on the Big Island has 32,845 acres of Hawaiian Home Lands under lease at $3.79 an acre. Kekaha Sugar, an Amfac subsidiary, leases the lion's share of Kauai's 18,569 acres of Hawaiian Home Lands, while less than 5% is leased to native Hawaiians.

In addition the federal, state and county governments have illegally, and with little or no compensation, taken large tracts of Hawaiian Home Lands for their own use. The Lualualei Naval Reservation alone constitutes one-fifth of all homestead lands on Oahu, where over 5000 native Hawaiians remain on the waiting list – some for as many as 30 years.

The mismanagement of the Hawaiian Home Lands has become a rallying issue for a number of native Hawaiian groups. One of the fastest growing, Ka Lahui Hawaii, has adopted a constitution for a Hawaiian nation within the USA, similar to that of Native Americans on the mainland who have their own tribal governments and lands. They want all the Hawaiian Home Lands, as well as the title to much of the crown land taken during annexation, turned over to native Hawaiians.

Most other native Hawaiian groups are now calling for some degree of self determination, as well as monetary reparations and an apology for the role the US government played in the overthrow of the monarchy.

Although the US Congress has shown a willingness to examine the issues, the Bush administration has taken a hardline position. In 1992 the US Justice Department declared that native Hawaiians do not have the same legal standing as Native Americans on the mainland and further argued that the very funding of programmes targeted solely for native Hawaiians should be considered an illegal and discriminatory benefit.

'Agricultural' Golf Courses

In the late 1980s the state passed a controversial bill that allowed golf courses to be built on agriculture-zoned land.

This bill led to the gobbling up of major tracts of farm land by Japanese developers and the eviction of small leasehold farmers.

Hawaii is one of the few Pacific island chains where island-grown produce has been relatively abundant and the continued eviction of farmers who have been growing crops on the land for generations will no doubt make the islands more reliant on imported foods. One of the slogans of the resistance movement is: 'No can eat golf balls'.

Currently the state has 65 golf courses, but the proposed courses on the drawing board could more than double that number in the next few years. On the Big Island's Kona Coast alone, plans are in the works for a dozen new golf courses, including one on the cliffs above Kealakekua Bay that threatens to leach chemicals into the bay, which is not only a rare Marine Life Conservation District but one of the finest snorkelling spots in Hawaii.

Not surprisingly, attempts to control the development of new golf courses is one of the forefront issues confronted by environmentalists on the islands.

The Military Presence
Hawaii is the most militarised state in the nation.

In total, the military has a grip on 265,000 acres of Hawaiian land. The greatest holding is on Oahu, where 25% of the island is controlled by the armed forces and where there are more than 100 installations, from ridgetop radar stations to Waikiki's Fort DeRussy Beach.

Oahu is the hub of the Pacific Command which directs military activities from the west coast of the USA to the east coast of Africa. The navy, which accounts for 40% of Hawaii's military presence, is centred at Pearl Harbor, home of the Pacific Fleet.

Despite the sudden ending of the Cold War the military still spends $2.5 billion annually in the state. It pays out $500 million in contracted services and employs 19,000 civilians directly. There are 54,000 military personnel and an additional 63,000 military dependants living on the islands.

Hawaii's politicians, while otherwise liberal-leaning, generally embrace the military presence. The Chamber of Commerce of

Hawaii even has a special military affairs council that lobbies in Washington DC to draw still more military activity to Hawaii.

About 3000 nuclear weapons, some 10% of the US nuclear arsenal, are stockpiled in Oahu. Pearl Harbor has the most, while other nuclear weapons are based at Barbers Point navy base, Schofield Barracks army base and the Kaneohe Marine Corps Air Station.

POPULATION & PEOPLE
In the 1990 US census the population of Hawaii was calculated at 1,108,229. That figure included military personnel stationed on the islands but did not include the 140,000 visitors in Hawaii on an average day.

The state's population is relatively young, with a median age of 31. There is no ethnic majority in Hawaii: everyone belongs to a minority.

Hawaii's people are known for their racial harmony. Race is generally not a factor in marriage. Islanders have a 50/50 chance of marrying someone of a race different than their own and the majority of children born in Hawaii are *hapa*, or mixed blood. The result has been a unique rainbow of people and Hawaii has some of the most beautiful children anywhere.

In Hawaii, 32% of the population claims 'mixed ethnicity', with a majority of those having some Hawaiian blood.

As for the rest, haoles (Caucasians) and Japanese each account for approximately 22% of the population, followed by Filipinos (12%), Chinese (5%), Blacks, Koreans, Samoans and Puerto Ricans. There are 9400 full-blooded Hawaiians, less than 1% of the population.

For the island breakdown, 836,231 people live on Oahu, 120,317 on the Big Island, 91,361 on Maui, 50,947 on Kauai, 6717 on Molokai, 2426 on Lanai, and 230 on Niihau.

ARTS
Hula
Hula *halaus* (schools) have experienced an influx of new students in recent years. Some practice in public places, such as school grounds and parks, where visitors are

welcome to watch. Although many of the halaus rely on tuition fees, others receive sponsorship from hotels and shopping centres and give weekly public performances in return.

There are also numerous island-wide hula competitions; two of the biggest are the Prince Lot Hula Festival held each July in Oahu and the week-long Merrie Monarch Festival which begins on Easter Sunday in Hilo.

Music

Contemporary Hawaiian music gives centre stage to the guitar, most prominently the steel guitar, an instrument designed in 1889 by Joseph Kekuku, a native Hawaiian. The steel guitar is one of only two major musical instruments invented in what is now the USA. (The other is the banjo.) The steel guitar is usually played with slack key tunings and carries the melody throughout the song.

The ukulele, so strongly identified with Hawaiian music, was actually derived from a Portuguese instrument introduced to Hawaii in the 1800s. The word 'ukulele' is Hawaiian for 'jumping flea'.

Both the ukulele and the steel guitar were essential to the light-hearted, romantic music popularised in Hawaii from the 1930s to the 1950s. *My Little Grass Shack, Lovely Hula Hands* and *Sweet Leilani* are classic examples. Due in part to the 'Hawaii Calls' radio show, which for more than 30 years was broadcast worldwide from the Moana Hotel in Waikiki, this music became instantly recognisable as Hawaiian, conjuring up images of beautiful hula dancers swaying under palm trees in a tropical paradise.

Hawaii has many renowned slack-key guitar players, including Raymond Kane, Peter Moon, Sonny Chillingworth and Atta Isaacs Jr. If you want to pick up a recording, consider the classic *Hiilawe* by the late Gabby Pahinui, one of the true virtuosos.

The hottest new sound in Hawaii today is Jawaiian, a blending of Hawaiian music and Jamaican reggae. Top Jawaiian musicians include Bruddah Walta, Willie K, Brother

Noland, Kapena and Manao Company. Other popular contemporary Hawaiian musicians include vocalist Henry Kapono; the innovative Peter Moon Band; the rock band Kalapana; and Jerry Santos and Olomana, who blend Hawaiian and folk. For a more traditional Hawaiian sound, there's Makaha Sons of Niihau and the Brothers Cazimero.

Art

Many artists draw inspiration from Hawaii's rich cultural heritage and natural beauty.

Well-known Hawaiian painter Herb Kawainui Kane creates detailed oil paintings focusing on the early Polynesian settlers and King Kamehameha's life. His works are mainly on display in museums and at gallery collections in resorts.

Rocky Kaiouliokahihikoloehu Jensen does wood sculptures and drawings of Hawaiian gods, ancient chiefs and early Hawaiians with the aim of creating sacred art in the tradition of *makaku*, or 'creative artistic mana'. Jensen is the director of Hale Naua III, the Society of Hawaiian Artists.

Pegge Hopper paints traditional Hawaiian women in relaxed poses using a distinctive graphic design style and bright washes of colour. Her work has been widely reproduced on posters and postcards.

Some of Hawaii's most impressive crafts are ceramics, bowls made of native woods and baskets woven of native fibres. The goddess Pele is a source of inspiration for many Big Island artists – some even use molten lava as a sculpting material. Hawaiian quilting is another unique art form.

CULTURE

In many ways, contemporary culture in Hawaii resembles contemporary culture in the rest of the USA.

Hawaiians listen to the same pop music and watch the same TV shows as Americans on the mainland. Hawaii has discos and ballroom dancing, rock bands and classical orchestras, junk food and nouvelle cuisine. The wonderful thing about Hawaii, however, is that the American influences largely stand beside, rather than engulf, the culture of the islands.

Not only is traditional Hawaiian culture an integral part of the social fabric, but so are the customs of the ethnically diverse immigrants who have made Hawaii their home. Hawaii is more than just a meeting place of East and West; it's also a place where the cultures merge, typically in a manner that brings out the best of both worlds.

The 1970s saw the start of a Hawaiian cultural renaissance that continues today. Hawaiian language classes are thriving and there is a concerted effort to reintroduce Hawaiian words into modern speech. Hula classes concentrate more on the nuances behind hand movements and facial expressions than on the dramatic hip-shaking that sells dance shows. Many Hawaiian artists and craftspeople are returning to traditional mediums and themes.

Certainly the tourist centres have long been overrun with packaged Hawaiiana, from plastic leis to theme-park luaus, that seems almost a parody of island culture. But fortunately for the visitor the growing interest in traditional Hawaiiana is having an impact on the tourist industry and authentic performances by hula students and contemporary Hawaiian musicians are increasingly easier to find.

Official Hawaii
State flower: *pua aloalo* – hibiscus
State tree: *kukui* – candlenut tree
State bird: *nene* – Hawaiian goose

State marine mammal: humpback whale
State fish: *humuhumunukunukuapuaa* – rectangular triggerfish
State motto: *Ua mau ke ea o ka aina i ka pono* – 'The life of the land is perpetuated in righteousness'.
State song: *Hawaii Ponoi* – written by King Kalakaua; in use since Hawaii was a kingdom.
State nickname: The Aloha State
State flag: Designed for King Kamehameha I prior to 1816, it has the UK's Union Jack in the upper left-hand corner. Eight stripes of red, white and blue represent the eight largest islands.
State seal: The state seal incorporates the state motto and a heraldic shield flanked by Kamehameha I on one side and the Goddess of Liberty holding the Hawaiian flag on the other. It also has taro and banana leaves, ferns, a phoenix and the statehood year of 1959.

RELIGION
Hawaii's population is religiously diverse. In addition to the standard Christian denominations, Hawaii has about 100 Buddhist temples, scores of Shinto shrines and two dozen Hindu temples. There are also Taoist, Tenrikyo, Jewish and Muslim houses of worship.

Christianity has the largest following, with Catholicism being the predominant religious denomination in Hawaii. Interestingly, the United Church of Christ, which includes the Congregationalists who initially converted the islands, claim only about half as many members as the Mormons and one-tenth as many as the Catholics.

LANGUAGE
The unifying language of Hawaii is English, although it's liberally peppered with Hawaiian phrases, loan words from the various immigrant languages, and pidgin slang.

It's not uncommon to hear islanders speaking in other languages, as the main language spoken in one out of every four homes in Hawaii is a mother tongue other than English.

The Hawaiian language itself is still spoken among family members by about 9000 people. Closely related to other Polynesian languages, Hawaiian is melodic, full of vowels and repeated syllables, and phonetically simple.

Some 85% of all place names in Hawaii are in Hawaiian and as often as not they have interesting translations and stories behind them.

The Hawaiians had no written language until the 1820s when Christian missionaries arrived and wrote down the spoken language in roman letters.

Pronunciation

The written Hawaiian language has just 12 letters. Pronunciation is easy and there are few consonant clusters.

Vowel sounds are about the same as in Spanish or Japanese, more or less like this:

a	ah, as in 'father' or uh, as in 'above'
e	ay, as in 'gay' or eh, as in 'pet'
i	ee, as in 'see'
o	oh, as in 'go'
u	oo, as in 'noon'

Hawaiian has diphthongs, created when two vowels join together to form a single sound. The stress is on the first vowel, although in general if you pronounce each vowel separately, you'll be easily understood.

The consonant *w* is usually pronounced like a soft English *v* when it follows the letters *i* and *e* (the town Haleiwa is pronounced Haleiva) and like the English *w* when it follows *u* or *o*. When *w* follows *a* it can be pronounced either *v* or *w* – thus you will hear both Hawaii and Havaii.

The other consonants – h, k, l, m, n, p – are pronounced about the same as in English.

Glottal Stops & Macrons Written Hawaiian uses both glottal stops and macrons, although in modern print they are often omitted.

The glottal stop (') indicates a break between two vowels producing an effect similar to saying 'oh-oh' in English. A macron, a short straight line over a vowel, stresses the vowel.

Glottal stops and macrons not only affect pronunciation, but can give a word a completely different meaning. There are many words with the same spelling which have different meanings depending on the pronunciation. For example *ai* can mean 'sexual intercourse' or 'to eat', depending on the pronunciation.

All this takes on greater significance when you learn to speak Hawaiian in depth. If you're using Hawaiian words in an English-language context (this *poi* is *ono*), there shouldn't be much problem.

Compounds Hawaiian may seem more difficult than it is because many proper names are long and look similar. Many begin with *ka*, meaning 'the', which over time simply became attached to the beginning of the word.

When you break each word down into its composite parts, some of which are repeated, it all becomes much easier. For example: *Kamehameha* consists of the three compounds Ka-meha-meha. *Humuhumunukunukuapuaa*, which is Hawaii's state fish, is broken down into humu-humu-nuku-nuku-a-pu-a-a.

Some words are doubled to emphasize their meaning. For example: *wiki* means 'quick', while *wikiwiki* means 'very quick'.

There are some easily recognisable compounds repeatedly found in place names and it can be fun to learn a few. For instance, *wai* means 'freshwater' and Waikiki means 'spouting water', so named for the freshwater springs which were once there. *Kai* means 'seawater' – Kailua means 'two seas'. *Lani* means 'heavenly' – Lanikai means 'heavenly sea'. *Hana* means 'bay' – Hanalei means 'crescent bay'.

Shaka Sign Islanders greet each other with the shaka sign, which is made by folding down the three middle fingers to the palm and extending the thumb and little finger. The hand is then usually held out and shaken in greeting. It's as common as waving.

Common Hawaiian Vocabulary

Learn these words first: *aloha* and *mahalo*, which are everyday pleasantries; *makai* and *mauka*, commonly used in giving directions; and *kane* and *wahine*, often on toilet doors.

aina
land

akamai
clever

alii
chief, royalty

aloha
love, welcome, goodbye

aloha aina
love of the land

hala
pandanus

hale
house

hana
work; or bay, a compound in place names

haole
Caucasian

hapa
half; or person of mixed-blood

hapa haole
half-white, used for a person, thing or idea

Hauoli Makahiki Hou
Happy New Year

Hawaii nei
all the Hawaiian islands, as distinguished from the Big Island

hau
lowland tree with flowers resembling hibiscus

haupia
coconut pudding

heiau
ancient Hawaiian temple

holoholo
to walk, drive or ramble around for pleasure

holoku
a long dress similar to the muu-muu, but more fitted and with a yoke

hui
group, organisation

hula
traditional Hawaiian dance

ilima
native groundcover with a delicate yellow-orange flower

imu
underground earthen oven used in traditional luau cooking

kahuna
wise person in any field, commonly a priest, healer or sorcerer

kalua
traditional method of baking in an underground oven

kamaaina
native-born Hawaiian or a long-time resident; literally 'child of the land'

kane
man; also the name of one of four top Hawaiian gods

kapu
taboo, part of strict ancient Hawaiian social system; today often used on signs meaning 'Keep Out'

kaukau
food

keiki
child, children

kiawe
a relative of the mesquite tree introduced to Hawaii in the 1820s, now very common; its branches are covered with sharp thorns

koa
native hardwood tree often used in woodworking

kohola
whale

kokua
help, cooperation; 'Please Kokua' on a trash can is a gentle way of saying 'don't litter'

kona
leeward, or a leeward wind

lanai
veranda

lauhala
leaves of the hala plant used in weaving

lei
garland, usually of flowers, but also of leaves or shells

lei hulu
feather lei

lilikoi
passion fruit
limu
seaweed
lolo
stupid, crazy
lomi salmon
raw, diced salmon marinated with tomatoes and onions
lomilomi
massage
luau
traditional Hawaiian feast
mahalo
thank you
makai
towards the sea
malihini
newcomer, visitor
manini
convict tang (a reef fish); also used to refer to something small or insignificant
mano
shark
mauka
towards the mountains, inland
mele
song, chant
Mele Kalikimaka
Merry Christmas
muu-muu
long, loose-fitting dress introduced by the missionaries
nene
Hawaii's state bird, a native goose
ohana
family, extended family
ono
delicious; also the name of the wahoo fish
pakalolo
marijuana; literally 'crazy smoke'
pali
cliff
paniolo
Hawaiian cowboy
pau
finished, no more; *pau hana* means quitting time
puka
any kind of hole or opening

pupu
snack food, hors d'oeuvres; shells
puu
hill, cinder cone
tutu
aunt, older woman
ukulele
stringed musical instrument
wahine
woman
wikiwiki
hurry, quick

Pidgin

Hawaii's early immigrants communicated with each other in pidgin, a simplified, broken form of English. It was a language born of necessity, stripped of all but the most needed words.

Modern pidgin is better defined as local slang. It is extensive, lively and ever-changing. Whole conversations can take place in pidgin, or often just a word or two is dropped into a more conventional English sentence.

Even Shakespeare's *Twelfth Night* has been translated (by local comedian James Grant Benton) to *Twelf Nite O Wateva*. Malvolio's line 'My masters, are you mad?' becomes 'You buggahs crazy, o wat?'

Short-term visitors will rarely win friends by trying to speak pidgin. It's more like an insider's code that you're allowed to use only after you've lived in Hawaii long enough to understand the nuances.

Some characteristics of pidgin include: a fast, staccato rhythm, two-word sentences, no 'th' sound, use of loan words from many languages (often Hawaiian) and double meanings which trip up the uninitiated.

Some of the more common words and expressions:

blalah
big Hawaiian fellow
brah
brother, friend; also used for 'hey you'
broke da mouth
delicious

buggah
  guy
chicken skin
  goose bumps
coconut wireless
  word of mouth
cockaroach
  steal
da kine
  that kind of thing, whatchamacallit etc;
  used whenever you can't think of the word
  you want but you know the listener knows
  what you mean
geev em
  go for it, beat them
grinds
  food, eat; *ono grinds* is good food.
haolefied
  become like a *haole*
howzit?
  hi, how's it going?

how you stay?
  how are you?
humbug
  a real hassle
like beef?
  wanna fight?
mo' bettah
  much better, the best
slippahs
  flip-flops, thongs
stick
  surfboard
stink eye
  dirty look, evil eye
talk story
  any kind of conversation, gossip, tales
tanks
  thanks. More commonly *tanks brah*.
tree
  three. (Dropping the soft 'h' sound from
  'th' is common.)

Facts for the Visitor

VISAS & EMBASSIES

The conditions for entering Hawaii are the same as for entering any other state in the USA.

Canadians require only proof of Canadian citizenship. Visitors from other countries must have a valid passport and most people require a US visa.

However there is a reciprocal visa-waiver programme in which citizens of certain countries may enter the USA for stays of 90 days or less without first obtaining a US visa. Currently these countries are: the UK, New Zealand, Japan, Italy, Spain, Austria, the Netherlands, Belgium, Switzerland, France, Germany, Norway, Denmark, Sweden, Finland, Iceland, San Marino, Andorra, Luxembourg, Liechtenstein and Monaco. Under this programme you must have a return ticket that is nonrefundable in the USA and you will not be allowed to extend your stay beyond the 90 days.

Other travellers will need to obtain a visa from a US consulate or embassy. In most countries the process can be done by mail.

Your passport should be valid for at least six months longer than your intended stay in the USA and you'll need to submit a recent photo (37 x 37 mm) with the application. Documents of financial stability and/or guarantees from a US resident are sometimes required, particularly for those from Third World countries.

Visa applicants may be required to 'demonstrate binding obligations' that will insure their return back home. Because of this requirement, those planning to travel through other countries before arriving in the USA are generally better off applying for their US visa while they are still in their home country – rather than while on the road.

The validity period for US visitor visas depends on what country you're from. The length of time you'll be allowed to stay in the USA is ultimately determined by US immigration authorities at the port of entry.

Incidentally, the infamous prohibition against issuing visas to people who 'have been members of Communist organizations' has been dropped. An anachronism of the Cold War, it still appears on the unrevised visa applications although most consular offices have penned a line through the item.

Foreign Consulates in Hawaii

In Honolulu there are consulates from Australia, Austria, Belgium, Brazil, Chile, Cook Islands, Denmark, Finland, France, Germany, India, Italy, Japan, Kiribati, Korea, Malaysia, Mexico, Norway, Panama, Peru, Philippines, Portugal, Spain, Sweden, Switzerland and Thailand.

There are also government liaison offices for Tonga, American Samoa, Western Samoa, Palau, the Federated States of Micronesia and the Republic of the Marshall Islands.

Addresses and phone numbers are in the Oahu phone book yellow pages under 'Consulates'.

CUSTOMS

US Customs allows each person over the age of 21 to bring one litre of liquor and 200 cigarettes duty-free into the USA. Most fresh fruits and plants are restricted from entry into Hawaii and there's a strict quarantine on animals.

Agricultural Inspection

All luggage and carry-on bags leaving Hawaii for the US mainland are checked by an agricultural inspector.

You cannot take out gardenia, jade vine, mauna loa flowers or *mokihana* berries, even in leis, however most other fresh flowers and foliage are permitted. You can take out pineapples and coconuts but most other fresh fruits and vegetables are banned. Other things not allowed to enter mainland states include plants in soil, fresh coffee berries, cactus and sugar cane (except 'chews'). Seeds,

fruits and plants which have been certified and labelled for export aren't a problem.

MONEY
Exchange Rates

US$1	=	A$1.40
US$1	=	Y122.36
US$1	=	C$1.23
US$1	=	NZ$1.85
US$1	=	UK£0.62
US$1	=	HK$7.72

Currency
US dollars are the only accepted currency in Hawaii.

Foreign travellers will find it easier if their travellers' cheques are already in US dollars, but major currencies can be exchanged at Honolulu International Airport and larger banks. Restaurants, hotels and most stores accept US dollar travellers' cheques as if they're cash.

Plastic Money
All major credit cards are widely accepted throughout Hawaii, including at most hotels, restaurants, gas stations, shops and car-rental agencies, and even at larger grocery stores.

The majority of recreational and tourist activities in Hawaii can also be paid for by credit card.

Automatic teller machines (ATM) are another plastic alternative. We no longer take any travellers' cheques at all when we go to Hawaii, choosing instead to withdraw money from a bank account back home using ATMs. The small service charge works out cheaper than the 1% fee charged for travellers' cheques and there's no need to carry a bundle of cheques around.

Major banks such as Bank of Hawaii and First Hawaiian Bank have ATMs throughout Hawaii. Both of these banks are part of the Plus system and First Hawaiian Bank is also part of the Cirrus system. Plus and Cirrus are the two largest ATM networks in the USA and most ATM bank cards are affiliated with one or the other.

Costs
How much money you need for Hawaii depends on your travelling style. Some people get by quite cheaply while others rack up huge balances on their American Express cards.

The air fare to Hawaii is usually one of the

heftier parts of the budget. Fares vary greatly, particularly from the US mainland, so shop around. (Note that Hawaii stopovers are often thrown in free on trips between North America and Asian or Pacific countries.)

Flights between Hawaiian islands cost about $50 to $70 one way. Hawaii has only two ferry services, one of which operates between Lanai and Maui and the other between Molokai and Maui; both cost $25 one way.

It's a challenge to explore the islands without renting a car, except on Oahu where there's a good inexpensive bus system. Fortunately, Hawaii has lots of competition in the car-rental arena so if you shop around you can often find something for about $100 a week.

Camping is an alternative to paying for a hotel. Every island except Lanai has at least one state park with free camping as well as inexpensive county camping grounds. In addition, Maui and the Big Island have excellent national parks with free camping.

Currently each of the four main islands has at least one hostel-style place with dormitory beds for between $10 and $15 and either B&Bs or spartan hotels for around $40. For hotels with more standard middle-class amenities expect to pay nearly double that and if you've got your mind set on a 1st-class beachfront hotel get ready to pay upwards of $100 a night. For a splurge on a luxury hotel – and Hawaii has some of the world's finest – rates generally begin around $250.

If you're staying awhile, there are ways to cut accommodation costs. Weekly and monthly condo rental rates can beat all but the cheapest hotels. Besides having more space most condos are turn-key, which means virtually everything you'll need from towels and beach mats to a kitchen stocked with pots and pans is provided. Being able to prepare your own meals in a condo can save a bundle on your food bill.

Another cost-cutter is to travel in the low season, generally from April to mid-December, when accommodation rates are often discounted as much as 30%.

Since much of Hawaii's food is shipped in, grocery prices average 25% higher than on the mainland. Because of the shipping costs, bulky items like cereal have the highest mark-ups, while compact items such as canned tuna have the lowest. Food in local neighbourhood restaurants is a good value in Hawaii, with prices generally as cheap as you'll find on the mainland.

The good news for visitors is that lots of things in Hawaii are free. There are no parking or entrance fees at any beach or state park for instance, and most of the islands' historical sights can be explored for free.

Tipping

Tipping practices are the same as in the rest of the USA. In restaurants, waiters expect a tip of about 15% to 20%, while 10% is generally sufficient for taxi drivers.

Consumer Taxes

Hawaii has a 4.17% sales tax that is tacked onto virtually everything, including all meals, groceries, car rentals and accommodation. An additional 5% room tax brings the total tax added to all accommodation bills to 9.17%. Another tax targeted at visitors is the new $2-a-day 'road use' tax imposed upon all car rentals.

WHAT TO BRING

Hawaii has wonderfully balmy weather and a casual attitude towards dress so, for the most part, packing is a breeze.

At the lower elevations it's summer all year. Shorts, sandals and a T-shirt or aloha shirt are the standard day dress. If you don't intend to spend time at higher elevations, a light jacket or sweater will be the warmest clothing you'll need.

Pack light. You can always pick up something with a floral Hawaiian print when you get there and dress island style.

An aloha shirt and lightweight slacks for men, and a cotton dress for women, is pretty much regarded as 'dressing up' on the islands. Only a few of the most exclusive restaurants require anything dressier and some of them lend their own jackets at the door.

Hawaii does, however, have highland areas (called upcountry on the islands) as well as mountains, and most people get at least as far as the former. The upcountry can be a good 20°F cooler than the coast and when the fog blows in and the wind picks up, it gets quite nippy. If you intend to spend any time in the upcountry, plan on another layer of clothes.

The temperature on the mountain summits on the Big Island and Maui can dip below freezing. If you're going to be camping at high elevations, you need to be prepared for cold weather. A tent, winter-rated sleeping bag, rain gear and layers of warm clothing, preferably wool, are a must.

Camping on the beach is another matter entirely. A very lightweight cotton bag is the most you'll need. Public camping grounds require tents – and because of mosquitoes they're a good idea anyway. If you don't want to pack camping gear, it can be rented on Oahu, Kauai, Maui and the Big Island.

For hiking, bring footwear with good traction. Many people just wear sneakers, although walking on lava can be tough on the ankles. Serious hikers should consider lugging along their hiking boots.

You won't regret bringing binoculars for watching whales and birds, and a flashlight is useful to explore caves. We always carry a snorkel, mask and fins, but you can also buy or rent them there. Actually, you don't need to worry too much about what to bring, as just about anything you forget to pack you can easily buy in Hawaii.

TOURIST INFORMATION
Hawaii Visitors Bureau

The Hawaii Visitors Bureau (HVB) provides free tourist information from its domestic and foreign offices. Unless you request something special they usually just mail out general sightseeing brochures for the main islands and booklets containing member hotel and restaurant listings.

The central office (☎ 808-923-1811) is in the Waikiki Business Plaza, Suite 801, 2270 Kalakaua Ave, Honolulu, HI 96815.

HVB warrior marker

There are branch offices on Maui, Kauai and the Big Island (both Kona and Hilo). Information on these offices is in the individual island chapters.

There are also four toll-free numbers that can be called to receive tourist information. For a magazine-like booklet on all Hawaii, call (800) 257-2999. For a similar booklet on Maui, call (800) 525-MAUI. For Kauai, the number is (800) AH-KAUAI, and for the Big Island it's (800) 648-BIG1.

HVB offices outside Hawaii include:

Australia
c/o Walshes World, 92 Pitt St, 8th Floor, Sydney, NSW 2000 (☎ 02-235-0194)
Canada
205-1624 56th St, Delta, BC V4L 2B1 (☎ 604-943-8555)
Germany
c/o Hans Regh Associates, Postfach 930247, Elbinger Strasse 1, 6000 Frankfurt/Main 90 (☎ 069-704-013)
Hong Kong
Suite 3702A, W Tower, Bond Centre, Queensway (☎ 5-260-287)
Japan
Hibiya Kokusai Building, 11th Floor, 2-2-3 Uchisaiwai-cho, Chiyoda-ku, Tokyo 100 (☎ 03-3597-7951)
Korea
c/o Travel World, 2nd Floor, Westin Chosun Hotel, CPO Box 6445, Seoul 100-070 (☎ 02-778-0457)

Top: Chinese lion dance at Bishop Museum, Oahu
Left: Leis
Right: Tatto artist, Chinatown, Oahu

Top left: Surfer crossing sign, Haleiwa, Oahu
Top right: Surfing, Waikiki, Oahu
Bottom left: Boogie board acrobatics, Makaha Beach, Oahu
Bottom right: Windsurfer at Kailua Beach, Oahu

New Zealand
    c/o Walshes World, 87 Queen St, 2nd Floor, Dingwall Building, PO Box 279, Auckland 1 (☎ 793-708)
Singapore
    c/o Pacific Leisure, 149 Rochor Rd 05-06, Fu Lu Shou Complex, Singapore 0718 (☎ 338-1612)
Taiwan
    c/o Federal Transportation Co, 8th Floor, No 61, Nanking East, Road Section 3, Taipei (☎ 507-8133)
UK
    14 The Green, Richmond, London TW9 1PX (☎ 081-332-6969)
US mainland
    180 N Michigan Ave, Suite 1031, Chicago, IL 60601 (☎ 312-236-0632)
    Central Plaza, 3440 Wilshire Blvd, Room 502, Los Angeles, CA 90010 (☎ 213-385-5301)
    441 Lexington Ave, Suite 1003, New York, NY 10017 (☎ 212-986-9203)
    50 California St, Suite 450, San Francisco, CA 94111 (☎ 415-392-8173)
    1511 K St, NW, Suite 519, Washington, DC 20005 (☎ 202-393-6752)

Brochures and travel information on Molokai are available from Destination Molokai (☎ 553-3876, (800) 367-4753 from the USA and Canada, (0014-800) 126-922 from Australia), Box 960, Kaunakakai, HI 96748.

For a free guide to the state parks on all the islands, with a brief description of each park and camping information, contact the Division of State Parks (☎ 587-0300), Box 621, Honolulu, HI 96809.

USEFUL ORGANISATIONS
Information for Disabled Visitors
The Commission on Persons with Disabilities publishes the *Aloha Guide to Accessibility, Part I and II*, which contains detailed travel tips for physically disabled people.

The guides, which cover all the major islands, list hotels which have wheelchair access and specially-adapted rooms or facilities; beaches, parks, shopping malls and other attractions with appropriate accessibility and facilities; and medical equipment agencies, nursing services and transportation services for the disabled.

The two-publication set can be ordered by sending $3 via check or money order to the Commission (☎ 548-7606), 5 Waterfront Plaza, Suite 210, 500 Ala Moana Blvd, Honolulu, HI 96813. The publications are free if picked up at the commission office.

Information for Gay Travellers
The following information sources can help visitors get oriented to Hawaii's gay scene.

Island Lifestyle, (☎ 373-9000), Box 240515, Honolulu, HI 96824, is a 50-page monthly magazine for Hawaii's gay community. Annual subscriptions cost $24. Lifestyle also publishes *The Community Yellow Pages of Hawaii*, a directory of clubs, B&Bs, restaurants and other businesses that are hospitable to the gay community. It's available by mail for $4.

The *Gay Community News* (☎ 526-3000), Box 37083, Honolulu, HI 96837, a monthly newspaper, is available free around Honolulu or by subscription for $25 a year.

Pacific Ocean Holidays (☎ 923-2400, (800) 735-6600) Box 88245, Honolulu, HI 96830, arranges vacation tours for gay men and women. They also produce a small booklet called *Pocket Guide to Hawaii* which is geared to the gay community and costs $3.

Hawaiian Weddings
Weddings are big business in Hawaii and the process is fairly simple. Hawaii requires that the prospective bride and groom appear in person together before a marriage licence agent and pay $16 for a licence, which is given out on the spot. There are no residence or citizenship requirements and no waiting period.

The legal age for marriage is 18, or 16 with parental consent. Those under 20 may require proof of age. Women need a health certificate for rubella screening from a doctor. Full information and forms are available from the Department of Health (☎ 586-4544), Marriage License Office, Box 3378, 1250 Punchbowl St, Honolulu, HI 96801.

You can get a free booklet to help plan

your wedding, which includes details on official requirements, location suggestions and information on photography and limousine services, from Mother of the Bride (☎ 944-0404, (800) 257-4190), 6750 Hawaii Kai Drive, Suite 805, Honolulu, HI 96825. The Reverend M C Hansen (☎ 923-4876, (800) 942-4554) is one of several ministers who can provide a nondenominational service, starting around $60 for a simple weekday ceremony.

BUSINESS HOURS

The most common office hours in Hawaii are 8.30 am to 4.30 pm Monday to Friday. Shops in central areas and malls, as well as large chain stores, are usually open into the evenings and on weekends, and some grocery stores are open 24 hours.

HOLIDAYS & FESTIVALS

With its multitude of cultures and good year-round weather, Hawaii has a seemingly endless number and variety of holidays, festivals and sporting events. The lists given here include the highlights.

As dates for many events change a bit from year to year, it's best to check activity schedules in local papers or pick up the most recent calendar of events from the Hawaii Visitors Bureau. Water sports particularly are reliant on the weather and the surf, so any schedule is tentative.

January

New Year's Day is a national holiday. Fireworks displays are held in many of the larger towns and resorts on New Year's Eve and firecrackers are shot off nonstop through the night.

Chinese New Year begins at the second new moon after winter solstice (around mid-January to early February) with lion dances and strings of firecrackers. Honolulu's Chinatown is the centre stage.

The *Narcissus Festival*, part of the Chinese New Year celebrations, runs for about five weeks and includes arts & crafts, food booths, a beauty pageant and coronation ball. (Oahu)

Martin Luther King Day is a national holiday observed on the third Monday of the month.

Ka Molokai Makahiki, a modern-day version of the ancient makahiki festival, is held in Kaunakakai

in mid-January. The week-long celebration begins with a fishing contest using outrigger canoes and concludes with a tournament of traditional Hawaiian games and sporting events. There's also Hawaiian music and hula on the final day. (Molokai)

February

Presidents' Day, a national holiday, is observed on the third Monday.

Cherry Blossom Festival features a variety of Japanese cultural events including tea ceremonies, mochi pounding and taiko drummers. Activities occur on all islands.

March

St Patrick's Day, the 17th, is celebrated with a parade down Kalakaua Ave, Waikiki. (Oahu)

Prince Kuhio Day, the 26th, is a state holiday honouring Jonah Kuhio Kalanianaole, Hawaii's first delegate to the US Congress. On his native island of Kauai there's a week-long festival including canoe races, a royal ball, music and dance.

Easter falls in March or April.

The *Merrie Monarch Festival*, named after King David Kalakaua, is Hawaii's biggest hula competition and Hawaiiana festival. Held in Hilo, it starts on Easter Sunday and lasts for a week. (Big Island)

May

May Day, on the 1st, is Lei Day in Hawaii. Everybody dons a lei for this one. There are lei-making competitions on several islands and Oahu crowns a lei queen.

The *50th State Fair* at Aloha Stadium has livestock, commercial exhibits, food, crafts, rides and entertainment. It lasts for four weekends, beginning in late May. (Oahu)

Memorial Day, on the last Monday in the month, is a national holiday to honour war dead.

June

The *Festival of the Pacific* is a multicultural presentation of music, dances, sports competitions etc, held in Honolulu in late May or early June. (Oahu)

King Kamehameha Day, 11 June, is a state holiday celebrated on the day or the nearest weekend, with events on all islands. On Oahu the statue of Kamehameha is ceremoniously draped with leis and there's a parade from downtown Honolulu to Kapiolani Park. On the Big Island the Kamehameha statue in the king's hometown of Kapaau is draped with leis, while there's entertainment and a crafts fair at Coconut Island in Hilo.

The *King Kamehameha Hula & Chant Competition*, one of Hawaii's biggest hula contests, is held in Honolulu near the end of the month. (Oahu)

July

The *Puuhonua O Honaunau Cultural Festival* is held at the 'Place of Refuge' national historical park on the weekend closest to 1 July. The festival includes a 'royal court', a *hukilau* (net fishing with a seine), hula and traditional craft displays. (Big Island)

Independence Day, the 4th, is a national holiday celebrated with fireworks and festivities on all the main islands.

The *Prince Lot Hula Festival*, held at Moanalua Gardens on the third Saturday, features hula competitions from Hawaii's major hula schools. (Oahu)

The annual *Ukulele Festival* is held at the Kapiolani Park Bandstand near the end of the month. (Oahu)

August

Ka Himeni Ana is a contest of old-style Hawaiian singing without amplification. All the songs are pre-WW II and sung in Hawaiian. It's held at the University of Hawaii. (Oahu)

Admission Day, a state holiday on the third Friday, observes the anniversary of Hawaiian statehood.

The *Obon* season, which is celebrated around the islands in July and August, is marked by Japanese bon odori dances to honour deceased ancestors. The final event is a floating lantern ceremony at Waikiki's Ala Wai Canal on the evening of 15 August.

September

Aloha Week is a celebration of all things Hawaiian with parades, cultural events, contests, canoe races and Hawaiian music. Festivities are staggered throughout September and October, depending on the island. Oahu has a street fair in downtown Honolulu and a parade in Waikiki.

Labor Day is a national holiday observed on the first Monday.

October

Columbus Day is a national holiday on the second Monday.

November

Veterans' Day, the 11th, is a national holiday.

The *Kona Coffee Cultural Festival*, held in Kailua-Kona in early November, features a parade, a coffee-picking contest and cultural events. (Big Island)

Thanksgiving is a national holiday celebrated on the fourth Thursday.

The *Hawaii International Film Festival* features about 150 films from Pacific Rim and Asian nations. Films are shown throughout Oahu for a week around the end of November and on the Neighbor Islands the following week. The local papers print the schedules.

December

Bodhi Day, the Buddhist Day of Enlightenment, is celebrated on the 8th with ceremonies at Buddhist temples.

Christmas Day is a national holiday. Christmas festivals and craft fairs are held on all the islands throughout December.

Sporting Events

January

The *Hula Bowl* is the classic East/West college all-star football game held at Aloha Stadium, usually on the first or second Saturday of the year. (Oahu)

At the *Morey Boogie World Bodyboard Championships*, held mid-month, some of the world's top bodyboarders hit the Banzai Pipeline's towering waves. (Oahu)

February

The *NFL Pro Bowl*, the annual all-star game of the National Football League, is held at Aloha Stadium near the beginning of the month. (Oahu)

The *Great Aloha Run* is a popular 8.2-mile fun run from Aloha Tower to Aloha Stadium held on Presidents' Day. (Oahu)

The *Hawaiian Open Golf Tournament* at Waialae Country Club, a PGA event held early in the month, is Hawaii's biggest golf tourney with pros competing for a $1 million purse. (Oahu)

The *LPGA Women's Kemper Open*, held at Wailea in late February, is Hawaii's biggest international golf tournament for women. (Maui)

Buffalo's Big Board Surfing Classic, held at Makaha Beach, is a surf contest using old-time 12-foot longboards. Held over two weekends in late February or early March. (Oahu)

March

Oahu Kite Festival is a weekend event held at Kapiolani Park that includes stunt championships by the pros, with colourful kites dancing against the backdrop of Diamond Head. (Oahu)

The *Hawaii Ski Cup* and *Mauna Kea Ski Meet* are ski races down Mauna Kea – snow permitting. (Big Island)

April

The *Marui/O'Neill Invitational*, held at Hookipa

Beach early in the month, is the world's top international windsurfing competition and has a purse of nearly $200,000. (Maui)

The *Carole Kai International Bed Race & Parade* is an offbeat wheeled bed race from Fort DeRussy to Kapiolani Park. (Oahu)

The *Morey Boogie Bodyboard Championship* is held at Sandy Beach near the end of the month. (Oahu)

May

The *Kanaka Ikaika Molokai to Oahu Kayak Race* is a 32-mile kayak race across the treacherous Kaiwi Channel, from Kaluakoi Resort, Molokai to Koko Marina, Oahu. It's held in mid-May.

The *Keauhou-Kona Triathlon* is a half-Ironman with a mere 56-mile bike race and 13-mile run starting at Keauhou Bay. (Big Island)

July

On odd-numbered years sailboats in the *Transpacific Yacht Race* leave southern California on the 4 July weekend and arrive in Honolulu 10 to 14 days later. The race has been held since the turn of the century. (Oahu)

Parker Ranch Rodeo is held at Paniolo Park in Waimea on 4 July. (Big Island)

Makawao Statewide Rodeo is an old-fashioned rodeo in Makawao's cowboy country that lasts for a few days around the 4 July holidays. (Maui)

The *TDK/Gotcha Pro* is a professional surf meet for both board surfers and bodysurfers held at Sandy Beach, usually around mid-month. (Oahu)

The *Kilauea Volcano Wilderness Marathon and Rim Runs* at Hawaii Volcanoes National Park includes a 10-mile run around the rim of Kilauea, a 5½-mile race into Kilauea Iki Crater and a 26.2-mile marathon through the Kau Desert. It's held mid-month and draws an international crowd. (Big Island)

August

The *Hawaiian International Billfish Tournament* is the world's number one marlin tournament. Held in Kailua-Kona, it lasts a week, usually beginning in early August. (Big Island)

The *Summer Kite Festival*, sponsored by the Hawaii Kite Flyers Association, is held at Kapiolani Park. (Oahu)

September

The *Maui Channel Relay Swim* is a nine-mile six-person relay race from Lanai to Kaanapali on Maui, with more than 50 teams competing. It's usually held on the first Saturday of the month.

The *Hana Relay* is a 54-mile relay run from Kahului to Hana. (Maui)

The *Haleakala Run to the Sun* is a 36-mile marathon

to the top of Haleakala, beginning at dawn in Kahului. It's held late in the month. (Maui)

Bankoh Na Wahine O Ke Kai, Hawaii's major annual women's outrigger canoe race, starts at sunrise at Hale O Lono Harbor on Molokai and ends at Waikiki's Fort DeRussy on Oahu. It's held near the end of the month.

October

The *Bankoh Molokai Hoe* is Hawaii's major men's outrigger canoe race, held near mid-month. It starts after sunrise from Hale O Lono Harbor on Molokai and finishes at Fort DeRussy Beach on Oahu about five hours later. Teams from Australia, Tahiti, Germany and the US mainland join Hawaiian teams in this annual competition which was first held in 1952.

The *Ironman Triathlon*, held on a Saturday in mid-October, is considered by many the ultimate endurance race. This is the triathlon that started it all and remains the world's best known. The 2.4-mile swim, 112-mile bike race and 26.2-mile marathon begins and ends at Kailua Pier. (Big Island)

November

The *Makapuu Morey Boogie Bodyboard Championships* are held at Makapuu Beach early in the month. (Oahu)

The *Triple Crown of Surfing* covers three events that draw the world's top surfers to Oahu's North Shore: the Hard Rock Cafe World Cup of Surfing, the Marui Pipeline Masters and the Billabong Pro & Sunset Beach Women's Pro. The events begin in November and run throughout December, with the exact dates and locations depending on when and where the surf's up.

December

The *Honolulu Marathon*, Hawaii's biggest, is run mid-month along a 26-mile course from the Aloha Tower to Kapiolani Park. (Oahu)

The *Aloha Bowl* is the big collegiate football game held at Aloha Stadium on Christmas Day and televised nationally. (Oahu)

POST & TELECOMMUNICATIONS
Postal Rates

Postage rates for 1st-class mail within the USA are 29 cents for letters up to one ounce (23 cents for each additional ounce) and 19 cents for postcards. First-class mail between Hawaii and the mainland goes by air and usually takes three to four days.

International airmail rates are 50 cents for a half-ounce letter and 40 cents for a postcard to any foreign country with the exception of Canada (40 cents for a one-ounce letter and 30 cents for a postcard) and Mexico (35 cents for a half-ounce letter and 30 cents for a postcard).

The cost for parcels airmailed anywhere within the USA is $2.90 for two pounds or less, $5.45 for five pounds. For heavier items, rates differ according to the distance mailed.

Receiving Mail

You can have mail sent to you c/o General Delivery at any post office in Hawaii that has its own zip (post) code. Mail is usually held for 10 days before being returned to sender.

Telephone

The area code for all of Hawaii is 808, and it needs to be dialled with all Hawaiian phone numbers when calling from outside the state. If you're calling from abroad, the international country code for the US is '1'.

All numbers listed in this book beginning with 800 are toll-free numbers from the US mainland, unless otherwise noted. The same numbers are sometimes toll free from Canada as well.

Local calls within Hawaii cost 25 cents at pay phones, and there's no time limit. Any call made from one point on an island to any other point on that island is a local call. Calls from one island to another are long distance.

To call from one Hawaiian island to another from a pay phone, the cost for the first three minutes is $2, with additional minutes costing 27 cents from 8 am to 5 pm weekdays; 18 cents from 5 to 11 pm Sunday to Friday; and 11 cents at all other times.

To make an international call direct, dial 011, then the country code, followed by the area code and the phone number. You may need to wait as long as 45 seconds for the ringing to start.

In Hawaii pay phones are owned by a few different companies, including AT&T and MCI. The cost for calling overseas, including to the US mainland, will depend on the carrier you use.

If for example, you're at an AT&T pay phone using coins and dialling direct to Sydney, Australia, the cost is $5.39 for the first minute and $1.20 for each additional minute from 10 am to 11 pm, and $4.75 for the first minute and 85 cents for additional minutes from 11 pm to 10 am. To London, the cost is $4.81/1.19 for the first/additional minutes from 7 am to noon and from 8 pm to 1 am, and $4.36 for the first minute and 88 cents for additional minutes at all other times. To Vancouver the cost is roughly $3.50 for the first minute, plus 28 cents for additional minutes from midnight to 8 am, 67 cents from 8 am to 6 pm Monday to Saturday and 44 cents at other times. To New York the cost is roughly $2.25 for the first minute, plus 35 cents for additional minutes from 8 am to 5 pm weekdays and 20 to 25 cents at other times.

Most hotels add on a service charge of 50 cents to $1 for each local call made from a room phone and they also have hefty surcharges for long-distance calls. Public pay phones, which can be found in most lobbies, are always cheaper. You can pump in quarters, use a phone credit card, or make collect calls from pay phones.

In Waikiki there's a private long-distance phone service at the International Market Place. Rates are 45 cents a minute to the US mainland, $4 for three minutes to Canada and $8 for three minutes to most Pacific and European destinations.

TIME

Hawaii does not observe daylight saving time. When it's noon in Hawaii the time in other parts of the world is: 1 pm in Anchorage, 2 pm in Los Angeles, 5 pm in New York, 10 pm in London, 11 pm in Bonn, 7 am the next day in Tokyo, 8 am the next day in Sydney and Melbourne, and 10 am the next day in Auckland.

The time difference is one hour greater during those months when other countries observe daylight saving. For example from April to October when it's noon in Hawaii it's 3 pm in LA and 6 pm in New York; and from November to March when it's noon in Hawaii it's 9 am in Melbourne and 11 am in Auckland.

Hawaii has about 11 hours of daylight in mid-winter and almost 13½ hours in midsummer. In mid-winter the sun rises at about 7 am and sets about 6 pm. In mid-summer it rises before 6 am and sets after 7 pm.

And then there's Hawaiian Time, a euphemism for being late.

ELECTRICITY

Electricity is 110/120 V, 60 cycles, and a flat two-pronged plug is used, the same as everywhere else in the USA.

WEIGHTS & MEASURES

Hawaii, like the rest of the USA, uses the imperial system of measurement. Distances are in feet, yards and miles; weights are in ounces, pounds and tons. For those unaccustomed to the imperial system, there is a metric conversion table at the back of this book.

BOOKS & MAPS

Hawaii is said to be the most written-about place in the Pacific. There are books on just about every subject you can think of, from the origin of volcanoes to the history of *hula*. There are even reference books devoted to the books of Hawaii.

People

Keneti by Bob Krauss (University of Hawaii Press, Honolulu, 1988) is a biography of Kenneth 'Keneti' Emory, the esteemed Bishop Museum archaeologist who over the years sailed with writer Jack London, worked with anthropologist Margaret Mead and surfed with Olympian Duke Kahanamoku. Emory, who died in 1992, spent much of his life uncovering the ruins of villages and temples throughout the Pacific, recording them before they disappeared forever.

Paddling My Own Canoe by Audrey Sutherland (University of Hawaii Press, Honolulu, 1978) details the author's explorations in an inflatable kayak along the rugged and isolated north shore of Molokai. The book helped popularise wilderness kayaking in Hawaii.

Father Damien, the priest who worked in the leprosy colony on Molokai, is the subject of many books including *Holy Man: Father Damien of Molokai* by Gavan Daws (Harper & Row, 1973), *Damien the Leper* by John Farrow (Doubleday & Co, New York, 1954) and others.

Aloha Cowboy by Virginia Cowan-Smith & Bonnie Domrose Stone (University of Hawaii Press, Honolulu, 1988) is an illustrated account of 200 years of *paniolo* life in Hawaii.

History & Politics

Hawaiian Antiquities by David Malo (Bishop Museum Press, Honolulu, 1991), written in 1838, was the first account of Hawaiian culture written by a Hawaiian. It gives an in-depth history of Hawaii before the arrival of the missionaries.

Shoal of Time by Gavan Daws (University of Hawaii Press, Honolulu, 1974) is a comprehensive and colourful history covering the period from Captain Cook's 'discovery' of the islands to statehood.

Hawaii's Story by Hawaii's Queen by Queen Liliuokalani (Mutual Publishing, 1990), written in 1897, is an autobiographical account of Liliuokalani's life and the circumstances surrounding her 1893 overthrow.

The Betrayal of Liliuokalani: Last Queen of Hawaii, 1838-1917 by Helena G Allen (Mutual Publishing, Honolulu, 1990) is an insightful account not only of the queen's life but also of the missionary activity and foreign encroachment in Hawaii.

Fragments of Hawaiian History by John Papa Ii (Bishop Museum Press, Honolulu, 1983) is a first-hand account of old Hawaii under the *kapu* system. Ii lived in Kailua-Kona at the time of Kamehameha I.

Kauai, the Separate Kingdom by Edward Joesting (University of Hawaii Press, Honolulu, 1984) is the authoritative history book on Kauai, the only Hawaiian kingdom never conquered in battle.

The Hawaiian Kingdom by Ralph S Kuykendall (University of Hawaii Press, Honolulu) is a three-volume set written from 1938 to 1967. It covers Hawaiian history from 1778 to 1893 and is considered the definitive work on the period.

Six Months in the Sandwich Islands by Isabella Bird Bishop (University of Hawaii Press, Honolulu, 1964) is the personal account of a Victorian lady's travels around Hawaii in 1873.

The Dark Side of Paradise, Hawaii in a Nuclear World, by Jim Albertini, Nelson Foster, Wally Inglis & Gil Roeder (Catholic Action of Hawaii, Honolulu, 1980) is an enlightening, although a bit dated, exposé of the military presence in Hawaii.

Natural History

Hawaii: The Islands of Life (Signature Publishing, 1988) has strikingly beautiful photos of the flora & fauna and landscapes of areas being protected by the Nature Conservancy of Hawaii. The text is by respected Pacific author Gavan Daws.

The Many-Splendored Fishes of Hawaii by Gar Goodson (Stanford University Press, 1985) is one of the better little fish identification books, with good descriptions and 170 colour drawings.

Hawaii's Birds (Hawaii Audubon Society, Honolulu, 1989) is the best pocket-sized guide to the birds of Hawaii. It has colour photos and descriptions of all the native birds and many of the introduced species.

Mammals in Hawaii by P Quentin Tomich (Bishop Museum Press, Honolulu, 1986) is the authoritative book on the mammals in Hawaii, with interesting stories on how they arrived in the islands. He includes all species of whales and dolphins found in Hawaiian waters.

Trailside Plants of Hawaii's National Parks by Charles H Lamoureux (Hawaii Natural History Association, 1976) covers common trailside plants and trees in some depth. It's a good book to have if you'll be spending time hiking in the national parks.

Similarly, *Hawaiian Forest Plants* by Mark David Merlin (Oriental Publishing Company, Honolulu, 1976) has descriptions and colour photos of many of the plants encountered on Hawaii's forest trails.

Plants and Flowers of Hawaii by S H Sohmer & R Gustafson (University of Hawaii Press, Honolulu, 1987) has information on several hundred of the native plants of Hawaii, their habitat and evolution.

Flowers in Hawaii (Hakubundo, Honolulu), with text in both English and Japanese, is a good picture book of common flowers found in Hawaii.

Practical Folk Medicine of Hawaii by L R McBride (Petroglyph Press, Hilo, 1975) has descriptions of many native medicinal plants and their uses.

Maui – How It Came to Be by Will Kyselka & Ray Lanterman (University of Hawaii Press, Honolulu, 1980) is a readable geology book on the evolution of Maui from volcanic formation to present day.

Hawaiian Culture

The Kumulipo by Martha Beckwith (University of Hawaii Press, Honolulu, 1972) is a translation of the Hawaiian chant of creation. The chant of 2077 lines begins in the darkness of the spirit world and traces the genealogy of an *alii* (royalty) family, said to be the ancestors of humankind.

Hawaiian Mythology by Martha Beckwith (University of Hawaii Press, Honolulu, 1970) has comprehensive translations of Hawaii's old myths and legends.

Nana I Ke Kumu (Look to the Source) by Mary K Pukui, E W Haertig & Catherine A Lee (Hui Hanai, 1972, 2 vols) is a fascinating collection of information on Hawaiian cultural practices, social customs and beliefs.

The Legends and Myths of Hawaii (Charles Tuttle Co, Rutland, Vermont, 1985) is a collection of legends as told by King David Kalakaua. It has a short introduction to Hawaiian culture and history as well.

The Hula by Jerry Hopkins (APA Productions, Hong Kong, 1982) is a history of the hula and the musical instruments used in the dance. It also includes biographical sketches of some of hula's most important people.

Hawaiian Music and Musicians: An Illustrated History by George S Kanahele (University of Hawaii Press, Honolulu, 1979) is a history of the islands' music, including singers and composers and some of their songs and chants.

Niihau Shell Leis by Linda Paik Moriarty (University of Hawaii Press, Honolulu, 1986) explains the development of the unique Hawaiian craft of shell *lei* making by Niihauans and illustrates the various styles.

Hawaiian Petroglyphs, an artistically striking book by J Halley Cox (Bishop Museum Press, Honolulu, 1988), lists petroglyph sites and includes extensive photos and illustrations.

Fiction

A Hawaiian Reader, edited by A Grove Day & Carl Stroven (Mutual Publishing, Honolulu, 1959), is an excellent anthology with 37 selections, both fiction and nonfiction. It starts with a log entry by Captain James Cook and includes writings from early missionaries as well as Mark Twain, Jack London, Somerset Maugham, David Malo, Isabella Bird, Martha Beckwith and others. If you only have time to read one book about

Hawaii this inexpensive paperback is a great choice.

O A Bushnell is one of Hawaii's best-known contemporary authors. The University of Hawaii Press, Honolulu, has published his titles *The Return of Lono* (1971), a historical novel of Captain Cook's final voyage; *Kaaawa* (1972), about Hawaii in the 1850s; *The Stone of Kannon* (1979), about the first group of Japanese contract labourers to arrive in Hawaii, and its sequel *The Water of Kane* (1980).

Stories of Hawaii (Appleton, 1965) is a collection of 13 of Jack London's yarns about the islands.

Hawaii (Fawcett, 1986) is James Michener's ambitious historical novel of the islands, from their volcanic origins to their emergence as a state. This sweeping saga traces the Polynesian settlers, the arrival of the missionaries and whalers, the emergence of the sugar barons and the development of Hawaii's multiethnic society.

Outdoor Activities

Hawaiian Hiking Trails by Craig Chisholm (The Fernglen Press, Lake Oswego, Oregon, 1989) is a good, detailed hiking guide to Hawaii's best known trails. Chisholm illustrates each hike with a USGS map of the route. He also has trail guides to Kauai and the Big Island, both published in 1991.

The pocket-sized *Hawaii's Best Hiking Trails* by Robert Smith (Wilderness Press, Berkeley, California, 1991) combines the best trails from hiking guides that Smith has written to each of the main islands.

On the Na Pali Coast by Kathy Valier (University of Hawaii Press, Honolulu, 1988) is a guide for hikers and boaters in Hawaii's most spectacular state park. It has maps and narrative covering both ethnobotany and practical details.

The Beaches of Oahu (1977), *The Beaches of Maui County* (1989), *Beaches of the Big Island* (1985) and *Beaches of Kauai and Niihau* (1990) are by John R K Clark (University of Hawaii Press, Honolulu). These are comprehensive books detailing each island's coastline and every one of its beaches, including water conditions, shoreline geology and local history. The Maui edition includes Maui, Molokai, Lanai and Kahoolawe. If you're going to be spending a lot of time exploring beaches, these books are the ones to have.

The Divers' Guide to Hawaii by Chuck Thorne & Lou Zitnik (Hawaii Divers' Guide, Kihei, 1984) is a guide to the best shore dives on all the islands. It has comprehensive directions to sites, maps of entry points, what you'll see and hazards to expect, all written in a light and colourful style. Though it's geared for divers it's of some value to snorkellers as well.

Diving and Snorkeling Guide to the Hawaiian Islands by Doug Wallin (Pisces Books, New York, 1991) is a good guide to both diving and snorkelling on the four main islands. It has colour photos of sites and fish.

Let's Go Shore Dive'n' on the Kona Coast by Dick Dresie (DPD Associates) is a shore dive guide to the west coast of the Big Island. Dresie gives first-person accounts of his diving experiences in each spot.

Surfer's Guide to Hawaii: Hawaii Gets All the Breaks by Greg Ambrose (Bess Press, Honolulu, 1991) describes the top surfing spots throughout the islands. It's written in an entertaining style and is packed with info on everything you need to know about surfing in Hawaii.

Six Islands on Two Wheels by Tom Koch (Bess Press, Honolulu, 1990) is a comprehensive guide to cycling in Hawaii. Koch encourages you to bring your own bike to Hawaii and tells you how to outfit it, where to ride and what to expect.

Reference

The *Atlas of Hawaii* by the Department of Geography, University of Hawaii (University of Hawaii Press, Honolulu, 1983), is loaded with data, maps and tabulations covering everything from land ownership to seasonal ocean wave patterns. This 238-page atlas is the most comprehensive reference book of Hawaii.

Place Names of Hawaii by Mary Kawena Pukui, Samuel H Elbert & Esther T Mookini (University of Hawaii Press, Honolulu, 1974) is a glossary of 4000 Hawaiian place names. The meaning and background of each name is explained.

Hawaiian Dictionary by Mary Kawena Pukui & Samuel H Elbert (University of Hawaii Press, Honolulu, 1986) is the authoritative work on the Hawaiian language. It's in both Hawaiian-English and English-Hawaiian, with 30,000 entries. They also have a $3.95 pocket-size version with 6000 Hawaiian words.

There are many other Hawaiian language books on the market including grammar texts, conversational self-study guides and books on pidgin.

Bookshops

The four largest islands all have good bookshops with extensive Hawaiiana sections. Bookshop locations are listed under each island.

Ordering by Mail The following publishers will send catalogues of their books that can be ordered by mail:

Bess Press
  Box 22388, Honolulu, HI 96822 (☎ 734-7159)
Bishop Museum Press
  Box 19000-A, Honolulu, HI 96817 (☎ 848-4135)
Mutual Publishing
  2055 N King St, Suite 201, Honolulu, HI 96819 (☎ 924-7732)
Petroglyph Press
  201 Kinoole St, Hilo, HI 96720 (☎ 935-6006)
University of Hawaii Press
  2840 Kolowalu St, Honolulu, HI 96822 (☎ 956-8255)

Libraries

Hawaii has an excellent statewide library system. If you present identification (such as a driver's licence or passport), they'll issue you a free library card on the spot which can be used at all public libraries in the state.

Books can be checked out for three weeks and returned to any state library; for example you can check out a book on Kauai and return it on Molokai. Most of the larger libraries have comprehensive Hawaiiana sections.

Maps

If you're renting a car the guide booklets handed out by the rental agencies have simple maps showing the main roads. However if you really want to explore, a more detailed road map is invaluable.

Rand McNally and Gousha both put out good Oahu street maps, which have detailed Honolulu sections. The American Automobile Association (AAA) puts out good Honolulu and all-Hawaii maps which it distributes free to members. If you're a member of AAA or an affiliated automobile club outside the USA (such as the AA of the UK), you can either pick up these maps from your local office before you go or at 590 Queen St in Honolulu once you arrive.

The University of Hawaii (UH) Press publishes separate relief maps of Oahu, Kauai, Maui, the Big Island and Molokai/Lanai. Overall they're the best general maps for the Neighbor Islands as they not only cover roads but also beaches, historical sites and major hiking trails. UH maps, which cost $3, are available in bookstores and in many shops frequented by tourists.

The United States Geological Society (USGS) publishes topographical maps of Hawaii. Both full-island and detailed sectional maps are available, and there's also an individual USGS map for Hawaii Volcanoes National Park. Maps can be ordered by mail from the US Geological Survey, Box 25286 Denver Federal Center, Denver, Colorado 80225. Prices per map range from $2.50 to $4.

In Hawaii, USGS maps can be purchased on Kauai at Jungle Bob's in Hanalei, the Kauai Museum in Lihue, Outfitters Kauai in Poipu and the Kokee State Park museum; on Maui at Maui Expedition, 87 S Puunene Ave, Kahului; on Oahu at Pacific Map Center, 647 Auahi St, Honolulu; and on the Big Island at Hawaii Volcanoes National Park, Middle Earth Bookshoppe in Kailua-Kona and Basically Books in Hilo.

Nautical charts published by the National Oceanic and Atmospheric Administration can be ordered by mail from the NOAA Distribution Branch, National Ocean Service, Riverdale, Maryland 20737. They can also be ordered by phone (☎ 301-436-6990) using Visa or MasterCard. Upon request NOAA will send a complete list of charts available and addresses where they can be purchased around the world.

If you're looking for NOAA nautical chart maps after you arrive on the islands, you can find them at Pacific Map Center in Honolulu, Basically Books in Hilo and a number of the larger marine supply companies.

For those who want to dig a little deeper, the basement of Hamilton Library at the University of Hawaii, Manoa campus, has a great map room with thousands of esoteric maps on Hawaii and other Pacific islands. You can't buy them, but you can photocopy them.

MEDIA

Newspapers

Hawaii's two main daily papers are the *Honolulu Advertiser* which comes out in the morning and the *Honolulu Star-Bulletin* which comes out in the afternoon. On Sundays they jointly produce the *Star-Bulletin & Advertiser*.

For copies of either paper, contact the Circulation Department (☎ 538-6397), Box 3350, Honolulu, HI 96801. Single copies sent airmail to the US mainland cost $2.85 for a weekday copy and $6.75 for a Sunday copy. Prices vary to other countries.

The Honolulu papers are sold throughout Hawaii but the Neighbor Islands also have their own newspapers. The *Hawaii Tribune-Herald* in Hilo, *West Hawaii Today* in Kailua-Kona, the *Maui News* in Wailuku and the *Garden Island* in Lihue are each published five to six times a week.

Several mainland and international newspapers are also widely available, including *USA Today, Wall Street Journal* and the *Los Angeles Times*. Look for them in the larger hotels.

Magazines

Honolulu, Aloha and *Hawaii Magazine* are the largest general interest magazines about Hawaii. *Honolulu* is geared more towards residents and is published monthly by the Honolulu Publishing Co, 36 Merchant St, Honolulu, HI 96813. *Aloha* (Box 27810, San Diego, CA 92128) and *Hawaii Magazine* (Box 485, Mt Morris, IL 61054) have more visitor-oriented feature articles; both are published six times a year.

There are also numerous tourist magazines distributed free on the islands which are well worth picking up. They usually have simple maps, a bit of current event information, lots of ads and discount coupons for everything from hamburgers to sunset cruises.

TV & Radio

Hawaii has commercial TV stations representing the three major US networks, and cable network stations which include tourist information and Japanese language channels. Almost anything you can watch on the mainland you can watch in Hawaii.

For some local flavour, the evening news on Channel 2 ends with some fine slack-key guitar music by Keola and Kapono Beamer and clips of people waving the shaka sign.

Hawaii has about 50 AM and FM radio stations. There's a wide variety of programming, including some stations that feature Hawaiian music.

FILM & PHOTOGRAPHY

Both print and slide film are readily available on all the islands. If you're going to be in Hawaii for any length of time consider having your film developed there as the high temperature and humidity of the tropics greatly accelerate the deterioration of exposed film. The sooner it's developed, the better the results. Kodak and Fuji have labs in Honolulu, and island drug stores and camera shops often send in to those labs. Longs Drugs is one of the cheapest places for both purchasing film and having it developed. All the tourist centres have one-hour print processing shops; Fox Photo is the largest and reportedly does good work.

Don't leave your camera in direct sun any longer than necessary. A locked car can heat up like an oven in just a few minutes.

Sand and water are intense reflectors and in bright light they'll often leave foreground subjects shadowy. You can try compensating by adjusting your f-stop or attaching a polarising filter, or both, but the most effective technique is to take photos in the gentler light of early morning and late afternoon.

HEALTH

Hawaii is a very healthy place to live and to visit. As it's 2500 miles from the nearest industrial centre, there's little air pollution – other than that caused by volcanic activity. Hawaii ranks first of all the 50 US states in life expectancy, which is currently about 76 years for men and 81 years for women.

There are few serious health concerns. The islands have none of the nasties like malaria, cholera or yellow fever and you can drink water directly out of any tap, although all stream water needs to be boiled or treated.

No immunisations are required to enter Hawaii or any other port in the USA.

Be aware that there are many poisonous plants in Hawaii, so you should never taste a plant that you cannot positively identify as edible.

If you're new to the heat and humidity you may find yourself easily fatigued and more susceptible to minor ailments. Acclimatise yourself by slowing down your pace and setting your body clock to the more kicked-back 'Hawaiian Time'. Drink plenty of liquids.

If you're planning on a long outing or anything strenuous, take enough water and don't push yourself.

Predeparture Preparations

Health Insurance Foreign visitors should be warned that health care in the USA is expensive, and while Hawaii is the only one of the 50 states that has an extensive health-insurance programme, the coverage is limited to Hawaii residents.

Therefore, a travel insurance policy that covers medical expenses may be a wise idea. There are a wide variety of policies available and your travel agent should have recommendations. While you may find a policy that pays doctors or hospitals direct, be aware that many private doctors and clinics in Hawaii will demand payment at the time of service. If you have to make a claim later be sure you keep all documentation.

Check the small print because some policies exclude 'dangerous activities' like scuba diving, motorcycling, anything to do with parachutes and even trekking. You may want to get a policy that covers you for an emergency flight home; some policies even allow for a companion to travel home with you.

Medical Kit A small first-aid kit is a sensible thing to carry on your travels to cope with minor health problems or injuries, especially if you plan on camping or hiking into the backcountry.

A basic kit should have things like aspirin or Panadol for pain or fever; an antihistamine (such as Benadryl) for use as a decongestant, to relieve the itch from insect bites or to help prevent motion sickness; an antiseptic and antibiotic ointment or powder for cuts and grazes; calamine lotion to ease the irritation from bites and stings; Band-aids and bandages; scissors, tweezers, insect repellent and sunscreen.

Bring adequate supplies of any prescription medicine or contraceptive pills you may already be taking.

Medical Care

Hawaii has 25 acute care hospitals, 2600 physicians and 1200 dentists. While the rural islands of Molokai and Lanai have limited medical facilities (Lanai Community Hospital has but a single doctor on staff!), the other islands have fully-staffed hospitals with modern facilities. Still, for specialised care and serious illnesses, many islanders have more confidence in Honolulu hospitals than in Neighbor Island facilities.

Medical Problems & Treatment

Leptospirosis Visitors to Hawaii should be aware of leptospirosis, a bacterial disease found in freshwater streams and ponds. The disease is transmitted from animals such as rats, mongoose and wild pigs.

Humans most often pick up the disease by swimming or wading in freshwater contaminated by animal urine. Leptospirosis can exist in any fresh water, including idyllic-looking waterfalls and jungle streams, because the water may have washed down the slopes through animal habitats.

Leptospirosis enters the body through the nose, eyes, mouth or cuts in the skin. Wetland taro farmers, swimmers and backcountry hikers account for the majority of cases.

Symptoms can occur within two to 20 days after exposure and may include fever, chills, sweating, headaches, muscle pains, vomiting and diarrhoea. More severe symptoms include blood in the urine and jaundice. Symptoms may last from a few days to several weeks.

In 1990 there were 43 confirmed cases statewide. Because symptoms of leptospirosis resemble the flu and hepatitis, other cases have probably gone unconfirmed. Although deaths have been attributed to the disease they are relatively rare, with five fatalities in Hawaii between 1982 and 1990. Leptospirosis is not specific to Hawaii and can be found on the mainland as well.

Some precautions include wearing waterproof *tabis* when hiking and avoiding unnecessary freshwater crossings, especially if you have open cuts.

Leptospirosis can be serious, yet thousands of people swim in Hawaiian streams without contracting it. The state has posted warnings at many trailheads and freshwater swimming areas. Islanders have differing opinions on leptospirosis – some never swim in fresh water because of it, while others consider it such a long shot that they take no precautions at all.

Sunburn Sunburn is always a concern in the tropics, as the closer you get to the equator the fewer of the sun's rays are blocked by the atmosphere. Don't be fooled by what appears to be a hazy overcast day as those rays still get through.

Sunscreen with an SPF (sun protection factor) of 10 to 15 is recommended if you're not already tanned. If you're going into the water use one that's water-resistant. Snorkellers may want to wear a T-shirt if they plan to be out in the water a long time. You'll not only be protecting against sunburn but potential skin cancer and premature ageing of the skin.

Fair-skinned people can get both first and second degree burns in the hot Hawaiian sun and wearing a sun hat for added protection is a good idea. The most severe sun is between 10 am and 2 pm.

Prickly Heat Prickly heat is an itchy rash caused by excessive perspiration trapped under the skin. It usually strikes people who have just arrived in a hot climate and whose pores have not yet opened sufficiently to cope with greater sweating. Keeping cool but bathing often or resorting to air-conditioning may help until you acclimatise.

Heat Exhaustion Dehydration or salt deficiency can cause heat exhaustion. Take time to acclimatise to high temperatures and make sure you get sufficient liquids. Salt deficiency is characterised by fatigue, lethargy, headaches, giddiness and muscle cramps and in this case salt tablets may help. Vomiting or diarrhoea can deplete your liquid and salt levels.

Heat Stroke This serious, sometimes fatal, condition can occur if the body's heat-regulating mechanism breaks down and the body temperature rises to dangerous levels. Long, continuous periods of exposure to high temperatures can leave you vulnerable to heat stroke. Avoid strenuous activity in open sun (such as lengthy hikes or bike rides across lava fields) when you first arrive. The symptoms of heat stroke are feeling unwell, not sweating very much or at all and a high body temperature (102°F to 106°F). Where sweating has ceased the skin becomes flushed and red. Severe, throbbing headaches and lack of coordination will also occur, and the sufferer may be confused or aggressive. Eventually the victim may become delirious or convulse. Hospitalisation is essential, but meanwhile get patients

out of the sun, remove their clothing, cover them with a wet sheet or towel and then fan continually.

Altitude Sickness On the Big Island, people planning to go to the summits of Mauna Kea or Mauna Loa need to be aware of the possibility of Acute Mountain Sickness (AMS), which occurs at high altitudes due to lack of oxygen and is potentially fatal. While AMS can generally be avoided by making gains in elevation at a slow pace, Hawaii presents an unusual situation as most people who visit Mauna Kea summit do so by car. Many of those visitors drive straight up to nearly 14,000 feet from their hotels on the coast, a mere two-hour ride that offers no time to acclimatise. As a result AMS is a common problem for summit visitors, even though most cases are on the mild side. AMS symptoms include headaches, nausea, dizziness and shortness of breath, while confusion and lack of coordination and balance are real danger signs. With all but the mildest of symptoms, travellers experiencing signs of AMS should immediately descend to a lower elevation. For more information, see Precautions in the Saddle Road/Mauna Kea section in the Big Island chapter.

Fungal Infections The same climate that produces lush tropical forests also promotes a prolific growth of skin fungi and bacteria. Hot weather fungal infections are most likely to occur between the toes or fingers or in the groin.

Keeping your skin dry and cool and allowing air to circulate is essential. Choose loose cotton clothing rather than synthetics, and sandals over shoes. If you do get an infection, wash the infected area daily with a disinfectant or medicated soap. Rinse and dry well and then apply an antifungal powder.

Motion Sickness Eating lightly before and during a trip will reduce the chances of motion sickness. If you are prone to motion sickness try to find a place that minimises disturbance – near the wing on aircraft or close to midships on boats. Fresh air usually helps; reading or cigarette smoke doesn't. Commercial antimotion-sickness preparations, which can cause drowsiness, have to be taken before the trip commences; when you're feeling sick it's too late. Ginger is a natural preventative and is available in capsule form.

Cuts & Scratches Cuts and skin punctures are easily infected in Hawaii's hot and humid climate, and infections can be persistent. Keep any cut or open wound clean and treat it with an antiseptic solution. Keep the area protected but, where possible, avoid bandages which can keep wounds wet.

Coral cuts are even more susceptible to infection because tiny pieces of coral can get embedded in the skin. These cuts are notoriously slow to heal as the coral releases a weak venom into the wound.

Pesky Creatures Hawaii has no land snakes but it does have its fair share of annoying mosquitoes as well as centipedes which can give an unpleasant bite. The islands also have bees and groundnesting wasps which, like the centipede, generally pose danger only to those who are allergic to their stings.

This being the tropics, cockroaches are plentiful and although they don't pose much of a health problem they do little for the appetite. Condos with kitchens have the most problems. If you find that the place you're staying at is infested you can always call the manager or the front desk and have them spray poisons – which are no doubt more dangerous than the roaches!

While sightings are not terribly common, there are two dangerous arachnids on the islands: the black widow spider and the scorpion.

Black Widow Spiders Found in much of the USA, the black widow is glossy black with a body that's a half-inch in diameter, a leg span of two inches and a characteristic red hourglass mark on its abdomen. It weaves a strong, tangled web close to the ground and inhabits brushpiles, sheds and outdoor privies.

Its bite, which resembles the prick of a pin, can be barely noticeable, however it's followed in about 30 minutes by severe cramping in which the abdominal muscles become boardlike and breathing becomes difficult. Other reactions include vomiting, headaches, sweating, shaking and a tingling sensation in the fingers. In severe cases the bite can be fatal. If you think you've been bitten by a black widow, seek immediate medical help.

Scorpions The scorpion, confined principally to warm dry regions, is capable of inflicting a painful sting by means of its caudal fang. Like the black widow, the venom contains neurotoxins. Severity of the symptoms generally depends on the age of the victim and can even be fatal for very young children. Symptoms are shortness of breath, hives, swelling or vomiting. Apply diluted household ammonia and cold compresses to the area of the sting and seek immediate medical help.

While the odds of encountering a scorpion are quite low, campers should always check inside their hiking boots before putting them on!

Ciguatera Poisoning Ciguatera is a serious illness caused by eating fish affected by ciguatoxin, which herbivorous fish can pick up from marine algae. There is no ready way of detecting ciguatoxin, and it's not diminished by cooking. Symptoms of food poisoning usually occur three to five hours after eating.

Ciguatoxin is most common among reef fish (which are not commonly served in restaurants) and hasn't affected Hawaii's deep-sea fish such as tuna, marlin and *mahimahi*. The symptoms, if you do eat the wrong fish, can include nausea, stomach cramps, diarrhoea, paralysis, tingling and numbness of the face, fingers and toes, and a reversal of temperature feelings so that hot things feel cold and vice versa. Extreme cases can result in unconsciousness and even death. Vomit until your stomach is empty and get immediate medical help.

WOMEN TRAVELLERS

Women travellers are no more likely to encounter problems in Hawaii than anywhere else in the USA. We don't advise women travelling alone to hitchhike, but if you do, size up the situation carefully and don't hesitate to decline a ride from anyone who makes you feel uncomfortable. If you're camping, select your camping ground carefully, opting for popular, well-used camping areas, rather than more remote locales where you might be the only camper, as these lesser-used spots sometimes become impromptu drinking hangouts.

DANGERS & ANNOYANCES
Tsunamis

Tsunamis, or tidal waves, are not common in Hawaii but when they do hit they can be severe.

Tsunamis are generated by earthquakes or other natural disasters. The largest to ever hit Hawaii was in 1946, the result of an earthquake in the Aleutian Islands. Waves reached a height of 55.8 feet, entire villages were washed away and 159 people died. Since that time, Hawaii has installed a modern tsunami warning system which is aired through yellow speakers mounted on telephone poles around the islands. They're tested on the first working day of each month at 11.45 am for about one minute.

Though tsunamis which travel across the Pacific can take hours to arrive, others can be caused by earthquakes or volcanic eruptions within Hawaii. For these there may be little warning. Any earthquake strong enough to cause you to grab onto something to keep from falling is a natural tsunami warning. If you're in a low-lying coastal area when one occurs, immediately head for higher ground.

Tsunami inundation maps in the front of island telephone books show susceptible areas and safety zones.

Ocean Safety

Drownings are the leading cause of accidental death for visitors.

If you're not familiar with water conditions, ask someone. If there's no lifeguard around, local surfers are generally helpful. They'd rather give you the lowdown on water conditions than pull you out later. It's best not to swim alone in any unfamiliar place.

Shorebreaks Shorebreaks occur where waves break close to or directly on shore. They are formed when ocean swells pass abruptly from deep to shallow waters. If they are only a couple of feet high they're generally fine for novice bodysurfers to try their hand. Otherwise, they're for experienced bodysurfers only.

Large shorebreaks can hit hard with a slamming downward force. Broken bones, neck injuries, dislocated shoulders and loss of wind are the most common injuries, although anyone wiped out in the water is a potential drowning victim as well.

Rip Currents Rips, rip currents or riptides are fast flowing currents of water within the ocean, moving from shallow near-shore areas out to sea. They are most common in conditions of high surf, forming when water from incoming waves builds up near the shore. Essentially the waves are coming in faster than they can flow back out.

The water then runs along the shoreline until it finds an escape route out to sea, usually through a channel or out along a point. Swimmers caught up in the current can be ripped out to deeper water.

Though rips can be powerful they usually dissipate 50 to 100 yards offshore. Anyone caught in one should either go with the flow until it loses power or swim parallel to shore to slip out of it. Trying to swim against a rip current can exhaust the strongest of swimmers.

Undertows Undertows are common along steeply sloped beaches when large waves backwash directly into incoming surf. The outflowing water picks up speed as it flows down the slopes. When it hits an incoming wave it pulls under it, creating an undertow. Swimmers caught up in an undertow can be pulled beneath the surface. The most important thing is not to panic. Go with the current until you get beyond the wave.

Rogue Waves Never turn your back on the ocean. Waves don't all come in with equal height or strength. An abnormally high 'rogue wave' can sweep over shoreline ledges such as those circling Hanauma Bay on Oahu or tear up onto beaches like Lumahai on Kauai. Over the years, numerous people have been swept into the ocean from both.

You need to be particularly cautious during high tide and in conditions of stormy weather or high surf.

Some people think rogue waves don't exist because they've never seen one. But that's the point – you don't always see them.

Coral Most coral cuts occur when swimmers are pushed onto the coral by rough waves and surges. It's a good idea to wear diving gloves when snorkelling over shallow reefs. Avoid walking on coral, which can not only cut your feet, but is very damaging to the coral.

Jellyfish Take a peek into the water before you plunge in to make sure it's not jellyfish territory. These gelatinous creatures, with saclike bodies and stinging tentacles, are fairly common around Hawaii. They're most often found drifting near the shore or washed up on the beach. The sting of a jellyfish varies from mild to severe, depending on the variety. However, unless you have an allergic reaction to their venom, the stings are not generally dangerous.

In Hawaii, the Portuguese man-of-war is the worst type to encounter. Not technically a jellyfish, the man-of-war is a colonial hydrozoan, or a colony of coelenterates, rather than a solitary coelenterate like the true jellyfish. Its body consists of a translucent bluish bladder-like float, which in Hawaii generally grows to about four or five inches long. Known locally as 'bluebottles', they're most often found on the windward coasts, particularly after storms.

A man-of-war sting is very painful, similar to a bad bee sting except that you're likely to get stung more than once from clusters of incredibly long tentacles containing hundreds of stinging cells. Even touching a bluebottle a few hours after it's washed up on shore can result in burning stings.

If you do get stung, quickly remove the tentacles and apply vinegar or a meat tenderiser containing papain (derived from papaya), which act to neutralise the toxins. For serious reactions, including chest pains or difficulty in breathing, seek medical attention.

Fish Stings Incidences with venomous sea creatures in Hawaiian waters are rather rare. You should, however, learn to recognise scorpionfish and lionfish, two related fish which can inject venom through their dorsal spines if touched. Both are sometimes found in quite shallow water.

The Hawaiian lionfish, which grows up to 10 inches, is a strikingly attractive fish with vertical orange and white stripes and feathery appendages that contain poisonous

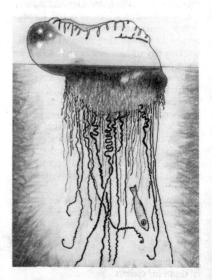

Portugese man-of-war

spines; it likes to drift along the reef, particularly at night. The scorpionfish is more drab in appearance, has shorter and less obvious spines, is about six inches in length, and tends to sit immobile on the bottom or on ledges.

The sting from either can cause a sharp burning pain, followed by numbness around the area, nausea and headaches. Immediately stick the affected area in water that is as hot as bearable (be sure not to unintentionally scald the area due to numbness) and go for medical treatment.

Cone Shells Cone shells should be left alone unless you're sure they're empty. There's no safe way of picking up a live cone shell as the animal inside has a long harpoon-like tail that can dart out and reach anywhere on its shell to deliver a painful sting. The wound should be soaked in hot water and medical attention sought.

A few species, such as the textile cone whose shell is decorated with brown diamond or triangular shapes, have a venom so toxic that in extreme cases the sting could even be fatal.

Sea Urchins *Wana*, or spiny sea urchins, have long brittle spines that can puncture the skin and break off, causing burning and possible numbness. The spines sometimes inflict a toxin and can cause an infection. You can try to remove the spines with tweezers or by soaking the area in hot water, although more serious cases may require surgical removal.

Eels *Puhi*, or moray eels, are often spotted by snorkellers around reefs and coral heads. They're constantly opening and closing their mouths to pump water across their gills, which makes them look far more menacing than they actually are.

Eels don't attack, but they will protect themselves if cornered by fingers jabbing into the reef holes or crevices they occupy. Eels have sharp teeth and strong jaws and may clamp down if someone sticks a hand in their door.

Sharks More than 35 varieties of sharks are found in Hawaiian waters, including the non-aggressive whale and basking sharks, which can reach lengths of 50 feet. As Hawaiian waters are abundant with fish, sharks in Hawaii are well fed and most pose little danger to humans.

Sharks are curious and will sometimes investigate divers, although they generally just check things out and continue on their way. If they start to hang around, however, it's probably time for you to go.

Outside of the rarely encountered great white shark, the most dangerous shark in Hawaiian waters is the tiger shark, which averages about 20 feet in length and is identified by vertical bars along its side. The tiger shark is not terribly particular about what it eats and has been known to chomp down on pieces of wood floating on the ocean surface.

Should you come face to face with a shark the best thing to do is move casually and quietly away. Don't panic as sharks are attracted by things that thrash around in water.

A Sea Life Park display suggests thumping an attacking shark on the nose or sticking your fingers into its eyes, which may confuse it long enough to give you time to escape.

Avoid murky waters. After heavy rains sharks sometimes come in around river mouths.

Sharks are attracted by blood. Some attacks on humans are related to spearfishing; when a shark is going after a diver's bloody catch, the diver sometimes gets in the way. Sharks are also attracted by shiny things and by anything bright red or yellow, which might influence your choice of swimsuit colour.

Unpleasant encounters with sharks are extremely unlikely however. According to the University of Hawaii Sea Grant College, only about 30 unprovoked shark attacks are known to have occurred in Hawaii since 1900; about a third of these were fatal. Nevertheless, in recent years, increasing numbers of both sharks and shark attacks have been reported. In late 1991 a woman swimming off Olowalu, Maui, was killed by a tiger shark and in 1992 a surfer who disappeared on Oahu's North Shore was also presumed to have been the victim of a shark attack after his board was recovered with a large bite taken out of it.

Theft & Violence

For the most part, Hawaii is a safe place to be.

However the islands do have notoriety for rip-offs from parked rental cars. The people who break into these cars are good at what they do; they can pop a trunk or pull out a lock assembly in seconds to get to loot inside. What's more, they do it not only when you've left your car in a secluded area to go for a long hike, but also in crowded parking lots where you'd expect safety in numbers.

It's best not to leave anything of value in your car any time you walk away from it. If for some reason you feel you must, at least pack things well out of sight *before* you've pulled up to the place where you're going to leave the car.

Other than rip-offs, most hassles encountered by visitors are from drunks. Be tuned in to the vibes on beaches at night and in places where young guys hang out to drink.

Overall, violent crime is lower in Hawaii than in most of the mainland cities. There are, however, some pockets of resentment against tourists, as well as against off-islanders moving in. Oahu tends to be worse than the other islands.

ACTIVITIES

Hawaii has an exhaustive variety of sports and recreational activities available to visitors. In addition to top conditions for practically all water sports, there are also fine opportunities for hiking, biking, jogging, tennis, golf, horseback riding, you name it. There's even snow skiing on the Big Island in winter.

Hawaii is a great place to learn to dive, surf or windsurf. Equipment rental is available on the main islands and most places that rent the equipment also give lessons to beginners. Hawaii has 750 miles of coastline and all of its 283 beaches are public up to the high water mark.

Except for sports competitions or specialised tours, few activities require advance planning before you get to Hawaii.

More detailed information is given in each island chapter.

Surfing

Hawaii lies smack in the path of all the major swells that race unimpeded across the Pacific, and the sport of surfing got its start in these islands hundreds of years ago with the early Hawaiians.

Hawaii has good surfing throughout the year, with the biggest waves hitting from November to February along the north shores of the islands. Summer swells, which break along the south shores, are usually not as frequent and nowhere near as large as the northside winter swells.

Oahu's north shore has Hawaii's top surf action. The winter swells at Waimea, Sunset Beach and the Banzai Pipeline can bring in 30-foot waves, creating the conditions that legends are made of. Waikiki has Oahu's top south shore surfing.

Maui and Kauai also have some excellent surfing spots. The Big Island and Molokai are not as notable, but it is possible to surf on both islands. See individual island chapters for more details.

Windsurfing

Maui has some of the world's best windsurfing action, with Hookipa Beach near Paia hosting the top international windsurfing competitions. Tamer spots can be found on other parts of the island.

Oahu also has lots of windsurfing activity, with some spots ideal for beginners and other locales boasting advanced wave-riding conditions. Oahu's Kailua Beach attracts the biggest crowd with its excellent year-round wind.

Though Maui and Oahu are by far the top two islands for windsurfing, Kauai also has some fairly good windsurfing spots. The Big Island doesn't rate as a windsurfing destination, although if you're there and want to windsurf there are a few beaches with reasonable conditions. It's possible to rent gear and take lessons on all four islands.

Although there are good windsurfing conditions in Hawaii year round, winter can have flat periods. In general, the best winds are from June to September.

Diving

There's good year-round diving in Hawaii. Under normal conditions, the leeward shores of the islands have the best diving most months of the year. The north shores are usually best in the summer.

Hawaiian waters have excellent visibility, with water temperatures ranging from 72°F to 80°F.

The marine life around the islands is superb. Almost 700 fish species live in Hawaiian waters, with nearly one-third of those found nowhere else in the world. Hawaiian reef fish are colourful and numerous. There are more than 20 different kinds of butterfly fish, plus rainbow-coloured parrotfish, wrasses, tangs, filefish and pufferfish, just to list a few. Divers often see spinner dolphins, green sea turtles, manta rays and moray eels. Though it's rare for divers to see humpback whales underwater, they do sometimes hear them singing.

Hawaii has underwater caves, canyons, lava tubes, vertical walls and sunken ships. There are all sorts of colourful sponges and corals, including the gem-like black coral.

There are numerous dive shops on the four largest islands, and they all have some excellent diving opportunities. All gear can be rented and prices are quite competitive.

Fishing

Hawaii has some of the world's best deep-sea fishing, with Kona holding most of the world records for Pacific blue marlin. For details, see the Activities section in the Big Island chapter.

In addition to ocean fishing, the state maintains four public freshwater fishing areas: in Kokee on Kauai, in Wahiawa and Nuuanu on Oahu and at Waiakea on the Big Island. Stocked game fish include rainbow trout, largemouth and smallmouth bass, bluegill sunfish, channel catfish, tilapia and carp.

Licences are required for freshwater fishing. A 30-day licence for nonresidents costs $3.75 (free for those aged 65 and older).

No licences are required for saltwater fishing when the catch is for private consumption. There are, however, seasons, size limits and/or other restrictions on taking *ula* (spiny lobster), crab, octopus *(hee* in Hawaiian, and also called tako or squid), *opihi* (a kind of limpet), *limu* (seaweed) and certain species of fish. Clams and oysters cannot be taken.

Also, seek local advice before eating your catch as ciguatera poisoning has become more common in recent years.

The booklets *Hawaii Fishing Regulations* and *Freshwater Fishing in Hawaii* may be obtained free from the Division of Aquatic Resources (☎ 587-0102), Department of Land & Natural Resources, 1151 Punchbowl St, Room 330, Honolulu, HI 96813.

Hiking

Hawaii has first-rate hiking opportunities. Like the islands themselves, the hiking options are incredibly varied, from desert treks to lush rainforest walks, and from beach strolls to snowline ridge trails.

The hikes range from short family-style nature walks to backpacking treks which last several days and require carrying food and gear.

Despite all the development on Hawaii, it's amazing how much of the islands are still in a natural state. There are places where you could walk for days without seeing another soul.

Hawaii's two national parks have hiking trails that have no parallels anywhere. Both have barren lunar-like landscapes as well as lush, tropical forests.

The Hawaii Volcanoes National Park on the Big Island has the distinction of containing both the world's most active volcano and largest mountain mass. The park has breathtaking hikes down into steaming crater floors and up to the snowcapped summit of Mauna Loa.

At Haleakala National Park on Maui the volcano is sleepier, but equally awe-inspiring. Hikes into the caldera of the world's largest crater can take half a day while hikes across its floor can take half a week.

Still, the premier hike in all of Hawaii is on Kauai's Na Pali Coast, where the Kalalau Trail follows an ancient Hawaiian footpath along the edges of the most spectacularly fluted coastal cliffs in Hawaii. The trail winds down into lush valleys where camping is allowed and waterfalls and ruins can be explored.

There are also hiking trails into other ancient valleys, such as Waipio on the Big Island and Halawa on Molokai. On Maui and the Big Island you can follow old 'king's trails' along footpaths worn through the lava by the bare feet of travellers over hundreds of years. Every island has ridgeline trails with panoramic views, as well as trails to secluded beaches and waterfalls. On some islands there are also trails in nature preserves where you can examine native plants and birds and enjoy lots of solitude.

Safety & Tips A number of Hawaii's hiking trails take you into steep, narrow valleys with gullies that require stream crossings. The capital rule here is that if the water begins to rise it's not safe to cross, as a flash flood may be imminent. Instead, head for higher ground and wait it out.

Flash floods are the biggest dangers on trails, followed by falling rocks. Be wary of swimming under high waterfalls, as rocks can get dislodged from the top, and be careful on the edge of steep cliffs as cliffside rock in Hawaii tends to be crumbly.

Darkness sets in soon after sunset in Hawaii and ridgetop trails are not the place to be caught unprepared in the dark. It's a good idea to carry a flashlight when you're hiking, just in case.

Jeans will protect your legs from the overgrown parts of the trail and tennis shoes or sturdy walking shoes are advisable on most hikes.

Some people prefer *tabi* (reef walkers) for hiking, as they have good traction and also offer some protection from leptospirosis (see the Health section). Tabis can be bought around the islands at shops that sell sporting goods and fishing supplies.

Hawaii has no snakes, no poison ivy, no poison oak and few dangers from wild animals. There's a slim possibility of meeting up with a large boar in the backwoods, but they're unlikely to be a problem unless cornered.

Hiking Information You can get free recreational maps of Maui, Molokai and the Big Island from the Division of Forestry & Wildlife (☎ 587-0166), 1151 Punchbowl St, Room 325, Honolulu, HI 96813. Though they're primarily geared for hunters, showing 4WD roads and trails into wilderness areas, these maps are useful for hikers as well. In addition, the forestry has trail descriptions and photocopies of topo maps for some wilderness trails on Oahu and Kauai that they'll send out on request – just let them know which islands you'll be hiking on. Information on USGS topo maps is in the Maps section.

The Oahu, Maui, Kauai and Big Island branches of the Sierra Club lead guided hikes. You can contact the central office (☎ 538-6616), Box 2577, 212 Merchant St, Room 201, Honolulu, HI 96813, for a schedule of upcoming hikes or simply look in the activity listings in local newspapers once you arrive.

Specific information on the various hiking trails is given in each island section.

Running

There are more than 100 road races, ranging from fun runs to triathlons, held in the islands each year.

Hawaii's best known races are the Honolulu Marathon held in December and the Ironman Triathlon held in Kona on the Big Island in October. For info on the former contact the Honolulu Marathon Association

(☎ 734-7200), 3435 Waialae Ave No 208, Honolulu, HI 96816; and for the latter: (☎ 329-0063) 75-170 Hualalai Rd, Suite D214, Kailua-Kona, HI 96740.

The Department of Parks & Recreation of the City & County of Honolulu (650 S King St, Honolulu, HI 96813) has a comprehensive schedule of annual running events that it will mail out upon request.

ACCOMMODATION

Hawaii has a wide variety of accommodation in all price ranges, including B&Bs, hotels and condominiums. There are also a handful of hostels and state park cabins that are quite inexpensive.

In Waikiki there are far more hotels than condos, although in Kihei and Kona the opposite is true. In most other major tourist destinations in Hawaii the number of hotels and condos are pretty evenly divided.

There are more than 73,000 hotel and condo rooms in the state. Oahu, which once boasted all of Hawaii's visitor accommodation and until 20 years ago still had 75%, has now slipped to about 50% as development continues full speed ahead on the Neighbor Islands.

The Big Island alone has more than 40,000 new hotel and condo units planned. If it all goes unchecked the once sleepy Kona Coast will surpass Waikiki in the next decade.

Most places to stay in Hawaii have different rates for high season and low season (also called peak season and off season). High season most commonly applies to the winter period of 15 December to 31 March. During this time many of the best-value places, particularly the smaller hotels and condos, are booked out well in advance.

During the low season period of April to mid-December many places drop their rates by 10% to 30%. The low season is not only cheaper but it's got the best weather.

Due to a slowdown in the economy and correspondingly low occupancy rates, there's a growing number of hotel discounts. Some hotels offer a third night free while a few of the larger chains, such as Outrigger

and Hawaiian Pacific Resorts, often throw in a free rental car. Before booking any hotel, it's worth asking if they're currently running any specials – some places actually have room/car packages for less than the 'standard' room rate! While a good travel agent at home may know about some of these discounts, many of the best deals are advertised only in Hawaii and to find them you'll need to pick up a Honolulu newspaper. The travel section of the Sunday *Star-Bulletin & Advertiser* is best.

At most hotels the rooms are basically the same, with rates usually corresponding to two variables: the view and the floor. An ocean view often costs 50% to 100% more than a parking lot view, which is sometimes euphemistically called 'garden view'. Also the higher you go, the higher the tariff; the higher floors are generally quieter, especially on busy roads.

The toll-free numbers given in this book usually can't be dialled within Hawaii. However, some hotels will accept collect calls from the Neighbor Islands – it never hurts to try.

If you have a Hawaii driver's licence, always ask about *kamaaina* (native-born or long-time resident) rates. Many middle and top-range hotels give residents big discounts.

The Hawaii Visitors Bureau (2270 Kalakaua Ave, Honolulu, HI 96815) will mail out on request a free annual accommodation guide listing member hotels with addresses and prices. It includes virtually all of Hawaii's resort hotels and most of those in the moderate range.

Except where noted, the rates given in this book are the same for either singles or doubles. A combined room and sales tax of 9.17% is added to the price of all accommodation, including B&Bs.

Camping

Hawaii has numerous camping grounds. In general, camping in the national parks is better than in the state parks, and the state parks are better choices than the county parks.

Though local people often unofficially camp in places other than the parks, it doesn't necessarily mean that you'll be welcome to join them. They may just be out for a weekend of fishing, or they may be homeless. Either way there could be some turf issues.

Over the years there have been some assaults and numerous thefts targeted at off-island campers. The violence has decreased in most places although a few camping grounds in rough areas, including the entire Waianae Coast of Oahu, are best avoided. The biggest hassles usually come from young local guys who have been drinking. People travelling alone, especially women, need to be particularly cautious.

Rip-offs still occur at some camping areas and you'll need to watch your valuables. Generally the less you look like a tourist the less likely you are to be targeted.

Pick your park carefully, especially the county parks. Some are well-established with caretakers and attract other campers, while others are pit stops along the road frequented mostly by drinkers.

For the most part the farther you are from population centres, the less likely you are to run into hassles. Thieves and drunks aren't big on hiking. Camping in the wilderness is generally safe on all the islands – a twisted ankle, a wild boar or a cross-eyed hunter are the biggest safety concerns.

More information on all the following parks can be found in the individual island chapters.

National Parks There are two national parks in Hawaii which allow camping: Haleakala National Park on Maui and Hawaii Volcanoes National Park on the Big Island. These two parks offer some of the finest camping opportunities on the islands and also provide spectacular hiking. There are no camping fees at either, getting a space is seldom a problem and both parks have drive-up and wilderness camping areas.

State Parks The five largest islands have state park camping grounds. They range from wilderness areas that you need to backpack into to developed roadside camping sites. State parks often have caretakers and better security than county parks.

Camping is allowed in the following places: on Kauai in Kokee, Na Pali Coast and Polihale state parks; on Oahu in Keaiwa Heiau, Malaekahana and Sand Island state recreation areas; on Molokai in Palaau State Park; on Maui in Polipoli Spring State Recreation Area and Waianapanapa State Park; and on the Big Island in Kalopa State Park and MacKenzie State Recreation Area.

Camping in the state parks is free by permit and tents are required. Developed camping grounds generally have picnic tables, barbecue grills, drinking water, toilets and showers, although the maintenance of the facilities varies greatly.

The maximum length of stay allowable under a permit at any one state park is five nights. Another camping permit for the same park will not be issued until 30 days have elapsed. Camping grounds are open seven nights a week, except on Oahu where they are closed on Wednesday and Thursday nights. In addition, parks in forested areas may be closed during periods of drought due to extreme fire danger.

Camping permits can be obtained on weekdays from any of the following Division of State Parks offices, either in person, by mail or by phone:

Oahu
   Box 621, 1151 Punchbowl St, Honolulu, HI 96809 (☎ 587-0300)
Big Island
   Box 936, 75 Aupuni St , Hilo, HI 96721 (☎ 933-4200)
Maui
   54 High St, Wailuku, HI 96793 (☎ 243-5354)
Kauai
   Box 1671, 3060 Eiwa St, Room 306, Lihue, HI 96766 (☎ 241-3444)

Note Applicants must be 18 and provide their address and phone number as well as an identification number (driver's licence, passport or social security number) for each camper in the group. Applications should be received at least seven days in advance, but are not accepted earlier than 30 days before the intended camping date on Oahu or one year on the Neighbor Islands.

Cabins The state has housekeeping cabins on the Big Island at Kalopa State Park and at Kilauea and Mauna Kea state recreation areas, and on Maui at Polipoli Spring State Recreation Area and Waianapanapa State Park.

The cabins are generally simple places with a kitchen, a common area, a bathroom and one to three bedrooms. They have basic furnishings, bedding, hot showers and some cooking and eating utensils. Polipoli, the most remote, has neither electricity nor refrigerators and you'll need a 4WD vehicle or hiking boots to reach it.

The housekeeping cabins are good value: $10 for one person, $14 for two, $19.50 for three, $24 for four, $27.50 for five and $30 for six. People staying in the cabins are subject to the same five-day limit as tent campers.

Reservations can be made at any of the state park offices and should be done as early as possible as the cabins are in high demand. Summer is the busiest time, but reservations often book up well in advance throughout the year. The state parks office does, however, get cancellations and if someone with a reservation doesn't pay their deposit in time the computer automatically bounces them and the site opens again.

Cabin cancellations and waiting lists are handled only on the island where the cabins are located. Even at the last moment it's worth calling to see if something has become available. If you're a little flexible you might be lucky – as we have been on occasion.

Reservations can be made in person, by phone or by mail, with 50% of the fee due within two weeks of making the reservation. Personal cheques are accepted if you're paying more than 30 days in advance, but otherwise you'll need a bank cheque or postal money order. The remainder is due in cash when you check in. Refunds are given with notice 30 days prior to the camping date.

In addition to the state-maintained cabins, there are concession-run cabins at Malaekahana State Recreation Area on Oahu and Kokee State Park on Kauai and A-frame shelters at Hapuna Beach on the Big Island (see those sections for reservation information).

County Parks All the counties have parks with camping areas, although not all are of equal standard. Some county parks have wonderful white sand beaches and good facilities, while others are little more than unappealing roadside rest areas that have been turned into 'beach parks' simply by plopping down restrooms. Just because camping is allowed doesn't mean you'd want to camp there, or even use the beach.

Maui, which has the lion's share of outer island hotels and condos, seems more dedicated to getting your dollar than encouraging camping. Camping is allowed at only two county parks, each for only three nights, and neither is recommendable. The fee is $3 per person per night.

Molokai has two county parks with camping areas, one which is delightfully set on Hawaii's largest white-sand beach. The fee is $3 per person per night.

The Big Island has 13 county camping grounds and a fee of only $1 per person per night.

Kauai has seven county camping grounds, including a couple of the nicest beachside camping spots in Hawaii. The fee is $3 per person per night.

Oahu has 13 county camping grounds, a couple of which are safe and recommendable. There are no fees.

Hostels

Hawaii has two hostels associated with the International Youth Hostel Federation (IYHF). Both are on Oahu; one is in Waikiki and one is in Honolulu near the University of Hawaii.

In addition, a number of private places

offering inexpensive hostel-style accommodation have sprung up in the past couple of years. Private 'hostels' are located on Kauai in Wailua and Haena; on Maui in Wailuku, Keanae and Kipahulu; on the Big Island in Kailua-Kona and Hilo; and on Oahu in Waikiki, Kailua and Waimea. Some of the places are quite nice, while others are mere crash pads. Rates for a dorm bed range from about $10 to $15, and private rooms are often available as well.

Most of these establishments are on the up and up, but we have heard complaints from people on Oahu where 'touts' are sent to the airport to pick up backpackers. Apparently some places promise more than they deliver – a $40 double room turns out to be a mattress on the floor and that sort of thing – so do your best to assess the situation before accepting a ride.

B&Bs

There are hundreds of B&Bs scattered around Hawaii. Some are modest spare bedrooms in family households, others are romantic and private hideaways, and a few are full-fledged inns. B&Bs cost as little as $35, although most average $50 or $60 and the most exclusive properties are $100 to $150. Many require a minimum stay of two or three days, and some give discounts for stays of a week or more. B&Bs vary greatly but for the most part they represent some of the best value accommodation to be found in Hawaii.

Because Hawaii state codes place restrictions on serving home-cooked meals, most B&Bs offer a continental breakfast or provide food for guests to cook their own. Some places do provide full home-cooked breakfasts – they just don't advertise it.

Most home-based B&Bs don't handle their own reservations, but sign up with B&B reservation services. Some of these agencies can also book whole houses, condos and studio cottages as well. All require at least part of the payment in advance and have cancellation penalties. These agencies include:

Bed & Breakfast Hawaii, Box 449, Kapaa, HI 96746, is one of the largest services. For $10 (including postage) they'll send you a guidebook-style directory from which you can select a B&B, or you can simply book by phone. There's a $10 booking fee (☎ 822-7771 on Kauai, 536-8421 on Oahu, (800) 733-1632)

Bed & Breakfast Honolulu, 3242 Kaohinani Drive, Honolulu, HI 96817, despite the name, handles reservations on all the islands and can provide sample lists of B&Bs, including a list of those that welcome gay travellers. There's a $10 fee per reservation (☎ 595-7533, (800) 288-4666)

All Islands Bed & Breakfast, 823 Kainui Drive, Kailua, HI 96734, books over 350 host homes throughout Hawaii and there's no fee (☎ 263-2342, (800) 542-0344)

Hawaii's Best Bed & Breakfasts, c/o Barbara Campbell, Box 563, Kamuela, HI 96743, based on the Big Island, specialises in booking up-market B&Bs throughout Hawaii (☎ 885-4550, (800) 262-9912)

Pacific-Hawaii Bed & Breakfast, 19 Kai Nani Place, Kailua, HI 96734, charges a $10 booking fee and a 4% surcharge for payment by credit card (☎ 262-7865, (800) 999-6026)

My Island, Gordon & Joann Morse, Box 100, Volcano, HI 96785, don't charge a fee but they book only on the Big Island (☎ 967-7216)

Condominiums

Condos are individually owned apartments that are fully furnished with everything a visitor needs from linen and towels to dishes and cutlery. Condos have more space than hotel rooms, generally with a living room and full kitchen, and many also have washer/dryers, sofa beds and a lanai (veranda). Most condos don't have a daily room-cleaning service.

Condos are usually booked through rental agents, although some complexes have their own front desk. If you're staying awhile or are travelling with several people, condos almost always work out cheaper than all but the bottom-end hotels. However, most condo units booked through rental agents have a three to seven-day minimum stay and many require deposits.

Condos often offer weekly and monthly rates. The general rule is that the weekly rate is six times the daily rate, and the monthly is three times the weekly.

As most condo agencies deal with specific

destinations, they are listed in the individual island chapters.

FOOD

Eating in Hawaii can be a real treat, as the islands' ethnic diversity has given rise to hundreds of different foods. You can find every kind of Japanese food, an array of regional Chinese cuisines, spicy Korean specialities, native Hawaiian dishes and excellent Thai and Vietnamese food. Even McDonald's serves up saimin and Portuguese sausage and Woolworth has sushi at the lunch counter.

Local Fruit

Pineapple Hawaii's number one fruit crop is the pineapple. Most Hawaiian pineapple are of the smooth cayenne type and weigh a good five pounds. Pineapples are fairly unique among fruits in that they don't continue to ripen after they're picked. Though they're harvested year round, the long sunny days of summer produce the sweetest pineapples.

Papaya Papayas come in several varieties. One of the best of those found in grocery stores is the Solo, a small variety with pale strawberry-coloured flesh. The flavour of papayas depends largely on where they're grown. Some of the most prized are from the Kapoho area of Puna on the Big Island and the Kahuku area of Oahu. Papayas, which are a good source of calcium and vitamins A and C, are harvested all year round.

Avocado Hawaii has three main types of avocado: the West Indian, a smooth-skinned variety which matures in summer and autumn; the rough-skinned Guatemalan which matures in winter and spring; and the Mexican variety which has a small fruit and smooth skin. Many of the avocados now in Hawaii are a hybrid of the three. Local fruit tends to be larger and more watery than the avocados grown in California.

Mango Big old mango trees are abundant in Hawaii, even in remote valleys. The juicy oblong fruits are about three inches in diameter and four to six inches long. The fruits start out green but take on deeper colours as they ripen, usually reddening to an apricot colour. Mangoes are a good source of vitamins A and C. Two popular varieties, Pirie and Haden, are less stringy than those usually found in the wild. Mangoes are mainly a summer fruit.

Starfruit The carambola, or starfruit, is a translucent yellow-green fruit with five ribs like the points of a star. It has a crisp juicy pulp and can be eaten without being peeled.

Guava The common guava is a yellow, lime-shaped fruit, about two to three inches in diameter. It has a moist, pink, seedy flesh, all of which is edible. Guavas can be a little tart but tend to sweeten as they ripen. They're a good source of vitamin C and niacin and can be found along roadsides and trails.

Lilikoi Passion fruit is a vine with beautiful flowers which grow into small round fruits. The thick skin of the fruit is generally purple or yellow and wrinkles as it ripens. The pulp inside is juicy, seedy and slightly tart. The slimy texture can be a bit of a put-off the first time, but once you taste it you'll be hooked.

Mountain Apple The mountain apple is a small oval fruit a couple of inches long. The tree is related to the guava, although the fruit is completely different with a crispy white flesh and a pink skin. It fruits in the summer and is common along trails.

Ohelo These berries grow on low shrubs common in lava areas. It's a relative of the cranberry, similar in tartness and size. The fruit is red or yellow and is used in jellies and pies.

Breadfruit The Hawaiian breadfruit is a large, round, green fruit. It's comparable to potatoes in carbohydrates and is prepared much the same way. In old Hawaii, as in much of the Pacific, breadfruit was one of the traditional staples. ■

Though you could spend a bundle eating out, you don't need to, as there are good, cheap neighbourhood restaurants to explore on all the islands.

Hawaii also has many restaurants run by renowned chefs which feature gourmet foods of all type, including traditional continental fare. Some of the best restaurants are at the top-end hotels, although a fair number of the more successful chefs have moved on to open their own places.

Many of these 'renegade chefs' specialise in what's been dubbed 'Pacific Rim' or 'Hawaii Regional' cuisine, which incorporates fresh island ingredients and borrows liberally from the islands' various ethnic groups. It's marked by creative combinations such as kiawe-grilled freshwater shrimp with taro chips, wok-charred ahi with island greens and Puna goat cheese, and Peking duck in a ginger-lilikoi sauce.

Fresh fish is readily available throughout the islands. Seafood is generally expensive at places catering fancy meals to tourists, but can be quite reasonable at neighbourhood restaurants.

Note In Hawaii, as in the rest of the USA, 'entree' refers to the main course or main dish of a meal and 'granola' is a kind of cereal.

Fish

Some of the most popular locally caught fish include:

Hawaiian Name	Common Name
mahimahi	a fish called 'dolphin', (not the mammal)
aku	skipjack tuna
ahi	yellowfin tuna
ono	wahoo
opakapaka	pink snapper
onaga	red snapper
uku	gray snapper
au	swordfish, marlin
akule	mackerel bigeye scad
papio or ulua	jack fish
kaku	barracuda
uhu	parrotfish
mano	shark

Fruit

Hawaii has an abundance of fruit including avocado, banana, breadfruit, starfruit, coconut, guava, lychee, mango, papaya, *lilikoi*, or passion fruit, and pineapple. Sweet Kau oranges are grown on the Big Island.

Watermelons grown on Molokai are so famous throughout the islands that the airlines had to create special regulations for passengers carrying them out of Molokai to prevent loose melons from bombing their way down the aisles.

Wild fruits which can be picked along trails include strawberry guava, common guava, thimbleberries, mountain apples, Methley plums and ohelo berries.

Hawaiian Food

The traditional Hawaiian feast marking special events is the *luau*. Local luaus are still commonplace in modern Hawaii for events such as baby christenings. In spirit, these luaus are far more authentic than anything you'll see at a hotel, but they're family affairs and the short-stay visitor would be lucky indeed to get an invitation to one.

The main dish at a luau is *kalua pig*, which is roasted in a pit-like earthen oven called an *imu*. The imu is readied for cooking by building a fire and heating rocks in the pit. When the rocks are glowing red, layers of moisture-laden banana trunks and green ti leaves are placed over the stones. A pig which has been slit open is filled with some of the hot rocks and laid on top of the bed. Other foods wrapped in ti and banana leaves are placed around it. It's all covered with more ti leaves and a layer of mats and topped off with dirt to seal in the heat which then bakes and steams the food. Anything cooked in this style is called *kalua*.

The process takes about four to eight hours depending on the amount of food. A few of the hotel luaus still bake the pig outdoors in this traditional manner and you can often go in the morning and watch them prepare and bury the pig.

Wetland taro is used to make *poi*, a paste pounded from the cooked taro corms. Water is added to make it pudding-like and its consistency is measured in one, two or three-finger poi – which indicates how many fingers are required to bring it from bowl to mouth. Poi is highly nutritious and easily digestible, but an acquired taste. It is sometimes fermented to give it a zingier flavour.

Laulau is fish, pork and taro wrapped in a ti leaf bundle and steamed. *Lomi* salmon (or *lomilomi* salmon) is made by marinating thin slices of raw salmon with diced tomatoes and green onions (spring onions).

Other Hawaiian foods include baked *ulu* – breadfruit, *limu* – seaweed, *opihi* – the tiny limpet shells which fishers pick off the reef at low tide, and *pipikaula* – beef jerky. *Haupia*, the standard dessert to a Hawaiian meal, is a custard made of coconut cream thickened with cornstarch or arrowroot.

In Hawaiian food preparation, ti leaves are indispensable, functioning like a biodegradable version of both aluminium foil and paper plates: food is wrapped in it, cooked in it and served upon it.

Many visitors taste traditional Hawaiian food only at expensive luaus or by sampling a dollop of poi at one of the more adventurous hotel buffets. Though Hawaiian food is harder to find than other ethnic foods, there are a few restaurants throughout the islands that serve the real thing and it's some of the cheapest food in Hawaii.

Local Food

The distinct style of food called 'local' usually refers to a fixed plate lunch with 'two scoop rice', a scoop of macaroni salad and a serving of beef stew, mahimahi or teriyaki chicken, generally scoffed down with chopsticks. A breakfast plate might have Spam (a type of fatty canned meat), eggs, kimchee and, always, two scoops of rice.

These plate meals are the standard fare in diners and lunch wagons. If it's full of starches, fats and gravies, you're probably eating local.

Snacks

Pupus is the word for all kinds of munchies or hors d'oeuvres. Boiled peanuts, soy-flavoured rice crackers called *kaki mochi* and sashimi are common pupus.

Another local favourite is *poke*, which is raw fish marinated in soy sauce, oil, chilli peppers, green onions and seaweed. It's good with beer.

Crack Seed Crack seed is a Chinese snack food which can be sweet, sour, salty or some combination of the three. It's often made from dried fruits such as plums and apricots, although more exotic ones include sweet and sour baby cherry seeds, pickled mangoes and *li hing mui*, one of the sour favourites. Crack seed shops often sell dried cuttlefish, roasted green peas, candied ginger, beef jerky and rock candy as well.

Shave Ice Shave ice is similar to mainland snow cones, only better. The ice is shaved as fine as powder snow, packed into a paper cone and drenched with sweet fruit-flavoured syrups. Many islanders like the ones with ice cream and/or sweet azuki beans at the bottom, while kids usually opt for rainbow shave ice which has colourful stripes of different syrups.

DRINKS

Tap water is safe to drink but water from freshwater streams should be boiled.

Cans of Hawaiian-made fruit juices such as guava-orange or passion fruit are stocked at most stores. If you're going for a hike and want to toss a couple of drinks in your daypack, the juices make a good alternative to sodas as they don't explode when shaken and they taste good even when they're not kept cold.

Alcohol

The drinking age in Hawaii is 21. It's illegal to have open containers of alcohol in motor vehicles and drinking in public parks or on the beaches is also illegal although it's a common scene. All grocery stores sell liquor as do most of the smaller food marts. Hawaii has one winery, Tedeschi Vineyards on Maui, which makes a good pineapple wine, grape wine and champagne.

PAKALOLO

Hawaii's pakalolo is considered to be some of the most potent anywhere, although the scene of years past when local guys hung out in beach parking lots and whispered 'buds' to people walking by has virtually disappeared. Authorities have been so successful in rooting out marijuana crops and arresting growers that pakalolo is reportedly less common on Hawaii's streets than dangerous drugs like 'ice' and heroin. The possession of marijuana is illegal on the islands; yachties entering Hawaii should be aware that federal authorities have been known to seize boats after finding even minute quantities of marijuana on board.

THINGS TO BUY

Hawaii has a lot of fine craftspeople and quality handcrafts. Woodworkers generally use beautifully grained native Hawaiian hardwoods, such as koa, to create calabashes and bowls. Traditionally Hawaiian bowls are not decorated or ornate, but rather are shaped to bring out the natural beauty of the wood. The thinner and lighter the bowl, the finer the artistic skill and the greater the value.

There are some excellent island potters, many influenced by Japanese styles and aesthetics. Good raku work in particular can be found throughout the islands at reasonable prices.

Lauhala, the leaves of the pandanus tree which were once woven into the mats that Hawaiians slept on, are now woven into placemats, hats and baskets.

Many music shops carry recorded traditional and contemporary Hawaiian music. Hula musical instruments such as nose flutes and gourd rattles are uniquely Hawaiian, as is kukui nut jewellery and oils.

Niihau shell leis, made from the tiny shells which wash up on the island of Niihau, are one of the most prized Hawaiiana souvenirs. Elaborate pieces can cost thousands of dollars.

Hawaii's island-style clothing is colourful and light, often with prints of tropical flowers. The classiest *aloha* shirts are of lightweight cotton with subdued colours (like those of reverse fabric prints). Women might want to buy a *muu-muu*, a loose, comfortable, full-length Hawaiian-style dress.

Foods are popular purchases. The standard souvenir is macadamia nuts, either canned or covered in chocolate. Kona coffee, macadamia nut butters, lilikoi or *poha* berry preserves and mango chutney all make convenient, compact gift items.

Pineapples are not a great choice in the souvenir department. Not only are they heavy and bulky, but they're likely to be just as cheap at home.

If you're into Japanese food, Hawaii is a good place to pick up ingredients that might be difficult to find back home. Most grocery stores have a wide selection of things like dried seaweed, mochi and ume plums.

Flowers such as orchids, anthuriums and proteas make good gifts if you're flying straight home. Proteas stay fresh for about 10 days and then can be dried.

Getting There & Away

AIR

Hawaii is a major Pacific hub and an intermediate stop on most flights between the US mainland and Asia, Australia, New Zealand and the South Pacific. Passengers on any of these routes can usually make a free stopover in Honolulu.

With the exception of a few flights from the US mainland that go directly to the Neighbor Islands, all flights to Hawaii land at Honolulu International Airport.

There are numerous airlines flying to Hawaii and a variety of fares are available. In addition to a straightforward return ticket, Hawaii can also be part of a Round-the-World or Circle Pacific ticket. So rather than just walking into the nearest travel agent or airline office, it pays to do a bit of research and shopping around first.

You might want to start by perusing the travel sections of magazines and large newspapers, like the *New York Times*, the *San Francisco Chronicle-Examiner* and the *Los Angeles Times* in the USA; the *Saturday Age* or the *Sydney Morning Herald* in Australia; and *Time Out* or *TNT* in the UK. Keeping in mind that air fares are constantly changing, the fares listed throughout this chapter should at least give you an idea of relative costs.

Round-the-World Tickets

Round-the-World (RTW) tickets, which allow you to fly on the combined routes of two or more airlines, can be an economical way to circle the globe. Tickets are usually valid for one year and you must travel in one general direction without backtracking.

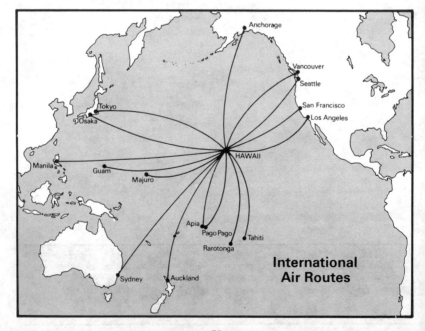

International Air Routes

While most US airlines restrict the number of sectors that can be flown within the USA, and a few heavily travelled routes (such as Honolulu to Tokyo) are blacked out by some airlines, stopovers are otherwise generally unlimited.

There's an almost endless variety of airline and destination combinations possible. Because of Honolulu's central Pacific location, Hawaii can be included on most RTW tickets.

Philippine Airlines in combination with TWA offers one of the cheapest tickets at US$1999, however the routing is more limited than with many other RTW tickets and only three stopovers are allowed in the USA.

If you want to explore the USA more thoroughly, TWA in combination with Singapore Airlines has a ticket for US$2570 that includes up to 12 stops in the continental USA, as well as Honolulu, Taipei, Hong Kong, Singapore, Bangkok, Bombay and London, among others. This ticket purchased in Australia costs A$3023 and can be written to originate from a number of cities, including Melbourne, Sydney and Perth, although domestic travel is not allowed between Australian cities.

Continental has a RTW fare with Malaysia Airlines which includes the US west coast, New York, London, Paris, Amsterdam, Frankfurt, Zurich, Dubai, Kuala Lumpur, Melbourne, Sydney, Auckland and Honolulu. There's a limit of four stops in the USA. The fare is UK£2127 from London, US$3198 from the USA. Continental also links up with Italia, KLM, Thai and Singapore airlines for other variations.

Bucket shops and travel agencies specialising in discount travel often have good deals on RTW tickets. Some of them also act as consolidators, piecing together itineraries using inexpensive one-way sectors that they buy in bulk from airlines. While consolidated RTW tickets usually have more limited itineraries than standard RTW tickets, and some may even require part of your trip to be made overland, the cost can be as low as US$1400. One US company

that specialises in consolidated tickets is Air Brokers International (☎ (800) 475-9041), 323 Geary St, San Francisco.

Circle Pacific Tickets

For Circle Pacific tickets, two airlines link up to allow stopovers along their combined Pacific Rim routes. Rather than simply flying from Point A to Point B, these tickets allow you to swing through much of the Pacific and eastern Asia taking in a variety of destinations – as long as you keep travelling in the same circular direction.

Continental Airlines links with Garuda allowing stops in places like Honolulu, Auckland, Melbourne, Sydney, Brisbane, Bali, Jakarta, Tokyo and the US west coast. Continental's link with Singapore Airlines allows you to stop in Melbourne, Sydney, Brisbane, Auckland, Christchurch, Tokyo, Taipei, Hong Kong, Bangkok, Singapore, Honolulu and the US west coast. Continental charges US$2268 for its Circle Pacific fare and also links with Thai Airways, Philippine Airlines, All Nippon Airways, Air France or Korean Air for other variations.

Canadian Airlines has Circle Pacific fares from Vancouver that include, in one combination or another, virtually all Pacific Rim destinations. Canadian's partners include Qantas, Air New Zealand, Singapore, Garuda, Cathay Pacific or Malaysia airlines, with fares costing C$2915 (US$2449).

Circle Pacific fares include four stopovers with the option of adding additional stops at US$50 each. There's a 14-day advance-purchase requirement, a 25% cancellation penalty and a maximum stay of six months.

As with Round-the-World tickets, there are a large number of airlines and destination combinations possible. Fares can vary a bit from country to country and restrictions may be somewhat different. From Hong Kong, for instance, Cathay Pacific's Circle Pacific fare works out to about US$2115.

Discount Fares from Hawaii

Hawaii is a good place to get discounted

fares to virtually any place around the Pacific. Fares vary according to the month, airline and supply and demand, but usually you can find a return fare to Los Angeles or San Francisco for around $300; to Tokyo for $450; to Auckland, Sydney, Hong Kong or Manila for $600; to Bangkok or Singapore for $700; and to Bali for $750. If you don't have a set destination in mind you can some-times find some great on-the-spot deals. The travel pages of Honolulu's Sunday *Star-Bulletin & Advertiser* have scores of ads by travel agencies advertising discounted over-seas fares.

Honolulu International Airport
Honolulu International is a modern airport that's continually undergoing expansion.

Air Travel Glossary
Apex Apex, or 'advance purchase excursion' is a discounted ticket which must be paid for in advance. There are penalties if you wish to change it.

Baggage Allowance This will be written on your ticket: usually one 20 kg item to go in the hold, plus one item of hand luggage. However, most US airlines allow passengers to check in two bags, each weighing up to 70 pounds, and carry on a third weighing 40 pounds.

Bucket Shop An unbonded travel agency specialising in discounted airline tickets.

Bumped Just because you have a confirmed seat doesn't mean you're going to get on the plane – see Overbooking.

Cancellation Penalties If you have to cancel or change an Apex ticket there are often heavy penalties involved, insurance can sometimes be taken out against these penalties. Some airlines impose penalties on regular tickets as well, particularly against 'no show' passengers.

Check In Airlines ask you to check in a certain time ahead of the flight departure (usually 1½ hours on international flights). If you fail to check in on time and the flight is overbooked the airline can cancel your booking and give your seat to somebody else.

Confirmation Having a ticket written out with the flight and date you want doesn't mean you have a seat until the agent has checked with the airline that your status is 'OK' or confirmed. Meanwhile you could just be 'on request'.

Discounted Tickets There are two types of discounted fares officially discounted (see Promotional Fares) and unofficially discounted. The lowest prices often impose drawbacks like flying with unpopular airlines, inconvenient schedules, or unpleasant routes and connections. A discounted ticket can save you other things than money – you may be able to pay Apex prices without the associated Apex advance booking and other requirements. Discounted tickets only exist where there is fierce competition.

Full Fares Airlines traditionally offer first class (coded F), business class (coded J) and economy class (coded Y) tickets. These days there are so many promotional and discounted fares available from the regular economy class that few passengers pay full economy fare.

Lost Tickets If you lose your airline ticket an airline will usually treat it like a travellers' cheque and, after inquiries, issue you with another one. Legally, however, an airline is entitled to treat it like cash and if you lose it then it's gone forever. Take good care of your tickets.

No Shows No shows are passengers who fail to show up for their flight, sometimes due to unexpected delays or disasters, sometimes due to simply forgetting, sometimes because they made more than one booking and didn't bother to cancel the one they didn't want. Full fare passengers who fail to turn up are sometimes entitled to travel on a later flight. The rest of us are penalised (see Cancellation Penalties).

On Request An unconfirmed booking for a flight, see Confirmation.

Although it's a busy place it's not particularly difficult to get around.

The airport has all the expected services, including snack bars, restaurants, newsstands, sundry shops, lei stands, gift shops, duty-free shops, a 24-hour medical clinic, and a mini-hotel for naps and showers. There are car-rental counters and hotel/condo courtesy phones in the baggage claim area. If you arrive early for a flight and are looking for something to do, the new **Pacific Aerospace Museum** ($2) in the main departure area is open from 8 am to 5 pm daily.

The free Wiki Wiki Shuttle (☎ 836-2505) connects the more distant parts of the airport, and links the main terminals with the interisland terminals. It runs between 7 am and 10 pm and is available streetside at the main

---

Open Jaws A return ticket where you fly out to one place but return from another. If available this can save you backtracking to your arrival point.

Overbooking Airlines hate to fly empty seats and since every flight has some passengers who fail to show up (see No Shows), airlines often book more passengers than they have seats. Usually the excess passengers balance those who fail to show up but occasionally somebody gets bumped. If this happens guess who it is most likely to be? The passengers who check in late.

Promotional Fares Officially discounted fares like Apex fares which are available from travel agents or direct from the airline.

Reconfirmation At least 72 hours prior to departure time of an onward or return flight you must contact the airline and 'reconfirm' that you intend to be on the flight. If you don't do this the airline can delete your name from the passenger list and you could lose your seat. You don't have to reconfirm the first flight on your itinerary or if your stopover is less than 72 hours. It doesn't hurt to reconfirm more than once.

Restrictions Discounted tickets often have various restrictions on them – advance purchase is the most usual one (see Apex). Others are restrictions on the minimum and maximum period you must be away, such as a minimum of 14 days or a maximum of one year. See Cancellation Penalties.

Standby A discounted ticket where you only fly if there is a seat free at the last moment. Standby fares are usually only available on domestic routes, although they're largely a thing of the past in the USA with the exception of a few commuter airlines.

Tickets Out An entry requirement for many countries is that you have an onward or return ticket, in other words, a ticket out of the country. If you're not sure what you intend to do next, the easiest solution is to buy the cheapest onward ticket to a neighbouring country or a ticket from a reliable airline which can later be refunded if you do not use it.

Transferred Tickets Airline tickets cannot be transferred from one person to another. Travellers sometimes try to sell the return half of their ticket, but officials can ask you to prove that you are the person named on the ticket. This is unlikely to happen on domestic flights, on an international flight tickets may be compared with passports.

Travel Agencies Travel agencies vary widely and you should ensure you use one that suits your needs. Some simply handle tours while full-service agencies handle everything from tours and tickets to car-rental and hotel bookings. A good one will do all these things and can save you a lot of money but if all you want is a ticket at the lowest possible price, then you really need an agency specialising in discounted tickets. A discounted ticket agency, however, may not be useful for other things, like hotel bookings.

Travel Periods Some officially discounted fares, Apex fares in particular, vary with the time of year. There is often a low (off-peak) season and a high (peak) season. Sometimes there's an intermediate or shoulder season as well. At peak times, when everyone wants to fly, not only will the officially discounted fares be higher but so will unofficially discounted fares or there may simply be no discounted tickets available. Usually the fare depends on your outward flight – if you depart in the high season and return in the low season, you pay the high-season fare. ■

lobby, the outlying gates (6-11 and 26-31) and the inter-island gates.

Money Thomas Cook has currency exchange booths spread around the airport, including at the international arrival area and the central departure lobby.

There's a Bank of Hawaii on the ground level across the street from baggage claim D. It's open from 8.30 am to 3 pm Monday to Thursday and to 6 pm on Fridays.

Baggage Storage Currently all baggage storage is in the parking garage on the ground floor opposite the main overseas terminal. It's open 24 hours a day and, depending on the size of the item, storage costs $2 to $5 a day.

For small items, there are baggage lockers at the same locale which cost $1 a day.

For information on either call 836-6547.

Airlines Serving Honolulu
The following airlines have scheduled flights to Honolulu International Airport on Oahu. The numbers listed for each airline are the local Oahu numbers; those that begin with 800 can be called toll-free from anywhere within the state.

Air Micronesia	☎ (800) 231-0856
Air Molokai	☎ 521-0090
Air New Zealand	☎ (800) 262-1234
Airline of the Marshall Islands	☎ 949-5522
All Nippon Airways	☎ 921-2800
Aloha Airlines	☎ 836-1111
Aloha IslandAir	☎ 833-3219
America West Airlines	☎ (800) 247-5692
American Airlines	☎ 833-7600
American Trans Air	☎ 833-0074
Canadian Airlines	☎ (800) 426-7000
China Airlines	☎ 955-0088
Continental Airlines	☎ 523-0000
Delta Air Lines	☎ (800) 221-1212
Garuda Indonesia	☎ 947-9500
Hawaiian Airlines	☎ 537-5100
Japan Air Lines	☎ 521-1441
Japan Air System	☎ 924-1515
Korean Air	☎ 923-7302
Malaysia Airlines	☎ 528-2999
Northwest Airlines	☎ 955-2255
Philippine Airlines	☎ (800) 435-9725
Qantas Airways	☎ (800) 227-4500
Singapore Airlines	☎ 524-6063
TWA	☎ (800) 221-2000
United Airlines	☎ 547-2211

To/From the US Mainland
Domestic air fares are constantly in flux. Fares vary with the season you travel, the day of the week you fly, your length of stay and the flexibility the ticket provides for flight changes and refunds. Still nothing determines fares more than business, and when things are slow, regardless of the season, some airlines will drop fares to fill the empty seats. There's a lot of competition to Honolulu from the major mainland cities and at any given time any one of the airlines could have the cheapest fare.

The airlines each have their own requirements and restrictions which also seem to be constantly changing. For the latest deals, either find a knowledgeable travel agent or just call the different airlines and compare.

When you call the airlines it's important to ask for the lowest fare, as that's not always the first one they'll quote. Each flight has only a limited number of seats available at the cheapest fares. When you make reservations the agents will generally tell you the best fare that's still available on the date you give them, which may or may not be the cheapest fare that the airline is currently offering. If you make reservations far enough in advance and are a little flexible with dates, you'll usually do better.

Typically the lowest return fares from the US mainland to Honolulu are about $600 to $750 from the east coast and $300 to $425 from the west coast. Though conditions vary, the cheapest fares are generally for midweek flights and have advance-purchase requirements and other restrictions. Sometimes tickets are non-refundable and non-changeable (though most airlines say they make allowances for medical emergencies if you have a note from a doctor).

As we were finishing up our research for this edition, we found a couple of airlines offering special immediate-purchase fares of $300 from the west coast to Honolulu. However most domestic airlines flying to

Honolulu were offering return fares of $370 from the west coast and $690 from the east coast. Those fares required a 14-day advance purchase, were for travel Monday to Thursday and had a 60-day maximum stay. After ticketing, the departure date could be changed up to 14 days prior to departure and the return date could be changed at any time; the fee for each change was $25. Although these fares were non-refundable, some of the airlines are now allowing this type of ticket to be 'reused' if you decide to cancel; with a 14-day advance notice and a $25 fee the old ticket can be exchanged like cash for the purchase of a new ticket.

For travellers wanting to stay longer, tickets with similar conditions that allowed a one-year stay and required a seven-day advance purchase were $100 more.

Most domestic airlines have a senior citizen voucher programme for people aged 62 and older. Under this programme you can buy a book of either four or eight coupons, which cost approximately $550 and $1000 respectively. Each coupon is good for a one-way ticket anywhere in continental USA; to go from the US mainland to Hawaii you use two coupons. From anywhere but the west coast these coupons can be one of the cheapest ways of getting to Hawaii.

The following airlines fly to Honolulu from both the US east and west coasts:

American	☎ (800) 433-7300
Continental	☎ (800) 525-0280
Delta	☎ (800) 221-1212
Northwest	☎ (800) 225-2525
TWA	☎ (800) 221-2000
United	☎ (800) 241-6522

Hawaiian Airlines (☎ (800) 367-5320) flies to Honolulu from Seattle, San Francisco, Las Vegas, Los Angeles and Anchorage. Depending on the season, the fare from Anchorage to Honolulu is $439 to $518 with a 14-day advance-purchase requirement and a 45-day maximum stay. Most of Hawaiian Airlines' west coast fares hover around $400 return, though they occasionally offer special fares for under $300. Usually a

Neighbor Island destination can be added on for $20 more.

America West Airlines (☎ (800) 247-5692) flies to Honolulu from Phoenix and Las Vegas. During the off-peak season, which is roughly from late August to mid-December and from mid-January to mid-June, midweek return fares are $418 for a ticket allowing a 30-day stay and requiring a 14-day advance purchase, and $518 for one allowing a 60-day stay with a seven-day advance purchase. It costs $40 more to fly on Fridays, Saturdays or Sundays. During peak season, fares are $518 for the 30-day ticket, $608 for the 60-day ticket.

Flight time to Honolulu is about 5½ hours from the west coast, 11 hours from the east coast.

To/From Canada

The cheapest return fares (in Canadian dollars) to Honolulu with Canadian Airlines International are $429 from Vancouver, $529 from Calgary or Edmonton, and $789 from Toronto. These fares require a minimum stay of seven days and allow a maximum stay of 15 days, have a 14-day advance-purchase requirement and are non-refundable and non-changeable.

For $100 more ($529 from Vancouver for instance) you can get a ticket that allows a 30-day stay and for an additional $100 ($629 from Vancouver) there's a third type of ticket that allows a maximum stay of 90 days. Both of these fares have a seven-day advance-purchase requirement, a $150 cancellation penalty and a $50 fee for date changes.

Fares on all three types of tickets are for midweek travel all year round except for a couple of weeks around the Christmas and New Year holidays.

The toll-free numbers for Canadian Airlines are (800) 663-0010 from British Columbia, (800) 263-6133 from Toronto's 416 area code and (800) 268-4910 from any other area code in Ontario.

To/From Central & South America

Most flights to Hawaii from Central and South America go via Houston or Los

Angeles, though a few of those from the eastern cities go via New York.

Continental has flights from about 20 cities in Mexico and Central America, including San Jose, Guatemala City, Cancun and Merida. Their lowest return fare from Mexico City to Honolulu is US$879, allows a maximum stay of 60 days and has a three-day advance-purchase requirement.

To/From Australia

Qantas flies to Honolulu from Sydney, Melbourne (via Sydney) and Brisbane, with return fares ranging from A$1013 to A$1279, depending on the season. These tickets have a 21-day advance-purchase requirement, a minimum stay of seven days and a maximum stay of 60 days. From Sydney and Melbourne, for approximately A$350 extra, you can also buy a return ticket to Honolulu that requires only a seven-day advance purchase, allows a stay of up to 90 days and includes a free stopover in Fiji. From Cairns, the cheapest fare to Honolulu currently available on Qantas costs from A$1281 to A$1550, depending on the season, requires a seven-day advance purchase and allows a 90-day stay.

United and Continental airlines also fly from Sydney and Melbourne to Honolulu and have fares that are comparable to those offered by Qantas.

To/From New Zealand

Air New Zealand has an Auckland to Honolulu return fare ranging from a low of NZ$1279 (February, October, November) to a high of NZ$1479 (December, January). These tickets have to be purchased at least 21 days in advance and within seven days of making reservations, and allow stays of up to two months. During slow periods, Air New Zealand sometimes runs discounted specials.

United Airlines has a return fare from Auckland to Honolulu for NZ$1299 that allows a two-month stay and has no advance-purchase requirement. United's next cheapest fare, NZ$1529, allows stays of up to six months.

To/From Fiji

Qantas and Air New Zealand have return fares from Nadi to Honolulu for F$1075 (US$721). The same fare is valid all year round, has a one-week minimum stay and a one-year maximum stay, and has no advance-purchase requirement or penalties for changes and cancellations.

The one-way fare from Nadi to Honolulu costs F$754 with a 14-day advance-purchase requirement.

To/From other South Pacific Islands

Hawaiian Airlines flies to Honolulu from Tonga, Tahiti, the Cook Islands, Western Samoa and American Samoa. Air New Zealand flies to Honolulu from Tonga, the Cook Islands and Western Samoa.

The lowest return fare from Tonga to Honolulu costs T$1076 (US$815), requires a 14-day advance purchase and allows a stay of up to one year. A one-way ticket costs T$656.

From Rarotonga on the Cook Islands, the cheapest return fare to Honolulu is NZ$1049 (US$571) during February, October and November; NZ$1249 in December and January; and NZ$1149 in other months. This ticket requires a 14-day advance purchase. The one-way fare is NZ$890 all year round.

From Pago Pago in American Samoa, the Honolulu return fare is US$589/689 in the low/high season, while the one-way fare costs US$345. From Apia in Western Samoa, the Honolulu return fare is WS$1247 (US$515) in the low season, WS$1347 in the high season. The one-way fare is WS$756.

In both American and Western Samoa, return tickets must be purchased within seven days of making reservations and are good for stays of up to one year. Low-season fares are valid from 6 January to mid-June and from mid-September to mid-December. The one-way fares given require a 14-day advance purchase.

From Papeete in Tahiti, the low-season return fare to Honolulu costs US$868 for a maximum stay of three months and US$907 for stays of up to one year. In high season, the fare is US$980/1060 respectively.

To/From Micronesia

From Guam to Honolulu, both Northwest and Continental have return fares from $776 to $876, depending on the departure date. On Northwest, the ticket allows a stay of up to one year and no advance purchase is required, while on Continental there's a maximum stay of 60 days and a seven-day advance-purchase requirement.

The cheapest nonstop one-way ticket from Guam to Honolulu is with Continental; it costs $478 and doesn't require an advance purchase.

The more exciting way to get from Guam, however, is to take Continental Air Micronesia's island hopper which stops en route at Chuuk (Truk), Pohnpei, Kosrae and Majuro before reaching Honolulu. It costs $632 one way. If you're coming from Asia this is a good alternative to a nonstop transpacific flight and a great way to see some of the Pacific's most remote islands without having to spend a lot of money.

To/From Japan

Northwest Airlines, United Airlines and Japan Air Lines fly to Honolulu from Osaka and Tokyo.

Northwest has the cheapest return fare from Japan to Honolulu, at Y145,000 (US$1104). The ticket is good for stays of two months and no advance purchase is required, though it must be bought within 24 hours of making the reservation. United Airlines' tickets good for a two-month stay cost about 10% more.

A one-way ticket from Japan to Honolulu costs almost as much as the return fare: Y144,600 (US$1101). For about the same amount of money you could instead fly from Japan to Guam (Y69,400) and then pick up a Continental Air Micronesia ticket that would allow you to stop at some of the Micronesia islands on your way to Honolulu.

To/From South-East Asia

There are numerous airlines flying directly to Hawaii from South-East Asia. The fares given are the cheapest ones that can be purchased directly from the airlines, though bucket shops in places like Bangkok and Singapore should be able to come up with deeper cuts. Also, if you're travelling to the USA from South-East Asia, tickets to the US west coast are not that much more than tickets to Hawaii and many allow a free stopover in Honolulu.

Northwest Airlines flies to Honolulu from Hong Kong, Bangkok, Manila and Singapore. From Hong Kong to Honolulu, return fares cost HK$7288 (US$941) from September to mid-June and HK$7988 (US$1032) the rest of the year. From Singapore to Honolulu, return fares cost S$2625 (US$1627). Both tickets are good for up to one year and have no advance-purchase requirements.

United Airlines flies to Honolulu from Manila, Hong Kong and Bangkok. Its cheapest excursion ticket from Manila is US$1043 and they have a one-way ticket for US$652. From Hong Kong, United charges US$1087 return; US$598 one way. Flights to Honolulu from Bangkok cost US$1070 return, US$538 one way. These tickets have no advance-purchase requirements and the return tickets are good for up to one year.

Flights from Manila to Honolulu on Philippine Airlines cost from US$557 to US$668 one way and from US$962 to US$1013 return, depending on the season. Tickets must be purchased seven to 14 days in advance and return tickets are valid for one year.

The one-way/return fares to Honolulu on Korean Airlines are: US$742/1122 from Bangkok, US$550/950 from Hong Kong and US$605/956 from Seoul.

To/From Europe

The most common route from Europe is west via New York or Los Angeles. If you're interested in heading east with stops in Asia, it may be cheaper to get a Round-the-World ticket instead of returning the same way.

American Airlines has one of the better London to Honolulu connections, combining two nonstop flights that connect in Los Angeles; the return fare is UK£494 (US$923) and allows a one-year stay. Its cheapest fare from Paris to Honolulu is

FF7945 (US$1209) and it's good for a stay of up to three months. From Frankfurt or Berlin, the fare is DM2172 (US$1599) and you can stay up to six months. All of these American Airlines fares are for Monday to Thursday travel and require a 21-day advance purchase.

On Continental, the cheapest London to Honolulu return ticket is UK£638 with a 14-day advance purchase and a stay of up to one year allowed. Continental's cheapest Paris to Honolulu return ticket costs FF7210, with a 21-day advance-purchase requirement, but it allows a maximum stay of only 21 days. From Munich or Frankfurt to Honolulu, Continental's cheapest return ticket is DM2589; no advance purchase is required and you can stay up to six months. All three fares are for mid-week travel.

You can usually beat these fares at bucket shops. Two of the best places in Europe for buying cheap tickets are London and Amsterdam, and they both have numerous, well-advertised bucket shops.

Two good, reliable agents for cheap tickets in the UK are: Trailfinders (☎ 071-938-3366), 46 Earls Court Rd, London W8 6EJ, and STA (☎ 071-937-9962), 74 Old Brompton Rd, London SW7 .

SEA

Travel agents, or shops that sell discount cruise tickets, are the best sources of information for transpacific cruises, though there are not many Hawaii-bound cruises to choose from.

Cunard (☎ (800) 221-4770) books the *Queen Elizabeth II* on five-day cruises between Ensenada (Mexico) and Hawaii from about $1770 one way, which includes a one-way air fare back from Honolulu to the US west coast. They also book the *Sagafjord* on South Pacific cruises which include Hawaii. Both cruises are infrequent, occurring only about once a year.

Royal Cruise Line (☎ (800) 227-4534) has a 16-day cruise to Hawaii which begins and ends in Los Angeles, goes via Ensenada, and includes about 11 days at sea and five days in Hawaii. The cheapest inside cabin costs $3200, based on double occupancy, for early bookings. A one-way eight-day version that includes the cruise from Ensenada to Honolulu, two nights in a Waikiki hotel and air fare from Honolulu to the US west coast, starts from $2300.

TOURS

There are a slew of package tours available to Hawaii. The basic ones just include air fare and accommodation, while others can be quite elaborate and include such things as lei greetings, car rentals, sightseeing tours and all sorts of recreational activities. If you're interested, travel agents can help you sort through the various packages.

For those with limited time, package tours can be the cheapest way to go. Costs vary, but one-week tours with air fare and no-frills hotel accommodation usually start around $499 from the US west coast, $699 from the US east coast, based on double occupancy. If you want to stay somewhere fancy or island hop, they can easily be double that.

Specialised Tours

In addition to traditional package tours, there are a number of study and adventure tours to Hawaii.

The University of Research Expeditions Program (☎ 510-642-6586), University of California, Berkeley, CA 94720, runs a couple of work/study tours a year assisting scholars in the field with such projects as surveying ancient petrogylphs or studying the ecology of plants that grow in lava. Most tours last for about two weeks, and rates range from $1100 to $1400, including food and simple accommodation but excluding air fare.

Island Bicycle Adventures (☎ 967-8603, (800) 233-2226), Box 458, Volcano, HI 96785, organises six-day bike tours of Kauai, Maui or the Big Island for $965, which include accommodation (based on double occupancy) and meals but not air fare. Bike rentals are about $100 more.

Hawaiian Island Windsurfing (☎ 572-5601, (800) 782-6105), 460 Dairy Rd,

Kahului, HI 96732, has customised tour packages for windsurfers which include windsurfing gear, car rental and accommodation. A one-week land package costs from $475 per person, based on double occupancy. The air fare from the US west coast can usually be added onto the package for about $325 to $400 more.

Elderhostel (☎ 617-426-8056), 75 Federal St, Boston, MA 02110, is a nonprofit organisation offering week-long educational programmes for those aged 60 or older. The organisation has its origins in the youth hostels of Europe and the folk schools of Scandinavia. There's a full range of ongoing programmes all year round. One Big Island programme, in conjunction with the Lyman Museum in Hilo, focuses on such topics as medicinal plants, Hawaiian culture through archaeology, the rainforest and endangered species. The fee is $400, which includes seven nights of accommodation, all meals and five days of classes. Other programmes are held at the Volcano Art Center and at Oahu colleges.

Oceanic Society Expeditions (☎ 415-441-1106, (800) 326-7491), Fort Mason Center, Building E, San Francisco, CA 94123, the environmental travel arm of Friends of the Earth, does eco-tours conducted with a noninvasive approach to viewing wildlife.

From Kona on the Big Island, the society offers a four-day humpback whale expedition for $975 including meals and accommodation aboard a 41-foot sailing vessel. The air fare to Hawaii is not included.

The tours operate from January to March. The boat sails among the endangered humpbacks, photographing them for identification and recording their underwater songs. Tours include snorkelling time off the Kona Coast.

LEAVING HAWAII
Customs Fee & Departure Tax

The USA must be one of the few countries in the world that charges for the 'privilege' of going through customs. Passengers flying into the USA from any destination except Canada and Mexico are charged a $10 customs fee. There's also a $6 departure tax to leave Honolulu International Airport for a foreign destination. Both of these fees are hidden taxes that are added on to the purchase price of your airline ticket.

Getting Around

AIR

The major airports handling inter-island traffic are at Honolulu (Oahu), Lihue (Kauai), Kahului (Maui), Kona and Hilo (both on the Big Island).

Smaller airports with scheduled commercial flights are: Waimea-Kohala (also called Kamuela), on the Big Island; Kapalua West Maui and Hana, both on Maui; Princeville, on Kauai's north shore; Molokai Airport and Kalaupapa (at the leprosy colony), both on Molokai; and Lanai.

Aloha Airlines and Hawaiian Airlines, the two major inter-island carriers, both have frequent flights in full-bodied aircraft between the five major airports.

The smaller airports are predominantly served by the two commuter airlines, Aloha IslandAir and Air Molokai, both of which use prop planes. However, Hawaiian Airlines also flies to Molokai, Lanai and Kapalua West Maui.

Air Fares

Hawaiian Airlines and Aloha Airlines both have a standard fare for flights between any two airports; with Aloha the fare is $68.95, with Hawaiian it's $69.95. (An exception is Aloha's commuter flight between Hilo and Kona which costs $28.) Return tickets are double the one-way fare.

Both airlines offer coupon booklets which contain six tickets good for inter-island flights between any two destinations. These tickets can be used by any number of people and on any flight without restrictions. With Aloha tickets you can combine the routes of both Aloha Airlines and Aloha IslandAir,

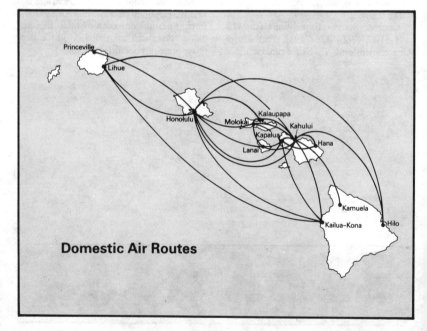

Domestic Air Routes

flying between any two airports served by either airline for a single ticket. You can buy the coupon books from the airlines at airport ticket counters for $305 with Aloha and $294 with Hawaiian, however, many travel agents discount the books by a good 10% and will also sell the coupons individually for $45 to $50 each.

Periodically there are other specials, with Hawaiian generally discounting a little deeper.

However, as this book goes to press, youth and senior fares, as well as the long-standing discounts on the first and last flights of the day between Honolulu and the main Neighbor Island airports, are not being offered.

Both Aloha and Hawaiian are professionally run operations. Until recently Aloha ranked at the top of the customer satisfaction list compiled by the US Transportation Department, with the fewest customer complaints among major US airlines. Hawaiian was generally found at the other end of the list.

In the latest reports, however, both airlines have gravitated towards the centre of the list and in deciding which to travel with you're probably just as well off going with whoever has the best deal and is leaving when you want to go.

Air Passes Both Aloha and Hawaiian airlines offer good-value passes allowing unlimited air travel for a specified number of consecutive days. The cheapest pass, which is good for five days, is roughly equivalent to the cost of a return air ticket.

The Hawaiian AirPass offered by Hawaiian Airlines is the most flexible. Reservations can be made in advance or you can fly on a space-available basis, and you're free to revise your itinerary at will. Anyone who possesses an inbound ticket to Hawaii can buy the pass once they arrive in the islands. Passes are non-refundable and will not be replaced if lost or stolen. The fare is: $139 for five days, $159 for one week, $199 for 10 days and $239 for two weeks. Passes are $20 cheaper for children and senior citizens.

Aloha Airlines has only a five-day pass,

which costs $139. Though you're allowed unlimited flights, you must make reservations for your entire itinerary in advance, and once the ticket is purchased, no changes are allowed. It's valid on flights by both Aloha Airlines and Aloha IslandAir.

Local Air Services
Hawaiian Airlines Hawaiian has about 250 flights a day between Honolulu, Lihue, Kahului, Kapalua West Maui, Kona, Hilo, Molokai and Lanai. They fly DC-9s between the main destinations and 50-passenger deHavilland Dash 7 aircraft to the smaller airports.

Reservation numbers for Hawaiian Airlines are:

Oahu	☎ 537-5100
Neighbor Islands	☎ (800) 882-8811
US mainland & Canada	☎ (800) 367-5320
American Samoa	☎ 669-1875
Western Samoa	☎ 21345
Cook Islands	☎ 239-1722
Tahiti	☎ 4215-00
Tonga	☎ 21-688

Aloha Airlines Aloha Airlines, which flies 737s between Honolulu, Lihue, Kahului, Kona and Hilo, has about 300 inter-island flights a day.

Reservation numbers for Aloha Airlines are:

Oahu	☎ 836-1111
Kauai	☎ 245-3691
Maui	☎ 244-9071
Big Island	☎ 935-5771
US mainland	☎ (800) 367-5250
British Columbia & Alberta	☎ (800) 663-9396
Rest of Canada	☎ (800) 663-9471
Sydney	☎ 02-236-0666
Tokyo	☎ 03-3216-5250
Osaka	☎ 06-341-7241
Hong Kong	☎ 05-251-365

Aloha IslandAir Aloha IslandAir serves Hawaii's smaller airports using 18-passenger deHavilland Dash 6 aircraft. As these prop planes fly lower than jet aircraft, you often get better views en route. Aloha IslandAir is part of the Aloha Airgroup that runs Aloha Airlines.

Aloha IslandAir has flights to Honolulu, Princeville, Molokai, Kalaupapa, Kahului, Hana, Kapalua West Maui, Lanai and Kamuela.

On some of the more remote sectors, flights are only once or twice daily, while the more popular routes have over a dozen flights a day.

Fares are $69.95 one way, except for the short flight between Molokai's two airports, and the flight between Kahului and Kapalua West Maui airports, both of which cost $20 each. In addition, the first morning flight out of (but not coming into) Honolulu to most destinations costs $49.95 and the two late-night flights from Kahului (11 pm and 1 am) to Honolulu cost $30.

Reservation numbers for Aloha IslandAir are:

Oahu	☎ 833-3219
Neighbor Islands	☎ (800) 652-6541
US mainland	☎ (800) 323-3345

Air Molokai Air Molokai is a small commuter airline serving Molokai with nine-seater Cessna prop planes. Flights between Molokai and Honolulu or Kahului cost $60 one way, $100 return. Air Molokai sometimes offers special discounts that drops the return fare to as low as $60 and occasionally offers a stand-by fare of $20. Flights to Kalaupapa from Molokai Airport cost $19 one way, $39 return.

Flights on Air Molokai can be like little sightseeing tours, as the planes fly lower and offer better views than the larger airlines. Sometimes you even end up in the co-pilot's seat! Another advantage is that your luggage is loaded and unloaded as you get on and off the plane – so it's rarely misplaced and there's no waiting at the carousel.

Reservation numbers for Air Molokai are:

Oahu	☎ 521-0090
Maui	☎ 877-0026
Molokai	☎ 553-3636

BUS

Oahu's excellent all-island public bus system, called TheBus, makes that island the easiest one to get around without a car. You can get almost anywhere in Oahu on TheBus and the fare is just 60 cents regardless of your destination.

The Big Island has a weekday public bus service between Kona and Hilo, and between Hilo and Hawaii Volcanoes National Park. There are a couple of other routes serving the Hilo area but they're geared primarily for commuters and the service is infrequent. While these buses will suffice to get you between major towns, they're not practical for short sightseeing hops back and forth in one day. There are also a couple of private shuttle buses serving the Kailua-Kona area.

Maui has no public buses, however there's a frequent (and free!) daily shuttle between Lahaina and Kaanapali, and other shuttles operate within the Kaanapali and Wailea resorts. Akina Bus Service operates a bus a few times a day between Makena and Kaanapali, stopping en route in Wailea and Kihei.

Kauai has a fledgling public bus service, which mainly goes between Kapaa and Lihue.

Molokai has no buses, but there's a mule train!

TAXI

All main islands have taxis, with the fares based on mileage regardless of the number of passengers. Rates vary, as they're set by each county, but average about $9 per five miles.

CAR

The minimum age for driving in Hawaii is 18 years. You can legally drive in the state as long as you have a valid driver's licence issued by a country that is party to the United Nations Conference on Road & Motor Transport – which covers almost everyone.

However, car-rental companies will generally accept valid foreign driver's licences only if they're in English. Otherwise most will require renters to show an international driver's licence.

Gasoline is about 25% more expensive in

Hawaii than on the US mainland, with the price for regular unleaded gasoline averaging about $1.50 a gallon.

Road Rules

Hawaiians drive on the right-hand side of the road just like on the US mainland and in Europe.

Drivers at a red light can turn right after coming to a full stop and yielding to oncoming traffic, unless there's a sign at the intersection prohibiting the turn.

Hawaii requires the use of seat belts for drivers and front-seat passengers. State law also strictly requires the use of child safety seats for children aged three and under, while four-year-olds must either be in a safety seat or secured by a seat belt. Most of the car-rental companies rent child safety seats, usually from $3 to $5 a day, but they don't always have them on hand so it's advisable to reserve one in advance.

Speed limits are posted and enforced. If you're stopped for speeding, expect to get a ticket, as the police rarely just give warnings. Cruising unmarked police cars come in the most unlikely models and colours!

Note that the word 'highway' is used very liberally in Hawaii. Just about every road of any distance gets to be called a highway, including some dinky little secondary roads and even a dirt road or two.

In this book we've given priority to using highway numbers because that's what you'll see on road signs. However, if you're asking directions keep in mind that islanders generally refer to roads by name and few pay attention to the route numbers – many

wouldn't even be able to tell you the route number of the road on which they live.

Horn honking is considered very rude in Hawaii unless required for safety.

Note In Hawaii, as in the rest of the USA, a paved road is one that's sealed (tarred) with asphalt (bitumen).

Rental

Rental cars are available on all the islands. The market is very competitive and rates are generally cheaper than on the mainland.

With most companies the weekly rate works out far cheaper per day than the straight daily rate. The daily rate for a small car, with unlimited mileage, is around $20 to $35, while typical weekly rates are $89 to $139. You're usually required to keep the car for a minimum of five or six days to get the weekly rate.

Rates vary greatly from company to company and within each company depending on season, time of booking, demand and current promotional fares. Call one week and you might find a weekly rate as low as $79. Call the same company a month later and the best deal might be double that. Sometimes you have to reserve a week or a month in advance for the best bargains, while at other times you can walk right into them.

At any given time any one of the rental companies could be offering the cheapest deal, so you can save money by taking a little time to shop around. Be sure to ask for the cheapest rate as the first quote given is not always the lowest.

It's a good idea to make reservations in advance for each destination. If you don't, the cheapest category of cars might be sold out altogether. With most reservations, there's no cancellation penalty if you change your mind.

Another advantage of advance reservations is that if you have a bottom-line car reserved and there are none in the yard when you show up, the upgrade is free.

The cheapest rates, which are the ones given in this book, are for economy class, which are usually small cars like the Geo

KEIKIS ARE BREAKABLE
BUCKLE UP HAWAII

Metro, Escort or Toyota Tercel, often with manual transmission. You're better off with manual transmission anyway if you're going to be climbing any hills, and Hawaii does have high country and mountains.

For daily rentals note that most cars are rented on a 24-hour basis so you could get two days use by renting at midday and driving around all afternoon, then heading out to explore somewhere else the next morning before the car is due back. Some companies even have an hour's grace period.

In Hawaii, rental rates generally include free unlimited mileage, though if you drop off the car at a different location from where you picked it up there's usually a fee added on and sometimes a mileage charge.

Having a major credit card greatly simplifies the rental process. Without one most places require prepayment by cash or travellers' cheques as well as a deposit, often around $100. Some even do an employment verification and credit check. Others don't do background checks though they reserve the right for the station manager to decide whether to rent to you or not.

Be aware that many car-rental companies are loathe to rent to people who list a camping ground as their address on the island. In addition, at least one company (Tropical) specifically adds 'No Camping Permitted' to their rental contracts.

Most car-rental companies officially prohibit use of their cars on dirt roads.

In addition to all rates, the state of Hawaii adds a $2-a-day tax to all car rentals.

Insurance

Collision damage waivers (CDW) are the ultimate rip-off and Hawaii used to have the ultimate hard sell. It got such a bad reputation that the state finally put some controls on 'coercive sales tactics'. Still the rental agencies will try to sell you the CDW for $10 to $15 a day, an amount that can be higher than the rental fee for the car itself! The CDW is not really even insurance (the companies already insure their cars) but rather a guarantee that the rental company won't hold you liable for any damages to their car

(though even here there are exclusions!). If you decline the CDW you are usually held liable for any damages up to the full value of the car.

If you have collision coverage on your vehicle at home it might cover damages to car rentals in Hawaii. Check with your insurance company before your trip.

A number of credit card companies now offer reimbursement coverage for collision damages if you rent the car with their card and decline the CDW. If yours doesn't, it may be worth changing to one that does. Be aware that some credit card coverage isn't valid for rentals of more than 15 days or for exotic models, jeeps, 4WD vehicles, vans and motorbikes.

Rental Agencies

Most of the following are international companies whose cars can be booked from offices around the world. The toll-free numbers given are valid from the US mainland, unless otherwise noted.

Budget (☎ (800) 527-7000) is at the main airports on Oahu, Kauai, Molokai, Maui and the Big Island as well as about 35 other locations around Hawaii. Eighteen to 20-year-olds can rent only if they have a major credit card in their name, and must pay a $20 per day surcharge! If you're at least 21 and don't have a credit card, Budget will accept a cash deposit, but only from 7 am to 4 pm on weekdays, and you'll need to show a round-trip air ticket and have a home phone number listed in your name – you'll also have to pre-pay the entire bill plus a $100 deposit.

Hertz (☎ (800) 654-3131) is at the main airports on Oahu, Maui, Kauai and the Big Island as well as at Princeville and Kapalua West Maui airports. Renters who don't have a credit card, but who are at least 25 years old, can call ahead to 'cash qualify'. To do this you'll need to have held your present job for at least one year and pay a $10 fee and, upon arrival in Hawaii, you'll have to prepay the total rental fee plus a 50% deposit.

Tropical (☎ (800) 678-6000; in Hawaii (800) 352-3923) is at or near the airports on Oahu, Kauai, Molokai, Maui and the Big Island. Tropical often has some of the cheaper rates on the islands, running specials for around $20 per day and $100 per week. Drivers without credit cards must sign a blank personal cheque imprinted with their name and address and have proof of employment (either a recent pay slip or a letter from their employer); final determination on whether to accept drivers without credit cards is made by the station manager. Tropical only rents to drivers who are at least 21 years old and those under age 25 are charged a $5 a day surcharge.

Dollar (☎ (800) 367-7006; in Hawaii (800) 342-7398) is at the airports on Oahu, Kauai, Molokai, Maui and the Big Island as well as numerous locations in Waikiki. Dollar's normal full rate for a compact car is $199 a week, though they commonly run specials for $99 per week if the rental starts on a Monday, Tuesday or Wednesday and $130 per week if it starts on other days.

Thrifty (☎ (800) 367-2277) is at or near the airports on Oahu, Kauai, the Big Island and Maui. If you don't have a credit card you have to deal directly with each location you're renting from, where approval is on a case-by-case basis. Thrifty often has good daily rates, however they rent child safety seats for a rather steep $6 a day and charge $15 a day for CDW.

Alamo (☎ (800) 327-9633) has booths at the Kona, Hilo and Lihue airports and near the Honolulu and Kapalua West Maui airports. They require a credit card of drivers aged 21 to 25 and then add on a $10 a day surcharge to the rental rates. Alamo doesn't rent to anyone under 21.

Avis (☎ (800) 831-8000) is at the main airports on Oahu, Maui, Kauai, Molokai and the Big Island. They don't rent to drivers under age 25.

National (☎ (800) 227-7368) is at the main airports on Oahu, Kauai, Maui and the Big Island and at three locations in Waikiki. They don't rent to people under age 25.

There are scores of smaller rental agencies as well, but this is one area where small is not necessarily better. For the most part the big companies have the better deals and the fewer hassles.

BICYCLE

It's possible to cycle around all the islands. However when you get away from coastal routes, there are some pretty hefty uphill climbs. Hawaii's roads also tend to be narrow, and many of the main coastal routes are rather heavily trafficked.

There are places to rent bicycles on the four largest islands. If you bring your own bike to Hawaii, you can transport it on inter-island flights for $20.

HITCHING

Hitchhiking is officially illegal on Maui, Molokai and Lanai, while on the other islands it's tolerated by the police. Results are mixed. We've met people who have waited on the roadside for hours with the only response from drivers being a few flipped fingers. We've also heard from people who have hitched around the islands and claim waits of only five to 10 minutes for most rides. Generally if you look like a traveller, and are not hitching with more than one other person, you stand the best chance of getting a ride. Hitchhikers should size up each situation carefully before getting in cars and women should be especially wary of hitching alone.

BOAT

Inter-Island Ferry There are only two inter-island passenger ferries in Hawaii. They are a good deal – about half the cost of flying – and during the winter you can often spot whales en route.

Expeditions on Maui runs a 24-passenger boat three times a day between Lahaina on Maui and Manele Boat Harbor on Lanai. The crossing, which takes an hour, costs $25.

The *Maui Princess* has twice-daily service between Kaunakakai on Molokai and Lahaina on Maui. It takes 75 minutes and costs $25.

Phone numbers and schedules are in the individual island sections.

TOURS

There are a number of companies doing half-day and full-day sightseeing bus tours on each island. There are also lots of specialised tours, such as whale watch cruises, bicycle tours down Haleakala, snorkel trips to Lanai and Zodiac cruises along the Na Pali Coast, just to mention a few. All these tours can be booked after arrival on Hawaii. For details on day tours, see the individual island chapters.

Overnight Tours

If you want to visit another island but only have a day or two to spare, it might be worth looking into 'overnighters', which are mini-packaged tours to the Neighbor Islands that include return airfare, car and a hotel. Rates depend on the accommodation you select, with a one-night package typically starting around $125 per person, based on double occupancy. You can add on additional days for an additional fee, usually for about $40 per person.

If you have an air pass the same tour companies also sell room/car packages minus the airfare (though the room/car packages offered directly by some of the hotels may work out cheaper).

The largest companies specialising in overnighters are: Island Escapes (☎ 944-8000 on Oahu, (800) 544-4421 from the Neighbor Islands), Roberts Hawaii (☎ 523-9323 on Oahu, (800) 348-3975 from the Neighbor Islands) and Akamai (☎ 971-3131 on Oahu).

These companies also sell one-day fly/drive packages, which include return airfare to another island and the use of a rental car, for around $95 per person for two people, or $120 for single travellers.

Helicopter

Helicopter tours are readily available from a number of companies on the main islands. They fly by some amazing places, such as over steaming (and sometimes erupting) volcanoes, along towering coastal cliffs and above inaccessible waterfalls. Prices vary depending on the destination and the length of the flight, with a 30-minute tour averaging about $100 per passenger.

Before you book one, be ready to make some inquiries. Be aware, for instance, that not every seat in all copters is a window seat. The most common configuration is two passengers up front with the pilot, and four people sitting across the back. The two back middle seats simply don't give the photo opportunities proclaimed in the brochures. It's like being a mid-seat rear passenger on a scenic drive – only there's no getting out at viewpoints! People are usually seated according to weight, so if you're dishing out a lot of money make sure it's clear where you're going to be sitting.

Cruises

American Hawaii Cruises (☎ 415-392-9400, (800) 765-7000) 550 Kearny St, San Francisco, CA 94108, has two cruise ships, the *Constitution* and the *Independence*, which make seven-day tours around Hawaii. The ships leave Honolulu each Saturday all year round and visit Kauai (Nawiliwili Harbor), Maui (Kahului Harbor) and the Big Island (Kona and Hilo) before returning to Honolulu.

Rates start at $995 for the cheapest inside cabin and go up to $4295 for the 'owner's suite'. The cheapest outside cabin is $1638. Fares are based on double occupancy.

Alternatives include a three-day cruise with a four-night hotel/car package from $779 and a four-day cruise with a three-night hotel/car package from $899.

These are full-fledged cruise ships, 682 feet long, with lavish buffet meals, swimming pools and the like. Each carries a crew of 325 along with 800 passengers.

Oahu

The images most commonly conjured up of Hawaii are those of Oahu – places like Waikiki, Pearl Harbor and Sunset Beach.

Oahu is by far the most developed of the Hawaiian islands and, quite appropriately, has long been nicknamed 'The Gathering Place'. The island is home to 836,000 people – more than 75% of the state's population. It's an urban scene, with highways, high-rises and crowds. If you're looking for a getaway vacation you'd best continue on to one of the Neighbor Islands.

Still, despite all its development, in terms of scenic beauty Oahu holds its own. It has fluted mountains, aqua-blue bays and valleys that look to be almost carpeted with pineapples and sugar cane.

Oahu has excellent beaches. Hanauma Bay is one of the finest, easily accessible snorkelling spots in the islands. The North Shore has Hawaii's top surfing action and windward Kailua is one of Hawaii's most popular windsurfing beaches.

Honolulu is a modern city with a blend of Eastern and Western influences. Cultural offerings range from Chinese lantern parades and traditional hula performances to ballet and good museums. Honolulu has the only royal palace in the USA, fine city beaches and parks and some great hilltop views. There's a wonderful variety of neighbourhood ethnic restaurants.

Oahu can be the cheapest Hawaiian island to visit. It's the only one you can get around easily without your own transport, thanks to the inexpensive, island-wide bus system. Oahu also has some of Hawaii's cheapest accommodation, including a couple of youth hostels and Ys.

Almost all of Oahu's hotels and tourist facilities are centred in Waikiki. Waikiki resembles a hybrid mix of Miami Beach and Tokyo, with a population density rivalling the latter. There's a lot happening in Waikiki, but to get a better feel for what Hawaii's all about you need to step out of it. There are plenty of places on Oahu worth exploring.

ORIENTATION

Almost all visitors to Oahu land at Honolulu International Airport, the only civilian airport on the island. It's at the western end of the Honolulu district, nine miles west of Waikiki.

If you're going to be doing any exploring at all, it's worth picking up one of the detailed road maps which are readily available at stores around Oahu.

H-1, the main south shore highway, is the key to getting around the island. H-1 connects with Hwy 93, which leads up the leeward Waianae Coast; with Hwy 72, which runs around the south-east coast; with the Pali (61) and Likelike (63) highways, which go to the windward coast; and with H-2, Hwy 99 and Hwy 750, which run through the centre of the island on the way to the North Shore.

By the way, H-1 is an *interstate* freeway – an amusing term to use to describe a road on an island state in the middle of the Pacific.

Rush-hour traffic is heavy heading toward Honolulu in the mornings and away from it in the evenings.

Directions on Oahu are often given by using landmarks, in addition to the Hawaii-wide mauka (inland side) and makai (ocean side). If someone tells you to go 'Ewa' (a land area west of Honolulu) or 'Diamond Head' (east of Honolulu) it simply means to head in that direction.

Facts

HISTORY

Oahu was the final island conquered by Kamehameha the Great in his campaign to unite all Hawaii under his sole rule.

Prior to that, however, it was not

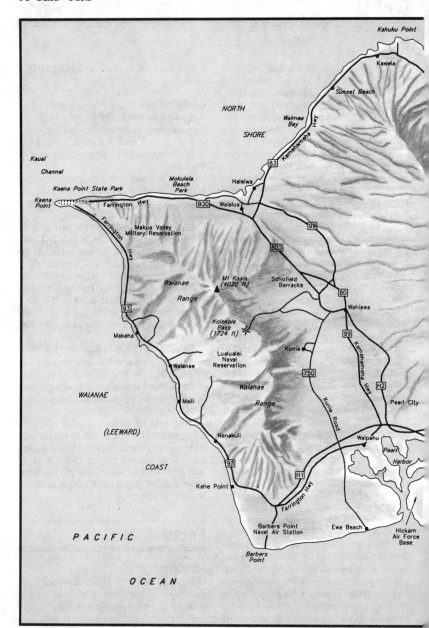

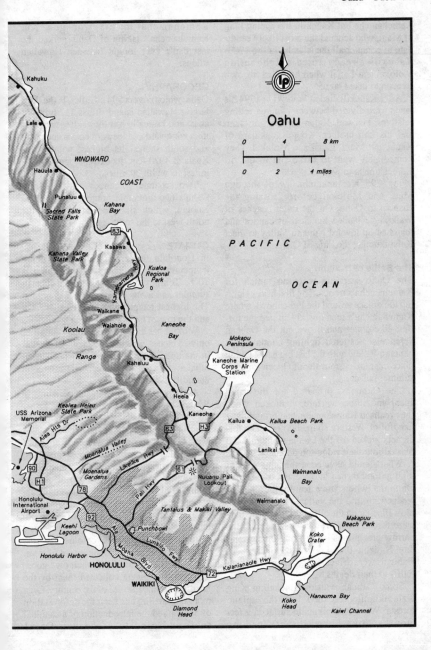

Kamehameha but Kahekili, the ageing king of Maui, who seemed the most likely candidate to conquer all the islands. In the 1780s Kahekili already ruled neighbouring Molokai and Lanai when he killed his own stepson to take Oahu.

After Kahekili died at Waikiki in 1794 his lands were divided between two quarrelling relatives. His son, Kalanikupule, got Oahu and his half-brother, King Kaeokulani of Kauai, got Maui, Lanai and Molokai. They immediately went to battle and in the rift Kamehameha moved in.

In 1795 Kamehameha swept through Maui and Molokai before crossing the channel to Oahu. On the quiet beaches of Waikiki he landed his fleet of canoes and marched up toward Nuuanu Valley to meet Kalanikupule, the king of Oahu.

The Battle of Nuuanu

The Oahu warriors were no match for Kamehameha's troops. The first heavy fighting took place around the Punchbowl, where Kamehameha's men quickly circled the fortress-like crater and drove out the Oahuan defenders. Scattered fighting continued up Nuuanu Valley, with the last big battle taking place near the current site of Queen Emma's summer palace.

The Oahuans, prepared for the usual spear-and-stone warfare, panicked when they realised Kamehameha had brought in a handful of Western sharpshooters. The foreigners picked off the Oahuan generals and blasted into their ridge-top defences.

What should have been the advantage of high ground turned into a death trap for the Oahuans when they found themselves wedged up into the valley, unable to redeploy. Fleeing up the cliffsides in retreat, they were forced to make their last stand at the narrow precipitous ledge along the current-day Nuuanu Pali Lookout. Hundreds of Oahuans were driven over the top of the *pali* (cliff) to their deaths.

Some Oahuan warriors, including King Kalanikupule, escaped into the upland forests. When Kalanikupule surfaced a few months later he was sacrificed by

Kamehameha to his war god Ku. Kamehameha's taking of Oahu marked the last battle ever fought between Hawaiian troops.

GEOGRAPHY

Oahu, which covers 594 sq miles, is the third largest Hawaiian island. It has 112 miles of coast and basically has four sides, with distinct windward and leeward coasts and north and south shores. Its highest point is Mt Kaala at 4020 feet. Its extreme length is 44 miles, its width 30 miles.

Two separate volcanoes arose to form Oahu's two mountain ranges, Waianae and Koolau, which slice the island from the north-west to the south-east.

CLIMATE

In Honolulu the average daily maximum temperature is 84°F, and the minimum is 70°F. Temperatures are a bit higher in summer and a few degrees lower in winter. The highest temperature on record is 94°F and the lowest is 53°F.

Waikiki has an average annual rainfall of only 25 inches, whereas the Lyon Arboretum in the upper Manoa Valley, north of Honolulu, averages 158 inches. Mid-afternoon humidity averages 56%.

Average afternoon water temperatures in Waikiki are 77°F in March, 82°F in August.

FLORA & FAUNA

Most of the islets off Oahu's windward coast are sanctuaries for sea birds, including terns, noddies, shearwaters, Laysan albatrosses, tropicbirds, boobies and frigate birds. Moku Manu (bird islands) off Mokapu Peninsula has the greatest variety of species.

Oahu has an endemic genus of tree snail, the achatinella. In former days the forests were loaded with these colourful snails, which clung like gems to the leaves of trees. They were too attractive for their own good, however, and hikers collected them by the handfuls around the turn of the century. Even more devastating has been the deforestation of habitat and the introduction of a cannibal snail and predatory rodents. Of 41 achatinella species, only 19 remain and all are endangered.

The *elepaio*, a brownish bird with a white rump, and the *amakihi*, a small yellow green bird, are the most common endemic forest birds on Oahu. The *apapane*, a bright red honeycreeper, and *iiwi*, a bright vermillion bird, are less common.

The only other native forest bird, the Oahu creeper, may already be extinct. This small yellowish bird looks somewhat like the amakihi, which makes positive identification difficult. The last Oahu creeper sighting was of a single bird in 1985 on the Poamoho Trail.

The most prominent urban birds are pigeons, doves, red-crested cardinals and common mynas. The myna, introduced from India, is a brown, spectacled bird that congregates in noisy flocks. Introduced game birds include pheasants, quails and francolins.

Oahu has wild pigs and goats in its mountain valleys. Brush-tailed rock-wallabies, accidentally released in 1916, reside in the Kalihi Valley. Although rarely seen, the wallabies are of interest to zoologists because they may be an extinct subspecies in their native Australia.

Oahu has some excellent botanical gardens. Foster Garden and the Lyon Arboretum both have unique native and exotic species, some of which have disappeared in the wild.

GOVERNMENT

The City & County of Honolulu is the unwieldy name attached to the single political entity governing all of Oahu.

Technically the City & County of Honolulu also includes the Northwestern Hawaiian Islands, which stretch 1300 miles beyond Kauai to Kure Atoll, but for practical purposes the City & County of Honolulu refers to the island of Oahu.

Like Hawaii's other counties, there are no municipal governments. Oahu is administered by a mayor and a nine-member council, elected for four-year terms. Frank Fasi is currently in his fifth term as mayor.

In this book we refer to beach parks as 'county' rather than using the awkward 'City & County of Honolulu' stamp that fills half the space on most public signs.

ECONOMY

In 1991 Oahu had a 3% unemployment rate. Tourism is the largest sector of the economy, accounting for about 30% of Oahu's jobs. It's followed by defence and other government employment which together account for 22% of all jobs.

One-fifth of Oahu is still used for agricultural purposes, mostly the production of sugar and pineapples. Production is declining, however, and employment in agriculture accounts for only about 2% of the workforce.

POPULATION & PEOPLE

The 1990 US census put Oahu's population at 836,231. Honolulu accounts for 377,059 people. Other sizeable population centres are Pearl City, Kailua, Aiea, Kaneohe, Waipahu and Mililani.

The population is 24% Japanese, 24% Caucasian, 18% part-Hawaiian (less than 1% pure Hawaiian), 11% Filipino, 6% Chinese and 2% Black, with numerous óther Pacific and Asian minorities.

Approximately 14% of Oahu's residents are members of the armed forces or their dependants.

TOURIST INFORMATION

The main office of the Hawaii Visitors Bureau (☎ 924-0266) is in Waikiki at 2270 Kalakaua Ave, Suite 801, Honolulu, HI 96815. It's loaded with free brochures and magazines, including those for the Neighbor Islands. Opening hours are from 8 am to 4.30 pm Monday to Friday.

Numerous free tourist magazines are available at the airport and all around Waikiki. They can be a good source of information, although most of it is paid advertising. *This Week Oahu* and *Spotlight Oahu* usually have the best discount coupons, *Waikiki Beach Press* has the most detailed section of entertainment and weekly events.

GENERAL INFORMATION
Official Oahu
Oahu is nicknamed 'The Gathering Place'. Its flower is the delicate native ilima, which is yellow-orange, the island's official colour.

Money
There are about 200 banks around Oahu and they can easily be found in the central areas of major towns. The Bank of Hawaii, Hawaii's largest bank, has a branch at the airport and at 2220 Kalakaua Ave in Waikiki.

Banks are generally open from 8.30 am to at least 3 pm Monday to Thursday and from 8.30 am to 6 pm Friday.

Automatic teller machines can be found at the Ala Moana Center, the airport, some Foodland supermarkets and many other places.

Post
There are 33 post offices on Oahu. The main Honolulu post office (☎ 423-3990) is at the side of the airport at 3600 Aolele St, opposite the inter-island terminal.

Ilima flower

The Waikiki post office is at 330 Saratoga Rd. There's a post office at the Ala Moana Center, one on the University of Hawaii campus and one in downtown Honolulu opposite Iolani Palace.

Media
The two English dailies are the morning *Honolulu Advertiser* and the afternoon *Honolulu Star-Bulletin*. They put out a joint Sunday paper, the *Star-Bulletin & Advertiser*. There's also one daily newspaper each in Korean, Chinese and Japanese/English.

Honolulu has 28 radio stations and 10 TV stations. In addition cable TV has a couple of channels featuring continuous visitor information.

Radio station KCCN features Hawaiian music on 1420 AM and 'island music', with a blend of more contemporary Hawaiian songs and reggae, on 100.3 FM. Da KINE (105.1 FM) also plays contemporary island music. Hawaii Public Radio is on KHPR (88.1 FM) and KIPO (1380 AM, 89.3 FM).

Bookshops
Honolulu Book Shops has a good selection of general, Hawaiiana and travel books. They're on the corner of Bishop and Hotel Sts in downtown Honolulu and in the Ala Moana, Hawaii Kai, Pearlridge and Kailua shopping centres.

Waldenbooks, a national chain, has shops in the Ward Warehouse, Kahala Mall, Koko Marina Shopping Center, Windward Mall, Pearlridge Center and in Waikiki at the Royal Hawaiian Shopping Center, the Waikiki Shopping Plaza and the Waikiki Trade Center. All have Hawaiiana and travel sections. The University of Hawaii Bookstore (☎ 956-4338) is in the university's Campus Center on 2465 Manoa Rd, Honolulu, HI 96822.

Libraries
Hawaii's statewide library system has its main library in downtown Honolulu, next to Iolani Palace. There are 21 other public libraries around Oahu, including ones in Waikiki, Kailua and Kaneohe.

Weather

The National Weather Service provides recorded weather forecasts for Honolulu (☎ 833-2849) and all Oahu (☎ 836-0121). They also record tides and surf conditions (☎ 836-1952) and a marine forecast (☎ 836-3921).

Night Sky

The Hawaiian Skyguide (☎ 948-0759) is a recording with information on the current stars and planets visible in the Hawaiian sky.

Emergency

Dial 911 for all police, fire and ambulance emergencies.

Hospitals with 24-hour emergency services include the Queen's Medical Center (☎ 538-9011), 1301 Punchbowl St, Honolulu; Straub Clinic & Hospital (☎ 522-4000), 888 S King St at Ward, Honolulu; Castle Medical Center (☎ 263-5500), 640 Ulukahiki, Kailua; Kahuku Hospital (☎ 293-9221), Kahuku; and Wahiawa General Hospital (☎ 621-8411), 128 Lehua St, Wahiawa.

Divers with the bends are sent to the UH Hyperbaric Facility (☎ 523-9155), 42 Ahui St, Honolulu.

A suicide and crisis line (☎ 521-4555) operates 24 hours a day.

ACTIVITIES
Swimming

Oahu boasts 60 beach parks, most of which have restrooms and showers. Nineteen are patrolled by lifeguards. The island's four distinct coastal areas have their own peculiar seasonal water conditions. When it's rough on one side, it's generally calm on another, so you can find places to swim and surf year round.

Oahu's south shore extends from Barbers Point to Makapuu Point and includes the most popular beaches on the island, including the white sands of Waikiki and Ala Moana.

The windward coast extends from Makapuu Point to Kahuku Point. Kailua Beach Park, Oahu's busiest windsurfing spot, also has good swimming conditions and is the best all-around beach on this side. Other nice beaches are at Waimanalo, Kualoa and Malaekahana.

The North Shore extends from Kahuku Point to Kaena Point. It has spectacular waves in winter, but can be as calm as a lake in summer.

The leeward Waianae Coast extends from Kaena Point to Barbers Point. It's the driest, sunniest side of the island, with long stretches of white sands. The most popular beach on this side is Makaha, which sees big surf in the winter but has suitable swimming conditions in summer.

The county maintains 17 community swimming pools, including ones in Kailua, Kaneohe, Pearl City, Wahiawa and Waipahu. Pools in the greater Honolulu area are at Palolo Recreation Center (☎ 733-7362), 2007 Palolo Ave; Manoa Valley Recreation Center (☎ 988-6868), 2721 Kaaipu Ave; Booth District Park (☎ 522-7037), 2331 Kanealii Ave; and McCully Recreation Center (☎ 973-7268), 831 Pumehana.

Surfing

Oahu has 594 defined surfing sites, nearly twice as many as any of the other Hawaiian islands. In winter, the North Shore gets some of Hawaii's most spectacular surf, with swells reaching 20 to 30 feet. This is the home of the Banzai Pipeline, Sunset Beach and some of the world's top surfing competitions.

Makaha is the top winter surf spot on the leeward Waianae Coast. The south shore gets its finest surfing waves in summer, with Waikiki and Diamond Head having some of the best breaks.

Surf News Network (☎ 531-SURF) has a recorded surf line reporting winds, wave heights and results of surfing contests, updated three times a day. KPOI, an FM rock music radio station, also provides surf reports (☎ 521-SURF) as does the National Weather Service (☎ 836-1952).

The county's Haleiwa Surf Center (☎ 637-5051), at Haleiwa Alii Beach Park, holds free surfing lessons from 9 am to noon

Saturdays and Sundays between early September and late May. Surfboards are provided.

H30 is a monthly newspaper that reports on surfing events and surf conditions and interviews surfers. It's free at surf shops around the island. One-year subscriptions, which cost $20 to the US and $55 overseas, are available from H30 (☎ 687-3800), 91-1052 Pohahawai St, Ewa Beach, HI 96706.

You can rent surfboards at the concession stands on the beach in Waikiki, at Surf-N-Sea (☎ 637-9887) in Haleiwa and at Local Motion (☎ 955-7873), 1714 Kapiolani Blvd.

Bodysurfing, Snorkelling & Boogie Boarding

The most popular boogie boarding place for beginners in Waikiki is at Kapahulu Groin.

Waimanalo Beach Park and nearby Bellows Beach Park have gentle shorebreaks good for beginning bodysurfers.

The two hottest (and most dangerous) spots for expert bodysurfers are Sandy Beach Park and Makapuu Beach Park in south-east Oahu. Other top shorebreaks are at Makaha on the Waianae Coast, Waimea Bay on the North Shore, and Kalama Beach in Kailua and Pounders in Laie on the windward coast.

For snorkelling, Hanauma Bay on the south shore is the best year-round spot. In summer, Pupukea Beach Park on the North Shore provides excellent snorkelling, while a favourite Waianae Coast location is the Makaha Caverns at Makaha Beach.

Equipment Rental If you're going to be doing much snorkelling or boogie boarding, you're better off buying your own equipment. However, there are plenty of places to rent them.

Titou Rentals (☎ 926-2060), 419 Nahua St, in the centre of Waikiki, rents snorkel sets for $5 a day, $15 a week. Boogie boards rent from $7.50 a day, $20 a week. They also rent other sports equipment, including surfboards and bicycles.

Snorkel Bob's (☎ 735-7944), 700 Kapahulu Ave, about a mile out of Waikiki, rents snorkel

sets for $15 a week. For $3 more you can return them to one of the Neighbor Islands. It's open from 8 am to 5 pm daily.

Surf-N-Sea (☎ 637-9887) in Haleiwa rents boogie boards for $3 for the first hour and $2 for each additional hour, and snorkel sets for $6.50 for half a day. It's open from 9 am to 6 pm daily.

In Kailua, Naish Hawaii (☎ 262-6068), 155A Hamakua Drive, rents boogie boards for $10 a day, snorkel sets for $7.50.

Windsurfing

Kailua Bay is Oahu's number one windsurfing spot. It has good year-round trade winds, and both flat water and wave conditions in different sections of the bay. Windsurfing shops set up vans at Kailua Beach Park on weekdays and Saturday mornings, renting boards and giving lessons. It's a great place for beginners.

Other good spots include Diamond Head for speed and jumps and Backyards for North Shore challenges. Fort DeRussy Beach is Waikiki's main windsurfing spot.

Naish Hawaii (☎ 262-6068, (800) 767-6068) – as in windsurfing champion Robbie Naish – sells and rents equipment, gives lessons and arranges windsurfing vacations. They're at 155A Hamakua Drive, Kailua, HI 96734. Introductory group lessons are $35 for three hours, while private lessons are $35 an hour. Rental rates vary with board and rig, starting at $25 for half a day.

The Kailua Sailboard Company (☎ 262-2555), 130 Kailua Rd, Kailua, HI 96734, rents boards for $20 per four hours, $27 a day and $95 a week. Three-hour beginner's lessons are $35. Call them for a wind report.

Waikiki Windsurfing (☎ 949-8952) at Fort DeRussy Beach rents windsurfing equipment for $30 for two hours, $40 with a lesson.

In Haleiwa, Surf-N-Sea (☎ 637-9887) rents windsurfing equipment for $12 for the first hour and $8 for each additional hour. Two-hour windsurfing lessons cost $38.

Diving

Top summer dive spots include the caves and

ledges at Three Tables and Shark's Cove on the North Shore and the Makaha Caverns on the Waianae Coast. On the south shore, Hanauma Bay has calm diving conditions most of the year. There are a number of other popular dive spots between Hanauma and Honolulu that provide good winter diving.

Aloha Dive Shop (☎ 395-5922) in Hawaii Kai has two- tank boat dives off Koko Head for $75. Half-day introductory dives at Hanauma Bay are $60. Divers can be certified in 2½ full-day sessions for $345. They offer free transport to and from Waikiki hotels. The shop, in the Koko Marina Shopping Center, Honolulu, HI 96825, sells and rents scuba and snorkelling gear. It's open from 8 am to 5 pm daily.

Leeward Dive Center (☎ 696-3414, (800) 255-1574) is at 87-066 Farrington Highway, Maili, HI 96792. They have dives to Makaha Caverns, the WW II minesweeper *Mahi* and an aeroplane wreck. Two-tank boat dives cost $72 day or night. Introductory dives cost $75, while snorkelling trips are $36.

Surf-N-Sea (☎ 637-9887), in Haleiwa, has boat dives for $65 for one-tank dives, $90 for two-tank dives. They can certify in PADI and offer introductory dives.

Snuba (☎ 922-7762), a sort of scuba diving for snorkellers, is available in Waikiki for $45, at Hanauma Bay for $65 (including transport from Waikiki) or aboard the *Barefoot* catamaran in conjunction with a three-hour cruise for $95. Snuba utilises long air hoses attached to a tank on an inflatable raft. The diver simply wears a mask and weight belt and can dive down as far as the air hose allows.

Kayaking

Kailua Sailboards (☎ 262-2555) in Kailua rents one-person kayaks for $25 a day and two-person kayaks for $39 a day.

Twogood Kayaks Hawaii (☎ 262-5656) in Kailua has kayak sales, rentals and lessons. Rentals cost $20 for half a day, $25 for a full day.

Surf-N-Sea (☎ 637-9887) in Haleiwa rents two-person kayaks for $25 half a day, $35 a full day.

Hiking

The trail that leads three-quarters of a mile from inside the crater of Diamond Head up to its summit is the most popular hike on Oahu. It's easy to get to from Waikiki and ends with a panoramic view of greater Honolulu.

Another nice short hike is the Manoa Falls Trail, just a few miles above Waikiki, where a quiet walk through an abandoned arboretum of huge trees leads to a nice waterfall.

The Tantalus and Makiki Valley area has the most extensive trail network around Honolulu, with fine views of the city and surrounding valleys. Amazingly, although it's just two miles above the city hustle and bustle, this lush forest reserve is unspoiled and offers quiet solitude.

On the western edge of Honolulu, the Moanalua Trail goes deep into the Moanalua Valley. You can hike it on your own or join a guided Sunday walk.

At Keaiwa Heiau State Park, north-west of Honolulu, the Aiea Loop Trail leads 4½ miles along a ridge with views of Pearl Harbor and Diamond Head to the south and the Koolau Range to the north and east.

The Kaena Point Trail is a coastal hike through a natural area reserve on the westernmost point of Oahu. On the windward side the Sacred Falls State Park trail goes up a narrow valley in the Koolau Range to a waterfall.

There are short walks from the Nuuanu Pali Lookout, along Nuuanu Pali Drive, around Hanauma Bay and along countless beaches.

All hikes are described in their respective sections.

Guided Hikes Notices of hiking club outings are run in the 'Bulletin Board' column which appears daily, except Saturday, in the *Honolulu Star-Bulletin*. By joining one of these outings you get to meet and hike with ecology-minded islanders.

It may also be a good way to get to the backwoods if you don't have a car, as they often share rides. Wear sturdy shoes and, for the longer hikes, bring lunch and water.

The Hawaiian Trail & Mountain Club (☎ 734-5515) meets for hiking at 8 am most Sundays on the mountain side of Iolani Palace. Usually anyone is welcome, although occasionally the number of hikers is limited and thus open to members only. The hike fee is $1.

Hikes range from three to 12 miles in length and from novice to advanced in difficulty, sometimes crossing private property on trails that are not generally open to the public. For a copy of the hiking schedule, send a stamped, self-addressed envelope to the club at Box 2238, Honolulu, HI 96804.

The Sierra Club (☎ 538-6616), in the Arcade Building, No 201, 212 Merchant St (Box 2577), Honolulu, HI 96803, leads hikes nearly every Sunday and sometimes on other days of the week as well. They range from an easy 1½-mile hike to Jackass Ginger to strenuous 10-mile treks. Most outings meet at 8 am at the Church of the Crossroads, 2510 Bingham St. The hike fee is $1.

The Hawaii Audubon Society (☎ 528-1432), 212 Merchant St, No 320, Honolulu, HI 96813, leads bird-watching hikes, usually on the third Sunday of each month. Binoculars and a copy of *Hawaii's Birds* are recommended.

The Hawaii Nature Center (☎ 955-0100) in Makiki leads hikes on Saturdays for $3. Trails range from the 2½- mile Makiki Loop Trail to a more difficult six-mile path up Mt Kaala, Oahu's highest point. Reservations are required.

The Lyon Arboretum (☎ 988-7378) leads guided hikes to various spots around Oahu on Saturday mornings a couple of times a month. It costs $8 and reservations are required.

Note Anyone who has hiked on Oahu should scrub their shoes and wash their socks and long pants before hiking on other islands to avoid transferring clinging *Clidemia hirta* seeds, which are practically invisible. This weed has infested much of Oahu, overrunning trails and choking out native plants, but it's not yet widely established on the Neighbor Islands. It's presumed that the patches of this invasive plant found along trails on Molokai and Maui hitchhiked there on an Oahuan hiker's boot.

Horse Riding

Sheraton Makaha Lio Stables (☎ 695-9511) in Makaha has one-hour rides in groups of up to eight people for $25 per person. The stables are closed on Mondays.

On Saturdays and Sundays, Kualoa Ranch (☎ 237-8515), 49-560 Kamehameha Highway, Kualoa, has two-hour trail rides at 9 and 11.30 am for $35 and one-hour trail rides at 1.30 pm for $25. These are geared for English-speaking riders and reservations are required. On weekdays there are afternoon rides that include lunch and a visit to a fishpond for $60, with commentary in Japanese. Bookings are made by calling at 10 am the same day, with openings on a space-available basis.

The Turtle Bay Hilton (☎ 293-8811) has 45-minute trail rides for $26.

Tennis

Oahu has 175 county tennis courts. If you're staying in Waikiki, the most convenient locations are the 10 lighted courts at Ala Moana Beach Park (☎ 522-7031), the 10 unlighted courts at the Diamond Head Tennis Center (☎ 971-7150) at the Diamond Head end of Kapiolani Park, and the four lighted Kapiolani Park courts opposite the Waikiki Aquarium. Court time is free on a first-come first-served basis.

With ground space at a premium, few Waikiki hotels have room for tennis courts. The Ilikai Hotel (☎ 949-3811, ext 6428) leads with five courts, rentals and a pro shop. Rates are $5 per hour per person for hotel guests, $7.50 for non-guests. The Pacific Beach Hotel has two courts and charges $5 per hour per person for guests, $8 for non-guests. The Hawaiian Regent has one court and charges $12 per hour per court for guests, $15 for non-guests.

The Honolulu Tennis Club (☎ 944-9696), 2220 S King St, has four tennis courts and two racquetball courts. The cost for non-residents is $10 per hour per person, with transport to and from Waikiki available at no extra charge. Reservations are requested.

The Sheraton Makaha Resort in Makaha (☎ 695-9511) has four courts for $10 per hour per court. The Turtle Bay Hilton in Kahuku (☎ 293-8811) charges $10 per person for a full day on one of its 10 courts.

Golf

Oahu has four 18-hole municipal golf courses: the Ala Wai Golf Course (☎ 296-4653) on Kapahulu Ave, mauka of the Ala Wai Canal near Waikiki; the Pali Golf Course (☎ 296-7254), 45-050 Kamehameha Highway, Kaneohe; the Ted Makalena Golf Course (☎ 296-7888), Waipio Point Access Rd, Waipahu; and the West Loch Golf Course (☎ 296-5624), 91-1126 Okupe St, Ewa Beach. Rates are $18 on weekdays and $20 on weekends and holidays. The earliest you can book is one week in advance. Start calling at 6.30 am to book the same day of the following week, as starting times are often filled by 7.30 am. The county also maintains the nine-hole Kahuku Golf Course (☎ 293-5842) in Kahuku.

At last count, Oahu had 16 private (and nine military) golf courses, but the number is rising, fuelling many a conflict between environmentalists and overseas developers.

The Sheraton Makaha (☎ 695-9511) claims to have the number one USGA-rated golf course on Oahu. The cost is $70 for nine holes and $140 for 18 holes for non-guests ($38 and $75 respectively for guests).

The Turtle Bay Hilton (☎ 293-8574) has an 18-hole golf course. Guests pay $68, while non-guests pay $99 on weekdays, $108 on weekends.

Running

Oahu is big on jogging. It's estimated that Honolulu has more joggers per capita than any other city in the world. Kapiolani Park and Ala Moana Park are two favourite jogging spots. There's also a 4.8-mile run around Diamond Head crater that's a pretty beaten track.

There are more than 100 road races each year, from one-mile fun runs and five-mile jogs to competitive marathons, biathlons and triathlons.

For an annual schedule of running events with times, dates and contact addresses, write to the Department of Parks & Recreation, City & County of Honolulu, 650 S King St, Honolulu, HI 96813.

Oahu's best-known race is the Honolulu Marathon held in December. For information send a stamped, self-addressed envelope to Honolulu Marathon Association, 3435 Waialae Ave, No 208, Honolulu, HI 96816.

The Department of Parks & Recreation holds a Honolulu Marathon Clinic at 7.30 am most Sundays at the Kapiolani Park Bandstand. It's free and open to everyone from beginners to seasoned marathon runners. Runners join groups of their own speed.

Cricket

The Honolulu Cricket Club plays on Sunday afternoons at Kapiolani Park, sometimes against visiting English teams. Visitors are welcome.

Skydiving

For $175, Skydive Hawaii (☎ 521-4404) will attach you to the hips and shoulders of a skydiver so you can jump together from a plane at 10,000 feet, freefall for 50 seconds and finish off with a couple of minutes of canopy ride. The more daring can take a three-hour lesson and then jump independently with a static line for the same price. Experienced skydivers are charged $55 for jumps. They take off daily (weather permitting) from Dillingham Airfield in Mokuleia.

Hang Gliding

Tradewinds Hang Gliding (☎ 396-8557), 380 H Haleloa Place, Honolulu, HI 96821, and Airsport (☎ 259-8192), 41-014 Ehukai, Waimanalo, HI 96795, both offer hang gliding lessons for beginners, taking off from Makapuu Point.

Organised Tours

For conventional sightseeing tours by van or bus, try Trans Hawaiian (☎ 735-6467), E Noa

Tours (☎ 599-2561), Polynesian Adventure Tours (☎ 833-3000) or Robert's Hawaii (☎ 523-5187).

Full-day circle-island tours usually cost about $40 to $50. Other tours go to places such as Diamond Head, the Nuuanu Pali Lookout, the Arizona Memorial and downtown Honolulu sights.

The Waikiki Trolley is a tourist trolley bus that runs between Waikiki and Honolulu. There are 17 stops, including the Ala Moana Center, Honolulu Academy of Arts, Iolani Palace, Hawaii Maritime Center, Bishop Museum, Chinatown and the Ward Centre. There's narration en route and passengers can get off at any stop and then pick up the next trolley, which comes by every half hour. It leaves from the Royal Hawaiian Shopping Center in Waikiki on the hour and half hour from 8 am to 4.30 pm. One-day passes cost $15 for adults, $5 for children aged 12 and under – a pricey alternative to the bus.

Gliding Glider Rides (☎ 677-3404) offers 20-minute flights in a glider from Dillingham Airfield in Mokuleia. While the coastline views are pretty they're not spectacular, and in winter the salt spray can hang in the air like a haze. Still, it is a nifty experience to be able to soar silently and the only other glider rides in Hawaii are given on Kauai and cost far more. Flights go daily between 10.30 am and 5.30 pm and cost $45 for one person and $70 for two.

Helicopter Papillon Hawaiian Helicopters (☎ 836-1566) leaves from Honolulu International Airport. Its cheapest flight costs $79, lasts 20 minutes and flies over Diamond Head, Waikiki, Honolulu and Pearl Harbor. The whole-island tour takes one hour and costs $187.

Cruises Sunset sails, dinner cruises and party boats leave daily from Kewalo Basin, just Ewa of Ala Moana Park. Rates are anywhere from $15 to $90, with dinner cruises averaging about $45. Many provide transport to and from Waikiki and advertise all sorts of come-ons and specials. Some of the cruising vessels are catamarans in name only; they're more like cattle boats in reality. You may prefer to go down to the harbour and check them out for yourself before buying a ticket.

The Hyatt Regency Waikiki's *Manu Kai* catamaran (☎ 923-1234) leaves from the beach at Waikiki. It has hour-long cruises during the day for $12, which includes one drink, and 1½-hour sunset cruises for $20 including pupus and mai tais.

There are also a few other catamarans leaving from Waikiki Beach for around the same price. The *Leahi* catamaran, in front of the Sheraton Waikiki, will sometimes give you half-price for the asking.

Hawaiian Cruises (☎ 947-9971) runs whale-watching cruises from January to April aboard the *Navatek*, a sleek modern ship. It leaves from Pier 6, near the Aloha Tower, at 8.30 am daily except Tuesday, comes back at 11 am, and costs $47 for adults and $23.45 for children.

Atlantis Submarines (☎ 973-9811) has a 65-foot, 46-passenger sightseeing submarine that descends 100 feet about a mile off Diamond Head. The tour lasts about 1¾ hours, including a catamaran ride to and from the sub. About 45 minutes are spent cruising beneath the surface around a ship and two planes that were sunk to create a dive site. Tours leave Hilton Hawaiian Village on the hour from 7 am to 5 pm daily and cost $82 for adults, $50 for children.

ACCOMMODATION

All but 10% of Oahu's nearly 40,000 visitor rooms are in Waikiki. Unlike on the Neighbor Islands, where there are multiple destinations, outside Honolulu there are only two resort hotels: the Sheraton Makaha on the Waianae Coast and the Turtle Bay Hilton, on the northern tip of the island.

The Waikiki/Honolulu area has a wide range of accommodation. The cheapest places to stay are the two AYH/IYHF-affiliated youth hostels. The one in Waikiki has dorm beds for $13, while the one by the university charges $10. In addition there are several casual hostel-type crash pads in

Waikiki with tightly squeezed dorm beds for about $15. After that, there are Ys for $25 to $30 and a few bottom-end Waikiki hotels that start around $40. Waikiki has lots of middle-range hotels in the $65 to $100 range as well as high priced luxury hotels.

The North Shore gets its fair share of surfers hanging out on a budget and Kailua attracts windsurfers. While neither place has hotels, you can find hostel-like accommodation, B&Bs and a few vacation rentals.

B&Bs have had a hard fight in Oahu. As more and more sprung up in the 1980s, complaints from neighbours in places like Kailua threatened to shut them all down. An agreement reached in 1989 allowed those in existence to remain open only if they were owner occupied and renting out no more than two bedrooms.

Unless otherwise noted, rates given throughout this book are the same for either singles or doubles and don't include the 9.17% room tax. Hotels often have different rates for the high and low seasons. The high season is generally from 15 December to 15 April, although it can vary by hotel a few weeks in either direction. The rest of the year is the low season.

To lure customers, some large chains like Outrigger and Hawaiian Pacific Resorts offer a free rental car if you request it at the time of booking. A few independent hotels occasionally throw in a car as well – it never hurts to ask whenever you book any hotel. If you had planned on renting a car, it can be a tidy savings.

If you're calling from outside Hawaii, add the 808 area code to all numbers. Numbers beginning with 800 are toll free from the US mainland and sometimes from Canada as well.

Camping

Camping is allowed at 12 county beach parks, one county botanic garden and four state recreation areas. The camping situation may change slightly in the future, as the state and county are in the process of shuffling a few parks. Kaiaka Park in Haleiwa was recently turned over to the county from the

state, and there are similar plans for Waimanalo State Recreation Area.

All county and state camping grounds on Oahu are closed on Wednesday and Thursday nights, ostensibly for maintenance, but also to prevent permanent encampments.

Although thousands of visitors use these camping sites each year without incident, Oahu has more of a reputation for trouble than other islands. Rip-offs, especially at roadside and beachfront camping grounds, are not uncommon.

Camping along the Waianae Coast is not recommended.

State Parks Camping is free by permit at Sand Island and Keaiwa Heiau, both in the greater Honolulu area; at Malaekahana, in Laie; and at the Waimanalo State Recreation Area.

Keaiwa Heiau is a good choice for an inland park, Malaekahana for a coastal park. Malaekahana is the only public park on Oahu with cabins (see the Windward Oahu section).

Camping is limited to five nights per month in each park. Permit applications must be submitted at least seven days and no more than 30 days before the first camping date. Applications may be made to the Division of State Parks by mail (Box 621, Honolulu, HI 96809), by phone (☎ 587-0300) or in person (1151 Punchbowl St, Room 310) between 8 am and 4 pm on weekdays.

County Beach Parks Camping is free at county beach parks but permits are required. Permits are not available by mail but can be picked up between 8 am and 4.30 pm on weekdays at the Department of Parks & Recreation (☎ 523-4525) on the ground floor of the Municipal Office building (650 S King St, Honolulu, HI 96813), the tall grey building on the corner of King and Alapai Sts. Permits are also available from any satellite city hall, including the one at the Ala Moana Center (☎ 973-2600), which is open Monday to Saturday. Other satellite city halls are in Kailua, Kaneohe and Wahiawa.

Camping is allowed at Mokuleia and

Kaiaka beach parks on the North Shore; Hauula, Swanzy, Kualoa, Bellows Field, Waimanalo and Makapuu beach parks on the windward coast; and Kahe Point, Nanakuli, Lualualei and Keaau beach parks on the Waianae Coast. Camping is allowed from 8 am Friday to 8 am Wednesday, except at Swanzy and Bellows Field beach parks, which are open only on weekends.

Kualoa, in one of Oahu's nicest beach settings, is the only county beach park with a caretaker and gates that are locked at night.

County Botanic Garden Hoomaluhia is an inland park in Kaneohe at the base of the Koolau Range. It has Oahu's safest camping and is unique among the county camping grounds in that it's operated by the botanic gardens division. Reservations can be made by mail. For an application, send a business-sized, self-addressed envelope to Hoomaluhia, Box 1116, Kaneohe, HI 96744.

Back-Country Camping The state forestry allows back-country camping along several valley and ridge trails, including three in Hauula on the windward coast and along the Waimano Trail north of Pearl City.

All back-country camping requires a permit from the Division of Forestry & Wildlife (☎ 587-0166), 1151 Punchbowl St, Room 325, Honolulu, HI 96813. Office hours are 7.45 am to 4.30 pm Monday to Friday. The forestry will send maps for these trails on request.

Fellow hikers on back-country trails are likely to be pig hunters.

Camping Supplies Omar The Tent Man (☎ 836-8785), 650A Kakoi St, Honolulu, HI 96819, rents six-person tents for $57 a week, frame backpacks or sleeping bags for $22 a week, and stoves or lanterns for $17 a week. Three-day rates for those items are $52, $17 and $14 respectively.

ENTERTAINMENT

The vast majority of Oahu's entertainment takes place in Honolulu, which includes but is certainly not limited to Waikiki.

For up-to-date entertainment information, check the free tourist magazines, especially the *Waikiki Beach Press*, and the free *Honolulu Weekly* newspaper. There are also listings in the *Honolulu Advertiser* and the *Honolulu Star-Bulletin*, the two daily newspapers. *Metropolis*, a free monthly newspaper dedicated to rock music, is found in music stores.

Honolulu has a lively gay scene, which is centred around the Kuhio District in Waikiki.

Oahu has more than 40 movie theatres, including a couple of drive-in theatres. Check the papers for details.

Call 527-5666 for a recorded listing of free performances and activities presented by the City & County of Honolulu.

For festivals, fairs and sporting events, see the Holidays & Festivals section in the Facts about the Country chapter. For details of specific venues, see the relevant town or city.

Luaus

Oahu's two main luaus, *Paradise Cove* and *Germaine's Luau*, are both huge impersonal affairs held nightly out in the Barbers Point area. Paradise Cove charges $39.50 with two drinks, Germaine's charges $44.50 with four drinks. Both include bus rides from Waikiki hotels (about one hour each way), buffet dinner, a Polynesian show and related hoopla. Children pay half-price. This area of Oahu is dry and dusty and the whole scene is a long way from most people's visions of paradise.

The other popular luau is at the *Royal Hawaiian Hotel* (☎ 923-7311). While the scale and setting of this beachside luau are nicer, it's a steep $60.

Hawaiiana

Some of the best Hawaiian entertainment can be found at community events, such as local festivals and the competitions between the hula schools. These generally take place outside Waikiki; check the papers for more information.

Some of the better contemporary Hawaiian musicians to look for are Jerry Santos and Olomana, Cecilio and Kapono, Kapono and

Keola Beamer, Kapena, Willie K, the Peter Moon Band, Brother Noland and the rock band Kalapana.

For a more traditional Hawaiian sound there's Makaha Sons of Niihau, Genoa Keawe and Haunani Apoliona, among others.

THINGS TO BUY

Honolulu is a large, cosmopolitan city with plenty of sophisticated shops. Chinatown has some quality antique shops and galleries. For crafts, the best deals are usually found at one of the craft shows that are held from time to time around the city (check the papers).

For kitsch souvenirs there are scores of shops selling fake Polynesian stuff, from Filipino shell hangings and carved coconuts to cheap seashell jewellery and wooden tiki-style statues.

If you just want to buy a carton of maca-damia nuts, Longs Drugs has better prices than places in Waikiki. There's a Longs, as well as 200 other stores at the Ala Moana Center, which boasts being the 'largest open-air shopping center in the world'.

For more local flavour, the Aloha Flea Market (☎ 486-1529), at Aloha Stadium out near Pearl Harbor, has more than 1000 sellers from 6 am to 3 pm Wednesdays, Saturdays and Sundays. Admission is 35 cents. A private shuttle bus (☎ 955-4050) leaves from Waikiki at 7.30, 9 and 10.30 am for a cost of $6 return.

At the county-run People's Open Market programme, farmers sell local produce for one hour a week at each of 21 locations around Oahu. Mondays and Wednesdays are set aside for the greater Honolulu area. For a schedule call 522-7088.

GETTING THERE & AWAY
Air

Most flights into Hawaii land at Honolulu International Airport, the only commercial airport on Oahu. All inter-island airlines that serve the Neighbor Islands also land at Honolulu.

See the Getting There & Away and Getting Around chapters in the front of the book for information.

GETTING AROUND
To/From the Airport

From the airport you can get to Waikiki by local bus (if your baggage is limited), by airport shuttle services, by taxi or by renting a car. A taxi to Waikiki from the airport will cost about $20. Most of the main car-rental agencies have booths in or nearby the airport.

The easiest way to drive to Waikiki from the airport is to take Hwy 92, which starts out as Nimitz Highway and turns into Ala Moana Blvd, leading directly into Waikiki. Although this route hits more local traffic, it's hard to get lost on it.

If you're into life in the fast lane, connect instead with the H-1 freeway heading east.

On the return to the airport from Waikiki, take note not to miss the poorly marked interchange where H-1 splits off to the airport. It takes 20 to 30 minutes to get from Waikiki to the airport via H-1 *if* you don't hit traffic.

Bus Travel time is about an hour between the airport and the far end of Waikiki on buses No 19 and 20. TheBus (see the Bus section) stops at the roadside median on the 2nd level, in front of the airline counters. Luggage is limited to what you can hold on your lap or store under your seat, the latter space comparable to the space under an airline seat.

Shuttle Bus The ride between Waikiki and the airport takes about 45 minutes by shuttle bus.

The Airport Motor Coach (☎ 926-4747) leaves the airport for Waikiki hotels about every 20 minutes, 24 hours a day, and costs $6. From Waikiki, service is from 5 am to 11.30 pm and costs $5 (call for pick up). Children's fares are half-price. Rates include two suitcases and one carry-on bag.

Bus

Oahu has a very good public bus system –

the only extensive one in Hawaii. It's called simply TheBus and it's easy to use.

TheBus has 61 routes covering most of Oahu. You can take the bus to watch windsurfers at Kailua or surfers at Sunset Beach or Makaha, visit Chinatown or the Bishop Museum, snorkel at Hanauma Bay or hike Diamond Head. Some of the island's prime viewpoints are beyond reach, however. TheBus doesn't stop at the Nuuanu Pali Lookout, go up to Tantalus or out to Kaena Point.

Each bus route can have a few different destinations. The destination is written on the front of the bus next to the number.

Buses generally keep the same number when inbound and outbound. For instance, the No 8 bus can take you either into the heart of Waikiki or out away from it toward Ala Moana – so note both the number and the written destination before you jump on.

When in doubt ask the bus driver. They're used to disoriented visitors and most drivers are remarkably patient and helpful.

Although TheBus is convenient enough, this isn't Tokyo – if you set your watch by the bus here you'll come up with Hawaiian Time.

In addition to not getting hung up on schedules, buses can bottleneck, with one packed bus after another cruising right by crowded bus stops. Saturday nights between Ala Moana and Waikiki can be a particularly memorable experience.

Overall the buses are in excellent condition – if anything they're too modern. Newer buses are air-conditioned, with sealed windows and climate-control, but are sometimes so out of 'control' that drivers wear jackets to keep from freezing!

Still, TheBus usually gets you where you want to go and as long as you don't try to cut anything close or schedule too much in one day it's a great deal.

Common Routes Buses No 8, 19 and 20 run between Waikiki and Ala Moana Center, Honolulu's central transfer point. There's usually a bus every 10 minutes or less. From Ala Moana you can connect with a broad network of buses to points mauka and Ewa.

Buses No 2, 19 and 20 will take you between Waikiki and downtown Honolulu.

Bus No 4 runs between Waikiki and the University of Hawaii.

Circle-Island Route It's possible to circle the island, beginning at Ala Moana Center. The No 52 Wahiawa-Circle Island bus goes clockwise up Hwy 99 to Haleiwa and along the North Shore. At the Turtle Bay Hilton, on the northern tip of Oahu, it switches signs to No 55 and comes down the windward coast to Kaneohe and down the Pali Highway back to Ala Moana. The No 55 Kaneohe-Circle Island bus does the same route in reverse. If you do it nonstop it takes about four hours.

For the south-east Oahu loop, from Waikiki it's bus No 58 to Sea Life Park and then No 57 up to Kailua and back into Honolulu.

Because you'll need to change buses, ask for a transfer when you first board. Transfers have time limits and aren't meant to be used as stopovers but you can grab a quick break at Ala Moana. Anytime you get off to explore along the route you'll need to pay a new 60-cent fare when you reboard.

Bus Fares The fare to anywhere is 60 cents – *exact change only*.

Monthly bus passes valid for unlimited rides in a calendar month cost $15 and can be purchased at Foodland supermarkets, satellite city halls and 7-Eleven stores.

Transfers are given free when more than one bus is required to get to a destination. Ask when you board.

Children under the age of six ride free.

While free bus passes for senior citizens have been discontinued, seniors 65 years and older can buy a $15 bus pass valid for unlimited rides during a four-year period. Senior citizen passes are issued only at TheBus office, 811 Middle St, Honolulu, and the process takes about 20 minutes.

Bus Schedules TheBus has a great telephone service. As long as you know where you are and where you want to go, you can call 848-5555 anytime between 5.30 am and 10 pm and they'll tell you not only which bus to catch but what time the next one will be there.

You can get printed timetables for some routes and a handy bus map from the satellite city hall in the Ala Moana Center.

If you're going to be using TheBus extensively it's well worth buying a bus guide, found in bookshops and at newsstands. *TheBus Guide* and *How to Get There on the Bus* are two good choices and cost about $3. Be sure to get the most up-to-date version.

Taxi

Metered taxis start with a flagfall fee of $1.75 and then notch up in 25-cent increments at a rate of $1.75 per mile. There's an extra charge of 30 cents per suitcase or backpack.

Taxis are readily available at the airport, but otherwise generally hard to find and you need to phone. Try Sida (☎ 836-0011), Charley's (☎ 955-2211), Americabs (☎ 521-6680) or the yellow pages.

Car

Budget (☎ 922-3600), National (☎ 831-3800), Hertz (☎ 831-3500), Avis (☎ 834-5536), Thrifty (☎ 836-2388), Dollar (☎ 831-2330) and Tropical (☎ 836-1041) all have desks at Honolulu International. Toll free numbers are in the introductory Getting Around chapter in the front of the book.

All things being equal, try to rent from a company with its lot inside the airport. The major companies, like Budget, National, Hertz and Avis, are all inside. Getting to their lots is quicker but, more importantly, on the way back all the highway signs lead to these in-airport car returns.

You can also rent cars in Waikiki at dozens of locations, most commonly in the lobbies of large hotels, but you usually get the best deals at the airport or with advance reservations.

Budget gives renters a coupon booklet with one free admission to the Bishop Museum, Polynesian Cultural Center, Queen Emma Summer Palace, a catamaran dinner cruise and other sights and eateries. You don't have to buy one to get one, so for a single traveller it's all free. This is a particularly good deal if you're only renting a car for a day or two and want to catch some of the sights.

In addition to the major chains, there are local rental companies. Some advertise come-on rates of around $13 a day, although few have cars available at that price. Still, the local companies are more likely to rent to people without credit cards and their rates, while not necessarily cheaper than the larger companies, are at least in the same ballpark.

The following advertise low rates, accept cash payments and are based in Waikiki: Waikiki Rent-A-Car (☎ 946-2181), 1958 Kalakaua Ave, near Sizzler steak house; United Car Rental/VIP (☎ 922-4605), 234 Beach Walk; and Discount Rent-A-Car (☎ 949-4767), 1920 Ala Moana Blvd, at the Inn on the Park.

At the other end of the price range, you can rent a Porsche, Mercedes, Corvette or other luxury car from A-1 Island Odyssey Rentals (☎ 923-0083), Five-0 Exotic Rentals (☎ 836-1028) or Stingray Hawaii (☎ 524-8388).

Moped

State law requires mopeds to be ridden by only one person and prohibits their use on sidewalks and on freeways. Both Budget and Island Scooters rent to drivers aged 18 and older.

Budget (☎ 922-3600) is the only major car-rental company that rents mopeds, charging $10 for four hours or $21 for 24 hours.

Island Scooters (☎ 946-0013) has several Waikiki locations, including one at 151 Uluniu Ave and another at 351 Saratoga Rd. They charge $13 for five hours and $19 for the period of 8 am to 5.30 pm. Renters need to have a credit card or a cash deposit of $60.

Bicycle

There's a lot more traffic on Oahu than on the other islands, which makes cycling seem a lot less appealing.

Titou Rentals (☎ 926-2060), 419 Nahua St in Waikiki, rents mountain bikes for $20/65 a day/week and cruisers for $15/50.

The Hawaii Bicycling League (☎ 735-5756), Box 4403, Honolulu, HI 96812, holds bike rides around Oahu nearly every Saturday and Sunday, ranging from 10-mile jaunts to 60-mile treks. Rides are free and open to the public.

Waikiki

Waikiki was once Hawaii's only tourist destination and it still accounts for nearly half of the visitor accommodation in the state. It has an amazing density of high-rise hotels along an attractive stretch of white sand beach.

Waikiki is crowded with package tourists from both Japan and mainland USA. It has 24,000 permanent residents and some 65,000 visitors on any given day, all in an area roughly 1½ miles long and half a mile wide. Waikiki has 450 restaurants, 350 bars and clubs, and more shops than you'd want to count. Its 34,000 hotel and condo rooms have a year-round occupancy rate of 85%.

While the beaches are packed during the day, at night most of the action is along the streets, where window shoppers, cruising pedicabs, time-share touts and prostitutes all go about their business. There's all sorts of music in the clubs and hotel lounges, from rock bands to Hawaiian guitar.

Visitors who are into city lights or singles scenes often find what they're looking for here, while many seasoned travellers and a fair number of Oahu residents avoid Waikiki like the plague.

In an effort to upgrade Waikiki's image, the beachfront Kalakaua Ave recently underwent an $11-million beautification project, while Waikiki hotels undertook their own half billion dollar face-lift. A few of the renovated hotels, like the Moana, are sights in themselves while most simply have new decor and higher rates.

Waikiki Beach has wonderful orange sunsets, with the sun dropping down between cruising sailing boats. It's the one time of day that the area approaches the romantic image that the travel brochures like to portray.

Just beyond Waikiki is Diamond Head, a landmark so dominant that it's used as a directional marker – people say 'go Diamond Head' instead of 'head east'.

History
At the turn of the century Waikiki was almost entirely wetlands. It had more than 50 acres of fishponds as well as extensive taro patches and rice paddies. Fed by mountain streams from the upland Manoa and Makiki valleys, Waikiki was one of Oahu's most fertile and productive areas.

By the late 1800s Waikiki's narrow beachfront was lined with private gingerbread-trimmed cottages, built by Honolulu's more well-to-do.

Robert Louis Stevenson, who frequented Waikiki in those days, wrote:

If anyone desires such old-fashioned things as lovely scenery, quiet, pure air, clear sea water, heavenly sunsets hung out before his eyes over the Pacific and the distant hills of Waianae, I recommend him to Waikiki Beach.

Tourism took root in 1901 when the Moana opened its doors as Waikiki's first real hotel. A tram line was constructed to connect Waikiki to downtown Honolulu and city folk crowded aboard for the beach. Tiring quickly of the pesky mosquitoes that thrived in the wetlands, these early beach-goers pressured to have Waikiki's 'swamps' brought under control.

In 1922 the Ala Wai Canal was dug to divert the streams that flowed into Waikiki. Old Hawaii lost out, as farmers had the water drained out from under them. Coral rubble was used to fill the ponds, creating what was to become Hawaii's most valuable piece of real estate. Water buffaloes were replaced by tourists.

Waikiki's second hotel, the Royal Hawaiian, was built in 1927 and became the

Top: Kite Festival, Kapiolani Park, Oahu
Bottom: Hanauma Bay, Oahu

Top: Iolani Palace, Honolulu, Oahu
Left: Father Damien's statue at State Capitol, Honolulu, Oahu
Right: Duke Kahanamoku's statue, Waikiki, Oahu

crown jewel of the Matson Navigation Company.

The Royal was the land component for cruises on the *Malolo*, one of the premier luxury ships of the day. The $7.5-million ship, built while the $2-million hotel was under construction, carried 650 passengers from San Francisco to Honolulu each fortnight. The Pink Palace, as the Royal Hawaiian was nicknamed, opened with an extravagant $10-a-plate dinner.

Hotel guests ranged from the Rockefellers to Charlie Chaplin, Babe Ruth to royalty. Some of the guests brought dozens of trunks, their servants and even their Rolls Royces.

The Depression put a damper on things and WW II saw the Royal Hawaiian turned into an R&R centre for servicemen.

Waikiki had 1400 hotel rooms in 1950. In those days surfers could drive their cars to the beach and park on the sand. In the 1960s tourism took over in earnest and by 1968 Waikiki had 13,000 hotel rooms. By 1988 that number had more than doubled.

The lack of available land has finally halted the boom. In a desperate attempt to squeeze in one more high-rise, St Augustine's Catholic Church, standing on the last speck of uncommercialised property along busy Kalakaua Ave, was nearly sold in 1989 to a Tokyo developer for $45 million. It took a community uproar and a petition to the Vatican to nullify the deal.

Orientation

Waikiki is bounded on two sides by the Ala Wai Canal and on another by the ocean. The eastern boundary varies according to who's drawing the line, but it's usually considered to be Kapahulu Ave.

There are two main roads: the coastal strip is Kalakaua Ave, named after King David Kalakaua; the main drag for Waikiki's buses is Kuhio Ave, named after Prince Jonah Kuhio Kalanianaole, a distinguished Hawaiian statesman.

City buses are not allowed on Kalakaua Ave, now a one-way street, and trucks are prohibited at midday. The avenue is no longer as congested as it was in years past,

but taxis and cars now tend to zoom by all the faster.

Walking along the beach is an alternative to using the crowded sidewalks. It's possible to walk the full length of Waikiki along the sand and the sea walls. Although it's rather hot and crowded at midday, it's pleasant at other times. The beach is quite romantic to stroll along at night, enhanced by both the city skyline and the surf lapping at the shore, and it's dark enough to see the stars. Cops patrol the beach on dune buggies after sunset and overall it's as safe as walking the streets.

Information

Tourist Information The Hawaii Visitors Bureau (☎ 924-0266) is at 2270 Kalakaua Ave, on the 7th floor of the Waikiki Business Plaza.

Freebie tourist magazines, such as *This Week*, *Spotlight* and the *Waikiki Beach Press*, can be found on street corners and in hotel lobbies throughout Waikiki.

The Waikiki Public Library (☎ 732-2777), 400 Kapahulu Ave, is open from 10 am to 5 pm Monday to Saturday and until 8 pm on Monday and Wednesdays. It's a relatively small library, but it does have daily newspapers from the Neighbor Islands and the mainland.

Money There's a Bank of Hawaii at 2220 Kalakaua Ave and a First Hawaiian Bank at 2181 Kalakaua Ave. The latter has some interesting Hawaiiana murals by Jean Charlot.

Food Pantry has an automatic teller machine that accepts many bank and credit cards.

Post The main Waikiki post office, 330 Saratoga Rd, is open from 8 am to 4.30 pm Monday to Friday, from 9 am to noon on Saturdays. There are branch post offices at the Royal Hawaiian Shopping Center, 2233 Kalakaua Ave; at Eaton Square, 444 Hobron Lane; and at Hawaiian Village, 2005 Kalia Rd.

Telephone Phone Line Hawaii (☎ 923-1214),

on the 2nd level of International Market Place, is a long-distance phone service open from 8.30 am to 11 pm daily. Three-minute calls to Canada cost $4, while those to most Pacific and European destinations are $8. Calls to anywhere in the USA cost 45 cents a minute.

Shopping Waikiki is as commercial as they come. There's no shortage of souvenir displays, swimsuit and T-shirt shops, quick-stop convenience marts or fancy boutiques. You won't have any problem finding beach mats or macadamia nuts. Everything's geared towards tourists, most of it bordering on either the tacky or the slick.

The prolific ABC discount marts (33 in Waikiki at last count) are quite often the cheapest places to buy candy, nuts, soda, suntan oil and other vacation necessities.

The Royal Hawaiian Shopping Center is Waikiki's biggest shopping centre, spanning three blocks along Kalakaua Ave in the centre of Waikiki. It has about 150 shops, restaurants and offices, including Aloha Airlines, Budget Rent A Car, American Express, Nene Travel, Fox Photo, Waldenbooks and about 25 eateries, from Baskin-Robbins to Chinese and Japanese restaurants. Most of its other shops are pricey speciality and jewellery stores. The centre is open from 9 am to 9 pm daily.

International Market Place is a collection of ticky-tacky shops and stalls set beneath a sprawling banyan tree. Although most of the stalls don't carry quality goods, if you're looking for inexpensive jewellery or T-shirts it might be worth a stroll. There's a food court with inexpensive food stalls on the north-western corner of the market place, but it too is predominately low quality.

Liberty House, a somewhat up-market department store with good quality clothing, is at the Waikiki Beachcomber Hotel.

For better deals, you need to leave Waikiki. Try the Ala Moana Center, the Aloha Flea Market or the craft shows that pop up around the city.

Grocery Stores The best place to get groceries in Waikiki is at the Food Pantry, 2370 Kuhio Ave, which is open 24 hours a day. Their prices are higher than those of the supermarkets, which are all outside Waikiki, but lower than those of the smaller convenience stores. Food Pantry, like most grocery stores, accepts credit cards.

The easiest supermarket to get to without a car is Foodland at the Ala Moana Center. There's a Times Supermarket at 3221 Waialae Ave, between 5th and 6th avenues, and a Foodland a few blocks away near the eastern intersection of King and Kapiolani Sts. There are grocery stores along Beretania St as well.

Film & Photography Fox Photo, with Waikiki branches in the Royal Hawaiian Shopping Center and at 2301 Kuhio Ave, does good quality one-hour photo processing.

To buy film and to have slides processed, Longs Drugs is a good choice. All their stores send out to Kodak, and most also do Fuji. Slides generally take two to three days, prints a day or two, and the cost is a dollar or two cheaper than the camera shops.

While there are no branches in Waikiki, there's a Longs on the top floor of the Ala Moana Center and another next to Times Supermarket at 3221 Waialae Ave.

Parking Parking in Waikiki is a hassle. Many of the hotels charge $6 to $10 a day at their parking garages.

At the west end of Waikiki the best bet is the free public parking lot at the Ala Wai Yacht Harbor.

On the east side, there's a small underground parking lot next to the Tradewinds Plaza on Lemon Rd, a couple of buildings down from Queen Kapiolani Hotel. It costs $2 for overnight parking and an additional $2 to park all day.

The zoo parking lot on Kapahulu Ave has meters and costs 25 cents an hour with a four-hour parking limit. If you like taking chances you can try your luck parking overnight at the zoo, when the police generally don't write tickets; however if you don't move out early enough in the morning you may be greeted with the sight of an officer placing a $25 ticket on your window. Trust us.

Emergency Dial 911 for all police, fire and ambulance emergency services.

Doctors On Call has six private clinics in Waikiki. They have doctors available 24 hours a day at the Hyatt Regency (☎ 926-4777), Diamond Head Tower, 4th floor, and during more standard hours at the Royal Hawaiian Shopping Center (☎ 923-4499), the Hawaiian Regent Hotel (☎ 923-3666) and Hilton Hawaiian Village (☎ 973-5252). Appointments aren't necessary. They have X-ray and lab facilities and even make house calls. A standard office visit costs around $50 and they honour many overseas travel insurance policies.

Dangers & Annoyances There's been a clampdown on the hustlers who used to push time shares and other con deals from every other street corner in Waikiki. They're not totally gone – there are just fewer of them (and some have metamorphosed into 'activity centres'). If you see a sign touting car rentals for $5 a day, you've probably found one.

Time-share salespeople will offer you all sorts of deals, from free luaus to sunset cruises, if you'll just come to hear their 'no obligation' pitch. *Caveat emptor*.

Waikiki Beaches

The two-mile stretch of white sand that runs from the Hilton Hawaiian Village to Kapiolani Park is commonly called Waikiki Beach, although sections along the way have their own names and characteristics.

In the early morning the beach belongs to walkers and joggers – and it's surprisingly quiet. Strolling down the beach toward Diamond Head at sunrise can actually be a meditative experience.

By midmorning it looks like a normal resort beach, with boogie board and surfboard concessionaires setting up shop and catamarans pulling up on the beach offering

$15 sails. By noon it is packed and the challenge is to walk down the beach without stepping on anyone.

Most of Waikiki's beautiful white sands are not its own. Tons of sand have been barged in over the years, much of it from Papohaku Beach on Molokai.

As the beachfront developed, landowners haphazardly constructed sea walls and offshore barriers to protect their property. In the process they blocked the natural forces of sand accretion, and erosion has long been a serious problem at Waikiki.

Sections of the beach are still being replenished with imported sand. Much of it ends up washing into the ocean, filling channels and depressions and altering the surf breaks.

Waikiki is good for swimming, boogie boarding, surfing, sailing and other beach activities most of the year. Between May and September, summer swells can make the water a little rough for swimming, although it's the best time for surfing.

Overall, Waikiki beaches aren't that good for snorkelling. The best of them is Sans Souci.

There are lifeguards and showers at most of the beaches.

Kahanamoku Beach Kahanamoku Beach, fronting the Hilton Hawaiian Village, is the westernmost section of Waikiki. It was named for Duke Kahanamoku, a surfer and swimmer who won Olympic gold in the 100-metre freestyle in 1912 and became a Hawaiian celebrity.

Kahanamoku Beach is protected by a breakwater at one end and a pier at the other, with a coral reef running between the two. It's a calm swimming area with a sandy bottom that slopes gradually.

Fort DeRussy Beach Fort DeRussy Beach, one of the least crowded Waikiki beaches, borders 1800 feet of the Fort DeRussy Military Reservation. Like all beaches in Hawaii, it's public. The federal government provides lifeguards.

The water is usually calm and good for

swimming. The swimming zone is marked by buoys and you can also snorkel there, although it's nothing to rush down for. While the beach is most popular with windsurfers, there's also boogie boarding and surfing.

A grassy lawn that gets at least sparse shade from palm trees provides an alternative to frying on the sand.

There's a beach hut, open daily from 9 am to 5 pm, where you can rent water sports equipment. Windsurfing equipment rents for $30 for two hours, $40 with a lesson. Boogie boards rent for $4 for the first hour and $3 for each additional hour, while snorkel sets cost $3 for one hour and $6 for three hours.

Gray's Beach Gray's Beach, the local name for the beach near the Halekulani Hotel, was named for a boarding house called Gray's-by-the-Sea that stood on the site in the 1920s. On the same stretch of beach was the original Halekulani, a lovely low-rise mansion that was converted into a hotel in the 1930s. About a decade ago, the mansion gave way to the present high-rise hotel.

Because the sea wall in front of the Halekulani was built so close to the waterline, the part of the beach fronting the hotel is often totally submerged.

The section of beach between the Halekulani and the Royal Hawaiian Hotel varies in width from season to season. The waters off the beach are shallow and calm.

Central Waikiki Beach The area between the Royal Hawaiian Hotel and the Waikiki Beach Center is the busiest section of the whole beach.

Most of the beach has a shallow bottom with a gradual slope. There's pretty good swimming, although there's a lot of activity, with catamarans, surfers and plenty of other swimmers in the water. Keep your eyes open.

Offshore are Queen's Surf and Canoe's Surf, Waikiki's best known surf breaks.

Waikiki Beach Center The area opposite the Hyatt Regency Waikiki is the site of the Waikiki Beach Center. There are restrooms,

showers, a police station, lockers and rental concessions.

The **Wizard Stones of Kapaemahu** – four boulders on the Diamond Head side of the police station – are said to contain the secrets and healing powers of four sorcerers, named Kapaemahu, Kinohi, Kapuni and Kahaloa, who visited from Tahiti in ancient times. Before returning back to Tahiti, they transferred their powers to these stones.

Just west of the stones is a bronze statue of Hawaii's most decorated athlete, Duke Kahanamoku (1890-1968), standing with one of his longboards. Considered the 'father of modern surfing' Duke, who made his home in Waikiki, gave surfing demonstrations on beaches from Sydney, Australia, to Rockaway Beach, New York. Many surfers took issue with the placement of the statue as Duke is standing with his back to the sea, a position they say he never would have taken in real life. In response the city moved the statue as close to the sidewalk as possible.

Star Beach Boys, a beachside concession stand, rents out surfboards for $8 for the first hour, $4 each additional hour, and boogie boards for $5 for the first hour and $3 for each additional hour. Private surf lessons, some by legendary beachboys like Rabbit Kekai, cost $25 an hour. They also give outrigger canoe rides for $5.

Kuhio Beach Park Kuhio Beach Park is marked on its east end by Kapahulu Groin, a walled storm drain with a walkway on top that juts out into the ocean from the end of Kapahulu Ave.

A low breakwater sea wall runs about 1300 feet out from Kapahulu Groin, paralleling the beach. It was built to control sand erosion and in the process two nearly enclosed swimming pools were formed. Local kids walk out on the breakwater, which is called The Wall, but it's very slippery and to the uninitiated can be dangerous.

The pool closest to Kapahulu Groin is best for swimming, with the water near the breakwater reaching overhead depths. However, because circulation is limited the water can get murky and sometimes collects a notice-able film of suntan oil.

The 'Watch Out Deep Holes' sign refers to holes in the pool's sandy bottom that can be created by swirling currents. They can take waders by surprise.

The park is named after Prince Kuhio, who maintained his residence on this beach. His house was torn down in 1936, 14 years after his death, in order to expand the beach.

Between the old timers who gather each afternoon to play chess and cribbage at Kuhio's sidewalk pavilions and the kids boogie boarding off the Groin, this section of the beach has as much local colour as tourist influence.

Kapahulu Groin Kapahulu Groin is one of Waikiki's hottest boogie boarding spots. If the surf's right you can find a few dozen boogie boarders, mostly teenage boys, riding the waves.

The kids ride straight for the wall and then veer away at the last moment, drawing 'oohs' and 'ahs' from the tourists who gather to watch them. If you want to join them, boogie boards can be rented from a stand at the side of the Groin for $5 an hour and $15 a day.

Kapahulu Groin is also a great place to catch sunsets.

Kapiolani Beach Park Kapiolani Beach Park starts at Kapahulu Groin and runs down to the Natatorium, past Waikiki Aquarium.

Queen's Surf is the name given to the wide midsection of Kapiolani Beach. The area in front of the pavilion is a popular beach with the gay community. It's a pretty good area for swimming, with a sandy bottom. The section of beach between Queen's Surf and Kapahulu Groin is shallow and has a lot of broken coral.

Kapiolani Beach Park is a relaxed place with little of the frenzy of activity found in front of the central strip of Waikiki hotels. It's a popular weekend picnicking spot for local families who unload the kids to splash in the water as they line up the barbecue grills.

There's a big grassy field to lay out on, good for spreading out a beach towel and unpacking a picnic basket. Free parking is available near the beach along Kalakaua Ave. There are restrooms and showers at the Queen's Surf pavilion.

The surfing area offshore is called Public's.

Natatorium The Natatorium, at the Diamond Head end of Kapiolani Beach, is a 100-metre-long saltwater swimming pool built after WW I as a memorial for soldiers who died in that war. There were once hopes of hosting an Olympics, with this pool as the focal point.

Waves bouncing off the Natatorium, which is now closed and in disrepair, create erosion problems. But because of its status as a memorial, sentiment has been against tearing it down.

Sans Souci Beach Down by the New Otani Kaimana Beach Hotel, Sans Souci is a nice little sandy beach away from the main tourist scene. It has outdoor showers and a lifeguard station.

Many residents come to Sans Souci for daily swims. A shallow coral reef close to shore makes for calm, protected waters and provides reasonably good snorkelling. More coral can be found by following the Kapua Channel as it cuts through the reef, although beware of currents that can pick up in the channel. Check conditions with the lifeguard before venturing out.

Royal Hawaiian Hotel
The Royal Hawaiian, Hawaii's first luxury hotel, is a neat place to walk through even if you're not staying there. With its pink turrets and Moorish/Spanish architecture, it's a throwback to the era when Rudolph Valentino was *the* romantic idol and travel to Hawaii was by luxury liner.

The hotel was originally on 20 acres of coconut grove but over the years the grounds have been chipped away by a huge shopping centre on one side and a high-rise mega-hotel on the other. The Royal Hawaiian is a survivor.

Inside, the hotel is lovely and airy with high ceilings and chandeliers and everything in rose colours. The small garden at the rear is filled with bird song, a rare sound in most of Waikiki.

Fort DeRussy

Fort DeRussy Military Reservation is a US Army post used mainly as a recreation centre for the armed forces. This large chunk of Waikiki real estate was acquired by the US Army a few years after Hawaii was annexed to the USA. Before that it was swampy marshland where Hawaiian chiefs hunted ducks.

The Hale Koa Hotel on the property is open only to military personnel and their families and guests. There's a public beach and a military museum on the grounds.

US Army Museum of Hawaii Battery Randolph, a reinforced concrete building built in 1911 as a coastal artillery battery, houses the army museum at Fort DeRussy. It once held two formidable 14-inch disappearing rifles with a 14-mile range that were designed to recoil down into the concrete walls for reloading after each firing. A 55-ton lead counter weight would then return the carriage to position.

The museum now houses weapons and exhibits on military history as it relates to Hawaii. There are some interesting historic displays on King Kamehameha, and the 19th-century overthrow of the monarchy, as well as WW II. It's open from 10 am to 4.30 pm daily, except Mondays, and admission is free.

Oceanarium

The Pacific Beach Hotel, at 2490 Kalakaua Ave, houses an impressive three-storey 280,000-gallon aquarium that forms the backdrop for three of their restaurants. Divers enter the Oceanarium to feed the tropical fish daily at 9 am, noon, and 1, 5.30, 6.30 and 8.15 pm.

Damien Museum

St Augustine's Church, off Kalakaua Ave and Ohua St, is a quiet little sanctuary in the midst of the hotel district. In the rear of the church a second building houses a modest museum honouring Father Damien, who lived and worked in the leper colony on Molokai. As a befitting tribute to Father Damien's life, the building also houses a lunchtime soup kitchen. Both operations are run by volunteers and admission to the museum is free. Opening hours are 9 am to 3 pm Monday to Friday, until noon on Saturdays.

Ala Wai Canal

Late in the afternoon outrigger canoe teams can be seen paddling up and down Ala Wai Canal and out to the Ala Wai Yacht Harbor.

Kapiolani Park

The nearly 200-acre Kapiolani Park, at the Diamond Head end of Waikiki, was a gift from King Kalakaua to the people of Honolulu in 1877. It was Hawaii's first public park and the king dedicated it to his wife, Queen Kapiolani.

In its early days horse racing and band concerts were the park's biggest attractions. Although the race track has gone the concerts continue and Kapiolani Park is still the site of all sorts of community activities.

The park contains the Waikiki Aquarium, the Honolulu Zoo, Kapiolani Beach Park, the Waikiki Shell, the Kodak Hula Show grounds and Kapiolani Bandstand. Parades marching through Waikiki usually end up at the park. It has sports fields, tennis courts, huge lawns and tall banyan trees.

The Royal Hawaiian Band presents free concerts from 2 to 3.15 pm nearly every Sunday at the Kapiolani Bandstand. Dance competitions, Hawaiian music concerts and other activities occur throughout the year.

The Waikiki Shell is an outdoor amphitheatre with symphony, jazz and rock concerts. For information on performances, check the papers or call the Blaisdell Center (☎ 521-2911).

Kapiolani is one of the top-rated kite-flying parks in the USA. Kite Fantasy, a kite shop at the nearby New Otani Kaimana

Beach Hotel, often gives kite demonstrations on the grassy lawns beyond the tennis courts.

It's a pleasant park and despite all the activities that go on, it's large enough to have a lot of quiet space.

Waikiki Aquarium This well-kept aquarium (☎ 923-9741) at 2777 Kalakaua Ave, which opened in 1904, has interesting displays that include tanks of black-tip sharks, moray eels, flash-back cuttlefish wavering with pulses of light, and rare Hawaiian fish with names like the bearded armorhead and the sling-jawed wrasse.

This is a great place to identify fish you've seen while snorkelling or diving. Separate tanks display fish common to Hanauma Bay, Kaneohe Bay, Waianae Reef, the Kona Coast and Hawaiian tide pools.

Other tanks display the exotic, such as the mudskippers of a mangrove swamp and the swaying tentacles of corals which help build Micronesian reefs.

In 1985 the aquarium was the first to breed the Palauan chambered nautilus in captivity. Four of these sea creatures, with their unique spiral, chambered shell, are on display.

There are also some giant clams from Palau that were less than an inch long when acquired in 1982 and now measure over two feet, the largest in the USA.

An outdoor tank re-creates a rocky Hawaiian shore and has some of the more common tropical fish found in inshore waters. There's also a touch tank for children, a mahimahi hatchery, green sea turtles and a pair of Hawaiian monk seals.

The aquarium will be closed for renovations until early 1993. The new admission fee, which has not yet been set, should be modest.

Honolulu Zoo The Honolulu Zoo is somewhat stark and artificial, with lots of small concrete cages. It has elephants, tigers, bears, white rhinos, storks, flamingos, giraffes, monkeys and Galapagos tortoises.

The zoo is in the midst of some long overdue upgrading and the completion of a new multimillion-dollar 10-acre African savannah exhibit should provide the beasts a more reasonable space to roam. In the meantime, a sign that reads 'This is the best zoo to be found for 2300 miles in any direction' is a slight exaggeration as Hilo's rainforest zoo, although smaller, is more natural and better.

Opening hours are 8.30 am to 4.30 pm daily. Admission is $3, but children under 12 years of age accompanied by an adult are admitted free.

In front of the zoo there's a large banyan tree which is home to hundreds of white pigeons – escapees from a small group brought to the zoo in the 1940s.

Art in the Park Local artists have been hanging their paintings on the fence around the zoo on weekends for more than 25 years. If you're looking for a painting, this is a good opportunity to buy directly from the artist. The artwork is on display from 10 am to 4 pm on Saturdays and Sundays.

Kodak Hula Show The Kodak Hula Show, off Monsarrat Ave near the Waikiki Shell, is a staged photo opportunity of hula dancers, ti-leaf skirts and ukuleles. The musicians are a group of older ladies who performed at the Royal Hawaiian Hotel in days gone by.

This is the scene in postcards where dancers hold up letters forming the words 'Hawaii' and 'Aloha'. The whole thing is quite touristy, although entertaining if you're in the mood, and it's free.

Kodak has been putting on this show since 1939. The benches are set up stadium-style around a grassy stage area with the sun at your back. The idea is for everyone to shoot a lot of film. It works. Even though Kodak doesn't monopolise the film market anymore, the tradition continues.

Shows are held from 10 to 11.15 am on Tuesdays, Wednesdays and Thursdays. Make sure you're on time because once it starts they only admit people between acts. The gates open at 8.30 am.

Dolphins
The Kahala Hilton, in the Kahala area

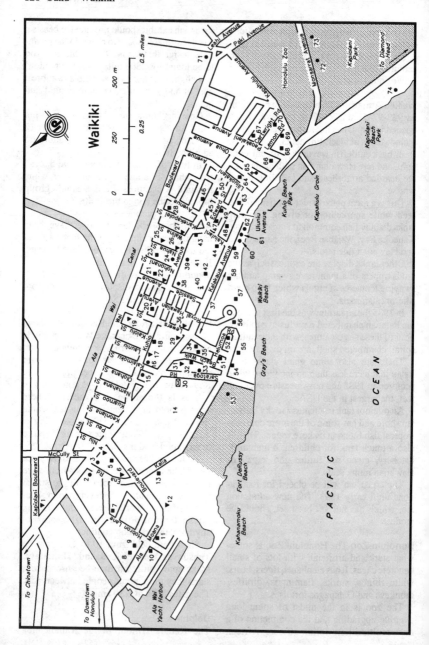

Waikiki

■ PLACES TO STAY

5	Polynesian Backpackers
7	Hawaii Hostel
8	Big Surf
9	Driftwood Hotel
10	Hawaii Prince Hotel
11	Ilikai Hotel
13	Hilton Hawaiian Village
18	Hotel Honolulu
20	Outrigger Waikiki Surf
21	Hawaiian Backpackers Hostel
23	Ilima Hotel
28	Waikiki Sand Villa Hotel
32	The Breakers
34	Outrigger Coral Seas
35	Niihau Apartment Hotel
42	Waikiki Beachcomber
43	Outrigger East Hotel
44	Sheraton Princess Kaiulani
45	Inter Club Hostel Waikiki
46	Continental Surf
47	Hale Aloha Hostel
48	Hyatt Regency Waikiki
49	Waikiki Prince Hotel
50	Royal Grove Hotel
51	Outrigger Waikiki Tower
52	Waikiki Parc Hotel
54	Outrigger Reef Hotel
55	Halekulani Hotel
56	Sheraton Waikiki
57	Royal Hawaiian Hotel
58	Outrigger Waikiki
59	Sheraton Moana Surfrider
63	Waikiki Circle Hotel
64	Pacific Beach Hotel
66	Hawaiian Regent
67	Ocean Resort Hotel Waikiki
68	Waikiki Beach Hotel
69	Waikiki Grand
70	Queen Kapiolani Hotel

▼ PLACES TO EAT

1	Hard Rock Cafe
4	Sizzler
6	California Pizza Kitchen & Singha Thai
12	Saigon Cafe
17	Hamburger Mary's
19	Zuke Bistro
22	Pizza Uno
25	Country Life Vegetarian Buffet
26	Patisserie
27	Food Pantry
29	Moose McGillycuddy's
31	New Tokyo Restaurant
36	Malia's Cantina

OTHER

2	Wave Waikiki
3	Pink Cadillac
14	Fort DeRussy
15	Kuhio Twins Theatre
16	Hula's Bar & Lei Stand
24	Scruples
25	Titou Rentals
30	Waikiki Post Office
33	Urasenke Tea Ceremony
37	Royal Hawaiian Shopping Center
38	Waikiki Trade Center
39	Kuhio Mall
40	Hawaii Visitors Bureau
41	International Market Place
53	US Army Museum
60	Board Rentals
61	Police
62	Wizard Stones
65	St Augustine's Church
71	Waikiki Library
72	Kodak Hula Show
73	Waikiki Shell
74	Waikiki Aquarium

beyond Diamond Head, has three Atlantic bottlenose dolphins in a lagoon as well as penguins, green sea turtles and tropical reef fish on display. Coached by trainers from Sea Life Park, the dolphins put on a short show for smelt and herring at 11 am and 2 and 4 pm daily. They jump and dive, stand on their tails, vocalise, hula dance, play volleyball and the like. The show is free and open to the public. Visitors are allowed a one-hour grace period of free parking in the hotel garage.

Places to Stay

Waikiki's main beachfront strip, Kalakaua Ave, is largely lined with high-rise hotels and $100-plus rooms. Many of these hotels cater to package tourists, driving the prices up for individual travellers.

Better values are generally found at the smaller and less pretentious hostelries on the back streets. There are hotels in the Kuhio Ave area and up near the Ala Wai Canal that are as nice as some of the beachfront hotels but half the price. If you don't mind walking 10 or 15 minutes to the beach you can save yourself a bundle.

In many hotels the rooms themselves are the same, only the views vary; generally the higher the floor, the higher the price. If you're paying extra for a view, you might want to ask to see the room first. Waikiki certainly doesn't have any truth-in-labelling laws governing when a hotel can sell a room as 'oceanview', for instance. Some 'ocean views' are merely glimpses of the water as seen through a series of high-rises.

Many of Waikiki's hotels have recently completed major renovations. While price hikes were planned upon the completion of these renovations, the economic downturn has put a lid on increases.

Waikiki has many more hotel rooms than condos. Most Waikiki condos are filled with long-term residents and there isn't the proliferation of vacation rental agents as in places like Kihei and Kona. The best way to find a condo is to look in the Vacation Rentals section of the daily paper, although the listings can be fairly meagre, particularly in the winter season.

Places to Stay – bottom end

Hale Aloha Hostel (☎ 926-8313), 2417 Prince Edward St, Honolulu, HI 96815, a member of AYH and IYHF, is a 50-bed hostel on a back street a few short blocks from Waikiki Beach. Dorm beds are $13. There are also three rooms for couples at $30, with small refrigerators and private bathrooms. For the private rooms, paid reservations are required and can be booked a maximum of three nights.

While posted office hours are from 8 to 11 am and 5 to 9 pm, the office is generally open all day until midnight. Dormitory lockout is from 11 am to 4 pm. There are four parking spaces available at $2 a day – a bargain for Waikiki. Occasionally you can be lucky as a walk-in, but at busy times reservations are often necessary two to three weeks in advance. Hostel membership is required. If you're not already a hostel member, cards can be purchased at the hostel near the university, but not in Waikiki. Both hostels are run by Thelma Akau and her family. MasterCard and Visa are accepted.

InterClub Hostel Waikiki (☎ 924-2636), 2413 Kuhio Ave, Honolulu, HI 96815, is one of a small Australian/American chain of hostels. There are 63 bunk beds, usually arranged five to seven to a room. To stay at InterClub you need a passport and an onward ticket to a destination outside the USA. Reservations aren't taken, so if they're full, show up in the morning and hang around until someone leaves. If you call from the airport and a bed is available, they'll usually hold it long enough for you to get there by bus. Office hours are from 8 am to midnight.

Guests are mostly backpackers, the staff include international travellers working for room and board, and lots of languages float in the air. Unlike the AYH hostel next door, you can come and go as you please all day and there are few rules. There's a TV lounge, a communal kitchen, a washer/dryer and $1 lockers. Try to get a bed in one of the rear units, as the rooms closest to the heavy traffic on Kuhio Ave can be very noisy. It costs $15 a night.

A number of small businesses providing hostel-like dormitory accommodation have popped up recently. They operate out of older apartment complexes, each unit of which is squeezed with bunk beds. While Oahu presently has few regulations regarding such businesses, that could change. It'd be a good idea to verify that the following three places are still in operation before showing up at the door.

Best bet is the *Hawaii Hostel* (☎ 941-0954), 403 Hobron Lane, Honolulu, HI 96815, which has converted a small apartment complex into a 48-bed hostel. Each apartment unit has its own kitchen and bathroom, four dorm beds in the front room, and a separate bedroom with a double bed that's usually rented to couples. This is a fairly quiet little niche in a neighbourhood of expensive high-rise condos. It's about a 15-minute walk to Fort DeRussy Beach. At present one of the units is reserved as a community TV lounge. Rates are $15 per person, $13 if you stay a week or more.

Polynesian Backpackers (☎ 949-3382), 1946 Ala Moana Blvd 212, Honolulu, HI 96815, has nine small studio rooms in the Hawaiian Colony building. Each room has four to six beds squeezed in, a table and a little kitchen, bathroom and shower. Some units have a double bed for couples as well as beds for singles together in the same room. It's all quite congested. All the rooms have air-con and cable TV and there's no curfew. The resident manager lives on site. Call ahead, otherwise the gates are locked. The rate is $15 per person.

Hawaiian Backpackers Hostel (☎ 845-6311), 419E Seaside Ave, Honolulu, HI 96815, is an older two-storey place in an alley off Seaside Ave. It's close to the main bus lines and about a 10-minute walk from Waikiki Beach. Guests have use of a kitchen and a TV lounge.

Perhaps in part because it's in the centre of a nightlife district, Hawaiian Backpackers tends to attract a partying crowd of travellers. Bunk beds in small dorms cost $15, there's no curfew and it's open 24 hours a day.

Waikiki Prince Hotel (☎ 922-1544), 2431 Prince Edward St, Honolulu, HI 96815, has 30 units next door to the Hale Aloha Hostel. Rooms are basic and not all that cheery, but the people working there make up for it with aloha spirit. They get an international crowd, with a lot of backpackers in the summer.

Standard rooms cost $39 a day, while rooms with kitchenettes cost from $42 to $49 a day. All rooms have cable TV and air-con. There are no room phones, but the staff are quite efficient at taking messages. Half a dozen parking spaces are available at $3 a day. The office is open from 9 am to 6 pm.

Waikiki Circle Hotel (☎ 923-1571), 2464 Kalakaua Ave, Honolulu, HI 96815, is a funky, circular building with a great location. It has 100 rooms on 13 floors, all with lanais. There are also phones, TVs and air-con. This older, locally owned hotel is a bit of a holdout, and you can't help but wonder how long it'll be before it's replaced by a slick high-rise.

While the rooms are nothing special, there's nothing wrong with them either – and

you can't beat this price and still be right across from Waikiki Beach. Singles/doubles cost $41/45, while rooms with an unobstructed view of the ocean cost $8 more.

So many retirees return each winter to the *Royal Grove Hotel* (☎ 923-7691), 151 Uluniu Ave, Honolulu, HI 96815, that it's difficult to get a room in season without reserving months in advance. Kitchenette units cost $43 in the old wing (with no air-con) and from $57 in the new wing (with air-con). Rooms without kitchenettes cost $38/42 in the old/new wing. There's a small pool.

Big Surf (☎ 946-6525), 1690 Ala Moana Blvd, Honolulu, HI 96815, on the western edge of Waikiki, is quite run down, the kind of place where the ceiling fans wobble and the TV picture fades to fuzz. Still, two people travelling together can have their own room with two twin beds, bathroom, fridge and small lanai for $39/45 in the low/high season, which may be a better option than cramped $15-dorm beds elsewhere. Very small one-person studios with no lanai cost $31/37 in the low/high season. Big Surf is not far from the YMCA (see Honolulu Places to Stay) and gets some Y overflow.

The *Driftwood Hotel* (☎ 949-0061, (800) 669-7719), 1696 Ala Moana Blvd, Honolulu, HI 96815, is next door to the Big Surf and opposite the ritzy Hawaii Prince Hotel. The 66 motel-style rooms have cinder-block walls and are lined up in rows with their entrances off a long outdoor corridor. The rooms are clean but rather basic. All have small refrigerators and some have lanais, although generally the lanai area is at the expense of room space. Rates are $65 to $85 during high season, $10 less during the low season, and $10 less again by the week.

Niihau Apartment Hotel (☎ 922-1607), 247 Beach Walk, Honolulu, HI 96815, is one of Waikiki's better condo bargains. However only about 20 of the 43 units are in the rental pool and winter residency is booked up far in advance. The units have kitchens, lanais and TVs. One-bedroom units cost $50, while two-bedroom units for up to four people cost $75. There's a three-night minimum stay, no pool and no parking.

Across the street is *Hale Pua Nui* (☎ 921-4398, (800) 367-8047 ext 467), 228 Beach Walk, Honolulu, HI 96815, an older four-storey building with 22 studio apartments. While they're not fancy each has everything most people would need – two beds, a kitchenette, cable TV and phone (50-cent local calls), and the beach is a five-minute walk away.

Rates are $55 in the winter and from 16 June to 15 September, $40 the rest of the year. There's a three-night minimum and stays must be paid in advance. There's no on-site parking and no air-conditioning.

Places to Stay – middle

Waikiki Sand Villa Hotel (☎ 922-4744, (800) 247-1903 from the mainland, (800) 342-1557 from the Neighbor Islands) is at 2375 Ala Wai Blvd, Honolulu, HI 96815, on the Ala Wai Canal, a 10-minute walk from Waikiki Beach. The 223 rooms have cable TV, refrigerators and small lanais, some with views across the golf course toward Manoa Valley. Ask for a corner unit, which has the best views. Standard rooms cost $56/70 in the low/high season. It's good value for this price range.

Continental Surf (☎ 922-2755, (800) 367-5004 from the mainland, (800) 272-5275 from the Neighbor Islands), 2426 Kuhio Ave, Honolulu, HI 96815, is a 140-room 21-storey hotel a few blocks from the ocean. Rates are $73 for standard rooms and $90 for rooms with kitchenettes, $10 less in the low season.

All rooms are the same size (small), so the ones with kitchenettes are a bit squeezed. The decor is uninspiring and things are a tad faded, but otherwise it's fine and many units have views of the ocean or the mountains. The higher you go, the better the view, and the rates are the same on all floors. When you reserve, ask if they're running their 'Affordable Waikiki' deal which includes a free Budget rental car.

Ocean Resort Hotel Waikiki (☎ 922-3861, (800) 367-2317 from the mainland, (800) 342-1560 from the Neighbor Islands), 175

Paoakalani Ave, Honolulu, HI 96815, has 451 rooms. It doesn't have a whole lot of character, with the orange vinyl from its Quality Inn days still predominant. However, it remains one of the cheapest of Waikiki's high-rise hotels and the new Japanese owners have sensibly painted over the orange striped wallpaper that once flashed across the bedroom walls. A few of the floors are designated for nonsmokers only.

Rooms cost from $72 to $109 in the older tower and from $93 to $137 in the spiffier Pali Tower. All are $10 cheaper in the low season.

Waikiki Hana (☎ 926-8841, (800) 367-5004), 2424 Koa Ave, Honolulu, HI 96815, is a 73-room hotel behind the Hyatt Regency. Rooms are rather small and simple and the mattresses, at least in the rooms we saw, seemed uncomfortably soft. Standard rooms cost $65/75 in the low/high season, and if you reserve in advance the rate includes a free Budget rental car.

The *Outrigger* (☎ 926-0679, (800) 733-7777 from the USA and Canada, (800) 125-642 from Australia), 2375 Kuhio Ave, Honolulu, HI 96815, has bought up Waikiki's middle-range hotels left and right and has recently put $125 million into renovating a number of them.

At last count the Outrigger had 21 Waikiki hotels. While many are pretty good deals, there's a wide range in price and quality. At any rate, with one phone call you can check on the availability of 25% of the hotel rooms in Waikiki! Ask for their 'Free Ride' package when you make reservations to get a free Dollar rental car for the length of your stay.

Outrigger Waikiki Surf (☎ 923-7671), 2200 Kuhio Ave, is one of the Outrigger's better deals. The 303 refurbished rooms are small but nice, each with a tiny refrigerator. Rooms cost from $70, kitchenette units from $75, and one-bedroom units for up to four people from $105. Rates are $5 less in the low season.

If you want to prepare your own meals consider the Outrigger's *Waikiki Surf East*, 422 Royal Hawaiian Ave, and *Waikiki Surf West*, 412 Lewers St, both right around the corner from the Waikiki Surf. Rates at both begin at $65/70 in the low/high season and all rooms have kitchenettes.

Closer to the beach, the 109-room *Outrigger Coral Seas* (☎ 923-3881), 250 Lewers St, has standard rooms for $65/75 in the low/high season, while kitchenette units are $10 more. Although the hotel is not much to look at from the outside, the rooms are rather nice.

The 439-room *Outrigger Waikiki Tower* (☎ 922-6424), 200 Lewers St, is a modern high-rise a few minutes' walk from the beach. Rooms have lanais and are comfortable and nicely decorated in pastels. The cheapest rates are for rooms from the 6th floor down, which cost $80/90 in the low/high season. Kitchenettes are $5 more.

Ala Wai Terrace (☎ 949-7384), 1547 Ala Wai Blvd, a bit off the main track at the western edge of the Ala Wai Canal, is the cheapest Outrigger property. Simply furnished studios in the older section cost $45/50 in the low/high season. One-bedroom units begin at just $5 more.

The Outrigger has two hotels right on the beach: the *Outrigger Reef Hotel*, with rooms from $120 to $225, and the *Outrigger Waikiki*, with rooms from $140 to $205. Despite the price, these are not luxury hotels – the tariff simply reflects the beachside locale.

Hotel Honolulu (☎ 926-2766, (800) 426-2766), 376 Kaiolu St, Honolulu, HI 96815, is Waikiki's only gay hotel. It's a quiet oasis on a side street a block from busy Kuhio Ave and the heart of the gay district. The three-storey hotel has the character of an unhurried inn, with helpful management, lots of hanging ferns and potted orchids and a peach-coloured cockatoo at the front desk. The 19 main units are decorated with flair, each with its own theme, such as 'Safari', 'Rangoon' or 'Norma Jean'. They are large and comfortable, with lanais, kitchens, ceiling fans and air-con. Studios cost $76 and one-bedroom units cost $98. There are also smaller, non-theme studios in an adjacent building for $64. This is a hotel for travellers, not a local hangout. While the guests are

predominantly gay, the hotel is not exclusively gay, and straights are also welcome.

Queen Kapiolani (☎ 922-1941, (800) 367-5004), 150 Kapahulu Ave, Honolulu, HI 96815, is a 313-room 19-storey hotel at the quieter Diamond Head end of Waikiki. It's an older hotel with an ageing regal theme – chandeliers, high ceilings and fading paintings of Hawaiian royalty.

Standard rooms cost $95/105 in the low/high season. However rooms are anything but standard and vary greatly in size, with some that are very pleasant and others so small they can barely squeeze a bed in. The simplest way to avoid a closet-size space is to request a room with two twin beds instead of a single queen. Also, be sure to get a room without interconnecting doors – they act like a sound tunnel to the next room. There are often special room and car packages for about $65 – check for ads in the Sunday *Star-Bulletin & Advertiser*.

Ilima Hotel (☎ 923-5200, (800) 367-5172), 445 Nohonani St, Honolulu, HI 96815, has studios that are large and light with lanais, full kitchen facilities, two double beds and tasteful rattan furnishings. Local phone calls and parking are free, a rarity in Waikiki. The lobby has an interesting mural of the god Ku and the goddess Hina in an ocean of eternal bliss.

Rates vary according to the floor, although the rooms themselves are essentially the same. High season rates start at $81/89 for singles/doubles in studios on the 4th floor and rise to $106/118 for studios on the 10th to 16th floors. There are 99 units, including some one and two-bedroom suites for $136 and $156 respectively. Everything's $12 less from April to mid-December. The hotel is in a less hurried section of Waikiki, a 15-minute walk from the beach.

Coconut Plaza (☎ 923-8828, (800) 882-9696), 450 Lewers St, Honolulu, HI 96815, is a quiet 90-room hotel near Ala Wai Blvd. Rooms are comfortable and have private lanais, microwaves and small refrigerators. High season rates range from $80 for a standard room to $110 for a deluxe. In the low season they are $10 lower and every seventh night is free.

The Breakers (☎ 923-3181, (800) 426-0494), 250 Beach Walk, Honolulu, HI 96815, is a low-rise hotel with 66 kitchenette units surrounding a well-used courtyard pool. This is one of the more pleasant places at the western end of town and the staff are friendly. Rooms cost from $85/88 for singles/doubles. Avoid the rooms closest to Saratoga Rd which has lots of traffic.

Waikiki Grand (☎ 923-1511), 134 Kapahulu Ave, Honolulu, HI 96815, is a 172-room hotel opposite the zoo. Although most of the rooms have been recently renovated, they are quite small and ordinary. Rates are $85 for a standard room, $95 for a room with a kitchenette.

The *New Otani Kaimana Beach Hotel* (☎ 923-1555, (800) 657-7949), 2863 Kalakaua Ave, Honolulu, HI 96815, is on Sans Souci Beach on the quieter Diamond Head side of Waikiki. It has 125 units, with rooms from $99 and studios with kitchenettes from $140.

Places to Stay – top end

The following hotels all have standard 1st class amenities and in-house restaurants. All are on the beach or across the street from it and all have swimming pools.

The new 298-room *Waikiki Parc Hotel* (☎ 921-7272, (800) 422-0450 from the USA, (008) 221-176 from Australia), 2233 Helumoa Rd, Honolulu, HI 96815, is across the street from its more up-market sister, the Halekulani. The comfy rooms have lots of nice touches, like ceramic tile floors, white shuttered lanai doors, remote-control TV and two phones. It has a pleasant, understated elegance. Standard rooms cost $135, while those with an ocean view cost from $195.

The *Hawaiian Regent* (☎ 922-6611, (800) 367-5370 from the USA or Canada, (0014-800) 125-666 from Australia), 2552 Kalakaua Ave, Honolulu, HI 96815, has 1346 rooms in a huge maze-like complex. Rooms are quite ordinary for the money, with rates ranging from $150 to $260.

The 715-room *Waikiki Beach Hotel*

(☎ 922-2511, (800) 877-7666), 2570 Kalakaua Ave, Honolulu, HI 96815, looks almost like a reflection of the bigger Hawaiian Regent across the street, and the rooms are just as nice, although cheaper. Prices start at $105/120 in the low/high season. The best value is the Mauka Tower, an annex off to the side of the main building, where the rates are at the low end and the rooms are larger, newer and quieter than in the main hotel.

The *Hyatt Regency Waikiki* (☎ 923-1234, (800) 228-9000), 2424 Kalakaua Ave, Honolulu, HI 96815, has twin 40-storey towers with 1230 rooms. There's a maximum of 18 rooms per floor, so it's quieter and feels more exclusive than other hotels its size. Rooms are nicely decorated in pastels with rattan furnishings and cost from $170 to $260, depending on the view. Between the towers there's a large atrium with cascading waterfalls and orchids, red torch ginger and other tropical vegetation.

The *Sheraton* pretty much owns a little stretch of the beach, boasting 4400 rooms in its Waikiki hotels. The toll-free numbers for all of Sheraton's Hawaii hotels are (800) 325-3535 from the USA and Canada, (008) 07-3535 from Australia and (008) 443-535 from New Zealand.

The 1150-room *Sheraton Princess*

Red torch ginger

Kaiulani (☎ 922-5811), 120 Kaiulani Ave, Honolulu, HI 96815, is the Sheraton's cheapest Waikiki property. Built in the 1950s by Matson Navigation to help develop Waikiki into a middle-class destination, from the outside it looks like an inner city housing project. From the inside it's nice enough, but pricey at $110 to $170. It's in the busy heart of Waikiki, across the street from the beach.

The 793-room *Sheraton Moana Surfrider* (☎ 922-3111), 2365 Kalakaua Ave, Honolulu, HI 96815, is a treat for anyone fond of colonial hotels. The Moana, built in 1901, was Hawaii's first beachfront hotel. It's recently undergone a $50-million historic restoration, authentic right down to the elegant carved columns on the porte-cochère.

Despite the fact that modern wings (the 'Surfrider' section) have been attached to the main hotel's flanks, the Moana has survived with much of its original character. The lobby is open and airy with high plantation-like ceilings, lounging sofas and reading chairs. The rooms in the original building have been closely restored to their turn-of-the-century appearance, undisturbed by modern additions such as central air-conditioning and soundproofing. The room furnishings are made from a different wood on each floor (koa on the 5th, cherry on the 6th), with TVs and refrigerators hidden behind armoire doors.

The staff are gracious and welcoming and the hotel's historic banyan-tree courtyard is the venue for some of Honolulu's best contemporary musicians. Rates in the historic wing range from $195 for city views to $270 for ocean views.

The pink Moorish-style *Royal Hawaiian Hotel* (☎ 923-7311), 2259 Kalakaua Ave, Honolulu, HI 96815, now a Sheraton property, was Waikiki's first luxury hotel. It's a beautiful hotel cool and airy and loaded with charm. The older section maintains the original character, with some of the rooms having quiet garden views. The older section is easier to book too, since most guests prefer the modern high-rise wing with its ocean views. Rates are from $235 to $425 in the historic wing, $375 in the tower.

Sheraton Waikiki (☎ 922-4422), 2255 Kalakaua Ave, Honolulu, HI 96815, is an impersonal 1850-room mega-hotel that looms over the Royal Hawaiian Hotel. The bustling lobby resembles an exclusive Tokyo shopping centre, lined with lots of expensive jewellery stores and boutiques with French names and designer labels. The hotel has central elevators that leave guests at some of the longest corridors in Hawaii. Rates start at $175 for a city view and climb to $355 for a luxury ocean unit.

Hilton Hawaiian Village (☎ 949-4321, (800) 445-8667), 2005 Kalia Rd, Honolulu, HI 96815, is Hawaii's largest hotel, with 2522 rooms. The ultimate in mass tourism, it's practically a package-tour city unto itself – all self-contained for people who never want to leave the hotel grounds. It's all quite busy and impersonal, right down to the roped-off lines at the front desk, which resembles an airline check-in counter.

The Hilton is on a nice beach, has some good if not inexpensive restaurants, and free entertainment and Friday-night fireworks. Rates start at $185.

Halekulani (☎ 923-2311, (800) 223-6800), 2199 Kalia Rd, Honolulu, HI 96815, is considered by many to be Waikiki's premier hotel. The 412 rooms are very modern and boast all amenities including deep soaking tubs, silent refrigerators and complimentary fresh flowers and home-made chocolates. It's all very sophisticated and elegant, a world of limousines and tuxedos.

Rooms with garden views are $245, while those fronting the ocean are $395. Suites cost from $550.

The *Kahala Hilton* (☎ 734-2211, (800) 367-2525), 5000 Kahala Ave, Honolulu, HI 96816, is in the exclusive Kahala residential area on its own quiet stretch of beach. This is where the rich and famous go when they want to avoid the Waikiki scene 10 minutes away.

Rather than formal opulence, the Hilton is subdued and private, with an appealing casualness. Staff who have been working there for decades and guests who return year after year know each other by name. The guest list is Hawaii's most regal: Charles and Di, King Juan Carlos and Queen Sofia, and the last five US presidents.

The older two-storey wing has rooms on the hotel's enclosed lagoon, with dolphins swimming just beyond the lanais. Prices range from $220 for a mountain view to $2200 for the presidential suite. (See the South-East & Windward Oahu map.)

Places to Eat

Waikiki has no shortage of places to eat, although the vast majority of the cheaper ones are easy to pass up. Generally the best inexpensive food is found outside Waikiki, where most Honolulu residents live and eat (see Places to Eat in the Honolulu section). Waikiki's top-end restaurants, on the other hand, are some of the island's best, although they'll quickly burn a hole in your wallet.

Breakfast Signs draped from buildings advertising breakfast specials for $2 to $4 are commonplace. The *Sandwich Island Coffee Shop, Eggs 'n Things, Moose McGillycuddy's, Malia's Cantina* and *Saigon Cafe* all have inexpensive breakfast specials.

Food Pantry at 2370 Kuhio Ave has a doughnut counter, while the nearby *Patisserie*, 2330 Kuhio Ave, has a full bakery serving Danish and other pastries. *McDonald's, Jack in the Box* and *Burger King* offer their standard quick, cheap breakfasts from just about every other corner. If you're really hungry and not too demanding on quality, the $4.45 all-you-can-eat breakfast buffet at *Perry's Smorgy* is a good deal.

For around $8 to $18 you can try one of the all-you-can-eat breakfast buffets that many of the larger hotels offer, but few are worth the money. Two noteworthy exceptions are the daily breakfast buffets at the oceanside *Shore Bird Broiler* ($6.95) in the Outrigger Reef Hotel and the *Parc Cafe* ($10.50) in the Waikiki Parc Hotel, which are both good value.

Or try one of the two romantic beachfront restaurants at San Souci Beach, at the Diamond Head end of Waikiki. You can get croissants and coffee at *Michel's* for as little as $5 or have a full breakfast served on fine china for less than most hotel buffets. Next door, the *Hau Tree Lanai* at the New Otani Kaimana Beach Hotel serves meals beneath the shade of a sprawling beachside hau tree. Prices are similar to Michel's and breakfast is served until 11 am.

For more details, see the individual restaurant listings.

Sunday Brunches Waikiki's most renowned Sunday brunch buffet is at *Orchid's* (☎ 923-2311) at the Halekulani Hotel. The grand spread includes sashimi, sushi, baron of beef, roast suckling pig, roast turkey, salads, fruits, and a rich dessert bar. There's a fine ocean view and a soothing flute and harp duo. The buffet lasts from 9.30 am to 2.30 pm and costs $27.50. Make advance reservations or be ready for a two-hour wait.

The Sunday brunch buffet at the *Parc Cafe* (☎ 921-7272) in the Waikiki Parc Hotel has eggs benedict, prime rib, fresh catch of the day and a wonderful array of salads such as Peking duck, green papaya and mixed greens. Tempting desserts, a frozen yoghurt bar and fresh fruit are also included. It's from 11 am to 2 pm. There's no ocean view and it's not as elaborate as the buffet at its sister hotel, the Halekulani, but the food is also superb and the price is $18.50.

The Sunday brunch buffet at the *Kahala Hilton* (☎ 734-2211), out beyond Waikiki in Kahala, is generally considered on par with the buffet at Orchid's. A relaxed affair, with beachside open-air setting, brunch is served from 11.30 am to 1.30 pm and costs $28. The restaurant will validate your ticket for free parking in the hotel garage.

Actually, our first choice for Sunday brunch would be to keep going beyond Kahala to *Roy's* in Hawaii Kai. Roy's doesn't offer a buffet, but rather has a brunch menu from 10 am to 2 pm on Sundays. Scrambled eggs with salmon ($12), crab cakes Benedict ($11.50), avocado and shrimp salad ($8.50) and 13 other dishes all come with a starter of fresh fruit and Danish pastries. In addition this is a fine time to order some of Roy's famous appetisers, which at $3 to $5 are half the usual price. Reservations are required.

Places to Eat – bottom end

For inexpensive bakery items try the *Patisserie*, 2330 Kuhio Ave, at the side of the Outrigger West Hotel. It's open from 6 am daily and has reasonably good pastries, croissants, bread and coffee. If you want to eat in, there's a small sit-down area where you can get standard breakfast items, sandwiches and salads.

With the opening of the *Saigon Cafe*, 1831 Ala Moana Blvd, 2nd floor, it's no longer necessary to bus to Chinatown for good Vietnamese food. The $2.95 shrimp rolls, which come with a tasty peanut sauce, make superb starters. Other treats are the green papaya salad and the frosty fresh fruit shakes. The combination rice noodle entree, which has barbecued pork and chopped-up spring rolls over a bed of rice noodles, cucumber, mint and lettuce, is a good main dish; it costs a reasonable $5.95, which is one of the higher priced items on the menu.

Breakfast starts at $1.95 for pancakes and eggs, and lunch plates begin at $3.95. Saigon is a popular haunt with travellers staying at the Ewa end of Waikiki. It's open from 6.30 am to 10 pm daily.

The *New Tokyo Restaurant*, 286 Beach Walk, is a popular local lunch spot with good, cheap Japanese food served in a pleasant setting. Oyako-ju, which is chicken, steamed egg and onions with a sweetened sauce over rice, costs $4.75. The yakizakana plate with grilled fish (often salmon!) is $5. Both are served with miso soup, pickles and rice. Other lunch specials cost from $5 to $9.50. Dinner is a far more expensive affair, with prices from $16 to $37. Lunch is served from 11.30 am to 2 pm except Sundays, dinner nightly.

Pizza Uno, 2256 Kuhio Ave, 2nd floor, is a busy pizzeria serving Chicago-style deep dish pizza, which has a thick pastry-like crust. One-person pizzas range from $4.75 for a plain cheese to $6.50 for one with chicken fajita toppings. The best deal is from 11 am to 3 pm weekdays, when the pizza of the day comes with a salad for $5.45. The restaurant also has burgers, pastas and a couple of chicken dishes. Avoid the lanai seating, as not only is the traffic below very noisy but you'll end up sucking in the exhaust from buses waiting at the traffic light.

Hamburger Mary's, 2109 Kuhio Ave, is an open-air restaurant and bar in the middle of the gay district. Burgers are good, ranging from $4.25 for a standard to $6.25 for an avocado special. A variety of salads served with multi-grain bread are about the same price and creative home-made soups, such as gazpacho and cinnamon fruit, cost $3.50 a bowl. It's open from 10 am to 11 pm daily.

Moose McGillycuddy's, 310 Lewers St, has 20 types of omelettes for $5 each, including such all-time favourites as the pina colada with pineapple, coconut and cheese and the Euell Gibbons' Memorial topped with Grape Nuts. From 7.30 to 9 am, two eggs, bacon, toast and orange juice cost $2.49.

Moose is popular with the college crowd and has an extensive menu of burgers, sandwiches, Mexican food, salads, pupus and drinks at moderate prices. It's open from 6.30 am to 10.30 pm daily, with breakfast served to 11 am. All drinks are half-price from 4 to 8 pm and there's music and dancing nightly.

Malia's Cantina, 311 Lewers St, opposite Moose, has reasonably good Mexican food, as well as sandwiches, burgers and salads. At lunch, from 11 am to 2 pm daily, an enchilada with rice and beans will set you back only $3.25, a burrito with rice and beans $5.25. At dinner the burrito dish is $9, although there are early bird specials from 5 to 6.30 pm for $6.25. Malia's also serves breakfast from 6.30 am and often has a special of two eggs and three pancakes for $2 until 9.30 am. At night, it's a popular bar and music spot.

Spaghetti! Spaghetti!, on the 3rd floor, Building A, of the Royal Hawaiian Shopping Center, attracts a crowd with its all-you-can-eat pasta buffet and salad bar. The pasta is not memorable, and the salad bar is limited, but you can eat your fill for $5 at lunch, $6 at dinner. It's open from 11 am to 10 pm daily.

Fatty's Chinese Kitchen, 2345 Kuhio Ave, is a hole-in-the-wall eatery in an alley opposite the Baskin Robbins ice-cream shop at Kuhio Mall. It serves up some of the cheapest food to be found in these parts, with two scoops of rice or chow mein plus one hot entree for only $2.50. Add on $1 for each additional entree. The atmosphere is local, with a dozen stools lining a long bar and the cook on the other side chopping away. Fatty's is open from 10.30 am to 10.30 pm daily.

Country Life Vegetarian Buffet, 421 Nahua St, run by the Seventh Day Adventist church, serves up a vegan buffet of hot dishes, salads, brown rice, fresh fruit and other foods free of animal fat and dairy products. The concept is certainly good, although many of the dishes could be more inspired and there's almost a weary soup-kitchen ambience. Almost everything is sold by the pound: $4.39 at lunch and $4.89 at dinner. This works out a bit pricier than you might expect, with a light lunch costing about $5 and something heartier closer to $8.

The two *Perry's Smorgy* restaurants, one at the Outrigger Coral Seas Hotel at 250 Lewers St and the other at 2380 Kuhio Ave on the corner of Kanekapolei St, specialise in cheap all-you-can-eat buffets. Breakfast, from 7 to 11 am, includes standards such as pancakes, eggs, ham, fresh pineapple, papaya and weak coffee. It's a tourist crowd and the food is strictly cafeteria quality, but you can't beat the $4.45 price. Lunch, from 11.30 am to 2.30 pm, costs $5.95. Dinner, from 5 to 9 pm nightly, costs $7.95. The Kuhio Ave restaurant has the better setting, with some rather pleasant outdoor tables.

The *Sandwich Island Coffee Shop* in the Waikiki Beach Hotel has a breakfast special of French toast, an egg, bacon and a pot of coffee for $3.50. Pass up the lackadaisical $10.50 breakfast buffet that's geared for Japanese pack-tourists who stay at the hotel and use breakfast coupons.

Eggs 'n Things at the Hawaiian Monarch Hotel, 1911 Kalakaua Ave, is an all-nighter, open daily from 11 pm to 2 pm. It specialises in breakfast fare, with prices starting at $2.25 for three pancakes with eggs.

Fast food is well represented in Waikiki: there are three *Burger King*, three *McDonald's* and six *Jack in the Box* restaurants. In addition to the standards, they add some island touches such as passion fruit juice, saimin and Portuguese sausage. All three chains usually have discount coupons in the free tourist magazines.

Cheap Kapahulu Restaurants There's a run of cheap neighbourhood ethnic restaurants along Kapahulu Ave, the road that starts in Waikiki near the zoo and runs up to the H-1 freeway. The following restaurants are grouped together about a mile up from Kalakaua Ave.

Ono Hawaiian Food, 726 Kapahulu Ave, is *the* place in the greater Waikiki area to get Hawaiian food served Hawaiian-style. It's a simple diner, but people line up outside waiting to get in. A kalua pig plate costs $5.25 and a laulau plate $5.60. Both come with pipikaula, lomi salmon and haupia with rice or poi. It's open from 11 am to 7.30 pm Monday to Saturday.

New Kapahulu Chop Suey, 730 Kapahulu Ave, serves big plates of Chinese food. The combination special lunch plate costs $3.75, the special dinner $4.50, while a score of other dishes are $3.50 to $5. It's a lot of food for the money and the restaurant is usually pretty crowded. Opening hours are 11 am to 9 pm daily.

Irifune's, 563 Kapahulu Ave, is a funky little joint complete with Japanese country kitsch and a waiting room that resembles the anteroom of a bordello. They don't use MSG in the kitchen and you can bring in beer from the nearby liquor store. The gyoza is good at $3.50, as is the garlic tofu with vegetables at $7.50. Kushiyaki or combo dinners, such as shrimp tempura and sashimi, are $8. It's open from 11.30 am to 1.30 pm Tuesday to Friday and from 5 to 9.30 pm Tuesday to Sunday.

KC Drive Inn at 1029 Kapahulu Ave, way

up the road near the freeway, features Ono Ono malts (a combination of chocolate and peanut butter that tastes like a liquid Reese's Cup) for $2.50 and waffle dogs (a hot dog wrapped in a waffle) for $1.75, as well as plate lunches, burgers and saimin for either eat-in or takeaway. It's been a local favourite since the 1930s, complete with car-hop service until just a few years back.

If you're on foot *Rainbow Drive-In*, at the intersection of Kapahulu Ave and Kanaina Ave, is much closer to central Waikiki, has similar food and just as much of a local following.

See also the listing for Keo's, in the same Kapahulu neighbourhood but with mid-range prices.

Places to Eat – middle

The very popular *Shore Bird Broiler*, at the Outrigger Reef Hotel, 2169 Kalia Rd, has a fine beachfront location and open-air dining. At one end of the dining room there's a big common grill where you cook your own order: fish costs $8, teriyaki chicken $10 and steak $12. Meals come with all-you-can-eat chilli, rice and a simple salad bar that includes slices of papaya and pineapple. The salad bar alone costs $6. Dinner is from 5 to 10 pm nightly. It's a busy place and unless you get there early expect to wait for a table – although this is scarcely a hardship, as you can hang out on the beach and watch the sun set while you wait.

Shore Bird also has an excellent-value buffet breakfast from 7.30 to 11 am daily, with slices off a round of ham, warm Danish pastries, granola, yoghurt, fruit, eggs and homefries for $6.95. There are usually coupons in the free tourist magazines that knock $1 off meal prices.

California Pizza Kitchen, at 1910 Ala Moana Blvd on the corner of Ena Rd, serves up an excellent thin-crust pizza cooked in a wood-fired brick oven. One-person pizzas range from $6 for a traditional tomato and cheese to $9 for more intriguing creations, such as their terrific tandoori chicken pizza which comes with a side serve of mango chutney. The restaurant also has a variety of pasta dishes, both traditional and exotic, for $6 to $10 and good green salads, with generous half-order portions for about $4. Opening hours are 11.30 am to 10 pm (to 11 pm weekends, from noon on Sunday).

Singha Thai, 1910 Ala Moana Blvd, is the place to go on the Ewa side of Waikiki for authentic Thai food in a somewhat upmarket atmosphere. For starters, the grilled beef salad and the hot and sour tom yum soup are tasty house specialities; each cost $7. Entrees such as the spicy garlic and pepper chicken or the pineapple shrimp curry cost from $10 to $14 at dinner, $7 to $10 at lunch. Lunch is served from 11 am to 4 pm Monday to Saturday, dinner from 4 to 11 pm nightly. Occasionally a troupe of Thai dancers performs at dinner.

The Honolulu branch of the *Hard Rock Cafe*, 1837 Kapiolani Ave, is just over the Ala Wai Canal beyond Waikiki. It's decorated with old surfboards and enlivened with loud rock music. A 1959 Cadillac 'woody' wagon hangs precariously over the bar. They serve good burgers from about $6 and other all-American food including barbecue ribs and milkshakes, but it's the trendy ambience as much as the food that draws the crowd. It's open daily from 11.30 am to 11 pm (11.30 pm weekends).

The *Oceanarium Restaurant* in the Pacific Beach Hotel, 2490 Kalakaua Ave, has standard fare with anything but standard views. The dining room wraps around an enormous three-storey aquarium filled with colourful tropical fish. At breakfast, hot cakes or oatmeal with papaya cost $5 and a full buffet is $12. They serve lunch and dinner as well. The more expensive Neptune (seafood) and Shogun (teppanyaki, sushi bar) restaurants in the same hotel also have views of the aquarium.

Keo's (☎ 737-8240), 625 Kapahulu Ave, is widely regarded as Hawaii's top Thai restaurant. It's decorated with sprays of orchids, original Thai paintings and dozens of photos of owner Keo Sananikone posing with celebrity diners, including the likes of Jimmy Carter, Stevie Wonder and Harrison Ford. Prices are surprisingly moderate considering the valet parking and the chic reputation.

House specialities are the Evil Jungle Prince dish ($9.95), spring roll appetisers ($6.95 for pork or tofu) and green papaya salad ($6.95). The most expensive items on the menu are seafood dishes at $15, so it won't break the bank to dine with the stars here. It's open from 5 pm nightly and is about a mile up Kapahulu Ave from Waikiki.

The *Parc Cafe* (☎ 921-7272) in the Waikiki Parc Hotel has continental-style dining in a pleasant setting. There are buffets for each meal, all attractively prepared with quality food on par with Waikiki's most expensive hotels. The daily breakfast buffet, from 7 to 10 am, includes breakfast meats, eggs, French toast, hot cakes, fresh fruit and pastries for $10.50. The lunch buffet, from 11.30 am to 2 pm, costs $14.50 on Wednesdays when it features Hawaiian food, $18.50 on Sunday when it begins at 11 am and is called brunch and $11.50 other days when it's centred around a sandwich bar and taco station.

At all meals there are at least a couple of hot dishes, salads, yoghurts and a dessert bar. The dinner buffet from 5.30 to 10 pm is a more elaborate event with entrees including fresh catch of the day, leg of lamb or prime rib, soup and a dozen tasty salads for $19.50.

The *W C Peacock & Co* in the Sheraton Moana Surfrider may be the only restaurant in Waikiki where you can look out across the lawn to see nothing but sailboats on the ocean and a few swaying coconut palms. The only 'modern' structure in view is a wing of the graceful 90-year-old Moana hotel, which screens out the high-rises along the beach and helps create an aura of being someplace timeless.

While the setting is a gem, the food is a bit more standard. The best deal is the $14.95 Sunset Special, from 5.30 to 6.15 pm daily, which consists of chicken teriyaki or cajun mahimahi, a small but select salad bar with leafy greens such as watercress, chicory and raddichio, as well as soup and a simple dessert. It's open for dinner only and meals other than the Sunset Special range from $17 to $35. Be sure to ask for a lanai table.

The *Surf Room* at the Royal Hawaiian Hotel has outdoor beachside dining, although it's rather crowded and the food is undistinguished. Breakfasts are an over-priced $9 to $16. At lunch, hot dishes range from fresh lemon pasta for $9.75 to grilled fresh fish for $15.50. They also have a reasonably good lunch buffet that includes sushi, turkey and beef roasts, fresh fruit, salads and desserts for $17.75. Dinner features fresh fish entrees around $30.

Roy's Park Bistro, at 1956 Ala Moana Blvd next to Sizzler steak house, was preparing to open when we were last in Waikiki. It's owned by chef Roy Yamaguchi, who is near-legendary in these parts for providing quality Pacific Rim cuisine at moderate prices. While it's apparently a more modest endeavour than his original restaurant in Hawaii Kai, it should be well worth checking out.

Places to Eat – top end

Zuke Bistro (☎ 922-0102), in the Coconut Plaza hotel at Ala Wai and Lewers, is a good place to go for fine seafood, with dishes ranging from shrimp scampi for $16 to fresh opakapaka in a ginger-cilantro sauce for $24. Add another $5 for a house salad. Although the setting off the hotel lobby is not terribly special, the food's excellent and the restaurant has a loyal following among Honolulu residents. It's open for dinner only.

The *Ilikai Yacht Club* in the Ilikai Hotel has open-air dining with a fine view of the yacht harbour. Dinners are served with soup or salad and warm breads that include some tasty popover-like cheese rolls. Prices range from $22 for scallop and shrimp fettucine to $30 for lobster Thermidor. A better deal is the Sunset dinner menu from 5.30 to 6.30 pm that offers a choice of three dishes, fresh mahimahi Normande amongst them, for $16.75. The food, while not outstanding, is nevertheless quite good and when there's a nice sunset it's a very romantic scene.

For fine dining Chinese food, the *Golden Dragon* in Hilton Hawaiian Village has both excellent food and a good ocean view. While the varied menu includes some expensive specialities there are many dishes, including ginger beef, sweet and sour almond duck and a deliciously crispy lemon chicken, that are reasonably priced from $11 to $13. It's open for dinner only, from 6 to 10 pm.

Michel's at the Colony Surf Hotel (☎ 923-6552), 2895 Kalakaua Ave, has been riding for years on its reputation as Oahu's most romantic restaurant. This is a bit overstated, although it's certainly nice – fine dining with crystal, china and chandeliers, all fronting Sans Souci Beach. The food is largely traditional French fare and prices are steep for the offerings. One speciality is opakapaka, which is ordered à la carte for $39 at dinner, $22 at lunch. Breakfast is a far more affordable affair. You can get coffee with two croissants for $5 or with Belgian waffles for $9.50.

It's open daily for breakfast from 7 to 11.30 am, lunch from 11.30 am to 2 pm and dinner from 5.30 to 10 pm. On Sundays, brunch replaces the lunch menu. When you make reservations be sure to ask for a window table, as it's a different experience without it.

La Mer (☎ 923-2311) in the Halekulani Hotel has a top reputation for both its creative French menu with Hawaiian influences and for its fine ocean view. The food is expensive and the dining formal. Men are required to wear jackets. It's open nightly from 6 to 9.30 pm.

The *Maile Restaurant* (☎ 734-2211), at the exclusive Kahala Hilton in Kahala, is considered by many to be the best restaurant in Oahu for traditional dishes, such as rack of lamb. The Maile sees Hawaii's greatest concentration of dignitaries and movie stars amongst its diners, although likewise prices are fit for a king! Roast duckling with Grand Marnier sauce, lychees and spiced peach wild rice croquettes is a speciality and costs $33. There's a complete dinner with appetiser, salad, main course, dessert and coffee for $62. Jackets are required (except on Sundays) and it's open from 6.30 pm nightly.

Other top-end Waikiki restaurants include *Baci* at the Waikiki Trade Center, 2255 Kuhio Ave, for Italian food; *Bali-by-the-Sea* at the Hilton Hawaiian Village for continental cuisine; and *Kyo-ya*, 2057 Kalakaua Ave, for good Japanese food served by kimono-clad waitresses.

Entertainment

The best updated entertainment listing for Waikiki is in the free *Waikiki Beach Press* tourist magazine, in its 'Honolulu City Lights' section. The other tourist magazines and the daily newspapers are also good sources of information.

Concerts The *Waikiki Shell* in Kapiolani Park has both classical and contemporary music concerts. Check the newspapers for information or call the Blaisdell Center box office (☎ 521-2911).

Hawaiiana Many major Waikiki hotels have Hawaiian-style entertainment, from Polynesian shows with beating drums and grass skirts to mellow duos playing ukulele or slack-key guitar.

The *Sheraton Moana Surfrider's* banyan courtyard has top local musicians performing on the veranda throughout the day. You can relax beneath the same old banyan tree where 'Hawaii Calls' broadcast its nationwide radio show from 1935 to 1975, and listen to the likes of Henry Kapono, Hookena, Jerry Santos and Olomana perform for free. While the music is ongoing, the best musicians generally play from 5 pm. It's open to the public, there's no cover charge and no one hassles you to buy drinks. Call 922-3111 for the updated schedule of performers, or just go check it out.

Of the splashy musical revues with hula dancers, the Brothers Cazimero are the best. They perform at 8.30 pm from Tuesday to Saturday at the *Royal Hawaiian Hotel* (☎ 924-5194), with cocktail seating from 8 pm for $30, which includes two drinks. There's an extra kamaaina show at 10.30 pm on Fridays and Saturdays for $15 that includes one drink; supposedly you have to have proof of Hawaiian residency but when we were there no one was checking. Or, cheaper still, have a drink at the bar and hear them across the lawn.

The Royal Hawaiian has a $60 beachside luau on Mondays, beginning with an open bar at 6 pm and continuing with a buffet-style dinner and a Polynesian show.

Doug Mossman, of *Hawaiian Eye* fame, hosts a luau at the *Waikiki Beachcomber Hotel* (☎ 395-0677) at 6.30 pm on Sundays and, when it's busy, on Tuesdays and Thursdays.

Movie Theatres Movie theatres in Waikiki include the Waikiki Twins (☎ 971-5033) on Seaside Ave near Kalakaua Ave; Waikiki 3 (☎ 971-5133) on Kalakaua near Seaside; and Kuhio Twins (☎ 973-5433) at 2095 Kuhio Ave. All show first-run Hollywood movies.

The *Hawaii Imax Theatre* (☎ 923-4629), 325 Seaside Ave, shows a 35-minute movie of Hawaii vistas on a 70-foot-wide screen. Shows are held on the hour from 11 am to 9 pm daily. The cost is $7.50 for adults, $5 for children.

Nightclubs & Discos In addition to the following listings, many of the major Waikiki hotels have a nightclub or disco with music and dancing.

Wave Waikiki (☎ 941-0424), 1877 Kalakaua Ave, has been one of Waikiki's hottest clubs since opening in 1980. Live bands play progressive rock, new wave or alternative music, with a disco between sets. Opening hours are 9 pm to 4 am nightly and the minimum age is 21. There's usually no cover charge before 10 pm, a $5 cover after.

The nearby *Pink Cadillac* (☎ 942-5282), 478 Ena Rd, is a popular dance spot, with a DJ playing progressive rock and new wave music. It pulls in the early-20s crowd with rock videos, dance parties and contests. It's open from 9 pm to 2 am nightly. The cover charge is usually $5 for ages 21 and older and $15 (yes, $15!) for ages 18 to 20.

Malia's Cantina (☎ 922-7808), 311 Lewers St, has live entertainment from about 10 pm to 4 am nightly, including local favourites such as Kapena, Bruddah Waltah and Willie K, often with a Jawaiian, rock or contemporary Hawaiian sound. The cover charge is usually $3.

Or check out the scene directly opposite Malia's, where *Moose McGillycuddy's* (☎ 923-0751), 310 Lewers St, has live rock, Jawaiian bands and dancing from 9 pm to 1.30 am nightly, from 8 pm on Fridays and Saturdays. There's usually a $2 cover charge on weekends and you have to be 21 to get in.

The *Jazz Cellar* (☎ 923-9952), 205 Lewers St, has live rock bands and dancing nightly from 9 pm to about 4 am. It's open to ages 18 and over and there's a cover charge that varies with the band.

For disco dancing to top-40 hits, there's *Spats* (☎ 923-1234) at the Hyatt Regency Waikiki and *Scruples* (☎ 923-9530), 2310 Kuhio Ave, both from about 9 pm to 4 am. Both have cover charges and are a bit dressier than the other places listed in this section.

Gay Scene The gay scene is centred around the Kuhio district, along Kuhio Ave from Kalaimoku to Kaiolu Sts.

Hula's Bar & Lei Stand (☎ 923-0669), 2103 Kuhio Ave, an open-air video dance club with tables under a big banyan tree, is a favourite place to meet, dance and have a few drinks. It's open from 11 am to 2 am daily.

Hamburger Mary's, 2109 Kuhio Ave, in the restaurant of the same name, is Honolulu's most popular gay bar. It's open from 3 pm to 2 am daily.

There are numerous other gay hangouts, although many of them come and go. To find out about the most happening spots, pick up the magazine *Island Lifestyle* or the newspaper *The Gay Community News*, free at Hula's or other gay-oriented businesses.

Comedy The *Honolulu Comedy Club* (☎ WACKY-98), atop the Ilikai Hotel, has stand-up comedians from Tuesday to Sunday. The 8 pm Sunday show is for non-smokers.

Tea Ceremony The *Urasenke Foundation of Hawaii* (☎ 923-3059), 245 Saratoga Rd, has tea-ceremony demonstrations on Wednesdays and Fridays, bringing a rare bit of serenity to busy Saratoga Rd. Students dressed in kimonos perform the ceremony on tatami mats in a formal tea-room.

It costs $2 to be served green tea and sweets, but you can watch the ceremony for free. Each demonstration lasts 30 to 45 minutes. The first sitting is at 10 am, the last at 11.30 am. Reservations are appreciated. Because guests leave their shoes at the door, they are asked to wear socks. The building is across the street from and makai of Waikiki's post office.

Free Entertainment For good fun, take an evening stroll along Waikiki Beach and catch a glimpse of the Hawaiian shows and luaus that take place at the beachfront hotels. You can wander into the Sheraton Moana Surfrider and listen to the music at the Banyan Veranda, watch the Brothers Cazimero from the beach in front of the Royal Hawaiian Hotel, check out the poolside performers at the Sheraton Waikiki and so on down the line.

Hilton Hawaiian Village (☎ 949-4321) shoots off fireworks from the beach at 8 pm on Fridays, preceded by a torch-lighting ceremony and a hula show that begin at 6.45 pm at the hotel pool.

The Royal Hawaiian Band performs from 2 to 3.15 pm most Sundays, with the exception of August, at the Kapiolani Park Bandstand.

Aunty Malia's Pau Hana Show performs free Hawaiiana entertainment from 5 to 6 pm on Fridays at Harry's Bar near the waterfall in the *Hyatt Regency Waikiki*. Aunty Malia also has a few displays of tapa, quilts and feather work on the 2nd floor of the hotel in a 'museum' called Hyatt's Hawaii.

A free Polynesian show is held at 7 and 8 pm nightly near the top of the escalator on the 2nd floor of *Kuhio Mall*. Dancers from a local hula troupe take turns performing on different nights. Many of the dancers are quite accomplished, while others are beginner students.

The *Royal Hawaiian Shopping Center* (☎ 922-0588) offers a variety of free events. On Mondays, Wednesdays and Fridays, hula lessons are given at 10 am and lei-making lessons at 11 am. On Tuesdays and Thurs-

days, coconut-frond weaving and Hawaiian quilting lessons are held at 9.30 am, ukulele lessons at 10 am. The Polynesian Cultural Center presents a free mini-show at 10 am on Tuesdays and Thursdays at the shopping centre, while Germaine's Luau presents a Polynesian show at the shopping centre at 1 pm on Tuesdays and Fridays. Check at the centre's information booth for the exact locations of each activity.

At 11 am daily the *Sheraton Moana Surfrider* offers free historical tours of the old Moana Hotel, which is on the National Register of Historic Places. Tours, which include titbits of old Waikiki history, leave from the lobby and are open to the public. You can also stroll through on your own. The 2nd floor has a display of memorabilia from the early hotel days, including scripts from 'Hawaii Calls', woollen bathing suits from the 1930s and old photographs.

Other free things, including the Kodak Hula Show, the Damien Museum, the Oceanarium and the US Army Museum, are detailed under Waikiki sights.

Honolulu

The first foreign ship to sail into what is now called Honolulu Harbor was the English frigate *Butterworth* in 1793. Its captain, William Brown, named the harbour 'Fair Haven'. Ships that followed called it 'Brown's Harbor'. In time the name 'Honolulu' (sheltered bay) came to be used for both the harbour and the seaside district that the Hawaiians had called Kou.

As more and more foreign ships found their way to Honolulu a harbourside village of thatched houses sprouted up and the town became Hawaii's centre of trade.

In 1809 Kamehameha I moved his royal court to Honolulu from Waikiki. On what today is the southern end of Bethel St, Kamehameha set up residence to keep an eye on all the trade that moved in and out of the harbour. From there sandalwood was shipped to Canton in exchange for weapons and luxury goods which Kamehameha loaded into his harbourside warehouses.

In the 1820s whaling ships began pulling into Honolulu for supplies, liquor and women. At the same time Christian missionaries began coming ashore to save souls. The Protestant mission and Episcopal and Catholic churches all established their Hawaiian headquarters in downtown Honolulu.

A century later luxury liners docked alongside Honolulu's Aloha Tower, bringing the first tourists to the islands.

All have left their mark. Downtown are the offices of the 'Big Five' corporations that were in control of most of Hawaii's commerce by the turn of the century. It's no coincidence that their lists of corporate board members – Alexander, Baldwin, Cooke and Dole – read like a roster from the mission ships.

The whalers left a different legacy. Hotel St, a line of bars and strip joints a few blocks from the harbour, remains the city's red light district.

By the early 1900s Honolulu had expanded into a sprawling cosmopolitan city, but the downtown area up from the harbour remains the heart of Honolulu.

Honolulu Today

Honolulu is the only major city in Hawaii. It has a population of 377,000 and is the state's centre of business, culture and politics. It's been the capital of Hawaii since 1845. Honolulu International Airport and Honolulu Harbor are Hawaii's busiest ports.

Honolulu is home to people from throughout the Pacific. It's a city of minorities, with no ethnic majority.

Honolulu's ethnic diversity can be seen on almost every corner – the sushi shop next door to the Vietnamese bakery, the Catholic church around the block from the Chinese temple, and the rainbow of school children waiting for the bus.

The main federal, state and county offices and the state's highest concentration of historic buildings are found in downtown Honolulu.

DOWNTOWN HONOLULU

Downtown Honolulu is a city that's grown up since the mid-1800s, and its older, most handsome buildings are all within walking distance.

The area is a hodgepodge of past and present. There's a royal palace, a modernistic state capitol, a coral-block New England missionary church and a Spanish-style city hall all within sight of one another. Downtown has both modern high-rises and stately Victorian-era buildings.

You can take in a Friday noon band concert on the palace lawn, lounge in the open-air courtyard of Hawaii's central library, or catch a view of it all from the top of the Aloha Tower.

Information

Downtown Honolulu is a hassle to drive around, not only because of traffic congestion but also because of the one-way streets and confusing intersections. During the week the best idea is simply to take the bus. Buses No 2, 19 and 20 run between downtown and Waikiki. On weekends the traffic is light and parking isn't difficult.

Lots of city bus routes converge downtown – so many that Hotel St, which begins downtown and crosses Chinatown, is for bus traffic only.

Post The downtown branch of the Honolulu post office is on the Richards St side of the Old Federal Building. It's open from 8 am to 4.30 pm Monday to Friday.

Shopping Honolulu's major shopping centre is the Ala Moana Center (see the Ala Moana section).

The Ward Warehouse on the corner of Ala Moana Blvd and Ward Ave has Waldenbooks, a Birkenstock shoe store, a few galleries and about 50 other shops and eateries. There's free garage parking. Buses No 8, 19 and 20 stop there.

Goodwill, 780 S Beretania St, has racks of used aloha shirts, jeans and muu-muus at reasonable prices. There's another thrift shop at St Andrew's Cathedral.

Parking There's metered parking along both sides of Punchbowl St and a limited number of metered spaces in the basement of the state office building on the corner of Beretania and Punchbowl Sts.

Walking Tours

Kapiolani Community College leads downtown walking tours with varied historical themes – from ghosts of old Honolulu to the revolution of 1893 and the crime beat of the 1920s. Schedules and a brief description of the tours are available from the Office of Community Services (☎ 734-9245), Kapiolani Community College, 4403 Diamond Head Rd, Honolulu, HI 96816. Advance registration is required. The cost is a reasonable $5 for adults and $2 for children aged five to 12.

For Chinatown walks, see the Chinatown section.

Iolani Palace

Iolani Palace is the only royal palace in the USA. It was the official residence of King Kalakaua and Queen Kapiolani from 1882 to

1891 and to Queen Liliuokalani, Kalakaua's sister and successor, for two years after that.

Following the overthrow of the Hawaiian kingdom in 1893, the palace became the capitol – first for the republic, then for the territory and later for the state of Hawaii.

It wasn't until 1969 that the current state capitol was built and the legislators moved out of their cramped quarters. The Senate had been meeting in the palace dining room and the House of Representatives in the throne room. By the time they left, the palace was in shambles, the grand koa staircase termite-ridden and the Douglas fir floors pitted and gouged.

After extensive renovations topping $7 million, the palace was largely restored to its former glory and opened as a museum in 1978. Visitors must wear booties over their shoes to protect the highly polished wooden floors.

Iolani Palace was modern for its day. Every bedroom had its own full bath with hot and cold water running into copper-lined tubs, a flushing toilet and a bidet. According to the tour guides, electric lights replaced the palace gas lamps a full four years before the White House in Washington got electricity.

The throne room, decorated in red and gold, features the original thrones of the king and queen, and a kapu stick made of the long, spiral ivory tusk of a narwhal. In addition to celebrations full of pomp and pageantry, it was in the throne room that King Kalakaua danced his favourite Western dances – the polka, the waltz and the Virginia reel – into the wee hours of the morning.

Not all the events that took place there were joyous. Two years after she was dethroned, Queen Liliuokalani was brought back to the palace and tried for treason in the throne room. In a move calculated to humiliate the Hawaiian people she spent nine months as a prisoner in Iolani Palace, her former home.

Guided tours leave every 15 minutes from 9 am to 2.15 pm Wednesday to Saturday and are well worth the admission of $4 for adults, $1 for children aged 5 to 12. Occasionally you can join up on the spot, but it's advisable

ONE ADMISSION
Iolani Palace
Honolulu, Hawaii
(1882)

This Souvenir Ticket is a partial facsimile of a dance card used at Royal Balls.
NON-REFUNDABLE
RETAIN THIS TICKET
43735

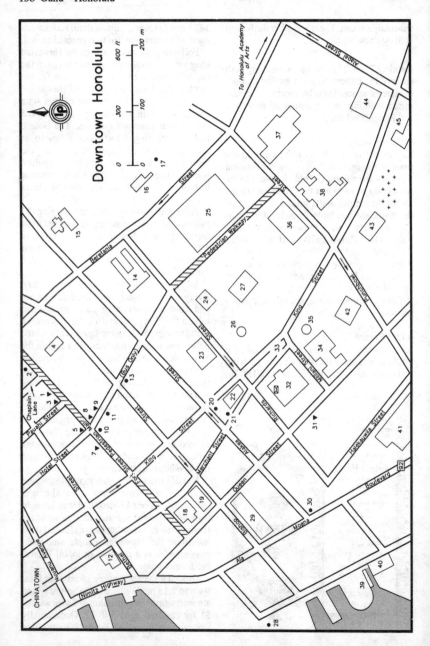

Downtown Honolulu

▼ PLACES TO EAT

1 Ba Le Restaurant
3 Tay Do Restaurant
5 Pizza Hut
7 Burger King
8 McDonald's
9 Taco Bell
31 Ba Le Sandwich Shop

OTHER

2 Hawaii Pacific College
4 Cathedral of Our Lady of Peace
6 Honolulu Publishing
10 Woolworth
11 Longs Drugs
12 Old Honolulu Police Station
13 Honolulu Book Shops
14 No 1 Capitol District
15 St Andrew's Cathedral
16 Washington Place
17 War Memorial
18 C Brewer Building
19 Alexander & Baldwin Building
20 Sierra Club
21 Used Books
22 Hawaiian Electric Co Building
23 YWCA
24 Iolani Barracks
25 State Capitol
26 Bandstand
27 Iolani Palace
28 Aloha Tower
29 Dillingham Building
30 Seaman's Home
32 Old Federal Building
33 Metered Parking
34 Aliiolani Hale
35 Kamehameha Statue
36 Hawaii State Library
37 State Office Building
38 Honolulu Hale (City Hall)
39 Falls of Clyde
40 Hawaii Maritime Center
41 Prince Kuhio Federal Building
42 Territorial Building
43 Kawaiahao Church
44 Honolulu Municipal Building
45 Mission Houses Museum

to make reservations by phoning 522-0832. Children under 5 are not admitted.

Palace Grounds Before Iolani Palace was built there was a simpler house on these grounds that King Kamehameha III used when he moved the capital from Lahaina to Honolulu in 1845. In ancient times it was the site of a heiau.

The ticket window and gift shop are in the former barracks of the Royal Household Guards. The barracks look oddly like the uppermost layer of a medieval fort that's been sliced off and plopped on the ground.

The domed pavilion on the grounds was originally built for the coronation of King Kalakaua in 1883 and is still used for the inauguration of governors and for concerts by the Royal Hawaiian Band.

The grassy mound surrounded by a wrought iron fence was the site of a royal tomb until 1865 when the remains of King Kamehameha II and Queen Kamamalu (who both died of measles in England in 1824) were moved to the Royal Mausoleum in Nuuanu.

The huge banyan tree between the palace and the state capitol is thought to have been planted by Queen Kapiolani.

Hawaii State Library
The central branch of the state-wide library system (☎ 548-4775) is on the corner of King and Punchbowl Sts. Located in a beautifully restored historic building, its collection of over half a million titles is the state's best and includes a good Hawaii and the Pacific section. The library's open-air garden courtyard is a wonderful place to sit and read.

Opening hours are from 9 am to 5 pm Monday, Wednesday, Friday and Saturday and from 9 am to 8 pm Tuesday and Thursday.

The **Hawaii State Archives** next door holds official government documents and an extensive photo collection. It's open to the public for research.

Queen Liliuokalani Statue
The statue of Hawaii's last queen stands between the capitol and Iolani Palace. It faces Washington Place, Liliuokalani's home, and place of exile for more than 20

years. The statue is holding the Hawaii constitution that Liliuokalani wrote in 1893, in fear of which American businessmen overthrew her; *Aloha Oe*, a popular hymn which she composed; and *Kumulipo*, the Hawaiian chant of creation.

State Capitol

Hawaii's state capitol is not your standard gold dome. Constructed in the late 1960s, it was a grandiose attempt at a 'theme' design.

Its two central legislative chambers are cone-shaped to represent volcanoes; the rotunda is open-air to let gentle trade winds blow through; the supporting columns represent palm trees; and the whole structure is encircled by a large pool symbolising the ocean surrounding Hawaii.

Unfortunately, the building not only symbolises the elements but has been quite effective in drawing them in. The pool draws brackish water; rain pouring in to the rotunda has necessitated the sealing of many of the skylights; and Tadashi Sato's 'Aquarius' floor mosaic, meant to show the changing colours and patterns of Hawaii's seas, got so weathered it had to be reconstructed.

After two decades of trying unsuccessfully to deal with all the problems on a piecemeal basis, the state has decided to close the facility and undertake a complete remodelling.

Until the remodelling is completed, which is expected to be sometime in 1993, visitors will have to be content viewing the building from the outside.

In front of the building is a statue of Father Damien, the Belgian priest who volunteered to work amongst the lepers of Molokai and died of the disease 16 years later, aged 49. The stylised sculpture was created by Venezuelan artist Marisol Escubar.

War Memorial

The war memorial is a sculptured eternal torch dedicated to soldiers who died in WW II. It sits between two underground garage entrances on Beretania St, directly opposite the state capitol.

Washington Place

Washington Place, the governor's official residence, is a large colonial-style building, with stately trees, built in 1846 by US sea captain John Dominis. The captain's son John married the Hawaiian princess who later became Queen Liliuokalani. After the queen was dethroned she lived at Washington Place in exile until her death in 1917.

A plaque near the sidewalk on the left side of Washington Place is inscribed with the words to *Aloha Oe*, the anthem composed by Queen Liliuokalani.

The large tree in front of the house on the right side of the walkway is a pili nut tree, recognisable by the buttress-like roots extending from the base of its trunk. In South-East Asia the nuts of these trees are used to produce oil.

St Andrew's Cathedral

King Kamehameha IV was attracted by the royal trappings of the Church of England and decided to build his own cathedral. He and his consort Queen Emma founded the Anglican Church of Hawaii in 1858.

The cornerstone was finally laid in 1867 by King Kamehameha V. Kamehameha IV had died four years earlier on St Andrew's Day – hence the church's name.

St Andrew's is on the corner of Alakea and Beretania Sts. The church is of French Gothic architecture, shipped in pieces from England. Its most striking feature is the impressive window of hand-blown stained glass that forms the western facade and reaches from the floor to the eaves. In the right section of the glass you can see the Reverend Thomas Staley, the first bishop sent to Hawaii by Queen Victoria, alongside Kamehameha IV and Queen Emma.

A thrift shop in the church grounds is open from 9.30 am to 4 pm on Mondays, Wednesdays and Fridays and from 9 am to 1 pm on Saturdays. If you're lucky you might find a $5 aloha shirt or muu-muu in your size. Used paperbacks are also a bargain and it appears Hawaii's Episcopalians have fairly good taste in literature, so you might spot something worth reading.

No 1 Capitol District

The elegant five-storey building on Richards St opposite the state capitol temporarily houses the offices of the state legislature. The building is owned by the Hemmeter Corporation, which after completing a multimillion-dollar renovation used the building briefly as their corporate headquarters. Chris Hemmeter is the developer behind Hawaii's largest fantasy hotels, including the Hyatt Regency Waikoloa and the Westin Kauai.

The stately building has something of the appearance of a Spanish mission, including courtyards and ceramic tile walls and floors. Built in 1928, it served as the YMCA Armed Services building into the 1980s.

Fort Street Mall

Fort St is a pedestrian shopping mall lined with benches, trees and an ever-growing number of high-rise buildings. It's not interesting in itself, but if you're downtown it's a place to eat – not as good as Chinatown, but a few blocks closer. Occasionally classical music flautists, folk guitarists or other street musicians perform along the mall, although these days most of the tunes are played by jackhammers.

Cathedral of Our Lady of Peace

The oldest Catholic cathedral in the USA is the Cathedral of Our Lady of Peace, at the Beretania St end of Fort St Mall. Built of coral blocks in 1843, it's older and more ornate than St Andrew's Cathedral.

Father Damien, who later served Molokai's leper colony, was ordained at the cathedral in 1864.

Aliiolani Hale

Aliiolani Hale (House of Heavenly Kings) was the first major government building built by the Hawaiian monarchy. It has housed the Supreme Court since its construction in 1874 and in earlier times was also home to the legislature. The building has a distinctive clock tower and was originally designed by Australian architect Thomas Rowe to be a royal palace, although it never was used as such.

It was on the steps of Aliiolani Hale, in January 1893, that Sanford Dole proclaimed the establishment of a provisional government and the overthrow of the monarchy.

Kamehameha Statue

The statue of Kamehameha the Great stands in front of Aliiolani Hale, opposite Iolani Palace. It was cast by Thomas Gould in 1880. This one is actually a recast, as the first statue was lost at sea near the Falkland Islands. The original statue, recovered after this second version was dedicated, now stands in Kohala, the Big Island birthplace of Kamehameha.

On 11 June, a state holiday honouring Kamehameha, both statues are ceremoniously draped with layer upon layer of 12-foot leis.

Honolulu Hale

City Hall, also known as Honolulu Hale, is largely of Spanish mission design with a tiled roof, decorative balconies, arches and

Kamehameha statue

pillars. Built in 1927, it bears the initials of C W Dickey, Honolulu's most famous architect of the day. The open-air courtyard in the centre of the building is sometimes used for concerts and art exhibits.

Kawaiahao Church

Oahu's oldest church, on the corner of Punchbowl and King Sts, was built on the site where the first missionaries constructed a grass thatch church shortly after their arrival in 1820. The original was an impressive structure that measured 54 feet by 22 feet and seated 300 people on lauhala mats.

Still, thatch wasn't quite what the missionaries had in mind so they designed a more typically New England-style Congregational church with simple Gothic influences.

Built between 1838 and 1842, the church is made of 14,000 giant coral slabs, many weighing more than 1000 pounds. Hawaiian divers chiselled the huge blocks of coral out of Honolulu's underwater reef.

Kawaiahao Church

The clock tower was donated by Kamehameha III and the clock, built in Boston and installed in 1850, still keeps accurate time.

Inside the church is breezy and cool. The rear seats, marked by *kahili* (feather) staffs and velvet padding, were for royalty and are still reserved for descendants of royalty today. The church is open to visitors from 8 am to 4 pm daily.

The **tomb of King Lunalilo**, the successor to Kamehameha V, is in the church grounds at the main entrance. Lunalilo ruled for only one year before his death in 1874 at the age of 39.

Around the back is a **cemetery** where many of the early missionaries are buried.

Mission Houses Museum

Three of the original buildings of the Sandwich Islands Mission headquarters still stand: the Frame House (built in 1821), the Chamberlain House (1831) and the Printing House (1841).

Together they're open to the public as the Mission Houses Museum (☎ 531-0481), 553 S King St. The houses are authentically furnished with handmade quilts on the beds, settees in the parlour and iron pots in the big stone fireplaces.

Tickets to the museum are sold in the coral-block Chamberlain House. Levi Chamberlain was the man appointed by the mission to buy, store and dole out supplies to the missionary families who each had an allowance. Account books show that in the late 1800s, 25 cents would buy either one gallon of oil, one pen knife or two slates.

The Chamberlain House was the early mission storeroom, a necessity as Honolulu had few shops in those days. Upstairs are hoop barrels and wooden crates packed with dishes and a big desk with pigeon-hole dividers and the quill pen Levi used to work on accounts.

The first missionaries packed more than their bags when they left Boston – they actually brought a pre-fabricated wooden house around the Horn with them! Designed to withstand cold New England winter winds, the small windows instead block out Honolulu's cooling trade winds, keeping the two-storey house hot and stuffy. The Frame House is the oldest wooden structure in Hawaii.

Inside the Printing House, an interpreter in period dress uses lead type to print pages of text in Hawaiian.

The Mission Houses are open from 9 am to 4 pm Tuesday to Saturday and from noon to 4 pm Sunday. Admission of $3.50 for adults and $1 for children (under age six free) includes a 45-minute guided tour of the three buildings.

The best day to visit is Saturday, the day of the living history programme. Costumed actors portray the missionary residents of 1831, as well as sea captains and native Hawaiians of the time.

Visitors can engage in lively debate with Hiram Bingham, Honolulu's first Christian minister, an opinionated and prejudiced evangelist. The actors don't step out of character or the period when they answer questions and show complete puzzlement about the existence of such things as cameras or the state of California.

On Saturdays tours are given every hour on the hour from 10 am to 3 pm. There's no extra fee for the living history programme. Tours on other days begin whenever a small group gathers.

If you're not into all that, a walk around the grounds and a peek inside open doors and windows is free.

Other Historic Buildings

The **Hawaiian Electric Company's** four-storey administration building, on the corner of Richards and King Sts, is of Spanish colonial architecture. It has an arched entrance way and some neat old lamps hanging from hand-painted ceilings. The entrance leads into the customer service department and it's OK to walk in and take a look.

Diagonally opposite, on Merchant St, is the **Old Federal Building**, another interesting edifice with Spanish colonial features. Completed in 1922, it holds a post office and customs house.

King Lunalilo's mausoleum

Also noteworthy is the three-storey **YWCA** at 1040 Richards St. It was built in 1927 and designed by architect Julia Morgan, who also designed William Randolph Hearst's San Simeon estate in California.

The **old Honolulu Police Station** (1931 to 1961), on the corner of Bethel and Merchant Sts, has beautiful interior ceramic tile work in earthen tones on its counters and walls. It now houses the state departments of Housing & Finance.

The four-storey **Alexander & Baldwin building** on the corner of Bishop and Queen Sts was built in 1929. The columns at the Bishop St entrance are carved with tropical fruit and the Chinese characters for prosperity and long life. Inside the portico are four interesting ceramic tile murals of Hawaiian fish.

Samuel Alexander and Henry Baldwin, both sons of missionaries, vaulted to prominence in the sugar industry and created one of Hawaii's 'Big Five' controlling corporations. The other four – Theo Davies, Castle & Cooke, Amfac and C Brewer – all have their headquarters within a few blocks of here.

The four-storey 60-year-old **Dillingham building** on the corner of Bishop and Queen Sts is of Italian Renaissance-style architecture with arches, marble walls, elaborate elevator doors and an arty brick floor. It's a study in contrasts, mirrored in the reflective glass exterior of the nearby 30-storey Grosvenor Center.

Hawaii Theatre

The neo-classical Hawaii Theatre, 1130 Bethel St, with its Art Deco neon signs, first opened in 1922 with silent films playing to the tune of a pipe organ. It ran continuous shows during the war but the development of mall cinemas in the 1970s was its undoing.

After closing in 1984, the theatre's future looked dim, even although it was on the Register of Historic Buildings. Theatre buffs came to the rescue forming a nonprofit group and purchasing the property from the Bishop Estate. They've since raised enough money to begin a $9.5 million restoration of the theatre, which is scheduled to be completed in mid-1994.

Honolulu Academy of Arts

The Honolulu Academy of Arts (☎ 532-8701), 900 S Beretania St, is an exceptional museum, with permanent Asian, European, American and Pacific art collections from ancient times to the present.

Just inside the door and to the right is a room with works by Monet, Cezanne, Gauguin, Van Gogh and Picasso. There is a welcoming place to sit in the middle of the room to take it all in.

The building is open and airy and has numerous small galleries around six garden courtyards. The Spanish Court has benches and a small fountain surrounded by Greek and Roman sculpture and Egyptian reliefs dating back to 2500 BC.

There are sculptures and miniatures from India, jades and bronzes from ancient China, Madonna and child oils from 14th-century Italy and quality changing exhibits. On our last visit we saw an excellent exhibit of some of John Webber's original drawings (including his recording of the death of Captain Cook!) on loan from such distant shores as the Royal Library in Stockholm and the Mitchell Library in Sydney.

The Hawaiian section is small but choice, with feather leis, tapa beaters, poi pounders and koa calabashes. The collection from Papua New Guinea, Micronesia and the South Pacific includes ancestor figures, war clubs and masks.

The museum is off the tourist track and seldom crowded. To top it all off, admission is free, although donations are appreciated.

It's open from 10 am to 4.30 pm Tuesday to Saturday and from 1 to 5 pm on Sundays. Docent-led gallery tours are given at 11 am Tuesday through Saturday and at 1 pm on Sundays. To join one, simply meet in the lobby. Tours for the hearing-impaired can be arranged by contacting the museum in advance.

The on-site **Academy Theatre** presents more than 400 programmes each year, including foreign and independent films, classical music concerts and art lectures. Movies cost $4, while tickets to musical performances vary but are quite reasonably priced. An events calendar is available at the museum. There's also a gift shop, library and lunch cafe (by reservation).

Aloha Tower

The top-floor observation deck of the Aloha Tower offers a sweeping view of Honolulu's big commercial harbour and downtown area. It is not really a 'pretty' view, but interesting nonetheless.

Built in 1926, the 10-storey Aloha Tower is a Honolulu landmark. For years it was the city's tallest building.

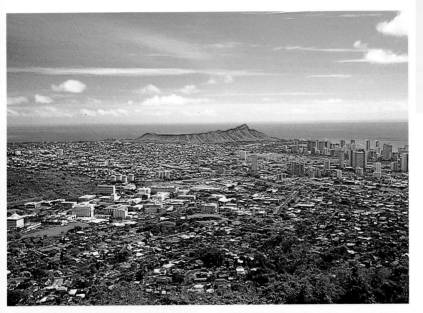

Top: View of Honolulu & Diamond Head from Round Top Drive, Oahu
Left: Manoa Falls, Oahu
Right: Divers at Koko Crater, Oahu

Top & Bottom: Mural at University of Hawaii, Honolulu, Oahu

Back in the days when all tourists arrived by ship, the four-sided clock tower greeted incoming passengers with the word 'Aloha'. Cruise ships still pull in beneath the tower, which houses the US Customs office.

Aloha Tower is at Pier 9, off Ala Moana Blvd at the harbour end of Fort St. The 10th floor observation deck is open from 8 am to 9 pm daily and admission is free. There's 30-minute free parking near the building entrance, which is at the 2nd-floor level. If you're walking take the outdoor escalator near the fountain to get up to the 2nd floor, where you pick up the elevator.

Hawaii Maritime Center

The Hawaii Maritime Center is at Honolulu Harbor's Pier 7 on the Diamond Head side of the Aloha Tower. The centre has a maritime museum; the *Falls of Clyde*, said to be the world's last four-masted four-rigged ship; and the berth for the double-hulled sailing canoe *Hokulea*.

The 60-foot *Hokulea* has made three voyages from Hawaii to the South Pacific, retracing the routes of the early Polynesian seafarers using traditional means of navigation, including wave patterns and the stars. In the third voyage, which lasted from July 1985 to May 1987, it sailed from Hawaii to Tahiti, the Cook Islands, New Zealand, Tonga and Samoa and from the Tuamotus back to Hawaii. When in port it's docked beside the museum, however it's presently undergoing preparations for a journey to Rarotonga.

Permanently on display is the 266-foot iron-hulled *Falls of Clyde*, which was built in Glasgow, Scotland, in 1878. In 1899 Matson Navigation bought the ship and added a deck house, and the *Falls* began carrying sugar and passengers between Hilo and San Francisco. It was later converted into an oil tanker and eventually stripped down to a barge.

After being abandoned in Ketchikan, Alaska, where it had been relegated to the function of a floating oil storage tank, the *Falls* was towed to Seattle. A group of Hawaiians raised funds to rescue the ship in

1963, just before it was scheduled to be sunk to create a breakwater off Vancouver. With the aid of the Bishop Museum, the *Falls* was eventually brought to Honolulu and restored.

The new museum has an interesting mishmash of maritime displays and artefacts, including a good whaling-era section and model replicas of ships. There's a reproduction of a Matson liner stateroom and interesting old photos of Waikiki in the days when just the Royal Hawaiian and the Moana hotels shared the horizon with Diamond Head. Both hotels belonged to Matson, who spearheaded tourism in Hawaii and ironically sold out to the Sheraton in 1959 just before the jet age and statehood launched sleepy tourism into a booming industry.

To get there by bus, take a bus No 19 or 20 from Waikiki. By car, it's off Ala Moana Blvd, about a mile west of Ward Warehouse. There's free parking for museum visitors on Pier 6, which is just east of the museum. The museum is open from 9 am to 5 pm daily and admission, which includes boarding the *Falls*, is $7 for adults, $4 for children aged six to 17 and free for kids under six.

Sand Island State Recreation Area

Sand Island is a 500-acre island on the western side of Honolulu Harbor. About a third of the island is a state park.

Sand Island is heavily used by locals, who camp and picnic there on weekends, as well as a growing number of homeless families who are encamped on a more permanent basis. It has little appeal to the casual visitor and you won't find many tourists.

The park is not reached from the downtown area, but by an access road a few miles west, off the Nimitz Highway. Sand Island Access Rd leads 2½ miles down to the park through an industrial area with a waste-water treatment plant, oil tanks, scrap metal yards and the like. The airport is directly across the lagoon and Sand Island is on the flight path.

The park has showers, restrooms and a white sand beach that is not particularly clean.

CHINATOWN

Chinatown proper is the area immediately west of downtown Honolulu, roughly bounded by Honolulu Harbor, Nuuanu Ave and River St.

A walk through Chinatown is like a journey to Asia. Although it's predominantly Chinese, it has Vietnamese, Thai and Filipino influences as well.

Chinatown is busy and colourful. It has a lively market that could be right off a back street in Hong Kong, fire-breathing dragons curl up the red pillars outside the Bank of Hawaii, and good, cheap ethnic restaurants abound. You can get tattooed, consult with a herbalist, munch on moon cakes or slurp a steaming bowl of Vietnamese soup. There are temples and shrines, noodle factories, antique shops and art galleries to explore.

Places to eat in Chinatown are listed near the end of the Honolulu section.

History

Chinese immigrants who had worked off their sugar cane plantation contracts began settling in Chinatown and opening up small businesses around 1860.

In December 1899 the bubonic plague

▼ PLACES TO EAT	13 Cebu Pool Hall
5 Doong Kong Lau Restaurant	15 Oahu Market
10 Ha Bien	16 Chinatown Marketplace
11 To Chau Restaurant	17 Antique Shops
14 Ba Le Sandwich Shop	18 Bank of Hawaii
21 Wo Fat	19 Meter Parking
22 La Tropicale Paris	20 Cindy's Lei Shop
28 Krung Thai	23 Shung Chong Yuein
	24 Nature Conservancy
OTHER	25 Hawaii Heritage Center
1 Entrance to Foster Botanic Garden	26 Meter Parking
2 Kuan Yin Temple	27 Chinese Chamber of Commerce
3 Izumo Taisha Shrine	29 Lai Fong Department Store
4 Taoist Temple	30 Pauahi Nuuanu Gallery
6 Sun Yat-Sen Statue	31 Pegge Hopper Gallery
7 Chinatown Cultural Plaza	32 Former Pantheon Bar
8 Hakubundo	33 Police Station
9 Armstrong Building	34 Hawaii Theatre
12 Island Tattoo Shop	35 Hawaii Pacific College
	36 Cathedral of Our Lady of Peace

Chinatown

broke out in the area. The 7000 Chinese, Hawaiians and Japanese who made the crowded neighbourhood their home were cordoned off and forbidden to leave.

As more plague cases arose, the Board of Health decided to conduct controlled burns of infected homes. On 20 January 1900 the fire brigade set fire to a building on the corner of Beretania St and Nuuanu Ave. The wind suddenly picked up and the fire spread out of control, racing toward the waterfront. To make matters worse, police guards stationed inside the plague area attempted to stop quarantined residents from fleeing. Nearly 40 acres of Chinatown burned to the ground.

Not everyone thought the fire was accidental. Just the year before, Chinese immigration into Hawaii had been halted by the US annexation of the islands, and Chinatown itself was prime real estate on the edge of the burgeoning downtown district.

Despite the adverse climate the Chinese held their own and a new Chinatown arose from the ashes.

In the 1940s, thousands of American GIs walked the streets of Chinatown before being shipped off to Iwo Jima and Guadalcanal. Many spent their last days of freedom in Chinatown's 'body houses', pool halls and tattoo parlours.

Orientation

Today Chinatown is where East meets East, as new Asian immigrants stake out their claim.

The stone block Armstrong building on the corner of River and King Sts houses Vietnamese and Thai businesses. Nearby, posters advertise Vietnamese movies like *The Moon Chasing Beauty* and *Gone With the Time*.

The part of Hotel St down by the river is the Filipino area, with the crowded Cebu Pool Hall and My Sista's Place bar.

Further along, the section of Hotel St around Nuuanu Ave is Chinatown's seamier side, where darkened doorways advertise 'video peeps' for 25 cents and the lounges have names like Risque Theatre and Club Hubba Hubba.

Chinatown is undergoing some urban renewal, particularly on its downtown edge. Although many of Chinatown's historic buildings have recently been renovated, others deemed less worthy have been razed, some for open space and others for affordable high-rise housing.

A new 'entranceway' to Chinatown on South Hotel St, near its intersection with Bethel St, includes a small park and two black marble lions flanking the road. As with all Chinese lion statues, the female is distinguishable as the one with her paw on her cub, the male with his paw on a ball.

Information

To get to Chinatown by car from Waikiki, take Ala Moana Blvd and turn at Smith St or Bethel St. Or take Beretania St and head makai down Nuuanu Ave or Maunakea St. Hotel St is open only to bus traffic.

Chinatown is full of one-way streets, traffic is tight and it's difficult to find a parking space. Cars line up at parking lots waiting for spaces to become available. Your best bet for metered parking is the lot off Smith St between Pauahi St and Beretania St.

You can avoid parking hassles by taking the bus. Buses No 2 and 20 run to Chinatown from Waikiki; get off at Maunakea St or Hotel St.

Walking Tours

Three organisations offer Chinatown walking tours. Reservations are not necessary.

The Chinatown Historical Society (☎ 521-3045) leads free walking tours Monday to Friday. From 10 am to noon the society tours the centre of Chinatown and from 1 to 3 pm visits local temples and Foster Garden ($1 entrance fee required). Meet at the sign in the Asia Mall, an enclosed section of the Chinatown Cultural Plaza on Maunakea St.

The Chinese Chamber of Commerce (☎ 533-3181) leads tours from 9.30 am to noon on Tuesdays for $5. Meet at the chamber office at 42 N King St.

The Hawaii Heritage Center (☎ 521-2749) leads tours of Chinatown from 9.30 am to 12.30 pm on Fridays for $4. Meet at the centre's office at 1128 Smith St.

While the guides do give some historical insights and may take you to a few places you're unlikely to walk into otherwise, it feels a bit touristy being led around in a group. All in all, Chinatown is a fun place to poke around on your own.

Oahu Market

The heart of Chinatown is Oahu Market, on the corner of Kekaulike and King Sts.

Everything the Chinese cook needs is on display: pig heads, ginger root, fresh octopus, quail eggs, salted jellyfish, slabs of tuna, jasmine rice and long beans, just to name a few items.

Oahu Market has been an institution since 1904. In 1984, the tenants organised and purchased the market themselves to save it from falling into the hands of developers.

Next door is Chinatown Marketplace, a smaller market that specialises in fresh fish.

Maunakea Street

Wo Fat, the distinctive pink restaurant on the corner of Hotel and Maunakea Sts, is a Chinatown landmark with a facade that somewhat resembles a Chinese temple. The oldest restaurant in Honolulu, it's been on this site since just after the Chinatown fire of 1900. Recent renovations stripped the interior of its once colourful Chinese decor and now it's only the exterior that's worth a glimpse.

Shung Chong Yuein, 1027 Maunakea St, sells delicious moon cakes, almond cookies and other pastries for less than 50 cents. This is the place to buy dried and sugared foods – everything from candied ginger and pineapple to candied squash and lotus root. They also sell boiled peanuts, which are actually quite good if you can resist comparing them to roasted peanuts.

Across the street is Cindy's Lei Shop, a friendly place with leis made of maile,

lantern ilima and Micronesian ginger in addition to the more common orchids and plumeria. Prices are very reasonable, starting at $3 for a lei of tuberose flowers. The colours and fragrances are heady.

Nuuanu Avenue

The Chinatown Police Station, on the corner of Hotel St and Nuuanu Ave in the Perry Block building (circa 1888), has been newly renovated with enough 1920s touches to resemble a set from 'The Untouchables'.

Just down the street is the Pantheon Bar, now abandoned, but noteworthy as the oldest watering hole in Honolulu and a favourite of sailors in days past.

Across the street, Lai Fong Department Store sells antiques, knick-knacks and old postcards of Hawaii dating back to the first half of the century. Even walking into the store itself is a bit like stepping back into the 1940s. Lai Fong's, which has been in the same family for over 65 years, also sells Chinese silks and brocades by the yard and makes silk dresses to order.

Note the granite blocks in the sidewalks on Nuuanu Ave. They were the discarded ballast used in the ships that brought tea from China in the 1800s.

Antiques & Arts

Chinatown is becoming trendy for antique shops and art galleries, the best of which are near the intersection of Pauahi St and Nuuanu Ave.

Pegge Hopper, whose prints of Hawaiian women adorn many a wall in the islands, has her gallery at 1164 Nuuanu Ave. Well-known island photographer William Waterfall's gallery is next door at 1160A Nuuanu Ave. In addition to his own works, the gallery features quality Balinese and Oriental arts & crafts.

The Pauahi Nuuanu Gallery, 1 N Pauahi St, has a quality collection of Hawaiian arts & crafts including works in koa, glass and ceramics.

There's also a handful of antique shops and galleries at the waterfront end of Maunakea St, including Bushido Antiques,

936 Maunakea St, which sells Japanese swords, Korean ceramics and Paul Jacoulet prints.

Chinatown Cultural Plaza

This plaza covers the better part of a block along North Beretania St from Maunakea St to River St.

The modern complex doesn't have the character of Chinatown's older shops, but inside it's still Chinatown, with tailors, acupuncturists and calligraphers alongside travel agents, restaurants and a Chinese newspaper press. One of the kiosks inside the Asia Mall section sells nuts, dried fruit and local honey at good prices. There's a post office and restrooms.

At a small courtyard statue of Kuan Yin, elderly Chinese light incense and leave mangoes. The lychee tree at the centre of the plaza blooms in July.

River St Pedestrian Mall

The River St pedestrian mall has covered tables beside Nuuanu Stream, where old men play mahjong and checkers. A statue of Chinese revolutionary leader Sun Yat-Sen stands at the end of the pedestrian mall near North Beretania St.

There are eat-in and takeaway restaurants along the mall, including Japanese food, Chinese food and the peculiarly named Kevin's Drive In, a hole-in-the-wall eatery serving plate lunches on a *pedestrian* walkway!

Other Shops

Chinatown herbalists are both physicians and pharmacists, with a wall full of small wooden drawers each filled with a different herb. They'll size you up, feel your pulse and listen to you describe your ailments before deciding which drawers to open, mixing herbs and flowers and wrapping them for you to take home and boil up together. The object is to balance Yin and Yang forces. Viet Hoa Chinese Herb Shop, 162 N King St, is one such shop.

There are half a dozen noodle factories in Chinatown. If you look inside you'll see clouds of white flour hanging in the air and thin sheets of dough running around rollers and coming out as noodles. Yat Tung Chow Noodle Factory, 150 N King St, next to Ba Le, makes nine sizes of noodles, from skinny golden thread to fat udon. None cost more than $1 a pound.

Tino Camanga, a former Big Island cowboy, has been tattooing Honolulu's sailors since 1946. He's one of the last survivors from the days when there was a tattoo shop on every block in town. His tiny shop is on River St near Hotel St.

Hakubundo, 100 N Beretania St, sells Japanese dolls, origami and calligraphy supplies.

Other cubbyhole shops sell teapots, bamboo steamers, dried lotus leaves, salted duck eggs and strands of freshwater rice pearls.

Taoist Temple

The Lum Sai Ho Tong Society was organised in 1889, one of more than 100 societies started by Chinese immigrants in Hawaii to help preserve their cultural identity. This one was for the Lum clan, who hail from west of the Yellow River. At one time the society had more than 4000 members, and even now there are nearly 900 Lums in the Honolulu phone book.

The society's Taoist temple on the corner of River and Kukui Sts honours the goddess Tin Hau, a Lum child who rescued her father from drowning and was later deified as a saint. Many Chinese claim to see her apparition when they travel by boat. The elaborate altar inside the temple is open for viewing when the street-level door is unlocked. The elderly caretaker is friendly, although he doesn't speak English.

Izumo Taisha Shrine

The Izumo Taisha Shrine, across the river on Kukui St, is a small wooden Shinto shrine built in 1923. During WW II the property was confiscated by the city of Honolulu and wasn't returned to its congregation until 1962.

Incidentally, the 100-pound sacks of rice

Izumo Taisha Shrine

that sit near the altar symbolise good health, while the ringing of the bell placed at the shrine entrance is considered an act of purification for those who come to pray.

Foster Botanic Garden

Foster Botanic Garden covers 20 acres at the northern end of Chinatown. The entrance is on Vineyard Blvd, opposite the end of River St. The garden took root in 1850 when German botanist William Hillebrand purchased five acres of land from Queen Kalama and planted the trees that now tower in the centre of the property.

Captain Foster bought the property in 1867 and continued planting the grounds. In the 1930s the tropical garden was bequeathed to the city of Honolulu, and it's now a city park.

The garden is laid out in groupings, including sections of palms, orchids, plumerias and poisonous plants.

If you've ever wondered how nutmeg, allspice or cinnamon grow, stroll through the Economic Garden. In this section there's also a black pepper vine that climbs 40 feet up a gold tree, a vanilla vine and other herbs and spices.

The herb garden was the site of the first Japanese language school in Oahu. Many Japanese immigrants sent their children there to learn to read Japanese, hoping to maintain their cultural identity and the option of someday returning to Japan. During the bombing of Pearl Harbor a stray artillery shell exploded into a room full of students. A memorial marks the site.

At the other end of the park the wild orchid garden is a beauty, and a good place for close-up photography. Unfortunately this side of the garden is skirted by the H-1 freeway, which detracts from what would otherwise be a peaceful stroll.

The garden's East African *Gigasiphon macrosiphon*, a tree with white flowers that open in the evening, is thought to be extinct in the wild. The tree is so rare that it doesn't have a common name.

The native Hawaiian loulu palm, taken long ago from the upper Nuuanu Valley, may also be extinct in the wild. The garden's chicle tree, New Zealand kauri tree and Egyptian doum palm are all reputed to be the largest of their kind in the USA. Oddities include the cannonball tree, the sausage tree and the double coconut palm with a single 50-pound nut.

Foster Garden is open from 9 am to 4 pm and admission costs $1 for those aged 13 and over. Trees are marked and a corresponding self-guided tour booklet is available at the entrance.

The Friends of Foster Garden provides volunteer guides who lead 45-minute walking tours at 1 pm on Mondays, Tuesdays and Wednesdays. Call 522-7065 for reservations.

Kuan Yin Temple

The Kuan Yin Temple, on Vineyard Blvd near the entrance of Foster Garden, is a bright red Buddhist temple with a green ceramic-tile roof. The ornate interior is richly carved and filled with the sweet pervasive smell of burning incense.

The temple is dedicated to Kuan Yin

Bodhisattva, goddess of mercy, whose statue is the largest in the prayer hall. Devotees burn paper 'money' for prosperity and good luck. Offerings of oranges, fresh flowers and vegetarian food are placed at the altar. The large citrus fruit that is sometimes stacked pyramid-style is the pomelo, considered a symbol of fertility because of its many seeds.

Hawaii's multiethnic Buddhist community worships at the temple and respectful visitors are welcome.

GREATER HONOLULU
Bishop Museum

The Bishop Museum (☎ 847-3511), 1525 Bernice St, is considered by many to be the best Polynesian anthropological museum in the world. It also has Hawaii's only planetarium.

One side of the main gallery, the Hawaiian Hall, has three floors covering the cultural history of Hawaii. The first floor, dedicated to pre-Western contact Hawaii, has a full-size pili-grass thatched house and numerous other displays from carved temple images to jewellery and weapons.

One of the most impressive holdings in the museum is a large yellow feather cloak made for Kamehameha I and passed down to subsequent kings. It was created entirely of the yellow feathers of the now-extinct mamo, a predominately black bird with a yellow upper tail. Around 80,000 birds were caught, plucked and released to create this cloak.

The 2nd floor is dedicated to 19th-century Hawaii and the top floor to the various ethnic groups that comprise present-day Hawaii. Like Hawaii itself, the top floor has a bit of everything, including samurai armour, Portuguese festival costumes, Taoist fortune-telling sticks and Queen Liliuokalani's royal coach.

The Polynesian Hall contains masks from Melanesia, stick charts from Micronesia and weapons and musical instruments from Polynesia.

The Cooke Rotunda features an exhibit detailing how ancient Pacific navigators were able to journey vast distances, tuning into the seas and the skies for direction.

The museum also has a natural history

section and large seashell, flora & fauna collections.

The Hall of Discovery is a hands-on centre aimed at getting kids interested in museums. There are Hawaiian toys to play with, pre-contact tools to try, large turtle shells to crawl under and petroglyph images to colour. The children's centre is open from noon to 4 pm weekdays, 9 am to 4 pm weekends.

In the Atherton Halau, craftspeople demonstrate Hawaiian quilting, lauhala weaving, lei making and other traditional crafts from 9 am to 3 pm. A daily hula show is presented at 1 pm.

Bishop Museum is well-respected, not only for its collections but for the ethnological research it has spearheaded. Beginning in the 1920s, supported by mainland philanthropy and Ivy League scholars, it organised teams of archaeologists and anthropologists and sent them to record the cultures of the Pacific islands before they were forever lost.

The most renowned of the researchers was Kenneth Emory, a local boy who spoke Hawaiian and thus had the linguistic underpinnings to understand all Polynesian dialects. For five decades he sailed schooners and mailboats to the far corners of the Pacific, cranking out film footage of native dancers, recording their songs, measuring their temples (both buildings and skulls!) and transcribing their folklore. Emory's treatises are the most important (and sometimes the only) anthropological recordings of many Pacific island cultures, from Lanai to Tuamotu. He was affiliated with the museum until his death at age 94 in January 1992.

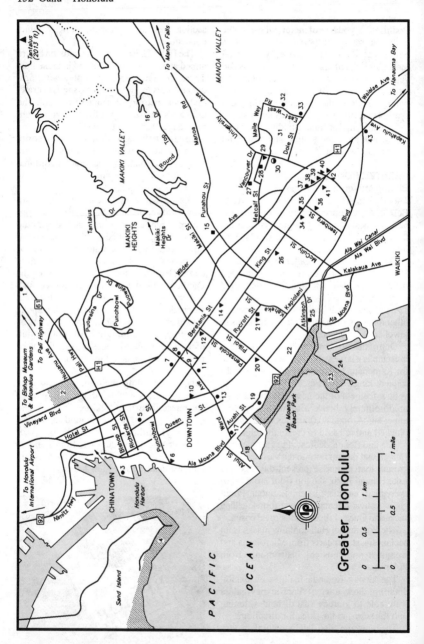

Greater Honolulu

Admission The Bishop Museum is open from 9 am to 5 pm daily. Admission of $5.95 for adults, $4.95 for children aged six to 17 (under age six free) includes all exhibits, demonstrations and the planetarium, although the latter is on a space available basis.

Planetarium shows are held at 11 am and 2 pm daily. On Fridays, Saturdays and the first Monday of each month there's an extra show at 7 pm. On clear nights this is followed by viewing from the observatory telescope. Reservations are recommended for the evening programmes. Admission to the planetarium alone costs $2.50.

Resources The museum library has nearly 100,000 books on the Pacific. It's open to the public from 10 am to 3 pm Tuesday to Friday and from 9 am to noon on Saturdays. The visual history collection (movies and old photographs) is open from 1 to 3 pm Tuesday to Thursday and from 9 am to noon on Saturdays.

The museum shop sells many books on the Pacific not easily found elsewhere as well as gift items. The museum cafeteria is open to 5 pm daily except Sunday.

Getting There & Away From Waikiki, take the No 2 School/Middle St bus to Kapalama St, walk towards the ocean and turn right on Bernice St. By car, take Exit 20B off H-1, go mauka on Houghtailing St and turn left on Bernice St.

Royal Mausoleum State Monument

The Royal Mausoleum contains the remains of Kings Kamehameha II, III, IV and V as well as King David Kalakaua and Queen Liliuokalani, the last reigning monarchs.

The only one missing is Kamehameha I, the last king to be buried in secret in accordance with Hawaii's old religion.

The original mausoleum building, which is usually locked, is now a chapel and the caskets are in nearby crypts. Other markers honour John Young and Charles Reed Bishop, husband of Bernice Pauahi Bishop.

The mausoleum, at 2261 Nuuanu Ave (just before the avenue meets the Pali Highway), is open from 8 am to 4.30 pm Monday to Friday.

Hsu Yin Temple

Part of the Chinese-Buddhist Association of Hawaii, the Hsu Yin Temple is on Kawananakoa Place, just across Nuuanu Ave from the Royal Mausoleum.

This temple is worth a quick look if you're visiting the Royal Mausoleum. At the altar are the standard offerings of Sunkist oranges and burning incense, while prints on the walls tell Buddha's life story.

Punchbowl

Punchbowl is the bowl-shaped remains of a long-extinct volcanic crater. At an elevation of 500 feet it sits a mile above the downtown district and offers a fine view of the city out to Diamond Head and the Pacific beyond.

Early Hawaiians called the crater Puowaina, 'Hill of Human Sacrifices'. It's believed there was a heiau at the crater and that the slain bodies of kapu breakers were brought to Punchbowl to be cremated upon the heiau altar.

Today it's the site of the 115-acre National Memorial Cemetery of the Pacific. The remains of Hawaiians sacrificed to appease the gods now share the crater floor with the bodies of more than 25,000 soldiers, more than half of whom were killed in the Pacific during WW II.

The remains of Ernie Pyle, the distinguished war correspondent who covered both world wars and was hit by machine gun fire in Okinawa during the final days of WW II, lies in section D, grave 109. His resting place is marked with the same style of flat granite stone that marks each of the graves.

A huge memorial at the head of the cemetery has eight marble courts representing different Pacific regions and is inscribed with the names of the 26,280 Americans missing in action from WW II and the Korean War. Two additional half courts have the names of 2503 soldiers missing from the Vietnam War.

For the best view of the city, walk to the lookout 10 minutes south of the memorial.

The cemetery is open from 8 am to 5.30 pm in winter and to 6.30 pm from early March to late September.

Getting There & Away The entrance into Punchbowl is off Puowaina Drive. There's a marked exit as you start up the Pali Highway from H-1; watch closely as it comes up quickly! From there, drive slowly and follow the signs as you wind through a series of narrow streets on the short way up to the cemetery.

By bus, take a No 2 from Waikiki to downtown Honolulu and get off at Beretania and Alapai Sts, where you transfer to a No 15 bus (which runs hourly on the half hour). Ask the driver where to get off. It's about a 15-minute walk to Punchbowl from the bus stop.

Ala Moana

Ala Moana means 'path to the sea'. Ala Moana Blvd (Hwy 92) connects the Nimitz Highway (leaving the airport) with downtown Honolulu and continues into Waikiki. Ala Moana is also the name of a land area just west of Waikiki, which includes Honolulu's largest beach park and a huge shopping centre.

Ala Moana Center Ala Moana Center is Hawaii's biggest shopping centre, with nearly 200 shops. When outer islanders fly to Honolulu to shop they go to Ala Moana. Tourists wanting to spend the day at a mall usually head there too. Ala Moana Center is Honolulu's major bus transfer point and tens of thousands of passengers transit through daily, so even if you weren't planning to go to the centre you're likely to end up there!

Ala Moana has a Sears, Liberty House, J C Penney, Longs Drugs, Foodland supermarket (open 7 am to 11 pm daily), Honolulu Book Shops, Sharper Image and Banana Republic chain stores. House of Music has a good selection of Hawaiian music on cassettes and compact discs.

Shirokiya is an authentic Japanese department store, from the chirping 'arigatos' as you walk in the door to the top-floor Japanese food market where sushi in little plastic containers sells for $3.

At the Crack Seed Center you can scoop from jars full of pickled mangoes, rock candy, salty red ginger, cuttlefish legs, roasted green peas and banzai mix.

There's a kite shop selling Molokai kites, a shop selling old Hawaiian stamps and coins, a couple of banks, a Thomas Cook currency exchange, a travel agency and a good food court with 20 ethnic fast-food stalls.

On the mountain side of the centre, near Sears, is a post office open from 8.30 am to 5 pm weekdays, to 4.15 pm Saturdays. Also at the ground level, but at the opposite end of the row, is a satellite city hall where you can get bus schedules and county camping permits. It's open from 9 am to 5.45 pm weekdays and from 8 am to 4.45 pm on Saturdays.

Ala Moana Beach Ala Moana Beach Park, opposite the Ala Moana Center, is a fine city park with much less hustle and bustle than Waikiki. The park is fronted by a broad white sand beach nearly a mile long which is buffered from the traffic noise of Ala Moana Blvd by a spacious grassy area with shade trees.

This is where Honolulu residents go to jog after work, play volleyball on the beach and enjoy weekend picnics. The park has full beach facilities, several softball fields and tennis courts, and free parking. It's a very popular park yet big enough to feel uncrowded.

Ala Moana is generally a safe place to swim and popular with distance swimmers. However the deep channel that runs the length of the beach can pose a danger at low tide, particularly to poor swimmers who don't realise it's there. A former boat channel, it drops off suddenly to depths of about 30 feet.

The 43-acre peninsula jutting from the Diamond Head side of the park is the **Aina Moana Recreation Area**, otherwise known as Magic Island. There's a nice walk around the perimeter of Magic Island and sunsets can be picturesque with sailboats pulling in and out of the adjoining Ala Wai Yacht Harbor. This is also a hot summer surf spot.

University of Hawaii
The University of Hawaii (UH) at Manoa, the central campus of the statewide college system, is east of downtown Honolulu and two miles north of Waikiki.

The university has strong programmes in astronomy (thanks to Mauna Kea), geophysics, marine sciences and Hawaiian and Pacific studies. The campus attracts students from islands throughout the Pacific.

Manoa Garden restaurant in Hemenway Hall is somewhat of a student hangout and sometimes has live music on Friday afternoons. Hemenway Hall and the Campus Center are behind Sinclair Library, which fronts University Ave opposite Burger King and the bus stop.

Two outside walls of the Campus Center have great Hawaiiana murals, with scenes based on photos from a classic August 1981 *National Geographic* article on Molokai. The Campus Center courtyard usually has live music a couple of days a week from noon to 1 pm.

Information The Information Center (☎ 956-7235) in the Campus Center can provide campus maps and answer questions. Free one-hour walking tours of the campus, emphasising art, history and architecture, leave from the Campus Center at 2 pm on Mondays, Wednesdays and Fridays.

Ka Leo O Hawaii, the student newspaper, lists lectures, music performances and other campus happenings. It can be picked up free at the university libraries and other places around campus.

Bulletin Boards Boards in front of Sinclair Library have notices of rooms for rent, cars and surfboards for sale, concerts and campus activities. Another board with only listings of rooms for rent is at the campus post office, opposite Hemenway Theatre. Although the listings are extensive, the majority are for rooms in shared student households and most advertisers are looking for long-term roommates.

Activities Hemenway Theatre (☎ 956-6468) in Hemenway Hall shows foreign flicks, select Hollywood movies and local surf films. Admission is $3.50 for non-students, $2.50 for senior citizens and children aged under 12. Printed schedules are available at the theatre and posted on the bulletin boards.

Hemenway Leisure Center (☎ 956-6468) in Hemenway Hall offers recreation and craft classes to the general public. Most classes, such as beginning hula, Hawaiian quilt-making, Afro-jazz dance, massage and ceramics, meet once or twice a week and cost from $30 to $80 for a month-long session. More useful to short-term visitors are the outdoor programmes, such as basic kayaking (two days, $60), deep sea fishing (one day, $85), beginning sailing (five days, $81) and guided hikes (half day $7, full day $10).

Attending University You can get information on undergraduate studies from the Admissions & Records Office (☎ 956-8975), Sakamaki Hall, 2530 Dole St, Honolulu, HI 96822, and on graduate studies from the Graduate Division (☎ 956-8544), Spalding Hall, 2540 Maile Way, Honolulu, HI 96822.

The summer session consists of two six-week terms. Tuition is $110 per credit for nonresidents and $55 per credit for residents. For the summer catalogue contact the Summer Session (☎ 956-7221, (800) 523-7866), Box 11450, Honolulu, HI 96828.

Getting There & Away Parking at UH is a hassle; you're better off arriving by bus and exploring on foot. Bus No 4 runs between UH and Waikiki, bus No 6 between UH and downtown Honolulu. If you do arrive by car, the East-West Center (entrance on East-West Rd, off Dole St) sells a daily pass for $2, although the parking lot fills early.

East-West Center

Adjacent to the university is the East-West Center (☎ 944-7111), 1777 East-West Rd, Honolulu, HI 96848, a federally funded educational institution established in 1960 by the US Congress. The centre's stated goal is the promotion of mutual understanding among the people of Asia, the Pacific and the USA.

Some 2000 researchers and graduate students work and study at the centre, examining development policy, the environment, culture and communication and other Pacific issues.

Free one-hour tours of the East-West Center's facilities and of the Japanese garden behind Jefferson Hall are held at 1.30 pm on Wednesdays. Meet at the Friends Desk on the garden level of Jefferson Hall. Reservations are not required, but you might want to call 944-7691 to confirm as the tour day has changed in the past.

Changing exhibits of Asian art and culture are displayed on the 1st floor of Burns Hall, which is on the corner of Dole St and East-West Rd. A single country or region is presented in each exhibit, with such themes as 'Cultural Portraits of Indonesia' and 'Silver, Silk: Khmer Artifacts'. Exhibits generally run about six weeks, with three weeks of down time between them. There's no admission charge.

The centre has other multicultural programmes open to the public. They include music performances ranging from Chinese lute music to ragtime, foreign films, international culture nights, and scholastic seminars on such topics as conflict resolution in Thailand or the homeless in Hawaii. Many of the activities are free, while others have fees up to $10. For the current listing, pick up the twice-monthly *Center Events* newsletter at Burns Hall or call 944-7283 for the schedule.

UPPER MANOA VALLEY

The Upper Manoa Valley, mauka of the university, ends at forest reserve land in the hills above Honolulu. There's a hike to Manoa Falls, trails through Lyon Arboretum and the touristy Paradise Park.

The road up the valley runs through a well-to-do residential neighbourhood. Not as exclusive as nearby Makiki Heights, in Manoa Valley the yards reflect the individual character of the residents rather than professional gardeners. Some yards are nicely planted with orange trees and flowering shrubs, others have tasteful Japanese touches such as stone lanterns, rock gardens and tiled roofs.

Paradise Park

Paradise Park (☎ 988-0200) is disappointing, with exotic birds in stark cages, a few hokey demonstrations, an animated dinosaur display and a tour-bus crowd. It's open from 9.30 am to 5 pm daily. Admission is a steep $15 for adults, $8 for children aged three to 12. There's a simple cafeteria-quality buffet at lunchtime for $10.

Manoa Falls Trail

The trail to Manoa Falls is a beautiful hike, especially for one so close to the city. The trail runs for three-quarters of a mile above a rocky streambed that leads up to the falls. It takes about 30 minutes one way.

Surrounded by lush damp vegetation and moss-covered stones and tree trunks, you get the feeling you're walking through a thick rainforest a long way from anywhere. The only sounds the birds have to compete with are the rush of the stream and waterfall.

There are all sorts of trees along the path, including tall *Eucalyptus robusta* trees with their soft, spongy, reddish bark, flowering orange African tulip trees and other lofty varieties that creak like wooden doors in old houses. Many of them were planted by the Lyon Arboretum, which at one time held a lease on the property.

Wild purple orchids and red ginger grow up near the falls. The ginger can be seen inside the fenced watershed area to the left of the falls. The falls are steep and drop about 100 feet vertically into a small shallow pool. The pool is not deep enough for swimming, and occasional falling rocks don't make it advisable anyway, but there are pools in the stream where you can at least get wet. The area is quiet and peaceful.

The trail is usually a bit muddy but not too bad if it hasn't been raining lately. Be careful not to catch your foot in the exposed tree roots – they're potential ankle breakers, particularly if you're moving with any speed. The packed clay can be slippery in some steep places, so take your time and enjoy the trail.

Aihualama Trail About 75 feet before Manoa Falls an inconspicuous trail starts to the left of the chain-link fence. This is the Aihualama Trail, well worth a little 15-minute side trip. Just a short way up you get a broad view of Manoa Valley.

After about five minutes you'll enter a bamboo forest with some massive old banyan trees. When the wind blows the forest releases eerie crackling sounds. It's a trippy forest, enchanted or spooky depending on your mood.

You can return to the Manoa Falls Trail or go on another mile to Pauoa Flats where the trail connects with the Puu Ohia Trail in the Tantalus area.

Lyon Arboretum

The Lyon Arboretum, 3860 Manoa Rd, is a great place to go after hiking to Manoa Falls if you want to identify trees and plants you've seen along the trail.

LYON ARBORETUM
University of Hawaii

Dr Harold Lyon, after whom the arboretum is named, is credited with introducing 10,000 exotic trees and plants to Hawaii. Approximately half of these are represented in this 124-acre arboretum, which is part of the University of Hawaii.

This is not a landscaped tropical flower garden, but a mature and largely wooded arboretum, where related species are clustered in a semi-natural state with trails meandering through.

The Hawaiian ethnobotanical garden has mountain apple, breadfruit and taro; ko, the sugar cane brought by early Polynesian settlers; kukui, which produced lantern oil; and ti, used medicinally since ancient times and for moonshine after Westerners arrived.

The arboretum also has herbs and spices and cashew, cacao, papaya, betel nut, macadamia nut, jackfruit and calabash trees, as well as greenhouses and classrooms.

Of the many short trails, the 20-minute walk up to **Inspiration Point** is a good choice. There are wonderful scents, stone benches along the way and lots of bird calls. The path loops through ferns, bromeliads and magnolias and passes by tall trees, including a bo tree, a descendant of the tree Gautama Buddha sat under when he received enlightenment.

Inspiration Point has a view of the hills that enclose the valley and it'd be a pleasant place to break out a picnic lunch.

The arboretum is open from 9 am to 3 pm Monday to Friday, to noon on Saturdays. They ask for a $1 donation. Free guided tours (☎ 988-7378 for reservations) are given at 1 pm on the first Friday and third Wednesday of each month and at 10 am on the third Saturday of each month.

The reception centre has a book and gift shop as well as helpful staff members who can give you maps and brochures of the garden and information on the arboretum's organised hikes, children's programmes and one-day workshops in cooking, horticulture and Hawaiian crafts.

Getting There & Away

From Ala Moana Center take the No 5 Manoa bus to the end of the line, which is at Paradise Park. From there it's a five-minute walk to the road's end, where the Manoa Falls Trail begins. Lyon Arboretum is at the end of the short drive off to the left just before the trailhead.

To get there by car, simply drive to the end of Manoa Rd. There's room to park at the trailhead, but don't leave anything valuable in the car. Parking is more secure at Lyon Arboretum.

TANTALUS & MAKIKI HEIGHTS

Just two miles from downtown Honolulu a narrow switchback road cuts its way up the lush green forest reserve land of Tantalus and the Makiki Valley. The road climbs up almost to the top of 2013-foot Mt Tantalus, with swank mountainside homes tucked in along the way.

Although it's one continuous road, the western side is called Tantalus Drive and the eastern side Round Top Drive. The 8½-mile loop is Honolulu's finest scenic drive, with great views of the city below.

The route is winding and steep, but it's a good paved road. Amongst the profusion of dense tropical growth, eucalyptus, bamboo, ginger and elephant-ear taro are easily identified. Vines climb to the top of telephone poles and twist their way across the wires.

A network of hiking trails runs between Tantalus and Round Top drives and throughout the forest reserve. The trails are seldom crowded, which seems amazing considering how accessible they are. Perhaps because the drive itself is so nice, the only walking most people do is between their car and the lookouts.

The Makiki Heights area below the forest reserve is one of the most exclusive residential areas in Honolulu and the site of a museum of contemporary art. There's bus service as far as Makiki Heights, but none around the Tantalus-Round Top loop drive.

Puu Ualakaa State Wayside Park

From Puu Ualakaa State Wayside Park you can see an incredible panorama of all

Honolulu. The park entrance is 2½ miles up Round Top Drive from Makiki St.

The sweeping view from the lookout extends from Kahala and Diamond Head on the far left, across Waikiki and downtown Honolulu, to the Waianae Range on the far right. The tan buildings inland on the left are the University of Hawaii at Manoa; below, and to the right, you can see clearly into the green mound of Punchbowl Crater; the airport is out on the edge of the coast; and Pearl Harbor is beyond that.

Although the best time for photos is usually during the day, this is also a fine place to watch evening settle over the city. Arrive at least 30 minutes before sunset to see the hills before they're in shadow.

The park gates are locked from 6.45 pm (7.45 pm in summer) to 7 am. For night (and anytime) views, there are a couple of scenic pull-offs before the park.

The Contemporary Museum

The Contemporary Museum (☎ 526-1322), 2411 Makiki Heights Drive, is a delightful modern art museum housed in a 1925 tropical-design estate with 3½ acres of wooded gardens.

The estate was built for Mrs Charles Montague Cooke, whose other former home is the present site of the Honolulu Academy of Arts.

You enter the museum through a covered courtyard with bronze gates and an arrangement of parabolic mirrors reflecting the view hundreds of times over.

Inside are galleries featuring quality changing exhibits of paintings, sculpture and other contemporary artwork by both national and international artists. A newer building on the lawn holds the museum's most prized piece, a vivid environmental installation by David Hockney based on his sets for *L'Enfant et les Sortilèges*, Ravel's 1925

opera. There's also an excellent cafe serving lunch and afternoon desserts.

The museum is near the intersection of Mott-Smith Drive and Makiki Heights Drive. The No 15 bus from downtown Honolulu gets you there.

It's open from 10 am to 4 pm Tuesday to Saturday, from noon to 4 pm on Sundays. Admission is free on Thursdays and $4 on other days. Children aged 14 and under are admitted free.

Meditation Center

The Honolulu Siddha Meditation Center, 1925 Makiki St, Honolulu, HI 96822, operated by followers of Gurumayi Chidvilasananda, has activities open to interested visitors.

Evening programmes that include chanting, sitar playing and a video of Gurumayi are held from 7.30 to 9 pm on Wednesdays and Saturdays. Visitors interested in that programme can share in a vegetarian dinner for $5 with advance reservations. On Tuesday evenings, you can join a hatha yoga session for $7. For registration and information call 942-8887.

Hiking Tantalus

A network of hiking trails crosses forest reserve land in the Makiki/Tantalus area, with numerous trailheads off Tantalus Drive and Round Top Drive.

Three of the hiking trails can be combined to make a 2½-mile loop through Makiki Valley.

The Puu Ohia Trail leads to the Nuuanu Valley Lookout and also connects with another trail that leads across to Manoa Valley.

Makiki Valley Loop Trail

Maunalaha and Kanealole, two of the three trails that form the Makiki Valley Loop Trail, start at the baseyard (field maintenance

---

In olden times, the slopes of Puu Ualakaa (Rolling Sweet Potato Hill) were planted with sweet potatoes, which were said to have been dug up and rolled down the hill for easy gathering at harvest time. The hill's other name, 'Round Top', dates to more recent times. ■

station) of the Makiki Forest Recreation Area. The Makiki Valley Trail crosses the upper Makiki Valley, connecting the Maunalaha and Kanealole trails.

The loop is through a lush and varied tropical forest that starts out in Hawaii's first state nursery and arboretum. In this nursery, hundreds of thousands of trees were grown to replace the sandalwood forests that had been levelled in Makiki Valley and throughout Hawaii in the 1800s. The new saplings were planted to stem the erosion and loss of watershed caused by the deforestation.

The **Maunalaha Trail**, which is three-quarters of a mile long, begins at the restrooms below the baseyard parking lot. It first crosses a bridge, passes taro patches and proceeds to climb the east ridge of Makiki Valley, passing Norfolk pine, bamboo and fragrant allspice and eucalyptus trees. There are some good views along the way.

Before reaching the Makiki Valley Trail junction you can find avocado trees on the right, which in early fall are ripe for the picking.

The mile-long Makiki Valley Trail is the left fork of the four-way trail intersection. The trail passes up and down through small

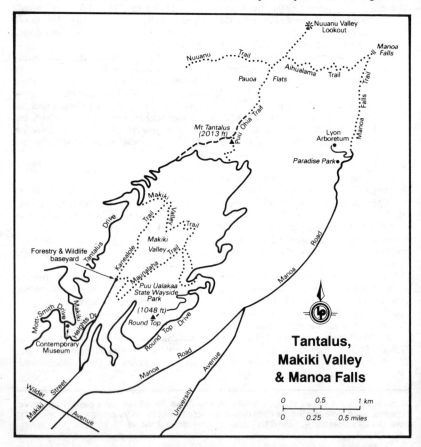

Tantalus,
Makiki Valley
& Manoa Falls

ravines and across gentle streams with patches of ginger. Near the Moleka Stream crossing are mountain apple trees (related to allspice and guava), which flower in the spring and fruit in the summer. Edible yellow and strawberry guavas also grow along the trail. There are some fine views of the city below.

The **Kanealole Trail** begins as you cross Kanealole Stream and then follows the stream down to the baseyard, three-quarters of a mile away. The trail leads down through a field of Job's-tears. The bead-like bracts of the female flowers of this tall grass are often picked to be strung in leis.

Kanealole Trail is usually muddy, so wear shoes with good traction and pick up a walking stick. Halfway down there's a grove of introduced mahogany.

Getting There & Away To get to the baseyard, turn left off Makiki St and go about half a mile up Makiki Heights Drive. Where the road makes a sharp bend, proceed straight ahead through a green gate into the Makiki Forest Recreation Area. Keep going until you come to the Forestry & Wildlife baseyard. There's a parking lot on the right just before reaching the office.

You can also take the No 15 bus, which runs between downtown and Pacific Heights. Get off near the intersection of Mott-Smith Drive and Makiki Heights Drive and walk down Makiki Heights Drive to the baseyard. It's a little less than a mile to the trailhead.

An alternative is to hike just the Makiki Valley Trail, which you can reach by going up Tantalus Drive two miles from its intersection with Makiki Heights Drive. As you come around a sharp curve, look for the wooden post marking the trailhead on the right. You can take this route in as far as you want and backtrack out or link up with other trails along the way.

Puu Ohia Trail
The Puu Ohia Trail leads up to a lookout with a view of Nuuanu reservoir and

valley. It's two miles one way and makes a hardy hike.

The trailhead is at the very top of Tantalus Drive, 3.6 miles up on the left from its intersection with Makiki Heights Drive. There's a large turn-off opposite the trailhead where you can park.

The Puu Ohia Trail leads through groves of bamboo and guava and past lots of eucalyptus, a fast growing tree that was planted to protect the watershed. About half a mile up, the trail reaches the top of 2013-foot Mt Tantalus (Puu Ohia).

From Mt Tantalus, the trail leads into a service road. Continue on the road to its end, where there's a Hawaiian Telephone building. The trail picks up again behind the left side of the building.

Continue down the trail until it leads into the Manoa Cliff Trail. Go left on the Manoa Cliff Trail a short distance until you come to another intersection where you turn right. This is the continuation of the Puu Ohia Trail which now leads down into Pauoa Flats and on to the lookout. The flats area can be muddy. Be careful not to trip on exposed tree roots.

You'll pass two trailheads before reaching the lookout. The first is Nuuanu Trail, on the left, which runs three-quarters of a mile along the western side of Upper Pauoa Valley and offers broad views of Honolulu and the Waianae Mountains.

The second is Aihualama Trail, a bit farther along on the right, which takes you the 1¼ miles to Manoa Falls through bamboo groves and huge old banyan trees. If you were to follow this route you could then hike less than a mile down the Manoa Falls Trail to Paradise Park and from there catch a bus back to town (see the Upper Manoa Valley section).

MOANALUA
In olden times Moanalua was a stopover for people travelling between Honolulu and Ewa as well as a vacation spot for Hawaiian royalty. In 1884 Princess Pauahi Bishop willed the valley to Samuel M Damon and it's now privately owned by his estate.

Moanalua Gardens

Moanalua Gardens is a large grassy park with grand shade trees. It's maintained by the Damon Estate as a public park and is a popular weekend picnic spot.

On the grounds, Kamehameha V's gingerbread-trimmed summer cottage overlooks a taro pond. Beyond it a Chinese-style hall is fronted by carp ponds and stands of golden-stemmed bamboo. The centre of the park has a grassy stage where the Prince Lot Hula Festival is held on the third Saturday in July. This is not a must-see spot, except during the festival, but it is a pleasant place for a quiet picnic if you're passing by.

To get there, take the Puuloa Rd/Tripler Hospital exit off Hwy 78 and then make an immediate right-hand turn into the gardens.

Moanalua Trail

The trail up Moanalua Valley is along a gravel and dirt road which was once a cobblestoned valley road. This is a dry area and there is only partial shade along the trail. There are both native and introduced plants, and lots of bird calls can be heard. Seven stone bridges remain along the path in various stages of disrepair.

The nonprofit Moanalua Gardens Foundation works to preserve Moanalua Valley in its natural state. Their efforts to raise public awareness of the valley's history and environmental uniqueness helped defeat plans that would have routed the new H-3 freeway through Moanalua Valley.

The foundation gives interpretive walks into Moanalua (Kamananui) Valley on the second Saturday and fourth Sunday of each month. The easy five-mile walks begin at 9 am and finish around noon and cost $2. Reservations are requested a week in advance (☎ 839-5334). If it's not crowded they may let you join in on the spot, but if fewer than 10 people reserve they usually cancel the hike.

If you want to hike the trail on your own, the Damon Estate requests that you first call the Moanalua Gardens Foundation for permission to enter.

If you follow the road all the way in, it's about four miles. It's also possible to branch off before the end of the road and take a trail up to the ridge. Numbered posts along the first half of the trail correspond to a self-guided brochure available from the Moanalua Gardens Foundation office (1352 Pineapple Place, Honolulu, HI 96819) for $2.50.

To get to the trailhead, take the Moanalua Valley/Red Hill exit off Hwy 78 (one exit past Moanalua Gardens). Stay to the right and then follow the Moanalua Valley sign uphill 1½ miles on Ala Aolani St to where the road ends at a parking lot. There are restrooms and drinking water in the little park at the trailhead.

PLACES TO STAY
Places to Stay – bottom end

Honolulu International AYH-Hostel (☎ 946-0591), 2323A Seaview Ave, Honolulu, HI 96822, is in a quiet residential neighbourhood near the University of Hawaii. The main house is a dormitory for Pacific Island students attending the university. Out the back, seven dorms with bunk beds can accommodate 40 travellers, with men and women in separate dorms. There are no rooms for couples.

Rates are $10 for IYHF or AYH hostel members and $13 for nonmembers. If you're not a member there's a two-night maximum stay. AYH membership is sold on site for $25. Office hours are from 7.30 to 9.30 am and from 5 to 11 pm. Guests must be out of the dorms from 10 am to 4.30 pm, although there's a TV lounge open during the day. Credit cards are accepted.

The bulletin board has useful information for new arrivals and there's a common-use kitchen and a laundry room. From Ala Moana, catch a No 6 or No 18 (University or Woodlawn) bus, get off on the corner of University Ave and Metcalf St and walk one block uphill to Seaview Ave. By car, take Exit 24B off the H-1 freeway, go mauka on University Ave and turn left at Seaview Ave.

Fernhurst YWCA (☎ 941-2231), 1566 Wilder Ave, Honolulu, HI 96822, has rooms for women only in a three-storey building about a mile from the university. There are 60 rooms, each intended for two guests, with two single beds, two closets with locks, a desk and dresser. Two rooms share a bathroom.

It costs $20 per person for YWCA members and $25 for nonmembers. If you get a room to yourself (easier during the low season), it costs $8 more. It's quite a good deal as rates include buffet-style breakfasts and dinners, except on weekends and holidays.

Payment is required weekly in advance and guests staying more than three days must become Y members ($25 a year). It costs $10 to rent linen, or you can bring your own. Reservations can be made by sending one night's rental as deposit by cashier's cheque or postal money order.

Fernhurst is near the intersection of Wilder and Punahou, on the No 4 bus line. It's a quiet community setting and there's a laundry room, security guard and a garden courtyard with a small pool. Office hours are 8.30 am to 10.30 pm.

The *Central Branch YMCA* (☎ 941-3344), 401 Atkinson Drive, Honolulu, HI 96814, on the Diamond Head side of the Ala Moana Center, has rooms for men only. Rates are $29 with community bath, $35.50 with private bath. It can be a bit difficult getting in as the Y generally stays full and they don't take reservations. Your safest bet is to call at 8 am when they set up a waiting list and again at around 11 am to check on your status. However, some days you can simply walk in at mid-afternoon and still find a room available.

The 115 rooms are simple but clean and guests receive YMCA privileges that include free use of the sauna, pool, gym and racquetball courts. There's a coin-operated laundry and a TV lounge for residents.

During the school year the *Atherton YMCA* (☎ 946-0253), 1810 University Ave, Honolulu, HI 96822, operates as a dorm for full-time University of Hawaii students only. During summer holidays (mid-May to mid-August) it's open on a space-available basis to non-students. Rates are $20 per day for a

room with a bed, dresser, desk and chair. Reservations are made by application (available by mail) with a $115 security deposit. The Y is next door to Burger King, directly opposite the university.

Sailors between ships can try their luck getting one of the 23 rooms at the *Seaman's Home* (☎ 538-6077) at the Marine Union Hall, 707 Alakea St, near Ala Moana Blvd. Just a few minutes' walk from Honolulu Harbor, it's open to both male and female sailors. The rooms are a bit spartan and the toilets are down the hall, but at $14 a night it's one of the city's best bargains.

Places to Stay – middle

The *Pagoda Hotel* (☎ 941-6611, (800) 367-6060 from the mainland, (800) 342-8434 from the Neighbor Islands), 1525 Rycroft, Honolulu, HI 96814, has two sections. The cheapest rooms, which are $73 studios in the apartment complex section, are run down and a bit on the seedy side. The more standard $78 hotel rooms are nicer and there's a central lobby. There's nothing special about this hotel, other than a nice restaurant with a carp pond, but it is one way to avoid jumping into the Waikiki scene.

Places to Stay – top end

Manoa Valley Inn (☎ 947-6019, (800) 634-5115), 2001 Vancouver Drive, Honolulu, HI 96822, is on a quiet side street near the University of Hawaii. The back porch and garden have views of the sunset and the high-rises of Waikiki, which is a 10-minute drive and a whole world away. The authentically restored Victorian inn is on the National Register of Historic Places.

All eight rooms are filled with period antiques, one with a four-poster bed, another with furnishings that belonged to the silent film star Frances Beaumont. Other nice touches include complimentary wine and cheese, lounging robes and fresh flower bouquets. There's lots of common space, a parlour and a billiard room. Rates are $95 for rooms with a shared bathroom and from $120 to $175 for rooms with a private bathroom. This includes a continental breakfast buffet.

Places to Stay – near the airport
If you've got some dire need to be near Honolulu International, there are three hotels outside the airport along a busy highway and beneath flight paths.

In addition, for long layovers or midnight flights there are two cheaper places where you can catnap or just take a shower. Both shower services provide towels, shampoo, razors and hair dryers and are open 24 hours a day.

The *Airport Mini Hotel* (☎ 836-3044), Terminal Box 42, Honolulu, HI 96819, is right in the airport's main terminal, between lobbies five and six. It has 17 small private rooms, each with a single bed and its own bathroom and shower. Overnight (eight-hour) stays are $30, a two-hour nap and shower costs $17.50 and showers only are $7.50. Reservations are taken for the overnight stays and MasterCard and Visa are accepted.

Nimitz Shower Tree (☎ 833-1411) is at 3085 N Nimitz Highway in an industrial area not far from the airport hotels. The private 'roomettes' are just a line of three-walled cubicles with curtains that can be drawn across the front. It's $25 per person for an overnight sleep and shower, or $7.50 for a shower only. They can store luggage ($1 per piece a day), provide free transport to and from the airport and have a courtesy phone in the baggage claim areas.

Holiday Inn-Honolulu Airport (☎ 836-0661, (800) 465-4329), 3401 N Nimitz Highway, Honolulu, HI 96819, on the corner of Rodgers Blvd and Nimitz Highway, has 310 rooms at $115. There's often a promotional rate that discounts the rack rate by about 20%.

Best Western Plaza Hotel-Honolulu Airport (☎ 836-3636, (800) 528-1234), 3253 N Nimitz Highway, Honolulu, HI 96819, is a comfortable, if undistinguished, mid-rise hotel with 268 rooms starting at $93.

The *Pacific Marina Inn* (☎ 836-1131),

2628 Waiwai Loop, Honolulu, HI 96819, is slightly further along in an industrial area. This lacklustre three-decker motel has rooms for $70/74 for singles/doubles.

All three hotels have swimming pools and provide 24-hour free transport to and from the airport, about 10 minutes away. The Holiday Inn and Best Western have restaurants, while a coffee shop and Sizzler steak house are nearby.

PLACES TO EAT
Honolulu has an incredible variety of good ethnic food. If you know where to look it can also be quite cheap. The trick is to get out of the tourist areas and eat where the locals do.

Around the University
There are some excellent restaurants in the area around the University of Hawaii at Manoa. The following listings are all within a 10-minute walk of the three-way intersection of King St, Beretania St and University Ave.

Coffeeline (☎ 947-1615), in the YWCA on the corner of University and Seaview Aves, is run by a politically active feminist group. In addition to good cheap food, there are lots of pamphlets on current progressive issues to read as well as conventional magazines and newspapers to browse through. A bowl of home-made soup costs $2, a French bread sandwich $3, and a cup of good coffee 75 cents. They also have muffins, scones, bagels and salads. Although there's some creative leeway in opening times, posted hours are 8 am to 8 pm Monday to Thursday, and to 11 pm on Friday evenings when there's an open mike.

Yakiniku Camellia, 2494 S Beretania St, has a tasty all-you-can-cook Korean lunch buffet for $9. It's good quality food and if you've got an appetite worked up it's a great deal. The mainstay is pieces of chicken, pork and beef that you select from a refrigerated cabinet and grill at your table. Accompanying this are 18 marinated and pickled side dishes, miso and seaweed soups, simple fresh vegetable salads and a few fresh fruits.

The mung bean and watercress dishes tossed with sesame seeds are sweet and mild. As for the kimchees, generally the redder they are, the hotter they are.

Dinner costs $14 and is essentially the same fare with the addition of sashimi. Everything is authentic; there's even a newspaper vending machine selling the Korean-language daily.

Chan's Chinese Restaurant, 2600 S King St, is the local place to go for inexpensive lunchtime dim sum. The chicken pies and curry turnovers, which cost 75 cents each, have a wonderful flaky crust and are potentially addictive. Chan's has noodles, chow mein and other Chinese dishes as well. Lunch specials are in the $4.50 to $5.75 range. It's open from 10.30 am to midnight daily.

Ezogiku Noodle Cafe, 1010 University Ave on the corner of Beretania St, dishes up miso ramen for $4.25, a gyoza, soup and rice meal for $4.75, and curries and cold noodles. While it's not gourmet quality, it is on par with similar fast-food noodle shops in Japan.

Across the street at 1091 University Ave, a branch of the Vietnamese restaurant *Ba Le* sells good inexpensive French rolls, croissants and sandwiches that range from a tasty vegetarian sandwich for $1.50 to a paté special for $3.

India Bazaar (☎ 949-4840), 2320 S King St, is a small cafe and food store selling inexpensive Indian food. There's a vegetarian thali that includes jasmine rice and three vegetable curries for $4.75 and chicken and shrimp thalis for $5.50 to $6. Side orders of papadams, chapattis, pakoras, samosas and raita are each under $1. It's open from 11 am to 9 pm Monday to Saturday.

Maple Garden, 909 Isenberg St, around the corner from South King St, is a popular local Sichuan restaurant with good food at honest prices. While chicken dishes tend to be fatty, the shrimp dishes are excellent. The house speciality, Eight Treasures, is a spicy combination of shrimp, diced tofu, peas and meats. There are about a dozen vegetarian dishes that cost $5 to $6, while most other dishes average $6 to $7. From 11 am to 2 pm

Monday to Saturday, there are a variety of lunch specials for around $4.

Chiang Mai (☎ 941-1151), 2239 S King St, serves northern Thai cuisine such as spring rolls, crispy noodles and chicken with eggplant. Their wonderful sticky rice, which is reminiscent of Japanese omochi, is served in its own little bamboo steamer. The Chiang Mai Evil Beef, with a spicy coconut sauce and fresh basil, is a recommendable speciality. There are two dozen vegetarian dishes for about $5.25 and most meat dishes are under $6.50.

The food is good, the decor pleasant enough, and unlike some of Honolulu's better known Thai restaurants, it's not impossible to get in on a weekend night – although it is still wise to call ahead for reservations. It's open from 11 am to 2 pm Monday to Friday and from 5.30 to 10 pm nightly. The menu is the same at lunch and dinner.

Down to Earth Natural Foods, 2525 S King St, is a fantastic natural foods supermarket. If it's healthy and you can eat it, you'll probably find it there. The store has everything from Indian chapattis and dahl to pure maple syrup and sesame oil on tap, as well as local organic produce and a dozen varieties of granola sold in bulk. It's a great place to shop and the healthier yoghurts and whole-grain breads that some of Honolulu's more with-it supermarkets sell are substantially cheaper at Down to Earth. It's open from 8 am to 10 pm daily.

Willows (☎ 946-4808), 901 Hausten St, a few minutes' walk from Down to Earth, has been a Honolulu attraction for 50 years, as much for the atmosphere as the food. You can even dine in thatched huts, although you usually need to reserve them in advance.

The Hawaiian Poi Dinner includes laulau, lomi salmon, poi, poki and haupia for $16 ($11 at lunch) and is a good alternative to being soaked at an impersonal luau. In addition, there's 'Poi Thursday', a weekly event with a Hawaiian lunch and Hawaiian entertainment from 11.30 am to 1.30 pm for $13. Except for Thursday lunch, you can also order off the menu, with fresh fish, scampi and curries some of the more popular items. There's also a Sunday brunch for $17.

Ala Moana Center

Ala Moana Center's central food court is a circus, with neon signs, 800 tiny tables crowded together and 20 fast-food stands circling it all. There's something for everyone, from salads to daiquiris, ice cream to pizza, and Chinese, Japanese, Korean, Hawaiian, Thai, Filipino and Mexican specialities.

If you've got the munchies, this is a good place to stop when you're between buses. It's like window shopping. If you come in here hungry you'll go crazy. It's open from 9.30 am to 9 pm Monday to Saturday and from 10 am to 5 pm on Sundays.

Kitchen Garden specialises in salads such as curried chicken, Thai peanut pasta, Waldorf, fruit, marinated vegetable and just plain green. The salads are fresh and healthy and range in price from $3.50 to $5.

Panda Express has Mandarin and Sichuan food. It's one of our favourites here, with dishes like spicy chicken with peanuts, broccoli beef and shrimp with garlic sauce. Combination plates with fried rice or chow mein and two entrees are $4.19, three entrees $5.19. The food is fresh and you can walk through and pick what looks best from the steamer trays.

Yummy Korean Bar-B-Q is a similar concept with Korean selections that include rice and a number of tasty pickled vegies and kimchees.

Patti's Chinese Kitchen, the busiest place in the food court, is a big-volume Chinese restaurant offering 20 to 30 dishes to choose from. It costs $4.05 for two selections, $4.95 for three selections, both of which include rice or noodles. If you really want to indulge you can get a whole roast duck for $9. It has a limited selection of dim sum and desserts, including almond cookies for 15 cents.

Two tasty skewers of chicken satay at *Little Cafe Siam* are $2. Big slices of acceptable pizza at *Sbarro* are $1.79 to $2.19, while a slice of pizza with salad costs $3.50.

Ward Centre

Ward Centre, a shopping complex at 1200 Ala Moana Blvd, has a bakery, a deli, a branch of *Keo's* Thai restaurant and about a dozen other dining spots.

Il Fresco (☎ 523-5191), on the ground level, has scrumptious Italian food with a Pacific Rim accent. The fresh-catch blackened ahi, which is seared on the outside and sashimi-raw on the inside, is a delicious preparation that melts in your mouth. The 'lite diner' portion at $12 provides a good-sized serving.

All dishes come in both light ($9 to $13) and regular ($13 to $18) portions. Salads, $5 to $10, include those with warm goat cheese, grilled tiger prawns or chicken with peanuts and sun-dried tomatoes. If you like spicy food, try the gazpacho soup. They also make good brick-oven pizzas with creative toppings and fine pasta dishes. It's open from 11 am weekdays and from 6 pm weekends, closing between 9.30 and 10.30 pm.

The food is a bit too Americanised at *Compadres*, but this hopping Mexican restaurant still draws a crowd. Two enchiladas with beans, rice and salad cost $10, while combination plates cost from $9 to $14. It's open from 11.30 am to 10.30 pm on weekdays, until midnight on weekends. Lots of margaritas and nachos are downed on late Friday afternoons, with the noise level rising as the daylight fades.

Mocha Java/Crepe Fever, on the ground level, is a popular hangout serving good coffees, crepes, croissants, sandwiches, desserts and other light eats. It's open from 8 am to 9 pm, except on Sundays when it closes at 4 pm.

Ward Warehouse

The *Old Spaghetti Factory* is the best deal at Ward Warehouse, the shopping complex on the corner of Ala Moana Blvd and Ward Ave. The restaurant is filled with old antiques, heavy woods, Tiffany stained glass – even an old street car.

At lunch you can get spaghetti with tomato sauce for $3.45, with clam sauce for $4.25, or with meatballs for $5.50. All meals come with warm sourdough bread and a simple green salad. At dinner they add coffee and ice cream and raise the prices by $1. To top it off, window tables have a view of the boat harbour across the street.

Horatio's specialises in seafood. Dinners, such as stuffed mahimahi for $15 and roasted garlic prawns or spicy Thai dungeness crab cakes for $17, include clam chowder or a choice of salads and are served from 5 to 10 pm nightly. The lunch menu, from 11 am to 5 pm daily except Sundays, has a sandwich special for $6 and quiche for $7, both with soup or salad. There's live music from 9 pm to midnight Wednesday to Sunday.

Dynasty II is a Chinese restaurant with fine dining and good food. While ordering from the dinner menu tends to be expensive, there's an all-you-can-eat lunch buffet from 11 am to 2 pm weekdays for a reasonable $8.45.

Stuart Anderson's is a steak house with lunches in the $6 to $9 range and dinners about double that. *Coffee Works*, open from 9 am to 6 pm, sells coffees and desserts such as carrot cake and apple pie.

Restaurant Row

Restaurant Row, a new and rather sterile complex on the corner of Ala Moana Blvd and Punchbowl St, caters largely to the downtown business crowd. There's a *Burger King*, a wine and deli shop, a bakery with cookies and pastries and about a dozen restaurants, the majority of which are quite pricey.

The most popular is the *Black Orchid*, a fine-dining restaurant co-owned by actor Tom Selleck, which has entrees ranging from roast duck for $18 to rack of lamb for $32. The Black Orchid has a sophisticated Art-Deco decor, serves reasonably good food and doubles as the venue for some good local jazz musicians.

Other restaurants in a similar price range include *Ruth's Chris Steak House*, an up-market mainland chain restaurant offering quality steaks; *Touch the East*, a ritzy Japanese bistro serving green tea linguine and high-priced sushi; and the more relaxed *Sunset Grill*, which features grilled fresh fish and meats.

The best value at Restaurant Row is *La Salsa*, which takes its name from its salsa table where customers can select from a variety of fresh-made salsas, ranging from the tame to the fire-eater. While there's no lard or preservatives in the food, in other ways it's near-authentic Mexican fare.

Burritos, either tofu or the traditional meat variety, cost $5, while combo plates with black beans and rice cost $8 to $10. If you're not up to a big meal there's a 'lite eaters' special of a single enchilada, rice and beans for $5. The horchata, a cinnamon-flavoured rice drink, is refreshing and costs a mere $1 for a huge glass.

Studebaker's, while a nightclub and not a restaurant, offers a simple buffet on weekdays from 4 to 8 pm which is 'free' with a $1 cover charge and a one-drink (from $3.50) minimum.

Fort St Mall

The Fort St Mall, on the edge of the downtown district, has a number of cheap restaurants within walking distance of Iolani Palace. It's convenient for downtown workers and sightseers, but not a draw if you're elsewhere around town.

Taco Bell, *McDonald's*, *Burger King*, *Jack in the Box* and *Pizza Hut* are all near the intersection of Hotel St and the pedestrian-only Fort St Mall.

Other Fort St Mall restaurants are a block away, between Pauahi St and Chaplain Lane. *Tay Do*, a Vietnamese restaurant, has lunch plates such as spicy lemon-grass chicken or barbecued pork that come with consomme, rice and salad for $5.25. It's open from 10 am to 6 pm weekdays, to 4 pm on Saturdays.

Ba Le, a branch of the Chinatown restaurant, has good inexpensive French bread, sandwiches, shrimp rolls and espresso. It's open from 7 am to 7 pm Monday to Friday, and from 8.30 am to 4 pm on Saturdays. There's another Ba Le on Queen St near the Old Federal Building, although it's open weekdays only.

Chinatown

Krung Thai (☎ 599-4803), 1028 Nuuanu Ave, is a friendly family-run Thai restaurant on the edge of Chinatown between the business and red-light districts. Lunch, the only meal served, is geared to the business community's 30-minute lunch breaks, with dishes ready in steamer trays. There are 13 hot dishes to choose from, including chicken Panang, shrimp squash curry and vegetarian curry. One item costs $2.95, two items $3.85 and all are served with brown rice or noodles. It's open from 10.30 am to 2.30 pm Monday to Friday.

Ba Le Sandwich Shop, 150 N King St, bakes crispy French bread and is a great place for a simple meal if you're in Chinatown. Baguettes can be purchased for 35 cents or as sandwiches for $1.50 vegetarian style, $2.50 with meat. The vegetarian sandwich is a tangy combo of crunchy carrots, daikon and cilantro (coriander leaves, also known as Chinese parsley) that's suitably filling. Sweet, strong French coffee with milk costs $1.50 hot or cold. There are also delicious croissants, shrimp rolls, Vietnamese manapua and soursop candies. It's open from 5 am to 7 pm daily.

The speciality at the Vietnamese restaurant *To Chau*, 1007 River St, is pho, a delicious soup of beef broth with rice noodles and thin slices of beef garnished with cilantro and green onion. It comes with a second plate of fresh basil, mung bean sprouts and slices of very hot red chilli to add at will. It's $3.70 for a regular bowl and $5 for an extra-large one.

The shrimp rolls with peanut sauce ($2.85) are good, and the restaurant also serves noodle and rice dishes, but just about everybody comes for the soup. To Chau is open from 8.30 am to 2 pm daily. It's so popular that even at 10.30 am you may have to wait for one of the 16 tables. It's well worth the wait.

Ha Bien, 198 N King St, next door to To Chau, is another popular Vietnamese restaurant with good inexpensive food. Although Ha Bien specialises in noodle and long rice dishes, the menu also includes spring rolls, soups and crepes. Most dishes cost from $4 to $6. It's open from 8 am to 6 pm daily.

Doong Kong Lau, on the River St pedestrian mall, has an extensive menu that includes the expected Chinese standards as well as more exotic preparations from the mountainous Hakka region of China. Meat dishes, including the house speciality, salt-baked chicken roasted in a paper bag, average about $6, while seafood plates are a few dollars higher.

Lunch specials are large, delicious and cost from $3.75 for an eggplant and rice meal to $5.75 for the shrimp and scallops in garlic sauce – both flavourful dishes. If you order noodles, splurge and pay the extra dollar for the cake noodles, pressed and cooked to a crisp on the edges. It's open from 9 am to 9.30 pm daily.

La Tropicale Paris on Hotel Street opposite the bus stop, has excellent all-natural ice cream with both traditional flavours and more intriguing local ones like lilikoi sorbet and pineapple ice cream. For something cross-cultural, try the coconut and red bean flavour.

Other Places to Eat

El Burrito, 550 Piikoi St (up from Ala Moana Center), could be a neighbourhood restaurant on a back street in Mexico City. It's a real hole-in-the-wall with about a dozen tightly squeezed tables and Oahu's most authentic Mexican food. Chicken enchiladas with rice and beans are $7.25 while other plates are priced from $6. It's a busy little place, with customers often waiting outside for tables. Inside it's noisy, crowded and alive with people laughing and chattering – often in Spanish. It's open from 11 am to 8 pm Monday to Thursday and to 9 pm on Fridays and Saturdays.

Mekong (☎ 521-2025), 1295 S Beretania St, is the original Keo's (now in Waikiki), and still has the original Thai cook. The menu is similar to that of Keo's, but Thai posters replace the artwork, you bring your own booze and prices are about a third less. The tasty spring rolls come with leaf lettuce, mint leaves and peanut sauce and cost $5.50.

The famous Evil Jungle Prince and most beef, chicken and vegetarian dishes are $6, while the most expensive item is the whole fish curry for $9.

It's open from 11 am to 2 pm on weekdays and from 5 to 9 pm nightly. If you're driving, consider *Mekong II* (☎ 941-6184), 1726 S King St, which has a similar menu and free parking in the rear.

For a cultured treat, try the *Contemporary Cafe* (☎ 523-3362) at the Contemporary Museum in Makiki Valley. It has a pleasant outdoor lawn setting and suitably creative food such as Malaysian shrimp salad with a gado-gado dressing for $9.75 or New Zealand mussels in a Thai curry with ginger and lime leaves for $8.25. Grilled eggplant or tempeh sandwiches cost $8 and meat sandwiches are $8.50, each served with a side of tabouli.

Lunch is from 11 am to 2 pm Tuesday to Saturday, from noon on Sundays. Desserts and beverages are available to 3.30 pm. Reservations are recommended, especially on Thursdays when admission to the museum is free.

The *Garden Cafe* (☎ 532-8734) is an open-air restaurant in the Honolulu Academy of Arts, 900 S Beretania St. It's run by volunteers who cook up something different every day and prices are quite moderate. It's open from 11.30 am to 1.30 pm Tuesday to Friday, 11 am to 3 pm on Saturdays, and for supper from 6.15 pm Thursdays. Call in the morning to see what's on the menu and to make reservations.

Auntie Pasto's (☎ 523-8855), 1099 S Beretania, has good Italian food at moderate prices. The $8 eggplant parmigiana is recommended. Pasta costs $4.95 with tomato sauce, $6.95 with creamy pesto or $5.95 heaped with fresh vegetables in a butter and garlic sauce. The parmesan cheese is freshly grated and the Italian bread is served warm.

Dishes and prices are the same at lunch and dinner. Although it's off the tourist track, this popular high-energy spot attracts a crowd. Even at lunch you may have to wait for a table, while dinner on weekends can have lines out the door. It's open from 11 am to 10.30 pm Monday to Friday and 4 to 10.30 pm on Saturdays and Sundays. Reservations are not taken.

The *Pagoda Floating Restaurant* at the Pagoda Hotel (☎ 941-6611), 1525 Rycroft, has good food and a serene setting in the midst of gardens, waterfalls and a carp pond. The breakfast menu (6.30 to 10 am) is extensive, with many choices from $3.50 to $6. There's a lunch buffet from 11 am to 2 pm for $8.95 on weekdays or you can order off the lunch menu for about $6. The nightly dinner buffet costs $17 ($14 from 4.30 to 5.30 pm) and features prime rib, Alaskan snow crab and tempura.

Yanagi Sushi (☎ 537-1525), 762 Kapiolani Blvd, and *Sada's* (☎ 949-0646), 1473 S King St, are two good places for sushi. Yanagi Sushi is open from 11 am to 2 pm and from 5.30 pm to 2 am daily (to 10 pm Sundays). Sada's is open from 11 am to 2 pm and from 5 to 11.30 pm Monday to Saturday.

ENTERTAINMENT

Honolulu has a thriving entertainment scene. The best updated entertainment listings are in the free *Honolulu Weekly*, which is readily found around the downtown and university areas. The free *Downtown Planet*, the *Waikiki Beach Press* and the Honolulu daily newspapers also have entertainment listings.

Classics & Concerts

Honolulu has a symphony orchestra, an opera company, ballet troupes, community theatre groups and chamber orchestras.

The *Blaisdell Center* (☎ 521-2911) at 777 Ward Ave presents musical concerts, Broadway shows and family events, with performers such as Sting, Steve Winwood, Dizzy Gillespie, the Honolulu Symphony, the Bolshoi Ballet, the Ice Capades and the Brothers Cazimero.

The *Academy Theatre* of the Honolulu Academy of Arts, and to a lesser degree the *East-West Center*, present quality multicultural theatre, films, lectures and concerts, such as performances by members of the

Beijing Opera and recitals of Japanese lute music.

Music & Dancing

The new *Pink's Garage* (☎ 537-1555), in a warehouse at 955 Waimanu St, is the hottest place in town. Stephen Stills, Nirvana, Metal from the Morgue, Smashing Pumpkins and Los Lobos have been headliners. Tickets are in the $10 to $20 range and many performances sell out in advance.

Anna Bannanas (☎ 946-5190), 2440 S Beretania St, not far from the university, rocks with a reggae/Jawaiian beat from 9 pm Wednesday to Sunday. It's particularly lively on Fridays and Saturdays when the house band, the Pagan Babies, plays roots dance music (African, reggae and soca). There's usually a cover charge of $3 or $4.

Moose McGillicuddy's (☎ 944-5525), 1035 University Ave, often has contemporary Hawaiian groups on Fridays and Saturdays.

Cafe Sistina (☎ 526-0071), a stylish Italian restaurant at 1314 S King St, has jazz on Friday and Saturday nights. The music starts around 10 pm and there's no cover charge. Wear black.

The *Black Orchid* restaurant (☎ 521-3111) in Restaurant Row, 500 Ala Moana Blvd, generally has jazz from about 6 to 10 pm, followed by top-40 dance music. It's a rather sophisticated crowd, there's a dress code and admission is $5 after 10 pm.

Rumours (☎ 955-4811) at the Ala Moana Hotel (410 Atkinson Drive), near the Ala Moana Center, has a video disco, karaoke, beach night, ladies night, contests and the like. The cover varies from free to $5.

Movie Theatres

For something progressive, there's the *Academy Theatre* (☎ 532-8768) at the Honolulu Academy of Arts, which showcases American independent cinema, foreign films and avant-garde shorts. Tickets are $4.

The *Hemenway Theatre* (☎ 956-6468) at the university leans toward more popular fare, including some good foreign films and select Hollywood offerings. General admission is $3.50.

The *Movie Museum* (☎ 735-8771), 3566 Harding Ave, shows classic oldies for film buffs. Tickets are $5.

Free Entertainment

Centerstage at the Ala Moana Center features local entertainment, with some sort of free performance on most days. The keiki dancers of the Young People's Hula Show perform at 9.30 am on Sundays and draw the biggest crowd. Other performers include the Royal Hawaiian Band, church choirs, ballet troupes and rock bands.

The Royal Hawaiian Band performs from 12.15 to 1.15 pm on Fridays (except August) on the lawn of the Iolani Palace.

The Celtic Pipes & Drums practise bagpipe and drum music from 7 to 9 pm on Wednesdays on the mauka side of the Honolulu Municipal Building.

For details on periodic music and dance performances in the courtyard of *Honolulu Hale* (City Hall) and other free performances sponsored by the City & County of Honolulu call 527-5666.

Other freebies include: the Honolulu Academy of Arts, the Contemporary Art Museum (on Thursdays) and the view from the top of the Aloha Tower.

Pearl Harbor Area

On 7 December 1941 a wave of more than 350 Japanese planes attacked Pearl Harbor, home of the US Pacific Fleet.

Some 2335 US soldiers were killed during the two-hour attack. Of those, 1177 died in the battleship USS *Arizona* as it took a direct hit and sank in less than nine minutes. Twenty other ships were sunk or seriously damaged and 188 aeroplanes were destroyed.

USS Arizona Memorial

Over 1.5 million people 'remember Pearl Harbor' each year by visiting the USS Arizona Memorial run by the National Park

Service. It is Hawaii's most visited attraction.

The visitor centre includes a museum and theatre as well as the off-shore memorial at the sunken USS *Arizona*. The park service provides a 75-minute programme that includes a 21-minute documentary film followed by a boat ride out to the memorial and back. Everything is free.

The film gives the history of the *Arizona* from the day it was launched to the day it went under, with a spiel emphasising military preparedness.

The 184-foot memorial, built in 1962, sits directly over the *Arizona* without touching it. It contains the *Arizona*'s bell and a wall inscribed with the names of those who went down with the ship. The average age of the enlisted men on the *Arizona* was 19.

From the memorial the battleship can be viewed eight feet below the surface. The ship rests in about 40 feet of water and even now oozes a gallon or two of oil each day. In the rush to recoup from the attack and prepare for war, the navy exercised its option to leave

the men in the sunken ship buried at sea. They remain entombed in its hull.

The visitor centre (☎ 422-2771; recorded information ☎ 422-0561) is open from 7.30 am to 5 pm daily except Thanksgiving, Christmas and New Year's Day. There's a snack bar and a souvenir shop.

Programmes run every 15 or 20 minutes from 8 am to 3 pm on a first-come basis. As soon as you arrive, pick up a ticket at the information booth; the number on the ticket corresponds to the time the tour begins. Summer months are busiest, with an average of 4500 people taking the tour daily, and the allotment of tickets is sometimes gone by 11 am. Generally the shortest waits are in the morning; if you arrive before the crowds you might get in within half an hour, but waits of a couple of hours are not uncommon.

Pearl Harbor survivors, who act as volunteer historians, are usually available at the front desk to give talks about the day of the attack.

There's a little open-air museum to keep you occupied while you're waiting. It has

Honolulu Star-Bulletin 1st EXTRA

HONOLULU, TERRITORY OF HAWAII, U. S. A., SUNDAY, DECEMBER 7, 1941 ★ PRICE FIVE CENTS

WAR !

(Associated Press by Transpacific Telephone)

SAN FRANCISCO, Dec. 7.—President Roosevelt announced this morning that Japanese planes had attacked Manila and Pearl Harbor.

OAHU BOMBED BY JAPANESE PLANES

SIX KNOWN DEAD, 21 INJURED, AT EMERGENCY HOSPITAL

interesting photos from both Japanese and US military archives showing Pearl Harbor before, during and after the attack. One photo is of Harvard-educated Admiral Yamamoto, the brilliant military strategist who planned the attack on Pearl Harbor even though he personally opposed going to war with the USA. Rather than relish the victory, Yamamoto stated after the attack that he feared Japan had 'awakened a sleeping giant and filled him with a terrible resolve'.

Another photo shows the Micronesian atoll of Bikini going up in a nuclear explosion in 1946. Ironically, a number of US battleships that the Japanese had missed at Pearl Harbor five years earlier – including the *Nevada* and the *Pennsylvania* – were nuked along with Bikini during the US atomic bomb test.

Getting There & Away The visitor centre is off Kamehameha Highway (Hwy 90) on the Pearl Harbor Naval Base just south of Aloha Stadium. Follow highway signs for the Arizona Memorial, not Pearl Harbor.

The private Arizona Memorial Shuttle Bus (☎ 926-4747) runs direct from Waikiki every 90 minutes between 6.50 am and 1 pm. The ride takes about 40 minutes and costs $2 each way.

By public transport, take the No 20 airport bus from Waikiki, which takes about 1¼ hours.

There are also private boat cruises to Pearl Harbor leaving from Kewalo Basin for about $20, but they should be avoided as passengers are not allowed to board the memorial.

Bowfin Park

If you have to wait an hour or two for your Arizona Memorial tour to begin, you might want to stroll over to the adjacent Bowfin Park.

The park contains a moored WW II submarine, the USS *Bowfin*, and the Pacific Submarine Museum, which traces the development of submarines from the turn of the century to the nuclear age.

The *Bowfin*, commissioned in May 1943, sank 44 ships in the Pacific before the end of

the war. The sub tour is self-guided, with a hand-held radio receiver that picks up recorded messages as you walk through. Admission of $6 for adults and $1 for children aged 12 and under includes entry to both the sub and the museum.

There's no charge to enter the park and view the missiles and torpedoes spread around the grounds, look through the periscopes or inspect the Japanese *kaiten*, or suicide torpedo.

The kaiten is just what it looks like: a torpedo with a single seat. As the war was closing in on the Japanese homeland, the kaiten was developed in a last-ditch effort to ward off an invasion. It was the marine equivalent of the kamikaze pilot and his plane. A volunteer was placed in the torpedo before it was fired. He then piloted it to its target. At least one US ship, the USS *Mississinewa*, was sunk by a kaiten. It went down off Ulithi Atoll in November 1944.

The park is open from 8 am to 5 pm daily.

PEARL CITY

Pearl City is the largest urban area in Hawaii outside Honolulu. It's home to about 45,000, including a lot of military people and civilians who work on the bases, but there's little of interest for visitors.

If you're just passing through and not going into Pearl City itself, stay on H-1 and avoid the parallel Kamehameha Highway (Hwy 90), as it's all stop-and-go traffic, fast food and malls.

Pearlridge Shopping Center is a massive mall that runs between H-1 and Kamehameha Highway. A swap meet is held a block west of the shopping centre on Saturdays, Sundays, Wednesdays and holidays at the drive-in theatre.

KEAIWA HEIAU STATE PARK

This park in Aiea, north of Pearl Harbor, covers 334 acres and contains an ancient medicinal temple, camping grounds, picnic facilities and a scenic loop trail. The park is open from 7 am to sunset for day visitors. As with all state parks there are no fees.

At the park entrance is Keaiwa Heiau, a

religious site built in the 1600s and used by Hawaiian *kahuna lapaau* (herbalist healers). The kahunas used hundreds of medicinal plants and grew many on the grounds surrounding the heiau. Among those still found here are noni, whose pungent yellow fruits were used to treat heart disease; kukui, whose nuts were an effective laxative; ulu, whose sap soothed chapped skin; and ti leaves, which were wrapped around a person to break a fever. Many of the medicinal plants around the heiau are marked.

The heiau is 100 by 160 feet, a single terraced stone structure. Not only did the herbs have medicinal value but the heiau itself was considered to possess life-giving energy. The kahuna was able to draw forth the powers from both.

People wishing to be healed still place offerings within the heiau. The offerings reflect the multiplicity of Hawaii's cultures: rosary beads, New-Age crystal pendants and sake cups sit beside flower leis and rocks wrapped in ti leaves.

Ohia Lehua Tree

Aiea Loop Trail

The 4½-mile Aiea Loop Trail begins at the top of the park's paved loop road next to the restrooms and comes back out at the camping ground, about a third of a mile below the start of the trail.

The trail starts off in a forest of eucalyptus and ironwood trees and runs along the ridge. Other trees along the way are Norfolk Island pines, edible guava and native ohia lehua, with its fluffy red flowers.

There are vistas of Pearl Harbor, Diamond Head and the Koolau Range. About two-thirds of the way along, the wreckage of a C-47 cargo plane that crashed in 1943 can be spotted through the foliage on the eastern ridge. The hike takes 2½ to three hours and is a fairly easy walk.

Camping

The camping area can accommodate 100 campers. Each site has its own picnic table and barbecue grill. Sites are not crowded together, but because they're largely open there's not a lot of privacy either. There's a

distant view of Honolulu's airport a couple of miles to the south.

If you're camping in winter make sure your gear is waterproof, as it rains a lot at this 880-foot elevation, although the temperature is usually pleasant. There are restrooms, showers, a phone and drinking water.

For Oahu, it's a good choice for a camping ground. There's a caretaker by the front gate, and the gate is locked at night for security.

Camping permits are limited to five nights per month and must be obtained in advance (see Camping in the Accommodation section at the start of this chapter). Like all Oahu public camping grounds it's closed on Wednesdays and Thursdays.

Getting There & Away

From Honolulu, head west on Hwy 78 and take the Aiea Stadium turn-off onto Moanalua Rd. Turn right onto Aiea Heights Drive at the first traffic light. The road passes the Aiea sugar refinery and winds up, through a residential area, 2½ miles to the park. The ride up the hill has good views of the city and Pearl Harbor.

South-East Oahu

Some of Oahu's finest scenery is along the south-east coast, which curves around the tip of the Koolau Mountains. Diamond Head, Hanauma Bay and the island's most famous bodysurfing beaches are all just a 20-minute ride from Waikiki.

East of Diamond Head, H-1 turns into the Kalanianaole Highway (Hwy 72), following the south-east coast up to Kailua. It passes the exclusive Kahala residential area, a run of shopping centres, and housing developments that creep up into the mountain valleys.

The highway rises and falls as it winds its way around the Koko Head area and Makapuu Point, with beautiful coastal views along the way. The area is geologically fascinating, with boldly stratified rock formations, volcanic craters and lava sea cliffs.

DIAMOND HEAD

Diamond Head is a tuff cone and crater that was formed by a violent steam explosion deep beneath the surface long after most of Oahu's volcanic activity had stopped.

As the backdrop to Waikiki it's one of the best-known landmarks in the Pacific. The summit is 760 feet high.

The Hawaiians called it Leahi and built a luakini heiau on the top where human sacrifices took place. But ever since 1825, when British sailors found calcite crystals sparkling in the sun and mistakenly thought they'd struck it rich, it's been called Diamond Head.

In 1909 the US Army began building Fort Ruger at the edge of the crater. They built a network of tunnels and topped the rim with cannon emplacements, bunkers and observation posts. Reinforced during WW II, it's been a silent sentinel whose guns have never fired.

Today there's a Hawaii National Guard base inside the crater as well as Federal Aviation Administration and civil defence facilities. Diamond Head is a state monument with interpretive plaques, picnic tables, restrooms and drinking water. The best reason to visit is to hike the trail to the crater rim for the panoramic view. The gates are open from 6 am to 6 pm.

Hiking Diamond Head

The trail to the summit was built in 1910 to service the military observation stations along the crater rim.

It's a fairly steep hike, with a gain in elevation of 560 feet, but it's only three-quarters of a mile to the top and plenty of people of all ages hike up. It takes about 30 minutes one way. The trail is open and hot and you might want to take along something to drink.

As you start up the trail, you can see the summit ahead at about 11 o'clock.

The crater is dry and scrubby with kiawe, koa haole, grasses and wildflowers. The little yellow-orange flowers along the way are native ilima, Oahu's official flower.

About 20 minutes up the trail you enter a long, dark tunnel. Because the tunnel curves you don't see light until you get close to the end. It's a little spooky, but the roof is high enough for you to walk through without bumping your head, and there is a hand rail. Your eyes should adjust enough to make out shadows but if you don't like walking in the dark, bring a flashlight.

The tunnel itself seems like it should be the climax of the long climb, but on coming out into the light you're immediately faced with a steep 99-step staircase. Persevere! After this there's a shorter tunnel, a narrow spiral staircase inside an unlit bunker and the last of the trail's 271 steps.

From the top there's a fantastic 360° view taking in the south-east coast to Koko Head and Koko Crater and the leeward coast to Barbers Point and the Waianae Mountains. Below is Kapiolani Park and the orange seats of the Waikiki Shell. You can also see the lighthouse, coral reefs, sailboats and even surfers waiting for waves at Diamond Head Beach.

Note Watch your footing at the top. There are some steep drops.

Getting There & Away Buses No 3 and 58, both of which run about twice an hour, stop at Diamond Head. It's about a 15-minute walk from the bus stop to the trailhead above the parking lot. Once you walk through the tunnel you're in the crater.

By car, take Monsarrat Ave (which goes by the zoo) to Diamond Head Rd and then take the right after Kapiolani Community College into the crater.

Diamond Head Beach

Diamond Head Beach is popular with both surfers and windsurfers.

Conditions at Diamond Head are suitable for intermediate to advanced windsurfers, and when the swells are up they really ride the waves – surfing more than sailing. Even as a spectator sport it's exhilarating.

The beach has showers but no other facilities.

Getting There & Away To get there from Waikiki, follow Kalakaua Ave to Diamond Head Rd. There's a parking lot just beyond the lighthouse. Walk east past the end of the lot and you'll find a paved trail down to the beach.

HANAUMA BAY BEACH PARK

Hanauma is a wide, sheltered bay of sapphire and turquoise waters set in a rugged volcanic ring. You shouldn't miss it, even if you only go to look.

Hanauma, which means 'curved bay', was once a popular fishing spot. It had nearly been fished out when it was designated a marine life conservation district in 1967. Now that the fish are fed instead of eaten, they swarm in by the thousands.

From the overlook you can peer into crystal waters and see the entire coral reef that stretches across the width of the bay. You can see schools of silver fish glittering, the bright blue flash of parrotfish and perhaps a lone sea turtle. To see an even more colourful scene, put on a mask, jump in and view it from beneath the surface.

The large sandy opening in the middle of the coral, called the Keyhole, is where most beginning snorkellers start. Divers and veteran snorkellers go beyond the reef to deeper parts of the bay.

Hanauma seems to get as many people as fish. With some two million visitors a year, it's often busy and crowded.

While it's for good reason that everyone's there, the heavy use of the bay has taken its toll. The coral on the shallow reef has been damaged by all the action, and the bread and peas that snorkellers feed the fish have increased fish populations in Hanauma well beyond what it can naturally support. In fact, many of these fish are not common to Hanauma, but are more aggressive types that have been drawn in by the feeding.

A master plan is under way that aims to normalise the fish distribution and reduce the number of beachgoers from 10,000 a day to 2000. The numbers have already been nearly halved by one new restriction that prohibits tour buses from dropping off passengers to use the beach, and fish feeding will be phased out in the next few years. In the meantime snorkellers shouldn't consider feeding the fish anything but fish food (which can be bought at the beach concession or the Foodland in Hawaii Kai).

Improperly discarded plastic fish food bags are another problem. Sea turtles that frequent the bay confuse the plastic for jellyfish, which they love to eat, and it kills them.

Hanauma is both a county beach park and a state underwater park. It has a grassy picnic area, lifeguards, showers, restrooms, changing rooms and access for the disabled. The bay is closed on Wednesdays until noon, but is otherwise open daily from 6 am to 7 pm from Memorial Day to Labor Day and from 7 am to 6 pm the rest of the year. Admission is free.

The snack bar sells hamburgers, hot dogs, and soda while snorkel sets can be rented at reasonable rates at the concession stand.

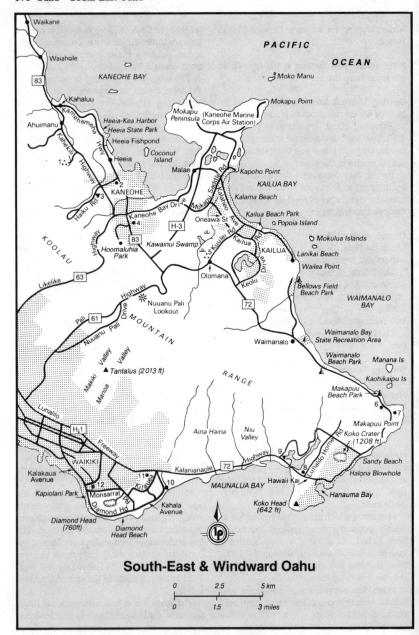

South-East & Windward Oahu

Paths lead along low ledges on both sides of the bay. Be cautious when the sea is rough or the tide is high, as waves can wash over the ledges.

More people drown at Hanauma than at any other beach on Oahu. Although the figure is high largely because there are so many visitors to the beach, people drowning in the Toilet Bowl or being swept off the ledges have accounted for a fair number of deaths over the years.

Toilet Bowl

A 15-minute walk out to the point on the left side of the bay brings you to the Toilet Bowl, a small natural pool in the lava rock. The Toilet Bowl is connected to the sea by an underwater channel, which enables water to surge into the bowl and then flush out from beneath.

People going into the pool for the thrill of it can get quite a ride as it flushes down four to five feet almost instantly. However, the rock around the bowl is slippery and hard to grip, and getting in is far easier than getting out. It definitely shouldn't be tried alone.

You can also get to the Toilet Bowl from above the parking lot. Go past the overlook wall at the left side of the parking lot and continue walking to the south-east for about 10 minutes. When you reach a small ravine bear left to get down to the Toilet Bowl, or bear right to view it from above.

Witches Brew

A 10-minute walk along the right side of the

bay will take you to the rocky point that juts out about two-thirds of the way down. Witches Brew is the name for the turbulent waters that swirl and churn in the cove on the southern side of this point.

There's a nice view of Koko Crater from there and green sand made of olivine can be found along the way.

Snorkelling & Diving

Snorkelling is good at Hanauma Bay year round. Mornings are better than afternoons, as swimmers haven't yet stirred up the sand.

The inner reef is an excellent place for novice snorkellers. The deepest water is 10 feet, although it's very shallow over the coral. It's well-protected and usually swimming-pool calm.

Hanauma's biggest attraction is the sheer number and variety of fish. It's got big rainbow parrotfish crunching off chunks of coral, moray eels, bright yellow butterfly fish, goatfish, Moorish idols and numerous other tropicals.

For confident snorkellers, it's better on the other side of the reef where there are larger coral heads, bigger fish and fewer people. Swim out to the red flag marking the channel on the right side of the beach and go out just beyond the boulders. Then snorkel down to the left parallel with the beach. There's a bit of a current in the channel, especially at low tide when you can feel it pull out as you come back in.

Don't swim outside the reef when the water is rough or choppy. Not only will the channel current be strong, but the sand will be stirred up and visibility poor anyway.

Divers have the whole bay to play in, with clear water and coral gardens, sea turtles and lots of fish. Beware of currents when the surf is up; surges in the Witches Brew, on the right hand side; and the Molokai Express, a treacherous current that runs just outside the mouth of the bay.

An interpretive board in front of the snack bar clearly illustrates water conditions in different parts of the bay and names the fish that can be seen.

Getting There & Away

Hanauma is about 10 miles from Waikiki along Hwy 72. There's free parking in a large parking lot, although it sometimes fills in the middle of the day and on weekends. Parking outside a marked space will result in a parking ticket.

TheBus runs a 'Beach Bus' (No 22) to Hanauma (and on to Sea Life Park). On weekdays the first bus leaves Waikiki from the corner of Kuhio Ave and Namahana St at 8.15 am, with subsequent buses leaving at 50 minutes past the hour until 3.50 pm. Buses leave Hanauma Beach Park for Waikiki at 10 minutes past the hour from 11.10 am to 5.10 pm. On weekends the buses are a little more frequent, although the times are more sporadic.

KOKO HEAD REGIONAL PARK

The entire Koko Head area is a county regional park. It includes Hanauma Bay, Koko Head, Halona Blowhole, Sandy Beach and Koko Crater.

Koko Head is backed by Hawaii Kai, an expansive development of condos, houses, shopping centres, a marina and a golf course – all overplanned and quite sterile in appearance.

Koko Crater and Koko Head are both tuff cones created about 10,000 years ago in Oahu's last gasp of volcanic activity.

Koko Head

Koko Head, not to be confused with Koko Crater, overlooks and forms the south-western side of Hanauma Bay.

The one-mile walk up the road to the summit has fine coastal views that light up nicely at sunset. The road starts near the highway at the Hanauma Bay entrance.

There are two craters atop Koko Head, as well as telecommunications facilities on the 642-foot summit. The Nature Conservancy maintains a preserve in the shallow Ihiihilauakea Crater, the larger of the two. The crater has a unique vernal pool and a rare fern, the *Marsilea villosa*. For information on work parties or weekend excursions to the preserve, call the Nature Conservancy (☎ 537-4508).

Lookouts & Halona Blowhole

Less than a mile past Hanauma is a lookout with a view of striking coastal rock formations and crashing surf.

Nearly a mile farther is the parking lot for Halona Blowhole, where water surges through a submerged tunnel in the rock and spouts up through a hole in the ledge. It's usually preceded by a gushing sound, as air is forced out immediately before the water.

Down to the right of the parking lot is Halona Cove, the beach where the risque love scene with Burt Lancaster and Deborah Kerr in *From Here to Eternity* was filmed in the 1950s.

Immediately before the blowhole, a small stone monument sits atop Halona Point. It was erected by Japanese fishers to honour those lost at sea.

Sandy Beach

Sandy Beach is one of the most dangerous beaches on the island if measured in terms of lifeguard rescues and broken necks. It has a punishing shorebreak, a powerful backwash and rip currents.

Nevertheless, the shorebreak is extremely popular with bodysurfers who know their stuff. It's equally popular with spectators, who gather to watch the bodysurfers being tossed around in the transparent waves.

Sandy Beach is wide and very long and, yes, sandy. It's frequented by sunbathers, young surfers and their admirers, and high school students cruising the parking lot. When the swells are big, board surfers hit the left side of the beach.

Not all the action is in the water – the grassy strip on the inland side of the parking lot is a popular area for flying kites. On Tuesday, Thursday, Saturday and Sunday afternoons, High Performance Kites (☎ 947-7097) sets up a van in the parking lot selling kites and offering free lessons. For beachcombers sifting through the sand will uncover white augers and other small shells.

The park has restrooms, showers, drinking water, a pay phone and lifeguards.

Koko Crater

According to Hawaiian legend, Koko Crater is the imprint left by the vagina of Pele's sister Kapo, which was sent here from the Big Island to lure the pig-god Kamapuaa away from Pele.

Inside the crater there's a neglected botanic garden with ageing plumeria trees that the county has plans to eventually revive. To get there, take Kealahou St off Hwy 72 opposite the northern end of Sandy Beach. Just over half a mile in, turn left at the road to Koko Crater Stables (no trail rides) and continue a third of a mile to the garden.

On the outside of the crater on the Hanauma side there's an unmaintained hiking trail. It follows an abandoned railroad track that once served a former army missile base on the 1208-foot summit.

Places to Eat

Koko Marina Shopping Center, on the corner of Lunalilo Home Rd and Hwy 72, has a *Sizzler* steak house, a *Taco Bell*, *Domino's Pizza*, a *Kentucky Fried Chicken*, a McDonald's and other restaurants as well as ice-cream, shave-ice and yoghurt shops.

For local flavour try *Yummy Korean Bar-B-Q*, which offers barbecue meat dishes accompanied with 'two-scoop rice' and four tasty marinated vegetable dishes or kimchees, including a terrific watercress and sesame variety, for around $5.

The shopping centre also has the Aloha Dive Shop, a Foodland supermarket, Waldenbooks, banks, drugstores, twin theatres and gas stations.

Roy's (☎ 396-7697) at Hawaii Kai Corporate Plaza on Hwy 72 not only serves some of Oahu's best food but has surprisingly moderate prices. Owner Roy Yamaguchi is a creative force behind the popular Pacific Rim cuisine, which emphasises fresh local ingredients and blends the lighter aspects of European cooking with Japanese, Thai and Chinese influences. A large exhibition kitchen sits in the centre of the dining room,

where Roy orchestrates an impressive troupe of sous cooks and chefs.

Starters include dim sum, imu-oven pizzas and a variety of salads. For entrees the crispy lemon-grass chicken has a delightful Cabernet curry sauce, comes on a bed of sauteed vegetables and is topped with red ginger and sprouts. It costs $12. Mesquite-smoked Peking duck with a mildly sweet ginger lilikoi sauce costs $15.25 and is another recommended dish. Daily fresh fish specials are reasonably priced between $18 and $22. For dessert, the Grand Marnier mousse is a treat big enough for two.

Roy's is top value, the food is attractively presented, the service attentive and the servings are a good size. It's open daily for dinner from 5.30 to 10 pm (to 11 pm weekends) and for brunch on Sundays from 10 am to 2 pm. Reservations are required for Sunday brunch and are advisable at other times.

MAKAPUU

The 647-foot Makapuu Point is the easternmost point of Oahu. A lighthouse marks its tip.

About 1½ miles north of Sandy Beach there's a lookout with a scenic view down onto Makapuu Beach, with aqua-blue waters outlined by white sand and black lava. It's an even more spectacular sight when hang gliders are taking off from the cliffs, Oahu's top hang gliding spot.

From the lookout you can see two offshore islands, the larger of which is Manana, otherwise known as **Rabbit Island**. This ageing volcanic crater is populated by feral rabbits and burrowing wedge-tailed shearwaters. They coexist so closely that the birds and rabbits sometimes even share the same burrows.

The island also looks vaguely like the head of a rabbit, and if you try hard you may see it, ears folded back. If that doesn't work, try to see it as a whale.

In front of it is the smaller **Kaohikaipu Island**, an island that won't tax the imagination – all it looks is flat.

There's a coral reef between the two

islands that divers sometimes explore, but to do so generally requires a boat.

Makapuu Beach Park

Makapuu Beach is one of Oahu's top winter bodysurfing spots, with waves reaching 12 feet and higher. It has the island's best shorebreak, but there are also dangerous currents to contend with. As with Sandy Beach, Makapuu is for bodysurfers who can handle rough water conditions. Surfboards are prohibited.

In summer, when the wave action disappears, the waters can be calm and good for swimming.

The beach is opposite Sea Life Park in a pretty setting, with cliffs in the background and a glimpse of the lighthouse. There are restrooms, showers, a lifeguard and drinking water. Two native Hawaiian plants are plentiful – naupaka by the beach and the yellow-orange ilima by the parking lot.

Sea Life Park

Sea Life Park (☎ 259-7933) is Hawaii's only marine park. Its 300,000-gallon aquarium is Oahu's best, with turtles, eels, eagle rays, hammerhead sharks and thousands of reef fish. A spiral ramp circles the aquarium, which is 18 feet deep, allowing you to see it from different depths.

In one of two outdoor amphitheatres, jumping dolphins and waddling penguins perform the standard marine life park tricks.

In the other, the Whaler's Cove, a 1500-pound false killer whale and a group of

Lionfish

dolphins give a choreographed performance. The dolphins tail walk, do the hula and give rides to a 'beautiful island maiden'. It borders on the kitsch.

There's a large pool of California sea lions and a smaller pool with harbour seals and a few rare Hawaiian monk seals. The turtle lagoon holds hawksbill, loggerhead and green sea turtles. Another section of the park has nesting red-footed boobies, albatrosses and great frigate birds, which are all sea birds indigenous to Hawaii.

Hanging from the ceiling of the park's little **Pacific Whaling Museum** is the skeleton of a 38-foot sperm whale that was washed up off Barbers Point in 1980. After the Coast Guard damaged a ship propeller unsuccessfully trying to tow the 20-ton mammal out to sea, they turned the carcass over to Sea Life Park. The park removed almost 38,000 pounds of flesh from the skeleton using many of the antique whaling tools that were on display in the museum. The whole process took the better part of two years.

In addition to harpoons, a trypot used to boil down whale blubber, and other whaling paraphernalia, the museum has a fine collection of whaling-era scrimshaw, from toys and bird cages to suggestive 'porno' pieces. The museum closes one hour before the rest of the park.

Sea Life Park is open from 9.30 am to 5 pm, with the last series of shows beginning at 3.15 pm. On Friday the park closes at 10 pm, with the last series of shows from 7 pm, followed by Hawaiian music at 8.30 pm. The Friday show often features top island musicians like Olomana and Kapena, and admission is the same as on other days – which makes it an ideal time to visit.

Admission is $14.95 for adults, $7.95 for children aged six to 12 and free for children under six.

You can visit the whaling museum and the park restaurant (sandwiches, salads, soba and other cafeteria-style food) without paying admission. You also get a free look at the seal and sea lion pools along the walk to the museum.

Public buses No 22, 57 Kailua/Sea Life Park and 58 Hawaii Kai/Sea Life Park stop at Sea Life Park. There's also a free shuttle bus (☎ 923-1531) from Waikiki three times a day.

WAIMANALO

Waimanalo Bay has the longest continuous stretch of beach in Oahu: 5½ miles of white sand stretching north from Makapuu Point to Wailea Point. A long coral reef about a mile out breaks up the biggest waves, protecting much of the shore.

Waimanalo has three beach parks with camping. The setting is scenic, although the area isn't highly regarded for safety.

Waimanalo Beach Park

Waimanalo Beach Park has an attractive beach of soft white sand and the water is excellent for swimming.

It's an in-town county park with a grassy picnic area, restrooms, changing rooms, showers, ball fields, basketball and volleyball courts and a playground. There's also camping allowed in an open area near the road but most of the campers are homeless families and it's not a scene that invites visitors.

The park has ironwood trees, but overall is more open than the state park and Bellows Field park up the road. The scalloped hills of the lower Koolau Range rise up mauka of the park and Manana Island and Makapuu Point are visible to the south.

Waimanalo Bay State Recreation Area

Waimanalo Bay State Recreation Area is about a mile north of the county beach park. For board surfers and bodysurfers this area has Waimanalo Bay's biggest waves.

Locals call the park Sherwood Forest because hoods and car thieves used to hang out there in the 1960s, and it hasn't totally shaken its reputation. Just as a park ranger in Honolulu was telling us that the incidence of crime on the windward coast is exaggerated, his co-worker told him of a friend, who just that weekend, while setting up camp at

Waimanalo, had watched someone drive off with his car!

Thievery aside, the park itself is quite appealing with camping sites on the beach under ironwood trees and barbecue grills, drinking water, showers and restrooms.

Bus No 57 stops in front of the park and it's a third of a mile walk in from the road to the beach and camping ground. The gate is open from 7 am to sunset.

Bellows Field Beach Park

The beach fronting Bellows Air Force Base is open to civilian beachgoers and campers on weekends only, from noon on Friday until 8 am on Monday. It's a long beach with fine, hard-packed sand in a natural setting of ironwood trees. The small shorebreak waves are good for beginner bodysurfers and board surfers.

There's a lifeguard, showers, restrooms and water. The 50 camping sites are under the trees. Permits are available from the county Department of Parks & Recreation.

The marked entrance is a quarter of a mile north of the state recreation area. Bus No 57 stops in front of the entrance road and from there it's 1½ miles to the beach.

Places to Eat

Bueno Nalo (☎ 259-7186) is between the state and county beaches, just north of Waimanalo's post office. It serves good homestyle Mexican food with combo plates priced around $9. The fresh fish tacos, a chalkboard item that's sometimes available, are *muy bueno*. It's open from 11.30 am to 9 pm daily, except Mondays.

There's a grocery store and a bakery next door to Bueno Nalo and a *McDonald's* just south of the state recreation area.

Pali Highway

The Pali Highway (Hwy 61) runs between Honolulu and Kailua, cutting through the spectacular Koolau Range. It's a scenic little highway with one of Oahu's best views.

Many Kailua residents commute to work this way, which wouldn't be a bad way to start the day!

Honolulu-bound traffic can be heavy in the morning, and outbound traffic heavy in the evening, although most day-trippers will be travelling against the traffic. City buses travel the Pali Highway but none stop at the Nuuanu Pali Lookout.

Up past the four-mile marker, look for two notches cut about 15 feet deep into the crest of the *pali* (cliff). The notches are thought to have been dug as cannon emplacements by Kamehameha I.

If it's been raining heavily, look up at the mountains to the left – every fold and crevice will have a lacy waterfall streaming down it.

The original route between Honolulu and windward Oahu was via an ancient footpath that wound its way perilously over these cliffs. In 1845 the path was widened into a horse trail and later into a cobblestone carriage road.

In 1898 the Old Pali Highway (as it's now called) was built following the same route. It was abandoned in the 1950s after tunnels were blasted through the Koolau Range and the present multi-lane Pali Highway opened.

You can still drive a loop of the Old Pali Highway (called Nuuanu Pali Drive) and hike another mile of it from the Nuuanu Pali Lookout.

Queen Emma Summer Palace

At the Pali Highway two-mile marker is the Queen Emma Summer Palace, which belonged to Queen Emma, the consort of Kamehameha IV.

Emma was three-quarters royal Hawaiian and a quarter English, a granddaughter of the captured sailor John Young who became a friend and adviser of Kamehameha I. The house is also known as Hanaiakamalama, the name of John Young's home in Kawaihae on the Big Island, where he served as governor.

The Youngs left the home to Queen Emma, who often slipped away from her formal downtown home to this cooler retreat. It's a bit like an old Southern plantation house, with a columned porch, high ceilings and louvered windows to catch the breeze.

The home was forgotten after Emma's death in 1885, and was scheduled to be razed in 1915, as the estate was being turned into a public park. The Daughters of Hawaii rescued it and now run it as a museum.

The house has period furniture collected from five of Emma's homes. Some of the more interesting pieces are a cathedral-shaped koa cabinet made in Berlin and filled with a set of china from Queen Victoria; feather cloaks and capes; and Emma's necklace of tiger claws, a gift from the Maharaja of India.

It's open from 9 am to 4 pm daily except holidays. Admission is $4 for adults, $1 for children aged 12 to 16 and 50 cents for those under 12.

Nuuanu Pali Drive

For a scenic side trip through a shady green forest, turn off the Pali Highway onto Nuuanu Pali Drive, half a mile past the Queen Emma Summer Palace. The 2½-mile road runs parallel to the Pali Highway and then comes back out to it before the Nuuanu Pali Lookout, so you don't miss anything by taking this side loop – in fact, quite the opposite.

The drive is through mature trees that form a canopy overhead, all draped with hanging vines and wound around with philodendrons. The lush vegetation includes banyan trees with hanging aerial roots, tropical almond trees, bamboo groves, impatiens, angel trumpets and golden cup, the latter a tall climbing vine with large golden flowers.

Judd Trail

If you want to get off the road and into the woods, you might try Judd Trail. The full trail is a 1½-mile loop, but most people just take it as far as Jackass Ginger, a little freshwater pool about 10 minutes in.

One mile up Nuuanu Pali Drive, there's a marked dirt parking lot on the right, just before a small bridge.

The trail starts below the parking lot and soon makes a stream crossing. The trail then runs parallel to the stream but goes uphill a bit, so you'll need to keep an eye out for the pool. Sometimes it's a good place for a dip, other times it's muddy; and the mosquitoes are hungry!

Trees along the way include large banyans, ironwood, *Eucalyptus robusta* and Norfolk pine.

Nuuanu Pali Lookout

Whatever you do, don't miss the Nuuanu Pali Lookout (Nuuanu Pali State Wayside) with its broad view of the windward coast from a height of 1200 feet. From the lookout you can see Kaneohe straight ahead, Kailua to the right and Chinaman's Hat (Mokolii Island) and the coastal fishpond at Kualoa Park to the far left.

This is *windward* Oahu – and the winds that funnel through the pali are so strong that you can sometimes lean against them. It gets cool enough to appreciate taking a jacket.

In 1795 Kamehameha routed Oahu's warriors up the Nuuanu Trail in his invasion of the island. On these steep cliffs Oahu's warriors made their last stand. Hundreds were thrown to their death over the pali as they were overcome by Kamehameha's troops. A hundred years later, during the construction of the Old Pali Highway, more than 500 skulls were found at the base of the cliffs.

The abandoned Old Pali Highway winds down from the right of the lookout, ending abruptly at a barrier near the current highway about a mile away. Few people realise the road is here, let alone venture down it. It makes a nice walk and takes about 20 minutes one way. There are good views looking back up at the jagged Koolau Mountains and out across the valley.

As you get back on the highway, it's easy to miss the sign leading you out of the parking lot and instinct could send you in the wrong direction. Go to the left if you're heading toward Kailua, to the right if you're heading toward Honolulu.

Windward Oahu

Windward Oahu is the island's eastern side, following the Koolau Range along its entire length. The mountains looming inland are lovely, with scalloped folds and deep valleys. In places they come so near to the shore that they seem almost to crowd the highway into the ocean.

The windward coast runs from Kahuku Point in the north to Makapuu Point in the south. (For the Waimanalo to Makapuu area, see the South-East Oahu section.)

The two main towns are Kaneohe and Kailua, both largely nondescript residential communities for workers who commute to Honolulu, about 10 miles away.

North of Kaneohe, the windward coast is rural Hawaii, where many Hawaiians struggle along, close to the earth, making a living with small papaya, banana and vegetable farms. It's generally wetter on the windward side, and the vegetation is lush and green.

The windward coast is exposed to the north-east trade winds. This is a popular area for anything that requires a sail – from windsurfing to yachting.

There are some nice swimming beaches on the windward coast – particularly Kailua, Kualoa and Malaekahana – although many more are silted and others are right in town in less than ideal settings. Swimmers should keep an eye out for stinging Portuguese man-of-war that are often washed in during storms. Most of the offshore islands that you'll see along this coast are bird sanctuaries.

Getting There & Away

Two highways cut through the Koolau Range to the windward coast. The Pali Highway (Hwy 61) goes straight into Kailua.

The Likelike Highway (Hwy 63) runs directly into Kaneohe and, although it doesn't have the scenic stops the Pali Highway has, it is in some ways more dramatic. Driving away from Kaneohe it feels like you're heading straight into the tall, fairy-tale mountains, which are often shrouded in clouds and laced with waterfalls. Then you suddenly shoot through a tunnel and emerge on the Honolulu side, the drama gone.

If you're heading both to and from windward Oahu through the Koolau Range, take the Pali Highway up from Honolulu and the Likelike Highway back for the best of both. (See the Pali Highway section for details on that drive.)

KAILUA

In ancient times Kailua was a place of legends. It was home to a giant turned into a mountain ridge, the island's first menehunes and numerous Oahuan chiefs.

But that's all history. Kailua today is an ordinary middle-class community, with one of Oahu's finest beaches, although little else of distinction to attract visitors. It's the third largest city in Hawaii, with a population of 36,800.

Ulupo Heiau

Ulupo Heiau is a large open platform temple, made of stones piled 30 feet high and 140 feet long. Its construction is attributed to

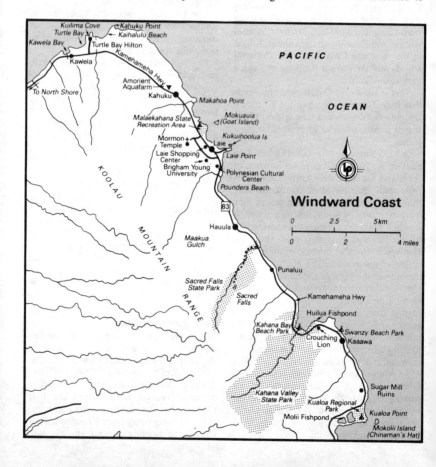

menehunes, the little people legends say created much of Hawaii's stonework, finishing each project in one night. Ulupo means 'night inspiration'.

If you walk out across the top of the heiau you get a view of Kawainui Swamp, one of the largest water-bird habitats in Hawaii. Legends say the swamp's ancient fishpond had edible mud at the bottom and was home to a *moo*, or lizard spirit.

Ulupo Heiau is one mile south of Kailua Rd. Coming up the Pali Highway from Honolulu, take Uluoa St, the first left after passing the Hwy 72 junction. Then turn right on Manu Aloha St and right again onto Manuoo St. The heiau is behind the left side of the YMCA.

Kailua Beach

Kailua Beach Park is at the south-eastern end of Kailua Bay. The white sand beach is long and broad and the water is a beautiful aqua. The park is popular for long walks, family outings and a range of water activities.

Kailua Bay is the top windsurfing spot in Oahu. Onshore trade winds are predominant and windsurfers can sail at Kailua every month of the year. In different spots around the bay there are usually a variety of water conditions, some good for jumps and wave surfing, others for flatwater sails. Several windsurfing companies, including Naish Hawaii (☎ 262-6068) and Kailua Sailboards (☎ 262-2555), rent boards and give lessons at the beach park each weekday and on Saturday mornings.

Kailua Beach Park has a gently sloping sandy bottom with waters that are generally flat and calm. Swimming is good year round.

The park has restrooms, showers, lifeguards, a snack shop, a volleyball court and large grassy expanses partly shaded with ironwood trees.

Kaelepulu Canal divides the park into two sections, although a sand bar usually prevents the canal waters from emptying into the bay. Windsurfing activities are on the west side of the canal; there's a small boat ramp on the east side.

The island offshore is **Popoia (or Flat) Island**, a bird sanctuary where landings are allowed. It's a popular destination for kayakers. Kailua Sailboards and Twogood Kayaks Hawaii (☎ 262-5656) rent kayaks on site.

While surfers do use the beach park at times, the surf is bigger at the northern end of Kailua Bay. **Kalama Beach**, an unimproved beach just north of the park, has gentle waves good for novice bodysurfers. Board surfers often go further north to **Kapoho Point** or further still to a break called **Zombies**.

To get to Kailua Beach Park, take buses No 56 or 57 from Ala Moana Center and transfer to a No 70 in Kailua. If you have your own transport, simply stay on Kailua Rd, which begins at the end of Hwy 61 and continues as the main road through town, ending right at the beach.

Lanikai

If you follow the coastal road as it continues east of Kailua Beach Park, you'll shortly come to Lanikai, a rather exclusive residential neighbourhood. It's fronted by Lanikai Beach, which is a gorgeous stretch of clear aqua waters and powdery white sand – at least what's left of it. Much of the sand has washed away as a result of the retaining walls built to protect the homes plopped right on the shore.

The sandy bottom slopes gently and the waters are calm, offering safe swimming conditions similar to those at Kailua. The twin Mokulua islets sit directly offshore.

From Kailua Beach Park, the road turns into the one-way Aalapapa Drive, which comes back around as Mokulua Drive to make a 2½-mile loop. There are 11 narrow beach access walkways off Mokulua Drive. For the best stretches of beach, try the one opposite Kualima Drive or any of the next three.

Places to Stay

Kailua has no hotels, but there are furnished beachfront cottages and vacation houses for rent. In addition, quite a few people rent out rooms in their homes. While a few of these can be rented directly from the owners, the majority are handled by B&B reservation services.

TC's (☎ 261-5766), 320A Uluniu St, provides hostel-style accommodation out of a contemporary two-storey house in a quiet residential neighbourhood. It's in a convenient location a few minutes' walk from the town centre, bus lines and inexpensive restaurants. The beach is about 15 minutes away.

There's one bedroom with four bunk beds, another with six bunk beds, and one private room with two single beds. The private room costs $35. Dorm beds cost $15 the first night, $13 thereafter, with bed linen provided. Guests have free use of the kitchen and washer/dryer and there's a pleasant exposed-beam living room with cable TV. The house is clean, the management is young and friendly, and the atmosphere is laid-back.

Akamai Bed & Breakfast (☎ 261-2227, (800) 642-5366), 172 Kuumele Place, Kailua, HI 96734, has two nice studio units in a private home about 10 minutes' walk from Kailua Beach. Each unit is modern and comfortable and has a refrigerator, microwave, coffeemaker, tiny bathroom, cable TV and private entrance. The larger room has a queen bed, the smaller has two twin beds that can be joined to make a king-size bed. Each room has a sofa-bed as well. The rate is $60 and includes a fruit basket and breakfast items. There's a laundry room and a pleasant courtyard with a pool. The minimum stay is generally three days.

Papaya Paradise Bed & Breakfast (☎ 261-0316), 395 Auwinala Rd, Kailua, HI 96734, is a 15-minute walk from Kailua Beach. Bob and Jeanette Martz, refired from the Army and home most of the time, rent two rooms off the side of their home. One room has a queen bed and a trundle bed, the other two single beds, both with private entrances through the garden courtyard, which has a pool. Each room has a bathroom, air-con, ceiling fan and TV. The rate is $65 for singles/doubles with a full breakfast, $60 without. There's a three-day minimum.

Pat's Kailua Beach Properties (☎ 261-1653) is at Kailua Beach Center, 130 Kailua Rd 110, Kailua, HI 96734. Pat handles about 30 vacation rentals, including studio cottages that start from $55 a day or $1100 a month. Two-bedroom places cost from $75 a day or $1700 a month and there are also larger luxury homes, some accommodating up to 10 people.

Most of the state-wide B&B agencies have listings of Kailua accommodation. The following two are home-based in Kailua and each book more than 50 different Kailua-area accommodation.

Pacific-Hawaii Bed & Breakfast (☎ 262-6026, (800) 999-6026), 19 Kai Nani Place, Kailua, HI 96734, has listings as low as $45, although most units are around $55. The four women who run the service have their own B&Bs as well. There's a $10 booking fee.

All Islands Bed & Breakfast (☎ 263-2342, (800) 542-0344), 823 Kainui Drive, Kailua, HI 96734, charges no booking fees. Typical rates are $50 to $60 for rooms in private homes and $60 to $70 for studio apartments.

Naish Hawaii (☎ 262-6068, (800) 767-6068), 155A Hamakua Drive, Kailua, HI 96734, books windsurfing vacations with accommodation in Kailua.

Places to Eat

Kailua has both fast-food eateries and some good-value restaurants. Near the intersection of Kailua and Kuulei Rds are *Pizza Hut*, *McDonald's* and a sandwich shop called *Gee A Deli*.

There are two good choices for Mexican food. The food is a bit tastier at *El Charro Avitia*, 14 Oneawa St, where two-item combos cost $8.50, three-item combos $10. At lunch, which is served weekdays from 11.30 am to 3 pm, prices are 20% cheaper. Across town, *Cisco's Cantina*, 123 Hekili St, has a reputation for serving big portions. Prices are similar to those at El Charro and it's open from 11 am to 10 pm daily.

Assaggio (☎ 261-2772), 354 Uluniu St, is a new restaurant serving good, moderately priced Italian food in a somewhat up-market setting. At lunch sandwiches are $5 to $6, although hot dishes are just a few dollars more. A good choice is the spicy chicken

Assaggio's, a combination of chunks of white chicken meat, pepperoncini, mushrooms and roasted bell peppers over a bed of pasta. A generous serving is $7.90 at lunch, $10.90 at dinner. Other dishes include a delicious eggplant parmigiana, shrimp scampi and calamari marinara. You can also get reasonably priced pizza at either meal.

Jaron's, 201A Hamakua Drive, is good for seafood, with fresh fish of the day priced around $20 at dinner. At lunch smoked turkey or Reuben baguette sandwiches are $7, eggplant parmesan or grilled chicken breast $9 and top sirloin or crab cakes $10. All dishes come with a green salad. They also have gourmet pizza and salads at lunch and dinner. It's open from 11 am to 10 pm.

An old standby is Buzz's, at 413 Kawailoa Rd near Kailua Beach Park, open daily for lunch from 11 am to 3.30 pm and for dinner from 5 to 10 pm. At lunch hamburgers are $6 and Thai chicken salad or fishburgers are around $8. Dinner prices range from $11 for beef kebab to $26 for steak and lobster, including a small, fresh salad bar. Credit cards are not accepted.

For fine dining try L'Auberge Swiss Restaurant (☎ 263-4663), 117 Hekili St, a romantic little restaurant serving good continental food at reasonable prices. Main dishes range from chicken piccata albergo for $13 to filet mignon for $18.50. There are also a few light dinners such as bratwurst and rosti ($9.75) and cheese fondue ($12). Meals come with soup or salad. It's open for dinner only and is closed on Mondays.

Entertainment
Jaron's (☎ 261-4600), 201A Hamakua Drive, has live jazz, blues, funk or pop bands from 10 pm to 1.30 am most nights of the week.

There's nightly jazz at Orson's (☎ 262-2306), 5 Hoolai St.

Someplace Else (☎ 263-8833), 33 Aulike St, has live entertainment, usually light rock and rhythm & blues, until 2 am Tuesday to Sunday.

The No Name Bar (☎ 261-8725), 131 Hekili St, has reggae, rock or blues music until 2 am nightly.

Fast Eddie's (☎ 261-8561), 52 Oneawa St, is open to 4 am nightly, with classic rock, blues, contemporary Hawaiian and Jawaiian groups.

KANEOHE
Kaneohe, with a population of 35,450, is Oahu's third largest town.

Kaneohe Bay, which stretches from Mokapu Peninsula all the way up to Kualoa Point, seven miles north, is the state's largest bay and reef-sheltered lagoon. Although inshore it's largely silted and not good for swimming, the near-constant trade winds that sweep across the bay are some of the best on the islands for sailing.

Two highways run north to south through Kaneohe. Kamehameha Highway is closer to the coast and goes by Heeia State Park. Kahekili Highway runs inland from the outskirts of Kaneohe, where it intersects the Likelike Highway, and goes north by Byodo-In. They merge into a single route, Kamehameha Highway (Hwy 83), just north of Ahuimanu.

Kaneohe Marine Corps Air Station occupies the whole of Mokapu Peninsula. H-3, the controversial new cross-island freeway now under construction, terminates at its gate.

Environmentalists opposed the H-3 project for years, as the freeway will cut through pristine valleys as well as open the more rural areas of the windward coast to further development. Windward residents complain that it will provide no relief to Kailua-Honolulu commuters, who have the biggest traffic congestion problems in the area. The H-3 freeway will end at Pearl Harbor, connecting military bases on both sides of the island. It's scheduled for completion at the end of 1994.

Hoomaluhia Park
The county's newest and largest botanic garden is Hoomaluhia, a 400-acre park in the uplands of Kaneohe. The park is planted with

groups of trees and shrubs from tropical regions of the world.

It's a peaceful, lush green setting, with a stunning pali as a backdrop. This is not a landscaped flower garden but more of a natural preserve. Trails lead up to the park's 32-acre lake (no swimming allowed).

The little visitor centre has small displays on flora & fauna, Hawaiian ethnobotany and on the history of the park that was originally built by the US Army Corps of Engineers as flood protection for the valley below. Ask for the free booklet detailing 30 of the labelled trees and shrubs in Pa Launa, the garden just beyond the visitor centre.

The park is at the end of Luluku Rd, which starts 2¼ miles down Kamehameha Highway from the Pali Highway. Buses No 55 and 56 go to Windward City Shopping Center opposite the start of Luluku Rd. It's 1½ miles up Luluku Rd from the highway to the visitor centre and another 1½ miles from the visitor centre to the far end of the park so, if you use the bus, expect to do some walking.

The park is open from 9 am to 4 pm daily (closed on Christmas and New Year's Day) and admission is free.

Free two-hour nature hikes are held at 10 am Saturdays and 1 pm Sundays. Moonwalks are held from 6.30 to 9 pm on nights nearest the full moon. Call the visitor centre (☎ 235-6636) for registration.

Valley of the Temples & Byodo-In

The Valley of the Temples is an inter-denominational cemetery in a beautiful setting just off the Kahekili Highway, 1½ miles north of Haiku Rd. The main attraction of the valley is Byodo-In, the 'Temple of Equality', which is a replica of the 900-year-old temple of the same name in Uji, Japan. This one was dedicated in 1968 to commemorate the 100th anniversary of Japanese immigration to Hawaii.

Byodo-In sits against the Koolau Range. The rich red of the temple against the verdant fluted cliffs is a pretty scene, especially when mist settles in on the pali.

The temple is meant to symbolise the mythical phoenix. Inside the main hall is a nine-foot gold-lacquered buddha sitting on a lotus. Wild peacocks roam the grounds and hang their tail feathers over the upper temple railings.

A carp pond fronts the temple, with cruising bullfrogs and cooing doves. A three-ton brass bell beside the pond is said to bring tranquillity and good fortune to those who ring it.

It's all very Japanese, right down to the gift shop selling sake cups, daruma dolls and happy buddhas. This scene is as close as you'll get to Japan without having to land at Narita.

Admission to the temple is $2 for adults, $1 for children under 12. It's open from 8.30 am to 4.30 pm daily.

On the way out, you might want to head up to the hilltop mausoleum with the cross on top and check out the view.

Heeia State Park

Heeia State Park is on Kealohi Point, just off Kamehameha Highway. It has a good view of Heeia Fishpond on the right and Heeia-Kea Harbor on the left.

Heeia Fishpond, which is owned by the Bishop Estate, is quite an impressive fishpond. It still remains largely intact, despite the invasive mangrove that grows along its walls. This introduced tree takes root between the rocks and has done more damage than hundreds of years of waves and storms.

Coconut Island, just offshore to the south-east of the fishpond, was a royal playground in times past. It was named for the coconut trees planted there by Princess Bernice Pauahi Bishop. In the 1930s it was the estate of Christian Holmes, heir to the Fleischmann Yeast fortune, who dredged the island, doubling its size to 25 acres. During the war the estate served as an R&R facility and had a brief stint as a hotel. In more recent times, air-brushed shots of Coconut Island were used in opening scenes for the *Gilligan's Island* TV series. The Hawaii Institute of Marine Biology of the University of Hawaii occupies a niche on the island, while the rest is privately owned.

You can walk around the grounds of Heeia State Park and take in the view but otherwise there's not much to do here. Friends of Heeia State Park have a little booth in the hall above the parking lot and can answer questions about the area.

Places to Stay

Windward Bed & Breakfast (☎ 235-1124), 46-251 Ikiiki St, Kaneohe, HI 96744, has two bedrooms in a cosy home filled with Old World furnishings, oil paintings, antique toys and other collectables. The Victorian Room has one double bed and costs $55, while the Circus Room has two twin beds and costs $50. Each room has a private bathroom. Originally from the Scottish Highlands, where his mother ran a B&B, host Don Munro gives guests the run of the house, provides beach towels and coolers, and serves complimentary afternoon tea and a continental breakfast. There's a small pool and a view of Kaneohe Bay.

The 56-unit *Schrader's Windward Marine Resort* (☎ 239-5711, (800) 735-5711), 47-039 Lihikai Drive, Kaneohe, HI 96744, is a spread of simple low-rise wooden buildings in a residential neighbourhood. The ambience is that of a local motel more than a resort, and prices seem high for what you get. So many of the guests are military families that there's a shuttle to the Kaneohe Marine Corps base. One-bedroom units range from $69 to $130, two-bedroom units from $99 to $190. All have refrigerators, microwaves, TVs and phones.

Camping Hoomaluhia has the best non-beach camping in Oahu. There are five camping areas, each with restrooms, cold showers and drinking water. The camping area farthest in is on an open grassy expanse with great views.

Camping is allowed from 9 am Thursday to 9 am Tuesday. Other than a few long weekends in summer the park seldom fills. There's no fee but reservations should be made two weeks (and not more than six months) in advance at the centre (☎ 235-6636) or with the county Department of Parks & Recreation. It's possible to do it all by mail. For an application send a business-size, self-addressed stamped envelope to Hoomaluhia, Box 1116, Kaneohe, HI 96744.

With a resident caretaker and gates that are locked to non-campers at 4 pm, they haven't had any safety problems since the park was opened to camping in 1982.

Places to Eat

The *Chart House* (☎ 247-6671) at Haiku Gardens has a lush, open-air setting with a picturesque view of a lily pond tucked beneath the Koolau Mountains. It's open for dinner from 5 pm nightly and for Sunday brunch. The food is standard steak and seafood dishes ($16 to $25) accompanied by a salad bar. The real attraction is the setting, and at night the gardens are flood-lit. Tell them you're a smoker and they'll sit you at a table near the railing with the best views.

You can also drop by Haiku Gardens in the daytime just for the view and to take a 10-minute stroll around the lily pond. From Kamehameha Highway turn left on Haiku Rd just past Windward Mall. After Haiku Rd crosses Kahekili Highway, Haiku Gardens is a quarter of a mile farther up, on the left.

Chao Phya Thai Restaurant in the Windward City Shopping Center, 45-480 Kaneohe Bay Drive at the intersection with Kamehameha Highway, is a family-run restaurant serving good, inexpensive Thai food. Nearly all dishes on the extensive menu are priced between $5.25 and $6.50. It's open for lunch from 11 am to 2 pm Monday to Saturday and for dinner from 5 to 9 pm nightly.

The Windward City Shopping Center also has a *Foodland* supermarket, *McDonald's*, and *Kentucky Fried Chicken*. *Burger King* and *Pizza Hut* are on the opposite side of the Kamehameha Highway.

The Windward Mall, on Kamehameha Highway at its intersection with Haiku Rd, is a large two-level mall with a Liberty House, Sears, JC Penny, Waldenbooks, a bank, a pharmacy and many other shops.

Eateries include *Arby's, Baskin-Robbins, Orange Julius, Marie Callender's, Carousel Yogurt* and *McDonald's*.

In addition, the Windward Mall's Food Court is sort of a mini Ala Moana with a line of food stalls selling hot cinnamon rolls, deli items, pizza by the slice and Japanese, Chinese, Mexican and Korean foods. *Patti's Chinese Kitchen* has good inexpensive buffet-style plate lunches. Prices range from $1.60 for a pint of chow mein to $9 for one of the hanging ducks. They have good Chinese pastries too, including coconut-filled gin doi and ten-cent almond cookies.

WAIAHOLE & WAIKANE

Waiahole and Waikane mark the beginning of rural Oahu. There are lots of nurseries and small farms, with coconut groves, banana fields and papaya and lemon orchards. Waikane has a couple of fruit stands and a little store on the side of the road.

Large tracts of Waikane Valley were taken over by the military during WW II for training and target practice, a use that continued up until the 1960s. The government now claims the land has so many live ordnances it can't be returned to the families it was leased from. Much of the inner valley remains off-limits.

The main 'attraction' in the area is Senator Fong's Plantation and Gardens, a tour bus stop where visitors pay $6.50 to take a tram through some rather elementary gardens. If you're curious, turn mauka onto Pulama Rd, one mile north of the intersection of Kamehameha Highway and Kahekili Highway. It's three-quarters of a mile to the gardens.

KUALOA

Kualoa Regional Park, a 153-acre county park on Kualoa Point, is bounded on its southern side by Molii Fishpond. From the road south of the park the fishpond is visible through the trees as a distinct green line in the bay.

Kualoa is a nice beach park in a scenic setting. The mountains looming precipitously across the road are, appropriately

enough, called Pali-ku, meaning 'vertical cliff'. When the mist settles it looks like a scene from a Chinese watercolour.

The main island offshore is **Mokolii**, which in more recent times has come to be known as Chinaman's Hat.

In Hawaiian legend, Mokolii is said to be the tail of a nasty lizard or a dog – depending on who's telling the story – which was slain by a god and thrown into the ocean.

Apua Pond, a three-acre brackish salt marsh on the point, is a nesting area for the endangered aeo (Hawaiian stilt). If you walk down the beach beyond the park you'll see a bit of **Molii Fishpond**, but it's hard to get much of a perspective on it. The rock walls are covered with mangrove, milo and pickleweed.

The park is largely open lawn with a few palm trees. It has a long thin strip of beach with shallow waters and safe swimming. The park has camping areas, picnic tables, restrooms, showers, a phone and a lifeguard. It's open for day use between 7 am and 8 pm, after which the gate is locked for security.

Lots of islanders camp here on weekends – so many, in fact, that at times they open a second camping ground on the bay side of the point. It's more shaded than the camping ground at the head of the beach. Camping is free from Friday to Tuesday nights with a permit from the county.

Kualoa used to be one of the most sacred places on Oahu. When a chief stood on the point, passing canoes lowered their sails in respect. The children of chiefs were brought here to be raised and it may also have been a place of refuge. It was at Kualoa that the double-hulled canoe *Hokulea* landed in 1987, following a two-year rediscovery voyage through Polynesia that retraced the ancient migration routes.

Kualoa Ranch

The horses grazing on the green slopes across the road from Kualoa Park belong to Kualoa Ranch. The ranch offers all sorts of activities from kayaking to target shooting but, except for horse riding that is open to the public with reservations, everything's packaged for Japanese honeymooners, who are shuttled in from Waikiki.

Back in 1850 Kamehameha III leased about 625 acres of this land for $1300 to Dr Judd, a missionary doctor who became one of the king's advisers. Judd planted the land with cane, built flumes and imported Chinese labourers to work the fields. His sugar mill trudged along for a few decades but went under just before the reciprocity agreement with the USA opened up mainland sugar markets.

You can still see the remains of the **mill's stone stack** and a bit of the crumbling walls a third of a mile north of Kualoa Park, right alongside the road.

KAAAWA

In the Kaaawa area, the road hugs the coast and the pali moves right on in. There's only enough space to squeeze a few houses in between the base of the cliffs and the road.

Swanzy, a neighbourhood beach park used mainly by fishers, is fronted by a shore wall. Across the road is a 7-Eleven store, a gas station and Kaaawa Country Kitchen, a takeaway restaurant with a couple of tables in front. Plate lunches cost around $4.50, fishburgers $1.80.

Crouching Lion

The crouching lion is a rock formation at the back of the restaurant of the same name, which comes up shortly after the 27-mile marker.

The rock is said to be a demigod from Tahiti who was cemented to the mountain during a jealous struggle between Pele, the volcano goddess, and her sister Hiiaka. When he tried to free himself by pulling into a crouching position, he was turned to stone.

To find him, glance at the inn's logo at the entrance to the parking lot. Then stand at the Crouching Lion Inn sign with your back to the ocean and look straight up to the left of the coconut tree. The lion is on a cliff in the background. The inn itself has a tour bus

ambience. Burgers, French fries and coleslaw are around $7.50 at lunch. Dinners are $15 to $20.

Continuing north, just past the inn you get a glimpse of Huilua Fishpond on the right.

Places to Stay

Plantation Spa (☎ 237-8685, (800) 422-0307), 51-550 Kamehameha Highway, Kaaawa, HI 96730, is a secluded eight-room health spa. It's geared for people who are undergoing transitions in their lives, and has attracted a number of TV 'soap' stars as the autographed photos on the wall attest. The exercise schedule includes aerobics, yoga and canoeing. The place is quite unpretentious and accommodation is rather simple. Rates are $1295/1990 a week all inclusive for singles/doubles.

KAHANA

In old Hawaii the islands were divided into *ahupuaa* – pie-shaped land divisions reaching from the mountains to the sea that provided everything the early Hawaiians needed for subsistence. Kahana Valley, four miles long and two miles wide, is the only publicly owned ahupuaa in Hawaii.

Kahana is a wet valley. Rainfall ranges from about 75 inches along the coast to 300 inches in the mountains. In pre-contact times Kahana Valley was planted with wetland taro. The overgrown remnants of more than 130 terraces and irrigation canals have been uncovered in the valley.

In the early 1900s, the area was planted with sugar cane, which was hauled north to the Kahuku Mill via a little railroad. The upper part of Kahana Valley was used as a military training jungle during WW II.

Kahana Valley was purchased by the state in 1965 from one of the Robinsons of Kauai (owners of Niihau) to preserve it from development.

Kahana Valley State Park

One mile north of the Crouching Lion Inn is the entrance to Kahana Valley State Park.

When the state purchased Kahana it also acquired tenants, many who had been living in the valley for a long time. Rather than evict a struggling rural population, the state created a plan which allows the 140 residents to stay on the land. The concept is to eventually incorporate the families into a 'living park', with the residents acting as interpretive guides. The development of the park has been slow and the 'living park' lives solely on planning documents. An information centre and restrooms, built a decade ago inside the park entrance, were only recently opened.

The park does have some trails, including a 1¼-mile loop trail, maintained by the Boy Scouts, that begins at the information centre. It starts along the old railroad route, passes a fishing shrine called Kapaeleele Koa, and leads to Keaniani Kilo, a lookout that was used in ancient times for spotting schools of fish in the bay. The trail then goes down to the bay and along the highway back to the park entrance. A trail map is available at the information centre.

Kahana Bay Beach Park
Opposite the entrance to Kahana Valley State Park is Kahana Bay Beach Park, a tree-lined park used primarily by island families.

Kahana Bay is set deep and narrow. The protected beach provides safe swimming, with a gently sloping sandy bottom. There are restrooms and a phone at the northern end of the park.

PUNALUU
Punaluu is more of a scattered little beach community than a town. It has a condo, a couple of restaurants and a beach park.

Punaluu Art Gallery, at 53-352 Kamehameha Highway just north of Punaluu Beach, sells locally made arts & crafts. It's open daily.

Punaluu Beach Park
Punaluu's narrow beach provides fairly good swimming, with its offshore reef protecting the shallow inshore waters in all but stormy weather. Be cautious in the area by the mouth of the Waiono Stream and in the channel leading out from it, as currents are strong

when the stream is flowing quickly or the surf is high.

Places to Stay
Pat's at Punaluu (☎ 293-8111, (800) 845-8799), 53-567 Kamehameha Highway, Box 359, Hauula, HI 96717, is a 136-room condo half a mile north of the 24-mile marker. Standard one-bedroom units cost $76 and are none too spiffy, but they're fairly large, with kitchens, TVs and a spare bed in the living room.

Countryside Cabins (☎ 237-8169), 53-224 Kamehameha Highway, Punaluu, HI 96717, is midway between the 25 and 24-mile markers. Rates are $30 a day or $500 a month. It's a modest older place; don't expect anything fancy. Manager Margaret Naai keeps the gate locked to keep her dog in, so call before you get there.

Places to Eat
Best bet in the area is the *Paniolo Cafe*, north of the 25-mile marker. Broiled chicken, rib and steak dinners cost $9 to $13, including rice, chilli and a salad bar. At lunch mahimahi sandwiches and burgers cost $7. They have a Hawaiian reggae band on Friday and Saturday nights and mellow Hawaiian music on Sundays. It's open from 11 am to 9 pm for meals, and to 2 am for weekend entertainment.

Pat's at Punaluu, at the condo of the same name, has sandwiches from 11 am to 5 pm for $7.50 to $9 and grilled meats at dinner for $15 to $18. Neither the food nor the atmosphere is special.

SACRED FALLS STATE PARK
Sacred Falls is a 1374-acre state park with a two-mile trail leading up the narrow Kaliuwaa Valley, which folds deeply into magical-looking mountains. The park is north of the 23-mile marker.

The trail begins across an old cane field and follows Kaluanui Stream through a narrow canyon. The upper end of the trail leads to an 80-foot waterfall beneath high, rocky cliffs. The falls are nice but not spectacular and there are lots of mosquitoes.

The hike is not terribly strenuous and takes about 1½ hours. There are a couple of stream crossings on the way that have slippery rocks and, more importantly, are subject to flash flooding. Even when it's sunny on the valley floor, a quick rain storm in the mountains can wash down suddenly.

The trail may be closed if the weather is sufficiently bad. Decisions are made daily and posted at the park. You can call 587-0300 to find out the status.

The falls may be sacred, but the hike isn't blessed. Although it's generally safe to hike, and thousands do, caution is definitely warranted.

In the past decade a number of hikers have been swept to their deaths in flash floods, at least one other killed by falling rocks and another by a slip over a ledge. Other hikers have been stranded during flash flooding, a few requiring rescue by helicopter.

Flash floods give little warning. Hikers caught in them here have reported hearing a sudden loud crack and then seeing a wall of water pour down the stream bed; they've had just five seconds to reach higher ground. If the water starts to rise or you hear a rumbling, get up on a bank and wait it out. Don't try to cross the stream if the water reaches your thighs. Use a walking stick.

An infamous incident occurred in 1984 when 25 hikers were ambushed at the falls and robbed at gunpoint in the worst of a rash of trail robberies. These days robberies don't seem to be a problem although thefts from parked cars are notorious and you shouldn't leave anything valuable in your vehicle here (or anywhere else, for that matter).

HAUULA

Hauula is a rather tired-looking town with a fine backdrop of hills and Norfolk pines. There's a 7-Eleven store and a few small eateries.

The in-town beach looks none too appealing for swimming but it occasionally gets waves big enough for local kids to ride. The beach is actually a county park that allows camping, although it's mostly local families that camp there.

The stone ruins of **Lanakila Church** (circa 1853) sit perched on a hill opposite Hauula Beach, next to the newer Hauula Congregational Church.

Trails

The Division of Forestry & Wildlife maintains three trails in the forest reserve behind Hauula: **Hauula Loop** (2½ miles), **Maakua Gulch** (three miles) and **Maakua Ridge** (2½ miles). All three trails are through a hunting area, and head into some beautiful hills. Hauula Loop and Maakua Ridge trails have good views, while the Maakua Gulch Trail crosses a stream and leads to a waterfall and pool.

The trailhead to all three is at a bend in Hauula Homestead Rd, about a quarter of a mile up from Kamehameha Highway. Camping is allowed along the trails. For information, trail maps and the required camping permits call the forestry at 587-0166.

LAIE

In ancient times Laie was thought to have been the sight of a *puuhonua* – a place where kapu breakers and fallen warriors could seek refuge. Today Laie is a Mormon town.

The first Mormon missionaries to Hawaii arrived in 1850. After an attempt to establish a Hawaiian 'City of Joseph' on Lanai failed amidst a land scandal the Mormons moved shop to Laie, and in 1865 they purchased 6000 acres of land. They cultivated the land and slowly expanded their influence.

In 1919 the Mormons constructed a **temple**, a smaller version of the one in Salt Lake City. It sits at the end of a promenade above their residential community at the foot of the Koolau Range. The temple is very stately and like nothing else on the windward coast. Although there's a visitor centre where eager guides will tell you all about Mormonism, tourists are not allowed to enter the temple itself.

Nearby is the Hawaii branch of **Brigham Young University**, with scholarship programmes bringing in students from islands throughout the Pacific.

Information

Laie Shopping Center, about half a mile north of the Polynesian Cultural Center, has restaurants, a coin laundry and a Bank of Hawaii.

Polynesian Cultural Center

The Polynesian Cultural Center (☎ 293-3333), called PCC by locals, is a 'nonprofit' organisation belonging to the Mormon Church. The centre draws about 900,000 tourists a year, more than any other attraction on Oahu with the exception of the USS Arizona Memorial.

The park has seven theme villages representing Samoa, New Zealand, Fiji, Tahiti, Tonga, the Marquesas and Hawaii. They have authentic-looking huts and ceremonial houses, many elaborately built with twisted sennit ropes and hand-carved posts. The huts hold weavings, tapa cloth, feather work and other handicrafts.

People of Polynesian descent in native garb demonstrate poi pounding, coconut frond weaving, dances, games and the like. There's also a re-creation of an old mission house and a missionary chapel representative of those found throughout Polynesia in the mid-1800s.

Many of the people working here are Pacific Island students at the nearby Brigham Young University, who earn their college expenses in this way while providing PCC a source of inexpensive labour. Not all students end up at the 'village' of their home islands. Apparently there are more Samoans than Hawaiians, for instance, so you may well find a Samoan student demonstrating Hawaiian weavings. People are amiable and you could easily spend a few hours wandering around chatting or trying to become familiar with a craft or two.

The admission price includes boat rides along the waterway that winds through the park, and the Pageant of the Long Canoes, a sort of trumped-up floating talent show at 1, 2, 3 and 4 pm.

The theme park is open from 12.30 to 6 pm daily except Sundays. The last half hour of the day ends with a grand finale canoe pageant that's worth catching if you've dished out the cost of admission.

Although PCC is interesting and is, to a surprising degree, sensitively presented, it is also very touristy and hard to recommend when the admission price is $25 for adults and $12.50 for children aged 5 to 11.

The 'Buffet-Show Plus' ticket, which costs $40.50 for adults and $23.50 for children, includes a buffet dinner and evening Polynesian show as well. The buffet is a mass production with uninspired cafeteria food. There's also a luau for an extra $10, with much the same food and the addition of an imu-baked pig.

The Polynesian song and dance show runs from 7.30 to 9 pm. It's partly authentic, partly Hollywood-style and much like an enthusiastic college production with elaborate sets and costumes.

Laie Beaches

The 1½ miles of beach fronting the town of Laie between Malaekahana State Recreation Area and Laie Point is used by surfers, bodysurfers and windsurfers.

Thatched hut

Pounders, half a mile south of the main entrance to PCC, is an excellent bodysurfing beach, but the shorebreak, as the name of the beach implies, can be brutal. There's a strong winter current. The area around the old landing is usually the calmest. Summer swimming is generally good and the beach is sandy.

From **Laie Point** there's a good view of the mountains to the south and of tiny offshore islands. The island to the left with the hole in it is Kukuihoolua, otherwise known as Puka Rock.

To get to Laie Point, head makai on Anemoku St, opposite the Laie Shopping Center, then turn right on Naupaka St and go straight to the end.

Malaekahana State Recreation Area

Malaekahana Beach stretches between Makahoa Point to the north and Kalanai Point to the south. The long narrow sandy beach is backed by ironwoods. Swimming is good year round, although there are occasionally strong currents in winter. It's a popular family beach and good for most water activities, including swimming, bodysurfing, surfing and windsurfing.

Kalanai Point, the main section of the state park, is less than a mile north of Laie and has picnic tables, barbecue grills, camping, restrooms and showers. Papaya trees heavy with fruit grow inland of the picnic and camping areas. It may be hard to find a ripe one however as they're picked regularly.

Mokuauia (Goat Island), a state bird sanctuary just offshore, has a nice sandy cove with good swimming and snorkelling. It's possible to wade over to the island – best when the tide is low and the water's calm. Be careful of the shallow coral and sea urchins.

You can also snorkel across to Goat Island and off its beaches. There's sometimes a rip current off the windward end of the island, although that's where the deeper water is.

Camping Malaekahana has the best camping grounds at this end of the windward coast. You can camp in the park's main Kalanai Point section for free if you have a

state park permit. Tent sites on this side are seldom crowded, although weekends and summer are busier.

You can also rent a cabin or camp for a fee in the Kahuku section of the park, which has a separate entrance off the highway three-quarters of a mile north of the main park entrance. This section of the park is secured at night.

An office at the Kahuku end handles the rentals. Check-in is from 3 to 5 pm and the gates are locked to vehicles between 6 pm and 8 am. There's a one-bedroom cabin for $25 for up to five people and four three-bedroom cabins for $40 for up to 10 people.

All are old, rustic and not well maintained but do have indoor bathrooms, refrigerators, stoves, hot water and musty mattresses on the floor. Linens and cookware are not provided.

Cabins are often booked solid on weekends, although mid-week arrivals can occasionally get a cabin on the spot. Tent camping in this section costs $3 per person. While reservations (☎ 293-1736) are preferred, except for holiday weekends in summer, walk-in campers can almost always get a tent site.

The state is set to build 'temporary' huts for homeless families on the Kahuku side of the park and it's unclear what effect that will have on the nearby camping.

Places to Stay

Laniloa Lodge (☎ 293-9282, (800) LANILOA), 55-109 Laniloa St, Laie, HI 96762, is a two-storey motel with 47 rooms surrounding a courtyard pool. While it's not special, it's comfortable enough and the management is friendly.

Each room has a lanai, cable TV, tub, air-con and mini-refrigerator. Rates are $79 for one or two people, $89 for three or four, and include a continental breakfast. They have a package deal which adds on a Thrifty rental car for $10 more.

It's also possible to find vacation rental signs in front of private houses around this area.

Places to Eat

Laie Chop Suey in the Laie Shopping Center is a local-style eatery with standard Chinese fare. Most dishes cost $4 to $6. Plate lunches with two dishes and rice cost $4 before 3 pm. It's open from 10 am to 8.45 pm Monday to Saturday.

The shopping centre also has a grocery store, a *Burger King* and a *Domino's Pizza*.

Laie's *McDonald's*, on the highway at the north end of PCC, has a little more character than the usual McDonald's. Originally built as a restaurant for the Laniloa Lodge next door, the building somewhat resembles a Polynesian longhouse with a peaked roof. Inside there's even a small waterfall. When the lodge's restaurant folded, McDonald's moved in.

KAHUKU

Kahuku is a former sugar town with little wooden cane houses lining the road. The mill in the centre of town belonged to the Kahuku Plantation which produced sugar here from 1890 until 1971 when it closed. The mill was a relatively small concern, unable to keep up with the increasingly mechanised competition of the bigger mills.

Kahuku Sugar Mill

A fledgeling shopping centre has been set up inside the old sugar mill, with small shops ringing the old machinery. The mill's enormous gears, flywheels and pipes have been painted in bright colours to help visitors visualise how a sugar mill works. The steam systems are red, the cane juice systems light green, hydraulic systems dark blue and so forth. It looks like something out of *Modern Times* – you can almost imagine Charlie Chaplin caught up in the giant gears.

The centre has not been wildly successful, but there's a restaurant, food mart, gas station and a handful of gift shops in the complex.

Amorient Aquafarm

Less than a mile north of the old mill is the Amorient Aquafarm. Founded in 1978, the farm has 143 one-acre ponds producing both saltwater and freshwater shrimp. The ponds are drained to harvest the shrimp.

You can get a fresh shrimp cocktail at the farm food stand for $4, shrimp tempura for $7.50, or you can take home live prawns for $10 a pound. Zoning rules restrict them to selling only what they raise but you can pick up drinks in town or at Tanaka's store just north of the farm.

Water birds are attracted to the ponds like kids to a candy store. They include night heron, coots, stilts, black swans, ducks and cattle egrets. If you're taking the circle-island bus and want a break, it stops right in front.

As you continue along to the North Shore there are papaya farms, banana trees, a university livestock station, and some high-tech windmills on the hill.

Turtle Bay Hilton

The Turtle Bay Hilton, the sole hotel in Kahuku, is not exactly welcoming, with its guard gate and parking fees. But the hotel does front shallow **Kuilima Cove**, which is one of the area's best swimming spots.

Parking costs $1 for the first half-hour and 50 cents for each additional half-hour – which seems a fleecing considering the hotel is out in the middle of nowhere.

Kaihalulu Beach

Kaihalulu is a beautiful curved white sand beach fronted by ironwoods and still largely in a natural state. Although a shoreline lava shelf and rocky bottom make the beach poor for swimming, it's good for beachcombing and you can walk east about a mile to Kahuku Point. Local fishers cast thrownets from the shore and pole fish from the point. The dirt road just in from the beach is also used as a horse trail.

To get there turn into the Turtle Bay Hilton and just before the guard booth turn right into an unmarked parking lot, where there are free spaces for beachgoers. It's a five-minute walk out to the beach. There are no facilities.

Places to Stay

The *Turtle Bay Hilton & Country Club*

(☎ 293-8811, (800) 445-8667), Kahuku, HI 96731, is a self-contained resort and the only 1st-class hotel on the windward and north shores. It's on Kuilima Point, between Turtle Bay and Kuilima Cove. All 486 rooms have ocean views. Room rates range from $160 to $305, with suites up to $1300. There's an 18-hole golf course, two pools, stables and 10 tennis courts.

Places to Eat

J-Jem Restaurant at the Kahuku Sugar Mill serves standard breakfast and lunch fare at moderate prices.

Ahi's Restaurant, on a dirt road south of the Kahuku Sugar Mill, is popular for seafood. Dishes include local prawns in various forms, including scampi, tempura and deep-fried. It's open from 11 am to 9 pm Monday to Saturday and has live Hawaiian entertainment on Fridays.

There are also a few restaurants at the *Turtle Bay Hilton*. The cheapest eats are at the Bay View Lounge, a drinking spot which sometimes has a taco bar for $5.49 from 5.30 to 8.30 pm. The Bay View sports a disco from 9 pm to 1 am on Fridays and Saturdays. The hotel's Palm Terrace has uninspired buffets for lunch (11 am to 2 pm) and dinner. The cost is $15.95, except dinner on weekends when it's $19.95.

Central Oahu

Central Oahu is the saddle between the Waianae Mountains on the west and the Koolau Mountains on the east.

Three routes lead north from Honolulu to Wahiawa, the town smack in the middle of Oahu. The freeway, H-2, is the fastest route and Highway 750, the farthest west, is the most scenic. Highway 99 catches local traffic as it runs through Mililani, a modern, nondescript residential community.

Most people just zoom up through central Oahu on their way to the North Shore. If your time is limited this isn't a bad idea. There are a few sights along the way and some nice

scenery, but Wahiawa doesn't really warrant much more than a zip through anyway.

From Wahiawa two routes then head north to Haleiwa on the North Shore. They are both fine scenic roads and if you're not circling the island you might as well go up one and down the other.

Highway 750

Highway 750 (Kunia Rd) adds a few miles to the drive through central Oahu but if you have the time it's worth it. Follow H-1 to the Kunia Rd/Hwy 750 exit, three miles west of where H-1 and H-2 divide.

After you turn up Hwy 750 you enter plantation lands, with sugar cane spreading out as the road leads up hill. This route runs along the foothills of the Waianae Range and the countryside is all agricultural from here to Schofield Barracks.

Up the road 2½ miles, a narrow strip of corn fields acts as a boundary between cane to the south and pineapple to the north. In these fields the Garst Seed Co grows three generations of corn each year, which makes it possible to develop hybrids of corn seed at triple the rate it would take on the mainland. The little bags placed over each ear of corn prevent them from being cross pollinated.

Further north is one of the most scenic pineapple fields in Hawaii. There are no buildings and no development – just red earth carpeted with long green strips of pineapples stretching to the edge of the mountains.

From the Hawaii Country Club up the road, there's a distant view of Honolulu all the way to Diamond Head.

Kunia

Kunia, a little town in the midst of the pineapple fields, is home to the field workers employed by Del Monte. If you want to see what a plantation town looks like turn west off Hwy 750 on Kunia Drive, which makes a 1¼-mile loop through the town.

Rows of green-grey wooden houses stand on low stilts. The simple buildings have corrugated tin roofs and there are chickens in the yards. People take pride in their little gardens, with bougainvillea and orange trumpet vines adding a splash of brightness to an already lush green area.

Kunia Drive intersects the highway at about 5½ miles north of the intersection of Hwy 750 and H-1 (there's a store and post office near the turn-off) and again at the six-mile marker.

Kolekole Pass

Kolekole is the gap in the Waianae Mountains that Japanese fighter planes flew through on their way to bomb Pearl Harbor. The flight scene was recreated here 30 years later for the shooting of the film *Tora, Tora, Tora.*

The Kolekole Pass, at an elevation of 1724 feet, sits above Schofield Barracks on military property. It can be visited as long as the base isn't on some sort of military alert.

Access is through Foote Gate, on Hwy 750, a third of a mile south of its intersection with Hwy 99. After entering the gate, take the first left onto Road A, then the first right onto Lyman Rd. The drive is 5¼ miles up past the barracks, golf course and bayonet assault course. The parking lot is opposite the hilltop with the big white cross, which is visible from miles away.

The five-minute walk to the top of the pass ends at a clearing with a view straight down to the Waianae Coast. The large ribbed stone that sits atop the ridge here is said to be the embodiment of a woman named Kolekole who took the form of this stone so as to become the perpetual guardian of the pass.

Along the side of the stone are a series of ridges, one of them draining down from a bowl-like depression on the top. Shaped perfectly for a guillotine, the depression has given rise to a more recent 'legend' that Kolekole served as a sacrificial stone for the beheading of defeated chiefs and warriors. The fact that military bases flank both sides of the pass has no doubt had a little influence on this one.

Just west of the pass the road continues through a Navy base down to the Waianae Coast, but you can't take it. The Navy base is a stockyard for nuclear weapons and there's no public access through their side.

WAHIAWA

Wahiawa is a GI town. Just about every fast-food chain you can think of is there – and as if that weren't enough, one local sit-down restaurant in the middle of town has even named itself 'Fast Food'. Tattoo parlours and pawn shops are the town's main refinements; if you're looking for a little excitement there are some rough and tumble bars.

To go through town and visit the botanic garden, healing stones and royal birthstones, take Kamehameha Highway (which is Hwy 80 as it goes through town, although it's Hwy 99 before and after Wahiawa). To make the bypass around Wahiawa, stick with Hwy 99.

Wahiawa Botanical Garden

The Wahiawa Botanical Garden, 1396 California Ave, is less than a mile east of the Kamehameha Highway. What started out in the 1920s as a site for forestry experiments by the Hawaii Sugar Planters' Association is now a 27-acre city park with grand old trees around a wooded ravine.

The park is a nice, shady place to take a stroll. Interesting 60-year-old exotics such as cinnamon, chicle and allspice are grouped in one area. Tree ferns, loulu palms and other Hawaiian natives are in another. The trees are identified by markers. The air is thick with birdsong.

The garden is open from 9 am to 4 pm daily. Admission to the park is free, as is a brochure describing some of the trees.

Healing Stones

One of the odder sights to be labelled with a HVB marker is the 'Healing Stones' caged inside a small concrete block 'temple'. It's next to the Methodist church on California Ave, half a mile west of its intersection with Kamehameha Highway.

The main stone is thought to have been the gravestone of a powerful Hawaiian chief. Although the chief's original burial place was in a field a mile away, the stone was

back to the 12th century. It was said that if a woman lay properly against the stones while giving birth, her child would be blessed by the gods. Many of Oahu's great chiefs were born at this site.

These stones are one of only two documented birthstone sites in Hawaii (the other's in Kauai). Many of the petroglyphs on the stones are of recent origin, but the eroded circular patterns are original.

To get to them from town, go three-quarters of a mile north on Kamehameha Highway from its intersection with California Ave. Turn left onto the red dirt road directly opposite Whitmore Ave. The stones are a quarter of a mile down through a pineapple field, amongst a stand of eucalyptus and coconut trees. If it's been raining, be aware that the red clay can cake onto your car tyres, and once back on the paved road the car may slide as if it's driving on ice.

WAHIAWA TO THE NORTH SHORE

Highways 803 and 99 both lead from Wahiawa through pineapple country and down across cane fields on the way to the North Shore.

Highway 803 (Kaukonahua Rd) is a slightly shorter way to Mokuleia than Hwy 99 and about the same distance to Haleiwa, although it by-passes some of the attractions. As Hwy 803 approaches Thompson Corner the road is lined with ironwood trees and has fine mountain and coastal views.

Highway 99 (Kamehameha Highway) passes the pineapple garden, from where it's 6½ miles to Weed Circle. At Weed Circle, you can go left to Mokuleia or right (Hwy 83) to Haleiwa.

About two miles north-west of Wahiawa on either road, you can see Kolekole Pass on your left.

Pineapple Garden

There's a pineapple demonstration garden in a triangle at the intersection of Hwy 99 and Hwy 80.

'Smooth cayenne', the commercial variety of pineapple grown in Hawaii, is shown in various growth stages. Each plant

moved long ago to a graveyard at this site. In the 1920s people thought the stone had healing powers and thousands made pilgrimages to it before interest waned. The housing development and church came later, taking over the graveyard and leaving the stones sitting on the sidewalk.

There are many stories about people who built above the old graveyard being beset with bad luck, divorces and other misfortunes.

A local group with roots in India who sees a spiritual connection between Hawaiian and Indian beliefs now visit the temple, so you might see coconuts, flowers or little elephant statues placed around the stones. The story is actually more interesting than the sight, however.

Royal Birthstones

Kukaniloko, a group of royal birthstones where queens gave birth, is just north of Wahiawa. The stones are thought to date produces just two pineapples. The first takes nearly two years to reach maturity, the second about one year more. Other commercial varieties grown in Australia, the Philippines and Brazil are on display, as well as many varieties of decorative bromeliads.

You can pull off to the side of the road and walk through on your own at any time.

Dole Pineapple Pavilion

The Dole Pineapple Pavilion is a gift shop on Hwy 99 less than a mile north of the pineapple garden.

You can get a cup of pineapple juice for 80 cents or a pineapple freeze for $1.50. They also sell pineapples ready to take home – three for $8.25. It's open from 9 am to 5.30 pm daily.

Dole's processing plant is across the street and pineapple fields surround the area. A few miles north the country changes from pineapple to cane fields, and broad views of the ocean open up.

North Shore

Oahu's North Shore is synonymous with surfing and prime winter waves. Sunset Beach, the Banzai Pipeline and Waimea Bay are among the world's top surf spots and draw some of the best international surfers.

Other North Shore surf breaks may be less well known but with names like Himalayas and Avalanche, they're not exactly for neophytes.

On winter weekends convoys of cars drive up from Honolulu to watch the action from the beach. You can beat much of the traffic simply by coming up on a weekday.

It's believed that the earliest Polynesians to arrive on Oahu were drawn to the North Shore by the region's rich fishing grounds, cooling trade winds and moderate rain. The areas around Mokuleia, Haleiwa and Waimea all once had sizeable Hawaiian settlements. Abandoned taro patches still remain in their upland valleys.

By the turn of the present century the

Oahu Railroad & Land Company had extended the railroad around Kaena Point and along the entire North Shore, linking the area with Honolulu and bringing in the first beachgoers from the city. Hotels and private beach houses sprang up, but when the railroad stopped running in the 1940s the hotels shut down for good. Sections of track are still found along many of the beaches.

Waikiki surfers started taking on North Shore waves in the late 1950s and big-time surf competitions followed a few years later. Each December there are three major surf competitions, known as the Triple Crown, with prize purses reaching six figures.

Surf mania prevails even in the restaurants, which serve up omelettes with names like 'Pumping Surf' and 'Wipe Out'. Half the North Shore population can be found on the beach when the surf's up.

Swimming

With the exception of Haleiwa Beach Park, North Shore beaches are notorious for treacherous winter swimming conditions. There are powerful currents along the entire shore. If it doesn't look calm as a lake, it's probably not safe for swimming or snorkelling.

During summer, waves along the whole North Shore can mellow right out. Shark's Cove is then a prime snorkelling and diving spot and Waimea Bay is a popular swimming and snorkelling beach.

WAIALUA

Waialua is a quiet little sugar town about a mile west of Haleiwa. Waialua Sugar Mill, the smaller of Oahu's two working sugar mills, is owned by Castle & Cooke.

Down by the mill the Sugar Bar, in an old Bank of Hawaii building, is the town's watering hole. The Sugar Bar has live local entertainment a few nights a week.

The most scenic route between Haleiwa and Waialua is along Haleiwa Rd.

Kukui Nut Factory

The Kukui Nut Factory, 66-935 Kaukonahua Rd, sells jewellery and skin oil products

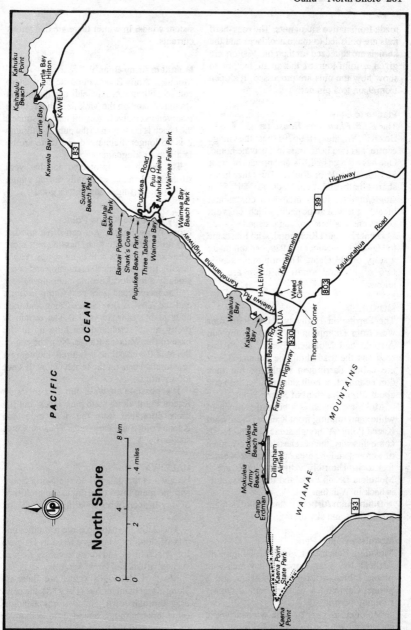

made from native kukui nuts. The rock-hard nuts are polished to make necklaces and the kernels are squeezed for their oil. Visitors are given a mini-tour of the small factory to show how the nuts are processed. It's open from 9 am to 5 pm daily.

Places to Stay

The *B&B Plantation House* (☎ 637-4988), Box 857, Waialua, HI 96791, near the village centre, has two bedrooms in a private home. One has a queen bed, TV and private bath for $65 for a single or double. The other has a shared bath and twin beds for $45/55 a single/double. Rates include a continental breakfast served at the patio, which looks out across endless fields of sugar cane.

Owner Nattalia Richmond, who first came to Hawaii by steamer in 1929, can tell many a story of old Oahu. The minimum stay is two nights and small children are not allowed.

MOKULEIA

The Farrington Highway (Hwy 930) runs west from Thompson Corner to Dillingham Airfield and Mokuleia Beach. (Both this road and the road along the Waianae Coast are called Farrington Highway, but they don't connect, as both sides reach a dead end about 2½ miles short of Kaena Point.)

Mokuleia Beach is a six-mile stretch of white sand running from Kaiaka Bay toward Kaena Point. Although some GIs and locals come this way, the beaches don't draw much of a crowd and the area has sort of a boonies feel to it. The only visitor facilities are at Mokuleia Beach Park, and the nearest store is back in Waialua.

Dillingham Airfield is the take-off site for glider rides and sky diving.

Mokuleia Beach Park

Mokuleia Beach Park, opposite Dillingham Airfield, has a large open grassy area with picnic tables, restrooms, showers and a phone. Camping is allowed with a county camping permit.

Mokuleia is popular with windsurfers in spring and autumn and is known for its con-

sistent winds. In winter there are dangerous currents.

Mokuleia Army Beach

Mokuleia Army Beach, opposite the western end of Dillingham Airfield, has the widest stretch of sand on the Mokuleia shore. Once reserved exclusively for military personnel, the beach is now open to the public, although it is no longer maintained and there are no facilities or lifeguards.

The beach is unprotected and has very strong rip currents, especially during winter high surf. Surfing is sometimes good.

Army Beach to Kaena Point

From Army Beach, you can drive another 1½ miles down the road, passing still more white sand beaches with aqua waters. You'll usually find someone shorecasting and occasionally a few local people camping.

The paved road goes past Camp Erdman and the YMCA Boy Scout Camp and then ends at old railroad tracks. The terrain is pretty much scrubland reaching up to the base of the Waianae Range. Near the end of the road the coastline is littered, including a few torched cars on the beach below. It's not too inviting.

It's possible to walk the 2½ miles to Kaena Point along state park lands, but it's more attractive from the other side (see Kaena Point State Park in the Waianae Coast section).

HALEIWA

Haleiwa is the gateway to the North Shore and the main town catering to the multitude of day-trippers who make the circle-island ride.

The 2500 townspeople are a multiethnic mix of families who have lived in Haleiwa for generations and more recently arrived surfers, artists and New-Age folks.

Most of Haleiwa's shops are lined up along Kamehameha Ave (Hwy 83), the main drag through town. Haleiwa has a picturesque boat harbour, bounded on both sides by beach parks. One side is known for its winter surfing, the other for the North Shore's safest year-round swimming.

The Anahulu River, which flows out along the boat harbour, is spanned by Rainbow Bridge, so nicknamed for its distinctive arches. Take a glimpse up the river from the bridge. It's still a lushly green scene and it's easy to imagine how it must have looked in ancient Hawaii when the riverbanks were lined with taro patches.

In the summer of 1832, John and Ursula Emerson, the first missionaries to the North Shore, built a grass house and missionary school beside the Anahulu River. They called the school Haleiwa. Over time the name, which means house (hale) of the great frigate bird (iwa), came to refer to the entire village.

Matsumoto's
For many people the circle-island drive isn't complete without lining up at Matsumoto's tin-roofed general store for shave ice.

Hawaiian shave ice is a bit like a snow cone, although better because the ice is finer. The cloyingly sweet syrups are no different, however. Shave ice at Matsumoto's costs from 80 cents for the small plain version to $1.50 for a large with ice cream and azuki beans.

Liliuokalani Protestant Church
The church opposite Matsumoto's takes its name from Queen Liliuokalani, who spent summer on the shores of Anahulu River and attended services here. Although the church dates from 1832, the current building was built in 1961. As late as the 1940s services were held entirely in Hawaiian.

Of most interest is the unusual seven-dial clock which Queen Liliuokalani gave the church in 1892. The clock shows the hour, day, month and year as well as the phases of the moon. The queen's 12-letter name replaces the numerals on the clock face. One hundred years later it still keeps accurate time. The church is open whenever the minister is in, which is usually in the mornings.

Shops & Galleries
Kaala Art, next to Cafe Haleiwa, has some nice tapa which is hand-made by a Tongan woman who lives on Oahu. The shop also sells hand-screened T-shirts, hand woven silk clothing from Thailand and tie-dyed and printed pareos, some from Bali and others made locally.

Wyland Gallery, 66-150 Kamehameha Ave, features paintings and sculptures of whales. Marine artist Wyland is best known for his many 'Whaling Wall' murals splashed on shopping centre walls around the islands.

Island Images, on the main road by the boat harbour, has prints of local and rural scenes, such as seascapes and plantation shacks.

Haleiwa Shopping Plaza has a Bank of Hawaii, the Haleiwa Super Market and restaurants. Across the street is the more colourful Fujioka's supermarket. The bulletin boards in front of both supermarkets are good places to check for rooms for rent, surfboards for sale and the like.

Surf-N-Sea (☎ 637-9887), 62-595 Kamehameha Highway, just north of Rainbow Bridge, rents surfboards, boogie boards, windsurfing equipment, dive gear and snorkel sets. They also offer surfing and windsurfing lessons, dive trips and sport fishing and sell new and used surfboards and sailboards.

Kaiaka Recreation Area
The 53-acre Kaiaka Recreation Area is on Kaiaka Bay, about a mile west of town. This would be a good place for a picnic as there are shady ironwood trees, but the beaches in town are better choices for swimming. Two streams empty out into the bay, muddying up the beach after heavy rainstorms. There's a view of the Waialua sugar mill and it's all quite peaceful and quiet. Kaiaka has restrooms, picnic tables, showers and seven campsites. Camping is by permit from the county.

Haleiwa Alii Beach Park
Surfing is king at Haleiwa Alii Beach Park. This is the site of several tournaments in the winter, when north swells can bring waves as high as 20 feet.

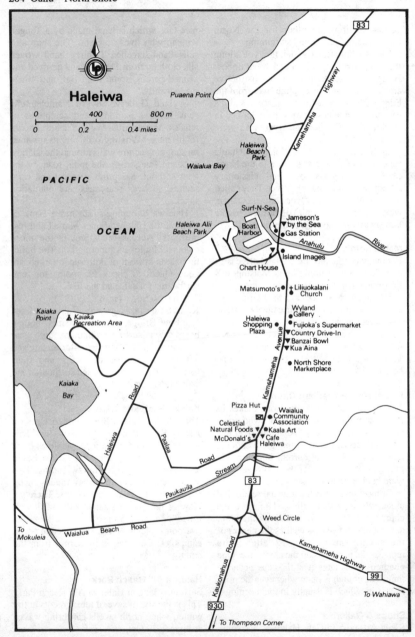

Haleiwa

PACIFIC

OCEAN

Puaena Point

Haleiwa
Beach
Park

Waialua Bay

Haleiwa Alii
Beach Park

Surf-N-Sea

Boat
Harbor

Jameson's
by the Sea

Gas Station

Anahulu

River

Island Images

Chart House

Matsumoto's

Liliuokalani
Church

Wyland
Gallery

Fujioka's Supermarket

Haleiwa
Shopping
Plaza

Country Drive-In

Banzai Bowl

Kua Aina

North Shore
Marketplace

Kaiaka
Point

Kaiaka
Recreation Area

Kaiaka
Bay

Haleiwa

Road

Paalaa

Road

Pizza Hut

Waialua
Community
Association

Celestial
Natural Foods

Kaala Art

McDonald's

Cafe
Haleiwa

Paukauila

Stream

Kamehameha

Avenue

83

Weed Circle

To
Mokuleia

Waialua

Beach

Road

Kaukonahua

Road

Kamehameha Highway

99

To Wahiawa

930

To Thompson Corner

0   400   800 m
0   0.2   0.4 miles

Kamehameha

Highway

83

When waves are five feet and under, lots of younger kids bring their boards out. Any time they're six feet or better there are also strong currents and it's more suited to experienced surfers. The county (☎ 637-5051) gives free surfing lessons here from 9 am to noon on Saturdays and Sundays from September to May.

The 20-acre park has restrooms, showers, picnic tables and a lifeguard tower. The shallow areas on the southern side of the beach are generally the calmest for swimming.

Haleiwa Beach Park

Haleiwa Beach Park is across the bridge over the Anahulu River, on the eastern shore of Waialua Bay. The beach is protected by a shallow shoal and a breakwater. The waters are usually very calm and see little wave action, although north swells occasionally ripple into the bay.

In addition to full beach facilities the 13-acre county park has basketball and volleyball courts, an exercise area, and a softball field. It also has a good view of Kaena Point.

The Anahulu River enters the bay just south of the beach, and if it's been raining hard the water may be full of sediment. It's not an overly attractive beach.

Places to Stay

There's no 'established' accommodation in Haleiwa, although people occasionally rent out rooms in their homes. Check the bulletin boards at the entrances of Haleiwa Super Market and Fujioka's Supermarket. The other option is camping which is allowed Friday to Tuesday nights at Kaiaka Recreation Area. For details on permits, see Camping in the Accommodation section at the start of this chapter.

Places to Eat

The *China Inn* in the North Shore Marketplace has filling meals at low prices. One entree is $2.50, two are $3.50 and three are $4.25, each including noodles or fried rice. If you select carefully the food is very good for the price. Cashew chicken and dishes with lots of vegetables are a good choice, but batter-dipped dishes are heavy on the batter. It's open from 9 am to 10 pm daily, except Mondays.

The *Coffee Gallery* in the North Shore Marketplace is a fine alternative to the burger and plate-lunch scene. It has steamed coffees, scones, Belgian waffles, lox and bagels and the like at quite reasonable prices. Breakfast is served from 6 to 11 am on weekdays and from 7 am on weekends. At lunch it's quiche, salads and sandwiches for under $5. They also make a good smoothie for $2.50 and there's open-air seating at the side of the cafe.

Cafe Haleiwa, on the right as you come into town, is a great inexpensive eatery, popular with surfers. Portions are huge and the food is good. It's a simple place with signed surfing photos on the wall and the kitchen at the end of the room. A large burrito filled with sauteed vegies and served with terrific home fries costs $4.95. You can get two large whole-wheat pancakes loaded with blueberries for $2 in a half order, a meal in itself. Daily specials include inexpensive fresh fish dishes. It's open from 6 am to 2 pm weekdays and from 7 am to 2 pm weekends. On weekends arrive early to avoid waiting outside in a queue.

Celestial Natural Foods, opposite Cafe Haleiwa, is a health-food store with bulk foods, trail mix, fresh produce, Alta Dena kefir and yoghurt and just about everything else you'd expect to find. Prices are reasonable. In the back of the store is *Galaxy Juice Works*, open from 10 am to 6 pm. You can get a bowl of vegetable chilli over brown rice for $1.75, sandwiches for $3 to $5, salads for $2 to $4, Tex-Mex food and smoothies.

Country Drive-In, opposite the Haleiwa Shopping Plaza, serves breakfast until 11.30 am. Two eggs, coffee and toast costs $2 or try a 'tube omelette' containing asparagus and cheese for $3.50. There are 21 different plate lunches, including some Korean dishes, for $4 to $4.75.

Banzai Bowl next door is a sit-down place with the same food at slightly higher prices.

Nearby *Kua Aina* is a popular sandwich and burger shop. Prices range from $3 for a cheese sandwich to $4.40 for a mahimahi sandwich.

Chart House (☎ 637-8005), at the boat harbour, has meat and seafood dinners from $16 to $30 from 5 pm nightly. The price includes the salad bar which has caviar, hearts of palm, artichoke hearts, fresh fruit and breads in addition to the usual greens. You can get the salad bar alone for $12.75, or on weekdays go for the early bird dinner from 5 to 6 pm which pairs prime rib, teriyaki chicken or fish with the salad bar for $14. Lunch, available from 11 am to 2.30 pm, includes sandwiches, salads and hot dishes in the $5 to $9 range.

Rosie's Cantina in the Haleiwa Shopping Plaza has reasonable Mexican food, although it's best to stick with traditional dishes. Two enchiladas cost $5.25, while combo plates with rice and beans are $7 for one item, $9 for two. Salads, which consist largely of brown-edged lettuce, are not recommended. Rosie's is open from 7 am to 10 pm.

Steamer's is also in the Haleiwa Shopping Plaza. At lunch, salads, fish sandwiches and burgers cost $6 to $7, while hot entrees cost a few dollars more. At dinner fresh fish is the speciality and costs $16. Lunch is from 11 am to 3 pm and dinner from 5.30 to 9.30 pm.

After dinner on Wednesdays through Saturdays, Steamer's becomes the North Shore's main dance spot. Weekdays tend to be an oldies scene, while on weekends rock, reggae and 'surf' bands are featured. The cover is usually $2.

Jameson's by the Sea (☎ 637-4336), north of the bridge, is Haleiwa's up-market seaside eatery. Seafood is a speciality. Dinner is served upstairs from 5 pm nightly, except Mondays, in a room with white tablecloths, ceiling fans and views across the boat harbour down to Kaena Point. Dishes such as seafood diablo or shrimp curry with mango chutney start around $16. It's more casual downstairs, where meals are served in the pub or out on the porch from 11 am to about 9 pm daily, with sandwiches and salads in the $7 to $10 range.

WAIMEA

Waimea Valley was once heavily settled. The lowlands were terraced in taro, the valley walls dotted with house sites and the ridges topped with heiaus. Just about every crop grown in Hawaii thrived in the valley, including a rare pink taro fancied by the alii.

Waimea Stream, now blocked at the beach, used to open into the bay and canoes could be paddled upstream to the villages. The sport of surfing was immensely popular here centuries ago, when the early Hawaiians rode the world's top waves on their long boards.

Deforestation above the valley contributed to a devastating flood in Waimea in 1894. In addition to water damage an enormous volume of mud washed through the valley, so much so that it permanently altered the shape of Waimea's shore. After the flood, most residents abandoned the valley and resettled elsewhere.

Waimea Bay Beach Park

Waimea Bay is a very beautiful, deeply inset bay with turquoise blue waters and a wide

---

When Captain Cook's ships sailed into Waimea to collect water in 1779, shortly after Cook's death on the Big Island, an entry in the ship's log noted how uncommonly beautiful and picturesque the valley was.

In 1792 Captain Vancouver, who had been an officer on one of Cook's vessels, anchored in Waimea. While three of his men were collecting water on shore they were attacked and killed. It's thought that their bodies were taken up to Puu O Mahuka Heiau on the ridge above the beach and sacrificed. When Vancouver returned a year later demanding justice, the high chief turned over three islanders. Although Vancouver doubted that they had anything to do with the murders, he had come to set an example so he ordered their execution. ∎

white sand beach almost 1500 feet long. Ancient Hawaiians believed its waters were sacred.

Waimea Bay's mood changes with the seasons: it can be tranquil and as flat as a lake in summer, and savage with incredible surf and the islands' meanest riptides in winter.

Waimea has Hawaii's biggest surf and holds the record for the highest waves ever ridden in international competition. As at Sunset Beach, the huge north swells bring out crowds of spectators who throng to watch Waimea surfers perform their near-suicidal feats on waves of up to 35 feet.

On winter's calmer days the boogie boarders are out in force, but even then sets come in hard and people get pounded. Winter water activities here are not for novices.

Usually the only time the water is calm enough for swimming and snorkelling is from June to September. The best snorkelling is around the rocks on the left of the bay.

Waimea Bay Beach Park is the most popular North Shore beach. There are showers, restrooms, picnic tables, a phone, and a lifeguard on duty daily. Parking is often tight.

Waimea Falls Park
Waimea Falls Park (☎ 638-8511), across the highway from Waimea Bay Beach Park, is a botanical garden, cultural preserve and tourist park in one.

The main park trail leads three-quarters of a mile up the Waimea Valley to a waterfall, passing extensive naturalised gardens that include sections of ginger, hibiscus, heleconia and medicinal plants. Along the way there are ancient stone platforms and terraces and some replicas of thatched buildings the early Hawaiians might have used.

Hula dances, Hawaiian games and other demonstrations are given during the day. A cliff diver plunges 60 feet into the waterfall pool five times a day to thrill spectators. Other than at dive times, the pool is a fine swimming hole.

The park can be pleasant to wander through and the valley is naturally pretty but the cost of admission is high at $14.95 for

adults, $8.95 for children aged six to 12. Those under six are admitted free. The best deal is to come at 4 pm when the rate drops to $6.50 for adults and $4.50 for children. Although the demonstrations stop at that point, the grounds are less crowded and more pleasant for strolling. The park is open from 10 am to 6 or 7 pm daily and there's an in-park restaurant called the *Proud Peacock*.

One-hour moonlight walks are held twice monthly at 8.30 pm on or near the full-moon night. There's no fee for the walks, although a donation of $5 per family is suggested. Bus No 52 stops at the highway, half a mile from the park entrance.

St Peter & Paul Church
The church of St Peter & Paul stands beneath the tall unassuming tower on the northern side of Waimea Bay. The structure was originally a rock-crushing plant built to supply gravel for the construction of the highway in the 1930s. After it was abandoned, the Catholic church converted it into Oahu's most unlikely chapel.

Puu O Mahuka Heiau State Monument
Puu O Mahuka is a long low-walled platform heiau perched on a bluff above Waimea. The largest heiau on Oahu, its construction is attributed to the legendary menehunes.

The terraced stone walls are a couple of feet high, although most of the heiau is now overgrown. This was an incredible site for a temple and it's definitely worth a ride up for the view. It's also a fine place to watch the sunset.

Walk up above the left side of the heiau from the parking lot for a view of Waimea Valley and Waimea Bay. The plateaus rising above the southern side of the valley are covered with sugar cane. To the west, you can see all the way out along the coast to Kaena Point.

For a vitamin-C-rich treat, check out the guava trees down past the end of the parking lot.

To get to the heiau, turn up Pupukea Rd at the Foodland supermarket. The marked turn-off to the heiau is about half a mile up the road and from there it's three-quarters of a mile in. On the drive up there's a good view of Pupukea Beach Park.

Pupukea Beach Park

Pupukea Beach Park is a long beach along the highway that includes Three Tables on the left and Shark's Cove on the right. In the middle is Old Quarry, where low tide exposes a wonderful array of jagged rock formations and tide pools. This is a very scenic beach, with deep blue waters, a varied coast and a mix of lava and white sand beach. The rocks and tide pools are tempting to explore but be careful because they're razor sharp and if you slip it's easy to get a deep cut.

The waters off Pupukea Beach are a marine-life conservation district.

There are showers and restrooms in front of the Old Quarry. The beach entrance is opposite the Shell gas station.

Three Tables Three Tables, at the western end of the beach, gets its name from the ledges rising above the water. In summer when the waters are calm Three Tables has good snorkelling and diving. It's possible to see some action by snorkelling around the tables, but the best coral and fish as well as some small caves, lava tubes and arches are in deeper water farther out. This is a summer-only spot, however. In winter dangerous rip currents flow between the beach and the tables. Beware of sharp rocks and coral.

Shark's Cove Shark's Cove is beautiful both above and below the water's surface. The naming of the cove was done in jest – sharks aren't a particular problem.

In the summer, when the seas are calm, Shark's Cove has good snorkelling and swimming conditions as well as Oahu's most popular cavern dive. A fair number of beginner divers take lessons here, while the underwater caves will thrill advanced divers.

To get to the caves, swim out of the cove and around to the right. Some of the caves are very deep and labyrinthine, so caution

should be used exploring them. There have been a number of drownings in the caves.

The large boulders out on the end of the point to the far right of the cove are said to be followers of Pele. She gave them immortality by turning them to stone.

Ekuhai Beach Park

The main reason people come to Ekuhai Beach Park is to watch the pros surf the world-famous **Banzai Pipeline**, a few hundred feet to the left of the park.

The Pipeline breaks over a shallow coral reef and can be a death-defying wave to ride.

At Ekuhai Beach itself, many board riders and bodysurfers brave a hazardous current and ride the waves. Water conditions mellow out in summer, when it's good for swimming.

Ekuhai Beach Park is opposite the Sunset Beach Elementary School but roadside parking isn't permitted and they do tow cars away. To get to the beach, continue past the school and turn in opposite the big roadside totem that marks a souvenir shop. Then turn left on the beach road and go down to the parking lot. There's a lifeguard, restrooms, showers and a phone.

Sunset Beach Park

Sunset Beach Park is near the nine-mile marker. This roadside beach is Oahu's classic winter surf spot with incredible waves and challenging breaks. It's such a big name you expect a big beach, but it's just a little roadside attraction without even a sign. All the action is in the water.

Winter swells create powerful riptides. Even when the waves have mellowed in the summer, there's still an along-shore current for swimmers to deal with.

Portable toilets and a lifeguard tower are the only facilities. Opposite the beach you can find two small grocery stores; Sunset Diner, a plate lunch eatery; and a pizza shop with sandwiches, New York-style pizza and reasonably priced breakfasts.

Backyards, the surf break off Sunset Point at the northern end of the beach, draws a lot of top windsurfers. There's a shallow

Top: Petroglyphs, Puako, Big Island
Left & Right: Puuhonua O Honaunau National Historical Park, Big Island

Top: Kailua Pier, Kona, Big Island
Bottom: Waipio Valley, Big Island

reef and strong currents to contend with, but Backyards has the island's biggest waves for sailing.

Places to Stay

Backpackers (☎ 638-7838), 59-788 Kamehameha Highway, Haleiwa, HI 96712, opposite Three Tables at Pupukea Beach, is pretty much a surfers' hangout. It has a few different set-ups, most of it beach-house casual. The main house has four bunk beds to a room for $14 a bed, while a three-storey house behind it has double rooms for $35 to $45. Both houses have shared bathrooms and kitchens. Expect clutter and ageing furniture, but if you're just looking for a place to crash you can't beat the price.

A small beachfront motel across the road has eight studios with TVs, kitchens and great views. Units on the bottom floor have dorm beds for $16, while those on the top are rented out like hotel rooms for $70 to $85.

The third property, a few hundred yards away, consists of nine cottages. Dorm beds are $16 while the entire cabin, which sleeps six to eight people, costs $95 to $135. They make a pick-up at 7 am every morning from the airport and charge $5 for the ride.

Ke Iki Hale (☎ 638-8229), 59-579 Ke Iki Rd, Haleiwa, HI 96712, has a dozen units fronting a beautiful white sand beach just north of Pupukea Beach Park. The rates are $125/770 by the day/week for a one-bedroom duplex and $145/1015 for small two-bedroom units. There are also a couple of streetside units for $80.

The Vacation Place (☎ 638-7947), 59-420 Kamehameha Highway, Haleiwa, HI 96712, is one large studio unit above the garage of Norman and Dianne Thomsen's home, near Ekuhai Beach Park. It has a king bed, queen sofabed, bathroom, kitchen area, private entrance, phone, TV and a lanai facing the mountains. Breakfast is not included. The rate is $65 for singles/doubles.

The bulletin board at Pupukea Foodland has notices of roommates wanted as well as an occasional vacation rental listing.

Waianae Coast

The Waianae Coast is the arid leeward side of Oahu.

In 1793 Captain Vancouver, the first Westerner to drop anchor there, found a barren wasteland with only a few scattered fishing huts. Two years later, however, Kamehameha invaded Oahu and many Oahuans who had been living in more desirable areas were forced to flee to the dry and isolated Waianae Coast.

Today it still stands separate from the rest of the island. There are no gift shops or sightseeing buses on the Waianae Coast. When you get right down to it, other than watching surfers at Makaha, there aren't a whole lot of sights to see.

Although developers are beginning to grab Waianae farmland for golf courses, for the time being leeward Oahu is the island's least touristed side. The area has a history of resisting development and a reputation for not being receptive to outsiders. In the past, visitors have been the targets of assaults and muggings. There's still a major problem with thefts from cars and camping sites, and although things aren't as hostile as they used to be, many locals aren't keen on sharing their space with tourists.

With the golf course developments resulting in the eviction of tenant farmers and growing numbers of homeless families living in tents on the beaches, the conflict could become more intense.

Overall, you need to be attuned to the mood of the people. This is the only place in Hawaii where the park brochures say camping opportunities are for *local* residents.

Farrington Highway (Hwy 93) runs the length of the leeward coast. There are long stretches of white sand beaches, some quite attractive, others littered with rubbish. In winter most have treacherous swimming conditions but at that time they also have some of the island's more challenging surfing. Although the towns themselves are

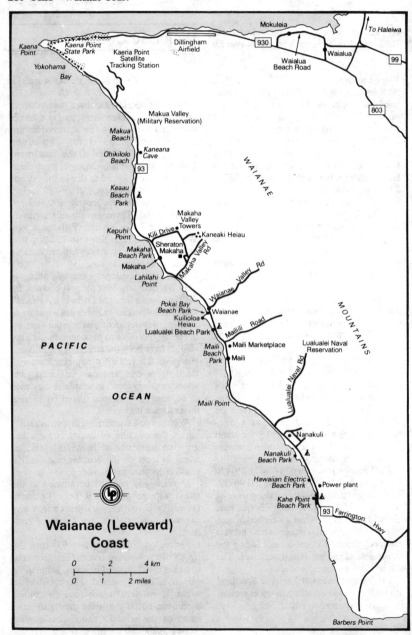

Waianae (Leeward) Coast

ordinary, the cliffs and valleys cutting into the Waianae Range form a lovely backdrop.

At road's end, there's an undeveloped mile-long beach and a fine nature hike out to scenic Kaena Point.

KAHE POINT
Kahe Point Beach Park
Despite the name, there's no beach at this park, just the rocky cliffs of Kahe Point. There are standard facilities and camping is allowed, but the park has little to recommend it.

Discarded TV sets, mattresses, household garbage and the occasional wrecked car make it over the cliffs to the rocky coast below. The backdrop is the smokestacks of the electric power plant across the way. Along the road in front of the park a sign welcomes visitors to the Waianae Coast.

Hawaiian Electric Beach Park
This sandy beach north of Kahe Point is more commonly known as Tracks, the name given to it by beachgoers who used to go there by train before the war. In summer this is a fairly calm place to swim, while in winter it's frequented by surfers.

To get there take the first turn-off after the power plant and drive over the abandoned railroad tracks.

NANAKULI
Nanakuli, with a population of 9500, is the biggest town on the Waianae Coast. The site of a Hawaiian Homesteads settlement, Nanakuli has one of the largest native Hawaiian populations on Oahu. The town has supermarkets, the Waianae District Court, a bowling alley, a movie theatre and a *McDonald's*.

Nanakuli is lined by a broad sandy beach park. There's swimming, snorkelling and scuba diving during the calmer summer season. In winter, high surf creates rip currents and dangerous shorebreaks.

To get to the beach park, turn left at the traffic lights on Nanakuli Ave. This is a community park with a playground, sports fields, full beach facilities and camping sites.

The area between here and Maili is dry scrubland and beach.

MAILI
Maili has a long grassy roadside park with an endless stretch of white sand beach. Like other places on this coast the water conditions are often treacherous in winter, but usually calm enough for swimming in summer. There's a lifeguard station, playground, beach facilities and a few castrated coconut palms to provide limited, although safe, shade.

As you come into Maili there's a 7-Eleven store, then Maili Cove condos and a little farther up Maili Marketplace which has the Leeward Dive Center, the only dive shop up this way.

Places to Stay
Maili Cove (☎ 696-4447), 87-561 Farrington Highway, Waianae, HI 96792, is a crescent-shaped three-storey condo right on both the highway and the beach in Maili. The large one-bedroom units cost $600 a week. All have lanais with ocean views and most have cable TV and phones. There's a pool.

Places to Eat
Salvatore's by the Sea at the Maili Market-place serves a good-value lunch buffet from 11 am to 3 pm Monday to Saturday for $6.95, or skip the hot dishes and have only the soup and salad bar for $5.95. There's a $10 champagne brunch on Sundays from 11 am to 3 pm. It's open from 7 am to 9 pm daily.

WAIANAE
Waianae has the local high school, a satellite city hall, supermarkets, a library, a police station, a protected boat harbour and fast food, including *McDonald's*, *Burger King*, *Taco Bell* and *Kentucky Fried Chicken*.

Pokai Bay Beach Park
Protected by Kaneilio Point and a long breakwater, Pokai Bay Beach Park has the calmest year-round swimming on the Waianae Coast. To get there, turn makai onto

Lualualei Homestead Rd at the traffic light just after the Waianae post office.

Waves seldom break inside Pokai Bay and the sea bottom slopes gently. Snorkelling is fair by the breakwater where fish gather around the rocks.

Local canoe clubs practice in the bay and you can watch them rowing in the late afternoon. There are full beach-park facilities and a lifeguard on duty daily. All in all for an in-town beach it's pretty nice.

Kaneilio Point is the site of **Kuilioloa Heiau**, partly destroyed by the army during WW II. It's been reconstructed by a Waianae group, but because some of the point had been lost, the heiau had to be moved mauka a bit and it's not exactly identical to the original.

MAKAHA

Makaha means 'ferocious', and in days past the valley was notorious for the bandits who used to hang out along the cliffs waiting for travellers to pass.

Today Makaha has world-class surfing, Oahu's best-restored heiau, a few condos and a Sheraton up in the valley.

Makaha Beach Park

Makaha Beach is broad, sandy and crescent-shaped, with some of the most daunting winter surf in the islands. Experienced surfers and bodysurfers both hit the waves here.

The beach is home to some major surf competitions. The most colourful is Buffalo's Big Board Surfing Classic held in February using old-style surfboards called 'tankers' which are sometimes 15 feet long and weigh more than 80 pounds. As surfers today go for small, light boards, most competitors are of an older generation of surfers.

When the surf's not up Makaha is a popular swimming beach. When the surf's up swimming is hazardous because of the dangerous rip currents and a strong shorebreak.

In summer the slope of the beach is relatively flat. In winter it's fairly steep. The beach sand is slightly coarse and of calcare-

ous origin with lots of mollusc shell fragments. As much as half of it temporarily washes away during winter erosion. Even then, Makaha is still an impressive beach.

Snorkelling is good offshore during the calmer summer months. Makaha Caves, out where the waves break furthest offshore, feature underwater caverns, arches and tunnels at depths of 30 to 50 feet. It's a popular leeward diving spot.

Makaha Beach has showers, restrooms, and a lifeguard on duty daily.

Makaha Valley

Up in Makaha Valley you'll find Kaneaki Heiau, a couple of condos and the Sheraton hotel and golf course.

If you turn mauka onto Kili Drive, opposite Makaha Beach Park, the drive up the valley is beside scalloped green cliffs.

An estimated 3000 wild peacocks live in the valley, including about 25 white ones. They come out in the early evening, sometimes gathering at the intersection by the Makaha Valley Towers condos, a mile up from the Farrington Highway.

At the Towers turn right onto Huipu Drive. Half a mile down on the left is Mauna Olu St, which leads a mile into Mauna Olu Estates and Kaneaki Heiau.

The Sheraton is at the intersection of Huipu Drive and Makaha Valley Rd. Most of the hotel activity is centred around its golf course.

Makaha Valley Rd comes back down to Farrington Highway through a residential neighbourhood.

Kaneaki Heiau Kaneaki Heiau, in the centre of Makaha Valley, was originally a Lono temple, dedicated to the god of agriculture. In its final days it was rededicated by Kamehameha I as a luakini war temple. It remained in use until the time of Kamehameha's death, in 1819.

Restoration, which was done by the Bishop Museum and completed in 1970, added two prayer towers, a taboo house, drum house, altar and god images. It was reconstructed in the traditional manner using ohia logs and pili grass shipped over from the Big Island.

The guard at the Mauna Olu Estates gatehouse lets visitors drive through to the heiau between 10 am and 2 pm daily except Mondays. It's occasionally closed if the weather is bad. You can call the gatehouse (☎ 695-8174) to inquire. Admission is free.

Places to Stay

The Waianae Coast doesn't have a lot of accommodation for short-term visitors. Apart from the Sheraton, all are condos and most require you to stay for at least one week.

Makaha Surfside (☎ 696-2105), Apollo Services, Box 27581, Honolulu, HI 96827, is a four-storey cinder-block apartment complex a mile south of Makaha Beach. Although it's mostly residential, some of the 450 units are rented out on a daily basis for $59. It's a very ordinary-looking complex although there are pools and barbecue grills.

Makaha Shores (☎ 696-8415), Hawaii Hatfield Realty, 85-833 Farrington Highway, Suite 201, Waianae, HI 96792, is a condo right on the northern end of Makaha Beach, with lanais overlooking the water. In winter, studios cost $550 for one week, $800 for two weeks or $1050 a month. In the low season they're $450 a week or $900 a month. A $45 cleaning fee is tacked on. There are one-bedroom units as well. It's tough to book in the high season, as a lot of retired people winter there.

At the *Sheraton Makaha Resort & Country Club* (☎ 695-9511, (800) 325-3535), 84-626 Makaha Valley Rd, Makaha, HI 96792, the theme is country club right down to the brochure that shows a young couple practising their putts in the bedroom. The 200 rooms have lanais and refrigerators. The hotel has an 18-hole golf course, an Olympic-sized pool, lighted tennis courts, horse riding and restaurants. Rates are from $110 to $170.

Up in Makaha Valley, there are two other large complexes: *Makaha Valley Plantation* and *Makaha Valley Towers*. Both give the impression they're under siege, with guards and gates to keep outsiders at bay. Of the two,

Makaha Valley Towers is the better value. Inga's Realty (☎ 695-9055), 84-1170 Farrington Highway, Makaha, HI 96792, handles 100 of the 586 units. Studios cost $1100 a month, one-bedroom units are $1300. The peacocks that hang out around the complex can be noisy in the mornings.

Places to Eat

The *Sheraton* has a poolside cafe with sandwiches and pizza, open from 11 am to 9 pm daily, and a snack bar off the pro shop. The main restaurant, the Kaala Room, serves more expensive fare, with breakfast and lunch from 7 am to 2.30 pm and dinner from 6 to 9 pm.

Cornet Village, on the corner of Farrington Highway and Makaha Valley Rd, has a store, a deli and a drive-in serving plate lunches. There's a 7-Eleven store on the opposite corner.

NORTH OF MAKAHA
Keaau Beach Park

Keaau Beach Park is another long open grassy strip, this time bordering a rocky shore, with camping, showers, drinking water, picnic tables and restrooms. A sandy beach begins at the very northern end of the park, although a rough reef, sharp drop and high seasonal surf make swimming uninviting.

Driving north along the coast you'll see low lava sea cliffs, white sand beaches and patches of kiawe. On the mauka side there are glimpses into a run of little valleys.

Kaneana Cave

Kaneana Cave, a massive cave on the right-hand side of the road about two miles north of Keaau Beach Park, was once underwater. Its size is the result of wave action wearing away loose rock around an earthquake crack and expanding the cavern over the millennia, as the ocean slowly receded.

It's a somewhat uncanny place – often a strong wind gusts near the cave while it's windless just down the road.

Hawaiian kahunas once performed rituals inside the cave's inner chamber. Older Hawaiians consider it a sacred place and won't enter for fear it's haunted by the spirits of deceased chiefs. From the collection of broken beer bottles and graffiti inside it's obvious not everyone shares their sentiments.

From Ohikilolo Beach, below the cave, you can see Kaena Point ahead. Ohikilolo Beach is sometimes called Barking Sands, as the sand is said to make a 'woofing' sound if it's walked on when very dry.

Makua

Scenic Makua Valley opens up wide and grassy, backed by a fan of sharply fluted mountains. It serves as the ammunition field of the Makua Military Reservation.

The makai road opposite the south end of the reservation leads to a little graveyard shaded by yellow-flowered be-still trees. This is all that remains of the Makua Valley community, forced to evacuate during WW II when the US military took over the entire valley for bombing practice. War games still take place in the valley, which is fenced off with barbed wire and signs that warn of stray explosives.

Makua Beach, the white sand beach opposite the reservation, was a canoe landing in days past. A movie set, of Lahaina as it was during the 1800s, was built on Makua Beach for the 1966 movie *Hawaii* which starred Julie Andrews and Max von Sydow. No trace of the set remains.

Satellite Tracking Station

Just before the start of Kaena Point State Park a road leads up to Kaena Point Satellite Tracking Station, operated by the US Air Force. The tracking station's domes and antennas sit atop the mountains above the point.

There are a couple of trails above the tracking station that can be hiked – one of them a two-mile ridge trail. You need to obtain a hiking permit in advance from the Division of Forestry & Wildlife (☎ 587-0166).

KAENA POINT STATE PARK

Kaena Point is the sharp, westernmost point of Oahu. Kaena Point State Park is an undeveloped 853-acre coastal strip that runs along both sides of the point.

Until the mid-1940s the Oahu Railroad ran up from Honolulu and around the point, carrying passengers on to Haleiwa.

The attractive mile-long sandy beach on this side of the point is Yokohama Bay, so named for the large numbers of Japanese fishers who came here during the railroad days.

Winter brings huge pounding waves and Yokohama is a popular surfing and bodysurfing spot. It is, however, best left to the experts because of the submerged rocks, strong rip currents and dangerous shorebreak.

Swimming is pretty much limited to the summer, and then only during calm conditions. When the water's flat, the rocky areas should provide half-decent snorkelling. There are restrooms and showers but no drinking water.

In addition to being a state park, Kaena Point has been designated a natural area reserve because of its unique ecosystem. The extensive dry, windswept coastal dunes that rise above the point are the habitat of many rare native plants. The endangered Kaena akoko that grows on the talus slopes is found nowhere else.

Nanaue

Hawaiian legend tells of a child named Nanaue who was born with a open space between his shoulders. Unknown to his mother, the child's father was the king of sharks who had taken on the guise of a man. Nanaue was born half human, half shark. He was human on land, but when he entered the ocean the opening on his back became a shark's mouth.

After a nasty spell in which many villagers were ripped to shreds by a mysterious shark, Nanaue was discovered and forced to swim from island to island as he was hunted down. For a while he lived near Makua and took his victims into Kaneana Cave via an underwater tunnel. ■

More common plants are the beach naupaka with white flowers which look like they've been torn in half; pau-o-Hiiaka, a vine with blue flowers; and beach morning glory, sometimes found wrapped in the parasite plant kaunaoa, which looks like orange plastic fishing line.

Sea birds common to the point include shearwaters, boobies and the common noddy, a dark-brown bird with a greyish crown.

Dirt bikes and 4WD vehicles have, until recently, created a great deal of disturbance in the dunes. It was only after Kaena Point became a natural area reserve in 1983 that vehicles were prohibited.

Recently the reserve has again become a nesting site for the Laysan albatross, and Hawaiian monk seals now occasionally bask in the sun there. Controversial on-again, off-again proposals to connect Farrington Highway around the point threaten it all.

Hiking

A 2½-mile (one way) coastal hike runs from Yokohama Bay to Kaena Point, following the old railroad bed. Along the trail are tide pools, sea arches, fine coastal views and the lofty sea cliffs of the Waianae mountain range. The hike is unshaded (Kaena means 'the heat'). Take plenty of water and don't leave anything valuable in your car.

Kaena Point

Early Hawaiians believed that when people went into a deep sleep or lost consciousness their souls would wander. Souls that wandered too far were drawn west to Kaena Point. If they were lucky they were met here by their *aumakua* (ancestral spirit helper) who led their soul back to their body. If unattended, their soul would be forced to leap from Kaena Point into the endless night, never to return.

On clear days Kauai can be seen from the point. According to legend, it was at Kaena Point that the demigod Maui attempted to cast a huge hook into Kauai and pull it next to Oahu to join the two islands. But the line broke and Kauai slipped away, with just a small piece of it remaining near Oahu. This is Pohaku O Kauai, a rock off the end of Kaena Point. ∎

Hawaii – The Big Island

The island of Hawaii, commonly called the Big Island, is nearly twice the size of all the other Hawaiian islands combined. Geographically, it's so incredibly varied that it resembles a mini-continent. Climates range from tropical to subarctic. Landscapes include one of just about everything: desolate lava flows, lush coastal valleys, high sea cliffs, rolling pastures, deserts and rainforests.

Geologically, it's the youngest Hawaiian island and the only one still growing. Kilauea, the most active volcano on earth, has added 300 acres of coastal land to the island since its latest series of eruptions began in 1983.

The Big Island has Hawaii's highest mountains, which rise almost 14,000 feet above sea level. Some people liken them to icebergs, not only for their seasonal snowcaps but because their summits are merely the tips of mountain masses that rise 32,000 feet from the ocean floor.

The mountains create a huge barrier that blocks the moist north-easterly trade winds and makes the leeward western side of the Big Island the driest region in Hawaii. The Kona and Kohala coasts, on this sunny western side, have the island's best beaches and water conditions.

The windward east coast catches the rain. Parts of it are planted in expansive fields of green sugar cane. The rest is a rugged coastline with pounding surf, lush tropical rainforests, deep ravines and impressive waterfalls.

The Hawaii Volcanoes National Park encompasses incredible volcanic sites. The park has excellent hiking and camping, ranging from black-sand beaches to the 13,679-foot summit of Mauna Loa. You can drive or cycle around the rim of Kilauea's huge caldera or walk across still-steaming crater floors.

The Big Island also has the largest privately owned cattle ranch in the USA and the world's top collection of astronomical observatories. The latter dot the summit of Mauna Kea, Hawaii's highest point at 13,796 feet.

The Big Island has many noteworthy historical sites, including Hawaii's best petroglyphs and some of its most important heiaus.

There are two distinct centres on the Big Island. Hilo, on the lush rainy east coast, is the island's only real city. It's the oldest city in Hawaii and it shows its age with character. But it's Kona, on the dry, sunny west coast that attracts the visitors. Kona has most of the island's accommodation and is the centre of most recreational activities, including excellent diving and deep-sea fishing.

The Big Island has some inviting small towns that remain unchanged by tourism. A couple of them even have old-fashioned hotels with old-fashioned room rates. Things move slower in these rural centres and there's a nice sense of community.

The Big Island is big on space and few places feel crowded. It attracts a lot of adventurous people. It's got cowboy country, traditional fishing villages, valleys with taro farmers and wild horses, and a fair number of alternative folks living off the land.

ORIENTATION

The Big Island's main airports are in Hilo and Kona. The Hilo Airport is in town.

Most visitors land in Kona at Keahole Airport. This can be a shock if you're expecting tropical greenery and waving palm trees – instead it looks more like a black lava wasteland, as if the island had been paved over in asphalt. Don't panic! This is but one face of the island and even here, if you look closer, you can catch a glimpse of some fine secluded white-sand beaches squeezed between the lava and the turquoise waters.

Hwy 19 runs along the Kona Coast. From the airport to Kailua-Kona, seven miles south, you'll pass endless masses of black lava accented with white coral graffiti and blazing bougainvillea. The Waikoloa resort area is 12 miles north of the Keahole Airport through similar scenery.

The Hawaii Belt Rd circles the island, taking in the main towns and many of the sights. Different segments of the road have different highway numbers and names, but it's easy to follow.

From Kona to Hilo, the northern half of the belt road is 93 miles and the journey takes about two hours nonstop. The southern Kona-Hilo route is 125 miles and takes approximately three hours.

Facts

HISTORY

By and large the history of the Big Island is the history of Hawaii. It's widely believed that the first Polynesian settlers landed on this island. It was on the Big Island that the first *luakini heiau* (temple of human sacrifice) was introduced and the *kapu* system of strict taboos which regulated all aspects of daily life came into being. It was also here, six centuries later, that the old gods were overthrown and replaced by those of the Christians.

English explorer Captain Cook died on the Big Island in 1779, a year after 'discovering' Hawaii, and this was where Kamehameha the Great rose to power.

The Kamehameha Era

Kamehameha I Kamehameha was born on the Big Island in 1758. As a young boy he was brought to Kealakekua Bay to live at the royal court of his uncle, Kalaniopuu, high chief of the island.

Kamehameha went on to become Kalaniopuu's fiercest general. To help him amass even more strength, Kalaniopuu appointed Kamehameha guardian of the war god, Kukailimoku, the 'snatcher of land'.

The god was embodied in a coarsely carved wooden image with a bloody red mouth and a helmet of yellow feathers. Kamehameha carried it into battle with him

and it was said that during the fiercest fighting the image would screech out terrifying battle cries.

Immediately after Kalaniopuu's death in 1782, Kamehameha led his warriors against Kalaniopuu's son, Kiwalao, who had taken the throne. Kiwalao was killed and Kamehameha emerged as ruler of the Kohala region and one of the three ruling chiefs of the Big Island. The other two were Kahekili of Maui and Kamehameha's cousin, Keoua.

However, Kamehameha's ambitions went beyond sharing control of the islands. In 1790, with the aid of a captured foreign schooner and two shipwrecked sailors, Isaac Davis and John Young, whom he used as gunners, Kamehameha attacked and conquered Maui.

Shortly after that, Kamehameha was in Molokai preparing for the invasion of Oahu when word reached him that Keoua, chief of the Kau region, was attacking the Hamakua Coast. Keoua had boldly pillaged sacred Waipio Valley where Kamehameha had ceremoniously received his war god a decade earlier.

As an angry Kamehameha set sail for home, Keoua's soldiers retreated to Kau,

Kamehameha the Great

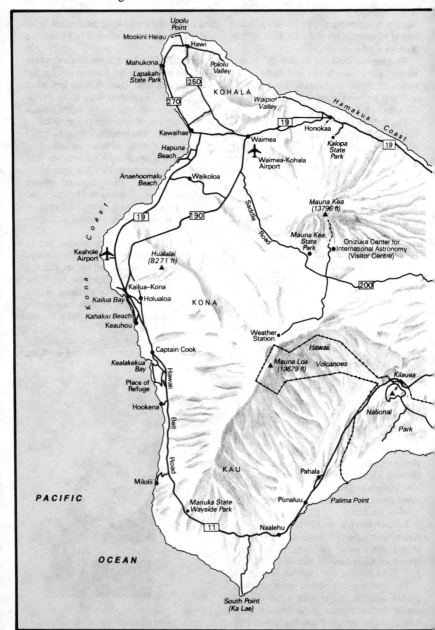

**Hawaii
The Big Island**

| 0 | 15 | 30 km |
| 0 | 10 | 20 miles |

passing beneath the slopes of Kilauea Volcano. The volcano erupted and many of the warriors were instantly killed as toxic fumes and ashes swept over them. It is the only known volcanic explosion in Hawaiian history to have resulted in such fatalities. Casts of the soldiers' footprints remain on the trail today.

Around this time Kamehameha was told by a prophet from Kauai that if he built a new heiau to honour his war god, Kukailimoku, he would become ruler of all the islands.

Kamehameha did so, completing Puukohola Heiau in Kawaihae in 1791. He then sent word to Keoua that his appearance was requested at the heiau for reconciliation. Keoua, well aware that this was a luakini temple, probably knew his fate was sealed.

Upon landing at Kawaihae, Keoua and his party became the heiau's first sacrifices. With Keoua's death, Kamehameha became sole ruler of the Big Island.

Over the next few years Kamehameha conquered all the islands (except for Kauai over which he established suzerainty) and named the entire kingdom after his home island, Hawaii.

End of an Era Kamehameha the Great established his royal court in Lahaina but later returned to his Kamakahonu residence, on the north side of Kailua Bay, where he died in May 1819.

The crown was passed to his hesitant son, Liholiho, and Kamehameha's favourite wife, Kaahumanu, a spirited woman who wasn't content to be kept in her place by the old traditions.

In Kamakahonu, six months after Kamehameha's death, Kaahumanu sat down with Liholiho to eat a meal, something strictly forbidden under the kapu system. This breaking of the kapus by royalty marked the demise of the old religion. Almost immediately, temples throughout the islands were abandoned and their idols burned.

On 19 April 1820, the ship *Thaddeus* sailed into Kailua Bay with Hawaii's first Christian missionaries aboard. They landed beside Kamehameha's recently desecrated heiau at Kamakahonu.

Their timing was perfect as the recent abandonment of the old religion had left a vacuum into which the missionaries readily moved.

GEOGRAPHY

The Big Island has an area of 4035 sq miles (10,451 sq km) and is growing as new lava spews into the sea. It's 93 miles long and 76 miles wide. The Big Island is the youngest Hawaiian island and the farthest east. Its southern tip, called South Point or Ka Lae, is the southernmost point in the USA.

The island was formed by five large shield volcanoes: Kohala, Hualalai, Mauna Kea, Mauna Loa and Kilauea. The last two are still active, with Kilauea having the distinction of being the most active volcano on earth.

Mauna Kea at 13,796 feet (4205 metres) is the highest point in the Hawaiian islands. It extends 19,680 feet below sea level to the ocean floor and when measured from its base is the highest mountain in the world.

Mauna Loa, just slightly lower at 13,679 feet (4169 metres) above sea level, makes up more than half the land mass of the Big Island and is the largest mountain mass in the world when measured from the ocean floor.

CLIMATE

Rainfall and temperatures vary more with location than with the seasons. The leeward north-west coast between Lapakahi and Waikoloa is the driest region in the state. Kawaihae, in the centre of this strip, averages less than 10 inches of rain a year.

On the windward side of Mauna Kea, near the 2500-foot elevation, 300 inches of rain falls each year. So much rain is squeezed out of the clouds as they rise up Mauna Kea and Mauna Loa that only about 15 inches of precipitation reaches the summits, much of it as snow. Heavy subtropical winter rainstorms in Hilo occasionally bring blizzards to the mountains, as low as the 9000-foot level.

Elevation makes enough of a difference that even within the city of Hilo, annual rainfall ranges from 130 inches on the shore to 200 inches on the higher slopes. Trivia buffs may be interested to know that Hilo has the world's largest measured raindrops, 4 to 8 mm in diameter!

Annual rainfall in Volcano is 101 inches. At Kailua-Kona it's 25 inches. Although winter is wetter than summer, location again is the key. In Kona seasonal rainfall variations are marginal. At Volcano it's about twofold.

The average daily high temperatures in January are 65°F at Hawaii Volcanoes National Park, 79°F in Hilo and 81°F in Kailua-Kona. In August, they are 71°F, 83°F and 85°F respectively. Night-time lows are about 15° less.

Vog

'Vog' is a word coined on the Big Island to define the volcanic haze that has been hanging over the island since Kilauea's latest eruptive phase began in 1983. It usually blows towards Kona and conditions can resemble city smog when the trade winds falter. Vog consists of water vapour, carbon dioxide and significant amounts of sulphur dioxide.

In 1991 an average of 275 tons of sulphur dioxide was being emitted from Kilauea daily, causing air quality problems on the Big Island and haze throughout Hawaii. The sulphur dioxide level exceeds standards set by the US Environmental Protection Agency an average of 22 days a year. While this shouldn't present health problems for short-term visitors, scientists are currently studying the link between vog and respiratory problems for residents.

FLORA & FAUNA

The nene, the endangered goose that is Hawaii's state bird, lives on the upland slopes of Mauna Kea, Mauna Loa and Hualalai. As recently as 100 years ago there were an estimated 25,000 nene on the Big Island. They now number just a few hundred. Still, they're a friendly species and you might come across them, particularly if you camp in the national park.

Nene

Other native birds include the endangered *palila*, a small yellow bird that survives solely on Mauna Kea's slopes, and the *io* (Hawaiian hawk), which also occupies the mountain slopes and lives only on the Big Island. Another endangered bird endemic to the Big Island is the *alala* (Hawaiian crow), which hangs on precariously with a single flock of only 10 birds remaining.

There are wild horses in Waipio Valley and feral cattle on the slopes of Mauna Kea. The Big Island also has wild pigs, goats and sheep.

Two varieties of silversword grow on the Big Island, one on Mauna Kea and the other on Mauna Loa. Related to their better-known Maui cousin, they grow in remote areas well off the beaten path.

GOVERNMENT
The Big Island is one county unto itself with an elected mayor and a nine-member council. Democrat Lorraine Inouye was elected to a four-year term as mayor in 1990.

Hilo is the county seat and political centre. Rivalry is ongoing between old established Hilo and boom-town Kona and there's even occasional talk of dividing the island into two counties. The biggest political issue on the island, as elsewhere in Hawaii, is rampant development.

ECONOMY
The Big Island's unemployment rate is about 5%. Employment is fairly diversified with the retail trade, government, hotels and construction industries employing about half of the workforce.

Agriculture accounts for a large sector of the economy and almost 15% of the workforce. The Big Island produces the vast majority of Hawaii's macadamia nuts, coffee and tropical flowers, as well as four-fifths of its fruit, including papayas, bananas and oranges. While sugar production is in decline, the Big Island is still the largest producer in the state, with about two billion tons of cane grown annually.

There's also a large, illicit underground agriculture in *pakalolo* (marijuana). Although it's on the decline, more than 90% of all marijuana confiscated in Hawaii is still from the Big Island. In 1991, approximately 700,000 plants were destroyed in police raids.

The Big Island has several sizeable cattle ranches. Spurred by Hawaii's population growth and tourist demands for steak dinners, the cattle business is booming.

Kona Coffee
Missionaries introduced the first coffee trees to Hawaii in 1827. By the early 1900s coffee was an important cash crop, planted throughout the islands.

The erratic rise and fall of coffee prices eventually drove coffee farmers out of business on the other islands. Only the coffee thriving in the upland areas of south Kona was of high enough quality to find a market during gluts in world markets.

Coffee production in Hawaii had dropped dramatically by 1980, when a rising interest in gourmet coffee sparked sales of the highly aromatic Kona coffee. Today, coffee farming is thriving among small growers. Kona coffee is the only commercially grown coffee in the USA and commands top prices.

Development

Growth is a big issue on the Big Island, which has more new hotel and condo developments planned than all the other islands combined. There are currently about 21,000 new hotel units and 23,000 condo units on the drawing board, most of them in the Kona and Kohala areas. Some are going up on beaches which are now totally undeveloped and secluded, while others are being built at existing Waikoloa resorts. To get an idea of the scale, in 1991 there were 74,000 visitor accommodation units in the entire state of Hawaii.

This rampant development raises many issues for environmentalists and Big Island residents. Besides threatening the finest stretch of secluded beaches anywhere in Hawaii, the developments present major infrastructure problems, from insufficient water and energy supplies to a serious lack of affordable housing.

POPULATION & PEOPLE

The population of the Big Island was 120,317 in 1990. Hilo has about a third of the island's population, but the Big Island's demographics are changing rapidly.

Between 1970 and 1980, North Kona (which includes Kailua-Kona) was the fastest growing district in the state with a growth rate of 185%. Between 1980 and 1990, neighbouring South Kohala took the honours as the state's most rapidly growing district, with its population doubling.

The Big Island's ethnic breakdown is 26% part-Hawaiian, 25% Caucasian, 22% Japanese, 12% mixed non-Hawaiian and 10% Filipino. Full-blooded Hawaiians make up just 1% of the population.

TOURIST INFORMATION

The Big Island has two Hawaii Visitors Bureau offices: 180 Kinoole St, Hilo, HI 96720 (☎ 961-5797) and 75-5719 W Alii Drive, Kailua-Kona, HI 96740 (☎ 329-7787).

You can receive a tourist information packet by calling (800) 648-2441 or by writing to B1G, Box 5900, Kamuela, HI 96743.

Free tourist magazines such as *This Week Big Island*, *Spotlight Big Island* and *Guide to the Big Island* are readily available at the airport, in hotel lobbies and around town. They're good sources of general information and include discount coupons for a range of activities and eateries around the island.

GENERAL INFORMATION
Official Hawaii

The Big Island's official flower is the *ohia lehua*, from a native tree that flourishes around lava flows. Ceremonial leis are made from its fluffy red pompom blossoms. The official colour is red.

Media

West Hawaii Today (☎ 329-9311), which is the Kona Coast newspaper, and Hilo's *Hawaii Tribune-Herald* (☎ 935-6621) are both published daily except Saturday. A single copy of *West Hawaii Today* may be

Ohia lehua flower

obtained by sending $3 to West Hawaii Today, Box 789, Kailua-Kona, HI 96745. The Friday issue usually has the biggest classified section.

The island has five AM and four FM radio stations and three cable TV stations. Commercial TV stations are relayed from Honolulu. Cablevision's Channel 6 features visitor information programmes.

Maps

The best map of the Big Island is the one put out by the University of Hawaii Press, which is available in shops in Kona and Hilo.

Libraries

There are public libraries in Kailua-Kona, Kealakekua, Holualoa, Hilo, Waimea, Pahoa, Pahala, Naalehu, Mountain View, Laupahoehoe, Kapaau, Honokaa and Keeau.

Weather

The National Weather Service has recorded forecasts for the Big Island (☎ 961-5582), for Hilo and vicinity (☎ 935-8555) and for water conditions (☎ 935-9883).

Hawaii Volcanoes National Park (☎ 967-7977) has recorded information on current volcano eruptions and viewing points.

Emergency

For ambulance or fire emergencies dial 961-6022. Each town has different telephone numbers for police: the Kona area is 329-3311, Hilo is 935-3311. The crisis line is 329-9111 in Kona, 969-9111 in Hilo.

The main hospitals are in Hilo (☎ 969-4111) and Kealakekua (☎ 322-9311).

ACTIVITIES

The vast majority of the Big Island's recreational activities take place on the west coast. In addition to those listed here, most of the Waikoloa-area resorts have a wide variety of activities, including water sports, cruises and dive trips. They generally charge higher-than-average rates and advertise mainly to their guests, but are usually open to the public as well.

Beaches

The Big Island has 313 miles of shoreline. What it doesn't have are the expansive stretches of sandy beaches that you'll find on Maui or Oahu. Most of the Big Island's beaches are sandy pockets bordering bays and coves.

The best spots are on the west coast. Kailua-Kona has a few good beaches, although the better ones are farther up along the Kona Coast around Waikoloa and Kohala. Anaehoomalu and Hapuna are beautiful, easily accessible public beaches. There are also a number of isolated gems dotting the coast that require a hike and are well worth the effort to get to.

Hilo is not as well endowed with beaches, although there are a few places to swim and snorkel on the east side of Hilo Bay.

The Puna and Kau districts have interesting black-sand beaches although generally unfavourable swimming conditions.

Kamoamoa Beach in Hawaii Volcanoes National Park is a gorgeous new black-sand beach pounded by rugged surf. The waters are too treacherous for swimming, but it's fun to walk on.

Swimming

The county has public pools at Honokaa High School in Honokaa, Kamehameha Park in Kapaau, Konawaena High School in Kealakekua, Kau High School in Pahala, Laupahoehoe High School in Laupahoehoe and at the Hoolulu Complex in Hilo. All county pools are free to the public for both lap swims and open pool use, which are scheduled at different hours.

There's a coastal saltwater pool with public access behind Kona by the Sea condos in Kailua.

Surfing

The Big Island is not one of the better islands for surfing, although local surfers do manage to catch waves in a number of places. Many of the island's surf spots are rocky and surfers new to the area should check out conditions before hitting the waves.

Honolii Cove, two miles north of Hilo, is

popular on the eastern side. In Kona, Kahaluu Beach in Keauhou and the area near the banyan tree before Magic Sands Beach in Kailua are favourite surfing locales.

Magic Sands Beach is also one of the best places on the Kona Coast for boogie boarding and bodysurfing.

One of the south coast's best surfing spots, Drainpipes, in the Kalapana area, was wiped out by the 1990 lava flow that engulfed Kaimu Beach.

Windsurfing

The Big Island is not a real hot spot for windsurfing. Most windsurfers head to Anaehoomalu Bay in Waikoloa, which has some of the better wind and water conditions. You can rent boards from Ocean Sports (☎ 885-5555), the beach hut in front of the Royal Waikoloan, for $19 an hour, and get a 1¼-hour lesson for $35.

Kawaihae Harbor and Hilo Bay are other spots that see some windsurfing activity.

Diving

The Big Island has excellent diving on the leeward Kona and Kohala coasts. Overall the best conditions are in spring and summer, although there are good, calm dive spots year round.

The Kona Coast has many good shore dives, including steep near-shore drop-offs with lava tubes, caves and diverse marine life. Diving is far more limited on the Hilo side where the season is basically from April to September.

A good reference is the book *Let's Go Shore Dive'n' on the Kona Coast* by Dick Dresie.

Kona has lots of dive operations. The cost of one-tank dives averages about $50, two-tank dives about $75. Several places offer introductory dives, night dives and certification courses.

One popular dive is Red Hill, an underwater cinder cone about 10 miles south of Kona. It has beautiful lava formations, including ledges and lots of honeycombed lava tubes nicely lit by streaks of sunlight.

There are also coral pinnacles and many brightly coloured nudibranchs.

Another good spot is off Kaiwi Point, south of Honokohau Harbor, where there are some respectable drop-offs and good marine life including huge eagle rays, sea turtles and large fish.

Kealakekua Bay has good coral and marine life in a very protected cove that's calm all year round. All in all, there are about 40 boat dives along the Kona Coast, including an aeroplane wreck off Keahole Point.

Jack's Diving Locker (☎ 329-7585, (800) 345-4807), Box 5306, Kailua-Kona, HI 96745, at the Coconut Grove Marketplace opposite the Kona Hilton, is a small, friendly operation and one of the best for introductory dives.

Kona Coast Divers (☎ 329-8802), 75-5614 Palani Rd, Kailua-Kona, HI 96740, is one of the larger operations. While they're quite professional they also have a reputation for being a bit regimented.

Dive Makai (☎ 329-2025), 74-5590 Alapa, Kailua-Kona, HI 96740, is a personable little operation run by husband-and-wife team Tom Shockley and Lisa Choquette. They are very conservation oriented and have a great word-of-mouth reputation.

Sea Paradise Scuba (☎ 322-2500, (800) 322-5662), Box 580, Kailua-Kona, HI 96745, is also environmentally oriented. They're based at Keauhou Bay and tend to head south, often to Red Hill or Kealakekua Bay.

Kohala Divers (☎ 882-7774), Box 4935, Kawaihae, HI 96743, at the shopping centre in Kawaihae, is another good operation. They organise trips up the Kohala Coast.

Live-Aboard Boat The *Kona Aggressor* (☎ 329-8182, (800) 344-5662), Live-Dive Hawaii, Box 2097, Kailua-Kona, HI 96745, is a 110-foot live-aboard dive boat that accommodates up to 18 people. All-inclusive one-week trips cost $1895, starting and ending each Saturday.

Dive Club The Kona Reefers Dive Club meets on the third Friday of the month and holds shore dives open to the public at 10 am on the third Sunday of the month. For more information, call club founder Roy Damron (☎ 325-5422).

Snorkelling

For snorkelling there are some good spots south of Kailua-Kona. Kahaluu Beach in Keauhou is teeming with fish and is the area's best easy-access snorkelling spot. The north side of the Place of Refuge is another fine drive-up snorkelling spot. While it takes a hike or boat ride to reach, there's terrific snorkelling in the calm, clear 30-foot-deep waters near Captain Cook's monument at the north end of Kealakekua Bay.

Snorkelling Cruises The most common snorkelling cruise is to Kealakekua Bay. Prices include snorkelling gear, beverages and pupus or picnic lunches.

Fairwind (☎ 322-2788) makes trips to Kealakekua Bay aboard a 50-foot trimaran. They start from Keauhou Bay which allows more snorkelling time than on boats leaving from Kailua. The morning trip leaves at 8.30 am, has 2½ hours of snorkelling and costs $56. The afternoon trip leaves at 1 pm and has 1½ hours of snorkelling for $36. They provide free transportation to the boat.

Royal Hawaiian Cruises (☎ 329-6411), also called Capt Cook VIII, goes to Kealakekua from Kailua Pier. There are two four-hour cruises a day, leaving at 8.30 am and 1.30 pm, that cost $50 for adults, $25 for children aged 5 to 12.

If you haven't tried it before, Kealakekua is a great place to try Snuba, which is a sort of scuba diving for snorkellers. It's a tankless operation, with an air hose attached to an air-filled raft that floats on the surface above you. Generally you get about 35 minutes underwater before you run out of air. The cost is an additional $40 with either Fairwind or Royal Hawaiian.

Captain Zodiac (☎ 329-3199) does four-hour tours aboard bouncy Zodiac rubber rafts. Departure is from Honokohau Harbor at 8 am and 1 pm daily, with pick-up possible at Kailua and Keauhou piers. The cost of $57 includes 45 minutes of snorkelling at Kealakekua Bay followed by visits to seacaves.

Kamanu Charters (☎ 329-2021) takes a 36-foot catamaran out of Honokohau Harbor to snorkel at Pawai Bay, just north of the Old Kona Airport. They take a maximum of 24 people, motoring down and using the sail on the way back. The 3¼-hour trips start at 9 am and 1.30 pm and cost $40 for adults, $22 for children 12 and under. They occasionally offer a sunset sail as well.

Snorkellers can sometimes tag along with divers on dive tours if space is available. Kohala Divers charges snorkellers just $15, while most others charge $25 to $35.

Snorkelling Rentals Snorkel Bob's (☎ 329-0770), off Alii Drive by the Kona Hilton, has snorkel sets starting at $15 a week ($29 a week with silicone masks). They also rent boogie boards and corrective-lens masks.

Kona Water Sports (☎ 329-1593) at Banyan Court in Kailua rents boogie boards for $4 to $7 a day or $16 to $28 a week and snorkel sets for $3/12 a day/week. They also have a few masks with corrective lenses at the same price.

Fairwind at Keauhou Bay rents snorkel sets for $5 a day.

The beach hut at Hotel King Kamehameha in Kailua rents snorkel sets and boogie boards for $5 a day and kayaks for $10 an hour.

B & L Bike & Sports on Pawai Place in Kailua sells good quality snorkelling equipment at reasonable prices in addition to swimwear and other sports gear.

Fishing

Kona is a world-renowned deep-sea fishing spot for Pacific blue marlin, spectacular fighting fish with long swords. Kona holds most of the world records, with at least one marlin topping 1000 pounds reeled in each year. Kona's also known for its record catches of ahi (yellowfin tuna).

Near Phillip Paolo's restaurant at Kailua's Waterfront Row, there's an interesting

Yellowfin tuna

'Granders Wall' lined with photos of anglers next to their 1000-pound marlin catches.

You can watch the boats come in and see the fish weighed at Kailua Pier and Honokohau Harbor, usually from around noon to 1 pm and 3.30 to 5 pm.

Kona has more than a hundred charter boats. The standard cost is around $90 to go out for half a day, sharing a boat with five others, and from around $350 to charter a whole boat for half a day. However, the tourist magazines usually advertise a few boats doing shared trips from around $50.

These centres each book several dozen boats:

Kona Charter Skippers Association, 75-5663 Palani Rd, Kailua-Kona, HI 96740 (☎ 329-3600, (800) 762-7546)

Kona Activities Center, Box 70, Kailua-Kona, HI 96745 (☎ 329-3171, (800) 367-5288)

Kona Coast Activities, Box 5397, Kailua-Kona, HI 96745 (☎ 329-2971, (800) 367-5105)

The Hawaiian International Billfish Tournament held in Kona each August is the Super Bowl of fishing tournaments and includes a week-long festival with a parade.

Hiking

Some of the Big Island's best and most varied hikes are in Hawaii Volcanoes National Park. The park trails lead across lava flows and steaming crater floors, through dense native forests and up to the peak of Mauna Loa.

On the northern tip of the island there are steep coastal cliffs and deep valleys reaching down from the Kohala Mountains that can be approached from either side. From the road's end on the north-west side, it's a 30-minute hike down to the beach at the bottom of Pololu Valley. On the south-east side you can take a 30-minute walk down into verdant Waipio Valley or backpack deep into remote Waimanu Valley.

North of Kona, you can hike in from the highway to secluded beaches, or explore portions of ancient footpaths and petroglyph fields. Efforts are under way by Na Ala Hele, a state-sponsored group comprised mostly of volunteers, to eventually re-establish the entire 50-mile historic trail system that once ran between Kailua and Kawaihae. Mauna Lani Resort and Lapakahi State Park have easy trails, marked with interpretive plaques, around ancient fishponds and through abandoned villages.

South of Kona, a trail leads to the spot where Captain Cook died at Kealakekua Bay. In the centre of the island, a strenuous hike leads to the summit of Mauna Kea with its observatory domes. On the slopes below, Kalopa State Park has short, easy forest trails.

All hikes are detailed in their respective sections.

Guided Hikes The Kona Hiking Club has hikes open to all trekkers on the first Saturday and third Thursday of each month (except in February when it's on Valentines Day). They vary in both location and difficulty. Most hikes take in a beach for picnics and swimming and the majority are on the west side of the island. Car pools leave from Kailua, with passengers contributing about $1 an hour for gas. Announcements are usually published in *West Hawaii Today* or you can phone 329-4179 for information.

Horse Riding

Ironwood Outfitters (☎ 885-4941) has rides through high mountain forest and grassland in the Kohala Mountains above Waimea, starting at the 4000-foot level. There are three rides: walking the horses from 8 to 9.30 am for $45, walking with some trotting from 2 to 3.30 pm for $45, and cantering from 10 am to 12.30 pm for $65.

Kings' Trail Rides O'Kona (☎ 323-2388) has rides at Kealakekua Ranch, a 21,000-acre working cattle ranch in South Kona at the 4200-foot level. It costs $50 for 1½-hour rides, $60 for two hours and $79 for a 4½-hour outing that includes two hours of riding, a tour of the ranch and lunch.

Mauna Kea Stables (☎ 882-7222) leaves from behind the Parker Ranch Shopping Center in Waimea. It costs $30 an hour or $55 for two hours of open-range riding. The stables is closed on Sundays.

For horse rides in Waipio Valley, see the Waipio section.

Tennis

The Old Kona Airport Beach Park in Kailua-Kona has four well-lit outdoor tennis courts and if you show up with racket in hand there's a good chance you'll find a partner. Hilo's Hoolulu Complex has five outdoor courts and three lighted indoor courts.

Other county courts that are lighted for night play are at Kailua Playground in Kailua, Greenwell Park in Captain Cook, Waimea Park in Waimea, Lincoln Park and Lokahi Park in Hilo, Papaaloa Park in the North Hilo district, Honokaa Park in Honokaa, Kamehameha Park in Kapaau, and Naalehu Park and Pahala School in the Kau district. All are free to the public.

The Mauna Lani Racquet Club (☎ 885-7765), which has hosted Davis Cup matches, has 10 courts and a schedule of clinics and round-robin tournaments. Court fees are $7 per person per hour and racquets can be rented.

The King Kamehameha, Kona Hilton and Kona Surf hotels in Kona have tennis courts open to the public at a fee.

Golf

The Big Island has about a dozen golf courses, including world-class courses in the Waikoloa area that are laid out on top of lava flows.

The Mauna Kea Beach Golf Course (☎ 882-7222), Francis Ii Brown Golf Course at Mauna Lani Resort (☎ 885-6655) and the Waikoloa Beach Resort Golf Club (☎ 885-6060), all 18 holes, are the big-time, big-buck courses. Mauna Kea and Francis Ii charge non-guests $130, while Waikoloa Beach Resort charges $95.

For more reasonably priced turf, the Hilo Municipal Golf Course (☎ 959-7711) on Haihai St in Hilo has 18 holes for $6 on weekdays, $8 on weekends.

Other courses include Naniloa Country Club (☎ 935-3000) in Hilo, nine holes, for $25 on weekdays and $35 on weekends; Volcano Golf and Country Club (☎ 967-7331) in Hawaii Volcanoes National Park, 18 holes, for $45; SeaMountain Golf Course (☎ 928-6222) at Punaluu, 18 holes, for $50; Waikoloa Village Golf Club (☎ 883-9621) in Waikoloa, 18 holes, for $68; and Kona Country Club (☎ 322-2595) in Keauhou, 36 holes, for $110 for 18 holes.

Skiing

Skiing in Hawaii is primarily a curiosity event. Snow does fall each winter on the upper slopes of Mauna Kea, although the timing is unpredictable. The ski season usually starts anywhere from early January to late February and can run for several months. There are good years and bad years (one year the ski season began in November and ended with a ski race on the Fourth of July). The last few years haven't been too good, however, with blame generally laid on El Nino weather patterns, global warming or the Kilauea Volcano eruptions.

Skiing Mauna Kea is not your standard sort of skiing. The altitude can be tough and the slopes can have exposed rocks. There are no ski lodges, lifts or other facilities.

When there's snow, Ski Guides Hawaii (☎ 885-4188), Box 1954, Kamuela, HI 96743, based in Waimea, can provide a full day of skiing for $150 per person. The cost includes use of ski equipment, transportation to Mauna Kea, lunch and a 4WD shuttle service up the mountain after each run.

Ski Shop Hawaii (☎ 737-4394), Box 8232, Honolulu, HI 96815, offers a similar service.

Sporting Competitions

The Ironman triathlon, held each October, combines a 2.4-mile ocean swim, 112-mile bike race and 26.2-mile marathon into one exhaustive endurance event. It begins and ends near the Kailua Pier in Kailua-Kona.

More than 1000 men and women from about 50 countries compete in the Ironman each year, with worldwide media coverage. The course record, set by Mark Allen in 1989, is eight hours, nine minutes and 15 seconds. For information contact the Ironman Triathlon World Championship (☎ 329-0063), 75-170 Hualalai Rd, Suite D214, Kailua-Kona, HI 96740.

The Kilauea Volcano Wilderness Marathon and Rim Runs are held at Hawaii Volcanoes National Park in July. There are three separate races that include a 10-mile run around the rim of Kilauea's caldera, a 5.5-mile race that goes down into Kilauea Iki Crater and a 26.2-mile marathon through the Kau Desert. Contact the Volcano Art Center (☎ 967-8222) for information.

The Big Island has numerous other road races. An annual race schedule listing marathons, fun runs and other sporting events is available from the Ironman office or can be picked up at B & L Bike & Sports in Kailua-Kona.

Organised Tours

Robert's Hawaii (☎ 935-2858) and Polynesian Adventure Tours (☎ 329-8008) have day-long circle-island tours for around $50.

Tours down into Waipio Valley and up Mauna Kea are listed in those sections.

Helicopter The most popular Big Island helicopter tour is a flight over Kilauea Volcano – especially when the volcano is acting up.

The cost largely depends on where you leave from. Flights from the Volcano Golf Course cost about $125, from Hilo about $150 and from Waikoloa about $250.

There are many companies, including: Volcano Heli-Tours (☎ 967-7578), which leaves from Volcano; Papillon (☎ 329-0551); Mauna Kea Helicopters (☎ 885-6400); Io Aviation (☎ 935-3031); and Kenai Helicopters (☎ 329-7424).

Kainoa Aviation (☎ 961-5591) leaves from Hilo and does tours of the volcano by helicopter and small aeroplane, the latter as cheap as $65.

It's a competitive market and it's worth checking the free tourist magazines for discount coupons and calling around to compare prices.

Keep in mind that the volcano area is often rainy even when it's sunny in Kona. If it's raining it's not worth going up, so if you're coming from the Kona side, call first to see what the weather's like.

Dinner Cruise Capt Beans' Cruises (☎ 329-2955), the high-profile boat with the yellow lights and orange sails, has a touristy dinner cruise in the evening. It leaves at 5.30 pm from Kailua Pier, takes two hours and costs $45, including meal, drink and a Polynesian show.

Whale Watching While the best whale watching is off Maui, you can spot whales from the Big Island as well. The season for humpback whales, which are the biggest attraction, usually starts around January and runs through March or April. However pilot, sperm and false killer whales and five dolphin species can be found in Kona waters all year round.

Naturalist Dan McSweeney of Whale Watch (☎ 322-0028) leads three-hour whale-watch cruises aboard a 31-foot boat leaving Honokohau Harbor at 9 am daily, and when business is brisk there's also a 1 pm tour. Hydrophones allow passengers to hear whale songs. The cost is $39.50 for adults, $29.50 for children aged 12 and under, including a light brunch. There's a 24-hour non-refundable cancellation policy.

Submarine Atlantis Submarines (☎ 329-6626, (800) 548-6262), based at Hotel King Kamehameha in Kailua, has one-hour rides in a submarine which dives down about 100 feet in a coral crevice in front of the Kona Hilton.

The sub has 26 side portholes and carries 46 passengers. It goes out 10 times a day and costs $79 for adults, $48 for children.

ACCOMMODATION

Because the island is so big, it's worth considering moving around and exploring from a couple of different bases.

Most of the island's accommodation is centred around Kailua-Kona, with the majority of the rooms in condos – although some of these are run like hotels with a front desk and daily rates. If you're staying a week or more, condos are usually a better deal than hotels.

Kailua has a new hostel with $14 dormitory beds. Otherwise, the cheapest places in the Kona area are mauka of Kailua, in small local hotels in the towns of Holualoa, Honalo and Captain Cook.

The Waikoloa area, north of Kona, has expensive seaside resorts. The Mauna Lani and Mauna Kea attract the rich who want elegant hideaways and not much excitement. Kona Village plays out the getaway fantasy in comfortable Polynesian thatched huts. The Hyatt Regency Waikoloa is loaded with splashy high-tech toys for those who desire constant titillation.

Rainy Hilo doesn't see a great many visitors and while choices aren't as varied as you might expect for a city, there are some good bottom-end to mid-range options, including a hostel-like lodge.

In the uplands, Volcano and Waimea have some delightful B&Bs as well as a couple of larger hostelries. There's a scattering of other B&Bs and guesthouses around the island, including some in fine country settings and scenic locales. This type of accommodation is becoming more common on the island and represents some of the best mid-range values.

Unless otherwise noted, the rate given is the same for either singles or doubles, and doesn't include the 9.17% tax. If calling from outside Hawaii, add the 808 area code to phone numbers.

Camping

At first glance, the list of Big Island camping grounds seems to read like some sort of 'Campers' Guide to Hell': Laupahoehoe Beach, where a village was washed away in a tidal wave; Halape Beach, where an earthquake sank the shoreline 30 feet; and Kamoamoa Beach, where a lava flow recently wiped out the nearby ranger station!

Actually there's little to worry about. Hawaii's lava isn't the rushing type which sweeps through camping grounds overnight and tsunami speakers have been set up to warn of approaching tidal waves.

Some of the best and safest camping is found in Hawaii Volcanoes National Park. Other good campsites are found on beaches, in upland forests and on the floor of lush Waipio Valley. There are also a few semi-secluded beaches where campers have been known to unofficially set up for a night or two.

State Parks Camping is allowed at Kalopa (temporarily closed; call for information), MacKenzie and Manuka state parks. There are no fees but permits are required.

There are A-frame shelters at Hapuna and self-contained housekeeping cabins at Mauna Kea, Kalopa and Kilauea.

With the exception of Hapuna, the system is computerised and reservations can be made at state park offices on any island. The Big Island office (☎ 933-4200) is at 75 Aupuni St (Box 936), Hilo, HI 96721. The maximum length of stay at any state park is five nights a month.

The A-frame shelters at Hapuna are single rooms with screened windows, a picnic table and wooden sleeping platforms for up to four people. Shared facilities include restrooms, cold showers and a pavilion with refrigerator, electric range, sink and tables. The cost is $15 per shelter per night.

The Hapuna shelters must be reserved through the concessionaire: Hawaii Untouched Parks & Recreation (☎ 882-1095), Box 390962, Kailua-Kona, HI 96739.

Cabin prices at the other three parks depend on the number of people, ranging from $10/17 for singles/doubles to $30 for six people. Cabins have kitchens with limited cookware and bathrooms with hot showers.

The cabins and shelters are popular and most require booking months in advance. Cancellations do occur, however, and if you're flexible with dates and lucky, you might be able to get a day or two without advance reservations. However, you'll have to register in person in Hilo if there's no time to do it by mail.

County Beach Parks The county allows camping at 13 of its beach parks: James Kealoha, Kolekole, Laupahoehoe and Onekahakaha, all near Hilo; Isaac Hale in Puna; Spencer, Keokea, Kapaa, Mahukona, Hookena and Milolii, all on the western side; and Whittington and Punaluu in Kau.

With the exception of Spencer, which is patrolled by a security guard, all the county parks can be rough and noisy areas, as they're popular among late-night drinkers.

Permits are required and are issued for specific parks and dates (it's no longer possible to get open permits). You can obtain permits by mail or in person from the Department of Parks & Recreation (☎ 961-8311), 25 Aupuni St, Hilo, HI 96720. Office hours are 7.45 am to 4.30 pm Monday to Friday.

Permits can also be picked up at the Parks & Recreation Office in the Yano Center in Captain Cook (☎ 323-3046), opposite the Manago Hotel. It's generally staffed from 8 am to noon and 1.30 to 4.30 pm (to 4 pm on Fridays).

A third spot, the community centre (☎ 885-5454) at Waimea Park in Waimea, also issues permits. However, the office is only open a few hours at a time and not every day, so it's best to call first.

Daily fees are $1 for adults and 50 cents for children aged 13 to 17 (free for children 12 and under). Camping is allowed for up to two weeks in each park, except June, July and August when it's limited to one week in each park.

Only about half of the county parks, generally those near towns, have drinking water. Some of the others have catchment water that can be treated for drinking, while others have only brackish water that is fine for showers but simply unsuitable for drinking.

Campers should also be aware that beach parks in the Puna and Kau areas are sometimes closed during winter storms.

Hawaii Volcanoes National Park The Hawaii Volcanoes National Park section has details on the park's three drive-up camping grounds and on trail shelters for backcountry hikers. They're all free and rarely filled.

Camping Supplies Pacific Rent-All (☎ 935-2974), 1080 Kilauea Ave, Hilo, HI 96720, rents pup tents for $7/28/56 a day/week/month, larger tents for $20/40/120, and cotton summer-weight sleeping bags for $7/21/42. It also rents Coleman stoves, lanterns, water jugs and other supplies. Opening hours are from 7 am to 5 pm on weekdays, 8 am to 5 pm on Saturdays and 9 to 11 am on Sundays.

ENTERTAINMENT

The Big Island entertainment scene is largely centred around the hotels in the Kona and Waikoloa area. Most offer Hawaiian music of some type, often duos or trios strumming guitars in the early evening, and some have dance bands, jazz groups and discos as well.

While not as lively as the west coast, Hilo has a few places with music and dancing. In addition, each spring Hilo hosts the weeklong Merrie Monarch Festival, the state's largest hula festival, which starts on Easter Sunday and features hula troupes from all the islands.

For the latest entertainment listings, check *West Hawaii Today*.

Luaus

Kona Village Resort (☎ 325-5555) has the most authentic luau in Hawaii. It's held on Friday nights, costs $58 and sometimes books out weeks in advance.

In Kona, luaus are held at the Hotel King Kamehameha on Sundays, Tuesdays and Thursdays and at the Kona Hilton on Mondays, Wednesdays and Fridays. In Waikoloa, the Hyatt Regency Waikoloa has a luau on Tuesdays and Fridays and the Royal Waikoloan has one on Sundays.

All Big Island luaus include a dinner buffet, cocktails and a Polynesian show.

Movie Theatres

Standard Hollywood movies are shown at the Prince Kuhio Plaza and Waiakea Shopping Plaza in Hilo, the Hualalai Theatres and World Square Theatre in Kailua, and on weekends at the Kahei Theatre in Hawi.

THINGS TO BUY

Kona coffee and macadamia nuts are the Big Island's most common souvenirs. If you're buying coffee, note that 'Kona blend' is only 10% Kona coffee. If you want the real thing make sure it says 100%. Prices change with the market, but it is one of the more expensive gourmet coffees, priced from around $10 a pound.

Supermarkets and discount stores (Longs, Pay'N Save) usually have the best deals on coffee. Rooster Farms produces an organically grown coffee which is sold at Kona Healthways in Kailua and a few other places.

Shops selling local arts & crafts are plentiful. Good places to start are at the Volcano Art Center in Hawaii Volcanoes National Park, Hale Kea in Waimea and galleries in the hillside village of Holualoa.

GETTING THERE & AWAY
Air

The Big Island has two main airports, in Kona and Hilo. Hawaiian Airlines (☎ (800) 882-8811) and Aloha Airlines (☎ 935-5771) connect both airports with the other main islands. Kona is by far the busiest of the two

and even has a few direct flights from the mainland with United Airlines.

There's also a small airport in Waimea, officially called the Waimea-Kohala Airport, but referred to as Kamuela by Aloha Island-Air (☎ (800) 652-6541), the only airline which serves it. Aloha IslandAir flies between Kamuela and Honolulu, Molokai, Lanai, Princeville and the Maui airports of Kahului, Hana and Kapalua West Maui. Many of these flights are only once a day and require a connection in Honolulu.

Fares for Aloha IslandAir and Hawaiian Airlines flights cost $69.95 one way. Aloha Airlines charges $68.95 one way. The main exception to these fares is the first and last flights to and from Honolulu on Hawaiian and Aloha airlines, which are $49.95. For information on other discounts see the Getting Around chapter in the front of the book.

Hilo Airport General Lyman Airport in Hilo is off Hwy 11, just under a mile south of its intersection with Hwy 19. It has a visitor information booth, newsstand, lei stand, restaurant, gift shops, taxi stand and car-rental booths.

Kona Airport Keahole Airport is on Hwy 19, about seven miles north of Kailua-Kona. It has a restaurant, car-rental booths, visitor information booth, mailbox, newsstands and a gift shop which sells the University of Hawaii Press map of the Big Island. For a relatively busy airport, it's surprisingly casual and all open-air (there's not enough rain to justify sealing it up!).

GETTING AROUND
To/From the Airport

Speedi Shuttle (☎ 329-5433) runs an airport shuttle service using seven-passenger vans. Fares from the airport for a single passenger are $12 to Kailua (up to the Hilton), $23 to the Kona Surf Resort in Keauhou and $27 to the Hyatt Waikoloa. The cost for each additional passenger is $2 to $4 depending on the distance. There's no set schedule. You can either call to reserve in advance or upon arrival use the courtesy phones found at the airline counters.

Bus

Hele-On is the county public bus. Service between Kona and Hilo is along the northern route of the Hawaii Belt Rd once in each direction Monday to Saturday. The bus leaves the South Kona town of Kealia at 5.45 am. Stops along the way include the Kona Surf Resort in Keauhou at 6.25 am, Waldenbooks in Kailua at 6.45 am, Parker Ranch Shopping Center in Waimea at 8.05 am and Honokaa at 8.30 am. It arrives in Hilo at the Mooheau bus terminal at 9.45 am.

The return trip leaves Hilo at 1.30 pm and arrives in Kailua at 4.30 pm. One-way fares are $5.25 between Kailua and Hilo, $3 between Kailua and Waimea and $4.50 between Waimea and Hilo.

Drivers accept only the exact fare. Bus tickets can be bought in sheets of 10 for $6.75, which are good for $7.50 worth of travel. Luggage and backpacks are $1 extra.

There are four other routes: Pahoa to Hilo, Laupahoehoe to Hilo, Waiohinu to Hilo via Volcano, and Hilo to the Waikoloa hotels. Each route runs at least once a day in each direction Monday to Friday. The Waikoloa bus, which leaves Hilo early in the morning for the Waikoloa area hotels and returns in late afternoon, is mostly used by commuting hotel workers, but if you're staying in Hilo it's convenient for a day's outing at the beach.

There's limited service around the city of Hilo for 75 cents per ride.

You can get a schedule and more information from Mass Transportation Agency (☎ 935-8241), 25 Aupuni St, Hilo, HI 96720.

Taxi

The taxi flag-down fee is $2. It costs $1.60 a mile after that. The approximate fare from Kona's Keahole Airport is $15 to Kailua, $35 to Waikoloa.

Car

The following companies have car-rental booths at Kona's Keahole Airport and at Hilo Airport:

	Keahole Airport	Hilo Airport
Budget	☎ 329-8511	☎ 935-6878
Avis	☎ 329-1745	☎ 935-1290
National	☎ 329-1674	☎ 935-0891
Hertz	☎ 329-3566	☎ 935-2896
Dollar	☎ 329-2744	☎ 961-6059
Thrifty	☎ 329-1730	☎ 935-1936
Tropical	☎ 329-2437	☎ 935-3385
Alamo	☎ 329-8896	☎ 961-3343

Toll-free numbers and more information are in the Getting Around chapter in the front of the book.

There are a couple of in-town local companies. World Rent-A-Car (☎ 329-1006), next to Sizzler in Kailua, has cars for $20.95 a day, $112 a week. You don't need a credit card if you take the CDW insurance at an additional $6 a day.

VIP Car Rental (☎ 329-7328), on Pawai Place in the industrial area in Kailua, advertises older cars at $16 a day, although availability at this rate seems to be very limited. VIP also accepts cash in lieu of credit cards.

Harper Car & Truck Rentals (☎ 969-1478), at 1690 Kamehameha Ave in Hilo, has 4WD vehicles adjusted for use at Mauna Kea's high altitude. Unlike other rental agencies, Harper puts no restrictions on going to the summit, although Waipio Valley and Green Sands Beach remain off limits. Isuzu Troopers cost $60 a day.

Hilo is a good place to gas up, as gas is cheaper there than in Kona.

Bicycle & Motor Scooter

Dave's Triathlon Shop (☎ 329-4522) in Kamehameha Square in Kailua rents mountain bikes for $15/90 a day/week.

Hawaiian Pedals (☎ 329-2294) in the Kona Inn Shopping Village in Kailua has mountain bikes for $20/63 a day/week, 18-speed touring bikes for $25 a day, tandem bikes for $35 a day and car bike racks for $5 a day.

Ciao (☎ 326-2426), which is in a kiosk opposite the Hotel King Kamehameha in

Kailua, rents scooters for $25 a day to 6 pm, $30 for 24 hours.

You can also rent motor scooters in Kailua for $20 from a concessionaire who sets up in the parking lot on Alii Drive in front of Huggo's. If you don't have a credit card, a $65 deposit and $4 CDW insurance is required.

The minimum age to rent motor scooters is 18.

Kona

Kona literally means 'leeward'. The Kona Coast refers to the dry, sunny west coast of the Big Island. However, to make matters a little more confusing, Kona also refers to Kailua, the largest town on the Kona Coast. The town's name is compounded Kailua-Kona by the post office and other officialdom to avoid confusion with Kailua on Oahu.

The weather is so consistent on this side of the island that the local paper usually just alternates two forecasts: 'Sunny morning. Afternoon clouds with upslope showers' or 'Sunny morning. Cloudy afternoon with showers over the slopes.'

The showers that hit the higher slopes rarely touch the coastline a couple of miles below. Because it sees so little rain, Kona is also called the Gold Coast. It's a good bet for a sunny vacation any time of the year.

KAILUA

In the 19th century Kailua-Kona was a favourite vacation retreat for Hawaiian royalty. These days it's the largest vacation destination on the Big Island.

It's got a lot to make it a drawing card. The weather is great, the setting on the leeward side of Mt Hualalai is pretty and it has both ancient Hawaiian and missionary-era historic sites. There are lots of places to stay and eat, as well as plenty of activities ranging from world-class deep-sea fishing to snorkelling cruises. Kailua is centrally

located and makes a perfect base for exploring the entire Kona coast.

To the south-east of Kailua are a couple of small hillside towns with a pleasant mix of local, alternative and artisan communities.

Kailua-Kona has long been one of our favourite places, but with all its recent growth it has lost some of its charm. Although people still come downtown in the evening to stroll along the sea wall and talk story under the banyan trees, much of the town's historic character has been stifled by trinket shops and mini-malls.

Most of Kona's condos are lined up along Alii Drive, the five-mile coastal strip that runs from the town's commercial centre at Kailua Bay south to Keauhou. Alii Drive sees a lot of power walkers, joggers and strollers, particularly in the cooler early morning hours.

Kailua has a few swimming, snorkelling and surfing spots, although the island's best beaches are up the coast to the north.

Information

Tourist Information The Hawaii Visitors Bureau (☎ 329-7787) is in the Kona Plaza. It's open from 8 am to noon and 1 to 4.30 pm Monday to Friday.

Money Both the Bank of Hawaii at the Hualalai Rd and Kuakini Highway intersection and the First Hawaiian Bank at the Lanihau Center have full-service branches with automatic teller machines.

Western Union has a money transfer service at the Typewriter Center (☎ 329-1255), which is near the laundromat on Pawai Place in the industrial area.

Post The main post office is in the Lanihau Center and there's a contract post office at the Kona Inn Shopping Village.

Bookshops Middle Earth Bookshoppe in the Kona Plaza and Waldenbooks in the Lanihau Center are both well-stocked bookstores with Hawaiiana and general travel sections.

The local daily, *West Hawaii Today*, is

readily available around town, as are the Hilo and Honolulu papers.

Resort Sundries at the Hotel King Kamehameha sells daily newspapers from the mainland.

Laundry There are coin laundries in the North Kona Shopping Center, on Kuakini Highway near Eclipse restaurant, and on Pawai Place in the industrial area.

Shopping Hotel King Kamehameha has a Liberty House department store and about 20 other shops.

The Lanihau Center on Palani Rd has the post office, Longs Drugs, Waldenbooks, a huge Food 4 Less supermarket, a bakery, Kentucky Fried Chicken, Express Pizza, a frozen yoghurt place and fast-food Chinese and Korean restaurants.

The Kona Coast Shopping Center on Palani Rd has a KTA supermarket, Pay'N Save, Sizzler steak house, Kona Healthways, World Rent-a-Car and a gas station.

The Kailua Candy Co on Kaiwi St is a friendly place that makes wonderful home-made chocolates using island fruits and nuts. They give free tours of their small operation, complete with mouthwatering samples, from 9 am to 3 pm Monday to Friday.

Film & Photography Longs Drugs in the Lanihau Center sells cameras and film and handles processing by major developers, including Kodak and Fuji. They do their own same-day print processing ($13 for 24 prints). However, if you can wait two days, the send-out service costs only $6 for 24 prints.

If you can't find camera accessories at Longs, try Kona Photo Center in the North Kona Shopping Center.

Parking The centre of Kailua can get quite congested and finding a parking space in town can be a challenge. There's free public parking in the lot behind Kona Seaside Hotel between Likana Lane and Kuakini Highway, at Hale Halawai Park, and for library users at the library off Hualalai Rd.

Just west of the library there are lots providing complimentary parking for patrons of the Kona Inn Shopping Village.

Hotel King Kamehameha, at the north end of Alii Drive, has a big pay-parking lot behind the hotel. The first 15 minutes is free and it's $1 per half hour after that. If you spend a few dollars in one of the hotel shops or restaurants you can get a voucher for free parking.

Kamakahonu & Ahuena Heiau

Kamakahonu, the beach at the north end of Kailua Bay, was the site of the royal residence of Kamehameha the Great.

Shortly after his death here in 1819, Kamehameha's successors came to Kamakahonu and ended the traditional kapu system, sounding a death knell for the old religion.

The ancient sites are now part of the grounds of the Hotel King Kamehameha. A few thatched structures along with carved wooden kii gods have been reconstructed above the old stone temple.

Ahuena Heiau, which was a place of human sacrifice, juts out into the cove and now offers protection to swimmers. The waters at Kamakahonu, which means 'eye of the turtle', are the calmest in Kailua Bay.

The hotel beach hut rents snorkels, kayaks and floats with windows. It's the only downtown swimming spot and it's popular with kids.

Hotel King Kamehameha

Be sure to take a stroll through the sprawling lobby of the Hotel King Kamehameha, which is full of museum-quality Hawaiiana displays. It includes items such as feather capes and leis, kapa beaters, quilts, war clubs, *pahoa* daggers, calabashes and gourd containers.

The musical instrument display has a nose flute, coconut shell knee drum, shell trumpet, bamboo rattles and hula sticks. Other displays are on traditional foods and fishing.

An interesting painting of King Kamehameha at Kailua Bay by Hawaiian artist Herb Kane can be viewed near the front desk.

Ahuena Heiau

The displays have interpretive plaques, but if you ask at the activity desk, they'll give you a free brochure that describes them in greater depth.

The hotel has guided historical and ethnobotanical tours free to the public. Some of the tours visit the indoor displays and others take in the hotel's historic grounds. Check at the hotel activity desk for the current schedule.

Kailua Pier

Kona has Hawaii's best deep-sea fishing and several world-class tournaments. Although most charter fishing boats now use the larger Honokohau Harbor north of Kailua, several still pull in each afternoon at Kailua Pier to hoist their catch on the scales. The Kona Coast is the world's number one fishing spot for Pacific blue marlin and some catches top 1000 pounds.

Kailua Bay was once a major cattle ship-ping area. Cattle driven down from hill ranches were stampeded into the water and forced to swim out to waiting steamers where they were hoisted aboard by sling and shipped to Honolulu slaughterhouses. Kailua Pier was built in 1915 and until the 1960s cattle pens were still in place.

Pa O Umi Point

In the 16th century the great King Umi moved his royal court from Waipio to Kona. He is thought to have landed at a lava out-cropping on the north-east side of Kailua Bay. This rocky point is called Pa O Umi, 'Umi's enclosure'.

A sea wall has been built over it but you can see just the tip of the lava point by looking over the wall in the area across the street from the Ocean View Inn.

The tiny sandy beach between Pa O Umi and Kailua Pier is **Kaiakeakua**, 'sea of the gods'. It was once Kamehameha's canoe landing.

Mokuaikaua Church

On 4 April 1820 Hawaii's first Christian missionaries landed at Kailua Bay, stepping out on to a rock that is now one of the footings for the pier. When the missionaries landed they were unaware that Hawaii's old religion had been abolished on this same spot just a few months before. They established Hawaii's first Christian church on Kailua Bay, a few minutes' walk from Kamehameha's ancient heiau and house site.

The Mokuaikaua Church was built in 1836 and is a handsome building with walls of lava rock held together with a mortar of sand and coral lime. The posts and beams are made from ohia wood, a strong termite-resistant wood which was hewn with stone adzes and smoothed down with chunks of coral. The pews and the pulpit are made of koa. The church steeple remains the highest structure in Kailua, at 112 feet.

There's usually an interpreter around to talk about the church's history from 9 am to noon and from 1 to 4 pm Monday to Saturday. A model of the brig *Thaddeus*, which brought those first Congregational missionaries, is on display in the back of the church.

Hulihee Palace

Hulihee Palace, a modest two-storey house, was built in 1838 by Governor 'John Adams' Kuakini as his private residence.

Kuakini was also the Mokuaikaua Church contractor and both buildings were of the same lava construction. The palace got its current look in 1885 when it was plastered over inside and out by King Kalakaua who had taken to a more polished style after his travels abroad.

The palace belonged to a succession of royal owners until the early 1900s when it was abandoned and fell into disrepair. The Daughters of Hawaii, a group founded in 1903 by daughters of missionaries, took it over and now operate the property as a museum.

Hawaiian royalty were huge people and everything inside the palace takes on those proportions, including a bed which is seven feet long.

Princess Ruth Keelikolani, who owned the palace in the mid-1800s, was indeed a lady of some presence, said to have weighed more than 400 pounds. She was an earthy woman, preferring to live in a big grass hut on the palace grounds rather than being confined within the palace.

After her death the wooden posts from her grass house were carved with designs of taro, leis and pineapples and used as posts in one of the beds upstairs.

The palace is furnished with antiques, many picked up on royal jaunts to Europe. Of the more Hawaiian pieces, there's an armoire made in China of Hawaiian sandalwood and inlaid with ivory. One table is inlaid with 25 kinds of native Hawaiian woods, some of which are now extinct. Kamehameha the Great's personal war spears are also on display.

The palace is open from 9 am to 4 pm daily. Admission costs $4 for adults, 50 cents for children, and includes a 30-minute tour. Although it's interesting enough, there's a bit of a haughty air about the place.

There's no charge to visit the gift shop or walk around the grounds. The stocked **fishpond** behind the palace once served as a queen's bath and before that was a canoe landing.

Sea Wall Walkway

A walkway along the sea wall begins behind the Hulihee Palace and continues south to the Kona Inn Shopping Village.

The wall is a nice place to sit and watch the surf breaking, people fishing, and boats pulling in and out of the harbour. It's typical Kona lava coastline with lots of sea urchins and scurrying black crabs camouflaged among the black rocks.

This is a quieter side of Kailua-Kona and it's possible to be totally unaware of all the traffic, shops and tourist attractions behind you.

St Michael's Church

The pink church opposite Waterfront Row is St Michael's. In the cemetery next to the church, a tiny grass hut marks the spot of an earlier thatched chapel, the first Catholic church on the Big Island.

Kealaokamalamalama Church

The green and white Kealaokamalamalama (path of the light) Church, is south and mauka of St Michael's Church. It is an independent Hawaiian Congregational church. The inside of the church is pleasantly Hawaiian with tropical flowers and a big rainbow painted on the wall.

Hale Halawai Park

Hale Halawai is a quiet oceanfront park with a few shady trees. As the coast is rocky and the sand full of coral chunks, it's not a sunbathing spot, but it is a fine place to sit and read the morning paper.

A prison and courthouse once stood at the site. Now there's a **pavilion** used by community groups for flea markets and pancake breakfasts. The park is your best bet for free public parking on the south side of the village centre.

Old Kona Airport Beach Park

The old Kona Airport, which was superseded by the current Keahole Airport in 1970, has been turned into a state recreation area and beach park. It's about a mile north of downtown Kailua, at the end of Kuakini Highway.

The old runway skirts a long sandy beach, but lava rocks run the length of the beach between the sand and the ocean. This makes for poor swimming conditions, but it's ideal for fishing and exploring tide pools. Some of the rocks have intriguing little aquarium-like pockets holding tiny sea urchins, crabs and bits of coral.

There are a couple of breaks in the lava that allow entry into the water, including one in front of the first picnic area.

A little cove, which can be reached by a short walk from the north end of the beach, is a good area for scuba divers and confident snorkellers. The reef fish are large and plentiful and in deeper waters there's good coral and a steep coral wall harbouring big moray eels and a wide variety of other sea creatures such as lionfish and cowries.

When the surf's up there's an offshore break that's popular with local surfers. In high surf it's too rough for other water activities.

While this local park is popular with families, picnickers, people drying reef fish and the like, the park is much too big to ever feel crowded. There are restrooms, showers and covered picnic tables on a lawn dotted with beach heliotrope and short coconut palms.

The Kailua end contains a new gym, soccer and softball fields and four outdoor, lighted tennis courts.

Directly behind the tennis courts there's a break in the wall marked 'Shoreline Public Access'. This leads into an exclusive subdivision, but the beach is public. If you walk along the beach a few minutes towards Kailua-Kona, you'll come to a sandy area with a big wading pool a few feet deep. It's a great place for kids.

Saltwater Pool

One of Kona's best-kept secrets is a saltwater swimming pool in a little lava outcrop so close to the ocean that waves lap in over the side. It's as large as most condo pools and it's open to the public.

The pool was once part of a retired admiral's private estate. By the time it was sold to developers (Kona by the Sea condos are here now) all coastline had become public domain.

Kona by the Sea (see the Kailua-Keauhou Condos map) has put in four public beach access spaces in its parking lot. A narrow path on the north side of the complex leads from the parking lot down to the pool.

The admiral had good taste. You float above the ocean and can glance over the edge and watch surfers riding into shore. Watch it when you're getting into the pool as the steps are slippery.

Magic Sands Beach Park

It's called Magic Sands, White Sands and Disappearing Sands, but it's all the same beach, midway between Kailua and Keauhou. In the winter when the surf is high, the sand can disappear literally overnight,

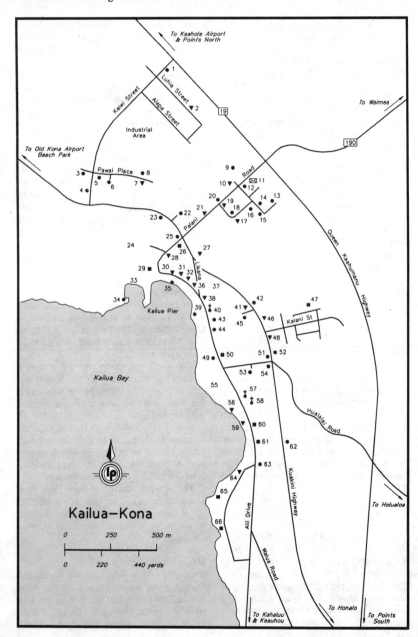

To Keahole Airport
& Points North

To Waimea

To Old Kona Airport
Beach Park

Kaiwi Street

Luhia Street

Alapa Street

Industrial
Area

19

190

Pawai Place

Queen Kaahumanu Highway

Palani Road

Likana

Kailua Pier

Kailua Bay

Kalani St

Hualalai Road

Kuakini Highway

Alii Drive

Wailua Road

To Holualoa

To Kahaluu
& Keauhou

To Honalo

To Points
South

Kailua–Kona

0   250   500 m

0   220   440 yards

■ PLACES TO STAY

26 Kona Seaside Hotel
29 Hotel King Kamehameha
47 Patey's Place
50 Kona Bay Hotel
60 Kona Islander Inn
61 Kona Alii
65 Kona Hilton
66 Hale Kona Kai

▼ PLACES TO EAT

2 Jennifer's Korean Barbecue
7 Su's Thai Kitchen
10 Sizzler
17 Kona Mix Plate
19 Burger King
21 Pizza Hut & Taco Bell
27 Kona Ranchhouse
28 Quinn's
30 Kona Amigos
31 Ocean View Inn
32 Cafe Sibu
36 Marty's Steak & Seafoods
38 Suzanne's Bakeshop
41 Jack in the Box
46 Eclipse
48 McDonald's
56 Waterfront Row
59 Jolly Roger
64 Huggo's

OTHER

1 Kaahumanu Plaza
3 Kailua Candy Co

4 Budget
5 B & L Bike & Sports
6 VIP Car Rental
8 Laundromat
9 Kona Coast Shopping Center
11 Post Office
12 First Hawaiian Bank
13 Bowling Alley
14 Lanihau Center
15 Waldenbooks
16 Longs Drugs
18 Hilo Hattie
20 Kona Coast Divers
22 North Kona Shopping Center
23 Kamehameha Square
24 Pay Parking
25 Gas Station (24-hour)
33 Kamakahonu Beach
34 Ahuena Heiau
35 Pa O Umi Point
37 Free Parking
39 Hulihee Palace
40 Mokuaikaua Church
42 Laundromat
43 Kona Plaza
44 Kona Marketplace
45 Kona Center
49 Kona Inn Shopping Village
51 Bank of Hawaii
52 7-Eleven Store
53 Library
54 Gas Station
55 Hale Halawai Park
57 St Michael's Church
58 Kealaokamalamalama Church
62 Hualalai Theatres
63 Jack's Diving Locker

leaving only rocks on the shore. And then just as magically it returns and again becomes a fine white-sand beach.

This is a very popular bodysurfing beach when the rocks aren't exposed. There's also a volleyball court, restrooms and picnic tables.

Places to Stay

In Kona, condos outnumber hotels many times over. Condos tend to be cheaper than hotels if you're staying awhile, although for advance reservations there are deposits and cancellation penalties to deal with. Unlike hotels, most condos have a three-day

minimum and during high season some have a seven-day minimum.

All Kona hotels and condos listed here have swimming pools unless otherwise noted.

Places to Stay – bottom end

The cheapest place to stay in town is *Patey's Place* (☎ 326-7018, (800) 972-7408 in Hawaii), 75-195 Ala-Ona Ona, Kailua-Kona, HI 96740, a new hostel-style accommodation. Dormitory beds cost $14, double rooms cost $35, and linen is provided. There's a TV room, lockers and free use of the kitchen. It's open 24 hours and is about a 10-minute walk from Kailua's downtown area.

One of the area's best deals is the *Kona Tiki Hotel* (☎ 329-1425), Box 1567, Kailua-Kona, HI 96745, on Alii Drive at the 1.5-mile marker. It's an older three-storey complex, which has 15 rooms, all with refrigerators and breezy oceanfront lanais. It's unpretentious, with a friendly management. Nice touches include complimentary coffee and breakfast pastries and a small seaside pool. Although it's right on the road the surf drowns out the sound of traffic.

Rooms have recently been refurbished and are quite pleasant. All but two have both a queen and a twin bed. Rates are $50 for standard rooms, $55 with kitchenettes, plus $5 more for a third person. The hotel is very popular with return visitors and generally books up in advance during the high season.

Kona Seaside Hotel (☎ 329-2455, (800) 367-7000 from the USA, (800) 654-7020 from Canada), 75-5646 Palani Rd, Kailua-Kona, HI 96740, has two sections. One's a modern six-storey building with private lanais and the standard amenities, priced from $70. The older refurbished Hukilau wing is simpler and has walls that carry sound, making the $64 rate a lesser value.

You can often get a cheaper local rate on both sections if you book within Hawaii. Discounted room rates, and a package that includes a free Budget rental car and room at $98 for two nights, are perpetually advertised in the Sunday Honolulu paper. To get the best deal skip the toll free number and call the local booking desk (☎ 922-1228).

For those who want to be right in the centre of town, there's Uncle Billy's *Kona Bay Hotel* (☎ 329-1393, (800) 367-5102 from the US mainland, (800) 442-5841 in Hawaii), 75-5739 Alii Drive, Kailua-Kona, HI 96740. The older cinder-block buildings lack charm but at $62 it's relatively cheap.

Three Bears' Bed & Breakfast (☎ 325-7563), 72-1001 Puukala St, Kailua-Kona, HI 96740, is a delightful cedar home seven miles north of Kailua centre, off Hwy 190. The home has a hillside location, sweeping views of the Kona coast and good conditions

for stargazing from the lanai. The two comfortable rooms have private baths, microwaves and cable TV. Owners Anne and Art are active in environmental issues, speak fluent German and know the island inside out.

For travellers with their own transportation, this would make a good base for exploring Kona, Waimea and the Waikoloa areas. Rates, which include a generous European-style breakfast and all the home-grown macadamia nuts you can crack, are $55 and $65 a night, with a two-day minimum stay, or $350 and $410 a week.

Kiwi Gardens (☎ 326-1559), 74-4920 Kiwi St, Kailua-Kona, HI 96740, is a B&B about three miles north of Kailua centre. Ron and Shirlee Freitas, who resettled here from the San Francisco area, rent three rooms in their contemporary home. One is a queen-bed room with a lanai and a sunset view for $60, another is a smaller double-bed room with wicker furniture for $50. These two rooms share a bathroom, although only one room is booked at a time unless there's a group travelling together. The third room is a master suite with a king brass bed, private bathroom and a lanai for $80.

All three rooms share a large common space with a big-screen TV, VCR, pool table and refrigerator. The house has a stylish Art-Deco theme, with antique aloha shirts on the walls, signed baseball cards, a vintage jukebox and the like. Breakfast includes coffee, juice, fruits from the yard and pastries.

Places to Stay – top-end hotels

The 460-room *Hotel King Kamehameha* (☎ 329-2911, (800) 367-6060), 75-5660 Palani Rd, Kailua-Kona, HI 96740, is located on Kailua Bay and the only beach in town. The sprawling koa-wood lobby is full of Hawaiiana displays and this is the site of King Kamehameha's former residence. Rates range from $115 to $195, $10 less in the low season.

Kona Hilton (☎ 329-3111, (800) 445-8667), Box 1179, Kailua-Kona, HI 96740, has an oceanfront location on the edge of

Left: Rainbow Falls, Hilo, Big Island
Right: Akaka Falls, Hamakua Coast, Big Island
Bottom: Kayakers at Keauhou Beach, Big Island

Top: Halemaumau Crater, Hawaii Volcanoes National Park, Big Island
Left: Mule-wagon tour, Waipio Valley, Big Island
Right: Hillside lava flow, Hawaii Volcanoes National Park, Big Island

town. There's no beach but there is a shallow saltwater pool built out of a tide pool that's deep enough for swimming. There are 452 rooms, with rates from $130.

Places to Stay – condominiums

Most of Kona's condos are quite nice, have complete kitchens and are fully furnished with everything from linen to cooking utensils. The general rule is that the weekly rate is six times the daily rate and the monthly rate is three times the weekly. However in the high season, if business is brisk, most places will offer only the daily rate, while in the off months of April, May and September you might be able to negotiate an even better deal.

If you wait until you arrive in Kona to look for a place, you can sometimes find a good deal in the classified ads of *West Hawaii Today*. However, this is risky during the high season as many places are booked up months in advance.

The *Kona Islander Inn* (☎ 329-3181, (800) 922-7866), 75-5776 Kuakini Hwy, Kailua-Kona, HI 96740, is an older development in the town centre. Some of the units are musty, particularly those on the bottom floor. Aston handles 67 of the 150 units and maintains a front desk, running them like a hotel. It's $84 for rooms with refrigerators, plus $10 more if you want a kitchenette.

The handful of Kona Islander Inn units rented by Hawaii Resort Management (next door on Alii Drive) are a better deal. They cost from $46/60 for low/high season, with a three-day minimum, and the units include hot plates and microwaves. The Kona Islander Inn has insufficient parking and finding a space can be a problem when it's full.

Kona White Sands is a two-storey building with 10 bargain units, all with kitchenettes and lanais. Studios cost $45/50 low/high and one-bedroom units cost $55/60 if booked through Hawaii Resort Management. The minimum stay is three days. There's no pool, but it's opposite White Sands Beach.

Kona Billfisher, mauka of the Hilton, has units that are large and quite well furnished

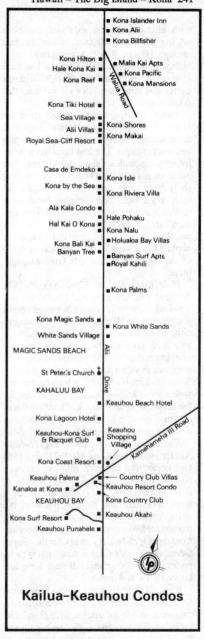

Kona Islander Inn
Kona Alii
Kona Billfisher

Kona Hilton
Hale Kona Kai
Kona Reef

Malia Kai Apts
Kona Pacific
Kona Mansions

Walua Road

Kona Tiki Hotel

Sea Village
Alii Villas
Royal Sea-Cliff Resort

Kona Shores
Kona Makai

Casa de Emdeko
Kona Isle
Kona by the Sea
Kona Riviera Villa

Ala Kala Condo
Hale Pohaku
Hal Kai O Kona
Kona Nalu
Kona Bali Kai
Holualoa Bay Villas
Banyan Tree
Banyan Surf Apts
Royal Kahili

Kona Palms

Kona Magic Sands
Kona White Sands
White Sands Village
MAGIC SANDS BEACH

Alii

St Peter's Church
KAHALUU BAY

Drive

Keauhou Beach Hotel

Kona Lagoon Hotel
Keauhou-Kona Surf & Racquet Club

Keauhou Shopping Village

Kamehameha III Road

Kona Coast Resort

Keauhou Palena
Country Club Villas
Kanaloa at Kona
Keauhou Resort Condo
KEAUHOU BAY
Kona Country Club
Kona Surf Resort
Keauhou Akahi
Keauhou Punahele

Kailua-Keauhou Condos

with kitchens, lanais, sofabeds and both ceiling fans and air-con. When booked through Hawaii Resort Management, one-bedroom units cost $60/75 for the low/high season, two-bedroom units $80/95. There's a three-day minimum. It's good value for this price range.

Malia Kai Apartments, inland from the Hilton on Walua Rd, has 21 units, each with three levels. The bottom level has a carport and washer/dryer. The 2nd floor has a lanai, living room with sofabed and kitchen. The 3rd floor has one main bedroom with sliding shoji doors separating it from another room with a sofabed. The complex has a nice garden courtyard with a small pool. The units aren't all that spiffy but if you're with a few people it could be economical. Rates are about $450 a week in the high season, $350 in the low season, through Triad Management.

Hale Kona Kai (☎ 329-2155), 75-5870 Kahakai Rd, Kailua-Kona, HI 96740, is a real find, right on the ocean in a quiet corner just beyond the Hilton. The 39 one-bedroom units aren't brand new, but they're comfortable and have standard features like full kitchens and cable TV. All have lanais with great ocean views and the sound of the surf. Rates are $75. It's $10 more for a corner unit with a wrap-around lanai and $10 more for the third and fourth person. There's a three-day minimum, a $150 security deposit and no Sunday or holiday check-in.

Kona Bali Kai (☎ 329-9381), 76-6246 Alii Drive, Kailua-Kona, HI 96740, is a 155-unit oceanfront complex midway between Kailua and Keauhou. Colony Hotels & Resorts (☎ (800) 777-1700) maintains a front desk here and handles many of the units, which range from mountain-facing studios for $90 a day to two-bedroom ocean-front units for $160. If you ask for the 'Super Saver' rate there's often a discount on these prices or a free upgrade. All units have full kitchens, TV and lanais.

Rentals handled by Kona Vacation Resorts are cheaper, costing $60/360/1080 a day/week/month for studios, $125/750/2250 for two-bedroom units. Either way, units are privately owned and are decorated according to the whim of the owner – some are quite nice, while others are a bit run down.

Alii Villas (☎ 329-1288), 75-6016 Alii Drive, Kailua-Kona, HI 96740, has 126 units and is a comfortable, quiet place with good ocean breezes. The units are large and each has a private lanai, cable TV and washer/dryer. Most have a phone and sofabed. One-bedroom units are $350 to $490 a week, depending on the season and unit. You can either contact Alii Villas directly or book through Hawaii Resort Management.

Sea Village (☎ 329-1000), 75-6002 Alii Drive, Kailua-Kona, HI 96740, is a condo near Alii Villas, but it's run more like a hotel and rates are higher. One-bedroom units are a pricey $90/106 in the low/high season and two-bedroom units are about $25 more. The minimum stay is three nights. There are tennis courts.

Kona Makai, on the ocean side of Alii Drive next to Alii Villas, has one-bedroom units with everything including washer/dryer, and cost from $80 through Kona Vacation Resorts. There's an exercise room and tennis courts.

Casa de Emdeko (☎ 329-2160), 75-6082 Alii Drive, Kailua-Kona, HI 96740, is a newer complex. The one-bedroom units are pleasant and have all the standard amenities although there's not much of an oceanfront view and the lanais line up at an angle facing other lanais. There are fresh and saltwater pools. Rates for one-bedroom units are $85/95 in low/high season through Hawaii Resort Management and from $75 through Kona Vacation Resorts.

Kona Reef (☎ 329-4780, (800) 367-7040), 75-5888 Alii Drive, Kailua-Kona, HI 96740, south of the Hilton, is a condo complex run like a hotel by Hawaiiana Resorts. It's modern, with all amenities including washer/dryers and private lanais. Rates are $105 to $125 for up to four people in a one-bedroom unit, which has a sofabed in the living room. In low season it's $10 less and the seventh night is free.

Royal Sea-Cliff Resort (☎ 329-8021,

(800) 922-7866), 75-6040 Alii Drive, Kailua-Kona, HI 96740, is modern and architecturally striking, with angular lines. The units are some of the nicest in Kona, with large balconies, stylish furnishings and very full kitchens. There are tennis courts, pools and a sauna. Aston runs it like a hotel with a front desk and there's no minimum stay. Studios are $135/155 in the low/high season. The units are ritzier than Aston's more expensive Kona by the Sea complex.

Vacation Rental Agencies Many condominiums can be booked through a few rental agencies, each handling different units within the complex. For condos with an address listed, you can write directly to the condo. Either they handle their own bookings or they'll pass correspondence on to the agents that do.

For the rest, units are handled by at least one of the three following agencies. They'll send their latest listings and rates upon request. It's worth comparing listings before booking.

Hawaii Resort Management, 75-5776 Kuakini Hwy, Suite 105C, Kailua-Kona, HI 96740 (☎ 329-9393, (800) 553-5035)
Kona Vacation Resorts, 77-6435 Kuakini Hwy, Kailua-Kona, HI 96740 (☎ 329-6488, (800) 367-5168 from the USA, (800) 800-5662 from Canada)
Triad Management, North Kona Shopping Center, 75-5629-P Kuakini Hwy, Kailua-Kona, HI 96740 (☎ 329- 6402)

Places to Eat

Kona has lots of restaurants, including fast food, good ethnic food and some fine oceanfront spots. It also has its fair share of mediocre tourist traps.

Places to Eat – bottom end

For a good cheap meal on the run try the *French Bakery* at Kaahumanu Plaza in the industrial area. This is Kona's best bakery, with good French bread, tempting strudels and hearty three-seed muffins. The Tongan bread, which costs $2.50 and is filled with cheese and vegetables, makes a good meal

and can be microwaved on request. Croissant sandwiches are also $2.50. It's open from 6 am to 4 pm Monday to Saturday.

The unassuming *Ocean View Inn* on Alii Drive has been a central Kona landmark for generations. This is where local folks come to eat local food. Complete breakfasts with coffee cost $2.75 to $5. Sandwiches are $1.50 to $2, burgers with French fries $4. You can get inexpensive Chinese, American and Hawaiian foods and it's a good place to try lomi salmon marinated with tomatoes and green onion or a side dish of poi. There's a view of Kailua Bay through the louvered windows.

The new *Kona Mix Plate* in Kopiko Plaza is a popular eatery with counter service and good-value local food. Mahimahi or calamari sandwiches, burgers and shrimp gyoza are all $3.50, while teriyaki, tonkatsu or barbecue chicken plates are about $5. It's open from 10 am to 8 pm Monday to Saturday.

For a healthy fast-food alternative *Kona Healthways*, a health-food store in the Kona Coast Shopping Center, has fresh green salads made with organically grown island produce for $3.25. It also has takeaway sandwiches, snacks, juices and yoghurt. Some of the locally grown items include dried shiitake mushrooms, Rooster Farms' organic coffee, macadamia nuts and spirulina.

The *Sizzler* in the Kona Coast Shopping Center has the best salad bar in town, with a good selection of vegies and fresh fruit plus pasta, soup and a tortilla bar for $7.50. This is also a family-style steak and seafood restaurant.

The *Royal Jade Garden* in the Lanihau Center has fair Chinese food at $4 to $5 for a combo plate served cafeteria-style from warmer trays. It's best to go around meal time when the food is fresher. You can also order from the menu for a few dollars more. It's open from 10.30 am to 10 pm daily.

Express Pizza in the Lanihau Center sells pizza by the slice for $1.50 to $2. Whole pizzas range from $8 to $18.

Suzanne's Bakeshop, on Likana Lane below the public parking lot, sells pastries, desserts and coffee and has a couple of tiny tables near the sidewalk where you can eat.

In addition to a couple of restaurants, Waterfront Row has a few small food stalls selling reasonably priced salads, tacos and sandwiches.

Kona also has a *McDonald's, Pizza Hut, Taco Bell, Burger King, Jack in the Box, Subway Sandwiches* and a *Kentucky Fried Chicken*.

Places to Eat – middle

Su's Thai Kitchen (☎ 326-7808), on Pawai Place in Kailua's industrial area, has good Thai food with flavourful curries. At dinner time, 5 to 9 pm daily, pad Thai costs $7, most curries are $8 and their speciality, volcano chicken with a sweet and sour sauce, is $13. At lunch, from 11 am to 2.30 pm weekdays, you can get pad Thai, tom yam soup or the curry of the day with rice for $6. The mood, like the food, is authentically Thai – there are about a dozen tables on a small outdoor lanai, which is lit by candles at night.

Cafe Sibu at Banyan Court serves delicious Indonesian food in a casual cafe setting. The combination plates for $11 to $12 offer three dishes (with choices like Balinese chicken, spicy Indian curry and shrimp satay) over brown rice. The huge gado gado, served over rice and covered with peanut sauce, costs $9.50. They also have a daily Italian dish, often garlic shrimp over linguine for $13, vegetarian dishes and good karma. It's open from 11.30 am to 9 pm daily.

Kona Ranchhouse (☎ 329-7061), up a driveway off Kuakini Highway, just south of Palani Rd, serves good breakfasts between 6.30 am and noon, from about $4. Lunch, which is served until 4.30 pm, is in the $6 to $10 range, while dinners are $9 to $20 and feature salads, seafood, barbecued meats and a few Mexican dishes. It's a popular place and evenings can be busy, so dinner reservations are a good idea, particularly on weekends. For a glimpse of paniolo Hawaii check out the old photos of island ranches hanging from the dining room walls.

Papagayos Mexican Grill (☎ 326-5660) in Kamehameha Square serves fairly good Mexican food, with both indoor and outdoor seating. Dishes range from a taco and enchilada served with rice and beans for $7.75 to sizzling fajitas for $12.50. Items are also served à la carte, with tacos for $3 and burritos for around $4. Papagayos is closed on Tuesdays, but otherwise it opens at 11 am, except on Sundays when it's open for dinner only.

For Korean food there's *Jennifer's Korean Barbecue* (☎ 326-1155), an airy, 2nd-floor restaurant in Kailua's industrial area. A dinner of yakiniku beef, chicken or pork cooked right at your table and served with rice, soup, salad and kimchee costs $12. Kitchen-prepared lunch plates with various meat and fish combinations cost $5 to $7. The plates are basically 'local food' with a Korean accent and include the requisite two scoops of rice and one scoop of macaroni salad. Opening hours are 10.30 am to 10.30 pm Monday to Saturday.

Quinn's, on Palani Rd opposite the Hotel King Kamehameha, serves dinner until 1 am. The crowd is mostly long-time residents who come for both the bar and the consistently good fish and steak dinners. For the setting, prices aren't cheap, but fish portions are huge.

Marty's Steak & Seafoods, an old stand-by on Alii Drive, is a 2nd-floor open-air restaurant that has sandwiches with salad and French fries for $5 to $6 at lunch, mahimahi and teriyaki chicken for $13 for dinner. At dinner all entrees include a rather limited salad bar.

Kona Amigos is a 2nd-floor open-air Mexican restaurant opposite the Kailua Pier. Between 4 and 6 pm they usually have early bird specials on food and drink and if you get a window seat you can watch fishers bring their boats into harbour and hoist up their catch of marlin and tuna. Prices are moderate and the food is on the bland side.

Jolly Roger, near Waterfront Row, serves ordinary American fare, but you can't get any closer to the water than their oceanfront tables. Breakfast dishes and lunch time sandwiches are $4 to $8 while dinners range from $9 to $14.

Huggo's is on the oceanfront beside the Hilton. The most popular meal is the $7.95 lunch time ribs special every Tuesday and Thursday from 11.30 am when there's usually a line of people waiting for tables. Dinner is largely seafood and steak with prices averaging about $20.

Places to Eat – top end

Phillip Paolo's (☎ 329-4436) on the upper floor of Waterfront Row has good Italian food, generous portions and attentive service in a fine-dining atmosphere complete with an ocean view. They're open for dinner only, from 4.30 pm daily. Dishes range from fettucine alfredo for $14 to steak capri or fresh fish of the day for $26. Garlic cheese bread topped with fresh basil comes with all meals. They sometimes have an early bird special for $10 that's one of the best food values in Kona.

The *Chart House* at Waterfront Row has a rather good salad bar, with fruit, clam chowder and bread for $12.75. Main dishes, which include the salad bar, range from $15.75 for teriyaki steak kabobs to $23 for shrimp scampi. When business is slow they sometimes offer an early bird special that includes fresh catch of the day and salad from the salad bar for $13.

Kona Inn, in the centre of the village, opened in 1929 as the Big Island's first hotel. It's now a shopping centre with a large and popular restaurant of the same name. Steak and seafood dinners are in the $15 to $30 range. Light meals are available from 11.30 am to midnight and include calamari sandwiches for $6 and steak sandwiches or jumbo fried shrimp for $10.

Jameson's by the Sea (☎ 329-3195) on Magic Sands Beach is a spin-off of the popular restaurant on Oahu's North Shore. Dinner entrees begin at $16, although the speciality is the fish of the day, usually priced at around $24. There's also a lunch menu at about half-price. The food is rather average fare and not overly inspired. The Yokohama soup at $3.75 is a savory exception. The oceanside tables are quite pleasant and about as close as you can get to the surf without getting your feet wet. It's open for lunch from 11 am to 3 pm Monday to Friday and for dinner from 5 to 10 pm daily.

Places to Eat – buffets

For a splurge, Kona Hilton and the King Kamehameha Hotel put on top-notch Sunday champagne brunches. Both include an array of appetizers from Alaskan crab legs to sushi, prime rib, numerous hot dishes, salads and desserts. The King Kamehameha has more extensive fruit and dessert selections, while the Hilton has a Haagen-Dazs sundae bar and a superior waterfront locale. Both charge $20. The Hilton brunch runs from 9 am to 1.30 pm, King Kamehameha's from 9 am to 1 pm.

The *Keauhou Beach Hotel* (☎ 322-3441) in Keauhou has a good seafood buffet from 5 to 9 pm Friday to Sunday for $20. Fried oysters, steamed clams, sashimi, crab legs, marlin and prime rib are featured.

Although the setting isn't as nice, the seafood buffet at King Kamehameha Hotel has basically the same offerings as the Keauhou one and is $4 cheaper at $16. It's open from 5 to 9 pm on Fridays and Saturdays.

Entertainment

Kona has no shortage of sunset views or happy hour come-ons at restaurants and bars all along Alii Drive.

The *Eclipse* restaurant and bar on Kuakini Highway has dancing from 10 pm to 1 am Wednesday to Sunday. It only plays mostly top 40 music with a little reggae mixed in. You have to be 21 to get in and there's a $4 cover charge on Fridays and Saturdays.

Papagayos at Kamehameha Square has live bands from 10 pm to 2 am Thursday to Saturday. *Philip Paolo's* at Waterfront Row has live jazz or Hawaiian reggae from 9 pm to 1.30 am on Fridays and Saturdays. *Huggo's* has live entertainment from 8.30 pm nightly.

Hualalai Theatres on Kuakini Highway shows standard Hollywood films. The *World Square Theatre* in the Kona Marketplace has mostly Hollywood movies and the occasional alternative film. World Square sells baked goodies from Aloha Cafe in Kainailu.

Luaus *Hotel King Kamehameha* (☎ 329-2911) has a luau on Sundays, Tuesdays and Thursdays on its beach in front of Ahuena Heiau. It begins with a lei greeting at 5.30 pm, followed by torch lighting, an imu ceremony, a buffet dinner and Polynesian show. The cost is $42 for adults, $15 for children aged from 6 to 10. If you just want to watch them bury the pig in the imu, they do that with a little commentary at 10.15 am on luau days.

The *Kona Hilton* has a less-authentic luau buffet and hula show from 6 to 9 pm on Mondays, Wednesdays and Fridays. It costs $44. One child under the age of 12 is free with each paying adult.

Getting Around

The red, white and blue Alii Shuttle (☎ 775-7121) makes a 45-minute run between Kailua village and Keauhou resort 10 times in each direction daily. The first bus leaves the Kona Inn Shopping Village at 8 am and the last bus returns from the Kona Surf Resort at 10 pm. This is a fine way to get to Kahaluu Beach Park if you're in Kailua without a car. The fare anywhere along the route is $1 each way.

KEAUHOU

Keauhou is the coastal area immediately south of Kailua-Kona. It starts at Kahaluu Bay and runs south beyond Keauhou Bay and the Kona Surf Resort.

Keauhou contains a planned community of three hotels, nine condo complexes, a shopping centre and a 27-hole golf course, all neatly spaced out with a country club atmosphere. Bishop Estate, Hawaii's largest private landholder, owns the land.

The area was once the site of a major Hawaiian settlement, supported by an abundance of fresh spring water. Several historical sites can still be explored, although they now share their grounds with the hotels and condos.

Information

Tourist Information Keauhou Visitors Association (☎ 322-3866), 78-6831 Alii Drive, Suite 234, Kailua-Kona, HI 96740, can mail out information and brochures on Keauhou.

Keauhou has a free on-call shuttle service (☎ 322-3500) that runs around the resort between 8 am and 4.30 pm daily.

Hawaiiana Keauhou senior citizens offer demonstrations on crafts and culture every Friday at 10 am in the outdoor courtyard at Keauhou Shopping Village. Some weeks they make leis and demonstrate lauhala weaving; other weeks they teach visitors to speak Hawaiian and provide Hawaiian entertainment.

Shopping Keauhou Shopping Village, the shopping centre on the corner of Alii Drive and Kamehameha III Rd, has a large KTA supermarket, newsstands, a contract post office and about 35 shops and restaurants. Keauhou Village Book Shop has a good collection of travel guides and books on Hawaii along with some mainland newspapers.

Penthouse, a clearance store for the upmarket Liberty House department store, is located in the Keauhou Beach Hotel. They have good-quality clothing at discounted prices and you can sometimes find a good selection of aloha shirts and Hawaiian print skirts. The best deals are on the first Sunday of the month when prices are slashed to make room for new stock. It's open daily except Tuesday and Wednesday.

Produce Sellers Island produce and flowers are sold along the roadside opposite the Keauhou Beach Hotel. In addition to organic vegetables, sellers have papayas, Kau oranges, mangoes, starfruit and anything else that's in season. The food is fresher and cheaper than you'll find in the grocery stores.

St Peter's Church

The little blue church on the north side of Kahaluu Bay is St Peter's Catholic Church.

It dates back to 1880 although it was moved from White Sands Beach to this site in 1912. Tidal waves have since attempted to relocate it on a couple of occasions.

This is Hawaii's most photographed 'quaint church' and it's still used for weekend services and weddings.

Just north of the church is what remains of the foundation of **Kuemanu Heiau**, a surfing temple. Hawaiian royalty, who surfed the waters at the north end of Kahaluu Bay, paid their respects at this temple before hitting the waves.

Between the heiau and the church there's a spring-fed pond where the alii used to bathe after surfing.

Locals keep up the surfing tradition, although high surf usually generates dangerous northward rip currents and it's not a good spot for beginners.

Kahaluu Beach

Kahaluu, 'the diving place', is the island's best easy-access snorkelling spot. The bay is like a big natural aquarium and it's a good place to learn to snorkel. It's not even necessary to go out over your head to enjoy it.

Large rainbow parrotfish, schools of silver needlefish, brilliant yellow tangs, butterfly fish and colourful wrasses are among the numerous tropicals easily seen here.

The fish are tame enough to eat out of your hand. If you hold out some bread or peas the frenzied swarms can give quite a rush!

There are lots of fish in the shallows but generally the deeper the water the better the coral and the larger the fish. Spotted moray eels are not that hard to find either.

An ancient breakwater, said to have been menehune-built, is on the reef and protects the bay. Still, when the surf is high Kahaluu can have strong currents that pull in the direction of the rocks near St Peter's Church and it's easy to drift away without realising it. Check your bearings occasionally to make sure you're not being pulled by the current.

A plaque by the picnic pavilion explains water conditions and gives a little information on marine life in the bay. Check it out before you go in.

A lifeguard is on duty daily. There's usually a snack van selling refreshments. Another van rents snorkel sets at $3 for the first hour and $1 an hour after that as well as 35mm underwater cameras for $12.50 an hour, plus film.

The park has a sandy beach, showers, restrooms, changing rooms, picnic tables and grills. It's a popular place and often draws a crowd.

Keauhou Beach Hotel

The grounds of Keauhou Beach Hotel, immediately south of Kahaluu Beach, contain some easily explored historical sites. A one-page brochure on the sites is available at the bell desk.

The ruins of **Kapuanoni**, a fishing temple that contains the remains of an old koa canoe, is on the north side of the hotel.

The reconstructed **summer beach house** of King Kalakaua is inland, beside a spring-fed pond once used as a royal bath. You can peek into the simple three-room cottage and see a portrait of the king in his European-style royal dress, a Hawaiian quilt on the bed and lauhala mats on the floor.

Other heiau sites are on the south side of the hotel. The remains of the seaside **Keeku Heiau**, just beyond the footbridge that leads to the Kona Lagoon Hotel, is thought to have been a luakini heiau.

There are some great **tide pools** nearby, in a low shelf of smooth *pahoehoe* lava, which are best explored when the tide is low. The pools contain numerous sea urchins, including spiny and slate pencil types, and small tropical fish.

When the tide is at its very lowest you can walk out onto a flat lava tongue that is carved with numerous **petroglyphs**. The site is directly in front of the northern end of the Kona Lagoon Hotel, with most of the petroglyphs about 25 feet from the shore. Other than at low tide the petroglyphs are submerged and cannot be seen.

The Keauhou Beach Hotel grounds also has a **fertility pit**, carved wooden god images, historic *kuula* stones sacred to fishers and an ancient house site or two.

Free historical walks are given by the hotel a couple of mornings a week. If you're interested, check with the bell hop for the schedule.

Keauhou Bay

Keauhou Bay, which has a launch ramp and space for two dozen small boats, is one of the most protected bays on the west coast.

Snorkelling is pretty good in the bay, but you have to watch out for the boat traffic. The only facilities are restrooms and showers.

A stone marking the site where Kamehameha III was born in 1814 is in a small garden just south of the harbourside dive shacks. The young prince was said to have been stillborn and brought back to life on this rock by a visiting kahuna.

To get to the bay turn makai off Alii Drive onto Kamehameha III Rd. Or, alternatively, drive down Kaleopapa Rd toward Kona Surf Resort. Continue to the end of the road instead of turning into the resort.

Manta Rays

If you're looking for something to do in the evening, you could go down to Kona Surf Resort and watch the manta rays that sometimes gather in the late evening at the rocky outcrop below the resort's saltwater pool. They're attracted by the spotlights that shine down onto the ocean which means they are less likely to make a showing around the full moon.

The wing tips of these impressive creatures often measure up to 12 feet across. It's hypnotic to watch the manta rays cruise around in the surf as their white underbellies flash against the dark waters.

Places to Stay

The 318-room *Keauhou Beach Hotel* (☎ 322-3441, (800) 367-6025), 78-6740 Alii Drive, Kailua-Kona, HI 96740, adjoins Kahaluu Beach Park. The grounds have interesting historical sites and tide pools to explore. Rates range from $91 to $145. Ask for the 'Mahalo Special' and you'll get a free rental car for the same rates.

Kona Surf Resort (☎ 322-3411, (800)

367-8011), 78-128 Ehukai St, Kailua-Kona, HI 96740, is a modern, sprawling, 553-room hotel oriented to Japanese package tourists. It has some interesting Polynesian carvings and decor, a little wedding chapel, tennis courts and both salt and freshwater pools. It's rather isolated on a rugged and rocky lava point on the south side of Keauhou Bay. Rates range from $109 to $185, $10 less in the low season. There's a daytime shuttle service between the hotel and Kailua-Kona village.

The *Keauhou Resort Condominiums* (☎ 322-9122, (800) 367-5286), 78-7039 Kamehameha III Rd, Kailua-Kona, HI 96740, has 48 units with full kitchens and washer/dryers. Although the units are about 20 years old they are well maintained and are the cheapest in Keauhou. One-bedroom units are $65/75 in the low/high season with a garden view, $75/85 with an ocean view. Add $20 more for a two-bedroom unit for up to four people. The minimum stay is five days. It's near the golf course and there's a pool.

At the other end of the spectrum is *Kanaloa at Kona* (☎ 322-9625, (800) 777-1700), 78-261 Manukai St, Kailua-Kona, HI 96740, operated by Colony Hotels & Resorts. It has 114 condo units ranging from $150 for a one-bedroom apartment with a golf course view to $275 for a three-bedroom unit with an ocean view. All units have lanais with wet bars as well as the standard amenities. The oceanfront units also have jacuzzis. There are three pools and two lighted tennis courts.

Other Keauhou condos are priced between the two and are largely booked through vacation rental agents. Kona Vacation Resorts (☎ 329-6488, (800) 367-5168), 77-6435 Kuakini Hwy, Kailua-Kona, HI 96740, handles units in most of them.

Places to Eat

The Terrace Restaurant is outdoors at the Kanaloa at Kona condos. It's got a poolside condo atmosphere but it's on the ocean and the food's OK. At lunch time, from 11 am to 2 pm, sandwiches and other dishes cost from

$6 to $9. Dinner, however, is about double that. To get there, turn makai off Alii Drive onto Kamehameha III Rd and then right onto Manukai St. Ask the gatekeeper where to park.

Drysdale's Two in the Keauhou Shopping Village is popular for sandwiches and burgers in the $5 to $7 range and is a hot spot for watching sports on TV. It's open from 10 am to at least midnight, with food service stopping at 11 pm.

Rocky's Pizza at the Keauhou Shopping Village sells pizza by the slice or the pie. The shopping centre also has a *Baskin-Robbins* ice-cream shop.

Keauhou Beach Hotel and *Kona Surf Resort* both have a few restaurants. At lunch *Pele's Court* in the Kona Surf Resort has a nice garden setting and offers a special that includes any sandwich on the menu, the soup of the day and fresh fruit for a reasonable $6.75.

For dinner Keauhou Beach Hotel has oceanfront dining and good buffets, served from 5 to 9 pm. On weekdays it features Chinese food for $13, while at weekends it features seafood for $20. There's also a Sunday champagne brunch buffet for $17.

Entertainment

Keauhou Beach Hotel's *Makai Bar*, an open-air thatched building right on the shoreline, has good sunset views and live Hawaiian music every evening except Sundays when there's jazz. Each night there's a different tropical drink for $4 and domestic beer for $3, served with free pupus. There's no cover charge.

The *Kona Surf Resort* presents a Polynesian show at its Nalu Terrace lounge from 5.30 to 6.30 pm on Tuesdays and Fridays. While the show is free, no doubt they appreciate you buying a drink.

Stand-up comics are showcased in a Kona Comedy Club performance at 8 pm on Tuesdays at the Kona Surf Resort.

The Kona Surf also occasionally hosts some big-name mainland jazz and blues musicians and some well-known Hawaiian musicians.

HOLUALOA

Holualoa is perched in the hills, 1400 feet above Kailua-Kona. The slopes catch afternoon showers so it's lusher and cooler than on the coast below.

Holualoa is an artist's community with craft shops, galleries and a community art centre. It's a friendly place with lots of aloha and is delightful to poke around.

Information & Orientation

This is pretty much a one-road village, with everything lined up along Hwy 180. There's a general store, a Japanese cemetery, an elementary school, a couple of churches and a library that opens a few days a week. Most shops are closed on Sundays and Mondays.

There are two places to stay. The Kona Hotel retains the small town character (and room rates!) of a bygone era, and Holualoa Inn is a lovely modern B&B off the main road.

From Kailua-Kona, it's a scenic four miles up Hualalai Rd to Holualoa. The landscape is bright with flowers, coffee bushes, and fruit trees of all kinds.

Kona's relentless development is creeping up this way. Older homes half-hidden by jungly gardens are being joined by a jumble of new houses. It's an enviable location, with a fine view of Kona's sparkling turquoise waters below.

Kimura Lauhala Shop

The Kimura Lauhala Shop (☎ 324-0053), at the intersection of Hualalai Rd and Hwy 180, sells items woven from lauhala, the lau (leaf) of the hala tree.

This was once an old plantation store which sold salt and codfish. During the Depression of the 1920s, Mrs Kimura started weaving lauhala hats and coffee baskets and taking them down to the plantations to sell.

Three generations of Kimuras still weave lauhala here. Their work is supplemented by the wives of local coffee farmers who do piecemeal work at home when it's not coffee season.

The hardest part, the Kimuras say, is preparing the lauhala, which is messy work,

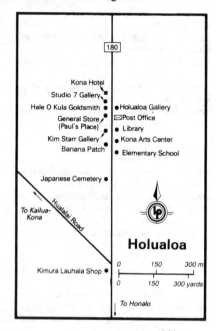

180

Kona Hotel
Studio 7 Gallery
Hale O Kula Goldsmith ●   ● Holualoa Gallery
General Store ●   ⊠ Post Office
(Paul's Place)   ● Library
Kim Starr Gallery   ● Kona Arts Center
Banana Patch   ● Elementary School

Japanese Cemetery ●

Hualalai Road

To Kailua-
Kona

Holualoa

Kimura Lauhala Shop ●

| 0 | 150 | 300 m |
| 0 | 150 | 300 yards |

To Honalo

times a week. Classes include pottery, batik, tie dye, basketry, weaving and painting.

Visitors who drop in to look around are offered Kona coffee. The centre is open from 10 am to 4 pm Tuesday to Saturday. There's also a small display area with items for sale including hand-blown glass, weavings, and baskets made of natural fibres like sea grass, coconut palm leaves and banana poka vine.

Banana Patch
This little gift shop, directly opposite the Kona Arts Center, has a select collection of art, jewellery and handcrafts at good prices. While it specialises in Balinese and other Indonesian crafts, there are also items from Sri Lanka, Ethiopia, Kashmir and the Big Island. Muriel Browne, who operates the shop, has picked up many of the items during her own travels overseas. Opening hours are 10 am to 4 pm Tuesday to Saturday.

Studio 7 Gallery
Studio 7 Gallery opened in 1980 to showcase the artwork of owner Hiroki Morinoue who works in watercolours, oils, wood block and 3D sculpture. His wife, Setsuko, is a potter and the gallery's director.

Studio 7 now exhibits some 30 top-notch artisans, about half of whom come from the Kona area. Works include ceramics, natural-dyed fabrics, sculpture, basketry, blown glass and pit-fired raku.

The gallery is like a little museum and the zen-like setting blends both Hawaiian and Japanese influences, with wooden walkways over lava stones. It's open from 10 am to 4 pm Tuesday to Saturday.

Places to Stay
If you want to be on the cool slopes above Kailua-Kona, Holualoa has two unique alternatives.

Kona Hotel (☎ 324-1155), Hwy 180, Holualoa, HI 96725, in Holualoa's town centre, is the best of the island's handful of cheap hotels. This old, local hostelry has high ceilings and some nice views. Rooms are basic with just a bed and dresser but are clean and priced at only $15/23 for

complicated by the sharp spines along the leaf edges. The easy part is the weaving. Once the lauhala is ready to weave, it takes a couple of hours to make a placemat which sells for around $8.

The most common items are placemats and open baskets, as well as hats of a finer weave. The shop, which is open from 9 am to 5 pm Monday to Saturday, also stocks baskets from China and the Philippines.

Kona Arts Center
The Kona Arts Center (Box 272, Holualoa, HI 96725) is in a ramshackle ex-coffee mill, with a tin roof and hot-pink doors.

Bob and Carol Rogers are the directors of this nonprofit organisation. She teaches crafts and he teaches visual arts. They've been there since 1965, nurturing the spirit as much as the art.

This is a community scene and everyone's welcome. It costs $20 a month to use the centre, which includes workshops up to five singles/doubles. Bathrooms are shared and down the hall.

Rumour has it that the mattresses in the street-side rooms are the most comfortable as the burly construction workers who sometimes stay during the work-week favour the ocean side. With only 11 rooms, getting a room here is pretty much hit and miss, although it's easier on weekends.

Holualoa Inn (☎ 324-1121), run by Desmond & Karen Twigg-Smith, Box 222, Holualoa, HI 96725, is a beautiful contemporary B&B atop 40 acres of sloping meadows with great views of the Kona Coast. The house was built as a getaway by Desmond's uncle, president of the *Honolulu Advertiser*, who at the time of construction owned a sawmill. The exterior is all western red cedar and the interior floors are red eucalyptus from Maui.

Although the house has 5000 sq feet, there are only four bedrooms, each of which has a private bath. There's a large swimming pool, a billiard room, a rooftop gazebo and a TV lounge. They serve a continental breakfast which includes their own home-grown Kona coffee and fruit from the garden. There are plans to add bungalows and a restaurant in the next couple of years. As it stands now, it's one of Hawaii's nicest finds. Rates are $100 to $150.

South Kona

Hwy 11 heads south out of Kailua-Kona through a number of small communities: Honalo, Kainaliu, Kealakekua, Captain Cook and Honaunau. These are unhurried upland towns surrounded by coffee farms and macadamia nut groves.

Side roads off Hwy 11 lead to Kealakekua Bay, Puuhonua O Honaunau National Historical Park (better known as the Place of Refuge) and the old fishing villages of Hookena and Milolii. South Kona is short on beaches but there are a couple of excellent spots for snorkelling and diving.

Kona coffee is the only coffee grown on a commercial scale in the USA. Almost the entire harvest comes from these upland towns, from Holualoa in the north to Honaunau in the south. The coffee trees thrive in the rich volcanic soil and the cloud cover that moves in nearly every afternoon.

During the coffee season buyers hang out signs announcing how much they'll pay for 'cherries', which are the red coffee berries. In a good year they may offer as much as 90 cents a pound.

Coffee trees must be hand-picked several times a year as not all the berries ripen at once. The harvesting season begins in August. Coffee farmers at the lowest elevations may finish harvesting by December, while those at the 2000-foot level might harvest into March.

HONALO

Honalo is the small village at the intersection of Hwy 11 and Hwy 180.

Daifukuji Soto Mission, in the village centre on the mauka side of Hwy 11, is a big Buddhist temple with two altars, gold brocade, large drums and incense burners. Visitors are welcome to view the inside. As with all Buddhist temples, leave your shoes at the door.

Fuku-Bonsai Center

About two miles north of Honalo village, on the mauka side of Hwy 180, is the Fuku-Bonsai Center, which consists of 3½ acres of bonsai trees – Hawaii's finest collection.

It's open daily from 8 am to 5 pm and costs $5 for adults, $2.50 for children.

Places to Stay

Teshima's Inn (☎ 322-9140) on Hwy 11 has 10 rooms in a building behind Teshima's restaurant. However, most are usually rented out on a monthly basis. The rooms are basic and on the dingy side. Each has its own bathroom and costs $20/30 for singles/doubles. Ask for Mrs Teshima at the restaurant.

Durkee's Coffeeland B&B (☎ 322-9142), Box 596, Holualoa, HI 96725, is a casual place in the hills between the villages of

Honalo and Holualoa. Chuck and Marilyn Durkee rent out two bedrooms with a shared bath in their house. One has a double bed and costs $45/55 for singles/doubles. The other has a queen bed, TV and a bit more space and costs $60, doubles only. Rates include breakfast on the lanai featuring their own home-grown coffee and fruit. It's $5 more for one-night stays. There's also a separate apartment beneath the house with two bedrooms and a kitchen for $70 for two people, $80 for three. The Durkees have a doberman and an African goose.

Places to Eat

Teshima's is an unpretentious restaurant that serves authentic Japanese food. The best deal is from 11 am to 2 pm when the lunch teishoku of miso soup, sashimi, sukiyaki, tsukemono (pickled cabbage), sunomono (vinegared cucumber, daikon, carrot) and rice costs $6.50, or $8 with the addition of fried fish. At dinner, from 5 to 10 pm, the same teishokus cost $8 and $11 respectively. There's a bar at the side of the restaurant.

KAINALIU

Kainaliu is a little town with positive energy. Aloha Cafe and the adjoining theatre and natural food store are the focal point.

Aloha Theatre, which is the home of the Aloha Community Players, presents performances with progressive themes and you can get a good feel for the community by attending one.

There are a couple of interesting shops in town. Kimura Store started out in 1926 as a country store and the Kimuras have been selling fabrics and dry goods there ever since. A more recent newcomer is Crystal Star Gallery, a New Age shop specialising in crystals, metaphysical books and the like.

Kona Coffee Roasters roasts and grinds Kona coffee beans and has a little lanai in the back where you can sip a cup of freshly brewed coffee.

Places to Eat

The *Aloha Cafe* is the place to eat in these parts and well worth the drive up from Kailua-Kona. The food is fresh, with some vegetarian dishes and good salads, as well as wonderful fresh fish specials. It has hearty sandwiches, fresh fruit smoothies, espressos and excellent carrot cake. A burrito or quesadilla with a side salad costs $7, while the most expensive dish, filet mignon, costs $16. The outside terrace has a distant ocean view. It's open from 8 am to 8 pm Monday to Saturday. If you come up for dinner in the winter bring a sweater as it gets cool in the evenings.

Next door is the *Aloha Village Store*, a fully stocked natural foods store.

A little farther south on the makai side of Hwy 11 is *Ohana Natural Foods*, a cooperative which sells organic produce, nuts, grains, fruit juices, dairy products and a good Hawaiian granola, all at reasonable prices. It's open daily except Sundays.

KEALAKEKUA

Kealakekua means 'path of the gods'. A series of heiaus once ran from Kealakekua Bay, a few miles south of town, north to Kailua-Kona.

These days Kealakekua is the banking centre for Kona's hill towns. The Kona Coast's hospital is on the north side of town, a quarter of a mile mauka of Hwy 11. The post office is on the corner of Hwy 11 and Halekii Rd.

Kealakekua has a good library, which is open from 10 am to 8 pm on Mondays, to 5 pm Tuesday to Friday and to 1 pm on Saturdays.

Next door to the library is the coral mortar and lava Kona Union Church, which dates back to 1854. The sign out the front proclaims 'Keepers of the Light, Lamp to Laser'.

Kahanahou

Kahanahou (☎ 322-3901) is a nonprofit native Hawaiian handcraft workshop, which sells hula instruments and native crafts such as nose flutes, split bamboo dancing sticks, hula drums and gourd masks at reasonable prices. It's at the north end of Kealakekua,

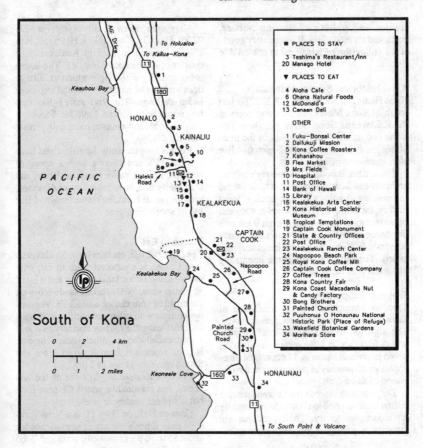

PLACES TO STAY

3 Teshima's Restaurant/Inn
20 Manago Hotel

PLACES TO EAT

4 Aloha Cafe
6 Ohana Natural Foods
12 McDonald's
13 Canaan Deli

OTHER

1 Fuku–Bonsai Center
2 Daifukuji Mission
5 Kona Coffee Roasters
7 Kahanahou
8 Flea Market
9 Mrs Fields
10 Hospital
11 Post Office
14 Bank of Hawaii
15 Library
16 Kealakekua Arts Center
17 Kona Historical Society Museum
18 Tropical Temptations
19 Captain Cook Monument
21 State & Country Offices
22 Post Office
23 Kealakekua Ranch Center
24 Napoopoo Beach Park
25 Royal Kona Coffee Mill
26 Captain Cook Coffee Company
27 Coffee Trees
28 Kona Country Fair
29 Kona Coast Macadamia Nut & Candy Factory
30 Bong Brothers
31 Painted Church
32 Puuhonua O Honaunau National Historic Park (Place of Refuge)
33 Wakefield Botanical Gardens
34 Morihara Store

South of Kona

0   2   4 km

0   1   2 miles

along the makai side of the highway. It's open weekdays from 8 am to 4 pm.

Mrs Fields Factory

Mrs Fields, on Halekii Rd just off Hwy 11, sells nuts and all the standard Mrs Fields cookies. Informal free tours of its small macadamia nut factory are conducted every half an hour or so from 9 am to about 3.30 pm on weekdays. The cracked nuts come down a chute where they are hand sorted, dried, graded, salted and vacuum packed. It's not all that dynamic, but if you're curious it only takes a few minutes to walk through and see

the process. Free samples are given, you can crack open your own macadamia nuts and the shop isn't at all pushy about sales.

Flea Market

A little farther down Halekii Rd on the right, a small flea market is held every Thursday and Saturday from 8 am to 2 pm. You can buy local produce and an assortment of other typical flea market merchandise.

Kealakekua Arts Center

The Kealakekua Arts Center on Hwy 11 is a new arts & crafts centre with a number of studios and galleries featuring pottery, batik and stained glass. It has a fairly good-sized collection of island art at reasonable prices.

Kona Historical Society Museum

Kona Historical Society (☎ 323-3222) is just south of Kona Meat Company and north of the Kealakekua Grass Shack gift shop. The stone and mortar building, built in the mid-1800s, was once a general merchandise store-cum-post office.

These days it houses the society's office, archives and little museum. There are some interesting displays of the area's local history, including old photos and bottles and other memorabilia. It's open from 9 am to 3 pm Monday to Friday and although there's no admission fee per se, donations are appreciated. The museum sells some interesting historical post cards.

Tropical Temptations

Tropical Temptations, at the south end of town, sells fruit dried without preservatives. The sign out the front tells local growers which fruit they're buying each day. It takes seven pounds of bananas, 11 pounds of pineapples or 15 pounds of papayas to make one pound of dried fruit.

They also sell macadamia nuts and roasted coffee beans dipped in chocolate and usually have samples to try. Their products are attractively packaged and make good gifts.

Places to Stay

Reggie's Tropical Hideaway (☎ 322-8888), Box 1107, Kealakekua, HI 96750, is in Kealakekua in an area thick with coffee and banana trees. While accommodation is island-style casual and doesn't have the polish of more expensive B&Bs, you're free to use the family hot tub. There's a room in the main house that has a private entrance, bath and deck and costs $60 and a small room with a double bed and shared bath for $40. There are also two separate cottages down the slope from the house. The largest has two bedrooms, full bath and kitchen and costs $100, a smaller one costs $75.

Merryman's Bed & Breakfast (☎ 323-2276), Box 474, Kealakekua, HI 96750, is in a quiet residential area in Kealakekua, a quarter of a mile above Hwy 11. The house is big and airy with ample windows, a large deck and lots of natural wood and exposed-beam ceilings. The 2nd storey has two bedrooms with shared bath for $55/65 a single/double and a master room with private bath for $70/80.

Rooms are pleasantly furnished and have private TVs and there's also a spacious common living area for guest use. Penny and Don Merryman, hospitable former Alaskans, provide guests breakfast on the lanai and free use of snorkelling gear.

Places to Eat

The Gallery Cafe, upstairs in the Kealakekua Arts Center, is a pleasant place to eat, with indoor and outdoor lanai seating and a bit of an ocean view. Well-stacked sandwiches on the bread of your choice cost $3.75. Vegetarian lasagne with salad and garlic bread costs $6, meat lasagne $7. They also serve various salads, enchiladas and other pastas. The cafe is open weekdays from 8 am to 8 pm and Saturdays from 11 am to 7 pm.

Peacock Restaurant, in front of the arts centre, has reasonably priced Chinese food but it's rather mediocre fare.

Canaan Deli, on Hwy 11, is a New York-style deli. It has a variety of sandwiches for about $5 to $6 plus spaghetti, pizza and 'loco moco'. There's a *McDonald's* nearby on Hwy 11.

Napoopoo Road

Napoopoo Rd leads makai from the north end of the town of Captain Cook, down to a coffee mill and Kealakekua Bay. The rural road passes coffee farms and a few banana and papaya orchards on the way down to coast.

At the fork, which is 2¾ miles from Hwy 11, bear to the left to go to St Benedict's Painted Church, or to the right to get to the coffee mill. All of these roads make nice short country drives.

Royal Kona Coffee Mill

Once a week Royal Kona Coffee Mill fires up its old roaster and cooks 500 pounds of coffee. After 20 minutes it's roasted down to 425 pounds. If you happen to go by on that morning, there's 75 pounds of coffee aroma in the air to greet you!

On any day you can stop and get a free cup of freshly brewed Kona coffee and learn a little about the coffee biz. They have a showroom with historical artefacts, a three-minute video about coffee picking and photos from the early 1900s.

In the early days donkeys (called Kona nightingales because of their braying) transported the coffee down Kona's stony hills, but in the 1950s they were replaced by jeeps. Photos from 1953 show coffee growers parading through town on lei-draped donkeys lamenting the mechanisation with such banners as 'Kona's reached a doleful pass, when our bray gives way to gas'.

A separate lanai area has displays of macadamia nuts in various stages. There's even a 1950s vintage macadamia nut husker with a Goodyear car tyre serving as the grinding wheel.

Coffee, seedlings and souvenirs are sold in the shop and both macadamia nuts and coffee are processed out the back. It's open from 9 am to 5 pm daily and admission is free.

KEALAKEKUA BAY

Kealakekua Bay is a large bay, a mile wide at its mouth. Napoopoo Beach Park and Hikiau Heiau are at the south end of the bay. The north end has a protected cove with one of the best snorkelling spots on the Big Island.

Steep sea cliffs separate the two ends of the bay and there's no land passage between them. The northern end can be approached only by sea or by a hike from the town of Captain Cook.

Kealakekua Bay is a state underwater park and marine life conservation district. Fishing is restricted and the removal of coral and rocks prohibited.

Captain James Cook, the first Westerner

to visit Hawaii, sailed into Kealakekua Bay at dawn on 17 January 1779. The beaches were lined with 10,000 onlookers and 1000 canoes sailed out to greet him.

Cook's tall ships with high sails appeared to fulfil a prophecy of the return of the god Lono who was to arrive on a floating island covered with tall trees.

On his first evening ashore, Cook was brought to Hikiau Heiau where the high priest performed a series of ceremonies recognising Cook as the incarnation of the god Lono.

Eleven days later at the heiau, Cook performed a burial service for sailor William Whatman who had died of a stroke. The inauspicious death of his mate raised a few questions about Cook's own mortality.

On 14 February, Cook was tragically killed in a scuffle at the north end of the bay. Ironically, the world's greatest navigator was such a poor swimmer that he apparently stumbled into the direction of an angry crowd rather than swimming a few metres out to a waiting boat.

An obelisk monument on the north side of the bay marks the spot where Cook died at the water's edge.

Napoopoo Beach Park

Napoopoo Beach Park is at the end of Napoopoo Rd, 4½ miles from Hwy 11.

The park's most predominant feature is **Hikiau Heiau**, the large platform heiau above the beach. The busy beach park has a boat landing, restrooms, showers and a couple of shacks near the heiau selling soft drinks and snacks.

The beach is rather rocky, and because it's small it often feels crowded. This is the less protected end of the bay and it can have dangerous water conditions when the surf is high and during periods of kona storms.

There's good snorkelling at Napoopoo, but the real prize is the cove at the northern end of the bay. Some people snorkel over from Napoopoo Beach when it's calm, but it's a long haul and only strong swimmers should consider it.

From the park you can continue four miles

south along a narrow road through scrub brush and lava flows to Puuhonua O Honaunau, the Place of Refuge. The road is bumpy, but paved and passable. Be careful if you pull over as there are roadside trenches partly concealed by grasses. Most of the stone walls, that run parallel to parts of the road, were built in the early 1900s to keep cattle from straying.

Captain Cook Monument Trail

If you're up to a hike, the trail to Captain Cook Monument and the cove at the north end of Kealakekua Bay makes a good day outing. Although you can expect to work up a sweat, you'll be rewarded with fantastic snorkelling, a natural bath once reserved for royalty and some historic sites to explore. To get to the trailhead, turn off Hwy 11 onto Napoopoo Rd and go down about 200 yards to the dirt road after the second telephone pole on the right.

A minute's walk down the dirt road, just before reaching a metal gate marked 'Private Property', there's a parting through tall grasses on the left which is the start of the trail. Don't expect a well-beaten path. Also, it's not a good hike to do in sandals.

Unless it's been recently cleared, the first half of the trail is like a jungle walk through shoulder-high elephant grass. Still, the path is fairly simple and in most places runs between two rock fences on an overgrown jeep road. When in doubt, stay to the left.

Eventually the coast becomes visible, the vegetation sparser and the trail easier to walk. The trail veers to the left along a broad ledge, leads through an old wooden gate and goes down to the beach. Once you're at the water, it's less than five minutes to the left to the monument marking Cook's deathplace.

The hike takes about 1¼ hours down, 1¾ hours up. It's not a particularly strenuous hike, but it is hot and largely unshaded, and it's uphill all the way back. On the return, about five minutes up from the beach, there's a small fork in the trail where there are lots of air plants; bear to the right and you'll be on your way back.

There are no facilities at the bottom. Be sure to take drinking water and snorkelling gear.

Snorkelling There's fairly easy entry from the rocks on the left side of the cement dock in front of the Captain Cook Monument. The water starts out about five feet deep and slopes gradually to about 30 feet. The cove is protected and usually very calm. Both coral and fish are abundant, there's great visibility and it's a terrific place to snorkel.

Snorkelling tour boats (see the Activities section) pull into the bay in the morning, but they don't come ashore and they generally leave before lunch time. Anyway, the cove is big enough so it doesn't feel crowded.

Exploring This area was once the Hawaiian village of Kaawaloa. Old lava stone walls still go all the way out to Cook's Point at the north end of the bay. There's a small **light beacon** on the point.

Queen's Bath, on the edge of the cove, is a small lava pool with brackish spring-fed water. It's a few minutes' walk from the monument in the direction of the cliffs. The water is cool and refreshing and this age-old equivalent of a beach shower is a great way to wash off the salt before hiking back. However, the mosquitoes can get a bit testy here.

A few minutes beyond the Queen's Bath, the path ends at the cliffs called **Pali-kapu-o-Keoua**, the 'cliffs sacred to the

Cup Coral

chief Keoua'. The cliffs contain numerous caves which were the burial places of Hawaiian royalty. It's speculated that some of Captain Cook's bones were placed here as well. As late as 1887 villagers from Kaawaloa were in the employ of King Kalakaua to maintain the burial grounds.

A few lower caves are accessible but they don't contain anything other than beer cans. The ones higher up are fortunately not as easy to get to and probably still contain bones. All are sacred and should be left undisturbed.

CAPTAIN COOK

The town named for the Pacific navigator is on Hwy 11 above the bay where he met his end. Captain Cook is a small unpretentious town with a few county and state offices, a shopping centre, a hotel and a couple of restaurants.

Kealakekua Ranch Center has a Sure Save supermarket, Ben Franklin store, a hardware store and Mexican and Chinese restaurants.

The Chevron gas station north of the Manago Hotel is open 24 hours.

As you continue south from town there are a handful of roadside coffee tasting rooms that sell locally grown coffee and provide free freshly brewed samples.

Kona Coffee

Captain Cook Coffee Company runs a little stand at the side of Hwy 11 at the south end of town. There's an outdoor lanai with a pretty view of Kealakekua Bay. They sell doughnuts and give out free coffee samples. A few coffee trees grow by the parking area.

If you just want to examine coffee trees, there's a pull-off for that purpose about a mile south, marked with an HVB sign. Coffee trees are planted in the front and macadamia trees beyond.

Coffee, a relative of the gardenia, has fragrant white blossoms in the spring. In the summer the trees have green berries, which turn red in the autumn as they ripen.

Kona Country Fair

Kona Country Fair is a large would-be flea market on a rather remote stretch between Captain Cook and Honaunau. It's been unable to fully operate because of water issues and essentially functions as another coffee tasting shop. There's also a snack shop selling overpriced sandwiches and reasonably good pastries. From the shop you can enjoy a broad vista of the south Kona Coast and there's a walk-through **lava tube** on the grounds that's worth a look. It's open from 9 am to 6 pm daily.

Places to Stay

Manago Hotel (☎ 323-2642), Hwy 11, Box 145, Captain Cook, HI 96704, is a family-run hotel that started in 1917 as a restaurant serving bowls of udon to salespeople on the then-long journey between Hilo and Kona. Those wanting to stay overnight were charged $1 for a futon on tatami mats. These days the basic rooms in the original roadside building show their age without much grace but rates are just $22/25 for singles/doubles. The furniture is rickety, the walls are thin and there are shared baths down the hall.

If you want comfort over character, go for one of Manago's 42 rooms in the newer wing at the rear. The motel-style rooms are ordinary but sufficient, with private baths and radios. The highlight is the unobstructed lanai view of Kealakekua Bay a mile below. Rates are $35 to $38 for singles, $38 to $41 for doubles; the higher rates are for better views. Weekly rates are six times the daily rate. There's a common TV room near the restaurant. Although it's pure local flavour, Manago draws a fair number of international travellers.

Doc Boone's Bed & Breakfast (☎ 323-3231), Box 666, Kealakekua, HI 96750, sits half a mile above Hwy 11 amidst a garden planted with tropical fruit trees and flaming red poinsettias. Doc is an MD who has delivered half the town's babies over the past few decades and the Boones welcome families. While the grounds have a pool, the cinder-block home is unpretentious and comfortably cluttered. The Boones are avid cyclists and snorkellers and like to show their guests around the area.

They have three rooms with shared bath upstairs that rent for $60 double, and an apartment downstairs that sleeps up to four for $85. However, they prefer to rent only one or two units at a time so they can get to know people better.

Adrienne's B&B (☎ 328-9726), RR1, Box 8E, Captain Cook, HI 96704, consists of three rooms in the home of Reginald and Adrienne Ritz-Baty, enthusiastic hosts who enjoy chatting about the island. Adrienne is a former national archery champion. All the rooms have private baths and cable TV. There's a hot tub on the lanai with a view of the distant coast, access to the kitchen and the washer/dryer and a collection of 1200 videos. Rates are $50 for singles and $60 or $70 for doubles and include a breakfast of home-made bread or muffins and fruit from the yard. They're on Hwy 11 about a mile south of the turn-off to the Place of Refuge.

RBR Farms B&B (☎ 328-9212, (800) 328-9212), Box 930, Captain Cook, HI 96704, on the slopes below Captain Cook, caters to the gay and lesbian community. Set amidst a small secluded coffee and macadamia nut farm, it's a comfortable getaway with total privacy, a small pool and a clothing-optional deck.

Rooms with shared bathroom cost $60/75 for singles/doubles, while the cottage with private bath, kitchen, living room and lanai costs $130 for two people, $180 for four. Accommodation includes a full poolside breakfast.

Places to Eat

Manago Restaurant, which is in the Manago Hotel, is a Japanese version of a meat and potatoes eatery, and is known for its pork chops. It's not health food, but the portions are large. Two big chops, rice, potato salad and side dishes such as tofu curd cost $7. Sandwiches and burgers are around $3. Breakfast is available from 7 to 9 am, lunch from 11 am to 2 pm and dinner from 5 to 7 pm. It's closed on Mondays.

HONAUNAU

Honaunau's main attraction is Puuhonua O Honaunau National Historical Park, commonly called the Place of Refuge, but there are other things to see in this area as well.

On Hwy 11, just south of Middle Keei Rd, Bong Brothers has a little shop where they sell their own coffee as well as organic and locally grown produce.

At Morihara Store, Hwy 160 connects with Hwy 11 and leads down to the Place of Refuge, passing Painted Church Rd, Wakefield Botanical Gardens and some fine rural scenery with grazing horses, stone walls and brilliant bougainvilleas.

Macadamia Nut Factory

The Kona Coast Macadamia Nut & Candy Factory, on Middle Keei Rd near Hwy 11, has a little display with a husking machine and a macadamia nut cracker. You can try it out, one nut at a time, and eat the final product.

The showroom overlooks the real operation out the back, where bags of nuts are husked and sorted. The shop sells both raw and roasted macadamia nuts as well as macadamia nut honey. They also sell edible rejects (mostly a bit over-roasted) for about $2 a pound.

St Benedict's Painted Church

This church is noted for its painted interior done by John Berchmans Velghe, a Catholic priest who came from Belgium in 1899.

He painted the walls with a series of Biblical scenes as an aid in teaching the Bible to natives who couldn't read. He designed the wall behind the altar to resemble the gothic cathedral in Burgos, Spain. The ceiling is a Hawaiian sky with clouds and birds.

When Father John arrived, the church was on the coast near the Place of Refuge. One of his first moves was to bring the church two miles up the slopes to its present location. It's not clear whether he did this as protection from tsunamis or just to be on the rise – both actual and symbolic – from the old gods of 'pagan Hawaii'.

The tin-roofed church still holds Sunday services, with hymns sung in Hawaiian. The grounds are lushly tropical and there's a majestic breadfruit tree out the front.

The church is on Painted Church Rd. Turn north at the one-mile marker on Hwy 160 and go a quarter of a mile.

Wakefield Botanical Gardens

Wakefield Botanical Gardens on Hwy 160 has free self-guided walks in their largely overgrown backyard. There are some interesting plants with names like snow on the mountain and Moses in the basket, as well as cactus, bonsai and more typical tropical flowers. The only price you pay is feeding the mosquitoes. The gardens are owned by island artist Arlene Wakefield.

Arlene also operates a restaurant here, open from 11 am to 3 pm. A bowl of vegetarian soup with chips and home-made salsa costs $4, other meals are in the $5.50 to $7 range, and there's also sandwiches, fruit salads and cold drinks. The macadamia nut pie for $2.25 should satisfy the strongest of sugar urges.

PLACE OF REFUGE

Puuhonua O Honaunau National Historical Park (☎ 328-2288) encompasses ancient temples, royal grounds and a puuhonua, a place of refuge or sanctuary. The park fronts Honaunau Bay.

Puuhonua O Honaunau is a tongue-twister of a name which simply means 'place of refuge at Honaunau'.

In old Hawaii, breaking any of the many kapus which strictly regulated all daily interactions was thought to anger the gods who might retaliate with a natural disaster or two. To appease the gods the offender was hunted down and killed.

Commoners who broke a kapu, as well as defeated warriors and ordinary criminals, could all have their lives spared by reaching the sacred ground of the puuhonua.

This was more of a challenge than it might appear. Since royalty and their warriors lived on the grounds immediately surrounding the refuge, kapu breakers were forced to swim through open ocean, braving currents and sharks to get to the puuhonua.

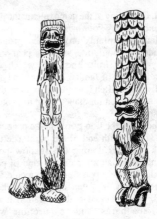

Tiki-Tiki

Once inside the sanctuary, priests performed ceremonies of absolution which apparently placated the gods. Kapu breakers could then return home with a clean slate.

Hale O Keawe Heiau, the temple on the point of the cove, was built around 1650. The bones of 23 chiefs were buried there. It's thought that the mana of the chiefs remained in their bones and added a spiritual power to those who came into the grounds. The heiau has been authentically reconstructed. The carved wooden statues that stand erect beside it are called kii and are said to embody the ancient gods.

The heiau is at the end of a large stone wall built around 1550. It's called the **Great Wall** and is more than 1000 feet (304 metres) long and 10 feet (three metres) high. The west side of the wall was the puuhonua and the east side was the royal grounds.

A self-guided walk corresponding to the park brochure passes by Hale O Keawe Heiau, two older heiaus, a petroglyph, legendary stones, a fishpond, lava tree moulds and a few thatched huts and shelters. The canoe on display is hand carved from koa wood.

There's also a stone board for konane, a game similar to checkers. The game pieces are small stones of black lava and white coral. Get a copy of the game rules at the park entrance and try your hand.

Medicinal plants around the grounds include the noni tree with its pear-sized warty-looking fruit. The fruit, which was eaten in times of famine, tastes as bad as it smells. More often it was used to make dyes or as a treatment for diabetes and high blood pressure.

Check out the **tide pools** in the pahoehoe lava at the south end of the park. The tiny black speckles dotting the shallow pools behind the heiau are pipipi, a kind of periwinkle. The tide pools near the picnic area farther south are even better. They have coral, black-shelled crabs, small fish and eels, sea hares, and sea urchins with rose-coloured spines.

Twenty-minute orientation talks are given at 10, 10.30 and 11 am and at 2.30, 3 and 3.30 pm daily. They're largely geared to people on tour buses who don't have time to see the whole park. There's good background information in the park brochure and the audio displays at the entrance.

Some of the rangers are native Hawaiians. You'll occasionally find one dressed in a malo or tapa demonstrating traditional pili grass thatching, feather cape weaving, canoe carving or kii statue making.

A programme in Hawaiian studies is held monthly, usually at 7.30 pm on the first Wednesday of the month, in the park's amphitheatre. A festival with traditional displays and food, hukilau (net fishing) and a 'royal court' is held on the weekend closest to 1 July. Local students compete in Hawaiian sports on the first Friday of February and November.

Admission is $1 per person, with a maximum of $3 per car, and is good for repeated visits over one week. Fees are generally collected between 8.30 am and 4.30 pm but visitors are free to enter and stroll the grounds until nightfall.

Honaunau Beaches

Place of Refuge Swimming is allowed at Keoneele Cove inside the Place of Refuge. The cove was once the royal canoe landing and it's shallow with a gradual decline. Snorkelling is best when the tide is rising, because not only is the water a bit deeper, but it brings in fish. Sunbathing is discouraged here.

South end of the Park Near the Place of Refuge visitors' centre there's a road leading a quarter of a mile south to a beach park with picnic tables and some quiet sandy patches.

Winter surf can be rough in this area. Unless the sea is flat it's best to stick to the Keoneele Cove area for swimming and snorkelling.

North end of the Park There's a terrific place to snorkel and dive just north of the Place of Refuge. From the park's parking lot, take the narrow road to the left with the 15 mph sign.

Go down about 500 feet and park just past the boat ramp. There's a little park mauka of the road. St Benedict's Painted Church was originally on this site.

Snorkellers step off a lava ledge immediately north of the boat ramp into about 10 feet of water. It then drops off fairly

Seaside idol

quickly to about 25 feet. There are some naturally formed lava steps that make it fairly easy to get in and out of the water.

Visibility is excellent, with good-sized reef fish and a fine variety of corals close to shore. The predatory crown of thorns starfish can be seen here feasting on live coral polyps.

For divers, there's a ledge a little way out that drops off about 100 feet.

In winter the water can get rough when the surf is high.

South on Highway 11

For about 15 miles south on Hwy 11 after the Place of Refuge turn-off, the road is narrow and winding with some fairly steep drops. Be careful when driving as there are sections that have no shoulder at all.

At night, sudden oncoming headlights and fog can make it particularly tricky, especially if you're tired from a long haul between Hilo and Kona.

HOOKENA BEACH

Hookena was once a bustling village with two churches, a school, court house and post office. King Kalakaua sent his friend Robert Louis Stevenson here in 1889 to show him a typical Hawaiian village. Stevenson stayed a week with the town's judge and wrote about Hookena in *Travels in Hawaii*.

In the 1890s Chinese immigrants began to move into the village setting up shops and restaurants. A tavern and a hotel opened and the town got rougher and rowdier.

In those days Big Island cattle were shipped from Hookena's landing to market in Honolulu. When the circle-island road was built, the steamers stopped coming and the townspeople moved away. By the 1920s the town was almost deserted.

These days Hookena is a tiny fishing community with a small county beach park. The storm-beaten remains of the landing are in front of the park restrooms.

Hookena is 2¼ miles down a narrow road from Hwy 11. The marked turn-off is between the 101 and 102-mile markers,

opposite the water tank that supplies the village with drinking water.

The beach has very soft black sand. The bay is backed by lava sea cliffs and there are trees for shade. When the winter surf is up, kids boogie board here.

When it's calm, you can snorkel straight out from the landing. It drops off pretty quickly, from 10 feet to about 30 feet, and there's lots of coral. Don't go too far out or you may encounter strong currents. Pygmy dolphins occasionally come into the bay, sometimes as many as 100 at a time.

There is water for showers but it is brackish and not suitable for drinking. A shack on the beach sells reasonably priced drinking coconuts, shave ice and soft drinks.

Hookena is a popular weekend picnic spot and camping is allowed with a permit from the county.

MILOLII

Milolii is the most traditional fishing village remaining in Hawaii. Families who have been fishing these waters for generations still set out in outrigger canoes each morning before dawn.

Milolii means 'fine twist'. Historically the village was known for its skilled sennit twisters who used bark from the olona shrub to make fine cord and highly valued fishing nets.

Milolii sits at the edge of an expansive 1926 lava flow that covered the nearby fishing village of Hoopuloa.

The village has about 125 residents and many of the homes are simple, shanty-like wooden structures. There's no running water or village-wide electricity, although a solar-powered desalinisation plant is being constructed. The state is also providing funds to tear down many of the old shacks and replace them with new houses.

Milolii fishers use an age-old method resembling aqua farming. They sail out to feed papaya and taro to opelu, a type of mackerel. After months of the fattening and taming process they return to net the fish.

Folks in Milolii have long-standing complaints with some commercial fishing boats that ply their fishing grounds and scoop up the opelu they've fattened. Things seem destined to get worse if the massive new Riviera resort complex planned for Kahuku, south of Milolii, builds its proposed 400-boat marina.

Milolii Beach Park, which is past the town's little boat ramp, has grills and a thatched picnic pavilion, but no drinking water. The village has just one ageing little store and it's only occasionally open.

Along the coast, tide pools of both red and black lava provide a splashy backdrop to white coral and colourful fish. When the waters are calm the snorkelling is good.

Camping is officially allowed in the beach park but it's right in the village and there's not a lot of space or privacy. This spot is also the village's playground and volleyball court. If you're thinking of camping, check it out first. Sentiments towards outsiders may be affected by the controversial Riviera development which some see as a threat to their privacy and lifestyle.

The turn-off to Milolii is just south of the 89-mile marker. It's five miles down a paved but steep and winding single-lane road that cuts across the lava flow. Use low gear or your brakes will smoke on this one.

MacFarms of Hawaii

Just before entering the Kau district, Hwy 11 passes through the largest macadamia nut orchard in Hawaii, 3800 acres belonging to MacFarms of Hawaii. The orchards were started by a partnership which included Jimmy Stewart, Julie Andrews and other Hollywood stars.

MacFarms has introduced biological insect controls, composting and the use of grazing sheep for weed control in an effort to go organic. The orchards annually produce about 10 million pounds of nuts that are husked, processed and packaged on site.

North of Kona

Hwy 19 (Queen Kaahumanu Highway) runs north 33 miles from Kailua-Kona up the Kona Coast to Kawaihae in the South Kohala district.

This is hot, arid country with a lava landscape. Along the road, clumps of brilliant-pink bougainvillea look striking against the jet-black rock, but otherwise the vegetation is mainly sparse tufts of grass that survive the dry winds.

Honokohau Harbor and a new historical park are just a couple miles north of Kailua-Kona. Tiny fishing villages once dotted this sparsely populated coast but most were wiped out by the tsunami of 1946.

There are beautiful secluded beaches and coves on the north Kona Coast that are hidden from the road and are accessible only by foot (or by boat). Once you hike in, you'll find white-sand beaches tucked between a sea of hardened lava and a turquoise ocean. A few of these beaches are nesting sites of the threatened Pacific green sea turtle.

The Big Island's fanciest resorts are farther north, in the Waikoloa area of the South Kohala district. They have fine art collections, some excellent restaurants and world-class golf courses.

South Kohala was an important area in Hawaiian history and there are heiaus, fishponds, petroglyphs and ancient stone-paved trails that can all be explored. There are wonderful drive-up beaches at the resorts and at the nearby Anaehoomalu and Hapuna beach parks.

From much of the coast you can look inland and see Mauna Kea, and to the south of it, Mauna Loa, both of which often have snowcaps in winter.

Hwy 19 is flat and straight and it's easy to zoom along but it's also a hot spot for radar speed traps, particularly on the stretch between the airport and Kailua. Most police cruise in their own unmarked cars, anything from Trans Ams to Broncos, and they're tough to spot.

The highway is part of the Ironman triathlon route and wide, smooth bike lanes border both sides of the road. Cyclists should be aware that when the air temperature is above 85°F, reflected heat from asphalt and lava can edge the actual temperature above

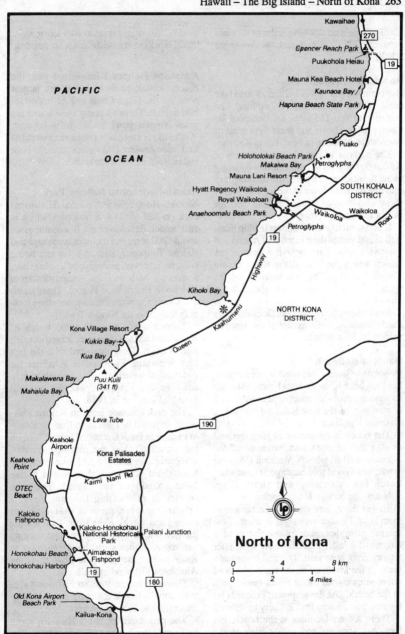

PACIFIC

OCEAN

Kawaihae

270

Spencer Beach Park

Puukohola Heiau

19

Mauna Kea Beach Hotel

Kaunaoa Bay

Hapuna Beach State Park

Puako

Holoholokai Beach Park

Makaiwa Bay

Petroglyphs

Mauna Lani Resort

Hyatt Regency Waikoloa

Royal Waikoloan

Anaehoomalu Beach Park

Petroglyphs

Waikoloa

SOUTH KOHALA
DISTRICT

Waikoloa

Road

19

Kiholo Bay

NORTH KONA
DISTRICT

Kona Village Resort

Kukio Bay

Kua Bay

Makalawena Bay

Mahaiula Bay

Puu Kuili
(341 ft)

● Lava Tube

Keahole
Airport

Kona Palisades
Estates

190

*Keahole
Point*

Kaimi Nani Rd

OTEC
Beach

Kaloko
Fishpond

● Kaloko-Honokohau
National Historical
Park

Palani Junction

Honokohau Beach

Honokohau Harbor

Aimakapa
Fishpond

19

*Old Kona Airport
Beach Park*

Kailua-Kona

180

North of Kona

0   4   8 km

0   2   4 miles

100°F. There's no drinking water or services between OTEC Beach and the Waikoloa hotels.

Honokokau Harbor

Honokohau Harbor was built in 1970 to take some of the burden off Kailua Pier. The majority of the 155 slips are occupied by charter fishing boats and these days most of Kona's catch comes in here, not to Kailua.

The harbour is about two miles north of Kailua on Hwy 19. In case you're wondering about the plaques in front of the coconut trees that line the road down to the harbour – they show who donated each of the 243 trees for this beautification project.

If you want to see the charter fishing boats pull in and weigh their catches of marlin and yellowfin tuna, park near the Texaco gas station and walk beyond the Kona Marlin Center building. The best time to see the weigh-ins is usually from about 4 pm onwards.

Inside the building the Fuel Dock deli sells sandwiches as well as delicious smoked marlin for $7 a pound.

Honokohau Beach

Honokohau Beach, just north of the harbour, has long been Kona's nudist beach, although its days are probably numbered as the beach is now part of the new Kaloko-Honokohau National Historical Park.

The beach is composed of large-grained sand, a mix of black lava, white coral and rounded shell fragments. Walking along the sand gives a good foot massage. It's not a bad beach for swimming and snorkelling, although the bottom is a bit rocky.

To get there, turn onto the harbour road from Hwy 19, then turn right in front of the marina complex and follow the road a quarter of a mile. Pull off to the right after the dry dock boat yard. The trail begins at a break in the lava wall on the right. It's about a five-minute walk along a well-beaten path to the beach. (As development proceeds on the new park, a new trail is likely to follow.)

There are no facilities at the beach, but there are showers and toilets back at the marina. You might want to take along some insect repellent in case the gnats are feasting.

Aimakapa Fishpond Just inland from the beach, Aimakapa Fishpond is the largest pond on the Kona Coast and an important bird habitat. There's a pretty view across the grass-fringed pond to the hills beyond. You're likely to see *aeo* (black-necked stilts) and *alae-keokeo* (Hawaiian coots), both endangered native waterbirds.

Kaloko-Honokohau National Park

Kaloko-Honokohau National Historical Park (☎ 329-6881) is a new park which is still under development. It encompasses about 1200 acres and includes Aimakapa and Kaloko fishponds, ancient heiau and house sites, burial caves, petroglyphs, a holua slide, a queen's bath and the oceanfront from Kaloko to Honokohau Harbor. There's also a one-mile segment of the ancient stone foot-path known as the **King's Trail**.

There's speculation that the bones of Kamehameha the Great were secretly buried near Kaloko. This, combined with the fact that Aimakapa Fishpond is a habitat for endangered waterbirds, was enough to help squeeze the national park designation through Congress in 1978.

The park entrance leads to Kaloko Fishpond, acquired in 1986 from Huehue Ranch in exchange for 300 acres of federal land on the mainland. Over the past two decades, mangrove has invaded and spread rapidly throughout Kaloko Fishpond and native birds abandoned the habitat. The park service is eradicating the mangrove, a labour-intensive process that involves cutting and torching the trees, then tearing the new shoots up one by one and burning the roots. Some stilts have returned to Kaloko, but mangrove is now invading Aimakapa Fishpond as well.

Plans call for the **Kaloko Fishpond** area to eventually have a centre for native Hawaiian crafts and cultural interpretation.

The park entrance is off Hwy 19, about half a mile north of the 97-mile marker. The park gates are open from 8 am to 3.30 pm daily.

Queen's Bath The queen's bath is a spring-fed pool with brackish water in the middle of a lava flow. Even though it's inland, the water level changes with the tide. At high tide more saltwater seeps in and the water rises.

You can get there by walking south for about 15 minutes from Kaloko Fishpond or inland from the north end of Honokohau Beach. The queen's bath is marked by stone cairns as well as Christmas berries, always a dead giveaway that fresh water is nearby.

Keahole Point/OTEC Beach

The turn-off to OTEC Beach and the Natural Energy Laboratory of Hawaii (NELH), a state hydroenergy research facility, is one mile south of the Keahole Airport.

At Keahole Point the sea floor drops steeply just offshore providing a continuous supply of both cold water from 600-metre depths as well as warm surface waters. These are ideal conditions for ocean thermal energy conversion (OTEC).

The OTEC system operates like a steam turbine, with the difference in temperature between the cold and warm waters providing the energy source. Electricity has been successfully generated at the site and research continues on ways to make this an economically viable energy source.

The nutrient-rich cold waters that are pumped up are also used in spin-off aqua-culture projects, such as the production of salmon, Maine lobster, abalone, edible and pearl oysters, seaweed and spirulina. Tours of the facility (☎ 329-0648) are by appointment.

From the highway it's about a mile in to OTEC (Wawaloli) Beach, where there are toilets, showers and drinking water. This windswept lava coastline is rocky and not very good for swimming.

When the waters are calm it's possible to dive nearby. If you follow the dirt road leading south from the beach there are a couple of small blowholes about a third of a

mile down. An inlet through the lava near the blowholes allows divers and confident snorkellers to get out to a steep wall drop that has interesting formations and marine life.

Farther down the dirt road is **Pine Trees**, one of the best surfing breaks in the Kona area. There's currently a struggle going on between Big Island residents who want Pine Trees to remain in a natural state and overseas developers who are targeting the area for a new resort.

Onizuka Space Center

The Astronaut Ellison S Onizuka Space Center (☎ 329-3441), at the Keahole Airport, pays tribute to the Big Island native who perished in the Challenger space shuttle disaster.

The little museum has a few exhibits about space and the role of astronauts, shows educational films and has a moon rock and one of Onizuka's space suits on display. Admission is $2 for adults, 50 cents for children. Opening hours are 8.30 am to 4.30 pm daily.

Lava Tube

There's a big open lava tube mauka of Hwy 19, north of the 91-mile marker and just before a speed limit sign. It might seem rather tame if you've been to Hawaii Volcanoes National Park, but interesting if you haven't.

The tube and the expansive lava flow that surrounds the airport are all from the last eruption of Mt Hualalai, in 1801.

Kua Bay

Kua Bay, also known as Maniniowali, has a beautiful secluded beach with turquoise waters and gleaming white sands. It's picture-postcard material.

It has a gentle slope and inviting waters for swimmers most of the year and for boogie boarders and bodysurfers in the winter. Although it's generally calm, winter storms can kick up currents in the bay.

The turn-off to the beach is just north of both the 88-mile marker and the grassy 341-foot Puu Kuili, the highest cinder cone on the makai side of the highway. Look for the stop sign and red gate at the head of the road.

The road down is rough and over loose lava stones. Some people do drive in about half a mile and park near the roadside, but if you park near the highway it only takes about 20 minutes to walk in.

At the end of the road there's a beaten path over the rocks to the south end of the beach.

Kua Bay is one of the nicest of the isolated Kona Coast beaches and you might not feel the need to go any farther. However, if you do want to explore, there's a trail leading along the coast to **Makalawena**, another beautiful stretch of beach about two miles to the south. It's backed by sand dunes and contains some fine coves with good swimming and snorkelling. Makalawena is in the midst of a coastal stretch that may eventually be turned into a state park.

You could also walk north from Kua Bay along the coast about a mile to **Kukio Bay**, which has a long stretch of white-sand beach and an absolutely lovely cove with good swimming. You're unlikely to have the place to yourself, however, as there's a large hotel under construction on the beach.

In the evenings donkeys come down from the hills to drink at the spring-fed watering holes and to eat the seed pods from the kiawe trees along the coast in this area. The donkeys are descendants of the pack animals that were used on coffee farms until the 1950s. They were largely forgotten until Hwy 19 went through in 1974.

The donkeys now need to cross the road and it's worth keeping an eye out for them at night as they don't always pay attention to the 'Donkey Crossing' signs on the highway!

Kona Village Resort

Kona Village Resort is the most unique of Hawaii's getaway hotels. The accommodation is in thatched Polynesian-style 'hales' on stilts that are spaced around a spring-fed lagoon and along the beach. The grounds have flowering tropical plants and trees, petroglyphs and lots of birds.

The resort is on the secluded **Kahuwai Bay**, surrounded by huge expanses of barren lava. There was a fishing village on the bay years ago but it got washed away in the 1946 tidal wave. When the resort opened in 1965 it was so isolated it had its own airstrip to shuttle in guests. The highway wasn't built for another decade.

Non-guest access is limited, but guided tours are given at 11 am Monday to Friday (no reservations required), and at 11.30 am and 1.30 pm on weekends with reservations. The turn-off is just before the 87-mile marker.

If you don't want to visit the resort but just want to go down to the coast, tell the guard at the gatehouse you want one of the beach access parking spaces. The access is at the south side of Kahuwai Bay. Unlike the sandy beach in front of the resort, this end of the bay is rocky and is mostly used by divers going spear fishing or people hiking along the coast.

Places to Stay The 125 free-standing cottages at *Kona Village Resort* (☎ 325-5555, (800) 367-5290), Box 1299, Kaupulehu-Kona, HI 96745, look like rustic thatched huts on the outside but are modern and very comfortable inside with high ceilings, rattan furnishings, ceiling fans and louvered windows.

The village is intended to be a getaway and the units do not have phones or TVs (the front office has both). It's all low-key and relaxed, although there are activities available including tennis, sailboats, glass-bottom boats and outrigger canoes. The meals are excellent and include seven-course dinners.

Daily rates range from $300 to $550 for singles, $390 to $640 for doubles, and include all meals and recreational activities. Despite the obvious irony of paying this kind of money to 'go native' there seem to be few unhappy campers here.

Places to Eat *Kona Village Resort* is open to non-guests except when the resort is at 100% occupancy.

The daily outdoor lunch buffet, held from 12.30 to 2 pm, costs $24. In addition there's expensive fine dining in the Hale Samoa, which is designed in the traditional New Hebrides style and is lined with lauhala matting. The 75-foot tapa cloth draped from the ceiling was a gift from the king of Tonga after his stay at the resort.

A better deal is to take in the resort's luau, the most authentic in Hawaii. It's Friday nights only, costs $58 and in peak season sometimes books out weeks in advance. Reservations are required for all dining.

Kiholo Bay

Halfway up the coast, near the 82-mile marker, there's a lookout which commands great views of Kiholo Bay. It appears like a little oasis in the midst of the lava, with intense blue waters and a line of coconut trees.

An inconspicuous trail down to the bay starts about 200 yards south of the 81-mile marker. It follows a 4WD road, the beginning of which has been blocked off by boulders to keep vehicles out. The hike down takes about half an hour.

Kiholo Bay is almost two miles wide and the south end of the bay has a lovely, large spring-fed pond called **Luahinewai**. It's refreshingly cold and fronted by a black-sand beach. There's also good ocean swimming when it's calm.

In ancient times Kiholo provided a respite along the King's Trail, a stone footpath that ran along the coast. It was a fishing village famous for a large fishpond built by Kamehameha. The fishpond was filled in by an 1859 lava flow.

Cattle were shipped from here in the 1890s and there was once a small hotel. Now there are a few private homes on the bay, including one owned by country & western singer Loretta Lynn.

Na Ala Hele, a state-affiliated group working on trail access issues, is restoring a 4½-mile stretch of the historic trail that runs between Kiholo Bay and Kona Village Resort.

WAIKOLOA BEACH RESORT

Just after crossing into the South Kohala district, a single turn-off leads to the Royal Waikoloan and Hyatt Regency Waikoloa hotels and to Anaehoomalu Beach Park. The road is just south of the 76-mile marker.

Petroglyphs

As you drive in there's a two-acre lava field etched with an impressive number of petroglyphs near the resort's golf course. It's off the road to the right, immediately before the Kings' Shops complex.

Many of the petroglyphs date back to the 1500s. Some are graphic (humans, birds, canoes); others cryptic (dots and lines). Western influences show up in the form of horses and English initials.

Although the footpath that leads through the petroglyphs is called the King's Trail, this section was actually a horse and cattle trail built in the late 1800s. The trail once connected Kailua with Kawaihae. It's possible to continue on the trail to a historical preserve at the Mauna Lani Resort, about two miles away. It's an unshaded walk over lava.

Anaehoomalu Beach

Anaehoomalu Beach is a long, sandy beach that curves along an attractive bay. The waters are popular for swimming and windsurfing and have a gently sloping sandy bottom. Winter weather can produce rip currents but most of the time the water is quite calm.

The south end of the beach has public facilities, with showers, toilets, changing areas and parking. The north end of the beach fronts the Royal Waikoloan hotel.

Both ends of the bay are composed of prehistoric lava flows from Mauna Kea, with rough *aa* lava to the north and smooth pahoehoe to the south.

The beach hut in front of the hotel has a good aerial photo showing the coral and rock formations in the bay and can give you the latest on water conditions. They rent windsurfing equipment for $19 an hour and give a 1¼-hour lesson for $40. Snorkel sets rent for $5 an hour or $15 a day. They also have a two-hour beginners scuba lesson in the hotel pool for $29 and offer boat dives, catamaran cruises, kayak rentals, glass-bottom boat rides and sailing.

Anaehoomalu was once the site of royal fishponds. Archaeologists from the Bishop Museum have found evidence of habitation dating back more than 1000 years.

There are two large fishponds just beyond the line of coconut trees on the beach. A short **trail** starts near the showers and winds by the fishponds, caves, ancient house platforms and a shrine. Interpretive plaques along the way explain the area's history. It's a nice little walk and this is a fine beach to drive up to if you're staying in Kona.

Hyatt Regency Waikoloa

The 62-acre Hyatt Regency Waikoloa is the most extravagant resort development on the Big Island. It has the air of a sophisticated theme park and islanders have nicknamed it 'Disneyland'.

The Hyatt had no beach, so it built its own. There's a four-acre saltwater lagoon stocked with tropical fish, a 'river' with a current for rafting and a dolphin pool.

Canopied boats cart guests between buildings along artificial canals and there's a modernistic tram that looks like it was intended for downtown Tokyo. Because the complex is so large both actually do function as public transport and the novelty of using and waiting for them wears off quickly.

There's free parking at the hotel, but you can also walk over from the Royal Waikoloan, a quiet 15-minute stroll up the lava coast. As you climb up the back steps of the Hyatt there are no clues as to what's on the other side of the fortress-like wall. Then suddenly you're in the midst of it all, crossing a rope walkway over sprawling swimming pools with cascading waterfalls and shrieking kids flying down a waterslide.

When it opened in 1988 the Hyatt billed it as the world's most expensive resort at a cost of $360 million. But for all the extravagance it's surprisingly casual and anyone can cruise around in the free boats and tram.

The Hyatt has a multimillion-dollar **art collection** along a mile-long walkway that runs in both directions from the front lobby.

The museum-quality pieces include extensive collections from Melanesia, Polynesia and Asia.

They're particularly big on Papua New Guinea, with war clubs and spears, spirit boards, carved fighting shields and a partial replica of a ceremonial house. There's a collection of Han pottery that dates back 2000 years, antique dolls and Noh masks from Japan, 18th-century Burmese puppets and huge cloisonne vases. They've even managed to slip in a little Hawaiiana section next to the Palace Tower.

The Hyatt holds free star-gazing with a Celstron-8 telescope a couple of times a week, but vacillate as to whether this is open to non-guests. Call 885-1234 for information.

Places to Stay

The 523-room *Royal Waikoloan* (☎ 885-6789, (800) 537-9800), Box 5000, Waikoloa, HI 96743, is a former Sheraton. While this is the 'budget' hotel in the Waikoloa area, with rooms beginning at $99 for a garden view, its beachside location is far superior to that of the Hyatt's. The hotel also frequently runs a 'Free Ride' deal that throws in a Budget rental car for the same $99 rate – very good value for the Waikoloa area.

Hyatt Regency Waikoloa (☎ 885-1234, (800) 228-9000), 1 Waikoloa Beach Resort, Waikoloa, HI 96743, a mega-hotel with 1241 rooms, was developed by Chris Hemmeter and is the most indulgent of his Hawaii fantasy resorts. Rates start at $235 for garden views and $305 for ocean views and go up to $3000 for the presidential suite. Add on a $12 porterage fee for the requisite privilege of having your baggage delivered to your room.

Places to Eat

The *Garden Cafe*, in the Royal Waikoloan, is a coffee-shop-style restaurant serving three meals a day. It has a relaxing setting with pleasant carp pools. Sandwiches are around $7 and hot dishes are about double the price.

The *Royal Terrace* in the Royal Waikoloan

has a nice Sunday champagne brunch from 9 am to 1 pm with omelettes, waffles, sashimi, jumbo shrimp, numerous salads and main dishes and good-quality desserts. It costs $18.75 for adults, $8.75 for children.

Cascades, in the Hyatt Regency Waikoloa, is open for breakfast from 6 to 11 am and for dinner from 5.30 to 10 pm. Both meals are buffet style. Breakfast, which has a few Japanese touches as well as the standard American dishes and pastries, costs $16 for adults, $8.50 for children. Dinner, which is a different ethnic buffet (Polynesian, Texas barbecue, Chinese etc) each night, is $21. It's a pleasant and somewhat casual setting overlooking a pond with exotic waterbirds. Ask for a swan-view table.

The Hyatt also has fine dining Japanese, Italian and continental restaurants. The most popular is *Donatoni's*, which has a reputation for serving the island's best Italian food. The cheapest dish on the menu is fettucine alfredo at $16, while more exciting seafood dishes such as the cioppino cost $29.

Entertainment

Both the *Hyatt Regency Waikoloa* and the *Royal Waikoloan* have luaus with Polynesian shows. The Royal Waikoloan luau, held on Sunday evening, is the smaller of the two. It has a pleasant lawn setting, a group that can strum good Hawaiian music, and costs $40 for adults, $20 for children aged under 12.

The Hyatt's luau is more theatrical. It is held in an outdoor theatre on Tuesdays and Fridays and costs $55 for adults, $35 for children.

The Kona Comedy Club brings national stand-up comics to the Royal Waikoloan's Vanda Lounge on Monday nights. On most other nights, the Vanda Lounge is a disco. A little more up-market is Spats, the disco at the Hyatt, which is open from 8.30 pm to 2 am on Fridays and Saturdays. There's no cover charge at either disco.

WAIKOLOA

Waikoloa village is a modern residential development and bedroom community for workers in the nearby resorts. Although there's not much of interest for visitors, the village has a store selling groceries and a golf course with a restaurant.

The 12-mile Waikoloa Rd runs through the village connecting Hwy 190 and Hwy 19.

Places to Stay

Waikoloa Villas is a modern low-rise condo development in Waikoloa village. One-bedroom units cost $115/135 in the low/high season, two-bedroom units cost $125/150 and three-bedroom units cost $165/185. Weekly rates, which are offered only in the low season, are six times the daily rate. Units have full kitchens, lanais, swimming pools and the like.

Waikoloa Villas is on the Waikoloa golf course, not the beach, and is booked through Hawaiian Islands Resorts (☎ 531-7595, (800) 367-7042), Box 212, Honolulu, HI 96810.

Places to Eat

The *Waikoloa Village Restaurant* (☎ 883-9644) at the golf course is open from 6.30 am to 2.30 pm daily, and from 5 to 9.30 pm nightly except Mondays. Breakfast costs around $5. Lunch includes sandwiches for $6 and broiled fish for $7.50. At dinner, fish, scampi or chicken costs around $15. Chef Bones Yuen has a good reputation and has been the executive chef for Hawaii's two most recent governors.

MAUNA LANI RESORT

After a brief encounter with coconut palms and bright bougainvilleas at the highway entrance, Mauna Lani Drive heads through a long stretch of lava with virtually no vegetation. Halfway along there's a strikingly green golf course sculptured into the black lava. Mauna Lani Bay Hotel is at the end of the road. The Ritz-Carlton Mauna Lani hotel and Holoholokai Beach Park are to the north.

Mauna Lani Bay Hotel

The hotel is ritzy but still low-key, a modern open-air structure centred around a breezy atrium which holds waterways, orchid sprays and full-grown coconut trees. A saltwater stream which runs through the hotel and outdoors into the sun holds small black-tipped sharks and a variety of colourful reef fish. The atrium is the venue for Hawaiian music and hula performed nightly from 5.30 to 8 pm, which makes it a nice time to visit.

The hotel has good beaches and historical sights and there's public access to both. A free, self-guided trail map is available at the concierge desk. The hotel is welcoming and relaxed, in contrast to some of the other resort hotels in the area. One-hour historical tours are given a couple of times a week and are free to the public. Call 885-6622 for the latest schedule.

Beaches The beach in front of the Mauna Lani Bay Hotel is protected but the water is rather shallow. There's a coral reef beyond the inlet that snorkellers might want to explore. Check at the hotel beach hut for water conditions.

There's also a spring-fed pool and a less-frequented cove down by the Beach Club restaurant, a 15-minute walk to the south.

An old **coastal foot trail** leads about a mile farther south to **Honokaope Bay**. It passes by a few historical sites, including a fishers' house site and other village remains. The southern end of Honokaope Bay is protected and good for swimming and snorkelling when the seas are calm.

Fishponds The ancient Kalahuipuaa fishponds are along the beach just south of the hotel in a shady grove of coconut palms and milo trees.

The ponds are stocked with awa, or milkfish. Water circulates from the ocean through traditional makaha sluice gates which allow small fish to enter but keep the older fattened ones from leaving. The fish sporadically jump into the air and slap down on the water, an exercise which knocks off parasites.

These are among the few continuously working fishponds in Hawaii and awa from here have been used to provide stock for commercial fisheries.

Historic Trail The Kalahuipuaa Trail begins at a parking area opposite the resort's little grocery store, which is mauka of the Mauna Lani Bay Hotel.

The trail meanders through a Hawaiian settlement that dates from the 1500s. There are cave shelters, a few petroglyphs and other archaeological and geological sites marked by interpretive plaques.

It's a neat little walk that ends at the fishponds and the beach. If you loop around the largest fishpond and head back the round trip is about 1½ miles.

Holoholokai Beach Park
Holoholokai Beach Park, north of the Ritz-Carlton Mauna Lani, is rocky with a mix of coral chunks and large pebbles. It's not a great bathing beach, although when the waters are calm there's reasonable snorkelling in the area and sometimes some good surf breaks in winter.

The park has showers, restrooms, picnic tables and grills and is open from 6.30 am to 7 pm.

The main reason for visiting is to walk the trail to the Puako petroglyphs. To get there, take Mauna Lani Drive and turn right at the rotary, then right again on the beach road immediately before the grounds of the Ritz-Carlton

Puako Petroglyphs With more than 3000 petroglyphs, the Puako petroglyph preserve has one of the largest collections of ancient lava carvings in Hawaii.

From the north end of the beach parking lot, a well-marked trail leads to the petroglyphs three-quarters of a mile away.

The human figures drawn in simple linear forms are some of Hawaii's oldest such drawings. Those with triangular shapes and curved forms are from more recent times.

The ageing petroglyphs are fragile as they're carved into an ancient lava flow which is brittle and cracking. Stepping on the petroglyphs can damage them, so be careful not to. The only safe way to record them is with a camera. If you want to make rubbings there are some authentically reproduced

Petroglyphs

petroglyphs just a minute's walk down the trail from the parking lot that have been made for that purpose.

Because of the sharp kiawe thorns along the trail, flip-flops (thongs) are not appropriate footwear for the walk – the thorns can easily pierce their soft soles and your feet.

Places to Stay

The *Mauna Lani Bay Hotel* (☎ 885-6622, (800) 367-2323), Box 4000, Kohala, HI 96743, is one of the finest hotels in the islands. Rates for the 350 rooms start at $260 for a garden view, $365 for an ocean view.

The luxury *Mauna Lani Point* condos at Mauna Lani Resort are booked through Classic Resorts (☎ 667-1400, (800) 642-6284), 50 Nohea Kai Drive, Lahaina, HI 96761. One-bedroom units start at $210/240 in the low/high season.

The new *Ritz-Carlton Mauna Lani* (☎ 885-2000, (800) 845-9905), 1 N Kaniku Drive, Kohala, HI 96743, on the rather rocky Pauoa Bay, has the requisite statuary on the grounds and art in the lobby. Rates for the 542 rooms start at $260 for a garden view, $365 for an ocean view.

Places to Eat

The best Sunday brunch in the Waikoloa area is at the Mauna Lani Bay Hotel's (☎ 885-6622) *Bay Terrace*. It starts out with a sushi and sashimi table, has waffles and omelettes to order, good meat and fish dishes, a variety of fruits and lots of salads including hearts of palm and green papaya. To finish it off there's a great-looking dessert table. It's in an open-air setting accompanied by a duo performing mellow Hawaiian music on the lawn. The buffet is served from 11.30 am to 2 pm and costs $21.50.

If you want a big splurge on the Big Island, dinner at the *Canoe House* next to the Mauna Lani Bay Hotel is a good place to go. Chef Alan Wong is renowned for his Pacific Rim cuisine, with dishes like kiawe-grilled Pacific spiny lobster and sheared ono on stir-fried asparagus. It's a romantic setting with open-air dining on the water, tropical decor and attentive service. Main dishes average $26 to $30 and appetizers cost $8 to $12. It's open for dinner only, from 6 to 9.30 pm.

For somewhere easier on the wallet, there's the *Beach Club*, a casual restaurant at the south end of Kaniku Drive. The restaurant fronts a small swimming cove. Sandwiches cost $6 to $7 and they also serve soup, chilli and salads. It's open for lunch only, from 11 am to 4 pm daily. Parking is marked for members and resort guests, but if the gate is open it doesn't seem to be a problem for non-guests.

PUAKO

Puako is a quiet one-road coastal village where everyone either lives on the beach or across the street from it.

Puako is lined with giant **tide pools**. The sea washes in and stays in the swirls and dips of the pahoehoe lava that forms the coastline. Some of the pools are deep enough to shelter live coral and diverse marine life. Snorkelling can be excellent, although the surf is usually too rough in winter. A narrow beach of pulverised coral and lava lines much of the shoreline.

The turn-off to Puako is marked on Hwy

19 and you can also reach Puako from Hapuna Beach Park along a passable route that's more patchwork than road.

Hoku Loa Church, which dates back to 1858, is about half a mile beyond the Puako Bay boat ramp. It's a plain plastered building with a few simple wooden pews. It's still used for Sunday services but at other times it's usually locked up tight.

The easiest beach access is to simply drive to the end of the road where a short dirt drive leads to the water. A couple of minutes' walk along the beach to the north will bring you to a few petroglyphs, a konane game board chinked into the lava and tide pools deep enough to cool off in.

HAPUNA BEACH STATE PARK

The long beautiful stretch of white sand along Hapuna Bay is the Big Island's most popular beach.

When it's calm, Hapuna Beach State Park has good swimming, snorkelling and diving. In the winter it's a hot bodysurfing and boogie boarding beach. The high winter surf can produce strong currents close to the shore and a pounding shorebreak. Waves over three feet should be left for the experts. Hapuna has had numerous drownings and many of the victims have been tourists unfamiliar with water conditions.

There's a tiny secluded cove with a small sandy beach about five minutes' walk to the north. Just follow the shoreline trail and you'll come across steps leading down to it. The water is calmer there and in winter there's less sand kicked up by the waves.

The 61-acre state park includes the beach, A-frame cabins for overnight stays and a landscaped park with picnic facilities, showers, restrooms, drinking water and telephone.

There's a snack bar, open from 10 am to 5 pm daily, which sells burgers, shave ice and ice cream, and a window at the side that rents out boogie boards and snorkel sets at $6 per four hours. A $60 deposit or a credit card is required for all rentals. As part of their agreement with the state the concessionaire staffs a lifeguard at the beach.

A new 350-room luxury hotel is being built adjacent to the northern end of the beach. Its construction has not been overly welcomed by beachgoers, who led an island-wide campaign initiative to 'Save Hapuna Beach' in the late 1980s. The initiative narrowly failed in a general election.

Hapuna to Mauna Kea

An easy trail runs along the craggy coast from the north end of Hapuna Beach to the south end of Kaunaoa (Mauna Kea) Beach. As part of the trail goes through stands of kiawe, watch out for sharp thorns that can easily puncture flip-flops (thongs). The walk takes about 20 minutes.

MAUNA KEA HOTEL & BEACH

In the early 1960s, Laurance Rockefeller obtained a 99-year lease on the land around Kaunaoa Bay from his friend Richard Smart, owner of Parker Ranch. Five years later he opened Mauna Kea Beach Hotel, the first luxury hotel on the outer islands.

Kaunaoa Bay is a gorgeous crescent bay with a white-sand beach. It has a gradual slope and fine swimming conditions most of the year. There's good snorkelling on the north side when it's calm.

Inside the hotel, a large collection of Asian and Pacific artwork is on display. Bronze temple toys from India are lined up opposite the elevators on the 5th floor. Thai guardian dogs, Hawaiian quilts and hanging batiks decorate other corners.

Their most prized possession is the 7th century pink granite meditating Buddha which sits in the north garden. It was taken from a temple in South India.

To use Mauna Kea Beach, ask at the gatehouse for one of the 30 beach access parking spaces allotted for non-guests.

Places to Stay

Mauna Kea Beach Hotel (☎ 882-7222, (800) 882-6060), Box 218, Kohala, HI 96743, has 310 rooms that start at $260. Throw in another $120 for an ocean view. For $68 more per person, breakfast and dinner are included.

Places to Eat

The *Mauna Kea Beach Hotel* has a good daily lunch buffet, with the likes of Alaskan crab legs, oysters on the half shell, eight hot entrees, either a tempura or pasta station, and good fruit and dessert offerings. On Sundays they add sushi and a Belgian waffle station. While the food is good the setting is not special. It's open from noon to 2.30 pm daily and costs $22.50. To find out what the hot entrees of the day are call 882-7222 (ext 68).

The *Batik Room* has a Sri Lankan theme with dishes ranging from Indian curry and fresh fish to Chateaubriand. It's open for dinner only with formal dining, dance music and dishes in the $30 range.

SPENCER BEACH PARK

Spencer Beach Park is a family beach park off Hwy 270, just south of Kawaihae. The shallow sandy beach is protected by a reef and by the jetty to the north. If anything, it's a bit too protected and the water tends to get silty.

The rocky south end of the beach past the pavilion is better for snorkelling, although entry is not as easy.

Spencer is a well-used beach park with a lifeguard and full facilities. Camping is allowed with a permit from the county. During the week, Hilo people who work on this side of the island sometimes camp here instead of commuting. On weekends quite a few families show up.

PUUKOHOLA HEIAU

The Puukohola Heiau National Historic Site, which is off the side of the road that leads down to Spencer Beach, contains the last major temple built in Hawaii.

In 1790, after his attempt at a sweeping conquest of the islands was thwarted, King Kamehameha sought the advice of Kapoukahi, a soothsayer from Kauai.

Kamehameha was told that if he built a temple to his war god here above Kawaihae Bay, then all of Hawaii would fall to him in battle. Kamehameha immediately began construction of Puukohola Heiau, completing it in 1791.

Kamehameha then held a dedication ceremony and invited his last rival on the Big Island, Keoua, the chief of Kau. When Keoua came ashore he was killed and brought up to the temple as the first offering to the gods. With Keoua's death Kamehameha had sole control of the Big Island, and he went on to fulfil the prophecy by conquering the other islands.

Puukohola Heiau, terraced in three steps, was covered with wooden idols and thatched structures, including an oracle tower, altar, drum house and the home of the high priest.

After Kamehameha's death in 1819, his son Liholiho and powerful widow Kaahumanu destroyed the heiau's wooden images and the temple was abandoned. These days only the basic rock foundation remains, but it's still an impressive site.

Puukohola means 'hill of the whales'. Migrating humpbacks can often be seen offshore during winter.

The visitors' centre (☎ 882-7218), which is open from 7.30 am to 4 pm daily, has a few simple displays and someone on duty to provide a brief introduction to the park. A free brochure describes the historic sites that are spread over the park's 77 acres. There are no entrance fees.

A trail to the heiau starts at the visitors' centre and takes less than 10 minutes to walk.

Just beyond Puukohola Heiau are the ruins of Mailekini Heiau, which predates Puukohola and was later turned into a fort by Kamehameha. Nearby, a heiau dedicated to shark gods lays submerged just offshore and you can still see the stone leaning post where the high chief watched sharks bolt down the offerings he made.

The path continues down by the creek to Kamehameha's former house site. Warbling silverbills, doves and mosquitoes frequent the kiawe woods, but there's not much to see.

The trail then leads across the highway to the site of John Young's homestead. Young, a shipwrecked British sailor, served Kamehameha as a military advisor and governor of the island. There's not much to see there either.

KAWAIHAE

Kawaihae has the Big Island's second largest deep-water commercial harbour. The harbour has fuel tanks and cattle pens and a little local beach park. There's not really much to attract visitors and most stop in Kawaihae just long enough to eat and fuel up on their way to somewhere else.

Kawaihae Center on Hwy 270 has two restaurants, an ice-cream and shave-ice shop, a 7-Eleven store and Kohala Divers.

Places to Eat

Cafe Pesto (☎ 882-1071) serves up good gourmet pizza, calzones, seafood pastas and salads. It's a class act with nasturtiums in the tossed salad and fresh basil leaves on the side. The Greek pizza is topped with feta cheese, fresh spinach, olives and peppers, while the Oriental pizza has sun-dried tomatoes, Japanese eggplant and roasted garlic. Both cost $10 for a small, $15 for a medium. Pizza of the day is available at $3 a slice until 4 pm. The cafe is on the lower level of the Kawaihae Center and is open from 11 am to 9 pm on weekdays, to 10 pm on weekends.

Tres Hombres Beach Grill, upstairs from Cafe Pesto, is a new restaurant serving Mexican food.

North Kohala

The north-west tip of the Big Island is dominated by a central range, the Kohala Mountains.

The leeward side of the mountains is dry and desert-like. The windward side is wet and lush with steep coastal cliffs and spectacularly cut hanging valleys.

North Kohala is often bypassed by travellers as it's off the main track, but it has a couple of impressive historical sites, a few sleepy towns to poke around in and a lovely valley lookout at the end of the road.

There are two ways to get to North Kohala, an inland road and a coastal road. You can make a nice tour by going up one and down the other.

WAIMEA TO HAWI (HWY 250)

Hwy 250 (Kohala Mountain Rd) runs north for 20 miles from Waimea to Hawi. This is a very scenic drive along the upland slopes of the Kohala Mountains. The road is lined in places with ironwood trees and goes through rolling green hills dotted with grazing cattle. At its northern end there's even a little llama farm.

As you head north, Maui rises out of the mist, with the crater of Haleakala showing up red. Mauna Kea is behind you. There are views of the coast and Kawaihae Harbor below and a scenic pull-off to take it all in.

There are also a couple of new subdivisions up this way, the largest being Kohala Ranch.

Hwy 250 peaks at 3564 feet before dropping down into Hawi.

Kohala Ranch

Kohala Ranch is a residential subdivision that was once part of a real ranch. A few years back it was zoned agricultural, subdivided into lots of three to 10 acres and sold to people looking to build second homes in the country.

Despite severe water shortages, a large tract of the 'ranch' has been re-zoned as urban. Thousands of new residential lots, a shopping village and a 27-hole golf course seem to be on the cards. If it all sells there may be 10,000 additional residents here in a few years, more than double the total current population of the entire North Kohala district.

Kohala Ranch Rd runs through the subdivision for six miles, connecting Hwy 250 and Hwy 270.

KAWAIHAE TO POLOLU VALLEY (HWY 270)

Hwy 270 (Akoni Pule Highway), which starts in Kawaihae, takes in the coastal sights of Lapakahi State Historical Park and Mookini Heiau and ends at a lookout above Pololu Valley.

There's a trail down to the valley floor, but even if you're not up for a hike the view from the lookout is worth the drive.

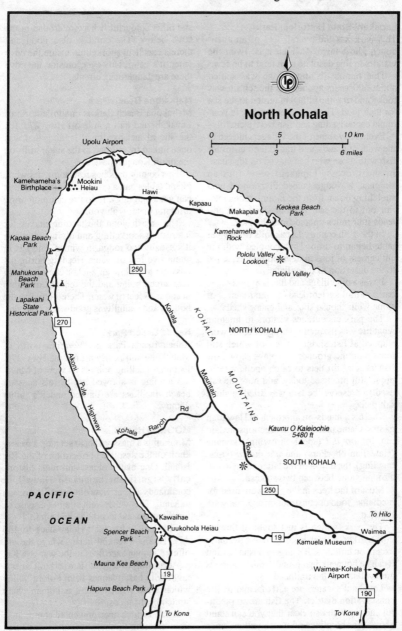

North Kohala

0   5   10 km

0   3   6 miles

Upolu Airport

Kamehameha's Birthplace → Mookini Heiau

Hawi

Kapaau

Makapala

Keokea Beach Park

Kamehameha Rock

Kapaa Beach Park

Pololu Valley Lookout

Mahukona Beach Park

Pololu Valley

Lapakahi State Historical Park

KOHALA

NORTH KOHALA

250

Kohala Mountain Road

MOUNTAINS

Akoni Pule Highway

Kohala Ranch Rd

Rd

Kaunu O Kaleioohie 5480 ft

SOUTH KOHALA

250

PACIFIC

OCEAN

To Hilo

Kawaihae

Puukohola Heiau

Waimea

Spencer Beach Park

Kamuela Museum

Mauna Kea Beach

19

Waimea-Kohala Airport

Hapuna Beach Park

19

190

To Kona

To Kona

Lapakahi State Historical Park

This park has the overall feel of an abandoned ghost town – which it is. Even the visitors in this desolate spot tend to be few.

This remote fishing village was settled about 600 years ago and as the terrain was rocky and dry, the villagers turned to the sea for their food. The cove provided a safe year-round canoe landing and fish were plentiful.

Eventually some of the villagers moved to the wetter uplands, and traded their crops for fish with those who had stayed on the coast. In the process, Lapakahi grew into an ahupuaa, a wedge-shaped division of land stretching down from the mountainous interior out to the sea. A stone-lined trail still leads four miles upland from the park.

In the 19th century Lapakahi's freshwater table began to drop. This, coupled with the enticement of jobs in developing towns, led to the desertion of the village.

It was a big village and this is a good-sized park. A trail system leads to the remains of stone walls, house sites and canoe sheds.

The park encourages visitors to imagine what life was like centuries ago. People worshipped at fish shrines, a few of which still remain on the grounds. Displays show how fishers used lift nets to catch opelu, a technique still practised today, and how the salt used to preserve the fish was dried in stone salt pans.

There's a hands-on approach to Hawaiian games. Game pieces and instructions are laid out for *oo ihe* (spear throwing), konane (Hawaiian checkers) and *ulu maika* (stone bowling), the object of the latter being to roll a round stone between two stakes.

Most of the trees in the park were used for medicine, food or construction and many are labelled.

The park, which is just south of the 14-mile marker, is open from 7 am to 4 pm daily except on holidays. It's largely unshaded and it can be hot walking around. Trail brochures are available at the trailhead.

Lapakahi's waters are part of a marine life conservation district. The fish are so plentiful and the water so clear that you can stand above the shoreline and watch yellow tangs and other colourful fish swim around in the cove below. The coral is also good and there's excellent snorkelling inside the cove when it's calm. However, outside the cove there are dangerous currents.

Mahukona Beach Park

Mahukona Beach Park is one mile north of Lapakahi and half a mile off Hwy 270. It's the site of an abandoned landing that was once linked by railroad to the sugar mills on the north Kohala coast.

This county park has restrooms, showers, picnic tables and a grassy camping area that can get a bit buggy. If you're camping bring drinking water with you.

The area beyond the landing makes for interesting snorkelling and diving, although it's usually too rough in winter. Entry is in about five feet of water. Heading north, it's possible to follow an anchor chain out to a submerged boiler and the remains of a ship in about 25 feet of water. There's coral on the bottom and visibility is good when it's calm.

Kapaa Beach Park

Kapaa Beach Park is 1¼ miles north of Mahukona and nearly a mile off Hwy 270. Its biggest selling point is its view of Maui.

Camping is allowed but there's no sand beach, facilities are limited and it's rather dumpy.

MOOKINI HEIAU

Mookini is a massive heiau set atop a grassy knoll on the desolate northern tip of the Big Island. One of the oldest and most historically significant heiaus in Hawaii, it commands a clear view out across the ocean to Maui. This windswept site has a sense of timelessness and a certain eerie aura.

Chants date Mookini Heiau back to 480 AD. This is a luakini heiau, where the alii offered human sacrifices to the war god Ku.

According to legend, it was built in one night with basalt stones from Pololu Valley which were passed along a human chain stretching 14 miles.

A kapu which once prevented commoners from entering the heiau grounds was lifted only a decade ago. Not many people come this way and it will probably just be you, the wind and the spirits here.

The heiau is 250 feet long, with rock walls reaching a good 25 feet high. The entrance through the wall into the heiau itself is on the west side. The long enclosure on the right immediately before the heiau entrance was the home of the *mu*, or body catcher, who secured sacrificial victims for the heiau altar. The large scallop-shaped altar on the north end of the heiau is thought to have been added by Paao, a Tahitian priest who arrived around the 12th century and introduced human sacrifice to Hawaiian worship.

The current kahuna nui priestess is Leimomi Mookini Lum, the most recent in a long line of Mookinis tracing their lineage back to the temple's first high priest.

To get there turn left off Hwy 270 at the 20-mile marker and go two miles down to Upolu Airport. At the airport turn left onto the road that runs parallel to the coast. Although it's usually passable, this red dirt road is rutted and bumpy and can get very muddy after heavy rains. After 1½ miles you'll come to a fork. The left road leads up to the heiau, a quarter of a mile farther.

Kamehameha's Birthplace

Kamehameha the Great was said to have been born on a stormy winter night in 1758 on this ruggedly desolate coast. If you continue straight ahead at the fork below the heiau for a third of a mile, you'll reach the stone enclosure that marks his birthsite.

According to one story, Kamehameha's mother was told by a kahuna that her son would become a destroyer of chiefs and a powerful ruler. The high chief of the island didn't take well to the prophecy and in a King-Herod-like scenario he ordered the newborn killed.

Immediately after birth, the baby was taken to Mookini Heiau for his birth rituals and then into hiding in the Kohala Mountains.

HAWI

Hawi (pronounced Hah-vee), with a popula-

tion of less than 1000, is the largest town in North Kohala. It has a post office, a couple of grocery stores and gas stations, a laundromat, a video arcade and a few restaurants.

North Kohala used to be sugar country and Hawi was the biggest of half a dozen sugar towns. Kohala Sugar Company, which had incorporated all of the mills, closed down its operations in 1975. Hawi now has more storefronts than stores and although some people are beginning to be drawn this way by the area's lower property values there's really not much happening.

The park on Hwy 250 in front of the post office is cool and shady with giant banyan trees. It would be a fine place for a picnic. Behind the park is the old sugar mill tower, a remnant of the town's former mainstay. You can still see the occasional strip of feral cane amongst the pastures outside town.

Places to Eat

Ohana Pizza on Hwy 270 has pretty good pizza and a variety of sandwiches. A cheese pizza or lasagne with salad and garlic bread costs $8. There's a bar and the place has a country & western feel.

Kohala Health Food & Nutrition Center, on Hwy 270 opposite Ohana Pizza, is a small health-food store that sells packaged health foods as well as organic fruit and vegetables.

KAPAAU

The statue of Kamehameha the Great on the front lawn of the North Kohala Civic Center may look familiar. Its lei-draped and much-photographed twin stands opposite the Iolani Palace in Honolulu.

The statue was made in 1880 in Florence, Italy, by American sculptor Thomas Gould. The ship delivering it sank off the Falkland Islands and another statue was cast. The duplicate made from the original mould arrived in 1883 and took its place in downtown Honolulu.

Later the sunken statue was recovered from the ocean floor and completed its trip to Hawaii. The original statue was then sent here, to Kamehameha's childhood home, where it stands watching the traffic trickle along in quiet Kapaau.

Kapaau has a new courthouse and police station and Kamehameha Park which includes a large, modern gymnasium and everything from a ball park to a swimming pool. The town has a little library, a Bank of Hawaii and a couple of interesting shops.

Still, it's an ageing town. The only crowd is at the senior centre, which is part of the civic centre. The senior citizens sometimes staff a table on the porch with visitor information.

Kalahikiola Church

Protestant missionaries Elias and Ellen Bond, who arrived in Kohala in 1841, built Kalahikiola Church in 1855. An earthquake damaged it in 1973 but it's since been restored and the church is still in use today.

If you want to take a look, turn mauka off Hwy 270 onto a narrow road half a mile east of the Kamehameha statue, near the 24-mile marker. The church is about half a mile up from the highway.

The land and buildings on the drive in to the church are part of the Bond estate, proof enough that the missionary life wasn't total deprivation.

If the doors of the church seem to be locked it's because they don't push or pull, but rather slide open.

Places to Stay

Island's End B&B (☎ 889-5265, (800) 332-4820), Box 1234, Kapaau, HI 96755, is a large plantation-era home with a pleasant front porch and a big old monkeypod tree in the yard. Owners Joyce and Peter Aros rent a couple of rooms in the main house with shared bath for $45/50 a single/double, including a full breakfast. There's also a detached studio with private bath for the same price. Each is furnished with a double bed and one also has a day bed that a child under 12 can use without any additional cost. Smoking is limited to the outdoors.

A more modest possibility are the rooms in the old girls school at the Bond Estate which are sometimes rented out on a nightly basis. While the accommodation is basic it's also quite inexpensive. For information call 889-5217.

Places to Eat

Don's Family Deli on Hwy 270 is the place to eat in Kapaau. Mahimahi sandwiches, quiche with salad or tofu burgers cost around $5. They also have meat and cheese sandwiches, Portuguese bean soup, and espresso.

For dessert you could walk down the street to *Tropical Dreams* for a scoop of gourmet ice cream or sorbet. Tropical Dreams also makes delicious macadamia nut butters in flavours such as Kona coffee, mocha java, or ambrosia with chunks of pineapple, currants and almonds. They're sold here and in speciality shops around the island and make a great gift.

Mit's Drive-In is just east of Kapaau Post Office, next to H Naito general store. Mit's has inexpensive breakfasts, plate lunches and burgers.

KAPAAU TO POLOLU VALLEY
Kamehameha Rock

Kamehameha Rock is on the right-hand side of the road, about two miles east of Kapaau, on a curve just over a small bridge. It's said that Kamehameha carried this rock uphill from the beach below to demonstrate his strength.

A road crew once attempted to move the rock to a different location, but although they managed to get it up onto a wagon the rock fell off – an obvious sign it wanted to stay where it was. Not wanting to upset Kamehameha's mana, the workers obliged.

Right around the corner is the Kohala Tong Wo Society, founded in 1886. Hawaii once had many Chinese societies which provided immigrants with a place to preserve their cultural identity, speak their native language and socialise. This is the last one remaining on the Big Island.

Makapala

The little village of Makapala has a few hundred residents. The last place to get anything to drink before Pololu Valley is just past the Episcopal retreat centre, where there's a soda machine on the left side of the road.

Keokea Beach Park

Keokea Beach Park is on a somewhat scenic rocky coast. There's no sandy beach and it's not great for water activities.

The park is most active on weekends and camping is allowed, with a county permit, on the grassy section below the pavilion. There are covered picnic areas, restrooms, showers, drinking water, barbecue grills and electricity.

The marked turn-off is about 1½ miles before Pololu Valley Lookout. The park is about a mile in from the highway.

There's an old Japanese cemetery on the way down to the park. Most of the gravestones are in kanji (Japanese script) and a few have filled sake cups in front of them.

Pololu Valley Lookout

Hwy 270 ends at a scenic viewpoint looking down into Pololu Valley and out along the steep scalloped coastal cliffs to the east. With its high vantage the lookout has the kind of strikingly beautiful angle that's rarely experienced without a helicopter tour.

Pololu was once thickly planted with wetland taro. Pololu Stream fed the valley, carrying heavy rainfall from the remote interior to the valley floor. When the Kohala Ditch was built, it siphoned off much of the water and put an end to the taro production. The valley slopes are now forest reserve land.

Pololu Valley Trail The trail from the lookout down to Pololu Valley only takes about 20 minutes to walk. It's steep and can be hot walking, but it's not overly strenuous. Much of the trail is packed clay that can be slippery when wet.

Cattle and horses roam in the valley. There's a gate at the bottom of the trail which keeps them in.

The black-sand beach fronting the valley stretches for about half a mile. Driftwood collects in great quantities and on rare occasions glass fishing floats get washed up as well.

Surf is usually high in winter and although it's a bit tamer in summer, there can be rip currents year round.

Kohala Ditch

Kohala Ditch is an intricate series of ditches, tunnels and flumes that lead from Waikaloa Stream in the rugged wet interior of the Kohala Forest Reserve out to the Hawi area. Waikaloa Stream is midway between Pololu and Waipio valleys.

The ditch was built in 1906 to irrigate Kohala sugar cane fields. The last Kohala cane was cut in the 1970s, but the ditch continues to be a source of water for Kohala ranches and farms.

It was engineered by a sugar man, John Hind, with the financial backing of Samuel Parker of Parker Ranch. Kohala Ditch runs 22½ miles and was built by Japanese immigrant labourers who were paid about $1 a day for the hazardous work. More than a dozen labourers died during the construction.

There were once miles of mule trails along the ditch which were used for maintenance, but the trails are now overgrown.

Much of the ditch runs through 19,000 acres of Kohala land which Castle & Cooke recently sold to a Japanese developer.

Waimea

Waimea has a pretty setting in the foothills of the Kohala Mountains at an elevation of 2670 feet. It's cooler than the coast, with more clouds and fog. The area has gentle rolling hills and frequent afternoon rainbows.

This is the headquarters of Parker Ranch, Hawaii's largest cattle ranch, which spreads across nearly one-ninth of the Big Island. Almost everything in Waimea is owned by, run by or leased by Parker Ranch.

Waimea has its cowboy influences, but it's rapidly growing and becoming more sophisticated. It's the main town serving the new subdivisions being developed on former ranches in the Kohala Mountains. While many of the newcomers are wealthy mainlanders, Waimea is also home to a number of the international astronomers who work on Mauna Kea.

Waimea has a handful of restaurants started by renegade chefs from the island's best hotels, with food so good that people regularly drive up from Kona.

While Waimea is a fine place to dine, it's not a big tourist town with a lot of action or sightseeing attractions. There are a couple of museums and the green pastures are scenic, but for most visitors Waimea is just a stopover on the drive between Kona and Hilo.

Information

Waimea is also referred to as Kamuela, which is the Hawaiian spelling of Samuel. Although some say the name comes from an early postmaster named Samuel Spencer, most claim it's for Samuel Parker of Parker Ranch fame. The result is the same: confusing. Address all Waimea mail to Kamuela.

The Waimea-Kohala Airport, which is usually called Kamuela by the airlines, is off Hwy 190, 1¾ miles south from the intersection of Hwy 19.

Parker Ranch

Parker Ranch claims to be the nation's largest privately owned ranch. It has 225,000 acres, 50,000 head of cattle and about 100 ranch hands. The ranch accounts for one-third of the beef produced in the state.

The first cattle to arrive in Hawaii were a gift to Kamehameha from British captain George Vancouver in 1793. Vancouver convinced the king to place a 10-year kapu on the killing of cattle to ensure the preservation of the herd.

The kapu worked but the cattle ran wild and multiplied so quickly that they became an uncontrollable and destructive nuisance to both crops and native forests. Feral cattle still roam Mauna Kea's slopes today.

Parker Ranch owes its beginnings to John

Palmer Parker, a 19-year-old from New England who arrived on the Big Island in 1809 aboard a whaler. He took one look at Hawaii and jumped ship.

Parker soon gained the favour of Kamehameha, who commissioned him to bring the cattle under control. Parker managed to domesticate some of the cattle and butchered others, cutting the herds down to size.

Later, Parker married one of Kamehameha's granddaughters and in the process landed himself a tidy bit of land. He eventually gained control of the entire Waikoloa ahupuaa clear down to the sea.

Descendants of the Mexican-Spanish cowboys brought over to help round up the cattle still work the ranches today. (The Hawaiian word for cowboy, 'paniolo', is a corruption of the Spanish word 'espanoles'.)

Parker Ranch Historical Homes

Parker Ranch has two historic homes open to visitors at **Puuopelu**, a mini-estate on the ranch. Tours are given of the estate's century-old manor as well as the more modest original Parker home which has been reconstructed next door.

Current Parker Ranch owner Richard Palmer Smart, the great-great-great grandson of John Palmer Parker, was raised at Puuopelu by his grandmother after his parents died at an early age. Smart took to the theatre and appeared in a number of Broadway performances, mainly musical comedies. Now in his 70s, he is still acting, occasionally at Kahilu Theatre in Waimea. His main residence is in Honolulu, although he sometimes stays at Puuopelu.

Puuopelu has an interesting collection of European art and antique Chinese vases. One room is French provincial with chandeliers, skylights and walls hung with paintings by French impressionists, including works by Renoir, Degas and Pissarro.

Next door is **Mana Hale**, originally built in the 1840s by John Parker in the hills seven miles outside Waimea. It's essentially of saltbox construction, a popular design in Parker's native Massachusetts where the sloping roof deflects winter's cold north-east winds. The house is simple and aesthetically striking with walls, ceilings and floors made entirely of koa. The interior of Mana Hale was dismantled board by board and rebuilt here at Puuopelu but the exterior is a replica.

Mana Hale is decorated with period furnishings and interesting old photos of the hardy-looking Parker clan.

The turn-off to the homes is on Hwy 190, about three-quarters of a mile south of its intersection with Hwy 19. Opening hours are 10 am to 5 pm Tuesday to Saturday and admission costs $7.50 for adults, $5 for children.

Parker Ranch Visitor Center

Parker Ranch Visitor Center, in the Parker Ranch Shopping Center, is a little museum of the ranch's history showcasing Parker family memorabilia such as portraits, lineage charts, quilts and dishes. There's a little cowboy hut with saddles and branding irons.

There are also stone adzes, lava bowls, poi pounders, tapa bed covers and other Hawaiian artefacts, although for Hawaiiana alone other Big Island museums have more extensive collections. Actually the museum is not terribly dynamic. Perhaps most interesting are the old photos and the 15-minute movie

on Parker Ranch, including footage of cowboys rushing cattle into the sea and lifting them by slings onto the decks of waiting steamers.

A separate room is dedicated to Duke Kahanamoku. Duke, who was of royal Hawaiian lineage, won Olympic gold in the 100-metre freestyle swim in 1912 and 1920 and is credited with introducing surfing to Australia in 1912. Duke went on to play small roles in Hollywood movies, was sheriff of Honolulu for 25 years and was the city's 'ambassador' until his death in 1968 at the age of 77. The museum holds many of his trophies, Olympic medals and mementoes, including a photo of Britain's Queen Mother Elizabeth, dancing the hula with Duke in a Honolulu restaurant.

A free glance of the Duke's room can be seen through the window on the left opposite Auntie Alice's restaurant.

The museum is open from 9 am to 5 pm daily. Admission costs $5 for adults, $3.75 for children. A ticket that includes this museum and the Parker Ranch Historical Homes costs $10 for adults, $7.50 for children.

At the back of the shopping centre, behind the parking lot, there's a picturesque view of

Waimea

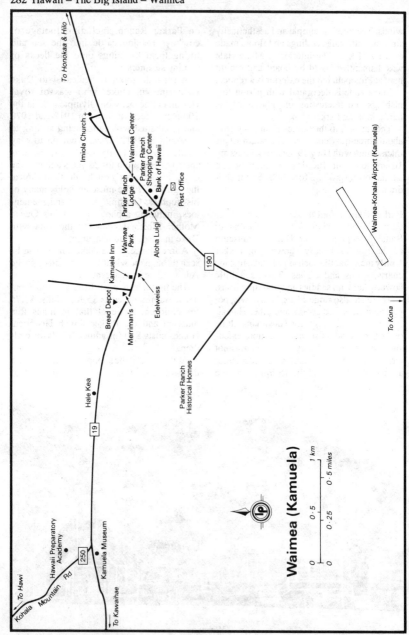

Waimea (Kamuela)

Mauna Kea rising above an old wooden corral and pastures.

Church Row

Waimea's churches are lined up side by side in an area called Church Row. Imiola Congregational Church is the oldest and the green steepled church next to it is Ke Ola Mau Loa Church, an all-Hawaiian church. Buddhists, Baptists and Mormons also have churches in the row.

Imiola Congregational Church Waimea's first Christian church was a grass hut built in 1830. It was replaced in 1838 by a wood and coral structure, built with coral stones carved out of the reef and carried inland on the backs of Hawaiian Christians. They named it Imiola, which means 'seeking salvation'.

The current building was constructed in 1857 and restored in 1976. The interior is simple and beautiful and it's built entirely of koa, most of it dating back to the original construction.

In the churchyard is the grave of missionary Lorenzo Lyons who arrived in 1832 and spent 54 years in Waimea. He wrote many of the hymns, including the popular 'Hawaii Aloha', that are still sung in Hawaiian here each Sunday. Also in the garden is the church bell, too heavy for the church roof to support.

Hale Kea

Hale Kea, on Hwy 19 between Hwy 190 and Hwy 250, is an 1897 estate which was formerly home for managers of Parker Ranch and later owned by Laurance Rockefeller. The main house has been restored with antiques and serves as the dining area for Hartwell's restaurant, while smaller guest cottages have been turned into shops selling quality gift items, including island-made crafts and artwork.

If you visit be sure to walk out the back to the gazebo for a view of a small waterfall flowing down a rocky ravine.

Kamuela Museum

There's a lot of history crammed into the Kamuela Museum (☎ 885-4724) at the junction of Hwy 19 and Hwy 250. The museum contains all sorts of Hawaiiana including tapa beaters, 18th-century feather leis braided with human hair, fish hooks made of human bones, a stone knuckle duster and a dog-toothed death cup. Some items are very rare and many once belonged to royalty. The museum has Kamehameha the Great's sacred chair and tables of teak and marble from Iolani Palace.

This museum is like one of those Chinese grocery stores that has one of everything – you just have to find it. The non-Hawaiian part of the collection ranges from a Tibetan prayer horn and stuffed moose heads from Canada to a piece of rope used on the Apollo II mission.

The future of the museum is a bit uncertain as it's up for sale. Opening hours are 8 am to 5 pm daily. Admission costs $5 for adults, $2 for children aged under 12.

Places to Stay

Waimea is upcountry and if you equate Hawaii with beach life and constant sun you may be disappointed making a base here. But if country settings and open spaces are what you're looking for, there are some fine choices.

Kamuela Inn (☎ 885-4243), Box 1994, Kamuela, HI 96743, is something in between an inn and a small hotel in both layout and atmosphere. The cheaper of its 20 rooms are rather small but comfortable. Standard rooms cost $54 to $67. Suites that have refrigerators and stoves and can sleep three cost $83. Free doughnuts and coffee are provided in the morning.

Parker Ranch Lodge (☎ 885-4100), Box 458, Kamuela, HI 96743, is a single-storey motel with 20 rooms. All have full baths, phones with free local calls, cable TV and good views of the hills out the back, complete with grazing horses. Rooms cost $78 with kitchenette, $68 without. Units numbered one to 10 are best as they have cathedral ceilings.

Hawaii Country Cottage (☎ 885-7441), Box 1717, Kamuela, HI 96743, is a B&B unit at the side of a contemporary home. It has double and single beds, a large living room with fireplace, Douglas fir floors and raised beam ceilings. The owner, Gale, has the 'tutu nene' business making the stuffed cotton nene found in gift shops around the island. There's a distant sunset view of the ocean and a stream running alongside the property. It's just a little way up Hwy 250. The rate is $75.

Waimea Gardens Cottages (☎ 885-4550, (800) 262-9912), Box 563, Kamuela, HI 96743, are two cottages on the property of Barbara and Charlie Campbell, near the intersection of Hwy 19 and Hwy 250. Both have hardwood floors, French doors, a deck and rustic charm. The older unit has a full kitchen. While the newer one has only limited cooking facilities, it has many other pleasant touches including a working fireplace. The units come stocked with a fruit basket, banana bread and Kona coffee.

The rate is $95 single or double, $15 more for a third person. Barbara also runs an up-market B&B service called Hawaii's Best Bed & Breakfasts and can book other accommodation on the island in this price range.

Puu Manu Cottage (☎ (800) 262-9912) has horses in the back pasture and a view of Mauna Kea through French glass doors. The cottage has skylights, raised beam ceilings, two bedrooms, a modern kitchen, a fireplace, phone and a stereo. It's $105 for two, but big enough to hold two couples ($135) comfortably. It's two miles east of Waimea in a pleasantly secluded area.

Hawaii Country, Waimea Gardens and Puu Manu cottages all have privacy, cooking facilities and TVs. Smoking is limited to the 'great outdoors'. Each has a three-day minimum.

If you don't mind being a few miles east of Waimea then *Mountain Meadow Ranch* (☎ 775-9376, (800) 535-9376), Myrna Makinster, Box 1361, Kamuela, HI 96743, is a real find. Located in a quiet eucalyptus grove off the Old Mamalahoa Highway, this pleasant seven-acre farm has gardens of citrus and macadamia nut trees and a simply splendid country setting. It would make a convenient base for exploring Waipio and the Hamakua Coast and is only about an hour's drive from Hilo.

There are two comfortably furnished rooms with double beds. Guests share a large tiled bathroom, a separate dry heat sauna and a lounge with a TV, VCR and a movie collection of classics and volcano documentaries. There's no minimum stay, children are accepted and a rollaway bed can be added to the room. Breakfast includes home-made breads and muffins and home-grown fruits. The cost is $45 single and $55 double, credit cards are accepted and there's a 10% discount for weekly stays.

Places to Eat

The *Bread Depot* in Opelo Plaza bakes its own breads and pastries and is a popular local lunch spot. They make good sandwiches for $4.50 and home-made soup or chowder for $3.50 a bowl. You can order food for either sit-down service or takeaway.

Auntie Alice's in the Parker Ranch Shopping Center has doughnuts, pies and coffee-shop-style meals. The huge cherry Danish makes a sweet treat for a dollar. You can get two eggs, home fries and toast for $3.50 and sandwiches and burgers in the $4 to $6 range. It's open from 6 am to 3 pm daily.

Aloha Luigi (☎ 885-7277), on Hwy 19 near its intersection with Hwy 190, serves generous portions of good Italian food. A half order of Caesar salad ($3.50) is like a regular-size serving elsewhere, while the full ($7) is large enough for two. The tasty eggplant Luigi is stacked with layers of cheeses much like a lasagne and costs $13. There are also large pizzas, from $11 for a plain cheese, and pasta dishes beginning at $6. Meals are served with home-made bread and pesto butter. It's open from 11 am to 9 pm daily except Sunday.

Merriman's (☎ 885-6822) in Opelo Plaza features Hawaiian regional cuisine, with a focus on fresh products from Big Island farmers. Chef Peter Merriman uses Waimea-grown strawberries, goat cheese from Puna, herbs from Kealakekua, freshwater shrimp from a local aquaculturist and field-raised veal from an upcountry ranch.

One of his specialities is wok-charred ahi, blackened-style on the outside and like sashimi on the inside. There are a couple of vegetarian meals, including stir-fried curried vegetables on brown rice for $12.50. Other dinner dishes range from chicken with green papaya curry for $14.50 to various meat and seafood preparations for around $25. While the menu is more limited, lunch provides an opportunity to dine quite inexpensively here. Either the grilled fresh fish of the day or a salad Nicoise, with island greens, artichokes and grilled fish cost only $6.75.

Opening hours are from 11.30 am to 1.30 pm weekdays, 5.30 to 8.45 pm nightly. At dinner, reservations are recommended.

Edelweiss (☎ 885-6800) on Hwy 19 has a reputation for good food, although heavy on the salt. German chef Hans-Peter Hager has built his following around such German-Austrian dishes as roast pork with sauerkraut and wiener schnitzel. Dinners cost $14.50 to $20. Lunches are lighter with burgers, sandwiches and salads starting at about $5. Lunch is from 11.30 am to 1.30 pm, dinner from 5 to 9 pm. It's closed on Sundays and Mondays.

Hartwell's (☎ 885-6095) has a number of atmospheric dining rooms spread through the old plantation house at the Hale Kea estate. The food can be good but it's not always consistent. The main dinner menu features fresh fish, island lamb, steaks and seafood priced between $20 and $25. A 'light supper' menu is also served between 5 and 6.30 pm, offering half a dozen entrees priced between $15 and $18. Lunch, from 11 am to 3 pm, features salads and sandwiches from $8 to $13. There's also a moderately priced Sunday brunch.

If you're just looking for something light, you could pick up a power bar, trail mix and juice at *Big Island Natural Foods* in the Parker Ranch Shopping Center.

The Waimea Center has a *KTA Supermarket*, a *McDonald's* and Chinese and Korean restaurants. *Cattleman's Steakhouse*, at the east end of the shopping centre, features steaks and a salad bar.

Entertainment
Waimea's entertainment scene is limited, perhaps because cowboys rise at dawn and astronomers work all night!

Kahilu Theatre at the Parker Ranch Shopping Center presents occasional plays, classical music concerts, dance troupes and other productions.

Getting There & Away
Waimea is 40 miles from Kona along Hwy 190. From Kona the road climbs out of residential areas into a mix of lava flows and dry grassy rangeland studded with prickly pear cactus. There's a little one-room church, broad distant coastal views, wide-open spaces and tall roadside grasses that have an incredible golden hue in the morning light.

If you come back on this road at night the highway reflectors light up like an airport runway to guide you along.

AROUND WAIMEA
Waimea to Honokaa
Hwy 19 heads east from Waimea to Honokaa through rolling hills and cattle pastures, with views of Mauna Kea to the south.

For a peaceful, scented backroad turn right off Hwy 19 onto the Old Mamalahoa Highway near the 52-mile marker. (If you're coming from Hilo, turn left at the 43-mile marker opposite Tex Drive Inn and then take the next immediate right.)

The 10-mile detour winds through hill country, with small roadside ranches, old wooden fences and grazing horses. This is an untourised Hawaii. Nobody's in a hurry on this road, if they're on it at all, and it's also a great alternative route for cyclists.

Mana/Keanakolu Road
To get closer to Mauna Kea for photography or views you could drive part way down Mana Rd, the start of a road which curves around the eastern flank of Mauna Kea. It begins off Hwy 19 at the 55-mile marker on the eastern side of Waimea. After 15 miles the road becomes Keanakolu Rd and continues about 25 miles before reaching

Summit Rd (the road leading up Mauna Kea) near the Humuula Sheep Station.

Only the first part of the Waimea section is paved. The entire road is passable on horseback or by 4WD vehicle but there are a couple of dozen cattle gates that must be opened and closed along the way. It's mostly ranchers and hunters that come this way and it's a long way from anywhere should you get stuck en route.

Keanakolu Rd passes along the new Hakalau Forest National Wildlife Refuge, which protects a portion of the state's largest koa-ohia forest. The forest provides habitat for the hoary bat and four endangered bird species. Only very limited access is allowed into the refuge itself. Call 969-9909 for information.

David Douglas Memorial A memorial to David Douglas, the Scottish botanist for whom the Douglas fir tree is named, is on Keanakolu Rd about halfway between Waimea and the Saddle Rd. Douglas died in 1834 at this spot.

The circumstances of Douglas' death are somewhat mysterious as his gored body was found trapped with an angry bull at the bottom of a pit. Hunters commonly dug such pits and camouflaged them with underbrush as a means of trapping feral cattle, but the probability of both Douglas and a bull falling into the same hole seemed highly suspicious. Fingers were pointed at Ned Gurney, an escaped convict from Botany Bay who had been hiding out in the area and who had been the last person to see Douglas alive.

Hilo authorities, unable to solve the case, packed both Douglas' body and the bull's head in brine and shipped them to Honolulu for further investigation. By the time the body arrived in Oahu, it was so badly decomposed that they buried Douglas' remains at the missionary church and the case was closed.

Hamakua Coast

The Hamakua Coast, the north-eastern coast of the Big Island, stretches 50 miles from Waipio Valley down to the city of Hilo.

From Waimea, it's 15 miles east on Hwy 19 to the town of Honokaa. If you detour there and drive nine miles north-west on Hwy 240 you'll reach Waipio Valley Lookout, one of the most spectacular valley views in Hawaii.

Much of the north end of the Hamakua Coast is owned by Hamakua Sugar and is planted in vast fields of green sugar cane. The rest of the Hamakua Coast is rugged with steep cliffs and luxuriant rainforests laced with streams and waterfalls. The Hawaii Belt Rd (Hwy 19) is an impressive engineering feat that runs along the wet windward slopes of Mauna Kea and spans deep green ravines with a series of sweeping cantilevered bridges. Hamakua's character comes out in its road signs: 'Slow Moving Cane Trucks' and 'Road Subject To Washout'.

Hwy 19 also passes small towns that are home to sugar cane workers and homesteaders and unmarked roads leading down to unfrequented beach parks. If you're just whizzing through on your way between Kona and Hilo, at the very least make time for Waipio Valley Lookout, majestic Akaka Falls and the Pepeekeo four-mile scenic drive.

HONOKAA

Honokaa's sugar mill opened in 1873 and sugar has been the mainstay of this town ever since. In the old days flumes carried the sugar cane down from the fields to the mill in town. Sugar cane fields still surround Honokaa and Hamakua Sugar Company maintains a working mill down by the bay.

Most of the residents are descendants of immigrants brought in to work on the sugar cane plantations. The Scots and English were the first to arrive. Then came the Chinese,

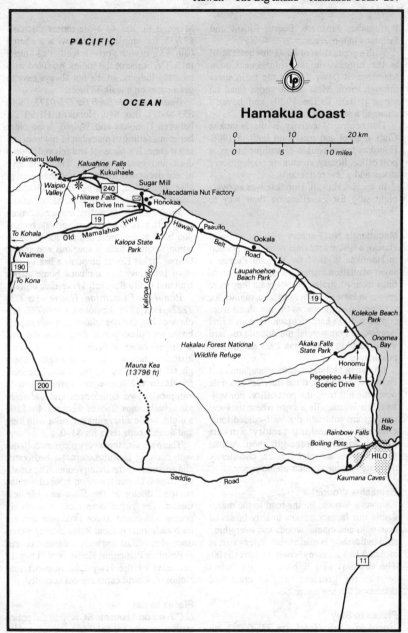

Hamakua Coast

PACIFIC

OCEAN

0   10   20 km

0   5   10 miles

Waimanu Valley

Kaluahine Falls

Kukuihaele

Waipio Valley

240

Sugar Mill

Macadamia Nut Factory

Hiilawe Falls

Tex Drive Inn

Honokaa

19

Old Mamalahoa Hwy

To Kohala

Waimea

190

To Kona

Kalopa State Park

Kalopa Gulch

Hawaii Belt Road

Paauilo

Ookala

Laupahoehoe Beach Park

19

Kolekole Beach Park

Hakalau Forest National Wildlife Refuge

Onomea Bay

Akaka Falls State Park

Honomu

Mauna Kea (13796 ft)

Pepeekeo 4-Mile Scenic Drive

200

Hilo Bay

Rainbow Falls

Boiling Pots

HILO

Saddle Road

Kaumana Caves

11

Portuguese, Japanese, Puerto Ricans and Filipinos in turn.

With a population of 2200, this quiet town is the biggest on the Hamakua Coast. Mamame St (Hwy 240) is the main street through town. Most of the shops lined up along it date to the 1920s and haven't changed a whole lot over the years.

The centre of activity is the Honokaa Club, a hotel and restaurant built in 1908. Honokaa has a couple of antique shops, a post office, library, swimming pool, grocery stores and a few restaurants.

In ancient Hawaii, Honokaa was an overnight stop for travellers on their way to Waipio.

Macadamia Nut Factory

Hawaii's first macadamia trees were planted in Honokaa in 1881 by William Purvis, a sugar plantation manager who brought seedlings from Australia. For 40 years they were grown in Hawaii, as in Australia, mainly for ornamental purposes, as the nut shells were considered too hard to crack. Hawaii's first large-scale commercial macadamia orchard was planted in Honokaa in 1924 and it's still producing.

Hawaiian Holiday has its macadamia nut factory on Lehua St, three-quarters of a mile down the hill from the post office. For visitors, this is basically a store where nuts and cookies are sold and the 'self-guided tour' consists of watching factory workers through windows in the gift shop. A little napkin of free samples is rather cheerlessly deposited on the counter upon request.

Kamaaina Woods

Kamaaina Woods, on the road to the macadamia nut factory, makes quality bowls of koa, milo and mango woods and everything sold in the shop is made there. Prices start at around $18 with many bowls well over $100. The thinnest and lightest-weight bowls require the greatest skill to craft and command the highest prices.

Places to Stay

Honokaa Club Hotel (☎ 775-0678), on Mamame St, has 14 basic rooms that cost $32/35 for singles/doubles with a shared bath, $35/39 with a private bath. It's $4 more for a TV. Some of the rooms are filled with monthly lodgers, so it's not always easy to get a room on a walk-in basis.

Waipio Wayside B&B (☎ 775-0275, (800) 833-8849), Box 840, Honokaa, HI 96727, between Honokaa and Waipio, is an older home in a setting of macadamia-nut trees and sugar cane. It's pleasant and relaxed, with a deck and garden gazebo. There are five nicely decorated theme rooms that vary in size and price, ranging from $50/55 a single/double for a room with shared bath up to $80/85 for the attractive master bedroom suite with natural wood and a private bath. If you book at the lower end ask for the Plantation Room, which is spacious and sunny. Owner Jackie Horne prepares a hearty, creative breakfast that includes home-grown fruit and richly flavourful Hamakua coffee.

Paauhau Plantation House (☎ 775-7222), Box 1375, Honokaa, HI 96727, is a classic 70-year-old plantation manager's house with plush period furniture and decor, a billiard room, a fireplace, and so much historic character that you might expect ghosts to come out of the walls. The bedrooms in the house are furnished with antiques, down comforters and old-fashioned bathrooms. Two of them rent for $105 a night, while a large master suite with king and double beds rents for $140.

There are also three very pleasant cottages with cooking facilities, separate bedrooms, and sofabeds in the living rooms. The smallest costs $75 but it's often booked for the contract doctor at the Hamakua Medical Center. The larger ones sleep four to six people and cost $90 for two, plus $15 for each additional person. Rates include a continental breakfast and there are tennis courts.

Paauhau Plantation House is off Hwy 19 just east of the Hwy 240 turn-off into Honokaa. Credit cards are not accepted.

Places to Eat

C C Jon's on Mamame St, next to the police station, is open for breakfast and lunch with hotcakes for $2, eggs, meat and toast for $3 and good fresh fish plates for about $5. It also has inexpensive sandwiches and loco moco.

Dairy Queen, on Mamame St, has the usual fast food, with hamburgers for $1.50, plate lunches from $4 and soft ice cream.

The *Honokaa Club*, on Mamame St, is the most popular place in town for dinner although the food's quite unexciting, with meals from $7 to $20.

Tex Drive Inn is up on Hwy 19 and if you're driving by in the morning, on your way from Waimea to Hilo, you might want to stop by for a couple of malasadas (50 cents each) and a cup of coffee. Malasadas are Portuguese pastries of sweet fried dough, rolled in sugar and served warm – like a doughnut without the hole. There's a drive-up window open from 6 am to 9.30 pm daily. There is a convenience store next door and a laundromat across the road.

KUKUIHAELE

About seven miles beyond Honokaa heading toward Waipio Valley, there's a loop road off Hwy 240 that leads off to the right and goes down to the tiny village of Kukuihaele.

The village's Last Chance Store is just that, as there's no food or supplies in Waipio Valley. At Last Chance you can get Alta-Dena yoghurt, crackers, canned food, beer and wine. Hard-boiled eggs cost a quarter, although most other items are marked up a bit more than at Honokaa grocery stores.

Farther down the road is Waipio Valley Artworks, which sells quality Hawaiian-made crafts, including a good selection of carved wooden bowls from the Big Island. A shop at the side of the store sells Tropical Dreams ice cream, sandwiches, soda and coffee.

Kukuihaele means 'travelling light' and refers to the ghostly night marchers who pass through on their way to Waipio.

This undeveloped rural area is now being focused on by developers. The financially strapped Hamakua Sugar Company is trying to sell 260 acres of plantation lands at Kukuihaele to a Japanese company for a golf course resort – the first on the Hamakua Coast.

Places to Stay

Hamakua Hideaway (☎ 775-7425), Box 5104, Kukuihaele, HI 96727, has two units, both with kitchens, that rent for $60 a night. Ask for the Cliffhouse, which has a fireplace, a sunken tub and a view down the coast to Waipio Valley.

WAIPIO VALLEY

Hwy 240 ends abruptly at the edge of cliffs overlooking Waipio Valley. The view is glorious. Waipio is the largest and southernmost of the seven spectacular amphitheatre valleys on the windward side of the Kohala Mountains. Waipio is a mile wide at the coast and nearly six miles deep. Some of the near-vertical pali wrapping around the valley reach heights of 2000 feet.

Everything is lushly green, a mix of tangled jungle, flowering plants, taro patches and waterfalls. The mouth of the valley is fronted by a black-sand beach and the Waipio Stream divides the beach in two.

From the lookout you can see the switch-back trail on the opposite cliff face which leads to Waimanu Valley and get glimpses of the rugged coastal cliffs that stretch out to the north-west.

The narrow, paved, mile-long road which leads down into Waipio Valley is so steep (25% grade) that it's restricted to all but hikers and 4WD vehicles. A couple of tour companies make the run daily, but the walk down is easier than it looks. There are restrooms and drinking water at the lookout.

History

Waipio means 'curving water' and is often referred to as the 'Valley of the Kings'. In ancient times it was the political and religious centre of Hawaii and home to the highest chiefs. Waipio was a very sacred place and the site of a number of important heiaus. The most sacred, Pakaalana, was also the site of one of the island's two major puuhonua or places of refuge.

Umi, the Big Island's ruling chief in the

early 1500s, is credited with laying out Waipio's taro fields, many of which are still in production today. Waipio is also the site where Kamehameha the Great received his fearsome war god, Kukailimoku.

According to oral histories at least 10,000 people – and possibly many times more – lived in Waipio during pre-contact times. It was the most fertile and productive valley on the Big Island.

In 1823 William Ellis, the first missionary to visit the valley, guessed the population to be about 1300. Later in that century immigrants, mainly Chinese, began to settle in Waipio. At one time the valley had schools, restaurants and churches as well as a hotel, post office and jail.

In 1946 the most devastating tsunami in Hawaii's history swept great waves far back into Waipio Valley. Afterwards, most people resettled 'topside' and Waipio has been sparsely populated ever since.

Waipio Valley Today

Taro remains important in Waipio. Many of the valley's 50 or so residents have taro patches and you may see farmers knee-deep in the muddy ponds.

Other Waipio crops include lotus (for its roots), avocados, breadfruit, oranges and limes. There are kukui and mahogany trees, huge elephant ears, Turk's cap hibiscus, air plants, ferns and vines. Pink and white impatiens climb the cliff walls along the road.

Most of Waipio Valley is owned by the Bishop Museum, which has been negotiating the sale of the land to the state's Department of Land & Natural Resources.

There's a rustic hotel in Waipio and camping is allowed near the beach. Spending a few nights in the valley is a chance to get closer to the spirit of old Hawaii.

Exploring Waipio Valley

The walk from the lookout to the valley floor and back is not terribly difficult, although if you're not in good shape you may notice some forgotten muscles the next day. It takes about 30 minutes to get down and about 45

minutes to go up. The road is carved into the cliffs at an angle that provides hikers with shade much of the way.

From the bottom of the hill, if you walk to the left for about five minutes there's a fair chance you'll see wild horses grazing along the stream. It's a picturesque scene set against the steep valley cliffs.

You'll also get a distant view of **Hiilawe Falls**, which with a sheer drop of more than 1000 feet is Hawaii's highest free-fall waterfall. Hiking to Hiilawe Falls is difficult as there's no real footpath and it's mainly bush-whacking. There are a lot of 'Private Property' signs and generally the farther back in the valley you go, the less friendly the dogs become.

According to legend the god Lono looked down from the heavens and discovered Kaikilani, the beautiful woman who was to become his wife, sitting beside Hiilawe Falls. Lono slid down to the falls on a rainbow – which is definitely the preferred way to get there.

In the 1970s an elaborate mirrored restaurant surrounded by a carp pond was built back in the valley. It looks straight on to Hiilawe Falls in one direction and out to the valley mouth in the other. Although the location was lovely the controversial restaurant wasn't allowed to open and it was later given to the Bishop Museum. It shines brightly beneath the falls and many Waipio residents consider it an eyesore.

Precautions

During heavy rains, streams in the valley can swell to the point where they become impassable, usually for just a few hours at a time, although occasionally for longer periods. It's dangerous to try to cross such streams when the water's above your thighs.

Because of all the feral animals roaming this Eden-like valley, precautions against leptospirosis are advisable (see the Health section). Taro farmers in Waipio have one of the highest incidence rates on the islands.

Don't drink from the Waipio Stream without first boiling or treating the water.

There are a couple of freshwater springs up from the beach that most people use for drinking water. You can get to one by turning left at the bottom of the hill upon entering the valley. Walk a few minutes to the first dirt path on the right, which leads down to a stream. The spring is at the bottom of the path, on the left, a few feet in.

As you walk around the valley you might come across wild horses or stray dogs along the road although both tend to veer off if you come too close.

Waipio Beach

It takes about 10 minutes to walk to the beach from the bottom of the hill. After heavy rains, the road can be like a slippery mud pie.

Waipio Beach is lined with ironwood trees that act as an effective windbreak against the strong wind that sometimes picks up here. It was an ancient surfing beach that occasionally still sees some action but there are usually rip currents and when the surf is high the waters can be outright treacherous.

Walk along the beach toward the stream mouth for a good view of **Kaluahine Falls** which cascade down the coastal cliffs to the east. It's easier to look at than to get to however, as the coast between Waipio Beach and Kaluahine Falls is loose lava rock and rather rough walking. The surf sometimes breaks up over the uppermost rocks so it can also be dangerous.

Local lore has it that ghost marchers periodically come down from the upper valley and march down the beach where there's a hidden entrance into the nether world, called Lua O Milu.

Waipio Tours

Waipio Valley Shuttle, which uses local drivers, first introduced tours into the valley about 20 years ago. The tour is via a 4WD vehicle, lasts about 1½ hours and is not terribly adventurous. It's more of a taxi ride for those who don't care to walk down. The driver points out waterfalls, identifies plants and throws in a bit of history. Sit as close to the driver as you can as it's nearly impossible to hear the spiel if you're bouncing around

in the back. Reservations (☎ 775-7121) can be made at the Last Chance Store in Kukuihaele. It costs $25 for adults, $12.50 for children aged under 11. The tours run on the hour from 8 am to 4 pm daily.

An alternative to the van tours is Waipio Valley Wagon Tours' (☎ 775-9518) 1½-hour jaunt through the valley in an open mule-drawn wagon. Tours are conducted by Englishman Peter Tobin who has been living in the valley with his Hawaiian wife for nearly a decade. He gives an interesting commentary on the valley's history as he wheels visitors along Waipio's rutted dirt roads and fords rocky streams.

Tours leave from Waipio Valley Lookout at 9 and 10.30 am and 12.30, 2 and 4 pm daily, except on Tuesdays. Passengers are taken to the valley floor by 4WD where they transfer to the wagon. It costs $35 for adults, half-price for children. Arrangements are made at their office in Honokaa, which is on Mamane St, east of the post office.

The third possibility for touring the valley is on horseback. Hawaii Resorts Transportation Company (☎ 775-7291) organises tours consisting of a van ride from the Hawaiian Holiday macadamia factory in Honokaa to the valley floor, followed by a 2½-hour trail ride. The cost is $65 and (weather permitting) the tour usually leaves at 9.30 am and 1.30 pm daily. Advance reservations are required. A second company, Waipio Naalapa Trail Rides (☎ 775-0419), runs a similar tour.

Switchback Trail to Waimanu Valley

The switchback trail leading up the northwest cliff face of Waipio Valley is an ancient Hawaiian footpath. Although it looks arduous, it really isn't all that bad if you're not carrying a heavy backpack. It's a well-beaten path, a few feet deep in places, almost like walking in a little trough.

Doing part of the trail makes a nice day hike if you're camping in Waipio. It takes about 1½ hours from the floor of Waipio Valley to the third ravine where there are little pools and a small waterfall. The trail is used by hunters as well as hikers and you might come across old timers on donkeys heading for the backwoods to hunt wild boar.

The trail continues up and down a series of ravines to Waimanu Valley. From Waipio to Waimanu it's about nine miles. About two-thirds of the way along there's a trail shelter.

Waimanu is a smaller valley than Waipio although it's similar in appearance. Now abandoned, it once had a sizeable Hawaiian settlement.

Most of Waimanu Valley is a national estuarine sanctuary which is managed by the state. Camping for up to six nights is allowed free by permit, which can be obtained at the Last Chance Store in Kukuihaele, the Division of Forestry & Wildlife office in Hilo or the state tree nursery in Waimea. For more information or to make reservations call 933-4221 on weekdays.

Places to Stay

Tom Araki's Hotel (☎ 775-0368), c/o Sueno Araki, 25 Malama Place, Hilo, HI 96720, is back to basics on the floor of Waipio Valley. It is about a 15-minute walk inland from the bottom of the hill, just on the other side of the stream. It once served Peace Corps instructors who trained new recruits in the valley before they went off on assignment in other Pacific and Asian jungles.

The hotel has five rooms in a straight line looking out on to a taro patch and it's all quite in keeping with its surroundings. The rooms are rustic and simple, but comfortable enough, and blankets and linen are provided. There's no refrigerator or electricity, but there is a communal kitchen with a gas stove, barbecue, sink, dishes and cooking utensils. Kerosene lanterns provide lighting. You'll have to carry in all your own food, and it's a custom to bring along a bottle of sake to pass the evening.

Tom is sometimes booked out and suggests making reservations at least three weeks in advance, although you can also take your chances and call upon arriving on the Big Island. Rates are $15 per person.

Waipio Tree House (☎ 775-7160), Box 5086, Honokaa, HI 96727, rates as the ulti-

mate getaway in Hawaii, as it's both a couple of miles back into Waipio Valley and 30 feet up a monkeypod tree! Owner Linda Beech, one of the more unusual hoteliers in Hawaii, is a vivacious woman who's been a journalist and a sit-com TV star in Japan and holds a doctorate in psychology. The tree house faces a waterfall and boasts skylights, a 360° view with screens all around and lots of Tarzan books. It has a double and single bed, a refrigerator, hot plate, electricity and running water. The cost is $150 a day, with a two-day minimum. There's also a cottage on the grounds called The Hale, which has a kitchen, living room and loft bedroom and rents for the same price. The cost includes 4WD transportation to and from the lookout. Bring your own food.

Camping Hamakua Sugar Company (☎ 776-1211) issues permits for camping on the section of Waipio Beach they control. Permits are free but must be picked up in person at their office, which is next to the post office in Paauilo, just off Hwy 19 about six miles south of Honokaa. The crux of the application seems to be a liability release and a promise to carry in a shovel to bury waste and to carry out your trash. The office is open from 7.30 am to 4 pm Monday to Friday.

KALOPA STATE PARK

Kalopa State Park is a few miles south-east of Honokaa and about three miles inland from the marked turn-off on Hwy 19.

This unfrequented park contains 100 acres of native rainforest as well as picnic sites and some pleasant log cabins that hold up to eight people. It's at an elevation of 2000 feet and cooler than the coast. Kalopa averages about 90 inches of rain a year.

The park has a pleasant hike leading to Kalopa Gulch in the adjoining forest reserve. Begin the hike along Robusta Lane, which starts on the left after the caretaker's house. It's about a third of a mile to the edge of the gulch through a thick forest of tall eucalyptus trees with mossy bark. The deep gulch was formed by melting glaciers that originated at Mauna Kea. A trail continues along the rim of the gulch for another mile and a number of side trails branch west off it back into the park.

Kalopa Park also has a nature trail that loops for three-quarters of a mile through an ancient ohia forest where some of the trees are more than three feet in diameter.

The woods are habitat for the elepaio, an easily spotted native forest bird. It's brown with a white rump, about the size of a sparrow, and it makes a loud whistle that mimics its name.

LAUPAHOEHOE POINT

Laupahoehoe means 'leaf of pahoehoe lava'. This flat peninsula-like point jutting out from the coastal cliffs was formed by a late eruption of Mauna Kea which poured lava down a ravine and out into the sea.

Laupahoehoe Point is midway between Honokaa and Hilo. A highway sign marks the steep winding road down to the point. There are views of the coastal cliffs on the way down and after heavy rains waterfalls come to life in all directions.

Tragedy hit Laupahoehoe on 1 April 1946 when tsunami waves up to 30 feet high wiped out the schoolhouse on the point, killing 20 children and four adults. After the tsunami the whole town moved uphill, although a few families have since settled back in. A monument on a hillock above the water lists those who died.

Laupahoehoe is a rugged coastal area and is not suitable for swimming. The surf is usually rough and pounding and can sometimes crash up over the rocks and onto the lower parking lot.

Inter-island boats once landed here. Many of the immigrants who came to work the sugar cane fields along the Hamakua Coast first set foot on the Big Island at Laupahoehoe.

The county beach park on the point has restrooms, campsites, showers, drinking water, picnic pavilions and electricity, and as it's off the highway it's relatively secluded. All this makes it convenient for camping, but makes it ideal for late-night partying too. Locals who use the park as a drinking hangout sometimes get fairly wasted and rowdy.

KOLEKOLE BEACH PARK

Kolekole is a grassy park beneath a big highway bridge and at the side of the Kokekole Stream which flows down from Akaka Falls. There are small waterfalls, picnic tables, barbecue pits, restrooms and showers, all which make the park a popular weekend picnic spot for families. Locals sometime surf here, but ocean swimming is dangerous. Camping is allowed with a permit from the county, although it can be busy on weekends and in summer.

To get to the park, turn mauka off Hwy 19 at the south end of the Kolekole Bridge, about three-quarters of a mile south of the 15-mile marker.

AKAKA FALLS

To get to Akaka Falls, turn mauka off Hwy 19 onto Akaka Falls Rd (Hwy 220), midway between the 13 and 14-mile markers. The road passes through the town of Honomu and then climbs up through fields of sugar cane, ending at the falls 3¾ miles away.

Honomu

Honomu is an old sugar town that might have been forgotten, if not for being on the route to Akaka Falls. As it is, things are pretty slow here.

Among the village's handful of old wooden buildings you'll find a gift shop, a place to get shave ice and Ishigo's store and bakery, which sells sandwiches and a few simple pastries.

Hideo Ishigo, a spry octogenarian who still does the baking at Ishigo's, often sits in front of the store during the afternoon. If you happen to stop by, he loves to talk story, has an intriguing photo collection of old-time Honomu and can tell you about little-known sights in the area.

Akaka Falls State Park

Akaka Falls State Park has the Big Island's most impressive easy-to-view waterfall. It shouldn't be missed.

The waterfall lookout is along a delightful half-mile rainforest loop trail that takes about 20 minutes to walk. The trail passes through dense and varied vegetation including massive philodendron vines, fragrant yellow and red gingers, hanging heliconia, hillsides of impatiens and cool bamboo groves. Look up and you'll even find orchids growing wild in the trees.

If you start the loop trail by going to the right you'll first come to the 100-foot **Kahuna Falls**. It's a nice waterfall but the real treat is still to come. Up ahead is **Akaka Falls** dropping a sheer 442 feet down a fern-draped cliff. Its mood depends on the weather – sometimes it rushes with a mighty roar and other times it cascades gently. Either way it's always beautiful. With a little luck you might even catch a rainbow in the spray.

One legend says that whenever a branch of the lehua tree lands on a particular stone at the top of the falls, it will begin to rain. If so, there are apparently a lot of loose lehua branches upstream! You might want to bring an umbrella.

PEPEEKEO FOUR-MILE SCENIC DRIVE

Between Honomu and Hilo there's a delightful four-mile side loop off Hwy 19. It's a drive through lush tropical jungle. The road crosses a string of one-lane bridges over little streams. In places it's almost canopied with African tulip trees, which drop their orange flowers on the road, and with passion fruit, guava and tall mango trees. The fruit can be picked up along the roadside in season.

The road is well-marked on the highway at both ends, with the south end about seven miles north of Hilo.

Hawaii Tropical Botanical Garden

If somehow the four-mile scenic drive isn't enough, there's also the Hawaii Tropical Botanical Garden (☎ 964-5233) along the way. The garden is a rainforest nature preserve with a lily pond, 1000 species of tropical plants and a couple of streams and waterfalls.

Visitors buy tickets at the little yellow building mauka of the road and are shuttled by van down to the valley garden at nearby Onomea Bay.

This nonprofit foundation charges $12 for adults and is free for children aged 16 and under. You're given a self-guided trail map and are free to wander as long as you like. It's open daily from 8.30 am to 5.30 pm, however, the last shuttle bus goes down to the valley at 4.30pm.

Hilo

Hilo, the county capital and commercial centre, is along a large crescent-shaped bay and has Hawaii's second largest port. The population is 38,000, which is nearly one-third the island's total.

In terms of lush, natural beauty, Hilo beats Kona hands down any day HiloHilo
Hilo, the county capital and commercial centre, is along a large crescent-shaped bay and has Hawaii's second largest port. The population is 38,000, which is nearly one-third the island's total.

In terms of lush, natural beauty, Hilo beats Kona hands down any day – the only catch is in finding a sunny one. During an average year in Hilo, measurable rain falls on 278 days.

Although the rain dampens some spirits, it feeds the waterfalls, gardens and jungle-like valleys. Flowers are big business in Hilo and orchids and anthuriums thrive in the area.

Many of Hilo's buildings are old and weathered and some of the small businesses within them look as if they've been there a hundred years. The street-side parking meters still take pennies.

Hilo is ethnically diverse, with a lot of people of Japanese and Filipino descent. There's also an alternative community that's been filtering in since the '70s, attracted by Hilo's affordability and the windward coast's scenic appeal.

Hilo is a survivor. Natural forces threaten it from both sides, tidal waves from one and lava from the other. Two devastating tsunamis

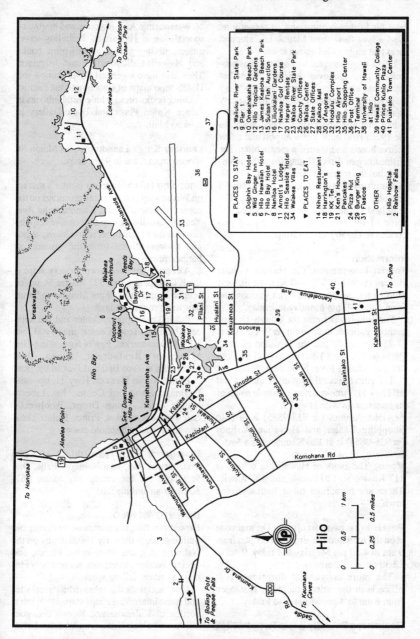

Hilo

PLACES TO STAY
- 4 Dolphin Bay Hotel
- 5 Wild Ginger Inn
- 6 Hilo Hawaiian Hotel
- 7 Hilo Bay Hotel
- 8 Hilo Bay Hotel
- 11 Arnott's Lodge
- 22 Hilo Seaside Hotel
- 34 Waiakea Villas

▼ PLACES TO EAT
- 14 Nihon Restaurant
- 18 Harrington's
- 19 KK Tei
- 21 Ken's House of Pancakes
- 24 Pizza Hut
- 29 Burger King
- 31 Fiascos

OTHER
- 1 Hilo Hospital
- 2 Rainbow Falls
- 3 Wailuku River State Park
- 9 Pier
- 10 Onekahakaha Beach Park
- 12 Hilo Tropical Gardens
- 15 James Kealoha Beach Park
- 15 Suisan Fish Auction
- 16 Naniloa Golf Course
- 17 Liliuokalani Gardens
- 20 Harper Rentals
- 23 Wailoa River State Park
- 25 County Offices
- 26 Wailoa Center
- 27 State Offices
- 28 Kaikoo Mall
- 30 d'Angoras
- 32 Hoolulu Complex
- 33 Hilo Airport
- 35 Hilo Shopping Center
- 36 Post Office
- 37 Terminal
- 38 University of Hawaii at Hilo
- 39 Hawaii Community College
- 40 Prince Kuhio Plaza
- 41 Puainako Town Center

have hit in this century and as recently as 1984 a lava flow from Mauna Loa stopped short just eight miles above town.

Hilo's reputation for wet weather has protected it from the invasive development that has spread elsewhere on the island. In many ways Hilo is the last remaining Hawaiian city unaffected by tourism.

Not that attempts haven't been made. In the 1970s Hilo built a new airport and a few deluxe hotels and started a media blitz. The airlines began direct flights from the mainland, but the tourists never showed.

'America's rainiest city' just couldn't compete with the sunny Kona Coast. The mainland flights have all been dropped and some of the hotels have been turned into condos or cheap local housing.

Information

Tourist Information The Hawaii Visitors Bureau (☎ 961-5797), 180 Kinoole St, near Hilo Hotel, is open from 8 am to noon and from 1 to 4.30 pm Monday to Friday.

For camping permits, the County Department of Parks & Recreation (☎ 961-8311) is at 25 Aupuni St and the Division of State Parks (☎ 933-4200) is at 75 Aupuni St. Both are near Wailoa River State Park.

The Hilo (General Lyman) Airport is just off Hwy 11, three-quarters of a mile south of its intersection with Hwy 19.

Aloha Airlines (☎ 935-9385) is in Hilo Shopping Center and Hawaiian Airlines (☎ 935-0858) is at 120 Kamehameha Ave.

Money The Bank of Hawaii has offices at 117 Keawe St, 120 Pauahi and 427 Kawili. There are numerous other banks around town.

Post Hilo has two post offices. The main one is on the road into the airport. It is open from 9 am to 4.30 pm Monday to Friday, 9 am to 12.30 pm on Saturdays.

The more convenient downtown post office is in the federal building. It is open from 8 am to 4 pm Monday to Friday.

Bookshops Basically Books (☎ 961-0144),

46 Waianuenue Ave, is a book and map store specialising in Hawaiiana, including travel guides, diving guides, out-of-print books and Hawaiian dictionaries and literature. They also have a general travel section and USGS topo maps of Hawaii and the Pacific.

Other bookstores include Waldenbooks in Prince Kuhio Plaza and Book Gallery in Kaikoo Mall.

Laundry King's Laundromat, 58 Mamo St, is open from 6 am to 9 pm daily.

Shopping Hilo has a great farmer's market on Wednesday and Saturday mornings on the corner of Mamo St and Kamehameha Ave. You can usually pick up four or five Kapoho papayas for $1 and other island fruits, vegies and flowers direct from the growers at bargain prices.

A convenient downtown grocery store is the KTA supermarket, 323 Keawe St, which is open from 7 am to 9 pm Monday to Saturday, to 6 pm on Sundays.

Puainako Shopping Center and the adjacent Puainako Town Center, on Hwy 11, has a KTA supermarket, Pay'N Save, Ting-Hao Mandarin Restaurant, Pizza Hut, McDonald's, Taco Bell and Jack in the Box.

Prince Kuhio Plaza on Hwy 11, opposite Puainako Shopping Center, has Liberty House, Sears, Longs Drugs, Woolworth, Safeway supermarket, Prince Kuhio Theatres and a one-hour photo place.

Emergency Hilo Hospital is at 1190 Waianuenue Ave, near Rainbow Falls. Dial 969-4100 for the emergency room, 961-6022 for an ambulance.

DOWNTOWN HILO

Downtown Hilo is a mishmash of classic old buildings from the early 1900s, many on the National Register of Historic Places, and ageing wooden storefronts, some newly renovated, others falling apart.

One short walk that takes in historical sites and some interesting shops starts at the intersection of Kalakaua and Keawe Sts, goes north-west along Keawe, up Wailuku Drive, along Kinoole St past Kalakaua Park and back down Kalakaua St.

If you wander a little further astray you can explore the backstreets, where there are little Japanese restaurants with faded kanji signs, barber shops with hand-pumped chairs and old pool halls.

The informative brochure *Walking Tour of Historic Downtown* is available free at the HVB office, the Lyman Museum and some hotels.

Keawe Street

The north end of Keawe St has been spruced up. The old welfare office has been turned into a Cajun restaurant and the old shops along the street have trendy new businesses.

Bears' Coffee is the place to hang out and sip a cup of espresso. The nearby Chocolate Bar makes home-made chocolates, specialising in dipped fruits and candy made to look like sushi.

The Big Island Gallery, on the corner, has a nice collection of island pottery, paintings and other arts & crafts.

Maui's Canoe

If you continue walking along Keawe St just beyond Wailuku Drive, you'll be on the Puueo St Bridge which crosses over the Wailuku River. The large rock in the river upstream on the left is called Maui's Canoe.

Legend has it the demigod Maui paddled his canoe with such speed across the ocean that he crash-landed here and the canoe turned to stone. Ever the devoted son, Maui was rushing to save his mother, Hina, from a water monster who was trying to drown her by damming the river and flooding her cave beneath Rainbow Falls.

Kalakaua Park

In the late 1800s King David Kalakaua established Hilo as the county seat. Kalakaua Park is a quiet downtown park with a **statue** of the king sitting beneath the shade of a banyan tree, holding a taro leaf and a hula drum. The park also has a **sundial** erected by the king in 1877, a **war memorial** and a

reflecting pool filled with carp and water lilies.

The most recent addition is a capsule containing a collection of 1991 mementoes which was buried during the total solar eclipse on 11 July 1991. It's intended to be opened on 3 May 2106 at the time of the next total eclipse.

The site of the king's former summer home, Niolopa, is opposite the park at what today is the Hilo Hotel.

Around Kalakaua Park

The old **federal building** opposite the park on Waianuenue Ave was built in 1919. It's of neo-classical design with high columns and a Spanish-tile roof. It houses the post office.

On the other side of the park, on Kalakaua St, the **East Hawaii Cultural Center** has taken over the old police station. The centre hosts quality art exhibits that change monthly. Admission is free and it's open 9 am to 4 pm Monday to Saturday. A performing arts centre is being installed upstairs.

Next door is the **Hawaiian Telephone Company building**, designed by Honolulu architect C W Dickey in the 1920s. It's of Spanish-mission influence with nice tile work.

Lyman Museum

Lyman Museum (☎ 935-5021), 276 Haili St, is a 1st-class museum and a great place to spend a rainy afternoon.

The ground floor features the **Island Heritage Gallery**. Displays show how adzes were made of volcanic clinkstone, how kukui nuts were skewered on coconut leaves to burn as candles and other aspects of life in Polynesian Hawaii. Exhibits include feather leis, tapa cloth and a house made of pili grass. Mana, kahunas and *awa* (kava) drinking are all succinctly explained.

The different lifestyles of those who came as indentured immigrants and stayed on to form Hawaii's multiethnic society are all given their due. Displays include costumes, cultural artefacts and insightful interpretive plaques. From Portugal there's a braginha, the forerunner of the ukulele. From China

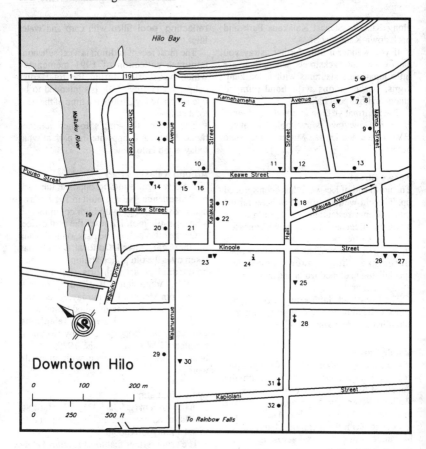

Hilo Bay

Wailuku River

Puueo Street

Shipman Street

Kamehameha Avenue

Keawe Street

Kekaulike Street

Kalakaua

Kinoole Street

Wailuku Drive

Downtown Hilo

Walanuenue

Kapiolani Street

To Rainbow Falls

Mamo Street

Kilauea Avenue

Haili

0   100   200 m

0   250   500 ft

there's a full-size Taoist shrine that was disassembled and carried aboard a ship in the luggage of Chinese emigrating to Hilo.

Upstairs in the **Earth Heritage Gallery** is the largest mineral collection in the Pacific. There are thousands of rocks, crystals and gemstones, as well as minerals that glow in the dark.

The **lava section** explains volcanic eruptions and lava formations with samples of spatter, olivine, Pele's tears and fine strands of Pele's hair. Other exhibits include native insects, birds, seashells and land shells. Hawaii has 1000 native land shell species found nowhere else on earth.

The museum is open from 9 am to 5 pm Monday to Saturday and from 1 to 4 pm on Sundays. Admission to the museum includes a tour of the adjacent Mission House and costs $4.50 for adults, $2.50 for people aged 6 to 18. Sign language tours are given on Tuesdays, Wednesdays, Fridays and Saturdays.

Mission House

Next door to the museum is the large missionary house built by the Reverend David Lyman and his wife Sarah in 1839. They had eight children of their own and in the attic

■ PLACES TO STAY

23 Hilo Hotel

▼ PLACES TO EAT

2 Lehua's
6 Abundant Life Natural Foods
7 Cafe Pesto
11 Karrots
12 Pescatore
14 Roussel's
16 Bears' Coffee
23 Fuji Restaurant
25 McDonald's
26 Kentucky Fried Chicken
27 Jimmy's Drive Inn
30 Dairy Queen

OTHER

1 Singing Bridge
3 Basically Books
4 Greenpeace Hawaii
5 Mooheau Bus Terminal
8 Farmer's Market
9 King's Laundromat
10 Bank of Hawaii
13 KTA Supermarket
15 Big Island Gallery
17 Hawaiian Telephone Company
18 Central Christian Church
19 Maui's Canoe
20 Federal Building/Post Office
21 Kalakaua Park
22 East Hawaii Cultural Center
24 Hawaii Visitors Bureau
28 Haili Church
29 Library
31 St Joseph's Church
32 Lyman Museum & Mission House

boarded a number of island boys who attended their church school.

The mission house tour is brief and informal, led by an enthusiastic guide. You get a good feel for the people who lived in this house. Things are faded and used, such as the very old patchwork quilts. The house has many of the original furnishings including Sarah Lyman's melodeon, rocking chair and china dishes. Some of the original wavy glass windows are still in place.

The mattresses are stuffed with wood shavings, a material which provided a bed for bugs as well (hence the expression 'Good night, sleep tight, don't let the bedbugs bite').

Tours of Mission House are given at 9.30, 10.30 and 11.30 am and 1, 2, 3 and 4 pm.

Churches

Haili St was once called Church Row for the churches which lined up along it. The three that remain, one Catholic and two Congregational, are worth a look.

St Joseph's Church, on the corner of Haili and Kapiolani Sts, is an attractive pink church of Spanish-mission style that looks as if it came right out of Southern California. It was built in 1919 and has an old cracked bell, stained glass windows and a columned entrance topped with angels.

Haili Church, at 211 Haili St, was built in 1859. It has straight lines and a boxy square tower, somewhat resembling a New England barn. Services are conducted in both Hawaiian and English.

The **Central Christian Church**, on the corner of Kilauea and Haili Sts, was built in the Victorian style in the early 1900s by Portuguese immigrants.

Hilo Library

Hilo has a good public library. It's on Waianuenue Ave, and is open from 9 am to 5 pm daily except Sundays, and until 8 pm on Mondays and Wednesdays.

The two large stones on the library's front lawn are the Naha and Pinao stones. The **Pinao Stone** was an entrance pillar to an old Hawaiian heiau.

The **Naha Stone**, from the same temple grounds, is said to weigh 2½ tons. According to legend any person who had the strength to budge the stone would have the strength to conquer and unite all the islands. Kamehameha I reputedly met the challenge and overturned the stone in his youth.

Wailoa River State Park

On 1 April 1946 Hilo Bay was inundated by a tsunami which had raced its way across the

Pacific from an earthquake in the Aleutian Islands. It struck at 6.54 am without warning.

Fifty-foot waves jumped the sea wall and swept into the city. They tore the first line of buildings off their foundations, carrying them inland and smashing them into the rows behind. As the waves pulled back, they sucked much of the splintered debris and a number of people out to sea.

By 7 am the town was littered with shattered buildings as far as the eye could see. The ground was not visible through the pile of rubble. Throughout Hawaii the tsunami killed 159 people and racked up $25 million in property damages. The hardest hit was Hilo, with 96 fatalities.

Hilo's bay-front 'Little Tokyo' bore the brunt of the storm. Shinmachi, which means 'New Town' in Japanese, was rebuilt on the same spot.

Fourteen years later, on 23 May 1960, an earthquake off the coast of Chile triggered a tsunami which made a beeline for Hilo at a speed of 440 miles per hour. A series of three tidal waves washed up in succession, each one sweeping farther up into the city.

Although the tsunami warning speakers roared this time, many people didn't take them seriously. The tiny tsunamis of the 1950s had been relatively harmless and some people actually went down to the beach to watch the waves.

Those along the shore were swept inland, while others farther up were dragged out into the bay. A few lucky ones who managed to grab hold of floating debris were rescued at sea. In the end there were 61 deaths and property damage of over $20 million.

Again Shinmachi was levelled, but this time instead of rebuilding, the low-lying bay-front property was turned into parks and the survivors relocated to higher ground.

All along Kamehameha Ave you can still see the kerbstone cuts which once led to streets or to the driveways of businesses that made up Shinmachi.

Park Attractions Wailoa River State Park, located on the grassy expanses where Shinmachi once stood, is reached from Pauahi St. The park has two **memorials**, one dedicated to the tsunami victims and the other to the area's Vietnam War dead.

Wailoa River flows through the park and most of **Waiakea Pond** is within the park boundaries. This spring-fed estuarine pond has both saltwater and brackish water fish species, mostly mullet. There's a boat launch ramp near the mouth of the river; only non-motor boats are allowed and fishing licenses are required.

The park's **Wailoa Center**, near the memorials, is a state-run art gallery with multimedia exhibits that change monthly. Photos of the tsunami damage are on display downstairs. It's open from 8 am to 4.30 pm on Mondays, Tuesdays, Thursdays and Fridays; from noon to 8.30 pm on Wednesdays and from 9 am to 3 pm on Saturdays. Admission is free.

Banyan Drive

Banyan Drive goes around the edge of the Waiakea Peninsula, which juts into Hilo Bay. The road skirts the Liliuokalani Gardens, the nine-hole Naniloa Golf Course and Hilo's bay-front hotels.

Banyan Drive is lined with sprawling **banyan trees** planted in the 1930s by royalty and celebrities, including the likes of Babe Ruth, Amelia Earhart and Cecil B De Mille. Plaques beneath the trees identify the planters.

Suisan Fish Auction

Local fishers sell their catch every morning except Sundays at Suisan Fish Auction, near the intersection of Lihiwai and Banyan Drive, on the western side of the Waiakea Peninsula.

The auction is a lively local scene where bids are shouted out in Hilo's unique blend of pidgin. Open to the public, it's best to get there by 8 am when the auction bell rings, as the whole thing wraps up in a matter of minutes.

Next door there's a fish market with the freshest fish on the island.

Liliuokalani Gardens

Hilo's 30-acre Japanese garden is named for Queen Liliuokalani, Hawaii's last queen. This waterfront park is filled with ponds and waterways complete with mullet that jump clear out of the water, little Japanese pagodas and covered sitting areas, stone lanterns, arched bridges and patches of bamboo.

The gardens are a monument of sorts to the Japanese presence in Hawaii. Many of the lanterns and pagodas that dot the park were donated by Japanese regional governments and sister cities in honour of the 100th anniversary of Japanese immigration to Hawaii.

It's a pleasant place to walk around, although after heavy rain you'll need to stick to high ground.

Coconut Island

Coconut Island, which is connected to land by a footbridge, sticks out into the bay opposite the Liliuokalani Gardens. The island is a county park with opportunities for picnicking, swimming and fishing. Hilo's Fourth of July fireworks display is shot off from the island.

In ancient times Coconut Island was called Moku Ola, 'island of life', in part due to the powers of a healing stone located there. Medical kahunas used the stone and invocations to cure the sick by ridding them of demonic spirits. Moku Ola also had pure spring water, which was said to bring good health, and a birthing stone which instilled mana to the children born there.

Beaches

Hilo is not a city for beach bums. Still, there are some decent beaches along Kalanianaole Ave, a four-mile stretch on the eastern side of Hilo. The road is basically a continuation of Kamehameha Ave, starting in front of the Hilo Seaside Hotel.

Onekahakaha Beach Park This park is a quarter of a mile off Kalanianaole Ave. The turn-off is just before the Hilo Tropical Gardens.

The park has a big sandy-bottomed **pool** formed by a large boulder enclosure. The water's just a foot or two deep in most places and it's popular with families with young children.

On the Hilo side of the park there's an unprotected cove that is sometimes used by snorkellers on calm days, but be careful as it has a seaward current. The park department cautions swimmers and snorkellers not to venture beyond the breakwater at any time.

There are camping sites, restrooms, showers and a picnic area shaded by big tropical almond trees. Campers usually set up their tents around the edge of the lawn near the tree line at the Hilo end of the beach. But at any rate, avoid low ground because when it rains in Hilo, it pours.

James Kealoha Beach Park Kealoha is a county park known locally as Four-Mile Beach because of the distance between the park and the downtown post office. It's just before the Mauna Loa Shores apartments and has camping, showers and restrooms.

For swimming and snorkelling most people go to the eastern side which is sheltered by an island and a naturally occurring rocky breakwater. It's generally calm there with clean, clear water and pockets of white sand.

The Hilo side of the park is open ocean and much rougher. You can sometimes find people net fishing there. It's also a popular winter surfing spot, although there are strong rip currents which run out to sea.

Richardson Ocean Park This park, just before the end of the road, has a small black-sand beach fronting Hilo's most favoured snorkelling site. The left side of the bay tends to be colder due to springs in the water. On the right side the springs are less common and the snorkelling is better.

The park has some overgrown footpaths through coastal vegetation to the west and a lava shoreline to the east which can be taken for short walks. There are restrooms, showers and picnic tables.

Rainbow Falls

Rainbow Falls is on the western side of Hilo, off Waianuenue Ave, just below the hospital.

Waianuenue, literally 'rainbow seen in water', is the Hawaiian name for this pretty 80-foot waterfall. The huge cave beneath the falls is said to have been the home of Hina, mother of Maui. The falls are usually seen as a double drop which flows together before hitting the large pool at the bottom.

The best time to see rainbows is in the mornings, although they're by no means guaranteed. Most people just look at the falls straight on from the viewpoint in front of the parking lot. However, when it's not overgrown, there's another spot with a better angle for catching rainbows in the mist. It's up on the left near the beginning of a short loop trail. The trail then continues for about five minutes past a giant banyan tree and through a lush jungle-like area before leading back to the parking lot.

The site has restrooms and drinking water.

Peepee Falls & Boiling Pots

Peepee Falls and Boiling Pots are up Waianuenue Ave, about 1½ miles past Rainbow Falls.

Peepee Falls drop from a sheer rock face and as the water runs downstream over a series of basalt depressions in the river, it swirls and churns into bubbling pools which have earned it the name Boiling Pots.

Boiling Pots is most interesting after periods of heavy rain when the water runs strongest.

Kaumana Caves

The Kaumana Caves were formed by an 1881 lava flow from Mauna Loa. As the flow subsided the outer edges of the deep lava stream cooled and crusted over in a tunnel-like effect. The hot molten lava inside drained out, creating these caves.

The caves are wet and mossy, thickly covered with ferns and impatiens. If you have a flashlight you might want to explore them, although they tend to be drippy.

The caves, which are marked, are on the right three miles up Kaumana Drive (Hwy

200). There's a parking area on the opposite side of the street.

Nurseries & Gardens

Most of the state's orchids are grown on the Big Island, earning it one of its nicknames 'The Orchid Island'. Hilo is the centre of activity and from here orchids, anthuriums and other tropical flowers are flown to florists around the world.

A number of Hilo's working nurseries open their greenhouses and gardens to visitors free of charge. Look for 'visitors welcome' signs along the road.

Hilo Tropical Gardens This pleasant little two-acre naturalised garden is conveniently located on the beach road. A moss-covered sign here quotes Kipling, 'Gardens are not made by sitting in the shade' and this garden is obviously the result of years of labour. Paths wind around lily ponds, orchids, azaleas, hibiscus, ginger and all sorts of tropical flowers. There's a flower and gift shop out the front, as well as a shop selling great home-made ice cream.

The garden is at 1477 Kalanianaole Ave, just past Onekahakaha Beach. It's open from 9 am to 4.30 pm daily. Admission costs $1 for adults and is free for children under 12.

Orchid

Rainbow Tropicals Rainbow Tropicals is on Mamaki St near Hwy 11, on the way to the zoo. There's a small shop and a large greenhouse loaded with anthuriums and other tropical flowers.

Nani Mau Gardens Nani Mau Gardens is a large commercial garden on the tour bus route. There are over 20 acres of flowering plants, including a lovely orchid section, and many of the plants are labelled. It's not terribly natural or charmingly overgrown, but rather is all fairly new with sculptured plantings, wide asphalt paths and tram rides. Still for those who enjoy formally manicured gardens, this ambitious project has much to offer. Nani Mau is about three miles south of Hilo.

The turn-off from Hwy 11 onto Makalika St is marked with a small HVB warrior sign. Admission is $5 for adults, $2.50 for teenagers and free for children aged 12 and under. Tram rides cost $3 per person. It's open from 8 am to 5 pm daily.

Panaewa Rainforest Zoo

Panaewa Rainforest Zoo, the only tropical rainforest zoo in the USA, is in a forest reserve which gets 125 inches of rain annually.

It's a respectable little zoo and good for an hour of strolling. Some impressive and healthy looking tigers, two of them born here, roam a large, natural pit-style cage. There are monkeys, alligators, giant anteaters, a pygmy hippo and feral pigs and sheep. Peacocks and guinea fowl have the run of the place. You can also see some of Hawaii's endangered birds, such as nene and the Hawaiian duck, hawk and owl.

To get there, turn off Hwy 11 onto Mamaki St (also called Kulani Highway), a few miles south of town. The zoo is one mile west of Hwy 11. It's open from 9 am to 4 pm daily and admission is free.

Mauna Loa Macadamia Nut Visitor Center

Mauna Loa Macadamia Nut Visitor Center is on Macadamia Rd off Hwy 11, about five miles south of Hilo. The nearly three-mile road to the centre cuts across row after row of macadamia trees, as far as the eye can see.

C Brewer Co, which owns Mauna Loa, produces most of the world's macadamia nuts. The large visitors' centre here caters to tour bus crowds and is essentially just a gift shop and snack bar.

To the side is a **working factory**, which has an outside walkway with windows that allows visitors to view the large, fast-paced assembly line inside.

The little planted area out behind the visitors' centre with its labelled fruit trees and flowering bushes is worth walking through if you've come this far. The centre is open from 8.30 am to 5 pm daily.

Places to Stay

Partially due to the weather, Hilo has no self-contained resorts. People don't come to Hilo to hang around a pool, but to visit the sights and then head on. Consequently, Hilo's best values are generally its bottom-end accommodation. The 'vacation rental' condo market that's so common on the Kona Coast is virtually nonexistent here.

Places to Stay – bottom end

Arnott's Lodge (☎ 969-7097), 98 Apapane Rd, Hilo, HI 96720, is the cheapest place to stay in Hilo and a good place for backpackers to meet. This hostel-style lodge has 32 beds in a converted apartment building. It costs $15 for a bunk bed in a room with two to four people, $26 for a single room and $36 for doubles, all with shared baths and kitchen facilities. Linen and towels are provided. There's a common room with a TV, a coin laundry and a ride board to help guests who don't have cars connect with those who do. The lodge rents beach bikes for $7 a day, mountain bikes for $12.

To get there, go east 1½ miles on Kalanianaole Ave from Hwy 11 and turn left onto Keokea Loop Rd. The lodge is about 100 yards down the road, on the right.

The *Dolphin Bay Hotel* (☎ 935-1466), 333 Iliahi St, Hilo, HI 96720, located on a hill just above downtown, is a gem. It's a very friendly, family-run place that, unlike many other small inns, welcomes travellers with children. All 18 apartment-like units have full kitchens, TVs and bathrooms, and all except the standard rooms have sunken bathtubs. Fresh-picked fruit from the backyard is available in the lobby, along with free morning coffee. This is one of the few hotels in Hilo with a continuously high occupancy rate and reservations are suggested.

There's a two-night minimum stay for the standard rooms, which cost $36/46 for singles/doubles. It's $8 for each additional person and $10 more for the superior rooms. They also have four large one-bedroom units for $67 and a two-bedroom unit for $77. Weekly rates are available.

The owner of the *Wild Ginger Inn* (☎ 935-5556, (800) 882-1887), 100 Puueo St, Hilo, HI 96720, has taken a formerly run-down motel and given it a bright face-lift. Rooms in this nonsmoking inn are simple but quite adequate and a good continental breakfast is included in the price. The rooms have either a double or two twin beds and private baths. The cost is $39 for singles or doubles.

Hilo Hotel (☎ 961-3733), 142 Kinoole St, Box 726, Hilo, HI 96720, is an old-fashioned downtown hotel built in the 1950s on the former site of King Kalakaua's summer home. Rooms are simple and a little faded, but otherwise fine. There's a community lounge with a TV, and complimentary malasadas and coffee in the morning. Rooms cost $45 with TV, $39 without.

Lihi Kai (☎ 935-7865), c/o Amy Gamble Lannan, 30 Kahoa Rd, Hilo, HI 96720, is a B&B in Amy's home perched on a cliff directly above Hilo Bay, two miles north of town. There's a small solar-heated swimming pool and a large living room with a wonderful ocean view. Rooms, which share a bath, cost $45/50 for singles/doubles with breakfast. There's a three-night minimum stay or an extra $5 charge.

If the rooms are booked, Amy might let you rough it in the teahouse for $20 or send you to her next-door neighbours, *Holmes' Sweet Home* (☎ 961-9089), 32 Kahoa Rd,

Hilo, HI 96720, who also have a couple of rooms for $45/50.

Places to Stay – middle

Hilo Seaside Hotel (☎ 935-0821, (800) 367-7000 from the US mainland, (800) 451-6754 in Hawaii), 126 Banyan Drive, Hilo, HI 96720 (formerly the Hukilau Hotel) is a 145-unit two-storey motel-style complex with a nice carp pond out the front. Rooms are on the small side and rather standard, although all have TV and a small refrigerator. You might want to avoid the rooms around the swimming pool, which can get a bit noisy.

Rates begin at $54 for the room only and $69 with a Budget rental car. However, if you book within Hawaii and ask for the special it's often as low as $95 for two nights with a car.

Uncle Billy's *Hilo Bay Hotel* (☎ 961-5818, (800) 367-5102 from the US mainland, (800) 442-5841 in Hawaii), 87 Banyan Drive, Hilo, HI 96720, is a 130-room lacklustre hotel. Rates range from $69 for a standard room to $79 for a room with an ocean view. Rooms cost about $10 less in the low season.

Waiakea Villas (☎ 961-2841, (800) 354-2017), 400 Hualani St, Hilo, HI 96720, has 147 units in a rambling complex that's pleasantly spread over 14 acres along Waiakea Pond. Some of the units are long-term rentals, while others are rented through the front desk like a hotel. Rooms are quite nice with a touch of tropical decor and are only mildly faded, which in Hilo is relatively spiffy.

Standard rooms cost $60/70 in the low/high season; however they often run specials for around $40; add $5 more for a phone, $10 more for a kitchen. The complex includes offices, shops and a couple of restaurants.

Places to Stay – top end

Hilo Hawaiian Hotel (☎ 935-9361, (800) 367-5004 from the US mainland, (800) 272-5275 in Hawaii), 71 Banyan Drive, Hilo, HI 96720, is a 285-unit high-rise hotel overlooking Coconut Island and Hilo Bay.

Rooms are comfortable and modern, although pricey at $99. If you want your lanai facing the ocean instead of the parking lot it's $21 more.

Naniloa Hotel (☎ 969-3333, (800) 367-5360 from the US mainland, (800) 442-5845 in Hawaii), 93 Banyan Drive, Hilo, HI 96720, is a 400-room high-rise – Hilo's largest. The rooms are quite nice, but cost $96 to $154 depending on the view. It's popular with Japanese tour groups.

Places to Eat

Hilo has lots of hole-in-the-wall restaurants and cheap places to eat. Many places have salad-to-dessert lunch specials for around $5. Even some of the best restaurants have weekday 'business lunches' for just a bit more than that.

Places to Eat – bottom end

Bears' Coffee, 106 Keawe St, is a nice place for a light lunch or breakfast. They have a wide selection of good pastries, from croissants and muffins to cheesecake and raspberry linzertorte. Bears' also sells deli sandwiches, burritos and build-your-own bagels with more than a dozen fillings. Everything, except the lox and bagel, costs less than $5. It's open from 7 am to 5 pm Monday to Friday, 8 am to 4 pm on Saturdays.

Miyo's (☎ 935-2273), at Waiakea Villas, is a home-style Japanese restaurant overlooking a lagoon. The atmosphere is relaxed and the food is good. At lunch, tempura with rice and soup, shabu shabu, tonkatsu or sesame chicken cost $4.75 to $6. The tempura and sashimi combo is $6. The same meals at dinner time are a dollar or two more. It's open Monday to Saturday from 11 am to 2 pm and 5.30 to 8.30 pm.

Jimmy's Drive Inn at 362 Kinoole St, next to Kentucky Fried Chicken, is a busy local eatery. They serve generous portions of inexpensive Korean, Japanese, Hawaiian and American food, although it all tends to blend in flavour. The Korean combo plate of kalbi, mundoo, barbecued chicken and kimchee

costs $5. Complete seafood dinners start at $5.75. Opening hours are 10 am to 9.30 pm Monday to Saturday.

Dick's Coffee House in the Hilo Shopping Center on Kilauea Ave is another inexpensive diner. Complete meals range from $4 for spaghetti to $7.25 for steak. At breakfast, omelettes with hash browns and toast start at $3. It's not exciting but it's cheap.

KK Tei, 1550 Kamehameha Ave, is a family restaurant with all the Japanese standards. At lunch time, oyako donburi (egg and chicken over rice) with miso soup and tea costs $4.25 and teishokus are $6.50. Dinners average a few dollars more. They're open from 11 am to 2 pm and 5 to 9 pm Monday to Saturday, but close up early on days when business is slow.

Karrots, a natural foods restaurant inside a fitness center at 197 Keawe St, is a good choice for healthy breakfasts and light lunches and dinners. Home-made granola costs $2, blueberry filled pancakes $4, sandwiches $3 to $4, and the intriguingly titled Marco Polo tofu and Evil Jungle Dude cost about $6. They also have fresh-squeezed 'carrot' juice, good 'carrot' muffins, smoothies and bagels. Opening hours are from 6.30 am to 8 pm weekdays, to 3 pm on Saturdays.

Abundant Life Natural Foods, 292 Kamehameha Ave, is a health-food store with a variety of products including cheeses, yoghurt, juices, bulk foods and organic produce. It's open from 8.30 am to 6 pm weekdays, to 5 pm on Saturdays and from 10 am to 3 pm on Sundays. Next door, *Oroweat Bakery Thrift Store* has slightly dated breads at discounted prices.

The city has an abundance of fast-food restaurants, including *McDonald's, Pizza Hut, Jack in the Box, Taco Bell* and the like. *Ken's House of Pancakes*, 1730 Kamehameha Ave, is open 24 hours daily.

Hilo's best ice cream can be found at *Hilo Homemade Ice Cream*, next to Hilo Tropical Gardens. Owner Fred Stoeber cheerfully scoops up his Hawaiian creations, including tasty poha berry, zesty ginger and other island flavours like lilikoi, coconut cream and macadamia nut. It's a mere $1 for a single scoop, $1.50 for a double. Opening hours are 10 am to 5 pm.

Places to Eat – middle

Soontaree's (☎ 934-7426) in the Hilo Shopping Center serves the Big Island's best Thai food. The complete lunch, which includes a main dish with rice and green papaya salad, is $7. Pad Thai is $5 at lunch, $7 at dinner. There's a vegetarian menu with dishes from $6 to $7 and fresh fish costs $8 to $9.

Soontaree does all the cooking, grows many of the herbs in her own garden and uses only natural ingredients and no MSG. Even the iced tea is a flavourful experience. If you like your Thai food spicy, order it hot, as medium is fairly mild. Opening hours are from 11 am to 2 pm Tuesday to Friday, 5.30 to 9 pm Tuesday to Sunday.

Lehua's (☎ 935-8055), 11 Waianuenue Ave, is popular and pleasantly up-market. There's a wide variety of dishes, including spinach lasagne, baby back pork ribs, steaks, cioppino and stir-fried vegetables over rice. A good-value choice is the charbroiled chicken with papaya salsa, which comes with salad, sourdough bread and potato and costs $7 at lunch, $10 at dinner. Lunch is from 11 am to 4 pm weekdays, to 3 pm on Saturdays. Dinner is from 5 to 9.30 pm daily (to 9 pm on Sundays).

Fiascos, 200 Kanoelehua Ave (Hwy 11), is a bustling place serving sandwiches, salads, pastas, fajitas and an array of meat dishes at moderate prices. There's also a rather ordinary salad bar with soup for $7. It's open from 11 am to 10 pm daily, to 11 pm on Fridays and Saturdays.

Traditional hula dance

Nihon Restaurant at 121 Lihiwai St, next to Liliuokalani Gardens, has a fine view of Hilo Bay and a good sushi bar. At lunch time there's a 'business special' for $8.25 which includes two entrees such as sashimi, tonkatsu or tempura along with nigiri rice, kappamaki, miso soup and tossed salad. Dinner teishokus are a few dollars more. They also have cheaper one-bowl dishes like donburi, soba and udon. Lunch is from 11 am to 2 pm and dinner is from 5 to 9 pm.

Cafe Pesto, a branch of the popular Kawaihae restaurant, has opened on Kamehameha Avenue in the newly renovated S Hata building, a classic 1912 building that once held the city's main department store. It serves good gourmet pizza and pasta dishes at moderate prices.

Fuji Restaurant in the Hilo Hotel, 142 Kinoole St, has a pleasant atmosphere and good Japanese food. The tempura teishoku costs $10 at lunch, $11 at dinner, and yakitori donburi is $7 at lunch, $7.75 at dinner. It's open from 11 am to 2 pm and 5 to 9 pm daily except Mondays.

Ting-Hao Mandarin Restaurant (☎ 959-6288), in Puainako Town Center on Hwy 11, is a popular Chinese restaurant. Vegetarian dishes such as broccoli with garlic and ma po tofu are in the $5 to $6 range, and Sichuan and Mandarin meat-based dishes cost $5 to $9. There's a daily lunch special for $4.60. No MSG is used. Opening hours are 11.30 am to 2.30 pm Monday to Saturday and 4.30 to 9 pm nightly.

Places to Eat – top end

Pescatore (☎ 969-9090), 235 Keawe St, is Hilo's best Italian restaurant. Lunch is a good deal, with an array of pasta dishes ranging from $6 for bolognese sauce to $9 for shrimp scampi alfredo. At dinner time, pasta dishes are about double, while meat and seafood plates cost $15 to $22. Lunch is from 11 am to 2 pm Monday to Saturday. Dinner is from 5.30 to 9 pm weekdays, to 10 pm weekends.

Harrington's (☎ 961-4966), right on Reeds Bay, is a small waterfront restaurant with wooden beam ceilings. Locally, it's a perennial favourite for special occasions and serves good seafood, steak and chicken dishes in the $14 to $19 range. It's open from 5.30 to 10 pm daily (to 9 pm on Sundays).

Entertainment

Lehua's, Hilo's trendiest night spot, has live rock & roll, soul or blues bands with dancing on weekends. The cover charge is $2.

There is a disco at *d'Angoras*, 101 Aupuni St, from 9 pm Thursday to Saturday, usually with a $3 cover charge, and a Dixieland jazz band on Sunday afternoons. *Fiascos*, on Hwy 11 near Banyan Drive, has a DJ and dancing to music from the '50s to '80s from 8.30 pm to 1 am on Fridays and Saturdays.

Harrington's has modern pop music, either guitar or keyboards, in its lounge from 5.30 pm nightly except Sundays.

Uncle Billy presents a hula show during dinner time, from 6 pm nightly, at the *Hilo Bay Hotel* restaurant.

The *Menehuneland Lounge* in the Hilo Hawaiian Hotel has a dance floor and live music nightly, mostly a mellow mix of contemporary and Hawaiian songs.

Movie Theatres The movie theatres at *Prince Kuhio Plaza* and at *Waiakea Shopping Plaza*, 88 Kanoelehua Ave, show standard Hollywood films.

Puna

Puna is the diamond-shaped easternmost point of the Big Island. Its main attractions are in lava: vast fields of it covering former villages, an ancient forest of lava tree moulds, lava tide pools and black-sand beaches.

Kilauea Volcano's active east rift zone slices clear across Puna. The most recent series of eruptions has been spewing lava since 1983. These days the highway into Puna ends abruptly at the 1990 lava flow that covers the former village of Kalapana.

Not surprisingly, Puna has Hawaii's cheapest real estate. The closer to the rift, the greater the volcanic activity and the cheaper the land gets.

While a growing number of people are drawn to Puna by the idea of homesteading, many have found it tough making a living off a lava flow. For years growing pakalolo has been one alternative.

The majority of all pot confiscated by Hawaii police is still taken in Puna. However, para-military raids, intense herbicide sprayings and helicopters with infrared sensors that allow authorities to see into people's homes have sharply curtailed the growing.

Deserved or not, Puna has the reputation of being less than friendly. If you're travelling the main roads you probably won't pick up on those vibes at all but if you're cruising around off the beaten path you may raise a suspicious eye.

Some crops take well to lava and Puna is a major producer of anthuriums, grows the best papayas in Hawaii, and grows many of the orchids that get credited to Hilo.

Puna is not known for its beaches and for

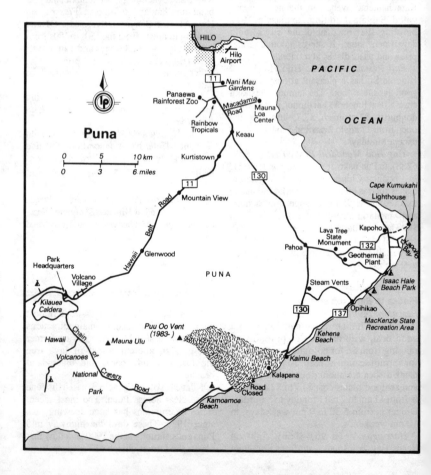

the most part waters along the coast are subject to strong currents and riptides.

Orientation

Keaau is the entrance to Puna, where Hwy 11 and Hwy 130 intersect. From there, Hwy 130 goes south 11 miles to Pahoa and then continues on to the coast.

Maps which show Hwy 130 winding down through Puna and up the Chain of Craters Road to Hawaii Volcanoes National Park were made obsolete in 1988 when a lava flow buried a large section of the road. The national park can now be entered only via the Hawaii Belt Rd (Hwy 11), which makes Puna more time consuming to visit, as you need to backtrack out the same way you go in. If you don't have a lot of time, Puna could easily be bypassed.

Hwy 11, on the way to the national park, passes through the towns of Kurtistown, Mountain View and Glenwood.

KEAAU

Keaau is the town at the northern end of Puna. Keaau Town Center, Puna's only shopping centre, is at the intersection of Hwy 11 and Hwy 130. It has a grocery store, post office, Dairy Queen and a good Mexican restaurant.

Keaau Natural Foods, opposite the shopping centre and open daily, has reasonably priced fruit and organic produce, baked goods and a full line of health foods.

PAHOA

Pahoa is the heart of Puna. It's a funky little town with raised wooden sidewalks, cowboy architecture and an untamed edge. There are influences from the '60s and '70s but there are other more timeless ones as well. One noteworthy building in the town centre is the Akebono Theater, which was built in 1917 and is one of the oldest theatres in Hawaii.

If you'd like to take a look at life on a lava flow as you're driving around, stop by Pahoa Realty on Main St and pick up their subdivision guide. Prices start as low as $4500 for a small lot (no electricity, water by catchment, gravel roads) in the Black Sand Beach subdivision, on Kilauea's active east rift zone.

Wild orchids grow like weeds along the roadsides around Pahoa and throughout Puna. There are fields of cultivated orchids and lots of anthurium nurseries as well. It may come as no surprise that the Hawaiian Hemp Company, which advocates the use of the hemp plant for various purposes, is based in Pahoa.

Places to Stay

The *Village Inn* (☎ 965-6444), 1 Main St, Pahoa, HI 96778, has five 2nd-storey rooms above Main St shops in an historic wooden building adjacent to the theatre. It's partly funky, slanted hardwood floors and all, and partly classy, with rooms furnished with authentic Victorian-era antiques. Rates are $40 for singles or doubles in rooms with shared bath, $60 for rooms with private baths. Credit cards are accepted.

Bamboo House (☎ 965-8322), Box 1546, Pahoa, HI 96778, a cottage rented by the

---

Puna & Pele

In the Hawaiian language there are several proverbial expressions that link Puna with the volcano goddess Pele. As an example, to express anger, someone might say *Ke lauahi maila o Pele ia Puna*, 'Pele is pouring lava out on Puna'.

Equally common are both historic and modern stories of a mysterious woman travelling alone through Puna. Sometimes she's young and attractive, other times she's old and wizened, and often she's seen just before a volcanic eruption. Those who stop and pick her up hitchhiking or show some other kindness are often protected from the lava flow.

After the 1960 lava flow in Kapoho, stories circulated about how the light keeper in the spared Kapoho lighthouse had offered a meal to an elderly homeless woman who had showed up at his door on the eve of the eruption. ■

owner of the natural food store, is on a side street in the centre of town. It's simple but clean, comfortable and pleasantly airy. There's one bedroom and a small living room with a queen-size sofabed and cable TV. The other half of the duplex cottage is being converted into a vacation rental as well, as is another building across the street. Rates are $45 per night, or $40 a night for three nights or more. There's no smoking allowed and credit cards are accepted.

Places to Eat

Luquin's is an authentic Mexican restaurant on Main St in Pahoa's town centre. A single taco or enchilada costs $2, while combination plates range from $4.50 to $6.50. Huevos rancheros with tortillas, rice and beans cost $4.25. It's open from 11 am to 9 pm daily.

Hana Ohana, on Main St near Luquin's, is an incense-scented metaphysical bookstore and espresso cafe. At breakfast, quiche with potatoes and toast, or a Belgian waffle with fresh fruit and whipped cream, cost $3.50. Vegetarian lunches are about $4. They serve Rooster Farms organic coffee and make good fruit smoothies. It's open Monday to Saturday, from 8 to 11 am for breakfast and to 5.30 pm for lunch.

Pahoa Natural Groceries, across from the Bank of Hawaii in the centre of town, is a well-stocked natural foods store with a full dairy section and bakery items. Sandwiches such as tofu and sprouts or jack cheese and avocado on sliced whole-wheat bread cost $2.60. It's open from 9 am to 9 pm daily (to 6 pm on Sundays).

For fresh fish sandwiches, you couldn't do better than *Paradise West* in the town centre. They have a good lunch menu, bottomless cups of coffee and free refills on soft drinks.

Pahoa also has a ribhouse restaurant, Chinese and Thai restaurants, a *Dairy Queen,* produce stands and an old grocery store where you'll find the local bulletin board.

Onward from Pahoa

The usual route after Pahoa is to make the triangle down Hwy 132 past Lava Tree State Monument, then Hwy 137 along the shore to the lava flow at Kalapana and back to Pahoa via Hwy 130. (At least for now, Madame Pele has stopped flowing at the very edge of a side road that connects Hwy 137 and Hwy 130.)

From Pahoa, Hwy 132 passes through tropical forest reserve. The area is very lush and junglelike, with ferns growing on the bark of trees and a thick ground cover of impatiens.

Lava Tree State Monument

The lava moulds at Lava Tree State Monument were created in 1790 when this former ohia rainforest was engulfed in pahoehoe from Kilauea's east rift zone. The lava was free-flowing and moved quickly, like a river flooding its banks.

As the molten lava ran through the forest, some of it began to congeal around the moisture-laden ohia trunks while the rest of the flow moved on through and quickly receded.

Although the trees themselves burned away, the moulds of lava which had formed around them remained. Now, 200 years later, there's a ghost forest of lava shells.

A 20-minute loop walk winds around the 'lava trees'. Some are a good 10 feet high, while others are short enough to look down into and shelter ferns within their hollows.

Be careful if you walk off the path as in places the ground is crossed by deep cracks, some hidden by new vegetation. It's thought one deep fracture, which was caused by an earthquake at the same time as the flow, may have drained much of the lava back into the earth.

The park is on Hwy 132, 2½ miles east from its intersection with Hwy 130. The mosquitoes can be wicked.

Geothermal Plant

A few miles south-east of Pahoa is a controversial geothermal operation that's experimenting with the production of electricity from hot (675°F) subterranean water rising from deep wells.

There are plans to eventually develop 20

geothermal plants, each of which would have about a dozen separate wells. The steam would generate up to 500 megawatts of electricity which would then be cabled directly to Oahu.

Greenpeace, the Rainforest Action Network and the Pele Defense Fund are three of many environmental groups opposing development of these geothermal energy projects. Not only are many of the wells being placed within a rare lowland tropical rainforest, but there are also concerns about the environmental hazards of extensive drilling into the world's most active volcano. In addition, many Hawaiians feel the proposed plant is sacrilegious and inviting Pele's wrath.

In June 1991 one of the wells experienced a serious blowout that spewed out noxious hydrogen sulphide gas in a roaring explosion that went uncontrolled for 31 hours. The fumes killed animals and caused nearby residents breathing difficulties and other health problems. Many had to be evacuated.

The project has been the focus of protesters, who have come from as far away as Israel and Japan. A number of lawsuits have been filed, including one by the Sierra Club Legal Defense Fund which has finally forced an environmental impact study to be undertaken, an action that should at least slow down the project for the next few years.

The Hawaii Geothermal Project's former visitors' centre, which once offered tours on the advantages of geothermal energy, is now locked and chained. It's on Pahoa-Pohoiki Rd, about a mile down from Hwy 132.

KAPOHO

Hwy 132 heads east through papaya orchards and long rows of vanda orchids to what was once Kapoho, a farming town of about 300 people.

On 13 January 1960 a fountain of fire half a mile long shot up in the midst of a sugar cane field just above Kapoho. The main flow of liquid pahoehoe lava ran toward the ocean. A slower moving offshoot of 'aa' lava crept toward the town, burying orchid farms in its path.

Earthen barricades were built and fire hoses frantically pumped water onto the lava, but none of the attempts to harden or divert the flow worked.

On 28 January the lava entered Kapoho and buried the town. A hot springs resort and nearly 100 homes and businesses disappeared.

One bizarre phenomenon occurred when the river of lava approached the sea at Cape Kumukahi. Within a few feet of the cape's lighthouse the lava parted into two flows and circled around it, sparing the lighthouse from destruction. If you want to take a look, the site is 1¾ miles down the dirt road which continues beyond the intersection of Hwy 132 and Hwy 137. However, the lighthouse has been replaced by a modern light beacon. Cape Kumukahi (first beginning) is the easternmost point in the state.

The most dominant landscape feature in the Kapoho area is an ancient 420-foot cinder cone. The hill is lush green with thick vegetation and has a small crater lake on top of it.

One of the earliest legends of volcanic activity in Kapoho goes back to the 1300s. It seems Kahavari, a young Puna chief, was holding a holua (sledding) contest on this hill. One of the spectators was an attractive woman who stepped forward and challenged the chief to a race.

Kahavari tossed the woman an inferior sled and charged down the hill, daring her to overcome him. Halfway down he glanced over his shoulder and found her close behind, racing down atop a wave on a sea of molten lava. It was of course Pele, who chased Kahavari clear out to sea where he narrowly escaped in a canoe. Everyone and everything in Pele's path was buried in the flood of lava.

Highway 137

Hwy 137 (Kalapana-Kapoho Beach Rd) is barely above water level, bordered by invasive milo and hala trees that look as if they plan to reclaim the road. In places it's so overgrown there's almost a tunnel effect, with just a lacy bit of light filtering in through the trees. The road sometimes floods during winter storms and high surf.

Kapoho Tidepools

Kapoho Tidepools are in the Kapoho Vacationland subdivision, a mile south of the lighthouse. To get there, turn makai off Hwy 137 onto Kapoho Kai Drive and then turn left on Waiopai. There is a sign for public access, but parking may be a hassle.

The network of tide pools are formed in lava basins, some of which are deep enough to swim and snorkel in.

Isaac Hale Beach Park

Isaac Hale Beach Park, which is on Pohoiki Bay on Hwy 137, has a shoreline of chunky lava rocks. This county park is small but on weekends there's usually a frenzy of local activity. Birthday picnics and fishing seem to be the biggest attractions.

The park has Puna's only boat ramp. Local kids like to swim near the ramp, which is somewhat protected by a breakwater, and there are sometimes surfers at the south side of the bay.

Camping is allowed, although you'll probably feel like you're in somebody's backyard as there's a fisher's house right on the shore. There's a warm freshwater spring south of the house.

The park has restrooms, but no drinking water or showers.

MacKenzie State Recreation Area

There's no beach at MacKenzie State Recreation Area but rather 40-foot cliffs with a surging surf that sometimes breaks three-quarters of the way up. There's good fishing from the cliffs for ulua, a jack fish that favours turbulent waters.

This 13-acre park on Hwy 137 is quiet and secluded, in a grove of ironwood trees. There's a soft carpet of needles underfoot. Both tent and trailer camping are allowed with a permit from the state. There are picnic tables, barbecue grills and pit toilets, but no drinking water.

An old Hawaiian coastal trail, called the King's Trail, passes through the park. It runs parallel to the ocean about 75 yards in from the cliffs. If you take it from the parking lot for about three minutes to the north-east you'll come across the opening of a long lava tube, which is marked by a low thicket of ferns.

Places to Stay

Champagne Cove (☎ 959-4487), c/o Drs Keith & Norma Godfrey, 1714 Lei Lehua St, Hilo, HI 96720, is an oceanfront home on Kapoho Beach with two three-bedroom units and a heated pool. The rate is $75 for two people, up to $95 for six and there's a three-day minimum stay.

OPIHIKAO

The village of Opihikao is marked by a little Congregational church and a couple of houses.

Kalani Honua Culture Center & Retreat, a New Age retreat centre emphasising the arts and Hawaiian culture, is 2½ miles south-west of Opihikao village, midway between the 17 and 18-mile markers. Workshops for such things as Iyengar Yoga, Kahuna Arts, massage and dance are offered. Visitors are welcome to take a look around. There's a cafe and gift shop at the office.

Places to Stay & Eat

Kalani Honua Culture Center & Retreat (☎ 965-7828, (800) 800-6886), RR2, Box 4500, Pahoa, HI 96778, caters mostly to groups, but also welcomes individual travellers on a space-available basis.

There are 31 rooms, most in two-storey cedar lodges which have exposed-beam ceilings, lots of wood and a screened common area with shared kitchen. Rates are $65/75 for singles/doubles with a private bath, $52/62 with a shared bath.

They also have cottages with one bedroom, bath and living room for $85. Tents can be pitched on the grounds for $13 per person. There's a sauna, pool and tennis court, which are free to guests and available to non-guests for a small fee.

The centre has a work scholar programme which provides room and board in exchange for 30 hours of work per week, with a two-month commitment required. This is a good opportunity to stay a few months in Hawaii without spending a lot of money.

The dining room, which serves buffet-style vegetarian meals, is open to the public. Breakfast costs $6, lunch $7 and dinner $11. Dining room hours are short: from 8 to 8.45 am for breakfast, 12.30 to 1.15 pm for lunch and 6.30 to 7.15 pm for dinner. The cafe at the office has juices, soup and sandwiches from 10 am to 6 pm daily.

KEHENA BEACH

Kehena Beach is a black-sand beach created by a 1955 lava flow. It's a nude sunbathing spot and occasionally an unofficial camping site. Coconut and ironwood trees offer shade along the beach.

When the water's calm swimming is usually safe, but during periods of heavy surf there can be powerful currents and dangerous undertows. In winter it's not unusual for dolphins to come close to the shore and swim with bathers.

Kehena is off Hwy 137, around the 19-mile marker. Look for cars parked at a pull-off and follow the path down. It is about a 15-minute walk. Don't leave valuables in your car.

End of the Road

Hwy 137 ends abruptly at the closed Black-sand Beach Drive Inn.

For years, the village of Kalapana sat precariously beneath Kilauea's restless east rift. When the current series of eruptions began in 1983 the main lava flow moved down the slope to the west of Kalapana. Much of the early flow passed through a series of lava tubes which carried the molten lava down to the coast and into the sea. After pauses in the eruption in 1990, the tubes feeding lava to the ocean cooled long enough to harden and block up. When the eruption started again, the lava flow was redirected towards Kalapana. By the end of 1990 the entire village, including 100 homes, was buried.

Today the road ends at Kaimu Beach at the eastern edge of Kalapana. Kaimu, formerly the most famous black-sand beach in Hawaii, is now buried under a sea of har-dened lava that flowed over the sand and clear into the bay. Opposite the beach, the drive-in restaurant where the tour buses used to park, was ironically spared. The rest of the coastal village and Harry K Brown Beach Park, which lay beyond, are gone.

Highway 130

From the edge of the most recent lava flow, a side road leads up to Hwy 130, which goes back to Pahoa. There are a couple of sights along the way.

Painted Church The Star of the Sea is a little white Catholic church noted for its interior murals painted in trompe l'oeil style to create the effect of being in a large cathedral. The illusion of depth is amazingly effective. There's also a nice stained glass window of Father Damien who was with the parish before he moved to the leprosy colony on Molokai.

The church, which was in the town of Kalapana, was moved just before lava flows swept over the site. It currently sits at the roadside along Hwy 130, waiting for a more permanent home.

Steam Vents At the 15-mile marker, 3½ miles south of Pahoa, for some less than obvious reason a big blue highway sign marks a scenic view. While the scenery is not particularly special, only a few minutes' walk away there are some low spatter cones with hollowed out natural steam baths inside, perfect for a sauna.

To get to the steam vents, take the path leading down from the scenic lookout. Where the path forks, bear right and walk to the last crater which has a little wooden bench inside.

Kau

The Kau district stretches from South Kona along the southern flanks of Mauna Loa, taking in the entire southern tip of the island all the way up to Hawaii Volcanoes National Park.

Kau is sparsely populated, with only about 5000 people and three real towns. Much of it is dry and desert-like. The highest temperature ever recorded in the state was in Kau in the town of Pahala: 100°F in April 1931. However Kau also has some lush areas in the foothills where sugar cane, macadamia nuts and most of Hawaii's oranges are grown.

Kau was the centre of devastation in the massive 1868 earthquake, the worst Hawaii has ever recorded. For five full days from 27 March, the earth was rattled almost continuously by a series of tremors and quakes. Then in the afternoon of 2 April the earth shook violently in every direction and an inferno broke loose from beneath the surface.

Those fortunate enough to be uphill watched as a rapidly moving river of lava poured down the hillsides and swallowed up everything in its path, including people, homes and cattle. Within minutes the coast was inundated by tidal waves and villages near the shore were swept away.

This deadly triple combination of earthquakes, lava flows and tidal waves permanently changed Kau's landscape. Huge cinder cones came crashing down the slopes and there was one landslide which covered an entire village. You can see the 1868 lava flow along the highway two miles west of the South Point turn-off. The old village of Kahuku lies beneath it.

MANUKA STATE WAYSIDE PARK

Manuka State Wayside Park is an eight-acre arboretum off Hwy 11 near the 81-mile marker. The trees and bushes planted here between the mid-1930s and the 1950s include 48 native Hawaiian species and 130 introduced species. Many are labelled, some with both Latin and common names.

Camping is allowed by permit in the three-sided covered shelter which has space for about five sleeping bags. It might be fine for an overnight break between Hilo and Kona, although it's quite close to the road. While camping under the trees looks tempting, it's prohibited. Facilities include restrooms and picnic tables and in season you can find ripe guavas opposite the entrance.

There's a 3½-mile loop trail leading north through an ohia forest that begins above the parking lot.

The park is in the midst of a natural area reserve which covers 25,550 acres and reaches from the slopes of Mauna Loa down to the sea where it takes in a couple of heiaus and other ruins.

HAWAIIAN OCEAN VIEW ESTATES

A few miles east of Manuka there's a new general store with a small deli. A post office, a plate lunch eatery, a Texaco gas station, a hardware shop and a real estate office are in the same little complex. For now, this is the commercial centre, such as it is, for Hawaiian Ocean View Estates and a couple of other isolated southside subdivisions.

There are a couple of small B&Bs in the area and a massive new resort development has been proposed for the barren Kahuku area between here and South Point.

Places To Stay

South Point Bed & Breakfast (☎ 929-7466), Box 6589, Captain Cook, HI 96704, is in Hawaiian Ocean View Estates, just mauka of Hwy 11. There are three comfortable units, each with a private entrance and bath. Rates, which include breakfast served on the lanai, are $45/55 a single/double for the two smaller rooms and $10 more for the larger unit, which has a kitchenette.

A bit more casual is *Bougainvillea Bed & Breakfast* (☎ 929-7089), Box 6045, Captain Cook, HI 96704, in Hawaiian Ocean View Estates, on the makai side of Hwy 11. Martie Nitsche rents out a few rooms in her home, each with a private bath and entrance, for $40/50 a single/double, including breakfast. There's an extra $5 charge for stays of only one night. Bicycles are available for guests to use and there's a swimming pool in the yard.

SOUTH POINT

South Point is the southernmost spot in the

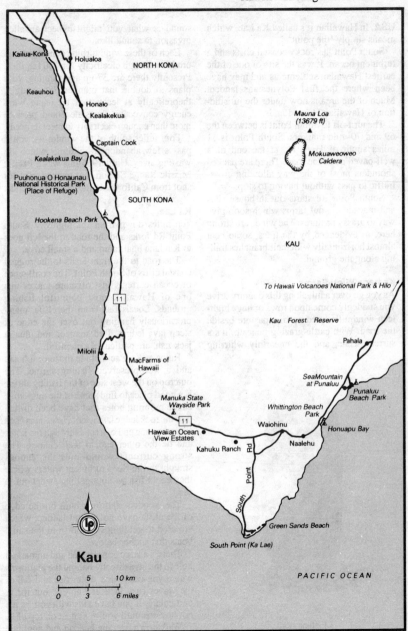

Kailua-Kona

Holualoa

NORTH KONA

Keauhou

Honalo

Kealakekua

Captain Cook

Kealakekua Bay

Puuhonua O Honaunau
National Historical Park
(Place of Refuge)

SOUTH KONA

Hookena Beach Park

Mauna Loa
(13679 ft) ▲

Mokuaweoweo
Caldera

KAU

To Hawaii Volcanoes National Park & Hilo

Kau Forest Reserve

Milolii

MacFarms of
Hawaii

Pahala

Manuka State
Wayside Park

SeaMountain
at Punaluu

Punaluu
Beach Park

Whittington Beach
Park

Waiohinu

Honuapu Bay

Hawaiian Ocean
View Estates

Kahuku Ranch

Naalehu

Green Sands Beach

South Point (Ka Lae)

PACIFIC OCEAN

Kau

South Point Rd

LP

| 0 | 5 | 10 km |
| 0 | 3 | 6 miles |

USA. In Hawaiian it's called Ka Lae, which means simply 'the point'.

South Point has rocky coastal cliffs and a turbulent ocean. It was the site of one of the earliest Hawaiian settlements and may have been where the first Polynesians landed. Much of the area is now under the jurisdiction of Hawaiian Home Lands.

The turn-off to South Point is between the 69 and 70-mile markers. South Point is 11 miles south of Hwy 11, at the end of a well-paved one-lane road. There are packed shoulders most of the way allowing cross-traffic to pass without having to stop.

South Point Rd starts out in house sites and macadamia nut farms which soon give way to grassy pastures. The winds are strong here, as evidenced by the trees, some bent almost horizontally with their branches trailing along the ground.

Kamaoa Wind Farms

As you go over a hill along this country drive you suddenly come upon rows of huge high-tech windmills lined up in a pasture beside the road. With cattle grazing beneath, it's a surreal scene, and the unearthly whirring

Fishing god

sound is what you might expect an alien invasion to sound like.

Each of these wind turbine generators can produce enough electricity for 100 families. Presently there are 37 up and running, with plans to double that number. It's thought, theoretically at least, that by using wind energy conversion the state could produce more than enough electricity to meet its needs.

Four miles south of the windmills, you'll pass a few abandoned buildings which are wasting away. Until 1965 this was a Pacific Missile Range Station that tracked missiles shot from California to the Marshall Islands.

Ka Lae

Ten miles down from the highway, South Point Rd forks and the road to the left goes to Kaulana boat ramp and a small cove.

The road to the right leads to the rugged coastal cliffs of South Point. The confluence of ocean currents just offshore makes this one of Hawaii's most bountiful fishing grounds. Locals fish from the cliffs, many precariously hanging out over the edge of steep lava ledges. Red snapper and ulua, a jack fish, are particularly plentiful.

Ruins at Ka Lae include those of a heiau and a well-preserved fishing shrine. The outcrop on the west side of the fishing shrine is a good place to find some of the numerous canoe mooring holes that have been drilled into the rock ledges. Ancient Hawaiians used to anchor one end of a rope through the holes and tie the other end to their canoes. The strong currents would pull the canoes straight out to deep turbulent waters where they could fish without getting swept out to sea.

The wooden platforms built on the edge of the cliffs have hoists and ladders which are used to get things to and from the small boats that anchor below.

There's a large unprotected and unmarked hole in the lava directly behind the platforms where you can watch water rise and fall as the waves rush in. Keep an eye out for it, particularly if you have kids with you, as it's not obvious until you're almost on top of it.

Walk down past the beacon and continue

along the wall to get to the southernmost point in the USA. There are no markers here, no souvenir stands, just crashing surf and lots of wind.

Green Sands Beach

If you want to explore the area more, go back to the fork and take the road to Kaulana boat ramp. Beside the ramp you'll find pockets of green sand sparkling in the sun. These are olivine crystals worn from the lava cliffs by a relentless and pounding surf.

The highest concentration of green sand in Hawaii is at Green Sands Beach, a 2½-mile hike away. To get there take the 4WD road heading north-east from the boat ramp. The walk is not difficult, though once you reach Green Sands you'll need to scramble down the cliffside to get to the beach. Pick a calm day to visit as during periods of high surf the entire beach can be inundated. A couple of minutes beyond Kaulana boat ramp the trail passes the site of **Kapalaoa**, an ancient fishing village.

WAIOHINU

After South Point, Hwy 11 winds down into a pretty valley and the sleepy village of Waiohinu, which sits nestled beneath green hills. On the right as you enter the town is the quaint little wooden Kauahaao Church, white with green trim, dating from 1841.

Shirakawa Motel is 500 feet ahead on the left and there's a monkeypod tree planted by Mark Twain in 1866 just past the hotel, on the same side of the road. The original tree fell in a typhoon in 1957 but hardy new trunks have sprung up and it's once again full grown.

Wong Yuen's Chevron gas station in the village centre is open from 8.30 am to 7 pm Monday to Saturday, to 6 pm on Sundays.

From Waiohinu the road runs beneath the lower slopes of Mauna Loa through sugar cane fields, cattle-ranch land and macadamia groves. Inland beyond the sugar cane fields is Kau Forest Reserve, which runs all the way up to Hawaii Volcanoes National Park.

Places to Stay

Shirakawa Motel (☎ 929-7462), Box 467, Naalehu, HI 96772, is a green weather-beaten motel with 13 basic units. The motel is plain, but the setting beneath the green hills is lovely. Rooms cost $27/33 for singles/doubles, $40 for a kitchenette unit. At dusk, flocks of myna birds fly through the area, squawking.

The *Nutt House* (☎ 929-9940), Box 852, Naalehu, HI 96772, is a B&B on an eight-acre macadamia nut farm half a mile from the village centre. There are two units, both with private entrances and bathrooms. The larger unit has over 1000 sq feet, with a spacious living room and an ocean view, and costs $55/65 for singles/doubles. A smaller second unit costs $45/55. Rates include breakfast on the lanai.

NAALEHU

Naalehu's claim to fame is being the southernmost town in the USA. It's two miles east of Waiohinu and a few inches to the south.

Modest as it is, Naalehu is the region's shopping centre. It has three grocery markets, a couple of restaurants, a gas station, a movie theatre, an elementary school and the Kau police station. If you happen to be around between 1 and 5 pm on Tuesday or Thursday you can even catch the tiny public library while it's open.

Naalehu closes up early, so you can't count on getting food or gas here if you're driving back to Kona from the Hawaii Volcanoes National Park at night.

Places to Eat

Naalehu Fruit Stand on Hwy 11 is a reasonably priced produce stand, health-food store and pizza and sandwich shop all in one. The ovens out the back bake bread in the morning and pizzas to order from 11 am. They have prepared sandwiches such as teri-tofu on home-made whole-wheat bread for $3 or you can get a sub with the works for a bit more. Macadamia nut cream cheese bars and many other pastries cost about a dollar. It's open from 9 am to 6.30 pm daily (to 5 pm on

Sundays) and there are a few picnic tables near the front steps where you can eat.

Naalehu Coffee Shop looks touristy with its gift shop and large dining room, but it's essentially a family-run local diner serving three meals a day. At breakfast, two thick slices of banana bread with home-made pineapple-papaya jam are $3. If you're coming from Kona, turn right just past the theatre.

WHITTINGTON BEACH PARK

Two miles beyond Naalehu there's a pull-off with a scenic lookout above Honuapo Bay. From the lookout you can see the cement pilings of the old Honuapo Pier, which was used for shipping sugar and hemp until the 1930s.

Honuapo Bay is the site of Whittington Beach Park and the turn-off is one mile from the lookout. Whittington has sheltered picnic tables, restrooms and showers.

There's really no beach at Whittington although there are tide pools to explore. The ocean is usually too rough and dangerous for swimming. Endangered green sea turtles, which can sometimes be seen offshore, apparently have been frequenting these waters for a long time, as Honuapo means 'caught turtle'.

Camping is allowed and it's far enough from the highway to offer a little privacy. Overall, it's a pretty good choice for a county camping ground but avoid setting up near the street light by the parking lot. The light is on all night and illuminates much of the lawn where tenting is allowed.

PUNALUU

Punaluu is a small bay with a black-sand beach that was once the site of a major Hawaiian settlement and in later days an important sugar port. The most visited section of the beach is the area fronting the Punaluu Black Sands Restaurant, which is lined with coconut trees and backed by a duck pond. The ruins of the Pahala Sugar Company's old warehouse and pier are a short walk away at the north end of the

beach. Sitting on a rise above it is the site of Kaneeleele Heiau.

Punaluu Beach Park, a county park just to the south, has restrooms, showers, drinking water, a picnic pavilion and camping. It's a flat, grassy area right on the beach and a nice place to camp although it's very open. At night you can drift off to sleep to the sounds of crashing surf. Be careful walking around as the area's black sands are used as nesting sites by hawksbill turtles.

The first turn-off you'll reach in Punaluu, if heading east, is the entrance to SeaMountain, Kau's only condo complex. To get to the beach park and restaurant take the turn-off marked Punaluu Park, which is less than a mile farther along Hwy 11.

Places to Stay

SeaMountain at Punaluu (☎ 928-6211, (800) 344-7675), Box 340, Pahala, HI 96777, is a comfortable condo complex with all the amenities you'd expect to find in Kona, but with none of the crowding. It has a pool, tennis courts, a golf course and new overseas owners who plan to develop it into a major five-star golf resort. In the meantime it's a low-key getaway.

The studios are big and almost as large as one-bedroom units elsewhere, while some one-bedroom units are two-level with cathedral ceilings. Some units have phones. Rates start at $83 for studios, $104 for one-bedroom units and $131 for two-bedroom units. Ocean views cost about $10 more. There's a two-day minimum stay.

Places to Eat

The *Punaluu Black Sands Restaurant* has a rather mundane lunch buffet from 10.30 am to 2 pm daily for $10.95. Tour buses start pouring in around 11.30 am. Dinner is from 5.30 to 8.30 pm Wednesday to Sunday, with dishes ranging from about $10 to $20.

The *Golf Course Broiler* at SeaMountain serves lunch from 10.30 am to 3.30 pm daily and breakfast on weekends. Prices are moderate, with burgers and simple dishes from $6 to $10.

PAHALA

Pahala is really two little towns side by side. Down by the mill it's still a working sugar town with old dusty shacks, cars rusting in the yards and 'Beware of Dog' signs. This part of town has a 1920s movie theatre, a little general store and big banyan trees.

The north side of town has tract homes, a hospital, bank, gas stations, a community centre and a modern grocery mart.

Kau Agribusiness, which runs the mill, has 15,000 acres of sugar cane planted for about 15 miles in either direction from Pahala. The production of sugar is in a gradual decline in these parts and they are diversifying with macadamia nut trees and oranges.

WOOD VALLEY RETREAT CENTRE

About four miles up the slopes from Pahala is remote Wood Valley and the Buddhist temple and retreat centre of Nechung Dorje Drayang Ling. The temple was built in the early 1900s by Japanese sugar cane labourers who lived in the valley.

In 1975 a Tibetan lama, Nechung Rinpoche, took up residence here and in 1980 the Dalai Lama visited to dedicate the temple. Since that time many Tibetan lamas have visited and conducted programmes. In addition to its teachings of Buddhism, the centre is also used by groups conducting Vipassana and Zen meditation, yoga classes and other New Age and spiritual programmes. If you're interested, the centre can send you a list of workshops for the coming year.

The retreat centre (☎ 928-8539), Box 250, Pahala, HI 96777, is a two-storey building with a meditation hall and private rooms on the upper floor. The ground floor has two dormitories, a kitchen/dining area and a library of books and videos on Buddhist culture. Guests are free to use the library and join in the morning service.

At times when there are no programmes going on, the centre is open to individual guests. Room rates are $20/35 for singles/doubles and dormitory beds cost $15. Weekly rates are six times the daily. For those seeking a peaceful retreat the temple is a special place.

TO HAWAII VOLCANOES NATIONAL PARK

Hawaii Volcanoes National Park begins 12 miles from Pahala. Hwy 11 crosses an 11-mile stretch of the park. There are no fees to drive through on the highway nor to explore the Mauna Loa side of the park.

Kilauea's south-west rift zone runs through this part of the Kau Desert, makai of the road. The rift runs for 20 miles, all the way from the summit of Kilauea down to the coast.

The Footprints Trail starts a quarter of a mile beyond the 38-mile marker. This three-quarter-mile trail leads to the cast footprints of a group of Hawaiians killed when a cloud of volcanic ash rained down over them in 1790.

Farther down Hwy 11, past Namakani Paio Campground, is Mauna Loa Rd. There are tree moulds near the turn-off, a hiking trail through a native forest and bird park a mile farther up, and the trailhead to the Mauna Loa summit at the end of the road.

You'll know you're getting closer to the centre of Hawaii Volcanoes National Park when the signs start reading 'Caution, Fault Zones. Watch for Cracks in Road'.

Hawaii Volcanoes National Park

Hawaii Volcanoes National Park is hands down the most unique park in the US National Parks system. It's a huge area which not only contains two active volcanoes, but terrain ranging from tropical black-sand beaches to the subarctic summit of Mauna Loa.

The centrepiece of the park is Kilauea Caldera, the sunken centre of Kilauea Volcano. This still-steaming crater, where molten lava boils just a few feet beneath the surface, is said to be the home of Madame

Pele, goddess of volcanoes. Both a foot trail and a paved road circle the caldera's rim.

The park's landscape is geologically awesome with dozens of craters and cinder cones, hills piled high with pumice, and hardened rivers of lava which have frozen rock-solid on the hillsides complete with ripples and waves. There are also native bird reserves, rainforests and fern groves which have either been spared by lava flows or grown over them.

The park is one of Hawaii's best places for camping and hiking. It has three free drive-up camping grounds as well as back-country camping, and 140 miles of amazingly varied hiking trails.

The park encompasses about a quarter of a million acres of land – more than the entire island of Molokai – and is growing. It even has a new black-sand beach, courtesy of Kilauea's most recent series of eruptions.

Kilauea's south-east rift has been actively flowing since 1983, taking everything in its path with it. The coastal road to Puna was blocked by lava in 1988. The Wahaula Visitor Center on the south coast went under the next year and the entire village of Kalapana, with more than 100 homes, was buried in lava in 1990. The current series of eruptions, which is the longest in recorded history, has spewed out nearly two billion cubic yards of new lava.

When there's action, Kilauea's flows generally show up best after dark. Then, lava tubes on the mountainside glow red in the night sky and lava lakes at the top of vents reflect light onto passing clouds.

Although many visitors expect to see lava fountains spurting up into the air, this is the exception rather than the rule. It's quite possible that without a helicopter ride you'll see no evidence of molten lava at all. But whenever Pele does put on one of her spectacular firework displays, cars stream in from all directions. In Hawaii, people generally run *to* volcanoes, not away *from* them.

Volcanic Formations

Hawaii's volcanoes are shield volcanoes, formed by repeated gentle eruptions, build-ing up over time as thin layers of lava are deposited one on top of another. As the mountains get higher and wider, long cracks break open down their gently stretched slopes. These are called fault zones, or rift zones, and lava eruptions may come from these cracks (as is currently the case with Kilauea) as well as from the summit crater.

Craters are formed when volcanic hills release their lava and collapse back into themselves.

'Pahoehoe' and 'aa' are Hawaiian words which are now used worldwide to describe the earth's two major types of lava. Pahoehoe is the rivers of lava which flow smooth and unbroken. When pahoehoe hardens it often twists into rope-like coils and swirls as the outer skin cools and stiffens while the hotter lava underneath continues to move a little.

Aa is rough and jumbled lava which moves so slowly that the tip of the flow hardens. It's only the molten lava pushing from behind that keeps the flow moving, with the lava at the front piling up and falling over itself, slowing rolling and clunking its way along.

Orientation

The park's main road is Crater Rim Rd which circles the moonscape sights of Kilauea Caldera. It's possible to take in the drive-up sites in an hour – and if that's all the time you have it's unquestionably worth it. Still, it's far better to give yourself a good three hours to allow time for a few short walks, and stops at the visitors' centre and museum.

The park's other scenic drive is the Chain of Craters Rd which leads south 23 miles to the coast, ending at the site of the most recent lava activity. Allow about three hours down and back to stop at all the scenic points along the way.

While you can get a good sense of the place in one full day, it would be easy to spend days, if not weeks, exploring this vast and varied park.

Information

The park's 24-hour hotline (☎ 967-7977) has recorded information on current volcanic

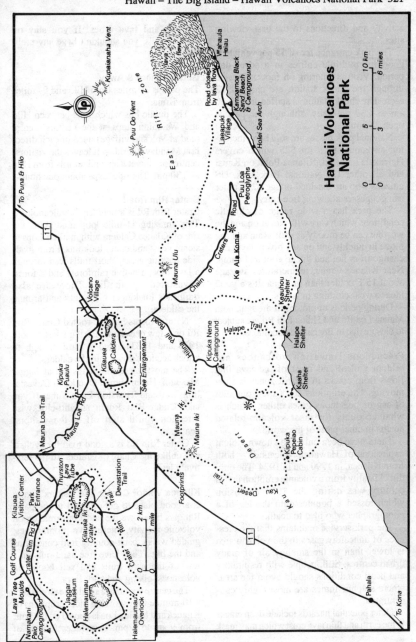

Hawaii Volcanoes National Park

activity and directions to the best viewing sites.

The park entrance fee of $5 per vehicle is good for multiple entries in a seven-day period. Visitors entering on foot or bicycle through the check station are charged $2 each. The check station is staffed from 8.30 am to 4.30 pm daily, although the park is open 24 hours.

National park passes are sold here, including an annual pass for $25 which covers Haleakala on Maui, Kilauea Point on Kauai and all other US National Park sites. US citizens who are disabled or age 62 or older can get passes allowing free entry.

The park has a wide range of climatic conditions which vary with elevation and the weather can be moody as well. Rain and fog move in quickly and on any given day it can change from hot and dry to cool and damp. Near Kilauea Crater, temperatures average about 15°F cooler than in Kona. It's a good idea to wear clothing in layers.

During periods of prolonged drought, both Mauna Loa Rd and Hilina Pali Rd are subject to closure due to fire hazard conditions.

Precautions Hawaiian volcanoes are seldom violent and most of the lava that flows from cracks in the rift zones is slow moving. The eruptions don't spew out a lot of ash or poisonous gases either, which is what accounts for most volcano-related deaths in other parts of the world.

There have been only two known violent explosions of Hawaiian volcanoes – both from Kilauea, in 1790 and in 1924. The only direct fatality from a volcanic eruption in this century was during the 1924 explosion which tossed a boulder onto the leg of a photographer who bled to death.

The park service maintains that the presence of unhealthy gases in the volcano area is lower than in the smoggy air of many urban centres. Still, people with respiratory and heart conditions should avoid the areas where sulphur fumes are most highly concentrated.

Other potential hazards include deep cracks in the earth and thin lava crust which may mask

hollows and lava tubes. If you stay on marked trails, you shouldn't have any problems.

Getting There & Away

The park is 29 miles from Hilo and 97 miles from Kona.

The public bus which runs between Hilo and Waiohinu stops at the visitors' centre (and at Volcano village) once in each direction Monday to Friday. It leaves the visitors' centre for Hilo at 8 am and returns from Hilo at 2.30 pm. The ride takes about one hour.

Crater Rim Road

Crater Rim Rd is a field trip in vulcanology. This amazing 11-mile loop road skirts the rim of Kilauea Caldera with marked stops at steam vents and crater lookouts. From roadside parking areas, short trails lead through a lava tube, a native rainforest and a forest devastated by pumice. There are also trailheads for longer hikes into and around the caldera.

Natural forces have re-routed Crater Rim Rd on a few occasions. Earthquakes in both 1975 and 1983 rattled it hard enough to knock sections down into the caldera.

The most interesting stops are at Jaggar Museum, Halemaumau Overlook, Devastation Trail and Thurston Lava Tube. If you take Crater Rim Rd in an anti-clockwise direction you'll start off at the visitors' centre.

Crater Rim Rd is a good road for cyclists and unlike the Chain of Craters Rd it's relatively level.

Kilauea Visitor Center The visitors' centre is a good place to get oriented to the park. Rangers here have the latest information on volcanic activity, interpretive programmes, guided walks, back-country trail conditions and the like. They have free hand-outs on a few of the park trails and sell books on volcanoes, hiking and park flora.

The centre contains a small **theatre** where a 10-minute film showing older eruptions of Kilauea and Mauna Loa is played on the hour from 9 am to 4 pm. It includes footage of rivers of lava flowing 20 miles an hour, a 13-mile-long curtain of fire and a 1900-foot fountain of lava.

In addition, commercial videos of the most recent eruptions run continuously in the centre's tiny museum where you'll also find a few volcano-related exhibits. The centre (☎ 967-7311) is open daily from 7.45 am to 5 pm and will store backpacks for park visitors.

Volcano Art Center The Volcano Art Center (☎ 967-7511), which is next door to the visitors' centre, sells island pottery, paintings, weavings, woodwork, stained glass and other arts & crafts. The work is high-quality, with many 'one-of-a-kind' items.

The centre is in a former Volcano House lodge, built in 1877. The nonprofit organisation which runs the place offers workshops on painting, crafts, vulcanology, music, dance and more. It's open from 9 am to 5 pm daily.

Sulphur Banks The first stop beyond the art centre is the Sulphur Banks, where the dayglo colours and piles of steaming rocks look like a landscape from another planet.

This is one of many areas where Kilauea lets off steam, releasing hundreds of tons of sulphuric gases daily. As the steam reaches the surface, it deposits sulphur around the mouths of the vents, giving them a froth of fluorescent yellow crystals. The putrid smell of rotten eggs is hydrogen sulphide.

Steam Vents There are a couple of open nonsulphurous steam vents at the next pulloff, although they're nothing special to look at. Rainwater which sinks into the earth is heated by the hot rocks below and rises back up as steam.

More interesting is the two-minute walk beyond the vents out to a part of the crater rim aptly called **Steaming Bluff**. The cooler it is, the more steam there'll be. A plaque on the rim tells a legend about the struggles between Pele and the pig-god Kamapuaa.

Jaggar Museum This museum is worth

stopping at both for its displays and for the fine view of Halemaumau Crater. Halemaumau sits within Kilauea Crater and is sometimes referred to as the 'crater within the crater'. Detailed interpretive plaques at the lookout explain the geological workings of volcanoes. There's also a good view of Mauna Loa to the west, 20 miles away.

The museum is named after Thomas A Jaggar, former head geologist at the Massachusetts Institute of Technology, and the first scientist to undertake in-depth studies of Kilauea. Jaggar led a group of geologists who lowered the first thermometer into Halemaumau's lava lake in the summer of 1911. It registered 1832°F before melting. Today an observatory at this site has Kilauea completely wired and it's the most studied volcano anywhere in the world.

Jaggar Museum is open from 8.30 am to 5 pm daily. It has photo displays, a section on Pele, seismographs, tiltmeters and printed updates showing the current status of volcanic activity. The museum also sells video tapes and books.

The museum is at **Uwekahuna Bluff**, the site of an infamous hut which once sat right on the ledge. Local kahunas are said to have tricked people into entering the building where they slipped through a false-bottomed floor to the crater pit below.

After leaving the museum you'll pass the south-west rift, where you can stop and take a look at the wide fissure slicing across the earth.

Halemaumau Overlook The next attraction is Halemaumau Overlook, where there's a five-minute walk to the crater rim. For at least 100 years (from 1823, when missionary William Ellis first recorded the sight in writing) Halemaumau was a boiling lake of lava which alternately rose and fell, overflowing and then receding.

This fiery lake attracted people from all over the world. Some observers compared it to the fires of hell while others saw primeval creation. Mark Twain wrote about staring down at:

...circles and serpents and streaks of lightning all twined and wreathed and tied together ... I have seen Vesuvius since, but it was a mere toy, a child's volcano, a soup kettle, compared to this.

In 1924 seeping water touched off a massive steam explosion which blew up the lava lake, causing huge boulders and mud to rain down and setting off a lightning storm. When it was over, the crater had doubled in size and the lava activity ceased. The crust has since cooled, although the crater still steams. The area is pungent with the smell of sulphur.

All of the Big Island is Pele's territory, but Halemaumau is her home. During special ceremonies the hula is performed in her honour here and throughout the year those wishing to appease Pele leave flowers, coins and bottles of gin at the crater rim.

Ohelo, a bush about two feet high with clusters of bright red berries, is one of the early takers to lava and grows near the site. Before eating any of the tart berries, which are said to personify Pele's sister Hiiaka, some should first be offered to Pele.

The Halemaumau Overlook is at the start of the **Halemaumau Trail**, which runs three miles across Kilauea Caldera to the visitors' centre. Although few people who aren't hiking the full trail venture past the overlook, it's an easy half-mile walk to the site of a 1982 lava flow and well worth the 30 minutes it takes to walk there and back. The spewed lava along the trail has amazing textures and colours and there's an eerie sense of the earth's raw power.

Devastation Trail After the Halemaumau Overlook, Crater Rim Rd continues across the barren Kau Desert and then through the fallout area of the 1959 eruption of Kilauea Iki Crater. Ash and pumice blown south-west of the crater buried a mile of Crater Rim Rd eight feet deep. The road had to be ploughed by tractors, much like clearing snow after a blizzard.

Devastation Trail is a half-mile walk across a former rainforest devastated by cinder and pumice from that eruption. Everything green was wiped out. What remains today are dead ohia trees, stripped bare and sun-bleached white, standing stark against the black landscape. It's so barren and desolate it could be the movie set for a post-nuclear scene.

The trail is over a wooden boardwalk, with parking lots on each end. The prominent cinder cone along the way is **Puu Puai**, 'gushing hill', formed during the 1959 eruption. The north-east end of the trail looks down into Kilauea Iki Crater.

The Chain of Craters Rd intersects with Crater Rim Rd opposite the parking area for Devastation Trail.

Thurston Lava Tube On the east side of the Chain of Craters Rd intersection, Crater Rim Rd passes through the rainforest of native tree ferns and ohia which covers Kilauea's windward slope.

The Thurston Lava Tube Trail is an enjoyable 15-minute loop walk which starts out in ohia forest, goes through an impressive lava tube and then through a fern grove. The cibotium tree ferns here grow to 20 feet high.

Lava tubes are formed when the outer crust of a river of lava starts to harden but the liquid lava beneath the surface continues to flow on through. After the flow has drained out, the hard shell remains. Thurston Lava Tube is a grand example – it's tunnel-like, and almost big enough to run a train through.

You'll probably hear a lot of birdsong along this walk. The apapane, a native honeycreeper, is easy to spot at the upper end of the trail. It has a red body and silvery-white underside and flies from flower to flower drinking from the yellow blossoms of the mamane tree and the red pompom-like flowers of the ohia tree.

Kilauea Iki Crater When Kilauea Iki burst open in a fiery inferno in November 1959 the whole crater floor turned into a bubbling pool of molten lava. Its fountains reached record heights of 1900 feet, lighting the evening sky with a bright orange glow for miles around. At its peak it gushed out two million tons of lava an hour.

From Kilauea Iki Overlook there's a good view of the mile-wide crater below. Today a trail runs across the crater floor. The hike is not dissimilar to walking on ice – here too there's a lake below the hardened surface, although in this case it's molten lava not water. For more information see Hiking Trails in this section.

Chain of Craters Road
The Chain of Craters Rd winds 23 miles down the southern slopes of Kilauea Volcano, ending abruptly at a lava flow on the Puna Coast. It's a good paved two-lane road, although there's no gas, food or other services along the way.

There are striking vistas of the coastline far below and for miles the predominant view is of long fingers of lava reaching down to the sea.

In some places the road slices through lava and in other places it's paved over it. You'll see both aa lava, which is crusty and rough, and pahoehoe lava, which is as shiny and black as fresh tar. You can sometimes find thin filaments of volcanic glass known as Pele's hair in the cracks and crevices.

In addition to endless lava expanses, the road takes in an impressive collection of sights, including a handful of craters that you can literally pull up to the rims of and peer into. Some of the craters are so new there's no sign of life, while others are thickly forested with ohia lehua, wild orchids and ferns.

The Chain of Craters Rd once connected through to Hwy 130 and Hwy 137 allowing traffic between the volcano and Hilo via Puna. Lava flows closed the road in 1969 but by 1979 it was back in service, re-routed slightly. Over the past few years flows from Kilauea's active east rift have again cut the link. This time the lava has buried a six-mile stretch of the road extending from a mile west of the former Wahaula Visitor Center clear across the former village of Kalapana to the east.

Hilina Pali Road
Hilina Pali Rd starts 2¼ miles down Chain of Craters Rd and leads five miles in to Kipuka Nene camping

ground. It's another 3½ miles to Hilina Pali, a lookout at 2283 feet with a view of the south-east coast. The end of the road is the trailhead for the Kau Desert Trail and for the Kaaha and Hilina Pali trails which lead down to the coast. They are all hot, dry back-country trails.

Mauna Ulu In 1969, eruptions from Kilauea's east rift began building a new lava shield which eventually rose 400 feet above its surroundings. It was named Mauna Ulu, 'growing mountain'.

By the time the flow stopped in 1974 it had covered 10,000 acres of parkland and added 200 acres of new land to the coast.

It also buried 12 miles of the Chain of Craters Rd in lava as deep as 100 metres. There's still a small portion of the old road left. You can drive up to the lava flow by taking the turn-off on the left 3½ miles down Chain of Craters Rd. Just beyond this is Mauna Ulu itself.

As you continue down the Chain of Craters Rd you'll be passing over Mauna Ulu's massive flows.

Ke Ala Koma About halfway along the road, at an elevation of 2000 feet, is Ke Ala Koma, a covered shelter with picnic tables and a superb ocean view. This would be a great place to unpack a lunch.

From here the road begins to descend along a series of winding switchbacks, some deeply cut through lava flows.

Puu Loa Petroglyphs The Puu Loa Trail leads to a field of petroglyphs carved into the lava by early Hawaiians. The site, about a mile in, is along an ancient trail between Kau and Puna and has one of the largest '-concentrations of petroglyphs in Hawaii. A boardwalk runs around a large group of them and offers some fine photo opportunities. Puu Loa (long hill) was also a place where Hawaiians brought the umbilical cords of their babies in the hope that burying them there would bring their children long lives.

The marked trailhead begins on the Chain

of Craters Rd midway between the 16 and 17-mile markers.

Holei Sea Arch About 2½ miles after the petroglyphs and just before the 19-mile marker, look for the sign marking the Holei Sea Arch. This rugged section of the coast has sharply eroded lava cliffs, called **Holei Pali**, which are constantly being pounded by crashing surf.

The high rock arch carved out of one of the cliffs is impressive, although the wave action has numbered its days. The ocean here is a deep rich blue.

Laeapuki Village A short trail leading to the site of the old Hawaiian fishing village of Laeapuki begins at the side of the road 2½ miles after the Holei Sea Arch. Look for a plaque marking the trailhead. The walk in to the coast only takes about five minutes.

The residents of this seaside fishing village turned to cattle and goat ranching in the 19th century and most of the ruins in the area are stone walls that date to the ranching era. In the 1920s Laeapuki was abandoned.

The coast fronting Laeapuki is of low lava sea cliffs. There are a few tiny picturesque coves with pockets of black sand, although they often get inundated when the surf is high and water conditions here are treacherous.

A **coastal trail** connects Laeapuki to Kamoamoa Black Sand Beach, three-quarters of a mile away.

Kamoamoa Beach Kamoamoa is Hawaii's newest black-sand beach, formed in the late 1980s when Kilauea's hot lava hit the ocean, exploded into a zillion tiny fragments and washed up on low sea cliffs here.

The white waves washing up on the beach create a striking contrast against the deep, radiantly black sand. The waves can be huge and break high and there are strong and dangerous currents.

As the lava flows have slowed, the beach's impressive mounds of sand are being reclaimed by the sea, and the rocky coastal cliffs are again re-emerging. Just how much

sand you'll find will depend upon what Madame Pele has been up to lately!

Kamoamoa Beach is one of the park's three drive-up camping grounds. It's also the site of an old Hawaiian village and the ruins of **Moa Heiau** are on the grounds. Most of the stone walls in the area are not from pre-contact time but were built by cattle ranchers in the 1880s.

Rangers staff a trailer that acts as a visitors' centre and there are restrooms. Drinking water is trucked in, but check with the ranger to see if it's drinkable without treatment, as the bacteria count is occasionally high.

End of the Road The Chain of Craters Road ends at a lava flow about a mile before the site of the former Wahaula Visitor Center, which was destroyed by lava in the summer of 1989.

It's still possible to visit that area via a 'trail' across the flow that leads to the nearby Wahaula Heiau. The heiau was mysteriously spared when the lava parted at its walls and flowed around it on the way to the sea. The site is now more impressive than ever and the 2½-mile round-trip hike is a hauntingly beautiful walk over crisp, shiny lava. The trail, which begins at road's end, is marked and easy to follow, although you need to watch your footing.

If you plan to visit the heiau, give yourself about 1½ hours and be sure to take a flashlight if it looks like you'll be cutting it close. Once the sun is down it gets dark quickly; between sharp jags of lava and the cracks and holes in the brittle surface, this is not a hike to do in the dark. Wear sturdy shoes with good traction and expect a hot walk if you hike in the middle of the day.

Wahaula Heiau Wahaula Heiau was the first luakini heiau built in Hawaii. Its construction is credited to Paao, a Tahitian high priest who migrated here in the 12th century. Paao not only introduced human sacrifice into temple ceremonies, but also the concept of mana, a divine power which could be held within temple grounds as well as by the royal chiefs who worshipped there.

A strict social system of kapus (taboos) were enacted to protect that mana. Commoners were forbidden to eat the same foods or walk the same grounds as chiefs for fear they would absorb the chiefs' mana. Those who broke the kapus were put to death.

Mana was an elusive element that could be lost. When a temple no longer had its mana it was abandoned and a new one built elsewhere. Wahaula Heiau never lost it – it was the last luakini temple where royalty worshipped before the Hawaiian gods were abandoned.

The heiau once had altars, idols and an oracle tower, although only the stone platform remains. The lava flow that left only twisted, rusting beams standing at the visitors' centre, 150 feet away, skirted around the main heiau and the high priest's house. Apparently it still has some mana left!

Mauna Loa Road

Mauna Loa Rd leads off Hwy 11 about 2¼ miles west of the visitors' centre. The world's highest active volcano, Mauna Loa has erupted more than 18 times in the past century. The last eruption began in March 1984 and lasted 21 days.

The **Mauna Loa Trail**, which climbs the slopes of Mauna Loa, begins at the end of the road, 13½ miles from Hwy 11. (For more details, see the Hiking Trails section.)

Lava Tree Moulds Near the start of Mauna Loa Rd there's a turn-off to some lava tree moulds. These tube-like holes were formed when a lava flow engulfed the rainforest that stood here. Because the trees were so waterlogged the lava hardened around them instead of burning them on contact. As the trees disintegrated, deep holes where the trunks once stood were left in the ground.

The first of the moulds are very close to the parking lot, making it easy to get a quick glimpse.

Kipuka Puaulu Kipuka Puaulu, a unique sanctuary for native birds and plants, is about 1½ miles up Mauna Loa Rd. A mile-long loop trail runs through this 100-acre oasis of native forest.

About 400 years ago a major lava flow from Mauna Loa's north-east rift covered most of the surrounding area. Pele spared this bit of land when the flow parted, creating an island forest in a sea of lava. In Hawaiian, it's known as a *kipuka*.

Kipuka Puaulu is a tiny and unique ecopreserve of rare endemic plants, insects and birds. The lava that surrounds the kipuka has served as a protective barrier against intruding species.

Koa is the largest of the trees here. The younger trees have fern-like leaves which are replaced with flat, crescent-shaped leaf stalks as the koa matures and rises above the forest floor. The tree provides habitat for ferns and climbing peperomia that take root in its moist bark.

Kipuka Puaulu is quiet, except for the chirpings of birds. The natives include the inquisitive elepaio and three honeycreepers – the amakihi, apapane and iiwi. The birds are sparrow size and brightly coloured. The honeycreepers have slender curved beaks that enable them to drink nectar from the flowers of native trees.

Also along the trail is a **lava tube** in the dark depths of which a unique big-eyed spider was discovered only a few years back.

Hiking Trails

The park has an extensive network of hiking trails, from sea level to over 13,000 feet. The hikes range from many short and easy ones to serious back-country treks. Trails strike out in a number of directions – across crater floors, down to secluded beaches, across the Kau Desert, through native forests and up to snow-capped Mauna Loa.

Crater Rim Trail The Crater Rim Trail is an 11-mile hiking trail which runs roughly parallel to Crater Rim Rd. On the north side the trail is along the crater rim, while on the south side it runs outside the paved road.

Because the vehicle road is designed to take in the main sights, you'll actually miss a few of them by hiking. If you have wheels of some sort, you might want to consider riding around the crater rim and saving your hiking legs for trails into areas inaccessible by car or bike.

Halemaumau Trail Diagonally across the road from the visitors' centre there are signs marking the way to a number of trailheads, including the Halemaumau Trail.

The first section of the Halemaumau Trail passes briefly through a moist **ohia forest**, with tall ferns and flowering ginger. It then descends about 500 feet to the floor of **Kilauea Caldera** and continues for three miles across the surface of this still-active volcano.

In ancient times the caldera was much deeper, but in the past century overflows from Halemaumau Crater as well as eruptions from the caldera floor have built it up.

The process is easy to visualise as the trail crosses flow after flow, beginning with one from 1974. It continues over flows from 1885, 1894, 1954, 1971, 1982 and each distinguished by a different shade of black. The trail is marked with ahu, or piles of lava rocks.

Shortly after breakfast on 30 April 1982, geologists at the Hawaiian Volcano Observatory watched as their seismographs and tiltmeters unexpectedly warned of an imminent eruption. The park service quickly closed off Halemaumau Trail and cleared hikers from the crater floor. Before noon a half-mile fissure began to spew a million cubic metres of lava!

This 1982 flow created a landscape which is both very barren and richly beautiful. Some of the spatter formed high brittle mounds, many with small hollow areas. They have incredible textures, unusual shapes and deep shades of black accented with rich shades of orange, rust and ochre. Sunlight glitters on tiny iridescent bubbles that have cooled in the lava. Ferns have already taken hold inside the cracks of steam vents which act like little terrariums.

The trail ends about 3½ miles from the visitors' centre at **Halemaumau Overlook**.

Needless to say there's no shade on the trail and it can be hot. Take water with you as there's none at the lookout.

Kilauea Iki Trail When Kilauea Iki Crater exploded in 1959, its lava fountains set a new height record of 1900 feet. When the ash finally settled, it covered the entire area south-west of the crater.

Kilauea Iki Trail begins near the parking lot of the Thurston Lava Tube and descends 400 feet to the crater floor. From there it goes clear across the mile-long crater, passing the main vent on the way. The crater floor is still steaming and there's molten lava beneath the hardened surface.

After you ascend the crater wall on the far side, you'll be on **Byron Ledge**, the ledge which separates Kilauea Iki from Kilauea Caldera. By looping around to the right, you can get back to the parking lot via the Crater Rim Trail which skirts the north rim of Kilauea Iki. Altogether this loop is about 3½ miles long.

If you want to check it out before hiking, there's a drive-up lookout half a mile north of the Thurston Lava Tube.

Footprints Trail The Footprints Trail is the beginning of the Mauna Iki Trail which leads to a network of trails through the Kau Desert. The trailhead is between the 37 and 38-mile markers on Hwy 11, nine miles south of park headquarters. The footprints are an easy three-quarter-mile hike in from the highway.

In 1790, a violent and massive explosion at Kilauea wiped out a regiment of soldiers retreating to Kau after attacking Kamehameha's sacred Waipio Valley. They were literally stopped in their tracks, suffocated by a rare cloud of poisonous gases. A shower of hot mud and ashes hardened around them, leaving a permanent cast of their footprints.

Two hundred years later, you can still count the toes in a few of the prints, although it takes some imagination these days as many have recently been damaged by vandals. Hoping a lower profile might stem the random vandalism, the park has removed the

Footprints Trail sign from the roadside trailhead. Still, it's a pleasant walk and a good trail to do with small children.

Halape Trail The 7¼-mile trail to Halape starts from Kipuka Nene camping ground off Hilina Pali Rd.

Halape was an idyllic beachfront camping ground bordered by coconut trees until 29 November 1975 when the strongest earthquake in 100 years shook the Big Island. Just before dawn, rock slides from the upper slopes sent most of the 36 campers running toward the sea, where the coastline suddenly sank. As the beach submerged beneath their feet a series of tsunamis swept the campers up, carrying them first out to sea and then tossing them back up on shore. Miraculously only two people died.

The earthquake left a fine **sandy cove** inland of the former beach. There are strong currents in the open ocean beyond the cove. Halape has catchment water, a pit toilet and a three-walled shelter.

Mauna Loa Trail Mauna Loa Trail begins at the end of Mauna Loa Rd, 13½ miles north of Hwy 11. It's about an hour's drive between the trailhead and the visitors' centre where overnight hikers are required to register (and where you can get more information on the trail).

This is a rugged 18-mile trail that ascends 6600 feet. The ascent is gradual but the elevation makes it a serious hike and it takes a minimum of three days.

There are two simple cabins available on a first-come, first-served basis. *Red Hill cabin* has eight bunks and *Mauna Loa summit cabin* has 12.

The trail rises out of an ohia forest and above the tree line seven miles to Red Hill at 10,035 feet. This leg of the hike takes four to five hours. From Red Hill there are fine views of Mauna Kea to the north and Haleakala on Maui to the north-west.

It's 11 miles and a full day's hike from Red Hill to the summit cabin at 13,250 feet. The summit has a subarctic climate and temperatures normally drop to freezing point at night all year round. Winter snow storms can last a few days and bring snow packs as deep as nine feet. Occasionally snow falls as low as Red Hill and covers the upper end of the trail.

It is important to acclimatise as altitude sickness is not uncommon. Common symptoms are headache, nausea and shortness of breath. For minor symptoms, deep breathing brings some relief, as does lying down with your head lower than your feet. If the symptoms are more serious get to a lower elevation immediately.

Hypothermia from the cold and wind is another hazard. A good windproof jacket, wool sweater, winter-rated sleeping bag and rain gear are all essential.

Back-country Hiking Hiking shelters and simple cabins are available along some of the longer back-country trails. There's no fee to use them.

In addition to the two cabins along the Mauna Loa Trail, there's a cabin at Kipuka Pepeiao along the Kau Desert Trail and coastal area shelters at Keauhou, Halape and Kaaha. All have limited water catchment, which should be treated. The visitors' centre keeps track of current water supplies and trail conditions.

All overnight hikers are required to register at the visitors' centre before heading out and upon returning. Essential backpacking equipment that the park recommends for any of the back-country trails includes a first aid kit, a flashlight with extra batteries, a minimum of two quarts of water, emergency food, a compass, broken-in boots, complete rain gear, cooking stove with fuel, sunscreen and a hat. For a more comprehensive checklist write to Hawaii Volcanoes National Park, HI 96718.

Volcano

The village of Volcano, about a mile east of the park, has two general stores with gas pumps, a post office, a takeaway diner, a restaurant and a growing number of B&B-type places to stay.

Places to Stay – Volcano Village

Yabuki Satoshi, who runs *Holo Holo In* (☎ 967-7950), Box 784, Volcano, HI 96785, is a former backpacker who has travelled the globe and settled in Volcano. The inn is only partially up and running as Yabuki works as an electrician full time and is still working out the logistics of running an inn single-handed. Still, he's built a large rambling house, put in 16 beds and taken a youth hostel management course, so if you're looking for a cheap place to stay it's worth checking out.

The four simple bedrooms are furnished with a combination of bunk beds and double beds. Rates are $15 per person and couples can have a room to themselves for $30. There are hot showers and a shared kitchen. Holo Holo In is a couple of blocks north of the Volcano village post office. To reserve, either write or call after 4.30 pm.

At *My Island B&B* (☎ 967-7216), Box 100, Volcano, HI 96785, Gordon and Joanne Morse rent out three bedrooms with shared bathroom in their home for $30/50 a single/double, including breakfast. It's a quarter of a mile past Kilauea Lodge, on the left after Wright Rd. Gordon is very outgoing and can pile you high with information on the Big Island which he proclaims is 'the *only* Hawaiian Island worth visiting'. The living room is full of books on volcanoes, from photo essays to geological tomes, a few written by former guests.

There are also three units separate from the house, each with a private entrance and bathroom. Two units cost $40/60 while an older unit, which is not quite as spiffy but is larger and has a kitchen, is $65. My Island also acts as a booking agent for other B&Bs around the island, most of which are in the $50 to $90 range.

Kilauea Volcano Kabins (☎ 967-7448) consist of four pleasant units built by Ron Ober, a skilled carpenter. Two of the units are in a modern duplex cabin. They have big picture windows looking out to a fern and ohia forest, electric heaters, queen beds, bathrooms with tubs, and a refrigerator, toaster oven and coffee pot. These comfort-able units are good value at $45/50 a single/double. Add $5 if you stay just one night.

There's also an adjacent house with two more units. The 1st-floor unit has a separate bedroom, a full kitchen, a living room with a sofabed and lots of natural wood. The upstairs is a big, open studio with wood-beam ceilings, a king bed, wood stove and a sofabed. Both cost $65 for two people and $10 extra for each additional person.

All units have phones with free local calls, and coffee and muffins are delivered in the morning. Ron is currently working on a Caribbean sailboat and the units are being handled by Volcano Comfort.

Volcano Comfort (☎ 967-7448) Box 605, Volcano, HI, 96785, is a spacious two-bedroom cottage next door to Steve and Donna Stephenson's home. It's a pleasantly rustic place with exposed-beam ceilings, a wood stove, full kitchen and 1½ baths. Steve, a high school science teacher, has plans to make the cottage handicapped accessible. Rates, which include a continental breakfast, are $65 for a single or double, $10 for each additional person.

Kilauea Lodge (☎ 967-7366), Box 116, Volcano, HI 96785, on the main road in Volcano village, has four delightfully renovated rooms in what was formerly a YMCA dormitory. They have the sort of country comfort you'd find in a fine inn, with working fireplaces (the only heat source), high ceilings, electric blankets, quilts and private bathrooms with tubs. The rate is $85.

A new building which has eight large cheery rooms and a common area with a large fireplace costs $85 for one or two people. Avoid rooms No 7 and 8 which are right off the common room and can get a bit noisy. There's also a two-room cottage for $105. Prices include a full breakfast from the menu in the lodge's restaurant.

The state maintains *Niaulani Cabin*, a housekeeping cabin, half a mile east of the national park. The cabin sits all by itself in the seven-acre ohia forest of Kilauea State Recreation Area, on Kalanikoa Rd near Volcano village. The cabin has two bedrooms, a living room, hot showers, a stove and refrigerator. Rates are $10/17 for singles/doubles, and up to $30 for six people, but it's a long shot getting in. For reservations contact the Division of State Parks (☎ 933-4200), Box 936, 75 Aupuni St, Hilo, HI 96721, where you also pick up the key.

Places to Stay – National Park
Namakani Paio Cabins are 10 dreary, windowless plywood cabins at the national park's Namakani Paio Campground. Each has one double bed, two single beds and electric lights, but there are no power outlets or heating. There are communal showers and restrooms. It can get cold at night so if you have a sleeping bag bring it along. (Or bring a tent as well and you can stay in the adjacent camping ground for free.)

Booking is done through Volcano House where you pay and pick up your bag of linen. The rate of $31 is for up to four people and there's a $15 deposit for keys and linen.

Volcano House (☎ 967-7321), Box 53, Hawaii Volcanoes National Park, HI 96713, is opposite the national park visitors' centre. Although it has an enviable location, perched right on the rim of Kilauea Caldera, most of the room views are disappointing. The lower-level rooms look out onto a walkway and even some of those on the upper floor have only a partial view of the crater.

The current hotel dates from 1941. Many of the rooms are plain and tired and noise carries through the louvered windows which open onto the hallway. Rates are $79 to $131.

Camping The park has three drive-up camping grounds. Camping is free and the camping grounds are seldom crowded, although things can pick up in summer. There's no registration or reservation system – it's simply on a first come, first serve basis. Camping is officially limited to seven days per camping ground per year. Rangers patrol the grounds and they're quite helpful and friendly.

Nights are crisp and cool at Namakani Paio (4000 feet) and Kipuka Nene (3000 feet).

Namakani Paio Campground is the busiest of the three camping grounds as it's about three miles west of the visitors' centre, just off Hwy 11. If you're on your way between Hilo and Kona it's a convenient place to stop for the night. The open tent sites are in a small meadow with little privacy, although it's surrounded by fragrant eucalyptus trees. It's about a one-mile hike to the Jaggar Museum and Crater Rim Trail.

Kipuka Nene Campground is about five miles down Hilina Pali Rd, off Chain of Craters Rd. Although it's the least developed of the camping grounds, there's still a water catchment system, toilets and a shelter with picnic tables. The area is bushy and grassy. True to the camping ground's name, a few friendly nene often hang out there.

Kamoamoa Campground is at the new black-sand beach of the same name. The camping sites are in a circle, with trees between sites to give a little privacy. There were originally nine sites but because of archaeological finds three have been closed off and the camping area occasionally fills.

Drinking water is trucked in, however the bacteria count is sometimes high, so plan on treating it. Nights are warmer here than in the other two camping grounds and you can hear the surf.

Places to Eat
If you're trying to see the park in a day, you can save time by bringing lunch and having a picnic wherever you are at noon. If you don't happen to be near the park entrance, it's a long haul from most points in the park out to a restaurant.

Volcano House (☎ 967-7321) serves up a cafeteria-quality breakfast buffet from 8 to 10.30 am for $8.75 and a lunch buffet from 11 am to 1.30 pm for $11. The quality of the food is better at dinner, with main courses from $15 to $25, although the service is indifferent.

While the dining-room view overlooking Kilauea Caldera is magnificent, it can be matched over in the adjacent snack shop where they serve sandwiches for $3 to $4 and have yoghurt, juice and coffee. The dining room is open for breakfast from 7 to 10.30 am, for lunch from 11 am to 1.30 pm and for dinner from 5.30 to 8 pm. The snack shop is open from 10.30 am to 4 pm.

The *Volcano Country Club Restaurant* at Volcano Golf Course serves continental breakfast from 7 to 10 am and lunch from 10.30 am to 3 pm daily. Simple hot lunches with a small salad and French fries cost around $7, while sandwiches with coleslaw or burgers with French fries are about $6. The food is essentially diner quality.

Volcano Store & Diner at the Chevron station in Volcano village has fairly inexpensive breakfasts, sandwiches and plate lunches for around $4 to $5. It's open from 8.30 am to 4 pm daily. You can eat at one of the five booths or order takeaway and have a picnic in the national park.

The best food in Volcano is at *Kilauea Lodge* (☎ 967-7366) which is only open for dinner, from 5.30 to 9 pm daily. Dinners of beef, seafood and chicken begin at around $17 and pasta dishes start at $13. For dessert there's home-made ohelo berry or macadamia nut pie for $3.75. The dining room has high wooden ceilings, island artwork and window tables looking out onto a fern forest. It also has a big stone fireplace, built in 1938 when this was a YMCA camp, which is embedded with an international collection of stones and coins.

Saddle Road/Mauna Kea

The Saddle Road, true to its name, runs between the two highest points on the island, with Mauna Kea to the north and Mauna Loa to the south.

The road passes over large lava flows and climbs through a variety of terrains and climates. At sunrise and sunset there's a gentle glow on the mountains and a light show on the clouds. In the early morning it's crisp enough to see your breath and if you take the spur road up to Mauna Kea you'll reach permafrost.

Although most car-rental contracts prohibit travel on the Saddle Rd, it's a paved road straight across. It's narrow and there are sections where the road's surface is a bit crumbly and potholed, but it's no big deal – particularly by island standards.

Locals looking for the rationale behind the car-rental ban come up with things like military convoys or evening fog. The crux of the matter seems to be that the rental agencies just don't want to be responsible if your car breaks down on Hawaii's most remote road.

The Saddle Rd is 50 miles long and has no gas stations or other facilities along the way. (Neither are there any gas stations on the 33-mile stretch of Hwy 190 between the Saddle Rd and Kona.)

Crossing the island on the Saddle Rd is a bit shorter than on the northern route of the Hawaii Belt Rd, but it's also a slower road and timewise there isn't much difference either way.

To the west, the Saddle Rd starts out in cattle-ranch land with rolling grassy hills and planted stands of eucalyptus trees. It's beautiful, but like the rest of the western side of the island it's changing. A new subdivision called Waikii Ranch has divided 3000 acres of the area's ranch land into million-dollar house lots and is marketing them to wealthy urban cowboys.

After about 10 miles the land starts getting rougher and the pastures and fences fewer. The military takes over where the cows leave off. Bradshaw Army Airfield comes up first, then the quonset huts of the Pohakuloa Military Camp. Most of the vehicles on the road are military jeeps and trucks, although in hunting season you'll come across a fair number of pick-up trucks as well.

MAUNA KEA
Mauna Kea is Hawaii's highest mountain and its 13,796-foot summit has a cluster of important astronomical observatory domes.

The unmarked Summit Rd which climbs up Mauna Kea is at the 28-mile marker, opposite a hunter's check station. It's a well-paved 6¼ miles to the visitors' centre. The road winds up a few thousand feet in elevation. If you've got a small car it's probably going to labour a bit, but it shouldn't be a problem making it up as far as the visitors' centre. A standard transmission is preferable.

Surprisingly, you don't really get closer views of Mauna Kea's peaks by driving up to the visitors' centre. The peaks actually look higher and the views are broader from the Saddle Rd. But you'll find nice vistas from the Summit Rd and you can often drive up above the clouds. Mauna Kea doesn't appear as a single main peak, but rather a jumble of peaks, some black, some red-brown, some seasonally snow-capped.

The Summit Rd passes through open range of grazing cattle. It's easy to spot Eurasian skylarks in the grass and if you're lucky you might see the endangered *io* (Hawaiian hawk) hovering overhead. Both make their home on the grassy mountain slopes. The io is found only on the Big Island. Mauna Kea is also home to the nene goose, as well as the *palila*, a small yellow honeycreeper which lives no where else in the world.

One of the more predominant plants here is mullen, which has soft woolly leaves and shoots up a tall stalk. In the spring the stalks get so loaded down with flowers that they bend over from the weight of what looks like big yellow helmets. Mullen was brought in by ranchers as a free-loading weed in grass seed.

Visitors' Centre

The visitors' centre (☎ 961-2180), officially the Onizuka Center for International Astronomy, was named for Ellison Onizuka, a Big Island native and one of the astronauts who died in the 1986 Challenger disaster.

The centre shows an interesting 10-minute video on Mauna Kea's observatories. There are also photo displays of the observatories and information on discoveries made from the summit. Note the astronomers aren't peering through little eyepieces or looking at the sky directly but rather are watching images relayed on computer monitors.

The centre also has exhibits of the mountain's history, ecology and geology.

If you're planning to go up to the summit, stop here first to check road conditions and pick up brochures.

The visitors' centre is open from 8 am to 5 pm on Saturdays and Sundays and 1 to 5 pm on Mondays and Fridays. The outdoor restrooms are always open and have running water.

For information on the visitors' centre's stargazing programmes and summit tours, see Organised Tours near the end of this section.

Summit Observatories

The summit of Mauna Kea has the greatest collection of state-of-the-art telescopes on earth and superior conditions for viewing the heavens. Nearing 14,000 feet, the summit is above 40% of the earth's atmosphere and 90% of its water vapour. The air is typically clear, dry and stable.

Not only are the Hawaiian Islands isolated, but Mauna Kea is one of the most secluded places in Hawaii. The air is relatively free from dust and smog. Nights are dark and free from city light interference. To further the cause, streetlights on the island have been converted to low-impact sodium. Rather than using the full iridescent spectrum, these orange lights use only a few wavelengths which the telescopes can be adjusted to remove.

Eight out of 10 nights are good for viewing. Only the Andes Mountains match Mauna Kea for cloudless nights, although air turbulence in the Andes makes viewing more difficult there.

The University of Hawaii (UH) holds the lease on Mauna Kea from the 12,000-foot level to the summit and UH receives observing time at each telescope as one of the lease provisions. Currently nine telescopes are in operation.

UH built the first telescope in 1968 with a 24-inch mirror. In comparison, the Maxwell telescope built in 1987 by the UK, Netherlands and Canada has a 590-inch mirror.

The UK Infrared Telescope (UKIRT) with

its 150-inch mirror, until recently the world's largest infrared telescope, can be operated via computers and satellite relays from the Royal Observatory in England. In 1988 UKIRT and the Canada-France-Hawaii Telescope jointly identified the most distant galaxy yet discovered. Its light is 12 billion years old.

NASA's Infrared Telescope has measured the heat of volcanoes on Io, one of Jupiter's moons. The most active of Io's volcanoes is now named after Pele.

Completed in 1992, the W M Keck Observatory, a project of Caltech and the University of California, is the world's largest and most powerful infrared and optical telescope. A price tag of $85 million makes it the world's most expensive as well.

Previously the sheer weight of the glass mirrors was a limiting factor in telescope design. The Keck telescope has a new honeycomb design with 36 hexagonal mirror segments, each six feet across, that function as a single piece of glass. Its capacity to receive light is greater than twice that of all Mauna Kea's other telescopes combined.

A second Keck observatory, a replica of the first, is now under construction. The telescopes will be interchangeable, and can function as one – 'like a pair of binoculars searching the sky'.

Driving to the Summit

Visitors may go up to the summit in daytime, but vehicle headlights are not allowed between sunset and sunrise because they interfere with observation. The Canada-France-Hawaii Telescope and the UH 88-inch Telescope have visitor galleries.

The paved road ends above the visitors' centre near Hale Pohaku, the stone buildings where scientists stay during the day. The road from the visitors' centre to the summit is accessible by 4WD only. Harper Car & Truck Rentals in Hilo is the only car-rental company that allows its jeeps to be driven to the summit.

The drive takes about half an hour. You should drive in the low range and loosen the gas cap to prevent vapour lock. The upper road can get iced over during winter. Be particularly careful on the way down and watch out for loose cinder.

About 4½ miles up is an area called **Moon Valley** where the Apollo astronauts rehearsed with their lunar rover before their journey to the real moonscape.

At 5½ miles up, look to the left for a narrow ridge with two caves and black stones. That's **Keanakakoi**, 'cave of the adze', an ancient adze quarry. From there high-quality basalt was quarried to make adze and other tools and weapons which were traded throughout the islands. For people interested in archaeology it's an impressive site. This is a protected area and nothing should be removed.

Precautions The summit air has only about 60% of the oxygen available at sea level and altitude sickness is not uncommon. Not only is the height a problem, but also the fact that visitors often don't take the time to properly acclimatise.

Unlike Nepal, for instance, where great heights are generally reached only after days of trekking, here you can zip up from sea level to nearly 14,000 feet by car in two hours.

Scuba divers who have been diving within the past 24 hours risk getting the bends by going to the summit. It's recommended that children under 16, pregnant women and those with a respiratory condition, or even a cold for that matter, do not go beyond the visitors' centre.

Even the astronomers who work up here never fully acclimatise and are always working oxygen-deprived in the summit's thin air. Anyone who gets a headache or feels faint or nauseous should head back down the mountain.

Mauna Kea can have snow flurries all year round and winter storms can dump a couple of feet of snow overnight.

Lake Waiau

Lake Waiau is a unique alpine lake which, at 13,020 feet, is the third highest lake in the

USA. It's inside the Puu Waiau cinder cone in a barren and treeless setting.

Lake Waiau is rather mysterious. It's a small lake, no more than 10 feet deep and set on porous cinder in desert conditions of less than 15 inches of rainfall per year. It's fed by melting winter snows and permafrost, which elsewhere on Mauna Kea quickly evaporates. Lake Waiau has no freshwater springs and yet it's never dry.

Hawaiians used to bring the umbilical cords of their babies and throw them in the lake to give their children the strength of the mountain.

Puu Poliahu

Just below the summit is Puu Poliahu, the home of Poliahu, goddess of snow.

Poliahu is said to be more beautiful than her sister Pele. According to legend, during conflicts over men, Pele would get miffed and erupt Mauna Kea, Poliahu would cover it over with ice and snow, then Pele would erupt again. Back and forth they went. The legend is metaphorically correct. As recent as 10,000 years ago there were volcanic eruptions through glacial ice caps here.

Because of its spiritual significance, astronomical domes have not been built on Puu Poliahu.

Mauna Kea Summit Trail

There's a six-mile hiking trail to the top of Mauna Kea which starts near the end of the paved road above the visitors' centre. Instead of continuing on the main 4WD road, take the road to the left. The trail begins up through wooden posts and more or less parallels the summit road. It's marked with posts and stone cairns.

The trail starts at 9200 feet and climbs almost 4600 feet. Because of the altitude it's quite strenuous and it's also easy to get sunburned. Take sunscreen and plenty of water along with you. Dress in layers of warm clothing. Give yourself a full day for this hike – most people take four to five hours to get to the summit.

It's a difficult hike, as you're walking on cinders, but there are incredible vistas and strange moonlike landscapes. The trail passes through the **Mauna Kea Ice Age Natural Area Reserve**. There was once a Pleistocene glacier here and scratchings on rocks from the glacial moraine can still be seen.

The ancient adze quarry **Keanakakoi**, at 12,400 feet, is two-thirds of the way up. **Lake Waiau** is a mile farther.

You might be tempted to hitch a ride from someone at the visitors' centre who's going to the summit and then walk down. But if you haven't spent the previous night in the mountains, there's a danger in doing this as you won't have as much time to acclimatise.

Organised Tours

Visitors' Centre Programmes The visitors' centre (☎ 961-2180) has summit tours at 2.30 pm on Saturdays and Sundays beginning at the University of Hawaii's 88-inch telescope. Most of the time is spent at the observatory's refrigerated dome, control room and catwalk.

The tour is free but you need to provide your own 4WD transportation to the summit. If you're lucky, you might be able to catch a ride up with someone from the visitors' centre, but you can't count on it. Children under 16 are not allowed because of altitude health hazards. Check in at the visitors' centre before 1.45 pm.

In addition, right at the visitors' centre, there's a free astronomy programme from 7 to 9 pm on Fridays and 6 to 10 pm on Saturdays. It starts with a lecture or video, and is followed by stargazing using an 11-inch telescope. Children are encouraged to come to this one.

Other Tours Pat Wright of Paradise Safaris (☎ 322-2366), Box AD, Kailua-Kona, HI 96745, conducts sunset tours of Mauna Kea summit for $100. The tour includes pick-up at West Hawaii hotels and stargazing from their own little telescope.

Waipio Valley Shuttle (☎ 775-7121) operates daytime tours that go to the summit of Mauna Kea. The tour costs $75 and leaves from Waimea.

Mauna Kea Astronomical Society makes a trip to Mauna Kea once a month, normally on the Saturday night closest to the new moon. The observation area is outside the visitors' centre where the group maintains permanent mounts and members bring their own telescopes. It's open to the public and meeting times are posted in local newspapers.

For information on snow skiing, see the Activities section at the beginning of the chapter.

Places to Stay

Mauna Kea State Park is seven miles west of Summit Rd, near the 35-mile marker. It has picnic tables, restrooms, a pay phone and 20 acres of shrubland. At an elevation of 6500 feet, the days are commonly cool and the nights cold.

The park has seven housekeeping cabins which are mostly used by hunters who hunt pigs, goats and game birds on the slopes of Mauna Kea. The cabins have basic kitchens, electric heating, bathrooms, hot showers and beds with the standard saggy mattresses.

As most hunting is restricted to weekends, it's the most difficult time to book the cabins. Nearby military manoeuvres can be noisy, but otherwise it's a good base for those planning to hike Mauna Kea or Mauna Loa.

For reservations, contact the Division of State Parks (☎ 933-4200), Box 936, Hilo, HI 96721. Rates are the same as for other park cabins: $10 for one person, $17 for two, up to $30 for six.

MAUNA LOA'S NORTHERN FLANK

The road to Mauna Loa starts just east of the Summit Rd and climbs 18 miles up the northern flank of Mauna Loa to a weather station at 11,150 feet. There are no visitor facilities at the weather station.

The narrow road is gently sloping, not paved but oil-packed, and passable in a standard car. It takes about 40 minutes to drive up. It might be wise to loosen your gas cap before you start in order to avoid vapour lock problems. Park in the lot below the weather station; the equipment used to measure atmospheric conditions is highly sensitive to exhaust.

The summit and domes of Mauna Kea are visible from here and when conditions are right you can see the 'Mauna Kea shadow' at sunset. It's a curious phenomenon in which Mauna Kea sometimes casts a blue-purple shadow behind itself in the sky.

Observatory Trail

The weather station is the trailhead for the Observatory Trail which connects up with the Mauna Loa Trail after three miles. From there it's 2½ miles around the western side of Mauna Loa's caldera, Mokuaweoweo, to the summit at 13,677 feet, or two miles along the eastern side of Mokuaweoweo Caldera to Mauna Loa cabin at 13,250 feet. The cabin marks the end of the 18-mile Mauna Loa Trail which starts down in the main section of Hawaii Volcanoes National Park.

The Observatory Trail is very steep and difficult. If you haven't been staying in the mountains, altitude sickness is very likely. The hike to the cabin takes four to six hours for strong hikers. Anyone who is not in top shape shouldn't even consider it.

Overnight hikers must register in advance with the Kilauea Visitor Center in Hawaii Volcanoes National Park. For details, see Hiking Trails in the Hawaii Volcanoes National Park section.

Continuing on to Hilo

Heading eastward from the hunter's check station below Mauna Kea's visitors' centre, the terrain along the Saddle Rd gradually becomes ohia-fern forest, shrubby at first, but getting thicker and taller as Hilo gets closer.

Red ohelo berries are fairly common in this area. These low shrubs are from the heath family, related to blueberries and cranberries. They're tart but edible.

Although most of the road is fine there's one winding stretch worthy of note as oncoming drivers often take to the centre of the road to cut curves. The last part of the highway is newly paved. As the road re-enters civilisation you can see Hilo Bay in the distance.

About four miles outside Hilo, Akolea Rd leads off to the left and connects in two miles to Waianuenue Ave, which passes Boiling Pots and Rainbow Falls (see the Hilo section).

Alternatively, stay on the Saddle Rd and you'll soon come to Kaumana Caves, a small county park on the left.

Maui

Maui has much to lure the visitor, including superb scenery and diverse landscapes. Most of the sunny west coast is lined with beautiful white-sand beaches and the island has world-class windsurfing and excellent conditions for most other water sports. The shallow coastal waters around Maui are central wintering grounds for North Pacific humpback whales, making it prime whale-watch country.

In the 1960s, Hawaii's first major development outside Waikiki was built on Maui. Since that time, Maui has become the most visited, the most developed and the most expensive of the Neighbor Islands. As might be expected, the resort action all centres around the beaches of West Maui.

The main tourist destinations – Lahaina, the Kaanapali area and the Kihei strip – are urbanised experiences. You have to be ready for high-rises, traffic and crowds.

Maui does have another side. It's quite easy to escape the West Maui scene by heading to the east coast or the uplands. Making a base in the small towns of Haiku, Kula, Makawao or Hana is a totally different experience. Those towns sit beneath Haleakala, the massive mountain that provides the scenic backdrop to all of East Maui. Its slopes hold native rainforests, eucalyptus groves and open pastures with large cattle ranches.

Haleakala Crater, with a summit of 10,023 feet, is the centrepiece of Haleakala National Park. The crater is an extraordinary landscape of spewed red cinders and grey lava hills. Haleakala is the world's largest dormant volcano, its crater so big that an entire city could fit inside. There are some incredible hiking trails across the crater floor, while sunrise at the summit is awe-inspiring.

Kula, at a cool 3000-foot elevation on Haleakala's western slopes, is Maui's gardenland. Flowers and vegetables which ordinarily don't have a chance in the tropics thrive up there. Upcountry has Hawaii's only winery, with a tasting room in a century-old jail. It's a lovely area for country drives.

The windward side of Haleakala is lush, wet and rugged. The famous Hana Highway runs down the full length of it, winding its way above the coast through tropical jungle and past roadside waterfalls. It's the most beautiful coastal road in Hawaii.

Artists and craftspeople have long been drawn to Maui, and many of Hawaii's New Age activities are centred here.

ORIENTATION

Most visitors to Maui land at the main airport in Kahului.

From Kahului, it's five miles to Paia down Hwy 36 and another 45 miles to Hana.

Upcountry (Kula) is 15 miles from Kahului on Hwy 37; though it's another 20 miles up to the summit of Haleakala.

It's about 10 miles to Kihei from Kahului along Hwy 350.

It's 25 miles from Kahului to Lahaina along Hwy 380 and Hwy 30. It's four miles more from Lahaina to Kaanapali.

Because of its figure-eight shape and the level of development, Maui has a more extensive road network than the other outer islands.

Islanders refer to highways by name, rarely by number. If you ask someone where Hwy 36 is, chances are they won't know – ask about the Hana Highway instead.

Most main roads are called highways whether they're a busy four lanes or just a paved country road.

Facts

HISTORY

Before Western contact, Maui had three major population centres: the south-east coast around Hana, the Wailuku area, and the district of Lele (Lahaina).

In the 14th century Piilani, chief of the Hana district, conquered the entire island. During his reign Piilani accomplished some impressive engineering feats. He built the island's largest temple, Piilanihale Heiau, which remains today, and an extensive road system around the island. Almost half of Maui's highways still bear his name.

The last of Maui's ruling chiefs was Kahekili. During the 1780s he was the most powerful chief in Hawaii, bringing both Oahu and Molokai under Maui's rule.

In 1790, while Kahekili was in Oahu, Kamehameha the Great launched a bold naval attack on Maui. Using foreign-acquired cannons and the aid of two captured foreign seamen, Isaac Davis and John Young, Kamehameha defeated Maui's warriors in a battle up in Iao Valley.

An attack on his own homeland by a Big Island rival forced Kamehameha to withdraw from Maui, but the battles continued over the years. When Kahekili died in Oahu in 1794, his kingdom was divided. In 1795, Kamehameha invaded all of Maui and this time he stayed.

In about 1800 Kamehameha established Lahaina as his main home and royal court. It remained the capital of Hawaii until 1845.

Whaling Days

Both the whalers and the missionaries arrived in Lahaina in the early 1820s. They were soon at odds.

Lahaina's first Protestant missionary, William Richards, converted Maui's Governor Hoapili to Christianity shortly after his arrival in 1823. Under Richards' influence, Hoapili began passing laws against drunkenness and debauchery.

After months at sea, the whalers weren't looking for a prayer service when they pulled into port. Ready for grog and women, they didn't take kindly to the puritanical influences of New England missionaries. To most sailors 'there was no God west of the Horn'.

In 1826 when the English captain William Buckle of the whaler *Daniel* pulled into port, he was outraged to discover Lahaina had a new 'missionary taboo' against womanising. Buckle's crew came to shore seeking revenge against Richards, but a group of Hawaiian Christians came to Richards' aid and chased the whalers back to their boat.

Following Captain Buckle's purchase of a Hawaiian woman, Richards wrote to Buckle's hometown newspaper reporting the details. A libel suit followed. Richards was summoned to Honolulu to be tried but he was acquitted.

In 1827, after Governor Hoapili arrested the captain of the *John Palmer* for allowing women to board his ship, a few cannonballs were shot into Richards' yard. The captain was released, but laws restricting liaisons between seamen and native women stayed.

After Governor Hoapili's death, laws against liquor and prostitution were no longer strictly enforced and whalers began to flock to Lahaina.

By the mid-1800s two-thirds of the whalers coming into Hawaii landed in Lahaina, which had replaced Honolulu as the favoured harbour. In 1846 almost 400 ships pulled into port.

By the 1860s the whaling industry started to fizzle. The depletion of the last hunting grounds in the Arctic and the emergence of the petroleum industry spelled the end of the US whaling era.

Whaling had been the base of Maui's moneyed economy. After the whalers left, Lahaina became all but a ghost town.

Sugar

As whaling was declining, sugar was on the

According to legend, the Polynesian demigod Maui was wandering the Pacific on a fishing expedition when his fish hook snagged the sea floor. He tugged with such a powerful force that the islands of Hawaii were yanked to the surface. He then claimed the island of Maui and made it his home. ■

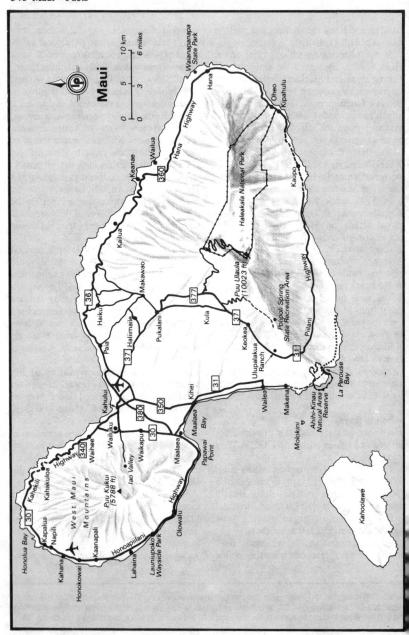

rise. Two of the first planters were Samuel Alexander and Henry Baldwin, sons of prominent missionaries.

In 1870 they began growing sugar cane on 12 acres in Haiku, and the next year they added another 500 acres. It was to be the beginning of Hawaii's biggest sugar company.

In 1876 Alexander & Baldwin began construction of the Hamakua Ditch to service the Haiku plantations 17 miles away. This extensive irrigation system turned Wailuku's dry central plains into green sugar land. Sugar remained the strength of the economy until tourism took over in the 1960s.

GEOGRAPHY

Maui, the second largest Hawaiian island, arose from the ocean floor as two separate volcanoes. Eventually lava flows and soil erosion built up a valley-like isthmus between the two, linking them in their present form. The flat isthmus provides a fertile setting for fields of sugar cane and has given Maui the nickname 'The Valley Island'.

The eastern side of Maui, the larger and younger of the two, is dominated by Haleakala which has a summit elevation of 10,023 feet. This dormant volcano has a massive crater-like valley containing numerous cinder cones and vents. Haleakala last erupted in 1790, which on the geological clock means it could just be snoozing.

The West Maui Mountains dominate West Maui, with Puu Kukui, at 5778 feet, the highest point.

The rainy north-east sides of both mountain masses are cut with deep ravines and valleys that lead down to the coast. White-sand beaches run along much of the island's western shoreline.

Maui's total land area is 728 sq miles.

Molokini

The largely submerged volcanic crater of Molokini lies midway between Maui and Kahoolawe. The crater rim has half eroded away, leaving a crescent moon shape that rises 160 feet above the ocean surface. Its land area is about 18 acres.

Molokini has transparent waters with abundant fish and coral, making it a popular snorkel and dive spot.

The US Navy used to shell Molokini for target practice and live bombs are still found on the crater floor. A few years ago demolition experts removed three which were in just 20 feet of water.

CLIMATE

Maui's west coast is largely dry and sunny. The south-east coast and the Kula uplands receive more rain and commonly have intermittent clouds.

Temperatures vary more with elevation than season. The variance between winter and summer is only about 7°F in most places. The average August temperatures (over a 24-hour period) are 77°F in Hana, 78°F in Lahaina and Kihei, 79°F in Kahului and 50°F at Haleakala summit.

The lowest temperature ever recorded at the summit of Haleakala was 14°F and temperatures hovering around freezing are the norm on winter nights. The mountain even gets an occasional winter snowcap.

Average annual rainfall is 69 inches in Hana, 13 in Kihei, 15 in Lahaina, 19 in Kahului and 44 at Haleakala summit.

Puu Kukui, the highest peak of the West Maui Mountains, gets 400 inches of rain a year. This is Maui's wettest spot, just five miles from the dry Wailuku plains.

FLORA & FAUNA

It's on Maui that you are most likely to see the endangered nene goose and the rare silversword plant. Haleakala is the habitat for both. Maui is also the best island for viewing humpback whales.

At least six birds native to Maui are found nowhere else in the world. They include the Maui parrotbill, Maui *nukupuu*, Maui creeper, Maui *akepa*, the crested honeycreeper and the *poouli*, all of which are endangered. The poouli was only discovered in 1973 by a group of University of Hawaii students working in the Hana rainforests.

Maui also has wild pigs, goats and game birds that are hunted.

Humpback Whales

After spending their summers up in Alaska, more than half of all humpback whales in the North Pacific come to Hawaii for the winter. The largest numbers are found in the shallow waters between Maui, Lanai and Kahoolawe.

Humpbacks have tail flukes with distinctive individual markings, making them easy to identify. The Pacific Whale Foundation has counted over 650 humpback whales off Maui in recent seasons.

The peak season for humpbacks in Hawaii is the same as for tourists from cold-weather climates. Some arrive as early as November and a few stay as late as May, with most in residence from January to March.

The western coastline of Maui from Olowalu to Makena (and the eastern shore of Lanai) are prime birthing and nursing grounds for mothers and newborns. Federal law protects these 'cow/calf waters', and prohibits boats and swimmers from approaching within 300 yards of the whales.

Humpbacks like to stay in shallow water when they have newborn calves, apparently as a safeguard against shark attacks. Maalaea Bay is a favourite nursing ground.

Humpbacks are highly sensitive to human disturbance and noise. Around Lahaina where the waters are buzzing with activity, they stay well offshore.

Because whales readily abandon waters where jet skiing occurs, it's one tourist activity that wears particularly thin on Mauians. 'Save a Whale – Harpoon a Jet Ski' is a common bumper sticker on the island. In early 1992 after a protracted legal struggle, the last jet ski company was forced out of Kaanapali waters and there are hopes that wintering whales will again become a common sight along that section of the coast.

For now the best bet for whale-spotting if you're in the Lahaina area, is to go south at least as far as Launiupoko Wayside Park. The stretches from Olowalu to Maalaea Bay and from Keawakapu Beach to Makena Beach are prime whale-watching spots.

GOVERNMENT

Maui County consists of the islands of Maui, Molokai, Lanai and uninhabited Kahoolawe. The county seat is in Wailuku. The county is governed by an elected mayor with a four-year term and a nine-member council with two-year terms. Linda Crockett Lingle, Hawaii's only Republican mayor, was voted into office in 1990.

ECONOMY

Maui's 1991 unemployment rate was just over 3%. The major industries are tourism, sugar cane and pineapple growing, cattle-grazing, and diversified agriculture, in that order.

Surprisingly, more land on Maui is used for grazing dairy and beef cattle than for any other purpose. For every acre of sugar, there are three acres of ranch land.

Kula is one of the state's major flower and vegetable producing regions, accounting for more than half of the cabbage, lettuce, onions and potatoes grown in Hawaii, and most of the proteas and carnations.

After Oahu, Maui captures the lion's share of Hawaii's tourist industry, accounting for roughly half the visitor accommodation on all the outer islands combined. Numbers, however, don't equate to bargains here. Maui has the highest room rates in Hawaii, averaging $140 a night, which is 40% higher than the state average.

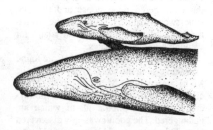

Humpback whales

POPULATION & PEOPLE

Maui has a population of 88,100. The Wailuku district, which includes the sister towns of Wailuku and Kahului, is home to half of the island's residents.

Ethnically, 26% of the population is Caucasian, 18% Japanese, 14% Filipino and 2% Hawaiian. About one-third of Maui's residents consider themselves to be of 'mixed blood', with two-thirds of these having some Hawaiian ancestry.

TOURIST INFORMATION

The Maui Visitors Bureau (☎ 871-8691) has its office at 250 Alamaha St (Box 1738), Kahului, HI 96732. If you call (800) 525-MAUI before you go, the bureau will send its 'travel planner,' a packet containing brochures and other promotional information.

For information on Kaanapali, contact the Kaanapali Beach Resort Association (☎ 661-3271), 45 Kai Ala Dr, Suite A-118, Lahaina, HI 96761. For information on Wailea, contact the Wailea Destination Association (☎ 879-1595, (800) 367-5246), 3750 Wailea Alanui, Wailea, HI 96753. Both organisations will mail out brochures on accommodation at their resorts.

GENERAL INFORMATION

Maui's nickname is 'The Valley Island'. Its official colour is pink; its flower is the *lokelani*, which is a type of rose; and the unofficial slogan is *Maui no ka oi* – 'Maui is the best'.

Media

Maui's main newspaper, the *Maui News* (☎ 244-3981), Box 550, Wailuku, HI 96793, comes out daily except Saturday. The Friday edition can be mailed to the US mainland for $2.75 (or three months' worth for $12). It can be ordered by calling (800) 827-0347.

Free tourist magazines such as *This Week Maui, Maui Gold, Maui Beach Press* and pocket-sized beach guides are full of ads, discount coupons, simple maps and general sightseeing information. They're everywhere – at the airport and in shopping malls, hotels and restaurants.

There are also some small community newspapers that focus on local issues, including the *Maui Press, Lahaina News* and *South Maui Times*.

Cable TV Channel 7 has ongoing programmes on Hawaii geared for visitors.

Maui has 10 radio stations. Station KPOA (93.5 FM) plays Hawaiian music from 1 am to 7 pm daily, with jazz in the evenings.

Books & Maps

The public library at Kahului is the best on Maui. There are other libraries in Wailuku, Lahaina, Hana, Kihei and Makawao.

For books on Hawaii, try Whalers Book Shoppe at The Wharf shopping centre in Lahaina or Waldenbooks in Kahului, Kihei, Lahaina and Kaanapali.

The best map to buy for getting around the island is the University of Hawaii Press map of Maui. In addition to covering roads, it marks beaches and major sights.

Weather

For recorded weather forecasts call 877-5111. For a more recreational forecast, including conditions at Haleakala and the road to Hana, sunrise and sunset times, tides and a marine forecast, call 871-5054.

Haleakala National Park (☎ 572-7749) has a recorded forecast. For surf and boating conditions call 877-3477.

Emergency

Dial 911 for police, ambulance or fire emergencies. The county crisis and help line is 244-7407.

Maui Memorial Hospital (☎ 244-9056) on Mahalani St in Wailuku has a 24-hour emergency service. The smaller Hana Medical Center (☎ 248-8294) also has 24-hour service.

ACTIVITIES

Beaches

Maui has lots of fine beaches and some of Hawaii's best windsurfing and board surfing. There are plenty of swimming, snorkelling and bodysurfing spots as well.

The north-west coast from Kaanapali up

to Honolua Bay and the south-west coast from Maalaea down through Kihei to Makena are largely fringed with white-sand beaches. This western side is dry and sunny and water conditions are generally calmer than on the windward northern and eastern coasts.

Most of the west coast beaches are backed by hotel and condo developments – good if you're looking to stay right at the beach, not so good if you prefer seclusion. Some of the best undeveloped beaches are Slaughterhouse Beach and Honolua Bay in the north and Makena's Big and Little beaches in the south.

Swimming

The county has a couple of swimming pools that are free to the public. In Wailuku, there's a new heated pool (☎ 243-7411) on the corner of Wells and Market Sts that's open from 9 or 10 am to 11.45 am and from 1 to 4.30 pm daily, as well as from 7 to 9 pm on Mondays and Fridays.

The pool at the War Memorial Center at Baldwin High School in Wailuku is open from 9 am to 4 pm daily, except on Thursdays when it opens at 10.30 am, Sundays when it opens at 1 pm, and Saturdays when it's closed between 11.45 am and 1 pm. In summer it's open from 6.30 to 9 pm most nights of the week.

Surfing

For surfing, Honolua Bay is tops in winter. Maalaea Bay has a very fast break, best during south swells. Hookipa Beach near Paia has surfing almost year-round, with incredible winter waves. The peak surfing season is November to March.

Lots of people give surfing lessons for beginners, including Andrea Thomas of Maui Surfing School (☎ 875-0625), Kaanapali Windsurfing School (☎ 667-1964), Hawaiian Sailboarding Techniques (☎ 871-5423) and Maui Mistral (☎ 871-7753).

Lessons typically take 1½ to two hours and cost $40 to $60. Most places 'guarantee' that students of all ages will be surfing at the end of the lesson.

Surfboards, as well as boogie boards, can be rented at numerous locations, including many of the windsurfing shops.

Fun Rentals (☎ 661-3053), 193 Lahainaluna Rd, Lahaina, rents standard surfboards for $20/100 a day/week, long boards for $25/120 and boogie boards for $6/25.

Hi-Tech Surf Sports (☎ 877-2111), 444 Hana Highway, Kahului, rents surfboards for $12 a day and boogie boards for $8 a day.

Windsurfing

Maui is a mecca for windsurfers. Some of the world's best windsurfing is at Hookipa Beach in Paia, though it's suitable for experts only. Spreckelsville Beach in Paia is for intermediate and advanced windsurfers. Kanaha Beach in Kahului is good for beginners, as are parts of the Kihei area. In Maalaea Bay, winds are usually strong and blowing offshore towards Kahoolawe, good for advanced speed sailing. When kona winds blow in the winter, the Maalaea-Kihei area is often the only place windy enough to sail and becomes the main scene for all windsurfers.

Maui is known for its consistent winds and windsurfers can find action in any month. Though trade winds can blow at any time of the year and flat spells can also hit anytime, generally the windiest time is June to September and the flattest from December to February.

The Maui Boardsailing Association has developed a 'sail safe' programme with windsurfing guidelines. Brochures are available at the windsurf shops. You can receive their newsletter by becoming a member for $10 (MBA, Box 356, Paia, HI 96779).

Most windsurfing shops are based in Kahului. Three of the largest are:

Hawaiian Island Windsurfing – gives lessons as Windsurfing West, 460 Dairy Rd, Kahului, HI 96732 (☎ 871-4981, (800) 231-6958)

Maui Windsurf Company – 520 Keolani Place, Kahului, HI 96732 (☎ 877-4816, (800) 872-0999)

Windrigger Maui – gives lessons as Maui Mistral, 261 Dairy Rd, Kahului, HI 96732 (☎ 871-7753, (800) 345-MAUI)

All three shops rent boards and rigs for $45/250 a day/week, which includes swapping privileges that let you try out different equipment.

They also give windsurfing lessons for all levels, including small classes for beginners at Kanaha Beach that last two to three hours and cost $55 to $60, including equipment. None give lessons on Sundays or holidays.

All three shops sell gear and book package tours for windsurfers.

A smaller operation, Kaanapali Windsurfing School (☎ 667-1964), rents windsurfing equipment and gives beginner lessons on Kaanapali Beach. The cost is $30 for a one-hour lesson, $40 for two hours and $50 for three.

Diving & Snorkelling

Some dive and snorkel boat tours go along the Maui shoreline, but the most popular tours by far are to the sunken volcanic crater of Molokini and to the island of Lanai. Although some dive boats take snorkellers, and vice versa, in general you're better off going out on a tour that's geared for the activity you're doing.

For snorkelling from the beach, the best

spots are Black Rock at the Sheraton in Kaanapali; Olowalu, south of Lahaina; around the rocky points of Wailea and Makena beaches; and in summer only, Honolua Bay and Slaughterhouse Beach on the north-west shore. Kapalua Bay is generally calm for snorkelling year-round. Hawaiian Reef Divers and Maui Dive Shops have free snorkelling maps.

Molokini Molokini is Maui's most popular snorkelling tour. The fish are tame and numerous and the water is clear.

Though the snorkelling is great, a score of tour boats crowd the islet everyday. All of this activity has taken a toll on the reef, sections of which are dying, partly from dropped and dragged anchors that have carved swaths in the coral.

Morning is the best time to snorkel Molokini as winds pick up in the afternoon. The fish are given their breakfast call by boat captains who drop in loaves of bread to start the action.

For divers, Molokini has walls, ledges, white-tipped reef sharks, manta rays, turtles and a wide variety of other marine life.

Black coral was once prolific in Molokini's deeper waters. Most of it, however, made its way into Lahaina jewellery shops before Molokini was declared a conservation district in 1977.

Lanai Lanai also has clear waters, but without the crowds. The most common destination is Hulopoe Bay.

Hulopoe is a big beautiful beach that was once secluded but now has a luxury hotel at its northern end. The reef at the southern end harbours large schools of fish and is good for snorkelling.

For divers, the nearby Cathedrals has intriguing geological formations, including caves, arches and connecting passageways.

Dive Shops & Boat Dives Maui has numerous dive operations. Maui Dive Shops (☎ 871-2111), whose main office is at 279 Wakea Ave, Kahului, HI 96732, is the most prolific with branches around the island:

Kahana	–	Kahana Gateway (☎ 669-3800)
Kihei	–	Azeka Place II (☎ 879-3388)
		Kamaole Center (☎ 879-1533)
		Kihei Town Center (☎ 879-1919)
Lahaina	–	Lahaina Cannery Mall (☎ 661-5388)
Wailea	–	Wailea Shopping Village (☎ 879-3166)

Maui Dive offers introductory dives for beginners for $59; two-tank dives for $65 off Maui, $85 at Molokini; night dives for $89; and five-day certification courses for $325.

Lahaina Divers (☎ 667-7496, (800) 657-7885), 710 Front St, Lahaina, HI 96761, has two-tank dives for $85 to either Lanai or Molokini, and one-tank introductory or night dives for $65. They also offer certification courses, book dive vacations, dive Kahoolawe and lead advanced dives, including drift and deep-water dives.

Hawaiian Reef Divers (☎ 667-7647), 129 Lahainaluna Rd, Lahaina, HI 96761, has half-day trips to either Molokini or Lanai costing $75 for two-tank dives, $69 for intro dives and $49 for snorkelling, including continental breakfast and a deli-style lunch. Lanai night dives, held on Wednesday and Saturday, cost $65. It costs $55 for a one-tank dive for either a certified or beginner diver along the Maui coast.

Underwater photographer Ed Robinson has a dive company called Hawaiian Watercolors (☎ 879-3584), Box 616, Kihei, HI 96753.

Snorkelling Tours & Rentals Numerous snorkelling cruises leave for Molokini daily from Maalaea Harbor. Boats are usually out from about 7 am to noon and cost about $45 to $60 including lunch or snacks and snorkelling gear.

Competition is heavy, so deals and discount coupons are easy to come by. Tickets are sold at activity booths around the island.

Snorkelling gear can be rented at reasonable prices from most dive and windsurfing shops and at inflated prices at hotel beach huts.

Snorkel Bob's rents full snorkel sets for $15 a week. There are two locations: 34

Keala Place in Kihei (☎ 879-7449) and Napili Village Hotel in Napili (☎ 669-9603).

Fun Rentals (☎ 661-3053), 193 Lahainaluna Rd, Lahaina, rents snorkel sets for $2.50 a day, $15 a week.

Hiking

Haleakala National Park has some extraordinary trails across the moonscape-like Haleakala Crater, varying from half-day walks to overnight treks. In the separate Oheo section of the park, which is south of Hana, there's a trail to two impressive waterfalls.

Polipoli Spring State Recreation Area in Maui's Upcountry has an extensive trail system in cloudforest. One, the Skyline Trail, leads up to (or down from) Haleakala summit.

Several pull-offs along the Hana Highway lead to short nature walks. There's a pleasant coastal trail between Waianapanapa State Park and Hana Bay.

The scenic Waihee Ridge Trail branches off the Kahekili Highway north of Wailuku. From La Perouse Bay, on the other side of the island, there's a hardy hike over lava south along the coastline. And, of course, Maui has many white-sand beaches perfect for strolls. Hikes are detailed in their respective sections.

Sierra Club The Maui branch of the Sierra Club, Box 2000, Kahului, HI 96732, leads hikes an average of once a month. Notices can be found in the local papers. The fee is $2 for hikers over age 14.

The group also has frequent service trips to help rid the island of invasive exotic plants, such as myconia and banana poka. The latter, a not-so-benign relative of the edible passion fruit vine, has run rampant over native forests on the Big Island and Kauai, but is kept relatively controlled on Maui thanks in large part to the Sierra Club. Eradication tactics include bagging fruit and seedlings, pulling up vines and spraying herbicide on the roots.

Cycling

Each morning groups of cyclists gather at the top of Haleakala for the thrill of coasting 38 miles and 10,000 feet down.

Cruiser Bob's (☎ 667-7717, (800) 654-7717) is the original group (started in 1982). The other main companies are Maui Downhill (☎ 871-2155, (800) 535-2453) and Maui Mountain Cruisers (☎ 572-0195, (800) 232-6284).

Generally it's an all-day affair (eight to 10 hours) starting with a hotel pick-up at around 3 am, a van ride up the mountain for the sunrise and about 3½ hours of biking down the mountain. It's not a nonstop cruise as cyclists must pull over for cars following behind. The going rate is $99, which includes bikes, helmets, transportation and meals.

Bikes are said to be special models with safety brakes and each group is followed by an escort van. Pregnant women, children under 12 and anyone less than five feet tall are usually not allowed to ride.

Horse Riding

Maui has lots of ranch land and opportunities for trail rides. The most unusual ride meanders down into Haleakala Crater via Sliding Sands Trail.

Pony Express (☎ 667-2200) is in a eucalyptus grove on Haleakala Crater Rd, 2½ miles up from Hwy 377. Rides across the rolling meadows of Haleakala Ranch, with views from 4000 feet down to the ocean, cost $30 for one hour, $50 for two hours, and are held weekdays only. A half-day Haleakala Crater ride leaves at 9.30 am, takes four hours, covers 7½ miles, is open to novice riders and costs $110 including a picnic lunch on the crater floor. A full-day version covers 12 miles, goes to Kapalaoa Cabin and costs $130. There are no Sunday rides.

Charles Aki Jr (☎ 248-8209), c/o Kaupo Store, Kaupo, HI 96713, arranges overnight pack trips from his home in Kaupo into Haleakala Crater. The cost is $150 to $200 per person, depending on the number of people (two to six), and includes camping equipment or cabin fees and meals. It costs $25 less if you bring and fix your own food. As Charles is a working cowboy, trips require advance notice and a deposit.

Thompson Ranch (☎ 878-1910) in Keokea has 1½-hour trail rides for $35 and two-hour rides for $40. Six-hour trips looping through Haleakala Crater cost $150 with lunch. Overnight crater trips can be arranged with three months' notice.

Makena Stables (☎ 879-0244), on the old Makena Rd in Makena, has trail rides to wooded and grassy areas of Ulupalakua Ranch daily except Sundays. The sunset ride costs $75 from 3 to 5 pm, or $95 from 2 pm. There's also an outing from 9 am to 2.30 pm that includes four hours of riding and a tour of the winery for $115.

Rainbow Ranch (☎ 669-4991) in Napili offers one-hour introductory rides for beginners for $30, two-hour sunset rides for $50, a three-hour picnic ride for $60, and more. For $7.50 they'll pick you up and drop you back in Lahaina.

Hana Ranch Riding Stables (☎ 248-8211) has guided trail rides along the Hana coast. It's closed on Sundays.

Tennis

The county maintains tennis courts at each of these places: Kahului Community Center, Kahului; Kalama Park, Kihei; Hana Ball Park, Hana; Eddie Tam Memorial Center, Makawao; Pukalani Community Center, Pukalani.

In Lahaina the county has two courts at the civic centre and four at Maluuluolele Park. In Wailuku there are seven courts at the Wailuku Community Center and four at the War Memorial. All county courts are free to the public and lit for night play.

Maui Community College in Wailuku has four courts open after school hours.

The Makena Tennis Club (☎ 879-8777) in Makena, the Napili Kai Beach Club (☎ 669-6271) in Napili, The Tennis Club (☎ 669-5677) in Kapalua, the Royal Lahaina Tennis Ranch (☎ 661-3611), and the Maui Marriott (☎ 667-1200) in Kaanapali charge $8 to $12 per person.

The Wailea Tennis Club (☎ 879-1958) is

Maui's largest tennis facility. The club likes to call itself 'Wimbledon West' as it has three grass courts, a stadium court for exhibitions and a cafe serving strawberries and cream. It costs $15 per person to play on hard courts, $20 on grass courts. Wailea guests are charged $5 less. Racquets can be rented for $5 a day.

Though rates listed for all clubs are per-day fees, most places guarantee only the first hour and courts are subject to space availability after that.

Golf

Maui has 13 golf courses open to the public. They include, in order by listing, one municipal, four private and eight resort courses. All are 18-hole par 71, 72 or 73 courses except Maui Country Club which is 9-hole, par 37.

Waiehu Municipal Golf Course – north of Wailuku; charges green fees of $25 plus $7 per person for a shared cart (☎ 243-7400)

Silversword Golf Course – Kihei; charges $65 for greens and cart, $40 after 2 pm (☎ 874-0777)

Pukalani Country Club – charges $60 including a cart (☎ 572-1314)

Sandalwood Golf Course – Maui's newest golf course, in Waikapu, next to the Waikapu Valley Country Club (☎ 242-7090)

Maui Country Club – Spreckelsville; open to the public Monday only and charges $45, including a cart, for either nine or 18 holes (☎ 877-0616)

Kapalua Golf Club – has three courses; green fees are $70 for resort guests, $110 for non-guests, including a shared cart, fees are lower after 2 pm (☎ 669-8044)

Kaanapali Beach Resort – has two courses, the Royal Kaanapali North and South; fees are $100 for greens and cart (☎ 661-3691)

Wailea Golf Club in Wailea – has two courses; fees are $50 for Wailea guests and $100 for the general public at the Orange Course, $10 more at the Blue Course, plus $15 for a mandatory shared cart (☎ 879-2966)

Makena Golf Course – Makena, charges $100 with a cart; there's also a $60 twilight rate (☎ 879-3344)

Organised Tours

Maui has many sightseeing tour companies. Tours to Hana and Haleakala are most popular, followed by Iao Valley, Lahaina and full-island tours.

Grayline-Maui (☎ 877-5507, (800) 367-2420), one of the largest companies, has a $25 tour to Upcountry, Haleakala, Lahaina and Iao Valley aimed at day visitors to Maui. It leaves Kahului Airport daily at 8.30 am, returning at 5 pm. Grayline also has a Hana tour for $70 and a Haleakala tour that costs from $20 to $34. The cost of the latter tour depends on the pick-up point, with Kahului the cheapest and Kapalua the most expensive.

Polynesian Adventure Tours (☎ 877-4242) has tours of Hana for $63 and of Haleakala, central Maui and Iao Valley for $50. There's also a Haleakala sunrise tour for $46. Children under 12 are charged about 75% of the adult fare.

Helicopter & Biplane Numerous helicopter companies fly out of the heliport at Kahului Airport for trips around the island. Some cross the channel and tour Molokai's spectacular north shore as well.

Most companies advertise in the free tourist magazines. Prices are highly competitive, with many running perennial specials, offering free use of video cameras and the like.

One of the cheapest is Sunshine Helicopters (☎ 871-0722, (800) 544-2520) which offers a 20-minute tour over the waterfalls of Waihee Valley for $59, a 35-minute tour of Haleakala and Hana for $99 and half a dozen longer tours.

Alexair (☎ 871-0792, (800) 871-0792) has similar rates. Unlike many of Maui's larger helicopter companies, it flies four-passenger Hughes 500 helicopters in which everyone has a window seat.

At Papillon (☎ 877-0022, (800) 367-7095), one of Hawaii's largest helicopter companies, prices range from $95 for a 30-minute tour of West Maui to $350 for a full-day outing that includes a circle-island flight and a jeep tour of Hana. There's also a one-hour tour for $185 that includes Molokai's north shore.

Biplane Barnstormers (☎ 878-2860) offers open-cockpit biplane rides for one or two passengers, either for scenic tours or aerobatic flights.

Cruises Maui has enough dinner cruises, sunset sails, deep-sea fishing and charter sailboats to fill a book. Most leave from Lahaina or Maalaea, a few from Kihei and Kaanapali.

You can get current rates and information from activity booths all around Maui or from the tourist magazines – or just go down to Lahaina Harbor where the booths and the boats are lined up and check out the scene for yourself.

Atlantis Submarines (☎ 667-2224) is a 65-foot sub that carries 46 passengers down to a depth of 150 feet in the waters off Lahaina and Kaanapali to see coral and large fish. Tours leave from Lahaina Harbor via a catamaran six times a day and cost $79 for adults, $48 for children.

If you want some of the effect at half the price, try Nautilus Submarine (☎ 667-7647), which despite its name is not a submarine but essentially a glass-bottom boat with a submerged lower deck with underwater windows. It leaves Lahaina Harbor five times a day and costs $40 for adults, $20 for children.

Whale Watching From January to the end of March is the peak humpback whale-watching season, though there are usually whales around Maui for a month or so on either side.

In season, whale-watch cruises are heavily advertised and you'll have no trouble finding one. Whale-watch boats range from double-hulled sailboats to 92-foot cruise vessels. Most leave from Maalaea or Lahaina harbours, a few from Kihei and Kaanapali. A two to three-hour tour usually costs $20 to $40 for adults, half-price for children. Some companies have hydrophones to hear whale songs, some claim to donate a portion of the ticket price to whale conservation groups, and some guarantee whale sightings or give another boat tour free.

Many of the boats that take snorkellers to Molokini in the morning go out whale watching in the afternoon. During the season there's a good chance of spotting whales on the snorkelling trip to Molokini itself.

The Pacific Whale Foundation (☎ 879-8811) has 2½-hour cruises leaving from both Maalaea and Lahaina harbours. It costs $27.50 aboard a 49-passenger power boat from Maalaea or a 109-passenger catamaran from Lahaina, and $30 aboard a 26-passenger sailboat from Lahaina. The fare for children is $15. Each boat goes out three times a day when it's busy. They guarantee whale sightings or you get another free trip. A portion of the profits go to the foundation's marine conservation projects.

To Other Islands Trilogy Excursions (☎ 661-4743, (800) 874-2666) sails a catamaran from Lahaina to Lanai's Hulopoe Bay. The boat leaves in the morning on Saturday and Sunday only, returning around 4 pm. It costs $125, which includes breakfast, a barbecue lunch, snorkelling and a land tour of Lanai. Children aged 3 to 12 are half-price.

Island Marine Activities (☎ 661-8397), 505 Front St 225, Lahaina, HI 96761, has numerous day tours to Molokai, which range from a self-drive tour for $69 to a mule ride to Kalaupapa for $179. Essentially it links up activities on Molokai with return passage between Lahaina and Kaunakakai aboard the *Maui Princess*. The prices are about the same as piecing the activities together yourself, with the advantage that it comes as a convenient package.

ACCOMMODATION

Other than camping, the cheapest places to stay on Maui are the Banana Bungalow and Northshore Inn in Wailuku, both of which have dorm beds for $15, and the Pioneer Inn in Lahaina, which has simple rooms with shared bath for $30. There are a couple of other places with cheap beds but they're in remote locales: the Maui YMCA Camp Keanae on the way to Hana and the Seven Pools Hikers' Lodge in Kipahulu.

Maui has a number of studio units, self-contained cottages and apartments that rent from about $50. Some of the better deals are found in the Haiku-Paia area. There are also a number of B&Bs around the island, offering some very pleasant places to stay for around $75.

Kihei has the highest concentration of middle-range accommodation, largely condos. Other mid-range accommodation can be found in Kahului, Lahaina and Honokowai. The lower end of the mid-range is about $50 to $80, but it's easy to spend well over $100 a night and not be in anything exclusive.

Maui's two biggest resort developments are Kaanapali Beach Resort and the newer Wailea Resort. Both have luxury hotels and condos. Prices at the cheapest condos start around $125. The beachfront hotels start at around $150 in Kaanapali and $175 in Wailea, though the most exclusive hotels have room rates that are double that.

Rates can be substantially lower during the low season (mid-April to mid-December) and you get to pick and choose. During the high season, the better condo deals usually require reservations far in advance.

Condominiums

Maui has many more condo units than hotel rooms. Some condo complexes are booked only through rental agents. Others operate more like a hotel with a front desk, though even then some of their units are usually handled by rental agents.

Overall, the best rates are through the agents, but you usually have to deal with security deposits and they sometimes slip in cleaning fees. For a short stay it may not be worth the hassle.

Most agents require deposits within one to two weeks of booking, with full payment within 30 days prior to arrival. Cancellation policies vary, but there will be a hefty charge (or no refund at all) for cancelling within the last month. The minimum stay is usually four to 14 days, depending on the place and season.

Each of the agents listed here handles a number of condo complexes and will send

listings with rates making it possible to compare values.

AA Oceanfront Condominium Rentals, 2439 S Kihei Rd 206A, Kihei, HI 96753 (☎ 879-7288, (800) 488-6004 from the USA and Canada)

Bello Realty, Box 1776, Kihei, HI 96753; handles a variety of Kihei condos, including some units at Kihei Alii Kai from $55/75 in the low/high season (☎ 879-3328, (800) 541-3060)

Condominium Rentals Hawaii, 2439 S Kihei Rd 205A, Kihei, HI 96753 (☎ 879-2778, (800) 367-5242)

Hawaiian Apartment Leasing Enterprises, 479 Ocean Ave No B, Laguna Beach, CA 92651 (☎ 714-497-4253, (800) 472-8449 from California, (800) 854-8843 from the rest of the USA and (800) 824-8968 from Canada)

Kihei Maui Vacations, Box 1055, 1325 S Kihei Rd 213, Kihei, HI 96753 (☎ 879-7581, (800) 542-6284 from the USA and (800) 423-8733 ext 4000 from Canada)

Kumulani Rentals, Box 1190, Kihei, HI 96753 (☎ 879-9272, (800) 367-2954)

Leisure Properties, Box 985, Kihei, HI 96753 (☎ 879-6770, (800) 888-MAUI)

Maui Condo & Home Realty, 2511 S Kihei Rd, Kihei, HI 96753; (☎ 879-5445, (800) 822-4409 from the USA, (800) 648-3301 from Canada)

Maui Network, Box 1077, Makawao, HI 96768 (☎ 572-9555, (800) 367-5221 from the USA, (800) 423-8733 ext 260 from Canada)

Camping

Maui has fewer camping options than the other islands. Waianapanapa State Park and Haleakala National Park are good choices.

In addition to the federal, state and county camping grounds listed here, there's also a church-sponsored camping ground at Olowalu, which is described in that section.

State Parks Polipoli and Waianapanapa, the only state parks with camping areas, both have tent sites and cabins. Permits are required, the maximum length of stay is five nights at each site, and tent camping is free.

Polipoli, in Upcountry, has one primitive cabin and a primitive road into it, which often requires a 4WD. Due to high fire hazard, Polipoli is sometimes closed. Waianapanapa, near Hana, has 12 housekeeping cabins that are very popular and must be reserved well in advance. If you can get one, the cabins are great value at $10/17 for singles/doubles.

Cabins can be reserved through the Division of State Parks (☎ 243-5354), State Office Building, 54 High St, Wailuku, HI 96793. Office hours are from 8 to 11 am and from noon to 4.15 pm weekdays.

County Parks On Maui there are only two county parks that allow camping, Baldwin and Rainbow. They're both in the Paia area and neither's a prize.

Permits cost $3 per day (50 cents for children), limited to three consecutive nights at each camping ground. Tents are required.

Permits are available by mail or in person from the Department of Parks & Recreation (☎ 243-7389), County of Maui, 1580 Kaahumanu Ave, Wailuku, HI 96793. The office is in the Wailuku War Memorial Center at Baldwin High School.

Haleakala National Park Tent camping is allowed at Hosmer's Grove, which is at the crater section of the park, and at Oheo Gulch on the coast south of Hana. They are both fine sites, though Oheo has no drinking water. There are no fees or permits required.

Tent camping is also allowed inside the crater and there are cabins as well. Full details are in the Haleakala section.

Each camping ground has a limit of three days a month.

Camping Supplies Fun Rentals of Maui (☎ 661-3053), 193 Lahainaluna Rd, Lahaina, rents tents from $20 a day, and backpacks and sleeping bags for $5 a day.

ENTERTAINMENT

Maui's entertainment scene is second only to Oahu's, with a wide variety of music from rock, jazz and disco to mellow Hawaiian guitar. Maui has its own symphony orchestra and there are occasional concerts by New Age musicians.

Casanova in Makawao usually has the hottest bands and brings in top-name musicians. Otherwise, most of the action is in Lahaina and at the resort hotels, especially in Kaanapali and Wailea. If you're into jazz, saxophonist Gabe Baltazar is not to be missed if he's doing a gig.

For the best updated entertainment information, see the 'Maui Scene' in the Thursday issue of the *Maui News*. The free *Maui Beach Press* also has entertainment listings.

Hawaiiana

Luaus are held regularly in Lahaina, Kaanapali, Wailea and Kihei. All include a buffet dinner with some Hawaiian foods and a Polynesian show and cost from $38 to $48. The Old Lahaina Luau in Lahaina puts on one of the more authentic productions.

There are free hula shows at 6.30 pm nightly at the Kaanapali Beach Hotel in Kaanapali; at 1 pm on Sundays at the Lahaina Cannery Mall in Lahaina; at 1.30 pm on Tuesdays at the Wailea Shopping Village in Wailea; and at 10 am on Thursdays at the Kapalua Shops in Kapalua.

The Napili Kai Beach Club in Napili has a Friday dinner show that features hula dancing by local children.

THINGS TO BUY

For local arts & crafts, some of the best deals are at the Lahaina Arts Society's gallery in Lahaina's old courthouse and at the Maui Crafts Guild in Paia.

Maui Blanc, Maui's own pineapple wine, is a quality wine that makes a good gift. It sells for about $7 a bottle at liquor and grocery stores around the island.

Proteas are a Maui speciality. The best deal is to buy direct from the Upcountry farms where they are grown.

Several businesses sell food and flowers, including leis, proteas, papayas, pineapples and Maui onions, which are agriculturally pre-inspected and delivered to the airport for you to pick up on your way out. Two places are Airport Flower & Fruit (☎ 877-6131), at 460 Dairy Rd near the airport, and Take Home Maui (☎ 661-8067), 121 Dickenson St, Lahaina.

GETTING THERE & AWAY
Air
The main airport is in Kahului. There are two commuter airports: Kapalua West Maui Airport and Hana Airport.

Airline phone numbers are given in the Getting Around chapter in the front of the book.

Kahului Airport Hawaiian Airlines and Aloha Airlines fly directly to Kahului from Honolulu, Lihue (Kauai), and Hilo and Kona (Big Island). Both airlines fly at least hourly to and from Honolulu and Kauai, and a few times daily from Big Island airports. Aloha also flies once a day to Lanai. One-way fares are $68.95 on Aloha and $69.95 on Hawaiian, except for the first and last flights out of Honolulu which are $49.95. Return fares are double.

Aloha IslandAir flies to Kahului from Honolulu, Princeville (Kauai), Molokai, Lanai and Kamuela (Big Island). One-way fares are $69.95. Two exceptions are: flights between Kahului and Kapalua West Maui, which cost $20, and the two late-night flights to Honolulu (discounted in that direction only), which leave Kahului Airport at 11 pm and 1 am and cost only $30.

Air Molokai connects Kahului to Molokai and Lanai. The fare is $59.90 one way, $99.90 round trip, though sometimes there are heavily discounted specials.

From the US mainland, Kahului Airport is served by United, American and Delta.

Kahului Airport has car-rental booths, a snack bar, restaurant, visitor information booth, lei stand, gift shop and newsstand.

Kapalua West Maui Airport This is a small airfield with a single 3000-foot runway. Hawaiian Airlines services Kapalua from Honolulu with about a dozen daily shuttle flights in 50-passenger Dash 7s, the largest plane the airport can handle. The first one leaves Honolulu about 7 am and the last one at 5 pm.

Aloha IslandAir also has numerous daily flights from Honolulu as well as flights from Hana, Princeville, Molokai, Lanai and Kamuela.

The fares for both airlines are $69.95 one way, $139.90 return.

The airport is between Kapalua and Kaanapali, both about two miles away.

Hana Airport Aloha IslandAir flies to Hana daily from Honolulu, Princeville, Molokai, Lanai, Kahului, Kapalua and Kamuela.

The fares are $69.95 one way.

Ferry
The *Maui Princess* (☎ 553-5736 on Molokai, 661-8397 on Maui, (800) 833-5800 from the mainland), 505 Front St, Suite 225, Lahaina, HI 96761, runs twice daily between Molokai and Maui. The boat leaves Kaunakakai at 5.45 am and 3.55 pm and leaves Lahaina's Pier 3 at 7 am and 5 pm. The one-way fare is $25 for adults, $12.50 for children.

Expeditions (☎ 661-3756) runs a ferry four times daily between Maui and Lanai. The boat leaves Lahaina Harbor at 6.45 and 9.15 am and 3.15 pm, arriving an hour later. The boat leaves Manele at 8 and 10.30 am and 4.30 pm. There's also an evening sail, which leaves Lahaina at 5.45 pm (at 8.30 pm on Thursdays) and leaves Manele at 6.45 pm (9.30 pm on Thursdays). The one-way fare is $25 for adults and $20 for children aged 2 to 11.

GETTING AROUND
To/From the Airport
Trans-Hawaiian has a shuttle bus that leaves Kahului Airport on the hour between 7 am and 6 pm daily and goes to Lahaina and Kaanapali hotels. It costs $13. The return service is slightly less frequent, and to get back to the airport reservations (☎ 877-7308) are required.

Akina Bus Service (☎ 879-2828) serves the Kihei-Wailea area with an airport shuttle bus from Kahului Airport. It costs $10. The bus leaves Kihei on the hour, the airport on the half-hour, between 8 am and 6.30 pm. Reservations are required.

From the Kapalua West Maui Airport, the Kaanapali Trolley (☎ 667-7411) runs a free airport shuttle bus to the Kaanapali hotels an average of 13 times a day. The first bus leaves the airport at 8 am, the last at 5 pm.

Bus

Maui has no public bus service, but there are several private shuttles in West Maui.

The Lahaina Express makes numerous runs daily between Kaanapali Beach Resort and Lahaina. Both Kaanapali and Wailea have shuttle services around their resorts. The Lahaina Cannery Mall operates a shuttle bus between its shopping centre and the Honokowai area, with stops at Kaanapali hotels. All four shuttles are free. Details are in the respective sections.

Akina Bus Service (☎ 879-2828) operates a bus between the Maui Prince in Makena and Whalers Village in Kaanapali four times a day, stopping at Wailea and Kihei en route. The full run takes 1¾ hours one way. The cost is $10 return for adults, $5 for children aged under 12.

Taxi

Taxi fares are regulated by the county. Including the minimum flagdown of $1.40, the first mile totals $2.80. Each additional mile is $1.40.

Approximate one-way fares from the airport are $6 to Kahului, $14 to $22 to Kihei, $34 to Lahaina and $40 to Kaanapali.

Car

Avis (☎ 871-7575), Budget (☎ 871-8811), National (☎ 871-8851), Thrifty (☎ 871-7596), Tropical (☎ 877-0002) and Dollar (☎ 877-2731) all have booths at Kahului Airport.

The only car-rental booth operated at the Kapalua West Maui Airport on a regular basis is Budget (☎ 669-7044). However, National, Dollar, Avis, Hertz and Alamo all have offices on Hwy 30 in nearby Kaanapali and pick up at the airport. Dollar is the only rental agency for Hana Airport.

More information on the national chains, including toll-free numbers, is in the Getting Around chapter in the front of the book.

Klunker's (☎ 877-3197), at 456 Dairy Road in Kahului, will rent to drivers without credit cards, accepting a $100 deposit ($250 if you don't take the CDW insurance) in lieu. Their cars are three to six years old and rent for $50 for three days, $100 per week. The optional CDW insurance is $5 a day. There's a three-day minimum.

In Lahaina, Rainbow Rent-A-Car (☎ 661-8734), 741 Wainee St, will rent to drivers without credit cards, accepting a $100 deposit and payment in advance. Rates for Toyota compacts are $24.50 a day, $140 a week. Rainbow also has Suzuki Samurai jeeps for $45 a day.

Bicycle & Moped

Fun Rentals (☎ 661-3053), 193 Lahainaluna Rd, Lahaina, rents several types of bicycles, ranging from $20 to $50 a day and from $60 to $300 a week. Mopeds cost $10 for two hours, $35 for 24 hours and $130 a week. The shop is open from 8.30 am to 5 pm Monday to Saturday, 8.30 am to 3 pm on Sunday.

Rainbow Rent-A-Car (☎ 661-8734), 741 Wainee St, Lahaina, rents Honda scooters at $15 for three hours, $25 for 24 hours. It's open from 7.30 am to 5 pm daily.

Kukui Activity Center (☎ 875-1151) at the Kukui Mall in Kihei rents bicycles for $10/50 a day/week and Honda Elite 50 cc scooters for $25/99 a day/week. They provide a free shuttle service in the Kihei-Wailea area and are open from 7.30 am to 6 pm daily.

For other bicycle rentals, see the yellow pages of the Maui phone book.

Hitching

Hitching is illegal in Maui County, but if you want to give it a go, then do what most hitchhikers in these parts do: just stand at the side of the road and 'look' like you want a ride. The correct stance should be enough; there's no need for a thumb.

Lahaina

Lahaina was a royal court for Maui chiefs and the bread basket, or more accurately the breadfruit basket, of West Maui. After Kamehameha I unified the islands he set up his base in Lahaina and the capital remained there until 1845. Hawaii's first stone church, first missionary school and first printing press were all in place in Lahaina by the early 1830s.

The whaling years reached their height in Lahaina in the 1840s with hundreds of ships pulling into port each year. The town took on the whalers' boisterous nature, with dance halls, bars and brothels. Hundreds of sick or derelict sailors, who had either been abandoned or jumped ship, roamed the streets. Herman Melville was among the multitudes that landed there.

These days Lahaina's streets are jammed with tourists. The old wooden shops that once housed saloons and provision stores are full of boutiques and galleries.

While there are plenty of interesting historical sites to see, Lahaina is abuzz with commercial activity and if you're expecting something quaint and romantic you may well be disappointed. The coastal setting and mountain backdrop *is* pretty, however, and it's easy to see why people have been drawn here. There are soft breezes off the water and fine sunset views of Lanai.

Orientation

The focal point of Lahaina is its bustling small-boat harbour, which is backed by the old Pioneer Inn and Banyan Tree Square. Half of Lahaina's sights are clustered around this area.

The main drag and tourist strip is Front St, which runs along the shoreline.

If Front St seems too hectic, stroll up a block or two to the residential streets, where you'll find Lahaina's quieter and more Hawaiian side.

Most of Lahaina's major attractions are historical sites. Sightseeing spots include homes of missionaries, prisons for sailors and graveyards for both.

Information

Lahaina is best explored on foot, though because the town is long and narrow, you may end up walking a fair distance. The Lahaina Restoration Foundation puts out a free walking-tour map.

Money There's a Bank of Hawaii in the Lahaina Shopping Center, and a branch of the First Hawaiian Bank on the corner of Wainee and Papalaua Sts.

Post The post office substation in the Lahaina Shopping Center is open from 8.15 am to 4.15 pm Monday to Friday. There's often a long wait for a parking space and a long queue inside.

The main post office where you pick up mail sent general delivery (poste restante) to Lahaina is near the civic centre, on Hwy 30 between Lahaina and Kaanapali. Hours are 8 am to 4 pm Monday to Friday, 10 am to noon on Saturdays.

There's also a little contract post office at The Wharf shopping centre which opens from 9.30 am to 4.30 pm Monday to Friday and 10 am to 1 pm on Saturday.

Library The Lahaina public library (☎ 661-0566), 680 Wharf St, is open from 9 am to 5 pm on Mondays, Tuesdays, Wednesdays and Saturdays and from noon to 8 pm on Thursdays.

Shopping The Wharf, a shopping centre on Front St near Pioneer Inn, has over 50 shops and restaurants, as well as a triple-screen movie theatre. Upstairs, the Whalers Book Shoppe & Coffee House is a pretty good bookstore with cafe tables out the front where you can have Kona coffee and pastries. A few doors down, Earth & Company has a large selection of save-the-whale paraphernalia. A percentage of the proceeds goes to Greenpeace Hawaii.

Lahaina Shopping Center, bordering Front, Wainee and Papalaua Sts, has a post

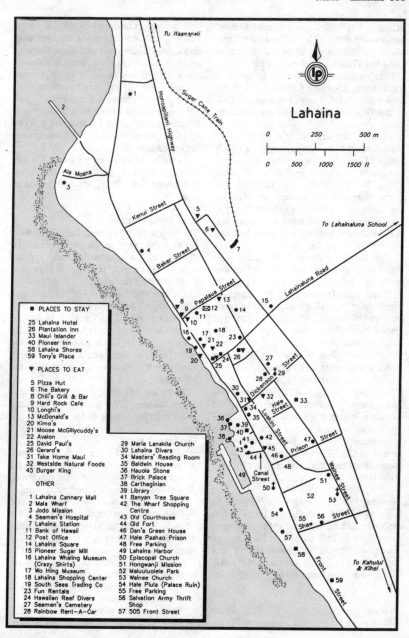

Lahaina

PLACES TO STAY
- 25 Lahaina Hotel
- 26 Plantation Inn
- 33 Maui Islander
- 40 Pioneer Inn
- 58 Lahaina Shores
- 59 Tony's Place

PLACES TO EAT
- 5 Pizza Hut
- 6 The Bakery
- 8 Chili's Grill & Bar
- 9 Hard Rock Cafe
- 10 Longhi's
- 13 McDonald's
- 20 Kimo's
- 21 Moose McGillycuddy's
- 22 Avalon
- 25 David Paul's
- 26 Gerard's
- 31 Take Home Maui
- 32 Westside Natural Foods
- 45 Burger King

OTHER
- 1 Lahaina Cannery Mall
- 2 Mala Wharf
- 3 Jodo Mission
- 4 Seamen's Hospital
- 7 Lahaina Station
- 11 Bank of Hawaii
- 12 Post Office
- 14 Lahaina Square
- 15 Pioneer Sugar Mill
- 16 Lahaina Whaling Museum (Crazy Shirts)
- 17 Wo Hing Museum
- 18 Lahaina Shopping Center
- 19 South Seas Trading Co
- 23 Fun Rentals
- 24 Hawaiian Reef Divers
- 27 Seamen's Cemetery
- 28 Rainbow Rent-A-Car
- 29 Maria Lanakila Church
- 30 Lahaina Divers
- 34 Masters' Reading Room
- 35 Baldwin House
- 36 Hauola Stone
- 37 Brick Palace
- 38 Carthaginian
- 39 Library
- 41 Banyan Tree Square
- 42 The Wharf Shopping Centre
- 43 Old Courthouse
- 44 Old Fort
- 46 Dan's Green House
- 47 Hale Paahao Prison
- 48 Free Parking
- 49 Lahaina Harbor
- 50 Episcopal Church
- 51 Hongwanji Mission
- 52 Maluuluolele Park
- 53 Wainee Church
- 54 Hale Piula (Palace Ruin)
- 55 Free Parking
- 56 Salvation Army Thrift Shop
- 57 505 Front Street

office, Thai and Japanese restaurants, McDonald's, Bank of Hawaii, Nagasako Super Market, a pharmacy, a 24-hour coin laundry and a Ben Franklin department store.

Lahaina Square, off Wainee St opposite the Lahaina Shopping Center, has a Foodland supermarket, Denny's restaurant, Jack in the Box and Baskin-Robbins ice-cream store.

Lahaina Cannery Mall, a former pineapple cannery, is a large shopping centre with a 24-hour Safeway supermarket, Longs Drugs, Waldenbooks and about 50 other shops. Restaurants include Marie Callender's, Burger King, Compadres Mexican restaurant, Sir Wilfred's Espresso Cafe and an inexpensive Greek takeaway restaurant. It's on the northern side of town between Front St and Hwy 30.

The Salvation Army Thrift Shop, 135 Shaw St, is open from 9 am to 6 pm Monday to Friday, and until 4 pm on Saturdays.

South Seas Trading Post, 851 Front St, stands apart from all the gaudy tourist shops on Front St. It sells Fijian and Tongan tapa, Papua New Guinea face masks and Marshallese stick charts, as well as interesting things from Burma, Thailand and Bali. The collection depends on the owners' last jaunt abroad, but is always intriguing.

Dan's Green House, at 133 Prison St, sells 'fuku-bonsai', created when the roots of the common house plant *schefflera* (octopus tree) wrap around a lava rock becoming quasi-bonsai. They are treated for export and cost from $25. Dan's has live cockatoos and a couple of monkeys and is a hangout for local kids.

Parking Finding a space for your car in Lahaina can be a challenge. Front St has on-street parking but there's always a line of cruising cars. Your best bet is the corner of Front and Prison Sts where there's free public parking with a three-hour limit. There's also free parking opposite 505 Front St.

Pioneer Inn
The old green and white Pioneer Inn is the most prominent landmark in town. It's got a whaling-era atmosphere with swinging doors, ship figureheads and signs warning against womanising in the rooms. The downstairs saloon is Lahaina's most popular watering hole. Lively country-and-western bands play all afternoon and evening.

Pioneer Inn has creaky stairs leading up to the cheapest rooms in Lahaina and you can still find brawny tattooed men hanging over the top balcony railings.

Actually, the two-storey Pioneer Inn was built in 1901, long after the whaling boom had passed, but nobody seems to notice or care.

Banyan Tree Square
The largest banyan tree in the USA covers most of the space in the park next to the Pioneer Inn. It's so sprawling that it appears to be on the verge of pushing the old courthouse clear off the block.

The tree was planted in 1873 to commemorate the 50th anniversary of the first missionary arrival in Lahaina. It has 16 major trunks and scores of horizontally stretching branches reaching across the better part of an acre. Local kids like to swing Tarzan-style from the aerial roots through the branches.

There are shaded benches and walkways under the tree. It's a good place to take a break from the crowds on Front St.

Old Courthouse
Beyond the banyan tree is the old courthouse, built in 1859. It once served as the government centre with a customs house, post office and governor's office upstairs.

The old jail in the basement is now used by the Lahaina Arts Society and the cells that once held drunken sailors now display artwork. The society is a nonprofit collective. Artists kick in a 30% commission, which covers operating expenses. As that's roughly half of the commission charged by private galleries, you'll find some of the best prices in Lahaina here.

All the exhibits are by island artists, and include paintings, blown glass, pottery, woodcarvings and some quality native basketwork. Many of the baskets are composed entirely of Maui fibres such as wattle, watsonia, philodendron, draco, ape and fishtail palm.

The society also sponsors community art classes. A number of well-known Maui artists got their start here. It's open from 10 am to 4 pm daily.

Old Fort

The Canal St corner of Banyan Tree Square has a reconstructed section of coral wall from a fort built in 1832 to keep rowdy whalers in line.

At one point the fort had 47 cannons, most of them salvaged from foreign ships which sank in Hawaiian waters.

Each day at dusk a sentinel beat a drum to alert sailors to return to their ships. Those that didn't make it back in time ended up imprisoned in the fort. In 1854 the fort was dismantled and its coral blocks used as building materials for the new prison.

Canal St

Canal St, bordering Banyan Tree Square, used to be part of a canal system that ran through Lahaina. An enterprising American consul officer built this initial section of the canal in the 1840s to allow whalers easier access to fresh water supplies – for a fee of course.

Because of problems with mosquitoes, most of the canal system was filled in long ago. Incidentally, Hawaii had no mosquitoes at all until the whalers brought them in from North America in their water barrels.

Lahaina Harbor

The four cannons on the waterfront opposite the old courthouse were raised from the wreck of a Russian ship that went down in Honolulu Harbor in 1816.

They point directly at Lahaina's crowded small-boat harbour which is filled with glass-bottom boats, windjammers, sport fishing boats, whale-watchers and sunset sailboats. Booths lining the edge of the harbour sell tickets for most of the cruises,

as do the ubiquitous activity booths around town.

The Carthaginian

In 1972, the 960-ton *Carthaginian*, one of the last square-riggers in Hawaii, was on its way from Maui to Honolulu for repairs when it hit a reef outside Lahaina Harbor and sank. The wooden-hulled *Carthaginian* belonged to a class of swift brigantines which made freight runs between New England, Hawaii and China in the 19th century.

The *Carthaginian* that now sits in Lahaina Harbor is a replica, with a steel hull, built in Kiel, Germany in 1920. After being brought to Lahaina in 1973, the 97-foot brig had to be completely restored and all the masts and yards handcrafted – a process which took seven years.

Though the best view of the ship is from the outside, you can also board the boat for $3. Below deck there's a tiny theatre where films on whales are shown continuously. It's open from 9 am to 4 pm daily.

Masters' Reading Room

The Masters' Reading Room, on the corner of Front and Dickenson Sts, is the office of the Lahaina Restoration Foundation (☎ 661-3262), the group most instrumental in preserving Lahaina's past. They restored the Baldwin Home, Wo Hing Temple and Hale Pai and have been involved in a number of other historical projects.

During the whaling years the building was a reading room for sea captains. From here they could keep an eye on happenings in the harbour across the road. The original construction of coral and stone blocks has been preserved.

Baldwin House

The Baldwin House, next door to the Masters' Reading Room, is the oldest building in Lahaina, built in 1834. It was home to the Reverend Dwight Baldwin, a missionary doctor. The exterior of the coral and rock building once resembled the Reading Room but it's been plastered over. The walls beneath the plaster are a full 24 inches thick, which keeps the house cool all year round.

It took the Baldwins 161 days to get to Hawaii from their native Connecticut. The house still holds the china and chairs they brought with them around the Horn, as well as other period furnishings.

The entrance fee of $3 ($5 per couple) includes a brief tour. It's open from 9.30 am to 4.30 pm daily.

Library Area

The entire area surrounding the library was once the site of a royal taro field. It was also the location of the first Western-style building in Hawaii, the **Brick Palace**, erected by King Kamehameha I so he could keep watch on arriving ships. The modest two-storey structure was built around 1800 by two Botany Bay convicts. All that remains today is the excavated foundation on the ocean side of the Lahaina public library.

Hauola Stone is a water-worn lava stone on the shoreline to the right as you face the ocean. The Hawaiians believed this flat seat-shaped stone emitted healing powers to those who sat on it.

If you walk north down Front St past the library there's a row of interesting **turn-of-the-century buildings** along the street, best appreciated from the sea-wall sidewalk.

Wo Hing Temple

The Wo Hing Temple, which is now a museum, was built in 1912 by the Chinese community in Lahaina. The two-storey building, on Front St, functioned largely as a meeting hall, though for a period after WW II it was also used as a home for elderly Chinese men.

As Lahaina's ethnic Chinese population declined, so too did the building. It was restored and turned into a museum by the Lahaina Restoration Foundation in 1983. There are cultural artefacts and period photos downstairs and a Taoist shrine upstairs.

The tin-roofed cookhouse next door (built detached because of the danger of fire) has been set up as a little theatre which shows fascinating films taken in Hawaii by Thomas Edison in 1898 and 1905.

Against the wall there's a collection of little opium bottles found during the clean-up of the grounds.

Entrance to both the temple and theatre, which are open from 9 am to 4 pm daily, is free.

Lahaina Whaling Museum

Lahaina Whaling Museum is a display of whaling era artefacts along one wall of the Crazy Shirts store at 865 Front St. It's authentic and free.

The collection includes antique harpoons, harpoon guns, ship logs, scrimshaw and photos of the *Carthaginian* sinking outside Lahaina Harbor in 1972. The figurehead hanging from the ceiling in the front of the store was salvaged from the ship. It had been carved in 1965 to prepare the *Carthaginian* for its feature role in the movie *Hawaii*, the adaptation of James Michener's epic novel.

Outside on the back porch there's a rusty old cannon and anchor, and a whaler's trypot used for boiling down blubber.

Holy Innocents' Episcopal Church

The interior of Holy Innocents' Episcopal Church, 561 Front St, is colourfully decorated with a Hawaiiana motif.

Paintings on the front of the koa altar depict a fisherman in an outrigger canoe and Hawaiian farmers harvesting taro and breadfruit. Above the altar is a Hawaiian madonna and child. A Lahaina mother and infant were the models for the painting.

Until the turn of the century the church property was the site of a vacation home belonging to Queen Liliuokalani, Hawaii's last reigning monarch.

Hale Piula

A couple of steps and a grassy building foundation between the Episcopal Church and the 505 Front St shopping centre is all that remains of Hale Piula, Lahaina's attempt at a royal palace.

The palace was never completed as Kamehameha III decided to move the capital to Honolulu halfway through the project. Most of the stones used in the construction were later carted away and used to build the harbourside courthouse.

Maluuluolele Park

Maluuluolele Park, opposite Hale Piula, was once the site of a large pond containing a legendary *moo* (water dragon). An island in the centre of the pond was home to Maui chiefs and at times to King Kamehamehas I, II and III. It held an ornate burial chamber for royalty.

The park's name is literally 'the breadfruit shade of Lele' ('Lele' was the ancient name for Lahaina).

In 1918 the island was levelled and the pond filled in. Today, the park has basketball courts, tennis courts, a baseball field and not a hint of its fascinating past.

Wainee Church

Wainee Church, 535 Wainee St, was built in 1832. It was the first stone church in Hawaii, though it had problems standing.

The steeple and bell collapsed in 1858. In 1894 the church was torched by royalists because its minister supported the annexation of Hawaii. A second version burned to the ground in 1947, and the third was blown away in a storm a couple of years later. One could get the impression that the old Hawaiian gods didn't take kindly to the house of this foreign god.

The fourth version has been standing since 1953. It's now called Waiola Congregational Church and holds regular Sunday services.

The **cemetery** next door is more interesting than the church. Here lies Governor Hoapili, who ordered the original church built; Queen Keopuolani, once the highest ranking woman in Hawaii and wife of Kamehameha I; and the Reverend William Richards, Lahaina's first missionary. Some of the old tombstones have interesting inscriptions and photo cameos.

Hongwanji Mission

The Lahaina Hongwanji Mission, 551 Wainee St, was built in 1927. It's usually locked but the front doors are glass so you can glance in. Unlike Buddhist temples in Japan, this one has rows of wooden pews. Services are held each Sunday in English and once a month in Japanese.

Hale Paahao

Hale Paahao, or 'stuck-in-irons house', Lahaina's old prison, was built in 1852. The old harbourside fort was dismantled by convicts who carried the blocks here to construct the eight-foot-high prison walls.

Inside, one of the whitewashed cells has an authentic-looking 'old seadog' mannequin with a recorded story about 'life in this here calaboose'.

In another cell you'll find a list of offences and arrests for the year 1855. The top three offences were drunkenness (330 arrests), adultery and fornication (111) and 'furious riding' (89). Others include profanity, aiding deserting sailors, drinking awa and giving birth to bastard children. Hawaiians could collect bounties by turning in sailors that jumped ship or fooled around with local women. There's also a copy of a 16-year-old seaman's diary describing his time spent in the prison.

Admission is free and you can pick up a historical walking map at the visitor's register.

Seamen's Cemetery

The Seamen's Cemetery on Wainee St is next to Maria Lanakila Church, the first Catholic church on Maui.

It's basically a local cemetery, with only one seaman's tombstone actually identified. However, old records show that numerous sailors were buried here, including a shipmate of Herman Melville's from the *Acushnet*.

Pioneer Mill

It's hard to think of tourist-jammed Lahaina as a sugar town, but it is. The Pioneer Sugar Mill has been a prominent part of Lahaina for 130 years and its cane fields stretch for 17 miles along the coast.

The mill, which sits on both sides of

Lahainaluna Rd on the slopes above the town centre, is part of the Amfac Corporation.

This is still an operating mill where people work hard to make a living. Their dusty workplace contrasts sharply with the tourist playground below.

Lahainaluna Seminary

Lahainaluna Seminary, established by Christian missionaries in 1831, was the first US educational institution west of the Rockies.

One of the school's early graduates was David Malo, a respected Hawaiian philosopher. He became Hawaii's first native rights spokesperson, warning in his early writings in 1837 that Hawaii was about to be swallowed up by the masses of foreigners arriving on its shores. His book *Hawaiian Antiquities* is today one of the best accounts of ancient Hawaiian history and culture.

Lahainaluna is now Lahaina's public high school, considered one of the best in the state.

The school is at the end of Lahainaluna Rd, above the mill. You get a nice view of Lahaina with Lanai in the background from the school's lower parking lot.

Hale Pai

Hale Pai, the printing house in Lahainaluna's grounds, held the first printing press in Hawaii.

Though the main purpose of printing was to make the Bible available to Hawaiians, the press also produced the first botany book of the islands and Hawaii's first newspaper (in 1834).

Examples of early books are on display at Hale Pai. You can use a replica of the original Ramage press to hand print your own copy of a page from the first Hawaiian primer.

Admission is free though donations are appreciated. It's open from 10 am to 3 pm Monday to Friday.

Seamen's Hospital

In 1844, the building at 1024 Front St was leased by the US government and turned into a hospital for sick and abandoned seamen.

Officials at the hospital were notorious for embezzlement. Sailors who weren't sick and others long since dead were commonly signed onto the hospital books. A US warship with a board of inquiry sent to investigate the corruption mysteriously disappeared at sea on the return home.

The seamen's hospital has been completely restored and is now used as an office. A huge anchor on the lawn marks the site.

Lahaina Jodo Mission

A large bronze statue of Buddha overlooks the compound of Lahaina Jodo Mission, on Ala Moana, off Front St at the northern end of town. The statue was put up in 1968 in celebration of the centennial of Japanese immigration to Hawaii. With its back to the mountains, the statue looks out over the Pacific towards Japan.

Opposite the mission, in the sandy cemetery along the beach, the county has moved a number of graves that have been disinterred by high surf in the past few years.

Just to the north is the long Mala Wharf, constructed in the 1920s to allow inter-island ferries to land passengers directly ashore. It never made the grade. Rough seas prevented the ferries from pulling up alongside the pier, forcing them to continue shuttling passengers across the shallows of Lahaina Harbor in small boats.

The wharf is now crumbling and closed, though Mala does have a new launch ramp for small boats nearby.

Lahaina Beaches

Lahaina is not known for its beaches and wins no prizes for swimming areas. For the most part, the beaches are shallow and rocky. Your best bet is to go north to Hanakaoo Beach Park or to Kaanapali. If you don't have a car use the free trolley bus (see Lahaina's Getting Around section later).

Places to Stay

You couldn't be more in the middle of the action than at the *Pioneer Inn* (☎ 661-3636, (800) 457-5457), 658 Wharf St, Lahaina, HI 96761. It can be noisy from the traffic, the throngs of tourists and the raucous bar and band, but this two-storey turn-of-the-century hotel is loaded with character. There are 48 rooms, all on the 2nd floor surrounded by a porch-like lanai. Rooms in the original building face the harbour and are the cheapest and noisiest. They're basic, with slanting floors, but are clean and comfortable enough. Rates are $30 for rooms with shared bath, $35 and $42 with private bath. Rooms in the newer wing with air-con and private bath start at $70.

Lahaina Roads (☎ 661-3166, (800) 624-8203), 1403 Front St, Lahaina, HI 96761, is a 42-room condo at the northern end of Lahaina near the Lahaina Cannery Mall. All units are oceanfront with full kitchens, lanais, TVs and phones with free local calls. There's a swimming pool. One-bedroom units cost from $75 in the low season, $95 in the high season. The minimum stay is three days.

The *Lahaina Hotel* (☎ 661-0577, (800) 669-3444), 127 Lahainaluna Rd, Lahaina, HI 96761, is a restored turn-of-the-century hotel, a project of Crazy Shirt owner Rick Ralston, who also restored the Moana Valley Inn in Honolulu. Ralston spent over $3 million on this 13-room hostelry. The rooms are small but delightfully atmospheric – each has hardwood floors, wallpaper, antique furnishings and lanais. Modern conveniences include air-con, private bath, telephone and piped in music, but no TV. Room rates are $89 and $99, while suites are $129. Prices are the same for a single/double and include a continental breakfast. Children under the age of 15 are not allowed.

The *Plantation Inn* (☎ 667-9225, (800) 433-6815), 174 Lahainaluna Rd, Lahaina, HI 96761, is an elegant two-storey Victorian-style inn with hardwood floors, antique furnishings, stained glass and a tiled pool. The 18 rooms and suites range from $99 to $175. It's classy and comfortable, and arguably the nicest place to stay in Lahaina. Guests pay half-price for the breakfast buffet at Gerard's, the renowned French restaurant at the front of the inn.

Maui Islander (☎ 667-9766, (800) 367-5226), 660 Wainee St, Lahaina, HI 96761, is a sprawling 372-unit hotel set back a few blocks from Front St. Rooms have cable TV, air-con and ceiling fans. There's a pool and tennis court. Rates are $83/95 in the low/high season for a room with a refrigerator, and $95/107 (for up to three people) for a studio with kitchen. It's standard middle-class fare, without a great deal of character.

Lahaina Shores (☎ 661-4835, (800) 642-6284), 475 Front St, Lahaina, HI 96761, is a 155-room condo run like a hotel. It's on the beach next to the 505 Front St shopping centre, on the south side of town. Mountain-view studios cost $95/105 for up to three people in the low/high season, one-bedroom units cost $120/145 for up to four people. Add on another $20/30 low/high for an ocean view. There's a small pool.

Tony's Place (☎ 661-8040), 13 Kauaula Rd, Box 11475, Lahaina, HI 96761, is off Front Street, a five-minute walk south of Lahaina Shores. Owner Tony Mamo rents out three of the four bedrooms in his modest home. Rooms are $50/60 a single/double, with a two-night minimum. Breakfast is not included but guests are allowed kitchen privileges. Tony accepts MasterCard and Visa.

Camping The nearest camping ground is in Olowalu, five miles south of Lahaina. Details are in the Olowalu section.

Places to Eat – bottom end
Westside Natural Foods & Deli, 136 Dickenson St, sells organic produce, yoghurts and kefir, fresh juice and trail mix. The deli makes non-dairy burritos for $3.25, salads for $4.95 a pound and good smoothies, carrot juice and vegie sandwiches. It's open from 7.30 am to 9 pm, except on Sundays when it's open from 9 am to 7 pm.

The Bakery, on Limahana Rd on the northern side of town, is Lahaina's best bakery. In addition to fresh breads, pastries and muffins, they bake the quiches and pastries served in many of Lahaina's restaurants. Whole-wheat croissants are 95 cents and huge sticky buns $1.50, while sandwiches made to order on a choice of breads cost $4.50. It's open from 6 am to 4 pm Monday to Saturday, 6 am to noon on Sunday. To get there, turn mauka at the Pizza Hut off Hwy 30.

Moose McGillycuddy's, 844 Front St, looks touristy but you'll find lots of locals here too. Breakfast is from 7.30 to 11 am with 21 different omelette plates at $5.95. The early-bird special served from 7.30 to 9 am is eggs, bacon, toast and orange juice for $3. At lunch time, burgers and sandwiches are $5 to $7. At dinner, which is served until 10 pm, dishes average $10 to $14, though from 4.30 to 5.30 pm there's an early-bird dinner with mahimahi or barbecued chicken for $7.95.

The Pioneer Inn has two dining rooms. Breakfast ($4 to $6.50) and lunch (sandwiches from $4 to $7) are served in the *Old Whaler's Saloon*. Dinner, which is served in the *Snug Harbor* restaurant just off the lobby, includes a simple salad bar. Prices range from $12.50 for Polynesian chicken to $17 for scampi, though when the mood strikes they run their 'Peg-Leg' special of steak or mahimahi, salad bar and a cocktail for $12.95.

Pancho & Lefty's at The Wharf has acceptable Mexican food. Two tacos or two enchiladas with rice and beans cost $8, burritos $10 and fajitas $14. Meals come with home-made chips and salsa. It's open from 10 am to 11 pm daily with the same menu at lunch and dinner. There's a happy hour from 3 to 6 pm daily featuring $1 draught beers and large $2.75 margaritas.

Musashi in Lahaina Shopping Center has Japanese food. At lunch time, oyako domburi costs $4.50 and tonkatsu or sukiyaki costs $6.50. Each comes with miso soup, pickles and rice. Dinners range from $10 to $17.

JJ's, 505 Front St, has an ocean view and good food. At lunch, sandwiches and burgers with fries cost $7 and fresh fish of the day costs $10. Dinners feature dishes such as kiawe chicken for $15 and catch of the day for $19, and include a Caesar salad. It's open daily from 10 am to midnight.

The *Hard Rock Cafe*, 900 Front St, has good burgers and sandwiches including a veggie burger, club sandwich or a bacon-guacamole cheeseburger for $7. All come with fries and green salad. There are also a few hot dishes, such as steak, barbecue chicken and fajitas for $11 to $15. It's open daily until midnight.

Chili's Grill & Bar, 900 Front St, serves Americanised Mexican food, burgers, salads and grilled meats. Two tacos cost $6, a good-sized chicken salad $7 and fajitas $11. There's a $4 'kiddie menu' for keikis under age 12. It's open from 11 am to 10 pm weekdays, 11 am to 11 pm on weekends.

Kimo's, 845 Front St, is a popular ocean-front restaurant with a sunset view. Lunch is mainly sandwiches in the $6 to $10 range, while dinner features seafood and steaks for $14 to $30, including green salad, fresh warm carrot muffins, sour bread rolls and rice.

Take Home Maui (☎ 661-8067), 121 Dickenson St, sells fresh fruit by the pound, as well as salads, sandwiches, bagels, smoothies and good coffee. There are a couple of tables on the porch; it's all quite casual. They also sell agriculturally pre-inspected pineapples that they'll deliver to the airport. A box of six pineapples costs $18.50. It's open from 7 am to 5.30 pm daily.

Lahaina has several fast-food restaurants, including *Burger King* at 632 Front St, not far from the banyan tree. *Pizza Hut* on Honoapiilani Highway has a lunch-time pizza special for around $3. *Denny's*, in Lahaina Square, is a family-style chain restaurant open 24 hours a day.

Places to Eat – top end

David Paul's Lahaina Grill (☎ 667-5117), at 127 Lahainaluna Rd in the historic Lahaina Hotel, serves excellent Pacific Rim cuisine in an intimate setting. This new restaurant is already one of the most popular fine dining spots in Maui. The spicy tequila shrimp and firecracker rice at $21 is the signature dish, but the cheapest entree on the dinner menu, vegetarian saute at $13, is also a tasty treat and one of the heartier meals. Lunch is a reasonable $7 to $13 and includes such items as crab and shrimp tacos with blue corn tortillas, served on a sizzling platter. It's open for lunch from 11 am to 2.30 pm weekdays and for dinner from 6 to 11.30 pm nightly.

Longhi's (☎ 667-2288), 888 Front St, has such a following that it's often hard to get in the front door. At lunch, sandwiches cost from $7, pasta from $8 and seafood dishes such as fresh ahi and prawns amaretto from $9 to $14. The same seafood dishes cost $20 to $24 at dinner, the pasta $13 to $21. The restaurant has an extensive wine list. It's open from 7.30 am to 10 pm.

Avalon (☎ 667-5559), 844 Front St, serves Pacific Rim cuisine outdoors on a covered patio. For starters, the summer rolls with Thai peanut sauce and the Indonesian satay are a treat. Excellent salads, including gado-gado over brown rice, cost from $7 to $10. Lunch entrees such as grilled chicken breast and Indonesian shrimp stir-fry cost $9 to $13. At dinner, creative vegetarian entrees are $9 to $15 and grilled meat and fish dishes are $18 to $27. Avalon is open from 11 am to midnight daily.

Gerard's (☎ 661-8939) serves traditional French country cooking in a pleasant setting at the Plantation Inn, 174 Lahainaluna Rd. The dinner menu is extensive and changes regularly but calamari, rack of lamb and comfit duck are house standards. À la carte entrees range from $22 to $36. Either a classical or jazz guitarist plays from 7 to 10 pm nightly. Gerard's also has a breakfast buffet from 7.30 to 10 am daily, with croissants, muffins, French toast, yoghurt, cereals, eggs florentine and breakfast meats for $9 ($4.50 for children). There's no lunch; dinner is from 6 to 10 pm.

Entertainment

Lahaina has lots of action, almost all of it on Front St.

The new *Studio 505* (☎ 661-1505), 505 Front St, is the hottest club in town. There's music and dancing from 9 pm nightly, sometimes dance videos but usually live rock, reggae or Jawaiian bands. Stephen Stills and Henry Kapono, who are partners in the club, occasionally perform here. The cover charge is $5, and except on Sundays and Mondays

the dress code specifies a collar shirt, long pants and shoes.

There's a good dance floor at *Longhi's* (☎ 667-2288), 888 Front St, where rock bands play from 10.30 pm to 1 am on Fridays and Saturdays. The cover charge is usually $3 and there's no dress code.

At *Moose McGillycuddy's* (☎ 667-7758), 844 Front St, loud rock or reggae bands play from 9.30 pm on Thursdays, Fridays and Saturdays and there's a video disco with a DJ from 9 pm Sunday to Wednesday. On live music nights, there's a $2 or $3 cover charge.

Cheeseburger in Paradise (☎ 661-4855), 811 Front St, has two groups nightly, one from 4 to 7 pm and the other from 8 to 11 pm. Expect easy-listening sounds, Jimmy Buffet style.

The *Pioneer Inn* has live music daily in its Old Whaler's Saloon from 3.30 to 7.30 pm and then again from 9 pm to 1 am. The music varies but is usually bluegrass, country, blues, jazz or contemporary pop.

There's a free keiki hula show at 1 pm on Sundays at the Lahaina Cannery Mall.

Luaus The Old Lahaina Luau (☎ 667-1998), on the beachfront at 505 Front St, has a buffet dinner with open bar, Hawaiian music and a show from 5.30 to 8.30 pm Tuesday to Saturday. The cost is $46 for adults, $23 for children aged 12 and under.

Cinemas & Theatres Lahaina Cinemas (☎ 661-3347) has three screens at The Wharf shopping centre.

The Hawaii Experience Domed Theater, 824 Front St, shows a 40-minute film about Hawaii on a giant screen on the hour from 10 am to 10 pm daily. It costs $5.95 for adults, $3.95 for children 12 and under.

Things to Buy

Lahaina has numerous arts & crafts galleries, some with high-quality collections and others which are mediocre. Lahaina Arts Society is a members' collective with a gallery in the old harbourside courthouse selling art and craftwork at good prices.

'Art Night', held from 6.30 to 9 pm on

Fridays, is the time when Lahaina galleries schedule their openings, occasionally with entertainment and hors d'oeuvres.

Getting Around

The Lahaina Express (☎ 661-8748) is a bright green trolley bus that shuttles between The Wharf shopping centre in Lahaina and the Kaanapali resort. There's no charge, and it makes a run about every 40 minutes. The first bus leaves The Wharf for Kaanapali at around 9.30 am, the last at 9.25 pm.

LAHAINA TO MAALAEA

The stretch between Lahaina and Maalaea has pretty mountain scenery, but during winter most people are craning their necks to look seaward as they drive along. This is a whale-watch road.

Launiupoko State Wayside Park

Launiupoko State Wayside Park is most popular as a picnic spot and as a place to watch the sun set behind Lanai. There are showers, toilets, picnic tables, changing rooms and a pay phone. It's 2½ miles south of Lahaina.

Olowalu

There's little to mark Olowalu other than Olowalu General Store and a seemingly misplaced expensive French restaurant named *Chez Paul*.

Olowalu Beach was the site of an infamous massacre in 1790. After a skiff was stolen from the US ship *Eleanora* and burned for its iron nails and fittings, Captain Simon Metcalfe retaliated by tricking the Hawaiians into sailing out in their canoes to trade. He then gunned them down with his cannons, killing an estimated 100 people.

When the water is calm, there's good snorkelling around the 14-mile marker, south of the general store. The coral reef here is large and shallow and there's a sandy beach to lay on, though be careful for kiawe thorns.

Olowalu means 'many hills' and the setting is lovely with cane fields backed by the West Maui Mountains.

Camping *Camp Pecusa* (☎ 661-4304), 800 Olowalu Village, Lahaina, HI 96761, run by the Episcopal Church, has a low-profile 'tentground' available to individuals on a first-come, first-served basis. It's located at the side of a cane field, half a mile south of the Olowalu General Store, on the makai side of the road. Camping is on dirt, but in shade and along a beach.

The camping ground has solar-heated showers, outhouses, water and picnic tables. A caretaker lives on the grounds, making this the most secure place in Maui to camp. No alcohol is allowed and there's a seven-night maximum stay. While reservations are generally not necessary they can be made by sending a non-refundable prepayment of $3 per person per night.

Papawai Point

The whole area between Olowalu and Makena are humpback cow/calf waters, and whale watching from the shore can be fantastic.

There are a couple of inconspicuous roadside lookouts just south of the 10-mile marker, but they are unmarked and difficult to pull into and out of when there's heavy traffic. Your best bet is to drive a little farther to Papawai Point, which is a clearly marked scenic lookout with a big parking lot.

Because the point juts into the waters at the western edge of Maalaea Bay, a favoured humpback nursing ground, it's a good sighting spot. Papawai Point is also good for sunsets, with Lanai, Kahoolawe and Molokini visible.

That popular bumper sticker 'I Brake For Whales' has particular significance around this stretch of road. Though they are usually spotted farther offshore, humpbacks occasionally breach as close as 100 yards from the coast. Forty tons of whale suddenly exploding straight up through the water can be a real show stopper! Unfortunately, some of the drivers whose heads are jerked oceanward by the sight slam on their brakes and others don't, with rear-ender potential.

LAHAINA TO KAANAPALI

On the stretch from Lahaina to Kaanapali the

driving can be aggressive and traffic often jams up, particularly during morning and late-afternoon rush hours.

Wahikuli State Wayside Beach Park

The state has a wayside park on a narrow strip between the highway and the ocean, two miles north of Lahaina. With a gift for prophecy, the Hawaiians aptly named this coastal stretch Wahikuli or 'noisy place'.

The beach is mostly backed by a black-rock retaining wall, though there's a small sandy area. If you don't mind the traffic noise, the swimming conditions are usually fine. There are showers and restrooms.

Across the street is Lahaina's civic centre, police and fire stations and main post office.

Hanakaoo Beach Park

Hanakaoo Beach Park is a long sandy beach just south of Kaanapali Beach Resort. Like all public beaches there's free parking.

The park has full facilities and a lifeguard on duty daily. The beach has a sandy bottom and water conditions that are usually quite safe for swimming. However southerly swells, which sometimes develop in the summer, can create powerful waves and shorebreaks, while the occasional kona storm can create rough water conditions in winter.

You can snorkel down by the second clump of rocks on the south side of the beach park or walk a few minutes north to the Hyatt and snorkel out by the green buoy.

Hanakaoo Beach is also called Canoe Beach, as the Lahaina, Kahana and Napili canoe clubs all store their canoes here. You can see them paddling up and down the coast in the early mornings and late afternoons. It's a pretty scene.

Kaanapali

Kaanapali is a high-rise resort community. Despite the opulence of some of its hotels, the overall development is rather ordinary – there's as much LA influence as Hawaiian.

In the late 1950s Amfac, owner of the Pioneer Sugar Mill, earmarked 600 acres of relatively barren sugar cane land for development as the first resort outside Waikiki. The first hotels, the Royal Lahaina and the Sheraton Maui, opened in 1962.

Now Kaanapali Beach is lined with six luxury hotels, each with their own shops and restaurants. The resort also includes six condominiums, two 18-hole golf courses, about 40 tennis courts and the Whalers Village shopping centre.

Kaanapali has three miles of white-sand beach and pleasant views across the Auau Channel to Lanai and Molokai.

While Kaanapali is not a 'getaway' in the sense of avoiding the crowds, it has its quieter niches. The north side of Black Rock and the condos up around the golf course are less bustling than the central beach area.

Information

Parking All Hawaii beaches are public and most resort developments are required to provide free beach access parking. Kaanapali, with all its space, could be more generous, particularly at its northern end.

The Sheraton, fronting the most desirable beach, provides only five spaces for beach access. If they're taken (as they usually are), they'll hit you for $1 per half hour.

There are a dozen free beach access spaces between the Westin and the Whaler, and 11 between Maui Marriott and Kaanapali Alii.

The Hyatt has 10 free beach access spaces. They also have free 'self parking' for hotel visitors on the south side of the hotel.

The Whalers Village shopping centre charges $1 for two hours and 50 cents for each additional hour.

Sugar Cane Train

The old train that once carried sugar cane from the fields to the mill has been restored and now takes passengers on a joy ride through the cane fields between Kaanapali and Lahaina.

At the Kaanapali end, the train can be boarded on the mauka side of Hwy 30 off

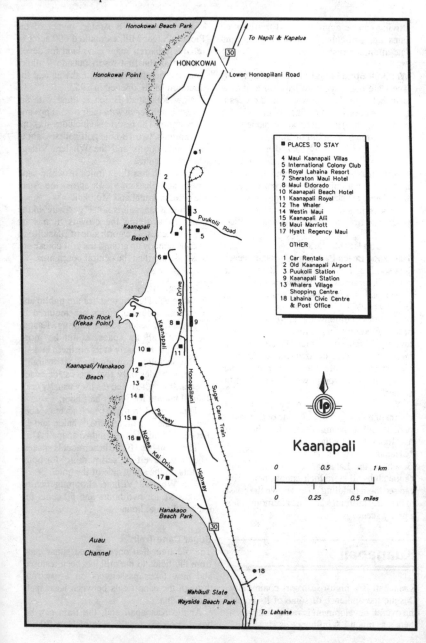

Kaanapali

PLACES TO STAY

4 Maui Kaanapali Villas
5 International Colony Club
6 Royal Lahaina Resort
7 Sheraton Maui Hotel
8 Maui Eldorado
10 Kaanapali Beach Hotel
11 Kaanapali Royal
12 The Whaler
14 Westin Maui
15 Kaanapali Alii
16 Maui Marriott
17 Hyatt Regency Maui

OTHER

1 Car Rentals
2 Old Kaanapali Airport
3 Puukolii Station
9 Kaanapali Station
13 Whalers Village
  Shopping Centre
18 Lahaina Civic Centre
  & Post Office

Puukolii Rd. To get to the Lahaina station, turn up Hinau St off Hwy 30 at Pizza Hut

The railroad's free double-decker bus runs between Banyan Tree Square and the Lahaina terminal, while the free Kaanapali Trolley services the Kaanapali station.

The train (☎ 661-0089) makes the six-mile journey six times a day between 9 am and 4 pm. It takes about half an hour each way and costs $10 for the return trip or $7 one way. Children aged three to 12 are half-price. It's a touristy scene right down to the singing conductor.

Beach Walk

A mile-long beach walk runs between the Hyatt and the Sheraton. Both the Hyatt and the Westin have some striking garden artwork and landscaping to stroll through.

The 17-foot-high bronze sculpture 'The Acrobats' in front of the Hyatt is noteworthy and makes a nice photo silhouetted against the sunset. Done by Australian John Robinson, it's a copy of the one standing in front of the Tower of London.

If you stroll in the early evening you'll often be treated to beachside entertainment, most notably in front of the Marriott, which performs its luau on the lawn right beside the beach walk.

Hyatt Regency Maui

The Hyatt's lobby and grounds contain the most tasteful art collection on the island.

The $2 million collection was acquired by the Hyatt's developer, Chris Hemmeter. It includes Ming vases, Balinese paintings, Hawaiian quilts, ceremonial drums and New Guinea artefacts, storyboards and war shields.

There's a bronze sculpture of King Rama battling with the King of Demons, from Thailand; a large wooden Buddha, lacquered and gilded, from Mandalay; and a spirit figure from the Misingi village in Papua New Guinea.

Even if you're not into big hotels, it's hard not to be impressed with the lobby atrium. It's light and lush, with macaws and white cockatoos perched in the tropical foliage.

Outside there are pools, waterfalls and gardens with swans, flamingoes and black-footed penguins.

Unlike most of the other Kaanapali hotels, the Hyatt has free parking and seems to welcome visitors. You're free to wander around and take in the sights and the concierge has a 25-page self-guided art tour booklet just for the asking.

The Hyatt has an 11 am 'Art & Garden Tour', and a 2 pm activity such as lei-making or hula lessons. Both are free, held daily and open to the public.

Westin Maui

The Westin Maui is another Chris Hemmeter project. It's landscaped with five free-form pools, rushing waterfalls, waterslides and artificial streams and ponds, complete with swans and crowned cranes.

Garden statuary is big here, both Oriental and European, with lots of Buddhas, vases and pairs of growling stone animals. The collection is a bit odd, especially the bronze dogs in menacing poses at the edge of the walkways.

Whalers Village

Whalers Village is a rambling three levels of more than 50 shops and restaurants, including Waldenbooks, Fox Photo 1-Hour Lab, Lahaina Divers, Sharper Image, Lahaina Printsellers (with engravings and antique prints), up-market clothing stores, and scrimshaw and seashell shops. Whalers Village has seven eateries, none particularly special.

Whaling Museum

The high point of Whalers Village is its small, but top-notch, whaling museum. A collection of period photos and detailed interpretive boards explain whaling history, from how whales were hunted to the uses of whale oil.

A lot of the character of the whalers comes through and you'll get a feel for how rough and dirty the work was. Wages were so low that sailors sometimes owed the ship money by the time they got home and had to sign up for another four-year stint just to pay off the debt.

There are harpoons, logs from whaling ships, all sorts of scrimshaw, a model of a whaling barque and a film on whales that plays on the hour from 10 am to 4 pm. The museum is on the 3rd level of Building G and is open from 9.30 am to 10 pm daily. Admission is free.

In addition, there's a full skeleton of a sperm whale on display at the entrance to Whalers Village.

Kaanapali Beaches

Kaanapali can be divided into two beaches, with Black Rock the dividing mark. The stretch south of Black Rock down to the Hyatt (and beyond to Hanakaoo Beach County Park) is officially Hanakaoo Beach. The stretch from Black Rock north to Honokowai is Kaanapali Beach. Since the resort was built, however, the whole thing is generally called Kaanapali Beach.

Kaanapali/Hanakaoo Beach The Hyatt has a shallow reef that makes for poor swimming but good snorkelling. One spot where fish can be thick is the buoy where the hotel catamaran ties up. The fish come to feed on bread thrown overboard by the crew and sea turtles are occasionally spotted in the area as well.

Much of the stretch in between the Sheraton and the Hyatt can be dangerous, particularly on the point in front of the Marriott where strong currents can pick up. As a general rule, waters are rougher in winter, though actually the worst conditions can occur in early summer if there's a southerly swell. Be careful in rough surf as the waves can pick you up and bounce you onto the coral reef that runs from the southern end of the Westin down to the Hyatt. Check with the hotel beach huts for present water conditions.

Black Rock Black Rock (Kekaa Point) is the rocky lava promontory that protects the beach in front of the Sheraton. This is Kaanapali's safest and best spot for swimming and snorkelling. According to traditional Hawaiian beliefs, Kekaa Point,

the westernmost point of Maui, is a place where the spirits of the dead leap into the unknown and are carried to their ancestral home.

You can snorkel alongside the southern side of Black Rock where there's some pretty nice coral and schools of fish that are used to being fed. However the real prize is the horseshoe cove cut into the tip of the rock, where there's more pristine coral, abundant tropical fish and a family of eagle rays.

There's often a current to contend with off the point, which can make getting to the cove a little risky, but when it's calm you can swim right around into the horseshoe and it's a delight. Check with the Sheraton beach hut or snorkellers in the water regarding current conditions. Black Rock is also a popular shore dive spot. If you want to see what the horseshoe cove looks like, take the path from the Sheraton beach to the top of Black Rock.

North of Black Rock To get to the north section of Kaanapali Beach, take the road makai of Puukolii Rd. Then instead of turning left into Maui Kaanapali Villas, turn right to the old airport. From the parking lot a short walk leads across the old runways down to the ocean.

This is the quieter end of Kaanapali and the site of a nice sandy beach, known locally as Prindle Beach. It's open ocean, but inshore is usually calm and good for swimming.

This is a good walking beach. If you walk north for about 15 minutes there's a reef around Honokowai Point with clear waters and good snorkelling when it's calm.

Places to Stay

All Kaanapali accommodation is either on the beach or within walking distance of it.

International Colony Club (☎ 661-4070, (800) 526-6284), 2750 Kalapu Drive, Lahaina, HI 96761, has 44 freestanding cottages spread over 10 acres. They are nice and spacious with big lanais, and have phones (free local calls) and cable TV. The complex is about 25 years old and was one of the first in Kaanapali, back when tastes were simpler

Top: Kahakuloa, Maui
Bottom: Jodo Mission, Lahaina, Maui

  Left: Ohio Gulch, Maui
 Right: Iao Needle, Iao Valley State Park, Maui
Bottom: Haipuaena Falls, Road to Hana, Maui

and things weren't as crowded. There are two heated swimming pools. One-bedroom units are $115, two-bedroom units are $125.

Maui Kaanapali Villas (☎ 667-7791, (800) 922-7866), 2805 Honoapiilani Highway, Lahaina, HI 96761, is an Aston property on the edge of Kaanapali, between Royal Lahaina Resort and the old airport. As is common with Aston properties, rooms are individually owned, and overall it's of a lower standard than other Kaanapali properties. Hotel rooms with refrigerators cost $99/119 in the low/high season and studios with kitchens start at $125/179.

Maui Eldorado (☎ 661-0021, (800) 535-0085), 2661 Kekaa Drive, Lahaina, HI 96761, is a low-rise condo complex up the hill from the beach. It has a slower pace and a friendlier atmosphere than the big resort hotels. The studios are big with kitchens completely set apart from the bedrooms. The units are individually owned so they vary, but some are quite nicely furnished with wallpapered bathrooms, wicker furniture and the like. Studios cost $135 and one-bedroom units cost $160.

The *Kaanapali Beach Hotel* (☎ 661-0011, (800) 733-7777), 2525 Kaanapali Parkway, Lahaina, HI 96761, has an enviable beachside location near Black Rock. The hotel's 430 rooms are spread across a number of three to six-storey wings. While it's an older complex, it's well maintained and is pleasantly low-key. The rooms have lanais, refrigerators and remote-control TV. Prices are $135 for a garden view, $180 for an ocean view. This is an Outrigger affiliate and the rate usually includes a free Dollar rental car if you ask for the 'Free Ride' special when making reservations. For those with a Hawaiian driver's licence, there's a $75 kamaaina rate.

Royal Lahaina Resort (☎ 661-3611, (800) 447-6925), 2780 Kekaa Drive, Lahaina, HI 96761, has 521 rooms on a broad beach on the north side of Black Rock. Standard rooms in the high-rise section cost from $120/150 in the low/high season. Cottages, which are nicely clustered and spread out down to the beach, cost from $130/160. If

they continue to run their 'Royal Ride' special, the rate includes a free rental car. The resort has 11 tennis courts and three pools.

The *Kaanapali Royal* (☎ 667-7200, (800) 367-7040) is a condo run by Hawaiiana Resorts. The units are large and comfortable. It's up the hill a few minutes from the beach and things are quite unhurried. One-bedroom units start at $150/185 in the low/high season for up to four people, two-bedroom units from $175/220.

The Whaler (☎ 661-4861, (800) 367-7052), 2481 Kaanapali Parkway, Lahaina, HI 96791, is a 360-unit high-rise condo that looks like a boxy apartment complex. Studios with garden views cost $170 high season, $155 low. Ocean views are $15 more.

The *Maui Marriott* (☎ 667-1200, (800) 228-9290), 100 Nohea Kai Drive, Lahaina, HI 96761, has 720 guest rooms in two long high-rises connected by walkways. Rates start at $179. It's not special for the money.

The *Sheraton Maui Hotel* (☎ 661-0031, (800) 325-3535), 2605 Kaanapali Parkway, Lahaina, HI 96761, got the prime beach spot, behind Black Rock. The 503-room hotel is large, sprawling and not very interesting. Garden rooms start at $185. The oceanfront cottages on the rocky point are $275.

The *Westin Maui* (☎ 667-2525, (800) 228-3000), 2365 Kaanapali Parkway, Lahaina, HI 96761, has 762 rooms. It has waterfalls flowing into free-form pools and a garden full of statues and vases. The hotel itself is not as special as the grounds, but then the Westin wasn't built from scratch but is a remake of the old Maui Surf. Rates start at $195 for rooms in the old wing, $330 in the new.

The 815-room *Hyatt Regency Maui* (☎ 661-1234, (800) 228-9000), 200 Nohea Kai Drive, Lahaina, HI 96761, is the premier hotel on Kaanapali Beach. It's loaded with artwork and there's a massive meandering swimming pool with a swim-through grotto and a 130-foot waterslide. Rates start at $230 for a standard Hyatt room, with rooms overlooking the ocean from $315.

Places to Eat

All of the Kaanapali hotels have restaurants, some formal and expensive, others casual poolside cafes.

The Marriott's *Moana Terrace* (☎ 667-1200) has a nightly buffet for $16 if you're seated between 5 and 6 pm, $19 after 6 pm. There are usually about half a dozen meat and fish dishes, as well as noodles, rice, potatoes, salads, fruits and a wide selection of desserts. It's fairly good value if you're hungry – on a par with the other Kaanapali hotel buffets and a few dollars cheaper. Dining is either indoors or in an open-air setting complete with a pair of hungry black swans begging from your table.

Nikko (☎ 667-1200) is a Japanese teppanyaki restaurant at the Marriott, open daily for dinner only. It has a pleasant atmosphere with authentic Japanese food cooked at your table and a good ocean view out the window. Complete dinners include an appetizer of shrimp in ginger sauce, miso soup, salad, rice and teppanyaki vegetables, with main dishes like sesame chicken ($20) and sukiyaki steak ($24). The best deal is one of the half dozen Samurai Sunset specials, which are served from 6 to 6.30 pm daily. The specials are complete dinners without the appetizer and salad, but served with green-tea ice cream. They cost from $13 for chicken to $18 for shrimp.

The *Lahaina Provision Company* at the Hyatt has a Chocoholic Bar, an all-you-can-indulge sugar rush of white and dark chocolate goodies served from 6.30 to 11.30 pm nightly. It's $4 with a meal, $6 alone.

Whalers Village The *Rusty Harpoon,*
Leilani's and *El Crab Catcher* all face the beach and all have burgers with French fries for around $7, chicken dinners for $13 and fresh fish, priced daily, that's almost double that. The mahimahi sandwich served at El Crab Catcher's poolside cafe has a generous portion of fish and comes with pasta salad for $8. At least one restaurant usually has some sort of early-bird dinner special for about $10.

Chico's serves American and Mexican food from 11.30 am to 2.30 pm and 5 to 10 pm daily. Combination plates, such as a taco and enchilada with rice and beans, cost $9.50, while burgers and sandwiches are a few dollars less.

Maui Yogurt is the cheapest place to eat in Whalers Village. A good garden salad topped with a scoop of fresh avocado costs $3.25 small, $4.25 large. Sliced-bread sandwiches cost $3.75, and there are also frozen yoghurts, juices and fruit.

Whalers Village also has a hot-dog stand and a Haagen-Dazs ice-cream shop.

Breakfast Buffets Kaanapali has a number of breakfast buffets. For the food alone, the Marriott is the best value. However if you consider the view, the Sheraton takes it hands down.

The breakfast buffet at the *Sheraton Maui* has traditional fare like cereal, bacon, eggs, biscuits, fruits, croissants and tempting cakes and pastries, as well as a few dishes such as musubi, miso and fresh salad for their Japanese diners. It's served in the 8th floor Discovery Room, which has an unbeatable view atop Black Rock – be sure to ask for a table with an ocean view. Breakfast is from 6.30 to 10.30 am and costs $13.75.

The *Maui Marriott* has a good breakfast buffet from 6.30 to 11 am daily at its Moana Terrace, including fresh fruits, juices, delicious strawberry blintzes, Belgian waffles and omelettes to order, yoghurt, cereals and an array of pastries. It costs $14 for a full breakfast or $10 for a continental breakfast which is everything minus the hot dishes. There's an outside patio but no ocean view.

The Westin's *Cooks on the Beach* also does a reasonably good breakfast buffet for $13.75 from Monday to Saturday, though there's nothing special about the setting.

The *Hyatt Regency Maui* has a mediocre breakfast buffet in a superb setting at Swan Court for $14.50. One side is open air and overlooks a large swan pond, waterfalls and a Japanese garden.

The bargain of the breakfast buffets is at the *Koffee Shop* off the lobby of the Kaanapali Beach Hotel. Here you can get fresh papaya and pineapple, eggs, sausage, steamer trays of pancakes and French toast, cereals, Danish, juice and coffee. While not a notable culinary experience, you can eat your fill for $5.95. Breakfast is from 6 to 10.45 am daily. There's also a cafeteria-quality lunch buffet for the same price from 11 am to 2 pm.

Entertainment

The Kaanapali hotels feature a variety of entertainment, including dance bands, pianists, Hawaiian music and Polynesian revues.

Spats at the Hyatt Regency Maui is Kaanapali's main disco. It's open from 10 pm to 2 am Tuesday to Thursday, with free admission, and from 10 pm to 4 am on Fridays and Saturdays with a $5 cover charge. There's a dress code of a collared shirt, slacks (jeans are OK if not faded or torn) and shoes for men.

Solo guitarists play mellow contemporary music at the side of the Hyatt's lobby from 6 to 10 pm nightly.

In the courtyard of the *Kaanapali Beach Hotel* there's a free hula show from 6.30 to 7.30 pm nightly, and Hawaiian music from 5.30 to 9.30 pm Saturday to Thursday.

The *Maui Marriott* has a comedy club at 8.30 pm on Sundays, with a $12 cover charge.

There's often contemporary or Hawaiian music outdoors in the evening at *El Crab Catcher* or *Leilani's* at Whalers Village.

Whalers Village has a free Polynesian show on its centre stage at 3 pm on Tuesdays and 12.30 pm on Saturdays.

Luaus The Kaanapali luaus all include an imu ceremony, open bar, buffet dinner and Polynesian show with music and dance. The rate for children is usually half-price. Reservations are required. Most of the shows are held outdoors, and you can get a look at them by walking along the beach.

The Hyatt Regency Maui (☎ 667-4420) has its 'Drums of the Pacific' luau from 5.30 to 8 pm on Monday, Wednesday, Friday and Saturday for $44.

The Kaanapali Beach Hotel (☎ 661-0011) has a luau from 5.30 to 8.30 pm on Fridays for $37.50.

The Sheraton Maui (☎ 661-3500) has a luau from 5 to 8 pm Monday to Saturday for $42.

The Royal Lahaina Resort (☎ 661-3611) has a luau from 5.30 pm nightly for $39.95.

The Maui Marriott (☎ 661-5828) has a luau from 5 to 8 pm nightly except Mondays for $45.

Astronomy You can look at the night sky through giant binoculars and a 16-inch telescope on the rooftop during the Hyatt Regency Maui's star-gazing programmes (☎ 661-1234, ext 3206), which are open to non-guests at 8 pm daily except on Wednesday and Saturday. The cost is $10 for adults, $5 for children under 12.

Getting There & Around

The Kapalua West Maui Airport is a 10-minute drive from Kaanapali Beach Resort.

The free Kaanapali Trolley (☎ 667-7411) goes between Kaanapali and the airport a dozen times a day. There's also a trolley run around Kaanapali Beach Resort, which stops at all the hotels, Whalers Village shopping centre, the golf courses and the sugar cane train's Kaanapali station. It runs from 7 am to 11 pm daily and makes one complete loop about every 30 minutes.

The free Lahaina Express (☎ 661-8748) makes daily runs between Kaanapali and The Wharf shopping centre in Lahaina. Stops in Kaanapali are at the Sheraton, Kaanapali Beach Hotel, Whalers Village and the Marriott. The first bus leaves Whalers Village at 9.15 am, the last bus at 9.45 pm.

The Lahaina Cannery Mall operates a free shuttle bus from about 9 am to 9 pm between its shopping centre in Lahaina and the Honokowai area. In Kaanapali, stops are made at the Whalers Village and most of the beachfront hotels.

Akina Bus Service (☎ 879-2828) operates a bus four times a day from Whalers Village to the Maui Prince in Makena, with stops in Kihei and Wailea. The first bus leaves the Maui Prince at 9 am, the last returns from

Whalers Village at 10 pm. The cost is $10 return for adults, $5 for children under 12.

North-West Maui

North of Kaanapali the road forks. The main road is Honoapiilani Highway (Hwy 30) and the parallel shoreline road is Lower Honoapiilani Rd.

If you just want to zip up to the beaches, bypassing the condos and resorts, stick to Hwy 30. Cyclists may want to come this way as well, as the highway has a wide shoulder lane marked as a bike route.

Napili Bay, Kapalua Beach, Slaughterhouse Beach and Honolua Bay are all fine beaches on Maui's curving north-west coast.

HONOKOWAI

To the degree that Kaanapali is a planned community, Honokowai is unplanned. It's basically a long stretch of condos squeezed between the shoreline and Lower Honoapiilani Rd.

Many of the condos were intended to be year-round housing for island residents but the growth in tourism makes daily and weekly rentals far more profitable. Indeed, the only reason most tourists are here is because the condos tend to be cheaper than at the nearby resorts.

For the most part, Honokowai lacks any sense of aesthetics. Though most of the condos are by the water, the sound of the surf isn't always strong enough to drown out the sound of the traffic.

While most of the shoreline is rocky with mediocre swimming conditions, Honokowai does have fine views of Molokai and Lanai.

Honokowai Beach Park

Honokowai Beach Park, largely lined with a submerged shelf of rock, has poor swimming conditions with shallow water and a rocky bottom. Most people staying here head to Kaanapali Beach. For snorkelling you can walk south to Honokowai Point (towards the

pink Embassy Suites) where there's a reef, marked by buoys in front of the hotel.

Places to Stay

Honokowai Palms (☎ 669-6130, (800) 669-0795), 3666 Lower Honoapiilani Rd, Honokowai, HI 96761, is a 30-unit two-storey cinder-block building. There's a little book exchange, a ping-pong table and a pool that's seldom crowded. One-bedroom condo units cost $60/65 for up to four people in the low/high season. Two-bedroom units cost $70/75 for up to six people. It's not much to look at from the outside, but it's one of the cheapest places around. Credit cards are not accepted.

Kaleialoha (☎ 669-8197, (800) 222-8688), 3785 Lower Honoapiilani Rd, Honokowai, HI 96761, is a 67-unit condo on the beach. Studios with mountain views cost $75. One-bedroom units with ocean views and lanais are $85 to $95. There's a three-night minimum.

Mahina Surf (☎ 669-6068, (800) 367-6086), is between Honokowai and Kahana at 4057 Lower Honoapiilani Rd, Honokowai, HI 96761. The three two-storey buildings are nicely spaced around a large grassy yard with a pool in the centre. All 56 units have ocean views and lanais. There's a three-night minimum. One-bedroom units cost $85 in the low season and $100 in the high season. It costs $15 more for two bedrooms.

On the other end of the scale is *Embassy Suites* (☎ 661-2000, (800) 362-2779), at 104 Kaanapali Place, Honokowai, HI 96761, on Honokowai Point, north of the Kaanapali resorts. You can't miss this pink giant, with its blue waterfall pouring down the front. Each of the 413 units is an 820-sq-foot suite with everything down to a 35-inch TV with VCR. Rates start at $195 for up to four people, including breakfast and evening cocktails. It's owned by Japanese pop singer Masao Sen.

Places to Eat

There aren't many choices for eating in Honokowai. Most people buy groceries at

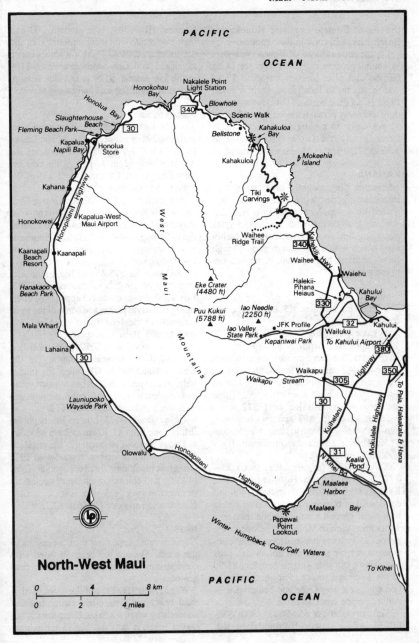

North-West Maui

0   4   8 km

0   2   4 miles

the *Food Pantry*, opposite Honokowai Beach Park, and cook in their condos.

On the southern end of Honokowai, next to a small grocery mart, *Fat Boys* serves up burgers and plate lunches for $5 to $7. If you're not up to local food, there a small *Pizza Hut* a little north of Fat Boys that sells only takeaway pizza. It's open from 11 am to 11 pm daily, to midnight on weekends. A farmer's market sets up in Honokowai from 7.30 to 11.30 am on Monday and Thursday.

KAHANA

Kahana is the unsightly high-rise stretch immediately north of Honokowai. It's geared for a wealthier crowd than Honokowai, with slicker condos and room rates averaging well above $100. There's a white-sand beach with a few places good enough for swimming, but there are better beaches to the north.

Places to Stay

The following are three of Kahana's cheaper condos.

Noelani (☎ 669-8374, (800) 367-6030), 4095 Lower Honoapiilani Rd, Kahana, HI 96761; has 50 nicely furnished units right on the beach. All units have lanais, phones with free local calls, sofabeds and VCRs, and all but the studios have a washer/dryer. There are two pools. Studios cost $77, one-bedroom units are $97 and two-bedroom, two-bath units for up to four people cost $130. There's a three-day minimum. It's a good deal for this area.

Kahana Reef (☎ 669-6491, (800) 253-3773), 4471 Lower Honoapiilani Rd, Kahana, HI 96761, is a four-storey, 88-unit condo. All units are oceanfront and are nicely furnished. There's a small pool on the ocean with a great view of Molokai. The studios are almost as large as one-bedroom units elsewhere and have single and double day beds and a tiny room with a single bed, for $85/90 in the low/high season. For another $5/10 you can get a very large one-bedroom unit. A third person costs $8 extra.

Kahana Villa (☎ 669-5613, (800) 535-0085), 4242 Lower Honoapiilani Rd,

Kahana, HI 96761, is a modern 100-unit high-rise condo with lanais, microwaves and the usual amenities. There's a tennis court, sauna and pool. One-bedroom units are $109 in the low season, $129 in the high season, including breakfast and daily maid service.

Places to Eat

The new Kahana Gateway shopping centre, which stretches between Hwy 30 and Lower Honoapiilani Rd half a mile north of the Kapalua West Maui Airport, is the best bet for places to eat. On the bottom end of the scale is the Gateway's *McDonald's*.

At the top end is *Roy's Kahana Bar & Grill* (☎ 669-6999), a branch of the renowned Roy's in Honolulu. The restaurant is centred around a large exhibition kitchen. Emphasis is on contemporary Hawaiian cuisine such as kiawe-smoked Peking duck with ginger lilikoi sauce for $15.25 and Big Island filet mignon with pan-crisped onions for $17.95. Roy's also serves excellent appetizers, interesting imu-style pizzas and some of the most scrumptious desserts found on Maui. It's open from 5.30 to 9 pm daily.

Powerhouse Bar & Grill (☎ 669-6950), a big 2nd-floor Mexican restaurant in the Kahana Gateway, is also open for dinner only, from 5 pm nightly. It has a varied menu and moderate prices. Combination plates with rice and beans cost about $12.

China Boat, 4474 Lower Honoapiilani Rd, is open from 11.30 am to 2 pm Monday to Friday and 5 to 10 pm daily. The standard array of Chinese dishes costs $8 to $17, though at lunch time there are special plates of kung pao chicken, Sichuan spice shrimp or sweet & sour pork with soup, egg rolls, fried wonton and rice for $6 to $7.75.

NAPILI

Napili is more appealing than the resorts to the south. Though the beach is lined with condos, they're small, low-rise and less congested.

Napili Beach is a beautiful, curving white-sand beach, with excellent swimming and snorkelling when it's calm. Occasionally big waves make it into the bay in the winter, attracting bodysurfers but also creating strong rip currents. To get to the beach turn down Hui Drive off Lower Honoapiilani Rd.

Napili Kai Beach Club, at the northern end of the bay, opened in 1962 with $10 rooms. It was the first hotel north of Kaanapali. To protect the bay and their investment, Napili Kai organised area landowners and petitioned the county to create a zoning bylaw restricting all Napili Bay buildings to the height of a coconut tree and limiting them to 25% of the property.

The law was passed in 1964, long before the condo explosion took over the rest of West Maui. It worked. Napili is the most relaxed niche on the whole coast. A fair number of retired people spend winters here.

The majority of Napili's condos are on the beach and for the most part away from the road and the sound of traffic.

Snorkel Bob's, in the Napili Village complex, rents full snorkel gear for $15 a week.

Places to Stay

Hale Napili (☎ 669-6184, (800) 245-2266), 65 Hui Road N, Napili, HI 96761, is an 18-unit condo on Napili Beach. The rooms have phones, microwaves and lanais. Garden studios cost $75, oceanfront studios are $95. There's a three-day minimum, credit cards are not accepted, and there's no pool.

The *Coconut Inn* (☎ 669-5712, (800) 367-8006), 181 Hui Rd F, Napili, HI 96761, up the hill from the beach, is more like a small apartment complex than an inn. The two-storey U-shaped building has 40 units, each with kitchen, TV and phone. It's a quiet, low-key place, with a shady garden courtyard and a small pool. Complimentary breakfast includes fruit, banana bread and cheese. The beach is a 15-minute walk away. Studios cost $85; one-bedroom units are $105 with lofts or $95 without. The one-bedroom units can accommodate up to four people, with the third and fourth persons charged $10 extra. There's a two-night minimum stay and during the low season all rates are $10 less.

Napili Sunset (☎ 669-8083, (800) 447-9229), 46 Hui Drive, Napili, HI 96761, has studios with garden views for $85 and one-bedroom beachfront units for $159, all with full kitchens. There's a three-day minimum.

Napili Surf (☎ 669-8002, (800) 541-0638), 50 Napili Place, Napili, HI 96761, is a motel-style, painted cinder-block construction at the southern end of Napili Bay. All 53 units are pretty spiffy, the grounds are well kept and there's a pool. Studios cost $94 with a view of the garden or $104 with a view of the ocean. One-bedroom units with ocean views are $142. There's a five-day minimum and credit cards are not accepted.

The *Napili Kai Beach Club* (☎ 669-6271, (800) 367-5030), 5900 Honoapiilani Rd, Napili, HI 96761, is a sprawling 180-unit hotel at the northern end of Napili Bay. The staff are friendly, almost pampering. The units are tasteful, with Polynesian decor and touches like shoji doors. Their Napili Kai Foundation works to preserve Hawaiian culture, mainly through teaching local children hula, history and Hawaiian arts & crafts. The catch here is the price: studios start at $155 without a kitchen, $175 with one.

Places to Eat

The Napili Plaza, at the junction of Napilihau St and Hwy 30, has a grocery store, a *Subway Sandwiches*, and *Koho Grill & Bar*, the best place in Napili for lunch and late-night munches. At Koho's, main dishes such as barbecue shrimp or catch of the day are about $10 with soup or salad, while a variety of burgers are all under $5. It's open daily to midnight.

The *Sea House Restaurant* at Napili Kai Beach Club is an open-air place above the bay, with a fine sunset view. Breakfasts are $5 to $10. Lunches such as burgers and French fries, fish & chips, and papaya stuffed with shrimp salad are $5.25 to $9. Dinners are in the $15 to $25 range with fish, steaks, rack of lamb and the like. Spotlights on the breaking surf provide a kaleidoscopic show and there's live Hawaiian music from 8 to 10 pm Saturday to Thursday. The Napili Kai Foundation dinner show is held at 6.30 pm on Fridays for $25, which includes dinner, dessert and a hula show by children aged six to 17; reservations are required (☎ 669-6271). The restaurant is open from 8 to 11 am, noon to 3 pm and 6 to 9 pm. On Sundays there's a champagne brunch from 8 am to 3 pm.

Whalers General Store in the Napili Village complex sells groceries, liquor, wrapped sandwiches and a few mediocre fast-food items.

KAPALUA

The Kapalua Bay resort development has the Kapalua Bay Hotel, luxury condos, restaurants and three golf courses.

The Kapalua Shops are a cluster of slick, pricey boutiques and gift shops in front of the hotel. The only one of particular interest is the South Seas Trading Post, which has quality Asian rugs and exotic imports. There's a free hula show at 10 am on Thursdays, and free parking under the shops.

Kapalua Beach

Kapalua Beach is a pretty white-sand crescent beach with a fine view of Molokai across the channel. The long rocky outcroppings at both ends of the beach make it the safest year-round swimming spot on this coast.

There's good snorkelling on the right side, where you'll find lots of large tangs, butterfly fish, wrasses and orange slate-pencil sea urchins.

Take the paved drive marked 'shoreline access' just north of Napili Kai Beach Club to get to a parking area with about 25 beach access spaces, restrooms and showers. A tunnel leads under the Bay Club restaurant to the beach.

Places to Stay

The *Kapalua Bay Hotel & Villas* (☎ 669-5656, (800) 367-8000) at 1 Bay Drive, Kapalua, HI 96761, is a luxury complex with hotel rooms from $215 up and one-bedroom condos from $275.

One-bedroom condos in the same resort development can be rented from Ridge Rentals (☎ 669-9696, (800) 326-6284), 10

Hoohui Rd, Suite 301, Kahana, HI 96761, for $115 in the low season, $165 in the high season.

Places to Eat

While the setting looks somewhat exclusive, the *Plantation House Restaurant* (☎ 669-6299), amidst the Plantation Course golf course, is actually the best place in these parts for sit-down breakfasts (8 to 11 am) and lunches (11 am to 4 pm). French toast made with Molokai bread costs $5, while three-egg omelettes with toast and rice are around $7. At lunch, wok-fried vegetables on rice or burgers and French fries cost $6. Dinner, from 5 pm, is not as good value, with meals in the $16 to $20 range. There's a view across the fairway to the ocean below.

The *Bay Club* (☎ 669-8008) is perched atop a promontory at the southern end of Kapalua Bay with a beautiful view in an open-air setting. It specialises in seafood and has a good reputation. At lunch time there's a salad bar with sashimi, sushi, cheeses, and fruits as well as green and pasta salads for $15. Sandwiches range from $6.50 for the daily special with a cup of soup, to $13 for the peppered sirloin steak sandwich. At dinner time, à la carte entrees range from $21 for a pasta dish to $38 for lobster. Dinner is a rather formal affair, though jackets are optional. Reservations are recommended for both lunch and dinner. It's open daily from 11.30 am to 2 pm and from 6 to 9 pm.

The *Grill & Bar* (☎ 669-5653), between the tennis club and the golf club, has a predictable country club atmosphere and an ocean view across the fairway. The best deal is at lunch, when you can get fresh fish dishes for $9 and burgers or sandwiches with French fries from $7. Dinners range from citrus chicken for $14 to Maine lobster for $30.

Pineapple Hill (☎ 669-6129), now a restaurant, is the former plantation home of David Fleming, the pineapple plantation manager after whom Fleming Beach is named. It's on a hill above a little pineapple patch and the golf course. There's a great view down to the ocean, which is especially nice at sunset. The menu ranges from baked chicken for $11 to the house speciality of shrimp Tahitian for $25. The restaurant opens daily at 4.30 pm for cocktails, 5 pm for dinner. To get there take Kapalua Drive up a mile-long drive through Norfolk pines.

HONOKAHUA

Honokahua's commercial centre – modest as it is – is set amidst the Kapalua Golf Course. It's comprised of the Honolua Store, a gas station and a small Catholic church out back. To get there turn up Office Rd, half a mile north of Kapalua Bay Hotel.

Fleming Beach Park

D T Fleming Beach Park on Honokahua Bay, about a mile north of Kapalua, is a developed park with restrooms, picnic facilities, showers and a pay phone.

The long sandy beach is backed by ironwood trees. There's good surfing and bodysurfing, with winter providing the biggest waves. The shorebreaks can be tough, however, and this beach is second only to Hookipa for injuries.

A sign warns of dangerous currents as there have been four or five drownings here in the last few years. The reef out on the right is good for snorkelling when it's very calm.

The Honokahua sand dunes just south of Fleming Beach were excavated in 1988 to build a new Ritz-Carlton hotel. After skeletal remains were found, the construction was halted, the bodies were reinterred and the hotel agreed to move its site mauka of the seaside graves. The Honokahua burial site is thought to contain the remains of over 1000 Hawaiians who were buried between 950 AD and the 1700s.

The Ritz-Carlton (scheduled to open in December 1992) marks the end of development on the West Maui coast. From here on it's rural Hawaii, with golf carts giving way to pick-up trucks and old cars with surfboards tied on top. The coast gets lusher, greener and more scenically rugged as you go along.

Places to Eat

The *Honolua Store* is an authentic old general store with high ceilings, old wooden shelves and a big ice chest full of beer. There's a cafeteria-style deli with local food like stew, beef tomato and fried chicken. Plate lunches are served from about 10 am to 3 pm, either 'hobo' style (a hot dish and rice for $3.25) or a full plate for $5. There are also sandwiches and a variety of good salads including Greek and chef's for around $4. Everything's takeaway.

HONOLUA & MOKULEIA BAYS

About a mile north of Fleming Beach are Mokuleia Bay (Slaughterhouse Beach) and Honolua Bay. The two bays are separated by the narrow Kalaepiha Point and together form the Honolua-Mokuleia Bay Marine Life Conservation District. Fishing is prohibited as is collecting shells, coral, rock or sand. In the winter both bays see heavy surf and sand erosion.

In winter Honolua Bay has perfect waves, often making the cover of surfing magazines. The bay faces north-west and when it catches the winter swells it has some of the best surfing in the world.

Slaughterhouse Beach (named for the slaughterhouse that once sat on the cliffs above) is a hot bodysurfing spot during the summer when the rocks aren't exposed. It's also a popular nude beach.

In summer there's excellent snorkelling in both bays. Both sides of Honolua Bay have good reefs with lots of different coral formations, though the mid-section of the bay is just sand. Honolua Stream empties into the bay and it can get murky after heavy rains.

When it's calm you can snorkel around Kalaepiha Point from one bay to the other. In addition to the coral and reef fish, you might get lucky and spot a sea turtle.

Access is by scrambling down the cliff. There are a few different pull-offs along the road where beachgoers park their cars and where rough paths lead down to the beaches. The paths are clay and can be slick when wet, so watch your footing. Don't leave valuables in the car.

Kahekili Highway
Farther north the road climbs, offering some nice coastal views. The beaches beyond here are open ocean with rough water conditions.

It's possible to continue around on the coastal road to Wailuku (see Kahekili Highway at the end of the Kahului-Wailuku section). The last stop for gas and provisions on this side of Wailuku is at the Honolua Store in Honokahua.

Kihei

Kihei extends six miles along Maui's southwest coast, on the leeward side of Haleakala. Maalaea Bay is to the north, the more exclusive Wailea resort to the south.

Kihei is fringed with sandy beaches its entire length and has near-constant sunshine. It has long attracted sunbathers, boogie boarders, windsurfers and Kahului families on weekend picnics.

The beaches have views of Lanai and Kahoolawe as well as West Maui, which because of the deep cut of Maalaea Bay looks like a separate island from here.

Twenty years ago Kihei was a long stretch of undeveloped beach with kiawe trees, a scattering of homes and a church or two. Over the past decade it's had the dubious distinction of being Maui's fastest growing community, with development continuing nonstop.

South Kihei Rd, which runs the full length of Kihei, is lined with condos, gas stations, shopping centres and fast-food places in such congested and haphazard disarray that it's the example most often cited by anti-development forces on other Neighbor Islands. Kihei is what no town wants to become.

While Kihei's 'condoville' character doesn't win any prizes for aesthetics, it has one advantage for visitors – the sheer abundance of condos means that Kihei's rates are among the cheapest in Maui.

The Piilani Highway (Hwy 31) parallels and bypasses the start-and-stop traffic of South Kihei Rd. Five crossroads connect the two.

Information

The Azeka Place shopping centre has the Kihei post office, a grocery store, an inexpensive Thai restaurant and a few other eateries. The new Azeka Place II, on the opposite side of the street, has a Bank of Hawaii, Fox 1-Hour Photo Lab, Liberty House department store and a Maui Dive Shop.

Kihei library (☎ 879-1141), 131 S Kihei Rd, is open from 9 am to 5 pm Wednesday to Saturday, and from noon to 8 pm on Tuesday. Keolahou Congregational Hawaiian Church, which was established in 1920 and is next to the library, has services in Tongan at 5.30 pm on Sundays.

Kihei Physicians (☎ 879-7781) is open daily in the Kihei Professional Plaza, 1325 South Kihei Rd, opposite the Star Market.

Maalaea Bay

Maalaea Bay runs along the south side of the isthmus between the two mountain masses of west and east Maui. Prevailing winds blow from the north funnelling between the mountains straight out towards Kahoolawe, creating midday gusts and some of Maui's best windsurfing conditions.

These are the strongest winds on the island. In winter, when the wind dies down elsewhere, windsurfers still fly along in Maalaea Bay.

The bay also has a couple of hot surfing spots. The Maalaea break, south of the boat harbour, freight trains right and is the fastest break on Maui. Summer's southerly swells produce huge tubes.

Maalaea Bay is fronted by a continuous three-mile stretch of sandy beach that runs from Maalaea Small Boat Harbor south to Kihei. There's beach access at several places along North Kihei Rd (Hwy 31).

The area near Maalaea harbour has a handful of moderately priced condo complexes and would make a convenient central base if not for ongoing problems with theft and other visitor-targeted crimes.

Kealia Pond

Kealia Pond, on North Kihei Rd two miles south of the intersection of Hwy 31 and Hwy 30, is a saltwater marsh and bird sanctuary. From the side of the road you can usually spot Hawaiian stilts, an endangered species, wading in the water. It's also a habitat for the Hawaiian coot.

Maipoina Oe Iau Beach Park

Maipoina Oe Iau Beach Park, at the northern end of Kihei, has a long white-sand beach. Swimming and sunbathing is best in the morning before the wind picks up. Windsurfing is best in the afternoon. Some of the windsurf shops give lessons here.

The park name means 'forget me not' and is dedicated to Maui's war veterans. It has full facilities.

Kalepolepo Beach Park

The waters off Kalepolepo Beach Park offer only mediocre swimming but this is one of the few places in Maui where you can see the stone wall remains of a fishpond.

Koieie Fishpond was built in the 16th century by King Umi of the Big Island. It was used to raise mullet for the alii.

In a story with an unusual menehune twist, Koieie Fishpond was said to have been built by regular-sized Hawaiians. After the workers protested that the work couldn't be done properly without the help of the menehune, the chief in charge angrily ordered that when the job was over the workers were to be cooked in an imu. The night before the last stone was to be placed, the menehune came down from the mountains and carried all the stones away. Only after the threats were withdrawn did the menehune return with the stones and rebuild the fishpond.

The park has restrooms, picnic tables and drinking water.

David Malo's Church

Another historic site at the northern end of Kihei is the church built in 1853 by David Malo, a noted philosopher and the first Hawaiian ordained to the Christian ministry. While most of the church was dismantled long ago, a three-foot-high section of the

Cormorant

church walls still stands. Eighteen pews are lined up inside the stone walls, where open-air services are held on Sunday mornings.

The church is at 100 Kulanihakoi St, about 250 yards past Koa Resort.

Kalama Park

Kalama Park, opposite the Kihei Town Center, is a local park with ball fields, tennis courts, volleyball, a playground, picnic pavilions, restrooms and showers. The park is long and grassy but the beach is shallow and unappealing for swimming.

Kamaole Beach Parks

Kamaole Beach is one long beach divided into three sections by rocky points. All three are pretty white-sand beaches, though sometimes powerful kona storms temporarily wipe out much of the sand.

Each section is along the roadside opposite

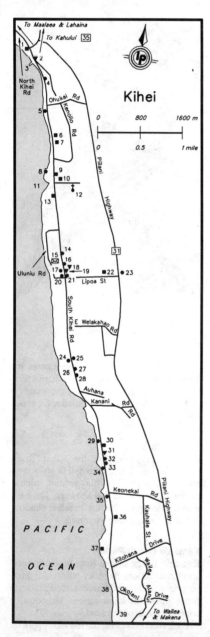

Kihei

■ PLACES TO STAY

1 Nani Kai Hale
6 Wailana Sands
7 Wailana Kai
9 Kihei Bay Surf
10 Koa Resort
13 Village by the Sea
22 Maui Sun
30 Kamaole Beach Royale
36 Kamaole Sands
37 Mana Kai-Maui

▼ PLACES TO EAT

2 Suda's Store
18 Shaka Pizza
19 Jack in the Box
31 New York Deli

OTHER

3 Kihei Wharf
4 Library
5 Maipoina Oe Iau Beach Park
8 Kalepolepo Beach Park
11 Koieie Fishpond
12 David Malo's Church
14 Longs Center
15 Post Office
16 Azeka Place II
17 Azeka Place
20 Star Market
21 Kihei Physicians
23 Silversword Golf Course
24 Kihei Fire Station
25 Kukui Mall
26 Kalama Park
27 Kihei Town Center
28 Snorkel Bob's
29 Kamaole Beach Park 1
32 Rainbow Mall
33 Kamaole Shopping Center
34 Kamaole Beach Park 2
35 Kamaole Beach Park 3
38 Keawakapu Beach
39 Beach Access

the condos and shopping centres, with full beach facilities and a lifeguard.

Water conditions vary greatly with the weather, but there's usually good swimming. Generally the beaches have sandy bottoms with a fairly steep drop which tends to create good conditions for bodysurfing as well.

For snorkelling, Kamaole No 3 is the best bet, though the Wailea beaches are far better.

Keawakapu Beach

Keawakapu Beach is bordered on the north end by the southernmost Kihei hotels and on the south end by Mokapu Beach and the up-market Wailea resort. It's more scenic and less crowded than the roadside Kihei beaches.

Keawakapu is a sandy beach with a sandy bottom. Snorkelling is fairly good at the rocky outcrop at the southern end.

As there's no reef off Keawakapu, the state has been working to develop an artificial reef here for the past 30 years. The original drop was piles of car bodies, the latest additions were old tyres embedded in concrete. About 1000 of these 'fish shelters' were dropped some 500 yards offshore in 1989.

There's a fine view from the beach and during the winter whales cavort offshore – sometimes quite close.

To get to Keawakapu, instead of continuing along the main road as it curves up to the left to Wailea, go straight ahead on S Kihei Rd until it ends. There are 25 public parking spaces and an outdoor shower.

Places to Stay

Kihei is packed with condos, but there are few hotels. In many places along South Kihei Rd, the traffic will challenge you to get a good night's sleep, so it's best to avoid rooms facing the road.

Condos *Wailana Sands* (☎ 879-2026), 25 Wailana Place, Kihei, HI 96753, is an older two-storey cinder-block building on a quiet cul de sac a block back from the beach. Though it looks like a simple motel, all 10 units have kitchens and those on the 2nd floor have lanais. There's a pool. Many Canadians return here each winter. Studios cost $35/50 in the low/high season, one-bedroom units $45/65 and two-bedroom

units $85/95. The minimum stay is four nights. Credit cards are not accepted.

Wailana Kai (☎ 877-5796), 34 Wailana Place (mailing address c/o Mary Caravalho, 255-E Alamaha St, Kahului, HI 96732), is next to Wailana Sands. This newer complex has 10 pleasant units, each with cable TV, full kitchen, a pool and everything you'd expect in a pricey condo except the price. One-bedroom units cost $55 in the low season and $65 in the high season. Two-bedroom units for up to four people cost $75/85 low/high. Credit cards are not accepted.

Kihei Bay Surf, 715 S Kihei Rd, is a condo complex directly opposite Kalepolepo Park with 118 studio units. Units are individually owned and furnished, some with queen-size beds, others with old-fashioned Murphy beds. Rates vary, hovering around $50/65 low/high, and reservations are handled through Maui Network and Kihei Maui Vacations (see the introductory Maui Accommodation section). There's a pool, tennis court, jacuzzi and laundry facilities. If you get a good unit it's good value.

Nani Kai Hale (☎ 879-9120, (800) 367-6032), 73 N Kihei Rd, Kihei, HI 96753, is a six-storey condo at a busy intersection. There's not much atmosphere, but it is on the beach and there's a pool. Two-bedroom, two-bath apartments cost from $95/125 low/high; one-bedroom apartments from $65/75. Oceanfront units average about $25 more. There are also a few studios that cost $50/65 and rooms without kitchens from $40/50. Units have phones with free local calls, ceiling fans and cable TV. There's a three-day minimum.

Village by the Sea, also known as *Kauhale Makai* (☎ 879-5445), 938 S Kihei Rd, Kihei, HI 96753, is a six-storey concrete-block complex. About half of the 160 condo units are vacation rentals. All have lanais and the standard amenities and while the location is not special the units are as nice as in more expensive condos nearby. Rentals are handled by Maui Condo & Home Realty, with studios going for $60/75 in the low/high season, one-bedroom units for $75/100.

The *Kamaole Beach Royale* (☎ 879-3131, (800) 421-3661), 2385 S Kihei Rd, Kihei, HI 96753, is a seven-storey condo opposite Kamaole Beach No 1, but back off the road. It's quiet with open rangeland behind and an ocean view from the top floors. Units are spacious and well-furnished with lanais, modern kitchens, washer/dryers, TVs and phones with free local calls. It's particularly good value during the low season when one-bedroom units cost $65, two-bedroom units $75. Both are $25 more in the high season. There's a cleaning charge ($35 minimum) for stays of four nights or less, and credit cards are not accepted.

Kihei Alii Kai (☎ 879-6770, (800) 888-6284), Box 985, 2387 S Kihei Rd, Kihei, HI 96753, opposite Kamaole Beach No 1, is a 127-unit complex with a pool, sauna and tennis courts. All units have a washer/dryer and cable TV. One-bedroom units cost $65/90 low/high, and two-bedroom units are $15 more for up to four people. The minimum stay is three days.

The *Koa Resort* (☎ 879-1161, (800) 877-1314), 811 S Kihei Rd, Kihei, HI 96753, has 54 very large units spread out over 5½ acres. All are fully equipped with a washer/dryer, lanai, cable TV etc. There are two tennis courts, a putting green, a jacuzzi and a swimming pool. The manager has a green thumb – check out the orange trumpet vines by the office. One-bedroom units cost $80/100 low/high and two-bedroom units are from $95/115. For this price category it's a good choice. The minimum stay is five days. Credit cards are not accepted.

Kamaole Sands (☎ 874-8700, (800) 992-7866), 2695 S Kihei Rd, Kihei, HI 96753, is its own condo city with 440 units in 10 buildings. The units are very large, quite nice and have all the modern amenities, but the complex is big and impersonal with lots of concrete and parking lots. The complex, which is directly opposite Kamaole Beach No 3, has a pool, jacuzzi and tennis courts. Aston, which books many of the units, charges $79/89 low/high for studio units and $110/125 for one-bedroom units.

Mana Kai-Maui (☎ 879-1561, (800) 525-2025), 2960 S Kihei Rd, Kihei, HI 96753, is a high-rise hotel/condo at the northern end of scenic Keawakapu Beach. Hotel rooms include breakfast for $90/95 low/high. One-bedroom apartments (without breakfast but with kitchen) cost $155/175 and have lanais with ocean views. All these rates include a rental car. There's a pool.

Hotels & B&Bs *Maui Sun* (☎ 875-9000, (800) 762-5384), 175 E Lipoa St, Kihei, HI 96753, is a new modern 231-room hotel in a quiet location between Silversword Golf Course and the centre of Kihei. Rooms are very comfortable, with a king bed or two double beds, a private lanai, a table and chair, remote-control TV and tasteful decor. There's a large free-form swimming pool and a whirlpool on the grounds. Rates are a reasonable $79 to $99 depending on the view, though as it's not on the ocean, the lower rates are a better value.

Ann & Bob Babson (☎ 874-1166, (800) 824-6409), 3371 Keha Drive, Kihei, HI 96753, rent out two upstairs bedrooms and a small apartment in their contemporary hillside home about a mile above Wailea. From the living room there's a wonderful view of Kahoolawe, Molokini and Lanai. One bedroom has a double bed and a mini-refrigerator and costs $55. The master bedroom, which has a private deck, wrap-around windows, a skylight and a jacuzzi, costs $60 to $85 depending on the season. If you want more privacy, the downstairs one-bedroom apartment with cooking facilities is the same price. Prices for the upstairs bedrooms include breakfast. All three have TVs, phones and private baths. There's a 10% discount on weekly stays and when things are slow the Babsons are negotiable with the rates. They also have a two-bedroom cottage on the property that rents for $75 to $120 a day, but it's often booked up in advance by monthly visitors.

Places to Eat
These Kihei restaurants are listed in order from north to south.

Margarita's Beach Cantina is a Mexican restaurant in Kealia Beach Shopping Plaza, 101 North Kihei Rd. At lunch, which is served from 11.30 am, either a taco, enchilada, or burrito with rice and beans costs $5. At dinner, combination plates are $8 to $11. There's a deck overlooking the beach and facing the sunset.

The snack shop adjacent to *Suda's Store*, 61 South Kihei Rd, has cheeseburgers and saimin for about $2 and plate lunches for under $5. Pizza is available from 3 to 9 pm. The 'Local Boy' version (medium $13.50) adds char siu to the cheese, green pepper, tomato and black olives.

Sub Paradise in the Longs Center makes a decent sub sandwich, with prices averaging around $4 for a six-inch sub. Hours are 9 am to 9 pm Monday to Saturday. There's a frozen yoghurt and shave ice shop next door.

Royal Thai Cuisine in Azeka Place is the best place in Kihei for Thai food. Though the servings are on the small side the food is tasty and the prices are inexpensive. At lunch, which is served weekdays from 11 am to 3 pm, there's a $5 daily special. At dinner, 5 to 9.30 pm nightly, pad Thai, curries and numerous other dishes cost $6 to $8.

Azeka Snack Shop next to the grocery store in Azeka Place has plate lunches for around $4, saimin or hamburgers for $1.75. It's open from 9.30 am to 4 pm daily. There's also a *Baskin-Robbins* ice-cream shop and an *International House of Pancakes* in Azeka Place.

Opposite Azeka Place there's a *Jack in the Box* with Art Deco decor. The fajita pita sandwich with chunks of white chicken meat, lettuce and salsa on pita bread is surprisingly good for fast food. There's often a discount coupon for the sandwich in the free tourist magazines.

Shaka Pizza (☎ 874-0331) at 1295 S Kihei Rd behind Jack in the Box, has the best pizza in town though it's takeaway only. An 18-inch cheese pizza costs $13, plus $1.75 for each topping, while a single slice of cheese pizza costs $1.50. There's also a variety of sandwiches served on Italian bread for

around $4. Shaka delivers ($10 minimum order) from 5 to 9 pm.

The Kihei Town Center has a 24-hour *Foodland* supermarket, *McDonald's* and a *Kentucky Fried Chicken*.

New York Deli in the Dolphin Plaza, 2395 South Kihei Rd, has sandwiches on French bread layered with a quarter pound of meat for $5 and tabouli, tortellini, Greek and other salads for about $3 for half a pound. You can get a cup of coffee and a doughnut next door at the *Kihei Bakery* for a mere $1. There are a couple of tables in front of the shops where you can chow down.

Paradise Fruit was once a landmark 24-hour alternative food store housed in a rambling old building at the southern end of Kihei. It's now moved into the Rainbow Mall. While but a shadow of its former funky self, the store sells produce and some health-food products and has a snack bar serving smoothies and sandwiches. Hours are 6 am to 10 pm daily.

Chum's in the Rainbow Mall has fairly good local food that is reasonably priced. Sandwiches and saimin cost about $5, while dishes like laulau or kalua pig cost $6.75. It's open for three meals daily, and there's often some sort of entertainment in the lounge at night.

Cinnamon Roll Fair in the Kamaole Shopping Center sells big hot cinnamon rolls drenched in sugar frosting for $2.

The beachside *Ocean Terrace* (☎ 879-2607) at the Mana Kai-Maui has a pleasant open-air setting with fine views of Kahoolawe, Molokini and Lanai. While the restaurant serves three meals a day, the best deal is between 5 and 6 pm when there are early-bird specials and sunset views.

At dinner, chicken teriyaki costs $16 ($10 during the early bird) while New York steak costs $20 ($11 early bird). Dinners come with chowder or salad, fettucine and bread. Breakfast is from 7 to 11 am and lunch is from 11.30 am to 2 pm. On Sundays there's a combined breakfast and brunch from 7 am to 1.30 pm. There's also a bar (good mai tais!) and a separate lanai serving sandwiches from mid-afternoon to about 9 pm.

Wailea & Makena

WAILEA

As soon as you enter Wailea you'll be struck by the contrast to the cluttery commercialism of Kihei. It has the feel of driving into a very exclusive suburb. Everything is green, manicured and precise.

While Wailea is the most up-market resort on Maui, a rash of newer and more densely clustered condo developments has taken away some of its former low-key charm. Wailea has a few swank hotels on the beach, a growing number of low-rise condo villas, two golf courses, a shopping centre and a tennis club nicknamed 'Wimbledon West'.

Wailea is fronted by two miles of attractive white-sand beaches. From Wailea and neighbouring Makena there are good views of Lanai, Kahoolawe and Molokini.

Information

If you're heading to Wailea beaches from Lahaina or Kahului, be sure to take the Piilani Highway (Hwy 31) and not South Kihei Rd. It's less than 10 minutes' drive this way, whereas the Kihei strip can be a tedious 30 minutes through congested traffic.

Wailea's main road is Wailea Alanui which after Polo Beach changes its name to Makena Alanui as it continues south to Makena.

A free shuttle bus runs every 30 minutes around the Wailea resort connecting the hotels, shopping centre, golf courses and tennis club. It operates from 6.30 am to 10.30 pm daily.

Wailea Shopping Village, in front of the Inter-Continental, has a First Hawaiian Bank, two restaurants, a little grocery store and a few boutiques and gift shops.

Wailea Beaches

Wailea's beaches begin with the southern end of Keawakapu Beach and continue south with Mokapu, Ulua, Wailea and Polo beaches. They all have beautiful white sand, free parking and beach facilities.

While Wailea's beaches generally have good swimming conditions, occasional high surf and kona storms can create dangerous shorebreaks and rip currents.

A pleasant mile-long beach walk runs along the shore connecting the beaches and the hotels that front them. Some of the luxury hotels are worth strolling through, most notably the new Grand Hyatt, which has $30 million of artwork and some rather elaborate artificial waterways on its grounds.

Ulua Beach Ulua Beach is between Maui Inter-Continental Wailea and Stouffer Wailea Beach Resort. The first road south of the Stouffer leads to the beach parking lot.

When it's calm, Ulua Beach has the area's best snorkelling. There's coral at the rocky outcrop on the right side of the beach and you can usually spot long needlefish, schools of goatfish, unicorn tangs and other tropicals. The water is very clear and snorkelling is best in the morning before the winds pick up.

When the surf's up there's usually good bodysurfing.

During WW II, US Marines trained for the invasion of Tarawa off this beach. Until the developers of Wailea resort moved in and named the beach Ulua, it was known as Tarawa Beach.

Wailea Beach Wailea is the largest and widest of Wailea's beaches. The inshore waters along the sandy beach slope gradually and are good for swimming. When the water's calm, there's good snorkelling around the rocky point on the left side of the beach. Divers entering the water at Wailea Beach can follow an offshore reef that runs down to Polo Beach. At times there's a gentle shorebreak suitable for bodysurfing.

Beach access is on the narrow road running between the Four Seasons Resort and the Grand Hyatt, which both front Wailea Beach.

Polo Beach Polo is fronted by a couple of condo developments and by the new Kea Lani Hotel, a large resort with an imposing design.

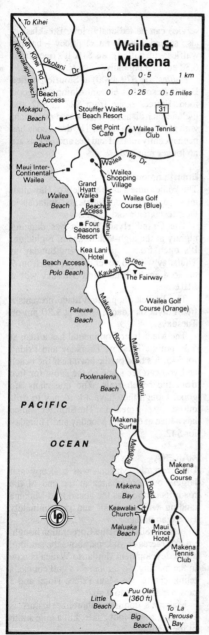

When there's wave action, boogie boarders and bodysurfers usually find a good shorebreak at Polo Beach. When the waters are calm, the rocks at the right end of the beach are good for snorkelling.

To get to Polo Beach, turn down Kaukahi St after the Kea Lani Hotel. The large beach parking lot is on the right before the end of the road; just beyond this is Makena Rd, which leads to the left. The walkway to Polo Beach is at the far end of the parking lot, as are the restrooms and showers.

Palauea Beach

Palauea Beach is along Makena Rd, a quarter of a mile south of Polo Beach. The kiawe brushland between the beach and the road is marked private property, though there are breaks in the fence where beachgoers cross. A fair number of people use the beach for surfing and bodysurfing. It's more secluded than Polo Beach, but otherwise much the same. You can walk to it from Polo Beach in about 10 minutes.

Places to Stay

The *Maui Inter-Continental Wailea* (☎ 879-1922, (800) 332-4246), 3700 Wailea Alanui Drive, Wailea, HI 96753, has 600 rooms spread across a number of low-rise buildings and a mid-rise tower. For Wailea, it's an unpretentious and pleasantly low-key operation. Garden-view rooms cost $145/175 low/high. An ocean view costs an extra $25. Sometimes there are discounted specials, though these are most common during the off-season.

The *Stouffer Wailea Beach Resort* (☎ 879-4900, (800) 992-4532), 3550 Wailea Alanui Drive, Wailea, HI 96753, is very much a luxury hotel. The grounds are lush, the 350 rooms are tastefully furnished with rattan and wicker and it's on a quiet beach. Rates range from $215 for mountain views to $1500 for the Aloha Suite.

The *Grand Hyatt Wailea* (☎ 875-1234), 3850 Wailea Alanui, Wailea, HI 96753, is a sprawling, extravagant affair. The lobbies are filled with sculptures and artwork and the grounds are covered with artificial waterfalls, a multimillion-dollar mosaic tile pool, fountains and the like. All 787 rooms have three telephones, an ocean view, marble baths, a minimum of 650 sq feet and a rate of at least $350.

The *Four Seasons Resort* (☎ 874-8000, (800) 332-3442), 3900 Wailea Alanui, Wailea, HI 96753, has opulence without much artwork. The 380 rooms front Wailea Beach and cost from $350.

Destination Resorts (☎ 879-1595, (800) 367-5246), 3750 Wailea Alanui Place, Wailea, HI 96753, books about 300 units in half a dozen complexes in the Wailea and Makena area. While they aren't cheap, most of the condos are quite nice and represent far better value than Wailea's luxury hotels. Studio and one-bedroom condos in Wailea begin at $120/140 in the low/high season.

Places to Eat

Ed & Don's at Wailea Shopping Village has a variety of sliced bread sandwiches for around $5.

Sandcastle (☎ 879-0606) at Wailea Shopping Village has sandwiches and salads for $6 to $9 from 11 am to 3 pm, while dinners range from $12 to $20.

Set Point Cafe (☎ 879-3244) is at the Wailea Tennis Club overlooking the exhibition court. Breakfast, served from 8 to 11 am, includes muffins, waffles and oatmeal with fresh fruit, all priced under $5. At lunch time, it's chowders, salads and sandwiches in the $6 to $8 range. Lunch is served until 2.30 pm on weekdays and until 2 pm on weekends.

The Fairway, up Kaukahi St amidst Wailea Golf Course, has outdoor tables and a distant ocean view. Breakfast costs $4 to $8. Sandwiches with French fries, which are served until closing at 6 pm, cost $6 to $7.

Cafe Kula in the Grand Hyatt is an open-air cafe overlooking the hotel gardens. Lunch is a sort of spa cuisine, with an emphasis on fresh vegetables and herbs. The menu changes daily but there's always a chicken dish for around $10, and fresh fish for around $13. The food is good and the meals are served with a crispy Italian potato bread. Portions, however, are on the small side and

service can be tediously slow. Breakfast is also served, but it's rather pricey – banana waffles with coffee costs $10. It's open from 6.30 am to 3 pm daily.

Raffles' (☎ 879-4900) at Stouffer Wailea Beach Resort has elegant dining and good food. Entrees range from $22 to $32 and include such dishes as wok-seared mahimahi with green papaya relish. The dress code has been recently relaxed and ties and jackets are no longer required.

Entertainment

The Wailea hotels have a variety of Hawaiian music, dance music, pianists and guitarists in their restaurants and lounges.

The Grand Hyatt Wailea has dancing nightly at the high-tech Tsunami nightclub. It's open from 9 pm to 2 am Sunday to Thursday with no cover charge, and from 9 pm to 4 am on Friday and Saturday with a $10 cover.

The Wailea Shopping Village presents a free Polynesian dance show at 1.30 pm on Tuesdays.

The Maui Inter-Continental has a luau at 5.30 pm on Tuesday, Thursday and Friday for $45. It's held on the lawn near the beach and you can see some of the show for free from the beach walk. The musicians are good, though they have a tendency to drift into sappy pop medleys. The Stouffer Wailea has a luau at 6 pm on Monday and Thursday for $42.

MAKENA

Until recently, Makena was a sleepy and largely overlooked area at the end of the road. Its centre was the abandoned Makena landing with its small and predominately Hawaiian village.

In the 1980s the Seibu Corporation bought up 1800 acres of Makena, above the landing, and a development similar to Wailea is now in the making. So far there's a golf course, a tennis centre, the Maui Prince Hotel and a new bypass road to it all.

Makena's dominant shoreline feature is Puu Olai, a 360-foot cinder hill a mile south of the landing.

Just beyond Puu Olai, Makena has two knockout beaches adjoining each other. They are commonly called Big and Little beaches or, together, Makena Beach.

These are two of the finest undeveloped beaches on Maui. Big Beach is a huge sweep of glistening sand and a prime sunset-viewing locale with straight-on views of Molokini and Kahoolawe. Little Beach is a secluded cove, Maui's most popular nudist beach.

In the late 1960s Makena was the site of an alternative-lifestyle free camping area, and took on the nickname 'Hippie Beach'. The tent city lasted until 1972 when police finally evicted everyone on health-code violations. More than a few of Maui's residents can trace their roots on the island to the camp at Makena Beach.

Long-term plans call for developing Big Beach into a state park with full facilities, but for now it remains totally undeveloped.

Makena Bay

To explore the old side of Makena, turn right down Makena Rd after Makena Surf condos and go about a mile to Makena Bay.

In the 1800s Makena was the busiest landing on this side of Maui. Cattle from Ulupalakua and other ranches were shipped to market in Honolulu from Makena landing. By the 1920s inter-island boat traffic had shifted to other ports on the island and Makena lost its economic base.

Keawalai Congregational Church was built here in 1855 with three-foot-thick walls made of burnt coral rock. A congregation of over 100 still meets for Sunday services held in a mix of Hawaiian and English. The church graveyard has a fine bayside view and the tombstones have interesting cameo photographs.

The sheltered cove is protected by two rocky outcrops and its waters are almost always calm. The showers and restrooms opposite the church are the nearest facilities to Big Beach.

Makena Rd ends shortly after the church at a cul de sac on the ocean side of Maui Prince Hotel.

Maluaka Beach

Maluaka Beach, at the southern end of Makena Bay, is the white-sand beach fronting the Maui Prince Hotel. The beach slopes down from an iceplant-covered sand dune. Rocky formations at each end of Maluaka might provide decent snorkelling, while the centre of the beach has a sandy bottom.

Big Beach

Big Beach is the sort of scene that people conjure up when they dream of a Hawaiian beach. It's very big, uncrowded, and there's absolutely no development on the horizon – not even a lifeguard tower.

The Hawaiian name for Big Beach is Oneloa, literally 'Long Sand.' This golden sand beach is well over half a mile long and as broad as they come, with clear turquoise waters.

Big Beach is about a mile past the Maui Prince Hotel. Look for the gravel parking lot after the roadside telephone. You can also park alongside the road and walk in, but thefts and broken windscreens have been commonplace in the area and the parking lot is a safer bet. Watch for kiawe thorns in the woods behind the beach.

Big Beach is open ocean and when there's heavy surf there are powerful rip currents and dangerous shorebreaks. There are no facilities.

Little Beach

Little Beach is hidden by a rocky outcrop

Lobster

which juts out from Puu Olai, the cinder cone that marks the north end of Big Beach.

A trail over the rock links the two and takes just a few minutes to walk. From the top of the trail there's a splendid view of both beaches.

Little Beach is a sandy cove which usually has a gentle shorebreak ideal for bodysurfing and boogie boarding. Snorkelling along the rocky point is good when the water is calm.

A trail continues a few minutes beyond Little Beach to an area where lava outcrops stick out into the clear deep water like giant fingers. When it's very calm divers and confident snorkellers sometimes explore these formations, which include some caves and abundant marine life.

Little Beach, also known as Puu Olai Beach, is a popular nudist beach despite posted signs to the contrary.

Beyond Makena

Makena Rd continues as a narrow paved road for 2½ miles after Big Beach. The road goes through the Ahihi-Kinau Natural Area Reserve before ending at La Perouse Bay.

Ahihi-Kinau The Ahihi-Kinau Natural Area Reserve covers 2045 acres and includes sections of Ahihi Bay and Cape Kinau.

Maui's most recent lava flow created most of the cape on its way to the sea in 1790. The reserve has lava tide pools, coastal lava tubes and all the *aa* lava you could ever want to see.

It has been designated a natural area reserve because of its distinctive marine life habitat and its unique geological features, such as *kipukas* in the midst of the flow and anchialine pools. The removal of any flora & fauna or lava is prohibited.

There are remains of a coastal Hawaiian village between lava flows at Ahihi Bay. The sites are marked by walled and terraced platforms.

La Perouse Bay In 1786 French explorer Jean Francois de Galaup La Perouse became the first Westerner to land on Maui. As he sailed into the bay that now bears his name,

scores of Hawaiian canoes came out to greet him and trade.

After leaving Hawaii La Perouse disappeared in the Pacific. While no-one knows his fate, some historians speculate that he and his crew may have been eaten by cannibals in the New Hebrides.

The paved road ends just short of La Perouse Bay. Though you may be able to drive all the way in on the 4WD road, you can also park where the asphalt ends and walk down to the coast. A 10-minute foot trail leads over the lava and along the water, passing a few tiny coves with sandy patches before reaching La Perouse Bay. The bay is rather rocky and marginal for most water activities, however there are some excellent hiking possibilities in the area.

King's Highway Coastal Trail From La Perouse Bay it's possible to continue on foot along the old King's Highway. This ancient trail follows the coastline across jagged barren lava flows, so hiking boots are a good idea. It's a dry area with no water and little vegetation so it can be very hot.

The first part of the trail is along the sandy beach at La Perouse Bay. Right after the beach it's possible to take a three-quarter-mile spur trail down to the lighthouse at the tip of Cape Hanamanioa.

Alternatively you can continue on the King's Highway as it climbs up through rough aa lava inland for the next two miles before coming back to the coast at an older lava flow. In that area there are a number of old Hawaiian house foundations and pebble and coral beaches.

Places to Stay

The *Maui Prince Hotel* (☎ 874-1111, (800) 321-6284), 5400 Makena Alanui, Wailea, HI 96753, turns inward in typical Japanese fashion. From the outside it looks like a fortress but the interior incorporates a fine sense of Japanese aesthetics. The five-storey hotel surrounds a courtyard with waterfalls and streams, carp ponds, raked rock gardens, orchids in planters and bougainvillea draped from the balconies. All 300 rooms have at least partial ocean views, from $210.

Places to Eat

Cafe Kiowai, the cafe in the Maui Prince Hotel, serves excellent food from a varied menu. At lunch time it features salads, sandwiches and hot dishes, ranging from a grilled chicken sandwich with taro chips for $6.75 to catch of the day for about $14. Dinners cost from $9 for a Thai shrimp pizza to $27 for filet mignon. The restaurant is open to 10.30 pm daily.

Hakone (☎ 874-1111) at the Maui Prince Hotel has kimono-clad waitresses, shoji screens and authentic Japanese food, including a good sushi bar. There are a number of full meals in the $25 to $30 range.

Prince Court (☎ 874-1111) at the Maui Prince has 'Hawaiian Regional Cuisine' prepared by Roger Dikon, one of the island's most creative chefs. Dishes range from fresh vegetables on onion pasta for $18 to lobster tail on a bed of spinach with caviar cream for $36. It's open from 6 to 10 pm daily. There's also an indulgent Sunday champagne brunch from 10 am to 2 pm, though it's a steep $25.

Kahului-Wailuku Area

Kahului and Wailuku are Maui's two largest communities and flow together to form the island's largest urban sprawl. This is where regular folks live, work and shop.

Kahului is the commercial centre. The main road, Kaahumanu Ave, is a collection of stores, banks and office buildings and a mile-long strip of shopping centres.

Kahului Harbor, Maui's deepwater commercial port, services barges, cargo ships and the occasional cruise liner. This one's geared for work – there are no charming wharfs or sailboats.

Kaahumanu Ave continues into Wailuku where it becomes Main St. Wailuku, the county seat, is the more distinctive and less hurried end of it all. It's an older town with

backstreets of small grocery stores, hole-in-the-wall ethnic restaurants and curio shops.

Maui's main airport is in Kahului. After landing, most people drive right out and don't come back until they're ready to leave. Unless you're up for mall shopping there's really not much in Kahului for visitors. Wailuku, on the way to Iao Valley State Park, has a few historic places of interest and makes for a good lunch break and stroll. It also has some of Maui's cheapest places to stay.

Information

The county and state office buildings are next to each other on High St in downtown Wailuku. Wailuku's post office is at 250 Imi Kala St, on the north side of town. Kahului's post office is on Puunene Ave.

Money The Bank of Hawaii has branches at 2105 Main St in Wailuku and 27 Puunene Ave in Kahului. Both have automatic teller machines.

Libraries Kahului has the best public library on the island. It's at 90 School St and is open from 9 am to 8 pm on Tuesday and Wednesday, and from 9 am to 5 pm on Thursday, Friday and Saturday.

The Wailuku library at 251 High St is open from 9 am to 5 pm on Tuesday, Wednesday and Friday and from 9 am to 8 pm on Monday and Thursday.

Emergency The Maui Memorial Hospital (☎ 244-9056) is at 222 Mahalani St in Wailuku.

Shopping Kaahumanu Shopping Center, on Kaahumanu Ave in Kahului, is the area's largest mall. It has Liberty House (and its Penthouse discount shop), Sears, Waldenbooks, Foodland supermarket, Holiday Theatres, pizza and taco stands and about 50 other shops and eateries.

Maui Mall on Kaahumanu Ave in Kahului has Longs Drugs, Woolworth, a one-hour photo-processing shop, Waldenbooks, Star Market supermarket and Maui Natural

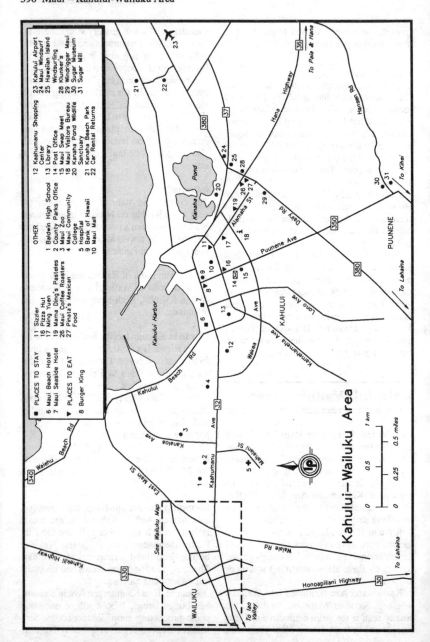

Kahului–Wailuku Area

PLACES TO STAY
6 Maui Beach Hotel
7 Maui Seaside Hotel

PLACES TO EAT
8 Burger King
11 Sizzler
16 Pizza Hut
17 Ming Yuen
19 Mama Ding's Pasteles
26 Maui Coffee Roasters
27 Pinata's Mexican Food

OTHER
1 Baldwin High School
2 County Parks Office
3 Maui Zoo
4 Maui Community College
5 Hospital
9 Bank of Hawaii
10 Maui Mall
12 Kaahumanu Shopping Center
13 Library
14 Post Office
15 Maui Swap Meet
18 Maui Visitors Bureau
20 Kanaha Pond Wildlife Sanctuary
21 Kanaha Beach Park
22 Car Rental Returns
23 Kahului Airport
24 Maui Windsurf
25 Hawaiian Island Windsurfing
28 Klunker's
29 Windrigger Maui
30 Sugar Museum
31 Sugar Mill

Foods, a standard mall-style health-food store.

Maui Swap Meet is held from 7 am to noon on Saturday on Puunene Ave, just south of the Kahului post office.

KAHULUI

In the 1880s Kahului became the head-quarters of Hawaii's first railroad, which was built to carry sugar down to the harbour. In 1900, in an attempt to wipe out an outbreak of bubonic plague, the settlement that had grown up around Kahului Harbor was purposely burned to the ground.

The present-day Kahului is a planned community developed in 1948 by Alexander & Baldwin. It was called 'Dream City' by sugar cane workers who dreamed of moving away from the mill camps to a home of their own. Their tract homes are at the southern end of town.

Kanaha Pond Wildlife Sanctuary

Kanaha Pond is a sanctuary for the endangered black-necked stilt, a wading bird that feeds along the marshy edges of the pond. It's a graceful bird in flight with long orange legs that trail behind. The total stilt population in all Hawaii is estimated at 1500.

Access to the pond is on Hwy 396, near the junction of Hwy 36. The parking lot is marked with an HVB warrior. There's an observation deck you can walk out on – a good site for spotting stilts, coots, ducks and black-crowned night herons.

Upon entering the sanctuary, if you close the gate behind you and walk in quietly you should be able to make sightings right along the shoreline. The pond is a respite in the midst of suburbia, right in the flight path for the airport and just beyond the highway where trucks go barrelling along.

If you'd like to hike on the service roads in the sanctuary you can do so by obtaining a permit from the Division of Land Management (☎ 243-5352), State Office Building, 1st Floor, 54 High St, Wailuku. Office hours are 7.45 am to 4.30 pm on weekdays.

Kanaha Beach Park

If you're stuck in Kahului, Kanaha Beach Park is OK, though most locals prefer the cleaner, clearer waters of Kihei.

Kanaha has a long white-sand beach and a nice view of the West Maui Mountains all the way up the coast to Hakuhee Point. There's a little roped-off swimming area, restrooms, showers, phones and lots of picnic tables under the shade of kukui, ironwood and kiawe trees. The airport noise can be annoying however.

Kanaha is a popular windsurfing spot and when the wind is right, it can be quite crowded. It's the best place in Maui for beginners and most of the windsurfing shops give their lessons here.

The beach access sign is down by the car-rental centres at the airport. Or from downtown Kahului take Amala Rd, the coastal road that runs makai of the Chevron storage tanks near the end of Kaahumanu Ave.

Maui Zoo & Botanical Garden

This is basically a weary little children's zoo with animals in small, confined cages. There are feral goats, pygmy donkeys, peacocks, swans, monkeys, and a flock of nene with goslings.

The 'botanical garden' part has a few labelled plants, but don't expect much.

Maui Zoo is between Kahului and Wailuku, a third of a mile down Kanaloa Ave off Kaahumanu Ave. It's open from 9 am to 4 pm daily and admission is free.

Places to Stay

Kahului's three hotels are all lined up on the main commercial strip in an area that hardly conjures up images of a vacation in Hawaii.

Maui Seaside Hotel (☎ 877-3311, (800) 367-7000 from the USA, (800) 654-7020 from Canada, (800) 451-6754 in Hawaii), 100 Kaahumanu Ave, Kahului, HI 96732, has two wings. The older wing, which used to be called the Hukilau Hotel, has rooms from $64/74 low/high season. The newer wing is a modern, air-con building that has comfortable, larger rooms with mini-refrigerators from $70/80. Add on about $15 more for a car/room package. With this Hawaiian-owned chain, you often get much better rates if you book within Hawaii – they commonly run discounted specials in the Sunday Honolulu papers.

Next door, the adjacent *Maui Beach Hotel* and *Maui Palms Hotel* are Hawaiian Pacific Resorts properties (☎ 877-0071, (800) 367-5004 from the mainland, (800) 272-5275 in Hawaii). Both are older, lacklustre and over-priced. Rates at the 103-room Maui Palms Hotel start at $57/67 in the low/high season. Rates at the 154-room Maui Beach Hotel are from $75/85. Free shuttle service is provided from the airport, but if you reserve in advance there's often a car/room package for the same price as the room only.

Places to Eat

The *Coffee Store*, a casual place in the Kaahumanu Shopping Center, roasts its own coffee right in the store and serves it straight or as espresso or cappuccino. Croissant sandwiches or quiche cost $3.50, lasagne is $4.50 and there are scrumptious pastries such as baklava and white-chocolate raspberry cheesecake. The shop has only a few cafe tables and gets very crowded at lunch time.

Koho Grill & Bar (☎ 877-5588) in the Kaahumanu Shopping Center is open daily for breakfast, lunch and dinner. This is one of the most popular eateries in town, despite its mall ambience. Full breakfasts such as omelettes with potatoes and toast, or French toast, are under $5. Most full meals, including lemon chicken, shrimp scampi, primavera fettucine and catch of the day are under $10. Burgers, soups, salads and sandwiches are also available.

Ming Yuen (☎ 871-7787), behind Maui Mall at 162 Alamaha St, has average Cantonese and Sichuan food. The weekday lunch special consists of an entree, rice and vegetables for $5.75, though ordering from the menu isn't much more. It's open from 11.30 am to 9 pm.

Down the street at 255 Alamaha St, *Mama Ding's Pasteles* has authentic Puerto Rican food at reasonable prices. It's open from 6.30 am to 2 pm on weekdays, and from 7.30 am to 1.30 pm on Saturdays.

Sir Wilfred's Espresso Cafe is the best place to have lunch in the Maui Mall. Sandwiches such as veggie-tofu burger or hot pastrami with pesto salad are $6. Breakfasts, served until 11 am, feature bagels, croissants and egg dishes. Hours are 9 am to 6 pm Monday to Friday, 9 am to 5.30 pm Saturday and 11 am to 5 pm Sunday. The Maui Mall also has a few fast-food restaurants, an ice-cream shop and an *International House of Pancakes*.

Pinata's Mexican Food, 395 Dairy Rd, has a fast-food atmosphere but serves up Mexican fare that's good value for the price. A taco, enchilada, rice and beans plate costs $5.65, a single burrito $3 and a bottle of Dos Equis $2.50. It's open from 10.30 am to 7 pm Monday to Saturday.

Maui Coffee Roasters, 444 Hana Highway, serves coffee of the day at 50 cents a cup or $1 for a large mug. It also has good steamed cappuccinos and scones and muffins. It's open from 7.30 am to 6 pm Saturday, and from 10 am to 3 pm Sunday.

There's a *Pizza Hut*, *Taco Bell*, *Jack in the Box* and *Sizzler* steak house lined up on Kamehameha Ave, and *McDonald's* is nearby on Puunene Ave.

Entertainment

The *Red Dragon Room* in the Maui Beach Hotel has a disco from 10 pm to 2 am on Friday and Saturday. There's a $3 cover charge.

Kahului gets standard Hollywood movies at Holiday Theatres (☎ 877-6622) in the Kaahumanu Shopping Center, and at Maui Theatre (☎ 877-3560) in the Kahului Shopping Center.

PUUNENE

Puunene is a working plantation village surrounded by sugar cane fields and centred around a mill run by the Hawaiian Commercial & Sugar Company. When the mill is in operation the air hangs heavy with the sweet smell of sugar.

The power plant next to the mill burns

residue sugar cane fibres called bagasse to run the mill machinery which extracts and refines the sugar. With a capacity of 37,000 kilowatts, it's one of the world's largest biomass power plants. Excess electricity is sold to Maui Electric.

Puunene's main attraction is the sugar museum opposite the mill.

Sugar Museum
The Alexander & Baldwin Sugar Museum tells the history of sugar in Hawaii. It explains how sugar cane grows and is harvested, complete with an elaborate working scale model of a cane-crushing plant.

What's most interesting here, however, are the images of people. The museum traces how Samuel Alexander and Henry Baldwin gobbled up vast chunks of Hawaiian land and fought tooth-and-nail with an ambitious Claus Spreckels to gain access to Upcountry water. They then dug extensive irrigation systems which made large-scale sugar cane plantations a possibility.

Representing the other end of the scale is a turn-of-the-century labour contract from the Japanese Emigration Company stating that the labourer shall be paid $15 a month for working 10 hours a day in the field, 26 days a month (minus $2.50 banked for return passage to Japan). There are interesting period photos and artefacts of plantation life.

The museum (☎ 871-8058), originally the home of the mill's superintendent, is near the intersection of Puunene Ave (Hwy 350) and Hansen Rd. It's open from 9.30 am to 4.30 pm Monday to Saturday. Admission is $3 for adults, $1.50 for children aged six to 17.

WAIKAPU
Honoapiilani Highway (Hwy 30), which runs along the east side of the West Maui Mountains, passes through the town of Waikapu a couple of miles south of Wailuku.

Waikapu's only sight is **Maui Tropical Plantation**, which features a touristy narrated tram ride past fields of sugar cane, pineapple and tropical fruit trees. The ride takes about 30 minutes and is overpriced at $8.

There's also a free-admission section that includes a gift shop, a nursery, a little taro patch and some exhibits, most fairly shallow in content. The poi exhibit, one of the better ones, has a few interesting historic photos.

If you're driving by you might want to make a quick stop, but it's not worth going out of your way.

WAILUKU
Wailuku sits beneath the eastern flank of the West Maui Mountains and is an interesting juxtaposition of old and new. While the central area serves as the county capital, complete with a few mid-rise government buildings, the backstreets are lined with a colourful hodgepodge of older shops and neighbourhood restaurants. Wailuku is unabashedly local – there's nothing touristy in the whole town.

It's a wonderful town for strolling. Begin on Market St, which has a handful of pawn shops, antique shops and galleries. The shops at the Main St end tend to be more refined while those farther north along Market St are intriguingly cluttered affairs. The most interesting shops are Traders of the Lost Art, which has ancestral carvings and primitive ritual art from Papua New Guinea, Oceania and the Antipodes; and Hula Moons, which specialises in Hawaiiana and glass and has some fairly inexpensive vintage aloha shirts.

Kaahumanu Church
Kaahumanu Church, on the corner of West Main and High Sts, dates from 1837, making it the oldest Congregational church in Maui. The present building was built in 1876 by missionary Edward Bailey.

The church was named in honour of Queen Kaahumanu who cast aside the old gods and burned temple idols, allowing Christianity to flourish. She visited Wailuku in 1832 and in her ever-humble manner requested that the first church be named after her.

The old clock in the steeple was brought around the Horn in the 19th century and it

still keeps accurate time. Hymns are sung in
Hawaiian at Sunday morning services.

Bailey House Museum

The Bailey House, a five-minute walk up Iao
Valley Rd from Kaahumanu Church, was
home to the family of missionary Edward
Bailey who came to Wailuku from Boston in
1837.

The building, also called Hale Hoikeike,
is the headquarters of the Maui Historical
Society, which has turned the former mission
house into a little museum.

There's a Hawaiiana section with tapa,
bottle gourds, calabashes and the like, as well
as period furnishings from the missionary
days. Bailey was a painter and engraver and
many of his works are on display.

One of the most interesting sights is a
surfboard used by Olympian Duke Kahanamoku; it can be seen above the parking lot at
the side of the shed. Compare it to today's
sleek fibreglass boards – this six-footer is

made of redwood and weighs in at a hefty
150 pounds!

The museum is open from 10 am to 4.30
pm Monday to Friday. Admission is $3 for
adults, $1 for children aged 6 to 12.

During the day from Tuesday to Saturday
Uncle Sol Kawaihoa teaches ukulele and
slack-key guitar at the museum.

Places to Stay

Banana Bungalow (☎ 244-5090, (800) 846-
7835), 310 Lower Market St, Wailuku, HI
96793, is a modest nonsmoking hostel with
cheap beds, a friendly management and lots
of international travellers. Private rooms are
simple but clean and freshly painted and cost
$32/39 for a single/double, while one of the
40 beds in the community rooms costs $15.
The community rooms have a combination
of single beds and bunk beds, and accommodate three or four guests per room. Bedding
is provided, but bring your own towel. All
guests share community showers and toilets.

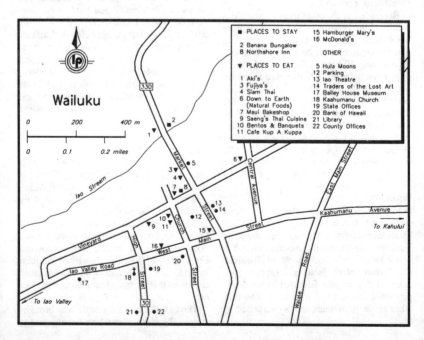

There's a TV room and coin laundry. Cooking is not allowed, but cheap breakfasts and dinners are served in the garden. Breakfast is to order, with eggs, pancakes and the like, whereas the daily dinner is posted each morning and guests who want to join sign up in advance. For $5 you get a hearty meal – anything from spaghetti to steak. Banana Bungalow organises activities for guests, including twice-weekly sunrise trips to Haleakala for $15, and rents boogie boards or snorkelling gear for $3 a day and sea kayaks for $20.

The 78-bed *Northshore Inn* (☎ 242-8999), 2080 Vineyard St, Wailuku, HI 96793, above Hazel's Cafe has simple rooms with small refrigerators and shared bathrooms, for $30/39 a single/double. A better deal are the community rooms, which have four to six bunks to a room and cost $15. Add on $1 to rent a cover sheet and another dollar if you want a blanket or towel. There's a community area with a TV near the front desk and free coffee.

Places to Eat

Wailuku has an excellent collection of good, reasonably priced restaurants. Within a few minutes' walk from the intersection of Vineyard and Market Sts there's Thai, Japanese, Hawaiian and just plain local food. As this is the government centre, there are a lot of good weekday lunch deals to be found, but most restaurants are closed at lunch time on Saturdays and Sundays.

Saeng's Thai Cuisine (☎ 244-1567), 2119 Vineyard St, has excellent food and a pleasant setting with open-air dining. While it's known for its curries, other dishes such as the Thai ginger shrimp and satay tofu are also delicious. Most dishes are in the $5.50 to $7.50 range and nothing on the extensive menu is over $10. It's open from 11 am to 2.30 pm on weekdays and from 5 to 9.30 pm nightly. The menu is the same at both lunch and dinner.

Two blocks away and run by a relative, *Siam Thai* (☎ 244-3817), 123 North Market St, also has good food. Though the atmosphere is more local in flavour, the food is nearly the same and the prices are a tad cheaper. The 'Evil Prince' fish, with tender slices of fresh mahimahi, is a good choice and costs $7.50. The menu also includes over a dozen vegetarian dishes that cost between $5.50 and $6. The hours are identical to Saeng's.

Bentos & Banquets (☎ 244-1124), at 85 Church St, has takeaway lunch specials from 10 am to 2 pm weekdays that are quite popular with local businesspeople. The menu changes daily, though a few dishes like roast pork, teriyaki steak and vegetarian tofu are standards. Most lunches cost $5.50 to $6.

The new *Cafe Kup A Kuppa*, next door at 79 Church St, has gourmet-quality food at cafeteria prices and is open from 7 am to 3 pm Monday to Friday. The hearty breakfast burrito is stuffed with eggs, chilli, potatoes and home-made salsa and costs $3.50. Two croissants or crepes with butter and jam cost a mere $2, while a Belgian waffle with fresh fruit, whipped cream and maple syrup costs $4.50. Lunch features a variety of salads and dishes like quesadillas for around $5 and there's an excellent fresh fish special a couple of times a week for $7.

Maui Bake Shop & Deli, a small family-run operation at 2092 Vineyard St, has good pastries, croissants and crispy French bread at reasonable prices. There are a few small tables where you can have a cup of espresso or one of the $3 sandwiches on a baguette. It's open daily at 5 am and except for Sundays stays open until 6 pm.

Fujiya's, 133 Market St, has a wide variety of Japanese dishes in the $5 to $9 range, including some good dinner teishoku combinations for $8.50. Hours are 11 am to 2 pm Monday to Friday and 5 to 9 pm Monday to Saturday. No credit cards accepted.

Aki's, a five-minute walk north from Fujiya's on Market St, serves Hawaiian food. Kalua pig with cabbage and salad costs $5, a small octopus with coconut milk is $3.35 and a side of poi is 80 cents. It's a local experience. Hours are 11 am to 10 pm Monday to Saturday.

Down to Earth, on the corner of Central and Vineyard Sts, is a well-stocked natural-food store with reasonable prices, fresh organic produce, bulk foods, a good dairy section, juices, and all the standard health foods including vitamins. There are also takeaway sandwiches, salads and pastries.

There's a *McDonald's* on Main St and a *Little Caesar's* pizza place at 1740 Kaahumanu Ave on the road to Kahului.

Entertainment

There's not a lot of nightlife in Wailuku. Most people head off to Casanova's in Makawao or to Lahaina.

Hamburger Mary's, 2010 Main St, is a popular evening spot for the gay community. There's a happy hour from 4 to 6 pm daily.

The Maui Community Theater (☎ 242-6969) presents plays at the old Iao Theatre.

IAO VALLEY ROAD

In 1790 Kamehameha I attacked Kahului by sea and quickly routed the defending Mauian warriors up into precipitous Iao Valley. Those unable to escape over the mountains were slaughtered along the stream. The waters of Iao Stream were so choked with bodies that the area was called Kepaniwai, or 'dammed waters'.

Today much of the upper valley along the stream is parkland. Iao Valley Rd leads into the scenic Iao Valley State Park, passing a few sights along the way.

Tropical Gardens of Maui

If you're looking for a botany lesson, Tropical Gardens of Maui has in-depth interpretive plaques explaining the background of many of the plants here. Otherwise it's not a spectacular garden. It's open from 9 am to 4.30 pm daily and admission is $4.

Kepaniwai County Park

Kepaniwai County Park is dedicated to Hawaii's varied ethnic heritage.

Like Hawaii itself, there's a little bit of everything mixed in, including a Hawaiian hale with a pili grass roof, a Filipino thatched house, a little New England missionary home and a Portuguese garden with a statue of the Virgin Mary overlooking a bubbling fountain and outdoor bread oven.

The manicured Oriental gardens with their pavilions, stone pagodas and miniature bridges over flowing water are the most prominent sights. Amidst the gardens is the Chinese pavilion, bright red and white with a green ceramic tile roof, and the requisite statue of Sun Yat-Sen. Nearby a bronze statue of Japanese sugar cane workers in traditional garb commemorates the centennial of Japanese immigration to the islands.

Iao Stream runs through this large park. It's bordered by many long picnic pavilions with barbecue pits and is a popular place for picnics and parties.

JFK Profile

A half mile after Kepaniwai Park you'll come to a bend in the road where there're often a few cars pulled over and people staring off into Pali Eleele, a gorge on the right. One of the rock formations on the cliff face looks surprisingly like John F Kennedy's profile. There's a pipe set up as a scope to help you find the obvious.

Iao Valley State Park

Iao Valley State Park is tucked up in the mountains three miles out of central Wailuku. The valley is named for Iao, the beautiful daughter of Maui and Hina.

Iao Needle, a rock pinnacle that rises 1200 feet from the valley floor, is said to be Iao's clandestine lover whom Maui captured and turned to stone.

Clouds often rise up the valley, forming a shroud around the top of Iao Needle. A stream meanders below and the steep cliffs of the West Maui Mountains form a backdrop.

Just before the bridge there's a walkway looping downhill by the stream. For photography, this is one of the nicest angles – capturing the stream, bridge and Iao Needle together.

Over the bridge, a short walkway leads up to a sheltered lookout with another fine view of Iao Needle. If you go a little bit farther along the trail that begins beyond the lookout rail you'll see it from a closer and completely different angle.

Coming down from the lookout, you can turn to the right and follow a well-beaten path 10 to 15 minutes upstream over rocks and tree roots and through yellow ginger. There are some pools deep enough for a dip – though the mosquitoes can be thick.

HALEKII & PIHANA HEIAUS

Halekii-Pihana Heiaus State Monument marks one of Maui's most important pre-contact historical sites.

Kahekili, the last ruling chief of Maui, lived here; and Keopuolani, wife of Kamehameha I and mother of Kamehamehas II and III, was born at this site. After the decisive battle of Iao in 1790, Kamehameha I came to these heiaus to worship his war god.

The two adjoining heiaus are atop a knoll and have a commanding view of the entire region, clear across the plains of central Maui and up the slopes of Haleakala. The temples were built with stones carried up from Iao Stream.

Halekii (literally, 'house of the idol'), the first heiau, has stepped stone walls and a flat grassy top. (Watch out for bullhead thorns if you're wearing flip-flops.) The pyramid-like mound of Pihana Heiau is directly ahead, a five-minute walk away.

Pihana is fairly overgrown with kiawe, wildflowers and weeds. Few people come this way and as you approach doves fly up from the bushes.

A certain spiritual essence still emanates from the site. Ignore the industrial warehouses and tract homes that have grown up around the base of the hill and concentrate instead on the vistas and the stones to imagine it all through the eyes of the Hawaiians 200 years back. It must have been an incredible scene.

From Hwy 340 (Waiehu Beach Rd), turn mauka onto Kuhio St, which is three-quarters of a mile south of the intersection of Hwy 340 and Hwy 330. Then take the first left off Kuhio St onto Hea Place and drive up through the gates. The heiaus are less than half a mile from Hwy 340.

KAHEKILI HIGHWAY

Kahekili Highway (Hwy 340) curves around the undeveloped north-eastern side of the West Maui Mountains. It's ruggedly scenic, with deep ravines, eroded red hills and rock-strewn pastures. The coastline is rocky lava sea cliffs and open ocean.

The route is pastoral and quiet with a couple of waterfalls, blowholes and one-lane bridges. It's common to spot cowhands on horseback, and egrets riding the backs of lazy cows. As a scenic coastal drive, it's second only to the road to Hana.

The northern end of the road is at Honokohau, the south at Wailuku, a distance of about 22 miles.

Like its counterpart to the south (the Piilani Highway around the southern flank of Haleakala), Hwy 340 is shown as a black hole on most tourist maps and car-rental agencies forbid use of their cars on it.

Much of the drive is very winding and narrow, often just one lane, with blind curves and the occasional sign warning of falling rocks. While most of the road is posted 15 mph, there are sections where it's a mere 5 mph. But taking it slowly is the whole point anyway.

The only part that's unpaved is a two-mile stretch around Kahakuloa. You'll have to drive very slowly to avoid hitting bottom, but it's no big deal. The last five miles to Honokohau is a regular two-lane road. Unless it's been raining a lot, it should all be passable in a car with no real challenge.

Waiehu & Waihee

Waiehu Beach Rd turns into Kahekili Highway at the northern end of Wailuku and heads through pineapple fields and the little towns of Waiehu and Waihee. Waihee Country Store is the last store until you reach Kapalua on the other side.

Waiehu Municipal Golf Course is down near the shore, bordered by two county beach parks that have poor swimming conditions and, other than for strolling and beach-combing, little appeal.

Rock Arch

From the direction of Wailuku, the road

climbs up into the mountains and the scenery just gets better.

There's a natural rock arch on the coastline that you can see by stopping at the little dirt turn-off that comes up at a bend midway between the five and six-mile markers.

Waihee Ridge Trail

A sideroad up to the Boy Scouts' Camp Mahulia is a pretty winding drive through open pasture that leads to the start of the Waihee Ridge Trail. The trail is one of our favourites, a peaceful seldom-trodden route offering varied scenery and breathtaking views of the interior.

Turn mauka just before the seven-mile marker where there's a road blocked by a yellow gate. Public access is permitted; look for the latch in the chain that allows the gate to open. Be sure to close the gate behind you before proceeding, as it keeps cattle within the range. It's a good one-lane paved road, but be prepared to stop for cattle on the road.

The trailhead is a mile up, on the left just before the camp, marked with a sign and a squeeze-through 'turnstile' through the fence. Another sign announces a $1000 reward for information leading to the arrest of cattle rustlers!

The trail is three miles one way, and takes about three hours round trip. Consider packing a lunch, as there's a picnic table with an unbeatable view at the end. It's a well-defined trail that crosses forest reserve land and though it's a bit steep, it's a fairly steady climb and not overly strenuous.

Starting at an elevation of 1000 feet, the trail climbs a ridge, passing from pasture to cool forest, much of it through groves of rainbow eucalyptus trees. Guava are also prominent along the trail and if you look closely, you can usually find thimble berries as well. From the three-quarter-mile post, panoramic views open up with a spectacular scene that sweeps clear down to the ocean along the Waihee Gorge and deep into the interior valleys. The ridge-top views are similar to those you'd see from a helicopter, however the stillness along this route can only be appreciated by those on foot. The

trail ends at the 2563-foot peak of Lanilili where there are great views in all directions, including Eke Crater at 4480 feet to the south-west.

Waterfalls & Tikis

Back on the highway, you'll pass a gentle waterfall on the left, rain permitting. Then at the pull-off just past the eight-mile marker a big waterfall flows into a pool in the ravine below.

Halfway between the nine and 10-mile markers, keep an eye out for a metal gate mauka of the road, where there are two carved wooden tiki images.

Kahakuloa

The village of Kahakuloa is at the base of a small green valley. Though there are only a few dozen simple homes, Kahakuloa (literally, 'the tall lord') has two churches. The little tin-roofed Catholic mission sits up a hill at the southern end of town, just off the road. On the valley floor is the green wooden Protestant church with its red-tiled roof, birds of paradise by the door and shell ginger out the front.

Up out of the valley at the northern edge of town there's a pull-off with a good view of the village and its boulder beach. The rise on the south side of Kahakuloa Bay is Kahakuloa Head, 636 feet high.

Bellstone

A rusting HVB sign marks Pohaku Kani, a large bellstone on the side of the road just past the 16-mile marker.

If you hit the bellstone with a rock on the Kahakuloa side where the deepest indentations are you might be able to get a hollow sound. It's pretty resonant if you hit it right, but it takes some imagination to hear it ring like a bell.

Pastures & Cliffs

The wide turn-off about half a mile beyond the 16-mile marker looks down over a clifftop plateau with a rugged coastline and crashing surf. The stretch of green turf practically invites you to walk from the road down to the cliffs along the coastline.

Though it's open and sunny, it would be a fine place to break out a bottle of wine and a picnic lunch.

This is hilly country, with rocky cattle pastures and tall sisal plants. There are a number of viewpoints and pull-offs where you can stop and explore.

Stone cairns are piled everywhere. They look like religious offerings, but most are just the creations of sightseers and are of no significance.

Blowhole

There's a blowhole visible from the road just past the 20-mile marker. After a sharp bend, look for a small pull-off marked by two white PVC posts on the mauka side of the road, opposite the area where the guardrail ends. Walk across the road and look down to the left for the blowhole. During the season, we've seen humpbacks breaching offshore in this area as well.

Nakalele Point Light Station

There's a walk out to the light station at the end of Nakalele Point about half a mile past the blowhole pull-off. The coastline has interesting pools, arches and other formations worn out of the rocks by the pounding of the surf. As elsewhere in Maui, don't leave valuables in your car at the parking area. The smashed glass from broken windshields is indicative of the break-ins that take place here.

As you continue north along the road, Molokai comes into view and the scenery is very lush on the way to Honokohau Bay.

Paia

Paia is an old sugar town with a fresh coat of paint.

As part of the original Alexander & Baldwin sugar plantation, Paia had about 8000 residents in the early 1900s, more than triple its present size. Most of the plantation camps were located up the slopes above the sugar mill.

The mill is still open though its heyday is past. During the 1950s many Paia residents moved to Kahului, shops closed and Paia began to collect cobwebs.

In the early 1980s windsurfers discovered nearby Hookipa Beach and Paia was dubbed the 'Windsurfing Capital of the World'.

Today Paia has as many windsurfers as sugar cane workers. They come from all over the world, including Germany, France, Australia and Japan, giving Paia more of an international feel than any other small town in Hawaii.

Paia has small grocery stores that have been in the same families for generations and offbeat shops selling bikinis and antique aloha shirts. Many of the old wooden storefronts are painted in bright tones of rose pink, sunshine yellow and sky blue, adding to the town's unique character.

For all its quaintness Paia is a town in flux. With the rising value of real estate, some of the mom and pop stores are giving way to boutiques and galleries, as younger generations find that selling the old shops is more tempting than carrying on the family business. A controversial plan to build Paia's first hotel on the edge of town could mean bigger changes are in the making.

The Hana Highway (Hwy 36) runs straight through the centre of Paia, which is the last real town before Hana and the last place to fill your car with gas. Baldwin Ave leads from the centre of town up to Makawao.

Information

Officially Paia is the area up Baldwin Ave around the sugar mill and Lower Paia is the section down on the Hana Highway. Most people call it all Paia.

Mana Natural Foods has a good bulletin board, with rooms for rent tacked up amid notices of such things as windsurfing lessons, tai chi classes and used mountain bikes for sale.

Hunt Hawaii in the Paia Town Center rents boogie boards and snorkel sets for $8/15 a day/week and windsurfing equipment for $35/175. Hi-Tech Sailboards on Baldwin Ave

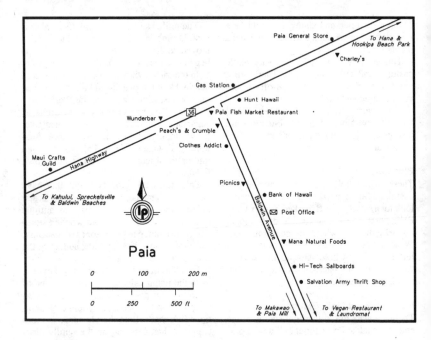

Paia General Store
To Hana &
Hookipa Beach Park
Charley's
Gas Station
Hunt Hawaii
Paia Fish Market Restaurant
Wunderbar
36
Peach's & Crumble
Clothes Addict
Maui Crafts
Guild
Hana Highway
Picnics
Bank of Hawaii
Post Office
To Kahului, Spreckelsville
& Baldwin Beaches
Baldwin Avenue
Mana Natural Foods
Paia
Hi-Tech Sailboards
Salvation Army Thrift Shop
0   100   200 m
0   250   500 ft
To Makawao
& Paia Mill
To Vegan Restaurant
& Laundromat

rents boogie boards for $8 a day. Both places also sell windsurfing equipment, though most of the larger windsurfing shops are based in Kahului.

There's a Salvation Army Thrift Store, a laundromat, a Bank of Hawaii and a post office on Baldwin Ave. The bank is open from 8.30 am to 3 pm Monday to Thursday, 8.30 am to 6 pm on Fridays. The post office is open from 8 am to 4.30 pm Monday to Friday, and from 10.30 am to 12.30 pm on Saturday.

Spreckelsville Beach
Spreckelsville Beach, by the golf course between Kahului Airport and Paia, is a hot windsurfing spot. It's one of the windiest places on the north shore, with the best wind conditions occurring in summer.

Spreckelsville is a long stretch of beach, a mix of lava outcrops and sandy stretches. Though much of the beach is rocky, there are a number of spots with reasonably good swimming.

To get there turn makai on Nonohe Rd, which runs along the west side of Maui Country Club. Turn right when the road ends and look for the beach access sign.

Baldwin Beach Park
Baldwin Beach Park is a big county park about a mile west of Paia. It has a long sandy beach with good bodysurfing. There are showers, restrooms, picnic tables and camping. The park also has a well-used baseball and soccer field, which tends to make it a rather congested and local scene.

The tent spaces are on a flat grassy spot by the road, surrounded by a chain-link fence. Even with the high visibility it's not a particularly secure place to stay and there have been some serious assaults on campers here.

Maui Crafts Guild
Maui Crafts Guild, on the left as you come into town, is a collective of Maui artists and craftspeople. It is the island's best crafts

Top: Pahoehoe & Aa lavas
Left: Makena Beach, Maui
Right: Kaupo, Maui

Top left: Black Rock, Kaanapali Beach, Maui
Top right: Blowhole off Kahekili Highway, North-west Maui
Bottom left: Haleakala Crater, Maui
Bottom right: Snow-capped Haleakala summit from Kihei, Maui

shop, with dyed cloth, woodwork, pottery, baskets, beadwork, shakuhachi flutes and more. Prices are much lower than in private galleries around the island. Guild members take turns staffing the store once a month.

Even if you're not looking to buy, it's worth a stop – it's almost a crafts museum. There's a view of the surrounding sugar cane fields from the top floor. It's open from 9 am to 7 pm daily.

Paia Mill

The century-old Paia Mill sits above town, less than a mile up Baldwin Ave. The power plant adjacent to the mill burns bagasse, the fibre residue of the sugar cane plant, producing steam power to run the mill.

The mill operates 24 hours a day, shutting down only four days a month. It's a whole little world of its own, and when you pass by at night it seems oddly surreal with all the lights glowing and the buzz of activity.

Rather than the more usual process of squeezing sugar cane by rollers, the Paia Mill flushes juice out of shredded sugar cane in a process resembling that of a drip coffee maker.

Mantokuji Buddhist Mission

Mantokuji is a Buddhist temple with an ocean view and a big gong in the yard. It's on the Hana side of town. The graves are decorated with colourful proteas, birds of paradise and anthuriums.

Hookipa Beach Park

Hookipa, which has long been one of Maui's prime surfing spots, has recently become Hawaii's premier windsurfing spot. It has good year-round action for both. Winter has the biggest waves for board surfers and summer has the most consistent winds for windsurfers.

Hookipa Beach attracts some of the world's top windsurfers, and is the site of the Marui/O'Neill Invitational in April and the Aloha Classic in October.

Between the strong currents, dangerous shorebreak and razor-sharp coral, it's definitely an area for experts. As a spectator sport, it's great – you're watching some of the best.

Hookipa is just before the nine-mile marker. There's usually a line of cars on the lookout above the beach. This county park has restrooms, showers, pay phones and picnic pavilions.

Places to Stay

As yet Paia has no hotels, but there are a number of smaller private places to stay. While most places are rented out through B&B-type services, you can also find them by checking bulletin boards around Paia and looking through the 'Vacation Rentals' column in the *Maui News* classifieds. If you're staying any length of time, you might be able to get a room of your own in a shared house for as little as $200 to $300 a month. Mana Natural Foods is a good place to ask around.

The following places are all near the eight-mile marker in Kuau, which is about two miles west of downtown Paia and the closest neighbourhood to Hookipa. (For accommodation on the east side of Hookipa, see the Haiku section.)

Mike Doherty (☎ 579-9430), 4 Kaiholo Place, Paia, HI 96770, rents out three studios as *North Shore Vacation Rental*. Each is a bit different but has a private bath, cooking facilities and one to three beds. This is essentially a windsurfer's crash pad – nothing fancy, but close enough to the beach that you can keep sails rigged in the yard, walk down the street and sail away. Studios are $45 a day, $280 a week and negotiable for longer stays.

The house next door, *Kaiholo Places* (☎ 579-9925), c/o Murray & Georgie Hunter, 10 Kaiholo Place, Paia, HI 96779, has a large studio in a converted garage with tile bath, fold-down bed, full kitchen and use of the washer/dryer. It rents for $50 a day. A deposit is required, usually $100. The studio is attached to a three-bedroom house that rents for $140 a day for up to six people, though it's often rented out a few months at a time.

Terry and Margit Tolman (☎ 579-9333), Box 1220, Paia, HI 96770, have two units called *Hookipa Haven*. A one-bedroom apartment on the 1st floor of their home rents for $55. It has a queen bed, kitchen, bathroom, private entrance and a hideaway bed in the living room. There's also a fully furnished two-bedroom cottage on the grounds that costs $75 for two people or $90 for four, though the walls open at the ceiling so there's no sound barrier between the rooms. There's a $150 deposit in the studio, $200 in the cottage, and optional phone service for $2 a day. Margit has a small vacation rental service and books other accommodation in the Paia and Haiku areas, starting at about $50 for studios.

Kuau Plaza (☎ 579-8080), 777 Hana Highway, 106, Paia, HI 96779, is a rundown 30-unit condo. Hotel-style rooms with TV cost $50/280 a day/week, and one-bedroom units with kitchen and TV are $60/350.

Places to Eat

Picnics, 30 Baldwin Ave, is a deli with takeaway or eat-in service. Sandwiches include all the usual selections, as well as more creative stuff like a vegetarian spinach nut burger with cheddar for $4.35. The Plantation Breakfast is cheese melted over scrambled eggs on toast, papaya-pineapple jam and Kona coffee for $3.45. Picnics also has both fruit and vegetable salads, pastries and espresso. There's a guide to the Hana Highway on the back of the menu, and they prepare picnic box lunches to take on the route. Hours are 7.30 am to 7 pm daily.

Peach's & Crumble Cafe & Bakery, on Baldwin Ave, has an array of pastries from $1 to $2.50 including scones, muffins, croissants and peach crumble squares. Sandwiches such as Mexican avocado, nutty vegie burger and smoked salmon cost $3.50 to $5. There are also daily specials like enchilada pie or lasagne, espressos and cappuccinos, and picnic lunches to go. It's open from 6.30 am to at least 6 pm daily.

The *Vegan Restaurant* (☎ 579-9144), 115 Baldwin Ave, serves vegetarian food free of dairy products. Salads and sandwiches cost from $4 to $6 and daily specials, such as Thai tempeh or tofu loaf, are $8 to $9. It's open from 4 to 8.30 pm Tuesday to Sunday.

Paia Fish Market Restaurant (☎ 579-8030), on the corner of Baldwin Ave and the Hana Highway, serves burgers and Mexican food, but the speciality is fish. The best deal is at lunch when the grilled fish sandwich on a whole-wheat bun costs $5. It's made with a slab of fresh fish of your choice – the selection usually includes ahi, marlin and mahimahi. At dinner the price jumps to $7. Another popular item, fresh fish & chips, costs $7 at lunch, $10 at dinner.

Charley's on the Hana Highway has pizza, pasta and meat dishes at moderate prices. Breakfast is served from 7 to 11.30 am, lunch from 11.30 am to 2 pm and dinner from 4 to 10 pm.

The new *Wunderbar* on the Hana Highway has a showpiece baby grand piano, Hawaii's longest monkeypod bar and Paia's most up-market food. Dinner features Italian, French, Spanish and German cuisines, including pasta for around $10, weinerschnitzel for $12.50 and other meat dishes from $14. At lunch, there's vegetarian lasagne for $7.50 and cold plates and continental specialities for around $10. The owners are German and have restaurants in Berlin and Nuremburg. The Swiss chef, Bernard Weber, formerly cooked for the king of Sweden. It's all quite European – there's even an outdoor beer garden serving schooners of brew.

Mana Natural Foods on Baldwin Ave is a large down-to-earth health-food store. It sells a variety of juices, yoghurts, kefir, bulk nuts, granola, cheeses, whole-wheat French bread and a large section of organic and commercial produce. It also has a few inexpensive takeaway hot dishes, like tofu enchiladas and curry vegetables. Mana is open from 9 am to 7 pm Sunday, 8 am to 8 pm other days, and like most grocery stores in Hawaii takes Visa and MasterCard.

Road to Hana

The Hana Highway runs from central Maui to the village of Hana and beyond to the

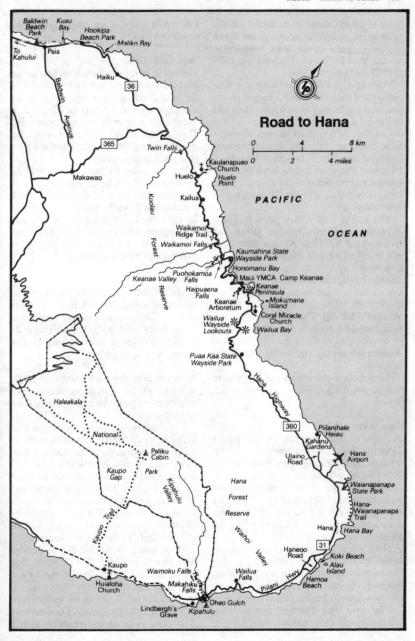

Road to Hana

0   4   8 km

0   2   4 miles

pools of Oheo Gulch. While all the islands have some incredible scenery, the Hana Highway ranks as *the* most spectacular coastal drive in Hawaii. The road was built in 1927 using convict labour.

The cliff-side road winds deep into lush valleys and back out above a rugged coastline, snaking its way around more than 600 twists and turns.

One-lane bridges mark dozens of waterfalls. Some are tiny and Zen-like, others sheer and lacy. The 54 bridges to Hana have 54 poetic Hawaiian names taken from the streams and ravines they cross – names like Heavenly Mist, Prayer Blossoms and Reawakening.

The valleys drip with vegetation. There are dense rainforests, bamboo groves and fern-covered hillsides. African tulip trees add bright splashes of orange.

It would take about two hours to drive straight through from Kahului to Hana. But this is not a drive to rush. If you're not staying over in Hana, get an early start to give yourself a full day. There are short trails to hike, mountain pools to dip in and a couple of historic sites to check out, all just a few minutes beyond the road for those with time to explore.

Remember to pull over if local drivers are behind you. They move at a different pace.

Paia to Hwy 360

A couple of miles past Paia the road passes Hookipa Beach, where there's a clifftop vantage point looking down onto some of Hawaii's top windsurfers in action.

After Hookipa, fields of sugar cane are replaced by rows of pineapples. You'll pass through Haiku, but there's not much to see. It's a spread-out little town, most of it up the slopes.

Hwy 365, which leads up to Makawao and other Upcountry towns, comes in just after the 16-mile marker. At this point the Hana Highway changes from No 36 to No 360 and the mile markers begin again at zero.

The road then changes dramatically, slicing through cliffs and becoming more of a mountain road than a highway. Hana is 35 scenic miles away.

Twin Falls

The trail to Twin Falls starts at the first bridge after the two-mile marker. Park on the shoulder after crossing the bridge and walk up along the side of the stream. It's about a five-minute walk to these double waterfalls. They're not terribly high, but when the water's rushing they're quite broad and it's a pleasant enough scene.

If you're going all the way down to Hana or Oheo you'll see better waterfalls, but if you're hanging around Paia these are worth checking out. Note that this is a popular spot for car break-ins. If you see a lot of windscreen glass on the ground, it's probably best to either pass it by or take everything out of your car and leave it unlocked.

Huelo

Huelo Rd, half a mile past the three-mile marker, is a passable dirt road that leads down to Kaulanapueo Church, a coral and stone church built in 1853. It's likely to be locked and if you're short on time this one can be easily bypassed.

Places to Stay There are a couple of B&Bs in Huelo. It's not the most practical site as a base for touring the island, but good for those seeking seclusion.

The *Halfway to Hana House* (☎ 572-1176), Box 675, Haiku, HI 96708, is a cosy studio unit at the side of the home of Gail Pickholz, a friendly host with a frisky Old English sheepdog. The studio has a private entrance and bath, a double bed, microwave, coffee pot, and an unobstructed view across treetops to the ocean. The cost is $55/65 for singles/doubles with breakfast, $50/58 without. There's a two-night minimum.

More remote is the *Tea House Cottage B&B* (☎ 572-5610), c/o Ann DeWeese, Box 335, Haiku, HI 96708, down a bumpy and unmarked dirt road. While the cottage is stylishly furnished, it's in an undeveloped setting and a bit adventurous. The electricity is provided by an alternative energy system and the bathhouse is outside and requires a flashlight. The cost is $55/65 for singles/doubles and includes breakfast. There's a two-night minimum. Ann is an artist who makes silk wall hangings.

Koolau Forest Reserve

After Huelo, the road winds and the vegetation becomes increasingly lush as the highway runs along the edge of the Koolau Forest Reserve.

Koolau, which means 'windward', is the windward side of Haleakala and catches the rain clouds. Most of this coast gets 60 to 80 inches of rain a year, while a few miles up on the slopes the annual rainfall is 200 to 300 inches.

The reserve is heavily forested and cut with numerous ravines and streams. From here there seems to be a one-lane bridge and a waterfall around every other bend.

Kailua

Kailua is home to many of the people who work for the East Maui Irrigation Company. They maintain the 75 miles of ditches and tunnels that bring water from the rainforests to the cane fields of dry central Maui. The century-old system is capable of carrying 450 million gallons of water a day.

Many of the dirt roads leading mauka from the highway are the maintenance roads for the **Koolau Ditch** which runs inland paralleling the highway.

If you want to take a closer look, stop at the small pull-off just before the bridge that comes up immediately after the eight-mile marker. Just 100 feet above the road you can see a section of the ditch, built of hand-hewn stone block, that meanders down the hillside and then tunnels into the rock face.

As you leave town, you'll notice Norfolk pines up on the hillside, followed by a grove of painted eucalyptus trees with rainbow-coloured bark, then a long stretch of bamboo and more painted eucalyptus.

Waikamoi Ridge Trail

Waikamoi Ridge Trail is a peaceful loop trail through tall trees with wonderful, fresh scents. You're welcomed by a sign: 'Quiet. Trees at Work'.

Pull off at the unmarked turn-off half a mile after the nine-mile marker. The trailhead is up on the left beyond the covered picnic table.

This is an easy trail, three-quarters of a mile long. The grand reddish trees with the huge climbing philodendron vines are eucalyptus *robusta*. (There couldn't be a better illustration of the etymology of philodendron, a Greek word meaning 'lover of trees'!) The trail also passes lots of hala, ferns and paper-bark eucalyptus trees.

Particularly if you're walking with children, keep an eye out for occasional metal spikes and tree roots that protrude along the path. From the ridge at the top there's a good view of the winding Hana Highway.

Waikamoi Falls

Waikamoi Falls is at the bridge just before the 10-mile marker. There's a waterfall and pool near the road. You can walk up to a higher waterfall beyond this, but the rocks can be slippery and the bottom waterfall is prettier anyway.

If you need drinking water, there's good spring water flowing from a pipe on the other side of the bridge. Past Waikamoi, bamboo grows almost horizontally out from the cliff side creating a canopy effect over the road.

Puohokamoa Falls

Puohokamoa bridge and waterfall, at the 11-mile marker, is another pretty waterfall that's just a few minutes' walk from the road. Because there's more parking space and a couple of picnic tables, it's more visited than the Waikamoi or Haipuaena waterfalls.

Haipuaena Falls

Haipuaena Falls, half a mile after the 11-mile marker, is a gentle little waterfall with a wonderful pool deep enough for swimming.

Most people don't know this one's here as you can't see the pool from the road. If you want to take a dip but don't have a bathing suit, this seems like a good choice.

There's space for just one car, on the Hana

side of the bridge. To reach the falls walk upstream for a couple of minutes. Wild ginger grows along the path and ferns hang from the rock wall behind the waterfall. It's an idyllic setting.

Kaumahina State Wayside Park

Kaumahina State Wayside Park is shortly after the 12-mile marker. A two-minute walk up the hill under the park's tall eucalyptus trees provides a broad ocean vista, with Keanae Peninsula to the south-east. The park has a large parking area, covered picnic tables and restrooms.

Honomanu Bay

For the next several miles, the scenery is particularly magnificent. This is one of those places where you keep grasping for superlatives as you round each bend.

Just after crossing the bridge at the 14-mile marker, an inconspicuous gravel road heads down to Honomanu Bay and a rocky black-sand beach. The water's usually too rough for swimming and it's mostly used by surfers and fishermen, though on very calm days it's possible to snorkel and dive there.

Keanae

Keanae is about halfway to Hana. The Maui YMCA Camp Keanae is midway between the 16 and 17-mile markers. There's a pay phone near the road.

Keanae Arboretum, the road to Keanae Peninsula, and the Keanae Peninsula Lookout come up in quick succession within the next half mile.

Keanae Arboretum This arboretum, three-quarters of a mile past the 16-mile marker, has six acres of trees and numerous ornamental and food plants displayed along a marked nature walk. One area has introduced tropical plants, including painted eucalyptus trees and thickets of golden-stemmed bamboo with green stripes that look like the strokes of a Japanese shodo artist.

The trail leads up past sections of heliconia, ti, banana, guava, breadfruit, ginger and other fragrant plants. The higher ground has dozens of varieties of Hawaiian taro in irrigated patches, separated by earthen walls that serve as footpaths. If you have extra time, you could follow an unfrequented trail about a mile up the stream past the taro patches to a rainforest.

Keanae Valley sits beneath the Koolau Gap in Haleakala Crater. It averages 150 inches of rain a year.

Keanae Peninsula The road down to Keanae Peninsula is just past the arboretum.

Lanakila Ihiihi O Iehova Ona Kaua (Keanae Congregational Church) is an attractive old (1860) stone church about half a mile down. This is one church made of lava rocks and coral mortar whose exterior hasn't been covered over with layers of whitewash. And rather than locked doors, there's a 'Visitors Welcome' sign.

Keanae is a quiet little village with colts and goats roaming freely. At the end of the road there's a scenic coastline of jagged rock and pounding waves. The rock island down the coast is Mokumana Island, a sea bird sanctuary.

Keanae Peninsula Lookout There's a good view of Keanae village, with its squares of planted taro fed by Keanae Stream, at an unmarked pull-off just past the 17-mile marker. Look for the mailbox under the tsunami speaker.

Keanae Peninsula was formed by a later eruption of Haleakala which flowed through Koolau Gap down Keanae Valley. Outlined with a black lava coastline, the peninsula still wears its birthmark around the edges. It's very flat, like a leaf floating on the water.

Places to Stay The *Maui YMCA Camp Keanae* is on a knoll overlooking the coast. On weekends the whole place is often rented to groups, but otherwise there's space for six women and six men at $8 each. Bunk beds with mattresses are provided but you have to bring your own sleeping bag and food. There's a three-night limit. The sign on the caretaker's door reads 'Check in Time 4 pm to 6 pm. Later? Forget it.' Checkout is at 9 am. While there's no pool, there's a swimming hole nearby in Palauhulu Stream. Reservations must be made in advance through the Maui YMCA office (☎ 242-9007), 95 Mahalani St, Wailuku, HI 96793.

Fruit Stands

Waianu Fruit Stand, just past the Keanae Peninsula Lookout, is open from 8.30 am to 4 pm daily. They have slices of fresh fruit, banana bread, coffee and shave ice as well as a 24-hour soda machine.

About a mile farther is Uncle Harry's snack shop, run by the family of the recently deceased Harry Kunihi Mitchell. Uncle Harry wrote 'Mele O Kahoolawe' (Song of Kahoolawe) and was a representative of the Hawaiian people in the Nuclear Free Pacific movement.

There's a picnic shelter beside a stream with a few displays – woodcarvings, poi pounders and other bits of Hawaiiana. Muffins, fruit, taro chips, hot dogs and soda are for sale from 9 am to 4 pm daily.

Wailua

Wailua Rd heads makai immediately after Uncle Harry's. The main attraction is **Our Lady of Fatima Shrine**.

The shrine, built in 1860, is also known as the Coral Miracle Church. The coral used in the construction came from a freak storm which deposited coral rocks up onto the beach. Before this, men in the congregation had been diving quite deep but were only able to bring up a few pieces of coral each time. After the church was completed another storm washed all the leftover piles of coral back into the sea. Or so they say.

The old church has just half a dozen little pews. The current congregation uses St Gabriel's Mission, the larger pink-shingled church next door.

From Wailua Rd you can get a peek of the long cascade of **Waikani Falls**, which is just to the left of Wailua Lookout up on the Hana Highway.

Wailua Rd ends half a mile down, though you might not want to go that far as driveways blocked off with logs and milk crates prevent cars from turning around.

Wailua Wayside Lookout

Back on the Hana Highway, just before the 19-mile marker, Wailua Wayside Lookout comes up on the right. It has a broad view into Keanae Valley, which appears to be a hundred shades of green. There are a couple of waterfalls and you can look up at Koolau Gap, a break in the rim of Haleakala Crater.

If you climb up the steps to the right you can get a good view of Wailua Peninsula, but there's a better view of it at a large paved turn-off just down the road.

Puaa Kaa State Wayside Park

Puaa Kaa State Wayside Park is midway between the 22 and 23-mile markers. A tranquil waterfall empties into a pool and then flows downhill into a ravine. This one's a treasure.

There are shaded picnic tables along the stream, a pool that you can swim in, restrooms and a pay phone.

Kahanu Gardens

Kahanu Gardens (☎ 248-8912) is run by Pacific Tropical Botanical Garden. To get there, turn makai onto Ulaino Rd just south of the 31-mile marker and drive 1½ miles to the entrance.

The 126-acre botanical garden on Kalahu Point has medicinal plants and ethno-botanical collections of hala, breadfruit and coconut trees. On the grounds is Piilanihale Heiau, the largest heiau on Maui. It was built by Piilani, the 14th-century Mauian chief who is also credited with building many of the coastal fishponds and taro terraces in the Hana area.

The garden is only open from 10 am to 2 pm Tuesday to Saturday. Admission is $5 for adults and free for children under 12.

Waianapanapa State Park

The road into Waianapanapa State Park is half a mile south of the turn-off to Hana Airport. This 120-acre park has 12 cabins, tent camping, picnic pavilions, restrooms, showers and drinking water.

The road ends at a parking lot above Pailoa Bay, which is surrounded by a scenic coastline of low rocky cliffs. There's a natural lava arch on the right side of the bay. A short path from the parking lot leads down to the small black-sand beach, which is unprotected and usually has strong rips. When it's very calm the area around the arch is said to be good for snorkelling. Check it out carefully, as people have drowned here.

Caves Some impressive lava-tube caves are just a few minutes' walk from the parking lot along a loop path. On the outside the caves are covered with ferns and flowering impatiens. Inside they're dripping wet and cool on even the hottest days.

Waianapanapa means 'glistening waters' and you might be tempted to take a dip. The clear mineral waters leave you feeling squeaky clean.

On certain nights of the year, the waters in the cave turn red. Legend says it's the blood of a princess and her lover who were killed in a fit of rage by the princess' jealous husband after he found them hiding together here. Less romantic types account it to swarms of tiny bright red shrimp called *opaeula* which occasionally emerge from subterranean cracks in the lava.

Hana-Waianapanapa Trail A coastal trail that parallels the ancient 'King's Highway' leads south about two miles from the park to Kainalimu Bay, just north of Hana Bay. Some of the original smooth lava stepping stones are still in place along the trail.

Past the cabins, the trail passes blowholes and the ruins of a heiau. There are gorgeous coastal views with cobalt blue water below craggy black lava outcrops. The most predominant vegetation is hala and beach naupaka, the latter with delicate white flowers that look as if they've been torn in half.

From the end of the trail it's about a mile farther to the centre of Hana.

Camping Tent camping is free with a permit and housekeeping cabins can be rented for $10/17 a single/double. Permits and reservations must be made in advance through any of the state parks district offices. Maui's (☎ 243-5354) is at 54 High St, Wailuku, HI 96793.

Hana

Hana is separated from Kahului by 54 bridges and almost as many miles. Its isolation has thus far protected it from development and though a line of traffic passes through each day not many visitors stay on.

Hana sits beneath the rainy slopes of Haleakala, surrounded by green pasture and a jagged black coastline. In ancient times it was the heart of one of Maui's largest population centres. The village itself was thought to have been reserved for the alii.

In the late 1800s, Chinese, Japanese and Portuguese labourers were brought in to work the newly planted sugar cane fields and Hana became a booming plantation town. A narrow-gauge railroad connected the fields to Hana Mill. In the 1940s Hana could no longer compete with larger sugar operations in central Maui and the mill shut down.

In 1943 Paul Fagan, a San Francisco businessman who owned Puu O Hoku Ranch on Molokai, purchased 14,000 acres in Hana. Starting with 300 Herefords, he converted the cane land into ranch land.

A few years later Fagan opened the six-room Hotel Hana Ranch as a getaway resort for his rich friends. Geographically and economically, Hana Ranch and the hotel became the hub of town.

Today Hana Ranch still has a few thousand head of cattle worked by Hawaiian cowhands. When the cattle are ready for Oahu stockyards, they're trucked all the way up the Hana Highway to Kahului Harbor. The trucks leave early in the morning to avoid traffic.

Hana is not a grand finale to the magnificent

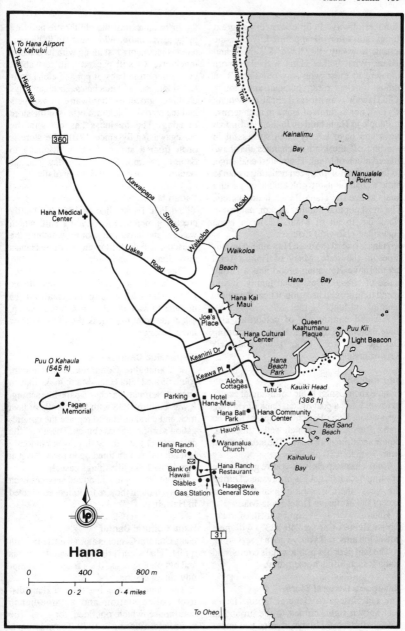

To Hana Airport & Kahului

Hana Highway

360

Hana-Waianapanapa Trail

Kainalimu Bay

Nanualele Point

Kawaipapa Stream

Waikoloa Road

Hana Medical Center

Uakea Road

Waikoloa Beach

Hana Bay

Puu O Kahaula (545 ft)

Hana Kai Maui

Joe's Place

Hana Cultural Center

Queen Kaahumanu Plaque

Puu Kii

Light Beacon

Keanini Dr

Keawa Pl

Hana Beach Park

Kauiki Head (386 ft)

Fagan Memorial

Parking

Aloha Cottages

Tutu's

Hotel Hana-Maui

Hana Ball Park

Hana Community Center

Red Sand Beach

Hauoli St

Hana Ranch Store

Wananalua Church

Kaihalulu Bay

Bank of Hawaii

Hana Ranch Restaurant

Stables

Gas Station

Hasegawa General Store

Hana

31

| 0 | 400 | 800 m |

| 0 | 0·2 | 0·4 miles |

To Oheo

Hana Highway. People expecting great things are often disappointed. While the setting is pretty, the town is simple and sedate. What makes Hana special is more apparent to those who stay on. There's an almost timeless rural character and though 'Old Hawaii' is an oft-used cliche elsewhere, it's hard not to think of Hana in such terms.

People in Hana hold on to their traditional ways and have largely been successful in warding off the kind of changes that have altered much of Maui. Their latest challenge, so far successful, has been resisting a plan to build a championship golf course on pasture lands above the Hana Ranch headquarters. The most popular bumper sticker, not just in Hana but in all of Maui, is 'Keep Hana Hawaiian – No Golf Courses'.

Hana is one of the most Hawaiian communities in the state. Many of Hana's 1800 people have Hawaiian blood and a strong sense of ohana, or extended family. If you spend time around here you'll hear the words 'auntie' and 'uncle' a lot.

A small community of celebrities also have homes in the Hana area, including George Harrison, Mike Love and Kris Kristofferson.

Information

Hana Ranch Center is the commercial centre of town. It has a post office, Bank of Hawaii, gas station, Hana Ranch Restaurant and the Hana Ranch Store which sells groceries, liquor and drugstore items. The store is open from 7 am to 6.30 pm daily.

Hana closes up early. If you're going to be heading back late, get gas in advance. During the week, there's nothing open for dinner except the exclusive Hotel Hana-Maui.

Hana Airport is 3½ miles north of town. Dollar Rent-A-Car (☎ 248-8237) will meet you at the airport if you've got a reservation.

The ball park has public tennis courts, and Hana Ranch offers horse riding.

Hasegawa General Store

The old Hasegawa General Store, Hana's best known sight, burned to the ground in 1990. After a brief hiatus, it relocated under the rusty tin roof of the old theatre building in the town centre. While some of its character was inevitably lost along with its eclectic inventory, it's still packed with just about everything from bags of poi and aloha dolls to fishing gear and machetes. Hasegawa has clothing, groceries, hardware, newspapers and the record which immortalised the store in song. The business has been in the Hasegawa family since 1910. The store is open from 8 am to 5.30 pm Monday to Saturday, 8 am to 3.30 pm Sunday. The gas station stays open until 5.30 pm daily.

Fagan Memorial

When Paul Fagan died in 1959 his family erected a memorial on Lyon's Hill, which was Fagan's favourite spot for watching the sunset. The huge hilltop cross is now Hana's most dominant landmark.

There's a trail up Lyon's Hill that's used by cyclists and joggers. It starts opposite the Hotel Hana-Maui and takes about 15 minutes to walk up. If you want to drive up, ask at the hotel front desk if you can borrow the gate key.

Wananalua Church

The Wananalua Congregational Church, south of the Hotel Hana-Maui, looks like an ancient Norman church in a park-like setting. It was built in 1838 with thick walls of lava rock and coral mortar to replace the congregation's original grass church. There's a little cemetery at the side with graves randomly laid out rather than lined up in rows. Even at rest, Hana folks like things casual.

About 50 people still attend services each Sunday, though they're no longer conducted in Hawaiian.

Hana Cultural Center

Hana Cultural Center is a small museum with quilts, Hawaiian artefacts, woodcarvings and old photographs. It's a friendly community-run operation.

The same grounds has the old Hana district police station and a three-bench courthouse which operated for over 100 years before closing in 1978. The museum is open from 10 am to 4 pm daily and a donation of $2 is suggested.

Hana Beach Park

Hana Beach Park is at the southern end of Hana Bay. It has a black-sand beach, snack bar, showers, restrooms, small boat ramp and picnic tables.

Hana folks often come down here with ukuleles, guitars and a few beers for impromptu parties in the evenings. You may even find one of Hana's celebrities joining in.

When water conditions are very calm, snorkelling and diving are good out in the direction of the light beacon. Currents can be strong and snorkellers shouldn't go beyond the beacon.

Surfers head to **Waikoloa Beach**, at the northern end of the bay.

Kauiki Head

Kauiki Head, the 386-foot cinder hill on the south side of Hana Bay, is said to have been the home of the demigod Maui and was the site of an ancient fort.

The islet at the tip of the point, which now holds a light beacon, is Puu Kii or 'image hill'. The name traces to a huge idol that the great king Umi erected here in the 16th century to ward off invaders. In 1780 the Mauian chief Kahekili successfully fought off a challenge by Big Island chiefs at Kauiki Head.

Queen Kaahumanu, the favourite wife of Kamehameha I and one of the most powerful women in Hawaiian history, was born in a cave here in 1768. It was Kaahumanu who destroyed the ancient kapu system and freed women from restrictive taboos.

A trail to a plaque noting her birth starts along the hill at the side of the wharf at Hana Beach Park. It leads through ironwood trees towards the light beacon, passing by a tiny red-sand beach. The walk to the rock where the plaque is mounted is only mildly interesting, but then again it's just five minutes. Watch where you step, as some of the trail is a bit crumbly.

Red Sand Beach

Red Sand Beach (Kaihalulu Beach), on the south side of Kauiki Head, is a local nudist beach. It's a gorgeous little cove with sand eroded from the red cinder hill and beautiful turquoise waters.

It's partly protected by a lava outcrop, though the currents can be dangerous if the surf is up. Water drains through a break on the left side which should be avoided.

The path to the beach is at the end of Uakea Rd beyond the ball park. It starts across the lawn at the lower side of the Hana Community Center, where a trail continues down to the beach, less than 10 minutes away.

Helani Gardens

Helani Gardens is a 70-acre drive-through botanical garden a mile north of town. This mature garden has clumps of bamboo, a fishpond and numerous flowering plants and trees. It's pleasantly funky and lush, but then again so is all of Hana. It's open from 10 am to 4 pm daily and admission is $2 for adults, $1 for children.

Places to Stay

Joe's Place (☎ 248-7033), Box 557, Hana, HI 96713, across the road from the Hana Kai Maui condos, has 12 rooms that cost $43 with shared bath, $55 with private bath. Rates are for one or two people. Most rooms have two single beds, though a few have double beds. Rooms are small and basic, though clean and comfortable enough. Guests have access to a community kitchen.

Aloha Cottages (☎ 248-8420), c/o Fusae Nakamura, Box 205, Hana, HI 96713, has one studio for $60, three two-bedroom units for $70 and a house for $75. All have kitchens. Most of the units are on Keawa Place, opposite the Hotel Hana-Maui.

Heavenly Hana Inn (☎ 248-8442), Box 146, Hana, HI 96713, is on Hwy 360, a mile north of town. It has four apartment-like units, each with two bedrooms, a lanai, bathroom and kitchenette. Everything's under one roof. From the outside it looks like a Japanese temple, with hanging paper lanterns and stone lions guarding the gate. Inside it's a hodgepodge of knick-knacks, antiques and Japanese touches. Rates are $75 a double, $105 for four people. The inn also books a beach cottage on Hana Bay for up to four adults and a family cottage in town for up to six people. Both cottages cost $75 a double, $100 for a full house. No credit cards.

Hana Plantation Houses (☎ 248-7248, (800) 657-7723), Box 489, Hana, HI 96713, has six units, all different. At the high end there's a three-bedroom home with hardwood floors, redwood walls and ocean views for $150. There's also a little Japanese-style studio with an efficiency kitchen and a jacuzzi on the deck for $70, as well as other units ranging from $90 to $150. All are about 10 minutes out of town. Rates are for up to two people; add $10 for each extra person.

Hana Bay Vacation Rentals (☎ 248-7727, (800) 657-7970), Box 318, Hana, HI 96713, manages about 10 cottages, cabins and homes in the Hana area. Prices range from $65 to $150 in the low season, $85 to $170 in the high season.

Hana Kai Maui (☎ 248-8426, (800) 346-2772), Box 38, Hana, HI 96713, just north of town, is a modern though not fancy 19-unit condo. Studios cost $110, one-bedroom units are $125. It has lanais with fine ocean views of Hana Bay, in earshot of the breaking surf.

Hotel Hana-Maui (☎ 248-8211, (800) 321-4262), Hana, HI 96713, is one of Hawaii's top getaway hotels. On 23 acres in the centre of town, the Hana-Maui is low profile, more like a plantation estate than a luxury hotel. Everything's very airy and open with Hawaiian accents from local art to quilt bedspreads. The 61 rooms are in one-storey cottages. They have bleached hardwood floors, tiled baths, a view over a private garden and French doors to trellised patios. Pampering has its price – rates start at $400/495 for singles/doubles, including all meals.

There's camping at Waianapanapa State Park, just north of Hana, and at Oheo Gulch, 10 miles south of Hana. If you plan to camp

at Oheo, you'll need to stock up on food and water in Hana.

Places to Eat

Tutu's, a fast-food grill at the beach park at Hana Bay, is open from 9.30 am to 4 pm daily. Hamburgers cost $2.20, vegie sandwiches $2.50 and mahimahi burgers $3.50. Tutu's also has plate lunches, ice cream, shave ice, and fruit and vegetable salads.

The *Hana Ranch Restaurant* is open for lunch from 11 am to 3 pm daily and for dinner on Fridays and Saturdays from 6 to 10 pm. At lunch, there's a salad bar for $7.95 or a buffet for $12.95. For dinner, meals range from $19 for baby back ribs to $37 for Pacific lobster tail, including a salad from the salad bar. At the side of the restaurant is a takeaway counter open from 6.30 am to 4 pm with standard breakfast fare for under $5, plate lunches for $5.25 and saimin, burgers and sandwiches.

Hotel Hana-Maui (☎ 248-8211) serves three meals a day. At lunch time (11.30 am to 2 pm), dishes such as teriyaki chicken with soba or a steak sandwich with Maui onion rings cost about $15 to $20. Dinner (from 6.30 to 8 pm) is prix fixe for $50, with main course dishes such as grey snapper with papaya basil relish. Meals are served in an open-air dining room with high beam ceilings and orchids on the tables. If you go on luau night, the price is the same, but meals are served on Hamoa Beach – complete with free punch, tasty appetizers and pleasantly low-key entertainment. Reservations are required.

Hana to Kipahulu

From Hana, the road continues on to Kipahulu, passing Oheo, the southern end of Haleakala National Park. It's an incredibly lush stretch, perhaps the most beautiful part of the entire drive. As it continues south from Hana, the road changes its name to the Piilani Highway.

The road from Hana to Oheo is narrow,

bumpy and winding. Between the hairpin turns, narrow bridges and drivers trying to take in all the sights, it's a slow-moving 10 miles.

You'll get extra coastal views by detouring along the 1½-mile Haneoo Rd loop, which runs past Koki and Hamoa beaches and a couple of ancient shoreline fishponds. The turn-off is half a mile south of Hana Ranch headquarters.

Koki Beach is at the base of a red cinder hill less than half a mile from the start of the loop. Most of Koki's sand washes away in winter, leaving a rocky shoreline. Local surfers who know the coastline sometimes surf here, but rocks and strong currents make it hazardous for newcomers.

The offshore rock topped by two coconut trees is Alau Island, a sea-bird sanctuary. The trees were planted years ago by a couple of Hana residents so they'd have coconuts to drink while fishing off the island.

A little farther is Hamoa Beach, a nice silvery grey sand beach. It's used by the Hotel Hana-Maui which provides a lifeguard and maintains showers and restrooms. There's public access down steps below the hotel's bus stop sign. When the surf's up, there's good surfing and bodysurfing. When seas are calm, swimming in the cove is good.

As the road continues south, there are waterfalls down the cliffs, breadfruit and coconut trees, orchids growing out of rocks and even a statue of the Virgin Mary tucked into a rock face on the side of the road.

Wailua Falls, three miles before Oheo, is particularly attractive with its 100-foot drop visible from the road. There's usually a couple of people at the waterfall pull-off selling hand-painted T-shirts and the like.

OHEO GULCH

Oheo Stream dramatically cuts its way through Oheo Gulch as a lovely series of waterfalls and wide pools, each one tumbling into the next one below. In fair weather you can swim in them. A two-mile trail runs up the stream bed.

There was once a large Hawaiian settlement spread throughout the Oheo area. The stone remains of more than 700 structures have been counted. These early villagers cultivated taro and sweet potatoes in terraced gardens.

One of the expressed purposes of the national park is to manage the Oheo area 'to perpetuate traditional Hawaiian farming and *hoonanea* – a Hawaiian word meaning to pass the time in ease, peace and pleasure'.

Not so long ago Oheo Gulch was dubbed 'Seven Sacred Pools', a tourism promotion idea. There are actually 24 pools from the ocean all the way up to Waimoku Falls and they were never sacred (although it was kapu for menstruating women to bathe in them).

Rangers hang out around the parking lot from 7.30 am to 4 pm daily to answer questions. There are restrooms near the parking lot but there's no drinking water at Oheo.

Kipahulu Valley

Oheo Gulch is part of the 11,000 acres of Kipahulu Valley that was jointly purchased by the Nature Conservancy and the state and added to Haleakala National Park in 1969.

The upper Kipahulu Valley is pristine native rainforest and home to endangered native plants and birds. The Maui parrotbill, which lives only here, has a habitat range of just over eight miles. Fewer than 500 of the birds survive. The entire population (30) of the Maui *nuku-puu*, Hawaii's most endangered honeycreeper, also lives in Kipahulu Valley. The nuku-puu was last seen on Kauai in 1985 and is believed to be extinct on Oahu. The parrotbill and nuku-puu are both beautiful birds, about five inches long, with bright yellow underbellies.

The upper part of the valley gets up to 300 inches of rain a year and is swampy with dense vegetation. In an effort to protect the habitat, no public access is allowed.

Lower Pools

A 20-minute path from the Oheo Gulch parking lot heads down to the lower pools and then loops back via the road. There are interpretive signs along the way and a ranger station is located near the start of the trail. A few minutes down, the trail comes to a broad grassy knoll with a beautiful view of the Hana coast. On a clear day you can see the Big Island across the Alenuihaha Channel, 30 miles away. It would be a fine place to break out a picnic basket.

The large freshwater pools along the trail are almost terraced one atop the other, connected by gentle cascades. They're usually calm and great for swimming, though the water's brisk. The second big pool below the bridge is a favourite.

If it's been raining heavily and the water is flowing too high and fast, the pools are closed and signs are posted by the ranger. Still, at any time, heavy rains in the upper slopes can bring a sudden torrent of rising waters. If the water starts to rise, get out. People have been swept from the pools by flash floods. The ocean below is not inviting at all – it's quite rough and is populated by grey sharks!

Actually, the biggest cause of injury here is from falls on slippery rocks. Another hazard is the submerged rocks and ledges in some of the pools. Check them out before diving in.

Oheo is home to a rare goby fish which spends the first part of its life in the ocean, but returns to breed in the upper stream. It works its way up the chain of pools and waterfalls by using its front fins as suction cups on the rocks.

Waterfall Trails

Opposite the parking lot is a trail leading up to Makahiku Falls (half a mile) and Waimoku Falls (two miles). The path passes large mango trees and lots of guava, forking after about 10 minutes.

Makahiku Falls is just off to the right. This is a long bridal-veil waterfall which drops into a deep gorge. Thick green ferns cover the sides of 200-foot basalt cliffs and the scene is quite rewarding for such a short walk.

To the left of the overlook there's a path in a ditch that goes up to the top of the waterfalls where there's a popular skinny-dipping pool. Around midday the pool is

quite enjoyable but by late afternoon the sun stops hitting it and the mosquitoes move in.

Rocks above the waterfall protect the pool as long as the water level isn't high. A cut on one side lets the water fall over the cliff. If the water starts to rise, get out immediately – a drop over this sheer 184-foot falls would obviously be fatal!

Waimoku Falls is a thin, lacy 400-foot waterfall dropping down a sheer rock face. The walk to the falls is made all the more special by three thick bamboo groves. When you come out of the first grove, you'll see the waterfall in the distance. By the time you emerge from the third thicket, you're there.

It takes about 45 minutes to hike the 1½ miles to Waimoku Falls from the Makahiku Falls viewpoint. There are a couple of stream crossings on the way. Don't attempt them if the water is high or rising.

The upper part of the trail is muddy with a boardwalk over sections of it. The mosquitoes which thrive along the stream bed can be pesky. There are ancient farm sites with abandoned taro patches along the way, though it takes a keen eye to recognise them.

The pool under Waimoku was partially filled in by a landslide, caused by the 1976 earthquake, and the pool's not very deep anymore. Anyway, swimming is not recommended due to the danger of falling rocks. There are concerns that heavy vibrations from helicopters hovering over the waterfalls are destabilising the rocks even more.

If you want to take a dip, there are better pools to swim in along the way. About 100 yards before Waimoku Falls you'll cross a little stream. If you go left for 10 minutes up the stream there's a beautiful waterfall and a little pool about neck deep. There's not really a trail but you can walk alongside the stream to get to it.

There's also a nice pool in the stream about halfway between Makahiku and Waimoku falls.

Places to Stay

There's an undeveloped camping ground on the south side of the park. This is Hawaiian style; free, with no unnecessary structures –

just a huge open coastal pasture. There are incredible places to pitch a tent on grassy cliffs right above the coast. All you will hear is the pounding surf.

Between its stunning scenery and the setting amidst the ruins of an old Hawaiian village, this is a powerful place. In winter there are usually only a handful of tents here. It gets quite a few campers in summer but apparently never fills to the point where people are turned away. There are pit toilets and a few picnic tables but *no* water. Permits aren't required though camping is officially limited to three nights each month.

KIPAHULU

The village of Kipahulu is less than a mile south of Oheo. Around the turn of the century Kipahulu was one of several sugar plantation villages in the Hana area. It had a working mill from 1890 to 1922. The mill closure was followed by attempts at growing pineapples before ranching took hold in the late 1920s.

Today Kipahulu has both exclusive estates and more modest homes. A scattering of impromptu fruit stands are set up along the roadside, some attended by elderly women who string leis and sell bananas and woven lauhala hats. This is the end of the line for most day visitors who have pushed beyond Hana.

Lindbergh's Grave

The Hana area was home to aviator hero Charles Lindbergh during the last years of his life. He began visiting in the 1960s, built a cliff-side home in Kipahulu in 1968 and died in Maui of cancer in 1974.

Lindbergh is buried in the graveyard of Palapala Hoomau Congregational Church. His simple grave is surrounded by a chain and marked with little US flags.

Would-be visitors sometimes get the location mixed up with the peach-coloured St Paul's Church, which sits on the highway three-quarters of a mile south of Oheo, but the dirt drive down to Palapala Hoomau Church is a quarter of a mile beyond that. Turn in at the metal gate just past the wooden

cistern at the end of the field. The short road in can get very rutted.

Palapala Hoomau Church, the walls of which are 26 inches thick, dates from 1864. It's dusty, with simple wooden pews and wax candles melting in the candelabra. The church is known for its window painting of a Polynesian Christ dressed in the red and yellow feather capes worn only by Hawaii's highest chiefs.

The churchyard is a peaceful place, with sleepy cats lounging around waiting for a nice warm car hood to sprawl out on.

Places to Stay

Seven Pools Hikers' Lodge (☎ 248-8000), Star Route 170, Hana Hwy, Kipahulu, HI 96713, provides suitably rustic accommodation in a peaceful, alternative environment. The lodge is a two-storey house, all open-air with screens and cross breezes. A simple room for two with a loft bed is $30, while futons in a community room are $15, plus $5 if you need linen. There are hot showers, flush toilets and cooking facilities. Papaya, avocado and bananas grow on the 13-acre grounds and are free for the picking. The friendly manager, Jim Bydoleki, can give you the low-down on natural pools nearby and other local sights to explore.

The lodge is just over a mile south of the national park entrance, on the mauka side of the road. Turn in to the driveway at Box 170 and then go left at the fork. On foot, it's about 10 minutes from the road. Since it's a new operation, it would be a good idea to call in advance just to be sure they're still up and running.

Getting There & Away

A lot of people leave Oheo in mid-afternoon to head back up the Hana Highway. Some of them, suddenly realising what a long trek they have ahead, become very impatient drivers.

You might want to consider leaving a little later, which would not only give you more sightseeing time, but allow you to avoid the rush. Getting caught in the dark returning north on the Hana Highway does have certain advantages. You can see the headlights of oncoming cars around bends that would otherwise be blind and the traffic is almost nonexistent.

There are no short cuts, but sometimes there is another option.

From Kipahulu, the Piilani Highway (Don't be misled by the term 'highway' – there's barely a road in places!) heads west through Kaupo up to Keokea in Kula. It's usually passable, but not always, and it shouldn't be done in the dark.

The best way to find out about current road conditions is to drive to the far end of Kipahulu and talk to people coming from the Kaupo direction. Most likely they've either just driven down from Kula or else have started up the road from Kipahulu, found road conditions bad and turned around.

Another way is to call the county public works department (☎ 248-8254) between 7 am and 3 pm on weekdays. After hours, try the county police department (☎ 248-8311).

For more details on the drive, see the Piilani Highway section.

Upcountry

Upcountry refers to the highland area of East Maui on the western slopes of Haleakala. You have to drive through Upcountry to get to Haleakala National Park, but it's well worth visiting for its own sake. This is some of Maui's finest countryside, with rolling hills, grazing horses and green pastures.

Upcountry is uncrowded and dotted with small towns. A fair chunk of the area is still occupied by ranches, with Haleakala Ranch covering vast spreads to the north, and Ulupalakua Ranch to the south.

Kula, in the centre of it all, has rich farmland where most of Maui's vegetables and flowers are grown. On the mountainside above Kula are the delightful cloudforests of Polipoli.

From Upcountry you can look across the central plains to the West Maui Mountains and get a good view of the Maui coastline and the neighbouring islands. There are landscaped gardens and a winery tasting room to visit. Daytimes are cooler in the Upcountry and nights can be downright brisk.

Paia to Makawao

Baldwin Ave (Hwy 390) runs seven miles from Paia on the Hana Highway up to Makawao. It starts amid sugar cane, passes the Paia Mill and then runs on through pineapple fields interspersed with little open patches where cattle graze.

There are two churches up Baldwin Ave. The **Holy Rosary Church**, with its memorial statue of Father Damien, comes up first on the right and the attractive **Makawao Union Church**, a stone block building with stained glass windows, is farther along on the left. The latter was built in 1916 and is on the National Register of Historic Places.

The roadside **Rainbow Park** is at the three-mile post. It has a covered picnic table, a portable toilet and camping, but it's in a low area that can get a bit soggy when it rains.

Kaluanui, the former nine-acre plantation estate of sugar magnates Harry and Ethel Baldwin, now houses a classy gallery and arts centre, **Hui Noeau Visual Arts Center**, on the left between the five and six-mile markers. Hui Noeau (☎ 572-6560) is a non-profit group offering community classes in printmaking, weaving, batik and dozens of other visual arts.

The two-storey pink plantation home with Spanish-style tile roof was designed by Honolulu architect C W Dickey in 1917. The 1st floor of the house features changing exhibits, while the stables at the back have been turned into a ceramics studio. This one's a mansion for the masses.

The remains of Maui's first mule-powered centrifugal sugar mill and some abandoned railroad tracks are near the entrance. The gallery is open from 9 am to 4 pm Tuesday to Sunday.

HALIIMAILE

Haliimaile is a little pineapple town in the midst of a large pineapple plantation. The main attraction is the big old general store,

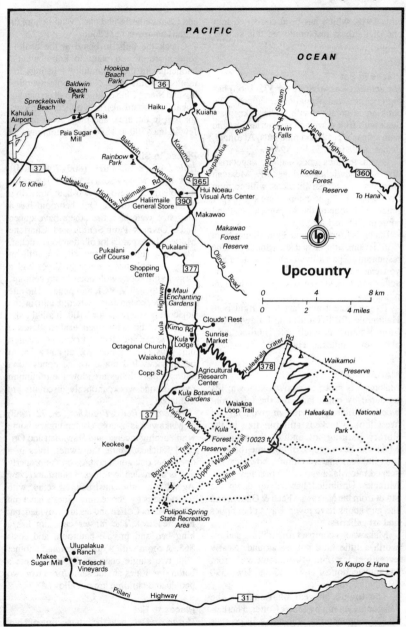

circa 1918, which has been converted into one of the best restaurants on this side of Maui.

Places to Eat

Haliimaile General Store (☎ 572-2666) has high ceilings and plantation-era appeal. The cooking is creative with dishes like roast duck with fruit glaze and vegetarian lasagne with spinach, pesto and pine nuts. At dinner, dishes range from $13 to $24.

Lunch features good salads, vegetarian dishes, sandwiches and a daily Mexican special such as fresh ahi tacos, with nothing over $10. For light eaters there's a 'gypsy lunch' with soup of the day, green salad and sourdough bread for $5.50.

Lunch is from 11 am to 3 pm, dinner from 6 to 10 pm. It's closed on Mondays. The restaurant has a Hollywood connection and you can rub elbows with some big-name actors and rock stars if you hit it on the right night.

To get there from Paia, turn right onto Haliimaile Rd, five miles up Baldwin Ave. From Kahului, turn left onto Haliimaile Rd about seven miles up Hwy 37.

MAKAWAO

Makawao is billed as a cowpoke town. It's bordered by ranch land and the false-front wooden buildings downtown give it an Old West look. Chickens still run free in the library parking lot and in the summer Makawao has a couple of big-time rodeos.

A little alternative culture, however, has seeped into Makawao in the past few years. Miracles Unlimited has set up down the street from the Makawao Feed & Garden and the gun shops have given way to boutiques and art galleries.

Makawao is compact for strolling and it's worth a little time poking around. Nearly everything is within a two-minute walk from the intersection of Hwy 365 and Hwy 390 (Baldwin Ave).

The town's newest pharmacy is the Dragon's Den run by Malik Cotter, a herbalist and acupuncturist, who also sells crystals and Chinese herbs and teas. Maui School of Yoga Therapy is next door.

Check the bulletin board at the health-food store if you want to know what's happening in the community – listings for things like Sufi dance classes, polarity training and Sierra Club outings to pull up banana poka. The board also has notices of rooms for rent in the area, and there are usually a few in the $300 to $350 per month range.

Places to Stay

Hale Lani (☎ 572-0020, (800) 788-MAUI) Box 1527, Makawao, HI 96768, is a comfortable three-bedroom, two-bath house in a quiet neighbourhood. One bedroom has a king-size waterbed, the others have queen beds. Owners Paul Santos and Charlene Mullens have paid a lot of attention to detail. There's a fully equipped kitchen with an array of appliances, a washer/dryer and a large living room with open-beam ceilings, a wood stove, TV, VCR and phone. The rate is $80. A second one-bedroom unit in the adjacent house rents for $100. It's light and airy, all cedar with open beams. It has a king-size bed and all the amenities of the first unit, plus a deck with a hot tub and a distant ocean view. It'd make a nice honeymoon suite. Unless things are slow the minimum rental is one week; monthly discounts are available.

Haleakala Bed & Breakfast (☎ 572-7988) in Makawao is a large contemporary home with burning incense and Hawaiian and Oriental touches. Mara, the owner, lives in a one-room octagonal cottage on the property and is interested in things Eastern and New Age. It's a rather unstructured setup, with reservations by phone only. Guests have run of the house. Coffee and tea are provided, but not breakfast. The master bedroom has a king bed and private bathroom and costs $65. A room with a queen bed and another with two single beds are $55 and share a bathroom. Rates are the same for one or two people and children are not allowed.

Places to Eat

Casanova Deli, near the intersection of Hwy

365 and Hwy 390, is a fine Italian deli, with all sorts of salads for $3.50 to $4 for half a pound and plates such as quiche and salad for $5. It also has good coffees, desserts and bread. Hours are from 8.30 am to 7.30 pm Monday to Saturday and 8.30 am to 6 pm Sunday.

Casanova Restaurant, next to the deli, is one of the most popular restaurants in the area. Delicious crispy crusted pizza baked in a kiawe-fired brick oven, as well as creative pastas, are served at cafe-style tables in the front dining room and average $9 to $13. In the back dining room things are more formal and a wider menu is offered, including fish and meat dishes for around $20. Desserts are superb, worthy of a splurge.

Polli's, at the intersection of Hwy 365 and Hwy 390, is an old stand-by serving Mexican food and big margaritas. Dinner combos cost from $9 to $14. You can also order vegetarian tacos or enchiladas that use soy-burger instead of meat; two tacos served with beans cost $5. It's open from 11.30 am to 10 pm (to 11 pm on weekends).

Kitada's Restaurant has been making inexpensive saimin for generations. It's open from 6 am to 1.30 pm daily except Sundays. It's on Baldwin Ave opposite the Makawao Steak & Fish House.

Down to Earth Natural Foods, opposite Casanova, is a health-food store with a large display of organic produce, bulk foods, juices, a deli with sandwiches and salads, a dairy section and all the standard natural-food grocery products.

Entertainment

Casanova (☎ 572-0220) is the hottest music spot on Maui, bringing in big names like Richie Havens, Los Lobos, the Hawaiian rock band Kalapana and other live groups on Fridays and Saturdays. There's entertainment from 9.45 pm nightly, usually rock, reggae, disco, jazz, rhythm & blues or Latin music. The cover charge is generally $3 to $10 for local bands and around $20 for international names.

Polli's (☎ 572-7808) has live music from 9 to 11 pm Thursday, Friday and Saturday. There's no cover charge.

HAIKU

Scenic back roads head out in all directions from Makawao and almost any one you choose to explore will make a prime country drive.

Some of those roads lead through Haiku, a scattered community that stretches north from Makawao down the slopes to the Hana Highway.

From Makawao, take Kaupakalua Rd (Hwy 365) north. After a mile, turn left onto Kokomo Rd, which passes through pineapple fields before reaching the modest two-store village that marks the centre of Haiku. Alexander & Baldwin grew their first 12 acres of sugar cane near Haiku and there was once a mill here.

Today Haiku is seeing a bit of a revival. Its rural character and its proximity to both Makawao and Hookipa have attracted a number of new residents ranging from windsurfers to artists and New Age folks. The area has some good-value places to stay and makes a fairly convenient base for exploring the whole island.

Places to Stay

Jan's Surf Resort (☎ 575-9505), 538 Kauhikoa Rd, Haiku, HI 96708, is about two miles inland from Hwy 36. Jan, a German windsurfer who has settled on Maui, rents six rooms in his contemporary house. The home is quite pleasant, with exposed high beam ceilings and the like. Most of the time it's shared by an international crowd, largely Europeans. A single room with shared bath costs $30, a double $35, with discounts possible on longer stays.

Pilialoha (☎ 572-1440), c/o Machiko & Bill Heyde, 255 Kaupakalua Rd, Haiku, HI 96708, is a delightful cottage in upcountry Haiku, about two miles from the centre of Makawao. Set in a eucalyptus grove, the terraced cottage has hardwood oak floors, floral cottons, a bedroom with a queen bed, and a second room with a single bed. There's a full kitchen, a washer/dryer, a phone, and a living room with VCR, cable TV and a queen hideaway bed. Machiko, an artist, has quilted and painted the pillows and added other charming touches. The cost is $75 for one or two people, $10 for each additional person. There's a two-day minimum stay and smoking is allowed outdoors only. Coffee, tea, fruit and home-made muffins and pastries are provided for breakfast; if you don't eat sugar, Machiko will bake with honey.

Haikuleana (☎ 575-2890), 69 Haiku Rd, Haiku, HI 96708, is an older plantation-style house that retains some graceful period touches. There's a central dining area and a sitting room with antiques and rattan and wicker furnishings. There are two rooms, one with a twin bed and one with a queen bed, and private baths with claw-foot tubs. Rates are $80 with a two-night minimum and include breakfast. Children under six are not accepted and smoking is not allowed. It's about 1⅓ miles up Haiku Rd from Hwy 36, next to the Haiku Chapel.

Akahi Farm (☎ 572-8795), 915 Kaupakalua Rd, Haiku, HI 96708, is a small secluded 55-acre retreat centre in Haiku. The centre sometimes has packages that include a room, vegetarian meals, hot tub, massage and other activities for about $1000 a week. There are Vipassana retreats and yoga, aikido and tai chi workshops held here that are occasionally open to individual travellers, though for the most part the centre is rented out to groups.

PUKALANI

Pukalani, on the way to Haleakala, is the biggest Upcountry town. It's a residential community with a population of 6000.

Pukalani is two miles from Makawao along Hwy 365. Midway between the two towns is a picture-perfect ranch scene with rolling pastures, horses and cattle grazing and a mountain backdrop. Beyond this the rows of pineapple start up again.

If you're coming from Kahului, the Haleakala Highway (Hwy 37) climbs for five miles through cane fields before turning into green grassy pastures below Pukalani. If you've been to the Big Island, the prickly pear cactus in the fields might look familiar. The seeds were introduced by cattle shipped to Maui from a Big Island ranch.

Places to Eat
Pukalani Terrace Shopping Center is south of the intersection of Hwy 365 and Hwy 37. It has a *Dairy Queen* with fast-food fare and a 24-hour Foodland supermarket with a salad bar, a deli section and a bakery that makes good croissants.

There's also a *McDonald's* a little farther up the highway, next to a convenience store that sells fried chicken and giant steak fries by the piece.

Pukalani Terrace Country Clubhouse (☎ 572-1325) is where Pukalanians head when they want to go out. It's located above the golf course, less than a mile past the shopping centre on Pukalani Rd. There's a reasonably good salad bar with soup that costs $7 alone or $3 with a meal. Meals range from complete Hawaiian plates (which include kalua pig, lomi salmon, poi and haupia) for about $8, to New York steak at $13. Hawaiian food is also served à la carte. Breakfast features omelettes, waffles and pancakes and costs about $5 with coffee. The dining room has a good view down to the ocean and is open from 7 am to 2 pm and 5 to 9 pm daily.

KULA
Kula is the agricultural heartland of Maui. The average elevation is 3000 feet. Crops such as lettuce, tomatoes, carrots, cauliflower and cabbage thrive in Kula's warm days, cool nights and rich volcanic soil. No gourmet cook in Hawaii would be without sweet Kula onions.

During the California Gold Rush in the mid-1800s, Hawaiian farmers in Kula shipped so many potatoes off to the miners that the area became known as 'Nu Kaleponi', the Hawaiian pronunciation for New California. In the late 1800s, Portuguese and Chinese immigrants moved in to farm the Kula area after they had worked off their contracts on the sugar plantations.

Kula grows most of Hawaii's proteas,

large bright flowers with an unusual flair. Some, like the pincushion varieties, are very delicate and others have spine-like petals.

Almost 90% of the carnations used in leis throughout Hawaii are grown in Kula, as are many of the chrysanthemums.

Hwy 377 (Haleakala Highway) and Hwy 37 (Kula Highway) are both scenic. Take your pick, or go up one and down the other.

Gardens

All of Kula is a garden, but if you want to take a closer look there are several established walk-through gardens.

Clouds' Rest Protea Farm, one mile along Upper Kimo Drive off Hwy 377, has a little garden area where many of the plants are identified by plaques. You can stroll through it for free from 8 am to 4.30 pm daily. Cut protea are on sale at rock-bottom prices at the farm, and by mail order for the usual shipped cost.

Sunrise Market, on Hwy 378 on the way to Haleakala, has a free roadside garden with a small but select group of proteas.

Kula Botanical Gardens is a mature garden of tropical plants, pleasantly overgrown and shady. It's on Hwy 37, three-quarters of a mile up from the southern intersection of Hwy 377 and Hwy 37. The garden is open from 9 am to 4 pm daily and admission is $3 for adults, 50 cents for children aged 6 to 12.

The more recently planted **Maui Enchanting Gardens** is sunny, open and orderly, with both tropical and cool-weather garden flowers. It's a colourful collection and most plants are labelled in both Japanese and English. It's on Hwy 37, just south of Omaopio Rd, and is open from 9 am to 5 pm daily. Admission is $3.50.

The University of Hawaii maintains a 20-acre **Agricultural Research Center** in Kula. It's there that Hawaii's first proteas, natives of Australia and South Africa, were established in 1965. You can walk through rows of their colourful descendants as well as dozens of new hybrids under development. The protea has more than 1400 varieties and is named after the Greek god Proteus, who was noted for his ability to change form.

There are now over 50 protea farms in Hawaii supplying the cut flowers to florists on the US mainland, Japan and Europe. The nearest is just across the street from the research centre.

You can visit the research centre until 3.30 pm weekdays after signing in at the office. It's free. Some sections of the garden are part of experiments in plant pathology and are closed to visitors. Avoid Fridays, which is the day pesticides are sprayed.

To get there, take Copp St (between the 12 and 13-mile markers on Hwy 37), turn left on Mauna Place; it's half a mile above town.

Octagonal Church

The distinctive octagonal Holy Ghost Church is a hillside landmark in Waiakoa village. The white church with its pink trim has a roof that glints silver in the sun. Built in 1897 by Portuguese immigrants, the ornate interior of the church looks like it came right out of Portugal, and much of it did. Because of termite problems, the church was dismantled and completely renovated in 1992.

Holy Ghost Church

Places to Stay

Kilohana Elua (☎ 878-6086), c/o Jody Baldwin, 378 Kamehameiki Rd, Kula, HI 96790, is a B&B on three nicely landscaped acres not far from the beginning of Haleakala Crater Rd. It's a delightful place with lots of atmosphere. Chickens roam the yard, there's a fine view from the back porch and a lava-rock fireplace graces the living room. There are three rooms, two with a shared bathroom for $65 and one with a private bathroom for $75. Rooms are furnished with antiques, and a breakfast of fruit, breads and Kona coffee is provided. There's a two-night minimum and children under age 16 are usually not accepted.

Ahinahina Farm Bed & Breakfast (☎ 878-6096), c/o Mike & Annette Endres, 210 Ahinahina Place, Kula, HI 96790, has two rentals about two miles west of the village of Waiakoa. One unit is a pleasant two-bedroom cottage with open-beam ceilings, a full kitchen, washer/dryer, TV, VCR, and a covered deck with a distant ocean view. There's also a studio that's closer to the main house, but still private. It has a queen bed, an efficiency kitchen, TV and deck. The studio costs $75 a night for a single/double, plus $10 if there's a third person. The cottage costs $90, plus $15 for each additional person over two. Rates include breakfast, children 12 and under are not accepted, and smoking is not allowed.

Kula Lodge (☎ 878-1535, (800) 233-1535), RR1, Box 475, Kula, HI 96790, on Hwy 377 has five cottages in the same complex as its restaurant. The units are pleasant, but not special, and the prices are a steep $140 for rooms with fireplaces, $120 without, plus $50 for each person beyond two.

Places to Eat

The dining room at the *Kula Lodge* is on a knoll with 180° wraparound windows and a splendid view of central and northern Maui and the ocean beyond. Breakfast features the standard items for about $5. The chef's creation is the best deal at lunch, with the entree of the day, soup or salad and coffee for $6.50.

Salads and sandwiches are about the same price. Dinner is more up-market, in the $14 to $22 range. The food is good, and the Portuguese bean soup is one of the best on the island. It's on Hwy 377, less than a mile before Haleakala Crater Rd (Hwy 378). Hours are 6.30 am to 9.30 pm.

The *Kula Sandalwoods Restaurant,* just past Kula Lodge on the mauka side of Hwy 377, is open from 7 am to 2 pm daily. Prices are similar to those at the lodge, though the food is not quite on par. They're renovating six cabins on the hill above the restaurant that will probably become vacation rentals.

Sunrise Market is a quarter of a mile up from the intersection of Hwy 378 and Hwy 377 on the way to Haleakala. You can pick up your morning coffee here along with bakery items, fresh and dried fruits and wrapped sandwiches. The store is open from 8 am to 4 pm daily. There's a nice little protea garden on the side of the store.

Kula Country Store, a quarter of a mile from the Octagonal Church, is a grocery store with a deli counter. Sandwiches range from $3 to $5. It's open from 7 am to 3 pm daily, with the deli closing at 1 pm.

POLIPOLI

Polipoli Spring State Recreation Area is high up in the Kula Forest Reserve on the western slope of Haleakala. The park is in a coniferous forest with picnic tables, camping and a network of trails. It's not always possible to get all the way to the park without a 4WD, but it's worth driving even part way up for the view.

Waipoli Rd, the road to the park, is off Hwy 377 just under half a mile before its southern intersection with Hwy 37.

Waipoli is a narrow switchbacking one-lane road. The drive is often through layers of clouds which drift in and out of groves of eucalyptus and past open rangeland. (Watch for cattle on the road.) When the clouds lift there are vast views across green rolling hills to the islands of Lanai and Kahoolawe.

Few people venture up this way. Except for the symphony of bird calls, everything is still.

When the clouds are heaviest, visibility is measured in feet. The road has some soft shoulders, but the first six miles are well paved. The road then enters the forest reserve and turns to dirt. When it's muddy, the next four miles up to the state park are not worth trying in a standard car.

The whole area was planted during the 1930s by the Civilian Conservation Corps (CCC), a Depression-era work programme. Several of the trails pass through old CCC camps. There are stands of redwood, ash, cypress, cedar and pines. It all looks somewhat like the northern California coast.

Because of fire danger caused by an ongoing drought, much of the park was closed to the public as we went to press. If the drought conditions persist, the closure probably will also. Call the state parks office (☎ 243-5354) for information on current conditions.

Waiakoa Loop Trail

The trailhead to the Waiakoa Loop Trail starts at the hunter check station five miles up Waipoli Rd. Walk three-quarters of a mile down the grassy spur road on the left to a gate marking the trail which starts out in pine trees.

Since a fire a few years back, the trail has not been maintained and it's no longer possible to do the whole three-mile loop. However, you can start from the left side of the loop and walk about two miles to where it connects with Upper Waiakoa Trail.

Upper Waiakoa Trail

The Upper Waiakoa Trail is a maintained seven-mile trail that begins off Waiakoa Loop. The trail starts at an elevation of 6000 feet, climbs 1800 feet up switchbacks and then drops back down 1400 feet.

It's stony terrain, but high and open and provides good views. Bring a full canteen of water.

The trail ends on Waipoli Rd between the hunter check station and the camping ground. If you want to start at this end of the trail, keep an eye out for the trail marker for Waohuli Trail, as Upper Waiakoa begins across the road.

Boundary Trail

The four-mile Boundary Trail begins about 200 yards beyond the end of the pavement. Park to the right of the cattle grate which marks the boundary of the Kula Forest Reserve.

This is a steep downhill walk that crosses ravines and goes down deep into the trees where there's eucalyptus, pine and cedar as well as a bit of native forest. In the afternoon the fog generally rolls in and visibility fades. The trail is marked and maintained.

Skyline Trail

It's possible to hike 8½ miles from the summit of Haleakala to Polipoli camping ground at 6200 feet. At Haleakala National Park, go past the summit and take the road to the left just before Science City.

The first 6½ miles is down Skyline Trail, a dirt road used to maintain the state park. It starts at the 9750-foot elevation in an open terrain of cinder and craters.

The tree line begins with a native mamane forest at 8500 feet, about three miles down. In the winter mamane is heavy with clusters of delicate yellow flowers that look like sweet-pea blossoms.

Skyline Trail merges into the Haleakala Ridge Trail and then the Polipoli Trail, which spurs half a mile to the camping ground.

There's solitude on this walk. If the clouds treat you kindly there are broad views as you pass from the barren summit into the dense cloudforest.

Places to Stay

Besides tent camping, Polipoli has one housekeeping cabin at $17 for two people, reserved through the state park system. Unlike the other state cabins, this one has gas lanterns but no electricity or refrigerator.

Come prepared as this is cold country and in the winter the temperature drops below freezing at night. There's drinking water and restrooms. It's a popular spot for pig hunters.

KEOKEA

Around the turn of the century, Keokea was home mainly to Hakka Chinese who farmed the remote Kula region.

Keokea is the last real town before Hana if you're swinging around the southern part of the island. It has two small stores with gas pumps (Fong Store/Shell and Ching Store/Chevron) and a coffee shop.

The village's green and white St John's Episcopal Church was built in 1907 to serve the Chinese community. 'St John's House of Worship' is written in Chinese above the door.

On a clear day there are good views of West Maui and Lanai from the roadside.

Places to Stay

Halemanu Bed & Breakfast (☎ 878-2729), c/o Carol Austin, 221 Kawehi Place, Kula, HI 96790, is in a lovely contemporary home set beneath the Kula Forest Reserve off Waipoli Rd. Accommodation is in a room with a queen bed, private bath, phone and deck. A TV and VCR are available in the loft. Carol writes the 'Word Has It' chat-style column in the *Maui News*. She's a very outgoing person who enjoys showing her guests around, and occasionally joins them for impromptu hikes and snorkel outings. There's a two-day minimum and the cost is $70 for one or two people.

Bloom Cottage (☎ 878-1425), RR2 Box 229, Kula, HI 96790, is a two-bedroom free-standing cottage in Keokea. There's a fireplace in the living room to ward off evening chills. The cottage also has a kitchen, a TV and a front porch. The rate is $85 for doubles, $10 for each extra person, with breakfast fixings provided. There's a two-night minimum stay. Smoking is not allowed.

Places to Eat

Upcountry folks gravitate to *Grandma's Coffee House* for sweet home-made pastries and dark roasted Maui coffee. It's a sunny, cheery place. You can also get espresso, saimin and sandwiches.

Alfred Franco's family has grown coffee on the slopes of Haleakala since 1918. Alfred started selling at flea markets, packing his coffee in little brown paper bags with felt-penned labels. In 1988 he set up a 103-year-old roasting machine and opened Grandma's. Demand for Maui coffee is high and the beans command a premium price, which has drawn more Upcountry growers to coffee. If you want to see coffee trees, just walk out to the side porch.

ULUPALAKUA RANCH

From Keokea, Hwy 37 winds south through ranch country with good views of Kahoolawe and the little island of Molokini. Even on overcast days you can often see below the clouds to sunny Kihei on the coast.

Tedeschi Vineyards, in the middle of Ulupalakua Ranch, is 5½ miles south of Keokea.

In the mid-1800s, Ulupalakua Ranch was a sugar plantation owned by whaling ship captain James Makee. The 25,000-acre ranch has been owned by Pardee Erdman and family since 1963. It's a working ranch with about 5000 head of cattle, 1000 Merino sheep and 100 head of Rocky Mountain elk.

Ulupalakua Ranch Store, opposite the ranch headquarters, is a small local store selling dungarees, bags of horse feed, a few groceries and Haagen-Dazs ice-cream bars. It's open from 9 am to 5 pm Monday to Friday, 10 am to 5 pm on weekends.

Tedeschi Vineyards

Tedeschi Vineyards (☎ 878-6058) is the only winery in Hawaii. The first grapes were planted in 1976. While waiting for the vines to mature, the vineyard began producing Maui Blanc, a pineapple wine. It's surprisingly light and dry and quite reasonably priced.

Tedeschi now makes four wines from grapes, including champagne and a blush zinfandel, which you can try out in the tasting room from 9 am to 5 pm daily. The little stone building is actually Captain Makee's old jail. Winery tours are given every half hour between 9.30 am and 2.30 pm.

Opposite the winery, you can see the remains of the three stacks of the Makee Sugar Mill, built in 1878. Maui artist Reems Mitchell, who carved the three mannequin cowboys perched on the steps of the Ulupalakua Ranch Store, lives in the mill. Actor Richard Chamberlain also has a home in the neighbourhood.

Piilani Highway

The Piilani Highway (Hwy 31) curves along the southern flank of Haleakala. From Tedeschi Winery it's 25 rugged miles to the town of Kipahulu, near Oheo Gulch, the southern end of Haleakala National Park.

Some day in an asphalt future this may well be a real highway with cars zipping along in both directions. For now, it's an unspoiled adventure.

In different sections the road is of broken pavement, gravel, dirt or stones. It takes a good two hours to drive it.

Signs such as 'Motorists Assume Risk of Damage Due to Presence of Cattle' and 'Narrow Winding Road, Safe Speed 15 mph' give clues that this is not your standard highway.

Road Conditions The hardest part is finding out if the road is currently open and passable. Tourist maps mark it impassable and rusting signs at the road's beginning imply the same. Car rental agencies say just being on it is a violation of their contract.

There are a couple of possibilities for getting info on road conditions. While the best is word of mouth from other drivers, you can also call the county's public works department (☎ 248-8254) between 7 am and 3 pm on weekdays. After hours, try the county police department (☎ 248-8311).

The trickiest section of the drive is usually down around Kaupo, where the road goes over three rocky creek beds. These are usually dry and pose little problem. But after hard rains, streams flow over the roads making passage difficult, if not dangerous.

Flash floods sometimes wash away portions of the road, making it impossible to get through until it's repaired.

The best way to approach the road is with an early morning start. Take something to munch, plenty to drink and check your oil and spare tyre. Go slow enough so you don't bottom out. If you break down it's a long haul to civilisation. The tow charge is said to be around $400. If all goes well it's possible to be soaking in one of Oheo's pools by early afternoon.

The road is pretty good for the first 10 miles after the winery. It's patchwork asphalt with a sprinkling of potholes. The next five miles is rougher. Around Kaupo there are some torturous climbs over rocky riverbeds. The strip between Kaupo and Kipahulu is the worst.

A 4WD is recommended, or at least a high riser with a manual transmission. Still, all said and done, we drove it in a low-slung small car and amazed ourselves by not scraping bottom even once. There were sections where we had to take it very slow, but other than being bounced and rattled, we had no problems.

Keokea is the last place on the Kula side to get gas and something to eat. In the Oheo Gulch area you might find a fruit stand, but there's no drinking water, gas stations or other services until Hana.

Tedeschi Vineyards to Kaupo

South from Tedeschi Vineyards, groves of eucalyptus trees and green pastures soon give way to a dryer and scrubbier terrain with pink-tipped grasses and wildflowers. It's open rangeland with cattle grazing alongside and moseying across the road.

A few miles south of the winery the road crosses an expansive lava flow dating from 1790, Haleakala's last eruption. This is the flow that covers the La Perouse area of the coast south of Makena. It's still black and barren all the way down to the sea.

Just offshore is the crescent island of Molokini with Kahoolawe beyond. The large grassy hills between here and the sea are volcanic cinder cones.

Painters sometimes set up their easels along the roadside to paint scenes of the grassy rock-strewn hills and the distant ocean. There's such a wide-angle view that the ocean horizon is noticeably curved.

As the road continues it runs in and out of numerous ravines and crosses a few bridges, gradually getting closer to the coast. Around the 28-mile marker keep an eye out for a natural lava sea arch. As you continue, there are a couple of black-sand beaches.

Kaupo

Kaupo Gap is a deep and rugged valley with the only lowlands on this section of the coast. The village of Kaupo is around the 35-mile marker. Don't expect a developed village in any sense of the word.

Kaupo is spread out and there's not much to see. This is home for the scattered community of paniolos who work the Kaupo Ranch, many of them third-generation ranch hands.

Kaupo General Store is on the east side of the gap. As the fading sign proclaims, it's the only store for 20 miles, though you shouldn't count on it being open.

Kaupo was once heavily settled. It has three heiaus from the 1700s and two churches from the 1800s. Loaloa Heiau is the biggest and is a registered national historical monument. All three heiau sites are mauka of the church.

Huialoha Church, less than a mile from the store, is down on the rocky black-sand Mokulau Beach. Mokulau means 'many small islands', named for the rocks just off-shore. The area was an ancient surfing site.

The picturesque whitewashed church was built in 1859 and was restored in 1978. It's surrounded by a stone wall and a few wind-swept trees.

From here the road curves in and then out at which point it's well worth a stop for the picturesque view looking back at the church across the bay. There used to be a landing in the bay for shipping Kaupo Ranch cattle and you can still see steps leading down into the water on a rock jutting out into the ocean.

This area is cool and forested, with sisal plants on the hillsides. The road winding into Kipahulu skirts the edge of rocky cliffs and the vegetation picks up, with hala and guava trees. The road surface is like heavy cobble-stones in places and in other sections loose and sliding.

Kipahulu

The pavement begins again at Kipahulu. The road is now flat and shaded with big mango trees (which drop fruit in season), banyans, bougainvillea, and wiliwili trees with their red tiger-claw blossoms.

For more details, see the end of the Hana to Kipahulu section.

Haleakala

Haleakala Crater is an awesome geological wonder. It resembles the surface of the moon, with a seemingly lifeless crater floor dotted with high majestic cinder cones. Haleakala is the world's largest dormant volcano, 7½ miles long and 2½ miles wide. It last erupted 200 years ago.

Haleakala National Park centres around the crater, offering views from its rim and hikes across the crater floor.

Haleakala (literally 'house of the sun') has long been considered Maui's soul. The summit is thought to be an energy vortex, a natural power point for magnetic and cosmic forces. In ancient times it was a spiritual centre for Hawaiian kahunas. When the planets aligned in 1987, Haleakala drew thousands of visitors observing the harmonic convergence.

Whether it's the lingering mana of the gods who once made their home here or the geological forces of the earth which still release an occasional tremor, Haleakala does emanate a sense of some omnipresent power.

The requisite pilgrimage to witness the sunrise at the rim of the crater can be an experience that borders on the mystical. Mark Twain called it 'the sublimest spectacle' he'd ever seen.

Morning is usually the best time for

viewing the crater. Later in the day warm air generally forces clouds higher and higher until they pour through the two gaps and into the crater.

Though sunrises get top billing, sunsets can be impressive too. Sometimes there's a high thin layer of cirrus clouds and a lower layer of fluffier clouds with colours on both levels. At other times, however, it's completely clouded over.

Haleakala National Park stretches from Haleakala Crater down to the pools of Oheo Gulch on the coast south of Hana. There are separate entrances to both sections of the park, but no passage between them. For information on the Oheo area, see the Oheo Gulch section.

Geology

In its prime, Haleakala probably reached a height of 12,000 feet before water erosion began to eke out two large river valleys. Eventually the valleys eroded into one another, forming what is known today as Haleakala Crater. The valley gaps, Koolau Gap on the north-west side and Kaupo Gap on the south-east, are dominant features in the crater wall.

Later eruptions have added numerous cinder cones to the floor of Haleakala. The yellow colours are from sulphur, the reds from iron oxide.

Information

It's a good idea to check out the weather conditions (☎ 572-7749 for a recorded forecast) before driving up. It's not uncommon for it to be cloudy at Haleakala when it's clear on the coast. A drizzly sunrise is a particularly disappointing nonevent after getting out of bed at 4 am. The *Maui News* prints a sunrise schedule.

You can call park headquarters (☎ 572-9306) to talk to a ranger or check activity schedules.

The park never closes. The pay booth at the park entrance opens after dawn, but you can drive through before that. Entrance passes, good for seven days, cost $3 per car or $1 per bicycle. Walk-ins and US citizens aged over 61 are allowed in free of charge. National park passes are valid.

There's no food for sale in the park. Bring something to eat, particularly if you're going up for the sunrise, so that a growling stomach doesn't force you to rush all the way back down the mountain before you've had a chance to explore the sights.

Activities Park rangers lead a guided two-hour hike that goes about a mile into the crater down Sliding Sands Trail (meet at the trailhead) from 10 am on Tuesdays and Fridays.

Guided hikes into Waikamoi Preserve leave from Hosmer Grove camping ground at 9 am on Mondays and Thursdays and last about three hours.

Nature talks are held at the summit building for 15 minutes at 9.30, 10.30 and 11.30 am daily. Crater rim walks of varying lengths are held during the summer. Other walks and activities vary with the season.

You can hike or ride a horse down into Haleakala Crater and come back the same

Legendary Past

Legend says that long ago the goddess Hina was having problems drying her tapa cloth because the days were too short. Her son Maui, the prankish demigod for whom the island is named, decided to take matters into his own hands.

One morning he went up to the mountain-top and waited for the sun. As it came up over the mountain Maui lassoed the rays one by one and held on until the sun came to a halt. When the sun begged to be let go, Maui demanded that as a condition for its release it hereafter slow its path across the sky.

The sun gave its promise, the days are longer and the mountain is known as House of the Sun. There's about 15 more minutes of daylight here than on the coast. ■

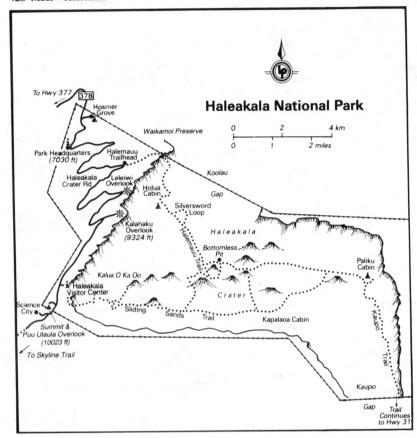

Haleakala National Park

day, or camp on the crater floor in a tent or cabin.

Bicycle tours down Haleakala via the park road and horse rides into the crater are detailed in the Facts section at the start of the Maui chapter.

Volunteer Programmes The national park service has a programme allowing volunteers to work at the park. Duties may be as varied as office work, leading hikes, fence construction, trapping predatory animals, controlling invasive plants, or cleaning pit toilets.

Competition is stiff; out of about 600 applications a year, only five people are accepted. There's a preference for volunteers with a background in natural sciences and a knowledge of practicalities like first aid. A three-month (40 hours a week) commitment is required. There's no salary or help with air fare, though barracks-style housing and a daily stipend of about $12 to help pay for food are usually provided. For information write to: Volunteers in Parks, Haleakala National Park, Box 369, Makawao, HI 96768.

Another group, the Student Conservation

Association (Box 550C, Charlestown, NH 03603), is basically a clearinghouse which sends five to eight people each year to work for three months as volunteers at Haleakala. The round-trip air fare to Hawaii, a weekly stipend of about $75 and accommodation are provided. Anyone over 18 may apply.

The Sunrise Experience

Sunrise at Haleakala is unforgettable. As you drive up in the dark, the only sights are lights: a sky full of stars, scattered city lights resembling a large connect-the-dots drawing, and a distant fishing boat or two on the dark horizon.

About an hour before sunrise, the night sky begins to lighten and turn purple-blue and the stars fade away. Interesting silhouettes of the mountain ridges appear.

Plan to arrive 30 or 40 minutes before the actual sunrise. The gentlest colours show up in the moments just before dawn. The undersides of the clouds lighten up first, accenting the night sky with pale silvery slivers and streaks of pink.

About 20 minutes before sunrise, the light intensifies on the horizon in bright oranges and reds, much like a sunset. Turn around for a look at Science City, whose domes turn pink.

Temperatures hovering around freezing and a cold wind are the norm at dawn. There's often a frosty ice in the top layer of cinders which crunches underfoot.

If you don't have a winter jacket or sleeping bag to wrap yourself in, take a warm blanket from your hotel. This will give you the option of sitting outside in a peaceful spot to take it all in rather than huddling for heat inside the crowded visitors' centre.

Everyone comes out for the grand finale. The moment the sun appears, the earth awakens and everything glows.

Every morning is different, but once the sun is up the silvery lines and the subtleties disappear. The best photo opportunities are before the sun rises.

Park Headquarters

Park headquarters, less than a mile from the park boundary, is open from 7.30 am to 4 pm daily. The office has brochures, provides camping permits and sells books on geology and flora & fauna. There are a few silverswords planted in front of the building and occasionally a pair of nene walk around the parking lot.

Hosmer Grove

Hosmer Grove is three-quarters of a mile before park headquarters. It has a pleasant half-mile loop trail that begins in the camping ground. The trail starts in a forest of introduced trees and then passes into Hawaiian shrubland.

The exotics in Hosmer Grove were introduced in 1910 in an effort to develop a lumber industry in Hawaii. They include incense cedar, Japanese sugi, Douglas fir, eucalyptus and various pines. Though the trees adapted well enough to grow, they didn't grow fast enough at these elevations to make tree harvesting practical. Thanks to this failure, there's a park instead.

Native plants include ohelo, pukiawe, mamane, pilo and sandalwood. There are wonderful scents along the trail and lots of bird calls.

Walking through either Hosmer Grove or the nearby Waikamoi Preserve, you might see the native iiwi or apapane, both fairly common sparrow-size birds with bright red feathers. The iiwi has a very loud, squeaking call, orange legs and a curved salmon-coloured bill. The apapane is a fast-moving bird with a black bill, black legs and a white under-tail. It feeds on the nectar of ohia flowers.

You might also see the melodious laughing thrush, also called the spectacle bird for the circles around its eyes that extend back like a pair of glasses, and the greenish Japanese white-eye, also with eye circles. These two are foreign species.

Waikamoi Preserve

Waikamoi Preserve is a 5230-acre reserve adjoining Hosmer Grove. In 1983 Haleakala Ranch conveyed the management rights of the land to the Nature Conservancy.

The area contains native koa and ohia

rainforest and is a habitat for Hawaiian forest birds, including a number of rare and endangered species. The yellow-green Maui creeper and the crested honeycreeper, while both endangered, are more common than some of the others. The beautiful crested honeycreeper is an aggressive bird that often dive-bombs apapane and chases them off branches.

The conservancy has hikes on the second Saturday of each month. Reservations are required and can be made by calling the preserve manager (☎ 572-7849).

The national park service leads guided hikes into the preserve from Hosmer Grove camping ground at 9 am Monday and Thursday.

Leleiwi Overlook

Leleiwi Overlook is midway between park headquarters and the visitors' centre. From the parking lot it's just a few minutes' walk out to the overlook, from where you can see the West Maui Mountains and both sides of the isthmus connecting the two sides of Maui. You also get another angle on Haleakala Crater.

In the afternoon if weather conditions are right you might see the Brocken spectre, an optical phenomenon that occurs at high elevations. Essentially, by standing between the sun and the clouds your image is magnified and projected onto the clouds. The light reflects off tiny droplets of water in the clouds, creating a circular rainbow around your shadow.

Kalahaku Overlook

Kalahaku Overlook is about a mile above Leleiwi Overlook. The lower section has a fenced enclosure containing lots of silversword, from seedlings to mature plants.

The upper section has an observation deck looking down into Haleakala Crater. Using the display here, you can clearly identify seven cinder cones on the crater floor below.

For photography, afternoon light is best. In the early morning you can get more favourable light by walking a few minutes down an unmarked path to the left of the observation deck.

Haleakala Visitors' Center

The visitors' centre, on the rim of the crater, is the main sunrise-viewing spot. It's open from shortly before sunrise to 3 pm daily.

The centre has good displays on geological and volcanic evolution and a recording explaining what you see looking out of the window into the crater floor 3000 feet below. Books on geology, plants and the national park are for sale here and there's usually a ranger on duty.

Summit

The Puu Ulaula (Red Hill) Overlook,. at 10,023 feet (3055 metres), is Maui's highest point. The octagon summit building at the overlook has wraparound windows and interpretive displays explaining the surrounding sights.

On clear days you can see the Big Island, Lanai, Molokai and even Oahu. The summit building is half a mile uphill from the visitors' centre.

The 37-mile drive from sea level to the summit of Haleakala is said to be the highest elevation gain in the shortest distance in the world. You can buy a certificate at the

Nene

The native nene, Hawaii's state bird, is related to and resembles the Canada Goose. It has been brought back from the verge of extinction (only 30 birds remained in 1951) by a captive breeding and release programme.

Currently, the nene population at Haleakala is holding steady at about 150. The birds generally nest in high cliffs surrounded by rugged lava flows with sparse vegetation.

Nene are rather curious. Many hang out where people do, from the crater floor cabins to park headquarters. Unfortunately they don't do well in an asphalt habitat and many have been run over by cars. ■

visitors' centre saying you've made the trip. The dollar for the certificate goes to help exterminate pests in the park, including cats, rats and mongoose.

Science City

On the Big Island's Mauna Kea, scientists study the moon. Here at Haleakala, appropriately enough, they study the sun.

Science City, just beyond the summit, is outside park headquarters and off limits to visitors. It's under the jurisdiction of the University of Hawaii, which owns some of the domes and leases other land for a variety of private and government research projects.

In addition to UH's solar observatory, the university's Institute of Astronomy operates a lunar ranging facility. Purdue University and the University of Wisconsin jointly operate a gamma ray telescope.

The most ominous tenant is the Air Force, which is involved in the beaming and catching of lasers. In the next phase of research the lasers will be beamed at a satellite orbiting in space. The beams will be bounced off the satellite's mirrors and aimed back down to an antenna farm planted above Kihei's Silversword Golf Course. It's all part of testing and research for the ill-conceived SDI 'Star Wars' project.

Two other defence-related facilities at Science City are a facility for satellite tracking and identification, and a deep-space surveillance system.

Places to Stay

Camping Free camping is allowed at three camping grounds in the crater section of the park and one on the coast at Oheo Gulch. Information on the Oheo Gulch area is at the end of the Hana section.

Hosmer Grove is a drive-up camping ground immediately after the park entrance. It has a picnic shelter, toilets, water and grills. Permits are not required, though there's a three-day limit per month. It's busier in summer than in winter and is often full on holiday weekends. It tends to be cloudy and a bit wet.

There are two backpack camping grounds

inside Haleakala Crater. One is at Holua cabin, four miles down Halemauu Trail, and the other is at Paliku at the trail's end. Both are below steep cliffs, though Holua is dry and barren while Paliku is lush and wet.

Permits are required for backpack camping. They can be picked up daily at the park headquarters from 7.30 am to 4 pm, or at the visitors' centre near the summit from sunrise to 3 pm, and are issued on a first-come first-served basis only. Camping is limited to three nights in the crater each month, with no more than two consecutive nights at either camping ground.

Each camping ground is limited to 25 people. Permits can go quickly if large groups show up, a situation more likely to occur in summer. In winter, the sites rarely fill up.

The camping sites have pit toilets and water. Fires are prohibited and you'll need to carry all your rubbish out.

Cabins There are three primitive cabins along trails in the crater, one each at Holua, Kapalaoa and Paliku. Each has a wood-burning stove, some cooking utensils, 12 bunks with mattresses (but no bedding), water and pit toilets. Hiking distances from the crater rim range from four to 10 miles.

Fees are $5 per adult and $2.50 per child under age 12, with a $15 minimum charge, plus a mandatory fee of $3 per person for firewood. There's a three-day limit, with no more than two consecutive nights in any cabin. Each cabin is rented to only one party at a time.

The problem here is the demand, which is so high the park service actually holds a lottery to award reservations! To enter, your reservation request must arrive by the last day of the month, three months prior to the proposed stay (that is, requests for cabins on any date in March must arrive by 31 December).

If you have alternative dates it increases your chances. You can send in your request with a letter or ask for a form. Don't send money until you're notified. The address is: Cabin Reservation Request, Haleakala

National Park, Box 369, Makawao, HI
96768.

Getting There & Away
Haleakala Crater Rd (Hwy 378) runs 11
miles from Hwy 377 up to the summit. It's a
good paved road but it's steep and winding.
You don't want to rush it.

The drive to the summit takes about 1¼
hours from Paia or Kahului, two hours from
Lahaina. If you need gas, fill up in Pukalani
as there are no services on Haleakala Crater
Rd.

On your return from the summit, much of
Maui unfolds below, with fields of sugar
cane and pineapple in patches on the valley
floor. The highway snakes back and forth,
with as many as four or five layers of switchbacks in view all at once.

Just south of the park there's a eucalyptus
grove with Pony Express stables where you
can go horse riding. Farther on is Sunrise
Market with its free protea garden and local
produce for sale.

HIKING THE CRATER
Hiking the crater floor offers a completely
different angle on Haleakala's lunar landscape. Instead of peering down from the rim,
you're looking up at the walls and towering
cinder cones. It looks so much like a moonscape that US astronauts trained here before
going to the moon.

The crater is a very still place to walk.
Cinder crunching underfoot is often the only
sound.

The trails inside the crater connect with
each other and are marked at junctions.

The weather at Haleakala can change suddenly from dry hot conditions to a cold
windswept rain. Though the general rule is
sunny in the morning and cloudy in the afternoon, fog and clouds can blow in at any time.

No matter what the weather is like at the
start of a hike, be prepared for temperatures
that can drop into the 50s (F) during the day
and the 30s at night, at any time of year.
Hikers without proper clothing risk exposure
to hypothermia.

The climate also changes radically as you
walk across the crater floor. In the four miles
between Kapalaoa and Paliku cabins, rainfall varies from an annual average of 12
inches to 300 inches. December to May is the
wetter season.

With the average elevation on the crater
floor at 6700 feet, the relatively thin air
means that hiking can be quite tiring. The
higher elevation also means that sunburn is
more likely. Take sunscreen, rain gear, a few
layers of clothing and a full canteen of
water.

Sliding Sands Trail
Sliding Sands, the summit trail into the
crater, starts at the south side of the visitors'
centre parking lot. The trail leads 9½ miles
to the Paliku camping ground and cabin,
passing Kapalaoa cabin at 5¾ miles. The
first six miles of the trail follows the south
wall of the crater.

From Kapalaoa to Paliku there's a gentle
descent and the vegetation gradually
increases. Paliku (6380 feet) is beneath a
sheer cliff at the eastern end of the crater. It
has heavy rainfall, in contrast to the crater's
barren western end. Here there are ohia
forests climbing the slopes and grassy
camping sites.

Sliding Sands-Halemauu Trail
One of the most popular day hikes for people
in good shape is the 12-mile hike which starts
down Sliding Sands Trail and returns via
Halemauu Trail. It's a strenuous full-day
outing.

Sliding Sands starts out at 9780 feet and
descends over loose cinders down to the
crater floor. If you hike it after catching the
sunrise you'll walk directly into a gentle
warmish wind and the rays of the sun. There
are great views on the way down but, except
for a few shrubs, there's no vegetation in
sight.

Four miles down, after an elevation drop
of 2500 feet, a spur trail leads north about a
mile to Halemauu Trail.

Once on Halemauu Trail it's possible to

Top: Outrigger canoe race, Molokai
Bottom: Guided Mule tours, Molokai

Top: Molokai's north coast from Kalaupapa Peninsula
Bottom: Halawa Valley, Molokai

take a short loop to the **Bottomless Pit.** Legends say the pit leads down to the sea, though the park service says it's just 65 feet deep. It's basically a large hole in the ground of limited interest.

About 1½ miles up the Halemauu Trail is the short **Silversword Loop,** which passes by silversword plants in various stages of development. If you're here in summer you should be able to see plants in bloom.

About a mile farther along Halemauu Trail is Holua cabin and camping ground. There's a large **lava tube** here that's worth exploring. At 6960 feet this is one of the lowest areas along this hike and there are impressive views of the crater walls rising a few thousand feet to the west. From the cabin it's four miles to the Halemauu trailhead.

Because of its steep descent, Sliding Sands Trail makes a better entry trail into the crater than a return trail. The Halemauu trailhead, at an elevation of 8000 feet, is an easier exit.

Halemauu trailhead is on Hwy 378, six miles below the visitors' centre (and the trailhead to Sliding Sands) and 3½ miles above park headquarters. If you haven't arranged to be picked up, you might try hitching.

Halemauu Trail
If you're not up for a long hike, you might try doing just part of the Halemauu Trail. Even hiking in the first mile to the crater rim gives a fine view of the crater with Koolau Gap to the east. It's fairly level up to this point.

If you were to continue on the trail and hike down the switchbacks to Holua cabin

Silversword

and back, the eight-mile round trip would make a fine, hardy day hike. From the trailhead to the bottom of the pali the trail descends 1400 feet. Once on the floor of the crater the trail follows the west wall for about a mile to Holua cabin at 6960 feet. The trail continues another six miles to Paliku cabin.

Halemauu trailhead, 3½ miles above park headquarters, is marked. There's a fair chance you'll find nene in the parking lot.

Kalua O Ka Oo Trail
Two miles down the Sliding Sands Trail (a descent of 1600 feet), a spur trail leads up the Kalua O Ka Oo cinder cone, about half a mile to the north.

Midway along Kalua O Ka Oo Trail are some silversword plants. From the visitors' centre to Kalua O Ka Oo and back it's a hardy three-hour hike. Because of the uphill climb

---

Silversword
The strikingly beautiful silversword with its pointed silver leaves is a distant relative of the sunflower. The plant grows for four to 25 years before blooming just once.

In its final year, it shoots up a flowering stalk sometimes as high as nine feet. During the summer the stalk flowers with hundreds of maroon and yellow blossoms. When the flowers turn to seed in late autumn, the plant dies.

The silversword, found only in Hawaii, was nearly wiped out in the early 1900s by grazing feral goats and by people who took them for souvenirs. It's making a comeback due to efforts by the park service who have fenced in sections of the park to protect the plants. ∎

back, this is a good hike to do early in the morning to avoid the midday heat.

Kaupo Trail

From Paliku camping ground on the eastern edge of the crater floor, it's possible to continue another nine miles down to Kaupo on the southern coast. The first 3½ miles of the trail drops 2500 feet in elevation before reaching the park boundary. It's a rocky trail through rough lava and brushland. The last 5½ miles pass through Kaupo Ranch property on a rough jeep trail as it descends the Kaupo Gap. There are fine coastal views along the way.

The 'village' of Kaupo is a long way from anywhere, with very little traffic. Still what traffic there is – largely sightseers braving the circle-island road – moves slow enough along Kaupo's rough road to start conversation. If you have to walk the final stretch, it's eight miles to Oheo Gulch and what will seem like hordes of people and traffic. If you do get caught in Kaupo, hikers are allowed to camp outside the walls at the Huialoha Church.

This is a strenuous hike and because of the remoteness and the ankle-twisting conditions it's not advisable to hike it alone. The national park service publishes a Kaupo Trail brochure that people considering the hike should pick up in advance.

Molokai

Molokai is the last stronghold of rural Hawaii. It manages to hold out in a sort of time warp: no packaged Hawaiiana, no high-rises, more farmers than tourists.

If you're looking for lots of action or anything slick, Molokai isn't the place. Instead, you can walk along Hawaii's largest beach with barely another soul in sight, or take the cliffside mule trail down to the old leprosy colony of Kalaupapa. Molokai has fine hikes and camping grounds, spectacular valleys, a wildlife park and a handful of historical sites.

Molokai is the most Hawaiian of the main islands, with almost 50% of its population of native Hawaiian ancestry. It's only sparsely populated, with but a handful of small towns.

According to ancient chants, Molokai is a child of Hina, goddess of the moon. This is a place to get in touch with basics.

In the morning you can sit on the edge of an 800-year-old fishpond and watch the sun rise over Haleakala on distant Maui. In the evening you can watch the sun set behind the silhouette of Molokai's royal coconut grove.

Molokai retains so much small-town character that at times it seems more like some forgotten outpost in the South Pacific than the island between the high-rises of Maui and Waikiki.

ORIENTATION

Molokai lies midway in the Hawaiian chain, 26 miles south-east of Oahu and nine miles north-west of Maui. Lanai is nine miles directly south.

The airport is on the island's flat central plains, more or less in the centre of Molokai.

Take a right turn when you leave the airport to get to Hwy 460. At the highway, to the left it's seven miles to Kaunakakai, the main town; to the right it's 13 miles to the Kaluakoi Resort on the west coast.

This one highway is Molokai's main road, stretching from east to west. From Kaunakakai westward it's called Hwy 460 (Maunaloa Highway). From Kaunakakai eastward it's Hwy 450 (Kamehameha V Highway).

Exploring Molokai

Molokai is not the place to explore dirt roads just to see what's there. People on Molokai spend a lot of time outdoors and their yards are extensions of their homes. Many dirt paths that seem like they could be roads are just driveways into someone's backyard. In addition, as on all the islands, there's a bit of pakalolo growing here and there as well. All in all, folks aren't keen on outsiders cruising their private turf.

On the other hand if there's a fishpond you want to see and someone's house is between the road and the water, it's usually easy to stop and strike up a conversation. Molokai people are generally receptive and friendly. If you ask permission first they'll usually let you cross their property. If you appear interested they might even share a little local lore and history – the old timers in particular can be fascinating to listen to.

Facts

HISTORY

Molokai had powerful sorcerers whose reputations were respected throughout the islands. Through carvings of poisonwood idols and other elaborate rituals, they were able to keep potential invaders at bay. For centuries, the battling armies of Maui and Oahu were careful to bypass Molokai.

By the 18th century, magic wasn't enough to keep things together. Internal dissent among the alii of Molokai, largely over access to valuable fishing grounds at Moomomi, led them to align with chiefs from other islands.

Oahu, Maui and the Big Island all got involved in the picture. Eventually the king of Oahu, Peleioholani, established his rule

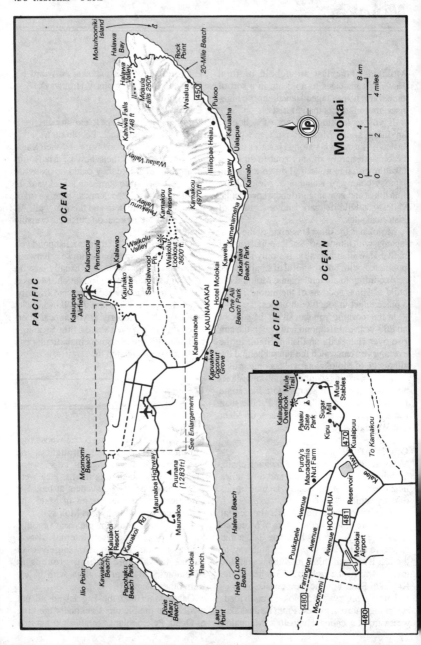

Molokai

over Molokai. When the daughter he left on Molokai was captured and killed by Molokai chiefs, Peleioholani hastily returned to the island and struck back with a vengeance. Molokai chiefs who were unable to flee to Maui were captured and roasted alive.

Oahu continued to rule over Molokai until 1785. Over the next decade warring Maui and the Big Island took alternate turns ruling Molokai until Kamehameha the Great finally united all the islands in 1795.

The first detailed description of the island was recorded by Captain George Vancouver, a British navigator, who anchored off Molokai in 1792. His guesstimate placed Molokai's population at around 10,000.

When the missionaries arrived in the 1830s they did a more detailed count, estimating Molokai's total population at 8700.

Molokai's largest settlements were on the rainy south coast of the eastern half of the island. The shallow waters and coastal indentations there were ideal for the construction of fishponds. In the valley wetlands, taro patches flourished.

The missionaries found the densest populations between Kamalo and Waialua and it is in this area that they established their first missions. Some of the churches still stand today.

Kalaupapa Peninsula had the island's other major settlement, with about 2500 people. The north shore valleys of Halawa, Pelekunu and Wailau were also populated. Molokai's central plains and dry western half were only lightly settled.

Ranching & Agriculture

Cattle and sheep, which were introduced in the mid-1800s, had a major impact on Molokai. Grazing resulted in widespread destruction of native vegetation, causing upland soils to wash down into the coastal fishponds, destroying the extensive centuries-old system of aquaculture.

In the 1850s Kamehameha V acquired the bulk of Molokai's arable land, forming Molokai Ranch. After his death the ranch became part of the Bishop Estate, which sold it off to a group of Honolulu business people in 1897.

A year later the American Sugar Company, a division of Molokai Ranch, attempted to develop a major sugar plantation in central Molokai. They built a railroad system to haul the cane, developed harbour facilities and installed a powerful pumping system to draw up water. By 1900 the well-water used to irrigate the fields had become so saline that the crops failed.

The company then got into honey production on such a scale that at one point Molokai was the world's largest honey exporter. In the mid-1930s an epidemic wiped out the hives and the industry.

In the meantime Molokai Ranch continued its efforts to find 'the crop for Molokai'. Cotton, rice and numerous grain crops all took their turn biting the red dust of Molokai.

Finally pineapple took root as the crop most suitable for the island's dry, windy conditions. In 1920, plantation-scale production began in Hoolehua. Within 10 years Molokai's population tripled to over 5000 as immigrant labour was introduced to work the fields.

In the 1970s competition from overseas brought an end to pineapple's reign on Molokai. Dole closed down its operation in 1976 and the other island giant, Del Monte, later followed suit. It brought hard times and the highest unemployment levels in the state.

Then cattle raising, long a mainstay, suddenly collapsed. In a controversial decision in 1985 the state, after finding an incidence of bovine tuberculosis, ordered every head of cattle on Molokai to be destroyed. Molokai Ranch has since restocked some of its herd, but the majority of the smaller 240 former cattle owners have given up.

Molokai Ranch still owns about one-third of Molokai, which is more than half of the island's privately held lands.

GEOGRAPHY

Molokai is Hawaii's fifth largest island. It is 38 miles long, 10 miles wide and roughly rectangular in shape, with a land area of 264 sq miles.

The western half of Molokai is dry and arid, with rolling hills and the gradually sloping range of Maunaloa (1381 feet). The island's highest point, Kamakou (4970 feet), is in the middle of the rugged eastern half.

Geologically Molokai is a union of two separate shield volcanoes that erupted to form two distinct islands. The rugged mountains of eastern Molokai captured the clouds. Heavy rainfall and stream erosion then cut deep valleys into its towering north face. Western Molokai formed into more modest hills and tableland. Later eruptions spilled lava into the channel that separated the two, forming the Hoolehua Plains and creating present-day Molokai.

Kalaupapa, on the north side of Molokai, seems to have been an afterthought by Madame Pele. An eruption from offshore Kauhako Crater created the flat lava peninsula long after the rest of Molokai had been formed. Kauhako Crater, at 400 feet, is Kalaupapa's highest point.

Molokai's north shore, from Kalaupapa to Halawa, is a wilderness area of coastal mountains and deeply cut valleys. They include the world's highest sea cliffs, which reach heights of 3300 feet with an average gradient of 58°. Hawaii's highest waterfall, Kahiwa Falls (1750 feet), drops from these cliffs.

The north shore is spectacular, but for the most part the steep slopes and rainforests are virtually inpenetrable. The main way to get into the valleys is by boat, however rough winter seas restrict that to the summer season.

CLIMATE

At Kaunakakai, the average daily temperature is 70°F in winter, 78°F in summer. The average annual rainfall is 27 inches.

FLORA & FAUNA

The two most dominant forest types on Molokai are kiawe in the dryer areas and ohia lehua in the wetter.

Along the banks of streams, once heavily cultivated with taro, forests of kukui and guava now dominate.

The axis deer that run free in Molokai are descendants of eight deer introduced from India in 1868 as a gift to King Kamehameha V. Feral pigs, introduced by the early Polynesian settlers, roam the upper wetland forests and feral goats inhabit the steep canyons and valley rims. All three cause havoc on the environment and are hunted game animals.

Native waterbirds include the common moorhen, Hawaiian coot and black-necked stilt, which are all endangered. Molokai has five native forest birds (mostly in the undisturbed upland forests) and the Hawaiian owl.

GOVERNMENT

Kalaupapa Peninsula is a county unto itself, called Kalawao, which is basically administered by the State Department of Health. The rest of Molokai, along with neighbouring Lanai, is swallowed up in the mire of Maui County.

In large part administrative decisions affecting Molokai are made on Maui. Since most community planning and development issues are decided at a county level, the island of Maui, with 12 times Molokai's population, has the clout.

ECONOMY

Molokai has a double-digit unemployment rate that's triple the state average. In an effort to bring the rates down, the state charters most of the seats on the early morning and late afternoon ferry runs to Lahaina for some 200 Molokai residents who commute to jobs on Maui, primarily in Kaanapali hotels.

Homegrown Economy

After the huge pineapple plantations left Molokai in the late 1970s, islanders began to more intensely develop small-scale farming.

Molokai has rich soil and some feel the island may have the potential to be Hawaii's 'breadbasket'. Recently, watermelon growers on Molokai have not only captured the Oahu market from mainland growers, but have begun to export to Canada as well. Other crops being grown in increasing quantities include dryland taro, macadamia nuts, sweet potatoes, string beans, onions and bell peppers.

The Kaunakakai area has one of the world's best growing conditions for seed corn. Hawaii's climate makes it possible to produce three generations of hybrids each year versus only one on the mainland. Corn for seed has been raised in Hawaii since the late 1960s and about half of the corn produced in the USA can now trace its roots to Molokai. Seed production is labour intensive – each ear of corn is bagged, tagged and eventually harvested by hand.

In 1991, coffee was planted on hundreds of acres of formerly fallow pineapple fields in Kualapuu.

Development

In 1981 a Maui County Committee was appointed to create a community plan to address future development on Molokai. The committee conducted hearings and surveys on Molokai and much to the surprise of Molokai residents the recommendations put forth in the final plan were tuned in to their own feelings on growth.

The Molokai Plan calls for the preservation of Molokai's rural lifestyle and the maintenance of agriculture as the basis of the economy. It also calls for all resort development to be limited to the western side of the island and to be low-rise. It recommends a number of environmental protection schemes, including conservation practices to reverse erosion, the maintenance of fishponds and the creation of marine conservation areas. The Molokai Plan has been widely accepted as the guiding code for land use on Molokai and is referred to whenever there are disputes over development – which is often.

You can pick up a lot of local antidevelopment sentiment walking around Kaunakakai. One faded poster in a shop window begins with the phrase, 'The thing about untouched beauty is that people want to instantly touch it...', while the hottest bumper sticker on pick-up trucks around town reads 'Molokai Is Too Small To Be Big'.

POPULATION & PEOPLE

Molokai's population is just under 7000. Molokai is the most Hawaiian of the islands outside of Niihau. Almost 50% of its people are Hawaiian or part-Hawaiian. Filipino is the next largest ethnic group, followed by the usual mixture.

The large Hawaiian population is in part due to the Hawaiian Homes Act of 1921 that awarded 40-acre blocks of land to people with at least 50% Hawaiian ancestry. The purpose of the act was to encourage homesteading among native Hawaiians who had become the most landless ethnic group in Hawaii. The first settlements under the act were made on Molokai.

TOURIST INFORMATION

Destination Molokai (☎ 553-3876 on Molokai, 941-0444 on Oahu, (800) 367-4753 from the USA and Canada, (0014-800) 126-922 from Australia), Box 960, Kaunakakai, HI 96748, handles tourist information on Molokai. There's no staffed office, but they mail out brochures.

GENERAL INFORMATION
Official Molokai

Molokai's official flower is the white kukui blossom, its official colour is green and its nickname is 'The Friendly Island'.

Money

The Bank of Hawaii in Kaunakakai is the largest of half a dozen banks and credit unions on the island. It's open from 8.30 am to 3 pm Monday to Thursday, to 6 pm on Fridays. Friendly Market has a Western Union money-transfer service.

Post

The post office in downtown Kaunakakai is open from 8 am to 4.30 pm Monday to Friday. There are also post offices in Hoolehua, Kualapuu, Maunaloa and Kalaupapa.

Media

Newspapers Molokai has two newspapers, both distributed free around the island. The

White kukui blossom

Molokai Dispatch (☎ 553-3293), Box 440, Kaunakakai, HI 96748, published on the 1st and 15th of each month, is a quality publication that stays on top of local issues; subscriptions to the mainland are available for $28 a year. The *Molokai Advertiser-News* (☎ 558-8253), Star Route, Box 329, Kaunakakai, HI 96748, is published each Friday.

The *Maui News* and the *Honolulu Advertiser* are sold at the airport and at C Pascua Store in Kaunakakai.

Maps

While by no means perfect, the best map of Molokai is the Molokai-Lanai map put out by the University of Hawaii Press and sold around town. A free island recreation map, useful for hikers and those who want to go off on jeep roads, is available from the Department of Land & Natural Resources, Division of State Parks, Box 1049, Wailuku, HI 96793.

Weather

For recorded weather and marine forecasts by the National Weather Service dial 552-2477.

Emergency

Dial 911 for police, ambulance and fire emergencies. Molokai General Hospital (☎ 553-5331) in Kaunakakai has 24-hour emergency service.

ACTIVITIES
Beaches

Papohaku Beach on the west coast is the broadest and longest white-sand beach in all of Hawaii. Though it's a great walking beach, it's not safe for swimming.

However, just a few miles south of Papohaku is Dixie Maru Beach, which has a small protected bay and is the West End's most popular family beach.

For something less frequented there's Kawakiu Beach north of Kaluakoi Golf Course. It's a crescent beach with fine coastal views and good swimming when the seas are calm.

Moomomi Beach, on the north coast, is another secluded coastal stretch, this one backed by expansive dunes.

The coast around Kaunakakai has shallow waters and a silted bottom. The public swimming pool in town is the best spot for swimming there.

At the south-eastern end of the island, the beach around the 20-mile marker offers some of Molokai's best swimming and snorkelling. Rock Point, not far from there, and Halawa Bay, at the end of the road, are popular surfing spots.

There are other beaches in remote places, but Molokai is the last place you'd need to torture yourself with washed-out roads or trips through jungles simply to get away from it all. For those who have ever fantasized about having a vast secluded beach to themselves, all that's needed is to drive up to the miles of white sands at Papohaku and start walking.

Snorkel sets and boogie boards can be rented from Kaluakoi Hotel or Molokai Fish & Dive.

Swimming

The Mitchell Pauole Center in Kaunakakai has a 25-metre pool open free to the public from 9 to 11.45 am daily except Thursdays and Sundays, and from 1 to 4.30 pm daily (also from 6 to 8.30 pm Wednesdays and Fridays in the summer). The lifeguard is friendly and welcomes anyone to come in and use the pool. It's not uncommon to have the pool to yourself, particularly in winter.

Hiking

Molokai has a variety of hiking opportunities. The hike to Moaula Falls in Halawa Valley, on the eastern side of the island, is the most popular.

The Nature Conservancy's Kamakou Preserve offers unique rainforest hikes in the island's rugged interior.

The Palaau State Park area has a couple of fine hiking opportunities. One, the hike down the mule trail to Kalaupapa, not only offers fine views but provides a way to get to the peninsula without dishing out a lot of money. A less frequented trail from the Kalaupapa Overlook provides a pleasant hour-long hike through a forest of fragrant eucalyptus and ironwood.

On the western side, there's the easy hike to secluded Kawakiu Beach from the Kaluakoi Golf Club. The expansive white sands of Papohaku Beach and Moomomi Beach offer fine walks as well.

All trails are detailed in their respective sections.

Tennis

The Mitchell Pauole Center has two good lighted tennis courts just beyond the pool. Like everywhere else in Molokai, you're not likely to find a crowd waiting.

The Kaluakoi Hotel in Kaunakakai has four lighted tennis courts, rents racquets and sells tennis balls.

Golf

Ironwood Hills Golf Club (☎ 567-6000) in Kalae is a casual course frequented by Molokai folks. Nonresidents are charged $10 for nine holes or $12 for 18 holes. Clubs can be rented for $5, pull carts for $2.

The Kaluakoi Golf Club has an 18-hole par 72 course. The hours are from 7 am to 6 pm. The resort has a driving range, putting green and pro shop. The cost for 18 holes including cart is $55 for hotel guests, $65 for non-guests; the second round is free, but there's a $15 cart fee.

Other Activities

Kaluakoi Hotel has some activities free to the public, including nature walks, leimaking, and movies at 8 pm each evening.

Organised Tours

Kukui Tours & Limousines (☎ 553-5133) has three-hour island tours for $16 to $20 per person (depending on pick-up point) that includes Kaunakakai and Maunaloa towns, Kaluakoi Resort, Purdy's macnut farm and the Kalaupapa Lookout. Seven-hour tours, which add on the ride through eastern Molokai to Halawa Valley, cost $28 to $36. There's a three-person minimum. Kukui also has vehicles with drivers that can be chartered at an hourly rate of $52 (or $71 for a stretch limo!) with a two-hour minimum.

Friendly Isle Tours (☎ 567-6177) has similar tours at similar prices.

Molokai Off-Road Tours & Taxi (☎ 553-3369) does 4WD mountain tours as well as standard tours.

Wagon Ride Molokai Horse & Wagon Ride (☎ 558-8380 daytime, 567-6773 in the evenings), Larry Helm, Box 56, Hoolehua, HI 96729, is a small local operation that combines a horse-drawn wagon ride from the beach at Mapulehu to Iliiliopae Heiau with coconut husking, net throwing demonstrations and hula lessons, followed by lunch at Hotel Molokai. It's touristy but most people seem to enjoy themselves. The ride leaves at 10.30 am and the cost is $35 for adults, $17.50 for children six to 12 (free for ages five and under). To get there look for a big mango grove, makai side, a quarter of a mile past the 15-mile marker on Hwy 450. There's also a 90-minute guided horseback ride for $42.

Helicopter While there have been helicopter tours from Molokai Airport in the past, the only helicopter tours of the island now fly from Maui.

The Activity Information Center (☎ 667-7777, (800) 624-7771) in Lahaina has one-hour flights that include West Maui, Molokai's North Shore cliffs and Kalaupapa for $160.

Sailing & Whale Watching Molokai Charters (☎ 553-5852), Box 1207, Kaunakakai, HI 96748, has a $30 two-hour sunset sail and a $40 four-hour midday sail that includes whale watching in season. There's also a full-day $75 trip to Lanai that includes five hours of sailing (and sailing lessons) plus three hours of anchoring off Lanai for snorkelling, swimming and lunch. All sailings are from Kaunakakai aboard *Satan's Doll*, a 42-foot sloop.

The 'whale-watching tour' aboard the *Maui Princess* (☎ 553-5736) is actually just a return crossing on the afternoon ferry to Lahaina and back. If you're travelling between Maui and Molokai anyway, you'll obviously do better to take the boat as a means of transportation at $25 one way. Otherwise, the $30 'tour' is the cheapest way to ply the waters, which are a frequented winter site for cavorting humpbacks. It leaves Kaunakakai pier at 3.55 pm and returns at 7 pm during the season, which is roughly from Christmas to Easter. Children pay half-price.

Joe Reich (☎ 558-8377), Box 825, Kaunakakai, HI 96748, has a 31-foot boat, the *Alyce C*, that can be chartered for fishing trips, whale-watching jaunts and inter-island runs.

ACCOMMODATION

Molokai has a total of three hotels and five condominium complexes.

The Kaunakakai area has two hotels, Pau Hana Inn and Hotel Molokai, and one condo, Molokai Shores. All three front a beach with a good view of Lanai, but with waters too shallow and silty for swimming.

Molokai's only resort is Kaluakoi, on the west coast. It has one hotel, a golf club, three condo complexes and white-sand beaches.

The Wavecrest condos are 13 miles east of Kaunakakai, on Molokai's wetter and lusher eastern side. Most of Molokai's handful of B&Bs are around this neck of the woods as well.

Unless otherwise specified, the rates given are the same for both singles and doubles.

Camping

Camping is allowed at Palaau State Park, at Waikolu Lookout, at the county beach parks of Papohaku and One Alii, at the Kapuaiwa Coconut Grove and at a few remote beaches owned by Molokai Ranch.

State Parks Camping is free at Palaau State Park. Permits are required and may be picked up at the Department of Land & Natural Resources office in Hoolehua or from Scott, the caretaker, who lives at the house immediately north of the mule stables. If you can't get a permit during business hours, it's OK to just set up camp and let Scott find you.

Free camping is also permitted at Waikolu Lookout, just outside Kamakou Preserve. For information contact the Division of Forestry & Wildlife (☎ 244-4352), Box 1015, Wailuku, HI 96793, on Maui. Otherwise, try to catch the ranger at the forestry baseyard on Oloolo St, which is a mile west of Kaunakakai off Hwy 460. The best bet is between 7 and 7.30 am or 3 and 3.30 pm.

County Parks The Department of Parks & Recreation (☎ 553-3204), Box 1055, Kaunakakai, HI 96748, issues camping permits for Papohaku and One Alii county parks from 8 am to 4 pm Monday to Friday at Mitchell Pauole Center in Kaunakakai. Permits cost $3 per adult and 50 cents per child per day. Camping is limited to three consecutive days. Both parks have restrooms, drinking water, showers and picnic areas.

Hawaiian Home Lands The Department of Hawaiian Home Lands (☎ 567-6296), Box 198, Hoolehua, HI 96729, on Puukapele Ave in Hoolehua issues permits for only one group each night for camping at Kapuaiwa

Coconut Grove, just west of Kaunakakai. The cost is $5 per night for the entire site. While it's usually booked by groups for parties, reunions and the like, individual travellers can stay when it's available.

Molokai Ranch Molokai Ranch (☎ 552-2767) allows camping at Kawakiu, Halena, Moomomi and Hale O Lono beaches. Camping is free at Kawakiu, which is the most accessible, and no permit is required.

At Halena, Moomomi and Hale O Lono, permits are required and camping is allowed only between 3 pm on Fridays and 5.30 pm on Sundays. These three camping areas are at the end of rough dirt roads (4WD vehicles are advisable) and entered via locked gates. There's a $5 charge for the gate key, plus a $50 refundable key deposit. The camping fee for non-Molokai residents is $10 per person per day. Halena Beach, which is the only one of the four camping areas with facilities, has a group pavilion that campers must rent for an additional $30 per night. Camping permits can be applied for in person from 7 am to 3.30 pm on weekdays from the Molokai Ranch office in Maunaloa, or by writing to Box 8, Maunaloa, HI 96770. Applications should be submitted at least one week in advance.

THINGS TO BUY
Craft fairs are held from 8 am to 4 pm on Saturdays at Kaluakoi Hotel. It's a good way to meet local artists who sell their own lauhala weavings, quilts, coconut fibre crafts, pottery, woodwork and other hand-crafts.

There are half a dozen shops in Kaunakakai selling T-shirts proclaiming Molokai's rural pride. With slogans like 'Keep Hawaiian Lands in Hawaiian Hands' and 'Molokai Mo Bettah', they make a good souvenir. Imamura's and Molokai Fish & Dive have some of the better prices.

Or you could take back the same stash islanders do when they leave Molokai: a home-grown watermelon and some Molokai bread from Kanemitsu Bakery.

GETTING THERE & AWAY
Air
Air Molokai (☎ 553-3636) flies to Molokai about half a dozen times a day from both Honolulu and Kahului and a couple of times a day from Lanai. Full fares are $60 one way, $100 return, however they're often discounted to as low as $60 return.

Aloha IslandAir (☎ 567-6115, (800) 652-6541) flies direct to Molokai 14 times a day from Honolulu, three times a day from Lanai, half a dozen times a day from Kahului and at least once a day from Kapalua West Maui and Hana. The one-way fare is $69.95.

Hawaiian Airlines (☎ 567-6510, (800) 882-8811) flies direct to Molokai four or five times a day from Honolulu and once each morning from Kahului. The one-way fare is $69.95.

Information on flights to and from Kalaupapa is in the Kalaupapa section.

Molokai Airport Molokai Airport, sometimes called Hoolehua Airport, has car-rental booths, a snack bar, a liquor lounge, restrooms, pay phones, and a visitor information booth that is occasionally staffed. The two Molokai newspapers can be picked up free and off-island papers are for sale.

Molokai Airport Lei Stand has good-looking leis at reasonable prices. The snack bar, which is open from 6.30 am to 6.30 pm daily, sells breakfast or lunch plates for $5 to $6, cheeseburgers for $3 and loaves of Molokai bread.

Ferry
The *Maui Princess* (☎ 553-5736 on Molokai, 661-8397 on Maui, (800) 833-5800 from the mainland), 505 Front St, Suite 225, Lahaina, HI 96761, runs between Maui and Molokai twice daily. The boat leaves Kaunakakai at 5.45 am and 3.55 pm. It leaves Lahaina's Pier 3 at 7 am and 5 pm. The journey takes about 75 minutes. The one-way fare is $25 for adults, $12.50 for children. This is not a leisurely ferry but rather a cruising 118-foot craft with airplane-style seats, and when the seas are choppy the ride can get a bit rough. However, not only

is this the cheapest way to get between Maui and Molokai, but during the season you can often spot whales en route.

There are no visitor facilities where the boat pulls in at Kaunakakai Wharf and it's a three-quarter-mile walk to the centre of town. All car rentals are at the airport.

GETTING AROUND

Taxi

Kukui Tours & Limousines (☎ 553-5133) provides 24-hour taxi service. The metered fee is $1.40 at flagdown plus $1.40 per mile, with a $5 minimum. Rides from the airport to Kaluakoi Resort (three-person minimum) or Kaunakakai (two-person minimum) is a set fee of $7 per person. The metered fare between the airport and Wavecrest condo is about $30 per taxi.

Friendly Isle Tours (☎ 567-6177) provides rides between the airport and Kaluakoi Resort or Kaunakakai for $8 per person, or to Wavecrest condo for $16, with a two-person minimum.

TEEM Cab Molokai (☎ 553-3433) has a 24-hour service with advance reservations. They accept collect calls from the Neighbor Islands and take credit cards.

Car

Renting a car on Molokai is just about essential if you intend to explore the island.

The car-rentals companies Budget (☎ 567-6877), Dollar (☎ 567-6156), Tropical (☎ 567-6118), and Avis (☎ 567-6814) all have booths at the airport. Tropical often has the best daily rate, around $20 with advance reservations. See the Getting Around chapter in the front of the book for toll-free numbers.

If you rent a 4WD, check first to see if that's what you're getting. Avis, for instance, rents jeeps for $59.95, but they're not 4WD. And even with a 4WD, rental contracts officially 'prohibit' driving on dirt roads.

There are gas stations in Kaunakakai, Maunaloa and Kualapuu.

Hitching

Hitching is officially illegal in Maui County.

It probably wouldn't be too difficult to get a ride between the airport and town, but hitching is fairly rare on Molokai and distant corners such as Halawa and the west coast beaches just don't get much traffic.

Kaunakakai

Kaunakakai, Molokai's biggest town, takes much of its character from what it doesn't have. There's not a single traffic light, no shopping centres and no fast-food stands.

Most of Molokai's businesses are lined up along Ala Malama St, the town's broad main street. The stores have old wooden false fronts that give Kaunakakai the simple appearance of a frontier town. There are a couple of restaurants, a bakery, post office, pharmacy and one of just about everything else a small town needs. The tallest point is still the church steeple.

Kaunakakai is a town that hasn't changed its face at all for tourism. It has an almost timeless quality and a nice slow pace.

Information

Since Molokai doesn't have a daily newspaper, bulletin boards around Kaunakakai are the prime source of news and announcements. The board next to the Bank of Hawaii is the most extensive.

The Mitchell Pauole Center contains the fire and police stations, a swimming pool, tennis courts and the county parks & recreation office where you pick up county camping permits.

Library Kaunakakai has a good public library (☎ 553-5483). It's open from noon to 8 pm on Mondays and Wednesdays and from 9 am to 5 pm on Tuesdays, Thursdays and Fridays. It carries the *Wall Street Journal, USA Today* and Neighbor Island papers.

Laundry The coin laundry behind Outpost Natural Foods is open from 7 am to 9 pm. It costs 75 cents for a cold wash, $1 for a hot wash.

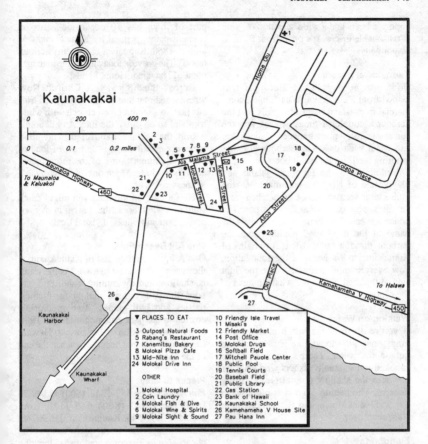

Kaunakakai

▼ PLACES TO EAT
3 Outpost Natural Foods
5 Rabang's Restaurant
7 Kanemitsu Bakery
8 Molokai Pizza Cafe
13 Mid–Nite Inn
24 Molokai Drive Inn

OTHER
1 Molokai Hospital
2 Coin Laundry
4 Molokai Fish & Dive
6 Molokai Wine & Spirits
9 Molokai Sight & Sound

10 Friendly Isle Travel
11 Misaki's
12 Friendly Market
14 Post Office
15 Molokai Drugs
16 Softball Field
17 Mitchell Pauole Center
18 Public Pool
19 Tennis Courts
20 Baseball Field
21 Public Library
22 Gas Station
23 Bank of Hawaii
25 Kaunakakai School
26 Kamehameha V House Site
27 Pau Hana Inn

Shops & Services Molokai Fish & Dive
(☎ 553-5926) no longer fills tanks or
arranges dive tours, but it does have fishing
supplies, knives, tabis, snorkel sets and
sports equipment. It's a pretty good place to
pick up T-shirts. They rent out snorkel sets
for $8 and boogie boards for $7, however the
most popular rentals are the coolers filled
with ice.

Molokai Drugs, besides being a pharmacy, is practically a department store. It has
snorkels, hardware, magazines and film. It's
open from 8.45 am to 5.45 pm Monday to
Saturday.

Molokai Sight & Sound sells cassettes,
including Hawaiian music, and rents videos
for $4 and VCRs for $8. They also do in-
house film processing; a 24-exposure roll of
prints costs $9.19 for overnight service,
$11.19 for one-hour service. They're open
from 9 am to 8.30 pm daily.

Misaki's and Friendly Market are the
island's major grocery stores. They're open
from 8.30 am to 8.30 pm Monday to Friday,
until 6.30 pm on Saturdays. Misaki's has the
island's cheapest wine prices but the selection is limited.

Molokai Wine & Spirits has lots of

imported beers and a wide selection of wine at reasonable prices. It's open from 9 am to 10 pm daily.

Kaunakakai Harbor

Gone are the days when pineapple was loaded from Kaunakakai Wharf, but a commercial inter-island barge still pulls into the harbour a couple of times a week and the commuter ferry plies between Kaunakakai and Maui each day. The harbour also has mooring facilities for small boats.

Molokai was the favourite island and playground of King Kamehameha V, who built a large vacation house of thatched grass on the shores of Kaunakakai Harbor. The house was called Malama, which today is the name of the main road leading from the harbour through town. All that remains of Kamehameha V's home is the foundation, now overgrown with grass. It's on the right side of the road before the wharf, mauka of the canoe shed.

Walking on Water

If you're down at the beach at night you might spot what looks like ghosts walking out on the water. There's no need to be spooked – it's actually fishers who walk far out onto the shallow coastal reef carrying lanterns. The fishing is good at night when the wind dies down and the lantern light stuns their prey.

Fishponds

Molokai's south-east coast is dotted with the largest concentration of ancient fishponds in Hawaii. Grazing by cattle and sheep introduced in the mid-1800s resulted in widespread erosion, and the clay that washed down from the mountains choked out the ponds. Over the years efforts have been made to revive a few of the fishponds, although without much commercial success.

One of the most impressive and easily visited is **Kalokoeli Fishpond**, behind Molokai Shores' condos.

Kapuaiwa Coconut Grove

The coconut grove one mile west of the main part of town has 10 oceanside acres of coconut palms planted by Kamehameha V around 1860. Kapuaiwa means 'mysterious taboo'. The grove is today under the management of Hawaiian Home Lands.

Across the highway is **Church Row** where a quaint white church with green trim sits next to a quaint green church with white trim and so on down the line. Any denomination that gets a handful of Hawaiian members gets its own little tract of land to put up a church. Some of the more recent arrivals include Mormons and Jehovah's Witnesses.

Half a mile up the road you might catch sight of a white horse that grazes in front of scarlet bougainvilleas, a visual treat.

One Alii Beach Park

One Alii, three miles east of Kaunakakai, is the beach park nearest to town. As the water is shallow and swimming conditions are poor, the park is used mainly for picnics, parties and ball games. Two memorials erected in the park commemorate the 19th-century immigration of Japanese to Hawaii. Camping is allowed near the beach at the end of the baseball field.

Places to Stay

Pau Hana Inn (☎ 553-5342, (800) 423-6656 from the USA, (800) 663-1118 from Canada), Box 546, Kaunakakai, HI 96748, is the closest hotel to the town centre. The cheapest of its 39 rooms are those in the long house at $45, which are small and simple but sufficient, with either two twin beds or a double bed, and a bathroom with shower. Try to get one of the end rooms on the ocean side – they're lighter and airier. There are four other room categories ranging from $75 for poolside units (which are no prize) to $125 for the beachfront suite. Pau Hana means 'work's over' and its bar is a popular drinking hole. It gets noisy on weekends when a live band plays until 1 am. Between the bar and the beach is an impressive 100-year-old Bengalese banyan tree.

Hotel Molokai (☎ 553-5347, (800) 423-6656 from the USA, (800) 663-1118 from

Canada), Box 546, Kaunakakai, HI 96748, about two miles east of town, has 55 units with a Polynesian design of sorts. The hotel is a bit funky, but overall the atmosphere is pleasant. However, for a good night's sleep, avoid the rooms next to the road where the 5 am ferry traffic zooms by. The 1st floor of the two-storey units can get noisy as well, as sound travels right through the floor. The rooms have small refrigerators, portable fans, louvered windows and lots of wood – some interior walls are even covered with wooden shake shingles! There's no TV, but sunsets and stargazing on the beach here are more rewarding than the nightly news anyway. Rates range from $59 for standard rooms up to $125 for up to six people in a family room with a loft.

Molokai Shores (☎ 553-5954, (800) 367-7042), Box 1037, Kaunakakai, HI 96748, about 1½ miles east of town, has 101 condo units, 40 of which are in the rental pool. Most are decorated quite nicely and each has a kitchen, sofabed, wooden louvered windows, lanai and ceiling fans. Ask for a unit on the top floor: they have cathedral ceilings and some have lofts. One-bedroom units hold up to four people, with rates for two at $85/95 in the low/high season. Two-bedroom units hold up to six people, with rates for four at $115/125 in the low/high season. Additional persons are $10 per day. If you stay a week during the low season or when things are slow, the seventh day is free. This is the nicest place to stay in Kaunakakai. There's a pool and coin-operated laundry on the premises.

Argyle Two B&B (☎ 553-5048), c/o Hannah & Will Johnstone, Box 295, 141 Kahinani St, Kaunakakai, HI 96748, is 1½ miles east of Kaunakakai, up the hill from Molokai Shores. The studio unit, which is detached from the main house, has two twin beds, a small refrigerator, a hot plate, cable TV and a bath with a tub. The owners spend half the year in Scotland, so the rental is available from the beginning of November to the end of March only. The rate of $55/60 single/double includes a full hearty breakfast with selections from a menu! Children are

not allowed and there's a three-night minimum. Will is a retired economist and Hannah, who grew up on Molokai, has recently written a book on Moomomi Beach ecology.

Camping Camping is allowed with a county permit at *One Alii Beach Park*, a roadside park on a shallow beach three miles east of Kaunakakai. While the campsites are near the water, they have no privacy and the only shade is cast by a few lone coconut trees. Still, because it's close to town, it tends to be more frequented than the more appealing county camping ground across the island at Papohaku Beach.

The other camping option for this area is *Kapuaiwa Coconut Grove* just west of Kaunakakai. However camping permits are issued to just one group each night and it's often booked up far in advance. The site has electricity, water, picnic tables, barbecue grills, restrooms and showers.

Places to Eat
Central Kaunakakai Until it burned down in 1991, the *Mid-Nite Inn* was the top eating and gathering spot on Molokai and served some of the freshest and cheapest fish in all Hawaii. Owner John Kikukawa is rebuilding and considering the inn's 60-year history as Molokai's favourite eatery, when it reopens it'll probably once again serve Molokai's best-value food.

Kanemitsu Bakery makes *the* Molokai bread that is shipped around the islands, plus other good breads, a variety of Danish pastries and doughnuts. The cinnamon apple crisp (70 cents) is a favourite. The restaurant in the back of the bakery serves three meals a day. At breakfast, which is served until 11 am, eggs, toast, coffee and ham will cost you $3.50. Burgers and sandwiches range from $1.35 to $3.20. Plate lunches cost about $4.50 and dinner specials, which include dessert, are about $6.25. It's open from 5.30 am to 8 pm every day but Tuesday.

Outpost Natural Foods has the standard collection of natural foods and vitamins as well as fresh produce, some of it organic.

Oasis Juice Bar inside the store makes good burritos for $2.25 to $3.25, while salads and sandwiches cost $3.50. They also have a daily special, such as vegie enchilada, lasagne or Korean barbecue tofu for $5. The juice bar is open from 11 am to 3 pm Monday to Friday. The store is open from 9 am to 6 pm Sunday to Thursday and 9 am to 3.30 pm on Fridays.

Molokai Drive Inn has $4 plate lunches, inexpensive hamburgers, and a breakfast of two eggs, bacon, toast and coffee for $3 served any time of the day. The food is takeaway but there are picnic tables at the side. This place used to be a Dairy Queen, but Molokai wasn't quite ready for fast food so the sign came down. It's open from at least 7 am to 10 pm daily.

Rabang's Restaurant has Filipino lunch plates such as turkey tail adobo, tripe or pig's feet for $3.50, as well as burgers, ice cream and shave ice. The food is not overly inviting. Opening hours are 10 am to 9 pm daily.

Coei's Lunch Wagon sets up at Bobo's Auto Service, opposite Misaki's, from 10.30 am Monday to Friday and is usually sold out by noon. Plate lunches of rice, macaroni salad and a choice of four entrees cost $3.50.

The *Molokai Pizza Cafe*, still in the planning stages when we were last there, is slated to open at the old Hop Inn site. It's expected to feature pizzas, pasta and submarine sandwiches.

Hotel Restaurants *Hotel Molokai* has an open-air restaurant right on the beach. When people want to 'go out' for dinner they put on their muu-muus and head here, however it's casual enough for you to feel equally at home in jeans. There's a fine sunset view with Lanai across the channel and water lapping at the shore. Breakfast is from 7 to 11 am, when you can get an order of hot cakes made with papaya batter for $3.75. At lunch, dishes such as beef stew, hamburger steak or mahi mahi are $5.50. Dinners, which include a salad bar, range from $8.50 for stew to $17 for coconut shrimp. The prime rib is best avoided. Lunch is from 11.30 am to 2 pm, dinner from 6 to 9 pm.

Pau Hana Inn serves rather standard fare. Breakfast, which is from 6.30 to 10.30 am, has Molokai bread French toast with ham and coffee for $4.75 and various egg dishes. At lunch, from 11.30 am to 2 pm, there's a soup and salad bar for $6 and a daily special that includes the salad bar for $7. If you're lucky the special could be teriyaki chicken; if you're not, it might be meatloaf. Dinner is from 6 to 9 pm and features meats and seafood from $10 to $17, but they do occasionally run cheaper specials. The dining room fireplace is sometimes lit on cool winter evenings.

Entertainment

The local band FIBRE (Friendly Isle Band Rhythmic Experience!) plays dance music from oldie standards and rock & roll to Hawaiian songs from 9 pm to 1 am on Fridays and Saturdays at *Pau Hana Inn*. The cover charge is $2. The action is out on the patio, with the band setting up under the big banyan tree.

The restaurant at *Hotel Molokai* has entertainment at dinner time and through the early evening. Most nights it's Kimo Paleka, who plays guitar and sings in English and Hawaiian, running the gamut from mellow folk music to hokey Don Ho favourites. He'll even sing 'The Cock-Eyed Mayor of Kaunakakai' on request. Sometimes visiting musicians just walk on stage. If you're lucky Clyde Sproat might be on the island. His salt-of-the-earth singing and ukulele playing is authentic Hawaiian folk music at its best.

Hotels aside, the baseball field in Kaunakakai is about the most active spot on the island. For some local flavour, you could go down and cheer on the Molokai Farmers as they compete against their high school rivals, the Lanai Pinelads.

East Molokai

The 28-mile drive from Kaunakakai to Halawa Valley is along the Kamehameha V Highway (Hwy 450) and takes about 1½ hours one way. It's a good paved road from start to finish. Check your gas gauge before starting off as there are no gas stations after Kaunakakai.

The road edges alongside the ocean for much of the drive, with the mountains of East Molokai rising up to the north. The terrain starts out relatively dry and becomes greener and lusher as you head east. It's all quite pastoral, with small homes tucked into the valleys, horses grazing at the side of the road and silver waterfalls dropping down the mountainsides.

The beaches along this stretch are mostly shallow and silted and not good for swimming until about the 20-mile marker. The last part of the road is narrow, with lots of hairpin bends and scenic coastal views, winding up to a clifftop view of Halawa Valley. One of Molokai's best hikes starts from the valley floor, following Halawa Stream to Moaula Falls.

KAWELA

Kakahaia Beach Park is a grassy roadfront park in Kawela, about five miles east of Kaunakakai, with a couple of picnic tables but little other reason to stop. Should you pull over, pick your spot carefully as the loaded coconut trees are like aerial bombers. The park is the only part of the Kakahaia National Wildlife Refuge open to the public. Most of the 40-acre refuge is mauka of the road. It includes marshland with a dense growth of bullrushes and an inland freshwater fishpond that has been expanded to provide a home for the endangered Hawaiian stilt and coot.

Farther inland is the Kawela puuhonua, a place of refuge that was used in ancient times by those running from the law or hiding from personal enemies. The stone ruins are on a high ridge separated by deep ravines and nearly impossible to get to.

In 1795 Kamehameha the Great invaded Molokai with such a large force that his war canoes were lined up for a full four miles along this coast. He quickly brought Molokai under his command. From here he went on to invade Oahu, the last battle in a campaign that united all the Hawaiian islands.

KAMALO

The biggest attraction in Kamalo, a small village about 10 miles east of Kaunakakai, is the roadside St Joseph's Church.

St Joseph's Church

Two of the four churches Father Damien built outside the Kalaupapa Peninsula on Molokai are still standing, including St Joseph's in Kamalo. This simple one-room wooden church built in 1876 has a steeple and bell, plain wooden pews and some of the original wavy glass panes. A statue of Damien and a little cemetery are at the side. Only the yellow tsunami-warning speaker brings the scene into the 20th century.

Across the road a short stroll leads to a self-service fruit hut. A little roadside signboard lists what produce is for sale each day commonly limes, coconuts and pomegranates. The stand itself is just 50 yards up the driveway.

Smith-Bronte Landing

About three quarters of a mile after the 11-mile marker, a small wooden sign makai of the road notes the site where pilot Ernest Smith and navigator Emory Bronte safely crash-landed their plane at the completion of the world's first civilian flight from the US mainland to Hawaii.

They left California on 14 July 1927, coming down in Molokai 25 hours and two minutes later. Oahu was the intended destination. A little memorial plaque is set amongst the kiawe trees and grasses where they landed.

Places to Stay

Glenn & Akiko Foster (☎ 558-8236), Star Route, Box 128, Kaunakakai, HI 96748, has a B&B cottage opposite St Joseph's Church. The rate of $60 includes breakfast items for meals you fix yourself. The simple cottage is quiet and private, in the midst of five acres of lime trees and away from both the main house and the road. It's studio-style with twin beds that convert into daytime couches, a bathroom with stall shower and a kitchen. They also rent two rooms with a shared bath in the main house for the same price.

UALAPUE

The Wavecrest condo development is at the 13-mile marker in Ualapue. Wavecrest has a small grocery store that is open from 8 am to 6 pm daily.

Shortly beyond Wavecrest you'll spot **Ualapue Fishpond** on the makai side of the road. Molokai once had more than 60 productive fishponds, constructed from the 13th century onwards. They were built of lava rock upon the reefs. Sluice gates allowed small fish into the pond where they were fed and fattened, but did not allow the large fish to swim back out the slats in the gate. The ready supply of fish could then be easily caught with a net as they were needed.

With state aid, Ualapue Fishpond has recently been restored by a native Hawaiian group, Hui O Kuapaa, and is once again stocked with mullet and milkfish.

Beyond this, look for the Ah Ping Store and its old gas pump at the roadside. The classic building, of faded green wood with red tin roof, was a Chinese-owned grocery store in the 1930s.

Places to Stay

Wavecrest Resort (☎ 558-8101, (800) 367-2980), Star Route, Kaunakakai, HI 96748, is a 126-unit condo complex that has about 20 units in the rental pool. Rates range from $66 for an oceanview unit to $76 for an ocean-front unit. There's a $15 charge on stays less than three nights. The condos are slightly faded, but fine. Each has a kitchen, sofabed, TV and lanai. Even if you fold out the sofabed, the living room is still large enough to move around. Breezes blow right through the oceanfront units and there are great views of Maui and Lanai from the lanai. The resort has a pool and tennis courts. If you're looking for a long-term rental, you can sometimes find a unit for about $750 a month in the local newspaper.

KALUAAHA

The village of Kaluaaha is about two miles past Wavecrest. The ruins of Molokai's first church are here, a bit off the road, mauka side, but visible if you keep an eye out. **Kaluaaha Church** was built in 1844 by Molokai's first missionary, Harvey R Hitchcock. There was recent talk of rebuilding the church, but the rusting old steel rods in the original structure thwarted the plan.

Our Lady of Sorrows Church is a quarter of a mile past the Kaluaaha Church site. The present Our Lady of Sorrows Church is a 1966 reconstruction of the original wooden-frame building built in 1874 by Father Damien.

From the church parking lot, there's a fine view of an **ancient fishpond** with the

---

Iliiliopae Heiau

Legend says Iliiliopae Heiau was built in one night by menehunes who brought *iliili* (stones) over the mountains from Wailau Valley. In return for their efforts each was given one *opae* (shrimp), hence the temple's name.

Lono, the god of harvest, and Ku, the war god, were both worshipped here. Human sacrifices were made at this heiau, always on the eve of a full moon. Drums were beaten to call all males to the temple where, upon the priest's direction, all fell prone and the victims to be sacrificed were brought to the platform. Amid chanting and rituals these victims, always male, were strangled to death and their bodies later burned.

One legend tells of a man, Umoekekaua, who lost nine of his 10 sons to sacrifice at Iliiliopae. He became so outraged that he went with his only remaining son to Pelekunu Valley to seek the aid of Kauhuhu, the Shark God. Kauhuhu sent a torrent of rain whose flood waters damaged the heiau and washed the priests responsible for the sacrifices into Pukoo Harbor where they were duly eaten by sharks. ■

high-rise-studded shores of West Maui providing an incongruous backdrop.

ILIILIOPAE HEIAU

Iliiliopae is the largest and best-known heiau on Molokai, and probably the oldest. Approximately 300 feet long and 100 feet wide, it is about 22 feet high on the east side and 11 feet high at the other end. It is strikingly level. It's believed the heiau may have originally been three times its current size, reaching out beyond Mapulehu Stream.

The path to the heiau is mauka of the highway, nearly half a mile past the 15-mile marker, immediately after a little bridge. It starts on a dirt drive on the east side of the creek. After a 10-minute walk a footpath leads off to the left, just before reaching a house. The heiau is two minutes farther.

Today Iliiliopae is silent except for the chittering of birds. African tulip trees line the trail to the site, a peaceful place with stones that still seem to emanate vibrations of a powerful past. A good place to sit and take it all in is on the north side, up the steps to the right of the heiau.

PUKOO

The village of Pukoo was once the seat of local government – complete with a courthouse, jail, wharf and post office – until the plantation folks built Kaunakakai and centred everything there. The population shifted away from Pukoo and it's been a sleepy backwater ever since. Now bit by bit islanders are beginning to move back to the Pukoo area and while it's not exactly suburbia you'll notice a handful of newer homes as the road continues.

Places to Stay

There are a couple of B&Bs near the 17-mile marker. While the area is delightfully rural, its isolation can also be a drawback, as it's about a 30-minute drive to Kaunakakai.

Honomuni House (☎ 558-8383), Star Route 306, Kaunakakai, HI 96748, is a guest cottage just beyond the Honomuni Bridge. This is the nicest B&B on the island. There are lush gardens and old taro terraces behind the cottage, making it a good place for people who like to hike and explore. The cottage is spacious with a kitchen, bath, separate sleeping space and outdoor deck and shower. The living room has a sofabed, TV and tables made of monkeypod wood from the grounds. Rates are $75 for two, plus $10 for each additional adult and $5 for each additional child. The weekly rate is $450. Fresh eggs, papayas, bananas and other fruits in season are free. Hosts Jan (a marine biologist) and Keaho (a teacher of Pacific studies) Newhouse live in a large house on the same grounds.

Manae House (☎ 553-3475), c/o Kehau & Lou McKee, Box 919, Kaunakakai, HI 96748, is a large hillside cottage built 30 years ago by Kehau's father as his retirement getaway. It's a somewhat funky plywood structure, suitably simple. The cottage has a sofabed and two cushion couches in the living room, two twin beds upstairs, a full kitchen, TV, stereo, phone and a washer. From the upper deck there are good views of Kahoolawe, Lanai and Maui, including a glimpse of the sunrise over Haleakala. It's on the mauka side of the road, about 100 yards up a rough private drive that the McKees intend to grade. The rate is $75 per night, plus $10 for each person beyond two. For stays of one week or more the daily rate is $65. Breakfast is not included and children are not allowed. They also have a second unit on the makai side of the road sitting amidst ti, likikoi and taro patches that is being fixed up for rent. It's a pretty basic structure, there's no ocean view and the rate will be the same.

Places to Eat

Neighborhood Store 'N' Counter in Pukoo is the only place to eat on the east side. At lunch time on weekdays you can order $6 plate lunches inside the tiny store and eat at outdoor picnic tables. The store, which is open from 9 am to 5 pm daily, also sells a few grocery items such as snack food, cereal and Spam.

WAIALUA

Waialua is a little roadside community

around the 19-mile marker. The attractive little Waialua Congregational Church, which marks the centre of the village, was built of stone in 1855. The nearby Waialua Beach is the site of Molokai's keiki surf meets.

Sugar Mill Remains

Look for the remains of a stone chimney and rusting metal boiler three quarters of a mile after the 19-mile marker. The ruins are about 50 feet mauka of the road, just before a stand of tall ironwood trees. This is all that remains of the Moanui Sugar Mill which processed sugar from a nearby plantation until it burnt down in the late 1800s.

Twenty-Mile Beach

A stretch of white-sand beach pops up right along the roadside at the 20-mile marker. There are places to park just beyond that. During the winter, when other Molokai beaches are rough, this is the area everyone directs you to for swimming and snorkelling.

However, when the tide is low the water is sometimes too shallow for snorkelling inside the reef. Snorkelling is much better beyond the reef, but unless it's very calm the currents can be dangerous.

Rock Point

The point of rocks sticking out as the road swings left just before the 21-mile marker is called, appropriately enough, Rock Point. It's a popular surfing spot and a place where local competitions sometimes take place.

Onwards to Halawa

After the 21-mile marker the road starts to wind upwards. Tall grasses just at the edge seem to be trying to reclaim the paved road. Ironwood trees and the tall spikes of sisal plants decorate the hillsides.

It's a good paved road – the only problem is there's not always enough of it. In places, including some cliff-hugging curves, it's really only wide enough for one car and you'll need to do some horn tooting.

The road levels out just before the 24-mile marker where there's a view of the ocean

with the offshore island of Mokuhooniki. Kanaha Rock is in front.

The fenced grassland you pass is part of Puu O Hoku Ranch, Molokai's second largest cattle ranch. A grove of sacred kukui trees on the ranch property marks the grave of Lanikaula, a famous kahuna of the late 16th century. Over the years many islanders claim to have seen the night lanterns of ghost marchers bobbing along near the grove.

After passing the 25-mile marker, the jungle begins to close in and the smell of the soil and eucalyptus fills the air. One and a quarter miles after the 25-mile marker there's a turn-off with a great panoramic view of Halawa Valley – if the viewpoint is overgrown, just walk down the road a little farther. In the winter, this is also a good place to watch for whales breaching off the coast.

There are lots of 'beep as you go' hairpin bends on the one-lane road that leads down to the valley, but the road is in good condition and the incline reasonably gradual.

HALAWA VALLEY

Halawa Valley once had three heiaus, two of which are thought to have been used for human sacrifice. Little remains of the sites. In the mid-1800s the fertile valley had a population of about 500 people and produced most of Molokai's taro as well as many of its melons, gourds and fruits. Taro production declined over the years, coming to an abrupt end in 1946 when a massive tsunami swept up Halawa Valley, wiping out the farms and much of the community. A second tsunami washed the valley clean in 1957. Only five families now remain in Halawa. Sunday services are still held in Hawaiian at the little church a couple of times a month.

One elderly Hawaiian man manages to collect a little money from tourists who follow the 'security parking' signs onto his property and leave their cars there while they hike to the waterfall. If his $5 fee seems steep, ask him about the history of the valley and get your money's worth in stories. He also sells soft drinks, candy, chips and bananas.

There's no indication that parking off to the right after reaching the valley floor is not equally safe. You could also park at the beach at the road's end.

Moaula Falls Trail

The hike to the 250-foot Moaula Falls is Molokai's most-hiked trail, although it's not the easiest to follow. The one-hour walk up is neither steep nor particularly strenuous, but it is often muddy and slippery. It's more suited to old sneakers than new white Reeboks. A walking stick would make a good companion.

The trail goes through a forest of lush tropical vegetation: giant mango trees, wild taro, ti, papaya and bananas. On the ground you might see the warty yellow fruits of the noni whose pungent odour is favoured by swarms of fruit flies. Stopping too long to observe this – or anything else – is a sure way to find out what the voracious mosquitoes favour.

The trail starts on a dirt road in front of the church. Go straight ahead on this road for about 10 minutes. At the last house the road becomes a footpath. About 100 yards farther the path splits. This split is easy to miss so keep an eye out for a white PVC water pipe crossing the trail here and for some rocks on either side of the trail that heads down to the right. Take this trail down to the stream.

You'll have to cross Halawa Stream, either by walking across stones that can be deceptively slippery when wet, or by stepping right into the water and walking on the streambed. If you wade across, choose your footing carefully as water depth can go from ankle-high to knee-high in one step. If it's been raining heavily, water levels can rise to the point where it's impossible to cross the stream safely.

The trail is blazed with orange markings. After crossing a narrow orange-bottomed brook (or mudflat, depending on water levels) the path will fork. Take the trail to the left which parallels the stream, usually within sound of it, although not always within sight. Along most of the trail there's a water pipe going up towards the falls, but

it does disappear in places. There are moss-covered stone walls along the way, most of which were built in the 1800s as cattle fences.

About halfway up you'll begin to hear the waterfall. Once it comes into sight there's another stream crossing, this one is a little more challenging. Use the metal water pipes to help climb down to the stream and cross over the boulders to the other side. Moaula Falls is less than five minutes straight up from here. Under the waterfall is a good-sized pool, at least 40 feet wide. Partly because the pool is so deep in the centre, the water is shockingly cold. Moaula translates as 'red chicken' and fittingly the water appears reddish.

If you plan on taking a dip here, it's best to first place a ti leaf in the water.

Legend has it that a moo, a giant lizard-like creature, resides in the pool. If the ti leaf floats she welcomes company and it's OK to swim. If it sinks, it's a warning she wants no visitors.

Halawa Beach Park

Halawa Beach was a favoured surfing spot for Molokai's chiefs and remains so today for local kids. When the water is calm the beach has good swimming. However, in the centre of the bay there's a channel through the reef that's subject to dangerous rip currents when the surf is heavy.

Halawa Beach Park has restrooms, showers and running water, however a sign warns that the water, which is piped down from the upper valley, does not meet health standards and needs to be treated before drinking. The old building before the park is a former village church that burned down a few decades ago.

Central Molokai

Central Molokai takes in the Hoolehua Plains, which stretch from windswept Moomomi Beach in the west to the former plantation town of Kualapuu in the east. The central part of the island also has forested interiors leading to Kamakou, the island's highest mountain and a unique nature preserve. On the northside of central Molokai is the Kalaupapa Peninsula, the site of the leprosy colony.

The most trodden route in central Molokai is the drive up to the Kalaupapa Overlook, where you'll find one of the prettiest views on Molokai. It takes about 20 minutes to drive the 10 miles from Kaunakakai.

Turning north off Hwy 460 onto Hwy 470 (Kalae Highway), the road starts in dry grasslands and climbs, passing the town of Kualapuu, a golf course, a restored sugar mill, a community of single-rooster dwellings, a mule stable and the trail down to the Kalaupapa Peninsula. The road ends at Palaau State Park, site of the Kalaupapa Overlook.

KUALAPUU

Kualapuu is the name of both a 1017-foot hill and the village that has grown up north of it.

At the base of the hill is the world's largest rubber-lined reservoir. It can hold up to 1.4 billion gallons of water, which is piped in from the rainforests in East Molokai for use on the island's dry western side.

Water use is a hot issue as both farmers and West End developers are concerned not only with the present supply, but also with who gets priority in the event of a drought. The reservoir is the sole source of water for the Hoolehua Plains and the towns on the West End. Much to the ire of local farmers, a new water-thirsty golf course designed for wealthy off-islanders is under construction in the Kipu area north of Kualapuu.

Del Monte set up headquarters in this area in the 1930s, and Kualapuu developed into a plantation town. The centre of Del Monte's activities covered the spread between Kualapuu and the nearby Hoolehua homesteads.

In 1982 Del Monte decided to phase out its Molokai operations and the economy came tumbling down. For a decade the old harvesting equipment sat rusting in overgrown fields. Now the old pineapple fields are being planted in long rows of coffee, and Kualapuu is banking on a new crop to spur its revival.

Kualapuu is a friendly village with a tiny post office and beauty salon tucked beside the general store. Gas pumps are out the front, and a restaurant and laundromat are across the street. Up the hill there's a little church but otherwise there is not much else to see or do in this town.

Places to Eat

The *Kualapuu Cookhouse* (☎ 567-6185) serves up good food. The meal of the day costs $6.50, a cup of chilli con carne $1.50 and burgers $2 to $3.50. Home-made pies are a speciality and on Fridays they make the best pizza on the island. Owner Nannette Yamashita is a weaver who has one of her works hanging in the state capitol building. The restaurant is open from 7 am to 8 pm Monday to Friday, to 3 pm on Saturdays.

KALAE
R W Meyer Sugar Mill

Four miles north of Hwy 460, in Kalae, is the sugar mill built by Rudolph W Meyer, an industrious German immigrant.

Meyer was on his way to the California gold rush when he dropped by Hawaii, married a member of Hawaiian royalty and in the process landed a tidy bit of property.

Meyer found his gold in potatoes which he grew and exported to the Californian miners. Other hats he wore were overseer of the Kalaupapa leprosy settlement and manager of King Kamehameha V's ranchlands.

In the 1850s Meyer established his own ranch and exported cattle from Palaau village. In one infamous incident, after finding his herd declining, he had all the men of Palaau charged with cattle rustling and sent off to a jailhouse in Honolulu.

Meyer later tried a number of crops including coffee, corn and wheat before settling on sugar. He built his sugar mill in 1878, around the time a reciprocity treaty gave Hawaiian sugar planters the privilege to export sugar free of duty to the USA. The mill operated for about 10 years.

A lot of time and money has gone into authentically restoring the mill, including the complete rebuilding of a 100-year-old steam engine and other rusting machinery abandoned a century ago. The mill, which is on the National Register of Historic Places, is the last of its kind. If you're into sugar mills, antique steam engines and that sort of thing you'll probably find it interesting.

Soon after the restoration, two mules were harnessed and sent circling to demonstrate the working mechanisms of the cane crushers. One of the mules, which apparently wasn't used to travelling in such fine circles, fell into the pit. The mule wasn't hurt, but the story might make some people think twice about descending a steep cliffside on the back of one of these creatures!

The sugar mill (☎ 567-6436) is open from 10 am to 2 pm Monday to Saturday. Admission is $2.50 for adults, $1 for students.

Meyer and his descendants are buried in a little family plot behind the mill. A museum that will feature Molokai's history and culture is under construction nearby.

Ironwood Hills Golf Course

There are no polo shirts with little alligators on them here. Ironwood Hills is a pretty casual golf course, with crabgrass growing in the sand pits and local golfers who actually look like they're having fun. Fees for non-residents are $10 for nine holes, $12 for 18. The course is a short way down the red dirt road at the tree-lined edge of the pasture immediately south of Meyer Sugar Mill.

Originally built by Del Monte for its employees, the course was maintained by Molokai residents after Del Monte left and is now managed by Molokai Golf, the company building the new exclusive Molokai Highlands Golf Club in nearby Kipu.

PALAAU STATE PARK

Palaau State Park is at the end of Hwy 470. The Kalaupapa Overlook is a few minutes' walk from the parking lot. A short trail in the opposite direction leads to a phallic stone. Both trails are marked and easy to follow.

The park has restrooms, campsites, picnic areas and lovely stands of paperbark eucalyptus.

Kalaupapa Overlook

Kalaupapa Overlook has a scenic overview of the entire Kalaupapa Peninsula from 1600-foot cliffs. It's like an aerial view without the aeroplane.

Interpretive plaques identify the landmarks below and explain Kalaupapa's history as a leper colony. The village where all residents live now is visible, but Kalawao, the original settlement and site of Father Damien's church and grave, can not be seen from here.

The lighthouse at the northern end of the island once had the most powerful beam in the Pacific. The 700,000-candlepower Fresnel crystal lens cast its light until 1986, when it was taken down and replaced by an electric light beacon.

Kalaupapa means 'flat leaf', an accurate description of the lava slab peninsula created when a low shield volcano poked up out of the sea, long after the rest of Molokai had been formed. The dormant Kauhako Crater, visible from the overlook, contains a little lake over 800 feet deep.

Kalaupapa residents use the term 'topside' to refer to all of Molokai outside their peninsula. From here it's obvious why.

Whether or not you get down to Kalaupapa itself, the overlook is a must. Because of the angle of the sun, the best light for photography is usually late morning to early afternoon.

Hiking There's an old trail that continues directly beyond the last plaque at the overlook. If you walk along it for a few minutes you'll come to a little offshoot path to the right, from where it's only about 50 metres to a spectacular clifftop view of the peninsula. You can see even more of the coast and get a peek into the valleys from there. Be careful approaching, as it drops off suddenly and the wind can be strong.

For one of Molokai's nicest forest walks, get back on the trail and follow it for another

30 minutes. Few people go this way and it's very peaceful. You walk on a carpet of soft ironwood needles through a thickly planted forest that goes from ironwood to eucalyptus, dotted here and there with Norfolk pine. These diagonal rows were planted during a 1930s reforestation project. The trees create a canopy over the trail and, as is generally true under ironwood and eucalyptus trees, there's little undergrowth to obscure the way.

There's no destination – the joy here is the woods. Eventually the trail winds down into a gully and peters out a little after that.

Phallic Stone Kauleonanahoa, literally 'the penis of Nanahoa', is Hawaii's premier phallic stone, poking up in a little clearing inside an ironwood grove. Nature has endowed it well but it's obviously been touched up by human hands.

Though it's said that women who spend the night here will return home pregnant, there apparently is no danger in just going to have a look.

Places to Stay
Camping Camping is free at Palaau State Park. The camping area is off the road in a grove of ironwood trees which is cool and shady in the summer, but can feel a bit dark and damp when it's rainy in winter. In winter you may well have the place to yourself and even in the summer you're unlikely to find a crowd.

Though you may hear a few trucks with boom boxes parking at the picnic grounds, it is generally very peaceful. The only other sounds are the roosters from the 'cock farm' and the braying of mules.

There are restrooms, cement picnic tables and fireplaces, but no showers. The tap is marked 'unfit to drink' and the water looks rather brown coming out of the tap.

KALAUPAPA PENINSULA
Kalaupapa Peninsula appears both strikingly beautiful and strikingly lonely. Set at the base of majestic and formidable cliffs, it has been a leprosy settlement for more than a century.

The trip to the peninsula – accessible only by mule, on foot or by small plane – is one of Molokai's major attractions. It's also a pilgrimage of sorts for admirers of Father Damien (Joseph de Veuster), the Belgian priest who devoted the latter part of his life to helping people with leprosy, before dying of the disease himself.

Kalaupapa Peninsula is a national historical park jointly managed by the State Department of Health and the US National Park Service. It is unique among historic parks in that many of the people whose lives are being interpreted are still living.

History
Ancient Hawaiians used Kalaupapa as a refuge when caught in storms at sea. The peninsula held a large settlement at the time of early Western contact and the area is rich in archaeological sites.

The first case of leprosy in Hawaii was diagnosed in 1835, one of many diseases introduced by foreigners, this one probably

Siloama – first church built on the peninsula

by Chinese labourers. Alarmed by the spread of the disease, in 1865 King Kamehameha V signed into law an act that banished people with leprosy to Kalaupapa Peninsula.

It was a one-way trip. Kalaupapa Peninsula is surrounded on three sides by some of Hawaii's roughest and most shark-infested waters and on the fourth by the world's highest sea cliffs. Once the afflicted arrived on Kalaupapa Peninsula there was no way out, not even in a casket. Hawaiians called leprosy *mai hookaawale*, which means separating sickness, a disease all the more dreaded because it tore families apart forever.

Father Damien arrived at Kalaupapa in 1873. He wasn't the first missionary to come, but he was the first to stay.

Damien nursed the sick, wrapped bandages on oozing sores, hammered coffins and dug graves. On the average he buried one person a day. He put up more than 300 houses – each little more than four walls, a door and a roof, but still a shelter to those cast here. He was a good carpenter. Some of the solid little churches he built earlier around the Big Island and Molokai still stand today.

The original settlement was in Kalawao, at the wetter eastern end of the peninsula. Some of the afflicted arrived in boats, whose captains were so terrified of the disease that they would not land but instead dropped patients overboard into the bay. Those who could, swam to shore.

Early conditions were unspeakably horrible. Before modern medicine, leprosy manifested itself in dripping, foul-smelling sores. Eventually there was loss of sensation and tissue degeneration that could lead to fingers, toes and noses becoming deformed or falling off altogether.

In 1888 Damien installed a water pipeline to the sunnier western side and the settlement moved to where it is today. Over the years, some 8000 people have come to Kalaupapa Peninsula to die. During Damien's time lifespans here were almost invariably short. Yet even in Damien's day leprosy was one of the least contagious of all communicable

diseases. All in all more than 1100 volunteers have worked with patients at Kalaupapa, but only Damien contracted leprosy. He died in 1889 at the age of 49.

Damien's work inspired others. Brother Joseph Dutton arrived in 1886 and stayed 44 years. In addition to his work with the sick, he was a prolific writer who kept the outside world informed on what was happening in Molokai. Mother Marianne Cope arrived a year before Damien died. She stayed 30 years, helping to establish a girls' home and encouraging patients to live life to the fullest. She is widely considered to be the mother of the hospice movement.

In 1909 a fancy medical facility called the US Leprosy Investigation Station opened at Kalawao. However, the hospital was so out of touch (requiring patients to sign themselves in for two years, live in seclusion and give up all Hawaiian-grown food) that even in the middle of a leprosy colony it attracted only a handful of patients. It closed four years later.

Although sulfone antibiotics have been used successfully to control leprosy since the 1940s, isolation policies in Kalaupapa weren't abandoned until 1969.

Kalaupapa Today

Today fewer than 100 patients live on Kalaupapa Peninsula. It's an old population, getting older, with only a few people younger than 50. Some of the elderly have become blind or weakened. Others fish or tend gardens, although lots of people just stay glued to their TVs.

Current residents are free to leave, but Kalaupapa is the only home most of them know. They have been given guarantees that they can stay in Kalaupapa Peninsula throughout their lifetimes. To minimise the impact on residents, the park requires all visitors to join a guided tour.

The state of Hawaii officially uses the term 'Hansen's Disease' for leprosy. Many Kalaupapa residents, who consider it a euphemism that fails to reflect the stigma they have suffered, continue to use the old term.

Things to See & Do

On typical tours the village looks semi-deserted. The sights are mainly cemeteries, churches and memorials. Places where residents go to talk story – the post office, store and hospital – are pointed out but no stops are made. Visitors are not allowed to photograph the residents. Kalaupapa is a tourist attraction but its people are not.

Stops are made in town at **memorials** for Father Damien and Mother Marianne and at a **mini-museum** where photographs of the original settlement are on display and books are for sale. The tours then go across the peninsula to Kalawao.

St Philomena Church (better known as 'Father Damien's Church') in Kalawao underwent a restoration for the centenary of Damien's death in 1989. You can still see where Damien cut open holes in the floor so that the sick who needed to spit could attend church and not be ashamed. The graveyard at the side contains Damien's gravestone and original burial site, although his body was exhumed in 1936 and returned to Belgium.

The view from Kalawao is one of the island's finest. It looks out on the pali of the north-east coast, each successive cliffside jutting out behind the one in front, each looking more like a shadow in the mist. The park boundaries include the Waihanau, Waialeia and Waikolu valleys, east of the peninsula.

The **rock island** just offshore is the legendary home of a giant shark. From some angles it looks like a shark's head coming straight up out of the water, while from other angles it looks like a dorsal fin.

Getting There & Around

The switchback mule trail down the pali (cliffs) is the only land route to the peninsula. No matter how you get there, you cannot wander around Kaluapapa Peninsula by yourself. You must take a guided tour.

Old state laws which require everyone who enters the settlement to have a 'permit' and which only allow entry to those 16 years of age and older are no longer required for medical reasons, but are still maintained to protect the privacy of the patients.

There's no actual paper permit. A reservation with either Damien Tours or Molokai Mule Ride is considered a permit.

Only guests of Kalaupapa residents are allowed to stay overnight. Unless you're on the mule tour, bring your own food and beverages. There are no stores or other public facilities for visitors.

Air Aloha IslandAir flights to Kalaupapa leave Molokai Airport at 8.50 and 9.45 am and come back at 2.35 and 4.20 pm. The cost is $20 each way. Flights leave Honolulu for Kalaupapa at 8.10 and 9.05 am and return to Honolulu at 2.35 and 4.20 pm. The cost is $66 one way, $132 return.

Air Molokai has an 8 am flight from Molokai Airport to Kalaupapa, coming back at 2 pm. The cost is $19 one way, $39 return. There are also flights to Kalaupapa from Kahului and Honolulu at about the same time that cost $66 one way, $105 return.

The 'airport' at Kalaupapa is just a runway on a grassy field and a covered waiting area with a few chairs, restrooms and a pay telephone.

On Foot The hike along the mule trail takes about one hour going down, a bit longer going up. It's best to begin hiking by 8.30 or 9 am, before the mules start to go down, to avoid walking in fresh dung. The narrow trail is rutted in places and can be slippery and muddy if it's been raining, but otherwise it's not terribly strenuous.

The trail starts on the right side of Hwy 470 midway between the mule stables and Kalaupapa Overlook. Don't be intimidated by the sign at the start of the path. If you have tour reservations, this is the trail in.

Tours Damien Tours (☎ 567-6171 or 567-6675 from 4 to 8 pm), Box 1, Kalaupapa, HI 96742, does the land tours for people who come to Kalaupapa on foot or by plane. Richard Marks, who runs Damien Tours, is a wonderful storyteller, an oral historian and the third generation of his family to be banished to Kalaupapa. He leads the best tour of Kalaupapa. Reservations must be made in advance and the cost is $20. The tours pick up visitors at both the trailhead and the airport.

Mule Ride One of the best-known outings in the islands is the mule ride down the pali to Kalaupapa. While the mules move none too quickly – actually, hiking can be faster – there's a certain thrill in trusting your life to these sure-footed beasts while descending 1600 feet on 26 narrow cliffside switchbacks.

The cost of $115 includes a van tour of Kalaupapa and a box lunch. The outing lasts from about 9 am to 3.30 pm and is restricted to people weighing no more than 225 pounds. The stables are on Hwy 470. A half-hour mini-lesson in mule riding is given before starting off down the trail.

Make reservations with Molokai Mule Ride, (☎ 567-6088, 537-1845 from Oahu, (800) 843-5978 from the mainland), Box 200, Kualapuu, HI 96757.

HOOLEHUA

Hoolehua is the dry plains area that separates eastern and western Molokai. Here, in the 1790s, Kamehameha the Great trained his warriors in a year-long preparation for the invasion of Oahu.

Hoolehua was settled as an agricultural community in 1924 as part of the Hawaiian Homes Act, which made public lands available to native Hawaiians. The land was divided into 40-acre plots. By 1930 more than half of Molokai's ethnic Hawaiian population was living on Hawaiian homesteads.

The first homestead was attempted closer to the coast at Kalanianaole, but it failed when the well water pumped to irrigate crops turned brackish. Many of these people then moved up to Hoolehua where homesteaders were already planting pineapple, a crop that required little water. As the two giant pineapple companies established operations in Molokai, homesteaders found it increasingly difficult to market their own pineapples and

were eventually compelled to lease their lands to the plantations.

These days there's a reliable water supply and crops, which are more diversified, include coffee, sweet potatoes, papaya and fresh herbs.

Information & Orientation

Three paved roads run east to west, with dirt crossroads going north to south. The post office and the Department of Land & Natural Resources office are on Puupeelua Ave (Hwy 481), just south of where it intersects with Farrington Ave (Hwy 480).

Farrington Ave is Hoolehua's main street with a fire station, Episcopal church and Molokai's high school. The Hawaiian Home Lands office is up on Puukapele Ave.

Puukapele Ave leads westward and merges into another paved road which deceptively appears to be a find, heading beachward, but the road ends at the Western Space & Missile Center, a radio recieving station for the US Air Force. Here a bunch of odd metal towers and wire cables look for all the world as if grown-up kids have been playing with a giant Erector Set.

Purdy's Macadamia Nut Farm

Tuddie Purdy runs the best little macadamia nut farm tour in all of Hawaii. Everything is Molokai scale. You can crack open macadamia nuts on a stone with a hammer and sample macadamia blossom honey scooped up with slices of fresh coconut.

Unlike tours on the Big Island that focus on processing, Purdy takes you into his orchard and explains how the nuts grow. A single macadamia tree can simultaneously be in various stages of progression – with flowers in blossom, tiny nuts just beginning and clusters of mature nuts. His 1½ acres of mature trees are over 60 years old and grow naturally: no pesticides, herbicides, fertilisers or even pruning.

Purdy, a Molokai native who left a job with Aloha Airlines to work his homestead, is as interesting as the orchard and can tell you a lot about the island.

Admission is free. Macadamia nuts

(roasted or raw) and honey are for sale. To get to the farm head north, turn left onto Farrington Ave from Hwy 470 and after one mile turn right onto Lihi Pali Ave, just before the high school. It's a third of a mile up, on the right.

The hours are from 9.30 am to 3.30 pm Monday to Friday, from 10 am to 3.30 pm on weekends.

MOOMOMI BEACH

Moomomi Beach, on the western edge of the Hoolehua Plains, is ecologically unique. It stands as one of the few undisturbed coastal sand dune areas left in Hawaii. Among its native grasses and shrubs are at least five endangered plant species that exist nowhere else on earth. It is one of the few places in the populated islands where green sea turtles still find a habitat suitable for breeding.

Evidence of an adze quarry and the fossils of a number of long-extinct Hawaiian birds have been unearthed here, preserved over time by Moomomi's arid sands. In 1988 the Nature Conservancy purchased 920 acres of Moomomi from Molokai Ranch and established Moomomi Preserve. Moomomi is not lushly beautiful, but windswept, lonely and wild.

To get there turn off Hwy 460, east of the airport, onto Hwy 481. Then turn left onto Hwy 480 (Farrington Ave) and head west. The paved road ends after about three miles. From there it's 2½ miles farther along a red dirt road that is in some areas quite smooth and in others deeply rutted. In places you may have to skirt along the edge of the road and straddle a small gully. It could be difficult going if it's muddy. People do make it down in standard cars, although the higher the vehicle the better.

A little over two miles after the paved road ends the road forks. Bear to the right and follow this road half a mile down to the beach. If it gets too rough there's a spot halfway down this last stretch where you can pull off to the right and park.

At the end of the road is Moomomi Bay with a little sandy beach used by sunbathers. The rocky eastern point that protects the bay

provides a perch for fishers. There are no facilities here, just the foundations of a bathhouse that burned down years ago. This area is part of the Hawaiian Home Lands.

The beautiful beach that people refer to as Moomomi is not here, but at Kawaaloa Bay, a 20-minute walk to the west. Kawaaloa is a broad white-sand beach. The wind, which picks up pretty steadily each afternoon, blows the sand into ripples and waves.

The high hills running inland are actually massive sand dunes. The coastal cliffs, which have been sculptured into jagged abstract designs by wind and water, are made of sand that has petrified because of the dry conditions.

The narrower right side of Kawaaloa Bay is partially sheltered, however the whole beach can be rough when the winter surf is up. A tattered old changing room and pavilion belonging to Molokai Ranch are at the east end of the bay. Kawaaloa collects a lot of drifting debris, some of it driftwood and some of it less romantic.

There's a fair chance you'll have Kawaaloa to yourself, but if you don't you can always walk farther on to one of the other sandy coves along the shore. Most of the area west of here is open ocean with strong currents.

Because of the fragile ecology of the dunes, visitors should stay along the beach and on trails only. Foot access is allowed via the route described, however visitors can also get a gate key from the Nature Conservancy and drive directly in to Kawaaloa Bay. To do that a permit application and key deposit are required. The conservancy also leads monthly guided hikes of Moomomi, usually on the fourth Sunday of the month.

The Nature Conservancy office (☎ 553-5236) is on Hwy 460 at the back of a former mortuary. The driveway is a third of a mile before Hwy 470 if you're heading west from Kaunakakai. The office hours are 8 am to noon Monday to Friday.

Molokai Ranch allows visitors to camp at the pavilion. A permit and gate key are required; for details see Camping in the front of the Molokai section.

KAMAKOU

The mountains that form the spine of Molokai's east side reach up to Kamakou, Molokai's highest peak (4970 feet). Over half of Molokai's water supply comes from the Kamakou rainforest.

Hawaiian women used to hike up to the top of Kamakou to bury the afterbirth of their babies, a process that assured their children would reach great heights in life. These days islanders come to the forest to pick foliage for leis as well as to hunt pigs, deer and goats.

The Nature Conservancy's Kamakou Preserve is a near-pristine forest that is home to more than 250 native plants and some of Hawaii's rarest birds. Just before the preserve entrance, Waikolu Lookout offers a panoramic view of remote Waikolu Valley, while a hike inside the preserve leads to another lookout, this one into the spectacular Pelekunu Valley.

Kamakou is a treasure, but it doesn't come easy. It is wilderness and is protected in that state in part because the rutted dirt road leading to it makes it challenging to get to.

To Kamakou Preserve

Coming from Kaunakakai on Hwy 460 turn right three-quarters of a mile after the three-mile marker, immediately before Manawainu Bridge. The paved road ends shortly at the Kalamaula hunter check box. The 10-mile drive from the highway to Waikolu Lookout takes about 45 minutes, depending on road conditions. During the rainy season vehicles leave tracks and the road gets progressively more rutted until it's again regraded in the summer.

A 4WD is best. In dry weather, some people do make it up to the lookout in a standard car. If it's been raining heavily it's not advisable to try. In places where it's narrow, if one person gets stuck the whole road is blocked. It's impossible to drive beyond Waikolu Lookout without a 4WD.

From the Kalamaula hunter check box, the road starts out fairly smoothly, but deteriorates as it goes along. Bear left at the first fork, about five minutes drive up the dirt

road, and from there just follow the main road all the way in.

Though there's no visible evidence of it from the road, the Kalamaula area was once extensively settled. It was here that Kamehameha the Great knocked out his two front teeth while grieving the death of a female high chief that he had come to visit.

The landscape starts off shrubby, dry and dusty, later turning to woods of eucalyptus with patches of cypress and Norfolk pines. The trees were planted in the 1930s by the Civilian Conservation Corps to stem the erosion and watershed loss that the area had suffered from the free range cattle policies of earlier times.

The Molokai Forest Reserve starts about 5½ miles in. A short loop road on the left leads to a former boy scout camp that's now used as a barracks for Nature Conservancy volunteers. After another 1½ miles there will be an old water tank and reservoir off to the left. Just past this a wooden sign marked 'Kakalahale' points to the right. (This is one of several 4WD roads used by hunters that lead south to the coast or to Kaunakakai. Once the roads leave forest reserve land they run across private property, often with closed gates along the way.) It's two miles more to the Sandalwood Pit and one mile past that to Waikolu Lookout and Kamakou Preserve.

Sandalwood Measuring Pit

Lua Moku Iliahi, or Sandalwood Pit, is a hull-shaped grassy depression marked with a sign, on the left side of the road. It takes a little imagination to get the whole picture as over the years water erosion has rounded the sides.

The sandalwood pit was dug in the early 1800s, shortly after the lucrative sandalwood trade began. In the frenzy to make a quick buck to pay for the foreign goods they craved, the alii forced the makaainana (commoners) to abandon their crops and work the forest.

The pit was dug out to the exact measurements of a 75-foot-long ship's hold and filled with fragrant sandalwood logs cleared from the nearby forest. When the pit was full, the wood was hauled down to the harbour for shipment to China. The sea captains made off like bandits and Hawaii lost its sandalwood forests.

After all the mature trees were taken, the makaainana pulled up virtually all the new saplings in order to spare their children the misery of another generation of forced harvesting.

Waikolu Lookout

Waikolu Lookout, at 3600 feet, provides a spectacular view into Waikolu Valley and out to the ocean beyond. Even if you're not able to spend time in Kamakou Preserve, the lookout is a fine destination in itself. If it's been raining recently you'll be rewarded with numerous waterfalls streaming down the sheer cliffsides. Waikolu means 'three waters' – presumably named for the three drops in the main falls. Morning is the best time for views as afternoon trade winds commonly carry clouds to the upper level of the canyon.

These steep mountains effectively prevent the rain clouds from entering Molokai's dry central plains. In 1960 a 5½-mile tunnel was bored into the western side of Waikolu Valley. It now carries up to 28 million gallons of water each day down to the Kualapuu Reservoir.

A grassy picnic and camping area is directly opposite the lookout. If you can bear the mist and cold winds that sometimes blow up from the canyon, this could make a good base camp for hikes into the preserve. The site has pit toilets but no water supply. For information see the Camping section in the front of the Molokai chapter.

Kamakou Preserve

In 1982 Molokai Ranch conveyed rights to the Nature Conservancy of Hawaii to manage the Kamakou Preserve, which starts immediately beyond Waikolu Lookout. Its 2774 acres of native ecosystems include cloudforest, bogs, shrubland and habitat for many species of endangered plants and animals.

Much of the preserve is forest of ohia lehua, a native tree with fluffy red blossoms whose nectar is favoured by native birds. The forest is home to two rare birds that live only on Molokai (Molokai creeper and Molokai thrush) and to the bright red apapane, the yellow-green amakihi and the pueo (Hawaiian owl), all natives. Other treasures are tree ferns, native orchids and silvery lilies.

The road deteriorates rapidly from the preserve entrance. Even with a 4WD, if you're not used to driving in mud and on steep grades it can be challenging. There are a few spots where it would be easy to flip a vehicle.

The Nature Conservancy asks visitors to sign in and out at the preserve entrance. Check out the sign-up sheet: on it people have written such entries as 'We've abandoned our car in the mud', 'The view into Pelekunu was breathtaking' or 'We found thimbleberries to eat along the way'.

Occasionally portions of the preserve are closed to the public. At such time notices are posted at Kaunakakai post office, Kalamaula hunter check box and the preserve entrance.

Hiking As Kamakou is a rainforest, trails in the preserve can be very muddy.

The best hiking trail is the **Pepeopae Trail**, which leads about 1½ miles to an overlook with a stunning view of Pelekunu Valley. The trail is along a raised wooden boardwalk over Pepeopae Bog. The boardwalk allows hikers access while protecting the fragile ecosystem from being trampled. Pepeopae is a nearly undisturbed Hawaiian montane bog, a mysterious miniature forest with stunted trees and dwarfed plants. The area gets about 180 inches of rain each year.

There are two ways to get to the Pepeopae Trail. The easiest is to walk from Waikolu Lookout about 2½ miles along the main jeep road to the trailhead. It's a nice forest walk that takes about an hour. There are some side roads along the way, but they're largely overgrown and it's obvious which is the main road. You'll eventually come to the 'Pepeopae' sign marking the start of the trail, which branches to the left.

The second and far muddier way is to take the **Hanalilolilo Trail**. It begins on the left side of the road about five minutes' walk past Waikolu Lookout, shortly after entering the preserve.

The Hanalilolilo Trail climbs 500 feet through a rainforest of moss-covered ohia trees and connects up with Pepeopae Trail after 1½ miles. If you approach via the Hanalilolilo Trail, turn left when you reach the Pepeopae Trail and you'll have about a half-mile walk up to the summit overlooking Pelekunu Valley.

From the Pelekunu Valley Overlook you get a view of majestic cliffs and if it's not clouded over you can see down the valley out to the ocean.

Pelekunu Valley is also under the steward-ship of the Nature Conservancy. The Pelekunu Valley Preserve covers nearly 6000 acres, extending from sea level up to a height of almost 5000 feet here at the valley's upper rim.

This inaccessible valley has one of the last perennial streams in Hawaii. It's an import-ant habitat for gobies and river shrimp that return from the ocean each year to swim up and lay their eggs in the fresh water of Pelekunu Stream.

Give yourself a good half day to do the entire hike from the Kamakou Preserve entrance and back. If you'd like to shorten the walk, consider one of the guided hikes led by the Nature Conservancy, as they enter the reserve in 4WD vehicles and start hiking from the Pepeopae trailhead. These guided hikes also give visitors insights into the history and ecology of the preserve.

The conservancy's hikes are conducted monthly, usually on the first or second Sat-urday. The cost of $5 for members and $15 for nonmembers includes transport to and from the preserve. As it's common for hikers to fly over from other islands to join in, the pick-up run includes the airport. Each hike is limited to 10 people and often fills up far in advance.

To get a hike schedule, make reservations or check road conditions contact the Nature Conservancy (☎ 553-5236), Molokai Pre-serves, Box 220, Kualapuu, HI 96757. If you're writing, include a stamped, self-addressed envelope.

West End

The Maunaloa Highway (Hwy 460) heads west from Kaunakakai, passes Molokai Airport, and then climbs into the high grassy rangeland of Molokai's arid western side.

Hwy 460 is about 17 miles long and the drive takes about half an hour from its start in Kaunakakai to its end at Maunaloa. It's a good paved road all the way, as are the roads to and around Kaluakoi Resort and down to Papohaku and Dixie Maru beaches. Most other West End roads, however, are privately owned dirt roads that are locked off to the public.

Molokai Ranch owns most of the land on this side of the island. Access is at the whim of the ranch, but generally requires special permission.

From Molokai's West End beaches, the twinkling lights of Oahu are just 26 miles away. The view is of Diamond Head to the left, Makapuu Point to the right.

West End Development
In the 1970s Molokai Ranch joined with Louisiana Land & Exploration Co to form the Kaluakoi Corporation. They proposed developing western Molokai into a major suburb of Honolulu, complete with a ferry service. The plan called for 30,000 private homes on the heretofore uninhabited west coast. A vocal antigrowth movement boomed quicker than the buildings could, and the plan was scrapped.

In its place a somewhat more modest master plan was drawn up for the develop-ment of Kaluakoi Resort that called for 1100 hotel units, 1200 condo units, 1000 single-family homes and a 15-acre shopping centre.

Only 200 of the condo units, one 18-hole golf course and one of the four planned hotels have thus far been built. The 290-room hotel never really took off and the occupancy rate has been so low that part of it has been turned into condos. The houselots have been subdivided but as of yet only a few dozen houses have been built, mostly exclusive homes scattered along the edge of the beach and up on the bluff.

The Japanese investment company that now owns Kaluakoi Resort wants to expand the golf course to 27 holes in the hope it will spur more interest from Japanese tourists who have thus far largely bypassed Molokai.

MAUNALOA

The long mountain range that comes into view on the left past the 10-mile marker is Maunaloa, which means 'long mountain'. Its highest point is Puunana at 1381 feet. Maunaloa is also the name of the town at the end of the road.

Maunaloa was the site of Hawaii's first hula school, had one of the most important adze quarries in the Hawaiian islands and was once a centre of sorcery.

According to legend, fire gods who roamed the heavens as shooting stars landed on Maunaloa, where they inhabited a grove of trees. Unsuspecting men who tried to cut down the possessed trees were poisoned upon touching the wood, until at last one of the gods explained to a kahuna how to cut the trees down. The kahunas were then able to carve the poisoned wood into images that harnessed the force of the gods. During the 17th century it became a powerful sorcery that could be sent off into the night to avenge enemies. It was potent stuff and none of Molokai's neighbours dared to violate Molokai's sovereignty in those days.

The town of Maunaloa, with its dusty tin-roofed houses, was built in the 1920s by Libby, McNeill & Libby. This little plantation town was the centre of their pineapple activities on Molokai. Dole, which acquired Libby, McNeill & Libby in 1972, closed down operations in Maunaloa in 1975.

Maunaloa has a cemetery, a church, an elementary school, a few backstreets and occasionally an unlocked road heading away from town that invites impromptu exploration, but basically that's it.

Currently about 400 people live in the area, most working for Molokai Ranch or at Kaluakoi Resort.

Information

Maunaloa Service, the only gas station in the West End (their motto is: 'Our view of Diamond Head is a gas'), is open from 7.30 am to 5.30 pm Monday to Saturday.

Maunaloa General Store, well-stocked with groceries and booze, is open from 9 am to 8 pm Monday to Saturday and from 10 am to 7 pm on Sundays. The little rural post office on the other side of the road is open from 8 am to 4.30 pm Monday to Friday.

The Molokai Ranch headquarters is on the right as you enter town.

Places to Eat

JoJo's Cafe (☎ 552-2803) with its long wooden bar, stools in front and mirrors behind, looks like an old-time saloon. In fact that's what it was, but things got so rowdy that the last two owners never bothered to renew the liquor licence and these days it's a quiet small town diner. If you want beer or wine with your meal, you can pick it up at the general store across the way and bring it in. Fish dishes are in the $11 to $14 range, while chicken at $9 is the cheapest dinner. Lunch features sandwiches, hamburgers and mahimahi burgers from $4 to $7. It's open from noon to 2.45 pm and from 5 to 7.45 pm daily except Wednesdays and Sundays.

Things to Buy

Big Wind Kite Factory sells designer kites of all shapes and styles. Owner Jonathan Socher's kites have a reputation throughout the islands for their creative flair. Many of the kites are made on site and if you're there at the right time you can watch the process. An extension of the kite factory is the Plantation Gallery next door: a gift shop with batik shirts and sarongs from Bali, horn scrimshaw from Molokai deer, silver jewellery, books on Molokai and the like. Both are open from 8.30 am to 5 pm Monday to Saturday and from 10 am to 2 pm on Sundays.

The nearby Molokai Red Dirt Shirts specialises in T-shirts with Molokai designs, while Dolly Hale, opposite JoJo's, sells handmade coconut fibre dolls.

SOUTH-WEST BEACHES

If you really want to get off the beaten track,

Top: Pineapple fields, Lanai
Bottom: Shipwreck Beach, Lanai

Top: Puu Pehe Rock, Lanai
Bottom: Moa (Polynesian jungle fowl), Kauai

there are a couple of remote beaches south of Maunaloa. Access is via rutted dirt roads across Molokai Ranch land and is restricted to weekends and holidays. Permits, which are required to visit these beaches, must be picked up in advance from Molokai Ranch headquarters and cost $10 per person plus a gate key deposit!

The most frequented spot is **Halena Beach**, a broad white-sand beach with a protective reef. About 1½ miles west of Halena is **Hale O Lono Beach**, the starting point of the Molokai-to-Oahu outrigger canoe race held each year during Aloha Week. Two miles to the east of Halena is the abandoned Kolo Wharf. Libby, McNeill & Libby shipped Maunaloa pineapples from Kolo until moving their operations to Kaunakakai Harbor in the 1950s.

Molokai Ranch allows camping for a fee at Halena and Hale O Lono. See Camping in the Accommodation section in the front of the Molokai chapter for information.

In 1989 a Japanese development company, Alpha Group, bought the entire undeveloped south-western tip of Molokai, from the southern end of Kaluakoi Resort around to Hale O Lono Beach. They then announced in Tokyo newspapers a plan to develop a massive resort rivalling Waikiki. Considering the scarcity of water and anti-development sentiments on Molokai, and a general cutback in Hawaii investments by Japanese banks, the development is unlikely to come to fruition any time soon.

MOLOKAI RANCH WILDLIFE PARK

In the late 1960s, Molokai Ranch began importing antelope in an effort to control the rapid spread of kiawe trees, which were encroaching onto their cattle pastureland. The antelope, which feed on kiawe in their native habitat, adapted so well to Molokai that the ranch later started importing other rare exotic animals to breed for game parks and zoos. When Kaluakoi Resort opened, Molokai Ranch began providing sightseeing tours for the resort's guests.

About 1000 animals from Africa, India, Asia and South America roam the park's 1000 acres. The more numerous animals are the eland, Indian blackbuck, oryx and greater kudu, all strikingly marked antelopes; Barbary sheep, with thick curved-back horns; and sika deer from Japan.

There are also a few zebras (including a rare all-white zebra born at the park in October 1991), giraffes, rheas and East African crowned cranes. Flocks of wild turkey, ring-necked pheasant, francolin, quail and other game birds have flown in on their own.

The park's grassy hillsides and scrubby kiawe trees look so convincingly like the Serengeti that both American and Japanese film companies have used it to fake African backdrops.

Tours around the park's rutted dirt roads last about 1½ hours. The best tours are those led by park manager Pilipo Solatorio, who treats the animals almost as pets and keeps up a lively commentary. When Pilipo honks his horn the animals come running.

Lots of stops are made for animal sightings and feedings, and for photography. The sliding door gets opened several times, so the best seats for viewing are closest to that door and at the front of the van. The front-seat passenger is apt to get nuzzled by a friendly eland – a large African antelope weighing a good 1500 pounds – which sticks its head in the window to be fed.

Tours of the ranch are held daily, weather permitting. They begin at 8 and 10 am and 1 and 3 pm, as long as there's a minimum of four passengers. It costs $30 for adults, $20 for children. Reservations can be made by calling 552-2767.

KALUAKOI RESORT

Off Hwy 460 at the 15-mile marker a road leads down to Kaluakoi Resort. The 6700-acre development includes Kaluakoi Hotel & Golf Club, the condominium complexes of Kaluakoi Villas, Paniolo Hale and Ke Nani Kai, largely undeveloped houselots and a beautiful windswept coast. Overall it's a low-keyed and unobtrusive development that's pleasantly quiet and uncrowded.

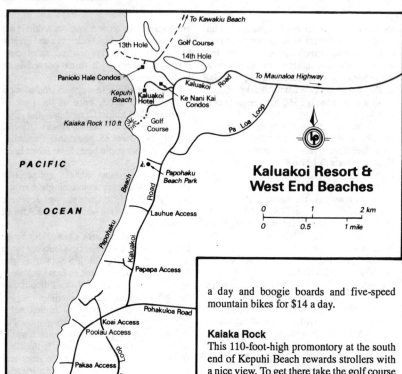

**Kaluakoi Resort &
West End Beaches**

a day and boogie boards and five-speed mountain bikes for $14 a day.

Kaiaka Rock

This 110-foot-high promontory at the south end of Kepuhi Beach rewards strollers with a nice view. To get there take the golf course road to its end from where a five-minute walk leads up Kaiaka Rock. At the top you'll find the remains of a boiler and a pulley that was once used to carry cattle down to waiting barges for transport to Oahu slaughterhouses. There was also a 40-foot heiau on the hilltop until 1967 when the US Army bulldozed it under. There have been on-again off-again plans to build a luxury hotel at Kaiaka Rock.

Places to Stay

Kaluakoi Hotel & Golf Club (☎ 552-2555, (800) 777-1700), Box 1977, Maunaloa, HI 96770, is run by Colony Hotels & Resorts. The rooms are fairly standard for a Sheraton-style hotel (which it used to be), but are on the small side, and cost $100 for a garden view, $125 for an ocean view. The hotel also has condo-style units that start at $135 for a

Kepuhi Beach

Kepuhi is the white-sand beach in front of Kaluakoi Hotel. During the winter the surf breaks close to shore, carrying a tremendous amount of sand to and fro. Experienced surfers like the northern end of the beach.

Swimming conditions are often dangerous here. Not only can there be a tough shorebreak, but strong currents can be present even on calm days. Check with the folks at the hotel beach hut on water conditions; if the hut's not open it's usually a sign that conditions are too dangerous for water activities. The hut rents snorkel sets for $12 studio, $155 for a one-bedroom. The hotel has an 18-hole golf course, tennis courts, pool, restaurant, tour desk and a couple of small stores.

About 100 units of the Kaluakoi Hotel are now under separate management and booked as *Kaluakoi Villas* (☎ 552-2721, (800) 525-1470), Box 200, Maunaloa, HI 96770. All the units have a private lanai, TV and kitchenette with a refrigerator, four-burner stove, coffeemaker and a basic supply of kitchenware. While the walls are on the thin side and the decor is lightly faded, they are pleasant enough and can be the island's best condo value if you get a discounted rate. Standard rates are $105 to $135 for studio units, $135 to $165 for one-bedroom units, but they commonly advertise specials in the Honolulu Sunday papers that halve those prices. Ask for a 2nd-floor unit, as they have cathedral ceilings and many have a peek of the ocean.

Paniolo Hale (☎ 552-2731, (800) 367-2984), Box 146, Maunaloa, HI 96770, is a 77-unit condominium. The units are airy and each has a kitchen, ceiling fans, TV, washer/dryer and screened lanai. Studios cost $95, single or double. One-bedroom, two-bath units cost $115 for up to four people, two-bedroom units with jacuzzi cost $145. Units with ocean views are $40 to $50 extra. The minimum stay is three nights and there's a 10% discount for weekly stays. The complex has a pool and barbecue grills. The office is open only from 8 am to 4 pm Monday to Friday and from 8 am to noon on Saturdays.

Ke Nani Kai (☎ 552-2761, (800) 888-2791), Box 126, Maunaloa, HI 96770, is a 120-unit condominium set back from the ocean. Each unit has a kitchen, lanai, washer/dryer, TV and sofabed. Units on the 2nd floor have high exposed-beam ceilings and are among the nicest on Molokai. The rates are $105 for up to two people in a one-bedroom unit, $125 for up to four people in a two-bedroom unit. Units with ocean views are $25 more, but it's a distant and partial view. There's a pool and two tennis courts. The minimum stay is two nights and

they often run a special that includes a free Tropical rental car.

Places to Eat

The only restaurant at the resort is the *Ohia Lodge* (☎ 552-2555) at Kaluakoi Hotel, but if you've been thinking that it's the place for a splurge meal on Molokai, forget it. The dining room is pleasant, and it's candlelit at night, but the food is ordinary and expensive for what you get.

Breakfasts are in the $6 to $9 range and sandwiches and light meals at lunch time are about the same. Prices step up at dinner, ranging from $13 for pasta alfredo to $21.50 for filet mignon. There's also a salad bar that costs $2.75 with entrees, $9.75 alone. Fridays is seafood buffet night for $25 and on Saturdays there's a prime rib buffet for $21. The hours are from 6.30 to 10.30 am, noon to 2 pm, and 6 to 9 pm.

The hotel's snack shop is open from 11 am to 5 pm. Burgers cost $3.50, a chicken plate $5, and the food's on the greasy side.

The hotel also has a sundries shop with wine, beer and some convenience foods at inflated prices. It's open from 9 am to 9 pm daily.

PAPOHAKU BEACH

Papohaku Beach lays claim to being Hawaii's largest white-sand beach. It's 2½ miles long and vast enough to hold the entire population of Molokai without getting crowded, although that would be an unlikely scenario. There's seldom more than a handful of beachgoers even on sunny days and at times you can walk the shore without seeing another set of footprints.

It's a beautiful beach and easy to get to, so why are so few people there? Well, for one, it can be windy. But the main drawback is the water itself which is usually too treacherous for swimming.

Yet for barefoot strolling it's a gorgeous stretch, with soft white sand gleaming in the sun and wisps of rainbows tossed up in the crashing surf – 'a beach to die for' as one islander said.

There are seven beach access points

marked with street signs just off Kaluakoi Rd south of Kaluakoi Hotel. All have outdoor showers at the end of paved parking lots. The first three lead to Papohaku Beach.

The first access is the most developed of the seven. This is Papohaku Beach Park, a grassy landscaped park with campsites, showers, changing rooms, restrooms, drinking water and thorny kiawe trees.

From the third access, Kulua (off Papapa Place), there's a broad view of the whole beach stretching north with the sun at your back. The large concrete tunnel at the end of the beach was used to load sand onto barges for shipping to Honolulu. The sand was used in construction and to build up Waikiki beaches until environmental protection laws put a halt to the sand mining operation in the early 1970s. There are a zillion miniature shells on this beach including lots of puka shells, most still without pukas. It's a nice place to catch the sunset.

The next three beach accesses are of rocky coastline, more suitable for fishing than other water activities.

Places to Stay

Camping Papohaku Beach Park is a choice site for camping, however the wind can pick up here. It's a beautiful spot, with the surf lulling you to sleep and the birds waking you up. Watch for thorns from the kiawe trees when you set up camp. Also, there are two sections of the camping area that are watered on different days of the week, so note the sign telling which days they water – there's nothing more depressing than finding your tent and belongings soaked!

For information on permits, see Camping in the Accommodation section in the front of the Molokai chapter.

DIXIE MARU BEACH

The beach at the end of the road is called Dixie Maru after a ship that went down in the area long ago. The Hawaiian name for the beach is Kapukahehu.

Dixie Maru is the most protected cove on the west shore and the most popular swimming area. There are usually a fair number of families here. The waters are generally calm except when the surf is high enough to break over the mouth of the bay.

MAKE HORSE BEACH

Make (pronounced 'mah-kay') Horse Beach supposedly takes its name from days past when wild horses were run off the cliff north of here. *Make* means 'dead'. This pretty little white-sand beach is a bit more secluded than the one in front of Kaluakoi Hotel. It's a good place for sunbathing but it's not safe for swimming.

To get there turn off Kaluakoi Rd onto the road to Paniolo Hale condos and then turn left as if going to the condo complex. Either park just beyond the condos and walk a quarter of a mile down to the golf course or drive the rutted dirt road to the end where there's a little spot to park. From there cross a narrow stretch of fairway and you're on the beach.

KAWAKIU BEACH

Kawakiu is a special place. It's a broad crescent beach of white sand and bright turquoise waters north of the Kaluakoi Resort complex.

In 1975 Kawakiu was a focus of Molokai activists who began demanding public access to private, and heretofore forbidden, beaches. The group, Hui Alaloa, marched to Kawakiu from Moomomi in a protest that convinced Molokai Ranch to grant public access to Kawakiu Beach.

To get there, turn off Kaluakoi Rd onto the road to Paniolo Hale, but instead of turning left down to the condos continue straight towards the golf course. Where the paved road ends, there's a place to pull over and park. There are restrooms and drinking water here at the 14th hole. It's the last chance to get water.

The red dirt road that continues down to the beach should be OK with a 4WD and might also be passable in a standard car. However, it's quite rocky in places and if you did bottom out or brush one of the rocks on the side it could put a dent in things. Anyway, why hassle driving when it's a pleasant half-hour hike down to the beach?

After the golf course the road passes through ranchland with kiawe trees. Trees that died during the drought of the mid-1980s now stand bleached white by the sun, making interesting silhouettes against the blue sky.

You'll come first to a rocky point at the southern end of the bay. Scramble around up here before descending to the beach and you can find old rock foundations and get a scenic view of the coast south to the sands of Papohaku Beach and north to Ilio Point.

When seas are calm, Kawakiu is generally safe for swimming, however that's more common in summer than winter. When the surf is rough, there are still areas where you can at least get wet. On the southern side of the bay is a little sandy-bottomed wading pool in the rocks. The northern side has an area of flat rocks over which water slides to fill up a shallow shoreline pool. On weekends there's usually a few families picnicking under the kiawe trees.

Places to Stay

Camping Molokai Ranch allows camping at Kawakiu Beach. Unlike at its other properties, permits aren't required – simply go down and camp. There's no water and no facilities.

Lanai

Until recently Lanai was a one-crop, one-company, one-town island. While the latter two still hold true, Castle & Cooke, which owns 98% of Lanai, is in the process of phasing out its pineapple operations.

For over half a century Castle & Cooke, through its Dole subsidiary, ran the island as its own private pineapple plantation. Nearly one-fifth of the world's pineapples came from Lanai. There are still millions of the spiked bushes planted row upon row in the red soil of Lanai's high central plateau, as far as the eye can see.

Now, in place of pineapples, Castle & Cooke is attempting to turn rural Lanai into an exclusive tourist destination. In 1991 they opened the second of two luxury resorts and an 18-hole golf course, and there are plans to follow with condos and a second course. For sleepy Lanai the pace of change has been dizzying.

Until April 1990 Lanai had but one hotel, with just 10 rooms. The few visitors who came this way were largely hunters, hikers and travellers trying to avoid the tourist scene on the other islands. With the opening of the two new luxury hotels, Castle & Cooke is gambling that enough wealthy visitors in search of seclusion will show up to make it pay off. On the surface, the hotels themselves, with 350 rooms combined, haven't altered things all that radically.

The centre of Lanai remains Lanai City – not a city at all, but merely a small plantation town. It's home to all but two dozen of Lanai's 2400 residents, most of whom work for Castle & Cooke.

While nearly one-sixth of the island is still planted in 'pine', as pineapple is called here, Lanai also has forested ravines, dry and dusty gullies, white-sand beaches and cool, foggy uplands. The island has some good archaeological sites and petroglyphs and the last native dryland forest in Hawaii.

Although Lanai is interesting to explore, many of the sights are a good distance from town, along rutted dirt roads that require a 4WD vehicle.

Lanai can be quite expensive to visit. One of the easiest ways to get a glimpse of it is to take the boat from Maui over in the morning, snorkel at Hulopoe Bay, which has the island's finest beach, and take the boat back in the afternoon.

ORIENTATION

Lanai has only one town, Lanai City, smack in the centre of the island. The town is laid out in a sensible grid pattern, which makes it easy to get around.

Outside Lanai City there are only three paved roads: Keomuku Rd (Hwy 44), which heads north-east towards Shipwreck Beach; Kaumalapau Highway, which heads west to Kaumalapau Harbor; and Manele Rd, which goes south to Manele and Hulopoe bays. Both Kaumalapau Highway and Manele Rd are marked Hwy 440, even though they are two distinct roads.

The airport is on Kaumalapau Highway, 3½ miles from town.

Dirt Roads

There are scores of dirt roads through Lanai's pineapple fields, with conditions varying from good to impassable. Castle & Cooke has traditionally graded the roads in the spring or whenever they got so rutted that the pineapple trucks had difficulty passing.

If you rent a 4WD vehicle, the car-rental agencies can tell you the current best routes to out-of-the-way sights. Often there are a few alternatives and they know which roads are washed out and which are easily passable. If you do go off the beaten path and get stuck, it can be a long walk back to the town. In addition the rental companies will hit you up for the towing and repair fees.

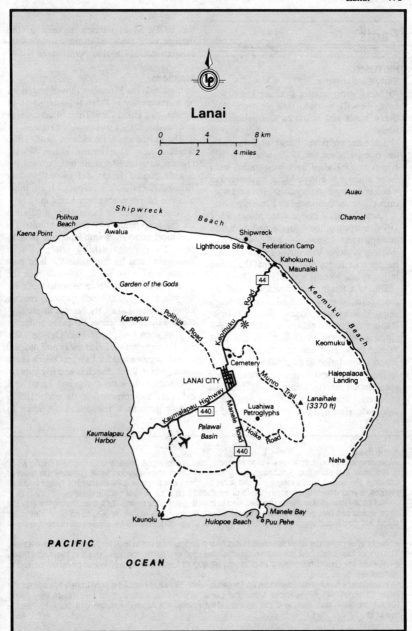

Facts

HISTORY
Early Settlements
Archaeological studies indicate Lanai was never heavily settled. Villages were relatively small and scattered throughout the island.

Since ancient times, Lanai has been under the rule of Maui. In 1778, when the Big Island chief Kalaniopuu was routed in a failed attempt to invade Maui, he decided to take his revenge on tiny Lanai and sent warriors under the command of Kamehameha.

Kamehameha's troops were brutal. They killed everyone they found and virtually depopulated Lanai. In 1792 when the Western explorer Vancouver sailed by Lanai he saw no villages and noted that the island might at best be only sparsely populated.

Due to a tough ocean swell that had, by the 1820s, already claimed a few foreign ships, visitors were largely dissuaded from landing on Lanai's shores. In 1823 the missionary William Ellis became the first Westerner to step ashore. He guessed the island's population to be 2000.

Though the early missionaries didn't spend much time on Lanai they still had an influence. They introduced the heretofore unknown crime of adultery to Hawaii and in the 1830s Maui women accused of the offence were banished to the barren northwestern side of Lanai as punishment.

Mormons
In the 1850s the Mormons moved in and set up a community at Palawai Basin, south of present-day Lanai City. Their intention was to establish a 'City of Joseph' in Hawaii.

The community floundered until 1861 when a new charismatic elder, Walter Gibson, arrived. Mormons from around the islands poured in, as did money to buy Palawai Basin. At the height of it all, there was one Mormon for every Lanaian.

Gibson, a shrewd businessman, handled the financial matters for the community. He was more concerned with land than preaching. Things got sticky when it was discovered that he had made the land purchases in his own name, rather than in the church's. In 1864, after refusing to turn over the title to his Lanai holdings to the mother church in Salt Lake City, he was excommunicated by church leader Brigham Young.

This didn't seem to faze Gibson. The Lanai congregation faded away and the 300 or so Mormons left for Laie on Oahu's north shore, where their church is centred today.

Gibson held onto the prime Lanai real estate he had cornered. In the early 1880s, Gibson became a friend and confidant to

---

Kaululaau
According to legend, Lanai was a land of spirits, and spirits alone roamed until the 15th century.

It was at this time that Kaululaau, the young prince of Maui, lived in what is today the town of Lahaina. He was a troublesome kid. After he had torn out breadfruit trees that his father had just planted, it was decided to banish him to uninhabited Lanai, an almost certain death.

Not easily intimidated, Kaululaau learned to trick the evil *akua* (spirits) of Lanai. During the day the akua would see him on the beach and ask where he spent his nights, hoping to ambush him in his sleep. He convinced them he slept in the surf, but when darkness fell he slipped off to the shelter of a cave.

Night after night, the akua returned to the beach and rushed out to look for Kaululaau in the waves. The longer they searched, the more exhausted they got, until finally the pounding surf overcame them. Kaululaau continued his pranks until at last all 400 of Lanai's akua had either perished or fled to Kahoolawe.

Kaululaau's family had given him up for dead, when Mauians noticed a light from a fire across the Auau Channel, which separates Maui and Lanai. When they went over to investigate they found Kaululaau alive and well and the island rid of spirits. Kaululaau was brought back to Maui a hero. ∎

King Kalakaua and came to hold a number of positions in Kalakaua's cabinet, including that of premier.

Sugar

Upon his death, Gibson left the land to his daughter, Talula Lucy. In 1888 she and her husband, Frederick Hayselden, established the Maunalei Sugar Company and developed a landing at Halepalaoa on Lanai's east coast. A water pumping station went up at nearby Keomuku, the surrounding area was planted with sugar cane and the whole shebang was connected by a little railroad. Over 400 Japanese labourers were brought in to work the fields. The sugar days were short lived, however. By 1901 the pumps were drawing saltwater, the sugar cane had died and the whole thing had folded.

This was not the first try at the sugar business on Lanai. In 1802 a Chinese man landed on Lanai with granite rollers to crush sugar cane and iron pots to boil down the syrup. He is credited with being the first person to attempt sugar production in Hawaii. Though this enterprise was a failure, it was Chinese know-how that became the base for sugar mills throughout Hawaii.

Cattle

After the dismal failure with sugar, the land was sold off to ranching interests. In 1910 the newly formed Lanai Company consolidated most of the holdings and established cattle ranching on a larger scale. The following year a New Zealander, George Munro, was hired to manage the ranch and a cattle landing was established at Manele Bay.

In 1917 the Baldwin brothers, sons of missionaries from Maui, purchased the Lanai Company. With the exception of a small haole-held ranch and about 500 acres held by Lanaians, the Baldwins owned the entire island.

Pineapples

In 1922 Jim Dole paid $1.1 million for Lanai, a mere $12 an acre. It was just enough for the Baldwins to buy the Ulupalakua Ranch that they had long coveted on Maui. Dole, who had already established pineapple production on Oahu, doubled his holdings of cultivable land by purchasing Lanai.

Dole's Hawaiian Pineapple Company poured $4 million into Lanai to turn it into a plantation island. It built the plantation town of Lanai City, dredged Kaumalapau to make it a deep-water harbour, put in roads and water systems, cleared the land and planted pineapples. By the end of the 1920s production was in full swing.

Dole had marketed his pineapples well, was producing bumper crops and the future looked rosy. Then the Great Depression hit the mainland and sales plummeted. The newly popular canned pineapples were suddenly seen as an exotic extra, one that most Americans could easily do without in hard times.

After an $8 million loss in 1932, a reorganisation took place. Castle & Cooke purchased much of the stock and eventually gained a controlling interest in Dole. They've been the dominant force on Lanai ever since.

GEOGRAPHY

Lanai is the sixth largest Hawaiian island. It's 18 miles long, 13 miles wide and shaped like a teardrop. It has an area of 140 sq miles.

Lanai lies nine miles south of Molokai and nine miles west of Maui. The name Lanai means 'hump'. When viewed from Maui it looks somewhat like the back of a whale rising out of the water.

The island was formed by a single volcano, Palawai, now long extinct. The large flat basin of Palawai crater is today covered with pineapples.

Lanai's terrain and climate are dominated by a ridge running from the north-west to the south-east. It reaches a height of 3370 feet at Lanaihale. From there, a series of ravines radiate down to the east coast, ending at a strip of coastal flats.

The western side of the ridge is a cool central plateau, containing the island's agricultural land. In the centre of it all is Lanai City at 1620 feet.

The south-west coast has sheer sea cliffs,

some higher than 1000 feet. North-west Lanai is dry and barren and slopes gently down to the coast.

CLIMATE

Lanai City has a mild climate. The lowest temperature on record is 46°F, the highest 88°F. Average temperatures range from 73°F in the summer to 66°F in the winter. Evenings can be brisk, commonly dipping down to around 50°F in winter.

Lanai is rather dry. Molokai and Maui to the north and east draw much of the rain out of the moisture-laden trade winds before they reach Lanai.

Annual rainfall averages 37 inches in Lanai City and 10 to 15 inches along most of the coast. The difference is great enough that when it's overcast in Lanai City, chances are that Shipwreck Beach or Manele Bay will be sunny.

As with the rest of Hawaii, October to April is the rainiest season. Even dry areas can get whacked with heavy rainfall during winter storms.

FLORA & FAUNA

Lanai has suffered the greatest loss of native forests, plants and birds of any of the main Hawaiian islands, the result of drastic overgrazing.

Lanai has about 8000 axis deer, descendants from a herd of eight brought to Molokai from India in 1868. The deer were introduced to Lanai in 1920 and are more prolific than on Molokai, the only other Hawaiian island where they roam free.

Mouflon sheep were introduced to Lanai in 1954 and inhabit the island's gullies and ridges. Both the deer and sheep are hunted.

Lanai has no mongoose, which eat the eggs of ground nesting birds, so introduced game birds thrive. Ring-necked pheasants, francolins, chukar partridges, quails, doves and wild turkeys are all hunted.

However the island has only two endemic birds remaining – the Hawaiian owl and the *apapane* (native honeycreeper) – and they are scarce.

Besides pineapples, the most noticeable types of vegetation are thorny kiawe trees and stately Norfolk Island pines. Lanai has a unique native dryland forest, under the protection of the Nature Conservancy.

GOVERNMENT

Lanai is part of Maui County. Historically Lanai has been treated as an extension of Maui, much as Niihau has been of Kauai. Lanai had at most only limited autonomy, with Maui kings maintaining suzerainty.

These days the control of the island is largely in the hands of Castle & Cooke. They own all but 2% of Lanai and thus the beaches, forests and most of the dirt roads around the island are on their property. Total county and state land accounts for just over 100 acres.

ECONOMY

Over 75% of Lanai's 1200 workers are employed by Castle & Cooke, either in their hotels or agricultural operations.

Pineapple production, which has long formed the backbone of Lanai's economy, is being phased out. While a few fields will be maintained for the image, the last commercial harvest will probably take place in 1993. Some of the pineapple fields are being converted on a limited basis to forage crops,

Abandoned church

papayas and macadamia nuts, but the importance of agriculture will be secondary at best.

As the pineapple economy is being replaced by a tourism-oriented service economy, it is resulting in major social and economic changes for Lanaians. There is a lot of apprehension, not only among laid-off pineapple workers but among shop owners who feel they may eventually lose their leases to tourist-based off-island businesses.

In terms of tourism, Lanai's greatest appeal has long been its unique rural character and its image as 'The Pineapple Island'. With the loss of that character, many people feel Lanai will be unable to attract enough tourists to keep the hotels in business. Indeed, the resorts have experienced very low occupancy rates and have already mounted millions of dollars in operating losses. Castle & Cooke argue that the losses can be stemmed if they receive approval to move to the next stage of development, the construction of a second golf course and 775 luxury homes. The homes are geared for the wealthy and the second-homers who have bypassed Lanai up to now. If it all develops according to plan, Lanai's population will more than quadruple to 10,000 before the end of the decade.

POPULATION & PEOPLE

Lanai has seen some dramatic rises and falls in its population. It had dropped well below 200 when Dole arrived in 1922.

Lanai's current population is 2450, about 1000 less than it was in the 1950s. With the exception of people staying at the Manele Bay Hotel, all but two dozen live in Lanai City. The largest ethnic group is Filipino (51%), followed by Japanese (18%), Caucasian (11%) and part-Hawaiian (9.2%).

Approximately a third of the people living on Lanai were born in the Philippines.

GENERAL INFORMATION

As there's no daily local newspaper, community notices are posted on bulletin boards outside the post office and the three grocery stores.

Official Lanai

Lanai's nickname is 'The Pineapple Island'. Its official flower is the kaunaoa. Its official colour is yellow.

Money & Post

The First Hawaiian Bank and the post office are both on Lanai Ave near 7th St. The post office is open from 8 am to 4.30 pm Monday to Friday, and for mail pick-up only on Saturdays from 9.30 to 10 am.

Library

Lanai's library is on Fraser Ave, adjacent to the school. It's a fairly large library with a good collection of newspapers, including *USA Today*, the *Los Angeles Times*, the *Wall Street Journal* and Neighbor Island papers. It's open from 8 am to 5 pm Monday to Friday.

Weather

For recorded weather forecasts and water conditions call 565-6033. For information on trails try the state's Department of Land & Natural Resources (☎ 565-6688) on 8th St.

Emergency

For all emergencies call 911. Lanai Community Hospital (☎ 565-6411) on 7th St has 24-hour emergency service.

ACTIVITIES

There's a new $3-million public recreation centre in Lanai City, next to the school, with a 75-foot-long pool, a playground, a basketball court and a couple of lit tennis courts.

The Cavendish Golf Course, a local nine-hole course just north of town, is the only free golf course in Hawaii and a popular recreation spot for islanders. The Lodge at Koele has an 18-hole designer golf course that's popular with tourists.

Lanai City Service rents snorkel sets for $5 a day.

Cockfighting, while not legal, is common on Lanai. The fights are held on Sundays but they're private and you generally won't find them unless you've been around for a while and made the right friends.

The two resort hotels offer a variety of activities including tennis, diving and horse riding, however the fees are generally quite high and many of the activities are limited to guests.

People go to bed early in Lanai and there's no real night life. The Lodge at Koele sometimes has a soloist singing Hawaiian songs in the evening. On rare occasions, the resort brings in an off-island band.

GETTING THERE & AWAY
Air
Aloha IslandAir (☎ 565-6744, (800) 652-6541 from the Neighbor Islands) flies daily to Lanai direct from Honolulu, Molokai, Kahului and Hana. The most frequent service is from Honolulu, with seven flights a day. The one-way fare is $69.95. For the same fare, you can also fly to or from any Aloha Airlines destination, with a transfer connection in Honolulu to Aloha IslandAir.

Hawaiian Airlines (☎ 565-6977, (800) 882-8811) flies direct to Lanai twice a day from Honolulu, at 10 am and 2.20 pm, with the morning flight connecting through Kapalua West Maui. The one-way fare is $69.95.

For information on discount tickets, see the Getting Around chapter in the front of the book.

Lanai Airport lacks the navigational equipment to allow instrument landings. When it's foggy, which sometimes happens for days on end during winter storms, planes are unable to land. However, far more common is a delay of a few hours.

Airport Lanai Airport is not much more than a runway. Hawaiian Airlines and Aloha IslandAir share a small wooden building, which also houses the restrooms. The only other amenities are a water fountain, a Coke machine and a pay phone. If you just need to call for a car, there's a free courtesy phone outside.

Still, for all its unpretentiousness there's a hustle of activity when the planes come in as

bell hops from the two resort hotels collect guests at a congested little baggage claim area and load them onto waiting vans.

Ferry
Expeditions (☎ 661-3756) operates a 24-passenger ferry between Lahaina on Maui and Manele Boat Harbor on Lanai. The boat departs Lahaina at the dock in front of Pioneer Inn at 6.45 am, 9.15 am and 3.15 pm daily. There's also a 5.45 pm sailing, except on Thursdays when it's at 8.30 pm. The boat departs Manele at 8 am, 10.30 am and 4.30 pm daily. There's also a 6.45 pm sailing, except on Thursdays when it's at 9.30 pm. The trip takes about an hour. One-way fares are $25 for adults and $20 for children aged 2 to 11.

This is a great way to get to Lanai. Though the ride can be jolting when the seas are rough, it's usually quite pleasant and during the winter there's a good chance of seeing whales.

GETTING AROUND
To/From the Airport
The Lodge at Koele and Manele Bay Hotel meet guests at the airport. Hotel Lanai will provide free pick-up at either the airport or the boat harbour for their guests; call when you get in.

Shuttle Bus
The resorts run a free shuttle bus between the Manele Bay Hotel and the Lodge at Koele for their guests. Non-guests can try their luck catching a ride. It runs once an hour on weekdays, every half hour on weekends.

Car
Two rental companies service Lanai. While there are no car-rental booths at the airport, both agencies provide free airport pick-up to their in-town offices; call from the airport when you arrive.

Oshiro Service & U-Drive (☎ 565-6952, (800) 678-6000), Box 516, Lanai City, HI 96763, which is affiliated with Tropical Rent a Car, is at 850 Fraser Ave. Cars cost $49.95 a day and 4WD vehicles cost $99.95 when booked directly to Oshiro. However if you book through Tropical before arriving, you can often get rates of about $35 for the cars, $75 for the 4WD. The station is open from 8 am to noon and from 1.30 to 5.30 pm Monday to Saturday, and on Sundays for those with reservations.

Dollar Rent A Car is handled through Lanai City Service (☎ 565-7227, (800) 342-7398 in Hawaii, (800) 367-7006 from the mainland), Box N, Lanai Ave, Lanai City, HI 96763, . Cars rent for $49.95 a day and 4WD vehicles for about $100, however if you reserve in advance through Dollar it's often about 25% cheaper. Lanai City Service is open from 7 am to 6 pm Monday to Friday and from 8 am to 6 pm on weekends.

The rental companies don't make it easy to explore Lanai. There are many dirt roads in fine condition that can easily be driven, yet both companies restrict all their cars to paved roads. They even impose a $100 fine if renters are found to have taken a car onto dirt roads! Oshiro tends to be the strictest in this matter.

Even with 4WD vehicles, which are allowed onto dirt roads, the rental companies insist you stick to the tamer roads, whereas locals readily explore everywhere.

Taxi

Both Lanai City Service and Oshiro Service provide taxi service. The cost is $5 per person between the airport and town and $10 per person between Manele and town. Oshiro's also provides customised tours at a flat rate of $33 an hour per vehicle.

Around the Island

LANAI CITY

Lanai City is nestled among Norfolk pines on a cool central plateau. It's wrapped on three sides by pineapples and on the fourth by the slopes of Lanaihale Mountain.

Lanai City is fairly classy for an old plantation town. Unlike Hawaii's working sugar towns, many of the homes in Lanai City are privately owned. Houses are brightly painted and have gardens with flowering trees and ornamental bromeliads,

Lanai City invites leisurely walking. The centre of town is Dole Park, a large grassy park lined with Norfolk pines. The park stretches six blocks from Fraser Ave to Lanai Ave, the two main roads in town.

Lanai's restaurants are on the north side of the park and the grocery stores are on the south side. To the west of the park are the post office, hospital and Hotel Lanai. To the east are the school and recreation centre, with houses spread out for five or six blocks on either side – and that's about it.

At sunset, walking through the town and looking at the pines silhouetted against the crimson sky can be a delight. On Sunday mornings a stroll by the Hawaiian church on the corner of 5th and Gay Sts will treat you to a fine melody of church music.

Strollers will find a pleasant short hike behind the Lodge at Koele. Simply take the road on the Lanai City side of the lodge to its end at the golf cart parking lot. From there take the path along the golf cart route for a 15-minute walk past stands of Norfolk pines, artificial ponds and golf course landscaping. It ends at a hilltop bench where there's a plaque with the poem 'If' by Rudyard Kipling.

While the new resorts are bringing change, this is still the place to come to unwind the clock. It's hard to imagine a town less hurried than Lanai City.

Lanai is an early riser. If the roosters don't rouse you the 5 am whistle will. Many shops close for siesta between noon and 1.30 pm.

Shopping

Richard's Shopping Center on 8th St is a fairly large grocery store for a small island. In addition to food, it also sells nonprescription medicines and camera film. It's open from 8.30 am to 5.30 pm Monday to Saturday, and stays open during lunch time on Fridays and Saturdays.

Pine Isle Market, also on 8th St, is the other major grocery store. It carries a bit of everything from Coleman lamps to watches.

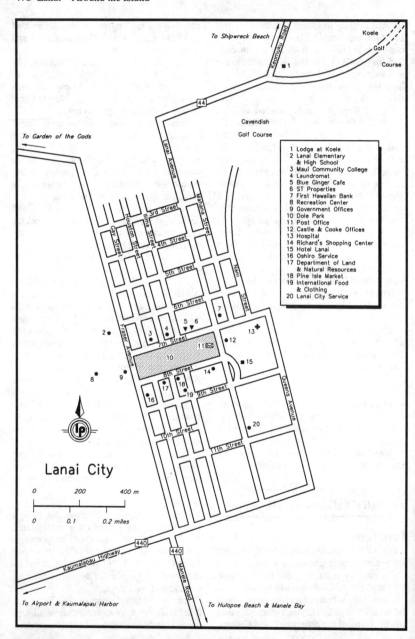

To Shipwreck Beach

Koele
Golf
Course

Keomuku Road

44

Cavendish
Golf Course

To Garden of the Gods

Lanai Avenue

Mahana Street

Nani Street

Houston Street
Gay Street
Ilima Street

3rd Street

4th Street

5th Street

6th Street

7th Street

8th Street

9th Street

10th Street

11th Street

Fraser Avenue

Queens Avenue

1 Lodge at Koele
2 Lanai Elementary
  & High School
3 Maui Community College
4 Laundromat
5 Blue Ginger Cafe
6 ST Properties
7 First Hawaiian Bank
8 Recreation Center
9 Government Offices
10 Dole Park
11 Post Office
12 Castle & Cooke Offices
13 Hospital
14 Richard's Shopping Center
15 Hotel Lanai
16 Oshiro Service
17 Department of Land
   & Natural Resources
18 Pine Isle Market
19 International Food
   & Clothing
20 Lanai City Service

Lanai City

0   200   400 m

0   0.1   0.2 miles

To Airport & Kaumalapau Harbor

Kaumalapau Highway

440

440

Manele Road

To Hulopoe Beach & Manele Bay

Pine Isle has a good selection of fresh and frozen meats and fish. Opening hours are 8 am to 5.30 pm Monday to Saturday.

The only grocery store that stays open weekdays during siesta is International Food & Clothing on Ilima St. It's open from 8.30 am to 5.30 pm, until noon on Saturdays and Sundays. It sells groceries, booze and some clothing. The *Honolulu Advertiser* and the *Maui News* can be bought at the store.

Lanai Art Studio, beside the community college, is the site of the community art programme and the place to purchase local art. The majority of the works on display are paintings of Lanai scenes. It's open from 9 am to 4 pm Monday to Saturday, 1 to 4 pm on Sundays.

Places to Stay

The *Hotel Lanai* (☎ 565-7211, (800) 624-8849), Box A119, Lanai City, HI 96763, was built by Dole in 1923 to lodge plantation guests. Not a whole lot has changed over the years except the rates. While the hotel has a weathered mountain lodge ambience, its rustic charm is hard to appreciate at $95 a night. The 10 rooms are simple: bed, dresser, nightstand, chair, stained curtains, old carpeting and painted wood walls that are anything but soundproof. Each has a private bathroom and the four front rooms have porches.

The *Lodge at Koele* (☎ 565-7300, (800) 321-4666), Box 774, Lanai City, HI 96763, is a low-rise 102-room hotel with the ambience of an overgrown plantation estate. Its lobby, called the Great Hall, is stuffed with an eclectic collection of antiques and upholstered furnishings. It also boasts of Hawaii's two largest stone fireplaces. Rooms cost from $295 to $350. Suites, which include butler service, cost from $475 to $975. Most rooms are quite nicely appointed and have VCRs, four-poster beds, private lanais, marble bathrooms and the like.

Lucille Graham rents two bedrooms with shared bath in her home as *Lanai Bed & Breakfast* (☎ 565-6378), Box 956, 312 Mahana St, Lanai City, HI 96763. The house is below Cavendish Golf Course. One room

has a double and single bed, the other a queen bed, and each costs $50 for one or two people. Rates include a full breakfast. Lucille, a retired nurse, knows the island well and can give you a lot of tips on where to explore. She has a fine collection of glass floats she's picked up on Lanai's shores.

Rudy Bosma, an expat from the Netherlands who manages Lanai City Service, rents out a few rooms with shared bath in his house. Called *Pineapple Isle Lodging* (☎ 565-7065), it's on Gay St in a residential area, just a few minutes' walk from the town centre. Rates are $25/50 for singles/doubles.

Lanai Realty (☎ 565-6597), Kathy Oshiro, Box 67, Lanai City, HI 96763, sometimes has a three-bedroom house for rent at $125 for two people, $150 for up to six, however it's often rented on a long-term basis. There's a two-night minimum.

Places to Eat

When locals want to go out, they head for *Hotel Lanai* which has good food, moderate prices and a dining room with high ceilings and hardwood floors. Breakfast costs no more here than at the simpler eateries in town, but on cool mornings when they light the dining room fireplace there's not another restaurant on Lanai that can match the atmosphere. Pancakes served with a dollop of fresh pineapple cost $3, omelettes with toast cost $4. The best lunch deal on Lanai is their fish of the day with French fries and vegetables for $5.50. They also make a good cheeseburger that comes with a big slab of fresh tomato and onion and is served with French fries for $4.50. Full dinners, which are largely meat and fish dishes, are in the $13 to $15 range. The salad bar, which is small but fresh and includes pineapple and oranges, is included with dinner or costs $4.95 alone. The tempting strawberry cheesecake served at Hotel Lanai comes from the same pastry shop the resorts use – only here it costs $3, at the Lodge at Koele $7.50. Breakfast is available from 7.30 to 9 am Monday to Saturday, to noon on Sundays. Lunch is from 11.30 am to 1.30 pm

Monday to Saturday and dinner is from 6.30 to 8.30 pm nightly.

S T Properties serves 1950s-style hamburgers – a bit heavy on the fat and sodium, but unquestionably the favourite burger among Lanaians. Burgers cost $1.50 to $2, lunch plates are around $4 and breakfast omelettes cost $4 to $5. There's an old-style counter where you can sit over coffee and watch the bacon sizzle on the grill. Opening hours are from 6.30 am to 12.30 pm daily.

The *Blue Ginger Cafe*, a combo bakery and cafe, makes doughnuts and a few sugary pastries and serves three meals a day. It's an unassuming place with a cement floor and vinyl chairs, but if you order right the food's good. Their best dishes are the Belgian waffles at breakfast for $4.25, an eight-inch pizza on boboli bread with vegetable toppings for $6.75, and fresh fish dishes. The cafe also serves $5-plate lunches and inexpensive hamburgers and saimin. Opening hours are from 5.30 am to 9 pm daily, with breakfast served until 10.30 am.

At the *Lodge at Koele*, the lobbyside Terrace Dining Room (☎ 565-7300) overlooks the hotel gardens. Breakfast costs from $8.25 for hotcakes to $12.25 for eggs benedict, while a cup of coffee costs $2. At lunch time, omelettes or sandwiches cost about $10, more elaborate dishes about $15. At dinner, main courses range from chicken for $16 to lobster tail for $26. Breakfast is served from 7 to 10 am, lunch from noon to 6 pm and dinner from 6 to 9.30 pm.

The Lodge's formal dining room is open for dinner only, with entrees such as venison from Lanai axis deer and grilled seafood in the $30 to $35 range. Add another $7.25 for a green salad or a bowl of soup.

You might want to check out high tea at the Lodge at Koele, served in the tearoom from 3 to 5 pm. A cup of tea costs $2 but the pastries are included free.

SHIPWRECK BEACH & KEOMUKU

Hwy 44 runs 8½ miles from town to the north-east coast. The highway is narrow, only about 1½ lanes wide, but it's well paved. To get to the highway, head north on Lanai Ave and bear right on Keomuku Rd (Hwy 44).

The road heads into hills and pastures with grazing cattle. The uplands here are often cool, with fog and cloud cover drifting in and out. The Lodge at Koele is on Hwy 44, a mile above town. A mile past the lodge is a paved road that leads off to the right to the Munro Trail.

The road to the trailhead is lined with Norfolk pines. It ends in half a mile at a cemetery with gravestones in Japanese and Filipino. Sake offerings are placed at some of the graves. Pinwheels, bunny rabbits and pink flamingoes adorn other sites where children are buried.

Back on Hwy 44, three miles out of town, there's a pull-off to the right with a beautiful view. Straight ahead is the undeveloped south-east shore of Molokai and its tiny islet of Mokuhooniki. The view to the right is of Maui and the Kaanapali high-rises.

From the lookout, the road starts down to the coast towards Molokai. The scenery is punctuated by interesting rock formations sticking up out of the eroded red earth, which are similar to those at Garden of the Gods. Later a shipwreck comes into view.

The paved road ends near the coast. The dirt road to the left leads to Shipwreck Beach and a former lighthouse. If you continue instead on the main road, it leads down the coast to Keomuku.

Shipwreck Beach

Shipwreck Beach is the name given to nine miles of Lanai's north-east shore. It starts at Kahokunui at the end of Hwy 44 and goes up to Polihua Beach. True to its name, there are a couple of shipwrecks as well as a shore that's good for beachcombing.

The dirt road that heads left from the highway ends after 1¾ miles at the site of a former lighthouse on a lava point. Only the cement foundations of the lighthouse remain.

When it's dry the road is usually passable by car, but you'll miss the beach walk. An alternative is to hike (or drive) in about half a mile from the end of the paved road, cut down to the beach and walk to the lighthouse from there. You can walk back by the road, which is quicker.

Lots of driftwood washes up on this windswept beach. Some of the pieces are identifiable sunbleached timbers from shipwrecks – hulls, side planks, perhaps even a gangplank if your imagination is active. There are also fishing nets, ropes and the occasional glass float.

It's likely to be just you and the driftwood, although about 20 minutes up the beach there's a cluster of small wooden beach shacks called Federation Camp, sometimes used by Filipino fishers. The lighthouse is 10 minutes farther.

The beach sand is a bit soft and sinks underfoot, making this a good walk for your calves. The sand gradually changes colours as you walk along. In some places it's a colourful, chunky mixture of rounded shells and bits of rock that look like a sort of beach confetti.

A low rock shelf lines much of the shore. It's shallow, murky water and not good for swimming or snorkelling.

Up on the slopes some of the beach morning glory (pohuehue) is entwined with an airplant that looks something like yellow-orange fishing line. This is kaunaoa, Lanai's official flower, a leafless parasitic vine.

Petroglyphs From the lighthouse, whitewash markings lead directly inland for about five minutes to some small petroglyphs. The simple figures are etched on large boulders on the right side of the path, down the slope past the 'Do Not Deface' sign.

The rocky path is through ground cover of flowering golden ilima and pink and yellow lantana. The former is native, while the latter was introduced to Hawaii just 30 years ago and has escaped from cultivation to become a major pest throughout the islands.

Keep your eyes open for animals. Up on the hill across the way we saw mouflon sheep – one male with curled-back horns and a harem of light brown females.

Up the Beach It's about 15 minutes farther

up the beach to a rusting WW II Liberty ship that has washed up on the reef. You can see the shipwreck clearly from the lighthouse.

This is the point where most people turn around and head back but it's possible to walk another six miles down to **Awalua**, which long ago was the location of a north shore landing. There's another shipwreck at Awalua but not much else. The beach is generally windy and it's a hot dry hike, although the farther down the beach you go, the prettier it gets.

Keomuku Beach

Keomuku Beach is the stretch of shore from Kahokunui, at the end of Hwy 44, south to Halepalaoa Landing.

The dirt road is likely to be either dusty or muddy, with deep ruts, however if you're lucky enough to catch it after it's been graded it's not so bad. Still, it's a 4WD road. When the tide is low, locals do much of the drive down on the beach sand rather than bump along on the road. The coast is not particularly attractive and there's not much to see though there are several historical sites and Maui is visible across the Auau Channel. There are scattered groves of coconuts along the way and lots and lots of kiawe.

Real diehards can go the full 12 miles down to **Naha**, at the end of the road. It may take as long as two hours one way, depending on road conditions.

Less than a mile down the road is **Maunalei**. An ancient heiau that once sat there was taken apart and its stones used to build a cattle fence by Frederick Hayselden, who later lost his shirt in the ill-fated Maunalei Sugar Company. Islanders believed the temple desecration was what caused the wells to turn salty and kill off the sugar cane Hayselden had planted.

Keomuku, 5¾ miles south of Hwy 44, was the centre of the short-lived sugar cane plantation. There's little left to see other than the old Ka Lanakila O Ka Malamalama Church, built in 1903 after Maunalei Sugar collapsed. The ruins of a couple of fishponds are along the coast, but not easily visible.

Another heiau at **Kahea**, 1½ miles south

of Keomuku, was also dismantled by Maunalei Sugar Co, this time to build a railroad to transport the sugar to Halepalaoa Landing. Kahea, meaning 'red stains', was a luakini heiau where human sacrifices were made.

Halepalaoa Landing, just south of Kahea, was used for several years by Club Lanai, who operated day outings from Maui. When passenger boats started making regular runs to Manele Bay, which has an unbeatable beach nearby, Club Lanai could no longer attract enough customers and it shut down. Still Halepalaoa has the best beach on this end of the island and it's an inviting spot to stop. The road onwards to Naha really doesn't offer much more scenery for the effort but should you want to continue it's about four miles farther.

MANELE BAY & HULOPOE BAY

Lanai's best beach, Hulopoe, is reached by a 20-minute drive down Manele Rd, a paved road that starts just south of town. The beach is 7½ miles south of the intersection of Manele Rd and Kaumalapau Highway.

Rows of pineapples line both sides of the road most of the way, but they're gradually being replaced by forage crops. You can often spot pheasants, quails and other colourful game birds in the fields. The birds tend to gather in this southern half of the island, where hunting's prohibited.

About 1½ miles down Manele Rd, a very wide dirt road comes in diagonally to the left. This is Hoike Rd, which leads to the Munro Trail and the Luahiwa Petroglyphs.

After four miles Manele Rd veers to the left and a mile farther there's a small pull-off with a pretty coastal view of both Manele Bay to the left and Hulopoe Bay to the right. The island beyond is Kahoolawe.

Manele Boat Harbor

Manele Harbor is a scenic, crescent-shaped natural harbour backed by sheer cliffs. Lanai folks like to fish from the stone breakwater that sticks out into the mouth of the bay.

Manele is a very protected harbour and a popular sailboat anchorage. Lanai is one of

the easier islands to sail to from Honolulu (although 'easy' is a relative term and the water can be rough).

In the early 20th century, cattle were herded down to Manele Bay for shipment to Honolulu. The remains of a cattle chute which was used to load them directly onto the ships can be seen by walking around the point to the right at the end of the parking lot.

Stone ruins from a Hawaiian fishing village and concrete slabs from the days of cattle ranching are up on the hill above the parking lot. The ruins are largely overgrown with kiawe and ilima.

Inside Manele Bay, coral is abundant near the cliffsides where the bottom quickly slopes off to about 40 feet. Beyond the western edge of the bay, near Puu Pehe Rock, is First Cathedrals, a popular dive site. Off the parking lot are restrooms, showers, drinking water, picnic tables and a little harbourmaster's office. If you arrive by boat, it's a 10-minute walk from Manele Bay to Hulopoe Beach.

Hulopoe Beach

Hulopoe Beach is a gently curving white-sand beach. It's long and broad and protected by a rocky point to the south. On the north side of the bay the Manele Bay Hotel sits on a low terraced area.

Even with the new hotel, it's a pretty quiet beach. Generally the most action is when the boats from Maui pull in with snorkellers.

Some of Lanai's best snorkelling is found on the left side of the bay, where there are lots of colourful coral and reef fish.

Also on that side, just beyond the sandy beach, there's a low lava shelf with tidepools worth exploring. One area has been blasted out, making a protected pool for children. Cement steps lead down to the pool from the rocks. It looks like every kid on Lanai rushed down to scrawl their name in the cement when it was poured in August 1951.

Hulopoe Beach has a landscaped park with solar-heated showers, restrooms, picnic tables, pay phones, barbecue grills, drinking water and campsites.

Both Manele and Hulopoe bays are part of

a marine-life conservation district in which the removal of coral and rocks is prohibited and many fishing activities are restricted. Water activities can be dangerous during kona storms, when strong currents and swells prevail.

Puu Pehe Cove

From Hulopoe Beach, a short path leads to the rocky point that juts out to the south. The peninsula of land separating Hulopoe and Manele bays is a volcanic cone that's sharply eroded on its southerly seaward edge. Here on the point the lava has rich rust-red colours with swirls of grey and black in fascinating patterns. The texture is bubbly and brittle – so brittle that huge chunks of the point have broken off and fallen onto the coastal shelf below. There's a small sea arch below the point.

Puu Pehe is the name of the cove to the left of the point as well as the sea stack just offshore. This islet, also called Sweetheart's Rock, has a tomb-like formation on top.

Places to Stay

The 250-room *Manele Bay Hotel* (☎ 565-7700, (800) 321-4666), Box 774, Lanai City, HI 96763, overlooking Hulopoe Beach, has spacious lobbies that are partially open air and adorned with artwork and antiques. There's a reading room with dark woods and leather-bound books, lots of Italian marble floors, and a central lounge with sofas, posh chairs and a grand piano. Rooms are quite pleasant, all with four-poster beds, lanais and

marble baths. Rates are $295 for a courtyard room, $395 for an oceanfront room and from $595 for suites.

Camping Surprisingly, even with the hotel up and running, camping is still allowed at three campsites right on Hulopoe Beach.

As long as the Koele Company (☎ 565-6661), Box L, Lanai City, HI 96763, continues issuing permits, here's how it goes. There's a $5 registration fee per campsite plus $5 per person per night. The maximum length of stay is seven days. Reservations can be made by mail or phone. Fees must be paid within five days of confirmation of the reservation.

Sometimes you can get permits without advance reservations if the camping ground's not full. The Koele Company, in the Castle & Cooke offices opposite the post office, issues permits Monday to Friday from 9 am to 4 pm.

Places to Eat

The *Manele Bay Hotel* serves breakfast in the Hulopoe Court from 7 to 11 am. The setting has a bit of everything: high ceilings with gaudy chandeliers, ornate Chinese vases and a view of the ocean. A continental breakfast will set you back $10, while à la carte items include croissants for $4, pancakes for $7.75 and coffee for $2.50. Lunch is at the poolside grill from 11 am to 5 pm, with light eats such as mahi sandwiches, crabmeat rolls and salads for $8 to $12. For dinner there's the Ihilani Dining Room, which is open air, somewhat elegant and quite pleasant. One of their best dishes is the tiger prawns cooked

---

Puu Pehe

Legend says an island girl, Puupehe, was so beautiful that her lover decided that they should make their home in a secluded coastal cave, lest any other young men in the village set eyes on her. One day the lover was up in the mountains fetching water when a kona storm suddenly blew in. He rushed down the mountain but by the time he arrived the waves had swept into the cave, drowning Puupehe.

The islanders brought a tapa cloth and prepared to bury the girl in the village. But Puupehe's lover slipped off with her body at night and carried it out to the rock where he built her a tomb. When he was finished, in his grief he jumped into the surging waters below and was dashed back onto the rock. The islanders recovered his body, wrapped it in the tapa they had prepared for Puupehe and buried him in the village. ■

in lemon oil and garlic for $27. Other main dishes range from $20 to $30.

KAUNOLU

Kaunolu was the site of an early Hawaiian fishing village abandoned in the mid-1800s. It has the greatest concentration of ruins on Lanai.

It was a vacation spot for Kamehameha the Great, who went there to fish the prolific waters of Kaunolu Bay. He also held tournaments and sporting events at Kaunolu. His house site was up on the bluff on the eastern side of the bay.

Kaunolu Gulch separates the two sides of the bay. Most of the house sites sit on the eastern side. The overgrown Halulu Heiau, on the western side, once dominated the whole scene. Beyond the ruins the Palikaholo sea cliffs rise more than 1000 feet.

The heiau included a puuhonua, a place of refuge where kapu breakers could find absolution and escape the punishment of death. There are a number of petroglyphs, some on the southern side of the heiau.

North-west of the heiau there's a high natural stone wall along the perimeter of the cliff. Look for a break in the wall at the cliff's edge where there's a sheer 90-foot drop. This is Kahekili's Jump, named after a Lanaian chief. There's a ledge below it that makes diving a bit death-defying. Apparently Kamehameha used to amuse himself by making upstart warriors jump from the cliff.

Dr Kenneth Emory of the Bishop Museum did an extensive survey of Kaunolu in 1921 and counted 86 house sites, 35 stone shelters and a number of grave markings, pens and gardens. These days most of the sites are simply too overgrown with kiawe to even recognise.

There are a couple of ways to get there. The easiest is to go south from Lanai City down Manele Rd. At three-quarters of a mile past the nine-mile marker, there's a sharp bend in the road. Rather than follow Manele Rd as it bears left, go straight ahead onto a dirt pineapple road. As you continue you'll see a small farm and then the lighthouse

marking Kaunolu will come into view. While a few fishers manage to make it down to Kaunolu in 4WD vehicles, it's a very rough dirt road and you may have to park at the edge of the pineapple fields and walk down.

KAUMALAPAU HARBOR

Kaumalapau, Lanai's commercial harbour, is about seven miles west of town. Once past the airport, the main traffic on Kaumalapau Highway is from the big trucks that haul pineapples down to the harbour, where the containers are loaded onto barges and shipped to the Dole cannery in Honolulu. It's fairly interesting to watch, although the harbour is not set up for visitors.

Local fishing boats also moor there. You'll sometimes find people fishing from the boulder jetty for awa (milkfish), a good eating fish and a common catch in the bay.

Scuba divers also use the bay, as the deep waters at Kaumalapau are extremely clear.

As along most of the south-west coast, Kaumalapau has sheer coastal cliffs.

NORTH-WEST LANAI

Polihua Rd (Awalua Highway) is a dirt road that continues from the end of Fraser Ave in Lanai City to Garden of the Gods and Polihua Beach. To get there go north up Fraser Ave and shortly after it turns to dirt turn right at the fence onto Polihua Rd. The dirt road passes through old pineapple fields for about 3½ miles, and then continues another two miles before reaching Garden of the Gods.

The section leading up to Garden of the Gods is a fairly well-maintained road that usually takes about 20 minutes from town. To get from Garden of the Gods to Polihua Beach is another matter. The road down to the beach is very rocky and narrow. Depending on when it's last been graded it could take anywhere from 20 minutes to an hour.

Kanepuu

The Nature Conservancy manages 462 acres at Kanepuu, a diverse native dryland forest that is the last of its kind.

Native plants include iliahi (Hawaiian sandalwood), olopua (an olive), lama (in the persimmon family), a morning glory, a native gardenia and fragrant vines of *maile* and *huehue*.

Dryland forests once covered 80% of Lanai and were also common on the leeward slopes of other Hawaiian islands, but feral goats and cattle did them in. Only this one remains. Credit goes to the naturalist and former ranch manager George Munro, who realised the need to protect this ecosystem and fenced hoofed animals out in the 1920s.

The Kanepuu Preserve is about six miles north-west of Lanai City. Castle & Cooke retains title to the land, but has given the Nature Conservancy an easement to the forest in perpetuity.

Garden of the Gods

There's no garden at Garden of the Gods but rather a dry and barren landscape of strange wind-sculptured rocks in rich shades of ochre, pinks and browns. The colours change with the light and are much nicer and gentler in the early morning and late afternoon.

How godly they appear depends on what you're looking for. Some people just see rocks, while others find the formations hauntingly beautiful.

Polihua Beach

Polihua Beach, on the north-western tip of the island, is a broad, 1½-mile-long white-sand beach. It has a great view of the entire south coast of Molokai. Though it's a gorgeous beach, strong winds kicking up the sand often make it uncomfortable and water conditions are treacherous all year round.

Polihua means 'eggs in the bosom' and refers to the green sea turtles that used to nest there en masse. After a long hiatus the now endangered turtles are beginning to return.

MUNRO TRAIL

Munro Trail is an 8½-mile jeep road that can either be hiked or driven in a 4WD vehicle. On foot, it's a full day's hike but if you're driving it takes about 1½ hours. While the road is in pretty good condition, drivers will need to watch out for sheer drops. The road can be dangerous when wet.

To start, head north on Hwy 44, the road to Shipwreck Beach. About a mile past the Lodge at Koele turn right onto the paved road that leads to a cemetery half a mile down.

Munro Trail starts at the left of the cemetery. It goes through sections planted with eucalyptus and up along the ridge where it's fern-draped and studded with Norfolk pines.

The trail is named after the naturalist George Munro, who planted the trees along this trail and around the island to provide a watershed. He selected species that draw moisture from the clouds and fog, both of which are fairly common in the high country (more so in the afternoon than in the morning).

Before the Munro Trail was upgraded to a jeep road it was a footpath. It's along this trail that islanders tried to hide from Kamehameha when he went on a rampage in 1778. Hookio Battleground, where Lanaians made their last stand, is just above Hookio Gulch, about 2½ miles in.

The trail passes a series of deep ravines that run down the eastern flank of the mountain. To the west are vistas of endless pineapple fields, in tidy ribbon-like rows.

The trail passes Lanaihale – at 3370 feet, the highest point on Lanai. On a clear day you can see all the inhabited Hawaiian islands except Kauai and Niihau from various points along the route. The trail ends in a pineapple field on Hoike Rd.

Hoike Rd is a little more than 1½ miles south of the intersection of Manele Rd and Kaumalapau Highway. Though it's not marked, it's obviously one of the big daddies of the pineapple roads.

Luahiwa Petroglyphs

The Luahiwa Petroglyphs are carved onto about two dozen boulders spread over three acres. This is Lanai's highest concentration of petroglyphs and includes a wide variety of forms thought to have been carved during different eras. There are lots of dogs in various poses, linear and triangular human figures and a canoe or two. Unfortunately many of the petroglyphs are quite weathered.

It's a little challenging to get there, but basically you turn onto Hoike Rd and then head for the water tower on the ridge. The boulders are near the head of a ravine north of the road, below the trees.

Kahoolawe

Kahoolawe is the uninhabited island seven miles off the south-west coast of Maui. It was used exclusively by the US military as a bombing target from WW II until 1990. While the bombing has now stopped the fate of the island remains up in the air.

The channel between Lanai and Kahoolawe, as well as the westernmost point of Kahoolawe itself, is named Kealaikahiki, meaning 'pathway to Tahiti'. When ancient voyagers made the journey between Hawaii and Tahiti they lined up their canoes at this departure point.

More than 500 archaeological sites have been identified on Kahoolawe. They include several heiaus and many koa shrines and kuula stones dedicated to the gods of fishermen. Puu Moiwi, in the centre of the island, has one of Hawaii's largest ancient adze quarries.

In 1981 Kahoolawe was added to the National Register of Historic Places as an archaeological area. For nearly a decade the island had the distinction of being the only such historic area being bombed.

Kahoolawe has become a symbol of the separation of Hawaiians from their land and a focal point in the growing Hawaiian rights movement.

GEOGRAPHY

Kahoolawe is 11 miles long and six miles wide, and has a land area of 45 sq miles. With the help of a vivid imagination, its shape can be seen as a crouching lion facing eastward.

A ridge runs diagonally across the island and the terrain is gently sloping. The highest point is the 1477-foot Lua Makika, at the site of the caldera that formed the island. It's a dry arid island with only 10 to 20 inches of rainfall annually.

Because of the windblown red dust on the island, Kahoolawe often appears to have a pink tinge when viewed from Maui, particularly in the afternoons when the winds pick up. At night it's pitch black, devoid of any light.

HISTORY
Prisoners & Opium

Since ancient times Kahoolawe has been under the rule of Maui.

From 1830 to 1848 Kaulana Bay, on the island's northern side, was used as a place of exile for Mauian men accused of petty crimes. (Female outcasts were sent to Kaena Point on the north-western tip of Lanai.)

Kahoolawe proved to be less of a 'prison isle' than intended. In 1841 some of the prisoners managed to swim to the Makena area of Maui where they stole food and canoes and paddled back with their booty. Later raids included one to Lanai where they picked up female prisoners and brought them back to Kahoolawe.

Kahoolawe's secluded south-western side was used for decades by smugglers bringing in illegal Chinese opium. To avoid detection, they'd unload their caches at Hanakanaea Bay (commonly known as Smugglers Bay) on arrival from China and come back later in small fishing boats to pick them up.

In recent times Smugglers Bay has served as the site of the US military base camp.

Overgrazing

Kahoolawe was once a green and forested island. It is now largely barren and pili grass and kiawe trees are the main forces in keeping the dry red soil from blowing away completely.

The first attempt at ranching was in 1858 by R C Wyllie, the Scotsman who developed a sugar plantation at Princeville in Kauai. Wyllie leased the entire island of Kahoolawe from the Territory of Hawaii, but the sheep he brought over were diseased and the venture failed. Those sheep that survived were left to roam freely, causing serious damage to native plants.

Over the years, the territory granted a series of leases to other ranchers. Cattle were first brought over around 1880 and sheep were also tried again. Land mismanagement was the order of the day.

By the early 1900s, feral goats, pigs and sheep had dug up, rooted out and chewed off so much of the vegetation that Kahoolawe was largely a dust bowl.

Kahoolawe Ranch

The most successful ranching operation on Kahoolawe was run from 1918 to 1941 by Angus MacPhee, former manager of Maui's Ulupalakua Ranch.

When MacPhee got his lease from the territory in 1918, Kahoolawe was overrun with goats and looked like a wasteland. MacPhee rounded up 13,000 goats which he sold on Maui and built a fence across the width of the entire island to keep the remaining goats at one end. He then brought in large redwood tanks to store water and planted grasses and groundcover.

Once the land was again green, MacPhee

created Kahoolawe Ranch Company in partnership with Harry Baldwin, a sugar plantation owner. Cattle were brought over and raised for the Honolulu market. Ranching Kahoolawe was not easy, but MacPhee was the only one to make it profitable.

Inez MacPhee Ashdown, Angus' daughter, has written her story in *Kahoolawe* (Topgallant Publishing Co, 1979). The book includes legends of Kahoolawe, as told to her by native Hawaiians, as well as ranch history.

A Bombing Target

In 1939, Kahoolawe Ranch subleased part of the island to the US Army for bombing practice and moved their cattle and ranchhands over to Maui.

After the bombing of Pearl Harbor in 1941, the military took all of Kahoolawe and began bombing the entire island. Ranch buildings and water cisterns were reduced to rubble.

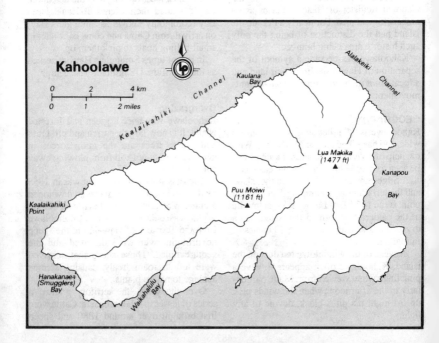

Of all the fighting that took place during WW II, Kahoolawe was the most bombed island in the Pacific – even though the 'enemy' never fired upon it.

After the war, civilians were forbidden from returning to Kahoolawe. MacPhee was never compensated for his losses.

In 1953 a presidential decree gave the navy official jurisdiction over the island. It stated that when Kahoolawe was no longer 'needed' that the live ordnances would be cleaned up and the island returned to the Territory of Hawaii.

Kahoolawe Movement

In the mid-1960s Hawaii politicians began petitioning the federal government to return Kahoolawe to the state. In 1976 a small group of Hawaiians set out in boats and occupied the island in an attempt to attract greater attention to the bombings. There were a series of occupations, some lasting more than a month.

During one of the 1977 crossings, group members George Helm and Kimo Mitchell mysteriously disappeared in the waters off Kahoolawe. Helm had been an inspirational Hawaiian-rights activist and with his death the movement Protect Kahoolawe Ohana sprang up. Helm's vision of turning Kahoolawe into a sanctuary of Hawaiian culture and identity became widespread among islanders.

In June 1977 two group members, Walter Ritte Jr and Richard Sawyer, were tried for trespassing on Kahoolawe and sentenced to six months in jail.

In a letter to President Jimmy Carter asking that the two men be pardoned, Daniel Inouye, US Senator from Hawaii, wrote:

...it was a form of protest against, what was to them, the unconscionable desecration of the land by the Navy's continued bombing of Kahoolawe. *Aloha aina*, love for the land, is an important part of the Native Hawaiian religion and culture...Kahoolawe has become a symbol of the resurgence of the Hawaiian people, a movement formulating for many Hawaiians a renewed respect for their culture and their history.

Kahoolawe Today

In 1980, in a court-sanctioned consent decree, the Navy reached an agreement with Protect Kahoolawe Ohana which allows the Ohana regular access to the island.

It also required the Navy to preserve archaeological sites, eradicate goats and control soil erosion.

Though the bombing continued, the decree restricted the Navy from using live ordnances on part of the island and from bombing historic sites. In 1982 the Ohana began to celebrate makahiki on Kahoolawe. The annual observances honour Lono, god of agriculture and peace.

Maui County, of which Kahoolawe is a part, adopted a planning document in 1982 calling for a 20-year phase-out of the military and development of Kahoolawe as an historical and cultural site, with Protect Kahoolawe Ohana as the stewards of the land. The Navy refused to recognise the document.

In what many Hawaiians saw as the ultimate insult to their heritage, the US military offered Kahoolawe as a bombing target to foreign nations during biennial Pacific Rim exercises. The exercises brought recognition of what was happening in Kahoolawe into a broader arena. An international movement against the bombing by environmentalist and union groups in New Zealand, Australia, Japan and the UK resulted in those countries withdrawing from the Kahoolawe exercises. With only the US and Canada willing to participate, the exercises stopped.

In the late 1980s Hawaii's first Hawaiian governor, John Waihee, and other state politicians became more outspoken in their demands that Kahoolawe be returned to Hawaiians. In October 1990 as Hawaii's two US senators, Daniel Inouye and Daniel Akaka, were preparing a congressional bill to stop the bombing, President Bush issued an order to halt military activities. The senators' bill, which became law the next month, requires the island to be cleared of munitions and restored to a pre-war condition. It also established a federally funded Kahoolawe Conveyance Commission to prepare recommendations on terms for the conveyance of the island to the state of Hawaii.

One major obstacle that remains is the cleaning up of live ordnance from the island, which federal studies estimate may cost $400 million. Proposals for the island's future range from establishing a marine sanctuary to making the island the centre for a new Hawaiian nation.

GETTING THERE & AWAY
There's no public access to the island. Unless you're a member of the Ohana, or on official business, it is nearly impossible to get to Kahoolawe.

Occasionally on weekends the Navy, which still oversees the island, opens the offshore waters surrounding Kahoolawe for fishing, boating and diving. The announcement is always accompanied by a statement that 'the US government will not be responsible for property damage, personal injury or death resulting from unexploded ordnance in the area'.

Kauai

If you're looking for lush scenery, Kauai is a great choice – the island is so richly green that it's nicknamed 'The Garden Island'.

Kauai is the oldest of the main Hawaiian land masses and arose from the sea as a high, smooth island. Over time heavy rains have eroded deep valleys, while pounding waves and falling sea levels have cut steep cliffs.

Kauai's central volcanic peak, Mt Waialeale, acts like a magnet drawing rain. The water flows down, feeding seven rivers, including Hawaii's only navigable one.

An impressive north-to-south rift slices the western end of the island, creating the Waimea Canyon.

The North Shore is lushly mountainous, with waterfalls, beautiful beaches and stream-fed valleys planted with taro. The north-west coast is lined by the steeply fluted Na Pali sea cliffs.

Movie makers looking for scenery bordering on fantasy have often found it in Kauai. *South Pacific* and *Raiders of the Lost Ark* were both filmed on Kauai's North Shore. Honopu Valley on the Na Pali Coast was the jungle home of King Kong.

Kauai is the least developed of the four major islands and most of its interior is mountainous forest reserve.

The Alakai Swamp is poised on a high, cliff-bound plateau, about 1000 feet below Mt Waialeale. There, clouds and mist that rarely lift promote a unique ecosystem where trees grow knee high.

Kauai is dry and sunny on its southern and western sides, with long stretches of white-sand beaches. Sugar cane fields cover

STOP PRESS

On 11 September 1992 Hurricane Iniki, the most powerful storm to strike Hawaii in a century, made a direct hit on Kauai. Packing gusts of 165 mph, Iniki felled thousands of trees, levelled sugar cane fields and caused serious damage to an estimated 50% of the buildings on Kauai. (To get a sense of how strong Iniki was, Hawaii's worst storm previously was Hurricane Iwa, which tore into Kauai in November 1982 with gusts of 117 mph.)

While some of the structures destroyed by Iniki were ageing wooden buildings, others were oceanfront wings of beach resorts that were battered by 30-foot waves. Most homes throughout the island had windows blown out, many lost roofs and others were simply laid to waste. A combination of powerful gusts and abrupt changes in atmospheric pressure caused some buildings to literally shatter as if hit by a bomb blast. Although nearly 100 people were injured by flying debris, quite amazingly only two people were killed.

As this book was going to press, Kauai was still in the initial stage of recovery. Roads were open, electricity was partially restored, a few phone lines were coming back on line and insurance agents and building inspectors were busy making damage assessments. Two areas hit particularly hard were Poipu on the South Shore and Princeville on the North Shore. However, even in these locales some hotels were open after the storm (housing relief workers) and many more were expected to open in the first quarter of 1993. A few of the most seriously damaged hotels won't be operating again until late 1993.

One spot of good news for visitors is that in the Wailua area most of the B&Bs weathered the storm without serious damage and the hostel, which did receive some damage, expects to be operating again early in 1993.

The visitors' industry has established a new toll-free number (☎ (800) 262-1400) to coordinate information about Kauai and answer questions. In addition, if you have a touch-tone phone and access to a fax machine, you can get a faxed updated listing of the status of Kauai accommodation by calling (800) OK-FAX-ME from the US mainland and (808) 941-3333 from elsewhere. ■

large portions of the island just inland from the coast in a semicircle from the north-east to the west.

Kauai's main attraction is its stunning natural beauty. There are hiking trails into some incredible places.

ORIENTATION

Kauai is roughly circular. A belt road runs three-quarters of the way around the island, ending at Haena in the north and Polihale in the west.

Most travellers arrive at the main airport in Lihue, the county capital, on the east coast. From Lihue the road runs north past the heiaus and waterfalls of Wailua and the town of Kapaa. It continues up to the sea-bird sanctuary of Kilauea, Princeville resort and the scenic North Shore communities of Hanalei and Haena. The road ends at the eastern edge of the Na Pali cliffs.

South of Lihue the road detours down to the resort beaches of Poipu before continuing west to Waimea. There, one road goes west to the arid Barking Sands region and another heads north along the Waimea Canyon into Kokee State Park.

Facts

HISTORY

Kauai was probably settled between 500 and 700 AD by Polynesians who migrated from the Marquesas Islands. Archaeological finds, including identical ring-shaped poi pounding stones found both in Kauai and the Marquesas, support the connection.

While in Hawaiian lore there are no direct references to the Marquesan culture, Kauai is often referred to as the home of a race of little people called menehunes. Legend after legend tells of happy Disneyland-type elves coming down from the mountains to produce great engineering works in stone.

It seems likely that when the first wave of Tahitians arrived in about 1000 AD they conquered and subjugated the Marquesans, forcing them into slavery to build the temples, irrigation ditches and fishponds now attributed to the menehunes.

The Tahitian term for 'outcast' is *manahune*. And the diminutive social status the Marquesans had in the eyes of their conquerors may have given rise to tales of a dwarf-size race.

The menehunes may have created the temples, but the Tahitian settlers created the legends. Fine stonework remains, but the true identity of Kauai's 'little people' is lost.

During the second wave of Tahitian migration, around the 12th century, a high chief named Moikeha arrived at Wailua with a fleet of double-hulled canoes. There, in the royal court, Moikeha was received by Kauai's ageing alii-nui (high chief), Puna.

Puna gave his daughter to Moikeha in marriage and upon Puna's death Moikeha became the alii-nui of Kauai. Moikeha introduced taro and sweet potatoes to Kauai and sent his son Kila back to Tahiti to fetch the pahu hula, a sharkskin drum for use in hula temples. This type of drum is still used in hula performances today.

Early Settlements

Kauai is the most isolated of the major islands, lying 72 miles from Oahu, its nearest neighbour. It was never conquered by another Hawaiian island and its history is one of autonomy.

Kauai was settled most intensively along river valleys near the coast, such as at Wailua, Waimea and Hanalei. Even valleys that were difficult to reach, like Kalalau and Nualolo on the Na Pali Coast, had sizeable settlements. When winter seas prevented canoes from landing on the northern shore, trails down precipitous ridges and sennit-rope ladders provided access.

When Captain Cook landed on Kauai in 1778 he estimated the island had 50 villages with a total population of about 30,000. Missionaries in the 1820s estimated it to be closer to 10,000. Historians tend to side with the missionaries and discredit Cook's estimates, but considering the diseases Cook's men left behind, it's possible both were correct.

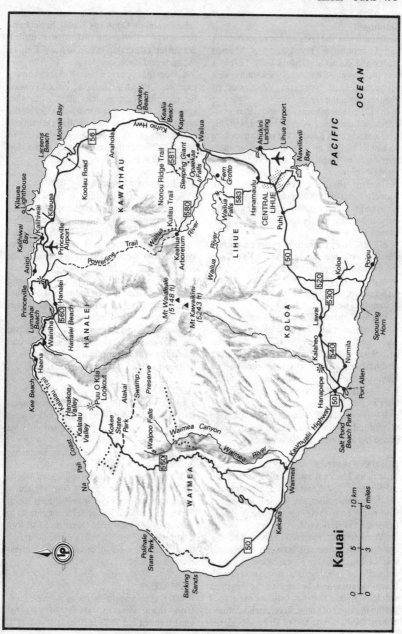

Kauai

Kaumualii

Kaumualii was the last chief to reign over an independent Kauai. Though he was a shrewd leader and Kauai's warriors were fierce, it was the power of Kaumualii's kahunas that protected him from the advances of Kamehameha the Great.

In 1796 Kamehameha, who had conquered all the other islands, sailed with his warriors towards Kauai. A mysterious storm suddenly kicked up at sea, forcing him to turn back to Oahu, and he never reached Kauai's shores.

During the next few years, both Kamehameha and Kaumualii continued to prepare for war by gathering foreign weaponry and trying to ally foreign ships to their cause.

In 1804 Kamehameha was once again on the shores of Oahu ready to attack Kauai. On the eve of the invasion an epidemic of what was probably cholera struck the island of Oahu, decimating his warriors and forcing yet another delay.

While Kamehameha's numerically superior forces had Kaumualii unnerved, Kaumualii's uncanny luck had a similar effect on Kamehameha. In 1810 they reached an agreement that recognised Kaumualii as the alii-nui of Kauai but ceded the island of Kauai to the Kingdom of Hawaii.

It was essentially a truce, and the plotting continued, with Kaumualii never fully accepting Kamehameha's suzerainty.

Russian Presence

In January 1815 a Russian ship was wrecked off Waimea, and Kaumualii confiscated the cargo. In November, the Russian-American Company sent their agent, Georg Anton Schaeffer, to retrieve it.

When Schaeffer arrived in Hawaii he saw opportunity in the rift between Kaumualii and Kamehameha. In Kauai he exceeded his authority by entering into an agreement with Kaumualii in which he claimed the Russians would provide a ship and military assistance for the invasion of Oahu. In return Kaumualii offered the Russians half of Oahu plus all the sandalwood on Oahu and Kauai. In September 1816 Hawaiian labourers under Schaeffer's direction began to build forts in Waimea and Hanalei.

Later that year when Russian naval explorer Otto von Kotzebue visited Hawaii he informed Kamehameha that the Russian government did not endorse Schaeffer's alliance. Kamehameha, tired of all the scheming, ordered Kaumualii to kick the Russians out. In May 1817 Schaeffer was escorted to his ship and forced to leave Kauai.

The End of a Kingdom

When Kamehameha died in 1819 he was succeeded by his son Liholiho, who didn't trust Kaumualii's loyalties any more than his father had. In 1822 Liholiho set off for Kauai in an 83-foot luxury schooner he had purchased from Western traders in exchange for sandalwood.

In Kauai he tricked Kaumualii into going out for a cruise. He then kidnapped him and took him to Oahu where Kaumualii was forced to marry Kamehameha's widow, Kaahumanu. In the grand scheme of royal design this served to bring Kaumualii into the fold. When Kaumualii passed away in 1824, so too did the kingdom of Kauai.

GEOGRAPHY

Kauai is shaped like a slightly compressed ball. It is 33 miles wide and 25 miles from north to south. The highest elevation is Mt Kawaikini at 5243 feet.

The fourth largest of the islands, Kauai has an area of 558 sq miles.

Kauai arose as a single volcano of which Mt Waialeale is the eastern rim. Moisture-laden trade winds blow into the deep North Shore valleys which channel the winds up to the top of Mt Waialeale. Near its 5148-foot summit cooler temperatures cause the moisture to condense, creating the heaviest rainfall on earth.

CLIMATE

Kauai's temperature varies more with location than season. Average coastal temperatures are 70°F in February and 77°F in August. At Kalalau Beach the temperature seldom drops below 60°F, while a few thousand feet above at Kokee State Park it dips into the 30s during winter nights. Kokee averages a crisp 55°F in February and 65°F in August.

Kauai's average annual rainfall is about 40 inches but variances are extreme. Waimea in the south averages 21 inches while Princeville in the north averages 85 inches. And Mt Waialeale in the swampy interior averages a whopping 486 inches, a world record.

Summer trade winds keep the humidity from becoming oppressive and bring in showers.

Winter is far less predictable. It's quite possible to have fairly continuous downpours for a week at a time in midwinter. Then again, it might be all blue skies and calm seas. We've experienced both.

FLORA & FAUNA

Kauai has the largest number of native bird species in Hawaii. It is the only major island free of mongoose, which prey upon the eggs of ground-nesting birds.

The greatest concentration of Kauai's native forest bird species is found in the remote Alakai Swamp. Many of those species are endangered, some having fewer than 100 birds remaining.

The Kauai oo, the last of four remaining species of Hawaiian honeyeaters, was thought to be extinct when a nest with two chicks was discovered in Alakai Swamp in 1971. The call of the oo was last heard in 1987 – that of a single male.

Alakai Swamp is unique in that it has 10 times as many native birds as introduced. (Elsewhere in Hawaii introduced birds outnumber the natives many times over.) Not only is the swamp inhospitable to exotic bird species, but due to its high elevation it is one of the few places in Hawaii where mosquitoes that transmit avian diseases do not flourish.

The ao, or Newell's shearwater, is a threatened sea bird that once nested on all the major Hawaiian islands; today it nests almost exclusively in the mountains of Kauai. The ao digs earthen burrows and lays just one egg each year. It has a call that sounds like a donkey braying.

The ao, which flies only between dusk and dawn, often fails to see utility wires strung across its path to the sea. Despite some success in a forestry programme that recovers some of the many birds that crash-land, the Sierra Club Legal Defense Fund estimates that over 1000 birds die in this way each year. They are preparing a lawsuit to block the electric company from stringing wires across Kalihiwai River Valley, one of the last clear valleys in Kauai.

Of Hawaii's two native mammals, the hoary bat lives in Kokee State Park and the Hawaiian monk seal occasionally hauls out on Kauai's more isolated beaches. Wild pigs, goats and black-tailed deer are non-native mammals that are hunted.

The most common tree in Kauai forests is the ohia lehua. Koa, guava, kiawe and kukui trees are also plentiful.

GOVERNMENT

Kauai County is composed of the islands of

Honeyeater

Kauai and Niihau. There is an elected mayor with a four-year term and a seven-member county council with two-year terms. Mayor JoAnn Yukimura, voted into her second term in 1990, ran on a pro-environment, controlled-growth platform.

ECONOMY

Kauai's unemployment rate is 4%; the labour force is 28,000. The service industry, including hotels, accounts for 33% of all workers. It is followed by wholesale and retail trade at 23%, government at 12% and agriculture at 5%.

The sugar industry still cultivates 38,000 acres on Kauai, but mechanisation has streamlined its labour force to 1000 employees. Other sizeable crops grown commercially are guava and taro. Attempts to diversify as sugar production declines have resulted in the introduction of new crops including seed corn, sunflower seed, macadamia nuts and coffee.

POPULATION & PEOPLE

According to the 1990 US census, the population of Kauai is 50,947. People of part-Hawaiian ethnicity make up 24% of Kauai's population, followed by Filipino (22%), Japanese (21%) and Caucasian (18%).

TOURIST INFORMATION

The Hawaii Visitors Bureau (☎ 245-3971), Lihue Plaza Building, Suite 207, 3016 Umi St, Lihue, HI 96766, is open from 8 am to 4.30 pm Monday to Friday. You can get a 'vacation planning kit' by calling (800) AH-KAUAI toll free from the USA.

Free tourist magazines such as *This Week Kauai*, *Spotlight Kauai* and *Kauai Beach Press* can be picked up at the airport, hotels and major shopping centres. All are loaded with ads and activity information.

GENERAL INFORMATION
Official Kauai

Kauai's flower is the mokihana, from a small tree of the citrus family found only on Kauai. Tiny anise-scented mokihana berries are

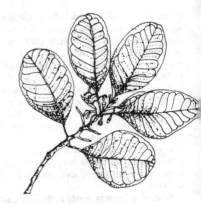

Mokihana flower

commonly combined with twists of fragrant maile leaves as a ceremonial lei. Kauai's colour is purple.

Money

Bank of Hawaii has branches in central Lihue, Kapaa, Princeville, Hanalei, Hanapepe and Waimea. The Lihue branch has an automatic teller machine. First Hawaiian Bank has automatic teller machines (Cirrus, Plus System) in its Lihue, Kapaa, Koloa and Waimea branches.

There are Western Union money transfer stations at the Star supermarket in the Kukui Grove Center in Lihue and at Princeville.

Media

Kauai's main newspaper, the *Garden Island* (☎ 245-3681), Box 231, Lihue, HI 96766, is published Monday to Friday, with a Saturday/Sunday weekend edition. The *Kauai Times* (☎ 245-8825), Box 3272, Lihue, HI 96766, is published on Wednesdays and Fridays. Both newspapers, as well as the Honolulu daily papers, can be purchased at stores all around Kauai.

Three four-colour feature magazines dedicated to Kauai are published on the island and can be purchased at bookstores or by subscription. They are: *The Sandwich Islands Magazine* and *Kauai Style*, both by

Top: Taro fields, Hanalei Valley, Kauai
Left: Na Pali cliffs from the Awaawapuhi Trail, Kauai
Right: Kilauea lighthouse, Kauai

Top: Hanalei Bay, Kauai
Left: Kalalau Valley, Kauai
Right: Waipoo Falls, Waimea Canyon, Kauai

Resort Publications, and *Kauai Magazine*, by Welcome Publications of Kauai.

Kauai has two AM and two FM radio stations. Commercial TV stations are relayed from Honolulu. KVIC shows a 90-minute video of Kauai sights 24 hours a day on cable Channel 3 or 12.

Bookshops

The Waldenbooks chain, which has travel, Hawaiiana and general interest books, has stores in the Kukui Grove Center in Lihue, the Kauai Village shopping centre in Waipouli and the Coconut Marketplace in Wailua. The Kauai Museum in Lihue sells Hawaiiana books.

Libraries

There are public libraries in Lihue, Hanapepe, Kapaa, Koloa and Waimea.

Weather

The National Weather Service has recorded local weather information (☎ 245-6001) and marine forecasts (☎ 245-3564).

KUAI radio (720 AM) broadcasts beach and surf reports and at 7.25 and 8.25 am reports weather conditions at Kokee State Park. To find out where the surf's up, dial KUAI's surf hotline (☎ 335-3611).

Emergency

Dial 911 for police, ambulance and fire department.

The main hospital is Wilcox Memorial Hospital (☎ 245-1100), 3420 Kuhio Hwy, Lihue. Kauai Veterans Memorial Hospital (☎ 338-9431), 4643 Waimea Canyon Drive, Waimea, is smaller but does have a hyperbaric chamber for divers who get the bends. Both hospitals have 24-hour emergency room services.

The local help-line (☎ 245-3411) provides crisis intervention services.

ACTIVITIES
Swimming

There are respectable beaches all around Kauai. For most water activities except surfing, the North Shore is tops in summer, the South Shore in winter.

Hanalei Bay is the island's most popular summer beach, while Poipu, on the South Shore, has a string of beautiful white-sand beaches that swimmers flock to in winter.

To the west, Salt Pond Beach Park is a popular family beach with protected swimming. Farther west, Kekaha, Barking Sands and Polihale have expansive white-sand beaches, though with open ocean and often treacherous water conditions.

The beaches around Lihue and Kapaa are generally not great for swimming. The safest bet is Lydgate Beach in Wailua, a large family park with a boulder retaining wall that creates a protected year-round swimming pool.

Donkey Beach, north of Kapaa, is a fine secluded beach hidden beyond a sugar cane field. Both Donkey Beach and the more spectacular Secret Beach in Kilauea are unofficial nudist beaches.

Many of Kauai's beaches have rough water conditions at various times of the year and caution is warranted. Kauai has an average of nine drownings a year, about half of those on the North Shore between October and May.

There are year-round lifeguards at Salt Pond Beach, Poipu Beach Park, Hanalei Bay, Kee Beach and Wailua Beach.

The county has two swimming pools free to the public. The pool in Kapaa Beach Park (☎ 822-3842) is open from 10 am to 5 pm daily, except on Wednesdays and Fridays when it opens at noon. The pool in Waimea (☎ 338-1271), next to the high school, is open from 10 am to 5 pm on Mondays, Tuesdays, Wednesdays, Saturdays and Sundays.

The pool at Kauai High School in Lihue is open to the public from 3 to 6 pm on Mondays, Wednesdays and Fridays and from noon to 5 pm on weekends.

Surfing

Kauai has 330 named surfing sites. Generally the best surfing is on the north coast in winter, the south in summer and the east during transitional swells.

Hanalei Bay is a very good spot for North Shore surfing, as well as boogie boarding and bodysurfing. Tunnels and Cannons are two other popular North Shore surf spots.

The area around the Sheraton at Poipu Beach is a top summer surf spot. Pakalas, which is near Makaweli, and Majors Bay at Barking Sands are two West Side favourites.

When the breaks are on the east coast, Kealia and the Coco Palms area can have good surf conditions.

Surfboards can be rented in numerous places.

Kayak Kauai, in the town centres of Hanalei (☎ 826-9844) and Kapaa (☎ 822-9179), rents surfboards for $15/60 a day/week and gives surfing lessons for $25 per hour ($12.50 for each additional person).

Hanalei Surf Company (☎ 826-9000), in the Hanalei Center in Hanalei, gives 1½-hour introductory surfing lessons for $45, which includes use of the surfboard for the rest of the day. They also rent surfboards for $15 a day, $65 a week.

Margo Oberg, a former World Cup surfing champion, gives surfing lessons at Poipu Beach. Arrangements can be made at the beach hut (☎ 742-6411) at the Kiahuna Plantation Resort.

Kauai Sea Sports (☎ 742-9303) in Poipu also gives lessons and rents surfboards. Surfboards cost $10/25 an hour/day from their beach huts on Poipu Beach, but are cheaper from their shop at Poipu Plaza.

Snorkelling & Boogie Boarding

On the North Shore, Kee Beach has good snorkelling most of the year. Nearby Tunnels Beach has excellent snorkelling in summer, but be cautious of currents.

On the South Shore, the section of Poipu Beach in front of the Stouffer Waiahai Beach Hotel is one of Kauai's best snorkelling spots for beginners. Another good snorkelling spot in Poipu is at the Koloa Landing. On the West Side, you can try Salt Pond Beach Park in Hanapepe.

For boogie boarding, Brennecke's in Poipu is Kauai's hottest spot, while on the North Shore Hanalei Bay attracts the biggest crowds.

Snorkel sets and boogie boards can be rented at lots of places. Most of the beach huts at the resort hotels charge about $5 an hour, while outside shops are much more reasonable.

Kayak Kauai, in the town centres of Hanalei (☎ 826-9844) and Kapaa (☎ 822-9179), rents snorkel sets for $8/20 a day/week, boogie boards for $6/25. It also gives boogie board lessons for $20 an hour.

Hanalei Surf Company (☎ 826-9000), in the Hanalei Center in Hanalei, rents snorkel sets for $8/34 a day/week, boogie boards for $7 to $10 a day, $30 to $42 a week.

Also in Hanalei, Sand People (☎ 826-6981) at the Hanalei Trader building and Pedal & Paddle (☎ 826-9069) at Ching Young Village rent snorkel sets or boogie boards for $7 or $8 a day, $25 a week.

Sea Sage (☎ 822-3841), on Hwy 56 in Kapaa centre, rents snorkel sets or boogie boards for $5 a day, $15 a week.

Snorkel Bob's, (☎ 245-9433), 4480 Ahukini Rd, Lihue, rents snorkel sets for $15 a week.

In Poipu, Kauai Sea Sports (☎ 742-9303) in the Poipu Plaza rents snorkel sets for $8/20 a day/week and boogie boards for $8/25.

Windsurfing

Beginner windsurfers usually start off at Anini Beach on the North Shore or at Nawiliwili Bay near the Westin. Tunnels Beach in Haena and Salt Pond Beach in Hanapepe are for the more advanced.

Hanalei Sailboards, (☎ 826-9000), Box 496, Hanalei, HI 96714, in the Hanalei

Center on Hwy 560, offers three-hour beginner classes at 9 am and 1 pm daily at Anini Beach for $60, including equipment. After two classes you can be certified. Standard boards and rigs cost $45 a day, $235 a week.

Sea Star Kauai (☎ 245-3732), opposite Kauai Community College in Puhi, rents boards for $50 a day, $200 a week.

Diving

Popular summer diving spots on the North Shore include Kee Beach, Tunnels and Cannons, all shore dives in Haena. Cannons is particularly special; it's a wall dive, with crevices and lava tubes sheltering all sorts of marine life.

Koloa Landing and Poipu Beach Park in Poipu are easy beach dives. On those rare days when kona winds blow from the south, east-side diving is good and Ahukini Landing becomes a favoured site. There are a number of offshore boat dives as well, including Niihau.

Dive shops give a free introductory scuba lesson in hotel pools at the Stouffer Waiohai and the Sheraton Kauai in Poipu, and the Coconut Beach Hotel in Wailua. For information check the hotel beach huts.

If you'd like to get underwater without loading down with dive equipment, you might consider snuba, in which you breathe through an air hose attached to a tank that floats on the water surface. Reefcomber Snuba (☎ 742-1007) offers snuba from Lawai Beach in Poipu for $49.

Kauai Sea Sports (☎ 742-9303), at Poipu Plaza in Poipu, is a personable dive operation. They take up to six divers out on small boats. An introductory dive at Koloa Landing costs $70 for one tank, $105 for two. Two-tank boat dives cost $85, one-tank night dives cost $65 and a three-day certification course is $295.

Sea Sage Diving Center (☎ 822-3841, (800) 659-3483), Kapaa Trade Center, 4-1378 Kuhio Hwy, Kapaa, HI 96746, has been around the longest – since 1973. They do two-tank boat dives for $75, a one-tank night dive for $65 and take snorkellers along for $60. One-tank introductory dives cost

$75 from shore, $90 by boat. There's also an open water certification course for $305. Other dive shops are:

Fathom Five Divers, Box 907, Koloa, HI 96756 (☎ 742-6991)
Aquatics Kauai, 733 Kuhio Hwy, Kapaa, HI 96746 (☎ 822-9213, (800) 822-9422)
Dive Kauai, 976 Kuhio Hwy, Kapaa, HI 96746 (☎ 822-0452)
Tropical Pacific Divers, Box 1481, Kapaa, HI 96746 (☎ 822-3133)
Polynesian Divers, 3470 Paena Rd, Lihue, HI 96766 (☎ 245-8887)

Kayaking

Kauai, with all its waterways, has some of Hawaii's best kayaking.

One particularly pleasant outing is up the Hanalei River which goes through the wildlife refuge and meanders deep into Hanalei Valley. The riverfront is lushly beautiful and often canopied by overhanging trees. The round trip is about nine miles. Another popular but quite busy route is up the Wailua River to the Fern Grotto, which is about seven miles for the round trip. Each takes three to four hours. Kayaking up the Hanapepe, Waimea and Huleia rivers is also popular.

Kayak prices include paddles, life vests and a car rack set-up.

Kayak Kauai, in the centre of Hanalei (☎ 826-9844) and Kapaa (☎ 822-9179), rents two-person kayaks for $48 to $65 a day. A credit card is required. In the summer they lead 13-hour guided sea kayaking trips along the Na Pali Coast for $115, overnighters for $150 and five-day expeditions for $750, equipment included. Ocean kayak lessons cost $25 per hour. Both shops are open from 8 am to 6 pm daily.

Outfitters Kauai (☎ 742-9667) in the Poipu Plaza in Poipu rents one-person kayaks for $35 a day and two-person kayaks for $65 a day. Guided kayak trips cost $48 along the South Shore and $105 along the Na Pali Coast. They prefer credit cards, but will accept a cash deposit.

Pedal & Paddle (☎ 826-9069) in the Ching Young Village in Hanalei rents one-person kayaks for $35 a day, two-person kayaks for $60. It's open from 9 am to 5 pm daily.

Sea Sage (☎ 822-3841) in Kapaa rents one-person kayaks for $25 and $35 a day. Island Adventure (☎ 245-9662) leads guided kayak trips up the Huleia River past the Menehune Fish Pond and the Huleia National Wildlife Refuge for $37.

Hiking

Kauai has some excellent hikes. The best known is the 11-mile Kalalau Trail along the rugged Na Pali Coast.

Kokee State Park is a hiker's paradise with the largest concentration of trails on Kauai. Some lead to spectacular views of the Na Pali Coast. Others include short nature walks, mountain stream trails and a muddy trek through the unique Alakai Swamp.

South of Kokee, trails lead deep into Waimea Canyon, forking into abandoned river valleys.

In the Kapaa-Wailua area there's a trail that goes across the chest of the Sleeping Giant mountain. A couple of ridge trails start at Keahua Arboretum in Wailua, including the Powerline Trail, which goes all the way to Princeville.

These hikes are all detailed in their respective sections.

The Kauai division of the Sierra Club offers weekly guided hikes for $3. Hikes are usually on weekends and range from strolls up the Sleeping Giant to overnighters in Waimea Canyon. Advance registration is required. For a hike schedule, send a stamped, self-addressed envelope to the Sierra Club, Box 3412, Lihue, HI 96766. On Kauai, updated information can be obtained by calling Micco Godinez at Kayak Kauai (☎ 826-9844).

Horse Riding

CJM Country Stables (☎ 742-6096) has rides in the Mahaulepu Beach area. There's a three-hour breakfast ride for $65, a two-hour morning ride for $47, a 1½-hour afternoon ride for $40 and sometimes a one-hour afternoon ride for $27. The stables are in Poipu, 1½ miles down the dirt road past the Hyatt hotel. They're closed on Sundays.

Pooku Stables (☎ 826-6777), just past Princeville Airport, has trail rides on Princeville Ranch lands. The cost is $27 for one hour, $48 for two hours and $75 for a three-hour picnic ride to a waterfall. They're closed on Sundays.

Tennis

County courts are free and open to the public at the following locations: Wailua Houselots Park and Wailua Homesteads Park, Wailua; Hardy Street, near the convention centre, Lihue; opposite Kauai Community College, Puhi; Kapaa New Park, Kapaa; near the fire station, Koloa; on the corner of Hwy 550 and Hwy 50, Kekaha; Kalawai Park, Kalaheo; and near Hanapepe Stadium, Hanapepe.

Kauai Community College in Puhi and Waimea High School in Waimea also have courts open to public use.

There are four courts at the Aston Kauai Beach Villas in Lihue free for public use, although condo guests have priority.

Coco Palms Resort in Wailua had the first clay courts in Hawaii. Clay courts cost guests/non-guests $10/12 per person per day, while hard-surface courts cost $7/9.

At Stouffer's Poipu Beach and Waiohai hotels, it costs $8/15 a day for guests/non-guests to use the tennis courts and fitness centre facilities. Kiahuna Tennis Club (☎ 742-9533) in Poipu charges $9 per person per hour. The Hyatt Regency Kauai in Poipu charges $20 per court hour.

Hanalei Bay Resort in Princeville charges $15 per court per day for non-guests but is free to guests. The Princeville Tennis Garden (☎ 826-9823) charges players staying in Princeville $9 and non-guests $12 for the first hour, with additional court time free if space is available.

Most places that charge fees have pro shops, rentals, lighting and lessons.

Golf

Kauai has one municipal, one local course and a growing number of resort golf courses.

Kukuiolono Golf Course (☎ 332-9151) in

Kalaheo is a nine-hole par 36 course on an old estate with a grand hill-top view and an earthy appeal. Green fees are just $5 and pull carts cost $5 more.

Wailua Municipal Golf Course (☎ 245-2163) is a county-owned 18-hole par 72 course. It's a highly rated public course and very heavily played. Reservations for two people or more are taken up to a week in advance. Green fees are $18 on weekdays and $20 on weekends.

Kauai's resort courses are highly rated, with Princeville resort's Prince course and the Kauai Lagoons' Kiele course considered the island's best.

Princeville resort has two courses: the 18-hole par 72 Prince (☎ 826-5000) and the 27-hole par 36 Makai (☎ 826-3580). Green fees for the Makai course are $70 for guests staying in Princeville and $90 for non-guests. Fees for the Prince course are $85/110.

The Kauai Lagoons Golf Club (☎ 246-5061, (800) 634-6400) next to the Westin Kauai has two 18-hole par 72 courses. The Kiele course costs $115 for Westin guests, $145 for non-guests, and the Lagoons course costs $80/100 for guests/non-guests.

The Poipu Bay Resort Golf Course (☎ 742-9489), an 18-hole course at the Hyatt Regency Kauai, charges Hyatt guests $85, non-guests $115.

Also in Poipu, the Kiahuna Golf Club (☎ 742-9595), an 18-hole par 70 course run by the Sports Shinko Group, costs $78. After 2 pm golfers can play until sundown for $45.

Organised Tours

Polynesian Adventure Tours (☎ 246-0122) has full-day tours that include Wailua, Fern Grotto, Waimea, Koloa, Poipu, Waimea Canyon and the Kalalau Lookout for $52.50 with pick-up in Lihue or Wailua ($57.50 from Poipu, $65 from Princeville). The same tour costs $39 without Wailua and the Fern Grotto. Half-day North Shore tours that include Hanalei, Haena and Kee Beach cost $32.50.

Kauai Mountain Tours (☎ 245-7224), Box 3069, Lihue, HI 96766, has 4WD vans for trips that go down backroads from Kokee State Park.

Glider & Biplane Tradewinds Glider Rides (☎ 335-5086; (800) 245-4337) has a 15 to 20-minute glider ride over Hanapepe for $75 for one person and $90 for two. A mile-high 35-minute ride along the coast to Poipu and into Hanapepe Valley costs $125/150. The combined passenger weight limit is 340 pounds.

They also offer rides in a new biplane, WW II-style with an open cockpit. Three passengers sit side-by-side in front, with the pilot in the back. The cost for a 30-minute tour around Lihue, Hanapepe Canyon and Poipu is $75 per person, or $125 for one person alone.

Rides leave from Burns Field near Port Allen, though the office is in Hanapepe next to the Green Garden Restaurant. There are no rides on Saturdays and Mondays.

Helicopter Many wilderness hikers resent the intrusiveness of helicopters, and local environmentalists have successfully stopped their landings on Na Pali Coast beaches. However these 'Kauai mosquitoes' that are an irritant to people on the ground no doubt offer some pretty spectacular views as they swoop deep into Waimea Canyon, run along the Na Pali Coast and seek out hidden waterfalls.

More than a dozen helicopter companies offer flights around Kauai. The free tourist magazines advertise most of them and often have discount coupons.

The going rate is about $80 for a basic 30-minute tour zooming by the main sights. There's usually some sort of 'ultimate splendour' tour that can add on 20 minutes and run up another $50. Most of the helicopter offices are either in Lihue near the corner of Hwy 56 and Ahukini Rd or out past the airport. A few operate out of Port Allen.

Nuisance low buzzes are supposedly controlled. There's a helicopter hotline (☎ 826-1182) to take complaints, run by Kauai helicopter owners and operators.

Cruises Like the other islands, Kauai has its fair share of catamaran picnic sails, sunset cruises and the like. It also has something the other islands don't: the spectacular Na Pali Coast.

More than a dozen boat companies have cruises down the Na Pali Coast. Most use small craft that can hug the coast and enter sea caves. The typical tour lasts four hours, goes down the coast as far as Nualolo, includes snorkelling when seas are calm and costs about $75.

The smoothest rides are generally in the summer. For most of the winter the seas are too rough for near-shore activities such as sea-cave exploration, and for a large part of the winter it's simply too rough for the boats to go out at all. Some companies then switch to the calmer southern shore for snorkelling cruises and whale-watching tours.

The rising popularity of the tours and subsequent boom in the number of boats cruising the coast has resulted in some fairly complex environmental issues. For instance, the tiny dock at the mouth of the Hanalei River, where most of the boats leave from, isn't suitable for the volume of activity the operations are creating. Fuel discharges have fouled the water and residents are unhappy about losing what was once a serene river setting. The state, under pressure from environmental groups, is on the verge of finally regulating the business. It is likely that the number of operators will be reduced in the future, and there may be further restrictions on landing rights on the Na Pali Coast as well.

The following four companies are all within a few minutes' walk of one another around Hwy 560 and Aku Rd in Hanalei, making it easy to shop and compare.

Captain Zodiac (☎ 826-9371, (800) 422-7824) uses Zodiac rafts.

Na Pali Adventures (☎ 826-6804) uses power catamarans which, while not as adventurous as Zodiac rafts, offer a far smoother ride.

Paradise Adventure Cruises (☎ 826-9999) uses both a six-passenger Boston Whaler and a 32-foot power catamaran.

Hanalei Sea Tours (☎ 826-7254, (800) 733-7997) uses both Zodiac rafts and power catamarans. If you want a quick look at the coast without spending much money, they have a 2½-hour mini-tour for $50 in addition to the longer tours.

Hanalei Sea Tours and Captain Zodiac are the two companies currently allowed to drop off and pick up backpackers along the Na Pali Coast. This summer-only service costs $60 one way to Kalalau Valley, $130 return to Milolii Valley.

ACCOMMODATION

Three areas in Kauai – Poipu, Princeville, and the strip from Lihue to Kapaa – have almost all the island's hotels and condos. Of the three Poipu is the most difficult area in which to find a moderately priced place to stay.

For the most part, Kauai's beach hotels are expensive. The cheapest begin around $75, although the majority are easily double that. Condos have the same price range but tend to be a better deal, particularly if you're travelling in a group.

The best accommodation deals on the island are found in the scattering of B&Bs that have sprung up in the past few years. The Wailua area has the greatest concentration, with prices averaging about $40/50 a single/double. Many are in fine homes that are very comfortable and scenically situated a few miles up the slope from the coast. Wailua makes a good base for exploring, as it's midway between the North Shore and Kokee State Park.

Other than camping grounds, the cheapest places are the dormitories at the YMCA in Haena at $12 per person, the dorm beds at the Sleeping Giant Guest House & Hostel in Wailua at $14 and the cabinettes at Kahili Mountain Park near Koloa at $20. Lihue has some local in-town hotels around $25 but they're quite dreary.

Camping

Kauai has some fine camping spots. Some are drive-up beach parks, some are in dense forest and others are at the end of day-long hikes into remote valleys.

Camping is allowed at three state parks, seven county parks, and at forest reserve trailside camps in Waimea Canyon and the Kokee area.

State Parks Camping is allowed at Kokee, Polihale and Na Pali Coast state parks with a permit. Permits are free and are issued from 8 am to 4 pm Monday to Friday from the Division of State Parks (☎ 241-3444), 3060 Eiwa St, Room 306, Lihue, HI 96766, and at state park offices on other islands.

Up to 10 people may be listed on each permit, but the person applying for the permit must show an ID (such as a driver's licence or passport) for each person. Permits may be obtained by mail if a photocopy of each camper's ID is sent. Permits must be applied for at least seven days in advance (at least a month in advance during the peak season of May to September) and may be applied for as early as a year in advance.

Camping is allowed for up to five consecutive nights at each state park within a 30-day period. The Milolii Valley section of Na Pali Coast State Park is accessible only by small boat, is only open May to September, and has a three-day limit.

County Beach Parks Camping is allowed at Haena, Hanalei, Anini, Hanamaulu, Niumalu, Salt Pond and Lucy Wright parks. Haena, Anini and Salt Pond are all on nice beaches and are good choices. Camping is allowed at Hanalei Beach Park on weekends and holidays only. Niumalu, near the commercial harbour, isn't really a tourist area and isn't recommended for camping.

All county camping sites have showers and restrooms, and most have covered picnic pavilions and barbecue grills, although there's a typical Hawaiian free style to them. Don't expect to find numbered sites or caretakers.

Permits, which are required, cost $3 per adult per day. Children under 18 are free. Permits can be issued for up to two weeks, with a limit of seven consecutive days at any one camping site. Camping is limited to a total of 60 days a year.

Permits are issued from 7.45 am to 4.30 pm Monday to Friday at the Division of Parks & Recreation (☎ 245-8821), 4193 Hardy St, Lihue, HI 96766, in the centre of the green row building behind Dairy Queen and the War Memorial Convention Center. Reservations can be made by mail, but the permits must be paid for and picked up in person at the Parks & Recreation office.

After hours and on weekends and holidays, you can get permits at the police station at 3060 Umi St in Lihue (use the yellow phone at the station entrance), but permits issued this way cost $5 per person. You can also just set up camp and wait for the ranger to come around and collect, which also costs $5 per person. However the rangers sometimes wake up campers as early as 4.30 am to collect, and if they determine the camping area is too full, campers without permits will be asked to move.

Waimea Canyon The Division of Forestry & Wildlife (☎ 241-3433) allows camping at five sites along trails in Waimea Canyon and at two sites (Sugi Grove and Kawaikoi) in the Kokee State Park area. Camping is limited to four nights in the canyon and three nights in the Kokee area within a 30-day period.

Camping permits and trail maps are issued free by mail or in person from the forestry office at 3060 Eiwa St, Room 306, Lihue, HI 96766 (the same office as the state parks). Simply send them a letter with the name and address of each camper, the camping area you want to stay at (Waimea or Kokee), and the nights you plan to camp.

Cabins Cabins run by private concessionaire are available in Kokee State Park; in Kahili Mountain Park, north of Koloa; and at the YMCA camp in Haena. See the relevant sections for more information.

Camping Supplies Jungle Bob's (☎ 826-6664) in the Ching Young Village shopping centre in Hanalei rents three-person dome tents for $30 a week, and $8 each additional night, and backpacks for $5/20 a day/week. It also rents camping stoves, sleeping pads, poncho-liner blankets and child carriers for $3 to $4 a day. They sell the same supplies they rent and have a selection of books, maps, snorkelling gear, freeze-dried foods and backpacking items. The store is open Monday to Saturday from 9 am to 6 pm in winter, 8 am to 7 pm in summer; on Sundays it opens an hour later and closes an hour earlier.

Outfitters Kauai (☎ 742-9667), 2827A Poipu Rd, Poipu, rents two-person dome tents for $15/75 a day/week, backpacks for $8/40 and light sleeping sets for $10 the first night, $5 each additional night. If you keep the gear three days the fourth day is free. They also sell topographical maps for Kauai and other camping and hiking supplies.

Kayak Kauai (☎ 826-9844), on Hwy 560 in Hanalei, rents two-person tents or backpacks for $8/30 a day/week, camping stoves for $4/16 and sleeping pads for $3/15.

ENTERTAINMENT

Most of the action is at the larger hotels in Poipu, Wailua and Princeville. Between them they have dance clubs with live bands, a handful of lounges with guitarists playing Hawaiian music and a couple of Polynesian dinner shows. The Westin Kauai and Coco Palms have torch-lighting ceremonies. The Kauai Hilton has a comedy club.

There's also weekend entertainment at the Roxy Theatre in Kapaa and live music at a couple of places in Hanalei.

The Coconut Beach Hotel in Wailua, Smith's Tropical Plantation in Wailua, Stouffer Waiohai Beach Hotel in Poipu and Tahiti Nui in Hanalei have luaus. All but the Tahiti Nui luau roast pigs imu style.

There are movie theatres in the Kukui Grove Center in Lihue, the Coconut Marketplace in Wailua and in Kilauea.

There's often a stage production of *South Pacific* running somewhere, usually at one of the hotels.

Free hula shows are presented a few times a week at the Coconut Marketplace in Wailua and weekly at the Kukui Village shopping centre in Waipouli and the Kiahuna Shopping Village in Poipu.

Check the local papers or free tourist magazines, especially the *Kauai Beach Press*, for updated entertainment information. For details of specific venues, see the relevant town sections.

THINGS TO BUY

Two good places to look for Niihau shell leis, island-made baskets, paintings and other arts & crafts are at Kilohana Plantation in Puhi and Ching Young Village in Hanalei. Both house a collection of galleries.

Farmers markets featuring locally grown fruits, flowers and vegetables are held at the Koloa Ball Park at noon on Mondays, Kalaheo Neighborhood Center at 3.30 pm on Tuesdays, Kapaa Ball Park at 3 pm on Wednesdays, Hanapepe centre at 4 pm on Thursdays and Vidinha Stadium in Lihue at 3 pm on Fridays.

GETTING THERE & AWAY
Air

Kauai's main airport is in Lihue. Both Aloha Airlines (☎ 245-3691) and Hawaiian Airlines (☎ (800) 882-8811) have direct flights to Lihue from Honolulu, Kahului on Maui, and Hilo and Kona on the Big Island.

The most frequent service is from Honolulu, with Hawaiian Airlines flying about once an hour and Aloha Airlines about twice an hour between 6 am and 8 pm. One-way fares to all islands are $68.95 on Aloha Airlines and $69.95 on Hawaiian Airlines. For information on discounts see the introductory Getting Around chapter in the front of the book.

United Airlines has a daily direct flight between San Francisco and Lihue.

Kauai also has a smaller airport in Princeville on the North Shore. Aloha IslandAir (☎ (800) 652-6541), which has the only commercial service to Princeville, flies from Honolulu, Molokai, Lanai, the Big Island airport of Kamuela, and the Maui airports of Kahului, Hana and Kapalua West Maui. Frequencies vary from twice a day for the

Kamuela flights to eight times a day on flights to and from Honolulu. One-way fares are $69.95.

Lihue Airport Until 1987, inter-island flights touched down in a Lihue sugar cane field. Now there's a big modern terminal, an airstrip that can handle direct flights from the US mainland and agricultural inspection for passengers leaving the state.

The airport has a restaurant, snack bar, cocktail lounge, flower shop, newsstand and gift shop. There's a stand loaded with activity brochures in the baggage-claim area. The car-rental booths are in front of the terminal, opposite the arrival and departure gates.

Princeville Airport This little airport on the North Shore is serviced by Aloha Island Air and Avis and Hertz car rentals, and has a cafe/lounge.

GETTING AROUND
Kauai has a very limited public bus service, but renting a car is almost essential for exploring the island in depth.

There's nothing tricky about Kauai's main roads, but if you plan on doing a lot of exploring, the best map is the *Hawaii, Maui & Kauai* Neighbor Island map produced by Compass Maps.

Surprisingly, Kauai has rush-hour traffic jams, especially in central Lihue and on the highway between Lihue and Kapaa. It can be an inconvenience but it's not unbearable.

Bus
The county has a small public bus service (☎ 246-4622) that operates between Kapaa and Lihue. The service is used mostly by the elderly and commuting college students.

There are half a dozen runs. The most useful for visitors is the Coconut Coast Shuttle, which stops at the airport on its thrice-daily runs between Kapaa and Kauai Community College. Another route is the Wailua Express, which goes to Wailua Homesteads once a day. There's also a Lihue shuttle that runs between Wilcox Hospital and Kukui Grove Shopping Center a few times an hour.

The cost for any ride is $1, paid to the driver. Transfers are free, but stopovers are not permitted. The buses are white with a green sugar cane motif. A bus schedule can be picked up from bus drivers or from the county Department of Transportation office, in the green row building behind the convention centre in Lihue.

Taxi
Taxis charge $2 at flagfall and then $1.75 a mile, metered in 25-cent increments. The fare from Lihue Airport is about $11 to the Coco Palms Resort in Wailua, $20 to the Hotel Coral Reef in Kapaa and $29 to Poipu.

Car
Budget (☎ 245-9031; 245-1901 toll free in Hawaii), Hertz (☎ 245-3356), Avis (☎ 245-3512), Alamo (☎ 246-0645), Dollar (☎ 245-3651), National (☎ 245-5636) and Thrifty (☎ 245-7388) have car-rental booths at the Lihue Airport.

Toll-free numbers are listed in the introductory Getting Around chapter in the front of the book.

Bicycle & Moped
Pedal & Paddle (☎ 826-9069) in Ching Young Village in Hanalei rents mountain bikes for $20/100 a day/week and beach cruisers for $15/65. Prices include helmets and car carriers. They also rent mopeds for $15 for three hours or $30 for an eight-hour day. A credit card or a $200 deposit is required. The store is open from 9 am to 5 pm daily.

Outfitters Kauai (☎ 742-9667) in the Poipu Plaza in Poipu rents mountain bikes from $28 to $38 a day and beach cruisers for $15 a day, with discounts for more than three days. All bikes come equipped with a helmet and a water bottle. They also have bicycle tours in the Waimea/Kokee area for $58. The store is open from 8 am to 5.30 pm.

Bicycle John (☎ 245-7579), 3148 Oihana Bay 15, Lihue, rents mountain-style 21-speed bikes for $25 a day, $65 for four days.

The shop, which also sells and repairs bikes, is open from 9 am to 5 pm Monday to Friday and from 10 am to 3 pm on Saturdays.

Kauai Downhill (☎ 245-1774, (800) 234-1774), Box 3322, Lihue, HI 96766, has a delightful sunrise bike tour down the Waimea Canyon road. The 12-mile ride takes about 1½ hours. The entire outing lasts about four hours, depending on your pick-up point, and costs $60 including a continental breakfast.

Hitching

Hitching is legal on Kauai as long as you're not standing on the road itself, but on the shoulder. Pick a place where there's room for a car to pull over safely.

Overall, Kauai tends to be hit and miss for hitching. Drivers on the North Shore are usually the most sympathetic, and occasionally will go out of their way to take hikers to the Kalalau trailhead. The usual precautions apply.

East Side

LIHUE

Lihue is the county capital, the island's commercial centre and the arrival point of most visitors to Kauai. Though it's the island's central town, its population is only 5500 and it's essentially a grown-up plantation town. It has inexpensive hotels and restaurants and the island's main shopping mall. There are a few sights of interest, but Lihue itself is ordinary, with no special charm.

Information

The Hawaii Visitors Bureau (☎ 245-3971), 3016 Umi St, on the 2nd floor of the Lihue Plaza, is open from 8 am to 4.30 pm Monday to Friday.

The government offices are centred around Rice, Umi and Hardy Sts.

Post & Money The post office is opposite the museum on Rice St, next to the Bank of Hawaii. The post office is open from 8 am to 4 pm Monday to Friday, 9 am to noon on Saturdays.

Library The Lihue Public Library (☎ 245-3617), 4344 Hardy St, is open from 9 am to 8 pm on Mondays, Tuesdays and Thursdays and from 9 am to 4.30 pm on Wednesdays, Fridays and Saturdays.

Laundry There are laundromats in the Rice Shopping Center and on Hwy 56 in Hanamaulu.

Kauai Museum

A few hours at the Kauai Museum (☎ 245-6931), 4428 Rice St, will give you a good overview of the island's history.

The displays begin with Kauai's volcanic genesis from the ocean floor, then move on to natural history and ecosystems. The first floor is Hawaiian history, with the likes of hula instruments, a hand-carved wooden canoe and a section on the short-lived Russian presence in Kauai.

Upstairs the sugar cane workers and missionaries arrive on the scene. A replica of a plantation worker's spartan shack sits opposite the spacious bedroom of an early missionary's house furnished with a four-poster koa bed and Hawaiian quilts. It is to these folks that Hawaii traces its multiethnic roots and vastly unequal distribution of land and wealth. The displays are accompanied by well-written interpretive presentations of life in old Kauai.

At the 'please touch' section visitors can tap a piece of tapa, pick up a stone poi pounder and shake gourd rattles. In another room a video about Kauai runs continuously and includes aerial views of the Na Pali Coast and Kauai's rugged, inaccessible interior.

The gift shop has an excellent selection of Hawaiiana books, as well as some koa bowls and other handcrafts. If you only want to visit the gift shop, which is inside the museum lobby, you can enter without paying anything.

The museum is open from 9 am to 4.30 pm Monday to Friday and from 9 am to 1 pm

Saturdays. Admission is $3 for adults and free for children aged under 18. If you run out of time, ask for a free re-entry pass when you leave.

Lihue Sugar Mill

The conveyer belt that crosses over Hwy 50 just south of its intersection with Hwy 56 transports crushed sugar cane to the Lihue Sugar Mill. The mill produces raw sugar crystals that are shipped to California to be refined. Molasses is also made here and on those days the air has an extremely sweet smell.

Old Lutheran Church

From the outside, the oldest Lutheran church in Hawaii is just one more quaint Hawaiian church. From the inside it's much more interesting.

German immigrants styled their church to resemble the boat that brought them from their homeland to Hawaii in the late 1800s. The floor has been built to slant like the deck of a ship, the balcony resembles a captain's bridge and ship lanterns hang from the ceiling. The current building was actually constructed in 1983, but it's an almost exact replica of the original 1885 church that was levelled by Hurricane Iwa in 1982.

The immigrants themselves now lie at rest in the church cemetery on a knoll overlooking the sugar cane fields in which they toiled.

The church is a quarter of a mile up Hoomana Rd, which is just south of the intersection of Hwy 56 and Hwy 50.

Wailua Falls

Wailua Falls is an 80-foot waterfall just north of Lihue. From Lihue, turn left onto Maalo Rd (Hwy 583), a narrow paved road that weaves through a sugar cane field. The road ends at the falls at precisely 3.94 miles – as the highway marker fastidiously proclaims.

Wailua, which means 'two waters', is usually seen as two falls. When the water is running strongly it becomes one wide rushing waterfall and you can watch fish being thrown out beyond the powerful waters for a flying dive into the pool below.

This is not a waterfall to explore from the top. A sign at the parking lot near a closed path reads, 'Slippery rocks at top of falls. People have been killed'. There are plenty of local stories told of people sliding off the rocks, some miraculously grabbing roots and being rescued and others not so lucky.

Back down the road a third of a mile, at a large dirt pull-off with a big tree, there's an eroded trail that leads to the base of the falls. The steep trail starts below the tree and can be very slippery when wet. Just below the head of the trail you can see another waterfall in the distance to the south. Once you get to the bottom, follow the trail along the riverbed. The condition of the trail varies greatly. Last time we were there, which was shortly after a major flood, the path was barely discernible. However, even if you have to do some scrambling, you should be able to make your way to the waterfall. It can be humid enough to steam up your glasses.

Wood roses used in dried floral arrangements are easy to find along the road. Look for vines bearing bright yellow flowers shaped like morning glories. They are especially thick around the bridge half a mile down the road from the waterfall.

Hanamaulu

Hanamaulu is a little village between Lihue and Wailua along Hwy 56. It was the birthplace of the legendary hero Kawelo. Hanamaulu has a good Japanese restaurant, a hole-in-the-wall post office and a doughnut shop that closes each day as soon as the doughnuts are gone.

Hanamaulu Beach Park Hanamaulu County Beach Park is three-quarters of a mile from the village centre. From Hwy 56 turn makai onto Hanamaulu Rd and then right onto Hehi Rd. Entering the park you'll drive under the arched trestle of an old abandoned railroad bridge, now topped with grass.

The park is at the inside of Hanamaulu Bay, a deep protected bay with a boulder breakwater partway across its mouth. It has camping with full facilities, but the park is

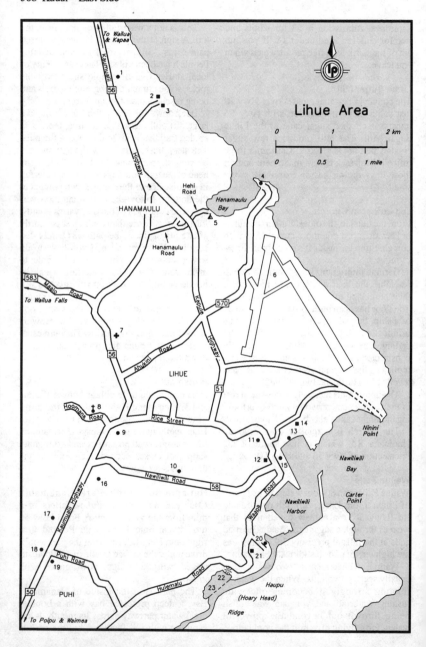

Lihue Area

To Wailua
& Kapaa

Kauai Highway

56

1

2
3

Hehi
Road

HANAMAULU

Hanamaulu
Road

Hanamaulu
Bay

4

5

6

570

583

Maalo Road

To Wailua Falls

56

7

Ahukini Road

Kapule Highway

LIHUE

51

Hoomana Road

8

Rice Street

9

10

Nawiliwili Road

58

11

12

13

14

15

16

Kaumualii Highway

17

18

Puhi Road

19

PUHI

50

To Poipu & Waimea

Hulemalu Road

Niumalu Road

20

21

22

23

Nawiliwili
Harbor

Nawiliwili
Bay

Ninini
Point

Carter
Point

Haupu
(Hoary Head)
Ridge

0   1   2 km

0   0.5   1 mile

feet above the shore, marking the northern entrance to Nawiliwili Bay. The road down to the lighthouse begins off Hwy 51, half a mile south of Hwy 570. Public access is through a guard gate on the Westin Kauai's property.

The 2½-mile drive from the gatehouse to the lighthouse skirts between the airport fence and the Westin's golf course. (If you hear popping sounds as you drive along, it's not your tyres going flat but timed explosions to scare birds away from the airport runway!) After two miles the pavement ends and the road continues as dirt. This section is sometimes too rough to pass in a low-slung car and you may have to hike the last 10 minutes of it. Not only is there a fine view from the lighthouse, but nearby is one of the few sections of accessible shore in the area where Hawaiians can still fish, pick opihi and gather limu as they've done for generations.

The Westin Kauai Hotel

The Westin Kauai is mammoth, with huge Chinese cloisonne vases, squawking parrots and fat pillars of pink faux marble. Art and antiques are everywhere, even on the men's restroom wall, where a distinguished Chinese gentleman of another century peers sideways across the row of urinals. Past the front desk are balconies looking onto a gigantic swimming pool with fountains spurting from the mouths of sculptured beasts.

The Westin offers one-hour rides around its manicured grounds in carriages pulled by Clydesdale horses ($21 per passenger) and boat rides around little islands stocked with exotic birds and monkeys ($14).

The Westin was not built from scratch, but was an up-market renovation of the old Kauai Surf Hotel. As the island's only highrise, the Surf's very construction led to public outcry, followed by a successful campaign that limited the height of all future hotels to that of a coconut tree.

The hotel is still controversial. Many islanders feel the Westin's bedazzling opulence is more befitting Las Vegas than Kauai.

close to town and is more of a local hangout than a visitor destination.

Ahukini Landing

If you've got some time to kill before your flight, you could drive down to the end of Hwy 570 to Ahukini Landing, 1½ miles beyond the airport. The road runs through sugar cane fields and crosses a series of narrow-gauge railroad tracks that were once used to bring sugar cane down to the landing. Ilima and chain of love grow along the road.

Ahukini State Recreation Pier is at the end of the road. It consists largely of old cement pillars and the decaying framework of the old pier. A wooden walkway runs out across it, providing a prime locale for pole fishing. At the head of the bay is Hanamaulu Beach.

Ninini Point

The lighthouse on Ninini Point stands 100

With all the island's natural beauty, Kauai is just about the oddest place to build artificial lagoons and electric waterfalls.

The Westin, off Hwy 51 at Nawiliwili Harbor, is on Kalapaki Beach, a white-sand beach sheltered by points and breakwaters. Swimming is usually good, even in the winter unless storms kick the surf up.

Nawiliwili Bay

Nawiliwili Bay is a deep-water port with a commercial harbour. The adjacent small boat harbour is picturesque, backed by the edge of the Haupu (Hoary Head) Ridge which ends at Carter Point. Several deep-sea fishing boats are based at the harbour.

Waapa Rd runs south from the Westin past the harbour and a couple of unexciting beach parks. It then connects with Hulemalu Rd, which leads up to an overview of the Menehune Fishpond.

If you continue about a mile past the fishpond and then turn right onto Puhi Rd, you'll come out to Hwy 50 at Puhi General Store.

Nawiliwili Beach Park Nawiliwili Beach Park is largely a parking lot facing an ocean retaining wall. From here you can look over at the Westin, the light beacon on Kukui Point and a long breakwater. If you drive to the far end of the parking lot you can also see the lighthouse on the more distant Ninini Point. The park is a local hangout and drinking spot.

There's no beach at the beach park, but if the waters in Nawiliwili Stream are not running strongly you could cross over to Kalapaki Beach in front of the Westin.

Right at the mouth of the stream is an old shelter under ironwood trees with a wooden sign reading 'Pine Tree Inn'. It's an impromptu neighbourhood open-air bar of sorts. Old-timers gather during the day with little ice chests to talk story and sometimes take out ukuleles and make music together. Occasionally someone has food to throw on the grill, but mostly they bring a few beers and drink until they're gone.

Niumalu Beach Park This county beach park is in a less affluent residential area and has been partly settled by homeless people who have set up tents and lean-tos. The park has a boat ramp used mainly for launching outrigger canoes. Camping is officially allowed, although it's not an area recommended for most visitors.

Menehune Fishpond Overlook

Half a mile up Hulemalu Rd there's a lookout on the left with a view of the Alakoko Fishpond, more commonly called the Menehune Fishpond. In the background is the misty Haupu Ridge.

The fishpond, created by a stone wall that runs along a bend in the river, was said to have been built in one night by menehunes. The stone wall is covered by a thick green line of mangrove trees. Morning is a good time for viewing as in the afternoon you look into the sun.

Huleai National Wildlife Refuge lies between the road and the fishpond. Once planted with taro and rice, the area now provides breeding and feeding grounds for endemic water birds. The refuge is not open to the public.

Grove Farm Homestead

The Grove Farm Homestead Plantation Museum, up Nawiliwili Rd (Hwy 58) 1¾ miles from Waapa Rd, is the preserved farmhouse built in 1864 by George Wilcox, son of the missionaries Abner and Lucy Wilcox. It's a bit like the house of an old aunt, rather musty and filled with memories. Rocking chairs sit on a covered porch. One room is lined with bookshelves stuffed with a home library, with koa calabashes and a model ship on top. In one corner a card table is set up, waiting for a foursome to sit down to a wild game of cribbage.

Tours are given at 10 am and 1 pm on Mondays, Wednesdays and Thursdays. Reservations are required (☎ 245-3202) and must sometimes be made a couple of weeks in advance. The cost is $3.

Kukui Grove Shopping Center

Kukui Grove Shopping Center, at the

intersection of Hwy 50 and Hwy 58, is Kauai's main shopping mall. The major department stores are Liberty House and its discount Penthouse branch, J C Penney, Sears, Woolworth and Longs Drugs. Close Outs, a clothing shop, has reasonably priced T-shirts, shorts and other casual wear. The centre also has Kukui Grove Cinema, Star supermarket, Bank of Hawaii, Waldenbooks, a one-hour photo shop, a video arcade and Stones Gallery, a quality art gallery with a coffee and dessert cafe. Other eateries include Kauai Cinnamons, which sells large hot cinnamon rolls for $1.50, Cisco's Mexican restaurant and a few fast-food joints.

Kilohana Plantation

Kilohana, 1½ miles south of Lihue on Hwy 50, is the 1930s sugar plantation estate of Gaylord Parke Wilcox, once head of Grove Farm Plantation. The Tudor-style mansion built by Wilcox was the most distinguished house on Kauai in its day.

The home has been restored, with most of the rooms turned into shops that sell artwork, antiques and handcrafts. It was a nice way to preserve the old estate and you get to look around without being charged an admission fee.

Visitors are free to wander through rooms full of antiques or even plop down in one of the overstuffed couches and read a book. The hallways hold cases of stone poi pounders and other Hawaiian artefacts, and Oriental rugs litter the hardwood floors. There's also a restaurant, Gaylord's, in a U-shaped courtyard setting around the lawn.

Many island galleries rent space at Kilohana, giving it the widest collection of arts & crafts on Kauai. On the 1st floor, a former cloakroom is now the Hawaiian Collection Room, which sells finely strung Niihau shell leis and scrimshaw.

The upstairs bedrooms have likewise been turned into shops, with displays laid out even in the bathrooms and closets. Sea Reflections sells mangrove and monkeypod carvings of dolphins and sharks handcrafted by the Kapingamarangi people of Pohnpei. Stones

Gallery sells quality contemporary paintings by Hawaiian artists, including Pegge Hopper. There's also a jewellery shop, Balinese clothing, and Japanese antiques and prints.

Kilohana (☎ 245-5608) is open from 9.30 am to 9.30 pm Monday to Saturday, until 5 pm on Sundays. The 35-acre grounds have gardens and a small working farm that you can explore. Turn-of-the-century carriages pulled by Clydesdale horses give 20-minute tours at $7 for adults and $4 for children. It's a bit touristy but more in tune with historical Kauai than the Westin's Clydesdale rides.

Places to Stay – bottom end

Lihue has some of Kauai's cheapest hotels. They are generally drab places and except for Motel Lani are filled mostly with local residents. You'll get a place to sleep but by no means are these vacation spots.

The *Motel Lani* (☎ 245-2965), 4240 Rice St, Box 1836, Lihue, HI 96766, is the best of the lot, though it's at a busy intersection. It has a dozen rooms for $25 to $35, very basic but clean and with mini-refrigerators. There's a two-day minimum or a $2 surcharge.

The *Hale Lihue Hotel* (☎ 245-3151), 2931 Kalena St, Lihue, HI 96766, has 20 rooms for $20/22/26 a single/double/triple, or $25/30/35 with a kitchenette. Rooms have twin beds, private showers and toilets, but zilch for atmosphere.

The *Tip Top Motel* (☎ 245-2333), 3173 Akahi St, Box 1231, Lihue, HI 96766, has 34 rooms in two simple two-storey cinderblock buildings. Rooms have twin beds, air-con, louvered windows and an ageing chest of drawers. Rates are $30/39 for singles/doubles.

Places to Stay – middle

Lihue has two older hotels near Nawiliwili Harbor that have recently been renovated, but neither is ideally located.

The three-storey *Garden Island Inn* (☎ 245-7227), 3445 Wilcox Rd, Lihue, HI 96766, has 21 small but tidy rooms with TVs, ceiling fans, mini-refrigerators and coffeemakers. It costs $50 for ground floor rooms, and $60 for rooms on the 2nd floor that have small private lanais. The hotel is near an industrial area and at the side of a rather busy road, but it is walking distance to Kalapaki Beach.

The *Kauai Inn* (☎ 245-2720, (800) 326-5242), 2430 Hulemalu Rd, Lihue, HI 96766,

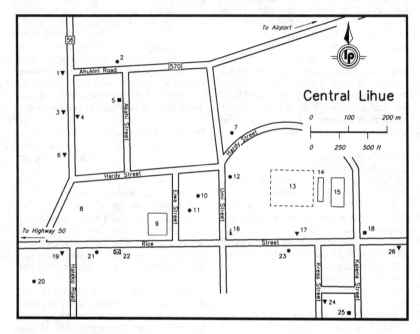

Central Lihue

■	PLACES TO STAY
5	Tip Top Motel
18	Motel Lani
25	Hale Lihue Hotel

▼	PLACES TO EAT
1	Kentucky Fried Chicken
3	Pizza Hut
4	Jack in the Box
6	McDonald's
17	Dairy Queen
19	Eggbert's
24	Hamura Saimin
26	Dani's Restaurant

	OTHER
2	Snorkel Bob's
7	Library
8	Lihue Shopping Center
9	Kauai Museum
10	State Offices
11	County Offices
12	Police Station
13	Baseball Park
14	County Parks & Recreation
15	Convention Hall
16	Hawaii Visitors Bureau
20	Lihue Sugar Mill
21	Bank of Hawaii
22	Post Office
23	Rice Shopping Center

is a 48-room, two-storey hotel near Niumalu Beach Park. The hotel has a musty history, but the rooms have been nicely renovated. Each has a refrigerator, microwave and remote control TV. The management is quite friendly and there's almost a condo ambience, with guests gathering around the pool for barbecues. Rates are $69 for standard rooms with queen beds, or $79 for slightly bigger rooms with king beds, and include a simple continental breakfast. Three units are accessible to the disabled.

Places to Stay – top end

The *Kauai Hilton* (☎ 245-1955, (800) 445-8667), 4331 Kauai Beach Drive, Lihue, HI 96766, has 350 rooms at $125 without ocean views, $160 with ocean views. The hotel is a standard Hilton and could easily be anywhere.

On the same property as the Hilton, the *Aston Kauai Beach Villas* (☎ 245-7711, (800) 922-7866), 4330 Kauai Beach Drive, Lihue, HI 96766, has one-bedroom condo units for $136/152 in the low/high season, for up to four people. Two-bedroom units cost $188/204 for up to six people.

The *Westin Kauai* (☎ 245-5050, (800) 228-3000), Kalapaki Beach, Lihue, HI 96766, is one of the 'fantasy hotels' designed by developer Chris Hemmeter. Rates begin at $195 for a courtyard view and climb to $320 for a beachfront unit, with suites up to $1800.

Places to Eat – bottom end

At *Hamura Saimin*, 2956 Kress St in central Lihue, you can get a big bowl of freshly made saimin for $3 and tasty skewers of barbecued chicken for only 80 cents. This little second generation family-run operation is a throwback to an older Kauai. It's open from 10 am until business dies down, which might be as early as 10 pm, but is more often around midnight on weekdays and 2 am on weekends. There are no separate tables, just a winding saimin bar where visitors and locals rub elbows as they slurp bowls of steaming hot saimin. The one rule of etiquette is written on the menu – 'Please do not stick gum under counter'!

Surprisingly, the *Wilcox Memorial Hospital cafeteria* on Hwy 56 is not a bad place to grab a cheap meal. It has a pretty good salad bar for 25 cents an ounce and a variety of hot dishes like seafood stir fry, laulau and fried chicken for $2 to $3, and poi and brown rice for under a dollar. It's open from 6.30 am to 7 pm daily, which makes it a good choice for mid-afternoon when most other restaurants have stopped serving lunch. To get there, use the main entrance and go straight through the hospital lobby.

The *Hanamaulu Restaurant & Tea House* (☎ 245-2511) on Hwy 56 in Hanamaulu has many faces. It has a sushi bar with a little carp pond, tatami-matted tearooms in a garden setting, a robatayaki and a no-frills dining room. Full dinner teishokus that include tempura, sushi and sashimi cost $12.50. An even better deal is the special plate lunch of miso soup, rice, shrimp tempura and teriyaki for $6.50 at lunch, $7.75 at dinner. Chinese dishes are available at similar prices. For a treat, try the kama as an appetizer from the robatayaki menu. Call in advance to reserve one of the tearooms – they really set the mood. It's open from 10 am to 1 pm Tuesday to Friday and 4.30 to 9 pm daily except Mondays.

Lots of working people start their day at *Dani's Restaurant*, at 4201 Rice St in Lihue. Omelettes, from cheese for $3.30 to kalua pig for $5, come with rice or toast. The waitress plops down a thermos of coffee as soon as you sit down – no extra charge. Dani's has Hawaiian, American and Japanese lunch dishes. The most expensive Western dish is the New York steak for $5.25. Breakfast is served from 5 to 11 am daily. Lunch is from 11 am to about 1.30 pm Monday to Saturday.

Stones, a gallery cafe in the Kukui Grove Shopping Center, has good coffees, scones, vegetable soup and other light eats. It's open from 9.30 am to 6 pm Monday to Wednesday, 8.30 am to 9 pm on Thursdays and Fridays, 8.30 am to 5.30 pm on Saturdays and 10 am to 4 pm on Sundays.

Chico's in the Kukui Grove Shopping Center has rather ordinary Mexican dishes at moderate prices. Many of the combo plates, which include rice and beans, are $9.

Kauai Chop Suey, in the Pacific Ocean Plaza opposite the Westin, has lots of standard Cantonese dishes for between $6 and $7. The menu is the same at lunch (11 am to 2 pm Tuesday to Saturday) and dinner (4.30 to 9 pm Tuesday to Sunday). Kauai doesn't have any really great Chinese restaurants, but this is one of the better ones.

Eggbert's, at 4483 Rice St in Lihue, is popular for omelettes and eggs Benedict. Expect to pay $6 to $8 with coffee. Eggbert's has burgers and other food too, but you're best off sticking with eggs. Breakfast is served from 7 am to 3 pm daily.

Hale O'Health in Lihue's Rice Shopping Center is a typical shopping centre health-food store and carries Alta-dena yoghurt, packaged granola and other standard items. They also have inexpensive wrapped sandwiches at lunch time.

The *Oroweat Thrift Shop* next to the Dairy Queen on Rice St in Lihue has day-old bakery products at discounted prices.

There's a *McDonald's, Jack in the Box, Pizza Hut* and *Kentucky Fried Chicken* clustered together on Hwy 56 and a *Burger King* and *Taco Bell* at the Kukui Grove Shopping Center.

Places to Eat – top end

Cafe Portofino (☎ 245-2121), in the Pacific Ocean Plaza, serves up authentic Northern Italian food. The $7 lunch buffet from 11 am to 2 pm Monday to Friday is a good deal and includes green salad, a couple of pasta dishes, frittatas and dessert. The restaurant is also open for dinner from 5 to 10 pm nightly, when home-made pasta, eggplant parmigiana and calamari dishes average $13 à la carte. For starters, the escargot maison at $7.50 is excellent.

Gaylord's (☎ 245-9593) at Kilohana Plantation has a pleasant open-air estate setting and attracts a crowd, though the food is more ordinary than its reputation would suggest. Lunch is served from 11 am to 3.30 pm daily

except Sundays, with sandwiches and salads for $9. Dinner is from 5 pm nightly, with entrees from $17 for baby back ribs to $35 for Alaskan king crab. On Sundays, there's a brunch from 9.30 am to 3 pm, with dishes from $10 to $14.

The best value at the Westin Kauai is the beachside *Duke's Canoe Club* (☎ 246-9599), an open-air restaurant with a waterfall and carp pond running through its centre. The casual downstairs grill, open from 11.30 am to 11 pm daily, has sandwiches and burgers from $6. The upstairs dining room, open from 5.30 to 10 pm, has a pretty good spinach and cheese ravioli for $10, meat dishes for around $15 and fresh fish for about $20. All meals come with a Caesar salad and banana muffins. The hula pie, a decadently huge slab of macnut ice cream in Oreo cookie crust with fudge topping, easily serves two and costs $4.

If you have a small fortune at hand, the Westin (☎ 245-5050) has a couple of good fine-dining restaurants. *Inn on the Cliffs* has elegant dining, superb views of Nawiliwili Bay and fresh fish dishes for about $25 a la carte. The *Tempura Garden* has excellent sushi and serves quality Japanese dinners in the $25 to $60 range. Both sometimes have a good-value early bird special.

Entertainment

The Westin Kauai has Hawaiian music, usually a soloist or trio, from 4 to 9 pm daily at *Cooks at the Beach*, a poolside restaurant and bar. The Westin's *Inn on the Cliffs* has a jazz trio in the lounge from 8 pm on Fridays and Saturdays.

Park Place (☎ 245-5775), in the Pacific Ocean Plaza opposite the Westin, is a trendy top-40 disco with a dress code and a minimum entry age of 21. They have a $2 drink special until midnight and dancing and pupus to 4 am.

Gilligan's (☎ 245-1955), a disco in the Kauai Hilton, is open from 9 pm Wednesday to Saturday. The minimum age is 21.

The *Club Jetty* at Nawiliwili Harbor is a rough and tumble bar that often has live rock music.

WAILUA

The three-mile stretch of Kuhio Highway (Hwy 56) from Wailua to Waipouli and Kapaa is largely a scattering of stores, restaurants, hotels and condos. Neither Wailua nor Waipouli have anything that resembles a town centre. Most of the area's sights are clustered around the Wailua River area.

Wailua was the site of Kauai's royal court and the birthplace of kings. There are 'Seven Sacred Heiaus' running from the mouth of the Wailua River up to the top of Mt Waialeale.

Six of the heiau sites are within a mile of the river mouth. Five are visible, while the sixth is abandoned in a sugar cane field on the northern side of the Wailua River. All date back to the early period of Tahitian settlement and are considered to be typical menehune construction.

Wailua State Park is a hodgepodge that includes most of the heiau sites, sections of the Wailua River bank, the Fern Grotto, the riverboat basin and a public boat ramp.

Wailua River, 11.8 miles long, is the only navigable river in Hawaii. Though most people travel the river on packaged riverboat tours, the more adventurous kayak or water ski on it.

Lydgate Beach Park

Lydgate is a popular family beach with protected swimming in a large seawater pool created with stone walls. It's great for kids but deep enough for adults to swim in too. The open ocean beyond often has strong currents and there have been many drownings on both sides of the river's mouth. The park has changing rooms, restrooms, showers, large picnic pavilions and drinking water.

Lydgate is makai of the Kauai Resort Hotel, down Leho Drive.

Hikina A Ka La Heiau

Hikina A Ka La (Rising of the Sun) Heiau is the long, narrow heiau aligned directly north to south at the far end of the Lydgate Beach parking lot.

The heiau is thought to have been built around 1200 AD. Boulders still outline the shape but most of the stones have long since been removed.

At the northern end of the heiau, a bronze plaque on a large stone reads 'Hauola, City of Refuge'. The mounded grassy area behind the plaque is all that remains of this former refuge for kapu breakers. The lucky ones who managed to reach Hauola had their lives spared.

The stone with bowl-shaped depressions 10 feet to the left of the plaque is an adze grinding stone. The stone hasn't always been in this upright position since to grind a correct edge it would have needed to be flat. There are also a couple of flat stone saltpans on the grounds.

If you look straight out across the bay you can see the remains of Aa Kukui Heiau on the point, in front of the red-roofed Lae Nani condos. Only the foundation stones are discernible, as the heiau site has been landscaped over in a carpet of condo grass. In ancient times torches were lit on the point at night to help guide outrigger canoes.

If you walk straight down to the beach while looking toward Aa Kukui Point you may find stones with petroglyphs on them, though they're often hidden under shifting sands.

Malae Heiau

Malae Heiau is in a thick clump of trees growing on the edge of a sugar cane field, a mere 40 feet in from the highway across from the Kauai Resort Hotel. Though this is the largest heiau on Kauai it's thickly overgrown with grasses and Java plum trees and almost impossible to explore.

In the 1830s the missionaries converted Deborah Kapule, the last Kauaian queen, to Christianity and she converted the interior of Malae Heiau into a cattle pen. Except for these alterations it's relatively well-preserved, thanks largely to its impenetrable overgrowth.

The whole area is state property and there are plans to eventually incorporate the heiau into the Wailua parks system. Java plums, by the way, are used in making wine. But should

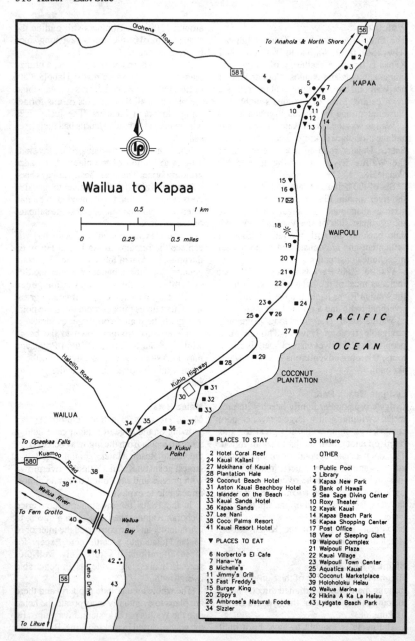

Wailua to Kapaa

0   0.5   1 km

0   0.25   0.5 miles

PACIFIC

OCEAN

KAPAA

WAIPOULI

COCONUT
PLANTATION

WAILUA

Aa Kukui
Point

To Anahola & North Shore

Olohena Road

Haleilio Road

Kuhio Highway

To Opaekaa Falls

Kuamoo Road

To Fern Grotto

Wailua River

Wailua
Bay

Leho Drive

To Lihue

■ PLACES TO STAY
2 Hotel Coral Reef
24 Kauai Kailani
27 Mokihana of Kauai
28 Plantation Hale
29 Coconut Beach Hotel
31 Aston Kauai Beachboy Hotel
32 Islander on the Beach
33 Kauai Sands Hotel
36 Kapaa Sands
37 Lae Nani
38 Coco Palms Resort
41 Kauai Resort Hotel

▼ PLACES TO EAT
6 Norberto's El Cafe
7 Hana-Ya
8 Michelle's
11 Jimmy's Grill
13 Fast Freddy's
15 Burger King
20 Zippy's
26 Ambrose's Natural Foods
34 Sizzler

35 Kintaro

OTHER

1 Public Pool
3 Library
4 Kapaa New Park
5 Bank of Hawaii
9 Sea Sage Diving Center
10 Roxy Theater
12 Kayak Kauai
14 Kapaa Beach Park
16 Kapaa Shopping Center
17 Post Office
18 View of Sleeping Giant
19 Waipouli Complex
21 Waipouli Plaza
22 Kauai Village
23 Waipouli Town Center
25 Aquatics Kauai
30 Coconut Marketplace
39 Holoholoku Heiau
40 Wailua Marina
42 Hikina A Ka La Heiau
43 Lydgate Beach Park

you be tempted to try the fresh fruit you'll find they're bitter enough to dry out your mouth!

Highway 580

Highway 580, also known as Kuamoo Rd, begins at the traffic light off Hwy 56 at Coco Palms Resort. It passes heiaus, historical sites, Opaekaa Falls and Wailua Homesteads before reaching Keahua Arboretum, the starting place for a couple of back-country trails.

Holoholoku Heiau

Holoholoku Heiau is just a quarter of a mile up Hwy 580, on the left. Like all the Wailua heiaus, this one was of enclosure-type construction, with walls built directly on the ground, rather than with terraced platforms. It was a luakini heiau and thus a place of human sacrifice.

This whole area used to be royal property and here in the yard against the flat-backed birthstone queens gave birth to future kings. Another stone, marked 'Pohaku Piko', was where the *piko* (umbilical cords) of the babies were left.

Above the temple where Hawaiian royalty were born, steps lead to a hilltop cemetery where Japanese labourers lie at rest.

Poliahu Heiau

Poliahu Heiau is perched high on a hill overlooking the meandering Wailua River. The heiau is named after the snow goddess Poliahu, one of Pele's sisters. This relatively well-preserved heiau is thought to have been a luakini type.

Poliahu Heaiu is immediately before the Opaekaa Falls lookout, on the opposite side of the road.

Bellstone

Immediately south of Poliahu Heiau, on the same side of the road, is a short dirt drive that leads to a bellstone. Because of the road angle it's easiest to approach coming downhill from Poliahu.

In old Hawaii, Wailua River was a naval entrance, and a bellstone at this lookout was thought to have been used by sentries to warn of attacks as well as to ring out announcements of royal births.

There are actually two stones at the end of the drive, one with an all-too-perfect petroglyph whose age is suspect. Archaeologists question just which stone may have been the bellstone. Although you can find depressions in the stones, they may well be the result of modern-day poundings by people trying to check out the resonance for themselves.

The path down from these rocks leads to a vista of the river. You can see cattle grazing on the banks below and hear the microphone narration from the passing riverboats.

Opaekaa Falls

Opaekaa Falls is a broad 40-foot waterfall, with the peaks of the Makaleha Mountains in the background. White-tailed tropicbirds can often be seen soaring in the valley below the falls. The turn-off to the viewpoint is clearly marked at 1½ miles up Hwy 580. For the best angle, walk up the sidewalk past the parking lot. From across the highway you can look down on Wailua River and Kamokila Hawaiian Village.

Kamokila Hawaiian Village

Kamokila (☎ 822-1192) is a re-created Hawaiian village with thatched huts set in a little clearing on the riverbank. There are taro patches, sleeping houses, an oracle tower and a women's menstrual house. Interpretive guides help explain it all in a tour that lasts about 40 minutes. The concept is good but they apparently don't get enough visitors to be able to fully carry it out and it's all a bit rundown. It's open from 9 am to 4 pm Monday to Saturday and costs $5 for adults and $1.50 for children.

Wailua Homesteads

In the Wailua Homesteads area, on the west side of the Sleeping Giant mountain, the government once gave 160-acre parcels to people willing to work the land. This mostly meant cattle grazing, though at one point Dole grew pineapples in the area. Today Wailua Homesteads is largely a mix of spacious residential lots and pastoral countryside reminiscent of Pennsylvania Quaker farmland.

The main through road is Hwy 581 (Kamalu Rd), which connects with Hwy 580.

Nounou Ridge (Sleeping Giant) Trail

The Nounou Ridge Trail goes up the Sleeping Giant to a summit on the giant's upper chest that affords views of both the east coast and the highland valleys. It's a well-maintained trail that takes 1½ to two hours for the round trip.

There are two trailheads, both marked. The trail on the western side is a shaded forest trail of tall trees and moss-covered stones. The trail on the eastern side is a little more open and a bit longer. It begins at the water pump site a mile up Haleilio Rd in Wailua Houselots.

The trail up the western side of the mountain starts on Hwy 581 (Kamalu Rd), near house No 1068. Walk through a metal gate marked as a forestry right of way and up along a small cattle pasture to the trailhead.

This is a wonderful trail to do early in the morning when it's relatively cool and you can watch the light slowly spread across the valley below. The eucalyptus at the trailhead soon gives way to a tall thick forest of Norfolk pines that were planted in a Civilian Conservation Corps (CCC) reforestation programme during the 1930s.

A few minutes up the trail there's a fork. Veer left up the path with the large rock beside it. The packed trail can get slippery when wet so look for a walking stick. Hikers sometimes leave them near the trailhead.

The trail passes through thick strawberry guava bushes that can grow up to 15 feet high. In places they create a canopied tunnel-like effect. The small red fruit is eaten whole: the sweetest of the guavas, it is considered a delicacy.

A few minutes below the summit, the eastern and western trails merge on the ridge. Continue up to the right past some hala trees. On the summit is a picnic table shelter that offers protection from the rain. Passing

showers can give some incredible valley rainbows. To the west there's a 180° view of Wailua and the Makaleha Mountains.

Below to the east you can see Kapaa, sugar cane fields, Wailua Houselots, Coco Palms and the Wailua River. To the right of the riverboat docks and mauka of the Kauai Resort Hotel there's a square dark-green area in the sugar cane field. This is Malae Heiau, now overgrown with Java plums.

If you go south across the picnic area the trail continues. About five minutes up there's a rocky area where you can sit and enjoy the view. The ridge continues up the giant's head. Should it tempt you, size it up carefully. It's sharp, and loose rocks and slides are visible.

Kuilau Ridge Trail

For the effort, the Kuilau Ridge Trail is one of the most visually rewarding trails on the island. The marked trailhead is on the right just before Hwy 580 crosses the stream at the Keahua Arboretum, 3.9 miles up from the junction of Hwy 580 and Hwy 581. Don't leave anything of value in your car.

The maintained trail starts up a wide dirt path that is also used by horses and the occasional dirt bike. There's a dense growth of native plants along the way, including koa trees, ohia lehua and thickets of ti, and there's plenty of birdsong as well. In the upper reaches there are hillsides covered with lush ferns and broad vistas of the mountains. A few thimbleberries grow wild along the trail and there are many trailside guava trees.

The hike climbs up to a broad ridge that offers views into valleys on both sides, right down to the coast. From the ridgetop you can see Kapaa to the east and the island's uninhabited central region to the west. It takes about 35 minutes to walk the 1¼ miles up to a grassy clearing where there are a couple of picnic tables and a great view that looks out onto Mt Waialeale due west.

Beyond the clearing, the Kuilau Ridge Trail continues as a narrow footpath offering even more spectacular views, ending in about a mile at the Moalepe Trail. If you don't want to go that far, at least walk a little of it, as some of the best vistas are along the next half mile of the trail, which continues to the right past the picnic area.

At the connection with the Moalepe Trail, if you go left you'll come to a viewpoint after about 10 minutes. If you go right on Moalepe you'll come out on Olohena Rd in Wailua Homesteads about 2¼ miles down.

Coco Palms

The Coco Palms Resort was built on the site of Kauai's ancient royal court, in the midst of a 45-acre coconut grove.

There's a Hawaiian design to it all, with thatched cottages and lagoons, and it looks a bit like a movie set. Like movie sets, the closer you get, the less authentic it appears – you begin to notice that the coconut palm pillars are made of cement and that sort of thing.

The hotel's outdoor **chapel** was originally built in 1954 for the movie *Sadie Thompson* with Rita Hayworth. The highest-profile wedding that took place at Coco Palms was between Elvis Presley and Joan Blackman in *Blue Hawaii*. A few faded decades later, about 700 people a year still come to the little chapel in the palms to be married.

Near the chapel is a small free **museum** with some Hawaiian artefacts that's operated by volunteers from Kauai Historial Society. It's open from 10 am to 3.30 pm on Mondays, Tuesdays and Thursdays and from 9 am to 1 pm on Sundays. The hotel leads walking tours of the grounds at 1 pm daily and there's a free torch-lighting ceremony at 7.30 pm.

Fern Grotto

Fern Grotto is Kauai's busiest tourist attraction. It's a riverboat tour complete with corny jokes and packaged sentimentality to the tune of Elvis's 'Hawaiian Wedding Song'.

The riverboats are big with wide flat bottoms – very simple, like covered barges. Some people compare them to cattle boats even before they pack the tourists on. The grotto itself is a large musty cave beneath a fern-covered rock face. It's pretty, but over-rated.

Smith's Motor Boat Service (☎ 822-4111)

and Waialeale Boat Tours (☎ 822-4908) both charge $10 for adults and $5 for children aged 4 to 13, and leave Wailua Marina every half hour between 9 am and 4 pm.

Smith's Tropical Paradise

Smith's Tropical Paradise (☎ 822-4654) at Wailua Marina has a loop trail through theme gardens and artificial 'villages'. It's open from 8.30 am to 4 pm daily. Admission is $5, with guided tram tours $4 more; it's half-price for children aged 3 to 12. In the evening there's a luau and Polynesian show.

Coconut Plantation

Coconut Plantation is a development with four hotels, one condominium and a shopping centre. It fronts a half-mile-long beach that's shaded by ironwood trees.

Water activities are restricted due to the low lava shelf that runs along most of the beach and the strong currents that prevail beyond. The sand on the beach is unique, each little piece polished to a high gloss.

While water conditions are mediocre, the beach makes for good strolling. The large grassy field between the Beachboy and the Coconut Beach Hotel is popular with egrets and the occasional kite flyer.

The beach hut at the Coconut Beach Hotel arranges a free introductory dive lesson in the pool every afternoon.

Coconut Marketplace The Coconut Marketplace is open from 9 am to 9 pm daily. It has 70 different shops, including Liberty House, a kite shop, a movie theatre, Fox Photo one-hour processing, art galleries, clothing stores with signs announcing perpetual 50%-off sales, and shops with names like 'Nik-Nak Shak' and 'Shells International'. There's also a Waldenbooks, with a good Hawaiiana section. Food places include steak and Mexican restaurants, a bakery, an ice-cream stand, several fast-food kiosks and a convenience store.

Free Polynesian-style hula shows take place at 4.30 pm on Mondays, Wednesdays, Fridays and Saturdays.

Places to Stay – B&Bs & Guesthouses

Some of the best accommodation on Kauai is at the Wailua B&Bs, which are more intimate and far better value than the area hotels. The listings in this section are all in the Wailua Homesteads area, which is about three miles from the coast in a rural country setting. All are roughly within a mile of the intersection of Hwy 581 and Hwy 580.

The *Sleeping Giant Guest House & Hostel* (☎ 823-6142, (800) 858-2295), 1320 Nahele Place, Kapaa, HI 96746, is off the north end of Kamalu Rd (Hwy 581). There are 16 bunk beds in a couple of rooms, as well as four rather spartan private rooms furnished with either two twin beds or a double bed. It costs $14 for a dorm bed, $35 for a room, with linen included. Bathrooms are shared and there's free use of the kitchen, TV room and lockers. The house is clean, there's no curfew, and Jack Schultz, who runs the place, organises day trips for $5. The outings generally alternate between the North Shore (also providing drop-off service for Na Pali Coast hikers) and Kokee State Park. There's a nightly barbecue for $6, breakfast for $2, a coin-op washer and dryer, and free airport pick-up. German and French are spoken.

Rosewood B&B (☎ 822-5216), Rosemary & Norbert Smith, 872 Kamalu Rd, Kapaa, HI 96746, is in a beautifully restored 80-year-old plantation home. Rosemary has a real estate business and Norbert is a landscaper. It's a wholesome family environment, with two cats, a mellow dog, a pre-teen daughter and a couple of teenage sons still at home. There's a newly renovated master bedroom with pastel wallpaper, soft carpeting and a comfortable king-size bed. The room has an attached tiled bath with a large sunken tub and a country view of grazing cattle and mountain backdrops. Another guest room has two twin beds and a queen bed. The rate for either room is $45/50 for singles/doubles. Guests can also opt to stay on the screened porch for $35 a double. There are plans to expand, and two separate guest cottages are under construction. Breakfast is served in the family kitchen. Smoking is not allowed.

The *House of Aleva* (☎ 822-4606), Ernest & Anita Perry, 5509 Kuamoo Rd, Kapaa, HI 96746, is a B&B right on Hwy 580, two miles up from Coco Palms. Ernest is a retired merchant seaman and Anita is a retired nurse who reads palms and makes ceramic Hawaiiana sculptures. They rent out two rooms with a shared bath in their home, at $35/50 for singles/doubles. The rooms have queen beds with comfortable mattresses, telephones and mini-refrigerators. The rate includes a full breakfast, which can be adapted for vegetarian and special diets. Guests are welcome to share the TV room, use the washer/dryer, borrow snorkelling equipment and make themselves at home. Photos of past guests, which line one wall, include a fair number of European travellers.

Lampy's Bed & Breakfast (☎ 822-0478), 6078 Kolopua St, Kapaa, HI 96746, has six rooms in a large house, each $45 for one or two people, continental breakfast included. There's an extra $5 fee if you stay just one night. Rooms have either queen beds or two twins. Four rooms have private bathrooms, while two share a bath. A couple of the units have private entrances, refrigerators and microwaves, whereas the others share a kitchen. There's a common room with TV and VCR. Lampy's is more business-like than some of the smaller B&Bs – local calls are 50 cents, laundry service is $5 a load, and snorkels are for rent rather than loaned free – but it's efficiently run, clean and comfortable.

Kauai's first B&B is still called *Kay Barker's B&B* (☎ 822-3073, (800) 835-2845), Box 740, Kapaa, HI 96746, though Kay has passed away and the place is now run by her son Gordon. While comfortable enough, the house is more modest than other Wailua B&Bs. There are four bedrooms, each with a private bathroom. The backyard looks out onto a field with grazing cattle and is beside the start of the Sleeping Giant trail. Rooms cost $35 to $50 for singles, $45 to $60 for doubles, breakfast included. A separate cottage costs $60/70. Smoking and social drinking are allowed.

Inn Paradise (☎ 822-2542), Major &

Connie Inch, 6381 Makana Rd, Kapaa, HI 96746, has three delightfully furnished units that include nice touches like Persian carpets on hardwood floors and quality Hawaiiana wall prints. Each has cable TV, a telephone, a refrigerator, a microwave and a private entrance. The three units are in a guesthouse that stands separate from the Inch's contemporary home. All share a lanai with an unspoiled view of pasture and mountains. The Prince Kuhio room, which has a king bed, is a great value at $50. The Queen Kapule suite has a separate living room with a fold-down murphy bed and costs $75 for up to two people. The King Kaumualii unit, which is equipped like a small house, has two separate bedrooms and a full kitchen and costs $100 for up to four people. Additional guests are $7 more. Rates include breakfast provisions and free use of a washer and dryer.

Royal Drive Cottages (☎ 822-2321), 147 Royal Drive, Kapaa, HI 96746, has two studio cottages on a quiet street just off Hwy 580. The cottages are simple, with almost a backwoods feel, but wholly adequate with two twin beds, phone, refrigerator, microwave, toaster and coffeepot. The cottages do have tin roofs and this is a wet island – some people find the sound of rain on tin romantic, while others might be kept awake by it. Rates are $60 for one person, $75 for two.

Places to Stay – Hotels & Condos

Wailua's hotels and condos all have swimming pools and the usual standard facilities, though they also tend to have an air of neglect and none are particularly special.

The *Kauai Sands Hotel* (☎ 822-4951, (800) 367-7000 from the USA, (800) 654-7020 from Canada), 420 Papaloa Rd, Kapaa, HI 96746, is part of the Hawaiian-owned Sand & Seaside hotel chain. The rooms have been renovated, although the bright striped wallpaper and turquoise and green decor give the overall ambience of a budget chain motel. Rates are $74 for standard rooms, $100 for rooms with kitchenettes. They're $10 cheaper in the low season, and you can often get a better rate by booking in Hawaii.

Kapaa Sands (☎ 822-4901, (800) 222-4901), 380 Papaloa Rd, Kapaa, HI 96746, has 24 condo units set up in either duplexes or fourplexes. All have kitchens, lanais, louvered windows to catch the breeze, and at least a partial ocean view. While the units are older and a bit faded, they are relatively good value at $75 for studios for one or two people and $99 for two-bedroom units for up to four people. Oceanfront units cost $10 more. There's a three to seven-day minimum stay.

The *Aston Kauai Beachboy Hotel* (☎ 822-3441, (800) 922-7866 from the USA, (800) 445-6633 from Canada), 484 Kuhio Hwy, Kapaa, HI 96746, is a standard hotel with 243 rooms from $98 to $118. Rates are $10 cheaper in the low season.

The *Islander on the Beach* (☎ 822-7417, (800) 847-7417), 484 Kuhio Hwy, Kapaa, HI 96746, has 200 hotel rooms in half a dozen three-storey buildings. Rooms are pleasant and have coffeemakers and refrigerators. Rates, which include a Tropical rental car, start at $105/95 in the high/low season. There's a poolside bar.

The *Kauai Resort Hotel* (☎ 245-3931, (800) 745-2824), 3-5920 Kuhio Hwy, Kapaa, HI 96746, is north of Lydgate Beach Park and next to the Wailua Golf Course. The rooms are small and the grounds are on the lacklustre side. Standard rooms cost $109 to $149, while studios cost $159 to $169. They're all $10 cheaper in the low season.

The *Plantation Hale* (☎ 822-4941, (800) 733-7777 from the USA, (800) 125-642 from Australia), 484 Kuhio Hwy, Kapaa, HI 96746, is on the highway side of Coconut Plantation. Now part of the Outrigger chain, the complex has 160 roomy one-bedroom units with modern furnishings, two doubles or one king bed in the bedroom, a queen sofabed in the living room, a separate full kitchen and two TVs. The rate of $105/120 in the low/high season is the same for up to four people, which makes it a good value for small groups. They often run discounts or throw in a free rental car.

The *Coco Palms Resort* (☎ 822-4921, (800) 338-1338), Box 631, Lihue, HI 96766, has a dated South Pacific motif, with older thatched-roof cottages and giant clam shell washbasins. Hotel rooms are $110 to $160, cottages (not recommended) are $175 to $270, suites are $160 to $330. All rooms have TV and refrigerators, but you pay for the resort's cliche charm. Honeymoon packages are big.

The *Coconut Beach Hotel* (☎ 822-3455), Box 830, Kapaa, HI 96746, a former Sheraton, is a 309-room hotel at the quieter north end of Coconut Plantation. The 4th floor rooms are the nicest, as they have high ceilings that make the room look a bit larger. Some of the lanais are amazingly small, with barely enough room to squeeze in a couple of chairs. Rates are $125 to $210, depending on the view.

Places to Eat

The *Sizzler* steak house, 4361 Kuhio Hwy, has a great salad bar with fresh fruits that rival those at any of the hotel buffets. It costs $7.49 and includes a taco bar, pasta bar, soups and cheeses. There's also a popular $7.99 breakfast buffet from 6 to 11 am on Saturday and Sunday mornings with food that ranges from waffles and fruit to salads and teriyaki chicken. It's rather classy looking for a Sizzler, with skylights and the like.

Perry's Smorgy in the Aston Kauai Beachboy Hotel is cafeteria style and quality, but at $4.95 for an all-you-can-eat breakfast that includes fresh papaya and pineapple, the price is hard to beat. The lunch buffet is from 11.30 am to 2.30 pm and costs $5.95 (except on Sundays when it's called brunch and costs $8.95). The dinner buffet is from 5 to 9 pm and costs $8.95. Prices include beverages and dessert.

Buzz's Steak & Lobster in the Coconut Marketplace has a pretty good salad bar, which at dinner costs $6.95 alone or $2.50 with entrees. There's usually an early-bird dinner from 5 to 6.30 pm, with teriyaki chicken or fish for $7. Otherwise most dinner entrees cost from $11 to $15. At lunch there's a soup, salad and sandwich bar for $6.75. Look for coupons in the free tourist magazines for discounts. It's open daily, from 11

am to 2.30 pm for lunch, 5 to 10.30 pm for dinner.

Cafe Espresso in the Coconut Marketplace is a bakery and cafe with a variety of coffees from $1.25 and croissants, muffins, pies, cakes and other pastries. It's open daily from 7 am.

The *Lagoon Dining Room* at Coco Palms Resort has a buffet lunch from 11 am to 2 pm for $11. It has fruits and vegies, and main dishes of average buffet fare. Tour groups start pulling in at 11.30 am and if you don't beat them you could find yourself in the midst of 100 hungry rushing groupies. The open-air restaurant looks out over the hotel's artificial lagoon and coconut grove.

Kintaro (☎ 822-3341), opposite the Sizzler, has Japanese dinners in the $13 to $17 range. The sushi is good but the tempura is mediocre. There's also a teppanyaki room where the chef prepares food at your table with 'flying' knives for a few dollars more. It's open from 5.30 to 9.30 pm Monday to Saturday.

Entertainment

Buzz's in the Coconut Marketplace has live contemporary music, sometimes Hawaiian but always mellow, in its lounge from 9 pm to midnight Wednesday to Saturday. There's no cover charge.

The *Kauai Resort Hotel* (☎ 245-3931) sometimes features good Hawaiian and contemporary musicians. It also has a dinner buffet with a Polynesian show on Monday, Wednesday and Friday nights for $18.

The *Coco Palms Resort* has a free torch-lighting ceremony nightly at 7.30 pm, with young men in malos running around the grounds lighting torches to the beating of drums. Coco Palms also has a Polynesian show at 9 pm in its Lagoon Dining Room. There's a cover charge and it's geared for an older crowd.

Smith's Tropical Paradise (☎ 822-4654) has a rather theatrical luau with cocktails, music and dinner at 7.30 pm Monday to Friday. It costs $43.75 for adults, $26 for children aged 7 to 13 and $17 for children aged 3 to 6.

The *Coconut Beach Hotel* (☎ 822-3455) has a luau nightly except Mondays that includes an open bar, dinner and a rather standard show. It costs $45 for adults, $26 for children aged 12 and under. You can catch a glimpse of it from the hotel parking lot.

The theatre in the Coconut Marketplace shows first-run Hollywood movies.

WAIPOULI

Waipouli is the name given to the strip between Coconut Plantation and Kapaa. Its biggest draw is its **shopping centres**, which are the region's largest and contain some of Kauai's best places to eat.

Waipouli Town Center has a Foodland supermarket (open 24 hours a day), a McDonald's and a Pizza Hut.

Kapaa Shopping Center has Kapaa's post office, a Big Save supermarket, a laundromat and a Burger King. The post office is open from 8.30 am to 4 pm Monday to Friday, from 10 am to noon on Saturdays.

Kauai Village

Kauai Village, Waipouli's newest and largest shopping centre, has a Pay'n Save drugstore, a Safeway supermarket, Waldenbooks and 40 other shops. Eateries include Papaya's Natural Foods, A Pacific Cafe, ice-cream shops, a Chinese restaurant and Subway Sandwiches.

The centre's Kauai Village Museum, near Papaya's, is a Hawaiiana gift and book shop. It displays a modest collection of Hawaiian artefacts and a pili-grass house.

There's free entertainment, usually quite local in flavour, near the courtyard waterfall from 6 to 8 pm on Fridays, and a keiki hula show at 4 pm on Saturdays.

Sleeping Giant

The Sleeping Giant is taking his eternal rest stretched out atop the Nounou Ridge with his head in Wailua and his feet in Kapaa. There's a marked viewpoint just north of the Waipouli Complex.

Legend says a friendly giant fell asleep on the hillside after eating too much poi at a luau. When his menehune friends needed his help they tried to awaken him by throwing stones at him, but the stones bounced from his full belly into his open mouth. As the giant swallowed the stones, he died and turned to rock.

Wailua Houselots, on the east side of the ridge, was the first subdivision on Kauai. It was originally divided into two-acre lots and had some spacious Hawaiian-style homes. Most of the lots have since been subdivided and the homes are now more typical standardised tract development.

A hiking trail runs across the ridge connecting Wailua Houselots and Wailua Homesteads (see the Wailua section). The giant's forehead, the highest point on the ridge, is 1241 feet.

Places to Stay

Mokihana of Kauai (☎ 822-3971), 796 Kuhio Hwy, has 80 studio units on the beach. While the rooms are rather plain, each has twin beds, a hot plate, a refrigerator and a lanai with an ocean view for $55. This is a time-share complex that rents to nonmembers on a space available basis. Not many visitors know about it, so when other places are full it's not uncommon to find a room or two available here.

The front desk at Mokihana also handles the 57 two-bedroom time-share units at nearby *Kauai Kailani I & II*. These units have full kitchens and cost $65 for doubles, plus $5 per additional person to a maximum of five. Ask for Kauai Kailani I as it's on the ocean.

You can also make advance reservations through Hawaii Kailani, (☎ 206-676-1434), 119 N Commercial, Suite 1400, Bellingham, WA 98225.

Places to Eat

The *King & I* (☎ 822-1642) in Waipouli Plaza is one of our favourite Kauai restaurants. It's casual, friendly and has excellent Thai food. The spring rolls served with fresh mint, cucumber, peanut sauce and lettuce leaves are not to be missed. They grow their own herbs; the green curry gets its colour from fresh basil, lime leaves and lemongrass. Most dishes cost between $6 and $8 and can be prepared mild, medium or hot. They have brown rice and a whole page of vegie dishes. The cooking is done by owner Cindy Choy, a former chef at Keo's, Honolulu's premier Thai restaurant. It's open daily from 4.30 to 9.30 pm, to 10 pm on Fridays and Saturdays.

The *Aloha Diner* in Waipouli Complex is the place to try authentic Hawaiian food. The laulau is pretty good and the lomi salmon excellent. You can order à la carte, or get complete lunches from about $6. Dinner costs about $10. It's open from 10.30 am to 3 pm and from 5.30 to 9 pm.

Papaya's Natural Foods (☎ 823-0191) in Kauai Village is a well-stocked health-food store with a cafe serving wholesome salads, hot dishes and desserts. The Garden Burger made of brown rice, sunflower seeds and cheese, served with tomato, lettuce and sprouts on a whole-wheat bun is recommended at $4.75. Grilled fish burgers are $6, spinach pies are $3.75 and deli-style dishes such as eggplant basmati rice and grilled chicken pasta are sold by the half pound. Breakfast, from 8 to 10.30 am, includes the likes of buckwheat pancakes, French toast with cream cheese and strawberries, artichoke frittata, granola and gourmet coffee. Papaya's closes at 9 pm on weekends, at 8 pm the rest of the week. Ethnic dinner specials are featured after 4 pm. Seating is at small outside tables.

Ambrose's Natural Foods, opposite Waipouli Town Center, sells local produce. Look for a tamale wagon that sometimes parks at the side selling authentic corn-husk tamales.

A Pacific Cafe (☎ 822-0013) in Kauai Village serves Pacific Rim cuisine at its best. French chef Jean-Marie Josselin has a creative menu with dishes like wood-grilled onaga in a hibiscus-ginger sauce, seared sirloin with lemon-grass peanut crust, Thai fish soup and sizzling squid salad. Starters and soups range from $4 to $9, main dishes are $15 to $23 and a daily chef's dinner of salad, starter and entree costs around $33. It's

a class act, with food presented on hand-crafted pottery. If you're saving one night for a splurge on Kauai, this is a good choice. Hours are 5.30 to 9.30 pm nightly. Reservations are suggested.

At the opposite end of the gastronomic scale are the slew of fast-food eateries along the highway. *Zippy's*, next to Waipouli Plaza, has a large menu, including burgers for $2.50 and plate lunches from $6 to $7. It's very much fast-food quality, but it is open 24 hours a day.

A fine alternative to fast food is the *Safeway* supermarket in Kauai Village which has a good salad bar that includes fresh fruits, guacamole, salsa and chilli at $3.50 a pound. Safeway also has a deli counter with a wide variety of pastas and salads, a bakery with French bread, a good produce section, and a fish counter with laulau, poi and eight kinds of poki. In addition, the store has some of the cheapest wine prices on the island.

KAPAA

Kapaa is an old plantation town with a small commercial centre that is still geared more towards local needs than tourism. It has a small hotel, a few restaurants and some clothing shops.

As unimposing as it appears, Kapaa is one of Kauai's largest towns. However most of the residential area is well inland of the centre. You can walk the main drag in 10 minutes.

The **Kapaa Beach Park**, off Niu St behind the ball field, has a beach, picnic tables and a public swimming pool.

The **Kapaa Public Library** (☎ 822-5041), 1464 Kuhio Hwy, is open from 9 am to 4.30 pm on Mondays, Wednesdays and Fridays and from noon to 8 pm on Tuesdays and Thursdays.

The classic-looking **Roxy Theater** was built in the 1930s with the help of Honolulu architect C W Dickey. It first opened with *Lady of the Tropics* starring Heddy Lamar and Robert Taylor: the tickets were 25 cents. These days it's a weekend entertainment spot featuring live music in an alcohol-free environment.

Places to Stay

The *Hotel Coral Reef* (☎ 822-4481, (800) 843-4659), 1516 Kuhio Hwy, Kapaa, HI 96746, has two sections. The older part has nine rooms for $41/46 singles/doubles, basic but clean, with standing fans, painted cinderblock walls and open-screen windows that don't act as much of a barrier to the traffic noise. There's almost a boarding house atmosphere, with a communal TV lounge downstairs. The newer wing has 16 rooms with refrigerators, lanais and ocean views for $75. There's no pool nor room TVs. Pastries and coffee are complimentary in the morning.

Keapana Center (☎ 822-7968, (800) 822-7968), 5620 Keapana Rd, Kapaa, HI 96746, is a relaxing New Age B&B with a scenic hilltop location three miles above Kapaa centre. There are three rooms with shared bath at $35/50 singles/doubles and two rooms with private bath at $50/65. The rooms are small and suitably simple and rates include continental breakfast and use of the hot tub. There's a common-use refrigerator and kitchen, a large airy lounge and a platform for sunrise stretching that faces a splendid view of the Anahola mountains. Metaphysical books are loaned free and massage is available for a fee.

Places to Eat

All these restaurants are on Hwy 56, within walking distance of its intersection with Olohena Rd (Hwy 581).

Fast Freddy's is an unpretentious local diner serving a Deuces Wild breakfast special of two pancakes, two eggs and two sausages for $2.22 from 7.30 am to noon Monday to Saturday. Except for the Deuces Wild, which always seems to get priority, Fast Freddy's has slow service. The restaurant reopens at 5.30 pm for dinner, when it has a reasonably good shrimp scampi for $10.95.

Michelle's is a small cafe serving homemade food. Breakfast includes espresso, croissants, muesli, scrambled eggs, and papaya with yoghurt. Lunch is mainly soups, salads and sandwiches from $4.50 to $6. The dinner menu includes entrees such as vegetable couscous, New Orleans gumbo and sauteed ahi priced in the $8 to $12 range. It's open from 7 am to 3 pm on Tuesdays, 7 am to 9 pm Wednesday to Friday and 8 am to 9 pm on Saturdays and Sundays.

Norberto's El Cafe (☎ 822-3362) has been in the neighbourhood a long time. Plates, such as enchiladas for $11.50 or fajitas for $13, include soup, rice and refried beans. Or order à la carte: a taco costs $3, a filling 'burrito outrageous' $6.50. You can wash it all down with margaritas or Mexican brew. Opening hours are 5.30 to 9 pm daily.

Hana-Ya is a little Japanese restaurant with a small sushi bar and a few tables. Oyaku donburi costs $5.95, soba costs $4.50 and other dishes are priced from $5 to $15.

Jimmy's Grill is the place where the crowd goes to have a few beers and watch the game on TV. Burgers and sandwiches with fries cost $6.50 to $8. It's open from 11 am to 10 pm daily. A couple of drinks are discounted during 'groovy hour', from 4 to 6 pm.

KAPAA TO KILAUEA

The drive from Kapaa to Kilauea is through fields of sugar cane in varying stages of growth, from newly planted seed cane to mature stalk. Beyond the fields, the jagged edges of the Anahola mountain peaks cut their way through the clouds. In the other direction there are glimpses of bright blue ocean and distant bays.

A couple of scenic lookouts just north of Kapaa are worth pulling over for. Sunsets can be particularly nice if there's a low tide with waves breaking over the shallows and fishers out with their throw nets.

Kealia Beach

The long, pretty beach at the 10-mile marker is Kealia Beach. During transitional swells, Kealia can be a good place for surfing. There are no facilities here.

After rain storms the beach tends to be littered with sugar cane cuttings that are carried down Kealia Stream, which empties at the south side of the beach.

Donkey Beach

Donkey Beach is best known as a nudist beach, though it's used by both clad and unclad sunbathers. This lovely windswept sandy beach is completely hidden from the road.

The trail to Donkey Beach begins about half a mile past the 11-mile marker, just before the guard rail starts. It's 10 minutes down a well-worn path beside a sugar cane field and through a narrow stretch of coastal ironwoods.

All the ironwood trees lean away from the shore and those right at the beach are so blown over they almost look like shrubs. Naupaka and ilima grow in the sand along the shadeless beach. There are no facilities. From October to May, high surf creates dangerous rip currents and a powerful shorebreak.

Anahola

Anahola is a small, somewhat scattered village, much of it along Anahola Bay. The wide bay was an ancient surfing site and has a break that's still popular with surfers today.

Anahola Beach Park, a county park on Hawaiian Home Lands, sits at the south side of the bay. It's been a source of contention over the last few years between county officials who want to maintain the park and native Hawaiians who want to take the land back. So far the county has prevailed and the beach park remains open to the public. To get there turn off Hwy 56 onto Kukuihale Rd at the 13-mile marker, and just less than a mile down, turn onto the dirt beach road.

Anahola's modest commercial centre consists of the Anahola post office, Duane's burger stand and a small general store grouped together at the side of Hwy 56, just south of the 14-mile marker.

Just to the north, on the mauka side of the road, is the quaint little **Anahola Baptist Church** backed by a picturesque mountain setting. A stand next door sells flower leis and shave ice.

Places to Stay *Mahina Kai* (☎ 822-9451), Box 699, 4933 Aliomanu Rd, Anahola, HI 96703, is a B&B on Anahola Bay that caters mainly for the gay community. Hosts Dale and Rick are well-travelled former Californians whose contemporary home has lots of Asian-Pacific aesthetics such as shoji doors, meditating buddhas and a little fountain courtyard. There's also a swimming pool and hot tub in a Japanese garden. It's a nice place to relax. There are three rooms with breakfast and private bathrooms at $80/115 singles/doubles, as well as a self-catering studio apartment that costs $125 for two people, $165 for four. The minimum stay is three days.

Places to Eat *Duane's Ono Burger* sells burgers and teri sandwiches for $3.65 to $6. Best deal is the basic burger, as more expensive burgers such as the 'teri' simply add a dollop of sauce on top. A huge order of fries costs $1.60. There are outdoor picnic tables. Opening hours are 10 am to 6 pm daily (from 11 am on Sundays).

Whaler's General Store, next door to Duane's, has boiled eggs for 30 cents, hot dogs two for a dollar, and cold beer. It's open daily from 7 am to 8.30 pm.

Hole in the Mountain

The Hole in the Mountain can't presently be seen from the HVB marker, as the hole closed during a landslide at the time of Hurricane Iwa. But just slightly north of the 15-mile marker, look back at the mountain down to the right of the tallest pinnacle and you'll be able to see the small hole that is slowly re-opening.

Legend says the original hole was created when a giant threw his spear through the mountain causing the water stored within to gush forth as waterfalls. After the hole closed, Hawaii began to experience one of the worst droughts in its history.

Koolau Road

The Koolau Rd is a peaceful drive through rich green pastures with white egrets and a smattering of bright wildflowers. Take it as a scenic loop off the highway or to get to Moloaa Beach or Larsens Beach. Both the road and the beaches are well off the tourist track. Neither beach has any facilities.

Koolau Rd connects with Hwy 56 half a mile north of the 16-mile marker (at Sunrise Fruit Stand) and again one-tenth of a mile south of the 20-mile marker.

Moloaa Beach To get to Moloaa Beach coming from the south, turn right onto Koolau Rd at the fruit stand and after 1¼ miles turn right onto Moloaa Rd. The road ends three-quarters of a mile down at a few beach houses.

Moloaa is very rural, with horses grazing on the hills above the crescent-shaped bay. Because it's not heavily frequented it's a pretty good beach for shelling.

The northern end of the beach before the rocky outcrop is somewhat protected for swimming though it's not all that deep. The whole bay can have strong currents when the surf is rough.

On the grassy hill north of the bay a trail leads to a point offering peeks into the coastal hills and valleys to the south. The trail is through flowering groundcover of pink and yellow lantana; sensitive plants whose leaves close when touched; and pau-o-Hiiaka, a trailing vine with small tulip-like blue flowers, related to the morning glory.

Larsens Beach The turn-off to Larsens Beach is off Koolau Rd, a little more than a mile down from the north intersection of Koolau Rd and Hwy 56, or just over a mile north of the intersection of Moloaa and Koolau Rds. Turn makai on the dirt road there and then take the immediate left. It's one mile to the parking area and then a five-minute walk downhill to the beach.

Larsens is a long golden sand beach, good for solitary strolls and beachcombing. While it's a bit shallow for swimming, snorkelling can be good when the waters are very calm, which is generally in the summer only. Beware of a current that runs westward along the beach and out through a channel in the reef.

If the tide is low, you may well see a few Hawaiian families on the outer edge of the reef collecting a seaweed called *limu kohu*. The seaweed found at Larsens is considered to be some of the finest in all Hawaii.

North Shore

Kauai's North Shore has an unhurried pace and incredible scenery. It has deep mountain valleys, ancient taro fields, one-lane bridges, white-sand beaches and the rugged Na Pali Coast.

It's lush and often wet. In winter that can mean days of rain on end, but in summer it usually means brief showers followed by rainbows. On bright full-moon nights you might even see a moonbow – a rainbow coloured with moonbeams.

Rainy days are almost dream-like. The tops of the mountains become shrouded in clouds that alternately drift and lift revealing a series of waterfalls that plunge down the face of the mountains.

The North Shore takes in the sea-bird sanctuary at Kilauea and a couple of small coastal villages before reaching the resort community of Princeville with its condos and golf courses.

But it's the area beyond, from Hanalei Bridge to Kee Beach at road's end, that best embodies the North Shore spirit. This is a part of Hawaii that has resisted mass tourism and stalled development. Its appeal is not in creature comforts but in stunning natural beauty. It attracts people tuned in to the environment. Over the years musicians like Graham Nash and Buffy Sainte-Marie and all sorts of artists have called Kauai's North Shore home.

KILAUEA

Kilauea is a former sugar plantation town whose main attraction is its picturesque lighthouse and sea-bird sanctuary at Kilauea Point. The sanctuary is the most visited site on the North Shore and shouldn't be missed.

Kolo Rd, the turn-off into Kilauea, is just past the 23-mile marker on Hwy 56. You pass a gas station with a health-food store attached, a post office with a mini-mart and then an Episcopal church, all in quick succession. Kilauea Rd starts opposite the church and ends two miles later at Kilauea Point.

The famed Kilauea Slippery Slide, built for the movie *South Pacific*, is on private property and is no longer accessible to the public due to concerns about legal liability.

Episcopal Church

The little Christ Memorial Episcopal Church attracts attention because of its striking lava rock architecture. It was built in 1941. The interesting lava rock headstones in the churchyard are much older, dating back to when the original Hawaiian Congregational church stood on this site.

Kong Lung Center

The Kong Lung Center, half a mile up Kilauea Rd, has a worthwhile crafts and clothing shop, a couple of good places to get a quick bite to eat and an expensive Italian restaurant. It also has a movie theatre showing first-run movies which halves its regular admission charge to $2.50 on Tuesdays and charges seniors only $1 everyday.

Quarry Beach

If you're looking for somewhere new to explore, you might try Quarry Beach at Kilauea Bay. Also known as Kahili Beach, it's the site of an abandoned rock quarry and former steamer landing. It's mostly used by fishers and local beachgoers, though when the surf is unusually high, surfers also take to these waters. Swimmers should be aware of strong nearshore currents when the surf is up.

Public access is down the second dirt road to the right after the Kong Lung Center. The drive is about 1½ miles long and the road, which starts off through a sugar cane field, is bumpy and rutted but usually passable if it hasn't been raining a lot. You have to wade across Kilauea Stream to get to the beach.

Kilauea Point

Kilauea Point, a national wildlife refuge, is the northernmost point of the inhabited Hawaiian islands. Topped by a lighthouse that was built in 1913, it's picture postcard material.

Four species of birds come to Kilauea to nest, leaving after their young have been hatched and reared.

Red-footed boobies are the most visible. They are abundant on the cliffs to the east where they build nests of sticks and leaves in the trees. Sea turtles can sometimes be seen swimming in the cove at the base of these cliffs. During winter, whales pass by off the point.

Wedge-tailed shearwaters arrive by April and stay through the summer, nesting in burrows that they dig into Kilauea Point. Another readily spotted species is the red-tailed tropicbird, which nests along the cliff edges. If you're lucky you'll spot a pair soaring in loops, performing their courtship ritual.

Laysan albatross are at Kilauea from about November to July. Some nest on Mokuaeae Rock, straight off the tip of the point. Inland, the grassy area to the west was cleared to attract more albatross. Some now nest there on the ground at the base of the trees. Looking out beyond the clearing you can see Secret Beach, divided into three scalloped coves by lava fingers.

Great frigate birds nest on the Northwestern Hawaiian Islands, not Kauai, though these aerial pirates do visit Kilauea Point during the winter to steal food from other birds. You won't see the distinctive red throat balloon that the male puffs out to attract females, however, as they're not here for courtship. Frigate birds have a distinctive forked tail and are beautiful when they soar.

The visitors' centre is open on weekdays at which time the staff allow you to use the binoculars at no charge; the centre has a telescope set up for bird-watching and it also sells books.

The cost for a single entry permit is $2, which includes an accompanying spouse, children and parents. US residents aged 62 and older may enter free.

The refuge (☎ 828-1414) is open from 10

Top: Waimea Canyon lookout, Kauai
Left: Kuilau Ridge Trail, Kauai
Right: Wailua Falls, Kauai

Left: Seaweed gatherers and snorkeller at Kee Beach, Kauai
Right: Na Pali Coast from Kalalau Trail, Kauai
Bottom: Secret Beach, Kauai

am to 4 pm daily. Even outside those hours it's worth driving to the end of Kilauea Rd for the picturesque view of the lighthouse and point.

Crater Hill

Crater Hill, a recent 100-acre addition to the refuge, is east of Kilauea Point. This 568-foot cliff is geologically younger than the rest of the area by a few million years. It's a nesting site for sea birds and has long been a favourite local spot for watching the sunset.

It's still possible to get a fine hilltop view of Kilauea Point and the coast from Secret Beach to Bali Hai by taking Iwalani Rd off Kilauea Rd, half a mile south of Kilauea Point. After a third of a mile, when Iwalani ends, go left and then left again at Makanaano Rd, which ends half a mile down at a cliffside cul de sac.

Volunteer naturalists lead one-mile **hikes** of Crater Hill at 10.15 am Monday to Thursday, and as more volunteers are trained the frequency of hikes is expected to increase. The hikes last 1½ to two hours and include an orientation to the ecology of the area. There is no charge, other than the Kilauea Point refuge fee, but reservations must be made by calling 828-1520. Visitors are not allowed to walk around the Crater Hill refuge property unaccompanied due to the presence of shearwaters who burrow into the hillside and whose fragile nests could be crushed by heavy feet.

Guava Plantation

The Guava Kai Plantation has 480 acres of guava trees that produce juice for Ocean Spray and a handful of other juice companies. A visitors' centre doles out small samples of guava juice and when the processing plant is in operation (mainly August to December and sporadically in the spring) you can get a glimpse of the process through viewing windows. As you go up the road through endless rows of guava trees it might seem like the fruit is too big to be the same guava growing wild in the woods. These guava trees are hybrids whose fruit grows to half a pound, twice the normal size.

There's a guava-products gift shop and a little deli selling guava ice cream and guava snacks. The plantation is open from 9 am to 5 pm. Admission is free.

To get there, turn mauka onto Kuawa Rd from Hwy 56, just north of the 23-mile marker and a quarter of a mile south of the Kolo Rd turn-off to Kilauea. The visitors' centre is about a mile from the highway.

Places to Eat

Jacques' Bakery, in an old sugar mill Quonset hut on Oka St off Kilauea Rd, is a good place to stop for breakfast on your way to the lighthouse. You can get a Danish pastry and a coffee for a mere $1 and eat it outside at an old rickety table. Simple foods are served from 6 am to 6 pm Monday to Friday. Hamburgers, mahimahi burgers or two eggs, meat and rice cost from $3 to $4. On weekends, they sell bread, pastries and coffee only.

Casa di Amici (☎ 828-1388), an Italian restaurant in the Kong Lung Center, serves up gourmet food at gourmet prices. Dinner main courses range from $15 for pastas to $24 for veal. Add another $4 to $6 for soup or salad. Dinner is from 5.30 to 9.30 pm Monday to Saturday, while lighter and less expensive foods are served from 11.30 am to 2.30 pm weekdays at lunch.

Kilauea Bakery, tucked behind Casa di Amici, sells a variety of whole-grain breads, French bread and pastries. From noon they also sell pizza by the slice for $2.25 and from 3 to 9 pm they sell whole pizzas – a 12-inch cheese costs $10. While the pizza is not outstanding, it's fairly good by Kauai standards and they load the mozzarella on. They also make some interesting speciality pizzas using tofurella and all sorts of toppings from fresh pineapple to smoked mahimahi. It's open from 7 am to 9 pm daily except Sundays.

The *Farmer's Market*, a grocery store with a good deli, is in the Kong Lung Center. The deli has a variety of sandwiches on whole-wheat bread, hummus rolls with sprouts and shredded carrots, and salads sold by the pound. The store is open from 9 am to 9 pm daily, the deli from 10 am to 2 pm.

Hale O Health, a small health-food store at the Shell station on Kolo Rd and Hwy 56, has wrapped sandwiches, taro chips, juices and vitamins. It's open from 10 am to 6 pm daily.

For a downhome treat, stop at *Banana Joe's*, the bright yellow shack on the mauka side of Hwy 56, just north of the Kolo Rd turn-off to Kilauea. Banana Joe and his sister Alex dish up a great frozen fruit frosty, made solely of frozen fruit that is squeezed through a processor and comes out as smooth as ice cream. The papaya and pineapple flavours are the best. A bowl of this ($1.50) and a granola bar ($1) make a nice snack. They also dry their own banana and jackfruit strips and sell fresh fruit from their six-acre plot of bananas, citrus and guava. The stand is open from 9 am to 6 pm daily and has a small bulletin board that usually has a few rooms for rent posted.

KALIHIWAI

Kalihiwai Rd was a loop road going down past Kalihiwai Beach, connecting with the highway at two points, until the tidal wave of 1957 washed out the bridge over Kalihiwai River. Now there are two Kalihiwai roads, one on each side of the river.

The Kalihiwai Rd on the Lihue side, half a mile beyond Kilauea, leads down a mile to **Kalihiwai Beach**. At the very end of the road you can still see the pillars that once supported the bridge. The river empties out into a wide, deep bay. The broad sandy beach is a popular spot for all kinds of activities including picnicking, swimming, bodysurfing, boogie boarding and, when the northwest swells roll in, some daredevil surfing along the cliff at the east end of the bay. The river is popular with kayakers. The beach has no facilities.

As you take Kalihiwai Rd back up to the highway, look to the left as soon as you see the 'Narrow Bridge' sign, to spot a picturesque waterfall that's nearly hidden in a lush little gully full of hanging vines.

Secret Beach

Secret Beach is a gorgeous golden sand beach backed by sea cliffs and jungle-like woods. The beach is well off the beaten path and access to it has changed frequently over the years, so very few visitors discover it. While tourists aren't exactly welcomed, the beach is mostly frequented by Kauai's alternative community and nude sunbathers, and unobtrusive visitors who can blend in are unlikely to encounter any problems.

To get there, turn down the Lihue-side Kahiliwai Rd and then turn right onto the first dirt road, which is a tenth of a mile from Hwy 56. The road ends at a parking area a third of a mile down, where you'll find a trashed car with 'Locals Only' spray-painted on the side.

The well-defined trail begins from the parking lot along a barbed wire fence that separates the woods from a horse pasture. After two minutes it leads downhill through ironwood trees and mixed jungle growth. All in all the trail only takes about five minutes and deposits you at the westernmost section of this long sandy beach.

While this part of the beach is quite idyllic, if you're up for a stroll or feel the need for even more privacy you can walk along the beach in the direction of Kilauea Lighthouse.

The beach has open seas, and high winter surf and dangerous currents prevail from

October to May. In summer water conditions are much calmer and swimming and snorkelling can be good.

Waterfalls

Back on Hwy 56, there's a pull-off on the right immediately before crossing the sweeping Kalihiwai Bridge. A brief stop will treat you to views of three waterfalls and lovely Kalihiwai Valley.

The most scenic waterfall is **Kalihiwai Falls**, seen by walking a third of the way onto the bridge ahead and looking up into the valley.

You can see a bit of another falls by simply walking to the side of the pull-off and looking down over the edge. For the third you must walk back along the road a minute or two toward Lihue. The falls is just above the road.

Kauai's native roosters – moa – hang out here. Like pigeons surrounding a park bench, they stare arrogantly with beady eyes at those who fail to offer a hand-out.

ANINI

Anini has a long beach and vast reef flats. To get there take the Kalihiwai Rd on the Hanalei side of the bridge and then bear left onto Anini Rd. It's about 1½ miles from the highway to the beach.

There has been talk of connecting Princeville and Anini by a direct coastal road. A grassroots group, Concerned Citizens to Save Anini, has managed to keep the road at bay. For now, Anini's dead-end street means little traffic, keeping the area unhurried and quiet.

Still, Anini is growing, and a number of new expensive private homes have been built across from the beach. A group of investors, including Sylvester Stallone, now own a sizeable chunk of Anini's privately held land. Stallone can sometimes be seen playing polo on the field across from the beach.

Anini Beach

Anini Beach Park is a long beach park divided into day-use, windsurfing and camping areas. It's a very pleasant spot, with gentle breezes and tropical almond shade trees. There are restrooms, showers, changing rooms, drinking water, picnic pavilions and a pay phone.

Anini has a good camping ground right on the water. It's spacious for a beach park and the camping sites are shaded by trees. It gets a little more crowded on weekends when locals, mostly families, come down.

In addition to the day-use area, you can also swim and snorkel in front of the camping area, though it's best when the tide is high. A pretty good spot is opposite the midpoint of Kauai Polo Club's fence.

Past the west end of the park Anini Channel cuts across the reef. While some people use the channel for water activities when the seas are calm, waters flowing off the reef create dangerous rip currents in the channel. The protected lagoon west of the channel provides good snorkelling and safer water conditions.

At the far end of Anini you can watch people walking way out onto the shallow reef of Anini Flats picking opihi, net fishing for bait fish and catching octopuses.

PRINCEVILLE

Princeville, Kauai's biggest development, traces its haole roots to Robert Wyllie, a Scottish doctor who later became foreign minister to Kamehameha IV. In the mid-1800s Wyllie bought a large coffee plantation in Hanalei and began planting sugar.

When Queen Emma and Kamehameha IV came to visit in 1860, Wyllie named his plantation and surrounding lands Princeville in honour of their young son, Prince Albert. The plantation later became a cattle ranch and in 1968 ground was broken for the Princeville Resort.

Today Princeville is a planned community spread over 11,000 acres on a promontory between Hanalei Bay and Anini Beach. It has 10 condo complexes, a luxury hotel, hundreds of private homes, a couple of championship golf courses, 22 tennis courts, restaurants, a shopping centre and even its own little airport.

While it all seems out of place on the North Shore, standing in sharp contrast to the free-spirited communities that lay beyond, Princeville's manicured grounds are spacious, the condos are low rise and the development is uncrowded compared to its counterparts on other islands.

Information

Princeville Center has a gas station, a supermarket, a kite shop, a camera shop, a Bank of Hawaii, a Western Union office, a Lappert's ice cream shop and several restaurants and boutiques. Foodland supermarket is open from 7 am to 11 pm daily.

Princeville Chevron is open from 7 am to 8 pm daily. If you're heading toward Kee Beach at the end of the road, this is the last place to buy gas.

Kuhio Highway changes from Hwy 56 to Hwy 560 at the 28-mile marker in front of Princeville Center. The 10-mile stretch from this point to Kee Beach at the end of the road is one of the most scenic drives in all of Hawaii.

Princeville Hotel

The Princeville Hotel, at the site of an old Russian fort, offers a splendid view of Hanalei Bay and the Bali Hai mountains. The luxury hotel was erected amidst a great deal of controversy in 1985. Locals, who were miffed at losing one of their favourite sunset spots, nicknamed the bluff-side building 'The Prison'. The hotel was indeed dark and inward-looking and it so failed to incorporate its surroundings that the owners closed it down in 1989. Over the next two years the hotel was gutted and virtually rebuilt. The newly reopened Princeville Hotel has a lobby with floor-to-ceiling windows offering 180° views of Bali Hai. It also has marble floors, pools of flowing water and a smattering of antiques and artwork, but the real attraction is the view. For a particularly fine vista check out the outdoor balcony just beyond La Cascata restaurant.

Powerline Trail

In the 1930s electric transmission lines were run along the mountains and a 13-mile maintenance route now known as the Powerline Trail was created. There is occasional talk of turning it into a real inland road connecting Princeville to Wailua.

The trail starts at the paved road running up from Pooku Stables, a third of a mile after the 27-mile marker on Hwy 56. The paved road ends at a water tank 1¾ miles up and even if you don't plan to hike it's a pretty drive. The road goes past large contemporary homes with grazing horses in their yards. There are fine mountain views and glimpses of Hanalei Bay.

The trail continues as a 4WD dirt road used mainly by hunters and the power company, passing a hunter check box and continuing all the way to the Keahua Arboretum. Wild orchids and hibiscus bloom along the trail.

Places to Stay

You can frequently find someone in Princeville renting out a bedroom in their condo or home, usually for about $35 to $45 a day. Most renters simply list their rooms on the bulletin board outside Foodland supermarket in the Princeville Center, though occasionally someone will run an ad in the newspaper.

Princeville has 10 condo complexes, some perched on cliffs, others by the golf course. While all of the complexes have some units that are vacation rentals, a fair number of Princeville's condo units are occupied as year-round housing.

Most condo complexes are represented by a number of different rental agents. Three agents with fairly extensive Princeville vacation listings are:

Blue Water Vacation Rentals, Princeville Center, Box 366, Princeville, HI 96714 (☎ 826-9229, (800) 628-5533)

Oceanfront Realty, Princeville Center, Suite 210, Box 3570, Princeville, HI 96722 (☎ 826-6585, (800) 222-5541)

Kauai Paradise Vacations, Box 1622, Hanalei, HI 96714 (☎ 826-7444, (800) 826-7782)

The *Hanalei Bay Resort* (☎ 826-6522, (800) 827-4427), Box 220, Hanalei, HI 96714, has both hotel-style rooms and condo units, some with fine views of Hanalei Bay. The hotel rooms range from $120 for a mountain view to $210 for an ocean view. One-bedroom condos with kitchen are $225 to $260, two-bedroom units are $340 to $450. There are pools and tennis courts. Not all of the units are rented out through the front desk, and cheaper prices are often available through the condo rental agents listed in this section.

The *Cliffs at Princeville* is a somewhat older complex in a rather ordinary location. Correspondingly the rates are among the cheapest in Princeville. The units are large and have one bedroom, front and rear lanais, two bathrooms and the usual amenities. If you get a well-maintained unit, they are one of Princeville's best values at about $75 a day, $500 a week, when rented from an agent. Colony Resorts (☎ 826-6219, (800) 777-1700) also handles a number of the units and maintains a front desk at the complex but it charges a steeper $110 to $195.

Sealodge is an older complex, but it's high on a cliff and many of the 86 units have great sunrise views looking across the expansive coral reef of Anini. If you leave the windows open the surf is guaranteed to give you nautical dreams. One-bedroom units generally cost from $85 to $115.

Hawaiian Islands Resorts (☎ 531-7595, (800) 367-7042), Box 212, Honolulu, HI 96810, manages the following three Princeville properties: the *Hale Moi* which has rooms for $80/$90 low/high season and studios for $100/110; the *Pali Ke Kua* which has rooms for $80/90 low/high season and one-bedroom units from $120/130; and the *Puu Poa* which has two-bedroom units from $185. Weekly rates are six times the daily rate.

The *Princeville Hotel* (☎ 826-9644, (800) 325-3535), Box 3069, Princeville, HI 96722, a Sheraton property, has 252 luxury rooms with modern amenities that run the gamut from original oil paintings with dimmer-controlled spotlights to electronic windows. Kid

you not – with the flick of a switch, liquid crystals turn the room windows from clear to opaque. Rates are $265 for a garden view, $375 for an ocean view and $2350 for the royal suite.

Places to Stay – B&B

At *Hale Ho'o Maha* (☎ 826-1130), Box 422, Kilauea, HI 96754, Kirby and Toby Guyer rent out the two bedrooms in their unassuming Princeville home. Guests are free to use the washer and dryer, barbecue grill, kitchen and beach equipment. One room costs $50, the other $65. Prices include breakfast and are the same single or double. Smokers and social drinkers are welcome.

Places to Eat

Princeville is a good place to eat out of a grocery store, as restaurant prices are quite high and food at the 'affordable' places is quite ordinary.

Zelo's Cafe in the Princeville Center is open from 10 am to about 9 pm, with burgers, sandwiches and salads from $5 to $8. Hot dishes include spinach lasagne with garlic bread for $8.50. Zelo's also serves espresso and cappuchino.

Chuck's Steak House in the Princeville Center has a very limited salad bar for $6.25 at lunch and $8.50 at dinner. Lunch is from 11.30 am to 2.30 pm weekdays only and features sandwiches. Dinners, from 6 to 10 pm nightly, range from $13 to $30, including the salad bar.

The signature dish at the *Pizza Burger*, in the Princeville Center, is a hamburger topped with pepperoni, mozzarella and pizza sauce for $4.75. There's also a conventional burger for $4 and a Hanalei buffalo burger for $5.30. The restaurant doubles as the local pizzeria, with 15-inch pizzas ranging from $12.75 for cheese alone to $23 topped with the works.

The *Bali Hai Restaurant* in the Hanalei Bay Resort has open-air dining with a wonderful view of Hanalei Bay and the Bali Hai mountains. At breakfast, macadamia nut waffles cost $6.25. At lunch, sandwiches with fries cost from $7 to $11. Dinners cost from $13 for stir fries over rice to $24 for lamb dijon. The food's good, but the view's the real attraction.

The *Beamreach* (☎ 826-9131), while one of Princeville's busier restaurants, has an uninspired location in the midst of a condo complex with no view. Standard steak, seafood and chicken dinners with salad and baked potato cost $15 to $24. The Beamreach is at Pali Ke Kua, off to the right on the way to the Princeville Hotel. It's open from 6 to 10 pm nightly.

While the *Cafe Hanalei* in the Princeville Hotel has an unbeatable view of Hanalei Bay, the daily breakfast buffet has rather mediocre fare at a steep $17.50. It features ordinary pastries, a selection of fruit and breakfast meats, a few undistinguished hot dishes and a waffle and omelette bar. At lunch, the blackened fish sandwich for $10 is one of the better choices. On Monday nights there's a Mexican dinner buffet for $20 and on Wednesday nights a Thai buffet for $22.50.

The Princeville Hotel also has a poolside cafe that serves continental breakfast and lunch, and an up-market Italian restaurant called *La Cascata* that specialises in seafood, with dishes averaging $25 à la carte.

Entertainment

At the *Hanalei Bay Resort*, the Kauai Boys play contemporary Hawaiian music in the Happy Talk Lounge from 6 to 9 pm on Tuesdays, Thursdays and Saturdays. A jazz band plays from 6 to 10 pm on Mondays, Wednesdays and Fridays and there's a lively jazz jam session from 3 to 7 pm on Sundays.

The Waioli Huuia Church Choir performs a mix of Hawaiian hymns and contemporary tunes for diners at 7 pm on Sundays at the Hanalei Bay Resort's *Bali Hai Restaurant*. Hula dancing is included and there's sometimes a second performance at 8 pm, depending on demand.

HANALEI VALLEY

Just beyond Princeville, Hanalei Valley Lookout provides you with a spectacular overview of the patchwork taro fields spread across the valley floor.

The Hanalei National Wildlife Refuge encompasses 917 acres of the valley, stretching up both sides of Hanalei River. The private taro farms in the refuge provide most of Hawaii's commercially grown taro as well as habitat for endangered water birds.

In the mid-1800s rice farming was introduced into Hanalei Valley to feed the Chinese labourers who worked the sugar cane fields. The rice grew so well that by the 1880s it became a major export crop. Now taro once again predominates and the old Hariguchi Rice Mill stands along the river slowly weathering away.

From the lookout, to the lower right, you can glimpse the North Shore's first one-lane bridge, opened in 1912. The road leading into the valley along the western bank of the river is Ohiki Rd. From Ohiki Rd there's a trail that climbs the first ridge on the right, going up to the twin peaks of Hihimanu, which in Hawaiian means 'beautiful.'

Hanalei Bridge

The seven one-lane bridges between Hanalei River and the end of the road not only link this part of the North Shore to the rest of the island, they also protect it from runaway development.

Big cement trucks and heavy construction equipment are beyond their limits. Even large package-tour buses are kept at bay.

Over the years developers have introduced numerous proposals to build a two-lane bridge over Hanalei River but North Shore residents have successfully beaten them all down.

While it's not a frequent occurrence,

Rules of the Road
The rules of the road on the North Shore dictate that when two cars approach an empty one-lane bridge from opposite directions, the car that reaches the bridge last yields to the entire line-up of approaching cars, rather than alternating one car in each direction. ■

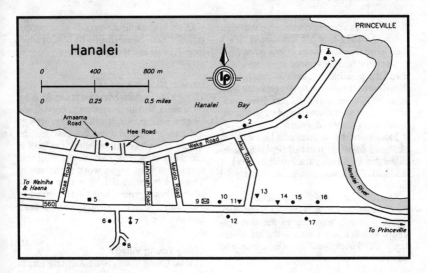

1 Pinetrees Beach Park
2 Beach Pavilion
3 Hanalei Beach Park
4 Wilcox Home
5 Hanalei Bay Inn
6 Hanalei School
7 Waioli Huiia Church
8 Waioli Mission House Museum
9 Post Office
10 Ching Young Village
11 Shell House
12 Hanalei Center
13 Hanalei Wake Up Cafe
14 Tahiti Nui
15 Kayak Kauai
16 Hanalei Trader
17 Hanalei Museum

raised for their meat and are the source of the buffalo burgers and kebabs found on Kauai menus.

Ohiki Road

If you want to go into Hanalei Valley, turn left onto Ohiki Rd immediately after Hanalei Bridge. The drive parallels the Hanalei River, starting in taro fields and later passing banana trees, bamboo thickets, hau trees, ferns and wild ginger. It dead ends after two miles.

Snow-white egrets are common alongside the road. Night herons and endangered Hawaiian water birds live in the valley too, including coots, stilts, the Hawaiian duck and the coot-like Hawaiian gallinule with its bright red bill.

during unusually heavy rains the road between the taro fields and the river can flood and the Hanalei Bridge closes until it subsides.

After the Hanalei Bridge, the valley widens. Buffalo belonging to Hanalei Garden Farms graze in the pastures to the right. Having shed their thick woolly fur for a short tropical coat, these creatures are

Okolehau Trail The Okolehau Trail offers ridge-top views of Hanalei and Waioli valleys. To reach the trailhead, go down Ohiki Rd about half a mile and turn right onto the unmarked paved road.

The hike starts up the 4WD power-line maintenance road to the left of the cemetery. It goes up through fragrant eucalyptus trees and past wild orchids. When you reach the

Norfolk pines you can continue up the ridge top to the 1272-foot Mt Kaukaopua. It's a little more than two miles to this point.

The trail becomes more strenuous as it rises. It's possible to continue through the Puu Ki area, following the ridge to the twin peaks of Hihimanu at 2262 feet. Give yourself an early start if you intend to go this far in and carry plenty of water.

Moonshiners who distilled a liquor called okolehao from the roots of ti plants established this trail during the Prohibition era of the 1920s. The ti they planted is still plentiful along the trail.

The literal translation of okolehao comes from *okole*, meaning 'buttocks', and *hao*, meaning 'iron', referring to the iron-bottomed still that was used. As the old-timers say, 'It'll knock you on your okole and how!'.

HANALEI

After the Hanalei Bridge, Hwy 560 runs parallel to the Hanalei River. The mile before Hanalei village is a very pastoral scene of taro patches and grassland. There's no development of any kind and no buildings in sight. Take away the telephone poles and asphalt and this is how it's looked for centuries.

Hanalei has a pleasant low-keyed village centre. Fitting its history, it has one museum depicting the modest lives of rural labourers and another of the more affluent missionary lifestyle. While there are a growing number of small businesses, Hanalei's three largest restaurants are still in weatherbeaten wooden buildings – it's that kind of town. The beaches are just off the main drag.

Hanalei is friendly, casual and slow. If you're in a hurry, you're in the wrong place.

Hanalei Trader

The first sign of town is Hanalei Trader, a green building on the right. It has the Hanalei Dolphin restaurant, Bali Hai Vacation Rentals, Sand People, Ola's and a shave ice stand.

Sand People (☎ 826-6981) sells beach clothing and rents boogie boards and snorkel sets for $7 a day.

Ola's has beautiful works in glass, wood, ceramic and other media by craftspeople from Hawaii and the mainland.

Hanalei Museum

Though the Hanalei Museum is closed as we go to press, and no-one seems to know if and when it will reopen, it still displays its sign and can be viewed from the outside. The simple green wooden building was built in the 1860s by Ho Pak Yet, a Chinese immigrant who began work at the age of 14 as an indentured labourer on the Big Island. Four generations of Hos lived in this house, which was a typical worker's home of the period.

Ching Young Village

The old Ching Young Store, since the turn of the century the North Shore's main general store, has evolved to become the Ching Young Village Shopping Center. It has a Big Save supermarket open from 7 am to 9 pm daily, a Bank of Hawaii, a camping and backpacking store, a health-food store, a few restaurants and a handful of other shops.

The original Ching Young Store now houses galleries, including that of the non-profit Artisans' Guild of Kauai. It's a good place to look for North Shore art, including watercolour paintings, pottery and photography.

Hanalei Center

Opposite the Ching Young Village is the old Hanalei elementary school, which has been renovated and turned into a small shopping complex called the Hanalei Center. The building is on the Hawaii Register of Historic Places.

The centrepiece is Hanalei Gourmet, a deli-cum-restaurant that has entertainment on Tuesday to Saturday nights. The centre also holds the dual-named Hanalei Sailboards/Hanalei Surf Company, which rents windsurfing equipment, surfboards, boogie boards and snorkel sets and gives windsurfing and surfing lessons.

Waioli Huiia Church

Hanalei's first missionaries, the Reverend and Mrs William Alexander, arrived in 1834 in a double-hulled canoe. Their church, hall and mission house are in the middle of town, set on a huge manicured lawn with a beautiful mountain backdrop. These folks knew how to pick property.

The picturesque Waioli Huiia Church is a favourite subject of area watercolourists. The green wooden church retains an airy Pacific feel with large stained-glass windows that open outwards and high ceilings. The doors remain open during the day and visitors are welcome to go inside. A Bible printed in Hawaiian in 1868 is on display on the old organ in the back corner of the room.

Waioli Mission Hall, to the right of the church, was built in 1836. The hall was formerly the church and was built of coral lime and plaster with a distinctive high-pitched roof to handle Hanalei's heavy rains. An old church graveyard is beside the hall.

Waioli Mission House Museum

The Waioli Mission House is behind the church and hall. According to the guides, the Alexanders spent their first three years living in a grass hut on these grounds, but couldn't handle living Hawaiian-style so they built this big New England house. It was home to other missionaries over the years, most notably Abner and Lucy Wilcox.

The main part of the house was built in 1837. It has all period furnishings, including braided rugs, lanterns, a spinning wheel and simple straight-backed chairs.

A large bookcase in the living room contains the original collection of Alexander's books. Of the two melodeon cases in this room only one contains a melodeon. The other came back empty after having been sent off to San Francisco in the late 1800s to be repaired. Such were the hardships of missionary life.

The house has old wavy glass panes, some nice simple woodwork and other interesting architectural features. For instance, the upstairs porch slopes, not from settling but

because it was built that way to let water run down during the valley's frequent torrential rains. The boy's bedroom on the 2nd floor has a central post that carries the weight of the 1st floor ceiling beneath it.

The original cookhouse was separate so that in the event of a kitchen fire the main house would be spared. With the advent of electricity it was linked to the main house. One corner still has iron pots hanging in the original fireplace, which was made of sandstone blocks cut in Waipa Valley, three miles away.

The museum's inconspicuous parking lot is just past the church. Turn left on the driveway before the school and then again at the second yellow hydrant. It's open from 9 am to 3 pm Tuesdays, Thursdays and Saturdays. Admission is free, though donations are welcomed. You're free to explore the garden area and taro patch out the back.

Hanalei Bay

Hanalei means 'crescent bay', and that it is – a large, perfectly shaped bay, one of the most scenic in all Hawaii. Weke Rd, which runs a mile along the bay between Waioli Stream and Hanalei River, can be reached by turning off Hwy 560 at Aku Rd.

Just after turning right onto Weke from Aku there's a public beach with a picnic pavilion. The more appealing Hanalei Beach Park is about half a mile farther, at the end of Weke Rd. Pinetrees Beach Park is in the opposite direction.

All three beaches have restrooms, showers, drinking water, picnic tables and grills. Hanalei Beach Park is the best place for catching the sunset as you can see Bali Hai from there. It's a popular summer anchorage for sailboats.

The big brown house with the wraparound porch mauka of the road midway between the pavilion and Hanalei Beach Park is the old Wilcox estate, home to descendants of early Hanalei missionaries Abner and Lucy Wilcox.

If the road names have a familiar sound, it means you're beginning to learn the names of Hawaiian fish – each road along the beach is named after a different one.

Hanalei Beach Park

Hanalei Beach Park is one of the North Shore's most popular beach parks. It has a grassy area and a long beach shaded by ironwood trees. The beach has a sandy bottom and a gentle slope. Swimming and snorkelling are good in summer, surfing in winter.

The remains of a narrow-gauge railroad track still lead up to the long pier that sticks out into the bay. A lifeguard is stationed on the beach through the summer and on weekends the rest of the year.

The mouth of the Hanalei River and a small boat ramp are at the eastern end of the park. That part of the beach is called Black Pot after the big iron pot that was hung there by local fishers for impromptu cook-outs. Camping is allowed on Fridays, Saturdays and holidays.

A snack truck arrives around noon every day but Monday, leaving when the sun hits the mountains. Drinking coconuts cost $2, sodas $1, and on some days they serve plates of spaghetti for $3.50.

The bluff north of the river mouth was once the site of the old Hanalei Plantation Hotel. It was followed by Club Med which, despite the spectacular angle on Hanalei Bay, was unable to make a go of it. More recently a Honolulu developer went bankrupt in the midst of building million-dollar condos and the property was sold to Princeville.

Pinetrees Beach Park

Pinetrees Beach Park, named by surfers, is actually shaded by ironwood trees.

From Weke Rd, turn either onto Hee Rd, which has the bigger parking lot, or Amaama Rd, which has the restrooms and showers. This section of the beach is also known locally as Toilet Bowls.

Pinetrees has some of the bay's highest winter surf and is the site of various surfing contests. One of the most interesting is the Pinetrees Longboard Surf Classic. Held around the beginning of March, it features an ageing group of surfers on the old-style 10-foot wooden boards used before the advent of fibreglass.

Places to Stay

Bed & Breakfast & Beach (☎ 826-6111), Box 748, Hanalei, HI 96714, is in a large house, a two-minute walk from the beach pavilion section of Hanalei Bay. There are four rooms plus an apartment, each furnished with queen beds. All have their own bath, either attached or just outside the room. The contemporary house has a wraparound 2nd-floor lanai and hardwood floors. Rates range from $55 to $75, with a two-night minimum, and include a continental breakfast.

Across the street, Mary and Dave Cunning (☎ 826-7949), Box 720, Hanalei, HI 96714, rent *Ohana Hanalei*, a pleasant studio unit attached to the side of their home. The rate is $60, with the seventh night free on weekly stays. The unit has its own entrance and bath, a queen bed, cable TV, phone, refrigerator, toaster oven and coffee maker.

Hanalei Bay Inn (☎ 826-9333), Box 122, Hanalei, HI 96714, formerly Mahikoa's Motel, has five simple units with kitchenettes. Despite the name, this ageing hostelry is not on the bay but rather located on Hwy 560, on the western side of the village. Rates are $59 to $65 a night for singles or doubles.

Bali Hai Vacation Rentals (☎ 826-4400, (800) 448-6333), Box 1220, Hanalei, HI 96714, represents about a dozen homes and cottages in the Hanalei area. Rates are from $550 to $2400 a week.

Places to Eat – bottom end

Hanalei Gourmet (☎ 826-2524) in the Hanalei Center has both a deli and a dining area for eat-in or takeaway meals. Breakfast includes reasonably priced muffins and pastries, as well as specials like bagels with lox and cream cheese for $6. Sandwiches cost from $4.75 for avocado or cheese to $6.75 for an Italian-style sub. They also make fairly good salads and soups, and sell sandwich meats and loaves of bread over the counter. The deli hours are from 8 am to 8 pm. The dining area has a nice view of the mountains and is open until 9.30 pm.

Hanalei Wake Up Cafe on Aku Rd serves a rich custard French toast topped with pineapple-coconut puree for $4.50, half a papaya with yoghurt and muesli for $4 and a quesadilla with eggs, cheese and salsa for $6.50. Servings are on the small side though the food is tasty. Opening hours are from 5.30 am to noon only.

Pizza Hanalei (☎ 826-9494) in Ching Young Village has the North Shore's best pizza. A cheese pizza with crisp whole-wheat crust topped with sesame seeds is $7.50. The spicy calzone-style pizzaritos are loaded with cheese and vegies, and make a good meal for $4.79. You can also buy slices of pepperoni or pesto pizza for $2.50 from 11 am to 4 pm daily. The restaurant closes at 9 pm.

Next door, *Hanalei Natural Foods* sells freshly squeezed juices, fruit, organic produce, wrapped sandwiches and salads and other health-food items. It's open from 8.30 am to about 8 pm daily.

The *Village Snack & Bake Shop* in Ching Young Village sells breakfasts, wrapped sandwiches, $6-plate lunches, bakery goods and coffee. It's open from 6 am to 5 pm daily.

Foong Wong on the 2nd floor in Ching Young Village has Sichuan and Cantonese dishes at moderate prices, but the food's not recommendable.

Tropical Taco parks its old green van at the Hanalei Trader building and dishes out Mexican food from about noon to 4 pm daily except Monday.

A counter at the side of the old Hanalei Museum sells standard plate lunches, sandwiches and cold drinks from about 10 am to 4 pm daily.

Places to Eat – top end

The *Shell House* (☎ 826-7977), on the corner of Hwy 560 and Aku Rd, serves breakfast from 8 to 11 am. Macadamia nut pancakes or Mexican omelettes are $7. Lunch, from 11 am to 4 pm, features hamburgers, sandwiches, and quesadillas in the $6 to $9 range. The varied dinner menu includes good fresh fish dishes – broiled, sauteed, or blackened in a spicy Cajun preparation. Fish dishes are $18 to $20, while most other dishes average $14 to $17. All include a salad or soup. Dinner is served from 5 to 10.30 pm daily.

The *Hanalei Dolphin* (☎ 826-6113) at Hanalei Trader is a steak and seafood restaurant. Entrees with salad range from $14 to $23. It's open from 6 to 10 pm daily.

The food is pretty good at *Tahiti Nui* (☎ 826-6277), on Hwy 560 near Aku Rd, though service can be slow. A big serving of fresh fish costs $17, including salad and a glump of white rice, while the daily chef's special costs $13.50. Dinner is from 6 to 9 pm except on Wednesdays and Fridays when there's a luau.

Entertainment

Hanalei Gourmet has live entertainment from 8.30 to 11.30 pm five nights a week. Tuesday is jazz night, Wednesday and Thursday are apt to see acoustic guitarists or rhythm & blues, and rock bands are usually booked for Fridays and Saturdays.

At *Tahiti Nui*, the Rainbow Rangers play country western music on Mondays from 9 pm to midnight and there's dancing to 1.30 am on weekends. Tahiti Nui also has a down-home, funky luau that can be fun, though it won't be everyone's cup of tea. The show is presided over by owner Aunty Louise, who lets out a few tunes in her native Tahitian as well as French and Hawaiian. It's essentially a family affair, with cousins and uncles performing. There's a lot of audience participation and the whole thing has the feel of a neighbourhood party. The luau is at 6.30 pm on Wednesdays and Fridays. It costs $35 for adults and $15 for children aged 5 to 11, including a rather ordinary buffet dinner. Drinks cost extra.

HANALEI TO WAINIHA
Waikoko Beach

The western part of Hanalei Bay, called Waikoko Beach, has a sandy bottom, is protected by a reef and is shallower and calmer than the middle of the bay. There are beachside places to park under ironwood trees around the four-mile marker, but no facilities.

Winter surfing is sometimes good off Makahoa Point, the western point of the bay, called Waikokos by surfers.

Lumahai Beach

Lumahai is the gorgeous mile-long stretch of beach where Mitzi Gaynor promised to wash that man right out of her hair in the 1958 musical *South Pacific*. It's a broad white sand beach with lush jungle growth on one side and tempestuous open ocean on the other.

It's a good beach for walking and exploring. Around some of the lava outcrops you can find green sand made of olivine.

There are two ways onto Lumahai. The first and most scenic is a three-minute walk that begins at a pull-off along a stone retaining wall three-quarters of a mile past the four-mile marker. Park in the direction of the traffic flow to avoid a ticket. The trail to the beach starts at an inconspicuous 'No Lifeguard' sign and goes down the slope to the left.

The lava point at this eastern end of the beach offers protection from the winds that often blow from the Princeville direction. These rocks are a rather popular place for sunbathing and for being photographed, but size it up carefully as people have been washed off by high surf and rogue waves. Lumahai has dangerous shorebreaks and is not a beach to turn your back on. It's particularly treacherous in winter, though there are strong currents all year round. Lumahai has been nicknamed Luma*die* by locals.

Back on the road, there are a couple of lookouts with views down onto Lumahai. The first is at the five-mile marker, though the next one that pops up around the bend is a better angle. It's easy to spot as it's marked with an HVB warrior.

The other access onto Lumahai Beach is along the road at sea level at the western end of the beach, just before crossing the Lumahai River Bridge. The beach at this end is lined with ironwood trees. Across the road is Lumahai Valley, open and flat with ranchland and grazing horses and cattle.

WAINIHA

Wainiha has the oldest general store in these parts and it's the last store on the North Shore that sells groceries and beer. It's open until 7 pm daily. There's a little sandwich shop at the side.

Ancient house sites, heiau sites and old taro patches reach deep into the Wainiha Valley. The valley is said to have been the last hideout of the menehunes. In fact as late as the mid-1800s, 65 people in the valley were officially listed as menehune on the government census!

Wainiha Powerhouse Road

Wainiha Powerhouse Rd begins shortly before the seven-mile marker. It leads up into Wainiha Valley, a narrow valley with steep green walls. It's a ride into an older Hawaii.

The road is lined with simple tin-roofed homes, old rusting cars and sleeping dogs. At 1½ miles up there's suddenly a manicured estate with a cool blue stream meandering through it. Shortly after this you arrive at the Wainiha hydroelectric plant. It was built in 1906 by McBryde Sugar Company and still pumps out juice today. Beyond the powerhouse the road turns to dirt and begins to feel more private.

Places to Stay

Tassa Hanalei (☎ 826-7298), Box 856, Hanalei, HI 96714, at the home of Ileah and Robert Van Hubbard, is a B&B in a quiet niche of Wainiha Valley. An airy studio cottage with glass doors looking out onto a fine mountain scene costs $90 per couple, $120 per family. It has a full kitchen, tables and chairs, a queen bed, a sofabed and a deck. Two newly built rooms that are attached to the main house and have private bathrooms and private entrances cost $70 single or double. Massage is available for $50, colonic therapy for $35.

HAENA

Haena has houses on stilts, little beachfront cottages, a few vacation homes, the YMCA camp, large caves, campsites and beautiful sandy beaches. It also has the only condo complex and restaurant beyond Hanalei.

Tunnels Reef

Tunnels is a big horseshoe-shaped reef that

has great diving and snorkelling when the water is calm, which is generally limited to the summer. There's a current as you head into deeper water. When conditions are right, you can start snorkelling near the east point and let the current carry you westward. It's more adventurous than Kee Beach and the coral is beautiful.

Tunnels was not named after the caves and other crevices in the underwater walls but by surfers for its tubular winter surf break at the outer corner of the reef. The beach is popular with both windsurfers and board surfers, though dangerous rip currents that prevail from October to May make it suitable for experts only.

To get there, look for cars parked at the side of the road near phone pole No 144, which is midway between the eight and nine-mile markers, opposite the beach access road. Or you can park at Haena Beach Park and walk along the beach to Tunnels.

Haena Beach Park
Haena Beach is a beautiful curve of white sand. To the right, you can see the horseshoe shape of Tunnels outlined by breaking waves. To the far left is Cannons, another good dive spot. Haena itself is not protected by reefs and has very strong rip currents and powerful shorebreaks from October to May.

The county beach park has camping sites, covered picnic tables, restrooms, showers and grills. There are usually a few hikers from the Kalalau Trail camping here. It's a bit over a mile to the trailhead and this is a safer place to park a car if you're going on to Kalalau.

A snack truck parked at Haena during the day serves up $5 plate lunches, chilli and rice, soft drinks and shave ice. On weekends another vendor sells $2 drinking coconuts near the entrance to the cave.

Maniniholo Dry Cave
Three large sea caves, which were part of the coast thousands of years back, are mauka of the road between Haena and Kee Beach. One is dry and two are wet.

According to legend, they were created when the goddess Pele dug into the mountains looking for a place on Kauai's North Shore to call home.

Maniniholo Dry Cave, across the road from Haena Beach Park, is a big broad cave that you can walk deep into. Dry is a relative term, as the dripping water that constantly seeps from the cave walls keeps the interior of Maniniholo damp and humid.

Limahuli
Limahuli is the last valley before the start of the Na Pali Coast. Much of it is still virgin forest.

The National Tropical Botanical Garden owns 1000 acres of the valley. The garden contains collections of Hawaiian ethnobotanical and medicinal plants and other rare and endangered native species. A trail passes old stone terraces planted with taro and various fruiting trees. Endemic trees along the way include the endangered Kokio hauheleula, which has a red hibiscus-like blossom, and the equally beautiful but more common ohia lehua tree.

The garden starts at a concrete driveway on the mauka side of the highway just before the stream that marks the Haena State Park boundary. It's open free to members for self-guided tours.

Wet Caves
Haena State Park includes the two wet caves and Kee Beach. The caves are near each other, less than a quarter of a mile from the end of the road, and usually marked with HVB warrior signs. The first, Waikapalae Wet Cave, is just a few minutes' walk uphill from the road along the rutted drive with the stop sign. The second, Waikanaloa Wet Cave, is at the side of the road.

Both are big, deep, dark and dripping with pools of very cold water. Divers sometimes explore them, but the caves can be dangerous and it's best to go with a local diver the first time.

Kee Beach
Kee Beach is commonly called 'the beach at the end of the road', which it is.

On the left side of the beach is the distinctive 1280-foot cliff that marks the start of the Na Pali Coast. Almost everyone calls it Bali Hai, its name in *South Pacific*. The Hawaiian name is Makana, which means 'gift'. A heiau and ancient hula school site is at its base.

Snorkelling is good at Kee Beach, which has a variety of tropical fish. A reef protects the right side of the cove and except on high surf days, it's usually calm. The left side is open and can have a powerful current, particularly in winter.

When it's really calm – generally only in summer – snorkellers cross the reef to the open ocean where there's great visibility, big fish, large coral heads and the occasional sea turtle. It makes the inside of the bay look like kid's stuff, but check it out carefully because breaking surf and strong currents can create some pretty dangerous conditions.

When the tide's at its lowest you can actually walk a great distance out on the reef without getting your feet wet and peer down into tidepools.

Showers, changing rooms, drinking water and restrooms are tucked back in the woods behind the parking lot and a lifeguard is on duty daily.

There are several ways to get views down the Na Pali Coast from Kee Beach. One way is to walk the first 30 minutes of the Kalalau Trail. Another is to take the short walk out around the point at the left side of the beach.

Or, walk down the beach to the right and look back as the cliffs unfold, one after the other. About 15 minutes down this way you'll come to a stream and the site of the former Taylor Camp.

In the late 1960s, a little free-style village of tents and tree houses sprang up on property owned by Elizabeth Taylor's brother. Reports of drugs, orgies and pipe organ music in the middle of the night eventually got the authorities down on their case. When the state tried to evict everyone on public health grounds, the campers challenged them in court claiming squatters rights. The 'squatters' eventually lost and the property was condemned and incorporated into the state park system. Taylor Camp remains part of North Shore folklore, though there's nothing left to see.

Kaulu Paoa Heiau

To walk out to Kaulu Paoa Heiau, take the path on the western side of the beach. The walk is shaded by tropical almond trees, which drop their edible nuts along the trail. Go around the private Allerton house and then follow the stone wall as it curves uphill. You can see the heiau almost immediately.

The overgrown section at the foot of the hill is one of the more intact parts of the heiau, but don't stop there. Walk up the terraces towards the cliff face. Surf pounding below, vertical cliffs above – what a spectacular site to worship the gods from!

Beneath the cliff face, large stones retain a long flat grassy platform. A thatched-roofed *halau*, a long house used as a hula school, once ran the whole length of the terrace. Here, dances to Laka, the goddess of hula, were performed. This was Kauai's most sacred hula school and students aspiring to learn hula came to Kaulu Paoa from all the islands.

Fern wreaths, rocks wrapped in ti leaves, leis and other offerings to Laka are still placed into the crevices of the cliff face. The site is sacred to native Hawaiians and should be treated with respect. Night hula dances are still performed on special occasions.

Lohiau's House Site

Lohiau's house site is just a minute's walk above the parking lot at Kee Beach. At the Kalalau Trail sign, go left along the dirt path to a vine-covered rock wall. This overgrown level terrace runs back 54 feet to the bluff and is said to have been the home of Lohiau, a 16th-century prince.

Legend says that the volcano goddess Pele was napping one day under a hala tree in Puna on the Big Island when her spirit was awakened by the sound of distant drums. Her spirit rode the wind in the direction of the sound, searching each island in turn until she finally arrived at Kee Beach. Here she found Lohiau above the heiau beating a hula drum, surrounded by graceful hula dancers.

Pele took the form of a beautiful woman and

captured Lohiau's heart. They became lovers and moved into this house. In time Pele had to go back to the Big Island, leaving a lovesick Lohiau behind. His longing quickly got the better of him and on this site he died from his grief.

Places to Stay

The *Kauai YMCA-Camp Naue* (☎ 246-9090), Box 1786, Lihue, HI 96766, in Haena, just before the eight-mile marker on Hwy 560, has a couple of rustic co-ed bunkhouses on the beach. It costs $12 for one of the 40 bunks, which have mattresses but no linen or blankets. To pitch a tent costs $10 for the first person and $7 for each extra person. There are hot showers, but the kitchen is reserved for groups only. While there are no lockers, the camp is a safe place and theft hasn't been a problem. Guests can stay a maximum of three nights. Check-in is officially until 6 pm, but usually allowed until it gets dark. They don't accept reservations, but unless there's a large group staying they can usually take everyone who shows up. Call ahead, however, as in summer and some other holiday periods the camp is commonly booked by children's groups and closed to travellers. It's a 15-minute walk to Tunnels Beach.

The *Hanalei Colony Resort* (☎ 826-6235, (800) 628-3004), Box 206, Hanalei, HI 96714, is an older condo complex that's a little faded but right on the beach on the east side of Haena. Each of the 49 units has two bedrooms, a kitchen and a lanai. There are no TVs. Rates are from $95 for a garden view to $170 for oceanfront in the low season, $115 to $190 in the high season. The rates are the same for up to four people and for weekly stays the seventh night is free.

Places to Eat

Charo's restaurant is on the beach, beside Hanalei Colony Resort. At lunch, it has hamburgers for $6, teriyaki chicken sandwiches for $8.50 and rather pricy Mexican food. At dinner, in addition to the Mexican dishes, there are steak and seafood dishes from $20. Lunch is served from 11.30 am to 4 pm, dinner from 6 to 9 pm. There's a piano bar nightly, but the splashy 'Tropical Fiesta' revue is gone, as Charo moved the show to Waikiki.

NA PALI COAST

Na Pali means simply 'the cliffs', and these are Hawaii's grandest example.

The Na Pali Coast is the rugged 22-mile stretch between the end of the road at Kee Beach in the north and the road's opposite end at Polihale State Park in the west. It has the most sharply fluted coastal cliffs in Hawaii.

Kalalau, Honopu, Awaawapuhi, Nualolo and Milolii are the five major valleys on the Na Pali Coast. These deep river valleys once contained sizeable settlements.

In the mid-1800s missionaries established a school in Kalalau, the largest valley, and

Koolau the Leper

Koolau was a paniolo (cowhand) who contracted leprosy in 1893. Rather than accept separation from his family and banishment to Molokai's leper colony, Koolau, his wife and young son hiked down into Kalalau Valley. Shortly after, a sheriff and deputy showed up to clear the valley of renegade lepers. Koolau was the only resister. That night, in the light of a full moon, the sheriff snuck up the valley hoping to take Koolau in his sleep. In self-defence Koolau shot the sheriff.

When word reached Honolulu, a shipload of soldiers was sent to land on Kalalau Beach. As they marched up the valley they met Koolau's gunfire. After two of the soldiers were shot off the ridge, and a third accidentally killed himself, they switched strategies. Just before dawn they blasted Koolau's hideaway with cannon fire, not knowing he had slipped through their lines the night before. From a nearby waterfall Koolau watched as the soldiers loaded up and set sail. They never returned. Koolau lived the rest of his days in the valley undisturbed.

Eventually the son, and then Koolau, died of leprosy. They are buried on a valley hillside. When his wife, Piilani, left the valley she found Koolau had largely been forgotten. A decade later a visiting reporter, John Sheldon, recorded her story. Jack London later wrote *Koolau the Leper*, a more fictionalised account. ■

registered the valley population at about 200. Influenced by Western ways, people began moving to towns and by the end of the century the valleys were largely abandoned.

The Na Pali valleys, with limited accessibility and abundant fertility, have long served as a natural refuge for people wanting to escape one scene or another. Koolau the Leper is the best known.

Getting There & Away

Precarious trails once led from the Kokee area to the valley floors below. In some places footholds were gouged into cliffsides and in others rope ladders were used. These trails no longer exist.

Only Hanakapiai, Hanakoa and Kalalau valleys can still be entered on foot, solely along the 11-mile Kalalau coastal trail.

The only other access is by boat. Landings are limited to Kalalau, Nualolo and Milolii valleys and are largely restricted to summer when the seas are calm. Milolii, part of Na Pali Coast State Park, has primitive camping. Currently, Hanalei Sea Tours and Captain Zodiac are the only companies licensed to drop off or pick up backpackers along the Na Pali Coast.

Kokee State Park has a drive-up lookout right on the rim of Kalalau, which is the only Na Pali valley you can look into without a hike or a helicopter. Kokee also has hardy hikes out to clifftops with gorgeous views of Honopu, Awaawapuhi and Nualolo valleys (see the Kokee State Park section later).

Kalalau Trail

Kalalau is Hawaii's premier trail. It's common to come across hikers here who have trekked in Nepal or climbed to Machu Picchu. The Na Pali Coast is similarly spectacular, a place of singular beauty.

The Kalalau Trail is basically the same ancient route used by the Hawaiians who once lived in these remote north coast valleys. The trail runs along high sea cliffs and winds up and down across lush valleys before it finally ends below the steep fluted pali of Kalalau. The scenery is breathtaking, with sheer green cliffs dropping into brilliant turquoise waters.

While hikers in good shape can walk the 11-mile trail in about seven hours, it's less strenuous to break it up and spend a night camping in one of the two valleys along the way.

In winter there are generally only a few people at any one time hiking all the way in to Kalalau Valley, while the trail is pretty heavily trodden in summer. As it's a popular hike for islanders as well as visitors, weekends tend to see the most use.

The hike can be divided into three parts: Kee Beach to Hanakapiai Valley (two miles); Hanakapiai to Hanakoa Valley (four miles); and Hanakoa to Kalalau Valley (five miles). The first two miles of the hike makes a popular day trip.

The trail is part of Na Pali Coast State Park. Camping is allowed in all three valleys, but is limited to five nights total, with no two consecutive nights in Hanakapiai or Hanakoa. State camping permits are required.

Kee Beach to Hanakapiai The two-mile trail to Hanakapiai has some excellent views of the coast. Morning is a good time to be going west, and the afternoon to be going east, as you have both the sun at your back and good light for photos.

The trail weaves through kukui and ohia trees and then back out to clearings with coastal views. There are purple orchids, wildflowers and a couple of tiny Zen-like waterfalls. The black nuts half buried in the clay are kukui, polished smooth by the scuffing of hundreds of hiking shoes.

Just a quarter of a mile up the trail you can catch a fine view of Kee Beach and the surrounding reef. After 30 minutes you get your first view of the Na Pali Coast. Even if you weren't planning on a hike, it's well worth coming this far.

Once you get to Hanakapiai Valley, there's a guide rope for crossing the stream.

Hanakapiai has a sandy beach in the summer. In the winter the sand washes out and it becomes a beach of boulders, some of them sparkling with tiny olivine crystals.

The western side of the beach has a small cave with dripping water and a miniature fern grotto.

The ocean is dangerous here, with unpredictable rips year round. It's particularly treacherous during winter high surf conditions, but summer trades also bring powerful currents. Hanakapiai Beach is matched only by Lumahai for the number of drownings on Kauai.

If you're just doing a day hike, it makes more sense to head up the valley to Hanakapiai Falls than it does to continue another couple of miles on the coastal trail.

Hanakapiai Falls The two-mile hike from Hanakapiai Beach to Hanakapiai Falls takes about 2½ hours for the round trip. Because of some tricky rock crossings, this trail is rougher than the walk from Kee to Hanakapiai Beach. Due to the possibility of flash floods in the narrow valley, this is a fair-weather hike.

The trail itself is periodically washed out by the flooding and sections occasionally get redrawn, but it should be easy to follow as it basically goes up the side of Hanakapiai Stream.

The trail starts on the western side of the stream above the pit toilets. About 50 yards up there's a picnic table, old stone walls and guava trees. If the guava is ripe it's a good place to stock up. There are also some big old mango trees along the way.

Ten minutes up from the trailhead you'll find thickets of green bamboo, interspersed with eucalyptus. Off to the left there's a picnic table shaded by horizontally leaning bamboo with wild ginger behind. It's Eden-like.

Along the trail is the site of an old coffee mill. All that remains is a little of the stack.

The first of four or five stream crossings is about 25 minutes up at a sign that warns: 'Hazardous. Keep away from stream during heavy rainfall. Stream floods suddenly.'

Be particularly careful of your footing on the rocky upper part of the trail. Some of the rocks are covered with a barely visible film of slick algae. It's like walking on glass.

The waterfall is spectacular, with a wide pool gentle enough to swim in. Directly under the falls the cascading water forces you back from the rock face, a warning from nature as rocks can fall from the top.

This is a very peaceful place to spend a little time meditating. It's a beautiful lush valley though it's not terribly sunny near the falls because of the incredible steepness.

Hanakapiai to Hanakoa Just 10 minutes up the trail from Hanakapiai to Hanakoa there's a nice view of Hanakapiai Beach, but then the trail goes into bush and the next coastal view is not for another mile. This is the least scenic part of the trail.

The camping site at Hanakoa is tucked into the valley about half a mile inland. Of the three camping areas, Hanakoa is the wettest. It also tends to have the most mosquitoes.

The valley is lovely and Hanakoa Stream has pools perfect for swimming. There's a waterfall about a third of a mile up the valley, but it's rough getting up there. The valley was formerly settled by farmers who grew taro and coffee, both of which still grow wild.

Hanakoa to Kalalau This is the most difficult part of the trail, although without question the most beautiful. Make sure you have at least three hours of daylight left.

About a mile out of Hanakoa Valley you'll reach the coast again and begin to get fantastic views of Na Pali's jagged edges. There are some very narrow and steep stretches along this section of the trail, so make sure your gear is properly packed and be cautious of your footing. A little past the halfway mark you'll get your first view into Kalalau Valley.

The large valley has a beach, a little waterfall, a heiau site, some ancient house sites and some interesting caves that are sometimes dry enough to sleep in during the summer.

A two-mile trail leads back into the valley to a pool in Kalalau Stream where there's a natural water slide. If you've a quick hand, you can try your luck spearfishing for prawns that live in the stream.

Valley terraces where Hawaiians cultivated taro until 1920 are now largely overgrown with Java plum and guava. Feral goats scurry up and down the crumbly cliffsides and drink from the stream.

Kalalau Valley has fruit trees, including mango, papaya, orange, banana, coconut, guava and mountain apple. During the 1960s and 1970s people wanting to get away from it all tried to settle in Kalalau, but forestry rangers eventually routed them out. It's still common to find a few folks hanging out in the valley, making flutes or otherwise whiling away the time.

Warnings & Information This is rugged wilderness and hikers should be well prepared. In places the trail runs along steep cliffs that can narrow to little more than a foot in width, which some people find unnerving. However, hikers accustomed to high country trails generally enjoy the hike and don't consider it unduly hazardous. The Sierra Club, which occasionally leads hikes into Kalalau, rates the trail as moderate to strenuous.

Accidents are not unknown. Most casualties along the Na Pali Trail are the result of people trying to ford swollen streams, walking in the dark on cliffside trails or swimming in treacherous surf. For someone who's cautious and in tune, it can be paradise.

There's no shortage of water sources along the trail, but all drinking water must be boiled or treated.

Bring what you need but travel light. You won't want to have extra shifting weight on stream crossings or along cliff edges. Shoes should have good traction; it's not a trail for flip-flops. If you bring a sleeping bag make it a light one.

The state parks office in Lihue can provide a Kalalau Trail brochure with a basic map. There is also information posted at the Kee Beach trailhead.

Break-ins to cars left overnight at Kee Beach are common. Some people advise leaving cars empty and unlocked. It might be safer to park at the camping ground at Haena Beach Park. Better yet, get a lift to the end of the road.

South Shore

Poipu is Kauai's main beach resort area. It's typically sunny and for the larger part of the year, including the winter, it has calm waters for swimming and snorkelling. During the summer the surf kicks up and the surfers move in.

The village of Koloa, three miles inland from Poipu, was the site of Hawaii's first sugar plantation. This sleepy town could have doubled for Dodge City before it got caught up in Poipu's boom. Now most of its shops are geared for tourists and it catches the overflow from neighbouring Poipu.

Poipu and Koloa are about 10 miles south of Lihue. To get there take Hwy 520 (Maluhia Rd) from Hwy 50 (Kaumualii Hwy).

Tree Tunnel

Immediately after turning down Maluhia Rd you enter the Tree Tunnel, a mile-long stretch of road canopied by swamp mahogany trees, a type of eucalyptus. Originally the tree tunnel was more than double this length but when Hwy 50 was re-routed south most of the tunnel was lopped off.

In 1982 Hurricane Iwa brought down many of the branches, temporarily destroying the tunnel effect, but by and large it's filled back in nicely.

The cinder hill to the right about two miles down Maluhia Rd is Puu O Hewa. From its top the ancient Hawaiians raced wooden holua sleds down paths covered with oiled pili grass. To add even more excitement to this popular spectator sport the Hawaiians crossed two sled paths near the middle of the hill. The paths were about five feet wide and if you strain your eyes you might be able to see the X on the hillside where they crossed.

Hewa means 'wrong' or 'mistake'. The hill's original name was lost when a surveyor jotted 'Puu O Hewa' (wrong hill) on a map he was making and it mistakenly went off to the printer like that.

The two grassy hills to the left of the road

are Mauna Kalika, or Silk Mountain. Two American entrepreneurs introduced Chinese silkworms here in the 1830s in an attempt to develop a Hawaiian silk industry. The climate proved unsuitable.

KOLOA

Hawaii's first sugar plantation was started in Koloa in 1835. The raw materials had arrived long before: sugar cane with the original Polynesian settlers and small-scale refinery know-how with the earliest Chinese immigrants. However large scale production didn't occur until William Hooper, an enterprising 24-year-old Bostonian, arrived in Kauai and made inroads with the alii.

With financial backing from Honolulu businesspeople, he leased land in Koloa from the king and paid the alii a stipend to free commoners from their traditional work obligations. He was then free to hire the commoners as wage labourers and Koloa became Hawaii's first plantation town.

Koloa Rd (Hwy 530) runs between Koloa and Lawai and if you're heading west it's the best way out of Koloa. Koloa Rd is a rural drive through sugar cane fields, pasture and tree-covered hills.

Sugar Exhibits

Any sugarologists in the crowd? The field at the intersection of Hwy 520 and Koloa Rd is for you.

In a tiny garden a dozen varieties of sugar cane have been labelled with interpretive markers. Some are noted for their high tonnage, others for high sucrose and some for their good ratooning abilities, though the different varieties have all grown to twist and clump together. Who knows, maybe there's a great new hybrid sprouting up amongst the tangles.

The stone stack in another corner of the field is a relic from one of Koloa's early mills and dates back to 1841.

In the centre of the field, the principal

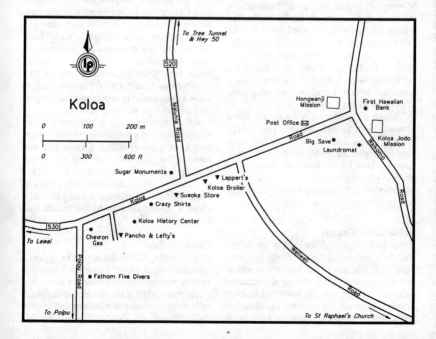

ethnic groups that worked the plantations are immortalised in a sculpture. The Hawaiian wears a malo and has a poi dog by his side. The Chinese, Korean, Japanese, Portuguese, Filipino and Puerto Rican groups are likewise in native field dress.

If you want to learn more about the history of sugar, there are informative plaques at the display.

Old Koloa

Koloa looks like an Old West town of wooden buildings with false storefronts. It was a thriving plantation town and commercial centre that largely went bust after WW II.

Its history is sugar but its present is tourism. The former fish markets, tailor shops, barber shops, Japanese bathhouses and beer halls are now boutiques, galleries and restaurants.

The building that houses Crazy Shirts was until recently the Yamamoto General Store. Moviegoers would line up at Yamamoto's for crack seed and soft drinks before the theatre across the street burned down. On the sidewalk in front of the store a lifelike sculpture of a craggy mechanic stands next to an ancient Texaco gas pump. The courtyard behind the store looks onto the former town hotel, where you'll find an interesting little display on Koloa's history.

Though it's pretty touristy Koloa is still a pleasant town to walk around. The 'newly quaint' shops are in stark contrast to a handful of old sugar shacks that still house cane workers farther down the street. The town is just beginning to boom beyond its old wooden buildings, with a couple of new construction projects underway.

Koloa Jodo Mission

Koloa Jodo Mission dates back to 1910. The Buddhist temple on the left is the original. Next to it is a newer and larger one where services are now held. During services the smell of incense and the sound of beating drums fills the air. It's still very Japanese but grass tatami mats and cushions have been replaced by wooden floors and folding chairs.

St Raphael's Catholic Church

St Raphael's is the oldest Catholic church on Kauai. Some of the first Portuguese immigrants to Hawaii are buried in the churchyard cemetery. The original building, built in 1856, was of lava rock and coral mortar with walls three feet thick. When the church was enlarged in 1936 it was all plastered over and it now has a more typical white-washed appearance. To get there from Koloa Rd, turn onto Weliweli Rd then right onto Hapa Rd. It's half a mile to the church.

Places to Stay

Kahili Mountain Park (☎ 742-9921), Box 298, Koloa, HI 96756, is a mile up a sugar cane road just beyond the seven-mile marker on Hwy 50. It's run by the Seventh Day Adventist church in a beautiful setting beneath Mt Kahili.

There are three categories of accommodation. Cabinettes, at the bottom end, are very simple structures on cement slabs and are rather dark and dank, though they cost only $20. More appealing are the cabins which are pleasantly spread out around the grounds. There are eight older rustic cabins for $35 and five new ones for $50. The new cabins, while not as quaint in appearance, are larger, spiffier and have screened porches.

All categories have a two-burner gas stove, a sink and a refrigerator, while cabins also have a table, chairs, dresser and hot water. Cabinettes hold four people, cabins hold up to seven. Rates given are for singles or doubles, with each additional person charged $4. It's an unbeatable value and only about a 20-minute ride to the beaches in Poipu.

Places to Eat

Sueoka Store, *Koloa Broiler* and *Lappert's* ice-cream store are in a row on Koloa Rd near its intersection with Maluhia Rd.

The snack shop at the side of Sueoka Store sells burgers, cheese sandwiches and saimin for $1.50 each and plate lunches for $3 to $4.

It's open from 10 am to 3 pm Monday to Saturday.

Koloa Broiler (☎ 742-9122) is in a funky old wooden building with a tin roof – a former soft drink bottling plant. The 'menu' is a display case of raw meat and fish. Diners get to be cooks, preparing their own orders over a communal gas grill. Sirloin steak is $10.95, mahimahi or barbecued chicken $9.95, burgers $6.75. A simple buffet of rice, beans and salad is included. It's open from 11 am to 10 pm daily.

Pancho & Lefty's (☎ 742-7377), behind the Chevron station, has standard Mexican food. Two enchiladas or tacos with rice and beans cost $7.95 and combination plates are $10 to $12. There's usually an afternoon happy hour until 6 pm featuring $1 Bud drafts. They also serve breakfast ranging from waffles to huevos rancheros. Hours are 8 am to 10 pm.

POIPU

Poipu is about three miles south of Koloa down Poipu Rd. Other than its lovely white-sand beaches, Poipu's most popular attraction is the Spouting Horn blowhole. To get to Spouting Horn, turn right off Poipu Rd onto Lawai Rd, just past Poipu Plaza, and continue for 1¾ miles.

Prince Kuhio Park

Prince Kuhio Park is about half a mile down Lawai Rd, across from tiny Hoai Bay. Here you'll find **Hoai Heiau** and a monument honouring Jonah Kuhio Kalanianaole, the Territory of Hawaii's first delegate to the US Congress. It was Prince Kuhio who spear-headed the Hawaiian Homes Commission Act, which provided homesteads for native Hawaiians. The remains of a fishpond and an ancient Hawaiian house platform are also on the grounds.

Baby Beach

There's a protected swimming area just deep enough for children off Hoona Rd, east of Prince Kuhio Park. Look for the beach access post at a little clearing between the road and the beach. Adults may want to walk west down the beach and swim out in front of the white house where there's a sandy break with fewer rocks and deeper water.

Lawai Beach

Lawai Beach is west of Prince Kuhio Park, just after the Beach House restaurant. It's a little rocky but during winter the water is usually quite clear and snorkellers can hand-feed the fish. When the surf's up in summer, the beach is inundated with surfers.

A concession stand opposite the beach rents boogie boards and snorkel sets.

Kukuiula Bay

Kukuiula Bay is a small boat harbour main-tained by the state. It's mostly used by fishing and diving boats. The beach is rocky and more suitable for pole fishing than other water activities. There are showers, restrooms, picnic tables, a launch ramp, nine mooring spaces and a concrete wharf.

Spouting Horn Beach Park

Spouting Horn is a blowhole that has its days. Sometimes it has a pretty good spout, other times it's simply a nonevent. The waves, the tides, and the overall force of the sea rushing into the lava tube decide how much water surges through the spout. The low whooshing that precedes the rushing water sounds like a whale breathing.

During the height of the day, tour buses pull in and out of the parking lot and there's often a small crowd with cameras clicking away. Jewellery and trinket stalls line the walkway from the parking lot down to the viewing area. You can avoid this scene simply by arriving in the late afternoon, which is also the best time to see rainbows that are sometimes cast in the spray by the sun.

Koloa Landing

Koloa Landing, at the mouth of Waikomo Stream, was once Kauai's largest port. It not only served as a shipping point for sugar grown on Koloa Plantation, but whalers also called at Koloa Landing to resupply provis-ions. In the 1850s local farmers shipped out oranges and sweet potatoes to California gold miners. The landing lost its importance after an island-wide road system was built, and it was abandoned in the 1920s. Other than a county boat ramp there's not much left to see.

Beneath the water it's another story. Koloa Landing is a popular snorkelling and diving spot. Its protected waters reach depths of about 30 feet and it's generally calm all year.

It has some underwater tunnels and a good variety of coral and fish. For the best sights swim out to the right after you enter the water.

The landing is off the western end of Hoonani Rd. A highway marker reading 5.08 (miles) marks the drive down to the landing.

Poipu Beach
The long stretch of white sand fronting the

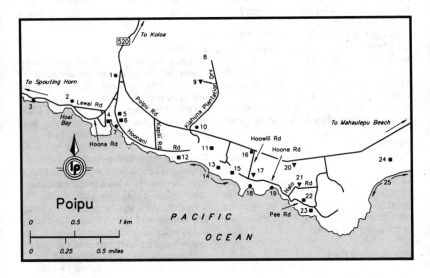

Sheraton, Kiahuna Plantation and the two Stouffer hotels is referred to as Poipu Beach. It's actually three attractive crescent beaches with narrow points or outcrops in between. The turquoise waters are good for swimming, bodysurfing, windsurfing, board surfing and snorkelling.

Cowshead, the rocky outcropping at the west end of the beach near the Sheraton, has Poipu Beach's best boogie boarding and bodysurfing breaks. Top surfing spots are Waiohai, which is off the east side of Poipu Beach, and First Break, offshore in front of the Sheraton. Slow, gentle waves more suitable for beginners can be found inshore along the beach.

You can rent gear and get information on water conditions at the beach huts fronting the Sheraton and Stouffer hotels. Snorkelling gear and boogie boards rent for $5 an hour or $15 a day, surfboards for $10/25. They also offer surfing lessons at 11.30 am and 2 pm daily for $30.

On the beach in front of the Stouffer Waiohai a section of the Kihahouna Heiau has been rebuilt by the resort.

Moir Gardens

Moir Gardens were part of the Moir Estate before it was turned into Kiahuna Plantation Resort.

The plantation house, now Plantation Gardens Restaurant, was a wedding gift to Hector and Alexandra Knudsen Moir when they married in 1933. It had previously been part of Hawaii's first sugar plantation, which was owned by Alexandra's father.

The Moirs were avid gardeners and created large flowering cactus gardens and water lily ponds. The garden paths are now open to the public and make for pleasant strolling.

Kiahuna Plantation Drive

African flame trees line Kiahuna Plantation Drive, the road leading to Kiahuna Golf Course and the club restaurant.

Kiahuna Shopping Center, on the corner of Poipu Rd and Kiahuna Plantation Drive, has a couple of places to eat as well as some art galleries and clothing shops.

Poipu Beach Park

Poipu Beach Park, at the end of Hoowili Rd, has a lifeguard station, shallow nearshore waters and safe swimming. That, combined with the playground equipment at the park, makes this one of the most popular weekend destinations for families on the South Shore.

Nukumoi Point extends into the water at the western side of the park, dividing it from the beach fronting the Stouffer Waiohai hotel. At low tide you can walk out on the point and explore tidepools that shelter sea urchins and small fish. For the best snorkelling head over to the Waiohai side of the beach, where there are swarms of near-tame fish.

Snorkel sets can be rented across the street at the mini-deli next to Brennecke's restaurant for $10/15 a day/week, boogie boards for $10/25.

Brennecke's Beach

Brennecke's has fantastic shorebreaks that make it the South Shore's best spot for bodysurfing and boogie boarding. It breaks very close to shore and is suitable for experienced riders only. While it's best when surf is highest, which is generally in the summer, there's some respectable action in winter as well. Beware of strong rips that are present with high surf. The beach is a pocket of sand barely 50 feet long and the waters can get crowded. For safety reasons fins are not allowed and surfboards are prohibited.

Brennecke's is off Hoone Rd, just down from Poipu Beach Park.

Shipwreck Beach

Shipwreck Beach, the sandy beach fronting the new Hyatt Regency Kauai, also sees some top bodysurfing and boogie boarding conditions. There are a couple of challenging nearshore surf breaks that attract local board surfers as well. The water conditions here are not for novices, and the pounding shorebreak and high surf make for treacherous swimming conditions along the entire beach.

Mahaulepu Beach

Secluded Mahaulepu Beach, a couple of miles beyond Shipwreck Beach, has lovely white sands, sheltered coves, tidepools, lithified sand dunes and sea cliffs.

At various times of the year Mahaulepu is good for surfing, windsurfing, boogie boarding and snorkelling. In pre-contact times the area was heavily settled and many important historic sites lie buried beneath the cane fields and shifting beach sands. Ghost marchers are said to still come in from the sea at night along the Mahaulepu coast.

The property is owned by Grove Farm and visitors are required to sign a waiver at the gate before being allowed to enter. The easiest way to get there is to drive past the Hyatt and continue on the dirt cane road for 1½ miles, at which point the road will be blocked by a yellow gate. Turn right, continue past the gravel plant and after a third of a mile you'll come to the gatehouse, which is open from 7.30 am to 6.30 pm daily. From there it's half a mile to the beach; bear right at the first fork and then take the middle road (which bears right) at a three-way fork near the road's end.

This will bring you to a popular windsurfing spot and a convenient place to explore from. One striking geological feature in the area is a cinder cone with a cave that you can walk deep into. To get there, walk west along the beach for about a third of a mile. After crossing a little stream, take the trail going inland which leads to the cave, a couple of minutes away. In the cave's centre you'll find an opening looking straight up to the heavens – it feels like sitting in a little volcano.

Or, instead of heading to the cave, walk east along the beach for about 10 minutes and you'll reach scenic Kawailoa Bay, which is surrounded by sand dunes to the west and protected by jutting sea cliffs to the east. The bay has a lovely beach and it's not uncommon to find a few Hawaiians netfishing in the waters along the shore.

It's also possible to get to the bay by car. Just bear left instead of right at the last turn. Camping is allowed at Kawailoa Bay with a permit from Grove Farm.

Places to Stay – bottom end
Since the YMCA closed down a few years

back, Poipu hasn't had anything in the budget range. It's an expensive tourist area and, unlike Princeville on the North Shore, it's difficult to find a room in a private home.

Places to Stay – middle
Koloa Landing Cottages (☎ 742-1470), 2704B Hoonani Rd, Poipu, HI 96756, have five cottages across the street from Koloa Landing. Each has a full kitchen, TV and telephone. Studios, which have a queen bed, cost $50. The cottages, which have both a queen bed and two twins, cost from $70 for two people in a smaller unit to $100 for four people in the largest unit. A cleaning fee of $20 for the studio, $40 to $60 for the cottages, is tagged onto the bill.

Poipu Plantation (☎ 742-6757, (800) 733-1632), 1792 Pee Rd, Koloa, HI 96756, consists of nine condo-style units and a couple of B&B rooms in a 1930s home. Best deals are the condos, which are modern and comfortable with tropical rattan furniture, TVs and full kitchens and cost from $70 to $80 for one-bedroom units, $85 for two-bedroom units. While not as spacious, the B&B accommodation is pleasant enough, includes breakfast and costs $70 for a room with a queen bed, $75 for a king, each with private bathroom. There's a coin-op washer and dryer on the grounds.

Garden Isle Cottages (☎ 742-6717), 2666 Puuholo Rd, Poipu, HI 96756, has 14 units in cottages above Koloa Landing and two Poipu houses. There's one studio for $53, another for $59 and others for $70 and $80, all with refrigerators. One-bedroom apartments with kitchens range from $90 to $125, and two-bedroom units cost $160. The rooms are decorated with abstract paintings and sculpture by owner/artist Robert Flynn. One of the houses is opposite the ocean on Hoona Rd, the other has a tiled lap swimming pool.

The *Poipu Bed & Breakfast Inn* (☎ 742-1146, (800) 552-0095), 2720 Hoonani Rd, Poipu, HI 96756, has four bedrooms, each with a private bathroom, TV and VCR. The decor is casually chic with white wicker, antique pine, chintz fabrics and an antique carousel horse in each room. Rates, which include a continental breakfast, are $90, $95, $110 and $125, the latter two for rooms with whirlpool tubs. It costs $5 less for singles, $10 more for one-night stands and $25 more a day around the Christmas/New Year holidays.

Sunset Kahili (☎ 742-1691, (800) 827-6478), 1763 Pee Rd, Poipu, HI 96756, is an older, well-maintained five-storey condo with a friendly manager. Each of the 36 units has an ocean view, a washer/dryer, cable TV and lanai. Rates are $90 for two people in a one-bedroom unit and $120 for up to four people in the two-bedroom units. The top floors are $5 more. The minimum stay is three nights, with prices dropping gradually the longer you stay. It can be difficult to book from January through March as a lot of retirees return each year to stay the winter.

Places to Stay – top end

The *Stouffer Poipu Beach Hotel* (☎ 742-1681, (800) 468-3571), 2251 Poipu Rd, Poipu, HI 96756, has 138 rooms, each with a stove, refrigerator and little lanai. Room rates are $100 to $175.

The *Stouffer Waiohai Beach Hotel* (☎ 742-9511, (800) 468-3571), 2249 Poipu Rd, Poipu, HI 96756, is more ordinary than the price would imply. The cheapest of the 430 rooms are $175 and they're small with almost no view. Oceanfront rooms jump to $275. Prices go up to $1500 for two-bedroom suites.

The *Sheraton Kauai Hotel* (☎ 742-1661, (800) 325-3535, from the USA and Canada, 008-073535 from Australia), 2440 Hoonani Rd, Poipu, HI 96756, has 455 rooms. The buildings tend to ramble but there are gardens and carp ponds in between. It's cheerier and more casual than the Waiohai but rates start at a steep $175 for a garden room, $275 for a beachfront room.

At the *Hyatt Regency Kauai* (☎ 742-1234, (800) 233-1234), 1571 Poipu Rd, Poipu, HI 96756, the new rich kid on the block, lagoonside rooms start out at a cool $270, while the best suites climb to $1800. The 600-room hotel is unmistakably Poipu's most elegant,

with airy lobbies adorned with antiques, and artificial lagoons and waterways spread around the grounds.

The *Kiahuna Plantation Resort* (☎ 742-6411), 2253 Poipu Rd, Koloa, HI 96756, is a 333-unit condo complex managed by Village Resorts. The rooms are rather average, but pleasant with big private balconies and the grounds include the Moir Gardens. Prices for one-bedroom units range from $155 (garden view) to $350 (oceanfront) for up to four people. Two-bedroom units are $290 to $400 for up to six people.

Places to Stay – vacation rentals

The Poipu Beach Resort Association (☎ 742-7444), Box 730, Koloa, HI 96756, has a brochure listing most of Poipu's accommodation. The following companies each handle about 100 vacation rentals in condos and private homes in the Poipu area, with rates that range from about $100 to $250 a night.

Suite Paradise, 2827 Poipu Rd, Poipu, HI 96756 (☎ 742-7400, (800) 367-8020)

R&R Realty & Rentals, 1661 Pee Rd, Poipu, HI 96756 (☎ 742-7555, (800) 367-8022)

Grantham Resorts, Box 983, Koloa, HI 96756 (☎ 742-7220, (800) 325-5701)

Place to Stay – camping

Camping is allowed at Mahaulepu Beach, with a permit from Grove Farm Co (☎ 245-3678), 3-1850 Kaumualii Hwy in Puhi, opposite Kauai Community College. The office is open from 7.30 am to 4.30 pm Monday to Friday. Permits are free and good for a maximum of two nights. There are no facilities, so you'll have to carry in everything you need, including water. They restrict the number of campers, but with the exception of weekends and summer vacation, it's not usually difficult to get a permit.

Places to Eat – bottom end & middle

Taqueria Nortenos in Poipu Plaza has cheap Mexican food. It's essentially a takeaway place with some indoor picnic tables. The meatless burrito is good value at $2.75, while an enchilada with rice and beans cost $4.25. The food is fine for the price.

Brennecke's, opposite Poipu Beach Park, is a touristy beachfront restaurant that serves good fish dishes. A fresh fish sandwich at lunch costs $10, a fish dinner about double that. Lunch is from noon to 4 pm, dinner from 4 to 10.30 pm daily.

A few dollars cheaper, though no bargain at $8, is the takeaway Hooker's Special of a fresh ahi burger with fries and soft drink. It's available from the sidewalk snack shop below Brennecke's restaurant, which is open from 10.30 am to 4 pm daily.

The *Flamingo Cantina* (☎ 742-9505), halfway up Nalo Rd, serves reasonably priced Mexican food. At happy hour, 3.30 to 5 pm, margaritas and beer are $1.75. There's a tostada, taco and burrito buffet for $7 during happy hour and $8.50 at dinner, which is from 5 to 9.30 pm daily. Other prices range from $8.75 for a taco salad to $13.50 for fajitas.

The *Pizza Bella* (☎ 742-9571) in the Kiahuna Shopping Village has pizzas from $9, lasagne, sandwiches and salads. Pizza is sold by the slice until 4.30 pm for $2.40. It's open from 11.30 am to 10 pm daily. They also home deliver.

A few shops down, *Shipwreck Subs* has takeaway vegetarian or meat submarine sandwiches at moderate prices.

The *Kiahuna Golf Club Restaurant* has open-air dining with a view of the fairways. Lunch, which is served to 3.30 pm, features sandwiches and salads. A good choice is the mahimahi sandwich with fries and coleslaw for $8. Breakfasts such as Mexican omelettes, banana pancakes or mahimahi and eggs are in the same price range. There's no dinner.

Keoki's Paradise (☎ 742-7534) in the Kiahuna Shopping Village doesn't look like much from the outside but inside it's open-air with seven waterfalls, lit torches, bamboo and hanging vines. While it's a bit contrived it somehow all works. The food is reasonably good and dishes range from teriyaki chicken for $13 to catch of the day for about double that. Meals include good home-made

muffins and a green salad. It's open for dinner only, from 5.30 to 10 pm daily.

Places to Eat – top end
Plantation Gardens (☎ 742-1695) at Kiahuna Plantation condos is in a former plantation home with a garden setting. Menu prices have recently been cut and if you're up for dining out this is a very good choice for Poipu. Entrees cost from $11 for vegetarian saute to $18 for shrimp scampi, while fresh catch of the day is a reasonable $15. Be sure to request a verandah or gardenside table. It's open from 5.30 pm daily.

The Sunday champagne brunch served from 10 am to 2 pm at the *Stouffer Waiohai* is widely considered Kauai's best. It's a steep $25 but it has everything from sashimi to an incredible dessert bar and live Hawaiian music.

For formal dining the Stouffer Waiohai's *Tamarind* restaurant and the Hyatt Regency's *Dondero's* have good reputations and some of the island's most expensive food.

Entertainment
Most Poipu entertainment is at the hotel nightclubs.

The *Poipu Beach Cafe* (☎ 742-9511) in the Stouffer Poipu Beach Hotel usually has reggae or Jawaiian music from 9 pm to midnight on weekends and top-40 bands from 8 to 11 pm during the week.

The *Sheraton Kauai Hotel* (☎ 742-1661) has live dance bands from 8 pm to midnight during the week, to 1 am on weekends. The Sheraton also has a luau on Wednesday nights for $42 adults, $24 children.

The *Stouffer Waiohai* has pianist Kimo Garner nightly in its Tamarind lounge.

West Side

The top destinations on Kauai's West Side are Waimea Canyon and Kokee State Park, both with ruggedly spectacular scenery.

It's 38 miles along Kaumualii Rd (Hwy 50)

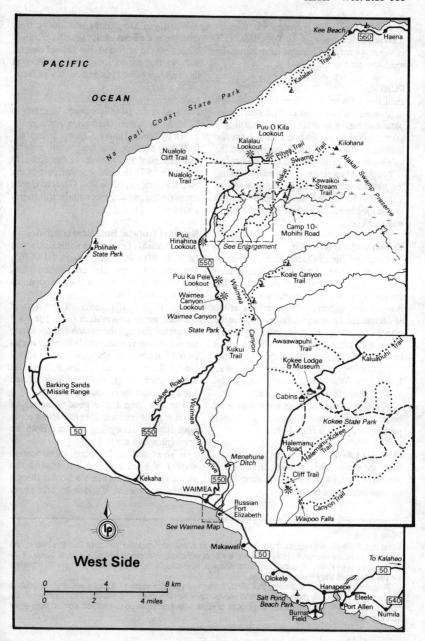

PACIFIC

OCEAN

Na Pali Coast State Park

Kee Beach

560

Haena

Kalalau Trail

Puu O Kila Lookout

Kalalau Lookout

Nualolo Cliff Trail

Pihea Trail

Kilohana

Alakai Swamp Trail

Alakai Swamp Preserve

Nualolo Trail

Kawaikoi Stream Trail

Puu Hinahina Lookout

Camp 10-Mohihi Road

See Enlargement

Polihale State Park

Puu Ka Pele Lookout

Koaie Canyon Trail

Waimea Canyon Lookout

Waimea

Waimea Canyon

State Park

Canyon

Kukui Trail

Barking Sands Missile Range

Kokee Road

Waimea Canyon Drive

50

550

Kekaha

Menehune Ditch

550

WAIMEA

Russian Fort Elizabeth

See Waimea Map

West Side

0   4   8 km

0   2   4 miles

Makaweli

Olokele

50

To Kalaheo

Hanapepe

Eleele

540

Port Allen

Numila

Salt Pond Beach Park

Burns Field

Awaawapuhi Trail

Kaluapuhi Trail

Kokee Lodge & Museum

Cabins

Kokee State Park

Halemanu Road

Halemanu-Kokee Trail

Cliff Trail

Canyon Trail

Waipoo Falls

from Lihue to Polihale State Park, the far-thest accessible point on the West Side. This is sugar country, with sugar cane lining the roadside most of the way.

PUHI

Puhi, two miles south of Lihue, is small enough to have an old-fashioned general store, complete with rural post office. The clerk still gets your groceries one item at a time from the shelves behind the counter and rings up the sale on an old hand-cranked cash register.

Peoples Market, in the adjacent parking lot, has smoothies for $2, local fruit and leis. Lappert's Aloha Ice Cream is next door. All are on the highway, opposite Kauai Community College.

Queen Victoria's Profile

The rock profile of Queen Victoria, part of the Haupu (Hoary Head) Ridge, can be seen from a marked viewpoint in front of the college. It takes some imagination, but here's how to find it. Start with your back at the HVB marker. Look across the highway at the phone pole, then over to the metal light pole in the background to the right. The queen's crowned head is under the arch of the lamp.

Supposedly she's shaking her finger at an imaginary William, saying 'Na, Willy, Willy', hence the harbour's name.

The Hawaiians had their own story long before the Europeans named this vague profile. They call it Hina-i-uka.

PUHI TO LAWAI

Shell ginger is fairly prominent along this stretch of road, its pink blossoms dangling in clumps from large bushes.

When you see banana and guava trees growing in the front yards of small tin-roofed homes you're in Omao, the first of several villages that are so small you zip through them almost before you notice they're there.

LAWAI

Lawai is at the 10-mile marker. Its claim to fame is the Lawai Gardens, started in the 1870s by Queen Emma. Chicago industrialist Robert Allerton later bought the property and expanded the gardens in the 100-acre estate. In 1971 the land became part of the National Tropical Botanical Garden. Queen Emma's original summer cottage still stands on the grounds.

National Tropical Botanical Garden

The National Tropical Botanical Garden (☎ 332-7361), Box 340, Lawai, HI 96765, propagates tropical and endangered plant species and does research in ethnobotanical and medicinal plants.

The twice daily tours of the Lawai Gardens are by reservation only. The two-mile walk through the garden and the estate takes 2½ hours and can get booked up pretty heavily in advance. The cost is a hefty $15, though the cause is good. A few dollars more buys membership, entitling you to see Limahuli Gardens on the North Shore.

The gift shop has a good selection of tropical plant books and there's also a room with displays of ongoing projects. Both are open from 7.45 am to 4 pm.

A short self-guided plant identification walk has been mapped out around the visitors' centre. This one's a freebie though it's of minor interest. If you do go, take a look

---

Hina-i-uka

Long ago Peleula, a princess from Oahu, sailed to Kauai to check out rumours that the island had the most handsome men in Hawaii. Hina, a Kauai princess, welcomed her with a royal banquet. At the banquet was Kahili, a young chief from Kilauea, who caught the fancy of both women. To compete for his affections they danced the hula.

Peleula's dance was stunning. But Hina, perfumed with the scent of Kauai's endemic mokihana berries, was absolutely mesmerising and she became Kahili's lover. The people of Kauai carved one ridge of the Haupu mountains into the image of Hina, with her finger up to warn off women from other islands. ■

at the traveller's palm at the entrance. It's so named because the base of each frond collects a reserve of water that can be tapped by thirsty travellers.

To get there from Hwy 50 take Koloa Rd south three-quarters of a mile and turn right onto Hailima Rd, which ends in half a mile at the visitors' centre.

KALAHEO

Kalaheo is essentially an old sleepy Portuguese community. Pig hunting is a popular pastime for people in this town, which accounts for all the hunting dogs in tiny backyard cages.

Kalaheo is in the midst of its own little development boom, not of hotels and condos but of private homes. Doctors and other highly paid professionals are buying up the cliffside oceanview lots below the golf course.

The town's main shops are clustered around the intersection of Hwy 50 and Papalina Rd. They include a couple of food marts, the post office and Kalaheo's restaurants. There's a laundromat behind the Kalaheo steak house on Papalina Rd.

Kukuiolono Park

Kukuiolono Park (☎ 332-9151) is a golf course with gardens and a scenic viewpoint. Kukuiolono means 'light of Lono', referring to the torches that were once placed on this hill to help guide canoes safely to shore.

From Hwy 50, turn left onto Papalina Rd in Kalaheo. Just short of a mile turn right onto Puu Rd and then make an immediate right turn up through an old stone archway into the park. A neat little Japanese garden is at the end of the parking lot.

On the knoll to the south-west, there's a green pavilion that looks down on a wide expanse of the south coast. To get there look for the satellite dish and head for the Norfolk pines. It's a 10-minute walk on a paved road across the golf course.

The ominous-looking gismo on the flat hill directly south of the pavilion is a navy signal beacon. Poipu is at the point on the left and to your back is Mt Kahili at 3089 feet.

The park gates are open from 6.30 am to 6.30 pm. The nine-hole golf course is open to the public on a first-come, first-served basis. Green fees are a mere $5. The little clubhouse has an inexpensive snack shop and a fine view clear down to the coast.

Puu Road Scenic Drive

Puu Rd is a scenic side loop with small ranches, sugar cane fields, bamboo clumps, grand mango trees and coastal views. It's a winding road, only one lane with some blind curves, but nothing tricky if you drive slowly. This is a quiet country road and it's quite possible you won't even encounter another car.

After leaving Kukuiolono Park, turn right onto Puu Rd. It's just over three miles back to Hwy 50 this way. About halfway along you'll look down on Port Allen's oil tanks and the sugar town of Numila with its now-closed mill.

Around another bend macadamia trees march in rows up the distant hills ahead. Down the slope to the left of the road are coffee trees, part of a total of 4900 acres that have been planted between Koloa and Hanapepe. Both the coffee and nuts belong to the McBryde Sugar Company and are an attempt to diversify crops on land that had formerly been planted only with sugar cane. The coffee is a joint venture with Hills Bros Coffee, and they've recently harvested their first crop.

Olu Pua Botanical Garden

The Olu Pua estate home, built in 1931 by Honolulu architect C W Dickey, was the headquarters of Alexander & Baldwin's Kauai Pineapple Plantation. It's been a getaway for dignitaries over the years and presidents Reagan, Carter, Ford and Nixon have all been guests of the estate. It's still a private home though the 12-acre gardens are open to the public for guided tours.

Olu Pua (☎ 332-8182) claims to have Hawaii's finest collection of tropical flowers. One section contains edible and useful plants, others are of palms, hibiscus and orchids.

Olu Pua is at the end of a long driveway mauka of the road immediately after the intersection of Hwy 50 and Hwy 540. Tours of the gardens are given five times a day on the half hour from 9.30 am to 1.30 pm. It costs $10 for adults, $5 for children aged 5 to 12.

Places to Stay

Classic Vacation Cottages (☎ 332-9201), c/o Dick & Wynnis Grow, Box 901, Kalaheo, HI 96741, has three units in Kalaheo, half a mile up from Hwy 50 and about 20 minutes from the beaches at Poipu. The studio, which costs $55, has a queen-size bed, a skylight and French doors to a little porch. A one-bedroom unit above the studio has high ceilings, a lanai and a peek at the ocean for $60. The third unit costs $58 and has a separate bedroom as well as a couple of twin beds in the living room, a good choice for a family. All have sofabeds, kitchens and cable TV. Guests have use of the hot tub and can borrow snorkelling equipment and boogie boards. Breakfast for two is $5 more and there's a two-day minimum stay.

Julie's Bed & Breakfast (☎ 332-9586), c/o Dave & Julie Akre, 3685 Waha Rd, Kalaheo, HI 96741, is a condo-like one-bedroom unit beneath a contemporary home, with a king bed, cable TV and a small kitchen. It's about two miles from the town centre, south of Kukuiolono Park. The cost is $65 with breakfast, $60 without, with a two-night minimum.

Black Bamboo (☎ 332-7518, (800) 527-7789), Box 1202, Kalaheo, HI 96741, is a B&B catering exclusively to gay and lesbian guests. The contemporary house, which is about half a mile south of Kukuiolono Park, has an airy tropical feel. There are four units with private entrances and bathrooms, a 40-foot lap pool, a hot tub and a common lounge. Rates are $65/85 for singles/doubles and include a continental breakfast. A unit with a kitchenette is available for $10 more.

Places to Eat

Brick Oven Pizza (☎ 332-8561) on Hwy 50 is a popular place and you may have to wait for a table, particularly at dinner time. A small cheese pizza costs $7.35, a large $15.20, with a choice of whole wheat or white crust. They also serve sandwiches, salads, wine and beer and are open from 11 am to 10.30 pm daily except Monday.

Camp House Grill on Hwy 50, opposite Menehune Food Mart, serves breakfast daily except Wednesday from 6.30 to 10.30 am. Dishes average about $5, though there's a $2 special which consists of eggs, bacon and toast until 8 am. Burgers and chicken sandwiches are $4 to $6 and hot dishes range from $6 to $10. Lunch and dinner are served from 11 am to 9 pm daily.

The *Bread Box* on Papalina Rd makes good whole-grain breads, tasty macnut rolls for $1.25 and coffee for just 25 cents. It's open Monday to Saturday from 6 am to noon, or until the bread sells out.

For meat and potatoes, the *Kalaheo Steak House* on Papalina Rd is open from 5.30 to 10.30 pm nightly, with dinner in the $12 to $17 range.

KALAHEO TO HANAPEPE

The **scenic lookout** that comes up soon after the 14-mile marker gives a view deep into Hanapepe Valley. The red clay walls of the cliffs are topped by bright green cane like a sugar frosting.

The same Robinson family that owns Niihau owns a lot of land around these parts and has a hideaway estate up in the valley.

Eleele Shopping Center, at the 16-mile marker, has a doughnut shop, Dairy Queen, Big Save supermarket, bank, post office, laundromat and gas station. Other than the shopping centre there's not much to the town.

Hwy 540 is an alternate route that leads off Hwy 50 just after Kalaheo and connects back to Hwy 50 at Eleele. It passes through rows of young coffee trees and swings by Numila, a former cane town with dusty wooden houses surrounding a defunct mill.

Port Allen on Hanapepe Bay is both a commercial harbour and one of Kauai's busiest recreational boat harbours. The state-run small craft harbour is protected by break-waters and has launch ramps, berthing and mooring spaces.

Glass Beach

Glass Beach, just half a mile east of Port Allen, is a cove piled high with colourful bits of glass that have been worn into smooth pebble-like pieces. The glass comes from an old abandoned dump site nearby and its weathering is the result of decades of wave action. At certain times of the year the glass is deep enough to scoop up by the handful, while at other times it's largely washed out to sea.

To get to the little cove, take the last left before entering the Port Allen commercial harbour, drive past the fuel storage tanks and then curve to the right down a cane road that leads 100 yards in to the beach.

HANAPEPE

Hanapepe is a step back in time, moving along at its own slow pace. The main street is lined with old wooden buildings, some with fading signs, a few recently smartened up. With its dusty feed store, boarded-up theatre and crackseed shop, the town is loaded with character.

Parts of *The Thorn Birds* was filmed here, because it so bears a resemblance to the dusty Australian outback of earlier days.

A new sign on Hwy 50, where you turn mauka onto Hanapepe Rd to get to the town centre, reads 'Welcome to Hanapepe, Kauai's Biggest Little Town'. A recent grant to spiff up Main St has brightened the town's face and provided seed money for half a dozen galleries to start up. Kauai Fine Arts, which occupies the former bowling alley, has an interesting collection of antique maps and prints, including works related to Captain Cook's explorations.

One sight you shouldn't miss is the **swinging bridge** that crosses the Hanapepe River. The path to it starts down the alley on the north side of Robert's, opposite Kauai Fine Arts.

The grounds of the First United Church of Christ, next to Robert's, is the site of a small farmers market on Thursday afternoons.

For a fine little **scenic side drive** through a niche of 'old Hawaii' turn mauka onto Awawa Rd at Seto's Market, which is on Hanapepe Rd at the west side of the river. The narrow road is bordered by cliffs on one side and by taro patches, corn fields and grazing horses on the other. After a mile Awawa Rd forks. If you take the dead end street to the left there's more rural scenery and lots of tall trees, some covered with passion fruit vines that drop the delicious ripe fruit onto the road. After three-quarters of a mile you'll have to turn around and come back to the 'main' road, where you can turn left and loop back to town along a dirt drive. However there's one tricky section where the road crosses a cement bridge. As the river flows *over* rather than under this bridge, you'll need to gauge the depth of the water on the bridge before deciding whether to continue. If it's only a couple of inches deep, you shouldn't have any problem crossing, but if it's more than that, turn around and return the way you came.

Salt Pond Beach

Kauai has long been known for its red alae salt, made by adding a little of its iron-rich earth to sea salt. The salt is made by letting seawater into shallow basins called salt pans and allowing it to evaporate. When dry, the salt crystals are scraped off. Native Hawaiians still make salt this way down on the coast south of Hanapepe.

Salt Pond Beach County Park is just beyond the salt ponds. It has a sandy beach, camping sites, covered picnic tables, barbecue grills, a pay phone, showers and a lifeguard on duty daily. Water in the cove gets up to 10 feet deep and is good for swimming laps. Four times across equals half a mile. Both ends of the cove are shallow and good for kids. If you camp at Salt Pond you'll probably get to talk story with Uncle Louie, a volunteer who watches over the park and knows just about everything there is to know about Hanapepe.

To get to Salt Pond Beach, turn left just

past the 17-mile marker onto Lele Rd, then right onto Lokokai Rd.

Places to Eat

Hanapepe Book Store, in the town centre on Hanapepe Rd, not only sells books and an eclectic collection of Hawaiiana, but is also an espresso cafe with coffees, croissants, scones and simple meals. The menu is chalk-board-style, changing daily, but includes the likes of vegie pot pie for $5.50, health burgers with taro chips for $6.50, Caesar salad and minnestrone soup. It's open from 7.30 am to 6 pm Monday to Saturday.

The *Green Garden Restaurant* on Hwy 50 is a large restaurant with a varied but not overly exciting menu. It's best known as the restaurant where the tour buses stop. Sand-wiches and hot plates cost $4 to $7, while dinners range from $8 for kabobs to $14.30 for steak and include soup, salad, rice, rolls and coffee. It's open from 7.30 am to 2 pm and from 5 to 9 pm daily except Tuesdays. Green Garden sells Taro Ko Chips, made from Hanapepe-grown taro, which is sliced thin and then fried into chips.

OLOKELE

Olokele exists for the Olokele Sugar Company. Of the 220 employees, mostly field labourers, 200 live in Olokele.

The road to the sugar mill, immediately after the 19-mile marker, is shaded by tall trees and lined with turn-of-the-century electric post lights. For a glance at real plantation life, take a drive down the road. Everything is covered with a layer of red dust from the sugar cane fields that completely surround the town. Rather than fight it, many of the houses are painted in beige-red tones.

MAKAWELI

Makaweli is headquarters for Gay & Robin-son, Niihau Ranch and Niihau Helicopters, all enterprises of the same Robinson family who owns Niihau. Quite a few native Niihauans live in this area, many of them working for the Robinsons. Once or twice a week an old military landing craft makes the 17-mile trip between Niihau and Makaweli Landing.

RUSSIAN FORT ELIZABETH

The remains of Russian Fort Elizabeth stand above the east bank of the Waimea River. Hawaiian labourers started building the fort in 1816 under the direction of Georg Anton Schaeffer, an agent of the Russian-American Company. The alliance between the Rus-sians and Kauai's King Kaumualii was short-lived and the Russians were tossed out in 1817, the same year the fort was com-pleted.

You can take a short walk through this curious period of Kauai's history following a self-guiding map found at the trailhead. The most intact part of the fort is the exterior lava rock wall. It's eight to 10 feet high in places and largely overgrown with scrub and colourful wildflowers. The seaward side was designed like the points of a star, but it takes some close observation to get the effect. A dozen markers point out where things used to be, such as the trading house, armoury and barracks.

The fort has a good view of the western bank of Waimea River where Captain Cook landed. Down the dirt road that continues past the parking lot there's a sandy area above the river mouth with a view of Waimea Pier and the island of Niihau. There are restrooms and a pay phone at the parking lot.

WAIMEA

Waimea (which means 'reddish water') was the site of an ancient Hawaiian settlement. It was at Waimea on 19 January 1778 that Captain Cook made his first Hawaiian landing. In 1820 the first wave of missionar-ies to Hawaii also landed at Waimea. In 1884 Waimea Sugar moved in and Waimea devel-oped into a plantation town.

Today Waimea is the biggest town on this side of the island. It has lots of small wooden buildings, some with false fronts, each with its own little history. The dominant building by the square is the First Hawaiian Bank, built in 1929 in the neo-classical style.

If you're on your way up to Waimea Canyon or out to the beaches, it probably doesn't make sense to give Waimea too much time. Most people just stop to eat and then move on.

If you do want to explore, Waimea Library, at the 23-mile marker, has a map of historical buildings that can be used for a self-guided walking tour. The library (☎ 338-1738) is open from 1 to 8 pm Mondays and Wednesdays and from 9 am to 5 pm Tuesdays, Thursdays and Fridays.

Waimea has an annual Captain Cook fair, around the last weekend in February, with carnival games, live music, pig-on-a-spit, cotton candy and lots of beer.

Waimea Canyon Drive heads north from town to Kokee State Park.

Lucy Wright Park

The Cook landing site is noted with a simple plaque on a nondescript rock on the western side of Waimea Bay. A well-worn path in the grass has been made by tourists who pull in and out like pilgrims.

The plaque is in Lucy Wright Park, on Ala Wai Rd, just over the Waimea Bridge. This county park has a ball field, picnic tables,

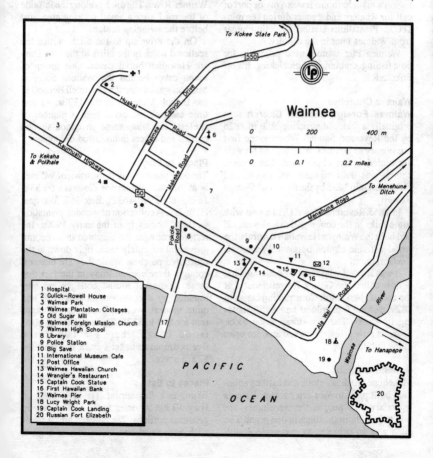

Waimea

1 Hospital
2 Gulick–Rowell House
3 Waimea Park
4 Waimea Plantation Cottages
5 Old Sugar Mill
6 Waimea Foreign Mission Church
7 Waimea High School
8 Library
9 Police Station
10 Big Save
11 International Museum Cafe
12 Post Office
13 Waimea Hawaiian Church
14 Wrangler's Restaurant
15 Captain Cook Statue
16 First Hawaiian Bank
17 Waimea Pier
18 Lucy Wright Park
19 Captain Cook Landing
20 Russian Fort Elizabeth

restrooms and showers. Camping is allowed on a flat grassy area, but it's at the side of the road in town and doesn't have much appeal.

Captain Cook Statue

The statue of Captain Cook in the centre of town is a replica of the original statue by Sir John Tweed that stands in Whitby, England. The Pacific's greatest navigator is all decked out in his best captaining finery with maps in hand.

Waimea State Recreation Pier

Until Port Allen was built, Waimea was the region's main harbour. It was a major port of call for whalers and traders during the mid-1800s. Plantations started exporting sugar from Waimea later in the century.

Waimea Pier is now used primarily for pole fishing, crabbing and picnicking. It's off Pokole Rd.

Waimea Churches

Waimea Foreign Mission Church was originally a thatched structure built in 1826 by the Reverend Samuel Whitney, the first missionary to Waimea. Whitney and his wife are buried in the churchyard. The present church was built of sandstone blocks and coral mortar in 1858 by the Reverend George Rowell.

In 1865 Reverend Rowell had a spat with some folks in the congregation and went off and built the **Waimea Hawaiian Church**, the wooden frame church opposite Wrangler's Restaurant.

It was Rowell who finished building what is now called the Gulick-Rowell House, at the end of Huakai Rd. Construction began in 1829, making it the oldest house still standing in Kauai. The two-storey stone block house is now privately owned and not open to the public.

Menehune Ditch

Menehune Ditch is a stone and earthen aqueduct built prior to Western contact. Kauai's legendary little people, the menehunes, are said to have built the ditch in one night. The ditch was an engineering masterpiece with rocks carefully squared and jointed to create a watertight seal.

When Captain Vancouver visited Waimea at the end of the 18th century he walked up the river valley atop the wall of the ditch that also served as a footpath. He estimated the walls to be 24 feet high. These days most of the ancient waterway lies buried beneath the road, but one section about two feet high can still be seen. The ditch still diverts water from the Waimea River along and through the cliff to irrigate the taro patches below.

To get there, turn at the police station onto Menehune Rd and go about 1⅓ miles up Waimea River. The ditch is along the left side of the road after a small parking area, just before the swinging bridge.

On the drive up to the ditch, notice the scattered holes in the cliffs to the left. They are Hawaiian burial caves. One group of seven caves behind the Waimea Shingon Mission was explored by Wendell Bennett of the Bishop Museum in the 1920s. At that time each of the caves held a number of skeletal remains, some in canoe-shaped coffins and others in hollowed-out logs.

Places to Stay

The only place to stay in the town of Waimea is at *Waimea Plantation Cottages* (☎ 338-1625, (800) 992-4632), Box 367, Waimea, HI 96796. A collection of wooden plantation workers' homes from the early 1900s, the restored cottages are clustered in a coconut grove and are cutely rustic right down to the tin-roofed porches. While they are pleasant enough, there's some irony in the fact that these up-market tourist cottages are surrounded by a neighbourhood of real, and quite modest, workers' cottages. Cottages rent for $95 to $225. To complete the plantation image, there's a two-storey five-bedroom manager's estate that rents for $2275 a week.

Places to Eat

Wrangler's Restaurant (☎ 338-1218) on Hwy 50 has a varied menu and serves up generous portions. The chicken breast sandwich with salad and home fries is a good choice at lunch for $5.25. At dinner, dishes range from $9.25 for cordon bleu to $17 for steak. They also have Mexican dishes, though this Hawaiian version of Mexican food won't suit too many people's taste. One local speciality that shouldn't be missed is the lilikoi pie, made daily by the manager's mother. The building was originally the Ako Store, built by Chinese shopkeeper Ah Go in 1909. It's open from 11 am to 9 pm Monday to Thursday, to 10 pm Fridays and Saturdays.

The *International Museum Cafe* (☎ 338-0403), in Waimea centre, has cafe tables set among an eclectic collection of art, antiques and old bottles. Vegetarian dishes are featured, though prices are a bit high, with a bowl of yoghurt and granola for $4.75 and sandwiches such as avocado or tuna salad for $5.50.

The *Kauai Kitchen*, next to the Big Save supermarket, has standard plate lunches for $4 to $5 and other dinner fare.

KEKAHA

Kekaha has great beaches, or rather it has one long glorious stretch. The road follows the beach for about two miles, with roadside parking all along the way. It's open ocean and when there's no swell there are usually people swimming. Niihau and its offshore island, Lehua, are visible from the beach.

There's a very inconspicuous shower just mauka of the highway between Alae Rd (Hwy 550) and Amakihi Rd, and restrooms and picnic tables farther in.

A few blocks inland from the beach is Kekaha Rd, the main village street, which runs parallel to the highway. It has a couple of grocery stores, a post office, a gas station, a Thai restaurant and a Lappert's ice-cream and sandwich shop. The village's most dominant feature is its working sugar mill, which is visible from the highway.

On its eastern end, Kekaha Rd comes out to Hwy 50 near the Kikiaola Small Boat Harbor. This state harbour has one launch ramp and eight mooring spaces.

Kekaha is the last town before the end of the highway. As you head towards Polihale, the inland cliffs get higher and the ravines

deeper. Corn and sunflowers planted for their seed grow in farms along the road. Cattle and cattle egrets feed in the pastures.

Places to Stay

Mindy's Bed & Breakfast (☎ 337-9275), 8842 Kekaha Rd, Kekaha, HI 96796, is the only alternative beyond Waimea other than camping, and is a good base for exploring Kokee. Mindy and Dave Heri have a cosy room at the side of their house, with a double bed, screened louvered windows, ceiling fan, private bath and a little deck. There's also cable TV, a microwave, refrigerator and coffeemaker. The cost is $40 single, $45 double, $5 more for stays of only one night and $5 less without breakfast. They also rent a one-bedroom apartment above their home for $55 single, $60 double, without breakfast.

Places to Eat

Toi's Thai Kitchen (☎ 337-9922) in the Traveler's Den on Kekaha Road serves good Thai food. A two-entree plate lunch that includes rice and green papaya salad costs $6 at lunch. At dinner a range of Thai dishes, both meat and vegetarian, average $8 to $9. Toi's is open from 11 am to 2.30 pm except Wednesday and Saturday and from 5.30 to 8.30 pm daily except Saturdays.

BARKING SANDS

Barking Sands Pacific Missile Range, a US Navy base, usually has one stretch of its beach open to the public. For a recorded message on current access, dial 335-4229.

The road in is at the 'Pacific Missile Range Facility' sign, less than half a mile after the 32-mile marker. At the gate they ask to see your driver's licence and then explain where you can go, which is usually the beach about two miles south of the gate, which locals call Majors Bay and the military calls RecArea No 3.

This broad curving sweep of fine golden sand is a good sunbathing and walking beach, though open and hot. The bush behind the beach offers no shade, but it hardly matters as the vegetation line is the DMZ line and you're forbidden to go beyond it anyway.

Majors Bay is a popular winter surfing spot. Like all West Side beaches the waters can be dangerous. There are no facilities. The purple-tinged island of Niihau can be seen on the horizon.

On very sunny days, when the wind is blowing off the water just right, the moving sands make sounds similar to barking dogs, hence the area's name.

The missile range facility provides the above-ground link to a sophisticated sonar network that tracks more than 1000 square miles of the Pacific. Established during WW II, it's been developed into the world's largest underwater listening device. The equipment is sensitive enough to pick up the songs of wintering humpback whales and the base has gathered the most comprehensive collection of humpback whale soundtracks recorded anywhere.

POLIHALE

Polihale is near-desert. When it's raining everywhere else, beachgoers head this way.

Polihale has a beautiful long white-sand beach with aqua-coloured water that often comes to shore in huge explosive waves. Expert surfers occasionally give Polihale a try, but strong rip currents make the waters treacherous for swimming.

Polihale State Park is about five miles from the military base. Turn left three-quarters of a mile north of the base entrance onto a wide dirt road that runs through sugar cane fields. The road is a bit bumpy but passable. Set your odometer at zero here.

At 3⅓ miles, at a large spreading tree in the middle of the road, a turn-off leads to the only safe swimming spot in the area. To get there turn left at the tree and then after a quarter of a mile follow the road up the hill to the right to the base of the dunes. Walk a couple of minutes to the north along the shore and you'll come to Queen's Pond, where a large semicircle of reef comes almost to shore creating a protected swimming pool. When the seas are relatively calm the reef blocks the longshore currents;

however when surf breaks over the reef and into the pool a dangerous rip current runs toward an opening at the southern end of the reef. Along the rest of the beach is open sea.

To get to Polihale State Park go back to the tree at the main road that runs through the sugar cane fields, turn left and continue down a mile. A turn-off on the left leads to a camping area with restrooms, outdoor showers, drinking water and a picnic pavilion. Farther down, other camping areas are in the dunes just above the beach amidst thorny kiawe trees.

At the very end of the beach is Polihale Cliff, marking the western end of the Na Pali Coast. Combined with the untamed ocean and vast expansive beach, it's a magnificent sight. Sunsets can be a meditative experience.

There's a terraced heiau towards the base of the cliff. It was originally on the seashore but shifting sands have since added about 300 feet of beach to the shore. The heiau is so overgrown that even after you tramp into the brush and find it, it's really hard to get a perspective on it. Wasps are another obstacle. If you're allergic to stings, forget about exploring this one.

WAIMEA CANYON

Waimea Canyon is nicknamed the 'Grand Canyon of the Pacific'. This may sound like promotional hype but it's not a bad description. It's smaller and 200 million years younger than the famed Arizona canyon, but Waimea Canyon is certainly grand.

The colourful river-cut gorge is 2785 feet deep. The river that runs through it, the Waimea-Poomau, is 19½ miles long, and is Kauai's longest. It seems incredible that such an immense canyon could be tucked inside such a small island.

The view of the canyon is usually a bit hazy. The best time to be there is a sunny day after it's been raining heavily. At such times, the earth's a deeper red and waterfalls cascade throughout the canyon. You can't beat it.

Waimea Canyon Drive

Waimea Canyon Drive (Hwy 550) starts in

Waimea. The road is about 19 miles long, ending at lookouts with terrific views into Kalalau Valley on the Na Pali Coast.

The views start about a mile up from Waimea and get better and better as the road climbs. There are plenty of little scenic lookouts where you can stop to take it all in. The one at 1¾ miles looks down on the Waimea River and the taro patches that the Menehune Ditch irrigates. About 2½ miles up there are good views across cane fields to Kekaha Beach with Niihau in the background. From there on in it's all canyon views.

WAIMEA CANYON STATE PARK
The southern boundary of Waimea Canyon State Park is about six miles up. Waimea Canyon Drive and Kokee Rd, both labelled Hwy 550, merge nearby. Kokee Rd, which climbs up from Kekaha, also has scenic views, but not of the canyon. After the two roads merge, the single road continuing north is called Kokee Rd.

Iliau Nature Loop
The marked trailhead for the Iliau Nature Loop is a quarter of a mile before the nine-mile marker. Just a hundred feet up the trail there's a bench with a scenic view, though for the best angle take a two-minute walk to the left where a cliffside bench provides a topnotch view into Waimea Canyon. After heavy rainfall waterfalls explode down the sheer rock walls across the gorge.

Iliau Loop starts at the first bench and takes about 10 minutes to walk. Iliau, a plant endemic to western Kauai, grows along the trail. The stalks are up to 10 feet high. Like its cousin the silversword, iliau grows to a ripe old age. Then for a grand finale it bursts open with blossoms and dies.

In 1989 a sandalwood replanting project was started along this trail to commemorate the bicentenary of Chinese immigration to Hawaii.

Scenic Lookouts
Waimea Canyon Lookout is a big turn-off where all the tour buses stop. The lookout offers a sweeping view of Waimea Canyon

from a perch of 3100 feet. The prominent canyon running in an easterly direction off Waimea is Koaie Canyon.

As you continue up the road Waipoo Falls can be seen from a couple of small unmarked lookouts before the 12-mile marker and then at the marked **Puu Ka Pele Viewpoint.** When the light is right a rainbow shows up in the spray of the 800-foot falls. Across the road from the viewpoint is a picnic area with barbecue pits, restrooms and water, as well as Camp Hale Koa, a Seventh Day Adventist camp.

Puu Hinahina Lookout, at 3640 feet, is a major turn-off between the 13 and 14-mile markers. There are two lookouts close to the parking lot. One has a fine view down Waimea Canyon clear out to the coast, while the other has a view of Niihau.

Waimea Canyon Trails
The trailhead for the **Kukui Trail** is a quarter of a mile before the nine-mile marker, the same as for the Iliau Nature Loop. Kukui Trail continues from the Iliau loop at a sign-in box and picnic table. It's a steep 2000-foot descent down the western side of Waimea Canyon, 2½ miles to the Waimea River. Wiliwili Camp is at the end of the trail.

The **Koaie Canyon Trail** begins at Kaluahaulu Camp, half a mile up the Waimea River from the end of the Kukui Trail. From there it runs east for three miles along the southern side of Koaie Canyon. There are some good swimming holes in the stream along the way and at the end of the trail. This trail should be avoided during stormy weather due to the danger of flash flooding.

The canyon's fertile soil once supported a Hawaiian settlement, long abandoned. The remains of a heiau and some house sites are still discernible. The Koaie Canyon Trail passes Hipalau Camp and ends at Lonomea Camp.

All four camping sites on these trails are part of the forest reserve system. Although they have simple open-air shelters, there are no facilities and the water needs to be treated before drinking.

During weekends and holidays, the trails are fairly heavily used by pig hunters.

KOKEE STATE PARK

The Kokee State Park boundary starts after Puu Hinahina Lookout. From about the 15-mile marker, you pass park cabins, a ranger station, Kokee Lodge, a museum and a camping ground one after the other. Kokee Lodge is not an overnight lodge but a restaurant and the concessionaire station for the nearby cabins.

Information

The ranger station in Kokee is currently not staffed though people at the museum can provide a little assistance, including an updated list of open trails. The museum also sells a map of park trails and occasionally has a few pamphlets as well.

Camping permits and more detailed trail maps must be obtained in advance at the state parks office in Lihue (☎ 241-3444). For cabin rentals, see Places to Stay.

At 7.25 and 8.25 am KUAI radio station (720 AM) announces the weather conditions at Kokee State Park.

Kokee Museum

The Kokee Natural History Museum (☎ 335-9975) is a good place to learn about Kauai's ecology. It has topographical maps and displays of local plants, birds, climate and geology. Check out the landslide photos showing how a 3000-foot side of Mt Waialeale collapsed into Olokele Canyon in 1981. Koa bowls, books and maps are sold at the museum. It's open from 10 am to 4 pm daily and admission is free.

According to legend Kanalohuluhulu Meadow opposite the museum was once a forested hangout for an evil akua (spirit) who enjoyed harassing people passing through on their way to Kalalau Valley. Distraught travellers appealed to the great god Kanaloa to protect them from the akua. Kanaloa responded by ripping out all the trees and declaring that they were never again to grow here, thus destroying the akua's hiding place. These days the meadow is full of good vibes.

The chickens running around this area are not the common garden variety, but moa, or jungle fowl. Early Polynesian settlers brought moa to Hawaii and they were once common on all the main islands. Now they remain solely on Kauai, the only island free from mongoose, who eat the eggs of ground-nesting birds.

Kalalau Lookouts

The two Kalalau Valley lookouts at the end of the road are not to be missed. From a height of 4000 feet you can see deep into the green depths of the valley straight out to the sea. Late afternoon rainbows sweep so deeply into Kalalau Valley that the bottom part of the bows curve back inward. Bright red apapane birds feed from the flowers of the ohia lehua trees near the lookout railings.

Kalalau Valley was once the site of a large settlement and was joined to Kokee by a very steep trail that ran down the cliffside. These days the only way into the valley is along the coastal trail from Haena.

The cone-shaped pinnacles along the valley walls look rather like a row of sentinels standing at attention. One legend says that rain has sculptured the cliffsides into the shape of the proud chiefs who are buried in the mountains.

The mushroom-shaped white dome and satellite dishes visible on the hill as you walk back to the parking lot are part of the Kokee Air Force station. There's drinking water at this first lookout.

Puu O Kila Lookout The paved road continues another mile to Puu O Kila Lookout. This is the last leg of the aborted Kokee-Haena Highway, which would have linked Kokee with the North Shore, thus creating an island circuit road. When you look at the cliffs at the end of the road it's easy to see why the plan was dropped.

The Pihea Trail that climbs the ridge straight ahead runs along what was to be the road.

From this lookout you get another view into Kalalau Valley and a glance inland toward the Alakai Swamp. A sign here points to Waialeale, the wettest spot on earth.

Kokee State Park Trails

Kokee State Park is the starting point for about 45 miles of trails, some maintained by the park service, others by the forestry. Pig and goat hunters use some of these trails during the hunting season.

Three of the trails – Nualolo, Awaawapuhi and Pihea – offer clifftop views into valleys on the Na Pali Coast. A couple of trails go into the swampy bogs of Alakai Swamp while others are easy nature trails.

Halemanu Road Trails Halemanu Rd, the starting point for several scenic hikes, is just north of the 14-mile marker. Whether or not the road is passable in a car often depends on whether it's been raining recently. Keep in mind that the clay roads provide no traction when wet and even if you're able to drive a car in, should it begin to rain driving out can be another matter!

The first hike is **Cliff Trail**, where a short five-minute walk leads to an overlook into Waimea Canyon. From there you can continue along **Canyon Trail**, a rather strenuous 1¾ miles one way that follows the canyon rim, passes Waipoo Falls and ends at Kumuwela Lookout with views down the canyon to the ocean beyond.

A little farther down Halemanu Rd is the start of **Halemanu-Kokee Trail**. This easy 1¼-mile (one way) nature trail passes through a native forest of koa and ohia trees that provide habitat to native birds. One of the common plants found on this trail is banana poka, a member of the passion fruit family and a serious invasive pest. It has pretty pink flowers but it drapes the forest with its vines and chokes out less aggressive native plants.

Nualolo & Awaawapuhi Trails The Nualolo and Awaawapuhi trails each go out to the very edge of sheer cliffs, peering down into valleys accessible only by boat. They connect via the Nualolo Cliff Trail. If you combine all three it makes for a hardy day hike. The valley views are extraordinarily beautiful.

The whole hike is about 10 miles of trails. Then you'll have to either hitch a ride or walk an additional two miles back down the road to where you started.

If you're only going to do one of the trails, we recommend Awaawapuhi, though it's a bit more strenuous than the Nualolo Trail. There are interpretive markers along the way and the views at the end are unbeatable.

Bring plenty of water as there's none along the way. Edible plants along the trail include blackberries, thimbleberries, guava and passion fruit (lilikoi).

Wild goats, prolific in the North Shore valleys, are readily spotted along the cliff walls. Capable of breeding at five months of age, the goats have no natural predators in Hawaii and their unchecked numbers have caused a fair amount of ecological damage.

The 3.8-mile Nualolo Trail starts between the cabins and Kokee Lodge. The trail begins in cool upland forest and descends 1500 feet, ending along a narrow ridge at a lookout on the rim of Nualolo Valley.

The Awaawapuhi Trail begins about 100 yards before the 17-mile marker. It descends 1600 feet, ending after three miles at a steep and spectacular pali overlooking Awaawapuhi and Nualolo valleys. The hike starts in ohia forest. About half a mile down the trail, the forest becomes dryer and koa begins to mix in with the ohia.

About 50 of the trees and plants along the trail are marked. A corresponding interpretive nature guide is available free from the forestry office. Awaawapuhi means 'valley of ginger'. Kahili, a yellow ginger, is seen at marker number nine.

The 2.1-mile Nualolo Cliff Trail is very scenic and offers numerous viewpoints into Nualolo Valley. There's even a picnic table where you can break for lunch along the way. The Nualolo Cliff Trail connects at the Nualolo Trail near the 3¼-mile mark and at the Awaawapuhi Trail near the 2¾-mile mark.

Kawaikoi Stream Trail The Kawaikoi

Stream Trail begins between the Sugi Grove and Kawaikoi camping grounds, off Camp 10-Mohihi Rd. It's a scenic mountain stream trail and the round trip is about 2½ miles. It starts out following the southern side of Kawaikoi Stream, then heads away from the stream and makes a loop, coming down the northern side of the stream before reconnecting with the southern side. If the stream is running high, don't make the crossings.

Kawaikoi Stream is popular for rainbow trout fishing, which is allowed during an open season in August and September. Fishing licences are required.

Camp 10-Mohihi Rd is up past the museum on the right. Like many of the dirt roads in Kokee, when it's dry, standard cars can usually make it down there. However, occasionally when it's really wet and rutted even 4WD vehicles have difficulty.

Pihea Trail The Pihea Trail starts from the Puu O Kila Lookout. The first mile runs along the ridge with views into Kalalau Valley. The beginning of the trail was graded in the 1950s, before plans to make this the last leg of the circle-island road were abandoned.

The Pihea Trail eventually turns inland and at about 1¾ miles crosses the Alakai Swamp Trail. If you turn left here you can continue on for about two miles through the Alakai Swamp to Kilohana Lookout. If you go straight instead, you will connect with Kawaikoi Stream Trail in about two miles.

Alakai Swamp Trail Alakai Swamp is inaccessible enough that even invasive plants haven't been able to choke out the endemic swamp vegetation and native bird species still have a stronghold.

There are parts of the swamp that receive sunlight so sparingly that the moss grows thick and fat on all sides of the trees. Most people that see this swamp see it from a helicopter but it's possible to walk through a corner of it by taking the Alakai Swamp Trail.

This 3½-mile trail starts off Camp 10-Mohihi Rd and goes through rainforest and bogs before reaching Kilohana Lookout on Wainiha Pali. If it's not overcast hikers will be rewarded with a sweeping view of Wainiha and Hanalei valleys. This is an extremely wet and muddy trail and there are plenty of stories of people slogging knee-deep in it.

If your car can't make it down Camp 10-Mohihi Rd, parking at Puu O Kila Lookout and approaching Alakai Swamp Trail via the Pihea Trail is probably your best bet.

Kaluapuhi Trail The Kaluapuhi Trail, a forest trail leading to a plum grove, is about two miles long. The marked trailhead starts at the highway a quarter of a mile past the 17-mile marker. This is a busy trail during midsummer when lots of islanders come up to pick the wild plums.

Places to Stay

Kokee Lodge (☎ 335-6061), Box 819, Waimea, HI 96796, manages the 12 cabins in Kokee State Park. The older cabins are a little tired and have just one large room with three beds for $35. Newer two-bedroom cedar cabins are $45 for up to seven people. The cabins have basic kitchens, linen, hot showers and wood stoves. State park rules limit stays to five days. The cabins are often booked up well in advance. However, cancellations do occur and you can sometimes get in if you're flexible.

The YWCA's *Camp Sloggett* in Kokee State Park has 39 beds, with a lodge that sleeps nine people and an annexe that sleeps 30. One group must rent the entire camp. The cost is $36 per night. For more than three people, there's an extra fee of $12 per adult and $6 per child. On weekends you must book both Friday and Saturday and the minimum cost per night is $72, which covers up to six people. Campers must bring their own sleeping bags. One box of wood is provided for the wood stove; additional boxes cost $5. Bookings are made through the YWCA (☎ 245-5959), 3094 Elua St, Lihue, HI 96766. The camp is about half a mile east of the park museum down a dirt road that's usually passable in an ordinary car.

Camping Kokee has one camping ground just past Kokee Lodge, above the meadow in a fairly uncrowded grassy area. There are restrooms, showers, water and picnic tables. Camping is free and allowed up to five nights, but state camping permits must be obtained in advance through the Lihue office.

If you want to get farther off the main track or extend your stay a few more days, there are also two forest reserve camping grounds, Kawaikoi and Sugi Grove, both off Camp 10-Mohihi Rd.

The camping grounds are at almost 4000 feet and nights are crisp and cool. This is sleeping bag and warm clothing country. The nearest store and gas station are in Waimea, 15 miles away.

Places to Eat

The *Kokee Lodge* (☎ 335-6061) has a monopoly on food north of Waimea. At breakfast, pancakes or French toast with coffee will cost about $6 and at lunch time, sandwiches with potato salad are $6 to $10. Dinners are in the $14 to $18 range. It's open from 8.30 am to 3.30 pm daily, and from 5.30 to 8.30 pm for dinner on Fridays and Saturdays only. You can also buy a few overpriced snack items and soft drinks at the gift shop in front of the restaurant.

Niihau

Niihau has long been closed to outsiders, earning it the nickname 'The Forbidden Island'.

No other place in Hawaii has more successfully turned its back on change than Niihau, which has no paved roads, no airport, no island-wide electricity and no telephones.

Niihau is a native Hawaiian preserve and the only island in the state where Hawaiian is still the primary language. The entire island, right down to the church, belongs to the Niihau Ranch, which is privately owned by the non-Hawaiian Robinson family. They are highly protective of Niihau's isolation.

Most of Niihau's 230 residents live in **Puuwai**, a settlement on the dry western shore, and make a living working the Robinson's ranch. Each house in the village is surrounded by a stone wall to keep grazing animals out of the gardens. It's a simple life.

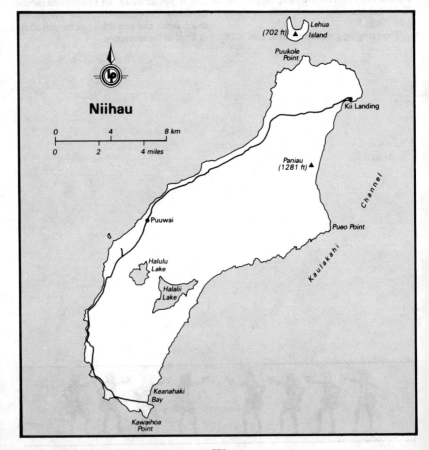

Water is collected in catchments; toilets are in outhouses.

Niihauans speak their own melodic dialect of Hawaiian. Business is conducted in Hawaiian, as are Sunday church services. Both of the Robinson brothers who manage the ranch speak Hawaiian fluently.

Children learn English as a second language when they go to school. Niihau has a two-room school house where two teachers and two educational aides teach from kindergarten through 12th grade to almost 50 students. Courses are taught solely in Hawaiian up to the fourth grade.

The island economy is based on sheep and cattle ranching, which on windswept Niihau is a marginal operation. Major droughts of the 1970s and '80s have taken a toll on the herds, and Niihau has been through some hard times.

A secondary income comes from the production of mesquite charcoal from the kiawe that flourishes in the dry, dusty environment. The mesquite is shipped off to restaurants both in Hawaii and on the mainland.

Niihau is 17 miles from Kauai via a weekly supply boat that plies between the two islands. The boat, an old WW II military landing craft, docks in Kauai at Makaweli, headquarters of Niihau Ranch and the Robinson family. Makaweli is also home to a settlement of Niihauans who prefer to live on Kauai, though many of them still work for the Robinsons.

Niihau is by no means a living history museum of Hawaiians stuck in time. Though it's got a foot in the past it takes what it wants from the present. The supply boat brings Cokes as well as poi, and the island has more dirt bikes than outrigger canoes.

Niihau residents are free to go to Kauai to shop, have a few beers (Niihau itself is dry) or just hang out. What they are not free to do is bring friends from other islands back home with them. Those Niihauans who marry people from other islands, as well as those whom the Robinsons come to see as undesirable, are rarely allowed to return.

Still, for the most part, Niihauans seem to accept that that's the way things are. Some

who leave are critical, but those who stay don't appear to be looking for any changes.

To outsiders, Niihau is an enigma. Some romanticise it as a pristine preserve of Hawaiian culture. Others liken its lifestyle to slavery.

The Robinsons see Niihau as a private sanctuary and themselves as the protectors of it all. It's that paternalism that sometimes rubs outside native Hawaiian groups the wrong way, though for the most part Niihauans don't seem to share those sentiments and resist interference.

HISTORY

Captain Cook anchored off Niihau on 29 January 1778, two weeks after 'discovering' Hawaii. Cook noted in his log that the island was lightly populated and largely barren, a description still true today. His visit was short, but it had a lasting impact.

It was on little Niihau that Cook first introduced two things that would quickly change the face of Hawaii. He left two goats, the first of the grazing animals that would devastate the native flora & fauna. And his men introduced syphilis, the first of the Western diseases that would decimate the Hawaiian people.

In 1864 Elizabeth Sinclair, a Scottish widow who was moving from New Zealand to Vancouver when she got sidetracked in Hawaii, bought Niihau from King Kamehameha V for $10,000. He originally tried to sell her the 'swampland' of Waikiki, but she passed it up for the 'desert island'. Interestingly, no two places in Hawaii today could be further apart, either culturally or in land value.

Mrs Sinclair brought the first sheep to Niihau from New Zealand and started the ranching operation that her great-grandsons continue today.

GEOGRAPHY

Niihau is the smallest of the inhabited Hawaiian islands. It is 18 miles long and six miles wide, with a total area of 70 sq miles. It has 45 miles of coast and the highest elevation is 1281 feet. The island is semi-arid, in the lee of Kauai.

Niihau's 860-acre Halalii Lake is the largest in Hawaii, though even during the rainy winter season it's only a few feet deep. In the summer it sometimes dries up to a mud pond. About 50% of Hawaii's endangered coots breed on Niihau – when there's enough water.

THINGS TO BUY

Niihauans create fine handcrafted necklaces made of tiny seashells painstakingly strung in spiral strands and intricate patterns. These Niihau shell leis are Hawaii's most highly prized and priced. They are sold in jewellery shops and craft galleries on the other islands, some for well over $1000.

The shells used in the necklaces are found mainly on Niihau beaches, where they are collected by sifting through the sand.

Smaller numbers of these shells can also be found on Kauai.

GETTING THERE & AWAY

The Robinsons have 'opened up' Niihau to tourism – via pricey helicopter flights.

Niihau Helicopters (☎ 335-3500), Box 370, Makaweli, HI 96769, runs tours at 9 am and 3 pm, as long as they have a minimum of four passengers. The tour costs $200 per person. The helicopter makes two brief stops, one at **Puukole Point** on the northern end of the island, and the other at **Keanahaki Bay,** on the southern end of the island where Captain Cook landed. They fly over much of Niihau, but avoid Puuwai village where people live.

The helicopter was purchased for emergency medical evacuations and the tours are said to be an effort to defray the cost.

Northwestern Hawaiian Islands

The Northwestern Hawaiian Islands stretch from Kauai nearly 1300 miles across the Pacific in an almost straight north-westerly line. They are also called the Leeward Islands.

There are 10 island clusters in all. They include atolls, each with a number of low sand islands formed on top of coral reefs, as well as some single rock islands and a reef that is mostly submerged.

Listed according to their order from Kauai, the clusters are Nihoa, Necker Island, French Frigate Shoals, Gardner Pinnacles, Maro Reef, Laysan Island, Lisianski Island, Pearl and Hermes Atoll, Midway Islands and Kure Atoll.

Together the 10 clusters have 33 named islands, all of which are small. Excluding Midway, the total land area is just under three sq miles, though the atoll lagoon areas are a hundred times that.

All the groups except Kure Atoll (a state sea bird sanctuary) and the Midway Islands are part of the Hawaiian Islands National Wildlife Refuge. The refuge, established in 1909 by US president Theodore Roosevelt, is the oldest and largest of the national wildlife refuges.

Visitors are not allowed on the islands unless they have permits, and these are granted only in the rarest of circumstances. Human activities are simply too disturbing to the fragile ecosystem. The only human habitation in the refuge is at Tern Island, and that is for wildlife researchers.

The Midway Islands, though geographically in the Hawaiian archipelago, are under the control of the US Navy and not part of the state of Hawaii. It has five islands, with a total land area of two sq miles, and a population of about 2000. Midway gained notoriety during WW II when the USA secured a major victory over Japan in a naval battle there in June 1942.

The other islands come under the political, though not the practical, jurisdiction of the City and County of Honolulu.

The Northwestern Hawaiian Islands, volcanic in origin, once jutted up high above sea level as the main Hawaiian islands do now. They are slowly slipping back into the sea, however, as a result of a sagging of the ocean floor and the forces of erosion.

The coral reefs appear like flower leis left floating on the water where the mountains once raised their heads.

FAUNA

The Northwestern Hawaiian Islands are home to around 15 million sea birds, all of which find room for at least a foothold. Endangered Hawaiian monk seals, green sea turtles and four endemic land birds also live there.

Sea Birds

Eighteen sea bird species nest on these islands, feeding on the abundant fish that live around the submerged reefs. They include frigate birds, boobies, albatrosses, terns, shearwaters, petrels, tropicbirds and noddies.

The sooty terns are the most abundant, numbering in the several millions. These screeching black and white birds also nest on the offshore islets of Oahu's windward coast.

Shearwaters and petrels lay their eggs in burrows that they dig in the sandy soil. The roofs of the burrows can easily collapse under the feet of nonobservant walkers, which is one reason why visitors are discouraged.

Land Birds

The Laysan duck, Laysan finch, Nihoa finch and Nihoa millerbird, endemic to Laysan and Nihoa islands respectively, are all listed as endangered or threatened species.

This is not because their numbers are declining but because these species exist in only one place on earth and are therefore susceptible to the introduction of new diseases and predators or the disruption of their habitat. One rat from a shipwrecked boat, weed seed from a hiker's boot or an oil slick washing ashore could mean the end of the species.

Monk Seals

The endangered Hawaiian monk seal, which exists only in Hawaii, uses Kure Atoll, the French Frigate Shoals and Laysan, Lisianski, Nihoa and Necker islands for pupping grounds. The seals are easily disturbed by human contact.

In the 19th century the seals were nearly hunted to extinction. Military operations in the area during and after WW II also resulted in a decline.

Fewer than 200 seal pups are born each year, many of which die from shark attacks. The total species population is around 1000.

FRENCH FRIGATE SHOALS

The French Frigate Shoals consist of 13 sand islands and a 135-foot rock, La Perouse Pinnacle, which was named after the French explorer who was almost wrecked on the reef. One of the sand islands, 37-acre Tern Island, is the field headquarters for the Hawaiian Islands National Wildlife Refuge.

Most of Tern Island is covered by an airfield left over from the days when the US Coast Guard had a loran (radio navigation system) station there. The old coast guard barracks now house two refuge managers, who work for the US Fish & Wildlife Service, and up to a dozen volunteers.

Tern Island is home to 17 species of sea birds and a lot of Hawaiian monk seals. Ninety percent of the green sea turtles that nest in the Hawaiian Islands nest at French Frigate Shoals.

LAYSAN ISLAND

Laysan Island is a classic example of how human interference can wreak havoc on island ecology.

Laysan is 1.45 sq miles in size, which though small is actually the largest of the

Northwestern Hawaiian Islands. From 1890 to 1904 Laysan was mined for guano – the phosphate-rich bird droppings used for fertiliser. Houses were built, mules were brought ashore as pack animals and ships docked to take the guano away.

There were once millions of birds on Laysan – mostly Laysan albatrosses, otherwise known as gooney birds. In addition to guano mining, albatross eggs were collected by the hundreds of thousands to be sold for their albumen, a substance used in photo processing.

As each albatross lays just one egg a year, an 'egging' sweep could destroy an entire year's hatch. Hunters also ravaged the island. In one six-month period alone, 300,000 birds were killed for their feathers, which were used by milliners to make hats for fashionable ladies.

Rabbits, introduced to Laysan first as pets for the workers' children and later for breeding, virtually destroyed the island's vegetation, and where they left off sandstorms took over. The loss of native food plants spelt the end of the Laysan flightless rail, Laysan honeycreeper and Laysan millerbird – all endemic land birds. The rabbits were finally exterminated in 1923.

There are now about 160,000 pairs of Laysan albatrosses on the island, still the world's largest colony. Albatrosses sometimes court and dance for five annual mating seasons before actually mating. Once they do mate, pairs stay together for life and sometimes live for 30 years.

The Laysan duck reached the brink of extinction as a result of the activities of rabbits and hunters. Their numbers were reduced to just six by 1911, but they're making a modest comeback. Laysan ducks swim in the brackish lagoon in the centre of the island, their only habitat. With a current population of about 300, they are one of the rarest ducks in the world.

The Laysan finch, the population of which was once as low as 100 thanks to the rabbits, is once again common on Laysan Island and has also been introduced to Pearl and Hermes Reef. Unlike its honeycreeper cousins on the main Hawaiian islands, which feed on nectar, the Laysan finch has become carnivorous and feeds on sea-bird eggs as well as the carcasses of dead sea birds.

There are also more than one million sooty terns nesting on Laysan.

NECKER & NIHOA

Necker and Nihoa, closest to the main Hawaiian islands, were probably settled more than a thousand years ago. Remains of stone temple platforms, numerous house sites, terraces and carved stone images have been found on the islands. Archaeological remains suggest that the early settlers were from the Marquesas.

Necker and Nihoa are not coral atolls but rugged rocky islands, each less than a quarter of a sq mile. Nihoa is the highest of the Northwestern Hawaiian Islands, with sheer sea cliffs and a peak elevation of 910 feet.

Two land bird species live only on tiny Nihoa and nowhere else.

The Nihoa finch, which like the Laysan finch is a raider of other birds' eggs, is hanging in there with a population of a few thousand. Attempts were made in 1967 to develop a back-up colony in case something happened to the birds on Nihoa. It failed when all 42 finches sent to the French Frigate Shoals died.

The grey Nihoa millerbird, related to the old world warbler family, is rare and secretive. It wasn't even discovered until 1923 and was so named because it eats miller moths. Approximately 400 birds remain.

Glossary

aa – lava which is rough and jagged

ahi – albacore (yellowfin) tuna

ahu – stone cairns used to mark a trail; or an altar or shrine

ahupuaa – a traditional land division, usually in a wedge shape from the mountains to the sea

aikane – friend

aina – land

akamai – clever

aku – skipjack tuna

akua – god, spirit, idol

akule – mackerel bigeye scad

alii – chief; royalty

aloha – the traditional greeting meaning love, welcome, goodbye.

amaama – mullet

amakihi – small yellow-green bird, one of the more common of the native birds

ao – Newell's shearwater (a sea bird)

apapane – bright red native Hawaiian honeycreeper

au – marlin

aumakua – ancestral spirit helper

auwe – Oh my! Alas!

awa – kava *(piper methysticum)*, made into an intoxicating brew; milk fish

awapuhi – wild ginger

bento – the Japanese word for a fixed box lunch

cilantro – coriander leaves (also known as Chinese parsley)

elepaio – a brownish forest bird with a white rump

hala – pandanus; the leaves are used in weaving mats and baskets

hale – house

hana – work; or bay, when used as a compound in place names

haole – Caucasian; literally 'without breath', it was formerly applied to any foreigner

hapa – half; person of mixed blood

hau – common indigenous lowland tree with spreading tangled branches; the flower resembles a hibiscus, the wood is often used for outrigger canoes

Hauoli Makahiki Hou – Happy New Year

haupia – coconut pudding

Hawaii nei – all the Hawaiian islands, as distinguished from the Big Island

heiau – ancient stone temple, a place of worship in Hawaii before Western contact

Hina – Polynesian goddess (wife of Ku, one of the four main gods)

holoholo – to walk, drive or ramble around for pleasure

holoku – a long dress similar to the muu-muu, but more fitted and with a yoke

holua – sled, or sled course

honu – turtle

hoolaulea celebration, party

huhu – angry

hui – group, organisation

hukilau – net fishing, with a seine, which involves a group of people; the word can also refer to the feast that follows

hula – traditional Hawaiian dance

hula halau – hula school or troupe

humuhumuukunukuapuaa – rectangular triggerfish

iiwi – a bright vermillion forest bird with a curved salmon-coloured beak

iliahi Hawaiian sandlewood

iliili stones

ilima – native groundcover with a delicate yellow-orange flower

imu – underground earthen oven used in traditional luau cooking

kahuna – wise person in any field, commonly a priest, healer or sorcerer

kahuna nui – high priest

kahili – a feather standard, used as a symbol of royalty

kalua – traditional method of baking in an underground oven (imu)

kamaaina – native-born Hawaiian or a long-time resident; literally 'child of the land'.

Kanaloa – god of the underworld

kane – man; also the name of one of four top Hawaiian gods

kapu – taboo, part of strict ancient Hawaiian social system

keiki – child, children

kiawe – a relative of the mesquite tree introduced to Hawaii in the 1820s, now very common; its branches are covered with sharp thorns

kipuka – an area of land spared when lava flows around it; an oasis

ko – sugar cane

koa – native hardwood tree often used in woodworking of native crafts

kohola – whale

kokua – help, cooperation

kona – leeward, or a leeward wind

konane – ancient Hawaiian board game similar to checkers

koolau – windward side

Ku – Polynesian god of many manifestations, including god of war, farming and fishing

kukui – the candlenut tree; this is the official state tree and a native to Hawaii; the oil from the nuts was once used in lamps

kupuna – grandparent

kuula – fishing shrine

lanai – veranda

lauhala – leaves of the *hala* plant used in weaving

laulau – wrapped package; pork or beef with salted fish and taro leaves wrapped in leaves and steamed

lei – garland, usually of flowers, but also of leaves or shells

lilikoi – passion fruit

limu – seaweed

lio – horse

lolo – stupid, crazy

lomi – raw, diced salmon marinated with tomatoes and onions

lomilomi – massage

Lono – Polynesian god of harvest, agriculture, fertility and peace

loulu – native fan palms

luakini – a type of *heiau* dedicated to the war god Ku and used for human sacrifices

luau – traditional Hawaiian feast

mahalo – thank you

mahimahi – this means 'dolphin', but this fish is unrelated to the mammal

maile – native twining plant with fragrant leaves often used in leis

makaainana – common people; literally 'people who tend the land'

makaha – sluice gates

makahiki – ancient annual four-month winter harvest festival dedicated to Lono when sports and celebrations replaced all warfare

makaku – creative artistic mana

makai – towards the sea

malihini – newcomer, visitor

malo – loincloth

mana – spiritual power

manini – convict tang (a reef fish); also used to refer to something small or insignificant

mauka – towards the mountains; inland

mele – song, chant

menehune – 'little people' who according to legend built many of Hawaii's fishponds, *heiaus* and other stonework

milo – a native shade tree with beautiful hardwood

moo – water spirit, lizard spirit, water lizard or dragon

mu – a 'body catcher', who secured sacrificial victims for the heiau altar

muu-muu – a long, loose-fitting dress introduced by the missionaries

naupaka – a native shrub, the delicate white flower of which looks like it's torn in half

Neighbor Islands – the term used to refer to the main Hawaiian Islands outside of Oahu

nene – a native goose; Hawaii's state bird

nisei – people of Japanese descent

noni – Indian mulberry; a small tree with yellow, warty, smelly fruit, used medicinally

nuku puu – a native honeycreeper with a bright yellow underbelly

ohana – family, extended family

ohia lehua – native Hawaiian tree; the

flowers, which are most often red, are tufted feathery pompoms

ohelo – low-growing native shrub with edible red berries related to cranberries, said to be sacred to Pele

okole – buttocks

olo – surf boards used by alii

ono – delicious; also the name of the wahoo fish

opae – shrimp

opakapaka – pink snapper fish

opihi – edible limpet

pahoehoe – type of lava which flows quickly and smoothly

pakalolo – marijuana; literally 'crazy smoke'

pali – cliff

palila – native honeycreeper

paniolo – a Hawaiian cowboy; the word is derived from 'espanole', as Hawaii's first cowboys were Mexican and Spanish

pau – finished, no more

Pele – goddess of fire and volcanoes, whose home is in Kilauea volcano

pho – a Vietnamese soup of beef broth, noodles and fresh herbs

piko – navel, umbilical cord

pili – a bunch grass, commonly used for thatching houses

pilikia – trouble

poha – gooseberry

poi – a staple food of the Hawaiian diet, poi is a gooey paste made from taro roots

Poliahu – goddess of snow

pua aloalo – hibiscus flower

puka – any kind of hole or opening

pupu – snack food, hors d'oeuvres; shells

puu – hill, cinder cone

puuhonua – place of refuge

saimin – a Japanese noodle soup

tabi – Japanese reef-walking shoes

talk story – to strike up a conversation, make small talk

tapa – cloth made by pounding and mashing the bark of the paper mulberry tree; used for early Hawaiian clothing. In Hawaiian: *kapa*.

taro – a plant, with green heart-shaped leaves, cultivated in Hawaii for its edible rootstock. The root is mashed to make *poi*. In Hawaiian, taro is pronounced *kalo*.

teishoku – Japanese word for fixed-plate meal

ti – common native plant; its long shiny 'multi-purpose' leaves are used for a variety of things, including plates and *hula* skirts. In Hawaiian: *ki*.

tutu – aunt, older woman

ukulele – a stringed musical instrument derived from the 'braginha', which was introduced to Hawaii in the 1800s by Portuguese immigrants

ulu – breadfruit

ulu maika – ancient Hawaiian game

wahine – woman

wana – sea urchin

wikiwiki – hurry, quick

Index

Keep in touch!

We love hearing from you and think you'd like to hear from us.

The Lonely Planet Newsletter covers the when, where, how and what of travel. (AND it's free!)

When...is the right time to see reindeer in Finland?
Where...can you hear the best palm-wine music in Ghana?
How...do you get from Asunción to Areguá by steam train?
What...should you leave behind to avoid hassles with customs in Iran?

To join our mailing list just contact us at any of our offices. (details below)

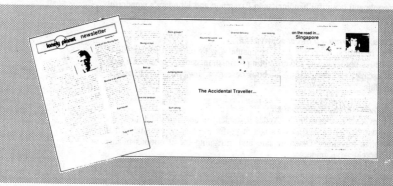

Every issue includes:

- *a letter from Lonely Planet founders Tony and Maureen Wheeler*
- *travel diary from a Lonely Planet author - find out what it's really like out on the road*
- *feature article on an important and topical travel issue*
- *a selection of recent letters from our readers*
- *the latest travel news from all over the world*
- *details on Lonely Planet's new and forthcoming releases*

Also available Lonely Planet T-shirts. 100% heavy weight cotton (S, M, L, XL)

LONELY PLANET PUBLICATIONS
Australia: PO Box 617, Hawthorn, 3122, Victoria (tel: 03-819 1877)
USA: Embarcadero West, 155 Filbert Street, Suite 251, Oakland, CA 94607 (tel: 510-893 8555)
UK: Devonshire House, 12 Barley Mow Passage, Chiswick, London W4 4PH (tel: 081-742 3161)

Guides to the Americas

Alaska – a travel survival kit
Jim DuFresne has travelled extensively through Alaska by foot, road, rail, barge and kayak. This guide has all the information you'll need to make the most of one of the world's great wilderness areas.

Argentina, Uruguay & Paraguay – a travel survival kit
This guide gives independent travellers all the essential information on three of South America's lesser known countries. Discover some of South America's most spectacular natural attractions in Argentina; friendly people and beautiful handicrafts in Paraguay; and Uruguay's wonderful beaches.

Baja California – a travel survival kit
For centuries, Mexico's Baja peninsula – with its beautiful coastline, raucous border towns and crumbling Spanish missions – has been a land of escapes and escapades. This book describes how and where to escape in Baja.

Bolivia – a travel survival kit
From lonely villages in the Andes to ancient ruined cities and the spectacular city of La Paz, Bolivia is a magnificent blend of everything that inspires travellers. Discover safe and intriguing travel options in this comprehensive guide.

Brazil – a travel survival kit
From the mad passion of Carnival to the Amazon – home of the richest and most diverse ecosystem on earth – Brazil is a country of mythical proportions. This guide has all the essential travel information.

Canada – a travel survival kit
This comprehensive guidebook has all the facts on the USA's huge neighbour – the Rocky Mountains, Niagara Falls, ultramodern Toronto, remote villages in Nova Scotia, and much more.

Central America on a shoestring
Practical information on travel in Belize, Guatemala, Costa Rica, Honduras, El Salvador, Nicaragua and Panama. A team of experienced Lonely Planet authors reveals the secrets of this culturally rich, geographically diverse and breathtakingly beautiful region.

Chile & Easter Island – a travel survival kit
Travel in Chile is easy and safe, with possibilities as varied as the countryside. This guide also gives detailed coverage of Chile's Pacific outpost, mysterious Easter Island.

Colombia – a travel survival kit
Colombia is a land of myths – from the ancient legends of El Dorado to the modern tales of Gabriel Garcia Marquez. The reality is beauty and violence, wealth and poverty, tradition and change. This guide shows how to travel independently and safely in this exotic country.

Costa Rica – a travel survival kit
This practical guide gives the low down on exceptional opportunities for fishing and water sports, and the best ways to experience Costa Rica's vivid natural beauty.

Ecuador & the Galápagos Islands – a travel survival kit
Ecuador offers a wide variety of travel experiences, from the high cordilleras to the Amazon plains – and 600 miles west, the fascinating Galápagos Islands. Everything you need to know about travelling around this enchanting country.

La Ruta Maya: Yucatán, Guatemala & Belize – a travel survival kit
Invaluable background information on the cultural and environmental riches of La Ruta Maya (The Mayan Route), plus practical advice on how best to minimise the impact of travellers on this sensitive region.

Mexico – a travel survival kit
A unique blend of Indian and Spanish culture, fascinating history, and hospitable people, make Mexico a travellers' paradise.

Peru – a travel survival kit
The lost city of Machu Picchu, the Andean altiplano and the magnificent Amazon rainforests are just some of Peru's many attractions. All the travel facts you'll need can be found in this comprehensive guide.

South America on a shoestring
This practical guide provides concise information for budget travellers and covers South America from the Darien Gap to Tierra del Fuego. The *New York Times* dubbed the author 'the patron saint of travellers in the third world'.

Trekking in the Patagonian Andes
The first detailed guide to this region gives complete information on 28 walks, and lists a number of other possibilities extending from the Araucanía and Lake District regions of Argentina and Chile to the remote icy of South America in Tierra del Fuego.

Also available:
Brazilian phrasebook, **Latin American Spanish** phrasebook and **Quechua** phrasebook.

Lonely Planet Guidebooks

Lonely Planet guidebooks cover every accessible part of Asia as well as Australia, the Pacific, South America, Africa, the Middle East, Europe and parts of North America. There are five series: *travel survival kits*, covering a country for a range of budgets; *shoestring guides* with compact information for low-budget travel in a major region; *walking guides*; *city guides* and *phrasebooks*.

Australia & the Pacific
Australia
Bushwalking in Australia
Islands of Australia's Great Barrier Reef
Fiji
Micronesia
New Caledonia
New Zealand
Tramping in New Zealand
Papua New Guinea
Papua New Guinea phrasebook
Rarotonga & the Cook Islands
Samoa
Solomon Islands
Sydney city guide
Tahiti & French Polynesia
Tonga
Vanuatu

South-East Asia
Bali & Lombok
Bangkok city guide
Myanmar (Burma)
Burmese phrasebook
Cambodia
Indonesia
Indonesia phrasebook
Malaysia, Singapore & Brunei
Philippines
Pilipino phrasebook
Singapore city guide
South-East Asia on a shoestring
Thailand
Thai phrasebook
Vietnam, Laos & Cambodia

North-East Asia
China
Mandarin Chinese phrasebook
Hong Kong, Macau & Canton
Japan
Japanese phrasebook
Korea
Korean phrasebook
North-East Asia on a shoestring
Taiwan
Tibet
Tibet phrasebook
Tokyo city guide

West Asia
Trekking in Turkey
Turkey
Turkish phrasebook
West Asia on a shoestring

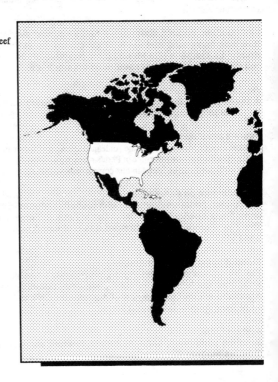

Middle East
Egypt & the Sudan
Egyptian Arabic phrasebook
Iran
Israel
Jordan & Syria
Yemen

Indian Ocean
Madagascar & Comoros
Maldives & Islands of the East Indian Ocean
Mauritius, Réunion & Seychelles

Mail Order

Lonely Planet guidebooks are distributed worldwide. They are also available by mail order from Lonely Planet, so if you have difficulty finding a title please write to us. US and Canadian residents should write to Embarcadero West, 155 Filbert St, Suite 251, Oakland CA 94607, USA; European residents should write to Devonshire House, 12 Barley Mow Passage, Chiswick, London W4 4PH; and residents of other countries to PO Box 617, Hawthorn, Victoria 3122, Australia.

Indian Subcontinent
Bangladesh
India
Hindi/Urdu phrasebook
Trekking in the Indian Himalaya
Karakoram Highway
Kashmir, Ladakh & Zanskar
Nepal
Trekking in the Nepal Himalaya
Nepal phrasebook
Pakistan
Sri Lanka
Sri Lanka phrasebook

Africa
Africa on a shoestring
Central Africa
East Africa
Kenya
Swahili phrasebook
Morocco, Algeria & Tunisia
Moroccan Arabic phrasebook
South Africa, Lesotho & Swaziland
Zimbabwe, Botswana & Namibia
West Africa

Mexico
Baja California
Mexico

Central America
Central America on a shoestring
Costa Rica
La Ruta Maya

North America
Alaska
Canada
Hawaii

South America
Argentina, Uruguay & Paraguay
Bolivia
Brazil
Brazilian phrasebook
Chile & Easter Island
Colombia
Ecuador & the Galápagos Islands
Latin American Spanish phrasebook
Peru
Quechua phrasebook
South America on a shoestring
Trekking in the Patagonian Andes

Europe
Eastern Europe on a shoestring
Eastern Europe phrasebook
Finland
Iceland, Greenland & the Faroe Islands
Mediterranean Europe on a shoestring
Mediterranean Europe phrasebook
Scandinavian & Baltic Europe on a shoestring
Scandinavian Europe phrasebook
Trekking in Spain
USSR
Russian phrasebook
Western Europe on a shoestring
Western Europe phrasebook

The Lonely Planet Story

Lonely Planet published its first book in 1973 in response to the numerous 'How did you do it?' questions Maureen and Tony Wheeler were asked after driving, bussing, hitching, sailing and railing their way from England to Australia.

Written at a kitchen table and hand collated, trimmed and stapled, *Across Asia on the Cheap* became an instant local bestseller, inspiring thoughts of another book.

Eighteen months in South-East Asia resulted in their second guide, *South-East Asia on a shoestring*, which they put together in a backstreet Chinese hotel in Singapore in 1975. The 'yellow bible' as it quickly became known to backpackers around the world, soon became *the* guide to the region. It has sold well over half a million copies and is now in its 7th edition, still retaining its familiar yellow cover.

Today there are over 100 Lonely Planet titles – books that have that same adventurous approach to travel as those early guides; books that 'assume you know how to get your luggage off the carousel' as one reviewer put it.

Although Lonely Planet initially specialised in guides to Asia, they now cover most regions of the world, including the Pacific, South America, Africa, the Middle East and Europe. The list of *walking guides* and *phrasebooks* (for 'unusual' languages such as Quechua, Swahili, Nepalese and Egyptian Arabic) is also growing rapidly.

The emphasis continues to be on travel for independent travellers. Tony and Maureen still travel for several months of each year and play an active part in the writing, updating and quality control of Lonely Planet's guides.

They have been joined by over 50 authors, 48 staff – mainly editors, cartographers, & designers – at our office in Melbourne, Australia and another 10 at our US office in Oakland, California. In 1991 Lonely Planet opened a London office to handle sales for Britain, Europe and Africa. Travellers themselves also make a valuable contribution to the guides through the feedback we receive in thousands of letters each year.

The people at Lonely Planet strongly believe that travellers can make a positive contribution to the countries they visit, both through their appreciation of the countries' culture, wildlife and natural features, and through the money they spend. In addition, the company makes a direct contribution to the countries and regions it covers. Since 1986 a percentage of the income from each book has been donated to ventures such as famine relief in Africa; aid projects in India; agricultural projects in Central America; Greenpeace's efforts to halt French nuclear testing in the Pacific and Amnesty International. In 1991 $68,000 was donated to these causes.

Lonely Planet's basic travel philosophy is summed up in Tony Wheeler's comment, 'Don't worry about whether your trip will work out. Just go!'